The Oxford Anthology of

TUDOR DRAMA

The Oxford Anthology of
TUDOR DRAMA

EDITED BY

GREG WALKER

OXFORD
UNIVERSITY PRESS

OXFORD
UNIVERSITY PRESS

Great Clarendon Street, Oxford, OX2 6DP,
United Kingdom

Oxford University Press is a department of the University of Oxford.
It furthers the University's objective of excellence in research, scholarship,
and education by publishing worldwide. Oxford is a registered trade mark of
Oxford University Press in the UK and in certain other countries

First Edition published in 2014

Impression: 1

Published in the United States of America by Oxford University Press
198 Madison Avenue, New York, NY 10016, United States of America

British Library Cataloguing in Publication Data
Data available

Library of Congress Control Number: 2013957001

ISBN 978–0–19–968112–9

Printed in Great Britain by
CPI Group (UK) Ltd, Croydon, CR0 4YY

PREFACE

THIS anthology is a companion volume to *The Oxford Handbook of Tudor Drama* (2012), which I co-edited with Thomas Betteridge. The essays in that collection provide a critical overview of the drama of the long Tudor century (1485–1603) and detailed case studies of most of the plays contained in this volume. The *Anthology* supplements these essays with the primary evidence of the play texts themselves, each newly edited from the earliest available manuscripts or Tudor editions. Like the *Handbook*, it is based on the belief that the drama of the Tudor period is best studied as a single body of work, rather than divided into potentially misleading categories such as 'medieval and Renaissance', 'pre- and post-Reformation', 'before and after Shakespeare'. As the Introduction will suggest, it also rejects the notion of a steady evolutionary process whereby drama in the period became increasingly more secular, sophisticated, experimental, and psychologically insightful to the point where it reached its apotheosis in the work of Shakespeare. While there is some evidence for each of these developments, they are not the only story to be told.

The quality of Shakespeare's work can speak for itself, but its canonical status in school and college syllabi, in scholarly and popular editions, in film and television adaptations, and in the theatrical repertoire can have the effect of casting everything before and around it into deep shadow. Set against the familiarity of *Hamlet* or *Twelfth Night*, everything else produced in the sixteenth century can seem awkward, old-fashioned, unfamiliar, and 'difficult'. In this collection I have tried to allow all the plays to speak for themselves, to make a claim for their own originality, their emotional appeal, their intellectual depth and engagement. Hence I print them all, even the earliest, in modernized spelling. For nothing reinforces the false assumption that Shakespeare is, as Jan Kott famously claimed, 'our contemporary', while his own contemporaries are not, more than the familiar scholarly practice of publishing his plays in modern English and those of his peers and predecessors in their original Middle or Early Modern English (what the historian Sir Geoffrey Elton wryly termed 'Ye Olde Englyshe Tea Shoppe Spellynge'). So I have kept the rich vocabulary, idioms, and phrasing of the original texts intact, but removed the unnecessarily defamiliarizing spelling, with what I hope is a light touch. Shakespeare's work can thus be seen in the context of the century of drama that preceded it, rather than as something different in kind from it and toward which that drama was necessarily leading. Similarly, the plays are printed in full, without disorientating cuts or use of extracts, on the grounds that they were carefully crafted by one or more hands (the term play*wright* is no accident) to be complete works with beginnings, middles, and ends, and so can be fully appreciated only if they are fully available to be viewed. (The principles behind the copy texts chosen and the addition of any extra materials are explained in the head-notes to each play.) The aim throughout is to provide versions of these plays that are readily accessible to readers, students, actors, and directors, in the hope that they will all become a more familiar part of college and university courses and the stage repertoire.

I am grateful to my *Handbook* co-editor Tom Betteridge for his help and advice, and for his preliminary notes on *Titus Andronicus* and *The Comedy of Errors*, which I have used when developing the apparatus for those texts here. I am also grateful to those friends and colleagues who have helped in matters great and small during the editorial process: George Bernard, Marie-Hélène Besnault, Michel Bitot, Sarah Carpenter, Anne Marie D'Arcy, Janette Dillon, Sarah Dunnigan, Jose Maria Perez Fernandez, Penny Fielding, Alastair Fowler, Alan Gillis, Jo George,

Richard Hillman, Kevin Jacklin, Claire Jowitt, James Loxley, Joanne Kantrowitz, Aaron Kelly, Tony Kushner, André Lascombes, Ken Millard, Ellie Rycroft, Kevin Sharpe, Randall Stevenson, Olga Taxidou, Greg Thompson, and Meg Twycross. I am especially grateful, as ever, to David Salter and Elaine Treharne for their friendship and advice well beyond the call of duty, to John J. McGavin for his heroic reading of parts of the typescript at various points and his invaluable advice, and to Sharon, Matt, Dave, and Tessa the dog for being there throughout.

CONTENTS

INTRODUCTION

Almost at the end of the long Tudor century, that archetypal Renaissance man, Prince Hamlet, can be found describing 'the purpose of playing', the nature and function of the dramatic enterprise, to a troupe of professional actors who are visiting Elsinore. His speech is frequently read as the blueprint for a new naturalistic theatre (implicitly Shakespeare's own), signalling definitively the rejection of an old, artificial, 'medieval' form of acting characterized by didacticism, allegory, mannerist gesture, and all the 'outward shows' of a passed Catholic age, in favour of a more realistic dramaturgy of individualized, 'rounded' characters, psychological depth, and ambiguity, a form of theatre pointing the way boldly to Protestant modernity. 'Suit the action to the word, the word to the action', the prince instructs the players, for the end of acting, 'both at the first and now, was and is, to hold as 'twere the mirror up to nature' (III.ii.21–22). So far, so seemingly naturalistic. But if we pause a little longer over Hamlet's account, and look at it, not with the assumptions of a post-Freudian modern reader about what constitutes 'nature' and the natural (whether in human behaviour or on the stage), but with those of late Tudor spectators, what he describes might seem less a manifesto for a revolutionary modern theatre and more a recollection of the kind of probing, socially engaged, allegorical dramaturgy that had dominated English stages for over a century. Read in full as it is printed in the First Folio of 1623, the prince's speech defines the ends and purpose of playing as, not simply to 'hold as 'twere the Mirrour up to Nature', but thereby,

> To shew Vertue her owne Feature, Scorne her owne Image, and the verie Age and Bodie of the Time his forme and pressure.[1]

This does not sound quite so much like Ibsen. The capitalization of the proper nouns and that use of 'his' to describe the age and body of the time might imply that Nature, Virtue, Scorn, and even The Time were not simply abstract notions, but named characters in the drama in Hamlet's mind. And in the moral interludes of the sixteenth century that is exactly what they—or figures very like them—would have been. Similarly, holding a mirror up to such things was no neutral act of observation, but a moral or satiric strategy. In an age when people did not have such ready access to accurate reproductions of their own image, and so were vulnerable to flattering descriptions of their own good looks, mirrors were indeed a rare opportunity to see oneself as the world saw one, and a valuable corrective to complacency or self-delusion. The interludes of the Tudor century thus regularly described themselves as mirrors or glasses, in which their audiences might see reflected the impostures of vice and the sins and follies of the age, and so, their prologues implied, learn to avoid them and to live better lives.

Such claims were always at least partly tongue in cheek. Even the most moralistic of morality plays was also there to entertain and engage its spectators. It was not simply a sermon for many voices. But it is illuminating to consider for a moment longer the suggestion that Hamlet's supposed manifesto for proto-modern drama might have more in common with the earlier moral plays than is usually allowed. In a play such as the late fifteenth-century morality *Mankind*, for example, characters named Mischief, New Guise (the new fashion), Nowadays, and Nought (worthlessness/evil) tempt the eponymous protagonist into sin, before he is ultimately redeemed

[1] *Mr William Shakespeares Comedies, Histories, and Tragedies, published according to the True Originall Copies* (London: Isaac Jaggard and Ed. Blount, 1623), p. 266.

through the agency of the virtue, Mercy, whom he had initially been persuaded to reject. The echoes with Hamlet's account of a drama that would reveal the truth about Nature (Mankind?), Virtue (Mercy?), Scorn (Mischief, Nought?), and The Time (Nowadays and New Guise?) seem ready and obvious. While *Hamlet* might in one sense be poised on the cusp of modernity, then, it still bears the baggage of a century or more of playmaking practice, and seems remarkably reluctant to part with it.[2]

To suggest that the drama of the end of the Tudor century might have had more in common with that of the beginning than is usually assumed is not to play devil's advocate for its own sake. The theatrical history of this period is characteristically told as a story of evolutionary change in which a development from simple, religious, didactic forms to complex, secular, open-ended ones was achieved through the gradual sophistication of dramatic technique energized by sudden moments of radical external change (the Reformation, the banning of religious drama, the building of the playhouses) or creative innovation (the 'genius' of Kyd, Marlowe, and Shakespeare). This account has been assailed from many quarters, and a rather more nuanced and critical approach is now adopted by most scholars.[3] Far more plausibly secular and religious drama evolved side by side, rather than the one having to emerge from the other, as that model suggested, and the various strands of dramatic tradition developed in complex dialogue rather than in evolutionary succession.

But the evolutionary model retains a curious hold on the critical imagination in a way that has few equivalents in other areas of literary history. It is not generally assumed that Spenser was a better poet than Chaucer simply because he wrote later, nor that the techniques of prose-writing had developed so markedly in the years separating them that the work of Charles Dickens can be studied only as a precursor to that of Graham Greene. Yet such assumptions still hover in the margins of many accounts of the drama of the Tudor century, to the point where everything prior to the 1590s can be found described as 'the pre-Shakespearean period'. This anthology seeks to bypass such accounts, and the assumptions on which they are based, and returns to the primary evidence of the plays themselves as works which were framed in relation to the needs of the communities which produced and used them. It allows readers to consider these plays afresh, not as representatives of either medieval or Renaissance, religious or secular, didactic or exploratory theatre (pairings that seem descriptive but actually carry an obvious critical agenda in which the second term is assumed to be superior or preferable to the first), but simply as plays, each of which was evidently highly successful in its own time, providing audiences with insights, provocations, and pleasures which they valued highly, and were often willing to pay good money to experience. It offers its readers the chance to sample a cross-section of the plays of the long Tudor century and make up their own minds about their merits or shortcomings, and to infer their own histories of continuity or change. For the richness of the material will support more than one story.

A comparison of the first play printed here, the York pageant of *The Fall of the Angels*, with the last, Shakespeare's *Comedy of Errors*, might, for example, suggest a contrast between a relatively short, simple, religious narrative and a much longer, more complex, secular one, between a piece that relatively few modern theatregoers will have seen, and one which many will have, and still more will be aware of. But there are other ways of considering that same

[2] Shakespeare himself had already brought Rumour onstage as a personified character in *2 Henry IV* in the late 1590s, and would do the same with Time in *The Winter's Tale*, as late as *c.*1610, so the uses of allegory were clearly well known and congenial to him.

[3] See, for example, the essays in Richard Beadle and Alan J. Fletcher, eds., *The Cambridge Companion to Medieval English Theatre*, 2nd edn. (Cambridge: Cambridge University Press, 2007).

pairing that are not so focused on demonstrating the greater sophistication and accessibility of the later play. Looked at afresh, might it not be the sheer intellectual ambition of the York playwright that is most striking? Here is a writer who was willing to tackle the deepest mysteries of theology and belief, to put himself in the mind of God, and try to reproduce His thoughts as He brought into being time, space, and the whole of universal creation in the space of just 162 lines of dramatic verse.[4] Set against such a sweeping theatrical ambition, Shakespeare's choice to use five acts to dramatize a series of short-lived comic misunderstandings between traders in a port in Asia Minor might suggest a distinct lack of artistic ambition rather than the hallmarks of future greatness.

Similarly, if we for a moment accept that formal innovation and imaginative creativity are the yardsticks by which we measure dramatic modernity and progress, might an observer innocent of the standard evolutionary narratives not be rather more impressed by Henry Medwall's interlude *Fulgens and Lucrece* (*c*.1490–1500), the third of the plays printed here, than with anything written in the avant garde, revolutionary 1590s? In *Fulgens* one finds, not only an elegant fusion of main plot and comic subplot and the integration of a serious philosophical debate about the nature and origins of nobility into a courtship narrative, but also in Lucrece arguably one of the most subtle and convincingly drawn female characters produced before 1600. Medwall also performs the bravura feat of having two of the main roles in the play seemingly taken by members of the audience, who apparently just 'step up' into the acting place and involve themselves in the action. Critics who are impressed by Shakespeare's audacity in having Richard III speak directly to his audiences, or by the way in which Marlowe plays with spectators' expectations in *Tamburlaine* or *Dr Faustus*, might pause for a moment over the thought that the largely uncelebrated Medwall had taken such ideas considerably further over a hundred years earlier. Not only that but he had also trumped Shakespeare's genre-bending inclusion of a comic messenger in the tragedy of *Titus Andronicus* or a clownish gravedigger in *Hamlet*, with his own addition of the scatological jousting game of 'fart prick in cule' ('fart prick in the arse') at the centre point of his characters' discussion of civic virtue—and this in a play probably written and performed for the household of Cardinal John Morton, Archbishop of Canterbury. The pageant-makers and interluders of the first decades of the Tudor century clearly would have had little to learn from their better-known successors about either formal innovation or ludic audacity.

I am not suggesting, of course, that we replace the traditional evolutionary model of the transition from *Mankind* to Marlowe with a new orthodoxy that sees the sixteenth century as a period of steady decline from the avant garde experimentation and meta-theatrics of the 1490s. But it would seem both intellectually and culturally beneficial periodically at least to consider the story from the other way around, and to ask, not only what had been achieved by the 1590s, but also what had been lost. Such an account would have to set the disappearance of the Mystery plays, the loss of the intimate familial association of playwright, performers, and audiences that was central to the household interludes (and the ready assumption that followed, that such plays not only could but should regularly confront their noble and royal patrons with both critical good counsel and merry mockery of their weaknesses and failings) against the manifest riches of the Elizabethan playhouse repertoires, the audacious provocations of Marlowe, and rich experimentation of the early Shakespeare.

Innovations there clearly were in the course of the sixteenth century, and critics have made good cases for the importance of individual writers, works, and formal innovations in the

[4] Greg Walker, '"In the beginning": Performing the Creation in the York Corpus Christi Play', in Thomas Betteridge and Greg Walker, eds. *The Oxford Handbook of Tudor Drama* (Oxford: Oxford University Press, 2012), pp. 36–54.

business of playing to the development of drama in the Tudor century. The first wholly secular play (*Fulgens and Lucrece*?), the first to be printed in England (perhaps *Fulgens* again, between 1512 and 1516), the first 'rediscovered' classical play performed in Britain (the 'goodly comedy of Plautus' played at court in Greenwich in March 1519?),[5] the first written in blank verse (*Gorboduc*), the building of the first commercial playhouses (of which more in a moment), the formation of the Queen's Men, a super-troupe drawn from the best actors of the age, in 1583,[6] the appearance of groundbreaking plays such as *The Spanish Tragedy* or *Tamburlaine*, which both embodied a new 'emotionalism',[7] and deployed 'questionable' characters whose motivation and character were ambivalent, and who thus became the subject of audience interest on their own terms rather than as emblems of wider themes or issues,[8] all of these marked important milestones in the story of theatre in the Tudor century. But most Tudor playwrights, and certainly all of those whose work appears in this anthology, brought something new and significant to the history of the stage, adding approaches, insights, themes, or techniques to the repertoire, and in turn neglecting or downplaying other things which were already there. John Heywood's audacious Lucianic playfulness in *The Play of the Weather*, William Stephenson's novel mixture of high academic humanism and low rustic comedy in *Gammer Gurton's Needle*, Richard Edward's emotionally fraught exploration of the ideals of male friendship in *Damon and Pithias*, Thomas Preston's powerful evocation of tyranny in *Cambises*, Jasper Heywood's importation of the sensationalism of Senecan tragedy in his translation of *Thyestes*, and John Lyly's coining of a new 'euphuistic' courtly idiom in *Endymion*, all were revolutionary interventions in their own moment in theatre history, and all were remembered and evoked by later writers.

Of the genuinely revolutionary moments in the sixteenth century, perhaps only two had an irreversible effect on the nature and direction of Elizabethan drama: the Reformation, which effectively, if gradually, killed off the kinds of religious drama that had dominated stages across the country for two centuries, and the building of the commercial playhouses in and around London in the last quarter of the century. As a consequence, English drama would of necessity be a largely secular affair, and its centre of economic and creative gravity would shift from the great provincial cities of the realm to London. We shall look briefly at each of these changes in what follows, starting with the second.

THE CONDITIONS OF PERFORMANCE

Until the summer of 1567, when John Brayne built the short-lived Red Lion playhouse in Whitechapel, east of London, there were no theatres, in the sense of dedicated, purpose-built commercial playhouses, in Britain. And there had not been for over a thousand years. Yet there were a number of long-standing rich, and diverse dramatic traditions stretching back at least two centuries, which had nurtured what we think of as 'theatre' (but which contemporaries tended, with Hamlet, to refer to by the non-site-specific term 'playing') in a host of spaces used also for other purposes. Sixteenth-century spectators might have seen plays in the great halls of palaces

[5] Janette Dillon, *The Cambridge Introduction to Early English Theatre* (Cambridge: Cambridge University Press, 2006), p. 148.

[6] Scott McMillin and Sally-Beth MacLean, *The Queen's Men and Their Plays* (Cambridge: Cambridge University Press, 1998).

[7] Andrew Gurr, *Playgoing in Shakespeare's London* (Cambridge: Cambridge University Press, 1987), pp. 136–7.

[8] Ruth Lunney, *Marlowe and The Popular Tradition in the English Drama before 1595* (Manchester: Manchester University Press, 2002), pp. 12, 38–51.

and manor houses, schools, colleges, and the academies of the London lawyers, the Inns of Court. They could have sat or stood in town halls, inn-yards, urban streets or rural churchyards, private gardens, or open fields to see biblical plays, saints plays, folk plays, interludes, moralities, contentious religious polemics, spectacular royal entries and ceremonial civic processions, humanist dramas, or revivals of the works of classical playwrights such as Plautus, Terence, and Seneca. And, as the century progressed, they might increasingly have been able to read the texts of some at least of the plays they had witnessed (or merely wished they had witnessed) in the privacy of their homes in printed editions.

This pre-playhouse drama was intimately connected to the groups and communities which produced and consumed it and the physical spaces in which it was performed. Indeed, even where entrance money was charged and some of the actors were paid, this was more obviously a communal than a commercial stage. The first three plays printed in this collection demonstrate the range of different communities that created and received drama in this period, and the types of drama they produced. The York pageant of *The Fall of the Angels* is the opening segment of the massive York Corpus Christi play, and is included here to give a sense of the scope and ambition of the religious drama produced by provincial towns and cities for much of the Tudor century. Designed by and for the civic community of the northern English city of York, it was performed annually on Corpus Christi day (probably a dozen or more times at different locations in the city streets) for at least a hundred and fifty years, until the play was finally suppressed by Protestant critics in the 1560s. It can thus legitimately claim to be the most popular and the longest lived of the plays included in this book, seen by more people over its performance life than ever saw *Hamlet* or *Tamburlaine* in the theatres. The second of the plays, Croxton's *The Play of the Sacrament*, is a drama intimately associated with the rural communities of fifteenth-century East Anglia. The surviving manuscript indicates a performance in the village of Croxton near Thetford in Suffolk, which may have been its regular home, or was possibly only one of a number of sites in which it was played around the county. Either way its name-dropping of local landmarks such as Babwell Mill, and its finale, in which actors and audience process into the local church, suggest the close connection between the play and its spectators' spiritual lives and worship. This was not escapist entertainment but an integral part of the life of the community.

Our third play, Henry Medwall's *Fulgens and Lucrece* (1490s), an example of that supremely flexible and versatile form of drama, the Tudor interlude, takes us indoors and to another kind of community, the aristocratic household: on this occasion that of the Cardinal Morton, for whom Medwall worked as a legal clerk or notary. The play shows every evidence of having been written for a community about which Medwall knew a great deal, both concerning its tastes, its sensitivities, and its sense of humour. It begins seemingly with two spectators berating the other guests for their rudeness in not thanking the Cardinal more vocally for the food that he has provided for them. These 'spectators' prove to be the characters A and B (so called as they were probably played by household members well known to the audience, and so didn't need 'play' names to identify them), but the episode reveals much, both about Medwall's confidence that he knew how far he could push his audience without really offending them, and about the occasion of the play, which was seemingly performed between what we would call lunch and dinner (but contemporaries called dinner and supper) on a feast day in the hall.

The play also reveals an acute awareness of, and attention to, the physical and symbolic topography of the hall in which it was played. Tudor halls varied in their dimensions and layout, but were fundamentally similar in their internal dynamics. These were generated by the relationship between the areas commonly known as the dais and the screens. The dais was a slightly raised area, frequently located at one end of the hall, on which the patron, his or her family, friends, and most honoured guests would sit to dine or watch a performance. The area around the dais was conventionally known as the 'high' end of the hall. Set against the dais symbolically, and frequently located opposite it at the other end of the room, were the screens, a partition masking a corridor leading to the outer doors and to the kitchens, storerooms, and other 'service' areas of the house. This partition, with its two doorways through which guests, servants, and performers would enter and leave the hall, was often also covered with a gallery for musicians, who might entertain the patron and their guests before, after, or during a meal or performance. In contradistinction to the dais, this area around the screens was popularly known as the 'low' end of the hall. Between screens and dais, along the other, longer sides of the room, were arranged benches and tables at which sat other guests, with those of highest status, or in greatest favour with the patron, nearest to the dais, and those of lesser note towards the screens. Around and behind the seated guests, and crowded in any free space around the screens doors, stood less favoured guests who were only there for the performance, servants attending upon the seated guests, other members of the household, and anyone else who wanted to see the show and had managed to inveigle his or her way in. In the middle of this space, in the rectangular area bounded by the benches to the sides and the dais and screens at either end, was the acting area for the interlude. This was generally referred to in play texts simply as the 'place', a seemingly loose appellation that nonetheless reveals a great deal about the acting styles and dramaturgy of this form of theatre. For this space was indeed just the place for acting. Bounded on all sides by a packed in, and no doubt demonstrative audience, and without major scenery or props to differentiate different locations in the hall (these would only come with the more lavish entertainments performed in college halls and the Inns of Court in the second half of the century) the early interludes made virtue of necessity and made no attempt to claim that the drama was set anywhere other than it actually was: in a hall full of spectators. So, even when the story is notionally set in ancient Rome, as *Fulgens and Lucrece* is, the characters nonetheless seem to have arranged to meet up in the here and now of Tudor England, to discuss their situation, before returning whence they came, through the screens doors, at the end of the show.[9]

The mixed yet hierarchically arranged audiences of the Tudor great halls provided playwrights such as Medwall with a wonderful resource to exploit. The interlude drama is thus full of incidents of comic or roguish characters pushing their way through the standing spectators at the screens end as they try to enter or leave the acting place, variously insulting them or claiming kinship with them as they go.[10] Characters habitually represent that section of the hall audience as a rowdy, raucous throng, there to enjoy the low comedy and vulgar spectacle, unlike the more dignified spectators seated on the benches, who are (probably equally playfully) addressed as if they were refined artistic connoisseurs, interested only in the serious intellectual and moral content of the play in hand. Medwall plays to these stereotypes perfectly, having his two comic servants step out from among the crowd standing around the screens seemingly to interrupt proceedings, while assuring the rest of the audience that the play will not suffer as a result of their intrusion. Indeed, B suggests, it might even be improved. The degree of playful irony inherent in this distinction between seated elite and standing vulgar viewers is, however, revealed when all alike are invited to enjoy the scatological pleasures of 'fart prick in cule', and are assumed to be all equally happy to do so.

[9] Greg Walker, 'The Cultural Work of Early Drama', in Beadle and Fletcher, *Cambridge Companion to Medieval English Theatre*, pp. 75–98.

[10] Greg Walker, *The Politics of Performance in Early Renaissance Drama* (Cambridge: Cambridge University Press, 1998), pp. 51–66.

STAGE BUSINESS

If theatre before the building of the playhouses was a matter for communal occasions, thereafter it was unequivocally a business, with its own novel rules of supply and demand. And audiences changed from communities to be served to markets to be courted and exploited. Before 1567, the demand for new plays was relatively modest. The great civic communities of the north and east of England and the more modest village audiences throughout the country seemed content to invest their energies in the annual performances of their own particular plays and those of their neighbours. Similarly the royal court, noble households, and colleges might commission a play from among their own number for feast days and festivals, supplementing these with visits from neighbouring players, or the touring commercial troupes that were regular visitors on well-established routes that criss-crossed the country. Those companies in turn might make do with a repertoire of around half a dozen plays that they could take with them on the road each year, alternating them to ensure they did not play the same one too many times at a given venue (unless, of course, they were asked to). Thus the company depicted in the affectionate parody of early Tudor practice in *The Play of Sir Thomas More* tells the hero that they have ready any one of seven interludes from which he can choose for the evening's performance, a set that may not have changed for years.[11]

After 1567, and still more obviously after 1576, when James Burbage, in collaboration with John Brayne, built a much more successful commercial playhouse, the Theatre, in Shoreditch, and others subsequently followed suit, the concentration of dramatic venues in and around the capital and the competition between them for a part of the same, albeit large, potential audience, called for a regular supply of new plays. This demand only increased when, in the early 1590s, the major acting companies settled themselves into specific playhouses (rather than progressing around the London venues), the Lord Admiral's Men at the Rose and the Lord Chamberlain's Men at the Theatre.[12] These companies developed their own regular clienteles, and so had to provide them with a varied repertoire of offerings, with the frequent addition of new material, if they were to keep them coming back on a weekly rather than a merely annual basis. The 1590s and 1600s thus saw the greatest demand for new material (of the 436 plays produced between 1560 and 1600 whose names we know, 266 were written in the 1590s),[13] a demand that was met by the rise of a new class of professional playwrights who, either individually or in collaboration, tried to feed this increasingly insatiable demand. But there is evidence that the problem of the new theatrical economy was identified much earlier, at a point when performances in London were still confined to inn-yards, houses, and other 'part-time' venues. For in 1572, an otherwise unknown writer, Rowland Broughton, was contracted to produce eighteen plays in the following thirty months (a seemingly impossible schedule which he indeed failed to deliver on): a sure sign that playing companies had identified a pressing new demand, and were seeking radical solutions to address it.[14]

By the late 1580s, then, English drama was for the first time primarily the preserve of theatres, professional playwrights, actors, and entrepreneurs rather than of the communities, part-time players, and largely peripatetic professional companies that had previously sustained it. But, although in many ways the professional playhouses mark a substantial departure in the nature

[11] William Shakespeare, *Sir Thomas More*, ed. John Jowitt (London: Arden Shakespeare, 2011).

[12] McMillin and MacLean, *The Queen's Men and Their Plays*, p. 6.

[13] Greg Walker, 'The Renaissance in Britain', in Patrick Collinson, ed., *The Short Oxford History of the British Isles: The Sixteenth Century* (Oxford: Oxford University Press, 2002), pp. 145–87, 155.

[14] McMillin and MacLean, *The Queen's Men and Their Plays*, p. 7.

and business of playing, in other respects they may have been less radically unsettling than we might assume. In their outward shape the playhouses may have gestured towards the circular theatres of the classical world, but in terms of their internal topographies of the stage and auditorium, in the Theatre, the Rose, and the Globe things were more domestic and familiar, echoing the special dynamics of the great hall playing spaces mentioned earlier. Both playhouse and hall relied upon what was essentially a thrust stage, bounded front and sides by seated and standing spectators, with a wall at the rear containing at least two doors through which actors might make their entrances and exits. Those doors had a substantial practical effect on the nature of the drama, allowing for the engineering of 'near misses' between characters who needed to be kept apart (the rival kings in *Tamburlaine*, the identical twins in *Errors*), with one character exiting one way as another arrives through the other door, and suggesting a stage area that was at the centre of a lively commerce between on- and offstage worlds, to which visitors and messages might come from rival directions, bringing news that would move on the plot, frustrate hopes, or suddenly resolve a dilemma. Similarly, in both the great hall and the playhouse, that rear wall was usually surmounted by a gallery in which musicians might be seated to play during the performance. So, while the administrative and commercial aspects of the theatre had changed fundamentally, the playhouse stages themselves, and the plays written for them, with their reliance on costume, rhetoric, and gesture rather than elaborate sets, and entrances and exits orchestrated through two doors, may have remained essentially familiar to spectators used to the great hall plays of aristocratic houses or colleges.

CRITICS OF THE DRAMA

The new theatres were not, of course, without their critics; many of whom represented the stage as the centre of new and chaotic practices. Such folk tended to criticize drama for what they claimed were two principal faults: one scholarly, its failure to conform to the classical principles of unity and decorum set out in Aristotle's *Poetics*, and the other ethical, its alleged scurrility and promotion of immorality. Both were objections of a fundamentalist kind, but each pointed in a different direction.

Writing in the 1580s, the poet and man of letters Sir Philip Sidney condemned contemporary playwrights on the first of those charges.

> All their plays be neither right Tragedies, nor right Comedies... [they] thrust in clowns by the head and shoulders to play a part in majestical matters, with neither decency nor discretion, so as neither the admiration and commiseration, nor the right sportiveness, is by their mongrel tragi-comedy obtained.[15]

In Sidney's neo-classicist view, tragedies should be consistently tragic and comedies comic, both in tone and content, so the kind of mingling of serious and comic matter evident in plays from *Fulgens and Lucrece* through to *The Comedy of Errors* (where the potentially tragic fate of Egeus frames the comic action) would have seemed to him an abomination, resulting in a mongrel drama that was neither one thing nor another. A handful of other scholars shared his concerns, but their views were always those of a minority divorced from actual dramatic practice. The mixing of styles and genres was the norm on Tudor stages, and always had been.[16] As Janette

[15] Sir Philip Sidney, *An Apology for Poetry*, ed. Geoffrey Shepherd (Manchester: Manchester University Press, 1973), p. 135.

[16] See Walker, 'The Renaissance in Britain', pp. 154–64.

Dillon has observed, 'generally, until well into the seventeenth century, the notion that different kinds of engagement belonged in different kinds of plays was alien' to Tudor playwrights,[17] even in the universities, where classically inflected works such as *Gammer Gurton's Needle* or *Damon and Pytheas* mixed high and low elements, clownage and majesty as vigorously as any popular interlude, appealing to spectators' emotions and bodies as well as to their minds. Indeed, as Kent Cartwright has shown, the most explicit defence of the 'mongrel' style against Sidney's strictures came not from a popular writer but from 'the premier academic playwright of the Elizabethan age', William Gager, in the preface to his Latin drama, *Ulysses Redux*, played at Christ Church, Oxford in 1592. There he justified his mixed style on the grounds that,

> Just as in living, so in writing my method is somewhat free and relaxed, a sort which pleases the learned less than the unskilled... For my part I have produced this tragedy, or play, or historical narrative, or whatever it is right and proper to call it, not according to the exacting standards of the *Art of Poetry* [the alternative title to Sidney's *Apology*], employed as some sort of goldsmith's balance, but rather have measured according to the exacting standards of popular taste, and I have poured it forth rather than composed it.[18]

It would be wrong, then, to take Sidney's eloquent exasperation at the mongrel nature of playhouse practice as speaking for any more than a minority of witnesses, even among scholars. Few if any of the spectators who crowded into the playhouses to watch *Titus Andronicus* are likely to have been troubled by the presence of the clownish messenger among the noble conspirators, just as they are unlikely to have worried greatly as the scene switched from Rome to the Goths' camp and back again in the course of the play, even though another of Sidney's objections was to the notion that different parts of the stage might represent different places, in clear defiance of the rules of geography and common sense. While entertaining in itself, Sidney's critique has little to tell us about the nature of the playhouse stage, for all his evident passion on the subject. And the same is true of much of the theologically driven criticism of its supposed immorality.

RELIGIOUS CHANGE AND DRAMATIC HISTORY

The middle of the Tudor century was probably the most turbulent period in English religious history. In the course of roughly forty years successive regimes instigated a series of changes to Church government, liturgy, and belief that overturned centuries of Catholic practice. First the government of Henry VIII (1509–47) removed the English Church from loyalty to Rome and made the king its supreme head, using this new authority to dissolve the monasteries, friaries, and nunneries, attack what it saw as abuses in the cults of the saints, pilgrimages, the use of images, and alter the number and interpretation of the sacraments. In the brief reign of Henry's successor, the boy king Edward VI (1547–53), further, more radical, Protestant reforms were introduced, dismissing the value of good works and prayers for the dead, denying the existence of purgatory and the central Catholic doctrine of transubstantiation. Under Edward's sister, the Catholic Queen Mary I (1553–8), these changes were reversed, obedience to Rome re-established, and doctrine and liturgy broadly returned to their pre-Reformation forms. Finally, following Mary's early death, in the reign of her sister Elizabeth I (1558–1603), the last and longest reigning

[17] Dillon, *Cambridge Introduction*, p. 157.

[18] Dana F. Sutton, ed. and trans., *William Gager: The Complete Works, ii: The Shrovetide Plays* (New York: Garland Press, 1994), p. 23, cited in Kent Cartwright, *Theatre and Humanism: English Drama in the Sixteenth Century* (Cambridge: Cambridge University Press, 1999), pp. 2–3.

Tudor monarch, a compromise Protestant settlement was re-imposed, the English Church was once more removed from Papal authority, and the Anglican Church established on essentially Calvinist lines.

The effects of these changes on the attitudes and beliefs of the generations of English men and women who lived through them can only be guessed at in most cases. Their effects upon artistic culture, and drama in particular, are, perhaps, clearer. In the post-Reformation period religious drama of all kinds became a political issue. For extreme reformers, the saturation of the urban cycle plays and moralities in the doctrines of good works and free will, the promotion of traditional beliefs and practices in the cycle plays, and their close association with the Catholic liturgy, made these plays entirely unacceptable in a reformed commonwealth. Equally, for traditionalists and more moderate Protestants, the polemical nature of Protestant drama, such as the work of John Bale, made it a liability at a time when central and local governments were struggling to control religious dissent and to promote conformity to the official doctrine of the moment. Hence central control and the eventual suppression of all religious drama became inevitable, with both the Marian and Elizabethan regimes banning the performing or publishing of plays that touched explicitly upon contentious matters of doctrine or religious practice. Thereafter discussion of spiritual issues had to be couched in secular terms, and references to divinity largely conducted through allusions to the classical gods, through euphemism and analogy.

Some reformers found even this new and supposedly unconfessional theatre unacceptable, however. Chief among their allegations was the charge of immorality. The playwright turned anti-theatrical pamphleteer Stephen Gosson voiced such objections in his *Plays Confuted in Five Actions* (1582), declaring boldly that,

> The groundwork of comedies is love, cozenage [*deceit*], flattery, bawdry, sly connivance and whoredom. The persons: cooks, queanes [*prostitutes*], knaves, bawds, parasites, courtesans, lecherous old men, [and] amorous young men.

Thus, even,

> the best play you can pick out is but a mixture of good and evil...The beholding of troubles and miserable slaughters that are in tragedies drive us to immoderate sorrow, heaviness, womanish weeping and mourning, whereby we become lovers of dumps [*depression*] and lamentation, both enemies to fortitude.[19]

Such criticism has led some modern scholars to detect a new sense of licentiousness and irresponsibility in the drama of the later Elizabethan period, marking it out from earlier plays. Kent Cartwright sums up the position in the form of a question,

> English drama at the beginning of the sixteenth century registers as allegorical, didactic, and moralistic, yet by the end of the century would be censured as emotional, fantasy-arousing, and even immoral. How could such a change occur?[20]

But the question is misleading, as it does not compare like with like. The observers for whom the early drama registers as didactic and moralistic are modern ones, while the censurers of the later plays were Tudor critics like Gosson. If we ask not what *we* make of the earlier drama but what its contemporaries made of it, then one finds religious critics making exactly the same objections to the moralistic plays of the 1500s as their successors made to the playhouse drama of the 1580s. Emotionalism, fantasy-arousal, and immorality were precisely the charges that critics levelled at

[19] Stephen Gosson, *Plays Confuted in Five Actions* (London, 1582), sig. C5 (verso).
[20] Cartwright, *Theatre and Humanism*, p. 1.

those Corpus Christi plays that might appear to modern eyes the epitome of pious, faith-filled performances. Thus the author of the fundamentalist tract, *A Treatise of Miracles Playing*, written probably in the later fourteenth century, denounced the performance of Passion plays as they evoked excessive weeping at the apparent suffering of the actor playing Christ rather than for the real sins of the spectators themselves, and encouraged indulgence in 'the lusts of the flesh and the mirth of the body', rather than a sober and penitent reflection on one's own fallen state.[21] Such fundamentalist, religiously inspired criticism was thus a constant through the Tudor century (and beyond) rather than a novel development of the 1580s.

It is drama itself, rather than any particular manifestation of it, that such religious fundamentalism finds troubling, precisely because of its capacity to expose dogma of all kinds to the uncertainties of performance and audience response. On stage any idea or truth-claim is forced to compete for spectators' attention and investment alongside other ideas and claims in an environment in which a multitude of values—spiritual, social, cultural, aesthetic, emotional, even comic—vie for valence and potency. Anyone who believes that certain truth-claims are so self-evidently true or primary that they must be protected from such challenges will always find their exposure in performance unacceptable, and articulate that view in moral and fundamental terms. Thus, for the author of the *Treatise*, having an actor perform Christ's Passion or his miracles was obviously a mockery of God, no matter how pious, faithful, or serious the inspiration behind the performance.

> Since [the] miracles of Christ and his saints were thus effectual (as by our belief we be certain), no man should use them in bourd [*play*] and play the miracles and works that Christ so earnestly wrought to our help, for whosoever does, he errs in belief, reverses [*contradicts*] Christ and scorns God.[22]

Gosson, writing two centuries later, repeats precisely the same injunction that no one should perform or watch the story of the Passion performed 'on the stage, where some base fellow that played Christ brings the person of Christ into contempt'.[23] Again the criticisms (in this case unchanging for two centuries) of an ideologically driven minority have little to tell us about the specifics of Tudor playhouse performances or their precursors or the attitudes of the majority of their audiences. For such evidence it is far more profitable to look to the plays themselves, their prologues, dialogue, and stage directions, which provide rich evidence of the assumptions of playwrights and companies about their own trade and the tastes and attitudes of their audiences.

THE ANTHOLOGY

This anthology will allow readers to look afresh at the riches of the long Tudor century of drama. The plays are printed in as close to chronological order of their first appearance as possible. But you are, of course, free to explore them in any order or combination, following your own tastes and inclinations. Those interested in plays which touch in various ways on contemporary political and social issues might find *Fulgens and Lucrece*, *Weather*, *Respublica*, *Cambises*, *Tamburlaine*, *The Three Ladies of London*, and *Titus Andronicus* a natural grouping to consider first. Those intrigued by the distinctive features of Tudor dramaturgy might wish to trace the presence of

[21] Greg Walker, *Medieval Drama: An Anthology* (Oxford: Blackwell, 2000), pp. 197–8, spelling modernized.
[22] Walker, *Medieval Drama*, p. 197.
[23] Gosson, *Plays Confuted*, sig. E6.

that most characteristic yet enigmatic Tudor stage figure, the Vice, from Merry Report in *Weather*, through his analogues in *Gammer Gurton's Needle*, *Respublica*, *Cambises*, and *The Three Ladies* to Aaron the Moor in *Titus*. Alternatively, a comparative study of the Croxton *Play of the Sacrament*, *Tamburlaine*, *Three Ladies*, *The Spanish Tragedy*, and *Titus* might provide the basis of an interesting investigation of Tudor attitudes to racial and regional otherness and prejudices of a number of kinds. Each of these last plays offers the promise of exoticisms of one sort or another, whether in the form of foreign locations (the court of Spain, the battlefields of Asia Minor, the streets of modern Turkey or ancient Rome) or of racial others (Jews, Moors, Italians, and Spaniards), but mixes that exoticism with local colour, in the form of recognizably English characters (a quack-doctor, village constables, country bumpkins, or London lawyers) and situations. This mixture of the exotic and the homely characterizes even the most domestic and provincial of the plays included here, *Gammer Gurton's Needle*, which finds room in its comic depiction of a Cambridgeshire village (itself quite exotic, perhaps, to some of its scholarly spectators), for the bizarre figure of Dicken the Bedlamite, whose knowledge of demonology and almost folkloric reputation for trickery does not seem to prevent him being a familiar and welcome visitor to the households he torments.

Many of the plays also provide insights into Tudor approaches to gender, whether in terms of the variations on heroic and unheroic masculinities represented in *Fulgens*, *Damon and Pythias*, *Endymion*, *Tamburlaine*, and *Errors*, or the various representations of high and low class, virtuous and variously flawed female figures in *Fulgens*, *Weather*, *Gammer Gurton*, *Respublica*, *The Three Ladies*, and *Errors*. Similarly, relations between the sexes are a significant theme of *Fulgens*, *Endymion*, *Tamburlaine*, *Three Ladies*, *The Spanish Tragedy*, and *Errors*. The Tudor stage was, of course, a stage without women, a theatre in which all of the female roles were representations generated by and refracted through male ideas and assumptions about what women want, what they should be, and what they actually are. It is not simply that such characters as Lucrece, Tamora the Goth, or Adriana of Ephesus are women who, owing to a quirk of contemporary theatrical practice, had to be acted by men until the Restoration, at which point they could emerge in their true colours in the hands of female actors. The fact that they would be acted on Tudor stages by men was a fundamental aspect of the process of their creation. Devised by male playwrights and performed by male actors, how these 'women' thought and spoke, how they behaved, even how they moved on stage, was based upon a set of cultural assumptions several stages removed from actual female experience. Thus when we hear Heywood's Laundress speak up boldly in support of hard-working women and criticize the pampered lifestyle of the Gentlewoman, or Adriana in *Errors* speak movingly of the anxieties and pressures of being a wife, we should resist the notion that this is an authentic insight into female experience in the period.[24] What it does reveal, most eloquently, is the range of attitudes that male writers could take to the representation of female experience, female agency, and character in this period, and the diversity of ways in which female characters could be presented to audiences.

Finally, the selection of plays should provide a sense of the sheer variety of ways in which the drama might address different audiences and issues, from the politicized interludes of the court and noble households to the commodified theatre of the playhouses, from the rich and demanding religious explorations of the York pageants and Croxton *The Play of the Sacrament*, to the holiday-humour humanism of school and college plays such as *Gammer Gurton* and *Damon and Pythias*. Some of the plays included here may, indeed, never have been performed at all, and may

[24] For a fascinating discussion of gender on an all-male stage, see Olga Taxidou, *Tragedy, Modernity and Mourning* (Edinburgh: Edinburgh University Press, 2004), pp. 19–20.

not have been designed to be. The two texts that are translations of Continental plays, for example, the anonymous *Everyman* and Jasper Heywood's *Thyestes*, each show some evidence of being produced for reading rather than performance. *Everyman*, a translation of the slightly earlier Dutch play *Elckerlijc* ('Everyone'), is included here not least to show that even the morality format allowed for a great deal of diversity. Unlike other examples of the genre such as *Mankind* or *Youth*, it has no comic vice figures to tempt the eponymous protagonist towards sin, and very little stage business to distract audiences from its theological 'message' that no one knows when death will come, so delaying concern for the health of one's soul may be a fatal error. A number of modern productions have shown that it can work very well on stage, but its first printer published it for sale as 'a treatise... in manner of a moral play', suggesting, perhaps, that he thought of it more as a moral dialogue for religious-minded readers than a script that actors might wish to perform. Similarly, Heywood's translation of Seneca's *Thyestes*, although it was influential in initiating the taste for Senecan tragedy on the playhouse stages that would lead to *The Spanish Tragedy*, *Titus Andronicus*, and *Hamlet*, may also have been intended as a scholarly exercise for the edification of like-minded readers, as its preparatory apparatus of commendatory epistles and verses 'from the translator of the book' might imply.

The Tudor century thus offers an extraordinarily rich dramatic legacy for readers, directors, and actors to explore. This anthology can only include a small sample of those riches, but it can gesture towards the wider picture. Its texts will touch upon the most abstruse questions of theology (what was there before there was Time?), the most sensitive of political issues (how should kings be advised?), and the most trivial of mundane concerns (the loss of a needle, the shaving of a drunken collier). They bring onstage figures and scenes that would have been very familiar to audiences from other aspects of their lives (the procedures of the English law courts, the debasement of the coinage, the small talk of farmers and craftsmen, or vulgar folk songs), and others which might have seemed very rich and strange (spectacular processions, fashionable courtly dances, acts of judicial or tyrannical punishment, the deeds of ancient heroes and potentates). At every turn they confound expectations of simplicity, didacticism, or dullness, revealing instead the kinds of vitality, vivacity, and willingness to challenge their spectators that must have excited their original audiences and kept them coming back for more. Hamlet's excitement at the arrival of the players in Elsinore reveals his own enthusiasm for their craft and for the repertoire of 'old' plays that they bring with them. I hope that the cross section of Tudor plays printed here suggests something of what it was that so moved him.

The York Pageant of *The Fall of the Angels*

(pre-1415–1569)

THE PLAY

The York *Corpus Christi Play* comprised up to forty-eight separate pageants, short playlets depicting individual episodes from the Old and New Testaments. Each pageant was sponsored and performed by one or more of the city's many trade and craft guilds, and performed on a separate pageant wagon (akin to a modern carnival float, and varying in complexity from a simple flat-topped cart to a flamboyant three-tiered representation of heaven, earth, and hell, depending upon the needs of the story and the wealth of the guild). As another name for 'craft' in this period was 'mystery', one also finds the York play, and other similar plays in northern and midland towns such as Chester, Wakefield, and Coventry, referred to as the 'mystery plays'. The York play is more properly termed a *Corpus Christi* play, though, as it was performed on Corpus Christi Day, the 'moveable' church feast falling on the first Thursday after Trinity Sunday (i.e. anywhere between 21 May and 24 June each year) which celebrates the miracle of the Mass, when, according to Catholic doctrine, the wine and bread of the Eucharist become literally the blood and body of Christ (*corpus Christi*). Its function was to represent and celebrate the body of Christ, both in the literal sense, by performing the life and sufferings of Jesus through the bodies of the various actors playing him in the New Testament pageants, and more symbolically in bringing together the civic community as a single body to perform and witness to their shared belief in the stories and doctrines represented.

The earliest full record of the play in the form we now have it comes from a civic document of 1415, but there is fragmentary and anecdotal evidence to suggest that the pageants were being performed from at least the later fourteenth century onwards. From that point they were played annually until the 1560s, when Protestants from the local church and civic authorities, troubled by the play's inherently Catholic underpinnings, brought about its suppression by the simple expedient of taking in the text for inspection and never returning it.

Beginning with an elliptical, theologically dense pageant representing the Creation and fall of Lucifer and the rebel angels (see below) and ending with the spectacular Last Judgement (representing Doomsday, the moment at the end of time when God would judge the living and the dead, sending the saved to heaven and the damned to hell for eternity), the York play made full use of the up to seventeen hours of daylight available on Corpus Christi Day to perform the whole of universal Christian history in a single day. The pageant wagons snaked their way in procession along a carefully planned route through the city, stopping at anything up to twelve separate stations or playing points, starting outside Holy Trinity Priory, near the city's south-western gate, Micklegate bar, and finishing on the Pavement, the central square at the heart of the city. Thus for one day each year the city became a huge living theatre, with pageants representing and mediating different aspects of Christian history through the streets from dawn to dusk.

When it was played at the first station at dawn (around 4.30 a.m.), *The Fall of the Angels* would have been able to make powerful use of the natural effects created by the rising of the sun as God divided the light from the darkness and gave life to the universe. The pageant, though brief, deals with some complex theological questions about the nature of time, space, and matter, and the chronology of creation both economically and lucidly (see Walker, 'In the Beginning'). It effectively counterpoints heavenly harmony, represented in the hymns of praise of the Good Angels, and hellish discord in the speeches of self-regard spoken by Lucifer and the Fallen Angels. Lucifer's rebellion is literally a thoughtcrime; no sooner does he voice his pride, but he falls into Hell (perhaps falling to street level by means of a trapdoor in the wagon, emerging through a lurid hell-mouth painted on the wagon-front) and is transformed into a devil (interrupting the eight-line stanza of the pageant with his stichomythic cries). As he complains at line 119, 'I said but a thought'. His crime is also an act of personification, an attempt to impersonate or resemble God—which begins a self-conscious exploration of the nature and aims of acting and pretence which runs through this and other civic cycle plays. The pageant was put on by the guild of Barkers (or Tanners), who prepared animal hides for manufacture into leather goods and so could provide the costumes and masks worn by the characters.

The York play was not printed in the Tudor period. I have used the facsimile of the surviving manuscript version in R. Beadle and P. Meredith, eds. *The York Play: A Facsimile of British Library Additional MS 35290, Together with a Facsimile of the Ordo Paginarum Section of the A/Y Memorandum Book* (Leeds: University of Leeds Publications, 1983) as the basis for this edition; and have consulted the modern editions by Beadle, Walker, and Beadle and King listed under further reading.

FURTHER READING

Beadle, Richard, *The York Plays: A Critical Edition of the York Corpus Christi Play* (2 volumes, London: Early English Text Society, 2009 and 2013).

—— and Alan J. Fletcher, eds., *The Cambridge Companion to Medieval English Theatre*, 2nd edn. (Cambridge: Cambridge University Press, 2008).

—— and Pamela M. King, *The York Mystery Plays: A Selection in Modern Spelling* Oxford World's Classics edn. (Oxford: Oxford University Press, 2009).

Davidson, Clifford, *From Creation to Doom: The York Cycle of Mystery Plays* (New York: AMS Press, 1984).

Happé, Peter, *English Drama Before Shakespeare* (Harlow: Longman, 1999).

King, Pamela M., *The York Mystery Cycle and the Worship of the City* (Cambridge: D. S. Brewer, 2006).

Walker, Greg, *Medieval Drama: An Anthology* (Oxford: Blackwell, 2000).

—— '"In the Beginning": Performing the Creation in the York *Corpus Christi Play*', in Thomas Betteridge and Greg Walker, eds., *The Oxford Handbook of Tudor Drama* (Oxford: Oxford University Press, 2012), 36–54.

[*Dramatis Personae:*

DEUS (God the Father),
TWO (GOOD) ANGELS (Cherubim and Seraphim),
TWO FALLEN ANGELS (Lucifer and Another).]

DEUS
Ego sum Alpha et O[mega]: vita,
Via, veritas, primus et novissimus.

I am gracious and great, God withouten beginning;
I am maker unmade, all might is in Me;
I am life and way unto wealth-winning;
I am foremost and first, as I bid, shall it be.
My blessing of blee shall be blending,
And hielding, fro harm to be hiding,
My body in bliss ay abiding,
Unending, withouten any ending.
Since I am maker unmade and most is of might,
And ay shall be endless and nought is but I,
Unto My dignity dear shall duly be dight
A place full of plenty to My pleasing at ply;
And therewith also will I have wrought
Many divers doings bedene,
Whilke work shall meekly contene,
And all shall be made even of nought.

But only the worthily work of My will
In My sprite shall inspire the might of Me;
And in the first, faithly, My thoughts to fulfil,
Banely in My blissing I bid that here be
A bliss all-bielding about Me,
In the whilke bliss I bide [th]at be here
Nine orders of angels full clear,
In loving ay-lasting at lout Me.

Tunc cantant angeli 'Te deum laudamus, te dominum confitemur'.

Here underneath Me now a nexile I neven,
Whilke isle shall be Earth. Now all be at once
Earth wholly, and Hell, this highest be Heaven,
And that wealth shall wield shall wone in these wones.
This grant I you, ministers Mine,
To-whiles ye are stable in thought,
And also to them that are nought
Be put to My prison at pine.

Of all the mights I have made, most next after Me
I make thee also master and mirror of My might;
I beild thee here banely in bliss for to be.
I name thee for Lucifer, also bearer of light.
Nothing here shall thee be dearing;
In this bliss shall be your bielding,
And have all wealth in your wielding,
Ay-whiles ye are buxomly bearing.

Tunc cantant angeli 'Sanctus, sanctus, sanctus, dominus deus sabaoth'.

1–2 **Ego . . . novissimus.** I am Alpha and Omega [the beginning and end], the life, the way, the truth, first and last. (Revelation 22:13, John 14:6.)
5 **way unto wealth-winning** access to happiness.
7 **My . . . blending** The blessing of My face will be shining.
8 **hielding . . . hiding** Radiating, shielding from harm.
13 **dight** ordained.
14 **to . . . ply** to shape to my pleasing.
16 **doings** deeds (i.e. the creation) completed.
17 **contene** continue.
18 **of nought** from nothing.
19–20 **But . . . Me** But only the precious labour of My will will be inspired in My spirit by My power.
22–23 **bid . . . Me** I order here to be about Me an all-protecting bliss [i.e. Heaven itself].
26 **at loute** to worship me.
26.1 **Tunc . . . confitemur'.** Then the angels sing "We praise Thee, God, we acknowledge Thee lord".
27 **nexile . . . neven** I speak into being a separate place/island.
28 **Whilke** Which.
30 **And . . . wones** And [all] who shall experience happiness shall live in these places.
31 **ministers mine** My servants.
32 **To-whiles** Whilst.
33 **to . . . nought** [I promise] to those who are evil that they shall . . .
34 **at pine** as a punishment.
35 **most next after** second only to.
39 **thee be dearing** harm you.
40 **your bielding** your dwelling place.
42 **Ay-whiles . . . bearing** All the time you are obedient.
42.1 **Tunc . . . sabaoth'.** Then the angels sing 'Holy, holy, holy, lord God of Hosts'.

FIRST ANGEL, SERAPHIM

Ah, merciful maker, full mickle is Thy might,
That all this work at a word worthily has wrought.
Ay loved be that lovely lord of His light,
That us thus mighty has made that now was right nought,
In bliss for to bide in His blessing.
Ay-lasting in love let us lout Him,
At bield us thus banely about Him,
Of mirth nevermore to have missing.

FIRST FALLEN ANGEL, LUCIFER

All the mirth that is made is marked in me!
The beams of my brighthood are burning so bright,
And I so seemly in sight myself now I see,
For like a lord am I left to lend in his light.
More fairer by far than my feers.
In me is no point that may pair;
I feel me fetous and fair,
My power is passing my peers.

ANGEL CHERUBIM

Lord, with a lasting love we love Thee alone,
Thou mightful maker that marked us and made us,
And wrought us thus worthily to wone in this wone,
There never filing of filth may full us nor fade us.
All bliss is here bielding about us.
To-whiles we are stable in thought
In the worship of Him that us wrought,
Of dear never there us more doubt us.

SECOND FALLEN ANGEL

O, what, I am fetous and fair and figured full fit!
The form of all fair-hood upon me is fixed;
All wealth in my wield is, I wote be my wit;
The beams of my bright-hood are bigged with the best.
My showing is shimmering and shining,
So bigly to bliss am I brought;
Me needs for to noy me right nought,
Here shall never pain me be pining.

ANGEL SERAPHIM

With all the wit that we wield we worship Thy will,
Thou, glorious God, that is ground of all grace;
Ay with steadfast steven let us stand still,
Lord, to be fed with the food of Thy fair face.
In life that is lelly ay-lasting,
Thy dale, lord, is ay daintily dealing,
And whoso that food may be feeling,
To see Thy fair face, is nought fasting.

FIRST FALLEN ANGEL, LUCIFER

Owe, certes, what I am worthily wrought with worship, iwis!
For in a glorious glee my glittering it gleams;
I am so mightily made my mirth may nought miss,
Ay shall I bide in this bliss through brightness of beams.
Me needs nought of noy for to neven,
All wealth in my wield have I wielding;
Above yet shall I be bielding,
On height in the highest of heaven.
There shall I set myself full seemly to sight,
To receive my reverence through right of renown;
Oh, what I am dear-worth and deft…

[*the rebel angels fall*]

[49] **At bield** To prosper.
[50] **to have missing** to lack.
[51] **marked** revealed.
[52] **brighthood** brightness.
[54] **lend** live.
[55] **feers** fellows.
[56] **point…pair** feature that may decay.
[57] **fetous** beautiful.
[58] **passing** surpassing.
[60] **marked** created.
[62] **never…us** no defiling of filth may corruptor diminish us.
[66] **Of…us** Of harm we need never have any fear.
[67] **figured full fit** very finely shaped.
[68] **fair-hood** beauty.
[69] **in my wield** under my control.
[70] **bigged with** as great as.
[71] **showing** appearance.
[72] **bigly** greatly.
[73] **Me…nought** I need not worry at all.
[74] **pain…pining** torment me.
[76] **ground** the foundation.
[77] **steven** voice.
[79] **lelly ay-lasting** truly everlasting.
[80] **Thy…dealing** Thy gift, Lord, is always generously given.
[81] **feeling** tasting.
[82] **nought fasting** not to go hungry.
[84] **glee** glow.
[85] **miss** fail.
[87] **Me…neven** I have no need to talk about harm.
[89] **Above…bielding** Still higher yet shall I be placed.
[93] **dear-worth and deft** worthy and noble.

...Oh! Deus! All goes down!
My might and my main is all marring
Help, fellows! In faith, I am falling.

SECOND FALLEN ANGEL

From Heaven are we hielding on all hand;
To woe are we wending, I warrant.

LUCIFER, DIABOLUS IN INFERNO

Out! Out! Harrow! Help, so hot it is here!
This is a dungeon of dole that I am to dight.
Where is my kind become, so comely and clear?
Now am I loathliest, alas, that ere was light.
My brightness is blackest and blue now,
My bale is ay beating and burning,
That gars one go gowling and gyrning.
Out! Ay wellaway! I well even in woe now.

SECOND DEVIL

Out! Out! I go wood for woe, my wit is all went now,
All our food is but filth we find us beforn.
We that were bielding in bliss, in bale are we
  burnt now.
Out on thee, Lucifer, lurdan, our light
  has thou lorn!
Thy deeds to this dole now has dight us,
To spill us thou was our speeder,
For thou was our light and our leader,
The highest of Heaven had thou hight us.

LUCIFER IN INFERNO

Wellaway! Woe is me now, now is it worse
  than it was!
Unthrivingly threep ye; I said but a thought.

SECOND DEVIL

Wee! Lurdan, thou lost us.

LUCIFER IN INFERNO

Ye lie! Out, alas!
I wist not this woe should be wrought!
Out on you, lurdans! Ye smore me in smoke.

SECOND DEVIL

This woe has thou wrought us.

LUCIFER IN INFERNO

Ye lie, ye lie!

SECOND DEVIL

Thou lies, and that shall thou buy!
We! Lurdans, have at you, let look!

CHERUBIM

A, lord, loved be Thy name that us this light lent,
Since Lucifer our leader is lighted so low,
For his unbuxomness in bale to be burnt.
Thy rightwiseness to reward on row
Ilke work after is wrought,
Through grace of Thy merciful might.
The cause I see it in sight,
Wherefore to bale he is brought.

DEUS

Those fools for their fairhood in fantasies fell,
And had main of My might that marked them
  and made them.
Forthy after their works were, in woe shall
  they well,
For some are fallen into filth that evermore shall
  fade them,
And never shall have grace for to girth them.
So passing of power them thought them,
They would not Me worship that
  wrought them;
Forthy shall My wrath ever go with them.

97 **hielding on all hand** tumbling down on all sides.
98 **wending** heading/travelling.
98.1 **in inferno** in the fire (of Hell).
99 **Out! Out! Harrow!** Alas! Help!
100 **dole** misery.
100 **to dight** appointed to.
101 **Where...clear?** What has become of my nature, once so comely and beautiful?
103 **blackest and blue** dark.
104 **ay beating** always kindling.
105 **gowling and gurning** howling and grimacing.
106 **Out! Ay wellaway!** Alas, O woe is me.
106 **well** wallow.
107 **go...woe** run mad with grief.
110 **Out on thee** Curse you.
110 **lurdan** villain.
110 **lorn** lost.
111 **has dight** have brought.
112 **To...speeder** You were the agent of our ruin.
114 **hight** promised.
116 **Unthrivingly threep ye** You chide [me] unhelpfully/unfairly.
119 **I...wrought!** I didn't know this would happen!
120 **smore** smother.
121 **that...buy** you'll pay for that.
122 **We!** Pah!
122 **let look!** look here.
124 **lighted** fallen.
125 **unbuxomness** disobedience.
125 **in bale** torment.
126-127 **Thy...wrought** Your justice [is] to reward every deed as it deserves.
131 **for their fairhood** because of their beauty.
132 **main of** power from.
133 **Forthy...were** Therefore, appropriate to their deeds.
135 **girth** shield.
136 **passing** excellent/superlative.

And all that Me worship shall wone here, iwis;
Forthy more forth of My work work now I will.
Since then their might is for-marred that ment
all amiss,
Even to Mine own figure this bliss to fulfil,
Mankind of mould will I make.
But first will I form him before
All thing that shall him restore,
To whilke that his talent will take.

And in my first making, to muster my might,
Since Earth is vain and void and mirkness emell,
I bid in My blissing ye angels give light
To the Earth, for it faded when the fiends fell.
In Hell shall never mirkness be missing.
The mirkness thus name I for night;
The day, that call I this light,
My after-works shall they be wissing.

And now in My blessing I twin them in two,
The night even from the day, so that they
meet never,
But either in a kind course their gates for to go.
Both the night and the day, do duly your dever,
To all I shall work be ye wishing.
This day work is done ilke a deal,
And all this work likes Me right well,
And bainly I give it My blessing.

140 **more forth** even more.
141–143 **Since . . . make.** Since the strength of these who intended evil is destroyed, in order to complete this bliss [i.e. to repopulate Heaven] . . . I shall make Mankind from the dust in My own image.
145 **restore** sustain.
146 **To . . . take.** To whatever his talents lead him.
147 **muster my might** demonstrate my power.
148 **vain . . . emell** empty and void, and everywhere in darkness.
152 **The . . . night** I name this darkness 'night'.
154 **My . . . wissing** By which they will know my later works.
155 **twin** divide.
157 **But . . . go** But each in their natural course to follow their own path.
158 **do . . . dever** duly do your duty.
159 **be ye wishing** you shall be (a) witness.
160 **ilke a deal** in every particular.

Croxton, *The Play of the Sacrament*

(1470–1530?)

THE PLAY

The Play of the Sacrament is the only surviving English example of a miracle play. More specifically it is one of the few surviving examples from Western Europe of a particular sub-genre of the miracle play, the anti-Semitic host-desecration play. In such plays the miracle of the mass and the transcendental truths of the Christian faith are represented in spectacular form when a consecrated host, the sacrament of the title, falls into the hands of a group or family of Jews who, in order to test whether it really is the body and blood of Christ as their Christian neighbours claim, subject it to a series of 'tortures'. The host confounds the Jews' doubts by responding to their attacks exactly as a human body would do, in some cases by bleeding so profusely that the blood floods out under a locked door and alerts the authorities, or, in this case, by symbolically repeating each of the events of Christ's passion in turn: being betrayed by the merchant Aristorius and handed over to the Jews, receiving the five wounds suffered by Christ on the Cross, being nailed to a post in a parodic crucifixion, being taken down and buried in an oven, and finally bursting forth once more in a symbolic resurrection, at each point subjecting the Jews, and their leader Jonathas in particular, to horrific injuries and humiliations.

Such plays are designed to demonstrate in the most spectacular and punitive ways the error of doubting the truth of the miracle of the Eucharist which stands at the heart of Catholic Christianity. Hence the repeated references here to the location and date of the miracle it represents (Heraclia in Aragon, in what is now eastern Spain, in 1461), which are a key part of its claim to authenticity as a narrative of Christian truth. But the Croxton play stands at a considerable remove from the more rebarbative European examples of the sub-genre. Most obviously, it ends, not in the massacre or brutal beating of the Jews, as happens in the surviving French and Italian versions, but in their conversion, in Christ's forgiveness and healing of Jonathas, and in a powerful demonstration of social unity as the newly converted Jews join the Christian characters and the members of the audience in a symbolic procession to the local parish church. Similarly the central characters are not the kinds of stereotyped 'good' Christians and 'bad' Jews that one might expect in an exercise in dramatic vilification. While Jonathas and his companions are subjected to some broad slapstick comedy, they are not without their dignity, while the Christian merchant, Aristorius, is in many ways the more problematic, morally compromised figure. The symbolic aim would seem to be a celebration of reconciliation within the community rather than the driving out of the scapegoat Jew.

As the central miracle celebrated in the play is that of the Mass, the play may have been intended, not as an attack on real Jews (of whom there were very few living openly in late-medieval or Tudor England) but to counter the heretical beliefs of a group of Christian heretics, the Lollards, who, among other unorthodox beliefs, denied the Real Presence of Christ in the host. The legend of the miraculous host is, however, a long-standing one, with versions circulating from as early as the 1430s which linked it with a number of different locations and dates.

At least one aspect of the play reflects another dramatic tradition, however. The comic double-act between the physician Master Branditch ('Brown-ditch') and his unruly servant Coll (whose name is both a diminutive form of 'Colin' and a slang form of '*cul*': arse) may reflect the folk traditions of the mummers' plays (but see Dutton, below, for an alternative view). A quack doctor frequently appeared in these locally produced fertility dramas to resurrect the hero or his adversary after he had been slain in combat. And a similar delight in comic lists of unlikely sounding cures and medicines seems to have been central to their performances too (for the mummers' plays see Axton, Brody, and Chambers, below). The inclusion of this scene may well reflect an attempt to tailor the play for a specifically English rural audience. The episode is not entirely irrelevant to the surrounding drama, however. Whereas Master Branditch brings only a parody of healing, Christ the true 'medicine for the soul' offers the real thing. Jonathas's immediate rejection of Branditch, then, acts as a foreshadowing of his later conversion by Christ.

The play was almost certainly intended for performance outdoors, probably in a town square or on a village green or in a churchyard. The text seems to require sizeable structures to represent the homes of Aristorius and Jonathas, and another to represent the parish church, with all the traffic between these locations occurring in the space in between them, referred too throughout simply as 'the place'. If the performance took place in the churchyard or close by, however, the local church itself could be used instead of the last structure, adding considerable resonance to the final scene in which the Bishop leads everyone in procession behind the Host to the altar. The text also calls for a number of spectacular special effects, including a bleeding host, a cauldron running with blood, and an exploding oven, each of which would have required a substantial investment from any company wishing to perform the play. Most spectacular of all, perhaps, and certainly the most difficult to interpret, is the call for an 'image' of the wounded Christ to emerge from the oven and speak. Whether this would have been a mechanical prop or an actor is unclear.

The play is conventionally associated, on the strength of the reference to a performance 'at Croxton' in the banns, with the village of Croxton near Thetford in Suffolk (the nearest of several Croxtons in East Anglia to Babwell Mill, near Bury St Edmunds, which is also mentioned in the text). But it may well have been designed for touring, and for performance by one or more companies in and around East Anglia. The banns themselves, and the claim that 'Nine may play it at ease' attached to the cast list suggest the play's adaptability to the differing demands of touring troupes. It cannot be accurately dated, but the repeated claim that the events depicted took place in 1461 provides a reliable earliest date for its composition. The surviving manuscript is mid-Tudor, and may date from the reign of Mary I, when traditional Catholic beliefs were briefly restored after the radical protestant experiments of Edward VI's reign. But the fact that someone copied out of a fair copy of the script at this time need indicate no more than a desire to record for posterity an important part of the region's Catholic heritage. The play itself seems rather earlier in tone and approach, and probably dates to the period in the later fifteenth or early sixteenth century, before the arrival of new ideas such as Erasmian scepticism and Reformation doctrinal debates would have made some of its apparent faith in spectacle as a medium of truth more problematic.

For all its idiosyncrasies, however, the play does point to other dramatic movements and genres of both earlier and later periods. As we have seen, there is at least a passing allusion to the mummers' plays in the double act of Branditch and his boy, and that kind of fluid, 'street' theatre in which actors would simply step out in front of the crowd and begin performances does seem evident elsewhere in the play. It begins, indeed, with an actor literally 'putting on' the role of

Aristorius as he speaks to the crowd. He begins talking in what seems to be his own persona, greeting the spectators and blessing them, 'Now Christ, that is our Creator, from shame he cure [*save*] us; / He maintain us with mirth that move upon the mould [*the earth*]; / Unto his endless joy might he restore us, / All those that in his name in peace well them hold'. And then moves to tell them about the merchant who is to be the subject of the play in the third person, 'For of a merchant most mighty thereof my tale is told; / In Heraclea is none such, whoso will understand'. But in the very next line he moves from the third to the first person, and, no doubt with a suitable gesture, *becomes* that merchant: 'For of all Aragon I am most mighty of silver and of gold' (ll. 1–7, see Dutton 2012), and proceeds from that point onwards in role. There are also pointers in the play to later drama, for Jonathas displays many of the anti-Semitic traits, and some of the theatrical complexities, that characterize later, better known, Jewish characters such as Marlowe's Barabas (*The Jew of Malta*) and Shakespeare's Shylock (*The Merchant of Venice*).

The play is preceded by the surviving set of banns, the brief advertisement which would tour the local villages in the days before a performance, drumming up interest ahead of the show.

The play text was not printed in the Tudor period, and survives in a single manuscript now in the library of Trinity College Dublin (TCD MS F.4. 20, ff. 338r–356r). For this edition I have used the facsimile in Norman Davis, ed., *Non-Cycle Plays and the Winchester Dialogues* (Leeds: Leeds University Publications, 1979), and have consulted the modern critical editions noted under further reading.

FURTHER READING

Axton, Richard, *English Drama of the Early Middle Ages* (London: Hutchinson University Library, 1974).

Bevington, David, ed., *Medieval Drama* (Boston: Houghton Mifflin, 1975).

Brody, A., *The English Mummers and Their Plays* (London: Routledge and Kegan Paul, 1970).

Chambers, E. K., *The Medieval Stage*, 2 vols. (Oxford: Oxford University Press, 1903).

Coldewey, John C., ed., *Early English Drama: An Anthology* (New York and London: Routledge, 1993).

Davis, Norman, ed., *Non-Cycle Plays and Fragments*, EETS S.S. 1 (Oxford: Early English Text Society, 1970).

Dillon, Janette, *The Cambridge Introduction to Early English Theatre* (Cambridge: Cambridge University Press, 2006).

Dutton, Elizabeth, 'The Croxton *Play of the Sacrament*' in Thomas Betteridge and Greg Walker, eds., *The Oxford Handbook of Tudor Drama* (Oxford: Oxford University Press, 2012), 55–71.

Lawton, David, 'Sacrilege and Theatricality: The Croxton *Play of the Sacrament*', *Journal of Medieval and Early Modern Studies*, 33 (2003): 281–309.

McMurray Gibson, Gail, *The Theatre of Devotion: East Anglian Drama and Society in the Late Middle Ages* (Chicago: University of Chicago Press, 1989).

Walker, Greg, '"And Here's Your Host...": Jews and Others in the Croxton *Play of the Sacrament*', in James Jordan, Tony Kushner, and Sarah Pearce, eds., *Jewish Journeys: From Philo to Hip Hop* (London: Valentine Mitchell, 2010), 47–65.

—— ed., *Medieval Drama: An Anthology* (Oxford: Blackwell, 2000).

The Names and Number of the Players

TWO VEXILLATORS ['flag-bearers', who appear only in the banns],
JESUS,
EPISCOPUS (a bishop),
ARISTORIUS, CHRISTIANUS MERCATOR ['Aristorius, a Christian Merchant'],
[PRESBITER,] ['a Priest': Isidore, chaplain to Aristorius],
CLERICUS ['Clerk': Peter Paul, servant to Aristorius],
JONATHAS, JUDEUS PRIMUS, MAGISTER ['the first Jew, Master'],
JASON, JUDEUS SECUNDUS ['the second Jew'],
JASDON, JUDEUS TERCIUS ['the third Jew'],
MASPHAT, JUDEUS QUARTUS ['the fourth Jew'],
MALCHUS, JUDEUS QUINTUS ['the fifth Jew'],
MAGISTER PHISICUS ['the Master Physician', Master Branditch of Brabant],
COLL, SERVUS ['Coll, the servant' (to Branditch)]

PRIMUS VEXILLATOR [*The Banns.*]
Now the Father and the Son and the Holy Ghost,
That all this wide world hath wrought,
Save [all] these seemly, both least and most,
And bring you to the bliss that He hath you to-bought!
We be full purposed, with heart and with thought,
Of our matter to tell the intent,
Of the marvels that were wondrously wrought
Of the Holy and Blessed Sacrament.
SECUNDUS VEXILLATOR
Sovereigns, and it like you to hear the purpose of this play
That [is] represented now in your sight,
Which in Aragon was done, the sooth to say,
In Heraclea, that famous city, aright:
Therein woneth a merchant of mickle might:
Sir Aristory was called his name,
Kenned full far with many a wight;
Full far in the world sprang his fame.
I [VEXILLATOR]
Anon to him there came a Jew,
With great riches for the nonce,
And woneth in the city of Surrey (this full true!)
The which had great plenty of precious stones.

3 **Save... most** [May God] save all these elegant (folk: i.e. the audience), both the highest and the lowest.
4 **you to-bought** bought for you.
5 **We... purposed** We fully intend.
6 **matter** story.
6 **intent** essence.
9 **Sovereigns... play** My masters, if you would like to hear the nature of this play.
11 **Aragon** The kingdom of Aragon in the east of modern Spain.
11 **the... say** to tell (you) the truth.
12 **aright** truly.
13 **woneth** lived.
13 **mickle might** great power.
15 **Kenned... wight** Known widely by many a person.
18 **for the nonce** at that time.
19 **Surrey** Syria.

Of this Christian merchant he freyned sore,
When he would have had his intent:
Twenty pounds and merchandise more,
He proffered for the Holy Sacrament.

II [VEXILLATOR]
But the Christian merchant thereof said nay,
Because his proffer was of so little value;
An hundred pounds but he would pay,
No longer thereon he should pursue.

But more of their purpose they gan speak,
The Holy Sacrament for to buy;
And all for the would be wreck,
A great sum of gold began down lay.

I [VEXILLATOR]
This Christian merchant consented, the sooth to say,
And in the night after, made him deliverance,
These Jews all great joy made they.
But of this betide a stranger chance:

They grieved Our Lord greatly on ground,
And put him to a [new] Passion;
With daggers gave him many a grievous wound;
Nailed him to a pillar; with pincers plucked him down.

II [VEXILLATOR]
And sith they took that blessed bread so sound
And in a cauldron they did him boil!
In a cloth full just they it wound,
And so they did him seethe in oil.

And then they put him to a new tormentry:
In a hot oven speared him fast.
There he appeared with wounds bloody;
The oven rove asunder and all to-brast.

I [VEXILLATOR]
Thus in our law they were made steadfast;
The Holy Sacrament showed them great favour.
In contrition their hearts were cast.
And went and showed their lives to a confessor.

21 **freyned sore** earnestly begged.
22 **When ... intent** When he tried to get what he wanted.
27–28 **An ... pursue** Unless he would pay £100, he would not take the matter further.
29 **gan** began (to).
31 **And ... wreck** And all because they wished to be revenged (upon Christ).
32 **down lay** (they) laid down.
34 **made him deliverance** he delivered (the Sacrament).
36 **But ... chance** But a far stranger event resulted from this.
37 **on ground** in (that) place.
43 **full just** very tightly.
44 **seethe** boil.
45 **tormentry** torment.
46 **speared** locked.
48 **rove** split.
48 **to-brast** burst.
52 **And ... confessor.** And went and confessed (the sins of) their (former) lives to a confessor (i.e. a priest).

Thus by miracle of the King of Heaven,
And by might and power given to the priest's mouth,
In an household were countered, iwys, eleven.
At Rome this miracle is known well couth.

II [VEXILLATOR]
This miracle at Rome was presented, forsooth,
In the year of our Lord 1461,
That the Jews with Holy Sacrament did woth,
In the forest said of Aragon.

Lo, thus God at a time showed him there,
Through his mercy and his mickle might;
Unto the Jews he gan appear
That they should not less his heavenly light.

I [VEXILLATOR]
Therefore, friends, with all your might
Unto your ghostly father show your sin.
Beth in no wanhope, day nor night;
No manner of doubts that Lord put in;

For that the doubts the Jews then in stood;
As ye shall see plead both more and less,
Was if the Sacrament were flesh and blood,
Therefore they put it to such distress.

II [VEXILLATOR]
And it please you, this gathering that here is,
At Croxton on Monday it shall be seen.
To see the conclusion of this little process,
Heartily welcome shall you been.

Now Jesu you save from trey and teen,
To send us his high joys of Heaven.
There might is withouten mind to mean.
Now, minstrel, blow up with a merry steven!

Explicit. *Here ends (the banns)*

55 **In . . . eleven** In one household, I know, eleven (people) were converted (to Christianity).
56 **well couth** very well known.
59 **woth** attack.
60 **said** aforesaid.
61 **Him** Himself.
63 **gan** did.
64 **less** lose.
66 **Unto . . . sin** Confess your sin to your spiritual father (i.e. your priest).
67 **Beth** Be.
67 **wanhope** despair.
68–72 **No . . . distress** Entertain no doubts about that Lord; for it was because the Jews doubted whether the Sacrament was (really his) flesh and blood that they harmed it so, as you, both high and low, shall see played (here).
73 **And** If.
75 **little process** short narrative.
76 **been** be.
77 **trey and teen** trouble and pain.
79 **withouten . . . mean** beyond the capacity of human thought to describe.
80 **steven** voice/noise.

Hereafter followeth the Play of the Conversion of Sir Jonathas the Jew by Miracle of the Blessed Sacrament.

ARISTORIUS MERCATOR

Now Christ, that is our Creator, from shame he cure us;
He maintain us with mirth that move upon the mould;
Unto his endless joy might he restore us,
All those that in his name in peace well them hold.
For of a merchant most mighty thereof my tale is told;
In Heraclea is none such, whoso will understand.
For of all Aragon I am most mighty of silver and of gold;
For, and it were a country to buy, now would I not wond!

Sir Aristory is my name,
A merchant mighty, of a royal array.
Full wide in this world springeth my fame,
Far kenned and known, the sooth for to say.
In all manner of lands, without any nay,
My merchandise runneth, the sooth for to tell:
In Genoa, and in Jenise, and in Geneway,
In Surrey, and in Saby, and in Salerno I sell;

In Antioch and in Alamain much is my might,
In Brabant and in Britain I am full bold,
In Calabria and in Cologne there range I full right,
In Dordrecht and in Denmark, by the cliffs cold;
In Alexandria I have abundance in the wide world.
In France and in Faro fresh be my flowers,
In Geldre and in Galice have I bought and sold,
In Hamborough and in Holland much merchandise is ours;

In Jerusalem and in Jericho among the Jews gentle,
Among the Chaldees and Catalans kenned is my coming;
In Raynes and in Rome to Saint Peter's temple
I am known certainly for buying and selling;

In Main and in Milan full merry have I been;
Out of Naverne to Naples much good is that I bring;
In Ponder and in Portingale much is my glee;
In Spain and in Spruce much is my speeding;

1 **he cure** (may) he save.
2 **move...mould** we who move upon the earth.
8 **For...wond!** For I would not hesitate to buy anything, even if it was a (whole) country!
10 **array** appearance.
12 **Far kenned and known** known far and wide.
13 **without any nay** without denial.
14 **runneth** is carried.
15 **Jenise** perhaps Génissac, near Bordeaux (France) and **Geneway** Geneva (Switzerland).
16 **Surrey** Syria, **Saby** Saba (an ancient city in pre-Islamic Arabia), **Salerno** (Italy).
17 **Antioch**, now Antakya in modern Turkey, **Almain** Germany.
23 **Geldre** Gelderland (Netherlands), **Galice** Galicia (Spain).
24 **Hamborough** Hamburg.
27 **Raynes** Reims (France).
30 **Naverne** the kingdom of Navarre (now part of France).
31 **Ponder** perhaps Pontevedra (Spain) and **Portingale** Portugal.
32 **Spruce** Prussia.
32 **speeding** prospering.

In Lombardy and in Lachborn, there led is my liking;
In Taryse and in Turkey, there told is my tale;
And in the Dukedom of Orion much have I in wielding:
And thus throughout all this world set is my sail.

No man in this world may wield more riches;
All I thank God of his grace, for he that me sent.
And as a lord's peer thus live I in worthiness,
My curate waiteth upon me to know mine intent,
And men at my wielding; and all is me lent
My will for to work in this world so wide,
Me dare they not displease by no condescent.
And whoso doth, he is not able to abide.

PRESBITER

No man shall you tarry ne trouble this tide,
But every man diligently shall do you pleasance;
And I unto my cunning to the best shall them guide
Unto God's pleasing to serve you to attreance.
For ye be worthy and notable in substance of good[s];
Of merchants of Aragon ye have no peer;
And thereof thank God that died on the Rood,
That was your Maker, and hath you dear.

ARISTORIUS

Forsooth, sir priest, your talking is good!
And therefore, after your talking I will attain
To worship my God that died on the Rood.
Never, while that I live, against that will I sayen.
But, Peter-Paul, my clerk, I pray thee go well plain
Throughout all Heraclea, that thou nay wond,
And wit if any merchant be come to this reign
Of Surrey or of Saba or of Shellisdown.

CLERICUS

At your will for to walk I will not say nay,
Smartly to go search at the water's side.
If any pleasant bargain be to your pay,
As swiftly as I can I shall him to you guide.
Now will I walk by these paths wide
And seek the haven, both up and down,

[33] **Lachborn** Luxembourg.
[34] **Taryse** perhaps Tharsia, or the biblical Tarsus (Asia Minor) or Tharshish.
[35] **Orion** perhaps Orléans (France).
[35] **much . . . wielding** I exercise great influence.
[41] **wielding** command.
[41] **all . . . lent** all (power) is given to me.
[43] **condescent** means.
[45] **tarry** delay.
[45] **tide** time.
[47] **And . . . guide** And I shall instruct them to the best of my wit/ability.
[48] **to attreance** at (your) command.
[51] **Rood** Cross.
[52] **hath** holds.
[54] **attain** endeavour.
[56] **sayen** speak.
[57] **go well plain** go without hesitation.
[58] **nay wond** do not delay.
[59] **wit** discover.
[59] **reign** realm.
[60] **Shellisdown** from, perhaps, Chelidonia (Lycia) or 'Calis-town' (Calais).
[63] **to your pay** pleasant for you.
[64] **him . . . guide** bring to you whoever offers it.
[66] **seek the haven** search the harbour.

To wit if any uncouth ships therein do ride
Of Surry or of Saba [or] of Shellisdown.

Now shall the merchant's man withdraw him, and the Jew Jonathas shall make his boast.

JONATHAS
Now, almighty Mahomet, mark in thy majesty,
Whose laws tenderly I have to fulfil,
After my death bring me to thy high see
My soul for to save, if it be thy will;
For mine intent is for to fulfil,
As my glorious god thee to honour.
To do against thy intent it should grieve me ill,
Or against thine law for to report.

For I thank thee highly, that hast me sent
Gold, silver and precious stones;
And abundance of spices thou hast me lent,
As I shall rehearse before you once:
I have amethysts rich for the nonce,
And beryls that be bright of blee,
And sapphire seemly, I may show you at once,
And Crystals clear for to see;

I have diamonds dear-worthy to dress,
And emeralds, rich I trow they be;
Onyx and agates both more and less,
Topazoons, smaragdies of great degree,
Pearls precious great plenty;
Of rubies rich I have great renown;
Crepalds and chalcedonies seemly to see,
And curious carbuncles here ye find mown.

Spices I have both great and small
In my ships, the sooth for to say:
Ginger, liquorice, and galingale,
And figs fat to please you to pay,
Pepper and saffron and spices small,
And dates whole, dulcet for to dress,
Almonds and rice, full every male;
And raisins both more and less;

67 **To . . . therein** To find out if any foreign ships ride (at anchor) there.
69 **Mahomet** a corruption of 'Mohammed', assumed here to be the god of the Jews.
69 **mark** distinguished.
70 **tenderly** diligently.
71 **see** seat/dwelling.
75 **ill** terribly.
76 **report** speak.
81 **for the nonce** now/ready at hand.
82 **blee** appearance.
85 **dear-worthy to dress** precious to set (in jewellery).
88 **Topazoons, smaragdies** Topazes, emeralds.
91 **Crepalds** Toadstones.
92 **find mown** may find.
98 **dulcet for to dress** sweet to prepare.
99 **male** sack.

Cloves, grains, and ginger green,
Mace, mastic that might is,
Cinnamon, sugar, as you may seen;
Long pepper, and Indies liquorice,
Oranges and apples of great a-price,
Pomegranates and many other spices,
To tell you all I have now, iwys,
And much other merchandise of sundry spices.

Jew Jonathas is my name;
Jazon and Jazdon they waiten on my will,
Masphat and Malchus they do the same,
As ye may know, it is both right and skill.
I tell you all, by dale and by hill
In Heraclea is no one so much of might,
Wherefore, ye owe tenderly to tend me till,
For I am chief merchant of Jews, I tell you by right.

But Jazon and Jazdon, a matter would I mean;
Marvellously it is meant in mind:
The belief of these Christian men is false, as I ween,
For they believe on a cake: me think it is unkind,
And all they say how the priest doth it bind,
And by the might of his word make it flesh and blood,
And thus by a conceit they would make us blind;
And how that it should be he that died upon the Rood.

JASON

Yea, yea, master, a straw for tales
That may not fall in my belief;
But, might we it get once within our pales,
I trow we should soon after put it in a proof.

JASDON

Now, by Mahomet so mighty, that ye done of move:
I would I wist how that we might it get!
I aver by my great God, and else mote I not 'chieve,
But wightly thereon would I be wreck!

[101] **grains** Grains of Paradise (*Amomum Meleguetta*).

[102] **mastic...is** strong gum-mastic.

[104] Long pepper is made from *Piper officinarum* (Davies, *Non-Cycle Plays*, p. 153).

[112] **skill** reasonable.

[113] **by...hill** i.e. everyone, wherever they live.

[115] **ye...till** you ought to listen attentively to me.

[117] **mean** mention.

[118] **it...mind** it sticks in my mind.

[119] **ween** think.

[120] **they...cake** they believe in a cake (i.e. the bread of the host), and that's unnatural.

[121] **bind** conjure.

[123] **conceit** trick.

[124] **how** (try to convince us) that.

[125-126] **straw...belief** I wouldn't give a straw for such unbelievable tales!

[127] **might...pales** if we could once get it (the Host) into our hands.

[128] **in a proof** to the test.

[129] **that...move** that which you talk of.

[130] **I...wist** I wish I knew.

[131] **aver** swear.

[131] **and...'chieve** or else may I never thrive.

[132] **wightly...wreck!** I'd eagerly be revenged on it (the Host)!

MASPHAT
Yea, I dare say faithfully that their faith [is false]:
That was never he that on Calvary was killed!
Or in bread for to be blood, it is untrue als'.
But yet with their wiles they would we were wiled.

MALCHUS
Yea, I am mighty Malchus, that boldly am built.
That bread for to beat bigly am I bent!
Once out of their hands and it might be exiled,
To help casten it in care would I consent.

JONATHAS
Well, sirs, then keep counsel I command you all,
And no word of all this be wist.
But let us walk to see Aristory's hall,
And afterward more counsel among us shall caste.
With him to buy and to sell I am of power prest;
A bargain with him to make I will assay.
For gold and silver I am nothing aghast
But that we shall get that cake to our pay.

Here shall Sir Isidore, the priest, speak onto Sir Aristory, saying on this wise to him; and Jonathas go down off his stage.

PRESBITER
Sir, by your leave, I may [no] longer dwell.
It is far past noon; it is time to go to church,
There to say mine evensong; forsooth as I you tell,
And sith come home again, as I am wont to work.

ARISTORIUS
Sir Isidore, I pray you walk at your will,
For to serve God it is well done.
And sith come again, and ye shall sup your fill,
And walk then to your chamber as ye are wont to doon.

Here shall the merchant men meet with the Jews.

JONATHAS
Ah, Peter-Paul, good day and well i-met!
Where is thy master, as I thee pray?

CLERICUS
Long from him have I not let
Sith I came from him, the sooth for to say.

135 **als'** also.
136 **they . . . wiled** they want us to be tricked.
138 **That . . . bent!** I'm determined to beat that bread!
139 **Once . . . exiled** If it might once be taken out of their hands.
140 **casten . . . care** cast it into torment.
141 **keep counsel** keep this secret.
142 **wist** known.
144 **more . . . caste** more discussion shall we have.
145 **prest** well capable.
146 **assay** attempt.
147–8 **For . . . pay.** I have no doubt that for gold and silver we will get that cake into our hands. (s.d.) **on this wise** in this way.
149 **dwell** stay.
152 **sith** then.
152 **as . . . work** as is my habit.
153 **at your will** as you please.
157 **well i-met!** Well met! (a greeting).
159–160 **Long . . . him** It's not been long since I left him.

What tiding with you, sir, I you pray,
After my master that ye do frain?
Have ye any bargain that were to his pay?
Let me have knowledge; I shall wit him to sayen.

JONATHAS

I have bargains royal and rich
For a merchant with to buy and sell;
In all this land is there none like
Of abundance of good, as I will tell.

Here shall the clerk go to Sir Aristory, saluting him thus:

CLERICUS

All hail master, and well mote you be!
Now tidings can I you tell:
The greatest merchant in all Surrey
Is come with you to buy and sell;
This tale right well he me told.
Sir Jonathas is his name,
A merchant of right great fame;
He would sell you, without blame,
Plenty of cloth of gold.

ARISTORIUS

Peter-Paul, I can thee thank!
I pray thee, richly array mine hall
As oweth for a merchant of the bank.
Let none default be found at all.

CLERICUS

Sickerly, master, no more there shall!
Stiffly about I think to stir,
Hastily to hang your parlour with pall
As longeth for a lord's peer.

Here shall the Jew merchant and his men come to the Christian merchant.

JONATHAS

All hail, sir Aristory, seemly to see,
The mightiest merchant of Aragon!
Of your welfare fain wit would we,
And to bargain with you this day am I bound.

ARISTORIUS

Sir Jonathas, ye be welcome unto mine hall!
I pray you come up and sit by me,

162 **frain** ask.
163 **to his pay** pleasing to him.
164 **I . . . sayen** (then) I'll know what to tell him.
169 **mote** might (i.e. good health to you!).
176 **blame** doubt.
180 **oweth for** befits.
181 **none default** no defect.
182 **Sickerly** Surely.
183 **Stiffly . . . stir** I'll set myself vigorously to the task.
184 **pall** fine tapestries/hangings.
185 **longeth** befits.
186 **seemly to see** splendid in appearance.
188 **Of . . . we** We are eager to know of your welfare (i.e. how are you?)

And tell me what goods ye have to sell,
And if any bargain made may be.

JONATHAS
I have cloth of gold, precious stones, and spices plenty.
With you a bargain would I make;
I would barter with you in privity.
One little thing, ye will me it take
Privily in this stound;
And I will sure you, by this light,
Never distrain you, day nor night,
But be sworn to you full right,
And give you [twenty pounds].

ARISTORIUS
Sir Jonathas, say me for my sake:
What manner of merchandise is that [ye] mean?

JONATHAS
Your God, that is full mighty, in a cake!
And this good anon shall you seen.

[ARISTORIUS]
Nay, in faith, that shall not been!
I will not for an hundred pound
To stand in fear my Lord to teen;
And for so little a value in conscience to stand bound!

JONATHAS
Sir, the intent is, if I might know or undertake
If that he were God Almight;
Of all my miss I will amend make
And doon him worship both day and night.

ARISTORIUS
Jonathas, truth I shall thee tell:
I stand in great doubt to do that deed;
To you that bear all for to sell,
I fear me that I should stand in dread!
For, and I unto the church yede,
And priest or clerk might me espy,
To the bishop they would go tell that deed,
And appeach me of heresy.

JONATHAS
Sir, as for that, good shift may ye make,
And, for a veil, to walken on a night

196 **in privity** privately.
198 **stound** place.
199 **sure** assure.
199 **by this light** (a mild oath.)
200 **distrain you** to oppose you.
201 **full right** completely.
203 **say** tell.
209 **to . . . teen** risk angering my Lord.
213 **Of . . . make** (If he were) I would make amends for all my sins.
216 **doubt** fear.
219 **and** if.
219 **yede** go.
222 **appeach** impeach/accuse.
223 **shift** provision (i.e. you can take precautions).
224 **for . . . night** to conceal the deed, do it at night.

When priest and clerk to rest been take;
Then shall ye be spied of no wight.

ARISTORIUS

Now say me, Jonathas, by this light,
What payment therefore would you me make?

JONATHAS

[Forty pounds], and pay it full right,
Even for that Lord's sake.

ARISTORIUS

Nay, nay, Jonathas, there-again
I would not for a [hundred] pound!

JONATHAS

Sir, here is your asking told plain;
I shall it tell in this stound.
Here is an [hundred pounds], neither more nor less,
Of dockets good, I dare well say.
Tell it ere you from me pass;
Me thinketh it a royal array!
But first, I pray you, tell me this:
Of this thing when shall I have deliverance?

ARISTORIUS

Tomorrow betimes, I shall not miss;
This night therefore I shall make purveyance.

Sir Isidore he is now at church,
There saying his evensong,
As it [is] his worship for to work.
He shall soon come home, he will not be long,
His supper for to eat.
And when he is busked to his bed,
Right soon hereafter he shall be sped;
No speech among you there be spread!
To keep your tongues, ye not let.

JONATHAS

Sir, almighty Mahomet be with you!
And I shall come again right soon.

ARISTORIUS

Jonathas, ye wot what I have said, and how
I shall walk for that we have to done.

Here goeth the Jews away, and the priest cometh home.

225 **to . . . take** have gone (to bed).
226 **of no wight** by no one.
229 **full right** immediately.
231 **there-again** to answer you.
233 **Sir . . . plain** Sir, here's what you ask for, openly counted out.
234 **tell . . . stound** count it out in this place (right here!).
236 **dockets** ducats.
238 **a royal array** a sight fit for a king!
241 **betimes** early.
241 **miss** fail.
242 **purveyance** provision/plans.
245 **worship . . . work** duty to do.
248 **busked** gone.
251 **ye not let** don't you fail.

PRESBITER
Sir, Almighty God mot be your guide,
And glad you whereso ye rest!
ARISTORIUS
Sir, ye be welcome home this tide.
Now, Peter, get us wine of the best.
CLERICUS
Sir, here is a draught of Romney Red;
There is no better in Aragon,
And a loaf of light bread;
It is wholesome, as sayeth the physician.

[*Exit Peter Paul.*]

ARISTORIUS
Drink off, Sir Isidore, and be of good cheer!
This Romney is good to go with to rest.
There is none preciouser, far nor near,
For all wicked meats it will digest.
PRESBITER
Sir, this wine is good at a taste,
And thereof have I drunk right well.
To bed to gone thus have I cast,
Even straight after this merry meal.

Now, sir, I pray to God send you good [night],
For to my chamber now will I [be]gone.
ARISTORIUS
Sir, with you be God Almight,
And shield you ever from your foe-en.

Here shall Aristorius call his clerk to his presence.

Ho, Peter! In thee is all my trust,
In especial to keep my counsel,
For a little way walken I must.
I will not be long; trust as I thee tell.

Now privily will I prove my pace,
My bargain this night for to fulfil.
Sir Isidore shall not know of this case,
For he hath often sacered, as it is skill.
The church key is at my will;
There is nothing that me shall tarry.

257 **glad you whereso** comfort you wherever.
258 **this tide** at this time.
260 **Romney** Rumney (Greek wine).
262 **light** white.
267 **wicked meats** harmful/over-rich foods.
270 **cast** decided.
275 **foe-en** foes.
280 **prove my pace** make my way.
283 **sacered . . . skill** consecrated: it is reasonable. (The priest has consecrated many wafers, so will not miss one.)

I will not abide, by dale nor hill,
Till it be wrought, by Saint Mary!

Here shall he enter the church and take the Host.

Ah, now have I all mine intent!
Unto Jonathas now will I fare,
To fulfil my bargain have I meant,
For that many will amend my fare,
As thinketh me.
But now will I pass by these paths plain;
To meet with Jonathas I would fain.
Ah, yonder he cometh in certain!
Me thinketh I him see.

Welcome, Jonathas, gentle and true!
For well and truly thou keepest thine hour.
Here is the Host, sacered new.
Now will I home to hall and bower.

JONATHAS

And I shall keep this trusty treasure
As I would do my gold and fee!

[*To the Host*:]

Now in this cloth I shall thee cover,
That no wight shall thee see.

Here shall Aristory go his way; and Jonathas and his servants shall go to the table, thus saying:

Now, Jason and Jasdon, ye be Jews gentle,
Masphat and Malchus, that might are in mind,
This merchant from the Christian temple
Hath got us this bread that makes us thus blind.
Now, Jason, as gentle as ever was the lind,
Into the foresaid parlour privily take thy pace;
Spread a cloth on the table that ye shall there find,
And we shall follow after to carp of this case.

Now the Jews go and lay the Host on the table, saying:

Sirs, I pray you all, harken to my saw:
These Christian men carpen of a marvellous case;

286 **abide** delay.
289 **fare** go.
291 **amend my fare** improve my situation.
298 **hour** appointment.
299 **sacered new** freshly consecrated.
306 **that... are** who are strong.
308 **that... blind** that deceives us.
309 **lind** linden tree (proverbially delicate).
312 **carp** discuss.
313 **saw** (wise) words.
314 **carpen** speak.

They say that this is Jesu that was attainted in our law,
And that this is he that crucified was.

On these words their law grounded hath he,
That he said on Sheer Thursday at his supper:
He brake the bread and said '*Accipite*',
And gave his disciples them for to cheer.
And more he said to them there
While they were all together and sum,
Sitting at the table so clear:
'*Comedite, corpus meum*'.

And this power he gave Peter to proclaim,
And how the same should be sufficient to all preachers.
The bishops and curates say the same,
And so, as I understand, do all his progenitors.

JASON

Yea, some men in that law rehearse another:
They say of a maiden born was he,
And how Joachim's daughter should be his mother,
And how Gabriel appeared and said '*Ave!*'
And with that word she should conceived be,
And that in her should light the Holy Ghost,
Against our law this is false heresy.
And yet they say he is of mights most.

JASDON

They say that Jesu to be our king,
But I wean he bought that full dear!
But they make a royal array of his uprising;
And that in every place is preached far and near.
And how he to his disciples again did appear,
To Thomas, and to Mary Magdalene,
And sith how he stied by his own power;
And this, ye know well, is heresy full plain.

MASPHAT

Yea, and also they say he sent them wit and wisdom
For to understand every language,
When the Holy Ghost to them came,

315 **attainted** convicted by.
317 **their...he** he has founded their religion. (The Jews here begin to list the tenets of the Apostles' Creed.)
318 **Sheer...supper** Holy Thursday, at his (Last) Supper.
319 ***Accipite*** Take.
322 **and sum** one and all.
324 ***Comedite, corpus meum*** Eat [this is] My body (Matthew 26:26.)
325 **Peter** St Peter.
328 **progenitors** probably 'successors' is intended here: probably those of St Peter (i.e. the popes).
329 **another** another story/part of the Creed.
330 **maiden** virgin.
331 **Joachim's daughter** Mary.
332 **Gabriel** the Angel Gabriel (at the Annunciation).
332 ***Ave!*** Hail!
334 **Light** alight/become manifest.
338 **he...dear!** he paid a high price for that!
339 **make...uprising** make a great fuss about his Resurrection.
343 **stied** ascended (into Heaven).
346–347 **For...came** see Acts 2:1–47 for the descent of the Holy Spirit upon the Disciples at Pentecost granting them the gift of speaking in tongues.

They fared as drunk men of piement or vernage;
And sithen how that he likened himself a lord of peerage:
On his Father's right hand he him set.
They hold him wiser than ever was Sibyl sage,
And stronger than Alexander that all the world did get.

MALCHUS

Yea, yet they say as false, I dare lay my head:
How they that be dead shall come again to Judgement,
And our dreadful Judge shall be this same bread,
And how life everlasting them should be lent.
And thus they hold, all at one consent,
Because that Philip said for a little gloss;
To turn us from our belief is their intent;
For that he said, '*Judicare vivos et mortuos*'.

JONATHAS

Now, sirs, ye have rehearsed the substance of [their] law,
But this bread I would might be put in a proof
Whether this be he that in Bozrah of us had awe.
There stained were his clothes; this may we believe,
This may we know: there had he grief,
For our old books verify thus:
Thereon he was judged to be hanged as a thief:
'*Tinctis Bosra vestibus*'.

JASON

If that this be he that on Calvary was made red,
Unto my mind, I shall ken you a conceit good:
Surely with our daggers we shall cess on this bread,
And so with clouts we shall know if he have any blood.

JASDON

Now, by Mahomet so mighty, that moveth in my mode;
This is masterly meant, this matter thus to move!
And with our strokes we shall fray him as he was on the Rood,
That he was undone with great reproof.

348 **piement or vernage** spiced or sweet wine.
349 **peerage** high birth.
351 **Sibyl** The Sibyl at Cumae, prophetess of the Roman world.
352 **get** conquer.
353 **lay** wager.
356 **should ... lent** should be granted to them.
358 **Philip** probably Philip the Evangelist, the forerunner of St Paul in spreading Christianity among the gentiles, see Acts 6:1–6, 8:4–8 and 26–39.
358 **gloss** commentary.
360 ***'Judicare vivos et mortuos'*** 'To judge the living and the dead', part of the Apostles' Creed. See I Peter 4:5, II Timothy 4:1.
362 **in a proof** to the test.
368 ***'Tinctis Bosra vestibus'*** Isaiah 63:1: '[Who is this that cometh from Edom] with dyed garments from Bozrah?' seen in the medieval period as a prophetic allusion to Christ.
370 **ken ... good** inform you about a good idea.
371 **cess on** strike at.
372 **clouts** blows.
374 **that to move** that persuades me (lit. moves (me) in my mind); that's masterfully said, to suggest such a plan!
375 **fray** attack.
376 **That ... reproof** (so) that he shall be ruined, with great shame.

MASPHAT

Yea, I pray you, smite ye in the midst of the cake,
And so shall we smite thereon wounds five!
We will not spare to work it wrack
To prove in this bread if there be any life.

MALCHUS

Yea, go we to then, and take your space,
And look our daggers be sharp and keen;
And when each man a stroke smitten has,
In the middle part thereof our master shall been.

JONATHAS

When ye have all smitten, my stroke shall be seen:
With this same dagger that is so stiff and strong,
In the midst of this print I think for to preen!
One lash I shall him lend ere it be long.

Here shall the four Jews prick their daggers in (the) four quarters, thus saying:

JASON

Have at it! Have at it, with all my might!
This side I hope for to seize!

JASDON

And I shall with this blade so bright
This other side freshly afeize!

MASPHAT

And I you plight I shall him not please,
For with this punch I shall him prick!

MALCHUS

And with this auger I shall him not ease:
Another buffet shall he lick!

JONATHAS

Now am I bold with battle him to black,
The middle part all for to preen,
A stout stroke also for to strike:
In the midst it shall be seen!

Here the Host must bleed.

Ah, out, out harrow! What devil is this?
Of this work I am in were!

379 **to . . . wrack** harm it/take revenge upon it.
381 **go . . . then** let's get on with it.
381 **space** place(s).
382 **look** be sure.
384 **shall been** shall strike his blow.
387 **In . . . preen!** In the middle of this embossed image I intend to strike. (The host is a wafer stamped with an image of Christ or a Cross rather than a conventional loaf.)
390 **seize** strike.
392 **freshly afeize** strike straight afterwards.
393 **I you . . . please** I promise you I shall not please him.
394 **punch** a carpenter's tool, like the auger (l. 395).
396 **lick** taste (i.e. feel).
397 **to black** blacken/make pale (with fear).
401 **out, harrow!** alas, help!
402 **Of . . . were!** I'm amazed by what's happening!

It bleedeth as it were wood, iwys!
But if ye help, I shall despair!

JASON
A fire, a fire, and that in haste!
Anon a cauldron full of oil!

JASDON
And I shall help it were in cast,
All the three hours for to boil.

MASPHAT
Ye[a], here is a furnace stout and strong,
And a cauldron therein doth hang.
Malchus, where art thou so long,
To help this deed were dight?

MALCHUS
Lo, here is three gallons of oil clear,
Have done fast; blow up the fire!
Sir, bring that ilk cake near,
Manly, with all your might.

JONATHAS
And I shall bring that ilk cake,
And throw it in, I undertake.

[The Host sticks to his hand.]

Out, out, it worketh me wrack!
I may not avoid it out of my hand!
I will go drench me in a lake.
And in woodness I gin to wake!
I run, I leap over this land!

Here he runneth wood with the Host in his hand.

JASON
Run, fellows, run, for Cock's pain,
Fast we had our master again!
Hold prestly on this plain
And fast bind him to a post.

JASDON
Here is an hammer and nails three, I say.
Lift up his arms, fellows, on high,
While I drive these nails, I you pray,
With strong strokes fast.

[They fasten the Sacrament to the post.]

403 **as ... iwys!** as if it was mad, I say!
404 **But if** unless.
407 **it ... cast** to throw it in.
412 **To ... dight?** to get this deed done?
415 **ilk** same.
419 **worketh me wrack!** does me pain!
420 **avoid** remove.
422 **in ... wake!** in madness I start to fall.
423.1 **runneth wood** runs mad.
424 **Cock's** God's (a euphemism).
425 **Fast we had** Let us capture.
426 **prestly** tightly.

MASPHAT
Now set on, fellows, with main and might,
And pluck his arms away in fight!
What? I see he twitch, fellows, aright!
Alas, bales breweth right bad!

Here shall they pluck the arm, and the hand shall hang still with the Sacrament.

MALCHUS
Alas, alas, what devil is this?
Now hath he but one hand, iwys!
Forsooth, master, right woe me is
That ye this harm have had.

JONATHAS
There is no more; I must endure!
Now hastily to our chamber let us go,
Till I may get me some recure.
And therefore charge you everyone
That it be counsel, that we have done.

Here shall the leach's man come into the place, saying:

COLL
Aha, here is a fair fellowship!
Though I be not shapen, I list to slip.
I have a master: I would he had the pip,
I tell you in counsel!
He is a man of all science
But of thrift, I may with you dispense!
He sitteth with some tapster in the spence;
His hood there will he sell.

Master Branditch of Brabant,
I tell you, he is that same man,
Called the most famous physician
That ever saw urine.
He seeth as well at noon as at night,

433 **in fight!** fiercely!
434 **aright!** careful!
435 **bales...bad!** things are getting even worse!
435.1 **Here...Sacrament** i.e. they pull off Jonathas' arm, leaving his hand still fixed to the post with the Host.
438 **right...is** I'm so sorry!
442 **recure** remedy.
444 **counsel** kept secret.
444.1 **leach's** doctor's.
446 **Though...slip.** I want to run away, though I'm not prepared.
447 **I...pip** I wish he were sick!
450 **But...dispense!** Except for thrift, I can be honest (i.e. dispense with politeness) with you!
451 **spence** wine-cellar.
452 **His...sell** He'd (even) sell his hood (for a drink) there.
456 Medieval physicians diagnosed diseases by examining the patient's urine.

And sometime by a candle-light
Can give a judgement aright
As he that hath none eyen.

He is also a bone-setter;
I know no man go the better!
In every tavern he is debtor,
That is a good tokening!
But ever I wonder he is so long;
I fear there goeth something a-wrong,
For he hath deserved to be hung;
God send never worse tiding!

He had a lady late in cure:
I wot by this she is full sure!
There shall never Christian creature
Hear her tell no tale!
And I stood here till midnight,
I could not declare aright
My master's cunning insight
That he hath in good ale.

By what devil aileth him so long to tarry?
A sick man might soon miscarry.
Now all the devils of Hell him worry!
God grant me my boon!
I trow best we make a cry:
If any man can him espy,
Lead him to the pillory;
In faith, it shall be done.

Here shall he stand up and make proclamation, saying this:

If there be either man or woman
That saw Master Branditch of Brabant,
Or ought of him tell can,
Shall well be quit his mead.
He hath a cut beard and a flat nose,
A threadbare gown and a rent hose;

459–460 **Can . . . eyen.** Can give as good a diagnosis . . . as he that has no eyes.
464 **tokening** sign.
467–468 **For . . . tiding!** i.e. it wouldn't be too bad if he has been hanged.
469 **late in cure** in his care recently.
470 **I . . . sure!** I know that by now she is well taken care of!
472 **Hear . . . tale!** i.e. she is dead.
473 **And** If.
479 **Now . . . worry!** Curse him!
480 **boon** request.
481 **cry** proclamation.
487 **ought . . . can** can report any news of him.
488 **Shall . . . mead** They'll be well rewarded.
490 **rent** torn.

He speaked never good matter nor purpose.
To the pillory ye him lead!

MASTER BRANDITCH
What, thou boy, what janglest here?

COLL
Ah, master, master, but to your reverence!
I wend never to a seen your goodly cheer,
Ye tarried hence so long.

MASTER BRANDITCH
What hast thou said in my absence?

COLL
Nothing, master, but to your reverence,
I have told all this audience;
And some lies among. [*Aside*]

But master, I pray you, how doth your patient
That ye had last under your medicament?

MASTER BRANDITCH
I warrant she never feel anointment.

COLL
Why, is she in her grave?

MASTER BRANDITCH
I have given her a drink made full well
With scammoly and with oxennell,
Lettuce, sage, and pimpernel.

COLL
Nay, then she is full safe!

For now ye are come, I dare well say
Between Dover and Calais the right way
Dwelleth none so cunning, by my fey,
In my judgement.

MASTER BRANDITCH
Cunning? Yea, yea, and with practice
I have saved many a man's life.

COLL
On widows, maids, and wife
Your cunning you have nigh spent.

MASTER BRANDITCH
Where is [my] budget with drink profitable?

493 **janglest** (are you) prattling (about)?
494–495 **but... cheer** only (things) respectful to you. I thought I'd never see your lovely face again.
500 **among** here and there.
503 **she... anointment** she feels no (more) annoyance/pain.
507 **scammoly** scammony (a purgative gum), **oxennell** oximel (mixed vinegar and honey), lettuce, sage, and pimpernel: all medicinal herbs.
511 **fey** faith. Ironic as Dover and Calais are separated by the English Channel.
516 **spent** knowledge (by implication also 'carnal knowledge').
517 **budget... profitable?** wallet (leather bottle) of medicinal drink?

COLL

Here, master, master, ware how ye tug!
The Devil, I trow, within shrugs,
For it goeth 'ribble-rabble'.

MASTER BRANDITCH

Here is a great congregation,
And all be not whole, without negation.
I would have certification:
Stand up and make a proclamation.
Have do fast, and make no pausation
But wightly make a declaration
To all people that help would have.

Hic interim proclamationem faciet.

COLL

All manner of men that have any sickness,
To Master Brantberkely look that you redress!
What disease or sickness that ever ye have,
He will never leave you till ye be in your grave.
Who hath the canker, the colic, or the lax,
The tertian, the quartian, or the burning access;
For worms, for gnawing, grinding in the womb, or in the boldyro;
All manner red eyen, bleared eyen, and the migraine also;
For headache, bone-ache, and thereto the toothache;
The colt-evil and the brosten men he will undertake,
All those that [have] the pose, the sneck, or the tissick.
Though a man were right hail, he could soon make him sick!
Inquire to the coal-cote, for there is his lodging,
A little beside Babwell Mill, if ye will have understanding.

MASTER BRANDITCH

Now, if there be either man or woman
That needeth help of a physician...

COLL

Marry, master, that I tell can,
And ye will understand.

518–519 **ware...shrugs** beware how you drink; I'm sure the devil is moving inside it.

520 **ribble-rabble** i.e. the gurgling of the liquid sounds like the devil growling.

521 **congregation** gathering (i.e. the audience).

522 **all...negation** not all of them are healthy, (I can say) without contradiction.

523 **I...certification** i.e. tell them who I am!

525 **Have do fast** get on with it.

526 **wightly** manfully/boldly.

527.1 ***Hic...faciet*** Here, for a time, he will make proclamation.

529 **redress** come.

532 **canker...lax** cancer, colic (stomach pains), and diarrhoea.

533 Tertian and quartian were terms for fevers which involved paroxysms every third or fourth day, respectively.

533 **burning access** internal pains.

534 **womb** stomach.

534 **boldyro** perhaps a euphemism for the genitals.

537 **The...undertake** He will take on colt-evil (swelling of the penis in horses) and burst men (men with hernias).

538 **pose...tissick** catarrh, a head-cold, or tuberculosis.

539 **right hail** perfectly healthy.

540 **coal-cote** coal-shed.

541 **Babwell Mill**, near Bury St Edmunds (Suffolk).

MASTER BRANDITCH
Knowest any about this place?
COLL
Yea, that I do, master, so have I grace!
Here is a Jew, hight Jonathas,
Hath lost his right hand.
MASTER BRANDITCH
Fast to him I would inquire.
COLL
'Fore God, master, the gate is here.
MASTER BRANDITCH
Then to him I will go near.
My master, well mot you be!
JONATHAS
What dost here, fellow? What wouldst thou han?
MASTER BRANDITCH
Sir, if you need any surgeon or physician,
Of your disease help you well I can,
What hurts or harms soever they be.
JONATHAS
Sir, thou art untaught to come in thus homely,
Or to 'pear in my presence thus malapertly.
Voideth from my sight, and that wightly,
For ye be miss-advised!
COLL
Sir, the hurt of your hand is known full rife,
And my master have saved many a man's life.
JONATHAS
I trow ye be come to make some strife.
Hence fast, lest that ye be chastised!
COLL
Sir, ye know well it cannot miss;
Men that be masters of science be profitable.
In a pot if it please you to piss,
He can tell if you be curable.
[JONATHAS]
Avoid, fellows, I love not your babble;
Brush them hence both, and that anon!
Give them their reward that they were gone!

Here shall the four Jews beat away the leach and his man.

548 **hight** named.
554 **What...han?** What are you doing here, fellow? What do you want?
558 **thus homely** so rudely (without proper formality).
559 **'pear** appear.
559 **malapertly** impertinently.
560 **voideth** vanish.
560 **wightly** quickly.
562 **full rife** very widely.
565 **Hence fast** Go away quickly.
567 **profitable** useful.
571 **Brush...anon!** Sweep them both out at once!
572 **reward** i.e. a beating.

JONATHAS

Now have done, fellows, and that anon,
For doubt of dread what after befall!
I am near 'mazed; my wit is gone!
Therefore, of help I pray you all.
And take your pincers that are so sure,
And pluck out the nails one and one;
Also in a cloth ye it cure
And throw it in the cauldron, and that anon.

Here shall Jason pluck out the nails and shake the hand into the cauldron.

JASON

And I shall rape me readily anon
To pluck out the nails that stand so fast.
And bear this bread and also this bone,
And into the cauldron I will it cast.

JASDON

And I shall with this dagger so stout
Put it down that it might plaw,
And stir the cloth round about
That nothing thereof shall be raw.

MASPHAT

And I shall manly with all my might,
Make the fire to blaze and bren,
And set there-under such a light
That it shall make it right thin.

Here shall the cauldron boil, appearing to be as blood.

MALCHUS

Out and harrow; what devil is herein?
All this oil waxeth red as blood,
And out of the cauldron it begineth to run.
I am so afeard I am near wood!

Here shall Jason and his company go to Sir Jonathas, saying:

JASON

Ah, master, master! What cheer is with you?
I cannot see our work will avail.
I beseech you, advance you now
Somewhat with your counsel!

574 **For...befall!** For fear of what may follow!
578 **and** by.
579 **it cure** cover it (the host).
581 **rape** hurry.
586 **plaw** boil.
590 **bren** burn.
592 **make...thin** i.e. boil it away.
594 **waxeth** grows.
597 **What...you?** How are you?
599-600 **advance...counsel!** Offer us some advice (what to do)!

JONATHAS

The best counsel that I now wot,
That I can deem, far and near,
Is to make an oven as red hot
As ever it can be made with fire;
And when ye see it so hot appear,
Then throw it into the oven fast,
Soon shall he staunch his bleeding cheer.
When ye have done, stop it; be not aghast.

JASDON

By my faith, it shall be wrought,
And that anon, in great haste.
Bring on firing, sirs. Hear ye nought?
To heat this oven be not aghast.

MASPHAT

Here is straw and thorns keen.
Come on, Malchus, and bring on fire,
For that shall heat it well, I wene.

Here they kindle the fire.

Blow on fast, that done it were!

MALCHUS

Ah, how this fire ginneth to bren clear!
This oven right hot I think to make.
Now, Jason, to the cauldron that ye steer,
And fast fetch hither that ilke cake.

Here shall Jason go to the cauldron and take out the host with his pincers, and cast it into the oven.

JASON

I shall with these pincers without doubt
Shake this cake out of this cloth,
And to the oven I shall it rout
And stop him there, though he be loath.
The cake I have caught here, in good sooth;
The hand is sodden, the flesh from the bones;
Now into the oven I will therewith.
Stop it, Jasdon, for the nones!

JASDON

I stop this oven, withouten doubt;
With clay I clome it up right fast,

601 **wot** know.
606 **it** the host.
607 **bleeding cheer** appearance of bleeding.
608 **stop it** block it (the oven) up.
609 **wrought** done.
611 **firing** kindling.
613 **keen** sharp.
615 **I wene** I say/believe.
619 **steer** go.
623 **to** into.
623 **rout** throw.
628 **Stop it** Seal it up.
628 **for the nones!** at once!
630 **clome** seal.

That none heat shall come out.
I trow there shall he heat and dry in haste!

Here the oven must rive asunder and bleed out at the crannies, and an image appear out with wounds bleeding.

MASPHAT
Out, out, here is a great wonder!
This oven bleedeth out on every side!

MALCHUS
Yea, the oven on pieces ginneth to rive asunder!
This is a marvellous case this tide!

Here shall the image speak to the Jews, saying thus:

JESUS
O mirabiles Judei, attendite et videte
Si est dolor [*sicut*] *dolor meus!*
Oh ye marvellous Jews,
Why are ye to your king unkind,
And I so bitterly bought you to my bliss?
Why fare ye thus foul with your friend?
Why pain you me and straitly me pined,
And I your love so dearly have bought?
Why are ye so unsteadfast in your mind?
Why wrath ye me; I grieve you nought?
Why will ye not believe that I have taught,
And forsake your foul negligence
And keep my commandments in your thought,
And unto my Godhead to take credence?

Why blaspheme you me? Why do ye thus?
Why put you me to a new tormentry,
And I died for you on the Cross?
Why consider not you what I did cry?
While that I was with you, ye did me villainy.
Why remember ye not my bitter chance,
How your kin did me advance
For claiming of mine inheritance?
I show you the straitness of my grievance,
And all to move you to my mercy.

632.1 **Here . . . crannies** The oven must split apart and bleed out of the cracks.

637–638 ***O . . . meus!*** O you strange Jews, behold and see if any sorrow is like my sorrow. (See Lamentations 1:12, 'Is it nothing to you, all ye that pass by? Behold, and see if there be any sorrow like unto my sorrow'.)

640 **unkind** unnatural/cruel.

641 **And . . . bliss?** And I so painfully redeemed you for (a place in) my Heaven.

642 **fare** behave.

643 **straitly me pined** tightly confined me.

656 **chance** fate.

657 **did me advance** treated me.

659 **straitness** severity.

JONATHAS
Tu es protector vitae mee; a quo trepidabo?
O Thou Lord, which art my defender,
For dread of Thee I tremble and quake!
Of Thy great mercy let us receive the shower;
And meekly I ask mercy, amends to make.

Here shall they kneel down all on their knees, saying:

JASON
Ah, Lord, with sorrow and care and great weeping,
All we fellows, let us say thus
With condolent heart and great sorrowing:
Lacrimis nostris conscienciam nostram baptizemus!

JASDON
Oh Thou Blessed Lord of mickle might,
Of Thy great mercy thou hast showed us the path,
Lord, out of grievous sleep and out of darkness to light,
Ne gravis sompnus irruat.

MASPHAT
Oh Lord, I was very cursed, for I would know thy Creed.
I can no 'mends make, but cry to thee thus:
O gracious Lord, forgive me my misdeed!
With lamentable heart: *misirere mei, Deus!*

MALCHUS
Lord, I have offended Thee in many a sundry wise.
That sticketh at my heart as hard as a core.
Lord, by the water of contrition let me arise:
Asparges me, Domine, isopo, et mundabor.

JESUS
All ye that desiren my servants for to be
And to fulfil the precepts of my laws,
The intent of my commandment know ye:
Ite et ostendite vos sacerdotibus meis.
To all you that desire in any wise
To ask mercy, to grant it ready I am.
Remember and let your wits suffice,
Et tunc non avertam a vobis faciem meam.
Know Jonathas, on thine hand thou art but lame,

661 ***Tu . . . trepidabo?*** You are the protector of my life, of whom should I be afraid? A variation of Psalm 27:1.

668 **condolent** contrite.

669 ***Lacrimis . . . baptizemus!*** With our tears may we baptize our conscience.

670 **mickle** great.

673 ***Ne . . . irruat*** May grievous sleep not seize [us].

674 **I was . . . Creed** I was truly cursed, for I wanted to test your Creed (rather than believe it by faith).

675 **'mends** amends.

677 ***misirere mei, Deus!*** Have mercy on me, God!

678 **sundry wise** different ways.

681 ***Asparges . . . mundabor*** [Sprinkle] me with hissop, [Lord,] and I shall be clean: a variation of Psalm 51:7.

685 ***Ite . . . meis*** Go show yourselves unto [my] priests (Luke 17:14).

689 ***Et . . . meam*** And then I will not turn My face from you. (See Psalms 27:9, 88:14, 143:7.)

And is through thine own cruelness.
For thine hurt thou mayest thyself blame:
Thou wouldst prove thy power me to oppress.
But now I consider thy necess:
Thou washest thine heart with great contrition.
Go to the cauldron, thy care shall be the less,
And touch thine hand to thy salvation.

JONATHAS

Oh Thou my Lord God and Saviour, Hosanna!
Thou King of Jews and of Jerusalem!
O thou mighty, strong Lion of Judah,
Blessed be the time that Thou were in Bedlam!
Oh Thou mighty, strong, glorious, and gracious oil stream,
Thou mighty conqueror of infernal teen,
I am quit of much cumbrance through thy mean,
That ever blessed mot thou been!

Alas that ever I did against thy will,
In my wit to be so wood
That I so ungoodly work should so grill!
Against my misgovernance thou gladdest me with good:
I was so proud to prove thee on the Rood,
And thou hast sent me lighting that late was lame.
To beat thee and boil thee I was mighty in mood,
And now thou hast put me from duress and disfame.

But, Lord, I take my leave at thy high presence,
And put me in thy mighty mercy.
The bishop will I go fetch to see our offence,
And unto him show our life, how that we be guilty.

Here shall the master Jew go to the Bishop,
and his men kneel still.

Hail, father of grace! I kneel upon my knee,
Heartily beseeching you, and entirely,
A swemfull sight all for to see
In my house appearing verily:
The Holy Sacrament, the which we have done tormentry,
And there we have put him to a new Passion;
A child appearing with wounds bloody:
A swemfull sight it is to look upon!

694 **necess** need.
701 **Bedlam** Bethlehem.
703 **infernal teen** hellish suffering.
704 **I … mean** I am relieved of much suffering through your mediation.
705 **mot thou been** may you be!
708 **That … grill!** That I should do such evil deeds so cruelly!
711 **that late** (I) who recently.
712 **mighty in mood** strongly determined.
713 **put** saved.
713 **disfame** shame.
720 **swemful** painful.

EPISCOPUS

Oh Jesu, Lord, full of goodness!
With thee will I walk with all my might.
Now, all my people, with me ye dress
For to go see that swemfull sight.
Now all ye people that here are,
I command you, every man,
On your feet for to go bare,
In the devoutest wise that ye can.

Here shall the bishop enter into the Jew's house, and say:

O Jesu, fili Dei,
How this painful Passion rancheth mine heart!
Lord, I cry to thee, *misirere mei*,
From this rueful sight thou wilt revert.
Lord, we all, with sorrows smart;
For this unlawful work we live in languor.
Now, good Lord, in thy grace let us be girt,
And of thy sovereign mercy send us thy succour,
And for thy holy grace forgive us our error.
Now let thy pity spring and spread!
Though we have be unrightful, forgive us our rigour,
And of our lamentable hearts, good Lord, take heed!

Here shall the image change again into bread.

Oh thou largifluent Lord, most of lightness,
Unto our prayers Thou hast applied!
Thou hast received them with great sweetness;
For all our dreadful deeds thou hast not us denied.
Full mickle ought thy name for to be magnified
With mansuate mirth and great sweetness,
And as gracious God for to be glorified,
For thou showest us great gladness.
Now will I take this Holy Sacrament
With humble heart and great devotion,
And all we will gone with one consent
And bear it to church with solemn procession.
Now follow me, all and some!
And all those that been here, both more and less,

728 **dress** prepare.
733 **wise** manner.
734 ***O . . . Dei*** O Jesu, Son of God.
735 **rancheth** wounds.
736 ***misirere mei*** have mercy on me.
737 **revert** change back.
739 **languor** distress.
740 **girt** clothed.
744 **rigour** cruelty.
746 **largifluent** bountiful.
747 **applied** (listened and) complied.
751 **mansuate mirth** gentle joy.
758 **all and some!** one and all!

This holy song, *O sacrum convivium,*
Let us sing all with great sweetness.

[They process to the church, singing.]

Here shall the priest, Sir Isidore, ask his master what this meaneth.

[PRESBITER]
Sir Aristory, I pray you, what meaneth all this?
Some miracle, I hope, is wrought by God's might.
The Bishop cometh in procession with a great many of Jews;
I hope some miracle is showed to his sight.
To church in haste will I run full right,
For thither, me think, he begineth to take his pace.
The Sacrament so seemly is borne in sight.
I hope that God hath showed of his grace.

ARISTORIUS
To tell you the truth I will not let;
Alas that ever this deed was dight!
An unlawful bargain I began for to beat:
I sold yon same Jews our Lord full right
For covetise of goods, as a cursed wight.
Woe the while that bargain I did ever make!
But you be my defensor in our diocesan's sight,
For an heretic I fear he will me take.

PRESBITER
Forsooth, nothing well-advised was your wit;
Wonderly was it wrought of a man of discretion
In such peril your soul for to put!
But I will labour for your absolution.

Let us hie us fast that we were hence,
And beseech him of his benign grace
That he will show us his benevolence
To make amends for your trespass.

Here shall the merchant and his priest go to the church, and the Bishop shall enter the church and lay the Host on the altar, saying thus:

[EPISCOPUS]
Estote fortes in bello et pugnate come antico serpente,
Et accipite regnum eternum, et cetera.

760 ***O sacrum convivium*** 'O sacred feast!' sung as part of the vespers for the feast of Corpus Christi.
770 **let** resist/hesitate.
771 **dight** done.
772 **beat** make.
774 **covetise** covetousness.
775 **Woe the while** Alas the time.
776 **But...sight** Unless you will be my protector when we come before the bishop.
778 **nothing** in no way.
779 **Wonderly** Unbelievably (stupidly).
782 **hie** hurry.
786–787 ***Estote...cetera.*** Be strong in battle and fight with the old serpent, and receive the eternal kingdom, and so on. (See Revelation 20:2: 'And [an angel] laid hold on the dragon, that old serpent which is the Devil and Satan, and bound him [for] a thousand years'.)

My children, ye be strong in battle ghostly
For to fight against the fell serpent
That night and day is ever busy;
To destroy our souls is his intent.
Look ye be not slow nor negligent
To arm you in the virtues seven.
Of sins forgotten take good advisement,
And knowledge them to your confessor full even.
For that serpent, the Devil, is full strong
Marvellous mischievous for man to mean,
But that the Passion of Christ is meant us among,
And that is in despite of his infernal teen.
Beseech our Lord and Saviour so keen
To put down that serpent, cumberer of man,
To withdraw his furious froward doctrine bedeen
Fulfilled of the fiend called Leviathan.
Give laurel to that Lord of might
That he may bring us to the joyous fruition:
From us to put the Fiend to flight,
That never he destroy us by his temptation.

PRESBITER [*To Episcopus*]

My father under God, I kneel unto your knee,
In your mighty miserichord to take us in remembrance;
As ye be material to our degree,
We put us in your moderate ordinance
If it like your highness to hear our grievance:
We have offended sorrowfully in a sin mortal,
Wherefore we fear us Our Lord will take vengeance
For our sins, both great and small.

EPISCOPUS

And in fatherhood, that longeth to my dignity,
Unto your grief I will give credence.
Say what ye will, in the name of the Trinity,
Against God if ye have wrought any inconvenience.

789 **fell** evil.
793 **the virtues seven** the seven cardinal virtues.
794 **Of... advisement** Think upon the sins (you have) forgotten.
795 **full even** completely.
796–797 **is... mean** is very maliciously inclined towards humanity.
798 **But that** Unless.
798 **meant** understood/spread.
799 **in despite of** to oppose.
802 **froward** perverse.
802 **bedeen** at once.
803 **fulfilled of** pursued by.
803 **Leviathan** see Isaiah 27:1: 'In that day the Lord with his sore and great and strong sword shall punish Leviathan the piercing serpent, even Leviathan that crooked serpent; and he shall slay the dragon that is in the sea.'
804 **laurel** honour.
805 **joyous fruition** i.e. of heaven.
809 **miserichord** mercy.
810 **material... kind** vital to (the wellbeing of) our kind.
811 **in... ordinance** under your gentle authority.
816 **longeth... dignity** belongs to my high office.
819 **inconvenience** offence.

ARISTORIUS

Holy Father, I kneel to you under *benedicite*,
I have offended in the sin of covetise;
I sold Our Lord's body for lucre of money,
And delivered to the wicked, with cursed advice.
And for that presumption, greatly I agrise
That I presumed to go to the altar
There to handle the holy sacrifice.
I were worthy to be put in burning fire.

But, gracious lord, I can no more
But put me to God's mercy and to your grace.
My cursed works for to restore,
I ask penance now in this place.

EPISCOPUS

Now, for this offence that thou hast done
Against the King of Heaven and Emperor of Hell,
Ever while thou livest good deeds for to done
And nevermore for to buy nor sell.
Chastise thy body as I shall thee tell
With fasting and praying and other good work,
To withstand the temptation of fiends of Hell;
And to call to God for grace look thou never be irk.

[*To Presbiter*]

Also, thou priest, for thy negligence,
That thou were no wiser in thine office
Thou art worthy imprisonment for thine offence;
But beware ever hereafter, and be more wise.

And all you [preachers] and curates that here be,
Of this deed you may take example
How that your pixes locked ye should see,
And beware of the key of God's temple.

JONATHAS

And I ask Christendom with great devotion;
With repentant heart in all degrees
I ask for us all a general absolution.

Here the Jews must kneel all down.

For that we kneel all upon our knees;
For we have grieved Our Lord on ground
And put him to a new painful Passion,

820 **under *benedicite*** under (the protection of your) blessing.
823 **with cursed advice** ill-advisedly.
824 **agrise** am horrified.
839 **irk** reluctant.
846 **pixes** the containers in which the Hosts were kept after consecration.
847 **beware of** keep carefully.
852 **on ground** in this place.

With daggers sticked him with grievous wound,
New nailed him to a post, and with pincers plucked him down.

JASON
And sith we took that blessed bread so sound
And in a cauldron we did him boil.
In a cloth full just we him wound
And so did we seethe him in oil.

JASDON
And for that we might overcome him with tormentry,
In an hot oven we speared him fast.
There he appeared with wounds all bloody;
The oven rave asunder and all to-brast!

MASPHAT
In his law to make us steadfast,
There spake he to us words of great favour.
In contrition our hearts he cast,
And bad take us to a confessor.

MALCHUS
And therefore all we with one consent
Kneel onto your high sovereignty;
For to be Christened is our intent
Now all our deeds to you showed have we.

Here shall the Bishop Christen the Jews with great solemnity.

EPISCOPUS
Now the Holy Ghost at this time mot you bliss
As ye kneel all now in his name!
And with the water of baptism I shall you bless
To save you all from the Fiend's blame.
Now, that Fiend's power for to make lame,
In the name of the Father, the Son, and the Holy Ghost,
To save you from the Devil's flame,
I Christen you all, both least and most.

SIR JONATHAS
Now, our father and bishop that we well know,
We thank you entirely, both least and most.
Now are we bound to keep Christ's law
And to serve the Father, the Son, and the Holy Ghost,

Now will we walk by country and coast
Our wicked living for to restore,
And trust in God, of mights most,
Never to offend as we have done before.

858 **full just** tight(ly).
861 **speared him fast** thrust him shut.
867 **bad take us** told (us to) take ourselves.
870 **Christened** baptized.
875 **blame** reproach/curse.
880 **well know** acknowledge.
884 **by country and coast** i.e. everywhere.
885 **to restore** atone for.

Now we take our leave at less and more;
Forward on our voyage we will us dress.
God send you all as good welfare
As heart can think or tongue express!

ARISTORIUS

Into my country now will I fare
For to amend mine wicked life;
And to keep the people out of care,
I will teach this lesson to man and wife.

Now take I my leave in this place.
I will go walk my penance to fulfil,
Now God, against whom I have done this trespass,
Grant me forgiveness if it be thy will.

PRESBITER

For joy of this, me think my heart do weep,
That you have given you all Christ's servants to be,
And him for to serve with heart full meek,
God, full of patience and humility.
And the conversation of all these fair men,
With hearts steadfastly knit in one,
God's laws to keep and him to serve bedeen,
As faithful Christians evermore for to gone!

EPISCOPUS

God omnipotent evermore look ye serve
With devotion and prayer, while that ye may.
Doubt it not, he will you preserve
For each good prayer that ye say to his pay.
And therefore in every due time look ye not delay
For to serve the Holy Trinity,
And also Mary, that sweet maid;
And keep you in perfect love and charity.

Christ's Commandments ten there be.
Keep well them; do as I you tell.
Almighty God shall you please in every degree,
And so shall ye save your souls from Hell.
For there is pain and sorrow cruel,
And in Heaven there is both joy and bliss,
More than any tongue can tell.
There angels sing with great sweetness.

To the which bliss he bring us
Whose name is called Jesus,

888 **at** of.
889 **we . . . dress** we will prepare ourselves for our journey.
904 **conversation** behaviour/actions.
905 **in one** together.
906 **bedeen** indeed.
908 **look** make sure that.
911 **to his pay** that pleases him.

And in worship of this name glorious
To sing to His honour *Te Deum Laudamus*.

FINIS.

Thus endeth the Play of the Blessed Sacrament, which miracle was done in the forest of Aragon, in the famous cite of Heraclea, the year of our Lord God 1461, to whom be honour, Amen.

927 ***Te Deum Laudamus*** We praise you, O God.

Fulgens and Lucrece

(1490–1500?)

HENRY MEDWALL

(1461–?1501)

THE PLAYWRIGHT

Fulgens and Lucrece is the earliest English play to which we can attach the name of an identifiable author. The first printed edition, produced by John Rastell at some point between 1510 and 1516, states on its title page that the interlude was 'compiled by master Henry Medwall, late chaplain to the right reverent father in God, John Morton, Cardinal and Archbishop of Canterbury'. And fortunately we know something about Henry Medwall from other sources. He was born on or around 8 September 1461 in Southwark, the suburb on the south bank of the river Thames, across London Bridge from the City. He was educated at Eton and King's College Cambridge, where he studied Arts and Civil Law, before he joined the household of Bishop John Morton of Ely, the man who would go on to become Henry VII's Lord Chancellor, a Cardinal and Archbishop of Canterbury. Medwall's main role in Morton's service was not, however, as a chaplain, but as a notary public, a drafter of legal documents and keeper of Morton's legal archive, so in this respect at least Rastell seems to have been mistaken. Medwall almost certainly wrote his plays for performance in Morton's household, though, so the suggestion that he was a chaplain might stem from an association with the choristers and choirboys of the archbishop's chapel, who perhaps provided many of his actors. Only two of his plays survive, although he may have written more. *Fulgens and Lucrece* was printed, as we have seen, by Rastell in the 1510s, and *Nature* by Rastell's son William in 1530.

Archbishop Morton died in 1500, and Medwall himself disappears from the records after 1501, suggesting that he may also have died around this time, at the relatively early age of forty.

THE PLAY

Medwall's humanist education and his interest in the law are both evident in *Fulgens*, which explores the familiar humanist topics of how best to serve the commonwealth and what qualities make up the virtuous citizen, and litters the discussion with legal terms such as 'replication' (l.2140, part of the process of pleas and counter-plea in a court case), 'judgement', 'sureties' (l. 623ff) and 'jointure' (l. 924ff). The play also reflects humanist educational values in that it is more interested in virtue and good conduct in this world than in notions of sin and salvation in the next. Thus it can also claim to be the earliest surviving secular play in English.

Medwall takes his plot from a scholarly treatise on aristocratic virtue: John Tiptoft, Earl of Worcester's English translation of Buonaccorso da Montemagno's *On True Nobility* (1428), which was printed by William Caxton in 1481. Its theme was traditional: does true nobility lie in birth and lineage or in personal virtue? Chaucer had discussed this in his *Wife of Bath's Tale*, written at the end of the fourteenth century, and a number of his shorter poems, so it was not a new theme, but it had gained new resonance and urgency with the rise of humanist studies in the European universities in the later fifteenth century. These universities created a new cadre of educated, ambitious, often low-born public servants who felt they were better suited to administer the commonwealth (a key term in *Fulgens*) than the generally less well-educated aristocrats who dominated the councils of princes, and voiced their frustrations with the status quo in treatises and lectures.

The argument that virtue is not inherited with a noble title but has to be striven for by each new generation may seem uncontentious to modern readers. But in the early Tudor period it remained controversial. While the principle might have been accepted, its practical implications were potentially revolutionary, and so had to be handled with care in a society still dominated by the great nobles and aristocrats for whom lineage and bloodlines were almost sacred. Medwall's awareness of the sensitivities at stake is evident in the way that he frames the discussion to minimize its apparent radicalism. Lucrece and Gaius, A and B, all issue apologies and disclaimers for the play's themes, claiming that it does not refer to or parody anyone in the audience, and concerns only matters long ago and far away in imperial Rome. (This was probably shrewd, as, although Morton, like Medwall, was a man of modest birth and family who had made his way in society on the strength of his academic ability, many of his guests would have been members of aristocratic families, and the possibility that the play's jovial satirical humour might, if not well-handled, cause genuine offence was clearly a worry.) Then, having chosen the solid and virtuous Gaius over the obviously decadent Cornelius, Lucrece is at pains to assure spectators that the choice had been a difficult one, that her judgement was based solely on her own 'fantasy', and that it should not be taken as a precedent for others to follow. Finally she agrees with the pro-noble servant B, that the ideal suitor would be a man of virtue who was also an aristocrat, as he would be worthy of more praise than 'many' (but perhaps significantly not 'all') who had more humble origins (ll. 780–86).

Medwall added to the social and political themes of his source a comic sub-plot of his own (perhaps the first real sub-plot, rather than merely a comic interlude, in English drama) in the courtship of Joan the Maid by the servants A and B. This mirrors the courtship of Lucrece by Gaius and Cornelius in a lower, more scatological register. And, in the play's most innovative feature, these servants seemingly step out of the audience as the play is about to begin, and get involved in the action.

'A' and 'B' are not the names of characters, but rather roles that were probably taken by members of Morton's household, who would effectively be 'playing themselves'. Thus they never refer to each other by a character name, but use vague terms such as 'what-called' ('whatever-your-name-is') to identify each other, safe in the knowledge that most of those present already knew who they were. One possibility is that one of the roles might have been played by the young Thomas More, the future Catholic martyr. More served as a page in the Archbishop's household during 1491–2, when he would have been around fourteen years old. In the biography of More written by his son-in-law, William Roper, there is a description of the boy's love of drama, relating how, 'though he was young of years, yet would he at Christmas-tide suddenly sometimes step in among the players and, never studying for the matter, make a part of his own there presently among them, which made the lookers on more sport than all the players beside' (Roper, p. 5). The coincidence that *Fulgens and Lucrece* (in which two characters do indeed seem to step in among the players and make parts of their own) was written for the same household has led to speculation that Roper's anecdote is a mangled recollection of More's having appeared in the play as one of the servants. But, as there is no hard evidence that *Fulgens* was played while More was in Morton's service, the suggestion must remain unproven.

The play would probably have raised eyebrows in the 1490s for its gender politics as well as its support for those able public servants without aristocratic lineage. In both the plot and the sub-plot women come out on top. Joan humiliates her would-be suitors both intellectually and physically, and Lucrece gets the husband she desires, rather than the noble suitor whom tradition and her father's preference support.

The play was probably designed for performance in the great hall of Lambeth Palace, the Archbishop of Canterbury's London home, spread over the course of a day's feasting and festivity. As the title page suggests, it is divided into two parts for performance at two separate times, probably accompanying dinner at midday and supper in the evening. The actors were probably, like Medwall, members of Morton's own household, with boys from the chapel choir perhaps taking the female parts, although broader comedy might be achieved if an adult male 'in drag' took the part of Joan. The broad scatological comedy of the A and B scenes, and the evident delight in such devices as the joust at 'fart prick in cule' (l.1165ff) ('fart prick in the arse') as well as the fashionable courtly bass dance (l.1819ff) and the moral matter of the main plot suggest the broad-mindedness of elite culture in this period.

The play survives in a single complete copy of the Rastell print, now held in the Huntington Library, San Marino, California (Huntington Library 62599). This edition is based upon that text. I have also consulted the modern scholarly editions cited under further reading.

FURTHER READING

Bevington, David, *From Mankind to Marlowe* (Cambridge, MA: Harvard University Press, 1962).

—— *Tudor Drama and Politics* (Cambridge, MA: Harvard University Press, 1968).

Boas, F. and A. W. Reed, eds., *Fulgens and Lucrece: A Fifteenth-Century Secular Play* (Oxford: Oxford University Press, 1926).

Craik, T. W., *The Tudor Interlude* (Leicester: Leicester University Press, 1958).

Godfrey, Bob, 'Nervous Laughter in Henry Medwall's *Fulgens and Lucrece*' in Andres Lascombe, ed., *Tudor Theatre* 3 (Amsterdam, 1996), 81–96 (which advances a case for re-dating the play to the 1510s).

Horner, Olga, '*Fulgens and Lucrece*: An Historical Perspective', *Medieval English Theatre* 15 (1993), 49–86.

Nelson, Alan H., ed., *The Plays of Henry Medwall* (Woodbridge: D. S. Brewer, 1980).

Norland, H. B., *Drama in Early Tudor Britain, 1485–1558* (Lincoln, NE: University of Nebraska Press, 1995).

Reed, A. W., *Early Tudor Drama: Medwall, the Rastells, and the More Circle* (London: Methuen, 1926).

Roper, William, *The Lyfe of Sir Thomas Moore, Knighte*, ed., E. V. Hitchcock, EETS, 197 (London: Early English Text Society, 1935).

Twycross, Meg, 'The Theatricality of Medieval English Plays' in R. Beadle and Alan J. Fletcher, eds., *The Cambridge Companion to Medieval English Theatre*, 2nd edn. (Cambridge: Cambridge University Press, 2008), 26–74.

Wright, Clare, 'Henry Medwall, *Fulgens and Lucres*' in Thomas Betteridge and Greg Walker, eds., *The Oxford Handbook of Tudor Drama* (Oxford: Oxford University Press, 2012), 177–92.

Here is contained a goodly interlude of Fulgens, senator of Rome, Lucrece his daughter, Gaius Flaminius, and Publius Cornelius, of the Disputation of Nobleness, and is divided in two parts to be played at two times. Compiled by master Henry Medwall, late chaplain to the right reverent father in God, John Morton, Cardinal and Archbishop of Canterbury.

[*Dramatis Personae:*

A and B (spectators, later servants to Gaius and Cornelius respectively),
FULGENS (Senator of Rome),
LUCRECE (daughter to Fulgens),
ANCILLA ('Maid' to Lucrece, named Joan),
PUBLIUS CORNELIUS (A nobleman, suitor to Lucrece),
GAIUS FLAMINIUS (a gentleman of lower social origins, a rival suitor to Lucrece).]

Intrat A dicens:

[A]
Ah, for God's will,
What mean ye, sirs, to stand so still?
Have not ye eaten, and your fill,
And paid no thing therefore?
Iwis, sirs, thus dare I say,
He that shall for the shot pay
Vouchsafeth that ye largely assay
Such meat as he hath in store.
I trow your dishes be not bare,
Nor yet ye do the wine spare,
Therefore be merry as ye fare!
Ye are welcome each one
Unto this house without feigning.
But I marvel much of one thing,
That after this merry drinking
And good recreation
There is no words among this press;
Non sunt loquele neque sermones,
But as it were men in sadness
Here ye stand musing,
Where-about I cannot tell,
Or some else damsel
For to dance and spring!

Tell me, what-called, is it not so?
I am sure here shall be somewhat ado,
And iwis, I will know it ere I go
Without I be driven hence.

Intrat B.

Intrat A dicens: Enter A, saying:.
2 **still** quiet.
3 **and your fill** and enough to fill you too.
5 **Iwis** I think/indeed.
6 **shot** bill.
7–8 **Vouchsafeth…store** Grants that you should sample widely the food he has provided for you.
9 **trow** believe.
10 **Nor…spare** And you are not holding back on drinking his wine.
14 **of** about.
17 **press** crowd.
18 ***Non…sermones*** 'There is no speech nor language [where their voice is not heard]' (Psalm 19:3).
21 **Where-about** about what.
22 A line, stating the first alternative, seems to be missing in the printed text. A jokes that the audience seem to be hoping for a pretty dancer to entertain them next.
24 **what-called** whatever you're called.
25 **somewhat ado** something happening.
27 **Without…hence** Unless I'm thrown out (first).
27.1 ***Intrat B.*** Enter B.

[B]
Nay, nay, hardily man, I undertake
No man will such masteries make,
And it were but for the manner sake!
Thou mayest tarry by licence
Among other men and see the play
I warrant no man will say thee nay.

A
I think it well even as ye say
That no man will me grieve.
But I pray you, tell me that again:
Shall here be a play?

B
Yea, for certain.

A
By my troth, thereof am I glad and fain.
And ye will me believe,

Of all the world I love such sport.
It doth me so much pleasure and comfort,
And that causeth me ever to resort
Where such thing is to do.
I trow your own self be one
Of them that shall play?

B
Nay, I am none.
I trow thou speakest in derision
To like me thereto.

A
Nay, I mock not, wot ye well,
For I thought verily by your apparel
That ye had been a player.

B
Nay, never a dell.

A
Then I cry you mercy:
I was to blame. Lo, therefore, I say
There is so much nice array
Amongst these gallants nowaday
That a man shall not lightly

Know a player from another man.
But now to the purpose where I began:
I see well here shall be a play, then.

B
Yea, that there shall, doubtless,
And I trow ye shall like it well.

A
It seemeth, then, that ye can tell
Somewhat of the matter.

B
Yea, I am of counsel.
One told me all the process.

A
And I pray you, what shall it be?

B
By my faith, as it was told me
More than once or twice,
As far as I can bear it away
All the substance of their play
Shall proceed this wise:
When th'empire of Rome was in such flower
That all the world was subject to the same,
Then was there a noble senator,
And as I remember, Fulgens was his name,
Which had a daughter of noble fame.
And yet, as th'author saith in very deed,
Her noble virtue did her fame exceed,

Albeit there was not one almost
Throughout all the city, young ne old,
That of her a did not boast.
And over that, her virtues manifold
In such manner wise were praised and told
That it was thought she lacked no thing
To a noble woman that was according.

Great labour was made her favour to attain

[28] **hardily** certainly.
[29–31] **No man . . . licence** No-one will be so bold (to try to throw you out), even if it were just for appearances' sake! You stay here with my permission.
[33] **say thee nay** refuse you.
[38] **fain** happy/eager.
[39] **And** If.
[42] **resort** come/go to.
[43] **to do** to happen.
[47] **like** liken.
[48] **wot** know.
[50] Because B is finely dressed, A mistakes him for an actor.
[50.1] **never a dell** not a bit (no way!).
[53] **array** fine clothing.
[54] **gallants** fashionable courtiers.
[55] **lightly** easily.
[62.1] **I . . . counsel** I am familiar (with the actors' plans).
[63] **all the process** the whole story (of the play).
[67] **bear it away** remember it.
[69] **wise** way.
[70] **in such flower** so flourishing.
[75] **in very deed** truly indeed.
[79] **a** he.
[83] **To . . . according** That was appropriate for a noble woman.

In the way of marriage, and among all
That made such labour were specially twain
Which more than other did busily on her call,
On the which twain she set her mind especial,
So that she utterly determined in her heart
The one of them to have, all other set apart.
One of them was called Publius Cornelius,
Born of noble blood, it is no nay.
That other was one Gaius Flaminius,
Born of a poor stock, as men doth say.
But for all that, many a fair day,
Through his great wisdom and virtuous behaviour,
He ruled the commonweal to his great honour.

And how so be it that the vulgar opinion
Had both these men in like favour and reverence,
Supposing they had been of like condition,
Yet this said woman of inestimable prudence
Saw that there was some manner of difference,
For the which her answer she deferred and spared
Till both their conditions were openly declared.

And yet to them both this comfort she gave:
He that could be found more noble of them twain,
In all goodly manner her heart should he have.
Of the which answer they both were glad and fain,
For either of them trusted thereby to attain

Th'effect of his desire. Yet, when they had do,
One of them must needs his appetite forego.
Hereupon was a-raised a great doubt and question.
Every man all after as he was affectionate
Unto the parties said his opinion,
But, at the last, in eschewing of debate,
This matter was brought before the Senate,
They to give therein an utter sentence
Which of these two men should have the
pre-eminence.
And finally they gave sentence and award
That Gaius Flaminius was to be commend
For the more noble man, having no regard
To his low birth of the which he did descend,
But only to his virtue they did therein attend,
Which was so great that of convenience
All the city of Rome did him honour
and reverence.

A

And shall this be the process of the play?

B

Yea, so I understand by credible information.

A

By my faith, but if it be even as ye say,
I will advise them to change that conclusion.
What? Will they affirm that a churl's son
Should be more noble than a gentleman born?
Nay, beware, for men will have thereof great scorn:
It may not be spoken in no manner of case.

B

Yes, such considerations may be laid
That every reasonable man in this place
Will hold him therein right well apaid,
The matter may be so well conveyed.

A

Let them convey and carry clean, then,
Or else he will repent that this play began.
Howbeit, the matter toucheth me never a dell,
For I am neither of virtue excellent
Nor yet of gentle blood. This I know well,
But I speak it only for this intent:
I would not that any man should be shent!
And yet there can no man blame us two,
Forwhy in this matter we have nought to do.

B

We? No, God wot, nothing at all,
Save that we come to see this play
As far as we may by the leave of the marshal.

92 **no nay** undeniable.
94 **stock** family.
97 **commonweal** commonwealth/state.
98 **vulgar** common people's.
99 **like** equal.
103 **spared** delayed.
109 **either** each.
110 **do** done.
111 **needs . . . forego** necessarily give up his desire.
113 **all . . . affectionate** according to his inclination.
117 **an utter sentence** a final judgement.
120 **commend** commended.
124 **of convenience** accordingly.
130 **churl's** poor man's.
133 **in no manner of case** under any circumstances.
134 **such . . . laid** such arguments may be put forward/discussed.
136 **apaid** contented.
137 **conveyed** presented.
138–139 **Let . . . began.** Let them go and carry themselves right off, then! [punning on B's 'conveyed']. Otherwise the creator of this play will regret it.
144 **shent** punished.
146 **Forwhy** because.
149 The marshal was the household officer responsible for organization and protocol within the great hall.

I love to behold such mirths alway,
For I have seen before this day
Of such manner things in many a good place
Both good examples and right honest solace.

This play in like wise I am sure
Is made for the same intent and purpose:
To do every man both mirth and pleasure.
Wherefore I cannot think or suppose
That they will any word therein disclose
But such as shall stand with truth and reason
In goodly manner according to the season.

A
Yea, but truth may not be said alway,
For sometime it causeth grudge and despite.

B
Yea, goeth the world so now a day
That a man must say the crow is white?

A
Yea, that he must, by God Almight.
He must both lie and flatter now and then
That casteth him to dwell among worldly men.

In some courts such men shall most win!

B
Yea, but as for the parish where I abide,
Such flattery is abhorred as deadly sin.
And specially liars be set aside
As soon as they may with the fault be spied,
For every man that favoureth and loveth virtue
Will such manner of folk utterly eschew,

Wherefore I can think these folk will not spare
After plain truth this matter to proceed
As the story sayeth. Why should they care?
I trow here is no man of the kin or seed
Of either party, forwhy they were bore
In the city of Rome as I said before.

Therefore, leave all this doubtful question
And praise at the parting even as ye find.

A
Yes, be ye sure, when they have all done
I will not spare to show you my mind.
Praise who will or dispraise, I will not
be behind.
I will jest thereon whatsoever shall befall,
If I can find any man to jest withal.

B
Peace! No mo words, for now they come!
The players been even here at hand.

A
So they be, so help me God and holydam!
I pray you, tell me where I shall stand.

B
Marry, stand even here by me, I warrant.
Give room there, sirs, for God avow,
They would come in if they might for you!

A
Yea, but I pray thee, what-called, tell me this:
Who is he that now cometh in?

B
Marry, it is Fulgens the senator.

A
Yea, is?
What, the father of the foresaid virgin?

B
Yea, forsooth, he shall this matter begin.

A
And where is fair daughter Lucrece?

B
She cometh anon. I say, hold thy peace!

Intrat Fulgens dicens.

FULGENS
Everlasting joy with honour and praise
Be unto our most dread Lord and Saviour,
Which doth us help and comfort many ways,
Not leaving us destitute of his aid and succour,
But letteth his sun shine on the rich and poor,

150 **mirths alway** pastimes always.
160 **season** occasion.
164 **That...white** proverbial, i.e. One must deny what is obviously true (that crows are black).
167 **That...men** He (who) wishes to live among men of the world.
168 **most win** prosper best.
172 **As...spied** As soon as their lies are noticed.
179 **forwhy...bore** because they were born.
182 **praise...find** praise at the end (of the play) according to your judgement.
185 **behind** slow (in speaking up).
188 **mo** more.
190 **holydam** the holy mother (i.e. the Virgin Mary).
192 **Marry** Indeed, used for emphasis.
193 **for God avow** I swear (to) God.
194 **if...you!** if you let them (i.e. if you were not holding things up).
197.1 **is?** is it? (You don't say!)
199 **forsooth** truly.
201 **hold thy peace!** be quiet!
s.d. ***Intrat Fulgens dicens*** 'Enter Fulgens, saying'.

And of his grace is ever indifferent,
Albeit he diversely commiteth his talent.
To some he lendeth the sprite of prophecy,
To some the plenty of tongue's eloquence,
To some great wisdom and worldly policy,
To some literature and speculative science,
To some he giveth the grace of pre-eminence
In honour and degree, and to some abundance
Of treasure, riches, and great inheritance.

Every man ought to take good heed
Of this distribution, for whoso doth take
The larger benefit, he hath the more need
The larger recompense and thank therefore to make.
I speak these words only for mine own sake
And for none other person, for I know well
That I am therein charged, as I shall you tell.

When I consider and call to my remembrance
The prosperous life that I have alway
Hitherto endured without any grievance
Of worldly adversity, well may I say
And think that I am bound to yield and pay
Great praise and thanks to the high King
Of whom proceedeth and groweth every good thing.

And certes, if I would not praise of boast
The benefits that he hath done unto me,
Yet is it well known of least and most
Throughout all Rome th'imperial city
What place in the Senate and honourable degree
I occupy, and how I demean me in the same.
All this can they tell that knoweth but my name.

To speak of plenty and great abundance
Of worldly riches thereunto belonging,
Houses of pleasure and great inheritance,
With rich apparel and every other thing
That to a worthy man should be according,
I am and ever have be in meetly good case,
For the which I thank Almighty God of his grace.

Then have I a wife of good condition
And right conformable to mine intent
In everything that is to be done.
And, howbeit that God hath me not sent
An heir male, which were convenient
My name to continue and it to repair,
Yet am I not utterly destitute of an heir,

For I have a daughter in whom I delight
As for the chief comfort of mine old age,
And surely my said daughter Lucrece doth hight.
Men sayeth she is as like me in visage
As though she were even mine own image
For the which cause nature doth me force
    and betide
The more to favour and love her in my mind.

But yet the principal and greatest occasion
That maketh me to love her as I do
Is this, which I speak not of affection,
But even as the truth moveth me thereto:
Nature hath wrought in my Lucrece so
That to speak of beauty and clear understanding
I cannot think in her what should be lacking.

And besides all that, yet a greater thing
Which is not oft seen in so young a damsel:
She is so discrete and sad in all demeaning,
And thereto full of honest and virtuous counsel
Of her own mind, that wonder is to tell
The gifts of nature and of especial grace.

Am not I greatly bound in this case
To God, as I rehearsed you before?
I were too void of all reason and grace
If I would not serve and praise him therefore
With due love and dread: he asketh no more.
As far as he will me grace thereto send,
The rest of my life therein will I spend,

207 **indifferent** impartial.
208 **Albeit...talent** Although he gives different gifts to different people. (See the account of the gifts of the Holy Spirit in I Corinthians 12.)
209 **lendeth the sprite** gives the spirit.
210 **plenty...eloquence** eloquence in many languages.
211 **worldly policy** political skill.
214 **degree** social status.
222 **charged** obliged (to do that).
229 **Of** From.
230 **certes** certainly.
230 **of boast** by boasting.
232 **of...most** by the highest and lowest alike.
235 **demean me** conduct myself.
241 **according** appropriate.
242 **be...case** been in (a) moderately good situation.
249 **repair** renew.
253 **doth hight** is named.
256 **force and betide** urge and prompt.
258 **occasion** cause.
267 **sad...demeaning** serious in her demeanour/behaviour.
271 **bound** obliged.
272 **rehearsed** told.

Albeit that I must partly intend
To the promotion of my daughter Lucrece
To some meetly marriage, else God defend!
She is my chief jewel and riches,
My comfort against all care and heaviness,
And also she is now of good and ripe age
To be a man's fere by way of marriage.

Wherefore, if I might see ere I die
That she were bestowed somewhat according,
Then were my mind discharged utterly
Of every great cure to me belonging.
It was the chief cause of my hither coming
To have a communication in this same matter
With one Cornelius. Came there none such here?

Intrat Publius Cornelius dicens.

CORNELIUS
Yes, now am I come here at the last.
I have tarried long, I cry you mercy!

FULGENS
Nay, no offence; there is no waste
Nor loss of time yet, hardily,
For this is the hour that ye and I
Appointed here to meet this other day.
Now show me your mind, let me hear what ye say.

CORNELIUS
Then will I leave superfluity away,
Forwhy ye know already my mind in substance.

FULGENS
I wot not whether I do, yea or nay.

CORNELIUS
Why, is it now out of your remembrance
That my desire is to honour and advance
Your daughter Lucrece, if she will agree
That I, so poor a man, her husband should be?

FULGENS
Ye need not, sir, to use these words to me,
For none in this city knoweth better than I
Of what great birth or substance ye be.
My daughter Lucrece is full unworthy
Of birth and goods to look so high,
Saving that happily her good condition
May her enable to such a promotion.

But, if this be your mind and such intent,
Why do ye not labour to her therefore?
For me seemeth it were right expedient
That we know therein her mind before
Ere ever we should commune thereof any more,
For, if she would to your mind apply,
No man shall be so glad thereof as I.

CORNELIUS
Suppose ye that I did not so begin
To get first her favour? Yes, trust me well!

FULGENS
And what comfort would she give you therein?

CORNELIUS
By my faith, no great comfort to tell,
Save that she abideth to have your counsel.
For, as she sayeth, she will nothing
In such matter to do without your counsel,

Nor otherwise than ye shall be content.
And thereupon it was my mind and desire
To speak with you of her for the same intent
Your good will in this behalf to require,
For I am so brent in love's fire
That nothing may my pain aslake
Without that ye will my cure undertake.

FULGENS
Sir, I shall do you the comfort that I can,
As far as she will be advised by me.
How be it, certainly, I am not the man
That will take from her the liberty
Of her own choice: that may not be!

278 **intend** attend.
279 **promotion** advancement/welfare.
280 **meetly . . . defend!** appropriate marriage, God forbid (it is) otherwise!
282 **heaviness** sorrow.
284 **fere . . . of** companion in.
286 **according** appropriately/as she deserves.
288 **cure . . . belonging** responsibility that I bear.
291 **Came . . . here?** Has no such (man) come here?
291.1 ***Intrat . . . dicens*** Enter Publius Cornelius, saying.
295 **hardily** certainly.
299 **leave superfluity away** avoid superfluous words.
300 **Forwhy** because.
300 **my . . . substance** the essence of what I want.
301 **wot** know.
308 **substance** wealth.
311 **condition** nature.
315 **me . . . it** it seems to me.
318 **to . . . apply** agree with your wishes.
320–321 **Suppose . . . favour?** Do you think that I would not have sought her opinion first of all?
331 **brent** burnt.
332 **aslake** quench.
333 **Without that** Unless.

But, when I speak with her, I shall her advise
To love you before other in all goodly wise.

CORNELIUS
I thank you, sir, with all mine heart,
And I pray you do it without delay.

FULGENS
As soon as I shall fro you depart
I will her mind therein assay,
For I shall think that every hour is twain
Till I may speak with you again. [*Exit Fulgens.*]

CORNELIUS
Now a wise fellow that had somewhat a brain,
And of such things had experience,
Such one would I with me retain
To give me counsel and assistance.
For I will spare no cost or expense,
Nor yet refuse any labour or pain
The love of fair Lucrece thereby to attain.

[*To the audience*]

So many good fellows as been in this hall,
And is there none, sirs, among you all
That will enterprise this gear?
Some of you can do it if ye lust!
But, if ye will not, then I must
Go seek a man elsewhere.

Et exeat [*Cornelius*]. *Deinde loquitur B.*

Now have I spied a meet office for me,
For I will be of counsel and I may
With yonder man.

A
Peace, let be!
By God, thou will destroy all the play!

B
'Destroy the play', quod a? Nay, nay,
The play began never till now!
I will be doing, I make God avow,
For there is not in this hundred mile
A feater bawd than I am one.

A
And what shall I do in the meanwhile?

B
Marry, thou shalt come in anon
With another pageant.

A
Who, I?

B
Yea, by Saint John.

A
What? I never used such thing before.

B
But follow my counsel, and do no more:

Look that thou abide here still,
And I shall undertake for to fulfil
All his mind withouten delay.
And whether I do so, yea or nay,
At the least, well dare I undertake
The marriage utterly to mar or to make.

If he and I make any bargain
So that I must give him attendance,
When thou seest me come in again,
Stand even still and keep thy countenance,
For when Gaius Flaminius cometh in
Then must thou thy pageant begin.

A
Shall any profit grow thereby?

B
Hold thy peace! Speak not so high,
Lest any man of this company
Know our purpose openly
And break all our dance!
For I assure thee faithfully,
If thou quit thee as well as I,
This gear shall us both advance. *Exit* [*B*].

344 **assay** test.
349 **retain** employ as a servant.
356 **enterprise this gear** take on this business.
357 **if ye lust** if you wanted to.
359 ***Et...B*** And [Cornelius] shall exit. Then B says.
360 **meet office** suitable job.
361 **and** if.
364 **quod a** says he.
366 **be doing** busy myself/get involved.
368 **A...one** A better pimp than I am.
371 **pageant** performance/trick.
372 **used such thing** did anything like this.
373 **counsel** advice.
379 **mar...make** ruin or bring to success.
380 **bargain** agreement.
383 **keep thy countenance** keep a straight face (don't reveal that you know me).
387 **high** loudly.
388 **Lest** In case.
390 **break...dance** i.e. spoil all our plans.
392 **thou quit thee** acquit yourself/perform.

A
Nay then, let me alone hardily!
If any advantage hang thereby
I can myself thereto apply
By help of good counsel.
This fellow and I be masterless
And live most part in idleness,
Therefore some manner of business
Would become us both well.

At the least wise it is merry being
With men in time of wooing,
For all that while they do nothing
But dance and make revel,
Sing and laugh with great shouting,
Fall in wine with revel routing.
I trow it be a joyful thing
Among such folk to dwell!

Intrat Fulgens, Lucrece et Ancilla, et dicat.

FULGENS
Daughter Lucrece, ye know well enough
What study and care I have for your promotion
And what fatherly love I bear to you,
So that I think in mine opinion
It were time lost and wasteful occupation
This matter to rehearse or tell you any more,
Sith ye it best know, as I said before.

But the special cause that I speak for
Is touching your marriage. As ye know well,
Many folk there be that desireth sore
And laboureth in that behalf with you to mell.
Ye know what is for you, ye need no counsel.
How so be it, if ye list my counsel to require.
I shall be glad to satisfy therein your desire.

LUCRECE
Truth it is, father, that I am bound
As much unto you as any child may be
Unto the father living on the ground,
And where it pleaseth you to give unto me
Mine own free choice and my liberty,
It is the thing that pleaseth me well,
Sith I shall have therein your counsel.

And now according to this same purpose,
What think ye best for me to do?
Ye know right well, as I suppose,
That many folk doth me greatly woo,
Among the which there be specially two
In whom, as I trow and so do ye,
The choice of this matter must finally be.

In that point your mind and mine doth agree.
But yet, right now ere I came here,
For Publius Cornelius ye advised me,
As touching ye would have me only rest there.
If that be your mind I shall gladly forbear
All other and only to him assent
To have me in wedlock at his commandment.

FULGENS
Nay, daughter Lucrece, not so I meant,
For though I did somewhat to him incline,
Yet for all that it is not mine intent
That ye should so thereupon utterly define,
But look whom ye will on God's blessing and mine.
For, trust ye me verily, it is all one to me
Whether Gaius Flaminius wed you or else he.

LUCRECE
Then, sith I have so great liberty
And so good choice, I were unfortunable
And also too unwise if I would not see
That I had him which is most honourable.
Wherefore, may it like you to be agreeable
That I may have respite to make inquisition
Which of these two men is better of condition?

FULGENS
I hold me content, that shall be well done.
It may be respited for a day or twain,
But in the meantime use this provision:

398 **masterless** without an employer.
407 **revel routing** riotous partying.
408 **trow** believe.
409.1 ***Intrat ... dicat*** Enter Fulgens, Lucrece, and the Maid, and (Fulgens) says.
414 **It ... occupation** It would be a waste of time.
420 **mell** deal.
422 **list ... require** want to know my advice.
426 **on the ground** on Earth.
440 **For** in favour of.
441 **As ... there** suggesting that you would prefer me to choose him.
448–449 **That ... mine** Finally decide on him. But, whoever you choose, you have God's blessing and mine.
450 **all one** all the same.
453 **I were unfortunable** I would be unfortunate.
460 **respited** postponed.

See that ye indifferently them both entertain
Till that your mind be set at a certain
Where ye shall rest now. Can ye do so?

LUCRECE
At the least, my good will shall I put thereto.

FULGENS
Then, sith I have business at home for to do,
I will go thither-ward as fast as I may.

LUCRECE
Is it your pleasure that I shall with you go?

FULGENS
Nay, I had leaver that ye went your way
About this matter.

Et exeat [*Fulgens*].

LUCRECE
Well, God be with you then!
I shall do therein the best that I can.

Et facta aliqua pausatione, dicat Lucrece

LUCRECE
I will not de-slander nor blame no man,
But nevertheless, by that I hear say,
Poor maidens be deceived now and then.
So great dissembling nowadays
There is conveyed under words gay,
That if...

ANCILLA
Peace, lady, ye must forbear!
See ye not who cometh here?

LUCRECE
Who is it, wot ye ere?

ANCILLA
It is Gaius Flaminius, perde,
He that would your husband be.

LUCRECE
Aye, good Lord! How wist he
For to find me here?

Intrat Gaius Flaminius.

GAIUS
Yes, good lady, where so ever ye go,
He that listeth to do his diligence
In such manner wise as I have do,
At the last he may come to your presence.
For, whosoever oweth obedience
Unto love, he hath great need
To attendance if he will speed.

LUCRECE
Sir, ye be welcome. What is your mind?

GAIUS
Why, fair Lucrece, is that your guise,
To be so strange and so unkind
To him that oweth you loving service?
I trow I have told you twice or thrice
That mine desire is to marry with you.
Have ye not heard this matter ere now?

LUCRECE
Yes, in very truth, I have heard you say
At diverse times that ye bear me affection:
To such an intent I say not nay.

GAIUS
What need ye then ask the question
What I would with you at this season?
Me seemeth ye should therein doubt no more
Sith ye know well mine errand before.
Iwis, your strangeness grieveth me sore,
But notwithstanding now will I cease,
And at this time I will chide no more
Lest I give you cause of heaviness.
I came hither only for your sake, doubtless,
To glad you and please you in all that I can,
And not for to chide with you as I began.

For, think it in your mind I am the man
That would you please in all that I may,
And to that purpose I will do what I can,
Though ye forbid it and say therein nay,
In that point only I will you disobey.
My heart shall ye have in all goodly wise
Whether ye me take or utterly despise.

465 **At the least** Of course.
469 **leaver** rather.
471.1 ***Et... Lucrece:*** And after a certain pause, Lucrece shall say:
472 **de-slander** slander.
474 **maidens** virgins.
475–476 **So... gay** There is so much deceit hidden under fine words nowadays.
479 **wot ye ere?** Do you know?
480 **perde** by God.
482 **How wist he** Did he know.
483.1 ***Intrat Gaius Flaminius*** Enter Gaius Flaminius.
485 **He... diligence** He who desires to do you diligent service.
489–490 **Unto... speed** He needs to come courting if he wants to prosper.
492 **guise** fashion/manner.
493 **strange... unkind** formal and unnatural.
504 **Sith... before** Since you already know my errand.

And to say that I will follow the guise
Of wanton lovers nowaday,
Which doth many flattering words devise
With gifts of rings and broaches gay
Their lemans' hearts for to betray,
Ye must have me therein excused,
For it is the thing that I never used.

Therefore I will be short and plain,
And I pray you heartily, fair Lucrece,
That ye will be so to me again.
Ye know well I have made labour and business
And also desired you by words express
That ye would vouchsafe in your heart
To be my wife till death us depart.

Lo, this is the matter that I come for:
To know therein your mind and pleasure,
Whether ye set by me any store
To th'effect of my said desire.
And nothing else I will require
But that I may have a plain yea or nay,
Whereto I may trust without delay.

LUCRECE
Me thinketh that by that that ye say,
Ye force not what mine answer be!

GAIUS
Ah, will ye take it that way?
My lady, I meant not so, parde.
Th'affirmative were most lief to me,
For, as ye yourself knoweth best,
That was and is my principal request.

But ye may say I am a homely guest
On a gentlewoman so hastily to call.

LUCRECE
Nay, nay, sir, that guise is best!
Ye cannot displease me withal,
And according to your desire I shall
Even as soon as I goodly may
Answer you therein without delay.

Howbeit, it cannot be done straightway
If I might get a realm thereby.
First will I my father's mind assay
Whether he will thereunto apply.
For, if he like you as well as I,
Your mind in this behalf shall be soon eased
If my said father can be content and pleased.

GAIUS
Gramercy, mine own sweet Lucrece.
Of you desire can I no more at all,
Save only that ye do your business
Upon your father busily to call,
So that whatsoever shall befall,
Within few days I may verily know
To what effect this matter shall grow.

LUCRECE
Ye shall know by tomorrow night
What my father will say thereto.

GAIUS
Then shall ye make mine heart full light
If it please you so to do.

LUCRECE
Yes, doubt ye not it shall be so,
And for that cause I will even now depart.

GAIUS
Now farewell then, mine own sweetheart.

Et exeat Lucrece [and Ancilla]. Deinde A accedens ad Gayum Flaminium, dicat ei sic:

A
Sir, ye seem a man of great honour,
And that moveth me to be so bold:
I rede you, adventure not over much labour
Upon this woman, lest ye take cold.

523 **lemans'** beloveds'.
524 **Ye . . . excused** You must excuse me from all that.
525 **never used** have never done.
528 **again** in return.
530 **express** openly.
531 **vouchsafe** grant (it).
532 **depart** divides us.
535 **set . . . store** place any value on me.
536 **th'effect** fruition.
540–541 **Me . . . be!** I think, from what you say, you don't really mind what my answer is!
544 **lief** desirable.
547 **homely guest** rude fellow.
550 **withal** with that.
552 **goodly may** reasonably can.
555 **If . . . get** (even) if I could gain.
557 **apply** agree.
561 **Gramercy** Thank you ('Grand merci').
562 **Of . . . all** I can ask nothing more of you.
566 **verily** truly.
567 **To . . . grow** How this matter will conclude.
570 **full light** completely happy.
574.1 ***Et . . . sic:*** And Lucrece [and the Maid] shall exit. Then let A approach Gayus Flaminius, saying to him thus:
577–578 **I . . . cold** I advise you, don't spend too much effort on this woman, in case you lose out.

I tell you, the matter is bought and sold;
Without ye take the better heed,
For all these fair words ye shall not speed!

GAIUS
Thinkest thou so in very deed?

A
Yea, so help me God, and I shall tell you why:
Sir, right now, this way as I yede,
This gentlewoman came even by,
And a fresh gallant in her company.
As God would, near them I stalked
And heard every word that they talked.

GAIUS
But spake they any word of me?

A
Nay, nay, ye were nothing in her thought.
They were as busy as they might be
About such a matter as ye have wrought.
And, by God that me dear bought,
Look what answer that ye now have,
Even the same words to him she gave.

Iwis, sir, I am but a poor knave,
But yet I would take on me a great pain
Your honesty in this matter to save,
Though it be unto me no profit nor gain.
But therefore I speak and have disdain
To see in a woman such dissemblance
Toward a gentleman of your substance.

GAIUS
Why, hast thou of me any acquaintance?

A
Yea, sir, and some time ye knew me,
Though it be now out of your remembrance.

GAIUS
By my faith it may well be,
But nevertheless I thank thee.
Me seemeth thou wouldst that all were well
Betwixt me and yonder fair damsel.

A
Yea, by God, I would fight in the quarrel
Rather than ye should lose your intent.

GAIUS
I pray thee, fellow, where dost thou dwell?

A
By my faith, I am now at mine own commandment;
I lack a master, and that I me repent.
To serve you and please I would be fain
If it might like you me to retain.

And of one thing I will, a certain:
I doubt not I shall do you better stead
Toward this marriage than some other twain,
And if I do not, let me be dead!

GAIUS
Well then will I do by thy rede,
And in my service thou shalt be
If thou canst find me any surety.

A
Yes, I can have sureties plenty
For my truth within this place.
Here is a gentleman that would trust me
For as much good as he has.

GAIUS
Yea, and that is but little, percase?

A
By my faith, go where he shall,
It is as honest a man as any in the realm.
I have no more acquaintance within this hall
If I would any friends assay.

[*Indicates B*]

By God, here is one best of all!
I trow he will not say me nay.
For he hath known me many a day.
Sir, will not ye for my truth undertake?

579 **bought and sold** already settled.
580 **Without** Unless.
584 **yede** made my way.
587 **would** wished it.
592 **wrought** attempted.
593 **me dear bought** redeemed me at great cost (to himself).
598 **honesty** reputation.
601 **dissemblance** deceptiveness.
608 **wouldst** hope.
611 **lose your intent** fail in your attempt.
614 **I me repent** I regret that.
617 **a certain** certainly.
618 **stead** service.
619 **some other twain** any two other men.
621 **do . . . rede** follow your advice.
623 **any surety** a testimonial to good character.
627 **For . . . has** With all the goods he has. (A either picks out a spectator, whom Gaius rejects, and he then turns to B, or A picks out B initially, sees him rejected, then picks him again at a different spot.)
628 **percase** perhaps.
634 **say me nay** deny me.
636 **for . . . undertake** attest to my honesty.

B

Yes, 'fore God, else I would I were bake!
Sir, my master, will ye believe me?
I dare trust him for all that I can make,
If ye find me sufficient surety.
As for his truth, doubt not ye.
I never could by him anything espy
But that he was as true a man as I.

He and I dwelled many a fair day
In one school, and yet I wot well
From thence he bare never away
The worth of an half-penny that I can tell;
Therefore he is able with you to dwell.
As for his truth, that dare I well say,
Hardily trust him therein ye may.

GAIUS

Upon your word I shall assay,

[*To A*]

And, sir, after thy good deserving
So shall I thy wages pay.
But now to remember one thing:
Me thought thou saidest at the beginning
That Lucrece favoureth better than me
Another lover. What man is he?

A

Cornelius I wean his name should be.

GAIUS

Ah, then, I know him well, by the Rood!
There is not within all this city
A man born of a better blood.
But yet Lucrece hath a wit so good
That as I think she will before see
Whether his conditions thereto agree,

And if they do not, fare well he!
But therein I have nought ado.
He shall not be dispraised for me
Without that I be compelled thereto.
I cannot let him for to woo
A woman being at her own liberty,
For why it is as free for him as for me.

I will forbear never the more
Till I know what shall be the end.
Go thy way unto Lucrece therefore,
And heartily me unto her recommend,
Praying her that she will me send
A ready answer of that thing
That she promised me at her departing.

A

Marry, I shall, without any tarrying.
I know mine errand well enough:
Ye shall see me appoint a meeting
Where she again shall speak with you.

GAIUS

Then shall I thy wit allow
If thou can bring that about.

A

Yes, that I shall do, have ye no doubt.

Et exeat Gaius Flaminius, et dicat B.

B

Now, by my troth, I would not have thought
That thou hadst been half so wise,
For thou hast this matter featly wrought
And conveyed it point device
To bring thyself to such a service;
I see well thou hast some wit in thy head!

A

Yea, a little. But hast thou sped?

B

Even likewise, have thou no dread,
I have gotten a master for my prow.
I never thrived as I shall do now!

A

No? Which way?

637 **'fore** before.
637 **bake** baked.
638 **make** earn.
646–647 **he... tell** both: A never stole anything, and (punning) he never learned anything at school.
651 **Upon... assay** I shall try him on your recommendation.
652 **after... deserving** as you deserve.
658 **wean** think.
659 **Rood** Holy Cross.
665 **fare well he!** It's 'goodbye' to him!
666 **therein... ado** I'll play no part in that.
668 **Without that** Unless.
669 **let... woo** prevent him from wooing.
681 **appoint** arrange.
683 **thy wit allow** praise your inginuity.
685.1 ***Et... dicat B:*** Let Gaius Flaminius exit, and B shall say:
688–689 **featly... device** neatly arranged and carried it off perfectly.
692 **sped** prospered.
694 **prow** advantage.

B

I shall tell thee how:
It is no mastery to thrive at all
Under a man that is so liberal.

There is now late unto him fall
So great goods by inheritance
That he wote never what to do with all,
But lasheth it forth daily askance
That he had no daily remembrance
Of time to come, nor maketh no store,
For he careth not which end goeth before.

And, by Our Lady, I commend him the more!
Why should he those goods spare,
Sith he laboured never therefore?
Nay, and every man should care
For goods, and specially such as are
Of gentle blood, it were great sin,
For all liberality in them should begin.

Many a poor man thereby doth win
The chief substance of his living.
My master were worthy to be a king
For liberal expenses in all his dealing!
I trow thou shalt see him come in
Like a rutter somewhat according
In all apparel to him belonging.
How much payeth he, as ye suppose,
For the making of a pair of his hose?

A

Marry, twelve pence were a fair thing.

B

Yea, by the Rood, twenty times told,
That is even twenty shillings for the making!

A

It cannot be so without a man would
Make them all with silk and gold!

B

Nay, by Jees, none earthly thing
But even the bare cloth and the lining!

Save only that there is in cutting
A new manner of fashion nowaday:
Because they should be somewhat strange,
They must be striped all this way
With small slips of colours gay,
A codpiece before almost thus large,
And therein resteth the greatest charge!

To speak of gowns and that good change,
Of them he hath store and plenty,
And that the fashions be new and strange,
For none of them passeth the mid-thigh.
And yet he putteth in a gown commonly
How many broad yards, as ye guess?

A

Marry, two or three?

B

Nay, seven and no less!

A

By my truth, that is like a lie!

B

But it is as true as ye stand there.
And I shall tell you a reason why:
All that doth that fashion wear,
They have wings behind ready to fly,
And a sleeve that would cover all the body!
Then forty pleats, as I think in my mind,
They have before, and as many behind.

A

Well, as for gentlemen, it is full kind
To have their pleasures that may well pay.

B

Yea, but then this grudgeth my mind:
A gentleman shall not wear it a day,

697 **is no mastery** takes no skill.
698 **liberal** generous.
702 **lasheth askance** throws it around every day as if.
704 **maketh no store** savings for the future.
705 **he...before** i.e. he cares for nothing.
708 **Sith...therefore?** Since he never worked for them?
709–710 **and...goods** if every man were to look after his wealth.
711 **were** would be (a).
712 **For...begin** For liberality should originate with them (the nobility).
714 **The...living** The greater part of his income.
718 **Like according** Looking something like a rutter (a gallant, from German 'ritter', knight, with implications of rutting: sexual predatoriness).
722 **fair thing** good price.
723 **twenty times told** that much counted out twenty times.
727 **Jees** Jesus.
731 **strange** newfangled.
734 **A...large** and with a codpiece in front, this large.
735 **resteth...charge** lies the greatest cost. (With a bawdy double entendre on 'the largest cannon'.)
736 **good change** sufficient change (of clothes).
739 Revealingly short gowns were fashionable in the late fifteenth century.
741 A 'broad yard' was a six-foot width of cloth.
743 **like** likely to be.
751–752 **full...pay** completely natural for those who can pay to get what they want.

But every man will himself array
Of the same fashion, even by and by
On the morrow after!

A

Nay, that I defy!
But then I marvel greatly why
You are not garnished after that guise.

B

There is never a knave in the house save I
But his gown is made in the same wise,
And, for because I am new come to service,
I must for a while be content
To wear still mine old garment.

A

Yea, but abide: to what intent
Doth thy master take in hand
To make him so much costly raiment?

B

Marry, that is easy to understand:
All is done for Lucrece's sake.
To wed her he doth his reckoning make.

A

I put case that she do him forsake
So that she be my master's wife.

B

By my faith, then I say it will make
Many a man to lose his life,
For thereof will rise a great strife.

A

Marry, I pray God send us peace!

B

By my faith, it will be no less
If my master have not Lucrece.
I can no more, God speed the right!
Lo, these folk will strive and fight
For this woman's sake,
And when they have done their uttermost,
I wean verily he shall speed best
That must her forsake!
He is well at ease that hath a wife,
Yet he is better that hath none, by my life!
But he that hath a good wife and will forsake her,
I pray God the Devil take her!

B

Now in good faith, thou art a mad knave.
I see well thou hast wedded a shrew!

A

The Devil I have!
Nay, I have married two or three
Sith the time that I her lost.

B

And keepest thou them all still with thee?

A

Nay, that would not quit the cost.
To say the truth, they find me most.

B

Then they have some manner getting
By some occupation, have they?

A

Sir, they have a pretty way!
The chief mean of their living
Is lechery . . . leach-craft I would say!
Wherein they labour night and day
And ease many a man in some case.

B

And where do they dwell?

A

At the Common Place;
There thou must them all find!
God's mercy, where is my mind?
By God, I shall be shent!
I should have gone to Lucrece
About my master's business;
Thitherward I was bent.

B

By my faith, my master is there
All the while that thou art here,
As I verily suppose.

754 **a day** (for more than) a day.
759 **garnished . . . guise** dressed in that style.
760 **knave . . . I** no servant except me.
767 **raiment** clothing.
770 **To . . . make** He runs up a bill with marrying her in mind (i.e. the dowry will repay all the initial expenditure).
771 **I . . . that** What if?
779 **I . . . right!** I know no more, may God favour the righteous!
783 **wean verily** truly believe.
794–795 **quit . . . most** repay the cost (of keeping them). To tell the truth, they mostly provided for me.
796 **manner getting** form of income.
798 **pretty** clever.
800 A's slip suggests that lechery rather than medicine ('leach-craft') may well be their trade, and that he is their pimp.
802 **in some case** in one way or another.
Common Place either the brothels of Southwark, haunt of 'common women' (prostitutes), or the court of Common Pleas (Westminster), i.e. they are always in court.
809 **bent** headed.

A

I shrew thy face, by Saint Mary!
With thy chattering thou dost me tarry
Even for the same purpose.

B

I say, when thou hast with Lucrece spoken,
I pray thee, will thou deliver me a token
In mine name to her maid?

A

Nay, ye must beware of that gear,
For I have been afore you there.

B

Why, hast thou her assayed?

A

Yea, yea, that matter is sped full.
I may have her and she will:
That comfort she me gave.

B

And hast thou no other comfort at all?
I trust to God then yet I shall
All this matter save.

Howbeit, I will not the matter begin
Without I were sure she were a virgin.

A

By my troth, this comfort shall
I put thee in:
I came never on her back in the way of sin.

Avoid the place A.

B

Then all is well and fine
If the matter be in that case!
I trust that within a little space
That wench shall be mine.
I tell you it is a trull of trust
All to quench a man's thrust
Better than any wine!

It is a little pretty mouset,
And her voice is as dulcet
And as sweet as reasty pork.
Her face is somewhat brown and yellow,
But for all that she hath no fellow
In singing hence to York.

But the worst that grieveth me,
She hath no leisure nor liberty
For an hour or twain
To be out of her mistress's sight.
I watched for her this other night,
But all was in vain.

Howbeit, I think that at the last
I shall come within two stones' caste
Of her, I ask no more.
And if I do so, then my mate
Shall have no lust therein to prate
As he did before.

Come in the maiden [Ancilla].

Cock's body, here she is!
Now welcome, by heaven's bliss,
Thee last that was in my thought.

ANCILLA

Tush, I pray you, let me go!
I have somewhat else to do,
For this hour I have sought

A man that I should speak withal
Fro my mistress.

B

What do you him call?

ANCILLA

Master Gaius, or his man.

B

Am not I he that ye would have?

ANCILLA

No, no, I would have another knave!

813 **shrew** curse.
817 **token** love-token.
821 **her assayed** tried her.
822 **sped full** successfully completed.
823 **and** if.
829 **Without** Unless.
831 A carefully ignores the possibility that he has known her sinfully from the front.
831.1 ***Avoid ... A***. A should leave the acting space.
833 **If ... case** If that's how things stand.
836 **trull of trust** trusty slut.
837 **thrust** thirst.
839 **It** She (baby talk).
839 **mouset** baby mouse.
841 **reasty** rancid.
844 **hence** from here.
849 **watched** waited.
852 **I ... caste** (If) I could only come within two stone's throws (of her). (As 'stones' was slang for testicles, there is an ejaculatory double entendre here.)
855 **lust ... prate** desire to chatter.
857 **Cock's** God's (euphemism).
859 **Thee ... thought** The very person I was thinking about!

B
Why, am I a knave, then?
ANCILLA
Nay, I said not so, perde.
But where trow ye these folks be?
B
I cannot verily say.
His man went even now from me
And I marvel greatly that ye
Met him not by the way,
For he is gone to speak with Lucrece
From his master.
ANCILLA
What, with my mistress?
Nay!
B
Yea, so I heard him say.
ANCILLA
God's mercy, and I was sent
Even hither for the same intent
To bring an answer
Of the errand that he is gone for,
Wherefore now there is no more
But I must go seek him there.
B
Nay, tarry here awhile gentle Joan,
For he will come hither anon.
ANCILLA
Tarry? Why should I so?
B
Marry, to laugh and talk with me.
ANCILLA
Nay, look where such giglets be,
For I am none of them, I warn thee,
That use so to do.
B
I mean nothing but good and honest
And for your weal, and you list
To assent thereunto.
ANCILLA
'For my weal', quod a? How may that be?
That is a thing that I cannot see.
B
Marry, this, lo, is mine intent:
I mean, if ye would be content
Or any wise agree

For to be my sacrament of penance...
Aye, God give it a very, very vengeance!
'Of wedlock' I would have said!
ANCILLA
Tush, by Saint James, ye do but mock,
To speak to me of any wedlock,
And I so young a maid!
B
Why, are ye a maid?
ANCILLA
Yea, else I were to blame.
B
Whereby wote ye?
ANCILLA
Marry, for I am!
B
Ah, that is a thing!
Hear ye not, sirs, what she sayeth?
So reasonable a cause thereto she layeth!
ANCILLA
A straw for your mocking!
Have ye none to mock but me?
B
Mock? Nay, so mote I thee,
I mean even good earnest!
Give me your hand and you shall see
What I will promise you.
ANCILLA
That way were not best for my prow!

Would ye handfast me forth with all?
Nay, by the Rood, first ye shall
Cheap or ever you buy!
We must first of the price agree,
For whosoever shall have me,
I promise you faithfully,

882 **more** alternative.
888 **look...be** (go and) look where the wanton women are (and talk to them).
892 **weal...list** benefit, if you wish.
900 **give...vengeance** curse it, doubly!
901 **would** should.
905 **maid** virgin.
906.1 **Whereby...am!** 'How do you know?' 'Because I am!'
909 **So...layeth!** So reasonable an argument she puts forward! (Ironic.)
912 **so...thee** if I may prosper!
916 **prow** profit/benefit.
917 **Would...all?** Would you betroth yourself to me just like that?
918–919 **first...buy!** always bargain before you buy!

He shall me first assure
Of twenty pound land in jointure.

B

Why, are ye so costly?
Nay, nay, then ye be not for me.
As pretty a woman as ye be
I can sometime buy
For much less wages and hire,
As for the season that I desire
To have her in company.

Therefore, if ye can find in your heart
To leave all such jointure apart
And take me as I am,
I shall do you as great a pleasure,
And thereto I will love you out of measure,
Else I were to blame.

ANCILLA

Yea, but our household shall be full small
But if we have somewhat else withal
Our charges for to bear.

B

Yea, God send us merry weather!
I may not wed and thrive all together;
I look not for that gear.

I shall tell you a marvellous case:
I knew twain married in a place

Dwelling together in one house,
And I am sure they were not worth a louse
At the beginning.
And ere ever the year were do,
They were worth an hundred or two!

ANCILLA

That was a marvellous thing!

But yet I can tell thee a greater marvel,
And I knew the persons right well:
Sir, I knew two, certain,

That when they were wedded, they had
in store
Scarce half a bed and no more
That was worth an haw,
And within a year or twain
They had so great increase and gain
That at the last they were fain
To shove their heads in the straw.

B

Tush, ye do but mock and rail!
And I promise you withouten fail,
If ye list to have me,
I woot where is an hundred pound in store,
And I owe never a grote therefore!

ANCILLA

All that may be;

I believe it even as ye say.
But ye tarry me here all day,
I pray you let me go.
And for my marriage, that is a thing
In the which I purpose to give a sparing
For a year or two.

B

'A year or two', quod a? Nay, God forbid!
Iwis, it had be time for you to wed
Seven or eight year ago.

And ye wist how merry a life
It is to be a wedded wife,
Ye would change that mind.

ANCILLA

Yea, so it is, as I understand,
If a woman have a good husband,
But that is hard to find!
Many a man blameth his wife, parde,
And she is more to blame than he!

923–924 **He...jointure.** He must first guarantee me £20 worth of land made over in jointure (i.e. legally owned in her name as well as her spouse's).
930–931 **As...company.** I can hire a woman as pretty as you are much more cheaply for as long as I want her.
939 **if** unless.
940 **Our...bear.** To cover our costs.
942–943 **all...gear!** at the same time. I'm not expecting that!
950 Whether 'pounds' or 'lice' is left uncertain.
957 **haw** a hawthorn berry (i.e. very little).
959–961 **so great...straw** i.e. the increase of children reduced them to hiding their heads in the bed-straw (or perhaps to eating it).
962 **rail** nag.
965 **woot** know.
966 A **groat** was a coin worth four pence.
972 **to give a sparing** to delay.
975 **had be** was.
977 **And ye wist** If you knew.
984 A seemingly unintentional slip?

B
As true as the Gospel now say ye.
But now tell me one thing:
Shall I have none other answer but this
Of my desire?

ANCILLA
No sir, iwis,
Not at this meeting.

B
Will ye now need be ago then?

ANCILLA
Take your leave honestly.

Et conabitur eam osculari.

See the man!
Let me alone, with sorrow!

B
Marry, so be it. But one word:
I will kiss thee ere thou go.

ANCILLA
The Devil's turd!
The man is mad, I trow!

B
So mad I am that needs I must
As in this point have my lust
Howsoever I do.

ANCILLA
Parde, ye may do me that request,
Forwhy it is but good and honest.

Et osculabitur. Intrat A.

A
Now a fellowship, I thee beseech,
Set even such a patch one my breach!

B
A wild fire thereon!

ANCILLA
God's mercy, this is he
That I have sought so!

A
Have ye sought me?

ANCILLA
Yea, that have I do!
This gentleman can witness bear
That all this hour I have stand here
Seeking even for you.

A
Have ye two be together so long?

ANCILLA
Yea, why not?

A
Marry, then all is wrong,
I fear me so now.

B
Nay, nay, here be too many witness
For to make any such business
As thou weanest, hardily!

ANCILLA
Why, what is the man's thought?
Suppose ye that I would be nought
If no man were by?

[A]
Nay, for God, I meant not so,
But I would no man should have to do
With you but only I.

ANCILLA
'Have to do', quod a? What call ye that?
It soundeth to a thing I wote ne'er what!

[A]
Aye, God's mercy!
I see well a man must beware
How he speaketh there as ye are,
Ye take it so strangely!
Nay, I mean nothing but well,
For by my will no man shall deal
With you in way of marriage,
But only I; this wise I meant!

ANCILLA
Yea, but though it were your intent,
Yet ye do but rage

To use such words unto me,
For I am yet at my liberty.

990 **ago** going.
991.1 ***Et... osculari.*** And he shall try to kiss her.
998 **Howsoever** Whatever (else).
1000.1 ***Et... A.*** And she shall be kissed. Enter A.
1001–1002 **Now... breach!** I beg you for fellowship's sake, put a similar patch on my breeches (i.e. kiss my arse)!
1003 **A... thereon!** Curse that!
1015 **weanest** imagine.
1017–1018 **Suppose... by?** Do you think I'd be wanton if no one was around (to witness)?
1023 **It... what!** I don't know what that implies!
1026 **there... are** when you're about.
1033 **rage** rave/speak madly.

A

Yea, that I know well.
But nevertheless, sithen I began
To love you long before this man,
I have very great marvel

That ever ye would his mind fulfil,
To stand and talk with him still
So long as ye have do.

B

'Before me', quod a? Nay, I make avow,
I moved this matter long before you:
How say ye thereto?

ANCILLA

I will nothing in the matter say
Lest I cause you to make afray,
For thereof I would be loath.

A

By cock's body, but whosoever it be
That weddeth her besides me,
I shall make him wroth!

B

Yea, but he that is so hasty at every word,
For a medicine must eat his wife's turd!

ANCILLA

Hold your tongues there I say,
For, and ye make this work for me,
Ye shall both disappointed be
As far as I may!

A

By my truth, but mark me well:
If ever thou with this man dwell
As a woman with her mate,
Thou shalt find him the most froward man
That ever thou sawest sith the world began!
For I dare undertake

That forty times on a day
Without any cause he will thee affray
And beat thee back and side!

ANCILLA

He shall not need so to do,
For he shall have forty causes and forty too,
If I with him abide.

A

Marry, that is a remedy according!
But I can tell thee another thing,
And it is no lie:
Thou mayest well be his wedded wife,
But he will never love thee in his life.

ANCILLA

Yet I know a remedy.

A

How so?

ANCILLA

Marry, I will love him as little again!
For every shrewd turn he shall have twain,
And he were my brother.

B

Iwis, Joan, he speaketh but of malice.
There is no man hence to Calais,
Whosoever be the t'other,

That can himself better apply
To please a woman better than I.

ANCILLA

Yea, so I heard you say!
But yet, be ye never so wroth,
There is never one of you both,
For all your words gay

That shall be assured of me
Till I may first hear and see
What ye both can do.
And he that can do most mastery,
Be it in cookery or in pastry,
In feats of war or deeds of chivalry,
With him will I go.

A

By my troth, that liketh me well.
There is no mastery that a man can tell
But I am meet thereto,
Wherefore that wager I dare well undertake!
Let me see, wilt thou go quoit for thy lady's sake,

1040 **his mind fulfil** satisfy his desire.
1044 **moved this matter** began (my) suit.
1048 **loath** unwilling.
1055 **and . . . me** if you argue over me.
1057 **may** can arrange it.
1058 **mark** understand.
1061 **froward** quarrelsome.
1063 **undertake** wager.
1065 **affray** attack.
1068 **too** more.
1076.1 **again** in return.
1077 **shrewd turn** mean act.
1078 **And** Even if.
1081 **Whosoever . . . t'other** Whoever he might be.
1091 **do most mastery** show most skill.
1097 **meet thereto** good at it.
1099 **go quoit** play at quoits.

Or what thing shall we do?

B

Nay, if thou wilt her with mastery win,
With boys' games thou mayest not begin;
That is not her intent.

A

What is best that we do, then?

B

Marry, canst thou sing?

A

Yea, that I can,
As well as any man in Kent.

B

What manner of song shall it be?

A

Whatsoever thou wilt choose thee,
I hold me well content.
And if I meet thee not at the close,
Hardily let me the wager lose
By her own judgement.
Go to now, will ye set in?

B

Nay, be the Rood, ye shall begin.

A

By Saint Jamie, I assent.
Abide, Joan, ye can good skill,
And if ye would the song fulfil
With a third part,
It would do right well, in my mind.

ANCILLA

Sing on, hardily, and I will not be behind,
I pray thee with all my heart.

Et tunc cantabunt.

B

I am so hoarse, it will not be.

A

'Hoarse', quod a? Nay, so mot I thee,
That was not the thing
And a man should the truth say:
Ye lost a crochet or two by the way,
To mine understanding.

B

Why, was I a minim before?

A

Yea, be the Rood, that ye were and more.

B

Then were ye a minim behind.
Let me see, yet sing again,

[*To Ancilla*]

And mark which of us twain
Pleaseth best your mind.

ANCILLA

Nay, nay, ye shall this matter try
By some other manner of mastery
Than by your singing.

B

Let him assay what mastery he will.

A

Marry, and my belly were not so full
I would wrestle with him a fair pull.
That were a game according
For such valiant men as we be!

B

I shrew thine heart and thou spare me.

Et deinde luctabuntur. [*B throws A*]

ANCILLA

Nay, by my faith, that was no fall!

B

Ah, then I see well ye be partial
When ye judge so.
Well, I shall do more for your love.
Even here I cast to him my glove
Ere ever I hence go,

On the condition that in the plain field
I shall meet him with spear and shield
My life thereon to jeopard.
Let me see and he dare take it.

Tunc projiciet cirothecam.

1110 **And . . . close** And if I'm not still in time and harmony with you at the end.
1113 **set in** set us off.
1116 **can good skill** are skilled (at singing).
1117–1118 **fulfil . . . part** complete the traditional three-part harmony. Joan will be the treble voice to accompany A and B's tenor and mean.
1021.1 ***Et tunc cantabunt.*** And they shall sing.
1126 **a crochet** a musical note, half a minim.
1128 **a minim before** a minim (half a semibreve) too quick?
1139 **pull** bout.
1140 **game according** suitable contest.
1142 **and** if.
1042.1 ***Et deinde luctabuntur.*** And then they shall wrestle.
1147 **cast to him** throw down (in formal challenge).
1149 **plain field** open field (of combat).

A
Yea, hardily, I will not forsake it.
I am not such a coward
But I dare meet thee at all assays;
When shall it be do?

B
Even straightways
Without further delay,
And I shrew his heart that fears
Either with cronal or sharp spears,
This bargain to assay.

A
And I beshrew him for me!
But abide, now let me see,
Where shall I have a horse?

B
Nay, we shall need no horse ne mule,
But let us joust at fart prick in cule.

A
By Saint Jamie, no force,

Even so be it! But where is our gear?

B
By my faith, all thing is ready [here]
That belongeth thereto.
Com forth, ye flower of the frying pan,
Help ye to array us as well as ye can.
And howsoever ye do,

See that ye judge indifferently
Which of us twain hath the mastery.

ANCILLA
Yes, hardily, that I shall.
I shall judge after my mind.
But see ye hold fast behind
Lest ye trouble us in all.

B
Tush, that is the least care of fifteen.
And if I do not, on my game be it seen!
Go to, bind me first, hardily.
So, lo, now, give me my spear,
And put me a staff through here;
Then am I all ready.

A
Abide, who shall help to harness me?

ANCILLA
That shall I do, so moot I thee,
With a right good will!

A
Soft and fair! Mine arm is sore,
Ye may not bind me strait therefore.

ANCILLA
Nay, no more I will.

I will not hurt thee for twenty pound.
Come off now, sit down on the ground,
Even upon thy tail.

A
Aye, good Lord, when will ye have do?

ANCILLA
Now all is ready: hardily, go to!
Bid him bale, bale!

A
[*To the audience*]

Fall to prayer, sirs, it is need,
As many of you as would me God speed,
For this gear standeth me upon.

B
Yea, and that shall thou find ere we depart,
And if thou spare me I shrew thy heart!
Let me see, come on!

Et projectus dicat A.

A
Out, out, alas for pain!
Let me have a priest ere I be slain
My sin to disclose.

1052.1 ***Tunc projiciet cirothecam.*** Then he shall throw down a glove.
1159 **cronal** a spear with a less-dangerous, divided head, used in jousting.
1165 **fart prick in cule** fart-prick-in-(the)-arse: a mock joust with the two men perhaps bound in squatting positions, hopping at each other with poles between their legs as spears. Once bound, they are helpless when Joan beats them.
1166 **no force** no worries!
1170 **flower...pan** a mock-romantic epithet for the (scullery?) maid, Joan.
1171 **array us** arm ourselves.
1177 **hold fast behind** keep your arse tight-shut.
1179 **least...fifteen** i.e. the least of my worries
1180 **on...seen!** the evidence will be seen on my 'game' (perhaps a variant of '*jambe*' (Old Fr.), leg or leggings).
1189 **strait** tightly.
1194 **have do?** have done? (i.e. stop it!).
1196 **bale** charge!
1198 **would...speed** wishes me well.
1199 **this...upon** the contest awaits me.
Et...A. And (having been thrown) A says:
1203 **Out!** Woe!
1205 **disclose** confess.

B
And because he sayeth so, it is need,
For he is not in clean life indeed:
I feel it at my nose…

Fo! Fo! etc.

Now ye are mine, lady!

ANCILLA
Nay, never the more.

B
No? Why so?

ANCILLA
For I am taken up before.

B
Marry, I beshrew your heart therefore!
It should better content me
That ye had be taken up behind!

ANCILLA
Nay, nay, ye understand not my mind
In that point.

B
It may well be,
But tell me, how meant ye then?

ANCILLA
Marry, I am sure to another man
Whose wife I intend to be.

B
Nay, I trow, by Cock's Passion,
Ye will not mock us of that fashion;
Ye may not, for very shame!

ANCILLA
Shame or not, so shall it be,
And because that for the love of me
Ye two have made this game,
It shall not be done all in vain,
For I will reward you both twain,
And else I were to blame.

Somewhat thereby ye must needs win,
And therefore to everych of you will I spin
A new pair of breaches!
Take thee that for thy dole!
And because he is black in the hole,
He shall have as much!

Et utroque flagellato recedit Ancilla.

A
Out, alas! What woman was this?

B
It is Lucrece's maid.

A
The Devil it is!
I pray God a vengeance take her!
How sayest thou, shall she be thy wife?

B
Nay, I had leaver she had eaten my knife!
I utterly forsake her.

Intrat Gaius.

GAIUS
How, sirs, who hath arrayed you this?

A
False thieves, master, iwis,
And all for your quarrel!

GAIUS
What? And this other man too?

A
Yea, and ye would our hands undo,
The matter we shall tell.

GAIUS
Yes, marry, will I. Now tell on:
Who hath you these wrongs done?

A
Marry, that I shall.

Cornelius' servants, which is your enemy,
Espied me going toward Lucrece's place,
That I could bring the matter to pass
Of that gentlewoman, as your desire was.
They laid await for me in the way,
And so they left me in this array.

GAIUS
Yea, but hast thou any deadly wound?
That is the thing that feareth my mind.

A
In faith, I was left for dead on the ground,
And I have a great gash here behind
Out of the which there cometh such a wind

1208–1209 **I…etc.** i.e. I can smell it! Phaw! (B complains about the smell).
1211.1 **taken up before** already promised (to another).
1218 **sure** promised.
1230 **everych** each.
1230–1231 **spin…breaches** i.e. she beats their buttocks.
1232 **for thy dole** for your share!
1234.1 ***Et…Ancilla.*** And, when both are beaten, the Maid withdraws.
1242 **who…this?** who's done this to you?
1243 **False** Wicked.

That if ye hold a candle thereto
It will blow it out! That will it do!

GAIUS
See to it betime by mine advice,
Lest the wound fester within.

A
Then have I need of a good surgeon,
For it is so deep within the skin
That ye may put your nose therein
Even up to the hard eyes.

Here is a man that quit him as well
For my defence as ever I see.
He took such part that in the quarrel
His arm was stricken off by the hard knee
And yet he slew of them two or three.

GAIUS
Be they slain? Nay, God forbid!

A
Yes, so help me God, I warrant them dead.

Howbeit I stand in great dread
That if ever he come in their way
They will cut off his arm or his head,
For so I heard them all three say.

GAIUS
Which, they that were slain?

A
Yea, by this day!
What needeth me therefore to lie?
He heard it himself as well as I.

GAIUS
Well then, ye lie both two! [*Exit B.*]
But now tell me, what hast thou do
As touching my commandment
That I bade thee do to Lucrece?
Spakest thou with her?

A
Yea, sir, doubtless,
And this is her intent:

She commendeth her to you by the same token
That with her father she hath spoken
According to your request,
And so she willeth you to be of good cheer,
Desiring you this night to appear,
Or tomorrow at the furthest,

And she will meet you here in this place
To give you a final answer in this case
Whereto ye shall trust.

GAIUS
That is the thing that I desire!
But said she so?

A
Yea, by this fire,
I tell you very just,

In so much that she bade me say
And warn you that ye should purvey
For your own business,

For then it shall determined be
Whether Publius Cornelius or ye
Shall have the pre-eminence.

GAIUS
All that purpose liketh me well,
But who shall be here more, canst thou tell?

A
Marry, here shall be Fulgens

And Publius Cornelius himself also,
With diverse other many mo
Beside this honourable audience.
Wherefore, if ye will your honour save
And your intent in this matter have,
It is best that ye go hence

For to study and call to mind
Such arguments as ye can best find
And make yourself all prest.

GAIUS
Thy counsel is good; be it so,
And even thereafter will I do,
For I hold it best.

Et exeat Gaius et A. Intrat B.

B
God's body, sirs, this was a fit!
I beshrew the whore's heart yet
When I think thereon,
And yet the strokes be not so sore
But the shame grieveth me more,

1264 **betime** quickly.
1269 **Even...eyes** Right up to the eyes.
1270 **quit him** performed.
1273 **stricken...knee** struck off near the knee.
1290 **commendeth her** commends herself.
1295 **furthest** latest.
1303 **purvey** provide.
1312 **mo** more.
1319 **prest** ready.
1322.1 ***Et...B.*** And let Gaius and A exit. Enter B.

Sith that it was done

Before so many as here be present.
But and I might take her,
By my troth I shall make her
This deed to repent!

[*Enter A.*]

A

Yet thou were as good hold thy peace,
For there is no remedy doubtless;
Therefore let it go.
It is to us both great folly and shame
This matter anymore to rehearse or name.

B

Well then, be it so.

And yet, because she hath made me smart,
I trust once to ride in her cart,
Be it shame or no.
I cannot suffer it patiently
To be rebuked openly
And to be mocked also.
Another thing grieveth me worst of all:
I shall be shent, that I shall,
Of my master too

Because I have been so long away
Out of his presence.

A

Nay, nay,

I have heard so much sith I went hence
That he had little mind to thine offence.

B

I pray you tell me why.

A

For, as I brought my master on his way,
I heard one of Lucrece's men say
That thy master hath been
All this hour at her place,
And that he his answer has,
This wise as I mean:

She hath appointed him to be here
Soon, in the evening about supper,
And then he shall have a final answer
What she intendeth to do.
And so then we shall know her intent,
For, as I understand, she will be content
To have one of them two.

But first she will needs know the certain
Whether is the most noble of them twain;
This she sayeth alway.

B

Why, that is easy to understand
If she be so wise as men bear in hand.

A

Yea, so I heard you say.

Let me see now, what is your opinion
Whether of them is most noble of condition?

B

That can I tell hardily:
He that hath most nobles in store,
Him call I the most noble ever more,
For he is most set by.

And I am sure Cornelius is able
With his own goods to buy a rabble
Of such as Gaius is!
And over that, if nobleness of kin
May this woman's favour win,
I am sure he cannot miss.

A

Yea, but come hither soon to the end of
this play
And thou shalt see whereto all that will weigh;
It shall be for thy learning.

B

Yea, come again who will for me,
For I will not be here, so mot I thee!
It is a gentlemanly thing

That I should await and come again
For other men's causes and take such pain!

I will not do it, I make God avow.
Why might not this matter be ended now?

1333 **thou . . . peace** you'd do better to keep quiet.
1340 **ride . . . cart** either a euphemism for sexual intercourse or a reference to the punishment of 'riding' prostitutes through the streets in carts. The implication might thus be: 'I'd like to be there when she gets what she deserves!'
1351 **had . . . to** has given little thought to.
1366–1367 **the certain whether** for certain which.
1370 **bear in hand** claim.
1375 A noble was a coin worth 80 pence.
1377 **set by** provided for/highly regarded.
1379–1380 **buy . . . is!** buy a crowd of men as good as Gaius!
1383 **miss** fail.
1385 **whereto . . . weigh** how it will conclude.
1386 **for thy learning** educational for you.

A
Marry, I shall tell thee why:

Lucrece and her father may not attend
At this season to make an end;
So I heard them say.
And also it is a courteous guise
For to respite the matter this wise
That the parties may

In the meantime advise them well,
For either of them both must tell
And show the best he can
To force the goodness of his own condition
Both by example and good reason.
I would not for a swan

That thou shouldst be hence at that season,
For thou shalt hear a royal disputation
Betwixt them ere they have do.
Another thing must be considered with all:
These folk that sit here in the hall
May not attend thereto:

We may not with our long play
Let them fro their dinner all day;
They have not fully dined.
For and this play where once over past,
Some of them would fall to feeding as fast
As they had been almost pined.

But no force, hardily, and they do.
Usher, get them good wine thereto,
Fill them of the best.
Let it be do or ye will be shent,
For it is the will and commandment
Of the master of the feast.

And therefore we shall the matter forbear
And make a point even here
Lest we exceed a measure,
And we shall do our labour and true intent
For to play the remnant
At my lord's pleasure.

Finis prime partis.
[Part Two]

Intrat A dicens.

A
Much good do it you everychone
Ye will not believe how fast I have gone
For fear that I should come too late!
No force, I have lost but a little sweat
That I have taken upon this heat
My cold courage to abate.

But now to the matter that I came for:
Ye know the cause thereof before;
Your wits be not so short.
Perde, my fellows and I were here
Today, when ye were at dinner,
And showed you a little disport

Of one Fulgens and his daughter Lucrece,
And of two men that made great business
Her husband for to be.
She answered to them both then:
Look which was the more noble man,
To him she would agree.

This was the substance of the play
That was showed here today,
Albeit that there was
Divers toys mingled in the same
To stir folk to mirth and game
And to do them solace,

The which trifles be impertinent
To the matter principal,
But nevertheless they be expedient
For to satisfy and content
Many a man withal.

For some there be that looks and gapes
Only for such trifles and japes,
And some there be among

1398 **guise** habit/practice.
1399 **respite** delay.
1404 **force** urge.
1406 **for a swan** even for a (whole) swan.
1408 **royal** splendid.
1409 **ere...do** before they're done.
1414 **Let** Keep.
1418 **pined** starved.
1426 **point** pause.
1429 **to...remnant** to perform the rest (of the play).
1430.1 ***Finis prime partis.*** The end of the first part.
1430.1 ***Intrat A dicens.*** A enters, saying.
1434 **No force** Never mind.
1452 **Divers toys mingled** various jests mixed.

That forceth little of such madness,
But delighteth them in matter of sadness
Be it never so long.

And every man must have his mind,
Else they will many faults find
And say the play was nought.
But no force, I care not,
Let them say and spare not,
For God knoweth my thought.

It is the mind and intent
Of me and my company to content
The least that standeth here,
And so I trust ye will it allow.
Aye? God's mercy, where am I now?
It were alms to wring me by the ear,

Because I make such digression
From the matter that I began
When I entered the hall.
For, had I made a good continuance,
I should have put you in remembrance
And to your minds call

How Lucrece will come hither again,
And her said lovers both twain,
To define this question:
Whether of them is the more noble man.
For thereon all this matter began:
It is the chief foundation

Of all this process both all and some,
And if these players were once come,
Of this matter will they speak.
I marvel greatly in my mind
That they tarry so long behind
Their hour for to break.

But what, sirs! I pray you everychone
Have patience, for they come anon.
I am sure they will not fail,
But they will meet in this place
As their promise and appointment was,
And else I have marvel.

Let me see, what is now o'clock?
Ah, there cometh one; I hear him knock.
He knocketh as he were wood!

[*To the audience*]

One of you go look who it is.

[*Enter B.*]

B

Nay, nay, all the many of them, iwis,
Cannot so much good.
A man may rap till his nails ache
Ere any of them will the labour take
To give him an answer.

A

I have great marvel on thee
That ever thou wilt take upon thee
To chide any man here!

No man is so much to blame as thou
For long tarrying.

B

Yea, God avow,
Will ye play me that?
Marry, that shall be amended anon:
I am late comen and I will soon be gone,
Else I shrew my cat.

Cock's body, sir, it is a fair reason.
I am come hither at this season
Only at thy bidding,
And now thou makest to me a quarrel,
As though all the matter were in peril
By my long tarrying.

Now God be with you, so mote I thee,
Ye shall play the knave alone for me!

A

What? I am afraid,
Iwis, ye are but lewd!
Turn again, all beshrewed,
Now are you fair prayed.

1463 **forceth little of** cares little for.
1464–1465 **matter . . . long** serious matter, however long it is.
1468 **nought** worthless.
1474 **the least** even the lowliest (spectator)
1477 **It . . . ear** It would be a good deed to tweak me by the ear.
1481 **made . . . continuance** got on with matters.
1490 **both all and some** all of it.
1495 **Their hour for to break** To miss their appointment.
1501 **And else I have marvel** I'd be amazed otherwise.
1504 **as he were wood!** as if he was mad!
1506 **many** crowd.
1520 **fair reason** good answer.
1527 **alone for me** for all I care!

B
Why then, is your anger all do?
A
Yea, marry, is it, lo.
B
So is mine too.
I have done clean.
But now, how goeth this matter forth
Of this marriage?
A
By Saint James, right nought worth.
I wot never what they mean,
For I can none otherwise think
But that some of them begin to shrink
Because of their long tarriage.
B
'Shrink' now, quod a? Marry, that were marvel!
But one thing of surety I can thee tell
As touching this marriage:

Cornelius my master appointeth him thereupon,
And doubtless he will be here anon,
In pain of forty pence,
In so much that he hath devised
Certain strangers freshly disguised
At his own expense

For to be here this night also.
A
'Strangers', quod a? What to do?
B
Marry, for to glad withal
This gentlewoman at her hither coming.
A
Ah, then I see well we shall have a mumming!
B
Yea, surely, that we shall!

And therefore never think it in thy mind
That my master will be behind
Nor slack at this bargain.
Marry, here he cometh, I have him aspied.
No more words, stand thou aside,
For it is he plain.

[*Exit A. Enter Cornelius.*]

CORNELIUS
My friend, where about goest thou all day?
B
Marry, sir, I came hither to assay
Whether these folk had been here.

And yet they be not come,
So help me God and holydam,
Of that I have much marvel,
That they tarry so.
CORNELIUS
Marry, go thy way
And wit where they will or no!
B
Yea, God avow, shall I so.
CORNELIUS
Yea, marry, so I say.
B
Yet in that point, as seemeth me,
Ye do not according to your degree.
CORNELIUS
I pray thee, tell me why.
B
Marry, it would become them well enough
To be here afore and to wait upon you,
And not you to tarry

For their leisure and abide them here,
As it were one that were led by the ear;
For that I defy!
By this mean you should be their drudge,
I tell you truth, I.

And yet the worst that grieveth me
Is that your adversary should in you see
So notable a folly.

1530–1531 **Turn . . . prayed.** Come back, curse you, now I've asked you nicely.
1532 **do** finished.
1534 **done clean** finished completely.
1536.1 **right nought worth** hopelessly.
1537 **mean** intend to do.
1539 **shrink** have second thoughts.
1540 **tarriage** delay.
1544 **appointeth him thereon** arranged to come here about that.
1548 **strangers** foreigners.
1552 **glad** entertain.
1554 **a mumming** an entertainment, generally involving masked visitors who engage the household in games and dancing.
1557 **behind** slow.
1561 **plain** plainly.
1562 **where . . . thou** where have you been?
1564 **folk** i.e. the missing 'mummers'.
1570 **wit . . . no!** find out whether they are coming to perform or not!
1574 **Ye . . . degree** You do not (act) according to your status.
1579 **abide** wait for.

Therefore withdraw you for a season.

CORNELIUS

By Saint John, thou sayest but reason.

B

Yea, do so hardily,
And when the time draweth upon
That they be come everychone
And all thing ready,
Then shall I come straightaway
For to seek you without delay.

CORNELIUS

Be it so, hardily.
But one thing while I think thereon,
Remember this when I am gone:
If it happen so
That Lucrece come in first alone,
Go in hand with her anon,
Howsoever thou do,
For to feel her mind toward me,
And by all means possible to be,
Induce her thereunto.

B

Then some token you must give me,
For else she will not believe me
That I came from you.

CORNELIUS

Marry, that is even wisely spoken.
Commend me to her by the same token:
She knoweth it well enough,
That as she and I walked once together
In her garden hither and thither,
There happened a strange case.
For at the last we did see
A bird sitting on a hollow tree,
An ash I trow it was.
Anon she prayed me for to assay
If I could start the bird away.

B

And did ye so? Alas, alas!

CORNELIUS

Why the Devil sayest thou so?

B

By cock's bones, for it was a cuckoo!
And men say among,
He that throweth stone or stick
At such a bird, he is like
To sing that bird's song.

CORNELIUS

What the Devil reck I therefore?
Hear what I say to thee evermore,
And mark thine errand well:
Sir, I had no stone to throw withal,
And therefore she took me her musk ball,
And thus it befell:
I cast it as straight as any pole,
So that it lighted even in the hole
Of the hollow ash.
Now, canst thou remember all this?

B

By God, I would be loath to do amiss,
For some time I am full rash
Ye say that ye cast it even in the hole
Of the hollow ash as straight as a pole.
Said ye not so?

CORNELIUS

Yes.

B

Well then, let me alone.
As for this errand, it shall be done
As soon as ye be go.

[CORNELIUS]

Farewell then, I leave thee here,
And remember well all this gear
Howsoever thou do.

Et exeat Cornelius.

B

Yes, hardily, this errand shall be spoken.
But how say you, sirs, by this token?
Is it not a quaint thing?

1600 **Go . . . anon** quickly talk to her.
1602 **feel** discover.
1609 **the same token** this token I'm about to tell you.
1613 **case** thing.
1622 **say among** commonly say.
1625 **To . . . song** to sing 'cuckoo' was popular slang for being a cuckold.
1626 **What . . . therefore?** What do I care about that?
1630 **took . . . ball** gave me her perfume ball.
1633 **lighted** landed.
1646.1 ***Et exeat Cornelius.*** And exit Cornelius.
1649 **quaint** strange.

I went he had been a sad man,
But I see well he is a madman
In this message doing.

But what choose he for me,
I am but as a messenger, perde;
The blame shall not be mine but his,
For I will his token report;
Whether she take it in earnest or sport
I will not thereof miss.

Be she wroth or well apaid,
I will tell her even as he said.

Intrat Lucrece.

God avow, here she is!
It is time for me to be wise.
Now welcome lady, flower of price:
I have sought you twice or thrice
Within this house, iwis.

LUCRECE
Me sir? Have ye sought me?

B
Yea, that I have, by God that bought me.

LUCRECE
To what intent?

B
Marry, for I have things a few
The which I must to you show
By my master's commandment.

Publius Cornelius is his name,
Your very lover, in pain of shame,
And if ye love him not ye be to blame.
For this dare I say,
And on a book make it good:
He loves you better than his own heart blood.

LUCRECE
His heart blood? Nay, nay.

Half that love would serve for me!

B
Yet sith he did you first see
In the place where he dwells,
He had loved you so in his heart
That he setteth not by himself a fart,
Nor by no man else.

And because ye should give credence
Unto my saying in his absence
And trust to that I say,
He told me tokens two or three
Which I know well as he told me.

LUCRECE
Tokens? What be they?

B
Let me see, now I had need to be wise,
For one of his tokens is very nice
As ever I heard tell.
He prayed you for to believe me
By the same token that ye and he
Walked together by a hollow tree.

LUCRECE
All that I know well.

B
Ah, then I am yet in the right way.
But I have some other thing to say
Touching my credence,
Which as I think were best to be spared,
For haply ye would not have it declared
Before all this audience.

LUCRECE
Nay, nay, hardily, spare not:
As for my deeds, I care not
If all the world it heard.

B
Marry, then shall I proceed.
He showed me also in very deed
How there sat a bird,

And then ye delivered him your musk-ball
For to throw at the bird withal,
And then as he said, ye did no worse
But even fair kissed him on the nock of
the arse.

1650 **I... man** I thought he was a serious fellow.
1653 **But... me** I don't care what he chooses (to do).
1659 **apaid** contented.
1661 **God avow** I swear to God!
1663 **flower of price** precious flower.
1673 **very** true.
1676 **on... good** swear it on a book (i.e. the Bible).
1683 **setteth... fart** doesn't care a fart about himself.
1688 **As... tell** Is as odd as any I've heard.
1693 **I... way** I'm right so far.
1700 **touching my credence** relating to my token of reliability.
1701 **spared** left unsaid.
1712 **no worse** nothing else.
1713 **on the nock** in the crack.

LUCRECE
Nay, there thou liest falsely, by my fay!

B
Truth, it was on the hole of th'arse I should say,
I wist well it was one of the two,
The nock or the hole.

LUCRECE
Nay, nor yet so.

B
By my faith, ye kissed him, or he kissed you,
On the hole of th'arse, choose you now;
This he told me sure.
Howbeit I speak it not in reproof,
For it was done but for good love
And for no sinful pleasure.

LUCRECE
Nay, nay, man, thou art far amiss!
I know what thine errand is,
Though thou be negligent.
Of thy folly thou mayest well abash,
For thou should have said the hollow ash:
That hole thy master meant.

B
By God avow, I trow it was!
I cry you mercy, I have done you trespass.

But I pray you take it in patience,
For I mistook it by negligence.
A mischief come thereon,
He might have sent you this gear in a letter!
But I shall go learn mine errand better,
And come again anon.

Et exeat [*B*].

LUCRECE
Yea, so do hardily!

Now forsooth, this was a lewd message
As ever I heard sith I was bore.
And if his master have thereof knowledge
He will be angry with him therefore.
Howbeit, I will speak thereof no more,
For it hath been my condition always
No man to hinder but to help where I may.

Intrat A.

A
Fair mistress, liketh it you to know
That my master commends me to you.

LUCRECE
Commendeth you to me?

A
Nay, commendeth you to him!

LUCRECE
Well amended, by Saint Sim!

A
Commendeth he to you, I would say,
Or else you to he: now choose ye may
Whether liketh you better!
And here he sendeth you a letter.

God's mercy, I had it right now!
Sirs, is there none there among you
That took up such a writing?
I pray you, sirs, let me have it again!

LUCRECE
Ye are a good messenger for certain!
But I pray you, sir, of one thing:

Who is your master? Tell me that.

A
Master what-call-ye-him... Parde, ye wot
Whom I mean well and fine!

LUCRECE
Yet I know not, so mot I go!

A
What? Yes, parde, he that would have you so.

LUCRECE
I suppose there be many of tho',
If I would incline!

But yet, know I not who ye mean.
I hold best that ye go again
To learn your master's name.

1714 **fay** faith.
1723 **good** respectable.
1725 **far amiss!** much mistaken!
1728 **abash** be ashamed.
1732 **done you trespass** caused you offence.
1735 **A... thereon** curse it!
1741 **bore** born.
1745 **condition** habit.
1750 **well amended!** well corrected! (A has still not got it right.)
1757 **took... writing?** picked up such a letter (A has lost it)?
1764 **so... go!** may I continue to walk/prosper (a mild oath).
1765 **he... so** he who wants you like this. (Presumably 'so' is accompanied by a gesture.)
1766–1767 **tho'... incline!** those (men who would like to do that), if I was willing!

A
By my faith, and I hold it best.
Ye may say I am a homely guest
In earnest and in game.

LUCRECE
Abide, I shall go to you near-hand:
What is your own name, I would understand?
Tell me that ere I go!
I trow thou canst not well tell.

A
By my faith, not verily well,
Because ye say so.

Et scalpens caput post modicome intervallum dicat.

By this light, I have forgotten!
Howbeit, by that time I have spoken
With some of my company,
I shall be ascertained of this gear.
But shall I find you again here?

LUCRECE
Yea, that thou shalt, happily!

Et exeat A. [*And enter Cornelius.*]

CORNELIUS
Now, fair Lucrece, according to th'appointment
That ye made with me here this day,
Because ye shall not find me there negligent,
Here I am come your will to obey,
And ready am I for myself to say
That, as touching the degree of noble condition,
Betwixt me and Gaius there may be no comparison.

And that shall I show you by apparent reason
If it shall like you that I now begin.

LUCRECE
Nay, ye shall spare it for a little season,
Till such time that Gaius your adversary come in,
For I will give you therein none audience
Till ye be both together in presence.
And in any wise, keep well your patience
Like as I have bound you both to the peace.
I forbid you utterly all manner of violence
During this matter, and also that ye cease
Of all such words as may give occasion
Of brawling or other ungodly condition.

CORNELIUS
There shall be in me no such abusion
In word nor deed, I you promise.

[*Enter B.*]

But now let me see, what occupation
Or what manner of pastime will ye devise
While that these folk doth tarry this wise?
Will ye see a basse-danse after the guise
Of Spain, while ye have nothing to do?
All thing have I purveyed that belongeth thereto!

LUCRECE
Sir, I shall give you the looking on.

CORNELIUS
Will ye do so? I ask no more.
Go soon and bid them come thence anon,
And cause the minstrels to come in before.

B
Marry, as for one of them, his lip is sore;
I trow he may not pipe, he is so sick.
Spele up tamborine, *ik bide yowe frelike!*

[*Enter the dancers,*] *et deinde corisabunt.*

LUCRECE
Forsooth, this was a goodly recreation.
But I pray you, of what manner nation
Be these goodly creators?
Were they of England or of Wales?

B
Nay, they be wild Irish Portingales
That did all these pleasures.

Howbeit, it was for my master's sake,

1773 **In earnest...game** in all things.
1774 **I...near-hand** I shall address you more closely (on a more personal matter).
1779 **Because...so** Now that you ask.
1779.1 ***Et...dicat.*** And, scratching his head, let him a little later say.
1782 **my company** my companions.
1783 **I...gear** I'll be correctly informed about the matter.
1797 **I...audience** I will not listen to you.
1798 **in presence** in my presence.
1804 **condition** behaviour.
1810 **basse-danse** a formal dance performed by one or two couples.
1813 **I...on.** I'll look at it.
1815 **thence** here.
1819 **Spele...frelike!** Flemish: 'Play up the tambourine (a pipe and tabor, not the modern tambourine), I bid you merrily!', presumably aimed at one of the Flemings who, along with French and Italian musicians, worked in early Tudor London.
1819.1 ***et...corisabunt*** and then they shall dance.
1824 **wild Irish Portingales** wild Irish Portuguese (a nonsensical 'nationality').

And he will deserve it, I undertake,
On the largest wise.

CORNELIUS
Go thyself; why stands thou so?
And make them cheer! Let it be do
The best thou canst devise.

B
Yes, they shall have cheer Heaven high!
But one thing I promise you faithfully;
They get no drink thereto.

Exeat [*B, dancers, and minstrels.*
Enter Gaius.] *Dicat Lucrece*:

LUCRECE
Lo, here this man is come now.
Now may ye in your matter proceed.
Ye remember both what I said to you
Touching mine answer; I trow it is no need
Any more to rehearse it.

CORNELIUS
No, in very deed,
For much rehearsal would let the speed
Of all this matter; it needeth no more.
Let us roundly to the matter we come for.

LUCRECE
Yea, that I pray you as heartily as I can.
But first me seemeth it were expedient
That ye both name some indifferent man
For to give betwixt you the foresaid judgement.

CORNELIUS
Nay, as for that, by mine assent,
No man shall have that office but ye.

GAIUS
And I hold me well content that it so be.

LUCRECE
Yea, but notwithstanding that ye thereto agree
That I should this question of noblesse define,
It is a great matter which, as seemeth me,
Pertaineth to a philosopher or else a divine.
Howbeit, sith the choice of this matter is mine,
I can be content, under certain protestation,
When that I have heard you, to say mine opinion.

Lo, this wise I mean and thus I do intend:
That whatsoever sentence I give betwixt you two
After mine own fantasy, it shall not extend
To any other person. I will that it be so,
Forwhy no man else hath therein ado.
It may not be noted for a general precedent,
Albeit that for your parts ye do thereto assent.

GAIUS
As touching that point we hold us well content.
Your sentence shall touch no man but us twain.
And sith ye shall give it by our own agreement,
None other man ought to have thereat disdain.
Wherefore all this doubt ye may well refrain,
And in that matter principal this time would be spent.

CORNELIUS
Then will I begin.

GAIUS
I hold me well content.

CORNELIUS
Sith ye have promised, fair Lucrece, heretofore
That to the more noble man ye will incline,
Vary not fro that word and I ask no more,
For then shall the victory of this cause be mine,
As it shall be easy to judge and define.
For every creature that any reason has
Me seemeth I durst make himself judge in this case,
Save that I fear me the beauty of your face
Should therein blind him so that he ne might
Equally discern the wrong fro the right.

And if he were half so wise a man indeed
As he reputeth himself for to be,
Upon your said answer he should not need
To gainsay in this matter or traverse with me.
My nobleness is known through all the city;

1827–1828 **he . . . wise** I dare say he deserves most of the credit.
1830 **make them cheer!** be hospitable to them (get them some food!).
1834 **They . . . thereto** B puns on cheer: food and drink, and a loud cheer of applause.
1834.1 ***Dicat Lucrece:*** and Lucrece says:
1840 **much . . . speed** too much discussion will hinder things.
1841 **roundly** quickly.
1845 **indifferent** impartial.
1851 **this . . . define** decide this question of nobility.
1853 **pertaineth** belongs.
1853 **divine** theologian.
1859 **fantasy** personal opinion.
1861 **Forwhy . . . ado** Because no other man is involved in it.
1868 **refrain** put aside.
1884 **traverse** argue.

He knoweth himself the nobleness of my kin,
And at that one point my process I will begin.

Among all th'histories of Romans that ye read,
Where find ye any blood of so great nobleness
As hath been the Corneliuses whereof I am
bred?
And if so be that I would therein hold my peace,
Yet all your chronicles beareth good witness
That my progenitors and ancestors have be
The chief aid and defence of this noble city.

How oft have mine ancestors in times of
necessity
Delivered this city from deadly peril,
As well by their manhood as by their policy?
What jeopardy and pain they have suffered in the
quarrel
Th'empire to increase and for the commonweal
It needeth not the specialties to rehearse
or name,
Sith every true Roman knoweth the same.

In every man's house that histories be rife
And written in books, as in some places be
The gests of Arthur, or of Alexander's life,
In the which stories ye may evidently see
And read how Carthage, that royal city,
By Scipio of Africa, my great grand-sire,
Subdued was and also ascribed to his empire.

And many other cities that did conspire,
Against the noble Senate making resistance,
As often as necessity did it require
They were reduced unto due obedience,
Either by the policy or by the violence
Of my said ancestors: th'histories be plain
And witness that I speak not these words in vain.

My blood hath ever taken such pain
To safeguard the commonweal fro ruin and decay,
That by one advice the Senate did ordain
Them to be named the fathers of the country,
And so were mine authors reputed alway,
For in every need they did upon them call
For help as the child doth on the father natural.

Howbeit, to pray them it was no need at all,
For of their own minds they were ready alway.
In token of the same, for a memorial
Of their deserts, the city did edify
Triumphal arches, whereupon ye may
To my great honour see at this day
Th'images of mine ancestors even by and by,
Because that their nobleness should never die.

In token also that they were worthy
Great honour and praise of all the country:
It is commanded and used generally
That every citizen that passeth that way
By the said images, he must obey
And to those figures make a due reverence,
And else to the laws he doth great offence.

Sith it is so then that of convenience
Such honour and homage must needs be do
To these dead images, then much more
reverence
To me should be given: I trow ye think so,
For I am their very image, and relic too
Of their flesh and blood and very inheritor
As well of their goods as of their said honour.

To me they have left many a castle and tower
Which in their triumphs they rightfully won.
To me they have also left all their treasure
In such abundance that I trow no man
Within all Rome sith it first began
Had half the store as I understand
That I have even now at once in my hand.

Lo, in these things my nobleness doth stand,
Which in mine opinion suffiseth for this intent.
And I trow there is no man through all this land
Of Italy, but if he were here present,
He would to my saying in this matter assent,

1891 **And . . . peace** Even if I kept silent about it (myself).
1895 **policy** political skill.
1900 **specialties** details.
1902 **In . . . rife** In the house of every man who keeps history books.
1904 **gests** deeds.
1904 **Alexander** Alexander the Great.
1907 **Scipio of Africa** Scipio Africanus.
1908 **ascribed** declared allegiance.
1916 **blood** family.
1918 **by one advice** with one voice.
1920 **mine authors** my forebears.
1921 **they** the senators.
1929 **by and by** one after the other.
1935 **obey** bow.
1936 **that** those.
1952 **stand** consist.

And give unto me the honour and pre-eminence,
Rather than make against me resistance.

[*To Gaius*]

I marvel greatly what should thy mind incense
To think that thy title therein should be good.
Parde, thou canst not say for thy defence
That ever there was gentleman of thy kin or blood!
And if there were one, it would be understood
Without it be thyself, which now of late
Among noble gentlemen playest check-mate.

LUCRECE

No more thereof, I pray you! Such words I hate,
And I did forbid you them at the beginning
To eschew th'occasion of strife and debate.

GAIUS

Nay, let him alone. He speaketh after his learning!
For I shall answer him to everything
When he hath all said, if ye will hear me,
As I think ye will of your equity.

CORNELIUS

Abide, I must make an end first, parde.
To you, sweet Lucrece, I would have said before
That, if ye will to my desire in this matter agree,
Doubtless ye shall bless the time that ever ye were
bore.
For riches shall ye have at your will evermore,
Without care or study of laborious business,
And spend all your days in ease and pleasant idleness.

About your own apparel ye can do none excess
In my company that should displease my mind.
With me shall ye do none other manner of business
But hunt for your solace at the hart and hind,
And sometime where we convenient game find
Our hawks shall be ready to show you a flight
Which shall be right pleasant and cheerful
to your sight.
And, if so be that in hunting ye have no delight,
Then may ye dance a while for your disport.
Ye shall have at your pleasure both day and night
All manner of minstrelsy to do you comfort.
Do what thing ye will, I have to support
Our charges, and over that I may sustain
At mine own finding an hundred or twain.

And as for him, I am certain
His ancestors were of full poor degree,
Albeit that now within a year or twain,
Because that he would a gentleman be,
He hath him gotten both office and fee,
Which, after the rate of his wretched sparing,
Suffiseth scarcely for his bare living.

Wherefore, sweet Lucrece, it were not according
For your great beauty with him to dwell,
For there should ye have a threadbare living
With wretched scarceness, and I have heard tell
That maidens of your age love not right well
Such manner of husbands, without it be they
That forceth little to cast themself away.

I mean specially for such of them as may
Speed better if they will, as ye be in the case.
And therefore, Lucrece, whatsoever he will say
His title against you to force and embrace,
Ye shall do your own self too great a trespass
If ye follow his part and incline thereto.
Now say what ye will, sir, for I have all do.

GAIUS

With right good will I shall go to,
So that ye will hear me with as great patience
As I have heard you: reason would so.
And whatsoever I shall speak in this audience,
Either of mine own merits or of his insolence,
Yet first unto you all, sirs, I make this request:
That it would like you to construe it to the best.

1964 **Without** Unless.
1965 **playest check-mate.** Strives to bring them down.
1969 **He . . . learning!** He speaks according to his (limited) knowledge!
1980–1981 **About . . . mind.** Nothing that you wear in my company (however excessive) will displease me.
1991 **have** have (enough money).
1993 **hundred or twain** 100 or 200 servants.
1998 **fee** salary.
1999 **after . . . sparing** thanks to his wretched parsimony.
2006–2007 **without . . . away** unless it is those (young women) who care little about throwing their lives away.
2008–2009 **such . . . case** those who could choose better, as you could now.
2011 **force and embrace** urge and (corruptly) support.
2014 **I . . . do** I'm finished.
2015 **go to** begin.
2017 **reason would so** reason demands it.

For loath would I be as any creature
To boast of mine own deeds; it was never my guise.
On that other side, loath I am to make any reporture
Of this man's folly or him to despise.
But, nevertheless, this matter toucheth me in such wise
That, whatsoever ye think in me, I must proceed
Unto the very truth thereof as the matter is indeed.

To make a great rehearsal of that ye have said
The time will not suffer, but, nevertheless,
Two things for yourself in substance ye have laid,
Which as ye suppose maketh for your noblesse,
Upon the which things dependeth all your process.
First, of your ancestors ye allege the noble gests;
Secondly, the substance that ye have of their bequests.

In the which things only, by your own confession,
Standeth all your nobleness: this said ye before.
Whereunto this I say under the correction
Of Lucrece our judge here, that ye are never the more
Worthy in mine opinion to be called noble therefore,
And without ye have better causes to show than these,
Of reason ye must the victory of this matter lose.

To the first part, as touching your ancestors' deeds,
Some of them were noble like as ye declare;
Th'histories beareth witness, I must grant them needs.
But yet, for all that, some of them were
Of contrary disposition like as ye are,
For they did no profit (no more do ye)
To the commonweal of this noble city.

If ye will the title of nobleness win,
Show what have ye done yourself therefore.
Some of your own merits let see bring in,
If ever ye did any sith ye were bore.
But surely ye have no such thing in store
Of your own merits whereby of right
Ye should appear noble to any man's sight.

But, nevertheless, I will you not blame,
Though ye speak not of your own deeds at all.
And to say the truth, ye may not for shame;
Your life is so voluptuous and so bestial
In following of every lust sensual
That I marvel no thing in my mind,
If ye leave your own deeds behind.

He weeneth that by his proud countenance
Of word and deed, with nice array,
His great oaths and open maintenance
Of thefts and murders every day,
Also his riotous disports and play,
His sloth, his cowardy, and other excess,
His mind disposed to all uncleanness:
By these things only he shall have nobleness.

Nay, the title of nobleness will not ensue
A man that is all given to such insolence,
But it groweth of long continued virtue,
As I trust, lady, that your indifference
Can well define by your sentence.
His ancestors were not of such condition,
But all contrary to his disposition.

And therefore they were noble withouten fail,
And did great honour to all the country.
But what can their said nobleness avail
To him that taketh a contrary way;
Of whom men speaketh every day
So great dishonour that it is marvel
The country suffereth him therein to dwell?

And, where he twitteth me of poor kin,
He doth me therein a wrongful offence.
For no man shall thanks or praising win
By the gifts that he hath of nature's influence.

2024 **reporture** declaration.
2030 **suffer** permit.
2031 **laid** claimed.
2032 **maketh** establish.
2033 **process** argument.
2034 **noble gests** heroic deeds.
2035 **substance . . . of** wealth . . . from.
2045 **I . . . needs** I must grant you that.
2048 **no profit** nothing useful.
2063 **behind** out of the account.
2064 **weeneth** believes.
2064 **countenance** looks/behaviour.
2065 **array** fine/foolish clothes.
2066 **maintenance** support.
2069 **cowardy** cowardice.
2086 **twitteth me of** mocks me for (my).

Likewise I think by a contrary sense
That if a man be born blind or lame,
Not he himself, but nature therein is to blame.

Therefore he doth not me therein reprove.
And, as for that point, this I wot well,
That both he and I came of Adam and Eve.
There is no difference that I can tell
Which maketh one man another to excel,
So much as doth virtue and goodly manner,
And therein I may well with him compare.

Howbeit, I speak it not for mine own praise,
But certainly this hath ever be my condition:
I have borne unto God all my days
His laud and praise with due devotion,
And next that I bear always
To all my neighbours charitable affection.
Incontinency and uncleanness I have had in
abomination,
Loving to my friend and faithful with all,
And ever I have withstand my lusts sensual.

One time with study my time I spend
To eschew idleness, the causer of sin.
Another time my country manly I defend,
And for the victories that I have done therein,
Ye have seen yourself, sir, that I have come in
To this noble city twice or thrice
Crowned with laurel as it is the guise.

By these ways, lo, I do arise
Unto great honour fro low degree,
And, if mine heirs will do likewise
They shall be brought to noblesse by me.
But, Cornely, it seemeth by thee
That the nobles of thine ancestors everychone
Shall utterly starve and die in thee alone.

And where he twitteth me on that other side
Of small possession and great scarceness,
For all that, lady, if ye will with me abide,
I shall assure you of moderate riches,
And that sufficient for us both, doubtless.
Ye shall have also a man according
To your own conditions in everything.

Now, Lucrece, I have showed unto you a part
Of my title that I claim you by,
Beseeching you therefore with all my heart
To consider us both twain indifferently,
Which of us twain ye will rather allow
More worthy for noblesse to marry with you.

LUCRECE
Sirs, I have heard you both at large.

CORNELIUS
Nay, abide Lucrece, I pray you heartily!
Sith he layeth many things to my charge,
Suffer that I may thereunto reply.

LUCRECE
Iwis, replication shall not be necessary
Without that ye have some other thing in store
To show for yourself than ye did before.

CORNELIUS
Why, lady, what thing will ye desire more
Than I have showed to make for nobleness?

LUCRECE
Yes, something there is that maketh therefore
Better than ye have showed in your process.
But now let me see what man of witness
Or what other proofs will ye forth bring
By the which either of you may justify his saying?

GAIUS
As for my part, I will stand gladly
To the common voice of all the country.

LUCRECE
And ye likewise, sir?

CORNELIUS
Yea, certainly,
I shall in no wise your word disobey.

LUCRECE
Then will I betwixt you both take this way:

2095 **came of** are descended from.
2098 **manner** conduct.
2102 **borne** given.
2106 **Incontinency** lack of restraint (especially sexually).
2108 **withstand** resisted.
2109 **One time** one part of the time.
2111 **manly** manfully/bravely.
2115 **Crowned ... guise** in formal triumph, crowned with laurel wreaths, in honour of military victory as is traditional.
2120 **Cornely** Cornelius.
2124 **scarceness** poverty.
2128 **according** who matches.
2129 **conditions** character.
2134 **will rather allow** decide is.
2136 **at large** freely (and fully).
2138 **layeth ... charge** alleges ... against me.
2140 **replication** a formal response.
2141 **Without** Unless.
2150 **stand** accept.

I shall go enquire as fast as I may

What the common fame will therein report,
And, when I have thereof a due evidence,
Then shall I again to you resort
To show you th'opinion of my sentence
Whom I will judge to have the pre-eminence.

CORNELIUS
Nay, fair Lucrece, I you require:
Let me not now depart in vain
Not knowing th'effect of my desire.

LUCRECE
Sir, although it be to you a pain,
Yet must ye do so even both twain.
Each of you depart hence to his own place,
And take no more labour or pain in this case.

For, as touching th'effect of my sentence,
I shall go write it by good advisement
Soon after that I am departed fro hence.
And then to either of you both shall be sent
A copy of the same, to this intent:
That of none other person it shall be seen,
Sith it concerneth but only unto you twain.

GAIUS
This is a good way as in my mind.
Are not ye, sir, content in like wise?

CORNELIUS
I wot ne'er, yet I will praise as I find
And as I have cause; that is ever my guise.

GAIUS
Well Lucrece, will ye command me any service?

LUCRECE
No service at all, sir. Why say ye so?
Our Lord speed you both where so ever ye go.

Et exeant Publius Cornelus et Gaius Flaminius [*and A*].

Now some maid, haply, and she were in my case,
Would not take that way that I do intend,
For I am fully determined with God's grace
So that to Gaius I will condescend,
For in this case I do him commend
As the more noble man, sith he this wise
By mean of his virtue to honour doth arise.

And for all that, I will not despise
The blood of Cornelius: I pray you think not so!
God forbid that ye should note me that wise,
For truly I shall honour them where so ever I go,
And all other that be of like blood also.
But unto the blood I will have little respect
Where tho' conditions be sinful and abject.

I pray you all, sirs, as many as be here:
Take not my words by a sinister way.

[*Enter B.*]

B
Yes, by my truth, I shall witness bear,
Where so ever I be come another day,
How such a gentlewoman did openly say
That by a churl's son she would set more
Than she would do by a gentleman bore.

LUCRECE
Nay, sir, then ye report me amiss!

B
I pray you tell me, how said ye then?

LUCRECE
'For God, sir, the substance of my words was this:
I say even as I said when I began,
That for virtue excellent I will honour a man
Rather than for his blood, if it so fall
That gentle conditions agree not withal.

B
Then I put case that a gentleman bore
Have goodly manners to his birth according.

LUCRECE
I say, of him is to be set great store:
Such one is worthy more laud and praising
Than many of them that hath their beginning
Of low kindred, else God forbid!
I will not affirm the contrary for my head;

For in that case there may be no comparison.

2156 **What...fame** What popular opinion.
2158 **resort** return.
2168 **touching** concerning.
2169 **advisement** advice.
2177 **I wot ne'er** I don't know.
2181.1 ***exeant*** exit.
2178 **case** situation.
2185 **to...condescend** in favour of Gaius... decide.
2191 **note...wise** interpret me in that way.
2195 **tho' conditions** the character.
2205 **'For** Before.
2209 **agree not withal** don't match them.
2212 **of...store** in him... placed great value.

But, nevertheless, I said this before,
That a man of excellent virtuous conditions,
Although he be of a poor stock bore,
Yet I will honour and commend him more
Than one that is descended of right noble kin
Whose life is all dissolute and rooted in sin.

And therefore I have determined utterly
That Gaius Flaminius shall have his intent.
To him only I shall myself apply
To use me in wedlock at his commandment,
So that to Cornelius I will never assent,
Although he had as great possession
As any one man in Christian region.

I shall in no wise favour or love his condition,
Howbeit that his blood requireth due reverence,
And that shall I give him with all submission.
But yet shall he never have the pre-eminence
To speak of very noblesse by my sentence.
Ye be his servant sir; go your way
And report to your master even as I say.

[*Exit Lucrece.*]

B

Shall I do that errand? Nay, let be!
By the Rood, ye shall do it yourself for me.
I promise you faithfully,

I would my master had be in Scotland
When he did put this matter in her hand
To stand to her judgement!
But, forasmuch as it is so,
That this wrong to him is do
By a woman, he must let it go
And hold him content.

But he is of such disposition
That when he heareth of this conclusion,
He will be stark mad;
Yea, by my troth, as mad as an hare![598]
It shall make him so full of care
That he will with himself fare
Even as it were a lad!

And so would not I, so mote I thee!
For this matter, and I were as he,
It should never anger me,
But this would I do:
I would let her go in the Mare name!

[*Enter A.*]

What now, sirs, how goeth the game?
What, is this woman go?

B

Yea, yea, man!

A

And what way hath she taken?

B

By my faith, my master is forsaken,
And needs she will agree
Unto thy master: thus she sayeth,
And many causes therefore she layeth
Why it should so be.

A

I marvel greatly whereof that grew.

B

By my faith, she said (I tell thee true!)
That she would needs have him for his virtue
And for none other thing.

A

Virtue? What the Devil is that?
And I can tell, I shrew my cat,
To mine understanding.

B

By my faith, no more can I.
But this she said here openly;
All these folk can tell.

A

[*To the audience*]

How say ye, good women? Is it your guise
To chose all your husbands that wise?
By my troth, then I marvel!

B

Nay, this is the fear, so mot I goo:
That men choose not their wives so

2226 **apply** dedicate.
2230 **Christian region** Christendom.
2241 **Scotland** i.e. far away.
2243 **stand to** abide by.
2251 Hares were proverbially mad, especially during spring, hence 'mad as a March hare'.
2252 **care** sorrow.
2253–2254 **fare...lad!** behave even like a madman!
2259 **in...name!** In the name of Mary (mild oath).
2266 **layeth** alleges.
2268 **whereof that grew** what caused that.
2279 **that wise?** that way?
2281 **so...goo** may I continue to walk: a mild oath.

In places where I have be.
For wives may well complain and groan,
Albeit that cause have they none
That I can hear or see.
But of wedded men there be right few
That will not say the best is a shrew;
Therein they all agree!

I warn you wedded men everychone
That other remedy have ye none
So much for your ease,
And ye would study till tomorrow,
But let them even alone, with sorrow,
When they do you displease.

A

Tush, here is no man that setteth a blank
By thy counsel or canneth thee thank:
Speak thereof no more!
They know that remedy better than thou.
But what shall we twain do now?
I care most therefore.

Me thinketh that matter would be wist.

B

Marry, we may go hence when we list;
No man sayeth us nay.

A

Why then, is the play all do?

B

Yea, by my faith, and we were once go
It were do straight way.

A

And I would have thought in very deed
That this matter should have proceed
To some other conclusion

B

Yea, thou art a master merry man!
Thou shall be wise, I wot ne'er when!
Is not the question

Of nobleness now fully defined:
As it may be so by a woman's mind?
What wouldest thou have more?
Thou toldst me that other day
That all the substance of this play
Was done specially therefore;

Not only to make folk mirth and game,
But that such as be gentlemen of name
May be somewhat moved
By this example for to eschew
The way of vice and favour virtue;
For sin is to be reproved

More in them, for the degree,
Than in other persons such as be
Of poor kin and birth.
This was the cause principal,
And also for to do with all
This company some mirth.

And, though the matter that we have played
Be not percase so well conveyed
And with so great reason
As th'history itself requireth,
Yet the author thereof desireth
That for this season

At the least ye will take it in patience.
And, if there be any offence
(Show us wherein or we go hence)
Done in the same,
It is only for lack of cunning,
And not he but his wit running
Is thereof to blame.

And glad would he be and right fain
That some man of stable brain
Would take on him the labour and pain
This matter to amend;
And so he willed me for to say.
And that done, of all this play
Shortly here we make an end.

[FINIS]

2288 **the best** even the best wife.
2293 **And** even if.
2297 **blank** blanc: a small French coin of little value, i.e. no-one values your advice, or will thank you for it.
2301 **therefore** about that.
2302 **would be wist** should be known/decided.
2303 **list** want.
2304 **sayeth us nay** forbids us.
2306–2307 **we . . . way** once we go it will finish immediately.
2311–2312 **thou . . . when!** you're chief among jokers; I don't know when you'll (ever) be wise!
2315 **As** As far as.
2326 **for the degree** because of their status.
2333 **percase . . . conveyed** perhaps so well performed.
2335 **As . . . requireth** as the story demands.
2342 **cunning** skill/wit.
2343 **wit running** over-eager brain.
2345 **right fain** very happy.

Everyman

(1490–1510?)

THE PLAY

Everyman is both an archetypal morality play and an odd example of the genre. Like *Mankind* and *Youth*, for example, it has a universal, eponymous hero, who learns through experience a general truth about humankind. Here that truth is the central Catholic belief that death comes to everyone, and when it does only our good works (good deeds), combined with God's grace, will win us a place in heaven. In the face of death, all our other worldly ties and attributes, our friends and family, even our bodily faculties and the five senses, will ultimately desert us. Even a life spent in good deeds cannot alone guarantee salvation. This profound religious truth is worked out through a series of scenes in which Everyman meets various representations of worldly and spiritual values, finding the former wanting and learning painfully from the latter the harsh truth about his former life. The play ends with a short sermon from an authority figure, in this case a Doctor of Divinity, who stresses the moral of the play once more and sends the audience off to live out its message.

At the same time as it displays these conventional features of the morality play, however, *Everyman* is also unique among late-medieval moral plays in that it has no true vice figures who seek to corrupt the hero, and so has none of the raucous, scatological comedy associated with the vices. Nor is there, strictly speaking, any real dramatic tension. Everyman's story is not the conventional roller coaster in which the hero is tempted and falls into sin before being finally reconverted to virtue and redeemed; rather, the play is a journey through fixed points representative of the ageing process itself. Everyman is surprised in the prime of his life by Death, who sends him on a journey towards his grave and the audit of his life before God which will follow. He calls upon all those things that have sustained him in his life thus far to accompany him on this grim pilgrimage towards death. But each of them in turn, friends, family, and material wealth, decline the offer and desert him. He finally turns to his long-neglected Good Deeds, who directs him to Knowledge and Confession as the guides who can steer him towards a good death. Through Confession, penitence, the mortification of his flesh, and the intervention of Priesthood (who administers the vital sacraments), Everyman is eventually prepared to meet his divine Judge. Finally, as he approaches his grave, his physical and mental faculties desert him. Beauty and Strength, Discretion, Five Wits, and finally Knowledge all depart, leaving him to descend into his grave with only Good Deeds beside him.

Everyman is a translation of an earlier dramatic source, the Dutch play *Elckerlijc* ('Everyone'), written at some point in the last quarter of the fifteenth century, and attributed to a Pieter van Diest. The title page of the first English printed edition, published at some point in the 1510s by the London printer Richard Pynson, describes it as 'The *Summoning* of Everyman', a formulation which suggests its highly clericist outlook, centred on the processes of the Church and its courts. Death is represented as a medieval summoner, serving writs of subpoena to God's court upon unsuspecting humanity, and Good Deeds is the chief witness who will testify on Everyman's behalf at his examination. In keeping with Augustinian theology, the hero's salvation will depend upon the combination of his own good works (worldly and spiritual), and God's grace (mediated through the sacraments of the Church). Five Wits' assertion (beginning at l.732) that neither an emperor on earth nor an angel in heaven has the power that even the lowliest priest has to manifest God in the bread and wine of the sacrament of the altar (through the miraculous process known as transubstantiation), reflects supreme confidence in the status and capacities of the Catholic clergy, just as Knowledge's reply, criticizing those clergy who fall short of the highest ideals of their calling, reflects the high standards demanded of the clergy by reformers within the Church and anticlerical critics and heretical movements such as Lollardy outside it. Finally the play's emphasis on the omnipresence of death and the need to learn to die well reflects the late medieval obsession with the *Ars Moriendi*, or 'Art of Dying', which was the subject of many treatises, tracts, and sermons.

Everyman was evidently a popular play, in textual form at least. It was published in a second edition by Pynson between 1525 and 1530. In 1528–29 a third edition appeared from the press of John Skot, and the same printer produced a fourth in the first half of the 1530s. The earliest surviving complete texts of the play are now in the British Library and the Huntington Library, California respectively. I have used the 1528–29 Skot edition as the base text for the version below, also consulting the modern critical editions listed among the further reading.

FURTHER READING

Bevington, David, *From Mankind to Marlowe: The Growth of Structure in the Popular Drama of Tudor England* (Cambridge, MA: Harvard University Press, 1962).

Bruster, Douglas and Eric Rasmussen, eds., *Everyman and Mankind* (London: Methuen, 2009).

Davenport, W. A., *Fifteenth Century English Drama: The Early Moral Plays and Their Literary Relations* (Cambridge: D. S. Brewer, 1982).

Hadfield, Andrew, '*The Summoning of Everyman*' in Thomas Betteridge and Greg Walker, eds., *The Oxford Anthology of Tudor Drama* (Oxford: Oxford University Press, 2012), 93–108.

Ladd, Roger A., '"My condition is mannes soule to kill": *Everyman*'s Mercantile Salvation', *Comparative Drama* 41 (2007), 57–78.

Mills, David, 'The Theatres of *Everyman*' in John A. Alford, ed., *From Page to Performance: Essays on Early English Drama* (East Lancing, MI: Michigan State University Press, 1995), 127–49.

Streitman, Elsa, 'The Middle Dutch *Elckerlijc* and the English *Everyman*', *Medium Aevum* 52 (1983), 111–14.

Tanner, Rod, 'Humour in *Everyman* and the Middle English Morality Play', *Philological Quarterly* 70 (1991), 149–61.

Walker, Greg, ed., *Medieval Drama: An Anthology* (Oxford: Blackwell, 2000).

Here begineth a treatise how the high Father of Heaven sendeth Death to summon every creature to come and give account of their lives in this world, and is in manner of a moral play.

[Dramatis Personae:

MESSENGER,
GOD,
DEATH,
EVERYMAN,
FELLOWSHIP,
KINDRED (Family),
COUSIN,
GOODS,
GOOD DEEDS,
KNOWLEDGE,
CONFESSION,
BEAUTY,
STRENGTH,
DISCRETION,
FIVE WITS (the Five Senses),
ANGEL,
DOCTOR (a Doctor of Theology, The Epilogue),
A PRIEST?]

MESSENGER
I pray you all give your audience,
And hear this matter with reverence;
By figure a moral play:
The Summoning of Everyman called it is,
That of our lives and ending shows
How transitory we be all day.
This matter is wondrous precious,
But the intent of it is more gracious
And sweet to bear away.
The story sayeth: Man, in the beginning
Look well, and take good heed to the ending,
Be you never so gay.
Ye think sin in the beginning full sweet,
Which in the end causeth the soul to weep
When the body lieth in clay.
Here shall you see how Fellowship and Jollity,
Both Strength, Pleasure, and Beauty,
Will fade from thee as flower in May;
For ye shall hear how our heaven King
Calleth Everyman to a general reckoning.
Give audience, and hear what He doth say. [*Exit*]

[GOD *speaketh*]

GOD
I perceive, here in My majesty,
How that all creatures be to me unkind,
Living without dread, in worldly prosperity.
Of ghostly sight the people be so blind;
Drowned in sin, they know me not for their God.
In worldly riches is all their mind;
They fear not My rightwiseness the sharp rod.
My love that I showed when I for them died
They forget clean, and shedding of my blood red.
I hanged between two, it cannot be denied;
To get them life I suffered to be dead.
I healed their feet, with thorns hurt was my head.
I could do no more than I did, truly.
And now I see the people do clean forsake me.
They use the seven deadly sins damnable,
As pride, covetice, wrath, and lechery

1 **give your audience** pay attention.
3 **By figure** in the form of.
6 **all day** always.
9 **to bear away** remember.
12 **Be ... gay** however happy you are (now).
13 **full** very.
18 **as flower** like flowers.
19 **heaven** heavenly.
20 'Everyman' is also 'every man'. Throughout, the play blurs singular and plural, making clear that the character reflects and embodies the situation of all humankind.
20 **reckoning** audit.
23 **unkind** unnatural.
25 **ghostly** spiritual.
28 **They ... rod** They do not fear the fierce punishment of my justice.
29 **love** the Skot text has 'law' here.
30 **and** and (the).
31 **two** the two thieves between whom Christ was crucified.
33 **healed** washed. See John 13:4–10.
35 **clean** completely.

Now in the world be made commendable,
And thus they leave of angels the
heavenly company.
Every man liveth so after his own pleasure,
And yet of their life they be nothing sure.
I see the more that I them forbear
The worse they be fro year to year.
All that liveth appaireth fast.
Therefore I will in all the haste
Have a reckoning of Everyman's person;
For, and I leave the people thus alone
In their life and wicked tempests,
Verily they will become much worse than
beasts.
For now one would by envy another up eat;
Charity they do all clean forget.
I hoped well that Everyman
In my glory should make his mansion,
And thereto I had them all elect.
But now I see, like traitors deject,
They thank me not for the pleasure that I to them
meant,
Nor yet for their being that I them have lent.
I proffered the people great multitude of mercy,
And few there be that asketh it heartily.
They be so cumbered with worldly riches
That needs on them I must do justice,
On every man living, without fear.
Where art thou, Death, thou mighty messenger?

[*Enter* DEATH].

DEATH

Almighty God, I am here at your will,
Your commandment to fulfil.

GOD

Go thou to Everyman
And show him, in my name,
A pilgrimage he must on him take
Which he in no wise may escape,
And that he bring with him a sure reckoning
Without delay or any tarrying. [*Exit*]

DEATH

Lord, I will in the world go run over all,
And cruelly out-search both greet and small.
Every man will I beset that liveth beastly
Out of God's laws, and dreadeth not folly.
He that loveth riches I will strike with my dart,
His sight to blind, and fro heaven to depart,
Except that alms be his good friend,
In hell for to dwell, world without end.

[*Enter* EVERYMAN]

Lo, yonder I see Everyman walking.
Full little he thinketh on my coming;
His mind is on fleshly lusts and his treasure,
And great pain it shall cause him to endure
Before the Lord, heaven King.
Everyman, stand still! Whither art thou going
Thus gaily? Hast thou thy Maker forgot?

EVERYMAN

Why askest thou?
Wouldest thou wit?

DEATH

Yea, sir, I will show you:
In great haste I am sent to thee
Fro God out of His majesty.

EVERYMAN

What, sent to me?

DEATH

Yea, certainly.
Though thou have forgot him here,
He thinketh on thee in the heavenly sphere,
As, ere we depart, thou shalt know.

39 **leave of** reject.
43 **fro** from.
44 **appaireth fast** quickly grows corrupt.
47 **and** if.
50 **For...eat** One person will eat another out of envy.
53 **mansion** home (i.e. heaven), see John 14:2: 'In my father's house are many mansions ...I go to prepare a place for you'.
54 **elect** chosen.
55 **deject** abject.
56 **meant** intended.
57 **being** existence.
59 **heartily** sincerely.
60 **cumbered** encumbered.
61 **needs** necessarily.
62 **fear** doubt.
69 **wise** way.
70 **a sure reckoning** an honest account (of himself).
73 **out-search** seek out.
74 **beastly** like beasts.
75 **folly** sin.
76 **dart** spear.
78 **Except that alms** Unless charitable giving.
79 **world without end** forever.
81 **Full...thinketh** he does not expect.
88 **Wouldest thou wit?** Do you (really) want to know?

EVERYMAN
What desireth God of me?
DEATH
That shall I show thee.
A reckoning he will needs have
Without any longer respite.
EVERYMAN
To give a reckoning, longer leisure I crave!
This blind matter troubleth my wit.
DEATH
On thee thou must take a long journey;
Therefore thy book of count with thee thou bring,
For turn again thou cannot by no way.
And look thou be sure of thy reckoning,
For before God thou shalt answer and show
Thy many bad deeds, and good but a few;
How thou hast spent thy life, and in what wise,
Before the chief Lord of Paradise,
Have ado that we were in that way,
For, wit thou well, thou shalt make none attorney.
EVERYMAN
Full unready I am such reckoning to give.
I know thee not. What messenger art thou?
DEATH
I am Death, that no man dreadeth,
For every man I rest, and no man spareth;
For it is God's commandment
That all to me should be obedient.
EVERYMAN
O Death, thou comest when I had thee least
in mind!
In thy power it lieth me to save;
Yet of my good will I give thee, if thou will be kind:
Yea, a thousand pound shalt thou have,
And defer this matter till another day.
DEATH
Everyman, it may not be, by no way.
I set not by gold, silver, nor riches,
Ne by pope, emperor, king, duke, nor princes;
For, and I would receive gifts great,
All the world I might get;
But my custom is clean contrary.
I give thee no respite. Come hence, and not tarry.
EVERYMAN
Alas, shall I have no longer respite?
I may say Death giveth no warning!
To think on thee it maketh my heart sick,
For all unready is my book of reckoning.
But twelve year, and I might have abiding,
My counting-book I would make so clear
That my reckoning I should not need to fear.
Wherefore, Death, I pray thee, for God's mercy,
Spare me till I be provided of remedy!
DEATH
Thee availeth not to cry, weep, and pray;
But haste thee lightly that thou were gone that
journey,
And prove thy friends if thou can.
For, wit thou well, the tide abideth no man,
And in the world each living creature
For Adam's sin must die of nature.
EVERYMAN
Death, if I should this pilgrimage take,
And my reckoning surely make,
Show me, for saint charity,
Should I not come again shortly?
DEATH
No, Everyman. And thou be once there,
Thou mayst never more come here,
Trust me verily.

101 **longer . . . crave** I beg (for) more time!
102 **blind** dark/uncertain.
102 **wit** mind.
104 **book of count** account book: the book recording Everyman's deeds. See the account of Doomsday in Revelation 20:12: 'And I saw the dead, great and small, standing in the presence of the throne, and the books were opened; and another book was opened, which is the book of life; and the dead were judged by those things which were written in the books, according to their works'.
105 **turn again** turn back.
109 **wise** manner.
111 **Have ado** Make sure.
112 **For . . . attorney** Understand well, you will have no attorney (to speak for you).
116 **rest** arrest.
121 **of my good** (some) of my wealth
123 **defer** if (you will) defer.
125 **set not** set (no store) by/do not value.
126 **Ne** Nor.
127–129 **For . . . contrary** For, if I would take such great bribes, I could gain the world, but my practice is completely the opposite.
135 **But . . . abiding** If I could only have a delay of twelve years.
141 **haste thee lightly** hurry quickly.
142 **prove** test.
143 **abideth** waits for (proverbial).
145 **of nature** because of their (fallen, mortal) nature.
148 **for saint charity** for holy charity's sake.
149 **Should . . . shortly?** Can't I return soon?
150 **And . . . there** Once you are there.

EVERYMAN

O gracious God in the high seat celestial,
Have mercy on me in this most need!
Shall I have no company fro this vale terrestrial
Of mine acquaintance that way me to lead?

DEATH

Yea, if any be so hardy
That would go with thee and bear thee company.
Hie thee that thou were gone to God's magnificence,
Thy reckoning to give before His presence.
What, wenest thou thy life is given thee,
And thy worldly goods also?

EVERYMAN

I had wend so, verily.

DEATH

Nay, nay, it was but lent thee.
For, as soon as thou art go,
Another a while shall have it, and then go there-fro,
Even as thou hast done.
Everyman, thou art mad! Thou hast thy wits five,
And here on earth will not amend thy life;
For suddenly I do come.

EVERYMAN

O wretched caitiff, whither shall I flee
That I might scape this endless sorrow?
Now, gentle Death, spare me till tomorrow,
That I may amend me
With good advisement.

DEATH

Nay, thereto I will not consent,
Nor no man will I respite,
But to the heart suddenly I shall smite
Without any advisement.
And now out of thy sight I will me hie.
See thou make thee ready shortly,
For thou mayst say this is the day
That no man living may scape away. *[Exit]*

EVERYMAN

Alas, I may well weep with sighs deep!
Now have I no manner of company
To help me in my journey, and me to keep;
And also my writing is full unready.
How shall I do now for to excuse me?
I would to God I had never been get;
To my soul a full great profit it had be,
For now I fear pains huge and great.
The time passeth. Lord, help, that all wrought!
For, though I mourn, it availeth nought:
The day passeth and is almost ago.
I wot not well what for to do.
To whom were I best my complaint to make?
What and I to Fellowship thereof spake,
And showed him of this sudden chance?
For in him is all mine affiance,
We have in the world so many a day
Be good friends, in sport and play.

[Enter FELLOWSHIP*]*

I see him yonder, certainly.
I trust that he will bear me company;
Therefore to him will I speak to ease my sorrow.
Well met, good Fellowship, and good morrow.

FELLOWSHIP

Everyman, good morrow by this day!
Sir, why lookest thou so piteously?
If anything be amiss, I pray thee me say,
That I may help to remedy.

EVERYMAN

Yea, good Fellowship, yea,
I am in great jeopardy.

153 **high seat** throne.
154 **most** greatest.
155 **vale terrestrial** this earthly valley (the mortal world).
156 **lead** guide.
157 **hardy** brave.
159 **Hie** Hurry.
161 **wenest...thee** do you think life is given to you (forever)?
163 **wend** thought.
165 **go** gone.
166 **Another...there-fro** Someone else shall have it, for a while, and then lose it (in turn).
171 **caitiff** slave.
179 **advisement** warning.
186 **keep** protect.
187 **My writing** (in the account book.)
189 **get** born/conceived.
190 **it...be** would have been.
192 **Lord...wrought!** Lord who created everything, help me!
194 **ago** gone.
198 **showed...chance?** told him about this unexpected event?
199 **mine affiance** my trust.
200–201 **We have...Be** We have been for so long.
205 **Well met...good morrow.** Good to see you...good morning.
208 **thee me say** tell me.

FELLOWSHIP
My true friend, show to me your mind;
I will not forsake thee to my life's end,
In the way of good company.
EVERYMAN
That was well spoken, and lovingly.
FELLOWSHIP
Sir, I must needs know your heaviness;
I have pity to see you in any distress.
If any have you wronged, ye shall revenged be,
Though I on the ground be slain for thee;
Though that I know before that I should die!
EVERYMAN
Verily, Fellowship, gramercy.
FELLOWSHIP
Tush, by thy thanks I set not a straw!
Show me your grief and say no more.
EVERYMAN
If I my heart should to you break,
And then you to turn your mind fro me
And would not me comfort when ye hear me speak,
Then should I ten times sorrier be.
FELLOWSHIP
Sir, I say as I will do indeed.
EVERYMAN
Then be you a good friend at need!
I have found you true here-before.
FELLOWSHIP
And so ye shall evermore.
For, in faith, and thou go to hell,
I will not forsake thee by the way.
EVERYMAN
Ye speak like a good friend! I believe you well.
I shall deserve it, and I may.
FELLOWSHIP
I speak of no deserving, by this day!
For he that will say and nothing do
Is not worthy with good company to go.
Therefore, show me the grief of your mind,
As to your friend most loving and kind.
EVERYMAN
I shall show you how it is:
Commanded I am to go a journey,
A long way, hard and dangerous,
And give a strait count without delay,
Before the high judge, Adonai.
Wherefore, I pray you, bear me company,
As ye have promised, in this journey.
FELLOWSHIP
This is matter indeed! Promise is duty;
But, and I should take such a voyage on me,
I know it well, it should be to my pain.
Also it maketh me afeard, certain.
But let us take counsel here, as well as we can,
For your words would fear a strong man.
EVERYMAN
Why, ye said if I had need
Ye would me never forsake, quick ne dead,
Though it were to hell, truly.
FELLOWSHIP
So I said, certainly,
But such pleasures be set aside, the sooth to say.
And also, if we took such a journey,
When should we again come?
EVERYMAN
Nay, never again, till the Day of Doom.
FELLOWSHIP
In faith, then will not I come there!
Who hath you these tidings brought?
EVERYMAN
Indeed, Death was with me here.
FELLOWSHIP
Now, by God that all hath bought,
If Death were the messenger,

216 **heaviness** sorrow.
220 **Though . . . before** Even if I knew in advance.
221 **Verily . . . gramercy.** Truly . . . many thanks (from the French, *grand merci*).
222 **by . . . straw** there's no need to thank me (literally, 'I don't care a straw for your thanks').
224 **break** open.
225 **then you to** then (if you were) to.
229 **at need** when I need (one).
230 **here-before** until now.
232 **and** (even) if.
235 **and** if.
237 **that will say and nothing do** who only speaks but does not act.
244 **strait count** strict account.
245 **Adonai** 'the Lord': a Hebrew name for God.
248 **This . . . duty** This is a serious business! A promise is a promise.
252 **let . . . counsel** let's discuss this.
255 **quick ne** alive nor.
258 **sooth** truth.
260 **again come** return.
261 **Doom** Judgement.
265 **bought** redeemed.

For no man that is living today
I will not go that loath journey,
Not for the father that begat me!

EVERYMAN
Ye promised otherwise, parde!

FELLOWSHIP
I wot well I said so, truly.
And yet, if thou wilt eat and drink and make good cheer,
Or haunt to women the lusty company,
I would not forsake you while the day is clear,
Trust me, verily.

EVERYMAN
Yea, thereto ye would be ready!
To go to mirth, solace, and play
Your mind will sooner apply
Than to bear me company in my long journey.

FELLOWSHIP
Now, in good faith, I will not that way.
But, and thou will murder or any man kill,
In that I will help thee with a good will.

EVERYMAN
O, that is a simple advice, indeed.
Gentle fellow, help me in my necessity!
We have loved long, and now I need;
And now, gentle Fellowship, remember me.

FELLOWSHIP
Whether ye have loved me or no,
By Saint Johan, I will not with thee go.

EVERYMAN
Yet, I pray thee, take the labour and so much for me
To bring me forward, for saint charity,
And comfort me till I come without the town.

FELLOWSHIP
Nay, and thou would give me a new gown,
I will not a foot with thee go.
But, and thou had tarried I would not have left thee so.
And as now God speed thee in thy journey,
For from thee I will depart as fast as I may.

EVERYMAN
Whither away, Fellowship? Will thou forsake me?

FELLOWSHIP
Yea, by my fay! To God I betake thee.

EVERYMAN
Farewell, good Fellowship! For thee my heart is sore.
Adieu forever; I shall see thee no more.

FELLOWSHIP
In faith, Everyman, farewell now at the ending;
For you I will remember that parting is mourning.

[*Exit*]

EVERYMAN
Alack, shall we thus depart indeed—
Ah, Lady, help!—without any more comfort?
Lo, Fellowship forsaketh me in my most need.
For help in this world whither shall I resort?
Fellowship here-before with me would merry make,
And now little sorrow for me doth he take.
It is said, in prosperity men friends may find,
Which in adversity be full unkind.
Now whither for succour shall I flee,
Sith that Fellowship hath forsaken me?
To my kinsmen I will, truly,
Praying them to help me in my necessity.
I believe that they will do so,
For kind will creep where it may not go.

[*Enter* KINDRED *and* COUSIN]

I will go say, for yonder I see them go.
Where be ye now, my friends and kinsmen?

270 **parde!** by God!
273 **haunt . . . company** keep the joyful company of.
274 **while . . . clear** while the sun shines (he intends this to mean 'ever', but unwittingly reveals he is indeed only a fair-weather friend).
276 **Yea . . . ready!** Oh yeah, you'd be ready for that!
278 **apply** focus upon.
283 **simple** foolish.
288 **Johan** John.
290 **bring me forward** escort me (part of the way).
291 **without** outside.
295 **speed** prosper.
297 **Whither away?** Where are you going?
298 **fay** faith.
298 **betake** commend.
300 **Adieu** Goodbye.
302 **mourning** sorrowful.
303 **Alack** Alas.
304 **Lady** i.e. the Virgin Mary.
306 **resort** go.
308 **take** show.
310 **full** completely.
312 **Sith** Since.
316 **kind . . . go** nature will crawl where it cannot walk (proverbial), i.e. family will always get there in the end, however difficult the journey.
317 **go say** (and) assay (test that maxim).

KINDRED
Here be we now, at your commandment.
Cousin, I pray you show us your intent
In any wise, and not spare.

COUSIN
Yea, Everyman, and to us declare
If ye be disposed to go any-whither;
For, wit you well, [we] will live and
die together.

KINDRED
In wealth and woe we will with you hold,
For over his kin a man may be bold.

EVERYMAN
Gramercy, my friends and kinsmen kind.
Now shall I show you the grief of my mind:
I was commanded by a messenger
That is a High King's chief officer;
He bade me go a pilgrimage, to my pain,
And I know well I shall never come again.
Also I must give a reckoning strait,
For I have a great enemy that hath me in wait,
Which intendeth me for to hinder.

KINDRED
What account is that which ye must render?
That would I know.

EVERYMAN
Of all my works I must show
How I have lived and my days spent;
Also of ill deeds that I have used
In my time, sith life was me lent,
And of all virtues that I have refused.
Therefore, I pray you, go thither with me
To help to make mine account, for
saint charity.

COUSIN
What, to go thither? Is that the matter?
Nay, Everyman, I had lever fast bread and water
All this five year and more.

EVERYMAN
Alas that ever I was bore!
For now shall I never be merry
If that you forsake me.

KINDRED
Ah, sir, what? Ye be a merry man.
Take good heart to you, and make no moan.
But one thing, I warn you, by Saint Anne:
As for me, ye shall go alone.

EVERYMAN
My Cousin, will you not with me go?

COUSIN
No, by Our Lady, I have the cramp in my toe.
Trust not to me for, so God me speed,
I will deceive you in your most need.

KINDRED
It availeth not us to 'tice.
Ye shall have my maid with all my heart;
She loveth to go to feasts, there to be nice,
And to dance, and abroad to start;
I will give her leave to help you in that journey,
If that you and she may agree.

EVERYMAN
Now, show me the very effect of your mind:
Will you go with me, or abide behind?

KINDRED
Abide behind? Yea, that will I, and I may!
Therefore, farewell till another day. [*Exit*]

EVERYMAN
How should I be merry or glad?
For fair promises men to me make,
But when I have most need, they me forsake.
I am deceived; that maketh me sad.

COUSIN
Cousin Everyman, farewell now,
For verily I will not go with you.
Also of mine own an unready reckoning
I have to account; therefore I make tarrying.

321 **not spare** don't hold back.
323 **any-whither** anywhere.
324 **wit you well** you know well.
325 **with you hold** stick with you.
326 **a man may be bold** both 'he may be frank with them' and 'he may have confidence in them'.
334 **that hath me in wait** who lies in wait for me.
335 **Which...hinder** Who intends to hinder/ambush me.
340 **ill** sinful.
341 **me lent** lent to me.
346 **lever fast** rather fast on.
348 **bore** born.
357 **God me speed** God bless me.
359 **It...'tice.** Trying to entice us won't help.
361 **nice** gay/flirtatious.
362 **abroad to start** to travel about.
363 **leave** permission.
365 **very effect** true intent.
367 **and I may** if I can.
375–376 **Also...account** And I have my own unprepared-for reckoning to make.

Now God keep thee, for now I go. [*Exit*]

EVERYMAN

Ah, Jesus, is all come here to?
Lo, fair words maketh fools fain;
They promise and nothing will do, certain.
My kinsmen promised me faithfully
For to abide with me steadfastly,
And now fast away do they flee.
Even so Fellowship promised me;
What friend were best me of to provide?
I lose my time here longer to abide.
Yet in my mind a thing there is:
All my life I have loved riches.
If that my Goods now help me might,
He would make my heart full light.
I will speak to him in this distress.
Where art thou, my Goods and riches?

[*Enter* GOODS]

GOODS

Who calleth me? Everyman, what haste thou hast!
I lie here in corners, trussed and piled so high,
And in chests I am locked so fast,
Also sacked in bags. Thou mayst see with thine eye
I cannot stir; in packs low I lie.
What would ye have? Lightly me say.

EVERYMAN

Come hither, Good[s], in all the haste thou may,
For of counsel I must desire thee.

GOODS

Sir, and ye in the world have sorrow or adversity,
That can I help you to remedy shortly.

EVERYMAN

It is another disease that greaveth me;
In this world it is not, I tell thee so.
I am sent for another way to go,
To give a strait count general
Before the highest Jupiter of all.
And all my life I have had joy and pleasure in thee.
Therefore, I pray thee, go with me;
For peradventure thou mayst before
God Almighty
My reckoning help to clean and purify;
For it is said ever among
That money maketh all right that is wrong.

GOODS

Nay, Everyman, I sing another song.
I follow no man in such voyages;
For, and I went with thee,
Thou should'st fare much the worse for me.
For, because on me thou did set thy mind,
Thy reckoning I have made blotted and blind;
That thine account thou cannot make truly;
And that hast thou for the love of me!

EVERYMAN

That would grieve me full sore,
When I should come to that fearful answer.
Up, let us go thither together.

GOODS

Nay, not so; I am too brittle, I may not endure.
I will follow [no] man one foot, be ye sure.

EVERYMAN

Alas, I have thee loved, and had great pleasure
All my life-days on good and treasure!

GOODS

That is to thy damnation, without leasing,
For my love is contrary to the love everlasting.
But, if thou had me loved moderately during,
As to the poor give part of me,
Then shouldest thou not in this dolour be,
Nor in this great sorrow and care.

EVERYMAN

Lo, now was I deceived ere I was ware,
And all I may wit miss-spending of time.

379 **fain** glad.
385 **were...provide** would best provide for me?
386 **lose** waste.
389 **Goods** property.
390 **full light** very happy.
398 **Lightly me say.** Tell me quickly.
400 **of...thee** I must ask your advice.
406 **strait count general** strict final (comprehensive) account.
407 **highest Jupiter** chief God.
410 **peradventure** perhaps.
412 **it...among** people always say.
419 **blind** illegible.
420 **make truly** clearly read.
423 **fearful answer** dreadful judgement.
425 **brittle** fragile/weak.
428 **on good** in goods.
429 **leasing** deception.
431 **during** during your life.
432 **As...me** (And done things such) as giving part of me (your wealth) to the poor.
433 **dolour** sorrow.
435 **ere...ware** before I knew it.
436 **And...time** And now I know that I have misspent my time.

GOODS
What, weenest thou that I am thine?

EVERYMAN
I had went so.

GOODS
Nay, Everyman, I say no.
As for a while I was lent thee;
A season thou hast had me in prosperity.
My condition is man's soul to kill;
If I save one, a thousand I do spill.
Weenest thou that I will follow thee?
Nay, fro this world not, verily.

EVERYMAN
I had wend otherwise.

GOODS
Therefore to thy soul Good[s] is a thief;
For, when thou art dead, this is my guise:
Another to deceive in this same wise
As I have done thee, and all to his soul's reproof.

EVERYMAN
O false Good[s], cursed thou be,
Thou traitor to God that hast deceived me
And caught me in thy snare!

GOODS
Marry, thou brought thyself in care,
Whereof I am glad;
I must needs laugh, I cannot be sad.

EVERYMAN
Ah, Good[s], thou hast had long my heartily love.
I gave thee that which should be the Lord's above.
But wilt thou not go with me indeed?
I pray thee truth to say.

GOODS
No, so God me speed!
Therefore farewell, and have good day. [*Exit*]

EVERYMAN
O, to whom shall I make my moan,
For to go with me in that heavy journey?
First Fellowship said he would with me gone;
His words were very pleasant and gay,
But afterward he left me alone.
Then spake I to my kinsmen, all in despair,
And also they gave me words fair;
They lacked no fair speaking,
But all forsook me in the ending.
Then went I to my Goods, that I loved best,
In hope to have comfort; but there had I least,
For my Goods sharply did me tell
That he bringeth many into hell.
Then of myself I was ashamed;
And so I am worthy to be blamed.
Thus may I well myself hate.
Of whom shall I now counsel take?
I think that I shall never speed
Till that I go to my Good Deed[s].
But, alas, she is so weak
That she can nother go nor speak.
Yet will I venture on her now.
My Good Deeds, where be you?

GOOD DEEDS
Here I lie, cold in the ground.
Thy sins hath me sore bound
That I cannot stir.

EVERYMAN
O Good Deeds, I stand in fear!
I must you pray of counsel,
For help now should come right well.

GOOD DEEDS
Everyman, I have understanding
That ye be summoned account to make
Before Messiah, of Jerusalem king;
And you do by me, that journey with you
will I take.

EVERYMAN
Therefore I come to you my moan to make.
I pray you that ye will go with me.

GOOD DEEDS
I would full fain, but I cannot stand, verily.

437 **weenest . . . thine?** do you believe I belong to you?
438 **went** thought.
441 **A season** (For) a time.
442 **condition** nature.
443 **spill** ruin.
448 **guise** habit.
449 **wise** way.
450 **reproof** ruin.
454 **Marry** Indeed.
454 **in care** into trouble.
457 **heartily** heart-felt.
461 **so . . . speed!** may God help me!
464 **heavy** sorrowful.
480 **speed** prosper.
483 **nother go** neither walk.
484 **venture on her** try her.
495 **And . . . me** If you'll take my advice.
498 **full fain** very willingly.

EVERYMAN
Why, is there anything on you fall?

GOOD DEEDS
Yea, sir, I may thank you of all!
If ye had perfectly cheered me,
Your book of count full ready had be.
Look, the books of your works and deeds eke,
Ah, see how they lie under the feet,
To your soul's heaviness.

EVERYMAN [*Trying to read the book*]
Our Lord Jesus help me,
For one letter here I cannot see!

GOOD DEEDS
Here is a blind reckoning in time of distress!

EVERYMAN
Good Deeds, I pray you help me in this need,
Or else I am forever damned indeed!
Therefore, help me to make reckoning
Before the Redeemer of all thing,
That king is, and was, and ever shall.

GOOD DEEDS
Everyman, I am sorry of your fall,
And fain would I help you, and I were able.

EVERYMAN
Good Deeds, your counsel I pray you give me.

GOOD DEEDS
That shall I do, verily,
Though that on my feet I may not go.
I have a sister that shall with you also,
Called Knowledge, which shall with you abide,
To help you to make that dreadful reckoning.

[*Enter* KNOWLEDGE]

KNOWLEDGE
Everyman, I will go with thee, and be thy guide,
In thy most need to go by thy side.

EVERYMAN
In good condition I am now in everything,
And am wholly content with this good thing,
Thanked be God my creator!

GOOD DEEDS
And when [s]he hath brought you there
Where thou shalt heal thee of thy smart,
Then go you with your reckoning and your Good
Deeds together
For to make you joyful at heart
Before the Blessed Trinity.

EVERYMAN
My Good Deeds, gramercy!
I am well content, certainly,
With your words sweet.

KNOWLEDGE
Now go we together lovingly
To Confession, that cleansing river.

EVERYMAN
For joy I weep; I would we were there!
But, I pray you, give me cognition,
Where dwelleth that holy man, Confession?

KNOWLEDGE
In the house of Salvation;
We shall find him in that place
That shall us comfort, by God's grace.
Lo, this is Confession. Kneel down and ask mercy,
For he is in good conceit with God Almighty.

EVERYMAN
O glorious fountain, that all uncleanness doth
clarify,
Wash fro me the spots of vice unclean,
That on me no sin may be seen.
I come with Knowledge for my redemption,
Redeemed with heart and full contrition;
For I am commanded a pilgrimage to take,
And great accounts before God to make.
Now, I pray you, Shrift, mother of salvation,
Help my Good Deeds for my piteous exclamation!

CONFESSION
I know your sorrow well, Everyman.
Because with Knowledge ye come to me,
I will you comfort as well as I can.

499 **is . . . fall?** has something (bad) befallen you?
500 **of all!** for all of it/above all!
501 **perfectly cheered me** treated me properly.
502 **had be** would have been.
503 **eke** also.
507 **For . . . see!** Not one letter can I read!
513 **ever shall** shall be.
515 **and** if.
523 **most** greatest.
528 **smart** pain/wound.
537 **would** wish.
544 **in good conceit** on good terms.
545 **clarify** purify.
552 **Shrift** Confession.

And a precious jewel I will give thee
Called penance, voider of adversity;
Therewith shall your body chastised be
With abstinence and perseverance in God's service.
Here shall you receive that scourge of me,
Which is penance strong, that ye must endure,
To remember thy Saviour was scourged for thee
With sharp scourges, and suffered it patiently.
So must thou, ere thou scape that
painful pilgrimage.
Knowledge, keep him in this voyage,
And by that time Good Deeds will be with thee.
But in any wise be sicker of mercy,
For your time draweth fast. And ye will saved be,
Ask God mercy, and He will grant truly.
When with the scourge of penance man doth him bind,
The oil of forgiveness then shall he find.

EVERYMAN
Thanked be God for His gracious work!
For now I will my penance begin.
This hath rejoiced and lighted my heart,
Though the knots be painful and hard within.

KNOWLEDGE
Everyman, look your penance that ye fulfil,
What pain that ever it to you be;
And Knowledge shall give you counsel at will
How your account ye shall make clearly.

EVERYMAN
O eternal God, O heavenly figure,
O way of rightwiseness, O goodly vision
Which descended down in a virgin pure
Because He would every man redeem,
Which Adam forfeited by his disobedience:
O blessed Godhead, elect and high Divine,
Forgive my grievous offence!
Here I cry Thee mercy in this presence.
O ghostly treasure, O ransomer and redeemer,
Of all the world hope and conductor,
Mirror of joy, foundator of mercy,
Which illumined heaven and earth thereby:
Hear my clamorous complaint, though it late be;
Receive my prayers unworthy in this heavy life
Though I be a sinner most abominable,
Yet let my name be written in Moses' table.
O Mary, pray to the Maker of all thing
Me for to help at my ending,
And save me fro the power of my enemy.
For Death assaileth me strongly.
And, Lady, that I may by mean[s] of thy prayer
Of your Son's glory to be partner,
By the means of His Passion, I it crave.
I beseech you help my soul to save.
Knowledge, give me the scourge of penance:
My flesh therewith shall give acquaintance.
I will now begin, if God give me grace.

KNOWLEDGE
Everyman, God give you time and space.
Thus I bequeath you in the hands of our Saviour.
Now may you make your reckoning sure.

EVERYMAN
In the name of the Holy Trinity,
My body sore punished shall be.
Take this, body, for the sin of the flesh!
Also thou delightest to go gay and fresh,
And in the way of damnation thou did me bring;
Therefore suffer now strokes of punishing.
Now of penance I will wade the water clear,
To save me from purgatory, that sharp fire.

GOOD DEEDS
I thank God, now I can walk and go,
And am delivered of my sickness and woe.
Therefore with Everyman I will go, and not spare:
His good works I will help him to declare.

KNOWLEDGE
Now, Everyman, be merry and glad;
Your Good Deeds cometh now; ye may not be sad.
Now is your Good Deeds whole and sound,
Going upright upon the ground.

558 **voider** remover. (The Skot text has, 'voice voider' here.)
561 **scourge of** whip from.
562 **strong** harsh.
568 **in... sicker** in all things be certain.
569 **draweth fast** is running out.
569 **And** If.
575 **lighted** lightened.
576 **knots** (in the whip).
578 **What... ever** However painful.
579 **at will** whenever you want (it).
585 **Which... by** (That) which Adam forfeited through.
590 **conductor** guide.
591 **foundator** founder/source.
596 **Moses' table** Moses' book (of saved souls).
602 **partner** a sharer.
613 **Take this** He scourges himself.
614 **go... fresh** appear elegant and smart.
615 **way** path.
625 **whole and sound** intact and healthy.

EVERYMAN
My heart is light, and shall be evermore.
Now will I smite faster than I did before.
DEEDS
Everyman, pilgrim, my special friend,
Blessed be thou without end.
For thee is preparate the eternal glory.
Ye have me made whole and sound,
Therefore I will bide by thee in every stound.
EVERYMAN
Welcome, my Good Deeds! Now I hear thy voice,
I weep for very sweetness of love.
KNOWLEDGE
Be no more sad, but ever rejoice.
God seeth thy living in His throne above.
Put on this garment to thy behove,
Which is wet with your tears,
Or else before God you may it miss
When ye to your journey's end come shall.
EVERYMAN
Gentle Knowledge, what do ye it call?
KNOWLEDGE
It is the garment of sorrow.
Fro pain it will you borrow.
Contrition it is,
That getteth forgiveness;
It pleaseth God passing well.
GOOD DEEDS
Everyman, will you wear it for your heal?

[EVERYMAN *puts on the robe*]

EVERYMAN
Now blessed be Jesu, Mary's son,
For now have I on true contrition.
And let us go now without tarrying.
Good Deeds, have we clear our reckoning?
GOOD DEEDS
Yea, indeed, I have [it] here.
EVERYMAN
Then I trust we need not fear.
Now friends, let us not part in twain.
KNOWLEDGE
Nay, Everyman, that will we not, certain.
GOOD DEEDS
Yet must thou lead with thee
Three persons of great might.
EVERYMAN
Who should they be?
GOOD DEEDS
Discretion and Strength they hight,
And thy Beauty may not abide behind.
KNOWLEDGE
Also ye must call to mind
Your Five Wits as for your counsellors.
GOOD DEEDS
You must have them ready at all hours.
EVERYMAN
How shall I get them hither?
KNOWLEDGE
You must call them all together,
And they will hear you incontinent.
EVERYMAN
My friends, come hither and be present,
Discretion, Strength, my Five Wits, and Beauty!

[*Enter* DISCRETION, STRENGTH, FIVE WITS, *and* BEAUTY]

BEAUTY
Here at your will we be all ready.
What will ye that we should do?
GOOD DEEDS
That ye would with Everyman go,
And help him in his pilgrimage.
Advise you, will ye with him or not in that voyage?
STRENGTH
We will bring him all thither,
To his help and comfort, ye may believe me.
DISCRETION
So will we go with him all together.
EVERYMAN
Almighty God, loved may thou be!
I give thee laud that I have hither brought

628 **smite** strike (myself).
631 **preparate** prepared.
633 **stound** circumstance.
638 **to thy behove** appropriate for you.
640 **miss** lack.
644 **borrow** redeem.
646 **getteth** brings.
647 **passing** exceedingly.
648 **heal** (spiritual) health/well-being.
651 **tarrying** delay.
655 **part in twain** become separated.
660 **hight** are named.
667 **incontinent** immediately.

Strength, Discretion, Beauty, and Five Wits.
Lack I nought.
And my Good Deeds, with Knowledge clear,
All be in company at my will here.
I desire no more to my business.

STRENGTH

And I, Strength, will by you stand in distress,
Though thou would in battle fight on
the ground.

FIVE WITS

And though it were through the world round,
We will not depart, for sweet ne sour.

BEAUTY

No more will I, unto Death's hour,
Whatsoever thereof befall.

DISCRETION

Everyman, advise you first of all;
Go with a good advisement and deliberation.
We all give you virtuous monition
That all shall be well.

EVERYMAN

My friends, harken what I will tell;
I pray God reward you in His heavenly sphere.
Now harken all that be here,
For I will make my testament
Here, before you all present.
In alms half my good I will give with my hands twain
In the way of charity, with good intent,
And the other half still shall remain
In queth, to be returned there it ought to be.
This I do in despite of the Fiend of hell,
To go quite out of his peril
Ever after and this day.

KNOWLEDGE

Everyman, hearken what I say:
Go to Priesthood, I you advise,
And receive of him, in any wise,
The holy sacrament and ointment together.
Then shortly see ye turn again hither;
We will all abide you here.

FIVE WITS

Yea, Everyman, hie you that ye ready were.
There is no emperor, king, duke, ne baron
That of God hath commission
As hath the least priest in the world being;
For of the blessed sacraments pure and benign
He beareth the keys, and thereof hath the cure
For man's redemption (it is ever sure!)
Which God, for our soul's medicine,
Gave us out of His heart with greet pain.
Here in this transitory life, for thee and me,
The blessed sacraments seven there be:
Baptism, confirmation, with priesthood good,
And the sacrament of God's precious flesh and blood,
Marriage, the holy extreme unction, and penance.
These seven be good to have in remembrance,
Gracious sacraments of high divinity.

EVERYMAN

Fain would I receive that holy body,
And meekly to my ghostly father I will go.

FIVE WITS

Everyman, that is the best that ye can do.
God will you to salvation bring,
For priesthood exceedeth all other thing.
To us holy Scripture they do teach,
And converteth man fro sin, heaven to reach.

683 **to my business** for my purpose.
686 **through** anywhere throughout.
687 **sweet ne sour** i.e. whatever the task.
688 **Death's hour** the moment of death.
689 **Whatsoever thereof befall** Whatever happens as a consequence.
692 **monition** forewarning.
702 **queth** bequest.
702 **there** where.
704 **go . . . of** escape free from.
708 **in any wise** however you can/whatever happens.
709 **holy . . . ointment** the Eucharist, received from the priest during the Mass, and Extreme Unction, the final sacrament, received immediately prior to death.
710 **turn** return.
712 **hie . . . were** hurry and prepare yourself.
714 **commission** (the same) authority.
715 **least** lowliest.
717 See Christ's words to St. Peter, 'And I will give unto thee the keys of the kingdom of heaven: and whatsoever thou shalt bind on earth shall be bound in heaven, and whatsoever thou shalt loose on earth shall be loosed in heaven', Matthew 16:19.
717 **cure** responsibility.
719 **medicine** healing.
723 **priesthood** Holy Orders.
724 **the . . . blood** the Eucharist.
728 **Fain** Eagerly.
728 **that holy body** i.e. the body of Christ in the Eucharist.
729 **ghostly** spiritual (i.e. the priest).

God hath to them more power given
Than to any angel that is in heaven.
With five words he may consecrate
God's body in flesh and blood to make,
And handleth his Maker between his hands.
The priest bindeth and unbindeth all bands,
Both in Earth and in heaven.
Thou ministers all the sacraments seven;
Though we kiss thy feet, thou were worthy!
Thou art surgeon that cureth sin deadly;
No remedy we find under God
But all only priesthood.
Everyman, God gave priests that dignity,
And setteth them in his stead among us to be.
Thus be they above angels in degree.

[*Exit* EVERYMAN *to receive the sacrament and extreme unction from the Priest*]

KNOWLEDGE
If priests be good, it is so, surely.
But when Jesu hanged on the cross with greet smart,
There he gave out of his blessed heart
The same sacrament in greet torment;
He sold them not to us, that Lord omnipotent!
Therefore Saint Peter the Apostle doth say
That Jesus' curse hath all they all
Which God their Saviour do buy or sell,
Or they for any money do take or tell.
Sinful priests giveth the sinners example bad:
Their children sitteth by other men's fires, I have heard;
And some haunteth women's company
With unclean life, as lusts of lechery.
These be with sin made blind.

FIVE WITS
I trust to God no such may we find.
Therefore, let us priesthood honour,
And follow their doctrine for our soul's succour.
We be their sheep, and they shepherds be,
By whom we all be kept in surety.
Peace! For yonder I see Everyman come,
Which hath made true satisfaction.

GOOD DEEDS
Methink it is he indeed.

EVERYMAN
Now Jesu be your alder speed!
I have received the sacrament for my redemption,
And then mine extreme unction.
Blessed be all they that counselled me to take it.
And now friends, let us go without longer respite;
I thank God that ye have tarried so long.
Now set each of you on this Rood your hand,
And shortly follow me.
I go before there I would be. God be our guide.

STRENGTH
Everyman, we will not fro you go
Till ye have done this voyage long.

DISCRETION
I, Discretion, will bide by you also.

KNOWLEDGE
And though this pilgrimage be never so strong,
I will never part you fro.
Everyman, I will be as sure by thee
As ever I did by Judas Machabee.

735–738 **God hath . . . make** Only priests have the power to consecrate the bread and wine at the mass. Not even angels have that power. The five words are '*Hoc est enim corpus meum*', 'This is my body', Christ's words at the Last Supper (see Matthew 26:26) spoken by the priest at the moment of consecration.
740 **bands** bonds.
742 It is not clear if Everyman addresses an onstage priest here, or is still speaking generally.
748 **setteth . . . be** places him (on Earth) as His representative among us.
749 **in degree** status/importance.
751 **smart** pain.
758 **Or . . . tell** Knowledge condemns those priests who take money for providing those sacraments which Christ gave freely.
760 **Their . . . fires** i.e. some men have priests' bastards in their houses, thinking they are their own children.
761 **haunteth women's company** frequent the company of women (for sex).
762 **as** such as.
769 **Peace!** Be quiet!
772 **alder speed** greatest aid.
778 **Rood** crucifix.
779 **shortly** quickly.
780 **before . . . be** where I want to be.
784 **strong** hard.
787 **Judas Machabee** Judas Maccabeus, see I Maccabees 2:4 and following.

EVERYMAN
Alas, I am so faint I may not stand!
My limbs under me do fold.
Friends, let us not turn again to this land,
Not for all the world's gold;
For into this cave must I creep
And turn to earth, and there to sleep.

BEAUTY
What, into this grave? Alas!

EVERYMAN
Yea, there shall ye consume, more and less.

BEAUTY
And what, should I smother here?

EVERYMAN
Yea, by my faith, and never more appear.
In this world live no more we shall,
But in heaven before the highest Lord of all.

BEAUTY
I cross out all this! Adieu, by Saint John!
I take my tap in my lap and am gone.

EVERYMAN
What, Beauty, whither will ye?

BEAUTY
Peace, I am deaf! I look not behind me,
Not and thou wouldest give me all the
gold in thy chest! [*Exit*]

EVERYMAN
Alas, whereto may I trust?
Beauty goeth fast away fro me.
She promised with me to live and die.

STRENGTH
Everyman, I will thee also forsake and deny.
Thy game liketh me not at all.

EVERYMAN
Why, then ye will forsake me all?
Sweet Strength, tarry a little space.

STRENGTH
Nay, sir, by the Rood of Grace!
I will hie me from thee fast,
Though thou weep to thy heart to-brast.

EVERYMAN
Ye would ever bide by me, ye said.

STRENGTH
Yea, I have you far enough conveyed.
Ye be old enough, I understand,
Your pilgrimage to take on hand.
I repent me that I hither came.

EVERYMAN
Strength, you to displease I am to blame,
Yet, promise is debt, this ye well wot.

STRENGTH
In faith, I care not.
Thou art but a fool to complain.
You spend your speech, and waste your brain.
Go thrust thee into the ground!

[*Exit*]

EVERYMAN
I had wend surer I should you have found.
He that trusteth in his Strength,
She him deceiveth at the length.
Both Strength and Beauty forsaketh me,
Yet they promised me fair and lovingly.

DISCRETION
Everyman, I will after Strength be gone.
As for me, I will leave you alone.

EVERYMAN
Why, Discretion, will ye forsake me?

DISCRETION
Yea, in faith, I will go fro thee,
For when Strength goeth before,
I follow after evermore.

EVERYMAN
Yet, I pray thee, for the love of the Trinity,
Look in my grave once piteously!

DISCRETION
Nay, so nigh will I not come.
Farewell, everyone!

[*Exit*]

789 **do fold** collapse.
793 **turn** return. See Genesis 3:19, 'dust thou art and unto dust thou shalt return'.
795 **consume** be consumed.
796 **smother** suffocate.
800 **cross out** reject.
801 **tap** distaff.
804 **Not and** Not (even) if.
809 **game** business.
811 **tarry ... space** wait a little time.
814 **to** until.
814 **to-brast** bursts.
816 **conveyed** escorted.
818 **take on hand** perform for yourself.
820 **to blame** reluctant.
821 **promise ... wot** 'a promise is a promise', as you know well.
825 **thrust thee** jump.
826 **I ... found.** I believed that I would find you more reliable.
828 **at the length** finally.

EVERYMAN
O, all thing faileth, save God alone:
Beauty, Strength, and Discretion;
For when Death bloweth his blast
They all run fro me full fast.

FIVE WITS
Everyman, my leave now of thee I take.
I will follow the other, for here I thee forsake.

EVERYMAN
Alas, then may I wail and weep!
For I took you for my best friend.

FIVE WITS
I will no longer thee keep.
Now farewell, and there an end.

[*Exit*]

EVERYMAN
O Jesu, help! All hath forsaken me.

GOOD DEEDS
Nay, Everyman, I will bide with thee.
I will not forsake thee indeed;
Thou shalt find me a good friend at need.

EVERYMAN
Gramercy, Good Deeds! Now may
I true friends see.
They have forsaken me, everyone;
I loved them better than my Good Deeds alone.
Knowledge, will ye forsake me also?

KNOWLEDGE
Yea, Everyman, when ye to Death shall go;
But not yet, for no manner of danger.

EVERYMAN
Gramercy, Knowledge, with all my heart!

KNOWLEDGE
Nay, yet I will not from hence depart
Till I see where ye shall be come.

EVERYMAN
Methink, alas, that I must be gone,
To make my reckoning and my debts pay,
For I see my time is nigh spent away.
Take example, all ye that this do hear or see,
How they that I loved best do forsake me
Except my Good Deeds, that bideth truly.

GOOD DEEDS
All earthly things is but vanity:
Beauty, Strength, and Discretion do
man forsake,
Foolish friends and kinsmen that fair spake;
All fleeth save Good Deeds, and that am I.

EVERYMAN
Have mercy on me, God most mighty,
And stand by me, thou mother and maid,
Holy Mary.

GOOD DEEDS
Fear not, I will speak for thee.

EVERYMAN
Here I cry God mercy!

GOOD DEEDS
Short our end, and 'minish our pain;
Let us go and never come again.

EVERYMAN
Into Thy hands, Lord, my soul I commend.
Receive it, Lord, that it be not lost.
As thou me boughtest, so me defend,
And save me from the fiend's boast,
That I may appear with the blessed host
That shall be saved at the Day of Doom.
In manus tuas, of mights most
Forever, *commendo spiritum meum!*

[EVERYMAN *and* GOOD DEEDS *descend into the grave*]

KNOWLEDGE
Now hath he suffered that we all shall endure.
The Good Deeds shall make all sure.
Now hath he made ending.
Me thinketh that I hear angels sing,
And make great joy and melody
Where Everyman's soul received shall be.

ANGEL
Come excellent elect spouse to Jesu;
Here above thou shalt go,
Because of thy singular virtue.
Now the soul is taken the body fro,
Thy reckoning is crystal clear.
Now shalt thou into the heavenly sphere,

843 **blast** trumpet.
849 **keep** protect.
870 **All...vanity** see Ecclesiastes 12:8, 'Vanity of vanities, saith the preacher; all is vanity.'
878 **Short** Shorten.
882 **boughtest** redeemed.
886 **mights most** greatest power.
886–887 ***In...meum!*** Into thy hands...I commend my spirit', Luke 23:46.

Unto the which all ye shall come
That liveth well before the Day of Doom.

[*Enter Doctor*]

DOCTOR
This moral men may have in mind.
Ye hearers, take it of worth, old and young,
And forsake Pride, for he deceiveth you
in the end.
And remember Beauty, Five Wits, Strength, and
Discretion,
They all at the last do Everyman forsake,
Save his Good Deeds there doth he take.
But beware; and they be small
Before God he hath no help at all;
None excuse may be there for Everyman.
Alas, how shall he do then?
For, after Death, amends may no man make,
For then mercy and pity doth him forsake.
If his reckoning be not clear when he doth come,
God will say: '*Ite, maledicti, in ignem aeternum!*'
And he that hath his account whole and sound,
High in heaven he shall be crowned.
Unto which place God bring us all thither,
That we may live body and soul together.
Thereto help the Trinity!
Amen, say ye, for saint Charity.

[FINIS]

Thus endeth this moral play of Every Man,
Imprinted at London in Paul's Churchyard by me,
JOHAN SCOT.

894 **elect** chosen.
897 **the body fro** from your body.
903 **Ye . . . young** You hearers, both old and young, believe (this moral) to be valuable.
907 **Save** Only.
908 **and . . . small** if they are (only) few.
915 ***Ite . . . aeternum!*** [Then he shall say also unto them on the left hand,] "Depart from me, ye cursed, into everlasting fire"; Matthew 25:41.

The Play of the Weather

(*c.*1533)

JOHN HEYWOOD

(*c.*1497–*c.*1578)

THE PLAYWRIGHT

John Heywood was born in Coventry in about 1497. By 1519 he was working at the court of Henry VIII as a chorister, 'player of the virginals' (a keyboard instrument), and court entertainer. Around 1522 he married Joan Rastell, daughter of the printer John Rastell, and sister of William Rastell, who would print Heywood's interludes in the 1530s. Through the Rastells he gained access to the group of Catholic intellectuals whose members included Sir Thomas More, many of whose cultural and religious views he seems to have shared. Unlike More, however, Heywood did not lose favour during the 1530s, when the religious reforms of the Henrician Reformation moved the Church of England in a Protestant direction. Despite his Catholicism, and his service in the household of Princess Mary (the daughter of Henry's 'divorced' first wife, Catherine of Aragon), Heywood continued to write and play for the court throughout the 1530s, and even produced interludes (including now lost works such as a *Masque of King Arthur's Knights* and an interlude *On the Parts of Man*) for evangelical patrons such as Thomas Cromwell and Archbishop Cranmer of Canterbury. Heywood was clearly a likeable and memorable figure. Strikingly tall, he was frequently described as 'merry': both sociable and witty. He made no secret of his opposition to the Reformation, however, and his interludes and poetry of this period voice eloquent appeals for religious toleration and moderation through the dangerous, fractious years of the Henrician Reformation (see Walker, *Politics of Performance*, chapter three, and *Writing Under Tyranny*, chapter six, and Axton and Happé, eds., *Plays*, introduction).

William Rastell began to print Heywood's plays in 1533, beginning with *Johan Johan*, a translation of a French dramatic fabliau, and *The Pardoner and the Friar*, a satirical attack upon religious controversy. Both of these plays were published anonymously, but *The Play of the Weather*, published late in 1533, and *The Play of Love* (1534) were both printed with Heywood's name on the title page. It is highly likely that *The Four PP* ('The Four 'P's') was also printed by Rastell at this time, but the earliest surviving edition of that play is William Middleton's, printed *c.*1544.

Despite being investigated in 1544, on suspicion of opposing Henry VIII's claim to be Supreme Head of the Church in England, Heywood continued to provide music and poetry for court entertainments throughout the 1540s and 1550s, and to publish a hugely popular series of proverb collections. Only when Elizabeth I passed the Act of Uniformity in Religion did he move to the Continent, where he lived in some poverty (his property having been confiscated by the Crown in his absence) until his death in Louvain, probably in 1578.

THE PLAY

The plot of *The Play of the Weather* is a simple one, involving a succession of suitors petitioning Jupiter, the king of the gods, with selfish and mutually contradictory requests for his or her preferred form of weather. In each 'scene' a new character arrives to sue for the kind of weather that best suits his or her trade or lifestyle: the Wind Miller for lots of wind to drive his mill, the Gentlewoman for mild weather to protect her delicate complexion, and so on, and implicitly to claim superiority for their own profession at the same time. Hence on one level the play is an 'estates satire' in the medieval tradition made famous by Chaucer's 'General Prologue' to *The Canterbury Tales*, which introduces characters representative of contemporary trades and 'estates' and uses them to explore, comically, the conflicting agendas of the various social classes and the sexes in the period. But the play has both older and more recent sources too. The device of introducing rival suitors to Jupiter, for example, was probably borrowed from the classical Greek satirist Lucian of Samosata's *Ikaromenippus*, in which the god is encountered listening to petitions from his mortal subjects, while Heywood may also have found examples of the comic treatment of the god in the dialogues of the Italian humanist Leon Battista Alberti (1404–72).

Beneath the conventional comedy of estates, though, the play also touches on contemporary political issues. It was probably written in 1533, a moment when all the issues upon which it touches (the powers of the sovereign, the problems of a rancorous parliament, the conflicting claims of the people, a king's marriage) were highly contentious. Henry VIII was claiming novel powers as Supreme Head of the Church in England (a claim that Heywood seems gently to mock in Merry Report's scatological joke with the Gentleman about the benefits of having a new head), the Reformation Parliament was bitterly divided between reformers and conservatives over the rights and powers of the Church, the realm was divided over religious reform, and the king had secretly married Anne Boleyn in the hope that his new Archbishop of Canterbury, Thomas Cranmer, would finally dissolve his marriage to Catherine of Aragon. For Heywood to produce a play at court that flirted with these issues, and in which Jupiter was a figure with obvious affinities with Henry VIII himself, was a bold political step. The play is ostensibly a discussion of the most trivial of subjects, the English weather, but it explores a serious question for all monarchs, and one which was pressing particularly upon Henry VIII in 1532–3: how can a king reconcile and satisfy all the contradictory demands of the subjects for whom he is responsible, especially when, as during the early years of the Reformation, they argue vociferously for mutually hostile ends? The god-king's final judgement, that the weather shall remain the same, thus rewarding everyone, if only for some of the time, perhaps reflects Heywood's own sense of the impossibility of the task.

The play is bold in dramatic terms too, not least in the creation of its central character, Merry Report. The latter is listed among the *dramatis personae* as 'the Vice', the first time that the title was used in this formal way. But he is more than just a figure of misrule in the manner of the morality vices. The audience is not invited to condemn his immoral behaviour from a Christian viewpoint; his engagement with them is more open, more like that of the clowns and fools of later sixteenth-century drama. Significantly it is he, rather than Jupiter, who is the play's master of ceremonies, directing the action and setting the tone for the various encounters which he oversees. Rather the pleasures of the play seem to lie in the diverse ways in which he interacts with, insults, or argues with each new suitor as he or she enters, as well as in the debates which the suitors have among themselves, such as the mock-schoolroom debate between the two Millers (in which they reach for ever more unlikely evidence), over which is the better element, wind or water, or the angry exchanges between the Gentlewoman and the Launder about which of them is the most useful to society.

The play itself needs only one major property, the curtained, canopied throne of state which Jupiter occupies for most of the play, and which must conceal the musicians who play a song 'within' the curtains at l. 178. Beyond that, the internal geography of the Tudor great hall itself, with its 'low end' around the screens entrance (through which the servants entered from the kitchens with food and drink for a banquet and through which the guests would leave at the end of the entertainment), and 'high end' around the dais where the patron sat and dined, could be exploited in the nuanced comedy of manners that the interlude demands (i.e. at l. 432 and following). Much of the fun to be had from the play thus comes from watching Merry Report alternately pastiche and transgress the numerous written and unwritten rules and forms of etiquette that determined how members of the various social classes might address each other and behave in the special circumstances of the Tudor royal court.

The cast requires ten actors with no doubling possible (the entire cast assembles onstage for the final scene), suggesting that Heywood could call upon the resources of the royal court to provide his actors. At least one child is required ('the least (smallest) that can play') for the role of Dick, the Boy; and it may well be that the entire cast (except Merry Report, who may have been played by Heywood himself) was made up of schoolboys and choristers.

The text printed here is based on the text published in 1533 by William Rastell, which was also the basis of the edition in my *Medieval Drama: An Anthology* (Blackwell, 2000). I have also consulted the edition in Axton and Happé's *Plays of John Heywood* (see further reading).

FURTHER READING

Axton, Richard and Peter Happé, eds., *The Plays of John Heywood* (Woodbridge: D. S. Brewer, 1991).

Bolwell, R. W., *The Life and Works of John Heywood* (New York: Columbia University Press, 1921).

King, Pamela M., 'John Heywood, *The Play of the Weather*', in Thomas Betteridge and Greg Walker, eds., *The Oxford Handbook of Tudor Drama* (Oxford: Oxford University Press, 2012), 207–23.

Reed, A. W., *Early Tudor Drama: Medwall, the Rastells, Heywood, and the More Circle* (London: Methuen, 1926).

Walker, Greg, *Plays of Persuasion: Drama and Politics at the Court of Henry VIII* (Cambridge: Cambridge University Press, 1991).

—— *The Politics of Performance in Early Renaissance Drama* (Cambridge: Cambridge University Press, 1998).

—— *Writing Under Tyranny: English Literature and the Henrician Reformation* (Oxford: Oxford University Press, 2005).

A new and very merry interlude of all manner weathers, made by John Heywood

The Players' Names:

JUPITER, a god,
MERRY REPORT, the Vice,
THE GENTLEMAN,
THE MERCHANT,
THE RANGER,
THE WATER MILLER,
THE WIND MILLER,
THE GENTLEWOMAN,
THE LAUNDER,
THE BOY, the least that can play.

JUPITER
Right far too long as now were to recite
The ancient estate wherein our self hath reigned,
What honour, what laud, given us of very right,
What glory we have had, duly unfeigned,
Of each creature which duty hath constrained,
For above all gods since our father's fall,
We, Jupiter, were ever principal.

If we so have been (as truth it is indeed)
Beyond the compass of all comparison,
Who could presume to show, for any mead,
So that it might appear to human reason,
The high renown we stand in at this season?
For, since that heaven and Earth were first create
Stood we never in such triumphant estate

As we now do; whereof we will report
Such part as we see meet for time present,
Chiefly concerning your perpetual comfort,
As the thing self shall prove in experiment,
Which highly shall bind you on knees lowly bent
Solely to honour our highness day by day.
And now to the matter give ear and we shall say.

Before our presence in our high parliament,
Both gods and goddesses of all degrees
Hath late assembled by common assent
For the redress of certain enormities
Bred among them through extremities
Abused in each to other of them all,
Namely to purpose in these most special:

Our foresaid father Saturn, and Phoebus,
Eolus and Phoebe, these four by name,
Whose natures not only so far contrarious,
But also of malice each other to defame,

Jupiter became chief of the Roman gods after he deposed his father, Saturn.
Launder a washer-woman.
Ranger a forest warden/gamekeeper
the...play the smallest who knows how to act. The Boy's name is Dick.
1 **Right...recite** It would take much too long now to tell you.
5 **Of** from.
6 **father's** i.e. Saturn. In Roman mythology, Jupiter usurped his father's place as king of the Gods in a bloodless coup. Zeus's displacement of Cronus in the Greek pantheon was more violent.
9 **compass** scope.
10 **mead** reward.
12 **at this season** at this time.
16–17 **Such...comfort** chiefly that part which concerns your perpetual well-being.
18 **As...experiment** As you shall see for yourself.
19 **highly** solemnly.
24 **late** recently.
26 **extremities** extreme (contrary) behaviour.
27 **Abused...all** committed by each of them against all the others.
28 **Namely...special** specifically in this case, especially (the following).
29–30 **Saturn** and **Phoebus** are the gods associated with cold and heat (the sun), respectively, **Eolus** Aeolus rules the winds and **Phoebe** the moon (associated with rain and the tides).
31 **contrarious** contradictory.
32 **defame** abuse.

Have long time abused right far out of frame
The due course of all their constellations,
To the great damage of all earthly nations,

Which was debated in place said before.
And first, as became, our father most ancient,
With beard white as snow, his locks both cold
and hoar,
Hath entered such matter as served his intent,
Lauding his frosty mansion in the firmament
To air and earth as thing most precious,
Purging all humours that are contagious.

Howbeit, he allegeth that of long time past
Little hath prevailed his great diligence.
Full oft upon earth his fair frost he hath cast
All things hurtful to banish out of presence,
But Phoebus, intending to keep him in silence,
When he hath laboured all night in his powers,
His glaring beams marreth all in two hours.

Phoebus to this made no manner answering;
Whereupon they both then Phoebe defied.
Each for his part laid in her reproving
That by her showers superfluous they have tried
In all that she may their powers be denied.
Whereunto Phoebe made answer no more
Than Phoebus to Saturn had made before.

Anon, upon Eolus all these did flee,
Complaining their causes each one arow,
And said, to compare none was so evil as he;
For when he is disposed his blasts to blow
He suffereth neither sunshine, rain, nor snow.
They each against other, and he against all three,
Thus can these four in no manner agree.

Which, seen in themselves, and further considering,
The same to redress was cause of their assembly.
And also that we, evermore being,
Beside our puissant power of deity,
Of wisdom and nature so noble and so free,
From all extremities the mean dividing,
To peace and plenty each thing atempering,

They have in conclusion wholly surrendered
Into our hands (as much as concerning
All manner weathers by them engendered)
The full of their powers for term everlasting,
To set such order as standeth with our pleasing.
Which thing, as of our part no part required,
But of all their parts right humbly desired,

To take upon us whereto we did assent.
And so in all things with one voice agreeable
We have clearly finished our foresaid parliament,
To your great wealth, which shall be firm and stable,
And to our honour far inestimable.
For, since their powers, as ours, added to our own,
Who can we say know us as we should be known?

But now, for fine, the rest of our intent
Wherefore as now we hither are descended,
Is only to satisfy and content
All manner people which have been offended
By any weather meet to be amended;

32–35 **malice . . . nations** As the gods argued, so their planets were thrown out of orbit, causing damage on Earth through their astrological influences.
33 **far . . . frame** beyond their normal limits.
36 **in . . . before** i.e. the heavenly Parliament.
37 **as became** as was proper.
39 **entered such matter** i.e. introduced a bill or petition to Parliament.
41–42 **To . . . contagious** Saturn claims that frost is the most beneficial weather for all earthly things as it kills off contagions.
44 **Little . . . diligence** his great efforts have achieved little.
46 **out of presence** from his presence (i.e. far away).
48 **he** Saturn.
49 **marreth all** ruin everything.
52 **laid . . . reproving** alleged against her.
53 **tried** found.
54 **In . . . denied** they see their powers (frost and sun) cancelled out by hers (rain), as far as she is able.
57 **flee** fly (to attack).
58 **each one arow** each in turn.
61 **suffereth** allows.
64–65 **Which . . . assembly.** It was this situation, when they considered it, that prompted them to assemble (in parliament) to correct it.
67 **puissant . . . deity** mighty divine powers.
68 **free** generous/noble.
69–70 **From . . . atempering** as I can find the mean between (harmful) extremes, and moderate things to bring peace and prosperity.
73 **engendered** created.
74 **full** total.
75 **with our pleasing** i.e. as shall please us/me.
76–77 **Which . . . desired** I did not ask for this responsibility, they all humbly asked me to accept it.
83–84 **For . . . known?** Since their powers are added to our own, who can claim to know us as we really are (in our full majesty)?
85 **for fine** in conclusion.

Upon whose complaints, declaring their grief,
We shall shape remedy for their relief.
And to give knowledge for their hither resort,
We would this afore proclaimed to be,
To all our people by some one of this sort,
Whom we list to choose here amongst all ye.
Wherefore each man advance and we shall see
Which of you is most meet to be our crier.

Here entereth Merry Report.

MERRY REPORT
Brother, hold up your torch a little higher.
Now I beseech you my lord, look on me first.
I trust your lordship shall not find me the worst.

JUPITER
Why, what art thou that approachest so nigh?

MERRY REPORT
Forsooth, and please your lordship, it is I.

JUPITER
All that we know very well, but what I?

MERRY REPORT
What I? Some say I am I *per se* I.
But, what manner I so ever be I,
I assure your good lordship, I am I.

JUPITER
What manner man art thou, show quickly.

MERRY REPORT
By god, a poor gentleman dwelleth here by.

JUPITER
A gentleman? Thyself bringeth witness nay,
Both in thy light behaviour and array!
But what art thou called where thou dost resort?

MERRY REPORT
Forsooth, my lord, master Merry Report.

JUPITER
Thou art no meet man in our business,
For thine appearance is of too much lightness.

MERRY REPORT
Why, cannot your lordship like my manner,
Mine apparel, nor my name neither?

JUPITER
To neither of all we have devotion.

MERRY REPORT
A proper likelihood of promotion!
Well then, as wise as ye seem to be,
Yet can ye see no wisdom in me.
But, since ye dispraise me for so light an elf,
I pray you give me leave to praise myself.
And for the first part I will begin
In my behaviour at my coming in,
Wherein I think I have little offended,
For sure my courtesy could not be amended.
And, as for my suit your servant to be,
Might ill have been missed, for your honesty;
For, as I be saved, if I shall not lie,
I saw no man sue for the office but I.
Wherefore, if ye take me not ere I go
Ye must anon, whether ye will or no.
And since your intent is but for the weathers
What skills our apparel to be frise or feathers?
I think it wisdom, since no man forbade it,
With this to spare a better, if I had it.
And for my name, reporting always truly
What hurt to report a sad matter merrily?

90 **declaring their grief** when they declare their grievances.
91 **shape** devise (a).
92 **And . . . resort** And to let them know that they should come here.
93 **We . . . afore** What I have already told you.
94 **some . . . sort** someone from this audience.
98 **Brother** the actor speaks to a servant holding a torch in the hall.
101 **what . . . nigh** Merry Report breaks courtly protocol by going straight to Jupiter rather than waiting to be summoned.
103 **what I?** i.e. who are you?
104 **I . . . I** I am I alone. Merry Report playfully quips that 'I' is singular, just as he is only himself, from '*a per se a*', the letter 'a' on its own.
107 **show** tell (me).
108 **dwelleth here by** who lives nearby.
109 **Thyself . . . nay** Your appearance argues that you are not.
110 **light** flippant.
110 **array** clothing.
111 **where . . . resort** where you live.
113 **no meet man** appropriate person for.
114 **too much lightness** too frivolous.
117 **To . . . devotion.** We like none of them.
118 **A proper likelihood** an excellent chance (ironic).
121 **so light an elf** so foolish a little rogue.
127 **suit** petition/request.
128 **Might . . . honesty** (rejecting my suit) through your fastidiousness might have been a bad mistake.
132 **will or no** want to or not.
133–134 **And . . . feathers?** And, since you're interested only in the weather, what does it matter whether I wear frise (coarse woollen cloth) or (luxurious) feathers?
136 **With . . . it** To wear this suit to save a better one (from wearing out)—if I had (a better) one, that is.

As by occasion, for the same intent
To a certain widow this day was I sent,
Whose husband departed without her witting
(A special good lover and she his own sweeting)
To whom at my coming I cast such a figure,
Mingling the matter according to my nature,
That when we departed, above all other things,
She thanked me heartily for my merry tidings!
And if I had not handled it merrily,
Perchance she might have take it heavily;
But in such fashion I conjured and bound her
That I left her merrier than I found her.
What man may compare to show the like comfort
That daily is showed by me, Merry Report?
And for your purpose at this time meant,
For all weathers I am so indifferent,
Without affection, standing so upright:
Sunlight, moonlight, starlight, twilight, torchlight,
Cold, heat, moist, dry, hail, rain, frost, snow,
  lightning, thunder,
Cloudy, misty, windy, fair, foul, above head or under,
Temperate or distemperate: whatever it be,
I promise your lordship all is one to me.

JUPITER

Well, son, considering thine indifferency,
And partly the rest of thy declaration,
We make thee our servant, and immediately
We will thou depart and cause proclamation,
Publishing our pleasure to every nation.
Which thing once done, with all diligence
Make thy return again to this presence.

Here to receive all suitors of each degree
And such as to thee may seem most meetly
We will thou bring them before our majesty.
And for the rest that be not so worthy;
Make thou report to us effectually,
So that we may hear each manner suit at large.
Thus see thou depart, and look upon thy charge.

MERRY REPORT

Now, good my lord god, Our Lady be with ye!
Friends, a fellowship, let me go by ye!
Think ye I may stand thrusting among you there?
Nay, by God, I must thrust about other gear.

Merry Report goeth out. At thend of this stave the god hath a song played in his throne ere Merry Report come in.

JUPITER

Now, since we have thus far set forth our purpose,
A while we will withdraw our godly presence
To enbold all such more plainly to disclose
As here will attend in our foresaid pretence.
And now, according to your obedience,
Rejoice ye in us with joy most joyfully,
And we our self shall joy in our own glory.

[Jupiter withdraws.] Merry Report cometh in.

MERRY REPORT

Now, sirs, take heed, for here cometh god's
  servant.
Avaunt, carterly caitiffs, avaunt!
Why, ye drunken whoresons, will it not be?
By your faith, have ye neither cap nor knee?
Not one of you that will make curtsy
To me that am squire for god's precious body!
Regard ye nothing mine authority?

139 **As... intent** It so happened, to prove this same point.
141 **departed... witting** died without her knowledge.
142 **(A... sweeting)** i.e. they were really in love.
143 **cast... figure** created such an impression.
144 **Mingling... nature** Mixing the (sad) news with my (merry) nature.
148 **heavily** sadly.
150 Double entendres litter this story. 'Cast', 'conjure', and 'handle' all have sexual connotations.
151 **What... comfort** Who could match me in offering such comfort.
154 **indifferent** impartial.
155 **affection** bias.
158 **under** underfoot.
160 **all... me** it's all the same to me.
164 **cause** make (a).
165 **publishing** making known.
167 **to this presence** to my presence here.
168 **degree** social class.
169 **meetly** appropriate.
173 **each... large** each kind of petition in full.
174 **look... charge** pay attention to your task.
176 **a fellowship** in fellowship (addressed to the spectators standing around the screens exit from the hall).
178 **I... gear** I must exert myself in other matters (with a sexual innuendo involving both 'thrust' and 'gear').
178.1 **At... throne** At the end of the next stanza (Jupiter) has a song played in his throne (by musicians within the curtain).
179 **set... purpose** described our intention(s).
181–182 **To... pretence** To encourage those who will come here to disclose their grievances... more fully.
187 **Avaunt... avaunt!** Get out of the way, unmannerly (lit. 'with the manners of a carter') wretches!
189 **have... knee?** haven't you got either caps (to take off) or knees (to bow with)?
191 **squire... body** Squire of the Body: a servant who attended to a king's bodily needs in his Privy Chamber.
192 **Regard ye nothing** Don't you respect at all?

No 'welcome home', nor 'where have ye been?'?
Howbeit, if ye asked, I could not well tell,
But sure I think a thousand mile from Hell.
And on my faith, I think, in my conscience,
I have been from Heaven as far as Heaven is hence,
At Louvain, at London, and in Lombardy,
At Baldock, at Barford, and in Barbary,
At Canterbury, at Coventry, at Colchester,
At Wansworth and Welbeck, at Westchester,
At Fulham, at Faleborne, and at Fenlow,
At Wallingford, at Wakefield, and at Walthamstow,
At Taunton, at Tiptree, and at Tottenham,
At Gloucester, at Guildford, and at Gotham,
At Hartford, at Harwich, at Harrow on the hill,
At Sudbury, Southampton, at Shooters' hill,
At Walsingham, at Witham, and at Warwick,
At Boston, at Bristol, and at Berwick,
At Gravelines, at Gravesend, and at Glastonbury,
Ing Jing-jang Jaybird, the parish of Butsbury.
The Devil himself without more leisure
Could not have gone half thus much, I am sure.
But now I have warned them, let them even choose,
For in faith I care not who win or lose.

Here the Gentleman, before he cometh in, bloweth his horn.

MERRY REPORT
Now by my troth, this was a goodly hearing!
I went it had been the gentlewomen's blowing,
But it is not so as I now suppose,
For women's horns sound more in a man's nose.

GENTLEMAN
Stand ye merry, my friends, everyone!

MERRY REPORT
Say that to me and let the rest alone.
Sir, ye be welcome, and all your many.

GENTLEMAN
Now in good sooth, my friend, God a mercy!
And, since that I meet thee here thus by chance,
I shall require thee of further acquaintance.
And briefly to show thee this is the matter:
I come to sue to the great god Jupiter
For help of things concerning my recreation,
According to his late proclamation

MERRY REPORT
Marry, and I am he that this must speed.
But first tell me, what be ye indeed?

GENTLEMAN
Forsooth, good friend, I am a gentleman.

MERRY REPORT
A goodly occupation, by Saint Anne!
On my faith, your mastership hath a merry life.
But who maketh all these horns, yourself or your wife?
Nay, even in earnest I ask you this question.

GENTLEMAN
Now, by my troth, thou art a merry one!

MERRY REPORT
In faith, of us both I think never one sad,
For I am not so merry but ye seem as mad.
But stand ye still and take a little pain,
I will come to you by and by again.

[*To Jupiter*]

195 **thousand . . . Hell** i.e. very far away.
197 **from . . . hence** as far from Heaven as Heaven is from here.
198 Louvain (in modern Belgium); Lombardy (Italy).
199 Baldock (Hertfordshire); Barford (perhaps the Cambridgeshire village of that name), Barbary (North Africa).
200 Canterbury (Kent); Coventry (Warwickshire); Colchester (Essex).
201 Wansworth Wandsworth (Surrey); Welbeck (Nottinghamshire); Chester (Cheshire).
202 Fulham (Middlesex); Faleborne ?Fulbourn (Cambridgeshire); Fenlow ?Farnlaw (Northumberland).
203 Wallingford (Berkshire); Wakefield (Yorkshire); Walthamstow (Essex).
204 Taunton (Somerset); Tiptree (Essex); Tottenham (at that time just north of London, in Middlesex).
205 Gloucester; Guildford (Surrey); Gotham (Nottinghamshire).
206 Hertford; Harwich (Essex); Harrow on the Hill (Middlesex).
207 Sudbury (Suffolk); Southampton (Hampshire); Shooter's Hill (near Greenwich).
208 Walsingham (Norfolk); Witham (Essex); Warwick.
209 Boston (Lincolnshire); Bristol; Berwick-upon-Tweed (Northumberland).
210 Gravelines (near Calais, France); Gravesend (Kent); Glastonbury (Somerset).
211 **Ing . . . Butsbury** the manors of Ginge Johiberd and Ginges Landri (Great and Little Blunts), where the Heywood family had lands.
214 **warned them** told them (of Jupiter's request).
217 **went . . . been** thought it was.
219 **For . . . nose** for women's horns (by implication, 'farts') smell worse than they sound.
222 **many** retinue.
223 **Now . . . mercy!** Truly . . . God bless you! (mild oaths).
229 **late** recent.
230 **Marry** Indeed.
230 **that . . . speed** who must help you.
235 **But . . . wife?** Merry Report puns insultingly. A cuckolded husband was said to grow horns as a result of his wife's adultery.
238 **never one sad** neither of us is serious.

Now, gracious god, if your will so be.
I pray ye let me speak a word with ye.

JUPITER
My son, say on; let us hear thy mind.

MERRY REPORT
My lord, there standeth a suitor even here behind,
A gentleman in yonder corner,
And, as I think, his name is master Horner.
A hunter he is, and cometh to make you sport,
He would hunt a sow or twain out of this sort!

Here he pointeth to the women [*in the audience*].

JUPITER
Whatsoever his mind be, let him appear.

MERRY REPORT
Now, good master Horner, I pray you come near.

GENTLEMAN
I am no horner, knave, I will thou know it.

MERRY REPORT
I thought ye had, for when ye did blow it,
Heard I never whoreson make horn so go!
As lief ye kissed mine arse as blow my hole so.
Come on your way before the god Jupiter,
And there for yourself ye shall be suitor.

GENTLEMAN
Most mighty prince and god of every nation,
Pleaseth your highness to vouchsafe the hearing
Of me, which, according to your proclamation,
Doth make appearance in way of beseeching;

Not solely for myself, but generally
For all come of noble and ancient stock;
Which sort above all doth most thankfully
Daily take pain for wealth of the common flock,

With diligent study always devising
To keep them in order and unity,
In peace to labour the increase of their living
Whereby each man may prosper in plenty.

Wherefore, good god, this is our whole desiring:
That for ease of our pains at times vacant
In our recreation, which chiefly is hunting,
It may please you to send us weather pleasant:

Dry and not misty, the wind calm and still,
That after our hounds yearning so merrily
Chasing the deer over dale and hill
In hearing we may follow and to-comfort the cry.

JUPITER
Right well we do perceive your whole request,
Which shall not fail to rest in memory.
Wherefore we will ye set yourself at rest
Till we have heard each man indifferently,
And we shall take such order universally
As best may stand to our honour infinite
For wealth in common and each man's singular profit.

GENTLEMAN
In Heaven and Earth honoured be the name
Of Jupiter, whom of his godly goodness
Hath set this matter in so goodly frame
That every wight shall have his desire, doubtless.

And first, for us nobles and gentlemen,
I doubt not in his wisdom to provide
Such weather as in our hunting now and then
We may both tease and receive on every side.

Which thing, once had for our said recreation,
Shall greatly prevail you in preferring our health,
For what thing more needful than our
preservation,
Being the weal and heads of all common wealth?

MERRY REPORT
Now I beseech your mastership, whose head be you?

GENTLEMAN
Whose head am I? Thy head! What sayest thou now?

247 **Horner** Horn-blower/cuckold.
249 **He would** (I bet) he would.
Perhaps the seating was segregated by gender.
253 **had** were.
254–255 **Heard...so.** I never heard any son-of-a-bitch blow a horn like that! I'd rather you kissed my arse than blow my (arse) hole like that.
261 **in...beseeching** in order to make a request.
263 **stock** lineage/ancestry.
265 **Daily...flock** Daily exert themselves for the good of the common people.
268 **increase...living** improvement of their prosperity.
271 **at times vacant** during our leisure time.
275 **yearning** crying out.
277 **In...cry** That we may follow closely to keep them in hearing and to encourage them as they cry.
280 **will ye** wish you (to).
283 **stand to** accord with.
284 **singular** individual.
287 **frame** order.
292 **tease and receive** chase and catch (the quarry).
294 **preferring our health** fostering our wellbeing.
296 **Being...wealth?** (As we are) the source of all common prosperity?

MERRY REPORT

Nay, I think it very true, so God me help,
For I have ever been, of a little whelp,
So full of fancies and in so many fits,
So many small reasons and in so many wits,
That, even as I stand, I pray God I be dead,
If ever I thought them all meet for one head.
But, since I have one head more than I knew,
Blame not my rejoicing; I love all things new!
And sure it is a treasure of heads to have store;
One feat can I now that I never could before.

GENTLEMAN

What is that?

MERRY REPORT

By god, since ye came hither
I can set my head and my tail together.
This head shall save money, by saint Mary,
From henceforth I will no apothecary,
For at all times when such things shall mister,
My new head shall give mine old tail a glister.
And, after all this, then shall my head wait
Upon my tail, and there stand at receipt.
Sir, for the rest I will not now move you,
But if we live, ye shall smell how I love you.
And, sir, touching your suit here, depart when it please you,
For be ye sure, as I can I will ease you.

GENTLEMAN

Then give me thy hand, that promise I take.
And if for my sake any suit thou do make,
I promise thy pain to be requited
More largely than now shall be recited.

[*Exit.*]

MERRY REPORT

Alas, my neck! God's pity, where is my head?
By Saint Ive[s], I fear me I shall be dead!
And if I were, methink it were no wonder,
Since my head and my body is so far asunder!

Entereth the Merchant.

Master Parson, now welcome, by my life!
I pray you, how doth my mistress, your wife?

MERCHANT

Sir, for the priesthood and wife that ye allege,
I see ye speak more of dotage than knowledge.
But let pass, sir, I would to you be suitor
To bring me, if ye can, before Jupiter.

[MERRY REPORT]

Yes, marry can I, and will do it indeed.
Tarry and I shall make way for your speed.

[*To Jupiter*]

In faith, good lord, if it please your gracious godship,
I must have a word or twain with your lordship.
Sir, yonder is another man in place
Who maketh great suit to speak with your Grace.
Your pleasure once known, he cometh by and by.

JUPITER

Bring him before our presence son, hardily.

MERRY REPORT [*To Merchant*]

Why, where be you? Shall I not find you?
Come away, I pray God the devil blind ye!

MERCHANT [*To Jupiter*]

Most mighty prince and lord of lords all,
Right humbly beseecheth your Majesty
Your merchant men through the world all,
That it may please you of your benignity,

In the daily danger of our goods and life,
First to consider the desert of our request
(What wealth we bring the rest to our great care and strife)
And then to reward us as ye shall think best.

300 **I...whelp** ever since I was a pup (i.e. child).
302 **reasons** thoughts.
303 **dead** (struck) dead.
304 **meet...head** able to be crammed into just one head.
307 **Sure...store** it's surely a great thing to have many heads!
312 **I...apothecary** I'll need no pharmacist.
313 **shall mister** shall be needed.
314 **glister** suppository.
316 **stand at receipt** stand ready to receive (whatever the suppository discharges).
317 **move you** reveal to you, with a pun on bowel movements.
320 **as...you** I'll help you as far as I can.
323–324 **requited more largely** rewarded more generously.
329 **Master Parson** Merry Report, perhaps deliberately, mistakes the Merchant's long coat for a priest's robes. The reference to his 'wife' is a further insult: priests should be celibate and could not marry.
332 **dotage** folly.
341 **Your...by** Once your pleasure is known, he could come to you at once.
342 **hardily** swiftly.
348 **benignity** benevolence.
351 **care** suffering.

What were the surplusage of each commodity
Which groweth and increaseth in every land,
Except exchange by such men as we be
By way of intercourse that lieth in our hand?

We freight from home things whereof there is plenty,
And home we bring such things as there be scant.
Who should afore us merchants accounted be?
For were not we, the world should wish and want

In many things, which now shall lack rehearsal.
And, briefly to conclude, we beseech your highness
That of the benefit proclaimed in general
We may be partakers, for common increase,

Establishing weather thus, pleasing your grace:
Stormy nor misty, the wind measurable,
That safely we may pass from place to place
Bearing our sails for speed most vailable;

And also the wind to change and to turn:
East, west, north, and south, as best may be set,
In any one place not too long to sojourn,
For the length of our voyage may lose our market.

JUPITER
Right well have ye said, and we accept it so,
And so shall we reward you ere we go hence.
But ye must take patience till we have heard mo,
That we may indifferently give sentence.
There may pass by us no spot of negligence,
But justly to judge each thing so upright
That each man's part may shine in the self right.

MERRY REPORT
Now sir, by your faith, if ye should be sworn,
Heard ye ever god speak so since ye were born?
So wisely, so gently his words be showed.

MERCHANT
I thank his Grace, my suit is well bestowed.

MERRY REPORT
Sir, what voyage intend ye next to go?

MERCHANT
I trust or mid-Lent to be to Chio.

MERRY REPORT
Ha, ha, is it your mind to sail at Chio?
Nay then, when ye will, by Our Lady ye may go,
And let me alone with this. Be of good cheer,
Ye may trust me at Chio as well as here.
For, though ye were from me a thousand mile
space,
I would do as much as ye were here in place.
For, since that from hence it is so far thither,
I care not though ye never come again hither.

MERCHANT
Sir, if ye remember me when time shall come,
Though I requite not all, I shall deserve some.

Exit Merchant.

MERRY REPORT
Now fare ye well, and God thank you, by Saint
Anne!
I pray you mark the fashion of this honest man:
He putteth me in more trust at this meeting here,
Than he shall find cause why, this twenty year.

Here entereth the Ranger.

RANGER
God be here! Now Christ keep this company!

MERRY REPORT
In faith, ye be welcome even very scantly.
Sir, for your coming what is the matter?

353 **What...commodity** (just think) what would be the excess of every commodity.
355 **Except exchange** if there was no trade.
356 **By...intercourse** Through the transportation and commerce.
359–361 **Who...rehearsal.** Who should be thought more important than us? For, if we did not exist, the world would lack many things, which I won't remind you of now.
363 **in general** to everyone.
364 **We...increase** We may be sharers, in the interests of common prosperity.
366 **measureable** moderate.
368 **Bearing...vailable** Keeping our sails (up), to make best speed.
372 **market** profit.
375 **mo** more (suitors).
376 **sentence** judgement.
378 **upright** properly.
379 **shine...right** be rewarded on its evident merits.
383 **is well bestowed** is in good hands.
385 **I...Chio?** I hope before mid-Lent (by the end of March), to be in Chios (an Aegean island).
386 **at** to.
391 **as...place** as if you were here yourself (i.e. by implication, nothing).
392–393 **For...hither.** The last sentence is presumably an aside.
395 **Though...some** although I won't give you all (you deserve), I shall give you some of it. (A suitably careful promise from a prudent merchant.)
397 **fashion** nature.
399 **casue why** reason to do so.
400 **God be here!** a blessing.
401 Merry Report's seemingly unprompted hostility to the Ranger may be the result of the latter's failure to show him any obvious respect on entering.

RANGER
I would fain speak with the god Jupiter.
MERRY REPORT
That will not be, but ye may do this:
Tell me your mind, I am an officer of his.
RANGER
Be ye so? Marry, I cry you mercy!
Your mastership may say I am homely.
But, since your mind is to have reported
The cause wherefore I am now resorted,
Pleaseth it your mastership it is so:
I come for myself and such other mo,
Rangers and keepers of certain places
As forests, parks, purlieus, and chases,
Where we be charged with all manner game.
Small is our profit and great is our blame.
Alas for our wages, what be we the near?
What is forty shillings or five mark a year?
Many times and oft where we be flitting,
We spend forty pence apiece at a sitting.
Now for our vantage which chiefly is windfall,
That is right nought; there bloweth no wind at all,
Which is the thing wherein we find most grief,
And cause of my coming to sue for relief,
That the god, of pity, all this thing knowing,
May send us good rage of blustering and
 blowing.
And, if I cannot get god to do some good,
I would hire the Devil to run through the wood,
The roots to turn up, the tops to bring under;
A mischief upon them, and a wild thunder!
MERRY REPORT
Very well said! I set by your charity
As much in a manner as by your honesty.
I shall set you somewhat in ease anon.
Ye shall put on your cap when I am gone,
For I see ye care not who win or lose
So ye may find means to win your fees.
RANGER
Sir, as in that ye speak as it please ye,
But let me speak with the god if it may be.
I pray you let me pass ye.
MERRY REPORT
Why, nay sir, by the mass, yea!
RANGER
Then will I leave you even as I found ye.
MERRY REPORT
Go when ye will, no man here hath bound ye.

Here entereth the Water Miller,
and the Ranger goeth out.

WATER MILLER
What the Devil should skill though all the world
 were dumb,
Since in all our speaking we never be heard.
We cry out for rain, the Devil sped drop will come.
We water millers be nothing in regard.

No water have we to grind at any stint;
The wind is so strong the rain cannot fall,
Which keepeth our mill-dams as dry as a flint.
We are undone, we grind nothing at all.

The greater is the pity, as thinketh me,
For what availeth to each man his corn,
Till it be ground by such men as we be?
Theirs is the loss if we be forborne.

For, touching ourselves, we are but drudges
And very beggars, save only our toll,
Which is right small, and yet many grudges
For grist of a bushel to give a quart bowl.

407 **may...homely** must think I am rustic/ill-mannered.
408 **mind** desire.
409 **wherefore...resorted** for which I have come here.
413 **parks...chases** parks (land enclosed for private hunting), forest-fringes (used as game reserves), and hunting grounds.
414 **be...game** are responsible for all kinds of game (animals and birds for hunting).
416 **what...near?** we're no nearer getting (proper wages)?
417 A mark was 13 shillings and 4 pence.
418 **flitting** travelling.
419 **apiece...sitting** each at one mealtime.
420 **windfall** perks. Rangers were entitled to collect and sell trees and branches blown down by the wind.
430 **set by** value/esteem.
433 **Ye...gone** the Ranger probably tries to put his cap back on here, but Merry Report, enjoying his new status, keeps him bareheaded (and so subservient) a while longer.
435 **So** so long as.
442 **What...skill** Would it matter.
444 **the...drop** not a single cursed drop.
445 **nothing in regard** held in no esteem.
446 **stint** rate.
448 **mill-dams** mill-races.
451 **what...corn** what use is corn to any man.
453 **forborne** neglected/ruined.
454 **touching** concerning.
455 **save...toll** except for our grinding fee.
456–457 **and...bowl** and yet many begrudge paying a two-pound bowl of grain as fee for each bushel (64 pounds) we grind for them.

Yet, were not reparations, we might do well:
Our millstones, our wheel with her cogs, and our trundle,
Our floodgate, our mill-pool, our water-wheel,
Our hopper, our axle-tree, our iron spindle.

In this and much more so great is our charge,
That we would not reck though no water were,
Save only it toucheth each man so large,
And each for our neighbour Christ biddeth us care.

Wherefore my conscience hath pricked me hither,
In this to sue, according to the cry,
For plenty of rain to the god Jupiter,
To whose presence I will go even boldly.

MERRY REPORT
Sir, I doubt nothing your audacity,
But I fear me ye lack capacity,
For, if ye were wise, ye might well espy
How rudely ye err from rules of courtesy.
What, ye come in revelling and rioting,
Even as a knave might go to a bear-baiting!

WATER MILLER
All you bear record what favour I have.
Hark how familiarly he calleth me knave.
Doubtless the gentleman is universal,
But mark this lesson, sir, you should never call
Your fellow 'knave', nor your brother 'whoreson',
For nought can ye get by it when ye have done.

MERRY REPORT
Thou art neither brother nor fellow to me,
For I am god's servant: mayest thou not see?
Would ye presume to speak with the great god?
Nay, discretion and you be too far odd.
By Our Lady, these knaves must be tied shorter.
Sir, who let you in, spake ye with the porter?

WATER MILLER
Nay, by my troth, nor with no other man,
Yet I saw you well when I first began.
How be it, so help me God and holy dam,
I took you but for a knave as I am.
But marry, now, since I know what ye be,
I must and will obey your authority,
And if I may not speak with Jupiter
I beseech you be my solicitor.

MERRY REPORT
As in that I will be your well-willer.
I perceive you be a water miller,
And your whole desire, as I take the matter,
Is plenty of rain for increase of water,
The let whereof, ye affirm determinately
Is only the wind, your mortal enemy.

WATER MILLER
Troth it is, for it bloweth so aloft
We never have rain, or at the most not oft.
Wherefore I pray you, put the god in mind,
Clearly forever to banish the wind.

Entereth the Wind Miller

WIND MILLER
How? Is all the weather gone ere I come?
For the Passion of God, help me to some!
I am a wind miller, as many mo be;
No wretch in wretchedness so wretched as we.
The whole sort of my craft be all marred at once,
The wind is so weak it stirreth not our stones,
Nor scantly can shatter the shitten sail
That hangeth shattering at a woman's tail.
The rain never resteth, so long be the showers
From time of beginning till four and twenty hours,
And end when it shall, at night or at noon,
Another beginneth as soon as that is done.

458 **were not reparations** were (it) not (for) repairs.
459 **trundle** horizontal wheel.
463 **reck...were** care if there was no water at all.
464–465 **Save...care** except that it concerns everyone (i.e. not just us), and Christ instructed us all to care for our neighbours.
466 **pricked me hither** prompted me (to come) here.
467 **cry** proclamation.
470 **doubt nothing** don't doubt.
471 **capacity** intelligence.
474 **rioting** quarrelling.
476 **record** witness (spoken to the audience).
477 **familiarly** presumptuously.
478 **universal** a know-all/all-powerful.
485 **too far odd** at variance.
486 **tied shorter** kept on a shorter leash.
489 **began** came in.
491 **took...knave** thought you were only a servant/common man.
495 **be my solicitor** i.e. speak on my behalf.
496 **well-willer** well-wisher.
500 **The...determinately** the hindrance to which, you firmly assert.
510 **marred** ruined.
512 **shattering** shaking.
515 **From...hours** i.e. all day and night.

Such revel of rain ye know well enough
Destroyeth the wind, be it never so rough;
Whereby, since our mills be come to still
standing,
Now may we wind millers go even to hanging.
A miller? With a murain and a mischief;
Who would be a miller? As good be a thief!
Yet in time past when grinding was plenty
Who were so like God's fellows as we?
As fast as God made corn, we millers made meal.
Which might be best forborne for common weal?
But let that gear pass. For I fear our pride
Is cause of the care which God doth us provide,
Wherefore I submit me, intending to see
What comfort may come by humility.
And now, at this time, they said in the cry
The god is come down to shape remedy.

MERRY REPORT
No doubt he is here even in yonder throne.
But in your matter he trusteth me alone,
Wherein I do perceive by your complaint
Oppression of rain doth make the wind so faint
That ye wind millers be clean caste away.

WIND MILLER
If Jupiter help not, it is as ye say.
But in few words to tell you my mind round,
Upon this condition I would be bound
Day by day to say Our Lady's Psalter:
That in this world were no drop of water
Nor never rain, but wind continual,
Then should we wind millers be lords over all.

MERRY REPORT
Come on and assay how you twain can agree;
A brother of yours, a miller as ye be.

WATER MILLER
By mean of our craft we may be brothers,
But while we live shall we never be lovers.
We be of one craft, but not of one kind:
I live by water and he by the wind.

Here Merry Report goeth out.

And, sir, as ye desire wind continual,
So would I have rain evermore to fall,
Which two in experience right well ye see
Right seld or never together can be.
For as long as the wind ruleth, it is plain,
Twenty to one ye get no drop of rain;
And when the element is too far oppressed,
Down commeth the rain and setteth the wind at rest.
By this ye see we cannot both obtain,
For ye must lack wind or I must lack rain.
Wherefore I think good, before this audience,
Each for our self to say ere we go hence.
And whom is thought weakest when we have finished,
Leave off his suit and content to be banished.

WIND MILLER
In faith, agreed. But then, by your license,
Our mills for a time shall hang in suspense.
Since water and wind is chiefly our suit
Which best may be spared we will first dispute.
Wherefore to the sea my reason shall resort
Where ships by means of wind try from port to port,
From land to land, in distance many a mile.
Great is the passage and small is the while.
So great is the profit, as to me doth seem,
That no man's wisdom the wealth can esteem.
And since the wind is conveyer of all,
Who but the wind should have thank above all?

518 **revel** excess.
521 **go...hanging** might as well hang ourselves.
522 **murain** plague.
523 **As...thief!** I might as well be a thief! (Ironic, as millers were proverbially associated with theft.)
524 **plenty** plentiful.
526 **meal** flour.
527 **Which...weal?** Which could best be done without for the common good? (i.e. God's growing or our milling?)
528 **But...pass.** But let's forget that business.
529 **care** suffering.
533 **shape** provide.
538 **clean caste away** completely ruined.
540 **mind round** opinion clearly and honestly.
542 **Day...Psalter** Daily to recite...the Rosary.
546 **assay** try (to discover).
549 **lovers** friends.
550 **kind** nature.
555 **Right seld** very seldom.
557 **Twenty to one** I'll give you odds of twenty to one.
558 **element** sky.
560 **both obtain** get what we want.
563 **for...say** speak up for himself (and his own craft).
566 **by your license** with your permission.
567 **hang in suspense** be put aside.
568 **is suit** are our chief concerns.
569 **spared** done without.
570 **resort** travel.
571 **try** sail.
573 **passage** journey.
573 **while** time.
575 **esteem** estimate.
576 **conveyer** mover.

WATER MILLER

Admit in this place a tree here to grow
And thereat the wind in great rage to blow;
When it hath all blowen, this is a clear case,
The tree removeth no hair's breadth from his place.
No more would the ships, blow the best it could,
Although it would blow down both mast and shroud.
Except the ship float upon the water,
The wind can right nought do: a plain matter.
Yet may ye on water without any wind
Row forth your vessel where men will have her 'signed.
Nothing more rejoiceth the mariner
Than mean cools of wind and plenty of water,
For commonly the cause of every wrack
Is excess of wind where water doth lack.
In rage of these storms the peril is such,
That better were no wind than so far too much.

WIND MILLER

Well, if my reason in this may not stand,
I will forsake the sea and leap to land.
In every church where God's service is,
The organs bear brunt of half the choir, iwys.
Which causeth the sound: or water or wind?
Moreover, for wind this thing I find:
For the most part, all manner minstrelsy
By wind they deliver their sound chiefly.
Fill me a bagpipe of your water full:
As sweetly shall it sound as it were stuffed with wool!

WATER MILLER

On my faith, I think the moon be at the full,
For frantic fancies be then most plentiful,
Which are at the pride of their spring in your head,
So far from our matter he is now fled.
As for the wind in any instrument,
It is no parcel of our argument.
We spake of wind that cometh naturally,
And that is wind forced artificially,
Which is not to purpose. But, if it were,
And water indeed right nought could do there,
Yet I think organs no such commodity
Whereby the water should banished be.
And for your bagpipes, I take them as nifils.
Your matter is all in fancies and trifles!

WIND MILLER

By God, but ye shall not trifle me off so!
If these things serve not, I will rehearse mo.
And now to mind there is one old proverb come;
'One bushel of March dust is worth a king's ransom.'
What is a hundred thousand bushels worth then?

WATER MILLER

Not one mite, for the thing self, to no man.

WIND MILLER

Why, shall wind everywhere thus be object?
Nay, in the highways he shall take effect,
Whereas the rain doth never good but hurt,
For wind maketh but dust, and water maketh dirt.
Powder or syrup, sirs, which like ye best?
Who liketh not the one may lick up the rest.
But, sure, whosoever hath assayed such sips,
Had lever have dusty eyes than dirty lips.
And it is said since afore we were born
That drought doth never make dearth of corn.
And well it is known to the most fool here,
How rain hath priced corn within this seven year.

578 **Admit...grow** Suppose for a moment that a tree was growing here.
583 **shroud** sail.
584 **Except** Unless.
585 **a plain matter** an obvious conclusion.
587 **where...'signed** wherever...assigned her to go.
588 **rejoiceth** pleases.
589 **mean cools** moderate gusts.
590 **wrack** (ship)wreck.
597 **bear...iwys** do half the choir's work, I know.
598 **or** (is it) either.
600 **all manner minstrelsy** all types of musician.
606 **at...spring** at their peak.
609 **parcel** part.
611 **that** i.e. wind used by musicians.
612 **to purpose** relevant.
614–615 **I...be** I think that organs are not so vital that water should be banished for their sake.
616 **take...nifils** consider them mere nothings.
618 **trifle...so!** put me off with trifles!
621 Dust (a sign of dry weather) in March is prized as it allows for the early planting of spring crops.
623 **the thing self** itself.
624 **object** objected to.
625 **take effect** find its true value/usefulness.
627 **dirt** mud.
630 **assayed such sips** i.e. tried licking up mud.
631 **lever** rather.
632 **it is** has been.
634 **the most** even the greatest.
635 **How...year** how rain has forced up the price of corn in the past seven years (by spoiling harvests).

WATER MILLER

Sir, I pray thee, spare me a little season
And I shall briefly conclude thee with reason.
Put case one summer's day without wind to be,
And ragious wind in winter days two or three:
Much more shall dry that one calm day in summer
Than shall those three windy days in winter.
Whom shall we thank for this when all is done?
The thank to wind? Nay, thank chiefly the sun!
And so for drought: if corn thereby increase,
The sun doth comfort and ripe all, doubtless.
And oft the wind so layeth the corn, God wot,
That never after can it ripe, but rot.
If drought took place as ye say, yet may ye see
Little helpeth the wind in this commodity.
But now, sir, I deny your principal:
If drought ever were, it were impossible
To have any grain, for, ere it can grow
Ye must plough your land, harrow, and sow.
Which will not be, except ye may have rain
To temper the ground; and after again
For springing and plumping all manner corn,
Yet must ye have water or all is forlorn.
If ye take water for no commodity,
Yet must ye take it for thing of necessity,
For washing, for scouring, all filth cleansing.
Where water lacketh, what beastly being!
In brewing, in baking, in dressing of meat,
If ye lack water, what could ye drink or eat?
Without water could live neither man nor beast,
For water preserveth both most and least.
For water could I say a thousand things mo,
Saving as now the time will not serve so.
And, as for that wind that you do sue for,
Is good for your windmill and for no more.
Sir, sith all this in experience is tried,
I say this matter standeth clear on my side.

WIND MILLER

Well, since this will not serve, I will allege the rest.
Sir, for our mills, I say mine is the best.
My windmill shall grind more corn in one hour
Than thy water mill shall in three or four:
Yea, more than thine should in a whole year
If thou mightest have as thou hast wished here.
For thou desirest to have excess of rain,
Which thing to thee were the worst thou couldst obtain,
For, if thou didst, it were a plain induction
To make thine own desire thine own destruction.
For in excess of rain at any flood
Your mills must stand still; they can do no good.
And when the wind doth blow the uttermost,
Our windmills walk a-main in every coast.
For, as we see the wind in his estate,
We moder our sails after the same rate.
Since our mills grind so far faster than yours,
And also they may grind all times and hours,
I say we need no water mills at all,
For windmills be sufficient to serve all.

WATER MILLER

Thou speakest of all and considerest not half.
In boast of thy grist thou art wise as a calf!
For, though above us your mills grind far faster,
What help to those from whom ye be much farther?
And of two sorts, if the one should be conserved,
I think it meet the most number be served.
In vales and wealds where most commodity is,
There is most people: ye must grant me this.
On hills and downs, which parts are most barren,

636 **season** time.
637 **conclude** refute.
638 **put case** consider this case.
639 **ragious** raging.
643 **The thank** (should) we give the thanks?
646 **layeth ... wot** blows flat the corn, God knows.
650 **your principal** your main claim (a debating term).
651 **ever were** prevailed all the time.
655 **temper** soften.
655 **after again** later on.
656 **springing** sprouting.
657 **forlorn** lost.
658 **no commodity** positively good thing.
661 **what beastly being** what a beastly life it would be.
662 **dressing of meat** preparing of food.
665 **most and least** the best and worst (i.e. every living thing).
669 **Is** It is.
670–671 **sith ... side** since all this is proved by experience, I'd say our argument stands clearly in my favour (i.e. I win!)
672 **allege the rest** put forward the rest of my argument.
677 **If ... here** (even) if you gained what you wished (for) here.
680 **induction** beginning.
685 **walk ... coast** work most strongly in every region.
687 **as ... rate** as we judge the state of the wind, we moderate our sails accordingly.
693 **grist** grinding.
696 **if ... conserved** if only one can be kept.
697–699 **I ... people** I think it should be the sort that serves the most people. In valleys and in fields, where the living is best, that's where most people are.

There must be few, it can no mo sustain.
I dare well say, if it were tried even now,
That there is ten of us to one of you.
And where should chiefly all necessaries be,
But there as people are most in plenty?
More reason that you come seven mile to mill,
Than all we of the vale should climb the hill.
If rain came reasonable, as I require it,
We should of your windmills have need no whit.

Entereth Merry Report.

MERRY REPORT
Stop, foolish knaves; for your reasoning is such
That ye have reasoned even enough and too much!
I heard all the words that ye both have had.
So help me God the knaves be more than mad!
Neither of them both that hath wit nor grace
To perceive that both mills may serve in place.
Between water and wind there is no such let,
But each mill may have time to use his fet.
Which thing I can tell by experience.
For I have of mine own not far from hence,
In a corner together, a couple of mills
Standing in a marsh between two hills,
(Not of inheritance, but by my wife.
She is feifed in the tail for terms of her life),
The one for wind, the other for water,
And of them both, I thank God, there standeth neither,
For, in a good hour be it spoken,
The water gate is no sooner open
But 'Clap!', sayth the windmill even straight behind.
There is good speed, the Devil and all they grind.
But whether that the hopper be dusty,
Or that the millstones be somewhat rusty,
By the Mass, the meal is mischievous musty!
And if ye think my tale be not trusty,
I make ye true promise; come when ye list,
We shall find mean ye shall taste of the grist!

WATER MILLER
The corn at receipt haply is not good?

MERRY REPORT
There can be no sweeter, by the sweet Rood.
Another thing yet, which shall not be cloaked,
My water mill many times is choked.

WATER MILLER
So will she be, though ye should burst your bones,
Except ye be perfect in setting your stones.
Fear not the ledger, beware your runner.
Yet this for the ledger or he have won her:
Perchance your ledger doth lack good pecking.

MERRY REPORT
So sayeth my wife, and that maketh all our checking.
She would have the mill pecked, pecked, pecked every day,
But, by God, millers must peck when they may.
So oft have we pecked that our stones wax right thin,
And all our other gear not worth a pin.
For with pecking and pecking I have so wrought,
That I have pecked a good pecking iron to nought.
Howbeit, if I stick no better till her,
My wife sayeth she will have a new miller.
But let it pass, and now to our matter.
I say my mills lack neither wind nor water;
No more do yours as far as need doth require.

701 **can . . . sustain** (the land) can sustain no more.
705 **as** where.
706 **More reason** (it is) more reasonable.
709 **need no whit** no need at all.
716 **let** hindrance.
717 **use his fet** perform its function.
719–721 **mine . . . hills** The allusion is punningly to his wife's genitals, sphincter, and buttocks.
722–724 **(Not . . . water** (I own them) not by inheritance, but through my wife, who is legally possessed of them via an entail (a lease, also punning: 'in her tail') for her lifetime. The one (mill) is for wind, the other for water.
725 **standeth neither** neither stands idle.
726 **in . . . spoken** (a mild oath).
728 **even straight behind** immediately after/right behind it.
732 **mischievous musty**! horribly smelly!
734 **list** like.
735 **We . . . grist!** If you don't believe me, you can eat the end result!
736 **at receipt haply** when it arrives, perhaps.
737 **Rood** Holy Cross.
738 **cloaked** hidden.
739 **choked** blocked. The speech is an extended double entendre suggesting Merry Report needs to perform better sexually to satisfy his wife, or she will look elsewhere for 'pecking'. ('Stones' = testicles (slang).)
740 **though . . . bones** no matter how hard you try.
741 **Except** Unless.
742 **Fear . . . runner.** Don't worry about your ledger (fixed lower millstone), look to your runner (the active upper stone).
744 **Yet . . . pecking.** But consider this about the ledger before you finish with it, maybe (it) hasn't been properly tooled with a pecker (and your grinding equipment isn't meshing properly).
745 **checking** argument(s).
748 **wax right thin** grow very threadbare.
749 **gear** stuff (slang: genitals).
751 **to nought** down to nothing.
752 **stick no better** don't persist any better with her.

But, since ye cannot agree, I will desire
Jupiter to set you both in such rest
As to your wealth and his honour may stand best.

WATER MILLER
I pray you heartily, remember me.

WIND MILLER
Let not me be forgotten, I beseech ye.

Both millers goeth forth.

MERRY REPORT
If I remember you not both alike,
I would ye were over the ears in the dike!
Now be we rid of two knaves at once chance.
By Saint Thomas, it is a knavish riddance.

The Gentlewoman entereth.

GENTLEWOMAN
Now good God, what a folly is this!
What should I do where so much people is?
I know not how to pass in to the god now.

MERRY REPORT
No, but ye know how he may pass into you!

GENTLEWOMAN
I pray you, let me in at the back side.

MERRY REPORT
Yea, shall I so, and your foreside so wide?
Nay, not yet! But, since ye love to be alone,
We twain will into a corner anon.
But first, I pray you, come your way hither
And let us twain chat awhile together.

GENTLEWOMAN
Sir, as to you, I have little matter.
My coming is to speak with Jupiter.

MERRY REPORT
Stand ye still a while, and I will go prove
Whether that the god will be brought in love.

[*To Jupiter*]

My lord, how now, look up lustily;
Here is a darling come, by saint Antony!
And if it be your pleasure to marry,
Speak quickly for she may not tarry.
In faith I think ye may win her anon,
For she would speak with your lordship alone.

JUPITER
Son, that is not the thing at this time meant.
If her suit concern no cause of our hither resort,
Send her out of place; but if she be bent
To that purpose, hear her and make us report.

MERRY REPORT
I count women lost if we love them not well,
For ye see god loveth them never a deal.
Mistress, ye cannot speak with the god.

GENTLEWOMAN
No, why?

MERRY REPORT
By my faith, for his lordship is right busy
With a piece of work that needs must be done.
Even now is he making of a new moon:
He sayeth your old moons be so far tasted
That all the goodness of them is wasted;
Which of the great wet hath been most matter,
For old moons be leaky, they can hold no water.
But for this new moon, I durst lay my gown,
Except a few drops at her going down,
Ye get no rain till her arising,
Without it need, and then no man's devising
Could wish the fashion of rain to be so good:
Not gushing out like gutters of Noah's flood,
But small drops sprinkling softly on the ground
Though they fell on a sponge, they would give no sound.

758 **rest** contentment.
763 **dike** ditch.
764 **at one chance** in one go.
770 **at...side** through the back door: with the obvious sexual connotations ('backside' is slang for arse).
771 **foreside** front-end.
778 **prove** (and) find out.
782 There may be a series of allusions here to Henry VIII's decision to marry Anne Boleyn on 5 January 1533 (hence the possible puns in the oaths to St Anne (l.812) and St *An*thony (l.781). Anne was heavily pregnant by this time, so the wedding could not 'tarry'.
786 **meant** intended.
787 **If...resort** if her suit does not relate to the cause of our coming here (i.e. the weather).
788 **if...bent** if she has come here.
790 **count** consider.
795 **making...moon** perhaps another allusion to Anne (who replaced the old queen/moon, Catherine of Aragon) and her potential to satisfy Henry and produce an heir.
796 **far tasted** used up.
797 **wasted** exhausted.
798 **Which...matter** Which has been the principal cause of the great 'wet' (storm).
800 **durst lay** dare bet.
801 **going down** setting/going to bed.
803 **Without it need** Unless it is necessary.
803 **devising** imagination.
805 **gutters** the downpours.
807 **Though** As though.

This new moon shall make a thing spring more in this while
Than an old moon shall while a man may go a mile.
By that time the god hath all made an end
Ye shall see how the weather will amend.
By Saint Anne, he goeth to work even boldly!
I think him wise enough, for he looketh oldly.
Wherefore, mistress, be ye now of good cheer,
For, though in his presence he cannot appear,
Tell me your matter and let me alone:
Mayhap I will think on you when you be gone.

GENTLEWOMAN
Forsooth the cause of my coming is this:
I am a woman right fair, as ye see,
In no creature more beauty than in me is,
And, since I am fair, fair would I keep me.

But the sun in summer so sore doth burn me,
In winter the wind on every side me,
No part of the year wote I where to turn me,
But even in my house am I fain to hide me.

And so do all other that beauty have,
In whose name at this time this suit I make,
Beseeching Jupiter to grant that I crave,
Which is this: that it may please him for our sake

To send us weather close and temperate,
No sunshine, no frost, nor no wind to blow.
Then would we jet the streets trim as a parrot;
Ye should see how we would set our self to show.

MERRY REPORT
Jet where ye will, I swear by Saint Quentin,
Ye pass them all both in your own conceit and mine.

GENTLEWOMAN
If we had weather to walk at our pleasure,
Our lives would be merry out of measure:
One part of the day for our apparelling,
Another part for eating and drinking,
And all the rest in streets to be walking,
Or in the house to pass time with talking.

MERRY REPORT
When serve ye God?

GENTLEWOMAN
Who boasteth in virtue are but daws.

MERRY REPORT
Ye do the better, namely since there is no cause.
How spend ye the night?

GENTLEWOMAN
In dancing and singing
Till midnight, and then fall to sleeping.

MERRY REPORT
Why, sweetheart, by your false faith, can ye sing?

GENTLEWOMAN
Nay, nay, but I love it above all thing.

MERRY REPORT
Now, by my troth, for the love that I owe you,
You shall hear what pleasure I can show you.
One song have I for you, such as it is,
And if it were better, ye should have it, by Jees!

GENTLEWOMAN
Marry sir, I thank you even heartily.

MERRY REPORT
Come on, sirs, but now let us sing lustily.

Here they sing.

GENTLEWOMAN
Sir, this is well done, I heartily thank you.
Ye have done me pleasure, I make God a vow.
Once in a night I long for such a fit,
For long time have I been brought up in it.

MERRY REPORT
Oft time it is seen both in court and town,
Long be women a bringing up and soon brought down.

813 **looketh oldly** looks old enough (to be wise).
816 **let me alone** leave it to me.
823 **on ... me** blows me on every side.
824 **wote I** do I know.
830 **close and temperate** mild and moderate.
832 **jet** strut about.
832 **trim** neat/pretty.
835 **pass** surpass.
835 **conceit** opinion.
837 **out of measure** immeasurably.
838 **apparelling** dressing.
842.1 **Who ... daws.** Those (who) boast of their virtue are merely fools.
843 **Ye ... cause.** You have no cause to boast of virtue (with the implication: because you have none).
851 **And if** Even if.
851 **Jees!** Jesus!
853 **Come on, sirs** addressed to the musicians who would accompany the song(s).
853.1 There is no indication of what song was sung here, although Heywood wrote many suitable songs and ballads.
856 **fit** stanza/bout. The line sets up the bawdy double entendre developed in the following speech.
859 **bringing up** educated/ 'persuaded to have sex/brought to orgasm'; **brought down** implies 'corrupted'.

So feat it is, so neat it is, so nice it is,
So trick it is, so quick it is, so wise it is!
I fear myself, except I may entreat her,
I am so far in love I shall forget her.
Now good mistress, I pray you let me kiss ye.

GENTLEWOMAN
'Kiss me', quoth a? Why nay, sir, I wiss ye!

MERRY REPORT
What, yes, hardily, kiss me once and no more.
I never desired to kiss you before.

Here the Launder cometh in.

LAUNDER
Why, have ye always kissed her behind?
In faith good enough if it be your mind.
And if your appetite serve you so to do,
By Our Lady, I would ye had kissed mine arse too!

MERRY REPORT
To whom dost thou speak, foul whore, canst thou tell?

LAUNDER
Nay, by my troth, I sir? Not very well.
But by conjecture this guess I have,
That I do speak to an old bawdy knave.
I saw you dally with your simper-de-cokket,
I rede you, beware she pick not your pocket.
Such idle housewives do now and then
Think all well won that they pick from a man.
Yet such of some men shall have more favour
Than we that for them daily toil and labour.
But I trust the god will be so indifferent
That she shall fail some part of her intent.

MERRY REPORT
No doubt he will deal so graciously
That all folk shall be served indifferently.
Howbeit, I tell thee truth, my office is such
That I must report each suit, little or much.
Wherefore, with the god since thou canst not speak,
Trust me with thy suit, I will not fail it to break.

LAUNDER
Then lean not too much to yonder giglet,
For her desire contrary to mine is set.
I heard by her tale she would banish the sun,
And then were we poor launders all undone.
Except the sun shine that our clothes may dry,
We can do right nought in our laundry;
Another manner loss if we should miss
Than of such nice by-sitters as she is.

GENTLEWOMAN
I think it better that thou envy me
Than I should stand at reward of thy pity.
It is the guise of such gross queans as thou art
With such as I am evermore to thwart;
Because that no beauty ye can obtain,
Therefore ye have us that be fair in disdain.

LAUNDER
When I was young, as thou art now,
I was within little as fair as thou,
And so might have kept me, if I had would,
And as dearly my youth I might have sold
As the trickest and fairest of you all.
But I feared perils that after might fall,
Wherefore some business I did me provide
Lest vice might enter on every side,
Which hath free entry where idleness doth reign.
It is not thy beauty that I disdain,
But thine idle life that thou hast rehearsed,
Which any good woman's heart would have
pierced.

860 **feat it is** elegant she is (baby talk).
860 **nice** wanton.
861 **trick** pretty.
862 **except** unless.
863 The bathos of **forget her** is intentional, part of Merry Report's cynical misogyny.
865 **quoth a?** says he?
865 **I wiss ye!** I tell you!
868 **behind** arse/afterwards, picking up on 'before'.
869 **if . . . mind** if that's what you like.
872 **To . . . tell?** Have you any idea to whom you are speaking?
876 **simper-de-cokket** a strumpet (perhaps 'simpering coquette' or 'always (*semper*) a coquette'?)
877 **rede** advise.
879 **well won** fair game.
883 **she . . . intent** she shall not get everything she wants.
889 **break** mention (but also 'ruin') it.
890 **giglet** strumpet.
896–897 **Another . . . is** it's a wholly more serious loss if we should be ruined than if such prim idlers as her are.
899 **I . . . pity** I should be the object of your pity.
900 **guise** habit.
900 **queans** whores.
901 **thwart** argue.
905 **within little** very nearly.
906 **would** wished.
908 **trickest** prettiest.
910 **some . . . provide** I found myself a trade.
911 **vice . . . side** proverbially idleness let in the other vices.
914 **rehearsed** described.

For I perceive in dancing and singing,
In eating and drinking and thine apparelling
Is all the joy wherein thy heart is set.
But nought of all this doth thine own labour get.
For hadst thou nothing but of thine own travail,
Thou mightest go as naked as my nail.
Methink thou shouldst abhor such idleness
And pass thy time in some honest business.
Better to lose some part of thy beauty
Than so oft to jeopard all thine honesty.
But I think, rather than thou wouldst so do,
Thou hadst lever have us live idly too.
And so, no doubt, we should, if thou mightest have
The clear sun banished, as thou dost crave.
Then were we launders marred, and unto thee
Thine own request were small commodity.
For of these twain I think it far better
Thy face were sun-burnt and thy clothes the sweeter,
Than that the sun from shining should be smitten
To keep thy face fair and thy smock beshitten.
Sir, how like ye my reason in her case?

MERRY REPORT

Such a railing whore, by the holy Mass,
I never heard in all my life till now!
Indeed, I love right well the one of you,
But, ere I would keep you both, by God's
    mother,
The Devil shall have the one to fetch the other!

LAUNDER

Promise me to speak that the sun may shine bright,
And I will be gone quickly for all night.

MERRY REPORT

Get you both hence, I pray you heartily.
Your suits I perceive and will report them truly
Unto Jupiter at the next leisure,
And, in the same, desire to know his pleasure;
Which knowledge had, even as he doth show it,
Fear ye not, time enough ye shall know it.

GENTLEWOMAN

Sir, if ye meddle, remember me first.

LAUNDER

Then in this meddling my part shall be the worst.

MERRY REPORT

Now I beseech Our Lord, the Devil thee burst!
Who meddleth with many, I hold him accurst.
Thou whore, can I meddle with you both at once?

Here the Gentlewoman goeth forth.

LAUNDER

By the Mass, knave, I would I had both thy stones
In my purse if thou meddle not indifferently,
That both our matters in issue may be likely.

MERRY REPORT

Many words, little matter, and to no purpose,
Such is the effect that thou dost disclose.
The more ye bib, the more ye babble,
The more ye babble, the more ye fable,
The more ye fable, the more unstable,
The more unstable, the more unable
In any manner thing to do any good.
No hurt though ye were hanged, by the holy Rood!

LAUNDER

The less your silence, the less your credence,
The less your credence, the less your honesty,
The less your honesty, the less your assistance,
The less your assistance, the less ability
In you to do ought. Wherefore, so God me save,
No hurt in hanging such a railing knave!

MERRY REPORT

What monster is this? I never heard none such.
For look how much more I have made her too much,
And so far at least she hath made me too little.

919–920 **nought . . . travail** you gain none of this through your own labour. If you had nothing except that you'd worked for.
925 **jeopard** jeopardize/risk.
925 **honesty** reputation.
927 **lever have us** rather have us (honest women).
930 **marred** ruined.
931 **small commodity** little advantage.
934 **smitten** stopped.
936 **reason** argument.
946 **leisure** free moment.
949 **time enough** in good time.
950 **meddle** i.e. take on the matter (but with sexual connotations too).
952 **thee burst** burst you!
953 **meddleth with many** deals (also 'has sex') with many (women).
957 **That . . . likely** so that both our requests might turn out equally (well).
960 **bib** talk.
961 **fable** lie.
962 **unstable** unstable/unreliable (you become).
965 **No hurt though** It wouldn't hurt if.
966 **credence** credibility.
967 **honesty** reputation.
968 **the . . . assistance** the less help you are (with Jupiter).
973–974 **For . . . little.** For, look how I have magnified her (with my 'more's), and how she has minimized me (with her 'less's).

Where be your launder? I think in some spittal!
Ye shall wash me no gear for fear of fretting;
I love no launders that shrink my gear in whetting.
I pray thee, go hence and let me be in rest.
I will do thine errand as I think best.

LAUNDER

Now would I take my leave, if I wist how.
The longer I live, the more knave you! *[Exit.]*

MERRY REPORT

The longer thou livest, the pity the greater,
The sooner thou be rid, the tidings the better!
Is not this a sweet office that I have,
When every drab shall prove me a knave?
Every man knoweth not what god's service is,
Nor I myself knew it not before this.
I think god's servants may live holily
But the Devil's servants live more merrily.
I know not what god giveth in standing fees,
But the Devil's servants have casualties
A hundred times mo than god's servants have.
For, though ye be never so stark a knave,
If ye lack money the Devil will do no worse
But bring you straight to another man's purse.
Then will the Devil promote you here in this world
As unto such rich it doth most accord.
First, '*pater noster qui es in celis*',
And then ye shall cense the sheriff with your heels.
The greatest friend ye have in field or town,
Standing a tip-toe shall not reach your crown.

The Boy cometh in, the least that can play.

[BOY]

This same is even he by all likelihood.
Sir, I pray you, be not you master god?

MERRY REPORT

No, in good faith, son, but I may say to thee
I am such a man that god may not miss me.
Wherefore, with the god if thou wouldst have ought done,
Tell me thy mind and I shall show it soon.

BOY

Forsooth, sir, my mind is this at few words:
All my pleasure is in catching of birds,
And making of snowballs and throwing the same,
For the which purpose to have set in frame,
With my godfather god I would fain have spoken,
Desiring him to have sent me by some token
Where I might have had great frost for my pitfalls,
And plenty of snow to make my snowballs.
This once had, boys' lives be such as no man leads.
O, to see my snowballs light on my fellows' heads,
And to hear the birds how they flicker their wings
In the pitfall, I say it passed all things!
Sir, if ye be god's servant or his kinsman,
I pray you help me in this if ye can.

MERRY REPORT

Alas, poor boy, who sent thee hither?

BOY

A hundred boys that stood together,
Where they heard one say in a cry
That my godfather, god almighty,
Was come from Heaven by his own accord,
This night to sup here with my lord.
And further he said, come whoso will,

975 **launder** laundry.
975 **spittle** spittle house/poor-hospital.
976 **gear** clothes (but also slang for genitals/penis).
977 **in whetting** with rubbing.
980 **wist** knew.
982 **the ... greater** more's the pity.
984 **office** job.
985 **drab** whore.
990 **standing fees** regular wages.
991 **casualties** casual tips and fees.
993 **stark** bold/hardened.
997 **As ... accord** as befits such rich thieves.
999 **First ... heels.** First (you'll say) 'Our Father who art in Heaven' (the *Paternoster*), next you'll be swinging your heels above the sheriff as if wafting him with incense. (Sheriffs were responsible for hanging thieves.)
1000 **greatest** tallest.
1001 **crown** head.

This speech is given, like the next, to Merry Report in the 1533 edition. But the first line might plausibly be either his or the Boy's. If the former, there is an ironic allusion to the 'greatest friend', since the Boy is so small. If the Boy is speaking, he is reassuring himself that Merry Report must be the god he is seeking.
1005 **may ... me** cannot do without me.
1007 **show it soon** reveal it to him.
1011 **frame** order.
1014 **pitfalls** traps (for birds).
1016 **This ... leads.** Once we have gained these things, a boy's life would be better than any man's.
1017 **light** land.
1018 **flicker** flutter.
1019 **passed** surpasses.
1024 **one** i.e. Merry Report himself.
1024 **cry** proclamation.
1027 **my lord** the patron of the feast, perhaps Henry VIII.

They shall sure have their bellies full
Of all weathers, who list to crave:
Each sort such weather list to have.
And when my fellows thought this would be had,
And saw me so pretty a prattling lad,
Upon agreement, with a great noise,
'Send little Dick!', cried all the boys,
By whose assent I am purveyed
To sue for the weather aforesaid.
Wherein I pray you to be good as thus,
To help that god may give it us.

MERRY REPORT
'Give boys weather', quoth a! Nonny nonny!

BOY
If god of his weather will give nonny,
I pray you, will he sell any,
Or lend us a bushel of snow or twain
And point us a day to pay him again?

MERRY REPORT
I cannot tell, for, by this light,
I cheaped nor borrowed none of him this night.
But by such shift as I will make,
Thou shalt see soon what way he will take.

BOY
Sir, I thank you. Then I may depart?

The Boy goeth forth.

MERRY REPORT
Yea, farewell, good son, with all my heart.
Now such another sort as here hath been
In all the days of my life I have not seen.
No suitors now but women, knaves, and boys,
And all their suits are in fancies and toys.
If that there come no wiser after this cry,
I will to the god and make an end quickly.

Oyez, if that any knave here
Be willing to appear
For weather foul or clear,
Come in before this flock,
And, be he whole or sickly,
Come show his mind quickly,
And if his tale be not likely
Ye shall lick my tail in the nock.

All this time, I perceive, is spent in waste
To wait for mo suitors: I see none make hast.
Wherefore I will show the god all this process,
And be delivered of my simple office.

[*To Jupiter*]

Now lord, according to your commandment,
Attending suitors I have been diligent;
And, at beginning as your will was I should,
I come now at end to show what each man would.
The first suitor before yourself did appear,
A Gentleman desiring weather clear,
Cloudy nor misty nor no wind to blow,
For hurt in his hunting. And then, as ye know,
The Merchant sued, for all of that kind,
For weather clear, and measurable wind,
As they may best bear their sails to make speed.
And straight after this there came to me indeed
Another man, who named himself a Ranger,
And said all of his craft be far brought in danger
For lack of living, which chiefly is windfall.
But he plainly sayeth there bloweth no wind at all,
Wherefore he desireth, for increase of their
fleeces,
Extreme rage of wind trees to tear in pieces.
Then came a Water Miller, and he cried out
For water, and said the wind was so stout
The rain could not fall, wherefore he made request
For plenty of rain to set the wind at rest.
And then, sir, there came a Wind Miller in,
Who said for the rain he could no wind win.

1029 **shall...full** have as much as they want.
1030 **who...crave** whoever cares to ask.
1036 **purveyed** sent (here).
1040 **Nonny nonny!** Hey ho!
1041 **nonny** the boy thinks Merry Report said that Jupiter will give boys 'none'.
1044 **bushel** barrel-full.
1045 **point** appoint.
1046 **cheaped** bought.
1047 **shift** means.
1051–1052 **Now...seen.** I've never seen such a group of people as this lot.
1054 **toys** fripperies.
1057 **Oyez** Hear ye!
1061 **whole** healthy.
1064 **nock** crack.
1065 **spent in waste** is wasted.
1068 **delivered** relieved.
1072 **would** wants.
1079 **bear** set.
1083 **living** income.
1085 **fleeces** perks.
1088 **stout** strong.
1092 **win** find.

The water he wished to be banished all,
Beseeching your grace of wind continual.
Then came there another that would banish all this:
A goodly dame, an idle thing, iwis.
Wind, rain, nor frost, nor sunshine would she have,
But fair, close weather her beauty to save.
Then came there another that liveth by laundry,
Who must have weather hot and clear her clothes to dry.
Then came there a boy for frost and snow continual,
Snow to make snowballs and frost for his pitfall,
For which, God wot, he sueth full greedily.
Your first man would have weather clear and not windy;
The second the same, save cools to blow meanly;
The third desired storms and wind most extremely;
The fourth all in water, and would have no wind;
The fifth no water, but all wind to grind;
The sixth would have none of all these, nor no bright sun;
The seventh extremely the hot sun would have won;
The eight and the last, for frost and snow he prayed.
By Our Lady, we shall take shame, I am afraid!
Who marketh in what manner this sort is led
May think it impossible all to be sped.
This number is small: there lacketh twain of ten,
And yet, by the Mass, among ten thousand men,
No one thing could stand more wide from the t'other.
Not one of their suits agreeth with another.
I promise you here is a shrewd piece of work!
This gear will try whether ye be a clerk.
If ye trust to me, it is a great folly,
For it passeth my brains, by God's body!

JUPITER

Son, thou hast been diligent and done so well,
That thy labour is right much thankworthy.
But be thou sure we need no whit thy counsel,
For in our self we have foreseen remedy,
Which thou shalt see. But first, depart hence quickly
To the Gentleman and all other suitors here,
And command them all before us to appear.

MERRY REPORT

That shall be no longer in doing
Than I am in coming and going.

Merry Report goeth out.

JUPITER

Such debate as from above ye have heard,
Such debate beneath among yourselves ye see.
As long as heads from temperance be deferred,
So long the bodies in distemperance be.
This perceive ye all, but none can help save we.
But, as we there have made peace concordantly,
So will we here now give you remedy.

Merry Report and all the suitors entereth.

MERRY REPORT

If I had caught them
Ere ever I raught them,
I would have taught them
To be near me.
Full dear have I bought them,
Lord so I sought them,
Yet have I brought them
Such as they be.

GENTLEMAN

Pleaseth it your Majesty, Lord, so it is:
We, as your subjects and humble suitors all,
According as we hear your pleasure is,
Are pressed to your presence, being principal
Head and governor of all in every place.
Who joyeth not in your sight no joy can have,
Wherefore we all commit us to your Grace
As Lord of Lords, us to perish or save.

JUPITER

As long as discretion so well doth you guide
Obediently to use your duty,
Doubt ye not we shall your safety provide.
Your griefs we have heard, wherefore we sent for ye

1098 **close** mild.
1105 **meanly** moderately.
1113 **Who marketh** Whoever considers.
1113 **sort is led** crowd behaves.
1114 **sped** helped.
1117 **more wide** further apart.
1120 **try . . . clerk** test if you are wise.
1122 **it . . . brains** it's beyond me.
1132 **Such . . . heard** Such debate above (in Heaven) as you heard about earlier (i.e. at ll. 25–63).
1133 **beneath** on Earth.
1134 **from . . . deferred** shun moderation.
1137 **there** i.e. in Heaven.
1140 **raught** reached.

To receive answer, each man in his degree.
And first to content, most reason it is,
The first man that sued. Wherefore, mark ye this:

Oft shall ye have the weather clear and still
To hunt in for recompense of your pain.
Also, you merchants shall have much your will:
For, oft times when no wind on land doth remain,
Yet on the sea pleasant cools you shall obtain.
And, since your hunting may rest in the night,
Oft shall the wind then rise and before daylight

It shall rattle down the wood in such case
That all ye rangers the better live may.
And ye water millers shall obtain this grace:
Many times the rain to fall in the valley
When at the self times on hills we shall purvey
Fair weather for your windmills, with such cools of wind
As in one instant both kinds of mills may grind.

And for ye fair women that close weather would have,
We shall provide that ye may sufficiently
Have time to walk in, and your beauty save.
And yet shall ye have, that liveth by laundry,
The hot sun oft enough your clothes to dry.
Also ye, pretty child, shall have both frost and snow.
Now, mark this conclusion, we charge you a-row.

Much better have we now devised for ye all
Than ye all can perceive or could desire.
Each of you sued to have continual
Such weather as his craft only doth require.
All weathers in all places if men all times might hire,
Who could live by other? What is this negligence,
Us to attempt in such inconvenience?

Now, on the other side, if we had granted
The full of some one suit and no mo,
And from all the rest the weather had forbid,
Yet who so had obtained had won his own woe.
There is no one craft can preserve man so,
But by other crafts, of necessity,
He must have much part of his commodity.

All to serve at once, and one destroy another,
Or else to serve one and destroy all the rest:
Neither will we do the one nor the other,
But serve as many or as few as we think best.
And where, or what time, to serve most or least,
The direction of that doubtless shall stand
Perpetually in the power of our hand.

Wherefore we will the whole world to attend,
Each sort on such weather as for them doth fall.
Now one, now other, as liketh us to send.
Who that hath it, ply it, and sure we shall
So guide the weather in course to you all,
That each with other ye shall whole remain
In pleasure and plentiful wealth, certain.

GENTLEMAN

Blessed was the time wherein we were born,
First for the blissful chance of your godly presence,
Next for our suit. Was there never man before
That ever heard so excellent a sentence

As your grace hath given to us all a-row;
Wherein your highness hath so bountifully
Distributed my part, that your grace shall know
Yourself sole possessed of hearts of all chivalry.

MERCHANT

Likewise we merchants shall yield us wholly
Only to laud the name of Jupiter
As god of all gods, you to serve solely,
For of everything, I see, you are nourisher.

RANGER

No doubt it is so, for so we now find,
Wherein your grace us rangers so doth bind
That we shall give you our hearts with one accord,
For knowledge to know you as our only lord.

1159 **in his degree** according to his status.
1160–1161 **And...this.** It is most reasonable to answer first the first man who petitioned. So listen to this.
1164 **much your will** much of what you want.
1169 **case** a manner.
1173 **self** selfsame.
1173 **purvey** send.
1182 **we...a-row** we instruct each one of you in order.
1187–1188 **All...other?** If men could arrange their own weather all of the time in all places, which of them could live together?
1188 **negligence** thoughtlessness.
1189 **Us...in** to try to persuade us to.
1194–1196 **There...commodity.** There is no trade that can sustain humankind sufficiently that it does not need others to provide the greater part of its needs.
1207 **Who...it** Let each of you use whatever weather comes to hand.
1209 **whole** united/harmonious.
1218 **Yourself...chivalry** You shall be the sole possessor of the hearts/loyalty of all noblemen.

WATER MILLER
Well, I can no more but, for our water
We shall give your lordship Our Lady's Psalter.

WIND MILLER
Much have ye bound us, for, as I be saved,
We have all obtained better than we craved.

GENTLEWOMAN
That is true, wherefore your Grace shall truly
The hearts of such as I am have, surely.

LAUNDER [*To the Gentlewoman*]
And such as I am (who be as good as you),
His highness shall be sure on, I make a vow.

BOY
Godfather god, I will do somewhat for you again.
By Christ, ye may hap to have a bird or twain.
And I promise you, if any snow come,
When I make my snowballs, ye shall have some.

MERRY REPORT
God thank your Lordship. Lo, how this is brought to pass;
Sirs, now shall ye have the weather even as it was!

JUPITER
We need no whit ourself any further to boast,
For our deeds declare us apparently.
Not only here on Earth in every coast,
But also above in the heavenly company
Our prudence hath made peace universally.
Which thing, we say, recordeth us as principal
God and governor of Heaven, Earth and all.
Now unto that Heaven we will make return
Where we be glorified most triumphantly.
Also we will all ye that on Earth sojourn,
Since cause giveth cause, to know us your lord only,
And now here to sing most joyfully,
Rejoicing in us; and in mean time we shall
Ascend into our throne celestial.

FINIS

Printed by W. Rastell.
1533
Cum privilegio.

1228 **give... Psalter** recite the Rosary in your name.
1241 **need no whit** do not need at all.
1242 **declare us apparently** clearly reveal our nature.
1243 **coast** region.
1246 **recordeth us as** reveals us to be.
1249–1251 **we... only** since you on Earth should follow the example of those in Heaven, (you should) acknowledge us as your only lord.
1254 ***Cum privilegio.*** (Printed) with (royal) permission.

Gammer Gurton's Needle

(1550–1560)

'MASTER S.' (WILLIAM STEPHENSON?)

THE PLAYWRIGHT

The authorship of *Gammer Gurton's Needle* is not certain, despite the clue provided by the title page of the 1575 printed edition that it was performed at Christ's College Cambridge, and 'made by Master S., Master of Arts'. Critical opinion has tended to identify 'Master S.' with William Stephenson, a student and fellow of Christ's College, perhaps working in conjunction with one John Bridges, the future bishop of Oxford, who was accused of writing the play by an opponent in a later exchange of polemical religious pamphlets known as 'The Martin Marprelate Controversy'. (For a detailed account of the play's possible authorship, see the introduction to Charles Whitworth's New Mermaid edition, listed under further reading.)

THE PLAY

Whoever wrote it, however, *Gammer Gurton* was clearly a product of Cambridge student drama, and is characterized by a mixture of attention to classical form with gleeful scatological humour and relatively tolerant contempt for the rural working class. The play borrows from classical comedy in its extravagant use of a formal five-act structure, and its occasional use of sophisticated verse forms, yet concerns the most trivial of subjects, the loss of an old woman's needle, which finally proves not really to have been lost at all. Like John Heywood's *Play of the Weather*, this play wrings a good deal of humour and social commentary out of its trivial scenario before returning things more or less to the state they were in before the play began. But, unlike *Weather*, *Gammer Gurton* does not seem to be using its surface banality to explore more serious matters beneath. Here the loss of a needle seems to be just that, and the humour lies in the various jealousies and anxieties that its apparent disappearance uncovers in the small community of neighbours living around Gammer (or 'godmother') Gurton's cottage, probably set in the village of Girton, Cambridgeshire, close to the university.

Like *Weather*, *Gammer Gurton* has its vice figure, here the more malicious Dicken (a variant of 'Dick', the diminutive form of 'Richard', but also a euphemism for 'devil'), the madcap roving beggar, who takes advantage of the fears and suspicions of Gammer, her neighbour Dame Chat, Hodge, and the curate, Doctor Rat, to trick them all into variously accusing or attacking each other in the course of the play, culminating in the comic tour-de-force of the stand-up fight between the two old women, Gammer Gurton and Dame Chat, and the beating up of Doctor Rat by Dame Chat, who, encouraged by Dicken, mistakes him for a thief come to steal her chickens. Only the appeal to Master Baily the Bailiff, the chief figure of civil authority in the local community, and his subsequent interviewing of all the 'suspects', brings matters to a happy conclusion. That Dicken is not seriously punished for his 'crimes' suggests that we should not take the play too seriously either, but rather enjoy it for the glimpses of everyday Tudor working-class rural society that it offers—or at least for the glimpses of how that society was seen and imagined by the scholars of Christ's College Cambridge.

As the title page reveals, the play was probably first performed in the great hall of Christ's College, and would, like the interludes performed at the royal court, have fitted readily into the space of the hall. The plot requires a relatively simple set with an open playing space or *platea* on the hall floor (or, perhaps, if we take the title page's use of the term 'played on stage' seriously, on a raised platform) with two structures, perhaps built against the screens at the lower end of the hall, to represent Gammer Gurton and Dame Chat's houses. Such structures, frequently referred to as 'houses' or 'mansions' in contemporary accounts, were quite common in the interlude drama of the mid-century and later, consciously echoing the *fons sceniae* of the Classical comic theatre, with its backdrop of a street front with doors for various locations. Much of the comedy of the play results from altercations between those outside these houses and those within, as when Doctor Rat is tricked into crawling into Dame Chat's house through a hole in the wall behind her oven and is then set upon by the owner and her companions. His cries for help are the only evidence of what is happening to him within, unless perhaps his legs still remain outside the hole and can be seen thrashing about in distress.

Much of the speech of these rustic characters is written in an approximation of local dialect. Thus Gammer Gurton, Hodge, and Tib use the personal pronoun 'Ich' rather than 'I', which is contracted to 'ch' at the beginning of compound words such as 'chould' (I would), 'chall' (I shall), 'cham' (I am), and so on. Similarly 'needle' is pronounced 'nee'le' throughout, to rhyme with 'feel', allowing Dicken at one point (l. 41) to pretend to mishear that Gammer has lost an eel. As befits their higher social status, Doctor Rat and Master Bailey do not use the 'Ich' form, neither does Dicken, who probably originates in another part of the country, or Dame Chat, who may have social aspirations above her class.

The text below is based on the 1575 edition, printed in London by Thomas Colwell. I have also consulted the modern edition, published in the New Mermaid series, and edited by Charles Whitworth listed under further reading.

FURTHER READING

Cartwright, Kent, *Theatre and Humanism: Drama in the Sixteenth Century* (Cambridge: Cambridge University Press, 2008), especially 75–99.

Craik, T. W., *The Tudor Interlude* (Leicester: Leicester University Press, 1958).

Fletcher, Alan J., '*Gammer Gurton's Needle*', in Thomas Betteridge and Greg Walker, eds., *The Oxford Handbook of Tudor Drama* (Oxford: Oxford University Press, 2012), 276–92.

Hutson, Lorna, 'Theatre', in Brian Cummings and James Simpson, eds., *Cultural Reformations: Medieval and Renaissance in Literary History* (Oxford: Oxford University Press, 2010), 227–46.

Nelson, Alan H., *Records of Early English Drama: Cambridge*, 2 vols. (Toronto: University of Toronto Press, 1989).

Robinson, J. W., 'The Art and Meaning of *Gammer Gurton's Needle*', *Renaissance Drama*, 14 (1983), 45–77.

Whitfield White, Paul, *Drama and Religion in English Provincial Society, 1485–1660* (Cambridge: Cambridge University Press, 2008), especially 114–21.

Whitworth, Charles, ed., *Gammer Gurton's Needle*, New Mermaid Edition (London: A. and C. Black, 1997).

A Right Pleasant and Merry Comedy entitled Gammer Gurton's Needle, Played on Stage not long ago in Christ's College in Cambridge.

Made by Mr. S. Master of Arts.
Imprinted at London in Fleet Street, beneath the conduit at the sign of St John the Evangelist
By Thomas Colwell

The Names of the Speakers in this Comedy:

DICKEN, the Bedlam,
TIB, Gammer Gurton's Maid,
COCK, Gammer Gurton's Boy,
DOCTOR RAT, the Curate,
DOLL, Dame Chat's Maid,
MUTES.
HODGE, Gammer Gurton's Servant,
GAMMER Gurton,
DAME CHAT,
MASTER BAILEY,
SCAPETHRIFT, Master Bailey's Servant,

God Save the Queen

THE PROLOGUE

As Gammer Gurton, with many a wide stitch
Sat piecing and patching of Hodge her man's breech,
By chance or misfortune as she her gear tossed,
In Hodge's leather breeches her needle she lost.
When Dicken the Bedlam had heard by report
That good Gammer Gurton was robbed in this sort,
He quietly persuaded with her in that stound
Dame Chat her dear gossip this needle had found;
Yet knew she no more of this matter, alas,

the Bedlam a present or former inmate of the hospital of St Mary of Bethlehem in London, a home for the mentally ill. When wholly or partially recovered, such inmates were released into the community to beg for their living. The term was also used more widely to describe strange or disturbed beggars.
Hodge diminutive of Roger.
Tib diminutive of Isabel.
Gammer Grandma/Old Mother.
Boy servant.
Dame Chat Mistress Gossip, a neighbour of Gammer Gurton ('Dame' is not an aristocratic title here).
Master Bailey the bailey or bailiff was the sheriff's officer, responsible for local policing duties.
Scapethrift Spendthrift. (Like Doll and the Mutes, Scapethrift is essentially an extra with no lines to speak.)
Mutes Unspeaking extras (to play Dame Chat's card-playing friends, bystanders, etc).
2 **piecing** mending.
2 **breech** breeches (trousers).
3 **her gear tossed** worked her needle.
6 **in this sort** in this way.
7 **persuaded...stound** persuaded her at that time.
8 **gossip** friend.

Than knoweth Tom our clerk what the priest sayeth at Mass.
Hereof there ensued so fearful a fray,
Mas' Doctor was sent for, these gossips to stay,
Because he was curate and esteemed full wise;
Who found that he sought not, by Dicken's device.
When all things were tumbled and clean out of fashion,
Whether it were by fortune or some other constellation,
Suddenly the needle Hodge found by the pricking,
And drew it out of his buttock, where he felt it sticking.
Their hearts then at rest with perfect security;
With a pot of good ale they struck up their plaudity.

The First Act: The First Scene
(Dicken.)

DICKEN

Many a mile have I walked, diverse and sundry ways
And many a good man's house have I been at in my days,
Many a gossips' cup in my time have I tasted,
And many a broach and spit have I both turned and basted.
Many a piece of bacon have I had out of their balks,
In running over the country with long and weary walks.
Yet came my foot never within those door cheeks,
To seek flesh or fish, garlic, onions, or leeks,
That ever I saw a sort in such a plight
As here within this house appeareth to my sight.
There is howling and scowling, all cast in a dump,
With whewling and puling, as though they had lost a trump;
Sighing and sobbing, they weep and they wail;
I marvel in my mind what the devil they ail.
The old trot sits groaning, with 'Alas and alas',
And Tib wrings her hands, and takes on in worse case.
With poor Cock, their boy, they be driven in such fits,
I fear me the folks be not well in their wits.
Ask them what they ail, or who brought them in this stay,
They answer not at all, but 'alack' and 'weilaway!'
When I saw it booted not, out at doors I hied me

[10] **than ... Mass** i.e. Tom, the parish clerk, does not understand the Latin of the service.
[11] **a fray** an argument.
[12] **Mas' Doctor** Master Doctor, i.e. the priest.
[12] **stay** restrain.
[14] **that ... device** something he wasn't expecting, through Dicken's devising.
[15] **tumbled and clean out of fashion** completely disordered.
[16] **constellation** astrological influence.
[20] **struck ... plaudity** celebrated/took their applause.
s.d. The 1575 text lists all the characters who will appear in a scene at the head of that scene.
[4] **a spit** skewer for spitting and turning meat over a fire.
[5] **had ... balks** stolen from the house-beams (where meat was hung to cure or smoke it).
[7] **cheeks** posts.
[9] **a sort** a group of people.
[11] **cast ... dump** thrown into sadness.
[12] **whewling and puling** moaning and whining (like a child).
[12] **trump** trump card, i.e. lost one of their best cards.
[14] **what ... ail** what the devil is upsetting them?
[15] **trot** hag.
[16] **takes ... case** makes even more fuss.
[19] **in this stay** into this state.
[20] **'alack'** 'alas' and **'weilaway!'** 'woe is me!'
[21] **When ... not** It didn't matter ('I could get nothing sensible out them').
[21] **I hied** I hurried.

And caught a slip of bacon when I saw that none spied me,
Which I intend not far hence, unless my purpose fail,
Shall serve for a shoeing-horn to draw on two pots of ale.

The First Act: The Second Scene
(Hodge. Dicken.)

HODGE

See, so cham arrayed with dabbling in the dirt;
She that set me to ditching, ich would she had the squirt!
Was never poor soul that such a life had.
Gog's bones, this filthy clay has dressed me too bad.
God's soul, see how this stuff tears;
Ich were better to be a bear-ward and set to keep bears!
By the Mass, here is a gash, a shameful hole indeed;
And one stitch tear further, a man may thrust in his head!

DICKEN

By my father's soul, Hodge, if I should now be sworn,
I cannot choose but say thy breech is foul be-torn.
But the next remedy in such a case and hap
Is to planch on a piece as broad as thy cap.

HODGE

Gog's soul man, 'tis not yet two days fully ended
Since my dame Gurton, cham sure, these breeches amended;
But cham made such a drudge to trudge at every need,
Chwould rend it, though it were stitched with sturdy pack-thread.

DICKEN

Hodge, let thy breeches go, and speak and tell me soon
What devil aileth Gammer Gurton and Tib her maid to frown?

HODGE

Tush man th'art deceived, 'tis their daily look,
They cower so over ye coals, their eyes be bleared with smoke.

DICKEN

Nay, by the Mass, I perfectly perceived as I came hither
That either Tib and her dame hath been by the ears together,
Or else as great a matter, as thou shalt shortly see.

HODGE

Now, ich beseech our Lord, they never better agree.

22 **caught a slip** grabbed a slice/cut.
24 **a shoeing-horn to draw on** a means to bring me.
1 **See...with** See what a state I'm in from.
2 **Ich...squirt!** I wish she had the shits!
3 **Was...soul** There was never so unfortunate a soul.
4 **Gog's** God's.
6 **bear-ward** bear-keeper.
7 i.e. in his trousers.
8 **And** If.
10 **foul be-torn** foully torn.
11 **next** best.
12 **planch...piece** slap on a patch.
15 **But...need** I'm given such hard work, made to walk here and there whenever an errand comes up.
16 **Chwould rend** I'd tear.
16 **sturdy pack-thread** thick, strong thread for tying packages.
17 **let...go** forget your breeches, and perhaps also literally, let go of them!
19 **'tis...look** they always look like that.
22 **hath...together** have been fighting.

DICKEN
By Gog's soul, there they sit, as still as stones in the street,
As though they had been taken with fairies or else with some ill sprite.

HODGE
Gog's heart, I durst have laid my cap to a crown Chwould learn of some prancome as soon as ich came to town.

DICKEN
Why Hodge, art thou inspired, or didst thou thereof hear?

HODGE
Nay, but ich saw such a wonder as ich saw not this seven year:
Tom Tankard's cow (by Gog's bones) she set me up her sail,
And flinging about his half acre fisking with her tail,
As though there had been in her arse a swarm of bees!
And chad not cried 'who-ah, whore!', she'd leaped out of his leas.

DICKEN
Why Hodge, lies the cunning in Tom Tankard's cow's tail?

HODGE
Well, chave heard some say such tokens do not fail,
But canst you not tell, in faith, Dicken, why she frowns or whereat?
Hath no man stolen her ducks or hens, or gelded Gib her cat?

DICKEN
What devil can I tell, man, I could not have one word;
They gave no more heed to my talk than thou wouldst to a lord.

HODGE
Ich cannot still but muse what marvellous thing it is;
Chill in and know myself what matters are amiss.

DICKEN
Then farewell, Hodge, awhile, since thou dost inward haste,
For I will into the goodwife Chat's, to feel how the ale doth taste. *[Exit.]*

The First Act: The Third Scene
(Hodge. Tib.)

HODGE
Cham aghast, by the Mass, ich wot not what to do;
Chad need bless me well before ich go them to.
Perchance some felon spirit may haunt our house indeed,
And then chwere but a noddy to venture where cha' no need.

[26] **had ... with** (their spirits) kidnapped by.
[26] **ill sprite** evil spirit.
[27–28] **durst ... prancome** dared to have bet my cap against a crown (five shilling) piece that I'd hear about some prank/bizarre event.
[29] **inspired** granted supernatural insight.
[31] **set ... sail** set off (like a boat in full sail).
[32] **flinging ... fisking** rushing around ... whisking.
[34] **And ... leas.** If I hadn't shouted ... she'd have leaped right out of his field.
[35] **the cunning** the inspiration (behind your foresight).
[36] **tokens** signs (by which the future can be predicted).
[37] **in faith** honestly.
[38] **gelded** castrated.
[40] **They ... lord** presumably ironic, as sensible folk would pay attention to lords.
[42] **Chill in** I'll go inside.
[44] **feel** test. Dame Chat's home evidently doubles as an alehouse.
[1] **wot** know.
[2] **Chad need** I have need to.
[4] **chwere ... need** I'd be just a fool to go where I have no need to.

TIB
Cham worse than mad, by the Mass, to be at this stay;
Cham chid, cham blamed and beaten all th'hours on the day,
Lamed and hunger starved, pricked up all in jags,
Having no patch to hide my back, save a few rotten rags.

HODGE
I say Tib, if thou be Tib, as I trow sure thou be,
What devil make ado is this between our dame and thee?

TIB
Gog's bread, Hodge, thou had a good turn thou wert not here this while.
It had been better for some of us to have been hence a mile!
My Gammer is so out of course, and frantic all at once,
That Cock, our boy and I, poor wench, have felt it on our bones.

HODGE
What is the matter, say on Tib, whereat she taketh so on?

TIB
She is undone, she sayeth, alas, her joy and life is gone.
If she hear not of some comfort, she is, [she] sayeth, but dead;
Shall never come within her lips one inch of meat ne bread!

HODGE
By'r Lady, cham not very glad to see her in this dump:
Chold a noble her stool hath fallen and she hath broke her rump.

TIB
Nay, and that were the worst, we would not greatly care
For bursting of her huckle-bone or breaking of her chair.
But greater, greater is her grief, as, Hodge, we shall all feel.

HODGE
Gog's wounds, Tib, my Gammer has never lost her nee'le?

TIB
Her nee'le!

HODGE
Her nee'le?

TIB
Her nee'le, by him that made me, it is true, Hodge, I tell thee.

HODGE
Gog's sacrament, I would she had lost th'heart out of her belly.
The Devil, or else his dame, they ought her sure ashame,
How a murrion came this chance, say Tib, unto our dame?

TIB
My Gammer sat her down on her pess and bade me reach thy breeches,
And, by and by, a vengeance on it, ere she had take two stitches
To clap a clout upon thine arse, by chance aside she leers,

5 **at this stay** in this state.
6 **Cham chid** I'm chided/told off.
7 **pricked ... jags** dressed all in tatters.
9 **trow** believe.
11 **thou had ... not** you were lucky you weren't.
15 **say ... on?** tell me, Tib, what upsets her so,
16 **undone** ruined.
20 **Chold a noble** I bet a noble (a coin worth six shillings and eight pence).
21 **and** if.
22 **huckle-bone** hip-bone/haunch.
28 **How a murrion** How the plague (murrain) ...? (a mild oath.)
29 **pess** cushion.
29 **bade me reach** told me to pass (to her).
31 **clap a clout** slap a patch.
31 **leers** glances.

And Gib, our cat, in the milk pan she spied, over head and ears.
'Ah, whore; out thief!', she cried aloud, and swapped the breeches down.
Up went her staff, and out leapt Gib at doors into the town;
And since that time was never wight could set their eyes upon it.
Gog's malison chave, Cock and I, bid twenty times light on it!

HODGE

And is not, then, my breeches sewed up; tomorrow that I should wear?

TIB

No, in faith Hodge thy breeches lie for all this never the near.

HODGE

Now a vengeance light on all the sort that better should have kept it:
The cat, the house, and Tib our maid the better should have swept it.
See where she cometh crawling. Come on, in twenty devils' way,
Ye have made a fair day's work have you not; pray you say?

The First Act: The Fourth Scene (Gammer. Hodge. Tib. Cock.)

GAMMER

Alas, Hodge, alas, I may well curse and ban
This day that ever I saw it, with Gib and the milk-pan;
For these and ill luck together, as knoweth Cock, my boy,
Have stack away my dear nee'le and robbed me of my joy,
My fair long, straight nee'le, that was mine only treasure.
The first day of my sorrow is, and last end of my pleasure.

HODGE

Might ha' kept it when ye had it, but fools will be fools still.
Lose that is fast in your hands ye need not, but ye will.

GAMMER

Go hie thee, Tib, and run, thou whore, to th'end here of the town.
Didst carry out dust in thy lap: seek where thou pourest it down,
And, as thou sawest me raking in the ashes where I mourned,
So see in all the heap of dust thou leave no straw unturned.

TIB

That chall, Gammer, swithe and tite, and soon be here again.

GAMMER

Tib, stoop and look down to the ground to it, and take some pain.

HODGE

Here is a pretty matter, to see this gear how it goes.
By Gog's soul, I think you would lose your arse and it were loose!
Your nee'le lost? It is pity you should lack care and endless sorrow!

33 **swapped** threw.
35 **was never wight** there was nobody.
36 **Gog's . . . it!** Cock and I have twenty times prayed God's curse on it!
38 **never the near** no nearer (to being mended).
41 **she** Gammer Gurton.
41 **Come . . . way** a mild oath: 'Come in, damn you!'
1 **ban** publicly curse.
4 **stack away** hidden/taken.
6 **is** i.e. this is.
7 **Might . . . still.** You might have . . . but fools will always be fools.
8 **fast** secure.
9 **hie** hurry.
13 **swithe and tite** fast and swift.
15 **Here . . . goes.** Here's a strange affair, to watch all this business unfold.
16 **and** if.
17 **care** sadness.

Gog's death, how shall my breeches be sewed, shall I go thus tomorrow?

GAMMER

Ah Hodge, Hodge, if that ich could find my nee'le, by the Rood,
Chould sew thy breeches, ich promise ye, with full good double thread,
And set a patch on either knee, should last these months twain.
Now God and good Saint Sith I pray, to send it home again.

HODGE

Whereto served your hands and eyes but this your nee'le to keep?
What devil had you else to do: ye kept, ich wot, no sheep!
Cham fain abroad to dig and delve, in water, mire, and clay;
Sossing and possing in the dirt still from day to day.
A hundred things that be abroad, cham set to see them weal,
And four of you sit idle at home and cannot keep a nee'le.

GAMMER

My nee'le, alas, ich lost it, Hodge, what time ich me up hasted
To save the milk set up for thee, which Gib our cat hath wasted.

HODGE

The Devil he burst both Gib and Tib, with all the rest!
Cham always sure of the worst end, whoever have the best!
Where have you been fidging abroad since you your nee'le lost?

GAMMER

Within the house and at the door, sitting by this same post,
Where I was looking a long hour before these folks came here.
But weilaway, all was in vain, my nee'le is never the near.

HODGE

Set me a candle, let me seek and grope wherever it be.
Gog's heart, ye be so foolish, ich think, you know it not when you it see.

GAMMER

Come hither Cock. What, Cock I say!

COCK

How, Gammer?

GAMMER

Go, hie thee soon and grope behind the old brass pan,
Which thing when thou hast done,
There shalt thou find an old shoe, wherein if thou look well,
Thou shalt find lying an inch of a white tallow candle,
Light it, and bring it tite away.

COCK

That shall be done anon.

GAMMER

Nay, tarry Hodge, till thou hast light, and then we'll seek each one.

HODGE

Come away, ye whoreson boy, are ye asleep; ye must have a crier?

19 **Rood** Holy Cross.
21 **months twain** two months.
22 **Saint Sith** Saint Osith, an early English martyr saint.
25 **Cham fain abroad** I'm obliged outdoors/far away.
26 **Sossing and possing** Splashing and bashing (digging).
27 **cham ... weal** I have to sort them out.
29 **what ... hasted** when I jumped up.
33 **fidging** fussing about, restlessly.
37 **grope** search.
39.1 **How** Yes/what is it?
44.1 **anon** immediately.
46 **ye ... crier?** do you need to be woken up by shouting? (Cock is slow to produce the light.)

COCK

Ich cannot get the candle alight, here is almost no fire.

HODGE

Chill hold thee a penny chill make ye come if ich may catch thine ears;
Art deaf, thou whoreson boy? Cock, I say, why, canst not hear?

GAMMER

Beat him not, Hodge, but help the boy, and come you two together.

The First Act: The Fifth Scene (Gammer. Tib. Cock. Hodge.)

GAMMER

How now, Tib, quick, let's hear, what news thou hast brought hither?

TIB

Chave tossed and tumbled yonder heap over and over again,
And winnowed it through my fingers as men would winnow grain:
No so much as a hen's turd but in pieces I tore it,
Or whatsoever clod or clay I found, I did not spare it,
Looking within and eke without, to find your nee'le; alas,
But all in vain and without help. Your nee'le is where it was.

GAMMER

Alas, my nee'le, we shall never meet, adieu; adieu for aye!

TIB

Not so, Gammer; we might it find if we knew where it lay.

COCK

Gog's Cross, Gammer, if ye will laugh, look in but at the door,
And see how Hodge lieth tumbling and tossing amidst the floor,
Raking there some fire to find among the ashes dead
Where there is not one spark so big as a pin's head.
At last in a dark corner two sparks he thought he sees,
Which were indeed nought else but Gib our cat's two eyes.
'Puff', quod Hodge, thinking thereby to have fire without doubt.
With that Gib shut her two eyes, and so the fire was out,
And by and by them opened, even as they were before.
With that the sparks appeared even as they had done of yore;
And even as Hodge blew the fire as he did think,
Gib, as she felt the blast, straightway began to wink,
Till Hodge fell off, swearing, as came best to his turn,
The fire was sure bewitched and therefore would not burn.
At last Gib, up the stairs, among the old posts and pins,
And Hodge he hied him after till broke were both his shins,
Cursing and swearing oaths were never of his making,
That Gib would fire the house if that she were not taken.

48 **catch** slap.
8 **adieu for aye!** farewell for ever!
19 **of yore** previously.
21 **wink** blink/close both eyes.
22 **fell off** gave up.
22 **as . . . turn** in words best suited to the task.
24 **up** ran up.
26 **were** which were.
27 **taken** caught.

GAMMER

See, here is all the thought that the foolish urchin taketh,
And Tib, methink, at his elbow almost as merry maketh.
This is all the wit ye have when others make their moan.
Come down Hodge; where art thou, and let the cat alone.

HODGE

Gog's heart, help and come up, Gib in her tail hath fire,
And is like to burn all if she get a little higher!
'Come down', quoth you? Nay, then you might count me a patch;
The house cometh down on your heads if it take once in thatch.

GAMMER

It is the cat's eyes, fool, that shineth in the dark.

HODGE

Hath the cat, do you think, in every eye a spark?

GAMMER

No, but they shine as like fire as ever man see.

HODGE

By the Mass, and she burn all, yous' bear the blame for me!

GAMMER

Come down and help to seek here our nee'le that it were found.
Down, Tib, on thy knees, I say; down, Cock, to the ground.
To God I make a vow, and so to good Saint Anne,
A candle shall they have apiece, get it where I can,
If I may my nee'le find in one place or in other.

HODGE

Now a vengeance on Gib light, on Gib and Gib's mother,
And all the generation of cats both far and near!
Look on the ground, whoreson, thinks thou the nee'le is here?

COCK

By my troth, Gammer, methought your nee'le here I saw;
But when my fingers touched it, I felt it was a straw.

TIB

See, Hodge, what's this, may it not be within it?

HODGE

Break it, fool, with thy hand and see and thou canst find it.

TIB

Nay, break it you, Hodge, according to your word.

HODGE

Gog's sides, fie it stinks; it is a cat's turd!
It were well done to make thee eat it, by the Mass.

GAMMER

This matter amendeth not, my nee'le is still where it was.
Our candle is at an end; let us all in quite,
And come another time, when we have more light.

30 **make their moan** complain.
34 **count...patch** consider me a fool.
39 **yous'** you shall.
45 **light** alight/land.
56 **all in quite** go in together.

The Second Act: First a Song

Back and side go bare, go bare;
Both foot and hand go cold:
But belly, God send thee good ale enough,
Whether it be new or old.

I cannot eat but little meat,
My stomach is not good;
But sure I think that I can drink
With him that wears a hood.
Though I go bare, take ye no care,
I am nothing a-cold;
I stuff my skin so full within
Of jolly good ale and old.
Back and side go bare, go bare;
Both foot and hand go cold:
But belly, God send thee good ale enough,
Whether it be new or old.

I love no roast but a nut brown toast,
And a crab laid in the fire,
A little bread shall do me stead,
Much bread I not desire.
No frost nor snow, no wind I trow,
Can hurt me if I would,
I am so wrapped, and thoroughly lapped
Of jolly good ale and old.
Back and side go bare, etc.

And Tib my wife, that as her life
Loveth well good ale to seek,
Full oft drinks she till ye may see
The tears run down her cheeks.
Then doth she troll to me the bowl,
Even as a malt-worm should;
And sayeth 'Sweetheart, I took my part
Of this jolly good ale and old'.
Back and side go bare, etc.

Now let them drink till they nod and wink,
Even as good fellows should do,
They shall not miss to have the bliss
Good ale doth bring men to:
And all poor souls that have scoured bowls
Or have them lustily trolled,
God save the lives of them and their wives,

8 **With...hood** as well as any hooded man—probably a friar or monk.
18 **crab** crab apple.
19 **do me stead** be enough for me.
23 **lapped** wrapped up.
30 **troll** roll/pass.
31 **malt-worm** lover of malt/great drinker.
39 **scoured** emptied (completely).

Whether they be young or old.
Back and side go bare, etc.

[The Second Act:] The First Scene
(Dicken. Hodge.)

DICKEN
Well done, by Gog's malt, well sung and well said.
Come on, mother Chat, as thou art true maid;
One fresh pot of ale let's see, to make an end,
Against this cold weather my naked arms to defend.
This gear it warms the soul, now wind blow on the worst,
And let us drink and swill till that our bellies burst.
Now were he a wise man by cunning could define
Which way my journey lieth, or where Dicken will dine.
But one good turn I have, be it by night or day,
South, east, north, or west, I am never out of my way.

HODGE
Cham goodly rewarded, cham I not, do you think?
Chad a goodly dinner for all my sweat and swink,
Neither butter, cheese, milk, onions, flesh, nor fish,
Save this poor piece of barley bread, 'tis a pleasant costly dish!

DICKEN
Hail fellow, Hodge, and well to fare with thy meat, if you have any?
But by thy words, as I them smelled, thy daintrels be not many.

HODGE
Daintrels, Dicken? Gog's soul man, save this piece of dry horse-bread,
Cha bit no bit this live-long day, no crumb come in my head.
My guts they yawl, crawl and all my belly rumbleth,
The puddings cannot lie still; each one over other tumbleth.
By Gog's heart, cham so vexed and in my belly penned,
Chould one piece were at the spittle-house, another at ye castle's end.

DICKEN
Why Hodge, was there none at home thy dinner for to set?

HODGE
Gog's bread, Dicken, ich came too late, was nothing there to get.
Gib (a foul fiend might on her light!) lick[ed] the milk-pan so clean,
See, Dicken, 'twas not so well washed this seven year, as ich wean.
A pestilence light on all ill luck! Chad thought yet, for all this,
Of a morsel of bacon behind the door at worst should not miss.
But when ich sought a slip to cut, as ich was wont to do,
Gog's soul Dicken, Gib our cat had eat the bacon too!

Which bacon Dicken stole, as is declared before.

12 **swink** labour.
15 **well to fare** good luck!
16 **as . . . daintrels** as I understood them . . . your dainties.
19 **yawl** cry out.
20 **puddings** sausages, i.e. the guts/intestines.
22 **at the spittle-house** in the hospital.
26 **wean** believe.
s.d. A helpful reminder to readers, printed as an indented line in the 1575 text.

DICKEN
'Ill luck', quod he; marry, swear it Hodge, this day the truth to tell,
Thou rose not on thy right side, or else blessed thee not well,
Thy milk slopped up, thy bacon filched; that was too bad luck, Hodge!

HODGE
Nay, nay, there was a fouler fault, my Gammer ga' me the dodge;
Seest not how cham rent and torn, my heels, my knees and my breech?
Chad thought, as ich sat by the fire, help here and there a stitch,
But there ich was pooped indeed.

DICKEN
Why Hodge?

HODGE
Boots not man to tell,
Cham so dressed amongst a sort of fools, chad better be in hell.
My Gammer, cham ashamed to say, by God, served me not well.

DICKEN
How so, Hodge?

HODGE
Has she not gone, trowest thou, and lost her nee'le?

DICKEN
Her eel, Hodge? Who fished of late, that was a dainty dish!

HODGE
Tush tush, 'her nee'le'! Her nee'le, her nee'le, man! 'Tis neither flesh nor fish.
A little thing with an hole in the end, as bright as any siller,
Small, long, sharp at the point, and straight as any pillar.

DICKEN
I know not what a devil you meanest, you bringst me more in doubt.

HODGE
Knowest not with what Tom Tailor's man sits broaching through a clout?
A nee'le, nee'le, a nee'le, my Gammer's nee'le is gone!

DICKEN
Her needle, Hodge, now I smell thee. That was a chance alone!
By the Mass, thou hadst a shameful loss and it were but for thy breeches.

HODGE
Gog's soul man, chould give a crown chad it but three stitches.

DICKEN
How sayest you, Hodge, what should he have again, thy needle got?

HODGE
By m'father's soul, and chad it, chould give him a new groat.

DICKEN
Canst thou keep counsel in this case?

32 **blessed . . . well** i.e. you've brought bad luck on yourself somehow.
34 **ga' . . . dodge** tricked me/disappointed me (worst of all).
37 **pooped** fooled.
37.2 **Boots . . . tell.** There's no point telling you.
38 **dressed** (badly) treated.
41 **eel** because 'needle' was colloquially pronounced 'nee'le', Dicken can pretend to miss-hear.
41 **Who . . . late** Whoever fished recently.
43 **siller** silver.
46 **broaching . . . clout?** mending holes in a cloth?
48 **smell** understand.
48 **That . . . alone!** That was rare (bad) luck!
49 **and . . . for** even if it was only for.
51 **what . . . got?** what should the one who finds your needle have in reward?
52 **groat** a coin worth four pence.
53 **keep counsel** keep a secret/your mouth shut.

HODGE
Else chwould my tongue were out.

DICKEN
Do thou but then by my advice, and I will fetch it without doubt.

HODGE
Chill run, chill ride, chill dig, chill delve, chill toil, chill trudge, shalt see;
Chill hold, chill draw, chill pull, chill pinch, chill kneel on my bare knee;
Chill scrape, chill scratch, chill skate, chill seek, chill bow, chill bend, chill sweat;
Chill stoop, chill stir, chill cap, chill kneel, chill creep on hands and feet;
Chill be thy bondman, Dicken, ich swear by sun and moon,
And ich cannot somewhat to stop this gap, cham utterly undone!

Pointing behind to his torn breeches.

DICKEN
Why, is there any special cause thou takest hereat such sorrow?

HODGE
Kirsten Clack, Tom Simpson's maid, by the Mass, comes hither tomorrow.
Cham not able to say between us what may hap;
She smiled on me the last Sunday when ich put off my cap.

DICKEN
Well, Hodge, this is a matter of weight, and must be kept close,
It might else turn to both our costs as the world now goes.
Shalt sware to be no blab, Hodge?

HODGE
Chill, Dicken.

DICKEN
Then go to,
Lay thine hand here. Say after me as thou shalt hear me do.
Hast no book?

HODGE
Cha no book, I.

DICKEN
Then needs must force us both
Upon my breech to lay thine hand, and there to take thine oath.

HODGE
I, Hodge, breechless,
Swear to Dicken, reckless,
By the cross that I shall kiss,
To keep his counsel close,
And always me to dispose
To work that his pleasure is.

Here he kisseth Dicken's breech.

DICKEN
Now, Hodge, see thou take heed,

54 **Do...by** If you just follow.
54 **fetch it** i.e. find the needle.
56 **draw** draw water (from the well).
59 **bondman** bound servant.
60 **And...gap** If I cannot find some way to mend this hole.
62 **Clack** Chatterbox.
65 **a...close** a serious matter...kept secret.
66 **It...goes** It may prove dangerous/costly for both of us, the way the world is these days.
67 **blab** tell-tale.
67.1 **go to** get on with it.
76 **To...is** To do whatever he wants.

And do as I thee bid;
For so I judge it meet;
This needle again to win,
There is no shift therein
But conjure up a sprite.

HODGE
What, the great devil, Dicken, I say?

DICKEN
Yea, in good faith, that is the way,
Fet with some pretty charm.

HODGE
Soft, Dicken, be not too hasty yet,
By the Mass, for ich begin to sweat.
Cham afraid of some harm.

DICKEN
Come hither then, and stir thee nat
One inch out of this circle plat,
But stand as I thee teach.

HODGE
And shall ich be here safe from their claws?

DICKEN
The master devil with his long paws
Here to thee cannot reach.
Now will I settle me to this gear.

HODGE
I say, Dicken, hear me, hear:
Go softly to this matter.

DICKEN
What devil, man, art afraid of nought?

HODGE
Canst not tarry a little thought
Till ich make a curtesy of water?

DICKEN
Stand still to it; why shouldst thou fear him?

HODGE
Gog's sides, Dicken, methink ich hear him!
And tarry, chall mar all.

DICKEN
The matter is no worse than I told it.

HODGE
By the Mass, cham able no longer to hold it,
Too bad: ich must beray the hall.

DICKEN
Stand to it, Hodge, stir not, you whoreson.

79 **meet** appropriate.
81 **There ... therein** There's no other effective course of action.
85 **Fet** Summoned.
86 **Soft** Hush!
90 **plat** drawn, like a plat (a plan or diagram) on the ground.
95 **settle ... gear** get down to business.
98 **afraid of nought** afraid of trifles.
99–100 **Canst ... water?** Can you not wait a moment while I take a short toilet break?
103 **And ... all.** If we hang around, everything's ruined.
106 **ich ... hall** I'll have to befoul the hall. (He soils his trousers.)

What Devil, be thine arse-strings brusten?
Thyself a while but stay,
The devil, I smell him, will be here anon.

HODGE

Hold him fast, Dicken, cham gone, cham gone!
Chill not be at that fray.

The Second Act: The Second Scene (Dicken. Chat.)

DICKEN

Fie, shitten knave, and out upon thee!
Above all other louts, fie on thee!
Is not here a cleanly prank?
But thy matter was no better,
Nor thy presence here no sweeter,
To fly I can thee thank.
Here is a matter worthy glosing,
Of Gammer Gurton's needle losing,
And a foul piece of work.
A man, I think, might make a play
And need no word to this they say,
Being but half a clerk.
Soft, let me alone, I will take the charge
This matter further to enlarge
Within a time short.
If ye will mark my toys and note,
I will give ye leave to cut my throat
If I make not good sport.
Dame Chat, I say, where be ye within?

CHAT

Who have we there maketh such a din?

DICKEN

Here is a good fellow maketh no great danger.

CHAT

What, Dicken? Come near, ye be no stranger.
We be fast set at trump, man, hard by the fire;
Thou shalt set on the king if thou come a little nigher.

DICKEN

Nay, nay, there is no tarrying: I must be gone again,
But first for you in counsel I have a word or twain.

CHAT

Come hither Doll! Doll, sit down and play this game,
And as thou sawest me do, see thou do even the same.

108 **brusten** broken.
1 **out upon thee!** curse/away with you!
7 **worthy glosing** worthy of interpretation/Scholarly 'glossing'.
11–12 **A...say** A man could make a play of all this, without adding a word to what was said.
16 **If...note** Just watch my tricks and learn (from them).
23 **We...fire** We're engrossed in a game of trump (a card game), sitting close to the fire.
24 **Thou...king** You can play the next card (the king), i.e. come closer and join the game.
27 Dame Chat asks Doll to play her cards for her while she talks with Dicken.

There is five trumps beside the queen, the hindmost you shalt find her.
Take heed of Sim Glover's wife, she hath an eye behind her.
Now Dicken say your will.

DICKEN

Nay, soft a little yet;
I would not tell it my sister, the matter is so great.
There I will have you swear by our dear Lady of Bullain,
St. Dunstan and St. Dominic, with the three kings of Collain,
That ye shall keep it secret.

CHAT

Gog's bread, that will I do,
As secret as mine own thought, by God, and the devil too.

DICKEN

Here is Gammer Gurton, your neighbour, a sad, heavy wight,
Her goodly fair red cock at home was stole this last night.

CHAT

Gog's soul, her cock with the yellow legs, it nightly crowed so just?

DICKEN

That Cock is stolen.

CHAT

What, was he fet out of the hens' roost?

DICKEN

I cannot tell where the devil he was kept, under key or lock,
But Tib hath tickled in Gammer's ear that you should steal the cock.

CHAT

Have I, strong whore, by bread and salt?

DICKEN

What, soft I say, be still.
Say not one word for all this gear.

CHAT

By the Mass, that I will,
I will have the young whore by the head, and the old trot by the throat.

DICKEN

Not one word, Dame Chat, I say, not one word, for my coat!

CHAT

Shall such a beggar's brawl, as it thinkest you, make me a thief?
The pox light on her whore's sides, a pestilence and a mischief.
Come out, thou hungry, needy bitch! Oh that my nails be short!

DICKEN

Gog's bread, woman, hold your peace, this gear will else pass sport.

29–30 **hindmost ... her.** You'll find the queen at the back (of the hand). Watch out for Sim Glover's wife; she has eyes in the back of her head! (She'll see your cards if you don't keep them hidden). (There is evidently a group of women playing, perhaps out of sight, in Chat's house.)

33–34 **Lady of Bullain** the shrine of the Virgin Mary in Boulogne (France), **St Dunstan**, the tenth-century Archbishop of Canterbury, **St Dominic** (1170–1221), founder of the Dominican order of friars, and **Collain**, the shrine to the three kings or magi in Cologne Cathedral.

37 **heavy wight** sorrowful person.

39 **so just** so regularly/accurately.

40.1 **fet** fetched/taken.

42 **tickled ... steal** whispered ... that you have stolen.

43 **strong** Here used as an intensifier: '(the) great whore!'

44 **for ... gear** despite all this matter.

45 **trot** hag.

47 **brawl ... me** broll (brat) ... make me out to be.

48 **light** land.

49 **needy** poor/wretched.

50 **pass sport** surpass/go beyond a joke.

I would not for an hundred pound this matter should be known,
That I am author of this tale, or have abroad it blown.
Did ye not swear ye would be ruled before the tale I told;
I said ye must all secret keep and ye said sure ye would.

CHAT
Would you suffer yourself, Dicken, such a sort to revile you,
With slanderous words to blot your name and so to defile you?

DICKEN
No, goodwife Chat, I would be loath such drabs should blot my name;
But yet ye must so order all that Dicken bear no blame.

CHAT
Go to, then, what is your rede? Say on your mind, ye shall me rule herein.

DICKEN
God-a-mercy to Dame Chat, in faith thou must the gear begin.
It is twenty pound to a goose turd my Gammer will not tarry,
But hitherward she comes as fast as her legs can her carry
To brawl with you about her cock, for well I heard Tib say
The cock was roosted in your house to breakfast yesterday,
And when ye had the carcass eaten, the feathers ye out flung;
And Doll your maid, the legs she hid a foot deep in the dung.

CHAT
Oh gracious God, my heart it bursts!

DICKEN
Well rule yourself a space,
And Gammer Gurton, when she cometh anon into this place,
Then to the quean let's see; tell her your mind and spare not.
So shall Dicken blameless be, and then, go to, I care not.

CHAT
Then, whore, beware her throat; I can abide no longer.
In faith, old witch, it shall be seen which of us two be stronger;
And Dicken, but at your request I would not stay one hour.

DICKEN
Well, keep it in till she be here, and then out let it pour.
In the mean while get you in, and make no words of this.
More of this matter within this hour to hear you shall not miss,
Because I know you are my friend, hide it I could not, doubtless.
Ye know your harm, see ye be wise about your own business.
So fare ye well.

CHAT
Nay, soft, Dicken, and drink. What, Doll, I say,
Bring here a cup of the best ale; let's see, come quickly away.

52 **or . . . blown** or that I've spread it around.
55 **such a sort** someone of that kind.
59 **Go . . . herein.** All right then, what's your advice? Tell me your opinion, and I'll follow your guidance.
60 **gear** matter.
61 **It is** I'll bet.
67.1 **Well . . . space** Control yourself for a moment.
69 **Then . . . see** Then let's deal with the whore.
73 **but . . . request** if you hadn't asked me to, I'd not restrain myself.

The Second Act: The Third Scene
(Hodge. Dicken.)

DICKEN

Ye see, masters, the one end tapped of this my short devise;
Now must we broach th'other too, before the smoke arise.
And by the time they have a while run (I trust ye need not crave it),
But look what lieth in both their hearts, ye are like, sure, to have it.

HODGE

Yea, Gog's soul, art alive yet? What Dicken, dare ich come?

DICKEN

A man is well hied to trust to thee. I will say nothing but mum.
But and ye come any nearer, I pray you see all be sweet.

HODGE

Tush man, is Gammer's nee'le found? That chould gladly weet.

DICKEN

She may thank thee it is not found, for if you had kept thy standing,
The devil he would have fet it out, even, Hodge, at thy commanding.

HODGE

Gog's heart, and could he tell nothing where the nee'le might be found?

DICKEN

Ye foolish dolt, ye were to seek ere we had got our ground,
Therefore his tale so doubtful was, that I could not perceive it.

HODGE

Then ich see well something was said; chope one day yet to have it,
But Dicken, Dicken, did not the devil cry 'Ho, ho, ho'?

DICKEN

If you hadst tarried where thou stoodst, thou wouldst have said so.

HODGE

Durst swear of a book, ch'heard him roar, straight after ich was gone.
But tell me, Dicken, what said the knave: let me hear it anon.

DICKEN

The whoreson talked to me, I know not well of what.
One while his tongue it ran and paltered of a cat,
Another while he stammered still upon a rat,
Last of all there was nothing but every word, 'chat, chat.'
But this I well perceived before I would him rid,
Between chat and the rat and the cat the needle is hid.
Now, whether Gib our cat have eat it in her maw,
Or Doctor Rat our curate have found it in the straw,
Or this Dame Chat your neighbour have stolen it, God he knoweth;
But by ye morrow at this time, we shall learn how the matter goeth.

1–2 **Ye...arise.** You've seen one end of the barrel tapped/one part of my plan begun. Now we need to begin the other, while the fire is still hot.

6–7 **A...sweet** A man does well to trust you. (Ironic) I'm saying nothing; but, before you get any closer, check everything's clean. (A reference to Hodge's beshitten trousers.)

8 **chould gladly weet** I'd gladly know.

9 **if...standing** if you'd stood your ground.

12 **ye...ground** you'd disappeared before we'd taken our places (for the summoning ritual).

13 **doubtful** unclear/inaudible.

14 **chope** I hope.

20 **paltered of** babbled about.

21 **upon** about.

HODGE
Canst not learn tonight man, seest not what is here?

Pointing behind to his torn breeches.

DICKEN
'Tis not possible to make it sooner appear,

HODGE
Alas, Dicken, then chave no shift but lest ich tarry too long,
Hie me to Sim Glover's shop, there to seek for a thong
Therewith this breech to 'tatch and tie as ich may.

DICKEN
Tomorrow Hodge, if we chance to meet, shalt see what I will say.

The Second Act: The Fourth Scene
(Dicken. Gammer.)

DICKEN
Now this gear must forward go, for here my Gammer cometh.
Be still a while and say nothing, make here a little roomth.

GAMMER
Good lord, shall never be my luck my nee'le again to spy?
Alas the while 'tis past my help; where 'tis, still it must lie.

DICKEN
Now Jesus, Gammer Gurton, what driveth you to this sadness?
I fear me, by my conscience, you will sure fall to madness.

GAMMER
Who is that? What Dicken, chave lost, man...fie, fie!

DICKEN
Marry, fie on them that be worthy, but what should be your trouble?

GAMMER
Alas, the more ich think on it, my sorrow it waxeth double;
My goodly tossing spurrier's nee'le chave lost, ich wot not where.

DICKEN
Your needle? When?

GAMMER
My nee'le. Alas ich might full ill it spare,
As God himself he knoweth, ne'er one beside chave.

DICKEN
If this be all, good Gammer, I warrant you all is safe.

GAMMER
Why, know you any tidings which way my nee'le is gone?

DICKEN
Yea that I do, doubtless, as ye shall hear anon,
A' see a thing this matter toucheth within these twenty hours,
Even at this gate, before my face, by a neighbour of yours;

33 **'tatch and tie** attach/fasten.
2 **roomth** room/space (spoken to the audience).
8 **fie...worthy** damn those who deserve it.
9 **waxeth** grows.
10 **My...nee'le** My swift-working spur-maker's needle.
11–12 **ich...chave** I cannot do without it...I've not got another one.
16 **A'...toucheth** I've seen something related to this business.

She stooped me down and up she took a needle or a pin:
I durst be sworn it was even yours, by all my mother's kin.

GAMMER
It was my nee'le, Dicken, ich wot, for here, even by this post
Ich sat what time as ich up start, and so my nee'le it lost.
Who was it, leave son? Speak, ich pray thee, and quickly tell me that.

DICKEN
A subtle quean as any in this town; your neighbour here, Dame Chat.

GAMMER
Dame Chat! Dicken, let me be gone, chill thither in post haste!

DICKEN
Take my counsel yet, ere ye go, for fear ye walk in waste.
It is a murrion crafty drab, and froward to be pleased,
And ye take not the better way, your needle yet ye lose it.
For when she took it up, even here before your doors,
'What, soft, Dame Chat', quoth I, 'that same is none of yours'.
'Avaunt,' quoth she, 'sir knave! What pratest thou of that I find?
I would ye hadst kissed me I wot where' (she meant, I know, behind.)
And home she went as brag as it had been a bode-louse,
And I after, as bold as it had been the goodman of the house:
But there, and ye had heard her, how she began to scold;
The tongue it went on pattens, by him that Judas sold!
Each other word I was a knave, and you a whore of whores,
Because I spake in your behalf and said the needle was yours.

GAMMER
Gog's bread, and thinks the callet thus to keep my nee'le me fro?

DICKEN
Let her alone, and she minds none other but even to dress you so.

GAMMER
By the Mass, chill rather spend the coat that is on my back!
Thinks the false quean by such a slight that chill my nee'le lack?

DICKEN
Sleep not your gear, I counsel you, but of this take good heed:
Let not be known I told you of it, how well so ever ye speed.

GAMMER
Chill in, Dicken, a clean apron to take and set before me,
And ich may my nee'le once see, chill sure remember thee.

The Second Act: The Fifth Scene
(Dicken.)

DICKEN
Here will the sport begin, if these two once may meet;

18 **She . . . took** She stooped and picked up.
21 **Ich . . . start** I was sitting when I jumped up.
22 **leave** beloved.
26 **a . . . pleased** a damned clever hag, and hard to please.
32 **as . . . been** as bold as if she were (either a 'body-louse', presumably happy to go anywhere, however intimate, or possibly a 'bode-de-lis' a town crier or herald embroidered with fleur-de-lis).
33 **And . . . goodman** And I followed . . . as if I was the master.
35 **The . . . sold!** Her tongue so clattered (as if it were wearing raised wooden clogs), by Jesus!
38 **thinks . . . fro?** does the slut think to keep my needle from me?
39 **and . . . so** if she wants to talk about you like that.
41 **chill . . . lack?** I'll accept the loss of my needle?
42 **Sleep . . . gear** Don't slack in your intention.

Their cheer, durst lay money, will prove scarcely sweet!
My Gammer sure intends to be upon her bones
With staves or with clubs, or else with cobblestones.
Dame Chat on the other side, if she be far behind
I am right far deceived, she is given to it of kind.
He that may tarry by it awhile, and that but short,
I warrant him trust to it, he shall see all the sport.
Into the town will I, my friends to visit there,
And hither straight again to see th'end of this gear.
In the mean time fellows, pipe up your fiddles, I say take them,
And let your friends hear such mirth as ye can make them.

[*Here a tune or song is played.*]

The Third Act: The First Scene
(Hodge.)

HODGE

Sim Glover yet grammercy, cham meetly well sped now,
Th'art even as good a fellow as ever kissed a cow!
Here is a thong indeed, by ye Mass, though ich speak it;
Tom Tankard's great bald curtal, I think, could not break it.
And when he spied my need to lie so straight and hard,
Has lent me here his nail to set the jib forward.
As for my Gammer's nee'le, the flying fiend go weet,
Chill not now go to the door again with it to meet.
Chould make shift good enough and chad a candle's end.
The chief hole in my breech with these two chill amend.

The Third Act: The Second Scene
(Gammer. Hodge.)

GAMMER

How, Hodge, mayst now be glad, cha news to tell thee;
Ich know who has my nee'le, ich trust soon shalt it see.

HODGE

The devil thou does! Hast heard, Gammer, indeed, or dost but jest?

GAMMER

'Tis as true as steel, Hodge.

HODGE

Why, knowest well where didst lose it?

GAMMER

Ich know who found it and took it up; shalt see ere it be long.

HODGE

God's mother dear, if that be true, farewell both nail and thong!

[2] **Their . . . sweet!** Their expression(s)/hospitality, I bet, will hardly be sweet!
[3] **be . . . bones** set upon her body.
[6] **given . . . kind** that way inclined by nature.
[1] **grammercy . . . now** God thank you, I'm well provided for now!
[4] **bald curtal** piebald horse with a docked/cut tail.
[5] **straight and hard** urgent and necessary.
[6] **to . . . forward** to help matters along.
[7] **the . . . weet** let the flying fiend go find it.
[9] **Chould . . . end.** I'd sort this out well enough if I had the remains of a candle (to see by).
[10] **chill amend** I'll mend.
[1] **How** Hello.
[5] **shalt** you shall.

But who has it, Gammer? Say on; chould fain hear it disclosed.

GAMMER
That false vixen, that same Dame Chat, that counts herself so honest.

HODGE
Who told you so?

GAMMER
That same did Dicken the Bedlam, which saw it done.

HODGE
Dicken? It is a vengeable knave, Gammer, 'tis a 'bomnable whoreson,
Can do mo things than that, else cham deceived evil.
By the Mass, ich saw him of late call up a great black devil!
'Oh,' the knave cried, 'Ho, ho', he roared and he thundered,
And ye'd been here, cham sure you'ld murrainly ha' wondered.

GAMMER
Was not thou afraid, Hodge, to see him in this place?

HODGE
No, and chad come to me, chould have laid him on the face,
Chould have promised him!

GAMMER
But Hodge, had he no horns to push?

HODGE
As long as your two arms! Saw ye never Friar Rush
Painted on a cloth, with a sidelong cow's tail
And crooked, cloven feet, and many a hooked nail?
For all the world, if I should judge, chould reckon him his brother.
Look even what face Friar Rush had, the devil had such another.

GAMMER
Now Jesus mercy, Hodge, did Dicken in him bring?

HODGE
Nay Gammer, hear me speak, chill tell you a greater thing:
The devil, when Dicken had him, ich heard him wondrous well,
Said plainly here before us that Dame Chat had your nee'le.

GAMMER
Then let us go and ask her wherefore she minds to keep it,
Seeing we know so much, t'were a madness now to sleep it.

HODGE
Go to her Gammer, see ye not where she stands in her doors?
Bid her give you the nee'le; 'tis none of hers, but yours.

The Third Act: The Third Scene
(Gammer. Chat. Hodge.)

GAMMER
Dame Chat, chwould pray thee fair, let me have that is mine!

10 **It...whoreson** He's a terrible rogue... an abominable son-of-a-bitch.
11 **else...evil** or I'm badly deceived.
14 **murrainly ha' wondered** been cursedly/absolutely amazed!
15 **him** i.e. the devil.
16 **and...face** if he'd come towards me, I'd have punched him in the face.
18 **Friar Rush** a devil from European folklore.
19 **sidelong** slanted/angled, but also huge.
28 **to sleep it** let the matter rest.
1 **that is mine** what's mine.

Chill not this twenty years take one fart that is thine;
Therefore give me mine own, and let me live beside thee.

CHAT

Why art thou crept from home hither to mine own doors to chide me?
Hence, doting drab, avaunt, or I shall set thee further!
Intends thou and that knave me in my house to murther?

GAMMER

Tush, gape not so on me, woman, shalt not yet eat me,
Nor all the friends thou hast in this shall not entreat me:
Mine own goods I will have, and ask thee no by-y'r-leave.
What woman; poor folks must have right, though the thing you aggrieve.

CHAT

Give thee thy right, and hang thee up, with all thy beggar's brood!
What, wilt thou make me a thief, and say I stole thy good?

GAMMER

Chill say nothing, ich warrant thee, but that ich can prove it well.
Thou fet my good even from my door, cham able this to tell.

CHAT

Did I, old witch, steal ought was thine? How should that thing be known?

GAMMER

Ich cannot tell, but up thou tookest it, as though it had been thine own.

CHAT

Marry, fie on thee, thou old gib, with all my very heart!

GAMMER

Nay, fie on thee, you ramp, thou rig, with all that take thy part!

CHAT

A vengeance on those lips that layeth such things to my charge.

GAMMER

A vengeance on those callet's hips whose conscience is so large.

CHAT

Come out, hog!

GAMMER

Come out, hog, and let me have right!

CHAT

Thou arrant witch!

GAMMER

Thou bawdy bitch, chill make thee curse this night.

CHAT

A bag and a wallet!

GAMMER

A cart for a callet!

[5] **set thee further** drive you away.
[6] **murther** murder.
[9] **by-y'r-leave** by your leave (with your permission).
[10] **though...aggrieve** even if it upsets you.
[14] **my good** because Gammer never names her needle, Chat believes she is talking about the chicken Dicken mentioned.
[15] **ought was thine?** anything of yours?
[17] **gib** tomcat.
[18] **you...part!** you shrew, you slut, with all who take your side!
[21] **Come out, hog!** Come on then, you pig (let's fight)!
[23] **A...wallet!** (rhetorically) 'Bring me a bag and satchel (for this wandering beggar-woman)!' (Satchels were traditional props for itinerant beggars.)
[23.1] **A...callet!** Bring me a cart to parade this whore in!

CHAT

Why, weanest thou thus to prevail?
I hold thee a groat I shall patch thy coat.

GAMMER

Thou were't as good kiss my tail,
Thou slut, thou cut, thou rakes, thou jakes; will not shame make ye hide thee?

CHAT

Thou scold, thou bald, thou rotten, [th]ou glutton, I will no longer chide thee,
But I will teach thee to keep home.

GAMMER

Wilt thou, drunken beast?

HODGE

Stick to her Gammer, take her by the head, chill warrant you this feast.
Smite, I say, Gammer; bite, I say, Gammer; I trow ye will be keen!
Where be your nails? Claw her by the jaws, pull me out both her eyen,
Gog's bones, Gammer, hold up your head!

CHAT

I trow, drab, I shall dress thee.
Tarry thou knave, I hold thee a groat I shall make these hands bless thee;
Take thou this, old whore, for amends, and learn thy tongue well to tame.
And say thou met at this bickering, not thy fellow, but thy dame!

HODGE

Where is the strong-stewed whore? Chill gi'er a whore's mark!
Stand out one's way that ich kill none in the dark!
Up Gammer, and ye be alive, chill fight now for us both.
Come no near me, thou scold callet, to kill thee ich were loath.

CHAT

Art here again, thou hoddy-peak? What, Doll, bring me out my spit.

HODGE

Chill broach thee with this, by m'father['s] soul; chill conjure that foul sprite:
Let door stand, Cock! Why, comes indeed? Keep door you whoreson boy!

CHAT

Stand to it you dastard, for thine ears, I's teach ye a sluttish toy.

HODGE

Gog's wounds, whore, chill make thee avaunt. Take heed Cock, pull in the latch.

CHAT

I' faith, Sir Loose-breech, had ye tarried, ye should have found your match.

GAMMER

Now, ware thy throat, losel, thou's pay for all.

HODGE

Well said, Gammer, by my soul!
House her, souse her, bounce her, trounce her, pull out her throat-bowl!

24 **I . . . coat.** I bet you a groat I'll beat you.

24.1 **Thou . . . tail** You'd do as well to kiss my arse.

25 **Thou . . . jakes** You slut, you cunt, you strumpet, you toilet/dunghill.

27 **keep home** stay at home.

28 **chill . . . feast** I'll back you to win this.

30 **eyen** eyes.

34 **thou . . . dame!** i.e. you met more than your match in this argument.

35 **strong-stewed** long-lived in the brothel.

35 **whore's mark** the brand given to a convicted prostitute.

39 **Art . . . hoddy-peak?** Are you back again, you blockhead?

39 **spit** skewer.

41 **Let door stand!** Guard the door!

41 **comes indeed?** is he coming?

42 **I's teach ye a sluttish toy** I'll teach you a dirty trick.

43 **pull in the latch** close the door.

45 **ware . . . all** watch your throat, you'll pay for all this, wretch!

CHAT
Comst behind me, thou withered witch? And I get once on foot,
Thou's pay for all, you old tar-leather, I'll teach thee what longs to it.
Take ye this to make up thy mouth, till time thou come by more.

HODGE
Up Gammer, stand on your feet. Where is the old whore?
Faith, would chad her by the face, chould rack her callet crown.

GAMMER
Ah Hodge, Hodge, where was thy help when vixen had me down?

HODGE
By the Mass, Gammer, but for my staff, Chat had gone nigh to spill you.
Ich think the harlot had not cared; and chad not come, to kill you.
But shall we lose our nee'le thus?

GAMMER
No Hodge, chould loath do so.
Thinkest thou chill take that at her hand? No, Hodge, ich tell thee, no.

HODGE
Chould yet this fray were well take up, and our own nee'le at home;
'Twill be my chance else some to kill, wherever it be or whom!

GAMMER
We have a parson, Hodge, thou knows, a man esteemed wise,
Mast' Doctor Rat, chill for him send, and let me hear his advice.
He will her shrive for all this gear, and give her penance strait.
We's have our nee'le, else Dame Chat comes ne'er within heaven gate!

HODGE
Ye, marry, Gammer, it ich think best. Will you now for him send?
The sooner Doctor Rat be here, the sooner we's ha[ve] an end.
And hear, Gammer: Dicken's devil, as ich remember well,
Of Cat, and Chat, and Doctor Rat, a feloneous tale did tell.
Chold you forty pound that is the way your nee'le to get again.

GAMMER
Chill ha' him straight. Call out the boy, we's make him take the pain.

HODGE
What, Cock, I say, come out! What, devil, canst not hear?

COCK
How now, Hodge? How does Gammer? Is yet the weather clear?
What would chave me to do?

GAMMER
Come hither, Cock, anon.
Hence swithe to Doctor Rat, hie thee that thou were gone,
And pray him come speak with me, cham not well at ease.

47 **And...foot** If I could just get up.
48 **old...it** old, dried sheepskin, I'll teach you what you deserve.
51 **would...crown** if I could have got hold of her face, I'd have raked her whore's (i.e. scabby with pox) scalp.
53 **spill** destroy.
54 **and...come** if I'd not been there.
58 **Chould...whom!** I wish this matter were settled... otherwise I'm sure I'll kill someone, and I don't care who!
61 **He...strait.** He'll take her confession about all this, and give her severe penance.
62 **We's** We shall.
68 **we's...pain** we shall make him do the job.
70 **Is...clear?** i.e. is it safe to come out?
72 **swithe** quickly.

Shalt have him at his chamber, or else at mother Bee's;
Else seek him at Hob Filcher's shop, for, as cheard it reported,
There is the best ale in all the town, and now is most resorted.

COCK
And shall ich bring him with me, Gammer?

GAMMER
Yea, by and by, good Cock.

COCK
Shalt see that shall be here anon, else let me have one the dock.

HODGE
Now Gammer, shall we two go in and tarry for his coming?
What, devil, woman, pluck up your heart, and leave off all this glomming.
Though she were stronger at ye first, as ich think, ye did find her!
Yet there ye dressed the drunken sow, what time ye came behind her!

GAMMER
Nay, nay, cham sure she lost not all, for, set th'end to ye beginning
And ich doubt not but she will make small boast of her winning.

The Third Act: The Fourth Scene
(Tib. Hodge. Gammer. Cock.)

TIB
See, Gammer, Gammer! Gib our cat, cham afraid that she aileth.
She stands me gasping behind the door, as though her wind her faileth.
Now let ich doubt what Gib should mean that now she doth so dote.

HODGE
Hold hither, ich [ho]ld twenty pound your nee'le is in her throat!
Grope her, ich say, me thinks ich feel it, does not prick your hand?

GAMMER
Ich can feel nothing.

HODGE
No, ich know there's not within this land
A murrainer cat than Gib is betwixt the Thames and Tyne.
Sh'as as much wit in her head almost as chave in mine!

TIB
Faith, sh'as eaten something that will not easily down;
Whether she got it at home or abroad in the town
Ich cannot tell.

GAMMER
Alas, ich fear it be some crooked pin;
And then, farewell Gib, she is undone and lost all, save the skin.

74 **Shalt have him** You'll find him.
76 **most resorted** the most popular (ale house). (The 1575 text gives this line to Cock, but the speech headings seem misaligned here.)
78 **one the dock** one (blow on) the arse.
80 **glomming** moping/looking glum.
82 **ye...her!** You bested her; and when you came up behind her, you sorted the drunken sow out!
83–84 **set...winning** if you judge by the whole battle, I'm sure she'll claim she won.
2 **stands me** stands there.
3 **let...dote** I've no idea what's wrong that she behaves so oddly.
4 **Hold hither** bring her here.
7 **murrainer** more cursed.
7 **betwixt...Tyne** between the river Thames in the south of England and the Tyne in the north.
8 **Sh'as** She has.
12 **save** except.

HODGE
Tib, your nee'le, woman, I say! Gog's soul, give me a knife
And chill have it out of her maw, or else chall lose my life.

GAMMER
What, nay Hodge, fie; kill not our cat; 'tis all the cats we ha' now.

HODGE
By the Mass, Dame Chat has me so moved ich care not what I kill, ma' God avow.
Go to, then, Tib to this gear; hold up her tail and take her,
Chill see what devil is in her guts, chill take ye pains to rake her.

GAMMER
Rake a cat, Hodge? What wouldst thou do?

HODGE
What, thinkst that cham not able?
Did not Tom Tankard rake his curtall to'er day, standing in the stable?

GAMMER
Soft, be content, let's hear what news Cock bringeth from Mast' Rat.

COCK
Gammer, chave been there as you bade, you wot well about what.
'Twill not be long before he come, ich durst swear of a book.
He bids you see ye be at home, and there for him to look.

GAMMER
Where didst thou find him, boy, was he not where I told thee?

COCK
Yes, yes, even at Hob Filcher's house, by him that bought and sold me,
A cup of ale had in his hand, and a crab lay in the fire.
Chad much ado to go and come, all was so full of mire.
And, Gammer, one thing I can tell, Hob Filcher's awl was lost,
And Doctor Rat found it again, hard beside the door-post.
I chould a penny can say something your nee'le again to fet.

GAMMER
Cham glad to hear so much, Cock, then trust he will not let
To help us herein best he can. Therefore, till time he come
Let us go in, if there be ought to get, thou shalt have some.

[The Fourth Act: The First Scene.]
(Doctor Rat. Gammer Gurton.)

DR. RAT
A man were better twenty times be a bandog and bark,
Than here, among such a sort, be parish priest,

13 **Tib** most editors amend 'Tib' to ''tis', which would make simpler sense, but the 1575 text's 'Tib' is not impossible. The speech would then have Hodge demand that Tib give him her needle, only to recall that she and Gammer don't have a needle between them, and change the call to one for a knife.
16 **God avow** God knows.
18 **rake her** purge her.
20 **to'er day** the other day (recently).
22 **as you bade** as you ordered me.
23 **of** on.
24 **him to look** to wait for him.
26 **by...me** a clumsy variant of 'by Christ'.
27 **crab lay** crab apple roasting (for him).
28 **Chad...mire.** I had much trouble going and coming back, the road was so muddy.
29 **awl** a sharp carpentry tool.
30 **hard beside** right next to.
31 **I...fet.** I bet you a penny he can try (assay) something to find your needle again.
32 **not let** not hesitate/fail.
34 **ought to get** anything to eat or drink.
s.d. **The Fourth Act** The 1575 text has: 'The Second Act: the Fourth Scene' here.
1 **a bandog** a guard dog.

Where he shall never be at rest one pissing while a day,
But he must trudge about the town, this way and that way,
Here to a drab, there to a thief, his shoes to tear and rent;
And, that which is worst of all, at every knave's commandment!
I had not sat the space to drink two pots of ale
But Gammer Gurton's sorry boy was straightway at my tail,
And she was sick, and I must come, to do I wot not what.
If once her finger's end but ache: trudge, call for Doctor Rat!
And when I come not at their call, I only thereby lose,
For I am sure to lack therefore a tithe pig or a goose.
I warrant you, when truth is known, and told they have their tale,
The matter whereabout I come is not worth a halfpenny-worth of ale;
Yet must I talk so sage and smooth, as though I were a gloser,
Else, ere the year come at an end I shall be sure the loser.
What work ye, Gammer Gurton? How! Here is your friend, Master Rat.

GAMMER
Ah, good Master Doctor, cha troubled, cha troubled; you chwot well that.

DR. RAT
How do ye, woman? Be ye lusty, or be ye not well at ease?

GAMMER
By Jees, Master, cham not sick, but yet chave a disease.
Chad a foul turn now of late, chill tell it you, by Jigs.

DR. RAT
Hath your brown cow cast her calf, or your sandy sow her pigs?

GAMMER
No, but chad been as good they had as this, ich wot well.

DR. RAT
What is the matter?

GAMMER
Alas, alas, cha lost my good nee'le!
My nee'le, I say, and wot ye what? A drab came by and spied it,
And when I asked her for the same, the filth flatly denied it.

DR. RAT
What was she that...?

GAMMER
A dame, ich warrant you! She began to scold and brawl.
Alas, alas! Come hither, Hodge. This wretch can tell you all.

The Fourth Act: The Second Scene
(Hodge. Doctor Rat. Gammer. Dicken. Chat.)

HODGE
Good morrow, gaffer vicar!

DR. RAT
Come on, fellow let us hear.

[3] **one pissing while** long enough to piss.
[8] **sorry** pathetic.
[12] **tithe...goose** animals given to the priest as tithe payments. One tenth of every parishioner's produce should be given yearly to the parish priest to supplement his income.
[15] **gloser** flatterer.
[17] **What work ye?** What are you doing?
[20–21] **Jees** and **Jigs** are colloquialisms for 'Jesus'.
[22] **cast** miscarried.
[1] **gaffer** literally 'godfather': a colloquial honorific title, the male equivalent of 'gammer'.

Thy dame hath said to me thou knowest of all this gear;
Let's see what thou canst say.

HODGE

By m'fay, sir, that ye shall.
What matter so ever here was done, ich can tell your ma'ship all.
My Gammer Gurton here, see now,
Sat her down at this door, see now;
And, as she began to stir her, see now.
Her nee'le fell in the floor, see now;
And while her staff she took, see now,
At Gib her cat to fling, see now,
Her nee'le was lost in the floor, see now.
Is not this a wondrous thing, see now?
Then came the quean, Dame Chat, see now,
To ask for her black cup, see now;
And even here at this gate, see now,
She took that nee'le up, see now.
My Gammer then she yede, see now,
Her nee'le again to bring, see now,
And was caught by the head, see now.
Is not this a wondrous thing, see now?
She tore my Gammer's coat, see now,
And scratched her by the face, see now.
Chad thought she'd stopped her throat, see now.
Is not this a wondrous case, see now?
When ich saw this, ich was wroth, see now,
And sturt between them twain, see now,
Else, ich durst take a book oath, see now,
My Gammer had been slain, see now.

GAMMER

This is even the whole matter, as Hodge has plainly told.
And chould fain be quit for my part, that chould,
But help us, good master, beseech ye that ye do,
Else shall we both be beaten, and lose our nee'le too.

DR. RAT

What would ye have me to do? Tell me that I were gone.
I will do the best that I can to set you both at one,
But, be ye sure Dame Chat hath this your needle found?

GAMMER

Here comes the man that see her take it up off the ground.
Ask him yourself, Master Rat, if ye believe not me;
And help me to my nee'le, for God's sake and saint charity.

DR. RAT

Come near, Dicken, and let us hear what thou can express.
Wilt thou be sworn thou seest Dame Chat this woman's needle have?

3 **m'fay** my faith.
17 **yede** went.
24 **wondrous case** amazing thing.
26 **sturt...twain** jumped between the two (to separate them).
30 **choud...choud** I want to be repaid for my part, that I would.
33 **that...gone** so that I can go (once it is done)
34 **at one** in unity.
38 **saint charity** holy charity.

DICKEN
Nay, by St. Bennet, will I not; then might ye think me rave.
GAMMER
Why, didst not thou tell me so even here, canst thou for shame deny it?
DICKEN
Aye, marry Gammer, but I said I would not abide by it.
DR. RAT
Will you say a thing and not stick to it to try it?
DICKEN
'Stick to it,' quoth you, Master Rat? Marry, sir, I defy it!
Nay, there is many an honest man, when he such blasts hath blown
In his friends' ears, he would be loath the same by him were known.
If such a toy be used oft among the honesty,
It may beseem a simple man [o]f your and my degree.
DR. RAT
Then we be never the nearer, for all that you can tell.
DICKEN
Yes, marry sir, if ye will do by mine advice and counsel.
If Mother Chat see all us here, she knoweth how the matter goes.
Therefore, I rede you three go hence, and within keep close,
And I will into Dame Chat's house and so the matter use
That, ere you could go twice to church, I warrant you hear news.
She shall look well about her, but I durst lay a pledge,
Ye shall of Gammer's needle have shortly better knowledge.
GAMMER
Now, gentle Dicken, do so, and, good sir, let us trudge.
DR. RAT
By the Mass, I may not tarry so long to be your judge.
DICKEN
'Tis but a little while man; what take so much pain?
If I hear no news of it, I will come sooner again.
HODGE
Tarry so much, good master Doctor, of your gentleness.
DR. RAT
Then let us hie us inward, and, Dicken, speed thy business.
DICKEN
Now sirs, do you no more but keep my counsel just,
And Doctor Rat shall thus catch some good, I trust.
But Mother Chat, my gossip, talk first withal I must,
For she must be chief captain to lay the Rat in the dust.
Good even, Dame Chat, in faith, and well met in this place!
CHAT
Good even, my friend Dicken, whither walk ye this pace?

41 **St. Bennet** St Benedict, the founder of the Benedictine order of monks.
41 **might . . . rave** you'd think I was mad.
44 **try** prove.
48 **the honesty** the honourable classes.
50 **never the nearer** no closer (to the truth).
53 **rede** advise.
53 **within keep close** stay hidden indoors.
58 **trudge** go.
63 If the text followed its regular divisions, Act Two, Scene Four should begin after this line.
68 **even** evening.

DICKEN
By my truth, even to you, to learn how the world goeth.
Heard ye no more of the other matter, say me now, by your troth?

CHAT
Oh yes, Dicken, here the old whore, and Hodge that great knave …
But in faith I would thou hadst seen, oh lord, I dressed them brave!
She bore me two or three souses behind, in the nape of the neck,
Till I made her old weesen to answer again, keck!
And Hodge, that dirty dastard, that at her elbow stands,
If one pair of legs had not been worth two pair of hands,
He had had his beard shaven, if my nails would have served;
And not without a cause, for the knave it well deserved.

DICKEN
By the Mass, I can thee thank, wench, you didst so well acquit thee.

CHAT
And th'adst seen him, Dicken, it would have made ye beshite thee
For laughter. The whoreson dolt at last caught up a club,
As though he would have slain the master devil Belsabub,
But I set him soon inward.

DICKEN
O Lord, there is the thing
That Hodge is so offended, that makes him start and fling.

CHAT
Why, makes the knave any moiling, as ye have seen or heard?

DICKEN
Even now I saw him last, like a madman he fared,
And sware by heaven and hell he would awreak his sorrow,
And leave you never a hen on live by eight of the clock tomorrow.
Therefore mark what I say, and my words see that ye trust,
Your hens be as good as dead if ye leave them on the roost.

CHAT
The knave dare as well go hang himself as go upon my ground.

DICKEN
Well yet take heed, I say, I must tell you my tale round,
Have you not about your house, behind your furnace or lead,
A hole where a crafty knave may creep in for need?

CHAT
Yes, by the Mass, a hole broke down even within these two days.

DICKEN
Hodge, he intends this same night to slip in there aways.

CHAT
O Christ, that I were sure of it, in faith he should have his meed!

74 **souses** blows.
75 **made keck!** made her old windpipe to reply 'argh!'.
76 **that…stands** that coward who stands behind her.
77 **If…hands** If his legs hadn't thwarted my hands (by running away).
80 **you…thee** you acquitted yourself so well.
81 **And th'adst** If you had.
81–82 **beshite…laughter** shit yourself with laughter.
84.1 **there…thing** that's the reason.
86 **makes…moiling** is he distressed?
88 **awreak** avenge.
89 **live** alive.
93 **round** to the end.
94 **furnace or lead** oven or cauldron.
95 **for need** if he needs to.
97 **there aways** through there.
98 **he…meed!** he'll get his reward!

DICKEN
Watch well, for the knave will be there, as sure as is your creed.
I would spend myself a shilling to have him swinged well.
CHAT
I am as glad as a woman can be of this thing to hear tell.
By Gog's bones, when he cometh, now that I know the matter,
He shall sure at the first skip to leap in scalding water,
With a worse turn besides. When he will, let him come!
DICKEN
I tell you as my sister, you know what meaneth 'mum'.
Now, lack I but my Doctor to play his part again.
And lo where he cometh towards, peradventure to his pain.
DR. RAT
What good news, Dicken? Fellow, is Mother Chat at home?
DICKEN
She is sir, and she is not, but it please her to whom.
Yet did I take her tardy, as subtle as she was.
DR. RAT
The thing that thou wentst for, hast thou brought it to pass?
DICKEN
I have done that I have done, be it worse, be it better.
And Dame Chat at her wit's end I have almost set her.
DR. RAT
Why, hast thou spied the needle? Quickly, I pray thee tell.
DICKEN
I have spied it, in faith, sir, I handled myself so well,
And yet the crafty quean had almost take my trump.
But, ere all came to an end, I set her in a dump.
DR. RAT
How so, I pray thee, Dicken?
DICKEN
Marry, Sir, will ye hear?
She was clapped down on the backside, by Cock's mother dear,
And there she sat sewing a halter or a band,
With no other thing save Gammer's needle in her hand!
As soon as any knock, if the filth be in doubt,
She needs but once puff and her candle is out.
Now I, sir, knowing of every door the pin,
Came nicely and said no word till time I was within;
And there I saw the needle, even with these two eyes,
Whoever say the contrary, I will swear he lies.
DR. RAT
O, Dicken, that I was not there then in thy stead!

100 **shilling** a coin worth twelve pence.
100 **swinged well** soundly thrashed.
105 **you...'mum'** you know what 'shhh' means.
107 Again, a new scene might be expected to begin after this line.
107 **peradventure** perhaps.
109–110 **it...tardy** depending upon whether she wants to see you. But I caught her napping.
111 **brought...pass** achieved it.
116 **almost...trump** almost defeated me.
117 **set...dump** left her depressed.
119 **clapped** set.
119 **Cock's** God's (euphemism).
120 **halter...band** collar or a neck-band.
124 **knowing...pin** knowing how to open every door.
125 **nicely** craftily.

DICKEN

Well, if ye will be ordered, and do by my rede,
I will bring you to a place as the house stands
Where ye shall take the drab with the needle in her hands.

DR. RAT

For God's sake do so, Dicken, and I will gage my gown
To give thee a full pot of the best ale in the town.

DICKEN

Follow me but a little, and mark what I will say.
Lay down your gown beside you, go to, come on your way.
See ye not what is here? A hole wherein ye may creep
Into the house and suddenly unawares among them leap.
There shall ye find the bitch-fox and the needle together.
Do as I bid you, man, come on your ways hither.

DR. RAT

Art thou sure, Dicken, the swill tub stands not here about?

DICKEN

I was within myself, man even now, there is no doubt.
Go softly, make no noise. Give me your foot, Sir John.
Here will I wait upon you till you come out, anon.

DR. RAT

Help Dicken, out alas, I shall be slain among them!

DICKEN

If they give you not the needle, tell them that ye will hang them.
Ware that, how my wenches, have ye caught the fox,
That used to make revel among your hens and cocks?
Save his life yet for his order, though he sustain some pain,
Gog's bread, I am afraid they will beat out his brain.

DR. RAT

Woe worth the hour that I came here,
And woe worth him that wrought this gear.
A sort of drabs and queans have me blessed;
Was ever creature half so evil dressed?
Whoever it wrought, and first did invent it,
He shall, I warrant him, ere long repent it.
I will spend all I have, without my skin,
But he shall be brought to the plight I am in.
Master Bailey I trow, and he be worth his ears,
Will snaffle these murderers and all that them bears,
I will surely neither bite nor sup
Till I fetch him hither this matter to take up.

129 **do . . . rede** follow my advice.

132 **gage** pawn.

144 Doctor Rat probably has his feet still outside the 'hole' in Dame Chat's wall, and his body within, thus the attack upon him is invisible, except for what we hear.

148 **yet . . . order** out of respect for his priesthood.

145–149 Dicken divides his lines between encouraging Dr Rat, calling to Dame Chat and her allies within, and turning to the audience in mock concern.

150 **Woe worth** curse.

153 **evil dressed** badly treated.

156 **without** except.

158 **and he be** if he is.

159 **snaffle** catch up/arrest.

The Fifth Act: The First Scene
(Master Bailey. Doctor Rat. [and Scapethrift.])

BAILEY

I can perceive none other, I speak it from my heart,
But either ye are in all the fault, or else in ye greatest part.

DR. RAT

If it be counted his fault, besides all his griefs,
When a poor man is spoiled and beaten among thieves,
Then I confess my fault herein, at this season;
But I hope you will not judge so much against reason.

BAILEY

And methinks by your own tale, of all that ye name,
If any played the thief, you were the very same.
The women they did nothing, as your words make probation,
But stoutly withstood your forcible invasion.
If that a thief at your window to enter should begin,
Would you hold forth your hand and help to pull him in,
Or you would keep him out? I pray you answer me.

DR. RAT

Marry, keep him out, and a good cause why.
But I am no thief, sir, but an honest learned clerk.

BAILEY

Yea, but who knoweth that when he meets you in the dark?
I am sure your learning shines not out at your nose;
Was it any marvel though the poor woman arose,
And start up, being afraid of that was in her purse?
Methink you may be glad that your luck was no worse.

DR. RAT

Is not this evil enough, I pray you, as you think?

Showing his broken head.

BAILEY

Yea, but a man in the dark, if chances do wink,
As soon he smites his father as any other man,
Because for lack of light discern him he ne can.
Might it not have been your luck, with a spit to have been slain?

DR. RAT

I think I am little better, my scalp is cloven to the brain.
If there be all the remedy, I know who bears the knocks.

BAILEY

By my troth, and well worthy besides to kiss the stocks!
To come in on the back side, when ye might go about,
I know none such, unless they long to have their brains knocked out.

[3] **griefs** injuries.
[4] **spoiled** robbed.
[5] **season** time.
[7] **of . . . name** from everything you have said.
[9] **make probation** prove.
[17] **at** of.
[19] **of** for.
[22–23] **if . . . smites** if his luck is out, might as easily hit.
[27] **If . . . knocks.** If that is your solution (to my complaint), I know who comes off worse.
[28] **By . . . stocks!** And you deserve to sit in the stocks too, by my faith!
[29] **go about** go the long way around (i.e. via the front door).

DR. RAT
Well, will you be so good sir, as talk with Dame Chat,
And know what she intended? I ask no more but that.

BAILEY
Let her be called, fellow, because of Master Doctor,
I warrant in this case, she will be her own proctor.
She will tell her own tale, in metre or in prose,
And bid you seek your remedy, and so go wipe your nose.

The Fifth Act: The Second Scene
(Master Bailey. Chat. Dr. Rat. Gammer. Hodge. Dicken.)

BAILEY
Dame Chat, Master Doctor upon you here complained
That you and your maids should him much misorder.
And taketh many an oath that no word he feigned,
Laying to your charge how you thought him to murder;
And on his part again, that same man sayeth further,
He never offended you in word nor intent.
To hear you answer hereto we have now for you sent.

CHAT
That I would have murdered him, fie on him, wretch;
And evil might he thee for it, our Lord I beseech!
I will swear on all the books that opens and shuts,
He feigneth this tale out of his own guts.
For this seven weeks with me I am sure he sat not down—
Nay ye have other minions in the other end of the town,
Where ye were liker to catch such a blow
Than anywhere else, as far as I know.

BAILEY
Belike then, Master Doctor, yon stripe there ye got not?

DR. RAT
Think you I am so mad, that where I was bet I wot not?
Will ye believe this quean before she hath tried it?
It is not the first deed she hath done and afterward denied it.

CHAT
What man, will you say I broke your head?

DR. RAT
How canst thou prove the contrary?

CHAT
Nay, how provest thou that I did the deed?

DR. RAT
Too plainly, by St. Mary. This proof I trow may serve, though I no word spoke.

Showing his broken head.

33 **fellow** to Scapethrift, his beadle.
34 **proctor** lawyer.
36 **go . . . nose** stop crying.
1–7 Perhaps as a reflection of his status and role in the play as the representative of social order, Master Bailey's opening speech forms a stanza of rhyme royal, rhyming ababbcc.
2 **should . . . misorder** did greatly ill-treat him.
9 **evil . . . thee** evil may he thrive! (i.e. Curse him!)
13 **minions** darlings/drinking companions.
14 **were liker** were more likely.
16 **Belike . . . not?** Perhaps . . . you did not receive your injury there (at Dame Chat's)?
17 **that . . . not?** that I don't know where I was beaten?
18 **tried** proved.

CHAT
Because thy head is broken, was it I that it broke?
I saw thee, Rat, I tell thee, not once within this fortnight.

DR. RAT
No marry, thou sawest me not, forwhy thou hadst no light;
But I felt thee for all the dark, beshrew thy smooth cheeks,
And thou groped me, this will declare, any day this six weeks.

Showing his head.

BAILEY
Answer me to this, Master Rat, when caught you this harm of yours?

DR. RAT
A while ago sir, God he knoweth, within less than these two hours.

BAILEY
Dame Chat, was there none with you, confess i'faith, about that season?
What, woman, let it be what it will, 'tis neither felony nor treason.

CHAT
Yes, by my faith, Master Bailey, there was a knave not far,
Who caught one good fillip on the brow with a door bar,
And well was he worthy as it seemed to me,
But what is that to this man, since this was not he?

BAILEY
Who was it, then? Let's hear.

DR. RAT
Alas sir, ask you that?
Is it not made plain enough by the own mouth of Dame Chat?
The time agreeth, my head is broken, her tongue cannot lie,
Only upon a bare 'nay' she sayeth it was not I.

CHAT
No marry, was it not indeed; ye shall hear by this one thing:
This afternoon a friend of mine for good will gave me warning,
And bade me well look to my roost and all my capons' pens,
For, if I took not better heed, a knave would have my hens.
Then I, to save my goods, took so much pains as him to watch,
And as good fortune served me, it was my chance him for to catch.
What strokes he bare away, or other what was his gains
I wot not, but sure I am, he had something for his pains.

BAILEY
Yet tells thou not who it was.

CHAT
Who? It was a false thief
That came like a false fox my pullen to kill and mischief.

BAILEY
But knowest thou not his name?

25 **forwhy** because.
26 **beshrew** curse.
33 **fillip . . . bar** a blow on the head with a bar used for securing doors.
35 Dame Chat still believes it was Hodge that she caught and hit.
38 **The time agreeth** the time (of the attack) was the same.
46 **other what else** what else were.
49 **my pullen . . . mischief** my poultry . . . distress.

CHAT

I know it, but what then?
It was that crafty cullion Hodge, my Gammer Gurton's man.

BAILEY

Call me the knave hither, he shall sure kiss the stocks.
I shall teach him a lesson for filching hens or cocks.

DR. RAT

I marvel, Master Bailey, so bleared be your eyes.
An egg is not so full of meat as she is full of lies!
When she hath played this prank to excuse all this gear,
She layeth the fault in such a one as I know was not there.

CHAT

Was he not there? Look on his pate, that shall be his witness.

DR. RAT

I would my head were half so whole, I would seek no redress.

BAILEY

God bless you, Gammer Gurton.

GAMMER

God aid you, master mine.

BAILEY

Thou hast a knave within thy house: Hodge, a servant of thine;
They tell me that busy knave is such a filching one,
That hen, pig, goose, or capon, thy neighbour can have none.

GAMMER

By God, cham much amoved to hear any such report.
Hodge was not wont, ich trow, to behave him in that sort.

CHAT

A thievisher knave is not on live, more filching nor more false.
Many a truer man than he has hanged up by the halse.
And thou, his dame, of all his theft thou art the sole receiver;
For Hodge to catch and thou to keep, I never knew none better.

GAMMER

Sir, reverence of your masterdom, and you were out a-door,
Chould be so bold for all her brags to call her arrant whore.
And ich knew Hodge so bad as thou, ich wish me endless sorrow,
And chould not take the pains to hang him up before tomorrow.

CHAT

What have I stolen from thee or thine, thou ill-favoured old trot?

GAMMER

A great deal more, by God's blessed, than ch'ever by thee got,
That thou knowest well, I need not say it.

BAILEY

Stop there, I say,
And tell me here, I pray you, this matter by the way.
How chance Hodge is not here? Him would I fain have had.

51 **cullion** rogue.
53 **filching** stealing.
58 **Look...pate** Look at his head.
62 **such...one** such a thief.
66 **A...live** There's no worse thief alive.
67 **halse** neck.
70 **reverence...chould** with reverence to your honour, if you weren't here, I'd.
72 **And...thou** If I knew Hodge was as bad as you are.
74 **ill-favoured** ugly.
75 **than...got** than I ever got from you.

GAMMER
Alas sir, he'll be here anon; ha' be handled too bad.
CHAT
Master Bailey, sir, ye be not such a fool, well I know,
But ye perceive by this lingering there is a pad in the straw.

Thinking that Hodge's head was broke, and that Gammer would not let him come before them.

GAMMER
Chill show you his face, ich warrant thee; lo now where he is.
BAILEY
Come on fellow, it is told me thou art a shrew, iwis.
Thy neighbours' hens thou takest, and plays the two-legged fox,
Their chickens and their capons too, and, now and then, their cocks.
HODGE
Ich defy them all that dare it say, cham as true as the best.
BAILEY
Wart not thou take[n]within this hour in Dame Chat's hens' nest?
HODGE
Take[n] there? No master, chould not do't for a house-full of gold.
CHAT
Thou, or the devil in thy coat, swear this, I dare be bold!
DR. RAT
Swear me no swearing, quean, the devil he give thee sorrow;
Is not worth a gnat, thou canst swear till tomorrow,
Where is the harm he hath? Show it, by God's bread!
Ye beat him with a witness, but the stripes light on my head!
HODGE
Beat me? Gog's blessed body, chould first, ich trow, have burst thee.
Ich think, and chad my hands loose, callet, chould have crust thee.
CHAT
Thou shitten knave, I trow thou knowest the full weight of my fist!
I am foully deceived unless thy head and my door-bar kissed.
HODGE
Hold thy chat, whore, you cryest so loud can no man else be heard.
CHAT
Well, knave, and I had thee alone, I would surely rap thy costard.
BAILEY
Sir, answer me to this, is thy head whole or broken?
CHAT
Yea, Master Bailey, blessed be every good token.
HODGE
Is my head whole? Ich warrant you, 'tis neither scurvy nor scald.

79 **ha'... bad** he's been too badly painted (by Dame Chat).
81 **ye... straw** you can see from this delaying that there's a toad in the straw. (Some hidden trick or trap.)
82 **where he is** here he comes.
83 **a shrew, iwis** a rogue, indeed.
89 **the... coat** i.e. someone who looks identical to you.
93 **Ye... head!** (You say) that you beat him, before witnesses, yet the scars seem to have landed on my head!
95 **chad... thee** if my hands were untied, I'd have beaten you over the head, whore!
99 **rap thy costard** beat your head.
101 **Yea... token.** That's it... blessed be each piece of good evidence.
102 **scald** scabbed.

What, thou foul beast, does think 'tis either pilled or bald?
Nay, ich thank God, chill not for all that thou maist spend,
That chad one scab on mine arse as broad as thy finger's end.

BAILEY

Come nearer here.

HODGE

Yes, that ich dare.

BAILEY

By our Lady, here is no harm,
Hodge's head is whole enough, for all dame Chat's charm.

CHAT

By Gog's blessed... However the thing he cloaks or smoulders,
I know the blows he bare away, either with head or shoulders.
Camest thou not, knave, within this hour, creeping into my pens,
And there was caught within my house, groping among my hens?

HODGE

A plague both on thy hens and thee! A cart, whore, a cart!
Chould I were hanged as high as a tree and chwere as false as thou art.
Give my Gammer again her washical thou stole away in thy lap!

GAMMER

Yea, Master Bailey, there is a thing you know not on, mayhap?
This drab, she keeps away my good, the devil he might her snare!
Ich pray you that ich might have a right action on her.

CHAT

Have I thy good, old filth, or any such old sow's?
I am as true, I would thou knew, as skin between thy brows.

GAMMER

Many a truer hath been hanged, though thou escape the danger.

CHAT

Thou shalt answer, by God's pity, for this thy foul slander.

BAILEY

Why, what can ye charge her withal? To say so, ye do not well.

GAMMER

Marry, a vengeance to her heart, that whore has stolen my nee'le.

CHAT

Thy nee'le, old witch, how so? It were alms thy skull to knock.
So didst thou say the other day that I had stolen thy cock
And roasted him to my breakfast, which shall not be forgotten,
The devil pull out thy lying tongue and teeth that be so rotten.

GAMMER

Give me my nee'le! As for my cock, chould be very loath
That chould hear tell he should hang on thy false faith and troth.

103 **pilled** plucked/shaved.
107 **charm** curse.
108 **smoulders** smothers (i.e. tries to hide).
109 **he bare away** took away with him.
113 **and chwere** if I were.
114 **washical** 'what's-it-called.' Hodge's failure to remember the word is necessary to maintain the confusion, with Dame Chat still thinking she is being accused of stealing the chicken.
115 **on, mayhap?** of/about, perhaps?
117 **a...her** a proper legal case against.
124 **It were alms** It would be an act of charity.

BAILEY

Your talk is such I can scarce learn who should be most in fault.

GAMMER

Yet shall ye find no other wight save she, by bread and salt!

BAILEY

Keep ye content awhile, see that your tongues ye hold,
Methinks you should remember this is no place to scold,
How knowest thou, Gammer Gurton, Dame Chat thy nee'le had?

GAMMER

To name you, sir, the party, chould not be very glad.

BAILEY

Yea, but we must needs hear it, and therefore say it boldly.

GAMMER

Such one as told the tale, full soberly and coldly,
Even he that looked on, will swear on a book,
What time this drunken gossip my fair long nee'le up took,
Dicken, master, the Bedlam, cham very sure ye know him.

BAILEY

A false knave, by God's pity; ye were but a fool to trow him.
I durst adventure well the price of my best cap
That when the end is known, all will turn to a jape.
Told he not you that, besides, she stole your cock that tide?

GAMMER

No master, no indeed, for then he should have lied,
My cock is, I thank Christ, safe and well a-fine.

CHAT

Yea, but that ragged colt, that whore, that Tib of thine,
Said plainly thy cock was stolen, and in my house was eaten.
That lying cut is lost that she is not swinged and beaten;
And yet, for all my good name it were a small amends.
I pick not this gear, hearest thou, out of my fingers' ends,
But he that heard it told me, who thou of late didst name:
Dicken, whom all men knows; it was the very same.

BAILEY

This is the case: you lost your nee'le about the doors,
And she answers again, she has no cock of yours.
Thus in your talk and action, from that you do intend,
She is whole five mile wide from that she doth defend.
Will you say she hath your cock?

GAMMER

No, marry, sir, that chill not!

131 **no other wight** no one else (to blame).

135 **To ... glad.** I'd rather not tell you who it was (who told me).

141 **trow** believe.

142 **durst adventure** dare to bet.

144 **that tide?** at the same time?

146 **a-fine** in conclusion.

149 **is ... swinged** is damned if she is not thrashed (and so taught a lesson).

150–151 **And ... ends** And even that would be little recompense for my lost reputation. I'm not making this up, you know!

157 **She ... defend** i.e. she is responding to a charge far away from/completely different to the accusation you are making.

BAILEY
Will you confess her nee'le?

CHAT
Will I? No sir, I will not!

BAILEY
Then there lieth all the matter.

GAMMER
Soft, master, by the way,
Ye know she could do little, and she could not say nay.

BAILEY
Yea, but he that made one lie about your cock stealing
Will not stick to make another, what time lies be in dealing.
I ween the end will prove this brawl did first arise
Upon no other ground but only Dicken's lies.

CHAT
Though some be lies, as thou belike have espied them,
Yet other some be true, by proof I have well tried them.

BAILEY
What other thing beside this, Dame Chat?

CHAT
Marry sir, even this:
The tale I told before, the self-same tale, it was his;
He gave me, like a friend, warning against my loss,
Else had my hens be stolen each one, by God's Cross!
He told me Hodge would come, and in he came indeed;
But as the matter chanced, with greater haste than speed,
This truth was said, and true was found, as truly I report.

BAILEY
If Doctor Rat be not deceived, it was of another sort.

DR. RAT
By God's mother, thou and he be a couple of subtle foxes.
Between thou and Hodge, I bear away the boxes.
Did not Dicken appoint the place where thou shouldst stand to meet him?

CHAT
Yes, by the Mass, and if he came, bade me not stick to spit him.

DR. RAT
God's sacrament, the villain knave hath dressed us round about!
He is the cause of all this brawl, that dirty shitten lout!
When Gammer Gurton here complained, and made a rueful moan,
I heard him swear that you had gotten her needle that was gone;
And this to try he further said he was full loath, howbeit
He was content with small ado to bring me where to see it.
And where ye sat, he said full certain, if I would follow his rede,
Into your house a privy way he would me guide and lead,

161 **she...nay** it's easy for her just to say no.
163 **Will...dealing** Won't hesitate to tell another (lie) when lies are so abundantly traded (as they are now).
164 **ween** believe.
175 **it...sort** it happened rather differently.
177 **I...boxes** I took the blows.
179 **not...him** not to hesitate to skewer him.
180 **hath...about** has fooled the lot of us.
184 **this to try** to prove this.

And where ye had it in your hands, sewing about a clout,
And set me in the back hole, thereby to find you out.
And whiles I sought a quietness, creeping upon my knees,
I found the weight of your door-bar for my reward and fees.
Such is the luck that some men gets while they begin to mell
In setting at one such as were out, minding to make all well.

HODGE

Was not well blessed, Gammer, to scape that scour? And chad been there,
Then chad been dressed belike as ill, by the Mass, as gaffer vicar!

BAILEY

Marry, sir, here is a sport, alone I looked for such an end.
If Dicken had not played the knave, this had been soon amend.
My Gammer here he made a fool, and dressed her as she was,
And goodwife Chat he set to school, till both parts cried 'Alas!'
And Dr. Rat was not behind, whiles Chat his crown did pare.
I would the knave had been stark blind, if Hodge had not his share.

HODGE

Cham meetly well sped already amongs, cham dressed like a colt;
And chad not had the better wit, chad been made a dolt.

BAILEY

Sir knave, make hast Dicken were here, fetch him wherever he be.

CHAT

Fie on the villain; fie, fie, that makes us thus agree!

GAMMER

Fie on him, knave, with all my heart, now fie and fie again!

DR. RAT

'Now, fie on him!' may I best say, whom he hath almost slain.

BAILEY

Lo, where he cometh at hand, belike he was not far.
Dicken, here be two or three thy company cannot spare.

DICKEN

God bless you, and you may be blessed, so many all at once.

CHAT

Come, knave, it were a good deed to geld thee, by Cock's bones!
Seest not thy handiwork? Sir Rat, can ye forbear him?

DICKEN

A vengeance on those hands light, for my hands came not near him.
The whoreson priest hath lift the pot in some of these ale wives' chairs,

193 **while . . . out** for meddling in trying to reconcile folk who have fallen out.

194–195 **Was . . . vicar!** Weren't you lucky to escape that assault, Gammer? If you'd been there, you'd have been treated as badly as Master Vicar was!

196 **alone . . . end** only I foresaw that it would turn out this way.

197 **played . . . amend** acted the trickster, this would soon have been sorted out.

198–201 **dressed . . . share** revealed her as she is (a fool), and he taught Dame Chat a lesson too, until each party cried 'alas'. And Dr Rat wasn't left out either, when Chat split his scalp. I imagine Dicken would have been blind if he couldn't arrange for Hodge to be tricked too.

202–203 **Cham . . . dolt.** I've been appropriately treated among the rest; I've been treated like a fool; and if I hadn't been too smart, I'd have been made to look an idiot.

204 **Sir knave** addressed to Scapethrift.

209 **two . . . spare** two or three people who can't wait to see you.

211 **geld** castrate.

212 **forbear him?** resist hitting him?

That his head would not serve him, belike, to come down the stairs.

BAILEY

Nay, soft, thou maist not play the knave and have this language too,
If thou thy tongue bridle a while, the better maist thou do.
Confess the truth as I shall ask, and cease awhile to fable.
And for thy fault I promise thee, thy handling shall be reasonable.
Hast thou not made a lie or two, to set these two by the ears?

DICKEN

What if I have? Five hundred such have I seen within these seven years;
I am sorry for nothing else but that I see not the sport
Which was between them when they met, as they themselves report.

BAILEY

The greatest thing, Master Rat, ye see how he is dressed?

DICKEN

What devil need he be groping so deep in good-wife Chat's hens' nest?

BAILEY

Yea, but it was thy drift to bring him into ye briars.

DICKEN

God's bread, hath not such an old fool wit to save his ears?
He showeth himself herein, ye see, so very a cox,
The cat was not so madly allured by the fox
To run into the snares was set for him, doubtless,
For he leapt in for mice, and this Sir John for madness.

DR. RAT

Well, and ye shift no better, ye losel, lither and lazy,
I will go near for this to make ye leap at a daisy.
In the king's name, Master Bailey, I charge you set him fast.

DICKEN

What, fast at cards or fast on sleep? It is the thing I did last.

DR. RAT

Nay, fast in fetters, false varlet, according to thy deeds.

BAILEY

Master Doctor, there is no remedy, I must entreat you, needs
Some other kind of punishment.

DR. RAT

Nay, by all hallows,
His punishment, if I may judge, shall be naught else but the gallows!

213–215 **A . . . stairs.** Curse those hands, for I never touched him. The bastard priest had probably drunk so much in an alehouse that he could not get down the stairs (and so fell and broke his own head).

218 **cease . . . fable** stop lying for a moment.

219 **handling** treatment.

220 **set . . . ears** set Gammer and Dame Chat to fighting.

224 **how . . . dressed?** what has happened to him?

226 **it . . . briars** it was your trick that got him into that mess.

228 **so . . . cox** so true a dupe.

229–231 **The . . . madness** The cat (in the well-known story of *Reynard the Fox*) wasn't tricked so well into the fox's trap as this priest was tricked (by me), for the cat at least was lured by the thought of mice, whereas this priest was lured simply by his own idiocy.

232–233 **and . . . daisy** if you can say no better for yourself than this, you good-for-nothing, lazy wretch, I will try to ensure you hang (proverbially 'to leap at a daisy'—picking up on Dicken's reference to leaping, above).

235 **What . . . last.** What, 'fast at cards' (to 'stick' or go without a card in a round) or 'fast asleep'? That (sleeping) was what I was doing just now (when you found me).

236 **varlet** knave.

237–238 **I . . . punishment** I must beg you, we need to find some other form of punishment.

238 **all hallows** all the saints.

BAILEY

That were too sore: a spiritual man to be so extreme.

DR. RAT

Is he worthy any better, sir, how do ye judge and deem?

BAILEY

I grant him worthy punishment, but in no wise so great.

GAMMER

It is a shame, ich tell you plain, for such false knaves [t']entreat.
He has almost undone us all, that is as true as steel;
And yet for all this great ado cham never the near my nee'le.

BAILEY

Canst you not say anything to that, Dicken, with least or most?

DICKEN

Yea, marry, sir, thus much I can say well: the needle is lost!

BAILEY

Nay, canst not thou tell which way that nee'le may be found?

DICKEN

No, by my fay, sir, though I might have an hundred pound.

HODGE

Thou liar lick-dish, didst not say the nee'le would be gitten?

DICKEN

No, Hodge, by the same token you were that time beshitten
For fear of Hobgoblin, you wot well what I mean.
As long as it is since, I fear me yet ye be scarce clean.

BAILEY

Well, Master Rat, you must both learn and teach us to forgive.
Since Dicken hath confession made, and is so clean shrive,
If ye to me consent, to amend this heavy chance,
I will enjoin him here some open kind of penance.
Of this condition, where ye know my fee is twenty pence,
For the bloodshed, I am agreed with you here to dispense;
Ye shall go quit, so that ye grant the matter now to run
To end with mirth among us all, even as it was begun.

CHAT

Say yea, Master Vicar, and he shall sure confess to be your debtor,
And all we that be here present will love you much the better.

DR. RAT

My part is the worst, but since you all here-on agree,
Go even to, Master Bailey, let it be so for me.

240 **That...extreme.** That would be too severe, a religious man (priest) to be so extreme.

242 **wise** way.

243 **for...[t']entreat** to plead on behalf of such lying rogues.

246 **with least or most?** i.e. in any way?

249 **fay** faith.

250 **Thou...gitten?** You lying scrounger, didn't you say the needle should be found?

252–253 **you...clean** you'd shat your trousers through fear of the bogeyman, so you'd no idea what I was saying. Even so long after the event, I'm not sure you've washed it all off.

255 **clean shrive** absolved.

256 **to...chance** to put right this sorrowful story.

257 **open** public.

258–261 **Of...begun.** Provided that you agree to drop the charges (about the bloodshed you have suffered)—for which you know I'd charge a 20 pence fee to pursue. (So I'll be losing money, but you'll be saving some.) I'll let you off (the charge of breaking into Dame Chat's house), provided you agree to let the matter end happily, just as it began.

BAILEY
How sayest thou, Dicken, art content this shall on me depend?

DICKEN
Go to, Master Bailey, say on your mind, I know ye are my friend.

BAILEY
Then mark ye well: to recompense this thy former action,
Because thou hast offended all, to make them satisfaction
Before their faces, here kneel down, and as I shall thee teach,
For thou shalt take an oath o[n] Hodge's leather breech.
First, for Master Doctor, upon pain of his curse,
Where he will pay for all, thou never draw thy purse,
And when ye meet at one pot, he shall have the first pull,
And thou shalt never offer him the cup but it be full.
To Goodwife Chat thou shalt be sworn, even on the same wise,
If she refuse thy money once, never to offer it twice;
Thou shalt be bound by the same here, as thou dost take it,
When thou maist drink of free cost, thou never forsake it.
For Gammer Gurton's sake, again sworn shalt thou be,
To help her to her nee'le again, if it do lie in thee;
And likewise be bound by the virtue of that,
To be of good bearing to Gib her great cat.
Last of all, for Hodge, the oath to scan,
Thou shalt never take him for fine gentleman.

HODGE
Come on, fellow Dicken, chall be even with thee now.

BAILEY
Thou wilt not stick to do this, Dicken, I trow?

DICKEN
No, by my father's skin, my hand down, I lay it;
Look as I have promised, I will not deny it.
But Hodge, take good heed now thou do not beshite me.

And g[i]ve him a good blow on the buttocks.

HODGE
Gog's heart, thou false villain, dost thou bite me?

BAILEY
What Hodge, doth he hurt thee ere even he begin?

HODGE
He thrust me into the buttock with a bodkin or a pin!
I say, Gammer, Gammer!

GAMMER
How now, Hodge, how now?

265 **Go even to** go on then.
268 **mark ye well** pay good attention.
272–275 **First . . . pull** a jovial 'punishment': when Dr Rat is paying for drinks, Dicken must never offer to pay; but when they share a tankard, the doctor must drink first.
276 **on . . . wise** in the same fashion (i.e. with the same seriousness).
281 **if . . . thee** if you are able.
284 **scan** summarize/complete.
285 **never . . . gentleman** never mistake him for (a) fine gentleman.
287 **stick** hesitate.
293 **bodkin** knife.
294.1 **how now?** what is it?

HODGE

God's malt, Gammer Gurton!

GAMMER

Thou art mad, ich trow.

HODGE

Will you see? The devil, Gammer!

GAMMER

The devil, son? God bless us!

HODGE

Chould ich were hanged, Gammer!

GAMMER

Marry, see, ye might dress us.

HODGE

Chave it, by the Mass, Gammer!

GAMMER

What, not my nee'le, Hodge?

HODGE

Your nee'le, Gammer, your nee'le!

GAMMER

No fie, dost but dodge?

HODGE

Cha' found your nee'le, Gammer, here in my hand be it.

GAMMER

For all the loves on earth, Hodge, let me see it.

HODGE

Soft, Gammer.

GAMMER

Good Hodge.

HODGE

Soft, ich say, tarry awhile.

GAMMER

Nay, sweet Hodge, say truth, and do not me beguile.

HODGE

Cham sure on it, ich warrant you; it goes no more astray.

GAMMER

Hodge, when I speak so fair, wilt still say me nay?

HODGE

Go near the light, Gammer, this; well, in faith good luck;
Chwas almost undone, 'twas so far in my buttock.

GAMMER

'Tis mine own dear nee'le, Hodge, sickerly I wot!

HODGE

Cham I not a good son, Gammer, cham I not?

GAMMER

Christ's blessing light on thee, hast made me forever!

297.1 **Marry . . . us.** Watch out, you might persuade us to do it (hang you). Gammer still does not see what Hodge is shouting about and pointing to in his backside.

299.1 **dost but dodge?** are you joking?

304 **it . . . astray** it'll not be lost again.

308 **sickerly I wot!** Truly I know!

HODGE
Ich knew that ich must find it, else chould a had it never.

CHAT
By my troth, Gossip Gurton, I am even as glad
As though I mine own self as good a turn had.

BAILEY
And I, by my conscience, to see it so come forth,
Rejoice so much at it as three nee'les be worth.

DR. RAT
I am no whit sorry to see you so rejoice.

DICKEN
Nor I much the gladder for all this noise.
Yet say, 'Grammercy, Dicken', for springing of the gin.

GAMMER
Grammercy, Dicken, twenty times; oh how glad cham!
If that chould do so much, your masterdom to come hither,
Master Rat, Goodwife Chat, and Dicken together:
Cha but one halfpenny, as far as ich know it,
And chill not rest this night till ich bestow it.
If ever ye love me, let us go in and drink.

BAILEY
I am content, if the rest think as I think?
Master Rat, it shall be best for you if we so do,
Then shall you warm you and dress yourself too.

DICKEN
Soft sirs, take us with you, the company shall be the more,
As proud comes behind, they say, as any goes before.
But now, my good masters, since we must be gone
And leave you behind us, here all alone;
Since at our last ending thus merry we be,
For Gammer Gurton's needle's sake, let us have a plaudity.

Finis Gurton.

Pursued and Allowed, etc.

318 **say...gin** say 'thank you, Dicken' (to me) for flushing out the quarry.
320 **your masterdom** i.e. Bailey.
323 **till...it** until I've spent it (on drinks for you all).
327 **dress** bandage yourself.
333 **a plaudity** a round of applause.
333.1 **Pursued and Allowed** examined and permitted to be printed.

Respublica

(1553–1554)

NICHOLAS UDALL

(1504–1556)

THE PLAYWRIGHT

Nicholas Udall (probably pronounced 'Yoo-dawl' or 'Yoo-dale') was born in Southampton in 1504 and educated at Winchester College and Corpus Christi College, Oxford. He became fellow of the college and university lecturer in Logic before moving into school-teaching as headmaster of first Eton and then Westminster, a post he held until his death on 23 December 1556. He also held a number of clerical appointments, including a period as a canon of Windsor. During the reign of Henry VIII he gained a reputation as a writer and translator, especially of Erasmian texts. In 1542 his translation of the *Apophthegms* of Erasmus (a collection of maxims and exemplary anecdotes) was printed by Richard Grafton, and in the following year he completed *The Paraphrases of Erasmus* (a translation of Erasmus's text of the New Testament) at the request of the reform-minded Queen Catherine Parr.

Udall's association with drama and pageant-writing was longstanding. In 1533 he had collaborated with the scholar John Leland to produce pageants for the coronation of Anne Boleyn. His *Thersites* (*c.*1537) was probably performed at court, and in 1538 he produced another, unknown play for the household of the evangelical Archbishop of Canterbury, Thomas Cranmer. His *Ralph Roister Doister*, a braggart comedy in the style of the classical playwright Terence, was probably performed before the young Edward VI in 1552. And he has also been linked with two other surviving mid-Tudor interludes, *Jack Juggler* and *Jacob and Esau*, although the attribution in each case is uncertain. He is associated with *Respublica* (a play performed at the court of Mary I, as its title page announces, during the first Christmas of her reign (1553–4), largely on stylistic grounds (the play echoes *Ralph Roister Doister* in a number of its linguistic features), although there is also some external evidence to support the attribution (see Walker, *Politics of Performance*, pp. 167–72). Certainly Udall, despite his apparent reformist sympathies, wrote a number of entertainments for the court of the Catholic Mary, and enjoyed considerable favour from the Queen, as a warrant of 13 December 1554 testifies. This document, issued in Mary's name, observes that 'our dearly beloved Nicholas Udall' had 'at sundry seasons convenient heretofore showed—and mindeth hereafter to show—his diligence in setting forth of dialogues and interludes before us for our regal disport and recreation'.

THE PLAY

The Plot of *Respublica* is relatively simple. Lady Respublica, already almost destitute at the start of the play, and looking for sound guidance, appoints as her chief minister someone she thinks is the good counsellor Policy (a concept roughly equating to 'political shrewdness'), but who is in reality the vice Avarice. Once appointed, Avarice finds jobs for his fellow vices Insolence, Oppression, and Adulation ('flattery'), who respectively pretend to be the political virtues Authority, Reformation, and Honesty. In these guises, the rogues plunder the commonwealth for their own profit, impoverishing the poor commons (represented by People) in the process, while pretending to bring about reform and reformation. Only with the arrival of the 'four daughters of God', Misericordia (Mercy), Veritas (Truth), Justicia (Justice), and Pax (Peace), is the deception discovered, and the vices are arrested, to be punished by the goddess Nemesis, announced as a figure for Mary Tudor. The latter brings about the restitution of the plundered goods to their former owners and the restoration of good order and prosperity.

As this plot summary suggests, *Respublica*, in its basic shape, is a story of the fall and regeneration of a central protagonist. It thus has something in common with earlier moralities such as *Everyman* or *Mankind*. But, like Skelton's *Magnificence* (*c.*1519) or John Bale's *King Johan* (1538), the play uses that framework to explore a deeper and more controversial political allegory, revisiting recent history in the guise of moral instruction.

Respublica, as the Prologue suggests, was almost certainly performed at court by child actors during the first Christmas of the reign of Mary I. Like *Gammer Gurton's Needle*, the play assumes a rather elitist disdain for the education and manners of non-courtly figures, here epitomized by People, a comic figure, who speaks with a thick rustic accent and tends to mispronounce any words of more than two syllables (hence he repeatedly refers to Respublica as 'Rice-Puddingcake'). But, unlike Gammer Gurton and her circle, People is an essentially affectionate portrait of an honest, if unschooled small farmer, who is shrewd enough to see through the lies of the vices when his social superiors cannot, and is punished and exiled by the villains as a result.

The first Christmas of Mary's reign was an anxious one for the Queen and her advisors. Her regime was less than six months old, and had been established in the teeth of an abortive Protestant coup aimed at crowning Lady Jane Grey in her stead. Mary was thus hardly secure on the throne, yet she was attempting to restore traditional Catholic beliefs and practices to the Church and considering how best to reverse the spoliation of Church property brought about by Henry VIII's dissolution of the monasteries and the Edwardian reformation. She was doing so, moreover, in the knowledge that a sizeable minority of her subjects would have preferred a Protestant sovereign, and most of the political nation had a vested interest in maintaining the status quo, as they had profited in lands and income from the dissolution. On one level, the events of the play tell the story of the seven years of the protestant boy-king Edward VI's reign from Mary's viewpoint, representing them as a period of famine and deprivation, in which self-seeking ministers had fleeced the country in the name of religious and social reform (hence the most direct and brutal of the vices personified, Oppression, takes the pseudonym 'Reformation'). The details of the vices' crimes also echo closely the economic events of the Edwardian period. The exportation of precious commodities for profit, avoidance of customs duties and taxes, the debasement of the coinage, and the forced exchange of episcopal lands and houses under political pressure: all of these things are a barely concealed commentary on the excesses of real mid-Tudor economic mismanagement and corruption (see Walker, *Politics of Performance*, pp. 181–8). The play is thus a daring political allegory as well as a lively example of the morality genre. It displays the flexibility of the form as a vehicle for exploring particular contemporary issues as well as timeless moral and religious truths.

FURTHER READING

Carpenter, Sarah, '*Respublica*', in Thomas Betteridge and Greg Walker, eds., *The Oxford Handbook of Tudor Drama* (Oxford: Oxford University Press, 2012), 514–30.
Edgerton, W. L., *Nicholas Udall* (New York: Twayne Publishers, 1965).
Greg, W. W., ed., *Respublica*, EETS original series, 226 (Oxford: Oxford University Press, 1952 for 1946).
Hunt, Alice, *The Drama of Coronation: Medieval Ceremony in Early Modern England* (Cambridge: Cambridge University Press, 2008), especially 111–145.
Rutledge, Douglas F., '*Respublica*: Rituals of Status Elevation and the Political Mythology of Mary Tudor', *Medieval and Renaissance Drama in England* 5 (1991), 55–68.
Schell Edgar T. and J. D. Shuchter, eds., *English Morality Plays and Interludes* (New York: Holt, Rinehart and Winston, 1969).
Walker, Greg, *The Politics of Performance in Early Renaissance Drama* (Cambridge: Cambridge University Press, 1998).

A Merry interlude entitled Respublica, made in the Year of Our Lord 1553, and the first year of the most prosperous reign of our most gracious sovereign, Queen Mary the First.

The Parts and Names of the Players:

THE PROLOGUE, a poet,
AVARICE, alias Policy, the Vice of the play,
INSOLENCE, alias Authority, the chief gallant,
OPPRESSION, alias Reformation, another gallant,
ADULATION, alias Honesty, the third gallant,
PEOPLE, representing the poor Commonty,
RESPUBLICA
MISERICORDIA, VERITAS, JUSTICIA, PAX (four ladies),
NEMESIS, the goddess of redress and correction, a goddess.

THE PROLOGUE

First, health and success, with many a good New Year,
Wished unto all this most noble presence here!
I have more, t'entreat you of gentle sufferance
That this our matter may have quiet utterance.
We that are th'actors have ourselves dedicate
With some Christmas device your spirits to recreate,
And our poet trusteth the thing we shall recite
May without offence the hearers' minds delight.
Indeed, no man speaketh words so well fore-pondered
But the same by some means may be misconstered;
Nor nothing so well meant but that by some pretence
It may be wrong interpreted from the author's sense.
But, let this be taken no worse than it is meant,
And I hope nor we nor our poet shall be shent.
But now of th'argument to touch a word or twain;
The name of our play is *Respublica*, certain;
Our meaning is (I say not as by plain story,
But, as it were in figure, by an allegory)
To show that all commonweals' ruin and decay
From time to time hath been, is, and shall be alway,
When Insolence, Flattery, Oppression,
And Avarice have the rule in their possession.
But, though these vices by cloaked collusion
And by counterfeit names hiden their abusion,
Do reign for a while to commonweal's prejudice,
Perverting all right and all order of true justice,
Yet Time trieth all, and Time bringeth truth to light,
That wrong may not ever still reign in place of right.
For, when pleaseth God such commonweals to restore
To their wealth and honour wherein they were afore,
He sendeth down his most tender compassion
To cause Truth go about in visitation.
Verity, the daughter of sage old Father Time,
Showeth all as it is, be it virtue or crime.
Then doth Justice all such as commonweal oppress,
Tempered with Mercy endeavour to suppress,
With whom anon is linked tranquillity and Peace,
To commonweal's joy and perpetual increase.

Commonty the common people.
four ladies The four 'Daughters of God' referred to in Psalm 84:11–12 ('Mercy and truth have met each other: justice and peace have kissed. Truth is sprung out of the earth: and justice hath looked down from heaven').
2 **presence here** i.e. all those present.
6 **device** clever, inventive entertainment.
9 **well fore-pondered** carefully thought about in advance.
10 **misconstered** misconstrued.
11 **nothing** nothing is.
14 **nor** neither.
14 **shent** shamed/punished.
15 **of...twain** to tell you a little about the plot of the play.
19 **commonweals'** commonwealths'/states'.
23 **cloaked collusion** concealed conspiracy.
24 **hiden** hide.
32 **visitation** a tour of inspection (specifically that conducted by bishops in their diocese to investigate and correct abuses).
33 **sage** wise.

But, shall boys (saith some now) of such high
matters play?
No, not as discussers, but yet the book doth say
'*Ex ore infantium perfecisti Laudem*',
For when Christ came riding into Jerusalem,
The young babes with th'old folk cried out all and some,
'Blessed be the man that in the Lord's name doth come!'
So, for good England's sake this present hour
and day,
In hope of her restoring from her late decay,
We children to you old folk, both with heart and voice,
May join all together to thank God and rejoice
That he hath sent Mary, our sovereign and queen,
To reform th'abuses which hitherto hath been;
And that ills which long time have reigned uncorrect,
Shall now forever be redressed with effect.
She is our most wise and most worthy Nemesis,
Of whom our play meaneth t'amend that is amiss.
Which to bring to pass that she may have time and
space,
Let us, both young and old, to God commend her
grace.
Now, if you so please, I will go, and hither send
That shall make you laugh well if ye abide th'end.

Finis.

Actus Primi. Scena Prima.

AVARICE

Now God-i-god everychone, both great and small,
From highest to lowest God-i-god to you all!
God-i-god... what should I say, even or morrow?
If I mark how the day goeth God give me sorrow!
But God-i-god each one, twenty and twenty score,
Of that ye most long for, what would ye have more?
Ye must pardon my wits, for I tell you plain,
I have a hive of humble bees swarming in my brain,
And he that hath the compass to fetch that I must fetch,
I may say, in counsel, had need his wits to stretch.
But now, what my name is, and what is my purpose,
Taking you all for friends, I fear not to disclose.
My very true unchristian name is Avarice,
Which I may not have openly known in no wise,
For though to most men I am found commodious,
Yet to those that use me, my name is odious.
For who is so foolish that the evil he hath wrought
For his own behoof he would to light should be
brought?
Or, who had not rather his ill doings to hide,
Than to have the same bruited on every side?
Therefore, to work my feat I will my name disguise,
And call my name Policy instead of Covetise.
The name of Policy is praised of each one,
But to rake grummle seed, Avarice is alone.
The name of Policy is of none suspected,
Policy is ne'er of any crime detected,
So that under the name and cloak of Policy
Avarice may work facts and scape all jealousy.
And now is the time come that, except I be a beast,
E'en to make up my mouth and to feather
my nest:
A time that I have waited for a great long space.
And now may I speed my purpose, if I have grace,
For, hear ye, sirrah; our great, grand-lady-mother,
Noble dame Respublica, she and none other,
Of the offals, the refuse, the rags, the parings,
The baggage, the trash, the fragments, the sharings,
The odd ends, the crumbs, the driblets, the chippings,
The patches, the pieces, the brokelets, the drippings,

41 ***'Ex... Laudem'*** 'Out of the mouth of infants and of sucklings thou hast perfected praise' (Matthew 21:16).
58 **hither send that** send out to you those who.
58 **abide** wait until.
Actus... Prima Act One, Scene One.
1 **God-i-god everychone** 'God give you good everyone!' Avarice mocks the lower-class, colloquial dialect which People will use later.
3 **even or morrow** evening or morning? Avarice voices the indifference to the times of the working day characteristic of Vice characters.
4 **If... sorrow!** God curse me if I know (or care) what time of day it is!
5 **twenty... score** twenty times twenty.
9 **the compass... fetch** the ability to plan what I must plan.
10 **in counsel** confidentially, just between us.
14 **I... wise** I don't want known publicly at all.
18 **behoof** benefit.
19 **ill** evil.
20 **bruited... side** talked about everywhere.
21 **work my feat** achieve my ends.
22 **Covetise** is here used as a synonym of Avarice.
24 **But... alone** But to bring in money, Avarice is uniquely skilled. ('Gromwell (lithospermum or stone-seed plant) seed', is a slang term for money.)
28 **work... jealousy** achieve great deeds and avoid suspicion.
29 **except... beast** unless I'm (as stupid as) a beast.
30 **make... mouth** provide (good) food for myself.
33 **sirrah** a variant of 'sir' used for servants and social inferiors.
38 **brokelets** broken pieces.

The fleetance, the scrapings, the wild waifs and strays,
The skimmings, the gubbins of booties and preys,
The gleanings, the casualties, the blind escheats,
The forging of forfeits, the scape of extracts,
Th'excess, the waste, the spoil, the superfluities,
The windfalls, the shreddings, the fleecings, the petty fees,
With a thousand things mo which she may right well lack,
Would fill all these same purses that hang at my back;
Yea and ten times as many mo bags as these,
Which should be but a flea-biting for her to lese,
That, if I may have the grace and hap to blind her,
I doubt not a sweet lady I shall find her.
To her it were nothing, yet many a small maketh a great,
And all thing would help me, whatever I may get.
Full little know men the great need that I am in.
Do not I spend daily of that that I do win?
Then age cometh on, and what is a little gold
To keep a man by dread that is feeble and old?
No man therefore blame me, though I would have more.
The world waxeth hard, and store, they say, is no sore.
Now the chance of thieves, in good hour be it spoken...
Out alas, I fear I left my coffer open!
I am surely undone; alas where be my keys?
It is gone that I have sweat for all my live days!
Woe worth all whoreson thieves, and such covetous knaves
That for their winding sheet would scrape men out of their graves! [*Exit*]

Actus Primi. Scena Secunda.
(Avarice, Insolence, Oppression, Adulation.)
Adulation, Insolence, Oppression intrant cantantes.

ADULATION
O noble Insolence, if I could sing as well,
I would look in heaven among angels to dwell.

INSOLENCE
Sing? How do I sing, but as other many do?

ADULATION
Yes, an angel's voice ye have to harken unto.

INSOLENCE
Yea, but what availeth that to high dignity?

OPPRESSION
By His arms, not a whit, as far as I can see.

INSOLENCE
Or what helpeth that thing to set a man aloft?

OPPRESSION
By His wounds, not a straw, so have I told you oft.

ADULATION
No, but ye are one of such goodly personage,
Of such wit and beauty, and of sage parentage,
So excellent in all points of every art...

INSOLENCE
Indeed, God and nature in me have done their part.

ADULATION
That if ye will put yourself forward to the most,
Ye may throughout the whole land rule all the roost.
How say you, Oppression? Is it not even so?

OPPRESSION
Thou sayst sooth, Adulation, so moot I go.
If he were disposed to take the charge in hand
I warrant him achieve to rule all the whole land.

ADULATION
Lo, master Insolency, ye hear Oppression?

INSOLENCE
I thank both him and thee, good Adulation,

39 **fleetance** flotsam/driftwood.
40 **gubbins...preys** left-over fragments of booty and spoils.
41 **gleanings...escheats** gatherings, tips and casual earnings, and secret confiscations.
42 **extracts** bribes paid to avoid fines.
45 **mo** more.
48 **lese** lose.
49 **hap** luck.
54 **Do...win?** Do I not spend everything I earn each day?
58 **waxeth** grows.
58 **store...sore** proverbial: having savings is no bad thing.
59–60 **Now...open!** Now, as for the possibility of thieves... ('In a good hour be it spoken' is a talismanic phrase intended to bring good luck, such as the modern 'touch wood'. But the mere thought of thieves prompts Avarice to imagine he has left his money chest unlocked at home, hence his cry of 'Out (oh no!), alas!')
62 **all...days** all the days of my life.
63 **Woe worth** A curse on!
s.d. The play follows neo-classical practice in listing at the outset of each scene the names of the characters appearing in the scene, regardless of when they actually enter the action.
intrant cantantes enter singing.
6 **His** Christ's (an oath).
7 **set...aloft** promote a man to high position.
16 **sayst sooth** speak (the) truth.
16 **moot I go** may I walk/prosper (a variant of the talismanic 'may I be blessed').
17 **charge** task/responsibility.

And long have I dreamed of such an enterprise,
But how or where to begin I cannot devise.

OPPRESSION
Wherefore serve friends, but your enterprise to allow?

ADULATION
And then must you support them, as they must maintain you.

OPPRESSION
And wherefore do friends serve, but to set you in?

ADULATION
Ye shall have all my help, whenever ye begin.

INSOLENCE
But we may herein nothing attempt in no wise
Without the counsel of our founder, Avarice.

ADULATION
He must direct all this gear, by His holy ghost.

OPPRESSION
For he knoweth what is to be done in each coast.
He knoweth where and how that money is to be had;
And yonder he cometh, methinketh more than half mad!

Enter Avarice.

Actus Primi. Scena Tertia. (Avarice, Insolence, Oppression, Adulation.)

AVARICE
It was a fair grace that I was not undone clean;
Yet my key was safe locked under nine locks, I ween.
But e'en as against such a thing my heart will throb,
I found knaves about my house ready me to rob.
There was such tooting, such looking, and such prying,
Such harkening, such stalking, such watching, such spying:
'What would ye, my masters?' 'We look after a cat.'
'What make ye hereabout?' 'We have smelled a rat.'
Now a wheal on such noses, thought I, by and by,
That so quickly can scent where hidden gold doth lie.
But had I not come when I did, without all fails,
I think they had digged up my walls with their nails.

INSOLENCE
Let us speak to him and break his chafing talk.

AVARICE
Such greediness of money among men doth walk,
That have it they will, either by hook or by crook.

OPPRESSION
Let us call to him, that he may this way look.

AVARICE
Whether by right or by wrong, in faith some care not.
Therefore catch that catch may hardily, and spare not.

ADULATION
All hail, our founder and chief master Avarice!

AVARICE
The devil is a knave, and I catch not a fleece...

ADULATION
When ye see your time, look this way your friends upon.

AVARICE
I doubt not to scamble and rake as well as one.

ADULATION
Here be that would fain be disciples of your art.

AVARICE
I will not be behind to get a child's part.

ADULATION
Now if ye have done, I pray you look this way back.

AVARICE
Who buzzeth in mine ear so? What, ye saucy Jack?

ADULATION
Are ye yet at leisure with your good friends to talk?

AVARICE
What, clawest thou mine elbow? Prattling merchant, walk!
Ye flatterabundus, you! You fleering clawback, you!

23 **Wherefore...allow?** What are friends for except to help in your schemes?
29 **gear** business.
30 **in each coast** in all places.
1 **It...clean** It was lucky I wasn't completely ruined.
2 **I ween** I'm sure.
3 **my...throb** Avarice claims an almost supernatural instinct, a throbbing of his heart, when thieves are around.
5 **tooting** peeping.
9 **a wheal...noses** i.e. a pox on them! A scabrous nose was taken as a sign of syphilis.
13 **break...talk** interrupt his anxious muttering.
14 **among...walk** is so common.
15 **by...crook** one way or another.
18 **catch that...not** i.e. I'd better do what I can, boldly, without delay.
20 **and...fleece** if I don't win some spoils.
22 **I...one.** I'm sure I'll fight and scrape up (coins) as well as anyone.
23 **Here...be** Here are folk who are eager to be.
24 **I...part.** I'll not be late, and so only get a small portion (of whatever is available to steal).
26 **buzzeth** mutters insistently
28 **Prattling merchant, walk!** Be off with you, prattling fellow!

You 'the crow is white' you! You 'the swan is black' you!
You 'John, hold my staff', you! You 'what is the clock?', you!
You *ait aio*, you; you *negat negoi* you!

ADULATION
I marvel you speak to me in such fashion!

AVARICE
Why troublest thou me, then, in my contemplation?

ADULATION
I came of right good love, not minding you to let.

AVARICE
Thou ne'er cam'st to any man of good love yet!

ADULATION
And these men's minds it was I should so do.

AVARICE
As false wretches as thine own self, and falser too!

INSOLENCE AND OPPRESSION
We have been loving to you and faithful alway.

AVARICE
For your own profits then, and not mine, I dare say;
And e'en very, you three it was, and others none,
That would have robbed me not yet half an hour gone!

INSOLENCE, OPPRESSION [AND] ADULATION
We never robbed any man, later or rather.

AVARICE
Yes, many a time and oft your own very father!

OPPRESSION
And to you have we born hearty favours alway.

AVARICE
And I warrant you hanged for your labours one day.

OPPRESSION
Adulation, even as our god we have always honoured you.

AVARICE
And e'en as your god I have aye succoured you.

OPPRESSION
We call you our founder, by all Holy Hallows!

AVARICE
Founder me no foundering, but beware the gallows!

INSOLENCE
I pray you, leave these words and talk friendly at last.

AVARICE
Content at your request, my fume is now well past;
And in faith, what saith our friend Adulation?

ADULATION
I wonder at your rough communication,
That ye would to me use words of such vehemence.

AVARICE
Faith man, I spake but even to prove your patience,
That if thou hadst grunted or stormed thereat...

ADULATION
Nay, few times do I use such lewd manner as that.

AVARICE
Come, shake hands, and forever we two be at one.

ADULATION
As for grudge, in me there shall never remain none.

AVARICE
Now, master Insolence, to your ghostly purpose.

INSOLENCE
We accorded a matter to you to disclose.

AVARICE
I understand all your agreement and accord,
For I lay in your bosoms when ye spake the word;
And I like well the advice of Oppression,
And eke of Flattery for your progression.

INSOLENCE
If there were matter whereon to work, I care not.

AVARICE
Ye shall have matter enough, be doing, spare not!

INSOLENCE
What, to come to honour and wealth for us all three?

AVARICE
Ah, then ye could be well content to leave out me!

INSOLENCE
No, for I know ye can for yourself well provide.

AVARICE
Yea, that I can, and for twenty hundred beside.

ADULATION
Oh, would Christ, good founder, ye would that thing open!

[32] Avarice's insults suggest (correctly) that Adulation is a flattering yes-man. Flatterandibus is mock Latin for 'full of flattery'; fleering clawback, 'mocking pesterer', the crow is white, etc and *ait aio....negat nego* ('what he says, I say, what he denies, I deny') are all proverbial suggestions that he'll agree to anything, however preposterous, to win favour.
[35] **not...let** not intending to hinder you.
[39] **alway** always.
[41] **e'en very** truly.
[43] **rather** earlier.
[49] **by...Hallows!** By all the holy saints!
[52] **fume** rage.
[56] **prove** test.
[61] **ghostly purpose** spiritual intentions (ironic).
[66] **eke** also.
[72] **beside** more.
[73] **ye...open!** Tell us about that!

AVARICE
Bones, knave, wilt thou have it ere it can be spoken?
OPPRESSION
For the Passion of God, tell it us with all speed!
AVARICE
By the Cross, not a word; here is haste made indeed.
INSOLENCE
Yes, good, sweet Avarice, despatch and tell at once.
AVARICE
Nay then, cut my throat; ye are fellows for the nonce!
Will ye have a matter before it can be told?
If ye will have me tell it, ye shall your tongues hold.
Whist! Silence! Not a word. Mum! Let your clatter cease.
Are ye with child to hear, and cannot hold your peace?
So sir, now: Respublica, the lady of estate,
Ye know now lately is left almost desolate.
Her wealth's decayed, her comfort clean ago,
And she at her wits ends what for to say or do.
Fain would she have succour and easement of her grief,
And highly advance them that would promise relief.
Such as would warrant her spirits to revive
Might mount to high estate, and be most sure to thrive.
INSOLENCE
so!
ADULATION
Well said!
OPPRESSION
Hah!
AVARICE
What is this? Hum? hah? hum?
INSOLENCE
On! Forth!
ADULATION
Go to!
OPPRESSION
Tell on!
AVARICE
Body of me!
ADULATION
Mum!
AVARICE
What say ye?
INSOLENCE
Hake.
ADULATION
Tuff.
OPPRESSION
Hem.
AVARICE
Who haken tuffa hum?
What say ye?
OPPRESSION
Nothing.
INSOLENCE
Not a word.
AVARICE
Nor you neither?
ADULATION
Mum.
AVARICE
Did ye speak or not?
INSOLENCE
No.
OPPRESSION
No.
ADULATION
No.
AVARICE
Nor yet do not?
INSOLENCE
No.
OPPRESSION
No.
ADULATION
No.
OPPRESSION
No.
INSOLENCE
No.
ADULATION
No.
AVARICE
That, that, that, that, that, that!
Sir, I intend Dame Respublica t'assail.
And so to creep in to be of her counsel.

74 **Bones, knave** By God's bones, you rogue.
78 **for the nonce** for the instant (i.e. 'you want everything now').
81 **Whist! . . . Mum!** all variants of 'hush!'.
82 **Are . . . hear** i.e. bursting, on the point of giving birth with eagerness and cannot be silent.
85 **clean ago** completely gone.
89 **Such . . . warrant** Who might promise.
92 **Forth!** Get on with it!
92.1 **Go to!** Forget it!
92.1 **Body of me!** a parodic oath.
93.1 **Hake** a cough.
93.1 **Tuff** Pah!
97 **That . . . that!** exclamations.
99 **to . . . counsel** to be her advisor.

I hope well to bring her in such a paradise
That herself shall sue me to have my service.
Then shall I have time and power to bring in you three.

OPPRESSION
Do this out of hand, founder, and first speak for me.
Bring me in credit, that my hand be in the pie,
And I get not elbow room among them, let me lie!

AVARICE
Nay, see all, Oppression, this eager elf,
Be not since more covetous than Covetous' self.
Soft, be not so hasty, I pray you, sir, soft awhile.
You will over the hedge ere ye come at the stile.

OPPRESSION
I would fain be shouldering and rumbling
among them.

AVARICE
Nay, I will help javels as shall wrong them.

ADULATION
I pray you, good founder, let not me be the last.

AVARICE
Thou shalt be well placed where to thrive very fast.

ADULATION
I thank you, master Avarice, with all my heart.

AVARICE
And when thou art in place, see thou play well
thy part.
When ye claw her elbow, remember your best friend,
And let my commendations be ever at one end.

ADULATION
I warrant you.

INSOLENCE
And what, shall I be left clean out?

AVARICE
No sir, ye shall be chief to bring all things about.
Ye shall amongst us have the chief preeminence,
And we to you, as it were, owe obedience.
Ye shall be our leader, our captain, and our guide.
Then must ye look aloft, with th'hands under the side.
I shall tell Respublica ye can best govern.
Be not ye then squeamish to take in hand the stern.
Then shall we assist you as friends of perfect trust,
To do and to undo and command what ye lust.
And when you have all at your own will and pleasure,
Part of your livings to your friends ye may measure,
And punish the proudest of them that will resist.

OPPRESSION
He that once winceth shall feel the weight of my fist.

ADULATION
Yea, we must all hold and cleave together like burrs.

AVARICE
Yea, see ye three hang and draw together like furs.

OPPRESSION
And so shall we be sure to get store of money,
Sweeter than sugar!

AVARICE
Sweeter than any honey.

INSOLENCE
Very well spoken, this gear will right well accord.

ADULATION
Did not I say ye were worthy to be a lord?

AVARICE
I will make Insolence a lord of high estate.

INSOLENCE
And I will take upon me well, both early and late.

OPPRESSION
But Insolence, when ye come to the encroaching
of lands,
Ye may not take all alone into your hands.
I will look to have part of goods, lands, and plate.

INSOLENCE
Ye shall have enough, each body after his rate.

ADULATION
I must have part too, ye must not have all alone.

INSOLENCE
Thou shalt be laden till thy shoulders shall crack
and groan.

ADULATION
I pray you, let me have a good lordship or two.

102 **bring in** find jobs for.
103 **out of hand** without hesitation.
106 **eager elf** naughty child.
108 **Soft** Hush, calm down.
109 **You . . . stile.** You want to be over the hedge before you come to the gate.
111 **javels** rogues.
117 **let . . . end** at the beginning or end of every sentence you speak, praise and recommend me.
123 **look . . . side** i.e. adopt a proud posture, perhaps with hands on hips.
125 **take . . . stern** take the tiller in hand (with bawdy innuendo).
127 **what ye lust** whatever you want.
129 **measure** hand out/divide among.
131 **winceth** kicks out (like an unruly horse).
133 **furs** thieves.
136 **this . . . accord** this business will suit us well.
140 **encroaching of lands** gathering up and enclosing of public land for private gain.
142 **plate** gold and silver.
143 **each . . . rate** everyone according to their fair share.

INSOLENCE
Respublica shall feed thee till thou wilt say 'Hoo!'
ADULATION
And I must have good manor places two or three.
INSOLENCE
But the chief and best lordship must remain to me.
OPPRESSION
Mass, and I will look to be served of the best,
Or else some folk somewhere shall sit but in small rest.
INSOLENCE
I must have castles and towns in every shire.
ADULATION
And I change of houses, one here and another there.
INSOLENCE
And I must have pastures and townships and woods.
OPPRESSION
And I must needs have store of gold and other goods.
INSOLENCE
And I must have change of farms and pastures for sheep,
With daily revenues my lusty port for to keep.
AVARICE
I would have a bone here rather than a groat,
To make these snarling curs gnaw out each other's throat.
Here be eager whelps, lo! To it boy, box him, Ball!
Poor I may pick straws, these hungry dogs will snatch all.
OPPRESSION
Each man snatch for himself; by God's I will be sped.
AVARICE
Lack who lack shall, Oppression will be corn-fed.
Is not dame Respublica sure of good handling
When these whelps, ere they have it, fall thus to scambling?
And me, their chief founder, they have since forgot.
INSOLENCE
Thou shalt have gold and silver enough to thy lot,
Respublica hath enough to fill all our laps.
ADULATION
Then I pray you, sir, let our founder have some scraps.
AVARICE
Scraps, ye doltish lout! Feed you your founder with scraps?
If you were well served, your head would have some raps!
ADULATION
I spake of good will.
INSOLENCE
Nay, fight not, good Avarice.
AVARICE
What any of us getteth, thou hast the chief price.
AVARICE
Then whatever ye do ye will remember me?
INSOLENCE, OPPRESSION [AND] ADULATION
Yea!
AVARICE
Well, so do then, and I forgive you all three.
INSOLENCE
But, when do we enter every man his charge?
AVARICE
As soon as I can spy Respublica at large
I will board her, and, I trow, so win her favour
That she shall hear me, and pay well for my labour.
Then will I commend the virtues of you three,
That she shall pray and wish under our rule to be.
Therefore, from this hour be ye all in readiness.
OPPRESSION
Doubt not of us; thou seest all our greediness.
INSOLENCE
If it be at midnight, I come at the first call.

They go forward, one after other.

ADULATION
Do but whistle for me, and I come forth withal.
AVARICE
That is well spoken. I love such a toward twig.

He whistleth.

ADULATION
I come, founder!
AVARICE
That is mine own good spaniel, Rig.
And come on back again; all three, come back again.

147 **Hoo!** Stop/enough!
148 **manor places** manor houses.
150 **Mass** By the Mass!
157 **my lusty...keep** to sustain my flamboyant lifestyle.
160 **box him, Ball!** Bring him down, Ball (a dog-fighting call).
162 **by...sped** I'll prosper, by God.
165 **scambling** fighting among themselves.
173 **chief price** best reward/portion.
177 **at large** free/in public.
178 **trow** swear.
186 **toward twig** eager/willing youth.

INSOLENCE
Our founder calleth us back. Oppression return then a-main!

Actus Prima. Scena Quarta
(Avarice, Adulation, Insolence, Oppression.)

INSOLENCE AND OPPRESSION
Come on, sirs, all three. And first to you, best be-trust,
What is your brainpan stuffed withal, wool or sawdust?
ADULATION
Why so?
AVARICE
What is your name?
ADULATION
Flattery.
AVARICE
E'en so, just?
ADULATION
Yea, or else Adulation, if you so lust.
Either name is well known to many a body.
AVARICE
An honest mome! Ah ye dolt, ye lout, ye noddy!
Shall Respublica hear your commendation
By the name of Flattery or Adulation?
Or when ye commend me to her, will ye say this:
'Forsooth, his name is Avarice or Covetise'?
And you that should have wit, is't your discretion
Bluntly to go forth, and be called Oppression?
And you, Insolence, do ye think it would well frame
If ye were presented to her under that name?
INSOLENCE
I thought nothing thereupon, by my holy dame!
OPPRESSION
My mind was another way, by my Christendom!
ADULATION
That thing was least part of my thought, by Saint Denys.
AVARICE
No, marry, your minds were all on your half-penny.
But my masters, I must on mine honesty pass,
And not run on head, like a brute beast or an ass;
For is not Oppression each-where sore hated?
And is not Flattery openly rehated?
And am not I, Avarice, still cried out upon?
ADULATION
Yes, I could have told you that a great while agone,
But I would not displease you.
AVARICE
And you, Insolence,
I have heard you ill spoken of a great way hence.
ADULATION
In my conscience, the devil himself doth love you!
AVARICE
But, changing your ill name, fewer shall reprove you,
As I mine own self, where my name is known
Am right sore assailed to be overthrown;
But, doing as I will now counterfeit my name,
I speed all my purposes, and yet escape blame.
INSOLENCE
Let us then have new names, each man without delay.
AVARICE
Else will some of you make good hanging stuff one day
OPPRESSION
Thou must new-Christen us.
INSOLENCE
First, what shall my name be?
AVARICE
Faith, sir, your name shall be monsieur Authority.
OPPRESSION
And for me what is your determination?
AVARICE
Marry, sir, ye shall be called Reformation.
ADULATION
Now, I pray you, devise for me an honest name.
AVARICE
Thou art such a beast, I cannot, for very shame.
ADULATION
If ye think good, let me be called Policy.
AVARICE
Policy? A rope ye shall! Nay, Hypocrisy!
ADULATION
Fie, that were as slanderous a name as Flattery.
AVARICE
And I keep for myself the name of Policy.
But, if I devise for thee, wilt thou not shame me?
ADULATION
Nay, I will make thee proud of me, or else blame me.

189 **a-main** at once.
1 **best be-trust** my best-trusted one.
3.1 **E'en so, just?** Is it now, really?
6 **mome** idiot.
6 **noddy** fool.
13 **would well frame** be well done.
18 **marry** indeed.
18 **half-penny** profits.
22 **openly rehated** hunted down.

AVARICE
Well then, for this time thy name shall be honesty.
ADULATION
I thank you Avarice... Honesty! Honesty!
AVARICE
'Avarice' ye whoreson? 'Policy' I tell thee!
ADULATION
I thank you Policy. Honesty! Honesty!
How say you, Insolence, I am now Honesty!
AVARICE
We shall at length have a knave of you, Honesty.
Said not I he should be called monsieur Authority?
ADULATION
O friend Oppression... Honesty! Honesty!
AVARICE
'Oppression'? Hah? Is the devil in thy brain?
Take heed, or in faith ye are Flattery again.
Policy, Reformation, Authority.
ADULATION
Hypocrisy, Defamation, Authority.
AVARICE
'Hypocrisy', hah? 'Hypocrisy', ye dull ass?
ADULATION
Thou namedst Hypocrisy even now, by the Mass!
AVARICE
'Policy', I said. 'Policy', knave: 'Policy'!
Now, say as I said.
ADULATION
Policy, knave, Policy.
AVARICE
And what callest thou him here?
ADULATION
Defamation.
AVARICE
I told thee he should be called 'Reformation'.
ADULATION
Very well.
AVARICE
What is he now?
ADULATION
Deformation.
AVARICE
Was ever the like ass born in all nations?
ADULATION
A pestell on him, he comes of the Asians!

AVARICE
Come on, ye shall learn to *sol fa*: 'Reformation'.
Sing on now: 'Re'.
ADULATION
Re.
AVARICE
'Refor'.
ADULATION
Reformation!
AVARICE
'Policy, Reformation, Authority.'
ADULATION
Policy, Reformation, Honesty.
AVARICE
In faith, ye ass, if your tongue make any mo trips
Ye shall both be Flattery and have on the lips.
And now, monsieur Authority, against I you call,
Ye must have other garments, and so must
ye all,
Ye must for the season counterfeit gravity.
INSOLENCE [AND] OPPRESSION
Yes, what else?
ADULATION
And I must counterfeit Honesty.
AVARICE
And I must turn my gown in and out, I ween,
For these gaping purses may in no wise be seen.
I will turn it e'en here. Come, help me Honesty.
ADULATION
Here at hand.
AVARICE
Why, how now? Play the knave, Honesty?
Help, what dost thou now?
ADULATION
I counterfeit honesty.
AVARICE
Why then, come thou; help me, my friend
Oppression...
What help call you that?
OPPRESSION
Fit for your discretion.
AVARICE
O, I should have said, help, Sir Reformation.
OPPRESSION
Yea, marry sir, that is my nomination.

66 **pestell** pestilence/plague.
67 ***sol fa*** sing out, note for note.
72 **have** have a punch.
73 **against** in preparation for when I call you.

80.1 A signal for some physical business. Adulation tries to pick his purses.
86 **afore close** wrapped around at the front.

AVARICE
And when you are in your robe, keep it afore close.

OPPRESSION
I pray you, master Policy, for what purpose?

AVARICE
All folk will take you, if they peep under your gown,
For the veriest caitiff in country or town.
Now go, and when I call, see that ye ready be.

INSOLENCE
I will.

OPPRESSION
And I will.

ADULATION
And so will I, Honesty. *Exit.*

AVARICE
Well, now will I depart hence also for a space,
And to board Respublica wait a time of grace.
Wherever I find her a time convenient,
I shall say and do that may be expedient.

Exit Avarice.

Actus Secundi. Scena Prima.
(Respublica.)

RESPUBLICA
Lord, what earthly thing is permanent or stable,
Or what is all this world but a lump mutable?
Who would have thought that I from so florent estate
Could have been brought so base as I am made of late?
But, as the waving seas do flow and ebb by course,
So all things else do change to better and to worse.
Great cities and their fame in time do fade and pass;
Now is a champion field where noble Troy was.
Where is the great empire of the Medes and Persians?
Where be th'old conquests of the puissant Grecians?
Where Babylon, where Athens, where Corinth so wide?
Are they not consumed with all their pomp and pride?
What is the cause hereof man's wit cannot discuss,
But of long continuance the thing is found thus.
Yet by all experience thus much is well seen,
That in commonweals, while good governors have been,
All thing hath prospered, and where such men do lack,
Commonweals decay, and all things do go back.
What marvel then, if I, wanting a perfect stay,
From most flourishing wealth be fallen in decay?
But like as by default quick ruin doth befall,
So may good government at once recover all.

Intrat Avarice cogitabundus et ludibundus.

Actus Secundi. Sena Secunda.
(Avarice, Respublica.)

AVARICE
Alas my sweet bags, how lank and empty ye be.
But, in faith and truth, sirs, the fault is not in me.

RESPUBLICA
Well, my help and comfort, O Lord, must come from thee.

AVARICE
And my sweet purses here, I pray you all see, see
How the little fools gasp and gape for grummle seed.

RESPUBLICA
If it be thy will, Lord, send some redress with speed.

AVARICE
But in faith, good sweet fools, it shall cost me a fall,
But I will shortly fill you, and stop your mouths all.

RESPUBLICA
O that it were my hap on friendly friends to light . .

AVARICE
Ha ha! Who is that same that speaketh yonder in sight?
Who is't? Respublica? Yea, by the Mary mass!

RESPUBLICA
Then might I be again as well as ere I was.

AVARICE
Hide up these pipes. Now I pray God she be blind!
I am half afraid lest she have an eye behind.
We must now change our copy: oh Lord, how I fray,
Lest she saw my toys and heard what I did say.

89 **veriest caitliff** truest villain.
2 **a lump mutable** a piece of changeable matter (as opposed to the unchanging celestial realm).
3 **florent** flourishing.
8 **champion** open, flat ('champaign').
19 **wanting . . . stay** lacking a true support/buttress.

s.d. ***Intrat . . . ludibundus.*** Enter Avarice, acting as if he is thinking.
9 **light** fall.
13 **pipes** bags/wallets.
15 **copy** manner.
15 **fray** am afraid.

RESPUBLICA
Is there no good man that on me will have mercy?
AVARICE
Remember now, my name is master Policy;
All thing, I tell you, must now go by Policy.
RESPUBLICA
Hark, methink I hear the name of Policy.
AVARICE
Who calleth, Conscience? Here am I, Policy.
RESPUBLICA
I pray you come to me if you be Policy.
AVARICE
Yea forsooth, yea forsooth, my name is Policy.
RESPUBLICA
I am sore decayed through default of Policy.
AVARICE
Yea, most noble Respublica, I know that well,
And do more lament it than any tongue can tell.
For, and if good Policy had had you in hand,
Ye had now been the wealthiest in any land.
But good Policy hath long been put to exile.
RESPUBLICA
Yea, God wot, ye have been barred from me a great while.
AVARICE
Yea, I have been put back, as one clean off-shaken,
And what can a man do, till he be forth taken?
RESPUBLICA
Well I feel the lack of your helping hand, by the Rood.
AVARICE
Alack, noble lady, I would I could do you good.
RESPUBLICA
Yes Policy, ye might amend all if you lust.
AVARICE
Yea faith, I durst put myself to you of trust;
But there be enough that for you could shift make.
RESPUBLICA
Yet none like to you, if you would it undertake,
And I will put myself wholly into your hand:
Metal, grain, cattle, treasure, goods, and lands.
AVARICE
Well, I will take some pain; but this to you be known,
I will do it, not for your sake, but for mine own.
RESPUBLICA
How say ye that, Policy?
AVARICE
This to you be known,
I will do all for your sake, and not for mine own.
RESPUBLICA
I thank you Policy.
AVARICE
Nay, I thank you, lady.
And I trust ere long to ease all your malady.
Will ye put yourself now wholly into my hands?
RESPUBLICA
Order me as you will.
AVARICE
Treasure, goods, and lands?
RESPUBLICA
Yea, every whit.
AVARICE
Well, I thank you once again.
But now, that you may think my dealing true and plain,
And because one cannot do so well as many,
Ye must associate me with mo company;
And first, by my will, ye shall set up Honesty.
RESPUBLICA
Marry, with all my very heart; but where is he?
AVARICE
Very hard to find; but I think I could fetch him.
RESPUBLICA
Call him straightways hither; see that nothing let him.
AVARICE
It were best if I shall go fetch men for the nonce,
To make but one voyage, and bring them all at once.
RESPUBLICA
Whom more than him?
AVARICE
Ye must 'stablish Authority.
RESPUBLICA
That must needs be done.
AVARICE
And eke Reformation.
We four will rule things of another fashion.

24 **default** lack.
30 **wot** knows.
32 **forth taken** picked up (again).
33 **Rood** Holy Cross.
34 **Alack** Alas.
35 **lust** desired.
37 **there ... make** there are sufficient people who could help you.
56 **let** hinders.
57 **men ... nonce** suitable men for the purpose.
61 **of another fashion** in a different fashion (to the current ruinous state of affairs).

RESPUBLICA
Policy, I pray you go fetch all these straightway.
AVARICE
Yes, for this your present case may bide no delay,
I will go and come with all festination.
RESPUBLICA
I like well this trade of administration:
Policy for to devise for my commodity;
No person to be advanced but Honesty,
Then Reformation, good wholesome laws to make,
And Authority see the same effect may take;
What commonweal shall then be so happy as I?
For this, I perceive, is the drift of Policy.

Intrat Avarice ad ducens Insolence, Oppression, and Adulation.

And behold where he is returned again since.
He showeth himself a man of much diligence.

Actus Secundi. Scena Tertia (Adulation, Avarice, Respublica, Insolence, Oppression.)

ADULATION
I will do her double service to another.
AVARICE
Ye double knave you, will ye never be other?
ADULATION
She shall have triple service of me, Honesty.
AVARICE
Ye quadruple knave! Will ye ne'er use modesty?
Thou drunken whoreson, dost thou not see nor perceive
Where Respublica stands, ready us to receive?
RESPUBLICA
What talk have they yonder among themselves together?
ADULATION
I have spied her now; shall I first to her thither?
AVARICE
Soft, let me present you.
RESPUBLICA
I ween they be in fear.
Policy, approach, and bring my good friends near.
AVARICE
Come on, my dear friends, and execute with good will
Such office as each of you shall be put until.
Dame Respublica it is that for you hath sent.
Come on, friends, I will you unto her grace present.
INSOLENCE [AND] OPPRESSION
To serve her we are prest, with heart and whole intent.
AVARICE
Madam, I have brought you these men for whom I went.
RESPUBLICA
Policy, I thank you; ye have made speedy speed,
Therefore ye be double welcome, and welcome friends indeed.
AVARICE
Madam, your grace to serve we all are fully bent.
ADULATION
And madam, ye shall find me double diligent.
RESPUBLICA
That is spoken of a good heart: but who be ye?
ADULATION
Forsooth, madam, my name is master Honesty.
RESPUBLICA
Honesty? Well said!
AVARICE
Madam, this is Honesty.
ADULATION
Yea forsooth, and please your grace, I am Honesty.
AVARICE
Madam he is for you; on my word regard him.
RESPUBLICA
Yes, and with large preferment I will reward him.
ADULATION
I thank your grace; and I will for you take such pain
That ere I deserve one, ye shall give me twain.
AVARICE
Honesty your tongue trippeth.
RESPUBLICA
How said ye, 'take such pain...'?
ADULATION
That ere ye give me one, I will deserve twain.
By your licence, madam, to take away this mote.

64 **festination** haste.
ad ducens leading in.
1 **double...another** twice as much service as anyone else. The vices play on the double entendre of 'service' as sexual intercourse.
12 **until** unto.
15 **prest** ready.
19 **bent** determined.
31 **take...mote** Adulation pretends to find a speck of dust on Respublica's coat.
32 **see a wem** permit a blemish.

AVARICE
Nay, Honesty will not see a wem on your coat.
Now unto you I commend Reformation.
RESPUBLICA
Of him is no small need now in this nation.
OPPRESSION
Well, now that ye bid me abuses to redress,
I doubt not all enormities so to repress
As shall redound to your wealth and honour at length.
RESPUBLICA
Thereto shall Authority aid you with his strength.
AVARICE
Yea, for Authority to govern is most fit.
INSOLENCE
If ye, dame Respublica, do me so admit,
I doubt not to hamper the proudest of them all.
RESPUBLICA
And among you destroy Avarice...?
ADULATION
Hem!
INSOLENCE ET OPPRESSION
We shall.
RESPUBLICA
Vanquish Oppression and Adulation,
For those three have nigh wrought my desolation.
AVARICE
Hem, sirs, hem there, keep your gowns close afore, I say;
Have ye forgotten now what I told you one day?
There is another too that would be chased hence.
RESPUBLICA
Who is that?
AVARICE
Lucifer's son, called Insolence.
RESPUBLICA
Ye say truth, and many naughty ones mo than he.
INSOLENCE AND OPPRESSION
If ye dare trust us...
INSOLENCE
All...
OPPRESSION
All shall reformed be.
RESPUBLICA
I thank you, and I trust you for my maintenance
To be administer for your good governance.
INSOLENCE
Then without fear or care ye may yourself repose.
OPPRESSION
And let us alone with all such matters as those.
RESPUBLICA
Then I leave you here on our affairs to consult.

Exit Respublica.

INSOLENCE
When you please in God's name.
OPPRESSION
We must both sift and bolt.
ADULATION
She is gone.
AVARICE
Well then, sirs, let us make no delay,
But about our market depart each man his way.
ADULATION
Nay, first let us sing a song to lighten our hearts.
AVARICE
Then are ye like, for me, to sing but of three parts.
Can Avarice's heart be set on a merry pin,
And see no gain no profit at all coming in?
INSOLENCE
We shall have enough to drive away all sorrow.
AVARICE
Then sing we on, bon voyage, and Saint George thee borrow.

Cantent, 'Bring ye to me and I to ye' etc, et sic exeant.

Actus Terci[i]. Scena Prima. (Respublica.)

RESPUBLICA
The good hope that my misters have put me in
To recover ruin that in me doth begin,
Hath so recomforted my spirits and mine heart
That I feel much easement of my great grief and smart.
Now I do less wonder that lost men, life to save,
Far from land do labour against the roaring wave,
For hope I see hath mighty operation
Against the mortal sting of drooping desperation.
Now, if I might but hear what Policy hath wrought,

s.d. **Hem!** Be careful!
52 **administer** governor/administrator.
s.d. **sift and bolt** sieve and search.
61 **be...pin** be so joyful.
64 **thee borrow** save you.

s.d. ***Cantent...exeant*** They sing...and so exit.
1 **misters** officers.
4 **smart** pain.
7 **mighty operation** great effectiveness.

Or some one good thing that my friends to pass had brought,
I would put no doubts, but all thing should be well.
Lo, where cometh Honesty! He will the truth tell.

Actus Terci[i]. Scena Secunda (Adulation, Respublica.)

ADULATION
Three hundred pound by year, and a good manor place.
Well, it is meetly well in so short time and space.
More will come right shortly; this gear doth gaily walk!
Bones, here is Respublica, what use I such talk?
I seek Lady Respublica.

RESPUBLICA
Lo, I am here.
And welcome, Honesty: what do my friends most dear?

ADULATION
Certes, madam, we rest nor day nor night, nor hour
To practice and travail for your wealth and honour.
But, O Lord, what a prudent man is Policy;
What a deep head he hath to devise and to spy.

RESPUBLICA
He is fine indeed.

ADULATION
Also Reformation:
How earnest he is in his operation.

RESPUBLICA
I think of him no less.

ADULATION
Now then, Authority,
The stoutest in his office that ever I did see.
I will no further praise them madam, for doubtless
They far surmount all praise that my tongue can express.
Ye may bless the time ye met with such as they be.
And I do my poor part.

RESPUBLICA
I doubt not, Honesty,
And condign reward shall ye all have for your pain.

ADULATION
I have scarce an house wherein myself to maintain.

RESPUBLICA
Honesty shall not lack.

ADULATION
I do not crave nor care.
We shall take but scraps and refuse that ye may spare.
We will not encroach the people's commodity;
We shall take only that may come with honesty.

RESPUBLICA
Christ's blessing have ye. But lo, yonder cometh People.

ADULATION
I had thought as soon to have met here Paul's steeple!

Actus Terci[i]. Scena Tercia. (People, Adulation, Respublica.)

PEOPLE
Where's Rice-Puddingcake? I pray God she be in heal.

ADULATION
Who? Rice-Puddingcake?

PEOPLE
Yea, *alese dicts* 'Common-weal'.

ADULATION
I know her not.

PEOPLE
Mass, you liest valsely in your heart!
She is this way, chew art a false harlot, you art!

ADULATION
I know 'Respublica'.

PEOPLE
Yea, marry, where is she?

ADULATION
She is busy now.

PEOPLE
Mass, ere Ich go chill her zee,
For this way she came.

[3] **this gear ... walk** this business prospers nicely.
[4] **what ... talk?** Why am I talking like this?
[7] **Certes** Certainly.
[7] **nor** neither.
[8] **practice and travail** work and toil.
[10] **deep head** profound mind.
[26] **Paul's steeple** the Steeple of St Paul's Cathedral.

[1] **Rice-Puddingcake** a mispronunciation of 'Respublica'.
[1] **in heal** in good health.
[2.1] ***alese dicts*** also known as.
[3.1] **valsely** falsely. People's rustic accent pronounces f's as v's.
[4] **chew art** you are.
[6.1] **ere ... zee** before I go, I'll see her.

RESPUBLICA

Let my People come to me.

ADULATION

God forbid else! Come on People, is this same she?

PEOPLE

Yea, Malkin, ist.

RESPUBLICA

People, what would you with me now?

PEOPLE

Marry, mistress madam, my lady, how do you?

RESPUBLICA

Even so so, People, I thank you with all my heart,
And I hope for better.

PEOPLE

Then let poor volk ha' zome part,
Vor we ignoram people, whom Ich do perzent,
Were ne'er zo i-poled, zo wrong[ed], and zo i-torment.
Lord Jiss Christ when he was y-pounced and y-pulled,
Was ne'er zo i-trounced as we have been of years late.

ADULATION

How so? who hath wrought to you such extremity?

PEOPLE

Nay, to tell how zo passeth our captivity.

RESPUBLICA

It passeth any man's imagination.

PEOPLE

You zay zooth, it passeth any man's Madge Mason;
Vor we think ye love us as well as ere ye did.

RESPUBLICA

My love towards you, my People, cannot be hid.

PEOPLE

And we think ye would fain we poor volk did well.

RESPUBLICA

And better than ere ye did, if how I could tell.

PEOPLE

And we think ye would we zelly poor volk should thrive.

RESPUBLICA

Yea, doubtless, as any like creature alive.

ADULATION

What need ye of her good will towards you to doubt?

PEOPLE

Peace thou, with zorrow, and let me tell my tale out.

RESPUBLICA

Say on, my good People; let me hear all your mind.

PEOPLE

Bum vay, we ignoram people beeth not zo blind
But we perceive there falleth of corn and cattle,
Wool, sheep, wood, lead, tin, iron, and other metal,
And of all things enough vor good and bad,
And as comedians vor us as ere we had.
And yet the price of everything is zo dear,
As though the ground did bring vorth no such thing nowhere.

RESPUBLICA

Indeed, I have enough if it be well ordered,
But few folk the better if I be miss-ordered.

PEOPLE

Nay, now you zay zooth, e'en thik same way goeth the hare:
Ill ordering 'tis hath made both you and we threadbare.

ADULATION

What naughty folks were they; can you their names rede?

PEOPLE

Yea, that I's can, a whole mass of 'em for a need.
There is virst and voremost Flattery, Ill a' thee,
As slipper, sugar-mouthed whore-cop as can be,
He fleereth on you, and beareth us fair in hand,
And there-while robbeth both you and we of our land.
Then cometh the sour, rough, crabbed child, Oppression;
He tumbleth whom a' lust out of possession.
Then is there the third, I's cannot 'member his name.

9 **Yea, Malkin, ist.** Yes, by Malkin [diminutive of Matilda], that's her.
11 **Even so so** Well enough/as you see me.
13 **we . . . perzent** we ignorant (i.e. unlearned) people, whom I represent.
14 **i-poled** fleeced (overtaxed)
15 **y-pounced and y-pulled** punched and pulled.
18 **captivity** People means 'capacity'
20 **zooth** truth.
24 **if . . . tell** if I knew how to.
25 **zelly** silly (simple/innocent).
28 **Peace** Be quiet.
30 **Bum vay** a colloquial contraction of 'by my faith'.
31 **there falleth . . . had** there is produced . . . as much as ever there was.
34 **comedians** he means 'commodious' (sufficient).
39 **thik** this.
39 **same . . . hare** now you're heading in the right direction!
41 **rede** advise me.
43 **Ill a' thee** Curse him.
44 **As . . . whore-cop** As slippery a sweet-talking bastard.
45 **fleereth . . . hand** mocks you and tricks us.
47 **crabbed child** ill-tempered youth.
48 **He . . . possession** He throws whoever he likes off their land.

What call ye thik same fellows, God give them a shame,
That beeth still climbing up aloft for premidence
And cannot be content with their state?

ADULATION

Insolence?

PEOPLE

Yea, thik same is he, 'Zorryless'!

RESPUBLICA

Nay, 'Insolence'.

PEOPLE

Well, he'll rule all the roost alone, cha heard it zaid,
Or else make the best of them aghast and afraid.
And zuch good men as could and would order you well,
He is so copped he nill not suffer [them] to mell.
If they nill not be ruled, then hence, out of favour!
Yea and perhaps corrupt 'em zore vor their labour.
Yet he and th'other twain work all after the vice
Of.. cha forget t'one name; t'other is Covetise.
Thik hungry whore-cop hath such a policate wit,
That he teacheth them to rake and scrape up each whit.
And zo these vour (but it shall never come out for me),
Volk think will never cease to spoil both you and we.
Vor sometime they face us, and call us peason knaves,
And zwareth God's bones they will make us all slaves.
Therevor chwas desirance your lady-dom to zee,
And to give you warning.

RESPUBLICA

Hear ye this, Honesty?

PEOPLE

Well and God amend all, and 'a be zo good a clerk...

RESPUBLICA

Hear ye this, Honesty?

PEOPLE

...Though tinkers should lack work.

RESPUBLICA

I am put in comfort all shall shortly amend.

ADULATION

It is in good way already, else God defend.

RESPUBLICA

Lo, People, hearest thou this? Be of good cheer.

PEOPLE

Yea, Ich hear his vair words; but what beeth we the near?

RESPUBLICA

People, understand ye that this is Honesty?

PEOPLE

Whether a' be true? Mass, cha zeen zome as zmooth as he
Have by trial be vound valse flatterers to be.

RESPUBLICA

I take this man for no such; this is Honesty.

PEOPLE

A gay, smolt, smirking whore-cop 'tis, zo mot I thee!

RESPUBLICA

Well credit my words, People: this is Honesty.

PEOPLE

When I's find it, chill believe it.

RESPUBLICA

T'is Honesty.

PEOPLE

I's cry him mercy, then.

RESPUBLICA

He and Authority,
Joining with Policy and Reformation,
Travail to restore th'old wealth to this nation.

PEOPLE

Wo then, chill war't all within two years as plenty
As 'twas any time within these years twice twenty.
But how may we know and see that this thing is true?

ADULATION

It shall prove at length by th'effect that shall ensue.

PEOPLE

Nay, and we shall alway be served but with shales,
Then chill believe e'en still that vair words beeth but tales.

ADULATION

The thing already to such forwardness is brought
That much to your benefit is already wrought.

PEOPLE

Yea? What any good act have ye already done?

51 **premidence** pre-eminence.
57 **copped** arrogant.
57 **he nill...mell** he won't allow them to do anything.
62 **policate wit** politic brain.
66 **face us** defy us openly.
66 **peason** peasant.
68 **Therevor...zee** That's why I was desirous to come and see your ladyship.
75 **what...near?** we're no closer (to a remedy)?
77 **Whether...true?** Whether that's true or not (I don't know)?
80 **smolt** smiling.
80 **zo...thee!** so may I thrive! (A talismanic self-blessing.)
86 **chill...plenty** I'll warrant everything will be as plentiful within two years.
90 **served...shales** fobbed off with shells/husks.
92 **already...brought** is already advanced so far.

ADULATION
It is but young days yet, things are but now begun.
The fruit of our doings cannot so soon appear.
But, People, ye shall feel it within seven year.
Ye know it is no small work from so great decay…

RESPUBLICA
People, he saith truth.

ADULATION
To set all in good stay.
Therefore, be ye quiet, and hope for a good end.

PEOPLE
Yes, chill tarry leisure I, and take what God shall send.

RESPUBLICA
Then People, let us twain depart in quietness,
For this talking here may hinder their business.

PEOPLE
Come on, I chill wait avore you, and be your man.
Exit.

ADULATION
And I will to my fellows as fast as I can.
Be they gone? Farewell they; God send them both the pip!
But in faith, People, I will have you on the hip.
I will be even with you for your broad carping.
Ah, ye peasant wretch, on us four to be harping!
And yet must we our matters handle discreetly,
Or else I fear it will end not very sweetly.
But now I would Avarice or else Insolence
Or Oppression were here, rather than six pence.
And lo, where Avarice cometh: a wolf in the tale,
As the proverb saith. What doth he after him hale?

Actus Terci[i]. Scena Quarta. (Avarice, [Adulation].)

AVARICE
Come on, sweet bags of gold, come on with a good will.
I on you so tender, and ye so froward still?
Come forward, I pray you, sweet bags; ah, will ye so?
Come or I must draw you, whether ye will or no.
I know your desire: ye would fain be in my chest;
When the belly is full, the bones would be at rest.
Be content awhile, I will couch you all up soon,
Where ye shall not be spied neither of sun nor moon.
What now, brother Honesty? What, pry ye this way?
Is there anything here that is yours, can ye say?
Look off from my bags, it is a pretty matter,
Ye can see no green cheese but your teeth will water.

ADULATION
In nomine patris, hast thou got all this since?

AVARICE
Why, thinkest thou I have sat idle since I went hence?
Nay, I have filled my little purses too, each one.

ADULATION
Hast thou so indeed? Thou art a fellow alone!

AVARICE
With old Angelots and Edwards I think I have.
Come forth. How say ye, sir? Peep out ye little knave.
How think you by this bunting? Is he full or no?
And his fellows all, doth not their skin stretch for woe?
Now these little buttons, no bigger than two nuts,
Have they not played gluttons, and filled well their guts?

ADULATION
But look who cometh yonder, puffing and tuffing.

AVARICE
Come the devil if him lust, staring and snuffing.

Actus Terci[i]. Scena Quinta (Oppression, Avarice, Adulation.)

OPPRESSION
In all my whole life was I never wearier.

AVARICE
Come near, on God's half; the mo knaves the merrier!
Where have ye lost your breath, in some coffer diving?

106 **the pip** a disease.
107 **I…hip** I'll bring you down.
108 **broad carping** public complaining.
114 **where…tale** he appears when you say his name, like the wolf in the tale (a variant of 'speak of the devil').
115 **What…hale?** What's he dragging behind him?
2 **I…still?** I behave towards you so kindly, and you are always stubborn (in return)?
7 **couch…up** hide you all away/tuck you up in bed.
11 **Look off from** Stop looking at.
12 **Ye…water** You cannot see anything tasty without salivating.
13 ***In nomine patris*** In the name of the father (said as an oath).
16 **Thou…alone!** You're unique!
17 **Angelots and Edwards** types of gold coin.
18 Said to his purses.
19 **bunting** plump little bird.
20 **for woe** until it hurts.
21 **little buttons** triflingly small things.
23 **tuffing** panting.
24 **if him lust** if he likes.
2 **on God's half** in God's name (on His behalf).

OPPRESSION

Shouldering amongst them for a piece of a living.

ADULATION

And what, are you now in any good hope to thrive?

OPPRESSION

Faith, if I lust I may wear mitres four or five;
I have so many half-bishoprics at the least.

ADULATION

By th'arms of Callis, then am I a very beast!

AVARICE

Why, what hast thou gotten to thy share in this space?

ADULATION

Three hundred pound by the year and one manor place.

AVARICE

Ah, the Passion of God! Three hundred pound and no more?

ADULATION

Is not that fair for him that had nothing before?

AVARICE

What, three hundred pound by years? Call thee Honesty?
Call thee a knave! Thou shamest our fraternity.
Three hundred pound? If some man had been in thy room,
A thousand pound a year ere this time might have come.
Three hundred pound a year? Against our next meeting,
Get more, or I shall give thee a homely greeting.

ADULATION

He here hath flitched the bishoprics already.

AVARICE

Yea, I can him thank, he hath been somewhat speedy.

OPPRESSION

But yet have I left many a good gobbet loose.
Change thou for the rest, give a feather for a goose.

ADULATION

Didst thou with any one of them make such exchange?

OPPRESSION

Yea, I almost left them never a farm nor grange.
I told them Respublica at their wealth did grudge,
And the fifth penny they had was for them too much.
So Authority and I did with them so chop
That we left the best of them a threadbare bishop.
To some we left one house, to some we left none,
The best had but his see place, that he might keep home.
We informed them and we deformed them,
We conformed them and we reformed them.

ADULATION

And what gave ye them in your permutations?

OPPRESSION

Bare parsonages of appropriations,
Bought from Respublica and first emprowed,
Then at the highest extent to bishops allowed,
Let out to their hands for four-score and nineteen year.

AVARICE

Lo, cousin Honesty, lo, do ye hear this gear?
Faith, your masship will thrive at the latter Lammas.

ADULATION

I now grant myself to have been a very ass,
But all is not yet gone, in case I have good luck.

OPPRESSION

No, there is yet enough left for a better pluck;
For some of them were aged and yet would not die,
And some would in no wise to our desires apply.
But we have rods in piss for them everychone,
That they shall be fleeced if we reign, one by one.

AVARICE

And how did all frame with our monsieur Authority?

OPPRESSION

At length he won the full superiority.

ADULATION

But the rude gross People at him repineth sore,
And against us all four with a wide throat doth he roar.
But soft, peace, me thinketh I hear him hem and hake.
If we meet here all four, we shall some order take.

[8] **Callis** Calais.
[15] **had ... room** had taken your place.
[17] **Against** In preparation for.
[18] **homely** rude/rough.
[19] **flitched** sliced up.
[21] **gobbet** chunk/portion.
[27] **chop** exchange (their good lands and properties for less good ones).
[30] **place** principal palace/manor house.
[33] **in your permutations** in exchange.
[34] **Bare ... appropriations** Poor livings based on parish tithes.
[35] **emprowed** enclosed (for private use).
[39] **latter Lammas** an imaginary date that will never come (Lammas was the feast day of 1 August).
[45] **we ... piss** we're preparing punishments.
[51] **hem and hake** cough and clear his throat.

Actus Terci[i], Scena Sexta.
(Insolence, Adulation, Oppression, Avarice.)

INSOLENCE
What, mine old friends all three? By my truth sirs, well found!
ADULATION ET OPPRESSION
Faith sir, most heartily welcome into this ground.
INSOLENCE
Bones, what have we here?
AVARICE
Aha!
INSOLENCE
Bags of money, I trow!
AVARICE
Have we? Nay I have, but none for you that I know.
Lo sir, thus might an honest man come to his harms.
I will lie down on them and keep them in mine arms.
INSOLENCE
Hast thou got all this? I myself have not so much.
AVARICE
Then have ye whole towns and castles; I have none such.
Yet will ye not deny, I judge in my fancy,
That ye got them by the drift of me, Policy?
INSOLENCE
I confess that.
OPPRESSION
All my lands are scarce so much worth.
AVARICE
They were less when I, Policy, first set you forth.
ADULATION
He hath purses with gold; would I had so many.
AVARICE
It were pity that such a goose should have any.
Your good mas'ship appointed me to crumbs and scraps,
But Policy will live by his neighbours, perhaps.
But thus I see: you would poll me and ye wist how.
Therefore I will go hoard it, I make God a vow;
I will make it sure under nine doors and nine locks,
And who but looketh that way shall sit in nine stocks.
INSOLENCE
Nay, first declare to us how thou didst all this get.
AVARICE
For your learning I will you a spectacle set.
But first get ye from me, and stand a good way hence;
This shall not lie within your reach, by your licence.
Nay, yet farther, lest ye take my bags for bloodings,
For such hungry dogs will slab up sluttish puddings.
ADULATION
Is it well now?
AVARICE
Yea, now hardily, stand there still,
And the names of my bags to you declare I will.
First and foremost, this bag is my very clear gain
Of leases encroached and forthwith sold again.
This bag is mine interest of this year's usury,
And this is of matters bolstered up with perjury;
This is bribes above my stipend in offices,
This fifth I have by selling of benefices;
This is my rents that my clerks yearly render me
To be and continue in office under me.
This same I got by sectorship of my mother;
A vengeance on her, old witch, for such another.
This bag have I kept of other sectorships whole,
Which the mad knaves would have scattered by penny dole;
This is of church goods scraped up without a law,
For which was as quick scambling as ever I saw,
Of their plate, their jewels, and copes we made them louts,
Stopping People's barking with linen rags and clouts;
They had th'altar cloths, th'albs and amices,
With the sindons in which were wrapped the chalices.
This ninth hath beguiled the king of his custom;
This tenth of selling counterfeit wares hath come.
Now this eleventh is of tallow, butter, cheese,
Corn, raw-cloths, leather by stealth sent beyond seas;
This twelfth is of grain, bell-metal, tin, and lead,
Conveyed out by creeks when Respublica was in bed.
This thirteenth I filled through facing out of daws,
Both from lands and goods by pretence of the laws.

1 **well found!** well met/good to see you!
17 **you...how** you'd strip me bare if you knew how.
25 **bloodings** blood puddings.
26 **slab...puddings** gobble up dirty sausages.
31 **usury** illegal money-lending at high interest (see the treatment of this practice in *The Three Ladies of London*).
34 **benefices** vicarages and other Church livings.
37 **sectorship** executorship (of a will).
40 **scattered...dole** scattered around in tiny portions.
42 **scambling** contention.
43 **Of...louts** We tricked them out of their jewels, etc.
45 **th'albs and amices** ceremonial shawls and surplices.
46 **sindons** shrouds.
47 **custom** customs duties (taxes on imported and exported goods).
50 **raw-cloths** unfinished cloth, sent for dyeing and finishing abroad.
53 **facing...daws** tricking fools.

Thus these thirteen small jobs are mine by Policy.
All men must shift for a poor living honestly.
If ere I bestow them, it shall be the next Lent,
To the prior of Prickingham and his convent.

ADULATION
Well now, we may come near, may we not, if we lust?

AVARICE
Ye are near enough: out of my reach I dare you trust.

ADULATION
Well, now let us sing, if it please Authority,
To refresh our spirits it is restority.

INSOLENCE
I reck not, for company's sake, to sing once more.

AVARICE
I have less mind to sing now than I had before.
Then had I no lust to sing because I was bare,
And now how to keep that I have got I do care.

OPPRESSION
Solace we must needs have, when that we are weary.

ADULATION
It prolongeth the life of man to be merry.

AVARICE
And if ye sing so much, Honesty, without fail
Thirst and you at length, I fear, will make a battle.
But go to, sing on, if there be no remedy.
And ye look at my bags, ye mar my melody!

Cantent, 'Hey nonny nonny, ho for money,' *etc.*

OPPRESSION
Now, about profit divide we ourselves abroad.

AVARICE
Yea, and hear ye, masters; while time is, lay on load;
Consider ye have but a time of hay-making,
And harvest is not mewed without pains-taking.
Now, time will not tarry, and therefore take good heed,
Despatch while time serves, and all your matters speed.
Time hath no rein nor bridle, but runneth apace.

INSOLENCE
Mark Policy's words, sirs, excellent in our case.

AVARICE
And time hath this one ungracious property,
To blab at length and open all that he doth see.
Then a daughter eke he hath, called Verity,
As unhappy a long-tongued girl as can be.
She bringeth all to light, some she bringeth to shame;
She careth not a groat what man hath thank or blame.
If men be praiseworthy, she doth so declare them,
And, if otherwise, in faith she doth not spare them.

OPPRESSION
We will feather our nests ere Time may us espy,
Ere Verity have power our doings to descry.

AVARICE
Remember this verse: *Ut sint omnia salva, Fronte capillata, post haec occasio calva.*

OPPRESSION
Make me understand that fine rag of rhetoric.

AVARICE
Lo here: a fine fellow to have a bishopric!
A verse of Latin he cannot understand,
Yet dareth he presume boldly to take in hand
Into a deanery or archdeaconry to chop,
And to have the livelihood away from a bishop!

OPPRESSION
To me show thy verse and leave this persuasion.

AVARICE
Forsooth, sir, it was of the goddess Occasion.
She weareth a great long tuffet of hair before
And behind hath not one hair, neither less nor more.
Whereby is taught you that when Occasion is
Ye must take it betime, or of your purpose miss.

ADULATION
Then, while Occasion doth now serve so well,
I pray you give ear to one thing that I must tell.

INSOLENCE AND OPPRESSION
What is that?

ADULATION
Monsieur, if ye hear People mumbling,

58 **prior...convent** either an imaginary priory (i.e. he'll never give them up) or a euphemism for a brothel (i.e. that's where he'll spend the profits).
62 **restority** a restorative or cordial.
63 **I reck not** I'm not averse.
72 **And** If.
Cantent They sing.
74 **while...load** gather as much as you can while you are able.
76 **mewed** safely gathered in.
81 **property** tendency.
82 **open** reveal.
84 **As...girl** As unfortunate a talkative girl.
86 **groat** a small coin.
90 **descry** reveal.
92 ***Ut...calva*** 'May they all be safe. [Chance/Occasion has] hair at the front, but she is bald behind' (Cato, *Disticha de Moribus*, 2.26), i.e. one has to grab Chance when she appears, if she passes you by, you will never be able to grab her by the hair.
104 **betime** quickly/early.

Ye must storm, and sharply take him up for stumbling.
Ye would not think what he said a little while since
Of us to Respublica, in mine own presence.

INSOLENCE
When I meet them next, I shall tell them both my mind.

AVARICE
And Policy to help you will not be behind.

ADULATION
Gentle Respublica was soon pacified,
But People was sturdy and would not be qualified.

AVARICE
Alas, good, poor, silly soul, bear her fair in hand
And ye may win her, as you lust, to use her land.

OPPRESSION
But of goddess Occasion one little more...

AVARICE
Marry, sir, even as I would have said before,
She standeth with winged feet on a rolling wheel,
To take flight ere any grass may grow on her heel.
And even while we stand jangling in this presence,
I dare say she is flown twice twenty-score mile hence.

OPPRESSION
Yea? Cock's bones, then adieu!

INSOLENCE
Farewell!

ADULATION
And I am gone!

Exeant currentes.

AVARICE
Faith and have after, as fast as I can, anon.
Now my God-almighties, as I did hither tug you,
So will I on my back to your lodging lug you;
And sure, if ye can be quiet there and lie still,
I will shortly bring you mo fellows, so I will.
I have a good benefice of an hundred marks;
It is small policy to give such to great clerks;
They will take no benefice, but they must have all.
A bare clerk can be content with a living small.
Therefore Sir John Lack-Latin, my friend, shall have mine.
And of him may I farm it for eight pounds or nine;
The rest may I reserve to myself for mine own share.
For we are good feeders of the poor, so we are,
And we patrons are bound to see (I do you tell)
The church patrimony to be bestowed well.
Other odd corners besides these I have many,
Which with all good speed shall increase your company.
Come on now therefore. In faith I do great wrong
To promise you lodging and keep you thence so long.

Exit.

Actus Quarti. Scena Prima (Respublica.)

RESPUBLICA
O, Lord, what may it mean to be thus born in hand
And yet none amendment to feel nor understand?
People doth daily and hourly to me resort,
Challenging my promise of relief and comfort.
I report to him as my rulers do to me,
People still affirmeth that they devourers be.
The more I do him cheer, the more he doth despair;
I say his wealth doth mend, he saith it doth appair.
What should I judge of this? May it be credible,
Or by any reason may it be possible,
That such four as those in whom I have put my trust,
Showing such face of friendship, should be men unjust?
I will know if People feel yet any redress
Of his former sores and of his rueful distress.
We shall meet soon, I doubt not, and talk together.

(*Enter People.*)

And lo, as I would wish, he approacheth hither.

Actus Quarti. Scena Secunda (Respublica, People.)

RESPUBLICA
Well met, People, what place go ye now unto?

112 **behind** slow.
121 **jangling** arguing.
123 **Cock's** God's (euphemism).
123.1 ***Exeant currentes.*** Exit running.
124 **have after** (I'll) follow.
130 **small policy** little sense.
133 A generic name for an unlearned priest.
134 **farm** rent.
1 **born in hand** deceived.
5 **I...me** I tell him what my ministers tell me.
8 **appair** gets worse.

PEOPLE

Ich am at the farthest, to zee how you do.
We twain must eftwhiles come physic either other,
Vor we beeth your children, and you beeth our mother.

RESPUBLICA

And how do you mend now in your thrift and your purse?

PEOPLE

As zour ale in summer, that is: still worse and worse.

RESPUBLICA

People, what should I say?

PEOPLE

Nay, Mass, I's cannot tell,
But we ignorams all would fain ye should do well.
And how feel you yourself? Better than ye did, trow?

RESPUBLICA

Till God send better hap, rather decay than grow.
This bringeth me in a conceit of zealousy. Rather
than much good, would I speak with Policy

PEOPLE

Was not he drowned, trow, last year, when Conscience was?

RESPUBLICA

I see him yonder appear; this cometh well to pass.

PEOPLE

Is this same he?

RESPUBLICA

Yea.

PEOPLE

And Ich heard not you zo zay.
Chould zware a' had be dead, or else clean run away.

Actus Quarti. Scena Tercia (Avarice, Respublica, People.)

AVARICE

O most noble lady, that I have not of late
Made to you relation how ye stand in state,
Hath not been of negligence nor to work by stealth,
But of my deep studies, devising for your wealth.

RESPUBLICA

To hear the truth thereof, I wished you to see.

PEOPLE

Doth you stud your brains, Mass' gent'man, pray you tell me,
For our lady, Rice-Puddingcake's commodity?

AVARICE

I devise what I can for the prosperity
Of this lady, Respublica, and her People.

PEOPLE

That lie, ere this, is flown as far hence as Paul's steeple.
I's pray God ye stud not as cha hard of zome elfs,
That study for the common profit of their own selves.

AVARICE

To study for both your wealths I am a debtor.

PEOPLE

Vay, then, as good ne'er a whit as ne'er the better.

AVARICE

I do nothing but compass therefore, without doubt.

PEOPLE

I' vay, then, thee fet too far a compass about,
Vor zome good might ha' be done in all this season.

AVARICE

So there is, if to perceive it ye had reason.

RESPUBLICA

Truly, I feel myself hitherto worse and worse.

PEOPLE

And I's veel the same, both in my ground and my purse.
Vive or zix year ago chad vour kine to my pale,
And at this prezent hour cham scarce worth a good cow-tail!
And that time chad a widge and her voal, and ten sheep,
Now I's can get nothing myzelf and my wife to keep.

[2] **Ich . . . farthest** This is as far as I am coming (i.e. I am coming here).
[3] **come physic other** heal/look after each other.
[4] **beeth** are.
[8] **ignorams** unlearned (people).
[9] **trow** I hope.
[10–12] **Till . . . Policy.** Until God send (me) better fortune, (I) rather decay than grow, and that prompts me to be suspicious. I'd give a lot to speak with Policy.
[17–18] **And . . . dead** If I'd not heard you say so, I'd have sworn Policy was dead.

[6] **stud your brains** a mangling of 'study with your brains'.
[11] **I's . . . elfs** I pray God you don't study as I've heard some villains do.
[14] **Vay . . . better.** Faith, it's as good to do nothing as to make nothing better.
[15] **compass** plan.
[16] **thee . . . about** you take too wide a path (People takes 'compass' to mean journey in an arc, as around the compass).
[20] **ground** land.
[21] **vour . . . pale** four cows on my small farm (lit. within my fences).
[23] **a widge . . . voal** a mare and her foal.

Then, and chad I be with the king's mass' constable,
Chould zet myself vorth pertly, and zo chwas able.
Now, vor lack of a sallet when my liege hath need,
Cham vain to take an hat of God's-good on my head.
And, vor God, my dame, this is but small amendment.
I's comport me to you: how thinketh your judgement?
'Compassing', ka? Gent'man, call ye the same compassing?
And whom shall we twain thank, you, for this compassing?

AVARICE
No sir.

PEOPLE
Now, by the compass that God compassed...

RESPUBLICA
Blame have they of God and man that this hath compassed.

PEOPLE
A small compass more now may zoon compass, by th'Rood,
To make forty thousand volks hair grow through their hood.

AVARICE
That is their own fault, not the fault of Policy.

RESPUBLICA
God above, He knoweth whose fault it is, and not I.

PEOPLE
But did not Ich daily give you warning?

RESPUBLICA
Doubtless.

PEOPLE
And did not Ich plain me to you?

RESPUBLICA
I grant no less.

PEOPLE
And when Ich made my moan, what would ye to me tell?

RESPUBLICA
As my hope was, that at length all thing should be well.

PEOPLE
'Compassing'? Ka!

RESPUBLICA
People, I put trust in other.

PEOPLE
Valse dezeivers of zimility, by God's Mother.

AVARICE
Well, suffer me then, for my declaration,
To fet Authority and Reformation,
That ye may both hear and charge them as well as me.

RESPUBLICA
With all my heart, good Policy, let it so be.
I pray you call them hither, if they may be got.

PEOPLE
And che hear 'em, I's can tell where they say true or not.

Actus Quarti. Scena Quarta
(Avarice, Insolence, Respublica, Oppression, People.)

AVARICE
The foulest, open-mouthed wretch that ere ye heard!

INSOLENCE
Couldst thou by no means make the peasant afeared?

AVARICE
No, but anon I trow we shall his mas'ship trim.
Convey her away, and then all we three chide him.
But whist, and come apace.

RESPUBLICA
I hear Policy's voice.

AVARICE
That I met you so well, I do much rejoice.
Lady Respublica, would you come her before?

INSOLENCE
Madam, God ye save.

OPPRESSION
And preserve for evermore.

RESPUBLICA
This is happy hap, ye come so soon together.

AVARICE
As I went, I met them both twain hasting hither.

25–28 **and chad...head** if I'd been called up by the King's constable (mustered to serve in a hue and cry or army), I could turn out well prepared. Now, for lack of a helmet, I'm forced to wear a hat of God's making (i.e. just his hair?)
30 **I's...you** I appeal to you.
31 **ka?** Pah?
36 **make...hood** i.e. be so poor they cannot afford to repair their hoods.
40 **plain me** complain.
44 **Valse...zimility** (They were) false deceivers, it seems.
46 **fet** fetch.
5 **whist...apace** hush and come quickly.
9 **happy hap** very fortunate.

RESPUBLICA
Never in better time.
INSOLENCE
Madam, what is your will?
OPPRESSION
Is there anything that you would say us until?
RESPUBLICA
People crieth out, and I am much aggrieved
That we feel ourselves in nothing yet relieved.
OPPRESSION
No, that is not true; many declare I can...
RESPUBLICA
Even in brief words, I pray you do it then.
PEOPLE
Pray you, let me s'pose with the same new-come gent'man.
INSOLENCE
No sir.
PEOPLE
Mass, but chill speak and che can spy my time when.
OPPRESSION
First, your priests and bishops have not as they have had.
RESPUBLICA
When they had their livings men were both fed and clad.
OPPRESSION
Yea, but they ought not by Scripture to be called lords.
RESPUBLICA
That they rule the church, with Scripture well accords.
OPPRESSION
They were proud and covetous and took much upon them.
PEOPLE
But they were not covetous that took all from them?
OPPRESSION
The coin eke is changed.
PEOPLE
Yea, from zilver to dross;
T'was told us vor the best, but poor we bear the loss.
When chad with zweat of brows got up a few small crumbs,
At paying of my debts Ich could not make my sums.
My landlord vor my corn paid me zuch sums and zuch,
When he should have it vor rent, it was but half zo much.
Zix pence in each shilling was i-struck quite away;
Zo vor one piece Ich took, cha was vain to pay him tway.
One would think 'twere brass, and zorrow have I else,
But Ich win most part on't was made of our old bells.
INSOLENCE
Yet, if ye mark it well, for one piece ye have three,
Which for your people is no small commodity.
PEOPLE
Well, I nill meddle in the same matter no more,
But I's reck not and 'twere zilver as t'was avore.
OPPRESSION
People, ye shall at length find it all for the best.
PEOPLE
Cha heard our parish clerk say, '*deum est*, Jus'lum west.'
RESPUBLICA
Undoubtedly I feel many things are amiss.
PEOPLE
Yea, I's can tell mo things yet, and me lust, by Jiss!
They have all the woods throughout the realm destroyed,
Which might have served long years, being well employed.
And then the great cobs have zo take the rest to hire,
That poor volk cannot get a stick to make a fire.
Then their great grazing hath made flesh so dear, I wot,
That poor volk at shambles cannot bestow their groat.
RESPUBLICA
I lament it, People. Alack, what may I do?

12 **us until** to us.
17 **s'pose** dispute (trade 'supposes' or arguments).
25 **The...changed.** Also, the coinage is devalued.
25.1 **dross** base metal.
32 **tway** two.
34 **Ich win** I believe.
34 **made...bells** i.e. bell-metal melted down to make coins.
37 **nill** will not.
38 **But...avore** But I don't believe it is silver as it was before.
40 ***deum*...west** perhaps, as Brandl suggests, a corruption of '*divites estis iuste fuistes*': 'you rich are as you were' (still rich).
42 **and...Jiss!** if I wanted, by Jesus!
45 **great...hire** great lords have so taken the rest into their own hands (by enclosure).
48 **cannot...groat** can't afford to buy anything from the butcher.

I myself, I fear, shall come to ruin too.
Policy, what comfort; when will you ease
my smart?

AVARICE
Ye are as safe even now, but for your false heart,
As any lady of your name in Christendom.

PEOPLE
If Ich had zo zaid, chad lied, by my holydom.

RESPUBLICA
Ye hear what People saith, which feel'th as I do.

AVARICE
But rude People's words will ye give credit unto?
Will ye judge yourself after his foolish jangling?
Ye were well enough till be began his wrangling.

INSOLENCE
Will ye believe People, that hath no manner of skill
To judge or to discern what thing is good or ill?
He is so headstrong he must be bridled with laws.

PEOPLE
Though zome be stark bedlams, yet wise volks beeth
no daws.

INSOLENCE
We have oft found People most disobedient
To orders most requisite and expedient.
Who such a maintainer of wrong opinions
As People in all countries and dominions?
Ye ought therefore to rebuke him at all hours,
For discouraging any ministers of yours.

OPPRESSION
Ye must tarry time ere we can your purpose serve.

PEOPLE
Yea, and then while the grass shall grow, the horse
shall starve.

INSOLENCE
Do ye not see this, by all experience plain,
That men from diseases recovered again
Do after sickness past remain a long time weak?

RESPUBLICA
People, hark, Authority doth good reason speak.

INSOLENCE
So ye, though oppressed with long adversity,
Yet, doubt not, are toward wealth and prosperity.

RESPUBLICA
Lo, People, to hope a while longer shall be best.

PEOPLE
Well, then, Ich am persuaged to do at your inquest.

INSOLENCE
Madam, mistrust not us, your painful ministers.

AVARICE
Never had lady more watchful officers.

OPPRESSION
For my part I will swear the Gospel book upon,
That if the laws I have made should every one
Redound to mine own singular commodity,
They could not be friendlier framed than they be.

INSOLENCE
Therefore, repose yourself Madam awhile,
and wink,
Ye are in better case toward than you can think.

AVARICE
We shall here remain and give People good counsel
Quiet for to be till Policy may prevail.

RESPUBLICA
He will do well with your good informations.

PEOPLE
Yea, vay, chill vollow their good exaltations.

RESPUBLICA
Then I leave you all here to God. I will depart.

Exit Respublica.

PEOPLE
Now how, destructions to 'member in my heart.

AVARICE
'Destructions'? Ye miser!

INSOLENCE
Ye peasant!

OPPRESSION
Ye lout!

INSOLENCE
Can ye naught else do but rage, and rave, and cry out?

OPPRESSION
And cannot tell on whom?

AVARICE
No more than can a daw.

51 **smart** pain.
57 **jangling** chattering.
62 **Though . . . daws.** Though some are complete madmen, wise folk are no fools.
65 **Who** Who is.
78 **persuaged . . . inquest** he means 'persuaded . . . request'.
79 **painful** i.e. we who take pains (on your behalf).
84 **friendlier framed** better drafted.
85 **wink** rest/close your eyes.
86 **in . . . toward** in a more promising state.
92 **destructions . . . heart** i.e. instructions to remember.
95.1 **daw** jackdaw/fool.

OPPRESSION
Crow against your betters!

INSOLENCE
And murmur against the law.
Let me hear thee prate as thou hast done heretofore…

AVARICE
Or trouble Lady Respublica anymore.

OPPRESSION
Thou canst not see, thou wretch, canst thou, when thou art well?

AVARICE
Is't part of thy play with such high matters to mell?

INSOLENCE
Doth it become thee to bark with such a wide throat?

AVARICE
And to have an oar in everybody's boat?

INSOLENCE
If thou do so again, it shall with thee be worse.

OPPRESSION
We shall wring and pinch thee, both by belly and purse.

INSOLENCE
I would advise you, friend, to grunt and groan no more.

OPPRESSION
Do the like again and thou shalt rue it full sore.

AVARICE
It were best for you, friend, all murmuring to cease.

PEOPLE
Bum vay, then chill e'en go home, and vair hold my peace.

INSOLENCE
Do so, by my rede, and fall to honest labour.

AVARICE
Hence, home, and be quiet, and thou shalt find favour.

PEOPLE
Then chill bid you varewell.

OPPRESSION
No words, but hence apace.
This was done as should be.

AVARICE
This was done in right place.

PEOPLE
But how, one word ere 'ch go, ye'll give volks leave to think?

OPPRESSION
No marry, will we not, nor to look, but wink.

PEOPLE
Yes, by Jiss, but chill lo, nay, ho there, thought is free!
And a cat, they zaith, may look on a king, pardee.

Exit.

INSOLENCE
Now where do we be come? I home! *Exit.*

OPPRESSION
And I abroad. *Exit.*

AVARICE
And I must see what feet about my door have trod.

Exit.

Actus Quinti. Scena Prima (Misericordia.)

MISERICORDIA
Wherein appeareth the graciousness of God
More than infinitely to exceed man's goodness,
But that He keepeth back the sharp stroke of His rod
When man would rage in most furious woodness?

Scarce any amends may man's eagerness appease,
Yea, and though He forgive, He will not soon forget;
Towards true penitence God's wrath forthwith doth cease,
And He their past sin behind His back doth set.

Of long sufferance He is, with weakness to bear
While any hope of amendment doth remain,
And, though He plague sinners to call them home by fear,
Yet His mercy and grace are aye ready again.

His grievous displeasure dureth not forever,
And why? *Quia miserationes eius,*
Which to show, He chiefly delighteth ever
Manent super omnia opera eius.

97 **prate** babble.
100 **mell** meddle.
109 **rede** advice.
115 **chill lo** I'll look!
116 **pardee** by God.

4 **woodness** madness.
12 **aye** always.
13 **dureth** endures.
14–16 ***Quia… eius.*** 'His tender mercies… are over all his works' (Psalm 144:9)

It grieveth Him sore when He must needs take vengeance;
His delight and glory is mercy to practice;
His tender compassion on true repentance
He hath still from the beginning sought t'excercise.

The mass of this world in His mercy did He frame,
The sky, earth, and sea His mercy replenished,
In His mercy did He after redeem the same,
When else remediless it must have perished.

In His mercy was Israel delivered
From the 'gyptian thraldom and captivity;
In His mercy the same through the Red Sea was led,
And through wilderness to a land of Liberty.

Sith that time all commonweals He hath protected,
And to such as with earnest prayer have made moan,
Me, Compassion, He hath quickly directed,
To revive and recover them every one.

Now lastly hath He heard the most doleful lament
Of woeful Respublica, His darling most dear.
Therefore me, Compassion, with speed He hath sent,
Her most sorrowful heart to recomfort and cheer.

I tarry her coming that I may her salute,
And lo, methinketh I see her appear in place,
Of friendship devoid, and of succour destitute.
I will hear her, and then give words of solace.

Actus Quinti. Scena Secunda (Respublica, Misericordia, Avarice, Adulation.)

RESPUBLICA

O Lord, hast Thou forever closed up thine ear?
Wilt Thou never more the desolate's prayer hear?
Wilt Thou still turn away Thy face from my distress?
Wilt Thou clean forsake me, and leave me comfortless?
The secret sighs and sobs and prayers of mine heart,
Shall they not forever Thine eyes to me convert?
I grant that mine offences have so much deserved,
But for whom save sinners is Thy mercy reserved?
Thou promised so, which hitherto hast been just.
Despair, Lord, I will not, nor Thy goodness mistrust.
Lo down on my distress, and for Thy glory sake,
Though I be ill worthy, yet mercy on me take.

MISERICORDIA

Now will I speak to her.

RESPUBLICA

Who maketh me afeared?

MISERICORDIA

No, I will thee comfort. God hath thy prayer heard.
And now, Respublica, be of good hope and trust.

RESPUBLICA

O Lord, now do I see that Thou art ever just.

MISERICORDIA

I am sent to recomfort thee, Respublica.

RESPUBLICA

O Lady Compassion, Misericordia.

MISERICORDIA

What say ye to me? What, woman, can ye not speak?
I am come down all your sorrows at once to break.
Speak, woman!

RESPUBLICA

Misericordia.

MISERICORDIA

Out comfortably,
Ye shall have now no more cause to speak desperably.

RESPUBLICA

My heart in God's mercy is so dilated,
That my very spirit to heaven is elated.
O Lady Compassion, welcome veriment!
Ever be God praised, that you to me hath sent.

MISERICORDIA

Now that I have put you in sure hope of relief,
I must go fet Verity, to try out all your grief.
Verity shall open how your decay hath grown,
And then the causers thereof shall be overthrown.

RESPUBLICA

Who be the causers thereof I cannot discern,
But yond cometh one of them that do me govern.

MISERICORDIA

What is his name?

RESPUBLICA

Policy.

MISERICORDIA

Policy is good;
He doth work you many good things, of likelihood.

26 **'gyptian thraldom** Egyptian slavery.
6 **convert** turn.
11 **Lo** Look.
25 **veriment** truly.
28 **try out** investigate.
29 **open** discover.

AVARICE

A vengeance upon him, and God give him his curse,
I am besieged now of every cutpurse.
I can go nowhere now, in city neither town,
But Piers Pickpurse playeth at organs under my gown.

MISERICORDIA

What talketh he?

AVARICE

Who speaketh yond? Respublica?

RESPUBLICA

What of the pickpurse?

AVARICE

Forsooth, Dame Respublica,
I said and we had two pillories mo t'were ne'er the worse,
For it is a light thing now to meet Piers Pickpurse.
God preserve you, right fair lady, and Christ you save,
Who are you, and what would ye in this country have?

RESPUBLICA

This same is the Lady Misericordia
Sent from God purposely.

AVARICE

Unto you, Respublica?

MISERICORDIA

Yea.

AVARICE

Then must ye needs be most heartily welcome.
We had ne'er more need of you, by my holydom.
There be in this country which, but ye comfort send,
Are full like to make both a mad and a short end.

MISERICORDIA

I will go to do that I said, Respublica,
And return with speed.

RESPUBLICA

Sweet Misericordia. *Exit Misericordia.*

AVARICE

Good Misericordia now, and lady most dear,
Christ blister on your heart; what make you here?

RESPUBLICA

Come back, Policy.

AVARICE

I come.

RESPUBLICA

Whither would ye now?

AVARICE

Convey myself hence honestly, if I wist how.

RESPUBLICA

When come ye, Policy? What look ye? Something lost?

AVARICE

Anon. If I tarry, it will turn to my cost.

RESPUBLICA

Ah, friend Policy.

AVARICE

Yea.

RESPUBLICA

Now shall I be in bliss,
Thanks to God.

AVARICE

We must find provision for this.

RESPUBLICA

Hah?

AVARICE

Did not I ere tell you that God would you save?
Ye may see now what it is good rulers to have.

RESPUBLICA

Ye say truth, but look, yonder cometh Honesty.

AVARICE

Pray God, Amen!

RESPUBLICA

Yes, look else.

AVARICE

What news bringeth he?

ADULATION

I should speak a word in th'ear of Policy.
If I may not so, I will speak it openly.

RESPUBLICA

I have not seen you a great while, Honesty.

ADULATION

O noble Lady Respublica, well you be.

RESPUBLICA

All shall be now, such news I have to me brought.

ADULATION

I hear it told for truth, Policy, all will be nought!

RESPUBLICA

Hearest thou any joyful news abroad or not?

36 **of** by.
37 **neither** nor.
38 **playeth . . . gown** i.e. has his fingers groping.
41 **and** if.
42 **light** common.
49 **There be** There are some folk.
54 **what . . . here?** what are you doing here?
56 **wist** knew.

ADULATION
Yea, I hear certain news, which are both breme and hot;
There is new start up a lady called Verity.

RESPUBLICA
Then am I all safe and sure of prosperity.
How was it spoken?

ADULATION
Thus in Latin gross and blunt:
'*Misericordia et Veritas sibi obviauerunt*',
That is, 'Mercy and Truth are both met together'.

RESPUBLICA
Then will it not be long ere they both come hither.

AVARICE
Hither? How so?

RESPUBLICA
Yea, both Mercy and Verity.

AVARICE
A pestle on them both, saving my charity.
But soft, brother Honesty, ye might mistake it;
Of which Verity was't, trow you, that they spake it?

ADULATION
Of the general Verity, old Time's daughter.

AVARICE
Faith, they were not our friends that first hither brought her.
Old Time's daughter? That shuttle-brained tall, long man,
That ne'er standeth still, but flyeth as fast as he can,
Much like as he swimmed or glided upon ice?

ADULATION
Yea.

RESPUBLICA
For all that, of wise men he is thought most wise.

AVARICE
I know him; he carrieth a clock on his head,
A sand glass in his hand, a dial in his forehead.

RESPUBLICA
Ye say truth, Policy, the same is very he.

AVARICE
Old Time the eavesdropper? I know him pardee,
An ancient turner of houses upside down,
And a common consumer of city and town.
Old Time's daughter, quod he? I shrew his naked heart;
Many of my friends hath he brought to pain and smart.
Compassion and that Truth come hither to you?

RESPUBLICA
Mercy, before ye came, promised so right now.

AVARICE
It is no time now, Honesty, to be idle.

ADULATION
Something breweth?

AVARICE
It is time for us to bridle.
Well, go your ways afore, in all haste, Honesty,
And tell Reformation and Authority
That both these ladies in all goodly fashion
Must be entertained here in this nation.
Madam Respublica, is't not your pleasure so?

RESPUBLICA
What else? In all the haste, Honesty, see ye go.

AVARICE
Say further that I would we four anon might meet
Her, or where they will, save in the open street.
And, hear you, Honesty?

ADULATION
What now?

AVARICE
A little near;
Provide in any wise that Verity come not here,
Let Insolence and Oppression keep her hence.

ADULATION
We shall all three therein do our best diligence.

AVARICE
Bid them well remember the world will wax queasy.
Some of us ere long may hap leap at a daisy,
Or put out the eye of Misericordia,
And without an eye play e'en plain trussing corda.

Exit Adulation.

RESPUBLICA
Policy, what is it that ye talk there so long?

72 **breme** loud/clear.
73 **new start up** newly sprung up.
76 ***Misericord . . . obviauerunt*** Mercy and Truth have met each other (Psalm 84:11).
80 **a pestle** a pestilence.
90 **dial** sundial.
95 **shrew** curse.
108 **where** anywhere.
114 **leap . . . daisy** be hanged.
115–116 **Or . . . corda.** Adulation puns that, without the 'i's' 'Misericordia' will be '*miser corda*': 'wretched hearts'. But 'corda/cord' hints also at the hangman's noose that he fears.

AVARICE
I send instructions that they may not do wrong.

RESPUBLICA
Said ye ought to him that may not be told to me?

AVARICE
Should we with every trifling trifle trouble ye?
Well then, ye look for these two ladies, I am sure.

RESPUBLICA
I trust they will not fail on me to do their cure.

AVARICE
I told you ever, did I not, that your wealth would frame.

RESPUBLICA
I shall reward your pains, or else I were to blame.

AVARICE
Then best I go now straight to my fellows and see...

RESPUBLICA
That things needful for us may not unready be?
Do so, I pray you.

AVARICE
Fare ye well, Respublica,
Till I see you next. *Exit.*

RESPUBLICA
Now Misericordia,
When shall be thy pleasure, bring hither Verity.

Enter Misericordia and Veritas.

Behold e'en with the word speaking, where they both be!

Actus Quinti. Scena Tercia (Misericordia, Veritas, Respublica.)

MISERICORDIA
I dare say Respublica thinketh the time long.

VERITY
Who can blame her, having endured so much wrong?
But, as meat and drink and other bodily food
Is never found to be so pleasant nor so good
As when fretting hunger and thirst hath pinched afore,
And as health after sickness is sweeter evermore,
So after decay and adversity overcome,
Wealth and prosperity shall be double welcome.

MISERICORDIA
How now, Respublica, have I not been long hence?

RESPUBLICA
Come ye first or last, ye bliss me with your presence.

MISERICORDIA
As I was commanded, I bring you Verity,
To help you, your People, and their posterity.

VERITY
Dear jewel Respublica, I do you embrace.

RESPUBLICA
I thank your goodness, and submit me to your grace.

MISERICORDIA
Embrace Verity forever, Respublica,
And cleave fast to her.

RESPUBLICA
Yes, Misericordia.

MISERICORDIA
Now please it you to declare, sister Verity,
How she may recover her old prosperity,
Her honour, her wealth, her riches, her substance
Her commons, her people, her strength, and her puissance.

VERITY
All this will be recovered incontinent,
And to better state also, by good government.

RESPUBLICA
No lady of my name upon earth, I esteem,
Hath had better administers than mine have been,
Policy, Reformation, and Authority.

MISERICORDIA
These three be very good.

RESPUBLICA
And the fourth, Honesty.

VERITY
But what if these which have had you and yours to keep,
Have been ravening wolves in the clothing of sheep?

RESPUBLICA
If I heard not you, Verity, such sentence give,
By no man's persuasion I could it believe.

VERITY
Ah, good Respublica, thou hast been abused.
Whom thou chosest are vices to be refused.
Whom thou call'st Honesty is Adulation,

122 **cure** duty.
123 **frame** be sorted out.
130 **e'en... be!** Even as I say their names, here they are!
21 **incontinent** without delay.

And he that in pretence was Reformation
Is indeed Oppression, and huge violence.
Whom thou call'st Authority is proud Insolence;
Then he that was Policy, the chief man of price,
Indeed is most stinking and filthy Avarice.
He first inveigled thee, and his purpose to frame,
Cloaked each of these vices with a virtuous name.

RESPUBLICA
Benedicite! Is this a possible case?

VERITY
Ye shall see it proved true before your own face.
They shall be convinced before you, one by one.

RESPUBLICA
O Lord, what marvel if my thirst were well-nigh gone?
But what redress shall I have hereof, and when?

MISERICORDIA
Such as may be most fit, and as soon as we can.
Justice and Peace are appointed to descend,
Th'one to keep you quiet, th'other you to defend.
As soon as we four sisters together shall be met,
An order for your establishment shall be set.
By the eternal providence it is decreed so.

RESPUBLICA
O most merciful Lord, all praise be Thee unto.

MISERICORDIA
I will leave you here with my sister Verity,
And learn of their coming with all celerity.

VERITY
Ye need not, for I know they be now very near,
And behold they begin already to appear.

Actus Quinti. Scena Quarta (Justicia, Veritas, Misericordia, Respublica.)

PEACE
Now once again in God let us two sisters kiss,
In token of our joining to make a perfect bliss.

JUSTICE
And now let us never be sundered any more,
Till we may Respublica perfectly restore.

VERITY
Let us meet them, sister Misericordia.

MISERICORDIA
And unto their sight present Respublica.

JUSTICE AND PEACE
All hail, most dear sisters Mercy and Verity,
And all hail, Respublica, with all sincerity.

RESPUBLICA
O, ye ladies celestial, how much am I bound
With thanks to fall flat before you on the ground,
That ye thus vouchsafe a forlorn creature
By your heavenly protection to recure.

JUSTICE
I, Justice, from heaven am come, you to visit.

PEACE
And I, Peace, forever with you to inhabit.

MISERICORDIA
And all we four sisters, to th'utmost of our power,
Shall restore, establish, and defend your honour.

JUSTICE
We shall first restore your most happy estate,
And suppress all them that had made you desolate.

VERITY
Verity shall all truth open as it is.

JUSTICE
I, Justice, shall redress what e'er is found amiss.

MISERICORDIA
I, Mercy, where the member may recured be,
Shall temper the rigour and slake extremity.

PEACE
I, Peace, when th'uncureable is clean cut away,
And th'ill made good, shall flourish forever and aye.

RESPUBLICA
And I, which cannot otherwise your goodness
deserve,
Shall your wholesome directions duly observe.
And what if Insolence shall come, or Avarice?

VERITY
Detest them, abhor them, and refuse their service.
I doubt not but they will be still haunting hither,
Till we four shall them four take here altogether.

MISERICORDIA
Now sisters, go we, and Respublica with us,
To be new apparelled otherwise than thus.

37 **chief...price** their principal.
41 ***Benedicite!*** Bless us all!
43 **convinced** convicted.
48 **quiet** in peace.
2 See Psalm 84: 11–13, 'Mercy and truth have met each other: justice and peace have kissed. Truth is sprung out of the earth: and justice hath looked down from heaven.'
3 **sundered** parted.
12 **recure** recover/restore.
32 **To...thus.** To be given new clothes very different to these.

JUSTICE
Come on, Respublica, with us to wealth from woe;
God hath given us in charge that it must be so.
VERITY
The blissful renovation ye shall reign in
Must from henceforth now immediately begin.

Cantent, 'The mercy of God' *et cetera, et exeant.*

Actus Quinti. Scena Quinta
(Avarice, Adulation.)

AVARICE
Such greedy, covetous folk as now of days been,
I trow, before these present days were never seen.
An honest man can go in no place of the street
But he shall, I think, with an hundred beggars meet.
'Give for God's sake!', 'Give for Saint Charity!';
'Give for our Lady's sake!', 'Give for the Trinity!';
'Give in the way of your good speed!'; 'Give, give, give, give!'
Find we our money in the street, do they believe?
If I had not a special grace to say nay,
I were but undone amongst them in one day.
But who cometh yond? Honesty? He cometh in haste.
ADULATION
I seek Policy.
AVARICE
Here, boy!
ADULATION
All is in waste!
AVARICE
How so?
ADULATION
We strive against the stream, all that we do!
AVARICE
Wherein?
ADULATION
That Verity come not this place unto.
For, wot ye what?
AVARICE
I shall when ye's have spake the word!
ADULATION
Justice and Peace too, with full consent and accord,
Are come down from heaven and have kissed together.
AVARICE
God give grace that they twain also come not hither.
ADULATION
As Mercy and Truth *sibi obviaverunt*,
So *Justicia et Pax osculatae sunt.*
AVARICE
Is it true; are they come?
ADULATION
And have kissed together.
AVARICE
Then carry in apace for fear of foul weather.
Have they kissed together?
ADULATION
Yea.
AVARICE
What needeth that?
Men should kiss women. And what point be they at?
ADULATION
All the four sisters, I do you t'understand,
Have already taken Respublica in hand.
They four progress with her in every border,
And mar all that ever we have set in order.
AVARICE
And what doth Insolence, or what saith he to that?
ADULATION
He stampeth, he stareth, and snuffeth sore thereat.
AVARICE
I advise him to storm, and to show himself stout;
They be women, and perchance may be faced out.
And Peace is an honest lady, and a quiet.
ADULATION
Verity and Justice are not for our diet.
AVARICE
Then Mercy is a good one. I like her well.
ADULATION
Yet oft turneth she her face away, and will not mell.
AVARICE
Well, fall back, fall edge, I am once at a point;
If Respublica come, t'adventure a joint.

36.1 ***Cantent . . . exeant.*** They sing . . . etc, and exit.
15 **wot ye what?** do you know what?
20 ***sibi . . . sunt*** 'Have met, so Justice and Peace have kissed' (Psalm 84).
22 **carry in apace** let's get indoors quickly.
27 **in every border** in all places.
32 **faced out** intimidated.
34 **not . . . diet** i.e. don't suit us.
38 **fall . . . joint** Whether the knife falls blade-up or blade-down, I've come to a point where I'll risk losing a limb.

ADULATION
She is fresh and gay, and flourisheth who but she?
AVARICE
Who brought it to such pass, will I tell her,
but we?
Or else, making these new ladies of her weary,
We should triumph and reign.
ADULATION
Oh never so merry.
AVARICE
Well, go to our company, I will remain here;
I may perhaps see Dame Respublica appear.
I will be in hand with her and make a good face.
ADULATION
And what shall I do?
AVARICE
Give warning in the mean space,
That Insolence shrinketh not, but play the stout man.
ADULATION
That I know he will do, for once I know he can.
AVARICE
And that you all three be prest to come hither
When need shall require we lay our heads
together.
Why, art thou here yet?
ADULATION
I am gone, with all my might. *Exit.*
AVARICE
And lo, where Respublica appeareth in sight.

(*Enter Respublica.*)

She is now at her nymphs, bearing up her train.
I will stand aside and listen a word or twain.

Actus Quinti. Scena Sexta (Respublica, Avarice.)

RESPUBLICA
O Lord, Thy mercies shall I sing evermore,
Which dost so tenderly Thy handmaid restore.
But what creature would suspicion have had
That my late administers had been men so bad?
Or who would have thought them counterfeits to
have been,
That had heard their words and their countenance seen?
And chiefly Avarice, which did the matter break?
AVARICE
That word toucheth me; now is time for me to speak.
RESPUBLICA
I thought him Policy, as just and true as steel.
AVARICE
I am glad that by me ye do such goodness feel.
RESPUBLICA
And that my wealth did grow, as it hath grown of late.
AVARICE
I ever told ye you should grow to this estate.
RESPUBLICA
Thou told me?
AVARICE
Yea, I told you so in very deed,
And highly I rejoice it doth so well succeed.
And *Salves festa dies* upon you, madam;
I am glad ye have got a new robe, so I am.
What saint in the calendar do we serve today,
That ye be so gorgeously decked and so gay?
RESPUBLICA
In rejoicing that I shall be clean rid of thee.
AVARICE
Nay, by this cross, ye shall never be rid for me.
RESPUBLICA
And of thy compeers.
AVARICE
Well, let them do as they lust,
I will ride upon Jill, mine own mare, that is just.
Other ways I shall do you service of the best.
RESPUBLICA
Thou wicked wretch, darest thou with me to jest?
AVARICE
What? I now see, *honores mutant mores.*
But as seemeth here, *raro in meliores*
RESPUBLICA
Thee, and all thy service, I do from me exile.
AVARICE
Is that the high reward ye promised me erewhile?

47 **mean space** meantime.
49 **stout** bold.
49 **prest** swift.
51 **art . . . yet?** are you still here?
53 **at** with.
4 **administers** ministers.
7 **which . . . break?** who started this business?
15 ***Salva festa dies*** Welcome festive day!
18 **decked** dressed.
22 **I . . . mare** I'll make my own plans (for my own benefit).
23 Again the sexual overtones of 'service' are implied.
26 ***honores . . . meliores*** 'honours change manners . . . and rarely improve them'.
28 **erewhile** not long ago.

Is not this a wise woman and minded to thrive,
That would me, Policy, out of the country drive!

RESPUBLICA
Thee and thy complices from me I shall out-cast.

AVARICE
Then I pray you, pay us for our pains that are past.

RESPUBLICA
Ye shall be paid.

AVARICE
Once I have done the best I can.
Authority also, he hath played the man;
Reformation hath done his part, I can tell;
If ye mistrust Honesty, faith ye do not well.
And as for Avarice, he is conveyed quite,
I bade him get him hence or I would him indict.
I, Policy, have made him to pluck in his horns,
I swear I would else lay him on prickles and thorns,
Where he should take no rest, neither day nor night,
So he had as lief be hanged as come in sight.

RESPUBLICA
I may say with Job, how vainly do ye cheer me,
When all the words ye give from truth doth disagree,
And with the wise man I may most justly say this:
'*Justicia tamen non luxit in nobis*.'
Or else with the prophet in most sorrowful mood,
'The fruit of our justice is turned into wormwood'.
Well, the best of you is a detestable vice,
And thou, for thy part, art most stinking Avarice!

AVARICE
Jesu, when were you wont so foul mouthed to be,
To give such nicknames? Ah, in faith, Dame Verity
Hath had you in schooling of late. Well, in God's name,
I am sorry for you, e'en sorry, that I am.
Iwis I have wrought to set you in good state,
And watched for that purpose both early and late.
And iwis if you would abide my framing,
And not thus to have fall to checking and blaming,
I would ere long of you have made such carpenter-work
That ye should have said Policy had been a clerk.
Nay, you should have seen how I would have you compact.

RESPUBLICA
Yea, no doubt, ye would have done some great and fine act.

AVARICE
I would have brought half Kent into Northumberland,
And Somersetshire should have wrought to Cumberland,
Then would I have stretched the county of Warwick
Upon tenter-hooks, and made it reach to Berwick.
A piece of the Bishopric should have come southward...
Tut, tut I tell you, I had wondrous feats toward.

RESPUBLICA
God hath placed me already in the best wise.

AVARICE
Yea, but yet not half so well as I could devise.
But, no force. Well then, I see ye will none of me.

RESPUBLICA
No.

AVARICE
Then ye can be content I depart from ye?

RESPUBLICA
Yea.

AVARICE
Well, yet and ye pray me, I will tarry still.

RESPUBLICA
No.

AVARICE
Well, speak me fair and woo me yet and I will.

RESPUBLICA
No hence, avaunt!

AVARICE
Have I had of you such a clog,

42 **as lief** rather.
43 The protagonist of the biblical book of Job.
46 ***Justicia . . . nobis*** Justice does not yet shine on us.
48 See Amos, 5:7, 'You that turn judgment into wormwood, and forsake justice in the land'.
55 **Iwis** I know.
57 **abide my framing** continue with my plans.
58 **checking** criticizing.
59 **such carpenter-work** such a masterpiece.
61 **compact** composed/brought together.
67 **Bishopric** Durham.
68 **I . . . toward** I was planning marvels.
69 **wise** manner.
71 **no force** no matter.
73.1 **and . . . me** if you ask me to.
75.1 **clog** a fetter used to tether cattle. Avarice suggests that Respublica used to want to keep him close to her.

And now you bid me avaunt, and make me a dog?

RESPUBLICA

Hence, at once!

AVARICE

Nay, tut, an ye will ha' us, ha' us.

RESPUBLICA

Out of my presence!

AVARICE

Well then, ye will not ha' us?

RESPUBLICA

No, avoid, I charge thee!

AVARICE

Then needs depart I must.
Adieu; in faith I would have served you of trust,
But, since Respublica hath put me to exile,
Where may I go keep myself secret for a while?
Is there never a good chaplain in all this town
That will for a while hide me under his gown?
Never a good farmer? Never a good merchant-man?
Well, I will go pick out some corner if I can.
But first will I monish my fellows of this gear,
And we scape this plunge, I care not for the next year.

Exit.

RESPUBLICA

Now will I to Justice and th'other ladies three,
And pray that these vices may all suppressed be.

Enter, People.

But lo, here cometh People; I will now turn again,
And first know of his good state by a word or twain.

Actus Quinti. Scena Septa (Respublica, People.)

RESPUBLICA

What, standeth he prying? Dareth he not enter?

PEOPLE

Ch'ould vain zee my lady, but I's dare not venture.

RESPUBLICA

Shrink not back from me, but draw to me, my dear friend.

PEOPLE

Chill virst know and ye be alone, zo God me mend.

RESPUBLICA

Come, here be none but thy friends, me believe.

PEOPLE

Well, then chill be zo bold to peek in, by your leave.

RESPUBLICA

How happeneth that thou hast so long been me fro?

PEOPLE

Marry, chill tell you. As soon as ye were ago,
Hither came a zort of court-nalls, hard men and zore,
They shaked me up, chwas ne'er zo rattled avore.
They vell all upon me, catch a word that might catch,
Well was him that at me, People, might get a snatch.
Chould have been at home rather than a new groat.
Ich may zedge to you, I's veared pulling out my throat.
They bade me pick me home and come at you no more.
And Ich did, they zware I's should be corrupt therefore.
Zo thick proud whore-cop, what call ye him?

RESPUBLICA

Insolence?

PEOPLE

Yea, even thick-same, he vair popped me to silence.

RESPUBLICA

And how is it with you now, better than it was?

PEOPLE

All beginneth now to come gaily well to pass.
We hear of your good vortune, that goeth about,
How ye beeth permounted, which maketh all us proud.
And Ich am able since to buy me a new coat,
And I's thank God chave in my purse a zilver groat.
Iwis Ich could not zo zay these zix years afore.

87 **monish . . . gear** warn . . . about this matter.
88 **And** If.
9 **a zort of court-nalls** a gang of courtiers.
11–13 **They vell . . . groat.** They fell upon me in a free-for-all, with prizes for everyone who could hit me: I'd rather have been at home then than have a new groat (a small coin, but a lot of money to People).
14 **zedge** say.
15 **at** to.
16 **And** If.
16 **corrupt** killed.
17 **Zo . . . whore-cop** So this proud bastard.
18 **popped** punched.
22 **permounted** promoted.
25 **Iwis . . . zay** Indeed, I couldn't have said that.

Whoever caused it, ill thank have they therefore.

RESPUBLICA
They will be here soon, bide you them here for a train.

PEOPLE
Mass, but I ninnat, would ye have 'em squat out on's brain?

RESPUBLICA
They shall not do thee harm the value of a point.

PEOPLE
Then, and you zay the word, Ich'll jeopard a joint.

RESPUBLICA
If they but offer thee wrong, they shall smart therefore.

PEOPLE
Nay, will ye be zo good to tie 'em up avore?
And what shall Ich zay to 'em?

RESPUBLICA
Nothing, but be a bait.
Till take them all here suddenly I may await. *Exit.*

PEOPLE
Well, it shall be do. Chould laugh and both my hands clap
To zee Rice-Puddingcake's enemies take in a trap.
And, az I pray, if zome of 'em come not yonder!
Chould my Lady had bid ne'er zo little longer.

Actus Quinti. Scena Octava
(Insolence, Adulation, Oppression, People, Avarice.)

INSOLENCE
Where is Avarice, how? He doth not now appear.

ADULATION
He bade me monish you that we might all meet here.

OPPRESSION
But see where People standeth.

ADULATION
What doth he here now?

OPPRESSION
About little goodness, I dare my word avow.

INSOLENCE
Let us speak unto him. People, wherefore and why,
Like a loitering losel standest thou here idly?

OPPRESSION
Thou comest to Respublica to make some moan.

ADULATION
Or else some complaint.

PEOPLE
You all see cham here alone.

INSOLENCE
Ye must have silver money must ye, gentleman?
You cannot be content with such coin as we can?

OPPRESSION
Yea, must burn wood and coal, must ye, all of pleasance?
Burn turfs or some of thy bedstraw, with a vengeance!

ADULATION
Ye must eat fresh meat, bought from the shambles, must ye?
Eat garlic and onions, and roots or grass and lust ye.

INSOLENCE
In faith, I will whip you for this, ye peasant lout!

ADULATION
And twig you.

INSOLENCE
Ere another year come about.

ADULATION
But see where Avarice cometh running very fast.

Enter Avarice.

AVARICE
I have trod and scud till my wind is almost past,
Yet my mates are not where...

INSOLENCE ET ADULATION
We be here come of late.

AVARICE
Be there not, trow ye, honester men in Newgate?

INSOLENCE
No words of reproach, brother mine, I rede you.

AVARICE
None but God-i-god eve, and God-i-god speed you.
Fare ye well again, and ye be falling out now.

INSOLENCE AND ADULATION
We mind it not.

AVARICE
'Twere more need to look about you.

[27] **for a train** as a trick (to act as a lure).
[28] **ninnat...brain?** will not. Would you have them bash out my brain?
[29] **point** a ribbon for fastening hose.
[34] **Till take** To catch.
[6] **losel** wretch.
[11] **wood and coal** i.e. more expensive fuels.
[14] **and lust ye** if you want to.
[18] **trod and scud** tramped and hurried.
[20] **in Newgate** i.e. in prison.
[21] **rede** advise.

INSOLENCE
How goeth all? Tell us.

AVARICE
My Lady is waxed froward.
Our names be all known, so there is array toward.

INSOLENCE AND OPPRESSION
God speed us well.

AVARICE
Once I am thrust out of service.

ADULATION
Alas, what may I do?

INSOLENCE AND OPPRESSION
Tell us thy best advice.

AVARICE
Nay, I cannot have you when I would, none of you all,
Therefore, shift for yourselves each one, for me you shall.

ADULATION
Nay, for the pash of God, tell us what best to do,
Ye know I was ne'er slack to resort you unto.

AVARICE
These ladies that are come for commonweal's relief,
Prepare to work us woe, and do us all mischief.

INSOLENCE
Nay, by His precious *populorum*, I swear,
Not the proudest of them all can hurt me a hair.

OPPRESSION
If they offer of us to make their gauds or toys,
They shall find, I trow, we are no babes nor boys.

AVARICE
To prevail against them with force I do despair.

INSOLENCE
Be that as be may.

ADULATION
I will fall to speaking fair.
But of all this trouble we may thank People, this wretch.

OPPRESSION
Faith, villain, if we scape, thou shalt an halter stretch.

ADULATION
But what remedy therewhile?

AVARICE
Faith, all will be nought.

ADULATION
Tell us what to do.

AVARICE
I will. They come, we are caught!

ADULATION
Whither shall I run?

AVARICE
Now sing a song, Honesty.

ADULATION
I am past singing now.

AVARICE
Yes one song, Honesty. Hey, hey, hey, hey!
I will be merry while I may.

Actus Quinti. Scena Nona
(Verity, Justice, Avarice, Respublica, Adulation, Misericordia, Peace, People, Insolence, Oppression.)

VERITY
Here they be, all four. This is an happy chance.

AVARICE
Take each man a lady, sirs, and let us go dance.

RESPUBLICA
I left People here for a train, to hold them talk.

AVARICE
Alas, that I could tell which way best hence to walk.
What be these fair ladies, and whether will they, trow?

JUSTICE
We arrest you sirs, all four, as ye stand in a row.
Not so hardy in your hearts our arrest to gainsay.

AVARICE
Nay, we are content, if ye let us go our way.

JUSTICE
No, not a foot, we must first your reckoning take.

AVARICE
I ne'er bought nor sold with you, reckoning to make,
Nor I know not who you be.

JUSTICE
Justice is my name.

AVARICE
Where is your dwelling?

25.1 **waxed froward** grown quarrelsome.
26 **array toward** a fight brewing.
30 **for...shall** for all I care.
31 **pash** passion.
35 ***populorum*** a nonsensical oath.
37 **If...toys** i.e. if they try to mess around with us.
42 **an halter stretch** i.e. be hanged.
7 **Not...gainsay.** Don't be so foolish as to try to resist.

JUSTICE

In heaven; and thence I came.

AVARICE

Dwell ye in heaven, and so mad to come hither?
All our hucking here is how we may get thither.

JUSTICE

I bring heaven with me, and make it where I am.

AVARICE

Then I pray you, let me be your prentice, madam.
I will be at your beck.

JUSTICE

Ye shall, ere ye depart.

AVARICE

I would learn how to make heaven, with all my heart.
Well, as for Lady Misericordia,
I remember I saw you with Respublica.

ADULATION

You, if you so please, may do much good in this land.
Many at this hour do need your good helping hand.

AVARICE

And ye came down from heaven too, I judge.

MISERICORDIA

Yea, sure.

AVARICE

Why, what folk are ye, that cannot heaven endure?
And what may I call you, Lady?

PEACE

My name is Peace.

AVARICE

Ye have long dwelt with us, we have been long in peace.

PEACE

Call ye it peace, sirrah, when brother and brother
Cannot be content to live one by another?
When one for his house, for his land, yea, for his groat,
Is ready to strive and pluck out another's throat?
I will in all such things make perfect union.

AVARICE

Then goodnight the lawyers' gain, by Saint Trunion!
Westminster Hall might go play if that came to pass.
Faith, we must serve you with a *supersedeas*.

VERITY

Well, leave vain prattling and now come answer to me.

AVARICE

I must hear first what ye say, and who ye be.

VERITY

I am Dame Verity.

AVARICE

What, the daughter of Time?

VERITY

Yea.

AVARICE

I know my master, your father, well afine.
Welcome fair Lady, sweet lady, little lady,
Plain lady, smooth lady, sometime Spital lady,
Lady long-tongue, lady tell-all, lady make-bate;
And I beseech you, from whence are ye come of late?

VERITY

I am sprung out of the earth.

AVARICE

What, ye do but jest?

VERITY

The book saith, '*Veritas de terra orta est*'.

AVARICE

Happy is he which hath that garden plot, I trow,
Out of which such fair blossoms do spring and grow.
Yet this one thing I say.

VERITY

What?

AVARICE

Ye are friend to few,
Prest to open all things and men's manners to show.

VERITY

If ye be true and just, that is your benefit.

AVARICE

True or untrue, just or unjust, it is your spite;
And glad ye are to take other folks in a trip,
Yet ye [...] now and then, your own self on the whip.
Well ye might be honest of your tongue, if you would.

VERITY

If your acts were honest, ye did but as ye should.

AVARICE

Who chargeth me with the crime of any vice?

14 **All...thither.** All our efforts here (on earth) are spent trying to get there (to heaven).
17 **beck** command.
33 **Westminster Hall** the home of the law courts.
34 ***supersedeas*** a writ to suspend a legal action.
38.1 **afine** indeed.
40 **Spital lady** hospital/leper-house-keeper.
41 **make-bate** cause-trouble.
44 ***Veritas...est.*** Psalm 84:12, 'Truth is sprung out of the earth (and justice hath looked down from heaven').
48 **Prest** eager.
52 A word or two is obliterated in the manuscript here.

VERITY
Thou callst thyself Policy, and art Avarice.
AVARICE
Nay, I defy your malice, I am Policy.
Ask of my fellows here, am not I Policy?
VERITY
Ladies, will ye all see him openly tried?
JUSTICE
If he be an ill one, let him be descried.
VERITY
What hast thou in thy bosom?
AVARICE
Nothing I, truly.
VERITY
Nothing truly got say; show it forth openly!
AVARICE
What should I show forth?
VERITY
That bag in thy bosom hid.
AVARICE
It lieth well, I thank you, as much as though I did.
VERITY
Nay, come on, out with it!
AVARICE
Lo, here 'tis for your fancy.
VERITY
Give it me.
AVARICE
Yea, nay, I defy that policy!
VERITY
Open it!
AVARICE
Yea, that each body might be catching?
Some's teeth, I think, water e'en since, to be snatching.
VERITY
We must needs see what it is.
AVARICE
'Tis a bag of rye.
VERITY
Rye? What rye?
AVARICE
A bag of rye.
VERITY
Such as men do eat?
AVARICE
A bag of rye flour, a great deal better than wheat.
VERITY
Let us see what rye it is. Pour it out in haste.
AVARICE
Yea, shall? I trow not. Indeed so might we make waste.
VERITY
There is no remedy, pour it out in my lap.
AVARICE
Nay, if there be no choice, I will use mine own cap.
VERITY
So, 'a bag of rye', quod thou?
AVARICE
Yea, so God me speed.
VERITY
Thou sayst even truth, 'tis a bag of rye indeed:
Usury, perjury, pitchery, patchery,
Pilfery, bribery, snatchery, catchery,
Flattery, robbery, cloutery, botchery,
Trumpery, harlotry, misery, treachery.
AVARICE
There is too, and please you, a little sorcery,
Witchery, bawdery, and such other grossery.
VERITY
And how gotst thou all this in thy possession?
AVARICE
Pardon me, and I will make my confession.
The world is hard, and the bag is but very small;
I got it where I could, to go on begging withal;
A plain, true dealing man that loveth not to steal,
And I durst not be bold to crave of commonweal.
VERITY
Now do off thy gown, and turn the inside outward.
AVARICE
Let me alone, and an Angel for a reward.
VERITY
Come, off at once. When? Come, off! No more gauds nor japes.
AVARICE
Must I needs whip over the chain, like Jackanapes?
RESPUBLICA
Out, in the virtue of God, what do ye here see?

61 **in thy bosom** hidden in your robes.
67–68 **Yea . . . snatching.** So everyone can grab some? Some folk are salivating already to snatch some.
73 **shall . . . waste.** Shall I? I don't think so. That way we might spill some.
90 **do** take.
91 **Angel** a gold coin.
92 **gauds** jests.
93 **whip . . . Jackanapes?** jump to order over my chain, like a trained monkey?

AVARICE
All this had been lost, Respublica, but for me.
RESPUBLICA
O Lord, where hast thou dragged up all these purses?
VERITY
Where he hath had for them many thousand curses.
RESPUBLICA
Where hast thou gotten them? Tell truth and do not lie.
AVARICE
Where no honest man could have gotten them but I;
In blind corners, where some would have hoarded them,
Had not I taken them with the manner and burdened them.
RESPUBLICA
And whither was it thine intent to convey them now?
AVARICE
I hid them, that I might bring them safely to you.
I durst not bear them openly, to God I vow.
Iwis ye have heard me blame pickpurses ere now.
And this is all yours.
VERITY
It is hers in very deed.
AVARICE
With sufferance I could get mo to help her need.
VERITY
How says ye, Respublica, now to Policy?
RESPUBLICA
I ne'er suspected him, nor had him in zealousy.
VERITY
E'en such-like counterfeits shall all the rest appear.
Sirs, do off your utmost robes, each one even here.
Now what these are ye see plain demonstration.
RESPUBLICA
Insolence! Oppression! Adulation!
O Lord, how have I be used these five years past?
PEOPLE
Nay, I's ne'er thought better of 'em, Ich, by God's vast.
Vey, madam, my Lady, such strussioners as these
Have oft made you believe the moon was a green cheese.
VERITY
Now ye see what they are, the punishment of this
Must be referred to the goddess Nemesis.
She is the most high goddess of correction,
Clear of conscience and void of affection;
She hath power from above, and is newly sent down
To redress all outrages in city and in town.
She hath power from God all practice to repeal
Which might bring annoyance to Lady Commonweal.
To her office belongeth the proud t'overthrow,
And such to restore as injury hath brought low.
'Tis her power to forbid and punish in all estates
All presumptuous, immoderate attemptates.
Her cognisance, therefore, is a wheel, and wings to fly,
In token her rule extendeth far and nigh.
A rudder eke she beareth in her other hand,
As directory of all things in every land.
Then pranketh she her elbows out under her side,
To keep back the heady and to temper their pride.
To her, therefore, dear sisters, we must now resort,
That she may give sentence upon this naughty sort.
She knoweth what is fittest for their correction;
Nemesis must therefore herein give direction.
JUSTICE
Then, People, while we Lady Nemesis do fet,
All these offenders in thy custody we set,
Them to apprehend and keep till we come again.
PEOPLE
And ye give me t'ority, chill keep 'em, that is plain.
INSOLENCE AND OPPRESSION
Shall People keep us, of whom we have been lords?
PEOPLE
Stand still, or by Jiss, chill bind you vast with chords.
Nay, sirs, Ich ha' you now in my custodity.
AVARICE
Mass, I will be gone, for mine own commodity.

101 **taken...them** caught them in the act, and accused them (of hoarding).
116 **strussioners** destroyers.
121 **affection** favouritism.
126 **To...belongeth** It is her mission.
129 **attemptates** enterprises.
130 **Her cognisance** Her heraldic badge or emblem.
134 **pranketh** sticks out.
137 **naughty sort** evil gang.
143 **t'ority** the authority.

PEOPLE

Zoft, whither wilt thou? Nilt thou not be ruled?
Stand still, skit-brained thief, or thy bones shall be coiled.
Yond be they coming now, Ich war't, that will tame ye.
A zee, art thou gone too? Come back and evil a' thee!

Actus Quinti. Scena Decima (Nemesis, Respublica, Misericordia, Veritas, Justicia, Pax, People, Insolence, Oppression, Adulation, Avarice.)

NEMESIS

Come forth, Respublica, our darling most dear.

RESPUBLICA

At your word, most gracious Lady, I am here.

NEMESIS

Are these your trusty men that had you in government?

PEOPLE

The skit-brains nold not be ruled, ne'er since ye went.

NEMESIS

People, why art thou bashful, and standest so far?
Be of good cheer now, and I warrant thee, come near.

PEOPLE

I nill come no nearer, cha not be haled up with states,
But I's cannot be fitchant enough amongst my mates.

NEMESIS

Come near when I bid thee.

PEOPLE

Marry, but I ninnat.
I nam not worthy to perk with you, no I nam not.

NEMESIS

Well, Respublica, are these your late governors,
Whom ye took for faithful and trusty counsellors?

RESPUBLICA

Yea, forsooth, madam.

AVARICE

These three be, but I am none,
For I was discharged nigh half an hour agone.

NEMESIS

Come first, stand forth here, thou, Adulation.

ADULATION

Speak a good word for me, Lady Compassion.

PEOPLE

Nay, she shall not need, I chill speak for thee myself.
Madam take good heed, for this is a naughty elf.

ADULATION

Nay, madam, the cause of all this was Avarice.
He forged us new names, and did us all entice.

OPPRESSION

We neither did nor could work but by his advice.

ADULATION

Because I got no more, he chid me once or twice.

INSOLENCE

Madam, only Avarice made us all to fall.

AVARICE

Yea? Fall to preaching? Nay, then will I tell all.
Madam, ere I had taught these merchants any while,
They were cunninger than I, all men to beguile.
And Verity saw mine were small purses and bags,
Tottering loose about me like wind-shaken rags.
But he that should have bagged that Insolence did win,
Must have made a poke to put five or six shires in!
He must have made wide sacks for castles, towns, and woods;
The canvas to make them of were worth ten times my goods.
Then Oppression here, to feather well his nest,
Cared not of their livelihood whom he dispossessed.
Bishops, deans, provosts, ye poor folk from the spital,
Lands with church and chapel, all was for him too little.
Poor I did not so, I scraped but little crumbs,
And here and there with odd ends patched up my sums.
Flattery got his thrift by counterfeit honesty,
Yet, by these ten bones, I bid him use modesty.
Therefore spare not him, he will ne'er come to good pass,
But I may well be mended, by the Mary Mass.

149 **coiled** beaten.
150 **Ich war't** I warrant.
151 **evil a' thee!** curse you!
7 **cha ... states** I've not been brought up among great ones.
8 **fitchant** nimble.
10 **perk** thrust myself forward.
29 **that** that which.
30 **a poke to** a pocket big enough.
40 Avarice swears on his fingers.

MISERICORDIA
Lady Nemesis, now have ye occasion
And matter to show your commiseration.
It is much more glory, and standeth with more skill,
Lost sheep to recover, than the scabby to spill.

JUSTICE
But how shall this redress be well prosecuted,
If Justice with Mercy shall be executed?
Straight Justice must such great enormities redress,
Severity must put men in fear to transgress.
Justice must give each man that he doth deserve.

MISERICORDIA
If offenders were not, wherefore might Mercy serve?

AVARICE
Stick hard to it, good sweet Lady Compassion,
We are else undone, by Cock's bitter passion.

MISERICORDIA
Verity, how say you? Have I not spoken well?

VERITY
Mercy in one place with Justice sometime may dwell,
And right well agree together. How say you, Peace?

PEACE
Where all thing is well amended, I do increase.

NEMESIS
Ladies, we have heard all your discrete advices,
And each one shall have some part of your devices;
Neither all nor none shall taste of severity,
But, as they are now known through Lady Verity,
So shall they receive our mercy or our ire,
As the wealth of Respublica shall best require.
Now, Adulation, what saith you in this case?

ADULATION
Nought in mine excuse, but submit me to your Grace.
Only this I promise, if I may mercy find,
Utterly forever to change my wicked mind.
I ne'er sought afore mine own private gain so much
But I will further Commonweal's ten times so much.

NEMESIS
Well, thou mayst become a worthy subject, it is plain.

ADULATION
Else, ye know at all times how to reach me again.

NEMESIS
Thou mightest swerve of frailty, thou mightest do to please,
Thou mightest do for fear, thou mightest do to live in ease.
Well, upon thy promise, for once we pardon thee;
Go, and see that from henceforth thou be perfect Honesty.

ADULATION
So long as shall please God to give me life and heal,
I shall most duly serve God and the Commonweal.

AVARICE
Now to thee, Avarice, have at thy petticoat.

NEMESIS
Now, the plague of commonweals, as all men do note,
Come forth Avarice: to spare thee will be no boot,
Thou must be plucked up e'en by the very root,
Because thou scrapest up whatever thou mightest get.

AVARICE
Indeed, I thank God there is no man in my debt.

NEMESIS
And because thou caughtst it by wrong contribution,
Thou shalt first and foremost make restitution.

AVARICE
Let me then, with pardon, go hence about it lightly.

NEMESIS
No, ye shall have help to see it done uprightly.
People, take this fellow...

AVARICE
God save me from this plunge.

NEMESIS
That he may be pressed, as men do press a sponge,
That he may drop out t'every man his lot,
To the utmost farthing that he hath falsely got.

PEOPLE
And ye bid me, chill squeeze him as dry as a kix.

46 **than...spill** than to lose the sick ones.
52 **If...serve?** What would be the point of Mercy, if there were no guilty folk (to pardon)?
56 **one** the same.
73 **swerve of frailty** err through weakness.
79 **Now...petticoat.** [Aside] Now it's your turn, Avarice, prepare yourself!
81 **no boot** no benefit (to anyone).
85 **caughtst...contribution** gained it unfairly.
87 **go...lightly** go off and do it quickly.
88 **uprightly** properly.
93 **kix** a stalk of straw.

AVARICE

Nay, the pash of God, I shall then die of the flix.

NEMESIS

Nay, thou shalt deliver him to the head officer
Which hath authority justice to minister.

PEOPLE

Chill 'liver him to the constable, and come again.

NEMESIS

Now, justice for these two that do here remain:
Because the fault of Insolence is heinous and great,
Lucifer's own fault, t'aspire to the highest seat;
And because Oppression hath wronged men so sore,
That he spoiled innocents of all they had, and more,
People shall deliver them unto safe custody,
Where they may no farther annoy anybody.
When the time may serve t'examine and try their cause,
Call them both before you, and judge them by the laws.

PEOPLE

And shall 'ch carry away these same two men also?

NEMESIS

Yea, go deliver them to an officer, go.
Now, darling Respublica, ye are in th'old good estate,
And they taken away that spoiled you of late.
Now cleave to these ladies, from heaven to you direct;
They from all corruption will you safe protect.
Well, I must go hence to another country now,
That hath of redress the like case that was in you.
I leave you for this time, immortal thanks to give,
To God and your sovereign, which do you thus relieve.

RESPUBLICA

Thanks be to Thee, O Lord, which hast this world wrought,
And hast me to this state from utter ruin brought.

PEACE

Now let us all together, both with heart and voice,
In God and in Queen Mary most joyfully rejoice.

VERITY

Praying that her reign, most graciously begun,
May long years endure, as hitherto it hath done.

MISERICORDIA

Pray we for her Council to have long life and health.

JUSTICE

Their sovereign to serve.

PEACE

And to maintain Commonwealth.

OMNES

Amen.

Cantent, et exeant.

FINIS.

94 **the flix** dysentery.
111 **to you direct** sent to you.
114 **That...you.** That has a similar need for reform.
124.1 OMNES All.
125.1 ***Cantent, et exeant.*** They sing, and exit.

Thyestes

(1560)

JASPER HEYWOOD
(1535–1598)

THE PLAYWRIGHT

Jasper Heywood was born in 1535, the son of the playwright John Heywood, author of *The Play of the Weather* and other interludes in the reign of Henry VIII (see the head-note to *The Play of the Weather*, this volume). He studied at Oxford University, gaining his BA in 1553, and an MA in 1558. He was elected a fellow of Merton College in 1554, but was forced to leave the college after a brush with authority in 1558. Later in the same year, however, he was offered a fellowship at All Souls, where he produced the translations of Seneca's Roman tragedies which are his greatest claim to literary fame. Heywood was, like his father, a devout Catholic, and so found it impossible to conform to the Protestant Elizabeth religious settlement. He thus left his fellowship and moved abroad, ending up in Rome, where he joined the Jesuit order in 1562. From 1564 he studied and taught theology at the Jesuit college in Dilingen, Bavaria, but was again often in dispute with his superiors. In 1580 he returned to Rome, where he was commissioned in 1581 to join the secret Jesuit mission to England designed to shore up Catholic support in the country and foment opposition to the Elizabethan government. Heywood worked in secret among the English gentry and aristocracy in the north, in the universities and in London, before being arrested in December 1583, when the boat in which he was returning to the Continent was driven aground near Queensborough (Kent) by a storm. Imprisoned and tortured in London, he was eventually exiled to France, from where he returned to Rome. He spent the remaining years of his life in the Jesuit house in Naples.

THE PLAY

Thyestes was the second of three tragedies translated by Heywood from the work of the Roman Stoic writer, Lucius Annaeus Seneca (Seneca the younger) (*c*.4BC–65AD) the first being *Troas* (1559), the third *Hercules Furens* (1561). It contains many of the characteristic features of Senecan tragedy that fascinated the early Elizabethans. The bloody feuds, excessive acts of violence, histrionic speeches, and obsession with ghosts and elemental forces of vengeance and malice, loosed from the underworld to blight successive generations of a cursed family, all spoke powerfully to the playwrights of Heywood's generation and their successors. The kinds of revenge plays popular in the 1590s and 1600s—Thomas Kyd's *Spanish Tragedy* (late 1580s?), Middleton's (or Tourneur's) *Revenger's Tragedy* (1606–7) and Shakespeare's *Titus Andronicus* (early 1590s)—the last of which borrows the plot line of the parent being forced unawares to eat their own children—*Richard III* (early 1590s) and *Macbeth* (*c*.1603–7)—all owe a profound debt to Seneca, and thus to Heywood, who, with his fellow translators, brought the playwright's works to the attention of an English-speaking readership.

The play follows the classical five-act structure and employs a Chorus that comments on the action (with varying degrees of partisanship and apparent knowledge of the characters' intentions) between the acts. Its subject concerns the playing out in the third generation of the curse placed on the house of Tantalus (son of Jupiter and the nymph Plouto), king of Lydia, when he tried to test the power of the gods. In an audacious act of violence of the kind that fascinated Seneca (who himself lived through the reigns of three emperors notorious for their cruelty, Caligula, Claudius, and Nero), Tantalus had killed his own son, Pelops, and served up his body as a meal for the gods. Jupiter saw the truth, however, and refused to eat. Restoring Pelops to life, he cursed Tantalus and his bloodline. Thus after his death the king was imprisoned in Tartarus, that part of the underworld reserved for the punishment of the wicked. There he was forced to stand, eternally thirsty and hungry, in a river whose water always evaded his grasp, beneath a tree whose fruit-laden branches remained forever just beyond his reach (a predicament that gives us the word 'tantalizing').

After the death of Tantalus, the Lydian throne remained wracked by evil and violence through successive generations. Pelops' sons, Atreus and Thyestes, conspired to murder their half-brother Chrysippus, and were exiled by their father for their crime. They fled to Mycenae, where they fought over the throne. Thyestes seduced Atreus' wife, Aerope, and persuaded her to steal for him a golden-fleeced ram, the pride of his brother's herd. Having secured the ram, he then proposed to Atreus that whoever had such a beast should become king. Thinking he had the ram safely hidden, Atreus agreed, only to discover that both it and his wife were now with Thyestes. The latter took the throne, but was later defeated and exiled in turn by Atreus. It is at this point in the story, with Atreus back in control of Mycenae, jealously ruminating on Thyestes' treachery and plotting further, more violent revenge, that the play begins.[1]

For the text edited here I have used the 1560 edition, printed 'in the house of' Thomas Berthelet, as the base text, from the copy now kept in the Huntington Library, San Marino, California, consulting also the version in *Seneca his Ten Tragedies* (1591), printed by Thomas Marsh, and the modern editions listed under further reading. Material from the 1591 edition is added within round brackets.

FURTHER READING

Flynn, Dennis, 'Heywood, Jasper (1535–1598)', *Oxford Dictionary of National Biography* (Oxford: Oxford University Press, 2004) <http://www.oxforddnb.com/view/article/13182>, accessed 6 June 2013.

Heywood, Jasper, *Thyestes*, New Mermaid edition, ed. Joost Daalder (London: Ernest Benn, 1982).

Seneca, *Thyestes*, ed. Jane Elder (Manchester: Carcanet New Press, 1982).

[1] As many of Heywood's readers would know from their schooldays, however, the tragic story would not end with the deaths of Thyestes and Atreus. Agamemnon and Menelaus, the sons of Atreus briefly mentioned in the play, would lead the Greek forces into the Trojan War, while Thyestes son, Aegisthus (conceived on his own daughter) continued the feud, conspiring with Agamemnon's wife Clytemnestra to kill him when he returned from Troy. Only when the conspirators are in turn killed by Clytemnestra's son Orestes and his sister Electra, and Orestes had propitiated the pursuing Harpies, spirits of vengeance, does the tragic cycle come to an end.

—— *Tragedies*, II (*Oedipus, Agamemnon, Thyestes, Hercules on Oeta, Octavia*), ed. John Fitch, Loeb Classical Library (New Haven, CT: Loeb, 2004).

Pincombe, Mike, 'Tragic Inspiration in Jasper Heywood's Translation of Seneca's *Thyestes*: Melpomene or Megaera?' in Thomas Betteridge and Greg Walker, eds., *The Oxford Handbook of Tudor Drama* (Oxford: Oxford University Press, 2012), 531–46.

de Vocht, H., *Jasper Heywood and his Translations of Seneca's 'Troas', 'Thyestes', and 'Hercules furens'* (Louvain: A. Uystpruyst, 1913).

Thyestes

The second Tragedy of Seneca, entitled Thyestes,
faithfully Englished by Jasper Heywood, Fellow of All Souls College, Oxford.
Imprinted at London in Fleet Street,
in the house late [of] Thomas Berthelet,
Anno 1560, 26 die Martii.

(THE ARGUMENT OF THIS TRAGEDY

Magaera, one of the hellish Furies, raising up Tantalus from Hell, incited him to set mortal hatred between his two nephews, Thyestes and Atreus, being brothers, and reigning as kings over Mycenae by interchangeable turns, that is to wit: Thyestes to reign the one year, and Atreus the other. Now Atreus, enraged with fury against his brother, partly for defiling and deflowering his wife, Aerope, by policy, and partly for taking from him a ram with a golden fleece, practiced with his servant how to be revenged of his brother. This Atreus therefore, dissembling a reconciliation and inviting Thyestes to Mycenae, secretly and unknown to him set before him at a banquet the flesh of his own children to eat. Afterwards, Atreus, having also given to his said brother the blood of his children in a goblet to drink, did lastly command the heads also to be brought in, at the doleful sight whereof, Thyestes, greatly lamenting, knowing he had eaten his own children, was wonderfully anguished. But Atreus, for that he had thus revenged himself, took therein great pleasure and delectation.)

[THE DEDICATORY EPISTLE]

To the Right Honourable Sir John Mason, knight, one of the Queen's Majesty's Privy Council, his daily orator Jasper Heywood wisheth health with increase of honour and virtue.

As bounden breast doth bear the poorest wight
That duty doth in trifling token send,
As he that doth with plenteous present quit
Of prouder price and glittering gold his friend.
Whoso repay'th with money's mighty mass
The good that he at other's hands hath found,
Remembrance of the benefit doth pass,
He thinks himself to him no longer bound.
The poor, whose power may not with price repay

Thomas Berthelet the former printer to Henry VIII.
26 die Martii 26 March.
Sir John Mason (1503–66) was Chancellor of Oxford University and a fellow of All Souls as well as a privy councillor. Heywood had been a friend of Mason's son Thomas, who died young (see Preface to this play, l.173). Daalder (1982 p. 3, n.) suggests that Mason's patronage may have got Heywood his All Souls' Fellowship.
daily orator one who prays for him daily.
1–4 **As bounden ... friend.** The poor man who sends only a modest token of his duty reveals as loyal a breast as he who can acknowledge his dedication to his friend with a more expensive, golden gift.
9 **with price** with equivalent value.

The great good gifts that he received before,
With thankful thought yet gogin gift doth sway,
Above the peise of pearl and gold great store.
If puissant prince at poor man's hand once took
A radish root, and was therewith content,
Your honour then I pray this little book
To take in worth that I to you present.
Which, though itself a volume be but small,
Yet greater gift it gives than wean ye might.
Though it a barren book be, throughout all
Full fruitless, yet not faithless sign in sight
It shows of him that for your honour prays
(As deeds of yours of him deserved have)
That God above prolong your happy days,
And make the skies your seat soon after grave.

THE TRANSLATOR TO THE BOOK

Thou little book my messenger must be
That must from me to wight of honour go.
Behave thee humbly, bend to him thy knee,
And thee to him in lowly manner show.

But do thou not thyself to him present
When with affairs thou shalt him troubled see;
Thou shalt, perhaps, so worthily be shent,
And with reproof he thus will say to thee,

'So proudly thus presume how darest thou,
At such a time so rashly to appear?
With things of weight thou seest me burdened now,
I may not yet to trifles give mine ear.'

Spy well thy time, when thou him seest alone,
An idle hour for thee shall be most meet,
Then step thou forth in sight of him anon,
And as behoves, his honour humbly greet.

But now take heed what I to thee shall tell,
And all by rote this lesson take with thee:
In everything thyself to order well
In sight of him, give ear and learn of me.

First, what or whence thou art if he would wit,
Then see that thou thy title to him show.

11–12 **With...store** The thankful thoughts of the poor giver add weight (sway) to the tiny (gogin) gift, giving it greater weight/value (peise) than great quantities of gold or pearl.

16 **in worth** as something valuable.

18 **than...might** than you might think.

2 **wight** man (i.e. Mason).

5–6 **do...see** don't present yourself when he's busy.

7 **shent** punished/rebuked.

21 **what...wit** if he should want to know what you are or who sent you.

Tell him thy name is in thy forehead writ,
By which he shall both thee and me well know.

Then when he hath once looked upon thy name,
If yet he shall neglect to read the rest,
Or if he chide and say thou art to blame
With trifles such to have him so oppressed,

Beseech him yet thereof to pardon thee,
Since thou art but thy master's messenger,
Excuse thyself and lay the fault in me,
At whose commandment thus thou com'st in there.

If my presumption then accuse he do,
If deed so rash of mine he do reprove,
That I thee dare attempt to send him to,
Beware thou speak nothing for my behove.

Nor do thou not excuse my fault in ought,
But rather yet confess to him the same,
And say there may a fault in me be thought,
Which to excuse it doubleth but the blame.

Yet with my boldness him beseech to bear,
And pardon give to this my enterprise,
A worthy thing in wight of honour were
A present poor to take in thankful wise.

For tell him, though thou slender volume be,
Ungreeing gift for state of honour guest,
So yet dost thou sign of duty bring with thee,
And pledge thou art of truly bounden breast.

And thou for him art come for to confess,
His beadman bound to be for his desert,
And how to him he grants he oweth no less,
Nor gives no more, but note of thankful heart.

In all the rest that he to thee shall say
Thy wit shall serve an answer well to make.
Thou hast thine errand, get thee hence away,
The gods thee speed, to them I thee betake.

THE PREFACE

It was the four and twentieth day of latest month save one
Of all the year, when flower and fruit from field and tree were gone,

28 **With . . . oppressed** To bother him with such trivia.
36 **behove** benefit.
43 **A worthy . . . were** It would be a worthy deed for a man of honour.
46 **Ungreeing** Unsatisfying/unsuitable.
50 **beadman** one who says prayers for another (in the Catholic tradition, using the beads of the rosary to count each prayer).
56 **betake** direct.
1–2 **the four . . . year** i.e. 24 November 1559.

And sadder season such ensued as dulls the doleful sprites
And muse of men that wonted were to wander in delights;
And weather such there was as well became the pensive pen
With sorry style of woes to write and eke of mischief, when
Aurora blushed with ruddy cheeks to wail the death again
Of Phoebus son: whom thunderbolt of mighty Jove had slain;
And clouds from high began to throw their dreary tears adown,
And Venus from the skies above on Friday foul to frown;
When (as at book with mazed muse I sat and pensive thought,
Deep drowned in dumps of drowsiness as change of weather wrought,)
I felt how Morpheus bound my brows and eke my temples stroke,
That down I sunk my heavy head and slept upon my book.
Then dreamed I thus, that by my side me thought I saw one stand
That down to ground in scarlet gown was dight, and in his hand
A book he bare: and on his head of bays a garland green.
Full grave he was, well steeped in years and comely to be seen.
His eyes like crystal shined, his breath full sweet, his face full fine,
It seemed he had been lodged long among the Muses nine.
'Good sir', quoth I, 'I you beseech (since that ye seem to me
By your attire some worthy wight), it may your pleasure be,
To tell me what and whence ye are'. Whereat a while he stayed,
Beholding me. Anon he spake, and thus (me thought) he said:
'Spain was,' quoth he, 'my native soil, a man of worthy fame
Sometime I was in former age, and Seneca my name'.
The name of Senec when I heard, then scantly could I speak.
I was so glad that from mine eyes the tears began to break
For joy, and with what words I should salute him I ne wist.
I him embraced; his hands, his feet and face full oft I kissed.
And as at length my trickling tears me thought I might refrain,
'O blissful day,' quoth I, 'wherein returned is again
So worthy wight. O happy hour, that liefer is to me
Than life, wherein it haps me so that I should Senec see!
Art thou the same that whilom didst thy Tragedies indite
With wondrous wit and regal style? O long desired sight!'
'And liv'st thou yet,' quoth I, 'indeed? And art thou come again
To talk and dwell as thou wert wont with men? And to remain
In this our age?' 'I live,' quoth he, 'and never shall I die.

3–4 **doleful... muse** the sorrowful spirits and thoughts.

7–8 **Aurora... slain** Aurora, goddess of the dawn, weeps for Phaethon, sun of Phoebus, the sun god, who lost control of his father's fiery chariot, forcing Jupiter (Jove) to slay him to bring the sun back to rest.

10 **Venus... frown** Friday was sacred to Venus, goddess of love and the morning star, and a day of ill omen.

11 **mazed muse** dull/confused inspiration. Heywood cannot write owing to the foul weather. Both his thoughts (muses) and divine inspiration (his Muse) are lacking.

12 **dumps** melancholy moods.

13 **Morpheus** god of sleep.

13 **eke... stroke** also stroked my temples.

16 **dight** dressed.

17 **bays** laurel, the crown of a 'laureate' poet.

20 **the Muses nine** the nine divine sisters who, in classical tradition, inspired writers and scholars.

23 **stayed** paused.

29 **I ne wist** I did not know.

33 **liefer** dearer.

34 **it... so** it is my (good) fortune.

35 **whilom** once.

The works I wrote shall still preserve my name in memory
From age to age. And now again I will revive the same,
And here I come to seek someone that might renew my name,
And make me speak in stranger speech, and set my works to sight,
And scan my verse in other tongue than I was wont to write.
A young man well I wot there is in th'isle of Britany,
(That from the rest of all the world aloof in seas doth lie)
That once this labour took in hand; him would I meet full fain,
To crave that in the rest of all my works he would take pain
To toil, as he in *Troas* did.' 'Is that your will?' quoth I.
I blushed, and said, 'The same you seek, lo, here I stand you by!'
'If thou,' quoth he, 'be whom I seek, if glory aught thee move
Of mine to come in after age, if Senec's name thou love
Alive to keep, I thee beseech again to take thy pen,
In metre of thy mother tongue to give to sight of men
My other works, whereby thou shalt deserve of them and me
No little thanks, when they themselves my Tragedies shall see
In English verse, that never yet could Latin understand.
With my renown perhaps thy name shall fly throughout this land,
And those that yet thee never knew shall thee both love and praise,
And say "God grant this young man well to live full many days,
And many happy hours to see in life; and, after grave,
Rest, joy, and bliss eternally above the skies to have,
That so translated hath these books."' 'To him,' quoth I, 'again
(If any be that so with thanks accepts a young man's pain)
I wish great good: but well I wot the hateful cursed brood
Far greater is, that are long since sprung up of Zoilus blood.
That red-haired, black-mouthed, squint-eyed wretch hath couched everywhere
In corner close some imp of his that sits to see and hear
What each man doth, and each man blames. Nor once we may him see
Come face to face, but, we once gone, then stoutly steps out he;
And all he carps that there he finds ere half he read to end,
And what he understands not, blames, though nought he can amend.
But were it so that such were none, how may these youthful days
Of mine, in thing so hard as this deserve of other praise?
A labour long,' quoth I, 'it is that riper age doth crave;
And who shall travail in thy books more judgment ought to have
Than I, whose greener years thereby no thanks may hope to win.
Thou seest dame Nature yet hath set no hairs upon my chin.
Crave this therefore of graver age, and men of greater skill.

43 **stranger** foreign (i.e. not Latin).
44 **scan** translate in language and poetic form.
45 **Britany** Britain.
49 ***Troas*** (*The Trojan Women*) was the first of Seneca's tragedies translated by Heywood.
50 **here...by** I stand here next to you.
51 **if...move** any glory at all inspires you.
65 **wot** know.
66 **Zoilus blood** the descendants of Zoilus, a notorious critic of Homer, hence malicious critics of any sort.
67–68 **hath...imp** who has hidden some offspring of his in every secret corner.
70 **we...he** once we have gone, then bravely he steps forward.
71 **all he carps** he criticizes everything.
72 **though...amend** although he can improve nothing.
75 **that...crave** that calls for a mature writer.
76 **who** (he) who.
77 **greener years** youth.
79 **graver age** some older, more serious writer.

Full many be that better can, and some perhaps that will.
But if thy will be rather bent a young man's wit to prove,
And think'st that elder learned men perhaps it shall behove
In works of weight to spend their time, go where Minerva's men
And finest wits do swarm, whom she hath taught to pass with pen.
In Lincoln's Inn and Temples twain, Gray's Inn and other mo,
Thou shalt them find whose painful pen thy verse shall flourish so
That Melpomen thou wouldst well ween had taught them for to write.
And all their works with stately style and goodly grace t'indite.
There shalt thou see the self same North, whose work his wit displays,
And Dial doth of Prince's paint, and preach abroad his praise.
There Sackville's sonnets sweetly sauced and featly fined be,
There Norton's ditties do delight, there Yelverton's do flee
Well pured with pen. Such young men three, as ween thou mightst again
To be begot as Pallas was, of mighty Jove his brain.
There hear thou shalt a great report of Baldwin's worthy name,
Whose Mirror doth of Magistrates proclaim eternal fame.
And there the gentle Blundville is by name and eke by kind,
Of whom we learn by Plutarch's lore what fruit by foes to find.
There Bavand bides, that turned his toil a Commonwealth to frame,
And greater grace in English gives to worthy author's name.
There Googe a grateful gains hath got: report that runneth rife,
Who crooked Compass doth describe and *Zodiac of Life*.
And yet great number more, whose names if I should now recite,
A ten times greater work than thine I should be forced to write.
A princely place in Parnass hill for these there is prepared,
Where crown of glitt'ring glory hangs, for them a right reward.
Whereas the laps of Ladies nine shall duly them defend,
That have prepared the laurel leaf about their heads to bend.

81 **if...prove** if you are determined to test a young man's mind.

83 **Minerva** the goddess of wisdom.

84 **pass with pen** surpass all others with the pen.

85 **In...mo** Heywood directs Seneca to the Inns of Court in London (Lincoln's Inn, the Inner and Outer Temple, and Gray's Inn), where lawyers were trained. They were centres of scholarship to rival the universities in this period.

87 **Melpomen...write** you'd think that Melpomena, the Muse of Tragedy herself had taught them how to write.

89 **North** Sir Thomas North, who translated Antonio de Guevara's advice book, *The Dial* ['clock'] *of Princes* from the Spanish in 1557.

91 **Sackville** Sir Thomas Sackville, the poet and co-author, with Thomas Norton, of the first English tragedy in the Senecan style, *Gorboduc*, performed in the Inner Temple at Christmas 1561–2. Norton's poems ('ditties') are praised in the next line.

91 **featly fined** elegantly refined.

92 **Yelverton** Christopher Yelverton, another poet and future playwright.

93 **pured** refined.

94 **begot...brain** the Greek goddess of wisdom, Pallas Athena (the Roman Minerva) was born directly from Zeus (Jupiter's) head.

95 **Baldwin** William Baldwin, who initiated the *Mirror for Magistrates*, a grand historical poem in the medieval *Fall of Princes* tradition, also contributed to by Sackville and others.

97 **Blundville...kind** Thomas Blundeville, who wrote *The Fruits of Foes* (printed in *Three Treatises* (1561)), partly translated from the Roman author Plutarch. Heywood calls him 'gentle' (aristocratic) in lineage/reputation (name) and nature (kind).

99 **Bavand** William Bavand, who translated *The Good Ordering of a Commonwealth*, by Joannes Ferrarius Montanus, in 1559.

99 **frame** design.

101–102 **Googe...*Life*.** Barnaby Googe, a poet who translated Pietro Angello Manzolli's *The Zodiac of Life* in 1560. Heywood suggests that he has gained the profit ('gains') of a widespread good reputation ('report that runneth rife') from the Compass (another name for the Zodiac).

105 **Parnass hill** Mount Parnassus, the home of the Muses (the 'Ladies nine').

And where their pens shall hang full high, and fame, that erst was hid,
Abroad in Brutus' realm shall fly, as late their volumes did.
These are the wits that can display thy Tragedies all ten,
Replete with sugared sentence sweet and practice of the pen.
Myself, I must confess, I have too much already done
Above my reach, when rashly once with *Troas* I begun,
And more presumed to take in hand than well I brought to end,
And little volume with mo faults than lines abroad to send.
And of that work what men report in faith I never wist,
But well I wot it may be thought so ill that little list
I have to do the like: whereof though mine be all the blame
And all to me imputed is that passeth in my name,
Yet (as of some I will confess that I the author was,
And faults too many made myself when I that book let pass
Out of my hands) so must I me excuse of other some.
For when to sign of Hand and Star I chanced first to come,
To printer's hands I gave the work, by whom I had such wrong,
That, though myself perused their proofs the first time, yet ere long,
When I was gone, they would again the print thereof renew,
Corrupted all, in such a sort that scant a sentence true
Now fly'eth abroad as I it wrote. Which thing when I had tried,
And fourscore greater faults than mine in forty leaves espied,
"Small thanks," quoth I, "for such a work would Senec give to me,
If he were yet alive, and should perhaps it chance to see."
And to the printer thus I said: "Within these doors of thine
I make a vow shall never more come any work of mine."'
'My friend,' quoth Senec therewithal, 'no marvel thereof is:
They have myself so wronged oft, and many things amiss
Are done by them in all my works. Such faults in every book
Of mine they make (as well he may it find that list to look),
That sense and Latin, verse and all, they violate and break,
And oft what I yet never meant they me enforce to speak.
It is the negligence of them, and partly lack of skill
That doth the works with pains well penned lull oft disgrace and spill.
But as for that, be nought abashed; the wise will well it weigh,
And learned men shall soon discern thy faults from his, and say,
"Lo, here the printer doth him wrong, as easy is to try,
And slander doth the author's name, and lewdly him belie."
But where thy years thou sayest lack skill, misdoubt thou not,' quoth he,

109 **erst** previously.
110 **Brutus' realm** Britain, reputedly founded by the mythical Trojan hero Brutus.
117 **I never wist** I don't know.
118–119 **little...like** I've little desire to try that sort of thing again.
119–120 **though...name** though I'm ultimately responsible for anything published under my name.
124 **Hand and Star** the shop sign of the printer, Richard Tottel, famous for publishing the anthology, *Songs and Sonnets* (aka *Tottel's Miscellany*) in 1557. Daalder speculates that Tottel's somewhat cavalier treatment of the poems by Wyatt, Surrey, and others in the *Miscellany* might support Heywood's claims to have been badly edited here.
128 **sort** way.
129 **tried** tested (by checking the published copy).
142 **spill** spoil/ruin.

'I will myself in these affairs a helper be to thee.
Each poet's tale I will expound, and other places hard.
Thou shalt (no doubt) find some that will thy labour well regard.'
And therewithal, 'O Lord,' he said, 'now him I think upon
That here but late too little lived, and now from hence is gone,
Whose virtues rare in age so green bewrayed a worthy wight,
And towardness tried of tender time, how lovely lamp of light
He would have been, if God had spared his days till such time when
That elder age had abled him by growth to graver man.
How thankful thing thinkst thou,' quoth he, 'would this to him have been,
If given to his name he might a work of thine have seen,
Whom during life he favoured so? But that may never be,
For gone he is (alas the while), thou shalt him never see
Where breathing bodies dwell again; nor never shalt thou more
Eftsoons with him of learning talk, as thou wert wont before.'
Yet wail no more for him,' he said, 'for he far better is.
His seat he hath obtained now among the stars in bliss.
And casting brighter beams about than Phoebus' golden gleed,
Above the skies he lives with Jove, another Ganymede,
In better place than Aquarie. Such grace did God him give.
But though the son be gone, yet here doth yet the father live;
And long might he this life enjoy in health, and great increase
Of honour and of virtue both, till God his soul release
From corpse to skies, with right reward to recompense him there
For truth and trusty service done to prince and country here.
His goodness, lo, thyself hast felt,' quoth he, 'and that of late,
When he thee failed not to help and succour thine estate.
To him it shall beseem thee well some token for to show,
That of thy duty which thou dost for his deserts him owe
Thou mindful art, and how thou dost thy diligence apply
To thank as power may serve, and with thy pen to signify
A grateful mind. And, though too light so little trifle be
To give to him that hath so much already done for thee,
Yet since thou canst none otherwise his honour yet requite,
Nor yet thy years do thee permit more weighty works to write,
This Christmas time thou mayest do well a piece thereof to end,
And many thanks in volume small, as thee becomes, to send.
And tell him how for his estate thou dost thy prayers make,
And him in daily vows of thine to God above betake.
But, for because the printers all have greatly wronged me,
To ease thee of thy pains therein, see what I bring to thee.'

152 **now...gone** Sir John Mason's son.
153 **bewrayed** revealed (him to be).
154 **And...time** if the promise of his youth had been realized.
161–162 **never...before** you shall never again discuss scholarship with him as you used to.
165 **gleed** torch.
166–167 **Ganymede...Aquarie** Ganymede, the beautiful youth taken to Olympus by Jove to be his cupbearer, was placed in the zodiac as Aquarius, bearer of water.
173 **of late** recently.
174 **estate** material well-being.
186 **betake** direct (your prayers).

He said, and therewithal began to ope the gilded book
Which erst I told he bare in hand, and thereupon to look.
The leaves within were fine to feel, and fair to look upon,
As they with silver had been sleeked, full clear to see they shone.
Yet far the letters did each one exceed the leaves in sight,
More glorious than the glitt'ring gold, and in the eye more bright.
The featly framed lines throughout in meetest manner stand,
More worthy work it was than might be made by mortal hand.
Therewith methought a savour sweet I felt, so fresh that was,
That beds of purple violets and roses far did pass.
No prince's perfume like to it, in chamber of estate,
I wist it was something divine did me so recreate.
I felt myself refreshed much, well quickened were my wits,
And often times of pleasure great had so joyful fits,
That waking now I will confess (you may believe me well!),
Great hoard of gold I would refuse in such delights to dwell,
As in that dream I had. Anon, me thought I asked him
What book it was he bare in hand, that showed and smelled so trim.
'These are,' quoth he, 'the Tragedies indeed of Seneca;
The Muse herself them truly writ, that hight Melpomena.
In Parnass' princely palace high she garnished this book,
The Ladies have, of Helicon, great joy thereon to look,
When walking in their aisles sweet the flowers so fresh they tread,
And in the midst of them me place, my Tragedies to read.
These leaves, that fine as velvet feel, and parchment-like in sight,
Of feat, fine fawns they are the skins, such as no mortal wight
May come unto, but with the which the Muses wont to play
In gardens still with grass full green, that garnished are full gay.
There fostered are these little beasts, and fed with Muses' milk,
Their whitest hands and feet they lick with tongue as soft as silk.
Their hair not such as have the herd of other common deer,
But silken skins of purple hue, like velvet fine they wear.
With proper featly framed feet about the arbours green
They trip and dance before these dames, full seemly to be seen,
And then their golden horns down in Ladies' laps they lay,
A great delight those sisters nine have with these fawns to play.
Of skins of them this parchment, lo, that shines so fair they make,
When aught they would with hand of theirs to written book betake.
This gorgeous glitt'ring golden ink, so precious thing to see,
Give ear, and whereof made it is I shall declare to thee.
Fair trees amid their paradise, there are of every kind,

192 **As . . . sleeked** As if they had been covered with a bright film of silver.
195 **featly** elegantly.
197 **a savour . . . felt** a sweet perfume I smelt.
198 **pass** surpass.
199 **No . . . . estate** i.e. there was nothing to compare to it, even in the finest rooms of a palace.
201 **quickened** enlivened.
202 **fits** moments/spells.
209 **garnished** decorated.
216 **still** always (not changed by the seasons).
222 **trip** skip.
226 **When . . . betake** Whenever they wish to write anything into a book.

Where every fruit that bough brings forth a man may ever find.
And dainties such as princes wont with proudest price to buy
Great plenty thereof may be seen, hang there on branches high.
The plum, the pear, the fig, the date, pomegranate wants not there,
The orange and the olive tree full plenteously do bear.
Yea, there the golden apples hang which once a thing much worth
To joy the wedding day of Jove the soil itself brought forth.
There Daphne stands transformed to tree, that green is still to sight,
That was sometime the loved nymph so fair of Phoebus bright.
Not far from fruit so rich that once did waking dragon keep
Doth Myrrha stand, with woeful tears that yet doth wail and weep.
Her tears, congealed hard to gum, that savour sweet doth cast,
It is that makes to leaf so fine this ink to cleave so fast.
But with what water is this ink thus made, now learn,' quoth he.
'The secrets of the sacred mount I will declare to thee.
Above the rest a cedar high, of haughty top there grows,
With bending branches far abroad on soil that shadow shows,
In top whereof do hang full high the pens of poets old,
And posies purtred for their praise in letters all of gold.
In shade whereof a banquet house there stands of great delight,
For Muses' joys. The walls are made of marble fair in sight,
Four-square, an ivory turret stands at every corner high;
The nooks and tops doth beaten gold and amel overlie.
In fulgent seat doth fleeing Fame there sit full high from ground,
And praise of Pallas' poets sends to stars with trumpets' sound.
The gate thereof, so strong and sure it need no watch nor ward,
A wondrous work it is to see, of adamant full hard,
With nine sure locks, whereof of one each lady keeps the key,
That none of them may come therein when other are away.
The floor within with em'ralds green is paved fair and feat,
The board and benches round about are made of pure black jet.
The lute, the harp, the citheron, the shawm, the shagbut eke,
The viol and the virginal, no music there to seek.
About the walls more worthy work than made by mortal hand,
The poets' painted pictures all in seemly order stand,
With colours such so lively laid, that at that sight I ween,
Apelles' pencil would bear back, abashed to be seen.
There Homer, Ovid, Horace eke, full featly portrayed be,

233 **wants not** is not lacking.

235–236 **thing...forth** the tree given by earth to the goddess Hera when she married Jupiter (Jove).

237–238 **Daphne...bright** the Nymph Daphnae was transformed into a tree to protect her from rape by Apollo.

240–241 **Myrrha...gum** Myrrha was transformed into the myrrh tree, which weeps pungent gum.

248 **purtred** portrayed.

252 **amel** enamel.

253 **fulgent** shining.

255 **watch nor ward** watchmen or guard.

262 **no...seek** i.e. no kind of music was lacking. The cithern, shawm, viol, virginals, and sackbut were common Elizabethan instruments.

266 **Apelles'...back** even Apelles, the legendary artist of the reign of Alexander the Great, would be reluctant to compare his work with this.

267 **Homer, Ovid, Horace** the Greek poet, Homer (*c.*8th century BC), reputed author of the *Iliad* and *Odyssey*; and the Romans Ovid (Publius Ovidius Naso, 43BC–17/18AD), best known for his *Metamorphoses*, and Horace (Quintus Horatius Flaccus, 65–8BC), author of the *Ars Poetica* and lyric and satiric poetry, were among the most celebrated of classical poets.

And there, not in the lowest place, they have described me.
There Virgil, Lucan, Palingene, and rest of poets all
Do stand, and there from this day forth full many other shall.
For now that house by many yards enlarged out they have,
Whereby they might in wider wall the images engrave,
And paint the pictures more at large, of hundreds, Englishmen,
That give their tongue a greater grace, by pure and painful pen.
In midst of all this worthy work there runs a pleasant spring,
That is of all the paradise the most delicious thing,
That round about enclosed is, with wall of jasper stone:
The ladies let no wight therein, but even themselves alone,
The water shines like gold in sight, and sweetest is to smell,
Full often times they bathe themselves within that blissful well.
With water thereof they this ink have made that writ this book,
And licensed me to bring it down for thee thereon to look.
Thou may'st believe it truly wrote, and trust in every whit,
For here hath never printer's press made fault, nor never yet
Came error here by miss of man. In sacred seat on high
They have it writ, in all whose works their pen can make no lie.
This book shall greatly thee avail, to see how printers miss
In all my works, and all their faults thou may'st correct by this.
And more than that, this golden spring, with which I have thee told
This ink so bright thus made to be, such property doth hold
That who thereof the savour feels, his wits shall quickened be,
And sprites revived in wondrous wise, as now it haps to thee.
Come on, therefore, while help thou hast,' he said, and therewithal
Even at *Thyestes* chanced first the leaves abroad to fall.
'Even here,' quoth he, 'if it thee please, begin. Now take thy pen;
Most dire debates describe of all that ever chanced to men,
And which the gods abhorred to see. The sum of all the strife
Now harken to. Thyestes keeps his brother Atreus' wife,
And ram with golden fleece. But yet doth Atreus friendship feign
With him, till time for father's food he hath his children slain
And dishes dressed,' he said, and then began to read the book.
I sat attent, and thereupon I fixed fast my look.
First how the Fury drave the sprite of Tantalus from hell
To stir the strife, I heard him read, and all expound full well.
Full many pleasant poet's tales that did me please I heard,
And evermore to book so fair I had a great regard.
Whereby I saw how oftentimes the printers did him wrong.

269 **Virgil, Lucan, Palingene** Virgil (Publius Vergilius Maro, 70–19 BC) was the greatest of Roman epic poets, famed for his *Aeniad*. Lucan (Marcus Anneus Lucanus, 39–65AD) was another epic poet, born in Cordoba in modern Spain. Palingene (Palingenius) is the contemporary Italian poet, Manzoli (1503–43), also mentioned at l.101 above. His inclusion in this august classical company is curious.

273 **at large** expansively/freely.

274 **painful** painstaking.

278 **even** only.

291 **the savour feels** smells the odour.

294 **at... fall** the book happened to fall open at (the beginning of) *Thyestes*.

Now Gryphius, Colineus now, and now and then among
He Aldus blamed, with all the rest that in his works do miss
Of sense or verse, and still my book I did correct by his.
The god of sleep had heard all this, when time for him it was
To dens of slumber whence he came again away to pass.
The kercher bound about my brows, dipped all in Limbo lake,
He straight unknit; away he fleeth, and I began to wake.
When round I rolled mine eyes about and saw myself alone,
In vain I 'Senec, Senec!' cried: the poet now was gone.
For woe whereof I gan to weep. 'O gods,' quoth I, 'unkind,
Ye are to blame with shapes so vain our mortal eyes to blind.
What goodly gain get you thereby, ye should us so beguile,
And fancies feed with joys that last, alas, too little while?'
I Morpheus cursed a thousand times that he had made me sleep
At all, or else that he me would in dream no longer keep.
And never were my joys so great, in sleep so sweet before,
But now as grievous was my woe, alas and ten times more,
Myself without the poet there thus left alone to see,
And all delights of former dream thus vanished to be.
Sometime I cursed, sometime I cried, like wight that waxed wood,
Or panther of her prey deprived, or tiger of her brood.
A thousand times my colour goes, and comes as oft again,
About I walked, I might nowhere in quiet rest remain.
In wondrous wise I vexed was, that never man I ween
So soon might after late delights in such a pang be seen.
'O thou, Megaera,' then I said, 'if might of thine it be,
Wherewith thou Tantal drawest from hell, that thus disturbeth me,
Inspire my pen with pensiveness, this tragedy t'indite,
And as so dreadful thing beseems, with doleful style to write.
This said, I felt the Fury's force enflame me more and more,
And ten times more now chafed I was than ever yet before.
My hair stood up, I waxed wood, my sinews all did shake,
And as the Fury had me vexed my teeth began to ache.
And thus inflamed with force of her, I said it should be done,
And down I sat with pen in hand, and thus my verse began.

308–309 **Gryphius . . . Aldus** the celebrated printers Sebastian Gryphius of Lyons and Jerome Avantius of the Aldine press (Aldus), each of whom published an edition of Seneca's *Tragedies*. Who Colineus was is unclear.

313 **kercher** the handkerchief or cloth, dipped in the waters of Lethe, the river of sleep that flows through the classical Hades.

314 **straight unknit** quickly untied.

318 **shapes so vain** false images.

327 **like . . . wood** like (a) man that grew mad.

332 **pang** sharp pain.

333 **Megaera** one of the Furies or Erinyes, classical spirits of revenge.

334 **Tantal** Tantalus.

338 **chafed** inflamed.

[*Thyestes* of Seneca]

The Speakers

TANTALUS [the ghost of Tantalus, King of Lydia, grandfather of Atreus and Thyestes, raised from Hades/Hell],
MEGAERA [one of the Furies (or Erinyes), spirits of vengeance],
ATREUS, King of Lydia,
SERVANT,
THYESTES, brother of Atreus,
PHYLISTHENES, oldest son of Thyestes,
[MESSENGER,
AGAMEMNON and MENELEUS, sons of Atreus (non-speaking roles),]
CHORUS.

The First Act
(Tantalus, Megaera)

[TANTALUS]

What Fury fell enforceth me to flee th'unhappy seat,
That gape and gasp with greedy jaw the fleeing food to eat?
What god to Tantalus the bowers where breathing bodies dwell
Doth show again? Is ought found worse than burning thirst of hell
In lakes alow? Or yet worse plague than hunger is there one,
In vain that ever gapes for food? Shall Sisyphus his stone,
That slipper, restless rolling peise, upon my back be borne?
Or shall my limbs with swifter swing of whirling wheel be torn?
Or shall my pains be Tityus' pangs, th'increasing liver still,
Whose growing guts the gnawing gripes and filthy fowls do fill,
That still by night repairs the paunch that was devoured by day,
And wondrous womb unwasted lieth a new-prepared prey.
What ill am I appointed for? O cruel judge of sprites,
Whoso thou be that torments new among the souls delights
Still to dispose, add what thou canst to all my deadly woe,
That keeper even of dungeon dark would sore abhor to know,
Or hell itself it quake to see, for dread whereof likewise

s.d. The play follows Continental, neo-classical practice in listing at the outset the names of the characters appearing in the scene, regardless of when they actually enter the action.

1 **fell** cruel.

1 **th'unhappy seat** the home of the unhappy, i.e. Hades, where Tantalus was imprisoned in Tartarus, its deepest realm.

2 **I...gape** i.e. Tantalus himself.

2 See head-note for details of Tantalus' 'tantalizing' punishment.

5 **alow** below.

6 **Sisyphus** Sisyphus was another denizen of hell. His punishment was to push a rock to the top of a mountain, only for it to roll down again as soon as it reached the top.

7 **slipper** unstable/slippery.

7 **restless rolling peise** unceasing rolling weight.

8 **whirling...torn** to be bound to a rolling wheel was the fate of Ixion, another inmate of Tartarus.

10 **Tityus...repairs** the giant Tytius was staked out in Hades while each day vultures ('gripes') pecked out his liver, only for it to grow back overnight.

11 **paunch** belly.

12 **womb** stomach.

13 **sprites** spirits/ghosts.

14–15 **that...dispose** who unceasingly delights in distributing new torments.

I tremble would; that plague seek out. Lo, now there doth arise
My brood, that shall in mischief far the grandsire's guilt outgo,
And guiltless make, that first shall dare unventured ills to do.
Whatever place remaineth yet of all this wicked land
I will fill up, and never once while Pelop's house doth stand
Shall Minos idle be.

MEGAERA

Go forth, thou detestable sprite,
And vex the gods of wicked house with rage of Fury's might.
Let them contend with all offence, by turns and one by one
Let swords be drawn, and mean of ire procure there may be none,
Nor shame; let fury blind inflame their minds and wrathful will,
Let yet the parents' rage endure, and longer lasting ill
Through children's children spread. Nor yet let any leisure be
The former fault to hate, but still more mischief new to see,
Nor one in one: but ere the guilt with vengeance be acquit,
Increase the crime. From brethren proud let rule of kingdom flit,
To runagates; and swerving state of all unstable things,
Let it by doubtful doom be tossed between th'uncertain kings.
Let mighty fall to misery, and miser climb to might,
Let chance turn th'empire up so down, both give and take the right.
The banished for guilt, when god restore their country shall,
Let them to mischief fall afresh as hateful then to all
As to themselves; let ire think nought unlawful to be done.
Let brother dread the brother's wrath, and father fear the son,
And eke the son his parent's power. Let babes be murdered ill,
But worse begot. Her spouse betrapped in treason's train to kill,
Let hateful wife await, and let them bear through seas their war,
Let bloodshed lie the lands about and every field afar;
And over conquering captains great, of countries far to see,
Let lust triumph. In wicked house let whoredom counted be
The light'st offense. Let trust that in the breasts of brethren breeds,
And truth be gone. Let not from sight of your so heinous deeds
The heavens be hid, about the pole when shine the stars on high,
And flames with wonted beams of light do deck the painted sky.
Let darkest night be made, and let the day the heavens forsake.
Disturb the gods of wicked house; hate, slaughter, murder make.
Fill up the house of Tantalus with mischiefs and debates.
Adorned be the pillars high with bay, and let the gates
Be garnished green, and worthy there for thy return to sight,
Be kindled fire. Let mischief done in Thracia once there light

19 **brood** the offspring of Tantalus and their cursed descendents, the house or lineage of his son Pelops.

23 **Minos** a judge in Hades.

26 **mean . . . none** let there be no possible means of moderating (or buying off) the anger.

33 **runagates** runaways (i.e. Thyestes).

33 **swerving** vacillating/falling to first one side then the other.

34 **doubtful doom** uncertain judgement.

35 **miser** the miserable/lowly.

36 **up so down** upside down.

41 **eke** also.

42–43 **Her . . . await** Let hateful wife lie in wait to kill her husband in a treacherous trap.

47 **light'st** least.

56–57 **mischief . . . manifold** Procne, queen of Thrace, fed their son to her husband, king Tereus. That crime will now be magnified threefold when Atreus, uncle to Thyestes' three sons, will feed them to their father.

More manifold; wherefore doth yet the uncle's hand delay?
Doth yet Thyestes not bewail his children's fatal day?
Shall he not find them where with heat of fires that under glow
The cauldron boils? Their limbs each one a-pieces let them go
Dispersed. Let father's fires with blood of children filed be.
Let dainties such be dressed; it is no mischief new to thee
To banquet so. Behold, this day we have to thee released,
And hunger-starved womb of thine we send to such a feast.
With foulest food thy famine fill, let blood in wine be drowned,
And drunk in sight of thee; lo now such dishes have I found
As thou wouldst shun. Stay, whither dost thou headlong way now take?

TANTALUS

To pools and floods of hell again, and still declining lake,
And flight of tree full freight with fruit that from the lips doth flee;
To dungeon dark of hateful hell let lawful be for me
To go, or, if too light be thought the pains that there I have,
Remove me from those lakes again, in midst of worser wave
Of Phleghethon to stand, in seas of fire beset to be.
Whoso beneath thy pointed pains by destinies' decree
Dost still endure, whoso thou be that underliest alow
The hollow den, or ruin who that fears and overthrow
Of falling hill, or cruel cries that sound in caves of hell
Of greedy roaring lions' throats, or flock of Furies fell
Who quakes to know, or who the brands of fire in direst pain
Half burnt throws off; hark to the voice of Tantalus again
That hastes to hell, and (whom the truth hath taught) believe well me;
Love well your pains, they are but small. When shall my hap so be
To flee the light?

MEGAERA

Disturb thou first this house with dire discord;
Debates and battles bring with thee, and of th'unhappy sword
Ill love to kings; the cruel breast strike through, and hateful heart,
With tumult mad.

TANTALUS

To suffer pains it seemeth well my part,
Not woes to work. I am sent forth like vapour dire to rise
That breaks the ground, or poison like the plague, in wondrous wise
That slaughter makes. Shall I to such detested crimes apply
My nephews' hearts? O parents' great of gods above the sky,
And mine, (though shamed I be to grant,) although with greater pain
My tongue be vexed, yet this to speak I may no whit refrain,

60 **a-pieces** dismembered.
61 **filed** defiled.
62 **Let . . . dressed** Let such delicacies be prepared.
67 **whither . . . take?** where are you running off to?
68 **still declining** forever receding from his grasp.
73 **Phleghethon** a river of fire in Hades.
74–75 **Whoso . . . endure** All you who endure your pains appointed by the Fates. (Tantalus addresses the sufferers in Tartarus whom he is intending to rejoin.)
75–76 **whoso . . . den** whoever crouches in a low hollow cave.
82 **hap** fortune.
84–85 **of . . . kings** (bring also) to kings an unhealthy love of the sword.
86.1–87 **To . . . . work.** It better suits my lot to suffer pains than to inflict woes.
88 **wise** manner.

Nor hold my peace. I warn you this, lest sacred hand with blood
Of slaughter dire, or frenzy fell of frantic fury wood
The altars stain; I will resist and guard such guilt away.
With stripes why dost thou me afright? Why threat'st thou me to fray
Those crawling snakes; or famine fixed in empty womb wherefore
Dost thou revive? Now fries within with thirst enkindled sore
My heart, and in the bowels burnt the boiling flames do glow.

MEGAERA

I follow thee; through all this house now rage and fury throw.
Let them be driven so, and so let either thirst to see
Each other's blood. Full well hath felt the coming in of thee
This house, and all with wicked touch of thee begun to quake.
Enough it is. Repair again to dens and loathsome lake
Of flood well known. The sadder soil with heavy foot of thine
Aggrieved is. Seest thou from springs how waters do decline
And inward sink; or how the banks lie void by droughty heat?
And hotter blast of fiery wind the fewer clouds doth beat?
The trees be spoiled, and naked stand to sight in withered woods
The barren boughs whose fruits are fled. The land between the floods,
With surge of seas on either side that wonted to resound,
And nearer fords to separate sometime with lesser ground,
Now broader spread, it heareth how aloof the waters rise.
Now Lerna turns against the stream, Phoronides likewise,
His pores be stopped. With customed course Alpheus drives not still
His holy waves. The trembling tops of high Cithaeron hill
They stand not sure; from height adown they shake their silver snow;
And noble fields of Argos fear their former drought to know.
Yea, Titan doubts, himself, to roll the world his wonted way,
And drive by force to former course the backward drawing day.

CHORUS

This Argos town if any god be found,
And Pisey bowers that famous yet remain,
Or kingdoms else to love of Corinth's ground,
The double havens, or sundered seas in twain;

If any love Taigetus his snows,
(By winter which when they on hills be cast,
By Boreas' blasts that from Sarmatia blows,
With yearly breath the summer melts as fast,)

93 **you** Megaera.
94 **wood** mad.
96 **stripes** strokes of the whip.
96–97 **Why...snakes** Why do you try to frighten me by threatening me with... snakes.
104 **Repair** Return.
114–115 **Lerna...Alpheus** Lerna, Phoronides, and Alpheus were classical Greek rivers.
116 **Cithaeron** Mount Cithaeron in Greece.
118 **Argos...drought** Argos, where the action of the play takes place, was scorched when Phaethon lost control of the chariot of the sun (see note to *Prologue*, l.8).
119 **Titan** the sun.
2 **Pisey bowers** the houses of Pisa (later Olympia) in Greece.
4 **double havens** the harbours of Cenchrae and Lechaeum on the isthmus of Corinth.
5 **Taigetus** a mountain range in the south of the Peloponnese peninsula, south of Argos.
7 **Sarmatia** the area stretching from north of the Balkans to what is modern southern Russia, the source of Boreas, the north wind.

Where clear Alpheus runs with flood so cold,
By plays well known that there Olympics hight;
Let pleasant power of his from hence withhold
Such turns of strife, that here they may not light,

Nor nephew worse than grandsire spring from us,
Or direr deeds delight the younger age.
Let wicked stock of thirsty Tantalus
At length leave off, and weary be of rage.

Enough is done, and nought prevailed the just
Or wrong. Betrayed is Myrtilus and drowned,
That did betray his dame: and with like trust
Born as he bare, himself hath made renowned

With changed name the sea, and better known
To mariners thereof no fable is.
On wicked sword the little infant thrown,
As ran the child to take his father's kiss,

Unripe for th'altars off'ring fell down dead,
And with thy hand (O Tantalus) was rent,
With such a meat for gods thy boards to spread.
Eternal famine for such food is sent,

And thirst; nor for those dainty meats unmild
Might meeter pain appointed ever be.
With empty throat stands Tantalus beguiled,
Above thy wicked head there leans to thee

Th[a]n Phineus' fowls in flight a swifter prey.
With burdened boughs declined on every side,
And of his fruits all bent to bear the sway,
The tree deludes the gapes of hunger wide.

Though he full greedy feed thereon would fain,
So oft deceived neglects to touch them yet:
He turns his eyes, his jaws he doth refrain,
And famine fixed in closed gums doth shet.

But then each branch his plenteous riches all
Lets lower down, and apples from on high
With lither leaves they flatter like to fall,
And famine stir, in vain that bids to try

10 **plays . . . hight** the place well known for the games called the Olympics (the river Alpheus flowed past Olympia).

12 **light** land/settle.

18–22 **Betrayed . . . is.** The Myrtoan sea, part of the Aegean, was named after Myrtilus, who betrayed his lord Oenomaus (rather than his dame, Hippodamia) to aid Pelops, but was in turn betrayed by Pelops and thrown into the sea that thereafter bore his name.

23 **infant** Pelops, slain by his father Tantalus and offered to the gods as food (see note to Tantalus in the list of speakers above).

33 **Phineus' fowls** the Harpies, half-women, half-birds, who befouled the food of Phineus as punishment for his defiance of the gods.

40 **shet** shut.

43 **lither** still more pliable (and so temptingly close).

His hands; which when he hath wrought forth anon
To be beguiled, in higher air again
The harvest hangs, and fickle fruit is gone.
Then thirst him grieves no less than hunger's pain;

Wherewith when kindled is his boiling blood
Like fire, the wretch the waves to him doth call,
That meet his mouth, which straight the fleeing flood
Withdraws, and from the dried ford doth fall,
And him forsakes that follows them. He drinks
The dust so deep of gulf that from him shrinks.

The Second Act
(Atreus, Servant)

[ATREUS]
O dastard coward, O wretch, and (which the greatest yet of all
To tyrant's check I count that may in weighty things befall)
O unrevenged! After guilts so great, and brother's guile,
And truth trod down, dost thou provoke with vain complaints the while
Thy wrath? All ready now to rage all Argos town throughout
In armour ought of thine, and all the double seas about
Thy fleet to ride; now all the fields with fervent flames of thine
And towns to flash it well beseemed, and everywhere to shine
The bright drawn sword. All under foot of horse let every side
Of Argos land resound; and let the woods not serve to hide
Our foes, nor yet in haughty top of hills and mountains high
The builded towers. The people all let them 'To battle' cry,
And clear forsake Mycenas town. Whoso his hateful head
Hides and defends, with slaughter dire let blood of him be shed.
This princely Pelops' palace proud and bowers of high renown,
On me, so on my brother too, let them be beaten down.
Go to, do that which never shall no after age allow,
Nor none it wished, some mischief great there must be ventured now,
Both fierce and bloody, such as would my brother rather long
To have been his. Thou never dost enough revenge the wrong
Except thou pass. And fiercer fact what may be done so dire
That his exceeds? Doth ever he lay down his hateful ire?
Doth ever he the modest mean in time of wealth regard?
Or quiet in adversity? I know his nature hard,
Untractable, that broke may be but never will it bend.
For which, ere he prepare himself, or force to fight intend,
Set first on him, lest while I rest he should on me arise.
He will destroy or be destroyed; in midst the mischief lies,
Prepared to him that takes it first.

51 **straight** at once.
1 **dastard coward** cowardly fool.
2 **tyrant's check** rebuke of kings.
13 **Mycenas town** Mycenae, a city in the kingdom of Argos.
13–14 **Whoso...hides** whoever tries to hide his (Thyestes') head.
20–22 **Thou...exceeds?** Thou (Atreus is speaking to and of himself) will never revenge the wrongs done to you unless you surpass them in return. And what act may be so fierce and dire that it exceeds his crimes?
24 **hard** to be hard.

SERVANT

Doth fame of people nought
Adverse thee fear?

ATREAS

The greatest good of kingdom may be thought
That still the people are constrained their prince's deeds as well
To praise as them to suffer all.

SERVANT

Whom fear doth so compel
To praise, the same his foes to be doth fear enforce again.
But who indeed the glory seeks of favour true t'obtain,
He rather would with hearts of each be praised than tongues of all.

ATREUS

The truer praise full oft hath happed to meaner men to fall,
The false but unto mighty man. What nill they, let them will.

SERVANT

Let first the king will honest things, and none the same dare nill.

ATREUS

Where lawful are to him that rules but honest things alone,
There reigns the king by other's leave.

SERVANT

And where that shame is none,
Nor care of right, faith, piety, nor holiness none stayeth,
That kingdom swerves.

ATREUS

Such holiness, such piety and faith,
Are private goods; let kings run on in that that likes their will.

SERVANT

The brother's hurt a mischief count, though he be ne'er so ill.

ATREUS

It is but right to do to him that wrong to brother were.
What heinous hurt hath his offence let pass to prove? Or where
Refrained the guilt? My spouse he stole away for lechery,
And reign by stealth; the ancient note and sign of empery
By fraud he got; my house by fraud to vex he never ceased.
In Pelop's house there fostered is a noble worthy beast,
The close kept ram, the goodly guide of rich and fairest flocks,

29.1–30 **Doth... fear?** Are you not afraid of arousing a bad reputation among the people?

31–32 **The... all.** The greatest good of a kingdom may be thought to be where the people are always/continually forced to praise and endure all their prince's actions.

33 **Whom... again.** He who is forced to praise (his prince) through fear will be driven by that same fear to be his prince's enemy.

37 **What... will.** What they don't wish to do ('nill they'), let them be forced to do.

38 **none... nill** then no one will dare to want anything else.

39–40 **Where... leave.** Where the king is only allowed to do honest things, there he rules only by the consent of others. (Atreus argues for the absolute right of kings, where whatever he wants to do is lawful, regardless of its morality.)

42 **where... swerves** where there is no shame, nor regard for right (etc)... where holiness provides no (self) restraint, there the kingdom totters.

43 **likes** pleases.

45 **The... ill.** Believe harming a brother to be an evil act, however evil that brother may be.

47 **What... prove?** What hideous crime has he turned down the chance to try out?

47–48 **Or... guilt?** Or when has he resisted a sin?

50 **By... got** He gained (the golden ram) the ancient symbol of kingship, through deception.

By whom throughout on every side depend adown the locks
Of glitt'ring gold; with fleece of which the new kings wonted were
Of Tantal's stock their sceptres gilt and mace of might to bear.
Of this the owner reigneth he; with him of house so great
The fortune fleeth. This sacred ram aloof in safety shet,
In secret mead is wont to graze, which stone on every side
With rocky wall encloseth round the fatal beast to hide.
This beast (advent'ring mischief great, adjoining yet for prey
My spoused mate), the traitor false hath hence conveyed away.
From hence the wrongs of mutual hate and mischief all up-sprung:
In exile wandered he, throughout my kingdoms all along,
No part of mine remaineth safe to me from trains of his.
My fere's deflowered, and loyalty of empire broken is;
My house all vexed, my blood in doubt, and nought that trust is in
But brother foe. What stayest thou yet? At length lo now begin.
Take heart of Tantalus to thee, to Pelops cast thine eye:
To such examples well beseems I should my hands apply.
Tell thou which way were best to bring that cruel head to death.

SERVANT

Through-pierced with sword let him be slain and yield his hateful breath.

ATREUS

Thou speakst of th'end, but I him would oppress with greater pain.
Let tyrants vex with torment more, should ever in my reign
Be gentle death?

SERVANT

Doth piety in thee prevail no whit?

ATREUS

Depart thou hence all piety, if in this house as yet
Thou ever wert! And now let all the flock of Furies dire,
And full of strife Erinyes come, and double brands of fire
Megaera shaking; for not yet enough with fury great
And rage doth burn my boiling breast. It ought to be replete
With monster more.

SERVANT

What mischief new dost thou in rage provide?

ATREUS

Not such a one as may the mean of wonted grief abide.
No guilt will I forbear, nor none may be enough despite.

SERVANT

What, sword?

ATREUS

Too little that.

SERVANT

What, fire?

53 **depend** hang.
64 **trains** plots.
65 **fere's** spouse is.
67 **What . . . yet?** What is still holding you back? (Atreus addresses himself again.)
69 **To . . . apply** It is entirely fitting that I respond to such examples.
80 **monster more** greater monstrosity.
81 **Not . . . abide.** Not one that can be suffered by only ordinary grief.

ATREUS

And that is yet too light.

SERVANT

What weapon then shall sorrow such find fit to work thy will?

ATREUS

Thyestes' self.

SERVANT

Than ire itself yet that's a greater ill.

ATREUS

I grant, a tumbling tumult quakes within my bosoms, lo,
And round it rolls. I moved am, and wot not whereunto.
But drawn I am; from bottom deep the roaring soil doth cry,
The day so fair with thunder sounds, and house as all from high
Were rent from roof and rafters cracks; and Lares turned about
Have wried their sight. So be't, so be't! Let mischief such be sought
As ye, O gods, would fear!

SERVANT

What thing seek'st thou to bring to pass?

[ATREUS] I note what greater thing my mind (and more than wont it was
Above the reach that men are wont to work) begins to swell,
And stayeth with slothful hands. What thing it is I cannot tell,
But great it is. Be't so; my mind now in this feat proceed,
For Atreus and Thyestes both it were a worthy deed.
Let each of us the crime commit. The Thracian house did see
Such wicked tables once; I grant the mischief great to be,
But done ere this. Some greater guilt and mischief more let ire
Find out. The stomach of thy son, O father, thou inspire,
And sister eke. Like is the cause, assist me with your power,
And drive my hand. Let greedy parent all his babes devour,
And glad to rent his children be, and on their limbs to feed.
Enough, and well it is devised; this pleaseth me indeed.
In meantime, where is he? So long and innocent wherefore
Doth Atreus walk? Before mine eyes already more and more
The shade of such a slaughter walks; the want of children cast
In father's jaws. But why, my mind, yet dread'st thou so at last,
And faint'st before thou enterprise? It must be done, let be.
That which in all this mischief is the greatest guilt to see,
Let him commit.

SERVANT

But what deceit may we for him prepare
Whereby betrapped he may be drawn to fall into the snare?
He wotes full well we are his foes.

ATREUS

He could not taken be

[87] **wot not whereunto** do not know ('wot not') to what end.

[90–91] **Lares . . . sight** the household gods ('Lares') have turned away their eyes.

[91] **So be't!** Let it be so!

[95] **stayeth . . . hands** is held back by my lack of action thus far.

[97] **were** will be.

[110] **before thou enterprise** before you begin the act.

[114] **wotes** knows.

Except himself would take. But now my kingdoms hopeth he;
For hope of this he would not fear to meet the mighty Jove,
Though him he threatened to destroy with lightning from above.
For hope of this, to pass the threats of waves he will not fail,
Nor dread no whit by doubtful shelves of Lybic seas to sail.
For hope of this (which thing he doth the worst of all believe,)
He will his brother see.

SERVANT

Who shall of peace the promise give?
Whom will he trust?

ATREUS

His evil hope will soon believe it well.
Yet to my sons the charge which they shall to their uncle tell
We will commit; that home he would from exile come again,
And miseries for kingdom change, and over Argos reign
A king of half. And though too hard of heart our prayers all
Himself despise, his children (yet nought woting what may fall,
With travels tired, and apt to be enticed from misery),
Requests will move. On th'one side his desire of empery,
On th'other side his poverty and labour hard to see,
Will him subdue and make to yield, although full stout he be.

SERVANT

His travels now the time hath made to seem to him but small.

ATREUS

Not so, for day by day the grief of ill increaseth all.
'Tis light to suffer miseries, but heavy them t'endure.

SERVANT

Yet other messengers to send, in such affairs procure.

ATREUS

The younger sort the worse precepts do easily harken to.

SERVANT

What thing against their uncle now you them instruct to do,
Perhaps with you to work the like they will not be a dread.
Such mischief wrought hath oft returned upon the worker's head.

ATREUS

Though never man to them the ways of guile and guilt have taught,
Yet kingdom will. Fear'st thou they should be made by counsel nought?
They are so born. That which thou call'st a cruel enterprise
And direly deemest done to be, and wickedly likewise,
Perhaps is wrought against me there.

SERVANT

And shall your sons of this

115 **my...he** he hopes to succeed me in my kingdoms.

119 **doubtful...seas** the treacherous sandbanks of the Libyan seas.

127 **nought...fall** knowing nothing (about) what may happen.

131 **full stout** very courageous/unyielding.

134 **'Tis...t'endure.** Injuries can be suffered easily (when they are inflicted), but they cannot be endured forever.

141 **made...nought** corrupted ('made...nought') by my advice/example.

Deceit be 'ware that work you will? No secretness there is
In their so green and tender years; they will your trains disclose.

ATREUS

A privy counsel close to keep is learned with many woes.

SERVANT

And will ye them, by whom ye would he should beguiled be,
Themselves beguile?

ATREUS

Nay, let them both from fault and blame be free.
For what shall need in mischiefs such as I to work intend
To mingle them? Let all my hate by me alone take end.
Thou leavest thy purpose ill, my mind; if thou thine own forbear,
Thou sparest him. Wherefore of this let Agamemnon here
Be minister; and client eke of mine for such a deed
Let Menelaus present be. Truth of th'uncertain seed
By such a practice may be tried: if it refuse they shall,
Nor of debate will bearers be, if they him uncle call:
He is their father, let them go. But much the fearful face
Bewrays itself. Even him that feigns the secret weighty case
Doth oft betray; let them therefore not know how great a guile
They go about. And thou these things in secret keep the while.

SERVANT

I need not warned be, for these within my bosom deep
Both faith and fear (but chiefly faith) doth shut and closely keep.

CHORUS

The noble house, at length, of high renown,
The famous stock of ancient Inachus,
Appeased and laid the threats of brethren down.
But now what Fury stirs and drives you thus,

Each one to thirst the other's blood again,
Or get by guilt the golden mace in hand?
Ye little wote, that so desire to reign,
In what estate or place doth kingdom stand.

Not riches make a king or high renown,
Not garnished weed with purple Tyrian dye,
Not lofty looks, or head enclosed with crown,
Not glitt'ring beams with gold and turrets high.

A king he is, that fear hath laid aside,
And all affects that in the breast are bred;

145 **'ware** aware.

146 **trains** plans.

147 **A . . . woes.** Suffering teaches you to keep secrets carefully.

153 Agamemnon and Menelaus are Atreus' sons.

158 Atreus considers telling his sons about his plans as a test. If they refuse to go, or acknowledge even kinship to Thyestes, then they may as well be his (Thyestes') sons, not Atreus' own, so he will disown them. But he subsequently persuades himself that not telling them is safer.

2 **Inachus** a river god, mythical founding king of Argos.

10 **weed . . . dye** robes decorated with purple dye from Tyre (purple was the colour worn by emperors).

14 **affects** emotions/passions.

Whom impotent ambition doth not guide,
Nor fickle favour hath of people led;

Nor all that west in metals' mines hath found,
Or channel clear of golden Tagus shows,
Nor all the grain that thr(e)shed is on ground,
That with the heat of Lybic harvest glows;

Nor whom the flash of lightning flame shall beat,
Nor eastern wind that smites upon the seas,
Nor swelling surge with rage of wind replete,
Or greedy gulf of Adria displease;

Whom not the prick of soldier's sharpest spear,
Or pointed pike in hand hath made to rue,
Nor whom the glimpse of sword might cause to fear,
Or bright drawn blade of glitt'ring steel subdue;

Who in the seat of safety sets his feet,
Beholds all haps how under him they lie,
And gladly runs his fatal day to meet,
Nor ought complains or grudgeth for to die.

Though present were the princes everychone,
The scattered Dakes to chase that wonted be;
That shining seas beset with precious stone
And Red Sea coasts do hold, like blood to see;

Or they which else the Caspian mountains high,
From Sarmats strong with all their power withhold;
Or he that on the flood of Danuby
In frost afoot to travel dare be bold;

Or Seres in whatever place they lie,
Renowned with fleece that there of silk doth spring;
They never might the truth hereof deny:
It is the mind that only makes a king.

There is no need of sturdy steeds in war,
No need with arms or arrows else to fight,
That Parthus wants with bow to fling from far,
While from the field he falsely feigneth flight.

Nor yet to siege no need it is to bring
Great guns in carts to overthrow the wall,
That from far off their batt'ring pellets sling.

18 **Tagus** the river Tagus in Seneca's native Spain, reputed to be lined with golden sand.

24 **Adria** the Adriatic.

30 **Beholds . . . lie** Considers all chance, good or bad, as beneath him.

33 **everychone** each one.

34 **Dakes** Dacians.

38 **Sarmats** the people of Sarmatia, stretching from north of the Balkans to the Vistula.

39 **Danuby** the river Danube.

41 **Seres** the people of East Asia.

47–48 **Parthus . . . flight** Parthian archers famously drew their enemies to pursue them by pretending to retreat, only to launch volleys of arrows as they did so.

A king he is that feareth nought at all.

Each man himself this kingdom gives at hand.
Let whoso list with mighty mace to reign
In tickle top of court delight to stand;
Let me the sweet and quiet rest obtain;

So set in place obscure and low degree,
Of pleasant rest I shall the sweetness know.
My life, unknown to them that noble be,
Shall in the step of secret silence go.

Thus, when my days at length are overpassed,
And time without all troublous tumult spent,
An aged man I shall depart at last,
In mean estate, to die full well content.

But grievous is to him the death that, when
So far abroad the bruit of him is blown,
That known he is too much to other men,
Departeth yet unto himself unknown.

The Third Act
(Thyestes, Phylisthenes)

[THYESTES]

My country bowers so long wished for, and Argos' riches all,
Chief good that unto banished men and misers may befall,
The touch of soil where born I was, and gods of native land
(If gods they be), and sacred towers I see of Cyclop's hand,
That represent than all man's work a greater majesty.
Renowned stadies to my youth, where noble sometime I
Have not so seld as once the palm in father's chariot won.
All Argos now to meet with me, and people fast will run;
But Atreus too. Yet rather lead in woods again thy flight,
And bushes thick, and hid among the brutish beasts from sight,
Like life to theirs; where splendent pomp of court and princely pride
May not with flatt'ring fulgent face allure thine eyes aside.
With whom the kingdom given is behold and well regard.
Beset but late with such mishaps as all men count full hard,
I stout and joyful was, but now again thus into fear
I am returned. My mind misdoubts, and backward seeks to bear

[55] **In . . . court** at the precarious pinnacle of the court.

[61] **are overpassed** have passed unnoticed (by those in power).

[66] **So . . . blown** When his reputation has spread so widely.

[68] **Departeth . . . unknown.** Dies without ever truly knowing himself.

[2] **banished . . . misers** miserable exiles.

[4] **sacred . . . hand** Argos was supposedly built by the Cyclopses, a race of one-eyed giants.

[6] **stadies to** stadia of.

[7] **not . . . palm** not so seldom as (i.e. more than) once won the prize (in races).

[10–12] **bushes . . . aside** in the forests the falsely shining face of the flattering courtier cannot distract and tempt one's eyes.

[13] **With . . . regard.** Carefully consider who it is that is offering you the kingdom (i.e. Atreus).

My body hence, and forth I draw my pace against my will.

PHYLISTHENES

With slothful step (what meaneth this?) my father standeth still,
And turns his face and holds himself in doubt what thing to do.

THYESTES

What thing, my mind, considerest thou? Or else so long whereto
Dost thou so easy counsel wrest? Whilt thou to things unsure
(Thy brother and the kingdom) trust? Fear'st thou those ills t'endure
Now overcome and milder made, and travails dost thou flee
That well were placed? It thee avails a miser now to be.
Turn hence thy pace while lawful is, and keep thee from his hand.

PHYLISTHENES

What cause thee drives, O father dear, thus from thy native land,
Now seen, to shrink? What makes thee thus from things so good at last
Withdraw thyself? Thy brother comes, whose ires be overpassed,
And half the kingdom gives, and of the house dilacerate
Repairs the parts, and thee restores again to former state.

THYESTES

The cause of fear that I know not thou dost require to hear.
I see nothing that makes me dread, and yet I greatly fear.
I would go on, but yet my limbs with weary legs do slack,
And other way than I would pass I am withholden back.
So oft the ship that driven is with wind and eke with oar,
The swelling surge, resisting both, beats back upon the shore.

PHYLISTHENES

Yet overcome whatever stays and thus doth let your mind,
And see what are at your return prepared for you to find.
You may, O father, reign.

THYESTES

I may; but then when die I mought.

PHYLISTHENES

Chief thing is power.

THYESTES

Nought worth at all if thou desire it nought.

PHYLISTHENES

You shall it to your children leave.

THYESTES

The kingdom takes not twain.

PHYLISTHENES

Who may be happy, rather would he miser yet remain?

THYESTES

Believe me well, with titles false the great things us delight;
And heavy haps in vain are feared. While high I stood in sight,

27 **shrink** turn away again.
29 **dilacerate** ripped apart (lacerated).
37 **let** hold back.
39.1 **when ... mought** when I might die.
41.1 **takes not twain** cannot accept two kings (either Atreus and Thyestes, or the division between Thyestes' heirs that Phylisthenes mentions).
44 **heavy haps** sorrowful events.

I never stinted then to quake, and selfsame sword to fear
That hanged by mine own side was. O how great good it were
With none to strive, but careless food to eat and rest to know?
The greater guilts, they enter not in cottage set alow;
And safer food is fed upon at narrow board alway,
While drunk in gold the poison is, by proof well taught I say,
That evil haps before the good to love it likes my will.
Of haughty house that stands aloft in tickle top of hill
And sways aside the city low need never be afright,
Nor in the top of roof above, there shines no ivory bright,
Nor watchman none defends my sleeps by night or guards my rest.
With fleet I fish not, nor the seas I have not backward pressed,
Nor turned to flight with builded wall; nor wicked belly I
With taxes of the people fed; nor parcel none doth lie
Of ground of mine beyond the Getes and Parthians far about,
Nor worshipped with frankincense I am, nor (Jove shut out)
My altars decked are; nor none in top of house doth stand
In garden trees, nor kindled yet with help of each man's hand
The baths do smoke; nor yet are days in slothful slumbers led,
Nor nights passed forth in watch and wine, without the rest of bed.
We nothing fear, the house is safe without the hidden knife,
And poor estate the sweetness feels of rest and quiet life.
Great kingdom is to be content without the same to live.

PHYLISTHENES

Yet should it not refused be, if god the kingdom give.

THYESTES

Nor yet desired it ought to be.

PHYLISTHENES

Your brother bids you reign.

THYESTES

Bids he? The more is to be feared there lurketh there some train.

PHYLISTHENES

From whence it fell yet piety is wont to turn at length,
And love unfeigned repairs again his erst omitted strength.

THYESTES

Doth Atreus then his brother love? Each Ursa first on high
The seas shall wash, and swelling surge of seas of Sicily

47 **careless** carefree.

48 **alow** lowly/humble.

49–50 **safer . . . say** eating at a humble table is always safer, while drinking from gold vessels (at court) risks poison. We know this well from experience.

57 **Nor . . . wall** I have not held rivers back with dams to help me fish.

58–59 **nor . . . about** I hold no lands in far-flung places (i.e. beyond the lands of the Getes in Dacia, or the Parthians in modern Iran).

60–61 **Nor . . . are** I'm not worshipped as a god while Jupiter himself is excluded.

62–63 **nor . . . smoke** no one has built (for me) gardens of trees in the tops of towers, or laboured to make my baths so hot that they smoke. (Thyestes cites the heights of extravagance that kings—or Roman emperors such as Seneca's own patron, Nero—might indulge in.)

70 **train** deception.

71 **from . . . length** familial piety (respect of blood) tends to return in time to the place from which it fled.

73 **Each Ursa** the constellations of the Great and Little Bear (Ursa Major and Ursa Minor).

74 **seas of Sicily** infamous for roughness.

Shall rest and all-assuaged be; and corn to ripeness grow
In bottom of Ionian seas, and darkest night shall show
And spread the light about the soil; the waters with the fire,
The life with death, the wind with seas, shall friendship first require,
And be at league.

PHYLISTHENES

Of what deceit are you so dreadful here?

THYESTES

Of everychone; what end at length might I provide of fear?
In all he can he hateth me.

PHYLISTHENES

To you what hurt can he?

THYESTES

As for myself, I nothing dread; you little babes make me
Afraid of him.

PHYLISTHENES

Dread ye to be beguiled when caught ye are?
Too late it is to shun the train in middle of the snare.
But go we on: this, father, is to you my last request.

THYESTES

I follow you; I lead you not.

PHYLISTHENES

God turn it to the best,
That well devised is for good. Pass forth with cheerful pace.

[Act Three:] The Second Scene
(Atreus, Thyestes)

[ATREUS]

Entrapped in train the beast is caught, and in the snare doth fall.
Both him and eke of hated stock with him the offspring all
About the father's side I see, and now in safety stands
And surest ground my wrathful hate. Now comes into my hands
At length Thyestes; yea, he comes and all at once, to me.
I scant refrain myself, and scant may anger bridled be.
So when the bloodhound seeks the beast by step and quick of sent
Draws in the leam, and pace by pace to wind the ways he went
With nose to soil doth hunt, while he the boar aloof hath found
Far off by scent, he yet refrains and wanders through the ground
With silent mouth; but when at hand he once perceives the prey,
With all the strength he hath he strives with voice, and calls away
His ling'ring master, and from him by force out breaketh he.
When ire doth hope the present blood, it may not hidden be.
Yet let it hidden be. Behold, with ugly hair to sight
How irksomely deformed with filth his foulest face is dight,

76 **Ionian seas** seas off the coast of Greece.
8 **leam** leash.
8 **to ... went** to follow his scent.
14 **doth hope** desires.
16 **dight** fashioned.

How loathsome lies his beard unkempt. But let us friendship feign.
To see my brother me delights, give now to me again
Embracing long desired for; whatever strife there was
Before this time between us twain, forget and let it pass,
Fro this day forth let brother's love, let blood, and law of kind
Regarded be; let all debate be slaked in either's mind.

THYESTES

I could excuse myself, except thou wert as now thou art.
But, Atreus, now I grant, the fault was mine in every part,
And I offended have in all. My cause the worse to be
Your this day's kindness makes indeed a guilty wight is he
That would so good a brother hurt as you, in any whit.
But now with tears I must entreat, and first I me submit.
These hands, that at thy feet do lie, do thee beseech and pray
That ire and hate be laid aside and from thy bosom may
Be scraped out and clear forgot. For pledges take thou these,
O brother dear, these guiltless babes.

ATREUS

Thy hands yet from my knees
Remove, and rather me to take in arms upon me fall.
And ye, O aids of elders' age, ye little infants all,
Me clip and coll about the neck. This foul attire forsake,
And spare mine eyes that pity it, and fresher vesture take
Like mine to see. And you with joy the half of empery,
Dear brother, take; the greater praise shall come to me thereby,
Our father's seat to yield to you, and brother to relieve.
To have a kingdom is but chance, but virtue it to give.

THYESTES

A just reward for such deserts, the gods, O brother dear,
Repay to thee. But on my head a regal crown to wear
My loathsome life denies, and far doth from the sceptre flee
My hand unhappy. In the midst let lawful be for me
Of men to lurk.

ATREUS

This kingdom can with twain full well agree.

THYESTES

Whatever is, O brother, yours, I count it mine to be.

ATREUS

Who would Dame Fortune's gifts refuse, if she him raise to reign?

THYESTES

The gifts of her, each man it wotes how soon they pass again.

ATREUS

Ye me deprive of glory great except ye th'empire take.

22 **slaked** quenched.

23–24 **I... part** I would try to excuse myself, but since you are so magnanimous, I must accept all the blame.

35 **clip and coll** embrace and hug.

36 **vesture** clothing.

44–45 **In... lurk.** Just let me hide myself among (ordinary) men.

THYESTES
You have your praise in off'ring it, and I it to forsake.
And full persuaded to refuse the kingdom am I still.

ATREUS
Except your part ye will sustain, mine own forsake I will.

THYESTES
I take it then, and bear I will the name thereof alone;
The rights and arms, as well as mine, they shall be yours each one.

ATREUS
The regal crown, as you beseems, upon your head then take,
And I th'appointed sacrifice for gods will now go make.

CHORUS
Would any man it ween? That cruel wight
Atreus, of mind so impotent to see,
Was soon astonied with his brother's sight.
No greater force than piety may be.

Where kindred is not, lasteth every threat,
Whom true love holds, it holds eternally.
The wrath but late with causes kindled great
All favour brake, and did 'To battle' cry,

When horsemen did resound on every side,
The swords each where then glistered more and more,
Which raging Mars with often stroke did guide,
The fresher blood to shed yet thirsting sore.

But love the sword against their wills doth suage,
And them to peace persuades with hand in hand.
So sudden rest, amid so great a rage,
What god hath made? Throughout Mycenas land

The harness clinked, but late, of civil strife,
And for their babes did fearful mothers quake;
Her armed spouse to lose much feared the wife,
When sword was made the scabbard to forsake

That now by rest with rust was overgrown.
Some to repair the walls that did decay,
And some to strength the towers half overthrown,
And some the gates with gins of iron to stay
Full busy were, and dreadful watch by night
From turret high did overlook the town.
Worse is than war itself the fear of fight.
Now are the threats of cruel sword laid down,

53 **bear... alone** I will have only the name of king (not the power itself).
1 **Would... ween?** Would anyone believe it?
3 **astonied** astonished/stupefied.
10 **each where** everywhere/on all sides.
11 **Mars** the god of war.
24 **with... stay** to shore up with iron-work.

And now the rumour whists of battle's sound,
The noise of crooked trumpet silent lies,
And quiet peace returns to joyful town.
So when the waves of swelling surge arise,

While Corus' wind the Brutian seas doth smite,
And Scylla sounds from hollow caves within,
And shipmen are with wafting waves afright,
Charybdis casts that erst it had drunk in,

And Cyclops fierce his father yet doth dread,
In Etna bank that fervent is with heats,
Lest quenched be with waves that overshed
The fire that from eternal furnace beats,

And poor Laertes thinks his kingdoms all
May drowned be, and Ithaca doth quake,
If once the force of winds begin to fall,
The sea lieth down more mild than standing lake.

The deep, where ships so wide full dreadful were
To pass, with sails on either side outspread,
Now fallen adown, the lesser boat doth bear,
And leisure is to view the fishes dead

Even there where late with tempest beat upon
The shaken Cyclads were with seas aghast.
No state endures; the pain and pleasure one
To other yields; and joys be soonest past.

One hour sets up the things that lowest be.
He that the crowns to princes doth divide,
Whom people please with bending of the knee,
And at whose beck their battles lay aside

The Medes, and Indians eke to Phoebus nigh,
And Dakes that Parthians do with horsemen threat,
Himself yet holds his sceptres doubtfully,
And men of might he fears, and chances great

(That each estate may turn) and doubtful hour.
O ye, whom lord of land and waters wide
Of life and death grants here to have the power,
Lay ye your proud and lofty looks aside;

29 **now... sound** now the sound of battle is hushed.

33 **Corus'... smite** the northwest wind blasts the seas off Calabria.

34–36 **Scylla** and **Charybdis** were a rock and a whirlpool on either side of the Straits of Messina, between Sicily and Calabria.

36 **casts... in** throws up again that which it has drunk.

41 **Laertes** King of Ithaca, and father of Ulysses.

50 **Cyclads** the Cyclades, a group of islands in the Aegean.

53 **One... be.** In a single hour the lowest things can become the highest.

57 **The... nigh** The Medes inhabited part of what is now northern Iran, the Indians are closer to the sun (Phoebus).

What your inferior fears of you amiss,
That your superior threats to you again.
To greater king each king a subject is.
Whom dawn of day hath seen in pride to reign,

Him overthrown hath seen the evening late.
Let none rejoice too much that good hath got,
Let none despair of best in worst estate.
For Clotho mingles all, and suffereth not

Fortune to stand, but fates about doth drive.
Such friendship find with gods yet no man might,
That he the morrow might be sure to live.
The god our things all tossed and turned quite
Rolls with a whirlwind.

The Fourth Act
(Messenger, Chorus)

[MESSENGER]
What whirlwind may me headlong drive and up in air me fling,
And wrap in darkest cloud, whereby it might so heinous thing
Take from mine eyes? O wicked house that even of Pelops ought
And Tantalus abhorred be.

CHORUS
What new thing hast thou brought?

MESSENGER
What land is this? Lieth Sparta here, and Argos, that hath bred
So wicked brethren? And the ground of Corinth lying spread
Between the seas? Or Ister else, where wont to take their flight
Are people wild? Or that which wonts with snow to shine so bright,
Hyrcana land? Or else do here the wand'ring Scythians dwell?

CHORUS
What monstrous mischief is this place then guilty of? That tell,
And this declare to us at large, whatever be the ill.

MESSENGER
If once my mind may stay itself, and quaking limbs, I will.
But yet of such a cruel deed before mine eyes the fear
And image walks. Ye raging storms, now far from hence me bear,
And to that place me drive to which now driven is the day
Thus drawn from hence!

CHORUS
Our minds ye hold yet still in doubtful stay.
Tell what it is ye so abhor. The author thereof show.
I ask not who, but which of them: that quickly let us know.

67 **greater king** Jupiter/God.
72 **Clotho** one of the Fates who control human destiny.
73 **fates...drive** whirls our fates about.
7 **Ister** the river Danube.
9 **Hyrcana** Hyrcania, a land south of the Caspian Sea.
11 **declare...large** tell us everything.

MESSENGER
In Pelops' turret high, a part there is of palace wide
That toward the south erected leans; of which the utter side
With equal top to mountain stands, and on the city lies,
And people proud against their prince (if once the traitors rise)
Hath underneath his batt'ring stroke. There shines the place in sight
Where wont the people to frequent, whose golden beams so bright
The noble spotted pillars grey of marble do support.
Within this place well known to men, where they so oft resort,
To many other rooms about the noble court doth go.
The privy palace underlieth in secret place alow,
With ditch, full deep, that doth enclose the wood of privety,
And hidden parts of kingdom old where never grew no tree
That cheerful boughs is wont to bear, with knife or lopped be,
But tax and cypress, and with tree of holm, full black to see,
Doth beck and bend, the wood so dark. Aloft above all these
The higher oak doth overlook, surmounting all the trees.
From hence with luck the reign to take accustomed are the kings,
From hence in danger aid to ask, and doom in doubtful things.
To this affixed are the gifts, the sounding trumpets bright,
The chariots broke, and spoils of sea that now Myrtoan hight,
There hang the wheels once won by craft of falser axle-tree,
And every other conquest's note; here lawful is to see
The Phrygian tire of Pelop's head, the spoil of en'mies here,
And of barbarian triumph left the painted gorgeous gear.
A loathsome spring stands under shade, and slothful course doth take
With water black, even such as is of irksome Stygian lake
The ugly wave, whereby are wont to swear the gods on high.
Here all the night the grisly ghosts and gods of death to cry
The fame reports; with clinking chains resounds the wood each where;
The sprites cry out; and everything that dreadful is to hear
May there be seen. Of ugly shapes from old sepulchres sent
A fearful flock doth wander there, and in that place frequent
Worse things than ever yet were known. Yea, all the wood full oft
With flame is wont to flash, and all the higher trees aloft
Without a fire do burn. And oft the wood beside all this
With triple barking roars at once. Full oft the palace is

[20] **utter** outward.
[20-23] **That...stroke** It faces the city... and could be used to smash the rebellious populace with artillery, if they ever rose in treason against their prince.
[32] **tax...holm** the yew, the cypress, and holm-oak: all trees of ill-omen.
[33] **beck** nod.
[35] **From...kings** From where kings traditionally seek blessings for a fortunate reign.
[36] **doom...things** (seek) judgement in difficult matters.
[38] **Myrtoan** the Myrtoan Sea (see Chorus I, l.18).
[39] **hang...axle-tree** Myrtilus betrayed his master Oenomaus by fixing wax axles to his chariot so that he crashed in the crucial chariot-race against Pelops.
[41] **tire** a crown or tiara from Phrygia, a land in modern Turkey.
[42] **of barbarian...gear** gorgeous clothes plundered in victories over the barbarians.
[44] **Stygian lake** the river Styx in Hades.
[54] **triple barking** the barking of Cerberus, the triple-headed dog who is guardian of Hades.

Afright with shapes, nor light of day may once the terror quell.
Eternal night doth hold the place, and darkness there of hell
In midday reigns. From hence to them that pray, out of the ground
The certain answers given are, what time with dreadful sound
From secret place the fates be told; and dungeon roars within
While of the god breaks out the voice. Whereto, when entered in
Fierce Atreus was, that did with him his brother's children trail,
Decked are the altars: who, alas, may it enough bewail?
Behind the infants' backs anon he knit their noble hands,
And eke their heavy heads about he bound with purple bands.
There wanted there no frankincense, nor yet the holy wine,
Nor knife to cut the sacrifice, besprinked with leavens fine.
Kept is in all the order due, lest such a mischief great
Should not be ordered well.

CHORUS

Who doth his hand on sword then set?

MESSENGER

He is himself the priest, and he himself the deadly verse
With prayer dire from fervent mouth doth sing and oft rehearse.
And he at th'altars stands himself; he them assigned to die,
Doth handle and in order set, and to the knife apply.
He lights the fires; no rites were left of sacrifice undone.
The wood then quaked, and all at once from trembling ground anon
The palace becked, in doubt which way the peise thereof would fall,
And shaking as in waves it stood. From th'air and therewithal
A blazing star, that foulest train drew after him doth go.
The wines that in the fires were cast with changed liquor flow,
And turn to blood, and twice or thrice th'attire fell from his head;
The ivory bright in temples seemed to weep and tears to shed.
The sights amazed all other men, but steadfast yet alway
Of mind, unmoved Atreus stands, and even the gods doth fray
That threaten him; and, all delay forsaken, by and by
To th'altars turns, and therewithal aside he looks awry.
As hungry tiger wonts that doth in Gangey woods remain
With doubtful pace to range and roam between the bullocks twain,
Of either prey full covetous, and yet uncertain where
She first may bite, and roaring throat now turns the t'one to tear,
And then to th'other straight returns, and doubtful famine holds:
So Atreus dire between the babes doth stand and them beholds,
On whom he points to slake his ire. First slaughter where to make
He doubts, or whom he should again for second off'ring take.
Yet skills it nought; but yet he doubts, and such a cruelty

58 **what time** at the time when.
65 **wanted** lacked.
66 **besprinkled with leavens** sprinkled with sacred leaves or touched with sacred fire.
75 **becked** shook/seemed to bow down.
75 **peise** weight.
82 **fray** frighten.
84 **awry** to either side.
85 **Gangey woods** woods on the banks of the river Ganges in India.
93 **skills it nought** it does not matter (which he chooses).

It him delights to order well.

CHORUS

Whom took he first to die?

MESSENGER

First place, lest in him think ye might no piety to remain,
To grandsire dedicated is. First Tantalus is slain.

CHORUS

With what a mind and count'nance could the boy his death sustain?

MESSENGER

All careless of himself he stood, nor once he would in vain
His prayers lose. But Atreus fierce the sword in him at last
In deep and deadly wound doth hide to hilts, and griping fast
His throat in hand, he thrust him through. The sword then drawn away,
When long the body had upheld itself in doubtful stay
Which way to fall, at length upon the uncle down it falls.
And then to th'altars cruelly Phylisthenes he tralls,
And on his brother throws, and straight his neck off cutteth he.
The carcass headlong falls to ground, a piteous thing to see,
The mourning head with murmur yet uncertain doth complain.

CHORUS

What after double death doth he and slaughter then of twain?
Spares he the child? Or guilt on guilt again yet heapeth he?

MESSENGER

As long-maned lion, fierce amid the wood of Armenie
The drove pursues and conquest makes of slaughter many one,
Though now defiled be his jaws with blood and hunger gone,
Yet slaketh not his ireful rage with blood of bulls so great,
But slothful now, with weary tooth, the lesser calves doth threat;
None otherwise doth Atreus rage, and swells with anger strained,
And holding now the sword in hand with double slaughter stained,
Regarding not where fell his rage, with cursed hand unmild,
He strake it through his body quite, at bosom of the child.
The blade goeth in, and at the back again out went the same.
He falls, and, quenching with his blood the altars' sacred flame,
Of either wound at length he dieth.

CHORUS

O heinous, hateful act!

MESSENGER

Abhor ye this? Ye hear not yet the end of all the fact;
There follows more.

CHORUS

A fiercer thing, or worse than this to see,
Could nature bear?

96 **Tantalus** Thyestes first son, named after his great-grandfather.
100 **griping** gripping.
102–103 **long . . . fall** remained upright, swaying this way and that for a long moment, uncertain which way to fall.
103 **uncle** Atreus himself.
104 **tralls** drags.
109 **child** Thyestes' third, unnamed son.
110 **Armenie** Armenia.
111 **drove** herd of cattle.
115 **None otherwise** in no other way (i.e. exactly like that).

MESSENGER

Why, think ye this of guilt the end to be?
It is but part.

CHORUS

What could he more? To cruel beasts he cast
Perhaps their bodies to be torn, and kept from fires at last?

MESSENGER

Would god he had, that never tomb the dead might overhide,
Nor flames dissolve, though them for food to fowls in pastures wide
He had out-thrown, or them for prey to cruel beasts would fling.
That which the worst was wont to be, were here a wished thing,
That them their father saw untombed. But O more cursed crime
Uncredible, the which deny will men of after-time:
From bosoms yet alive out drawn the trembling bowels shake,
The veins yet breathe, the fearful heart doth yet both pant and quake;
But he the strings doth turn in hand and destinies behold,
And of the guts the signs each one doth view, not fully cold.
When him the sacrifice had pleased, his diligence he puts
To dress his brother's banquet now; and straight asunder cuts
The bodies into quarters all, and by the stumps anon
The shoulders wide, and brawns of arms, he strikes off everychone.
He lays abroad their naked limbs and cuts away the bones.
The only heads he keeps, and hands to him committed once.
Some of the guts are broached, and in the fires that burn full slow
They drop; the boiling liquor some doth tumble to and fro
In mourning cauldron, from the flesh that overstands aloft
The fire doth fly and scatter out, and into chimney oft
Up heaped again, and there constrained by force to tarry yet,
Unwilling burns. The liver makes great noy upon the spit,
Nor easily wote I if the flesh or flames they be that cry,
But cry they do. The fire like pitch it fumeth by and by,
Nor yet the smoke itself so sad like filthy mist in sight
Ascendeth up as wont it is, nor takes his way upright,
But even the gods and house it doth with filthy fume defile.
O patient Phoebus, though from hence thou backward flee the while,
And in the midst of heaven above dost drown the broken day,
Thou fleest too late: the father eats his children, wellaway,
And limbs to which he once gave life with cursed jaw doth tear.
He shines with ointment shed full sweet all round about his hair,
Replete with wine; and oftentimes so cursed kind of food

131 **That . . . untombed.** That their father would see them unburied, which you think the worst possible crime, was something to be wished for (i.e. what Atreus actually did was much worse than that).

132 **of after-time** in the future.

135 **strings** entrails (from which auguries can be read).

141 **lays abroad** spreads out.

142 **The . . . once.** He keeps only the heads, and the hands, which once were dedicated to him (see III.ii.31, above).

143 **broached** skewered.

148 **makes great noy** cries our loudly/complains.

150 **fumeth** smokes.

153 **gods** household gods.

154 **Phoebus** the sun.

156 **wellaway** alas.

His mouth hath held that would not down. But yet this one thing good
In all thy ills, Thyestes, is: that them thou dost not know.
And yet shall that not long endure. Though Titan backward go
And chariots turn against himself to meet the ways he went,
And heavy night so heinous deed to keep from sight be sent,
And out of time from east arise so foul a fact to hide,
Yet shall the whole at length be seen; thy ills shall all be spied.

CHORUS

Which way, O prince of lands and gods on high,
At whose uprise eftsoons of shadowed night
All beauty fleeth, which way turns thou awry
And drawst the day in midst of heaven to flight?

Why dost thou, Phoebus, hide from us thy sight?
Not yet the watch that later hour brings in,
Doth Vesper warn the stars to kindle light.
Not yet doth turn of Hesper's wheel begin

To lose thy chair his well deserved way.
The trumpet third not yet hath blowen his blast
While toward the night begins to yield the day.
Great wonder hath of sudden supper's haste

The ploughman yet whose oxen are untired.
From wonted course of heaven what draws thee back?
What causes have from certain race conspired
To turn thy horse? Do yet from dungeon black

Of hollow hell the conquered giants prove
A fresh assault? Doth Tityus yet assay
With trenched heart and wounded womb to move
The former ires? Or from the hill away

Hath now Typhoeus wound his side by might?
Is up to heaven the way erected high
Of Phlegrey foes by mountains set upright;
And now doth Ossa Pelion overlie?

The wonted turns are gone of day and night.
The rise of sun nor fall shall be no more.

162 **Titan** the sun.

2 **eftsoons** quickly after.

7 **Vesper** the evening star; as is Hesper/Hesperus.

9 **chair** chariot.

10 **The...blast** The watchman has yet to blow his trumpet for the third time, signalling the hour.

12–13 **Great...untired.** The sudden, early arrival of night (and hence supper-time) surprises the ploughman, whose oxen are still fresh.

16–18 **Do...assault?** Are the giants launching another assault on Olympus (as they did in the ancient past)?

18 **Tytius** Tytius, potential leader of a giant army, was cursed to have his liver eternally pecked out by vultures (hence his 'trenched heart' and 'wounded womb').

19 **trenched** gouged.

21 **Hath...might** the monster Typhon was punished by Jupiter for attacking the gods, by having Mount Etna piled on his body. The Chorus asks if he has wriggled ('wound his side') free of the mountain.

24 **doth...overlie?** does Ossa lie on Pelion? (The giants launched their assault on Olympus from the valley of Phlegra in Thrace, piling mountains such as Ossa and Pelion on top of each other to reach the heavens.)

25 **wonted turns** usual rotations.

Aurora, dewish mother of the light,
That wonts to send the horses out before,

Doth wonder much again returned to see
Her dawning light: she wots not how to ease
The weary wheels, nor manes that smoking be
Of horse with sweat, to bathe amid the seas.

Himself, unwonted there to lodge likewise,
Doth setting sun again the morning see,
And now commands the darkness up to rise
Before the night to come prepared be.

About the pole yet gloweth no fire in sight,
Nor light of moon the shades doth comfort yet.
Whatso it be, god grant it be the night!
Our hearts do quake with fear oppressed great,

And dreadful are lest heaven and earth and all
With fatal mine shaken shall decay,
And lest on gods again and men shall fall
Disfigured Chaos, and the land away,

The seas and fires, and of the glorious skies
The wand'ring lamps lest nature yet shall hide.
Now shall no more with blaze of his uprise
The lord of stars that leads the world so wide

Of summer both and winter give the marks.
Nor yet the moon, with Phoebus' flames that burns,
Shall take from us by night the dreadful carks,
With swifter course o'er-pass her brother's turns

While compassless she fets in crooked race.
The gods on heaps shall out of order fall,
And each with other mingled be in place.
The wried way of holy planets all,

With path a-slope that doth divide the Zones,
That bears the signs and years in course doth bring,
Shall see the stars with him fall down at once.
And he that first not yet with gentle spring

The temperate gale doth give to sails: the Ram,
Shall headlong fall a-down to seas again,
Through which he once with fearful Helle swam.

28–30 **Aurora** Aurora, goddess of the 'dewy' dawn, is surprised to see the horses of her lover, Phoebus, the sun, return to her instead of taking their normal daily journey westward.

33 **Himself** Phoebus himself.

42 **decay** decline/sink down.

48 **The lord of stars** the sun.

51 **carks** troubles.

53 **While...race** as she pursues the curved course of her shorter orbit.

54 **The gods on heaps shall** The planets shall all together.

56–58 **The wried...bring** The curved courses of all the holy planets, with the circuit of the Zodiac that divides the heavens into constellations (each with its sign) and measures the progress of the years.

61 **the Ram** the constellation Aries.

63 **Helle** Helle and her brother Phrixus fled from death on the magical ram which would become the constellation Aries. But she fell into the sea off the Turkish coast, giving her name to the Hellespont.

Next him the Bull, that doth with home sustain
The Sisters seven, with him shall overturn
The Twins, and arms of crooked Cancer all.
The Lion hot (that wonts the soil to burn)
Of Hercules, again from heaven shall fall.

To lands once left the Virgin shall be thrown,
And levelled peise of Balance sway alow,
And draw with them the stinging Scorpion down.
So likewise he that holds in Thessal bow

His swift well-feathered arrows, Chiron old,
Shall break the same and eke shall lose his shot.
And Capricorn, that brings the winter cold,
Shall overturn, and break thy water pot,

Whoso thou be; and down with thee to ground,
The last of all the signs, shall Pisces fall.
And monsters eke in seas yet never drowned,
The water gulf shall overwhelm them all.

And he which doth between each Ursa glide
Like crooked flood, the slipper Serpent twined,
And lesser Bear by greater Dragon's side,
Full cold with frost congealed hard by kind;

And carter dull that slowly guides his Wain,
Unstable shall Boötes fall from high.
We are thought meet, of all men, whom again
Should hugy heap of Chaos overlie,

And world oppress with overturned mass.
The latest age now falleth us upon.
With evil hap we are begot, alas,
If, wretches, we have lost the sight of sun,

Or him by fault enforced have to fly.
Let our complaints yet go, and fear be past;
He greedy is of life that will not die,
When all the world shall end with him at last.

64–66 **the Bull...all** Taurus (the Bull), which houses the constellation of the Hyades (the seven stellified sister nymphs), will fall, bringing down Gemini (the twins, Castor and Pollux) and Cancer (the Crab).

67 **The Lion** Leo was created from the Nemean lion (killed by Hercules as one of his labours).

69–71 **To lands...down.** Illusions to the constellations Virgo, Libra, and Scorpio respectively.

72–73 **he...old** Chiron the centaur (who dwelt on the island of Pelion in Thessaly) became the constellation Sagittarius, the archer.

82 **Serpent** the constellation of the serpent, that curves between Ursa Major and Ursa Minor (the 'lesser Bear').

86 **Boötes** The constellation Boötes, supposedly the wagoner who drove the oxen in Ursa Major (also known as the Wain or Wagon).

90 **The...upon.** The end of days is upon us.

The Fifth Act
(Atreus alone.)

[ATREUS]
Now equal with the stars I go, beyond each other wight;
With haughty head the heavens above and highest pole I smite.
The kingdom now and seat I hold, where once my father reigned.
I now let go the gods, for all my will I have obtained.
Enough and well, yea, even enough for me, I am acquit.
But why enough? I will proceed, and fill the father yet
With blood of his, lest any shame should me restrain at all,
The day is gone, go to therefore, while thee the heaven doth call.
Would god I could against their wills yet hold the gods that flee,
And of revenging dish constrain them witnesses to be.
But yet, which well enough is wrought, let it the father see.
In spite of all the drowned day I will remove from thee
The darkness all, in shade whereof do lurk thy miseries.
And guest at such a banquet now too long he careless lies
With merry face; now eat and drunk enough he hath; at last
'Tis best himself should know his ills. Ye servants all, in haste
Undo the temple doors, and let the house be open all.
Fain would I see, when look upon his children's heads he shall,
What countenance he then would make, or in what words break out
Would first his grief; or how would quake his body round about
With sprite amazed sore; of all my work the fruit were this.
I would him not a miser see, but while so made he is.
Behold, the temple, opened now, doth shine with many a light,
In glitt'ring gold and purple seat he sits himself upright,
And stalling up his heavy head with wine, upon his hand,
He belcheth out. Now chief of gods, in highest place I stand,
And king of kings! I have my wish, and more than I could think.
He filled is, he now the wine in silver bowl doth drink.
And spare it not, there yet remains a worser draught for thee,
That sprung out of the bodies late of sacrifices three,
Which wine shall hide; let therewithal the boards be taken up.
The father, mingled with the wine his children's blood shall sup,
That would have drunk of mine. Behold, he now begins to strain
His voice and sings, nor yet for joy his mind he may refrain.

[Act Five:] The Second Scene
(Thyestes alone.)

[THYESTES]
O beaten bosoms, dulled so long with woe,
Lay down your cares, at length your griefs relent.
Let sorrow pass, and all your dread let go,
And fellow eke of fearful banishment,

9 **the gods that flee** the fleeing constellations.

25 **stalling** supporting.

Sad poverty, and ill in misery
The shame of cares. More whence thy fall thou hast
Than whither skills. Great hap to him from high
That falls it is in surety to be placed

Beneath. And great it is to him again
That pressed with storm, of evils feels the smart,
Of kingdom lost the peises to sustain
With neck unbowed, nor yet deject of heart,

Nor overcome, his heavy haps always
To bear upright. But now of careful carks
Shake off the showers, and of thy wretched days
Away with all the miserable marks!

To joyful state return thy cheerful face.
Put fro thy mind the old Thyestes hence.
It is the wont of wight in woeful case
In state of joy to have no confidence.

Though better haps to them returned be,
Th'afflicted yet to joy it irketh sore.
Why callest thou me aback, and hind'rest me
This happy day to celebrate? Wherefore

Bid'st thou me, Sorrow, weep without a cause?
Who doth me let with flowers so fresh and gay
To deck my hairs? It lets, and me withdraws.
Down from my head the roses fall away;

My moisted hair with ointment overall
With sudden maze stands up in wondrous wise.
From face that would not weep the streams do fall,
And howling cries amid my words arise.

My sorrow yet th'accustomed tears doth love,
And wretches still delight to weep and cry.
Unpleasant plaints it pleaseth them to move,
And flourished fair it likes with Tyrian dye

Their robes to rent; to wail it likes them still.
For sorrow sends (in sign that woes draw nigh)
The mind, that wotes before of after ill.
The sturdy storms the shipmen overlie,

When void of wind th'assuaged seas do rest.
What tumult yet or countenance to see

6–7 **More ... skills.** It matters more where you have fallen from than where you fell to.
14 **careful carks** troubling worries.
22 **Th'afflicted ... sore** It is troubling for the afflicted to enjoy life (even when their pains have ended).
26 **Who ... let** Who prevents me.
30 **maze** amazement.
35 **plaints** complaints.
35–37 **it pleaseth ... rent** they choose to tear their robes, coloured richly with dye of Tyre.
38–39 **For ... ill.** The mind sends us sorrow as a foreboding of coming evil.

Makest thou, madman? At length a trustful breast
To brother give, whatever now it be,
Causeless or else too late thou art adread.
I, wretch, would not so fear, but yet me draws
A trembling terror; down mine eyes do shed
Their sudden tears, and yet I know no cause.
Is it a grief, or fear? Or else hath tears great joy itself?

[Act Five:] The Third Scene
(Atreus, Thyestes)

[ATREUS]
Let us this day with one consent, O brother, celebrate.
This day my sceptres may confirm and I stablish my estate,
And faithful bond of peace and love between us ratify.

THYESTES
Enough with meat and eke with wine now satisfied am I.
But yet of all my joys it were a great increase to me
If now about my side I might my little children see.

ATREUS
Believe that here, even in thine arms, thy children present be.
For here they are, and shall be here; no part of them fro thee
Shall be withheld. Their loved looks now give to thee I will,
And with the heap of all his babes the father fully fill.
Thou shalt be glutted, fear thou not. They with my boys as yet
The joyful sacrifices make, at board where children sit.
They shall be called. The friendly cup now take of courtesy,
With wine upfilled.

THYESTES
Of brother's feast I take full willingly
The final gift. Shed some to gods of this our father's land,
Then let the rest be drunk. What's this? In no wise will my hand
Obey. The peise increaseth sore and down mine arm doth sway.
And from my lips the wafting wine itself doth fly away,
And in deceived mouth about my jaws it runneth round.
The table too, itself doth shake, and leap from trembling ground.
Scant burns the fire. The air itself with heavy cheer to sight,
Forsook of sun, amazed is between the day and night.
What meaneth this? Yet more and more of backward beaten sky
The compass falls; and thicker mist the world doth overlie
Than blackest darkness, and the night in night itself doth hide.
All stars be fled. What so it be, my brother, god provide,
And sons, to spare. The gods so grant that all this tempest fall
On this vile head. But now restore to me my children all.

16 **wise** way.
17 **The peise...sway.** The weight (of the cup) grows so great it pulls my arm downwards.
18 **wafting** turbulent/agitated into waves.
21 **with...sight** with sad face to see/a sorry sight to see.

ATREUS

I will, and never day again shall them from thee withdraw.

THYESTES

What tumult tumbleth so my guts, and doth my bowels gnaw?
What quakes within? With heavy peise I feel myself oppressed,
And with another voice than mine bewails my doleful breast.
Come near, my sons, for you now doth th'unhappy father call;
Come near, for, you once seen, this grief would soon assuage and fall.
Whence murmur they?

ATREUS

With father's arms embrace them quickly now,
For here they are, lo, come to thee. Dost thou thy children know?

THYESTES

I know my brother. Such a guilt yet canst thou suffer well,
O Earth, to bear? Nor yet from hence to Stygian lake of hell
Dost thou both drown thyself and us? Nor yet with broken ground
Dost thou these kingdoms and their king with Chaos rude confound?
Nor yet uprenting from the soil the bowers of wicked land
Dost thou Mycenas overturn? With Tantalus to stand
(And ancestors of ours, if there in hell be any one)
Now ought we both. Now from the frames on either side anon
Of ground, all here and there rent up, out of thy bosom deep
Thy dens and dungeons set abroad, and us enclosed keep,
In bottom low of Acheron. Above our heads aloft
Let wander all the guilty ghosts; with burning fret full oft
Let fiery Phlegethon, that drives his sands both to and fro,
To our confusion overrun and violently flow.
O slothful soil, unshaken peise, unmoved yet art thou?
The gods are fled!

ATREUS

But take to thee with joy thy children now,
And rather them embrace. At length thy children all, of thee
So long wished for (for no delay there standeth now in me),
Enjoy and kiss; embracing arms divide thou unto three.

THYESTES

Is this thy league? May this thy love and faith of brother be?
And dost thou so repose thy hate? The father doth not crave
His sons alive (which might have been without the guilt) to have,
And eke without thy hate; but this doth brother brother pray:
That them he may entomb, restore, whom see thou shalt straightway
Be burnt. The father nought requires of thee that have he shall,
But soon forgo.

ATREUS

Whatever part yet of thy children all
Remains, here shalt them have: and what remaineth not, thou hast.

47 **Acheron** a river of Hades, whose touch brought pain.

49 **Phlegethon** a river of fire in Hades.

56 **Is . . . league?** Is this your idea of an alliance?

THYESTES

Lie they in fields, a food out-flung for fleeing fowls to waste?
Or are they kept a prey for wild and brutish beasts to eat?

ATREUS

Thou hast devoured thy sons, and 'filed thyself with wicked meat.

THYESTES

O this is it that shamed the gods, and day from hence did drive,
Turned back to east! Alas, I, wretch, what wailings may I give?
Or what complaints? What woeful words may be enough for me?
Their heads cut off, and hands off torn, I from their bodies see,
And wrenched feet from broken thighs I here behold again.
'Tis this that greedy father could not suffer to sustain.
In belly roll my bowels round, and closed crime so great
Without a passage strives within, and seeks a way to get.
Thy sword, O brother, lend to me. Much of my blood, alas,
It hath. Let us therewith make way for all my sons to pass.
Is yet the sword fro me withheld? Thyself thy bosoms tear;
And let thy breasts resound with strokes. Yet, wretch, thy hand forbear,
And spare the dead. Whoever saw such mischief put in proof?
What rude Heniochus, that dwells by ragged coast aloof
Of Caucasus unapt for men? Or (fear to Athens) who
Procrustes wild? The father I oppress my children do
And am oppressed. Is any mean of guilt or mischief yet?

ATREUS

A mean in mischief ought to be when guilt thou dost commit,
Not when thou quit'st. For yet even this too little seems to me.
The blood yet warm even from the wound I should in sight of thee
Even in thy jaws have shed, that thou the blood of them mightst drink
That lived yet. But while too much to hast my hate I think,
My wrath beguiled is. Myself with sword the wounds them gave;
I strake them down; the sacred fires with slaughter vowed I have
Well pleased; the carcass cutting then and lifeless limbs on ground
I have in little parcels chopped, and some of them I drowned
In boiling cauldrons, some to fires that burnt full slow I put,
And made to drop their sinews all, and limbs atwo I cut
Even yet alive, and on the spit that thrust was through the same
I heard the liver wail and cry, and with my hand the flame
I oft kept in. But every whit the father might of this
Have better done; but now my wrath too lightly ended is.
He rent his sons with wicked gum, himself yet woting nought,
Nor they thereof.

66 **'filed** either 'defiled' or, more prosaically, 'filled'.

80 **Heniochus** a barbarian of the Heniochi, who lived in the Caucasus.

82 **Procrustes wild** the brigand Procrustes, who tortured his victims on a 'Procrustean bed'. If they did not fit it perfectly he hacked off their limbs until they did.

83 **Is...yet?** Is there any limit to his mischief?

84–85 **A mean...quit'st.** There are limits only when one commits a crime, not when one requites/revenges one.

94 **atwo** into two pieces.

THYESTES

O ye, enclosed with bending banks about,
All seas me hear; and to this guilt, ye gods, now harken well,
Whatever place ye fled are to. Hear, all ye sprites of hell,
And hear, ye lands, and night so dark that them dost overlie
With cloud so black, to my complaints do thou thyself apply.
To thee now left I am, thou dost alone me miser see,
And thou art left without thy stars. I will not make for me
Petitions yet, nor ought for me require, may ought yet be
That me should vail? For you shall all my wishes now foresee.
Thou, guider great of skies above, and prince of highest might
Of heavenly place, now all with clouds full horrible to sight
Enwrap the world, and let the winds on every side break out,
And send the dreadful thunder-clap through all the world about.
Not with what hand thou guiltless house and undeserved wall
With lesser bolt art wont to beat, but with the which did fall
The three upheaped mountains once, and which to hills in height
Stood equal up: the giants huge. Throw out such weapons straight,
And fling thy fires, and therewithal revenge the drowned day.
Let flee thy flames; the light thus lost and hid from heaven away
With flashes fill. The cause (lest long thou shouldst doubt whom to hit)
Of each of us is ill; if not, at least let mine be it,
Me strike! With triple-edged tool thy brand of flaming fire
Beat through this breast. If father I my children do desire
To lay in tomb, or corpses cast to fire, as doth behove,
I must be burnt. If nothing now the gods to wrath may move,
Nor power from skies with thunderbolt none strikes the wicked men,
Let yet eternal night remain, and hide with darkness then
The world about. I, Titan, nought complain, as now it stands,
If still thou hide thee thus away.

ATREUS

Now praise I well my hands,
Now got I have the palm! I had been overcome of thee
Except thou sorrowed'st so. But now even children born to me
I count, and now of bride-bed chaste the faith I do repair.

THYESTES

In what offended have my sons?

ATREUS

In that: that thine they were!

THYESTES

Set'st thou the sons for father's food?

ATREUS

I do, and (which is best)
The certain sons.

116 **three upheaped mountains** the mountains that the Giants piled up in their assault upon the gods: Pelion, Olympus, and Ossa.

117 **straight** immediately.

130 **I have . . palm!** The victory is mine!

THYESTES
The gods that guide all infants, I protest!

ATREUS
What, wedlock gods?

THYESTES
Who would the guilt with guilt so quit again?

ATREUS
I know thy grief, prevented now with wrong, thou dost complain.
Nor this thee irks, that fed thou art with food of cursed kind,
But that thou hadst not it prepared, for so it was thy mind,
Such meats as these to set before thy brother woting nought,
And, by the mother's help, to have likewise my children caught,
And them with such like death to slay. This one thing letted thee,
Thou thoughtst them thine!

THYESTES
The gods shall all of this revengers be,
And unto them for vengeance due my vows thee render shall!

ATREUS
But vexed to be I thee the while give to thy children all.

[Act Five:] The Fourth Scene
Added to the Tragedy by the Translator.
(Thyestes alone.)

[THYESTES]
King of Dytis' dungeon dark, and grisly ghosts of hell
That in the deep and dreadful dens of blackest Tartar dwell,
Where lean and pale diseases lie, where fear and famine are,
Where discord stands with bleeding brows, where every kind of care,
Where Furies fight in beds of steel, and hairs of crawling snakes,
Where Gorgon grim, where Harpies are, and loathsome Limbo lakes,
Where most prodigious ugly things the hollow hell doth hide,
If yet a monster more misshaped than all that there do bide,
That makes his brood his cursed food, ye all abhor to see,
Nor yet the deep Avern itself may bide to cover me,
Nor grisly gates of Pluto's place yet dare themselves to spread,
Nor gaping ground to swallow him whom gods and day have fled;
Yet break ye out from cursed seats and here remain with me;
Ye need not now to be afraid, the air and heaven to see.
Nor triple-headed Cerberus, thou needst not be afright
The day unknown to thee to see, or else the loathsome light.
They both be fled: and now doth dwell none other count'nance here
Than doth beneath the foulest face of hateful hell appear.

131–132 **now...count** now I know my children are my own (alluding back to Act II 154, where Atreus had suggested that if his own sons had shown any unwillingness to trap Thyestes he'd have doubted their paternity).

135.1 **protest** pray to in protest.

1 **King...dark** King of the dark dungeon of Dis, the underworld.

10 **Avern** Lake Averno, the gateway to Hades.

Come see a meetest match for thee, a more than monstrous womb,
That is of his unhappy brood become a cursed tomb.
Flock here, ye foulest fiends of hell, and thou, O grandsire great,
Come see the glutted guts of mine with such a kind of meat
As thou didst once for gods prepare. Let torments all of hell
Now fall upon this hateful head that hath deserved them well.
Ye all be plagued wrongfully, your guilts be small in sight
Of mine, and meet it were your pangs on me alone should light.
Now thou, O grandsire, guiltless art, and meeter were for me
With fleeing flood to be beguiled, and fruit of fickle tree.
Thou slewst thy son, but I my sons alas have made my meat.
I could thy famine better bear, my paunch is now replete
With food: and with my children three my belly is extent.
O filthy fowls and gnawing gripes that Tityus' bosom rent,
Behold a fitter prey for you to fill yourselves upon
Than are the growing guts of him: four wombs enwrapped in one!
This paunch at once shall fill you all. If ye abhor the food,
Nor may yourselves abide to bathe in such a cursed blood,
Yet lend to me your clinching claws, your prey awhile forbear,
And with your talons suffer me this monstrous maw to tear!
Or whirling wheels, with swinge of which Ixion still is rolled,
Your hooks upon this glutted gorge would catch a surer hold.
Thou filthy flood of Limbo lake, and Stygian pool so dire,
From choked charnel belch abroad, thou fearful fret of fire;
Spew out thy flames, O Phlegethon, and over-shed the ground;
With vomit of thy fiery stream let me and earth be drowned.
Break up, thou soil, from bottom deep, and give thou room to hell,
That night were day, that ghosts where gods were wont to reign may dwell.
Why gap'st thou not? Why do you not, O gates of hell, unfold?
Why do ye thus th'infernal fiends so long from hence withhold?
Are you likewise afraid to see and know so wretched wight,
From whom the gods have wried their looks and turned are to flight?
O hateful head, whom heaven and hell have shunned and left alone,
The sun, the stars, the light, the day, the gods, the ghosts be gone.
Yet turn again, ye skies, awhile, ere quite ye go fro me,
Take vengeance first on him whose fault enforceth you to flee.
If needs ye must your flight prepare, and may no longer bide,
But roll ye must with you forthwith the gods and sun aside,
Yet slowly flee, that I at length may you yet overtake,
While wandering ways I after you, and speedy journey make.
By seas, by lands, by woods, by rocks, in dark I wander shall,
And on your wrath for right reward to due deserts will call.
Ye scape not fro me so, ye gods, still after you I go,
And vengeance ask on wicked wight your thunderbolt to throw!

21 **grandsire great** i.e. Tantalus.
26 **Of** when compared to.
27–28 **meeter . . . tree** it would be more appropriate for me to suffer the punishments allotted to you.
30 **paunch** belly.
31 **extent** distended.
42 **fret** river/ribbon.
47 **unfold** open.

FINIS.

IMPRINTED AT
London in Fleet Street, in
the house late Thomas
Berthelet's.
Cum privilegio ad imprimendum solum.
ANNO. MDLX.

Cum . . . MDLX. With privilege for exclusive printing, the year 1560.

Cambises

(1560–1570)

THOMAS PRESTON

(1537–1598)

THE PLAYWRIGHT

Thomas Preston was born in Buckinghamshire and educated at Eton and King's College, Cambridge. He was elected scholar at King's in August 1533 and fellow in 1556, graduating BA in 1557 and MA in 1561. He came to the attention of Queen Elizabeth I in 1564, when she visited Cambridge. Preston acted in a performance of a 'tragedy of Dido' before the Queen, and subsequently took part in a formal disputation, in which he had the unenviable role of arguing *against* the idea that monarchy was the best form of government. Elizabeth seems to have been impressed by his performance, however, as she rewarded him with an annual pension of twenty pounds when he delivered a formal oration on her departure.

In 1572 Preston began formal study of civil law, graduating Doctor of Laws in about 1576. He may well have married his wife, Alice in 1581; for at this point he resigned his college fellowship (fellows had to be single men at this time). He returned to a major university role, however, in 1585 when he became Master of Trinity Hall, being the first married man to hold the position. In 1589 he became vice chancellor of the university, before becoming an advocate in the Court of arches in 1591. He died on 1 June 1598, leaving a substantial estate to his widow.

THE PLAY

Cambises was published by the London printer James Allde in 1569–70, but may have been written as early as 1560, almost certainly for performance at Cambridge University. It is based upon a story from the *Histories* of Herodotus, probably via the version to be found in the second book of Richard Taverner's *Garden of Wisdom* (1539).[1] In its time, like *Damon and Pithias*, it was a highly innovative attempt to explore the possibilities of the new, mixed genre of tragic-comedy, adding to the mix an element of chronicle history that looks forward to the history plays of Shakespeare and his contemporaries. Preston's slightly awkward attempt to mingle what the title page describes as the 'lamentable tragedy' of the main plot, with 'pleasant mirth', coupled with its versification, which uses the sombre and rather plodding 'fourteener' metre for the main characters and a kind of free verse for the Vice, seems to have become very old fashioned by the 1590s, however. Shakespeare has Falstaff parody Preston's style in Act II Scene 5 of *The First Part of Henry IV*, reddening his eyes with sherry and declaiming in 'a passion' speaking 'in King

[1] Richard Taverner, *The Garden of Wysdom* (London, John Harveye, 1539), sigs ci-cv^{v}.

Cambises' vein', and uses a similar style for Bottom the weaver's bombastic acting in *A Midsummer Night's Dream*. The fact that Shakespeare knew that he could get a laugh from parodying Preston's style over thirty years after the play was written does, however, suggest that it was well known, and remained popular, for a long period, and beyond the confines of the university culture which produced it. The fact that the printed edition offers a doubling scheme that it claims would allow the play to be performed by eight actors suggests that the Preston and/or Allde expected it to be taken up and played, perhaps by professional touring companies, in a range of different situations.

The play focuses, like many mid-Tudor tragedies, on issues of social and political justice and injustice. Its fascination with excessive violence and the mechanics of its representation also set it in a vivid tradition of sanguinary drama stretching back to the medieval Crucifixion pageants and the Croxton *Play of the Sacrament* to pseudo-Senecan dramas such as *The Spanish Tragedy*, Shakespeare's *Titus Andronicus*, and the bloody tragedies of the Jacobean period. The gruesome onstage flaying alive of the judge Sisamnes (performed, as the stage directions tell us, by the use of a false skin), and the histrionic onstage deaths of both Smirdis and Cambises himself (requiring the actors to wear hidden bladders filled with vinegar which could be burst at the requisite moment to look like blood), must have made witnessing the play, especially in the narrow confines of a college hall, an intense experience.

I have used the Allde edition of 1570 as the basis for the text, and have consulted the modern edition by T. W. Craik listed under further reading.

FURTHER READING

Cartwright, Kent, *Theatre and Humanism: Drama in the Sixteenth Century* (Cambridge: Cambridge University Press, 2008), especially 100–134.

Craik, T. W., ed., *Minor Elizabethan Tragedies* (London: J. M. Dent, 1974).

Dillon, Janette, *The Cambridge Introduction to Early English Theatre* (Cambridge: Cambridge University Press, 2006).

Happé, Peter, *English Drama Before Shakespeare* (London: Longman, 1999).

Lunney, Ruth R., *Marlowe and the Popular Tradition: Innovation in the English Drama before 1595* (Manchester: Manchester University Press, 2002).

Shepard, Alexandra, 'Thomas Preston (1537–1598)', *Oxford Dictionary of National Biography* (Oxford: Oxford University Press, 2004) <http://www.oxforddnb.com/view/article/22730>, accessed 6 June 2013.

Winkelman, Michael A., *Marriage Relationships in Tudor Political Drama* (Aldershot: Ashgate, 2005).

A Lamentable Tragedy mixed full of pleasant mirth, containing the Life of Cambises, King of Persia from the beginning of his Kingdom unto his Death, his one good deed of execution, after that many wicked deeds and tyrannous murders, committed by and through him, and last of all his odious death by God's justice appointed. Done in such order as followeth, by Thomas Preston.

[*Dramatis Personae:*

CAMBISES, King of Persia[2]
SISAMNES, the judge,
PRAXASPES, a counsellor,
LORDS and KNIGHTS, in attendance on the king,
QUEEN, wife of Cambises,
WIFE of Praxaspes,
AMBIDEXTER,
ATTENDANCE,
PREPARATION,
COMMONS' CRY
PROOF,
CRUELTY,
HUFF, RUFF, and SNUFF, ruffianly soldiers,
HOB and LOB, clownish countrymen,
VENUS,
PROLOGUE and EPILOGUE]

SMIRDIS, brother of the king,
OTIAN, his [Sisamnes'] son,
YOUNG CHILD, his [Praxaspes'] son,

WAITING-MAID, attending the Queen,
SHAME,
COUNSEL,
DILIGENCE,
SMALL HABILITY,
COMMONS' COMPLAINT,
EXECUTION,
MURDER,
MERETRIX, their companion.
MARIAN MAY-BE-GOOD, Hob's wife.
CUPID.

The Division of the Parts

Cambyses II (d. 522BC) was the son of Cyrus the Great, who founded the Persian Empire, and ruled it from 559 to 530 BC.
Small Hability 'Little Skill': a simple common man.
Commons' Cry the lamentation of the common people.
Commons' Complaint the protest of the common people.
Meretrix Latin for 'prostitute'.

COUNSEL, HUFF, PRAXASPES, MURDER, LOB, THE THIRD LORD: For one man.
LORD, RUFF, COMMONS' CRY, COMMONS' COMPLAINT, LORD SMIRDIS, VENUS: For one man.
KNIGHT, SNUFF, SMALL HABILITY, PROOF, EXECUTION, ATTENDANCE, SECOND LORD: For one man.
CAMBISES, EPILOGUE: For one man.
PROLOGUE, SISAMNES, DILIGENCE, CRUELTY, HOB, PREPARATION, THE FIRST LORD: For one man.
AMBIDEXTER, TRIAL: For one man.
MERETRIX, SHAME, OTIAN, MOTHER, LADY, QUEEN: For one man.
YOUNG CHILD, CUPID: For one man.

THE PROLOGUE *entereth.*

Agathon, he whose counsel wise to princes' weal extended,
By good advice unto a prince three things he hath commended:
First, is that he hath government and ruleth over men;
Secondly, to rule with laws, eke justice, sayeth he, then;
Thirdly, that he must well conceive he may not always reign.
Lo, thus the rule unto a prince Agathon squared plain.
Tully the wise, whose sapience in volumes great doth tell,
Who in wisdom in that time did many men excel,
'A prince,' sayeth he, 'is of himself a plain and speaking law:
The law, a schoolmaster divine', this by his rule I draw.
The sage and witty Seneca his words thereto did frame:
'The honest exercise of kings, men will ensue the same,
But, contrariwise, if that a king abuse his kingly seat,
His ignominy and bitter shame in fine shall be more great.'
In Persia there reigned a king, who Cyrus hight by name,
Who did deserve, as I do read, the lasting blast of fame;
But he, when Sisters three had wrought to sheer his vital thread,

s.d. As T. W. Craik notes, this doubling scheme, which suggests the play may be performed readily by eight actors, is not wholly accurate, as it omits Marian May-Be-Good and the Waiting-Maid, and seems to give a single role two names: 'Lady' and 'Queen'. That the 'Lady' might be the Queen's Maid seems ruled out by the claim that 'Lady' and 'Queen' can be played by the same actor.

1 **Agathon** perhaps the tragic poet of the fifth century BC who appears in Plato's *Symposium*. 'Agathon' means 'the good' in Greek, so Preston may be assuming that his work was a model of good counsel.

1 **whose counsel ... extended** he gave good advice for the well-being of princes and the commonwealths over which they ruled.

4 **eke** (and) also.

5 **he ... reign** he must understand well that he will not rule forever.

6 **squared plain** set out clearly.

7 **Tully** the rhetorician, philosopher and statesman Cicero (Marcus Tullius Cicero (106–43BC)).

9–10 **A prince ... divine** i.e. while a prince's word has the power of law, he should be instructed on how to act by the laws of the land.

10 **this ... draw** that is what I infer from his instruction.

11 **Seneca** Lucius Annaeus Seneca (Seneca the Younger, *c.*3BC–65AD), the playwright, philosopher, and politician.

11 **his ... frame** directed his words to the same end.

12 **The honest ... same** [Where] kings perform their roles virtuously, their subjects will be inspired to behave in the same way.

13 **kingly seat** throne/position.

14 **in fine** to put it briefly.

15 **Cyrus** Cyrus the Great (see the note to *Dramatis Personae*, above).

15 **hight** was called.

17 **Sisters three** the Three Fates, who controlled human destinies by cutting the threads of life at the moment of death.

As heir due, to take the crown Cambises did proceed.
He in his youth was trained up by trace of virtue's lore;
Yet, being king, did clean forget his perfect race before.
Then, cleaving more unto his will, such vice did imitate
As one of Icarus his kind: forewarning then did hate,
Thinking that none could him dismay, ne none his fact could see;
Yet at the last a fall he took, like Icarus to be.
Else, as the fish, which oft had take the pleasant bait from hook,
In safe did spring and pierce the streams when fisher fast did look
To hoist up from the wat'ry waves unto the dried land,
Then scaped, at last by subtle bait come to the fisher's hand;
Even so this King Cambises here, when he had wrought his will,
Taking delight the innocent his guiltless blood to spill,
Then mighty Jove would not permit to prosecute offence,
But, what measure the king did mete, the same did Jove commence
To bring to end with shame his race. Two years he did not reign.
His cruelty we will dilate, and make the matter plain,
Craving that this may suffice now your patience to win,
I take my way. Behold, I see the players coming in.

FINIS

First enter Cambises, the King, Knight, [*Lord*], *and Counsellor.*

CAMBISES
My counsel grave and sapient, with lords of legal train,
Attentive ears towards bend and mark what shall be sayen.
So you likewise, my valiant knight, whose manly acts doth fly
By bruit of Fame, that sounding tromp doth pierce the azure sky;
My sapient words, I say, perpend, and so your skill dilate.
You know that Mors vanquished hath Cyrus, that king of state,
And I by due inheritance possess that princely crown,
Ruling by sword of mighty force in place of great renown.
You know, and often have heard tell, my father's worthy facts,
A manly Mars' heart he bare, appearing by his acts.

20 **race before** previous path.
22 **As...kind** Like someone of Icarus' nature. (Icarus ignored his father's advice and flew too close to the sun on waxen wings, and fell to his death when the wax melted.)
22 **forewarning...hate** despising all warnings/advice.
23 **none...dismay** no one could hurt/defeat him.
23 **fact** deeds/crime(s)
25 **Else, as** Or, alternatively, Like.
28 Cambises is compared to the fish who many times escapes from the hook (and so comes to believe he is immortal), but at last falls victim to the angler's hook.
31 **Jove** Jupiter, king of the gods.
32 **what...commence** what Cambises did to others, Jove did to him.
33 **race** path/life.
33 **Two...reign.** He reigned for less than two years.
34 **dilate** describe in detail.
1 **My...train** My sober and wise advisors, with (you) lords trained in the law.
2 **towards bend** turn towards me.
2 **mark** note/pay attention to.
4 **bruit of fame** fame's report.
4 **sounding tromp** resonant trumpet.
6 **Mors** Death.
8 **in...renown** in the seat of great honour.
9 **facts** deeds.
10 **Mars** the god of war, i.e. warlike.

And, what, shall I to ground let fall my father's golden praise?
No, no, I mean for to attempt this same more large to raise.
In that that I, his son, succeed his kingly seat, as due;
Extend your counsel unto me in that I ask of you;
I am the king of Persia, a large and fertile soil;
The Egyptians against us repugn as varlets, slave and vile,
Therefore I mean with Mars' heart with wars them to frequent,
Them to subdue as captives mine: this is my heart's intent.
So shall I win honour's delight, and praise of me shall go.
My counsel, speak, and, lordings eke: is it not best do so?

COUNSEL

O puissant king, your blissful words deserve abundant praise,
That you in this do go about your father's fame to raise.
O blissful day, that king so young such profit should conceive,
His father's praise and his to win from those that would deceive.
Sure, my true and sovereign king, I fall before you prest,
Answer to give as duty mine, in that your grace request.
If that your heart addicted be the Egyptians to convince,
Through Mars' aid the conquest won, then deed of happy prince
Shall pierce the skies unto the throne of the supernal seat,
And merit there a just reward of Jupiter the Great.
But then your grace must not turn back from this pretenced will;
For to proceed in virtuous life, employ endeavour still.
Extinguish vice, and in that cup to drink have no delight;
To martial feats and kingly sport fix all your whole delight.

KING

My Counsel grave, a thousand thanks with heart I do you render,
That you my case so prosperous entirely do tender.
I will not swerve from those your steps whereto you would me train.
But now, my lord and valiant knight, with words give answer plain;
Are you content with me to go, the Mars' games to try?

LORD

Yea, peerless prince; to aid your grace myself will live and die.

KNIGHT

And I, for my ability, for fear will not turn back,
But, as the ship against the rocks, sustain and bide the wrack.

KING

O willing hearts, a thousand thanks I render unto you.
Strike up your drums with courage great; we will march forth even now.

12 **more . . . raise** to increase it still further.
16 **us . . . vile** insult us, (calling us) wretches, servile and low.
17 **frequent** visit.
19 **go** spread far.
25 **prest** swiftly/readily.
27 **convince** subdue.
29 **supernal seat** heavenly throne (lit. the throne above).
30 **of** from.
31 **pretenced** asserted.
32 **still** always.
41 **for my ability** as best I can.
42 **bide the wrack** endure the storm.

COUNSEL
Permit, O king, few words to hear, my duty serves no less;
Therefore give leave to Counsel thine his mind for to express.

KING
Speak on my Counsel; what it be, you shall have favour mine.

COUNSEL
Then will I speak unto your grace as duty doth me bind.
Your grace doth mean for to attempt of war the manly art;
Your grace therein may hap receive, with others for your part,
The dint of death: in those affairs all persons are alike.
The heart courageous often times his detriment doth seek;
It's best therefore for to permit a ruler of your land
To sit and judge with equity when things of right are scanned.

KING
My grace doth yield to this your talk, to be thus now it shall.
My knight, therefore prepare yourself Sisamnes for to call;
A judge he is of prudent skill; even he shall bear the sway
In absence mine, when from the land I do depart my way.

KNIGHT
Your knight before your grace, even here, himself hath ready prest,
With willing heart for to fulfil, as your grace made request. *Exit.*

COUNSEL
Pleaseth your grace, I judge of him to be a man right fit;
For he is learned in the law, having the gift of wit.
In your grace's precinct I do not view for it a meeter man.
His learning is of good effect, bring proof thereof I can;
I do not know what is his life, his conscience hid from me;
I doubt not but the fear of God before his eyes to be.

LORD
Report declares he is a man that to himself is nigh,
One that favoureth much the world, and sets too much thereby.
But this I say of certainty: if he your grace succeed
In your absence, but for a while, he will be warned indeed
No injustice for to frequent, no partial judge to prove,
But rule all things with equity, to win your grace's love.

KING
Of that he shall a warning have my hests for to obey;
Great punishment for his offence against him will I lay.

47 **what it be** whatever it is (you say).
50 **hap** chance to.
51 **dint** blow.
54 **when...scanned** if matters are considered wisely.
55 **to...shall** that's how it shall be.
57–58 **bear...mine** govern in my absence.
59 **hath ready prest** has already prepared himself.
63 **In...man.** I don't think there's a fitter man (for the role) in your realm.
65 **his life** manner of living.
67 **that...nigh** who loves himself, or possibly keeps himself very private.
70 **but** even if only.
71 **No...frequent** to do no injustice.
73 **hests** orders.

COUNSEL

Behold, I see him now aggress and enter into place.

SISAMNES

O puissant prince and mighty king, the gods preserve your grace.
Your grace's message came to me, your will purporting forth;
With grateful mind I it received according to mine oath,
Erecting then myself with speed before your grace's eyes,
The tenor of your princely will from you for to agnise.

KING

Sisamnes, this the whole effect the which for you I sent:
Our mind it is to elevate you to great preferment.
My grace, and gracious counsel eke, hath chose you for this cause:
In judgement you do office bear, which have the skill in laws.
We think that you accordingly by justice rule will deal,
That for offence none shall have cause, of wrong you to appeal.

SISAMNES

Abundant thanks unto your grace for this benignity;
To you, his counsel, in like case, with lords of clemency.
What so your grace to me permits, if I therein offend,
Such execution then commence, and use it to this end:
That all other by that my deed example so may take,
To admonish them to flee the same by fear it may them make.

KING

Then, according to your words, if you therein offend,
I assure you, even from my breast, correction shall extend.
From Persia I mean to go into the Egypt land,
Them to convince by force of arms and win the upper hand.
While I therefore absent shall be, I do you full permit
As governor in this my right in that estate to sit,
For to detect and eke correct those that abuse my grace.
This is the total of my will. Give answer in this case.

SISAMNES

Unworthy much, O prince, am I, and for this gift unfit;
But, sith that it hath pleased your grace that I in it must sit,
I do avouch unto my death, according to my skill,
With equity for to observe your grace's mind and will,
And nought from it to swerve, indeed, but sincerely to stay,
Else let me taste the penalty as I before did say.

KING

Well then, of this authority I give you full possession.

75 **aggress** approach.
77 **your will . . . forth** expressing your will.
79 **Erecting** Directing.
80 **agnise** discover.
86 **of . . . appeal** to accuse you of injustice.
91–92 **all . . . make** (if I offend) others may take example from my deeds that they avoid doing the same things themselves.
94 **I . . . extend** I assure you, from my very heart, that punishment will follow.
96 **convince** conquer.
103 **avouch** swear.
105 **swerve** deviate.

SISAMNES

And I will it fulfil also, as I have made profession.

KING

My Counsel, then, let us depart a final stay to make;
To Egypt land now forth with speed my voyage will I take.
Strike up your drums, us to rejoice to hear the warlike sound.
Stay you here, Sisamnes; judge, and look well to your bound!

Exeunt King, Lord, and Counsel.

SISAMNES

Even now the king hath me extolled, and set me up aloft.
Now may I wear the bordered guard and lie in down-bed soft;
Now may I purchase house and land, and have all at my will;
Now may I build a princely place my mind for to fulfil;
Now may I abrogate the law as I shall think it good;
If anyone me now offend, I may demand his blood.
According to the proverb old, my mouth I will up-make.
Now it doth lie all in my hand to leave or else to take,
To deal with justice to my bound, and so to live in hope.
But oftentimes the birds be gone while one for nest doth grope.
Do well or ill, I dare avouch some evil on me will speak.
No, truly, yet I do not mean the king's precepts to break.
To place I mean for to return my duty to fulfil. *Exit.*

Enter the Vice, [Ambidexter,] with an old cap-case on his head, an old pail about his hips for harness, a scummer and a pot-lid by his side, and a rake on his shoulder.

AMBIDEXTER

Stand away! Stand away, for the passion of God!
Harnessed I am, prepared to the field.
I would have been content at home to have bod,
But I am sent forth with my spear and shield.
I am appointed to fight against a snail,
And Wilken Wren the ancient shall bear:
I doubt not but against him to prevail,
To be a man my deeds shall declare.
If I overcome him, then a butterfly takes his part;

112 **look . . . bound** attend well to your responsibilities.
114 **bordered guard** an ornamental fringe around the clothing (i.e. here, fine clothes generally).
116 **place** house/palace.
119 **my . . . up-make** I will fill my mouth, i.e. have all I want.
123 **Do . . . speak.** Whether I act well or badly I'll wager some folk will speak ill of me.
125.1 **cap-case** bag.
125.1 **harness** armour.
125.1 **scummer** broad flat ladle for skimming froth from the top of pots and barrels.
128 **bod** stayed.
131 **shall bear** shall be my standard bearer.
134 **his part** his place (as the next opponent).

His weapon must be a blew-specked hen;
But you shall see me overthrow him with a fart,
So without conquest he shall go home again.
If I overcome him, I must fight with a fly;
And a black-pudding the fly's weapon must be.
At the first blow on the ground he shall lie;
I will be sure to thrust him through the mouth to the knee.
To conquest these fellows the man I will play!
Ha, ha, ha! Now ye will make me to smile,
To see if I can all men beguile.
Ha? My name? My name would ye so fain know?
Yea, iwis, shall ye, and that with all speed...
I have forgot it, therefore I cannot show.
Ah! ah! Now I have it! I have it, indeed!
My name is Ambidexter: I signify one
That with both hands finely can play;
Now with King Cambises, and by and by gone.
Thus do I run this way and that way;
For, while I mean with a soldier to be,
Then give I a leap to Sisamnes the judge;
I dare avouch you shall his destruction see.
To all kind of estates I mean for to trudge.
Ambidexter? Nay, he is a fellow, if ye knew all!
Cease for a while; hereafter hear more ye shall.

Enter three ruffians: Huff, Ruff, and Snuff, singing.

HUFF
Gog's flesh and his wounds, these wars rejoice my heart!
By his wounds, I hope to do well for my part!
By Gog's heart! The world shall go hard if I do not shift;
At some old carl's budget I mean for to lift.

RUFF
By His flesh, nose, eyes, and ears,
I will venture, void of all cares.
He is not a soldier that doth fear any doubt
If that he would bring his purpose about.

SNUFF
Fears that fear list, it shall not be I!
By Gog's wounds, I will make some neck stand awry.

142 **To...play!** I'll play the man to beat these fellows!
145 **fain** soon.
146 **iwis** indeed.
147 **show** tell you.
149 **Ambidexter** literally 'with both hands': implying the ability to double-deal.
154 **a leap** an unexpected movement or trick.
156 **To...trudge.** I mean to make my way to people of all classes (to deceive them?)
159 **Gog's** euphemism for 'God's', an oath.
161 **shift** make a living for myself.
162 **carl's budget** wretch's wallet.
163 **His** God's.
164 **venture** take the risk (of thieving).
167 **Fears...I!** Let them fear who want to (I won't)!
168 **I...awry** I'll break someone's neck.

If I lose my share, I swear by Gog's heart,
Then let another take up my part.

HUFF
Yet I hope to come the richest soldier away.

RUFF
If a man ask ye, ye may hap to say nay.

SNUFF
Let all men get what they can, not to lose I hope;
Where so ever I go, in each corner I will grope.

AMBIDEXTER
What and ye run in the corner of some pretty maid?

SNUFF
To grope there, good fellow, I will not be afraid.

HUFF
Gog's wounds, what art thou that with us dost mell?
Thou seemest to be a soldier, the truth to tell;
Thou seemest to be harnessed, I cannot tell how!
I think he came lately from riding some cow!
Such a deformed slave did I never see.
Ruff, dost thou know him? I pray thee, tell me.

RUFF
No, by my troth, fellow Huff, I never see him before.

SNUFF
As for me, I care not if I never see him more.
Come, let us run his arse against the post.

AMBIDEXTER
Ah, ye slaves! I will be with you at the host!
Ah, ye knaves! I will teach ye how ye shall me deride!

Here let him swinge them about.

Out of my sight! I can ye not abide!
Now, goodman pouch-mouth, I am a slave with you?
Now have at ye afresh again, even now!
Mine arse against the post you will run?
But I will make you from that saying to turn.

HUFF
I beseech ye heartily to be content.

RUFF
I insure you, by mine honesty, no hurt we meant.
Beside that again, we do not know what ye are.
Ye know that soldiers their stoutness will declare;
Therefore, if we have anything offended,

175 **and** if.
177 **mell** meddle/mix.
186 **I . . . host!** I'll sort you out, you and your army!
187.1 **swinge them about** thrash them.
189 **goodman pouch-mouth** mister big-mouth.
190 **have . . . afresh** take this too!
192 **I . . . turn** I'll make you think again about that.
194 **insure** assure.
196 **their . . . declare** cannot help but boast of their bravery.

Pardon our rudeness and it shall be amended.

AMBIDEXTER
Yea, God's pity, begin ye to entreat me?
Have at ye once again! By the mass, I will beat ye!

Fight again.

HUFF
Gog's heart, let us kill him. Suffer no longer.

Draw their swords.

SNUFF
Thou slave, we will see if thou be the stronger.

RUFF
Strike off his head at one blow;
That we be soldiers, Gog's heart, let him know!

AMBIDEXTER
O the passion of God, I have done, by mine honesty.
I will take your part hereafter, verily.

ALL
Then come, let us agree.

AMBIDEXTER
Shake hands with me, I shake hands with thee.
Ye are full of courtesy, that is the best;
And you take great pain, ye are a mannerly guest.
Why, masters, do you not know me? The truth to me tell.

ALL
No, trust us; not very well.

AMBIDEXTER
Why, I am Ambidexter, whom many soldiers do love.

HUFF
Gog's heart, to have thy company needs we must prove;
We must play with both hands, with our hostess and host,
Play with both hands, and score on the post;
Now and then with our captain, for many a delay,
We will not stick with both hands to play.

AMBIDEXTER
The honester man ye; ye may me trust!

Enter Meretrix, with a staff on her shoulder.

MERETRIX
What? Is there no lads here that hath a lust
To have a passing trull to help at their need?

206 **take your part** take your side.
210 **mannerly guest** polite fellow.
214 **to . . . prove** we must prosper with you in our company.
216 **score . . . post** add (it) to the tally (i.e. by double-dealing with hostess and host, run up debts in the inn and never pay them).
221 **trull** slut/prostitute.

HUFF

Gog's heart, she is come, indeed.
What, Mistress Meretrix, by His wounds, welcome to me!

MERETRIX

What will ye give me? I pray you, let me see.

RUFF

By His heart, she looks for gifts by and by!

MERETRIX

What, Master Ruff? I cry you mercy!
The last time I was with you I got a broken head,
And lay in the street all night for want of a bed!

SNUFF

Gog's wounds, kiss me, my trull so white;
In thee, I swear, is all my delight.
If thou should'st have had a broken head for my sake,
I would have made his head to ache.

MERETRIX

What, Master Ambidexter? Who looked for you?

AMBIDEXTER

Mistress Meretrix, I thought not to see you here now.
There is no remedy, at meeting I must have a kiss.

MERETRIX

What, man, I will not stick for that, by Jiss!

Kiss.

AMBIDEXTER

Go now, gramercy; I pray thee be gone!

MERETRIX

Nay, soft, my friend; I mean to have one.
Nay, soft, I swear; and if ye were my brother,
Before I let go, I will have another!

Kiss, kiss, kiss.

RUFF

Gog's heart, the whore would not kiss me yet!

MERETRIX

If I be a whore, thou art a knave; then it is quit.

HUFF

But hear'st thou, Meretrix? With who this night wilt thou lie?

MERETRIX

With him that giveth the most money.

HUFF

Gog's heart, I have no money in purse, ne yet in clout.

MERETRIX

Then get thee hence and pack, like a lout.

233 **Who . . . you?** Who invited you here?
235 **remedy** alternative.
236 **Jiss** euphemism for 'Jesus'.
237 **gramercy** thank you.
238 **soft** hush.
242 **then . . . quit** then we are even (I am revenged).
245 **clout** (my) clothes.
246 **get . . . lout** be off with you, like a wretch.

HUFF
Adieu, like a whore! *Exit.*

MERETRIX
Farewell, like a knave!

RUFF
Gog's nails, Mistress Meretrix, now he is gone,
A match ye shall make straight with me.
I will give thee sixpence to lie one night with thee.

MERETRIX
Gog's heart slave, dost think I am a sixpenny jug?
No, 'wis; ye lack, I look a little more smug!

SNUFF
I will give her eighteen pence to serve me first.

MERETRIX
Gramercy, Snuff, thou art not the worst!

RUFF
By Gog's heart, she were better be hanged to forsake me and take thee!

SNUFF
Were she so? That shall we see.

RUFF
By Gog's heart, my dagger into her I will thrust!

SNUFF
Ah, ye boy, ye would do it and ye durst.

AMBIDEXTER
Peace, my masters, ye shall not fight.
He that draws first, I will him smite.

RUFF
Gog's wounds, Master Snuff, are ye so lusty?

SNUFF
Gog's sides, Master Ruff, are ye so crusty?

RUFF
You may happen to see!

SNUFF
Do what thou darest to me!

Here draw and fight. Here she must lay on and coil them both; the Vice must run his way for fear [and] Snuff fling down his sword and buckler and run his way.

MERETRIX
Gog's sides, knaves; seeing to fight ye be so rough,
Defend yourselves, for I will give ye both enough!
I will teach ye how ye shall fall out for me.
Yea thou slave, Snuff; no more blows wilt thou bide?

252 **jug** tart/slut.
253 **'wis** indeed ('iwis')
253 **smug** decent/classy.
259 **and ye durst** if you dare.
263 **crusty** scabby.
265.1 **lay...them** set about them and beat them.
265.1 **buckler** small shield.
266 **seeing...rough** since you're so fierce (ironic).

To take thy heels a time hast thou spied?
Thou villains, seeing Snuff has gone away,
A little better I mean thee to pay!

He falleth down; she falleth upon him and beats him, and taketh away his weapons.

RUFF
Alas, good Mistress Meretrix, no more!
My legs, sides, and arms with beating be sore!

MERETRIX
Thou a soldier, and lose thy weapon?
Go hence, sir boy; say a woman hath thee beaten.

RUFF
Good Mistress Meretrix, my weapon let me have;
Take pity on me, mine honesty to save.
If it be known this repulse I sustain,
It will redound to my ignominy and shame.

MERETRIX
If thou wilt be my man, and wait upon me,
This sword and buckler I will give thee.

RUFF
I will do all at your commandment;
As servant to you I will be obedient.

MERETRIX
Then let me see how before me you can go.
When I speak to you, you shall do so:
Off with your cap, at place and at board,
'Forsooth, Mistress Meretrix,' at every word.
Tut, tut, in the camp such soldiers there be,
One good woman would beat away two or three.
Well, I am sure customers tarry at home.
Mannerly before, and let us be gone! *Exeunt.*

Enter Ambidexter.

AMBIDEXTER
O the Passion of God! Be they be still, or no?
I durst not abide to see her beat them so.
I may say to you I was in such a fright;
Body of me, I see the hair of my head stand upright!
When I saw her so hard upon them lay on,
O the Passion of God, thought I, she will be with me anon!
I made no more ado but avoided the thrust,

270 **To...spied?** Have you spotted your chance to run away?
275 **Thou** (Are) you.
280 **redound to** result in (lit. shout or echo to).
285 **how...go** how good you are at acting as my servant (lit. at walking ahead of me).
287 **at...board** when in public or at the meal table.
292 **Mannerly before** Walk before me decently.
292 **Exeunt** Both exit.
293 **still** quiet.
296 **Body of me** By my body! (A variant of the oath, 'God's body!')

And to my legs began for to trust;
And fell a-laughing to myself when I was once gone.
'It is wisdom', quoth I, 'by the mass, to save one!'
Then into this place I intended to trudge,
Thinking to meet Sisamnes the judge.
Behold where he cometh! I will him meet,
And like a gentleman I mean him to greet.

Enter Sisamnes.

SISAMNES
Since that the king's grace's majesty in office did me set,
What abundance of wealth to me might I get.
Now and then some vantage I achieve; much more yet may I take,
But that I fear unto the king, that some complaint will make.

AMBIDEXTER
Jesu, Master Sisamnes, you are unwise!

SISAMNES
Why so? I pray thee let me agnise.
What, Master Ambidexter, is it you?
Now welcome to me, I make God avow!

AMBIDEXTER
Jesu, Master Sisamnes, with me you are well acquainted.
By me rulers may be trimly painted.
Ye are unwise if ye take not time while ye may;
If ye will not now, when ye would ye shall have nay.
What is he that of you dare make exclamation,
Of your wrong-dealing to make explication?
Can you not play with both hands and turn with the wind?

SISAMNES
Believe me, your words draw deep in my mind,
In colour wise. Unto this day to bribes I have inclined;
More the same for to frequent, of truth, I am now minded.
Behold, even now unto me suitors do proceed.

SMALL HABILITY
I beseech you hear, good master judge, a poor man's cause to tender;
Condemn me not in wrongful wise that never was offender.
You know right well my right it is; I have not for to give.
You take away from me my due that should my corpse relieve.

300 **my...trust** relied on my legs (to run away).
302 **to save one** to look after oneself.
312 **agnise** know/understand.
316 **trimly painted** perfectly represented in order to deceive others (in modern terms, Ambidexter is suggesting he is the perfect spin-doctor).
318 **If...nay** If you don't act now it will be too late (lit. when you want to you'll be refused).
319 **What...exclamation** Who dares to complain about you?
322–323 **your...wise** your words persuade my mind powerfully by way of explanation.
324 **More...minded** truly, I intend to do that more often now.
327 **in wrongful wise** in an unjust manner.
328 **I...give** I have nothing with which to bribe you (you should hear my case rather as a matter of right).
329 **my due...relieve** the rightful income that should sustain my body.

The commons of you do complain from them you devocate;
With anguish great and grievous words their hearts do penetrate.
The right you sell unto the wrong, your private gain to win;
You violate the simple man and count it for no sin.

SISAMNES.

Hold thy tongue, thou prattling knave, and give to me reward,
Else, in this wise I tell thee truth, thy tale will not be heard.
Ambidexter, let us go hence, and let the knave alone!

AMBIDEXTER

Farwell, Small Hability, for helps now get you none;
Bribes hath corrupt him, good laws to pollute. [*Exeunt*]

SMALL HABILITY

A naughty man, that will not obey the king's constitute.
With heavy heart I will return, till God redress my pain. *Exit.*

Enter Shame, with a trump black.

SHAME

From among the grisly ghosts I come, from tyrants' testy train.
Unseemly Shame, of sooth, I am, procured to make plain
The odious facts and shameless deeds that Cambises King doth use.
All piety and virtuous life he doth it clean refuse;
Lechery and drunkenness he doth it much frequent;
The tiger's kind to imitate he hath given full consent.
He nought esteems his counsel grave as virtuous bringing-up,
But daily still receives the drink of damned vice's cup.
He can bide no instruction, he takes so great delight
In working of iniquity for to frequent his spite.
As Fame doth sound the royal trump of worthy men and trim,
So Shame doth blow with strained blast the trump of shame on him. *Exit.*

Enter the King, Lord, Praxaspes, and Sisamnes.

KING

My judge, since my departure hence, have you used judgement right?
If faithful steward I ye find, the same I will requite.

SISAMNES

No doubt your grace shall not once hear that I have done amiss.

PRAXASPES

I much rejoice to hear so good news as this.

Enter Commons Cry, running in, speak this verse;
[and] go out again hastily.

COMMONS' CRY

Alas! Alas! How are the commons oppressed

330 **you devocate** (that) you 'call down': probably a mistake for 'derogate', to destroy or take away the effect of the laws.
339 **constitute** mandate/commission.
340.1 **trump black** black trumpet.
341 **testy train** angry retinue.
342 **of sooth** truly.
345 **frequent** practice.
349 **bide** abide.

By that vile judge, Sisamnes by name!
I do not know how it should be redressed;
To amend his life no whit he doth frame.
We are undone and thrown out of door,
His damnable dealing doth us so torment.
At his hand we can find no relief nor succour;
God grant him grace for to repent!

Run away crying.

KING
What doleful cries be these, my lord, that sound do in mine ear?
Intelligence if you can give, unto your king declare.
To me it seemeth my commons all they do lament and cry
Out of Sisamnes, judge most chief, even now standing us by.

PRAXASPES
Even so, O king, it seemed to me as you rehearsal made;
I doubt the judge culpable be in some respect or trade.

SISAMNES
Redoubted king, have no mistrust, no whit your mind dismay;
There is not one that can me charge, or ought against me lay.

Enter Commons' Complaint, with Proof and Trial.

COMMONS' COMPLAINT
Commons' Complaint I represent, with thrall of doleful state,
My urgent cause erected forth my grief for to dilate.
Unto the king I will prepare my misery to tell,
To have relief of this my grief and fettered feet so fell.
Redoubted prince and mighty king, myself I prostrate here;
Vouchsafe, O king, with me to bear for this that I appear.
With humble suit I pardon crave of your most royal grace,
To give me leave my mind to break before you in this place.

KING
Commons' Complaint, keep nothing back; fear not thy tale to tell.
Whate'er he be within this land that hath not used thee well,
As prince's mouth shall sentence give, he shall receive the same.
Unfold the secrets of thy breast, for I extinguish blame.

COMMONS' COMPLAINT
God preserve your royal grace, and send you blissful days,
That all your deeds might still accord to give the gods the praise.
My complaint is, O mighty king, against that judge you by,
Whose careless deeds, gain to receive, hath made the Commons cry.
He, by taking bribes and gifts, the poor he doth oppress,

360 **To . . . frame** He does not try to reform his lifestyle at all.
366 **Intelligence** Information.
373–374 **with . . . dilate** and sorrowful slavery, brought forth to represent my urgent plight.
376 **fell** cruel.
378 **Vouchsafe** Grant/allow.
380 **my . . . break** to reveal my thoughts.
382 **Whate'er** Whoever.
387 **you by** who stands near you.

Taking relief from infants young, widows, and fatherless.

KING

Untrustful traitor and corrupt judge, how likest thou this complaint?
Forewarning I to thee did give of this to make restraint;
And hast thou done this devilish deed mine ire for to augment?
I sentence give, thou Judas judge, thou shalt thy deed repent!

SISAMNES

O puissant prince, it is not so! His complaint I deny.

COMMONS' COMPLAINT

If it be not so, most mighty king, in place then let me die.
Behold that I have brought with me both Proof and Trial true,
To stand even here, and sentence give what by him did ensue.

PROOF

I, Proof, do him in this appeal: he did the Commons wrong;
Unjustly he with them hath dealt, his greed was so strong;
His heart did covet in to get, he cared not which way.
The poor did lose their due and right, because they want to pay
Unto him for bribes; indeed, this was his wanted use;
Whereas your grace good laws did make, he did the same abuse.

TRIAL

I, Trial, here to verify what Proof doth now unfold,
To stand against him in his wrong, as now I dare be bold.

KING

How likest thou this, thou caitiff vile? Canst thou the same deny?

SISAMNES

O noble king, forgive my fact. I yield to thy mercy.

KING

Complaint and Proof, redress will I all this your misery.
Depart with speed from whence you came, and straight command by me
The execution-man to come before my grace with haste.

ALL

For to fulfil this your request no time we mean to waste.

Exeunt they three.

KING

My lord, before my grace go call Otian, this judge's son,
And he shall hear and also see what his father hath done.
The father he shall suffer death, the son his room succeed;
And, if that he no better prove, so likewise shall he speed.

PRAXASPES

As your Grace hath commandment given, I mean for to fulfil.

Step aside and fetch him.

390 **taking relief** taking away the sustenance.
396 **in place** here and now.
399 **appeal** accuse.
401 **want to pay** lack the means to pay.
403 **wanted use** usual practice.
407 **caitiff** wretch/slave.
410 **straight** immediately.
415 **his room succeed** take his place (as judge).
416 **speed** prosper.

KING

Accursed judge, couldst thou consent to do this cursed ill?
According unto thy demand, thou shalt for this thy guilt
Receive thy death before mine eyes. Thy blood it shall be spilt.

PRAXASPES

Behold, O king, Sisamnes' son before you doth appear.

KING

Otian, this is my mind, therefore to me come near:
Thy father here, for judgement wrong, procured hath his death,
And thou, his son, shalt him succeed when he hath lost his breath.
And, if that thou dost once offend, as thou seest thy father have,
In like wise thou shalt suffer death; no mercy shall thee save!

OTIAN

O mighty king, vouchsafe your grace my father to remit.
Forgive his fault; his pardon I do ask of you as yet.
Alas, although my father hath your princely heart offended,
Amends for miss he will now make, and faults shall be amended.
Instead of his requested life, pleaseth your grace take mine:
This offer I as tender child, so duty doth me bind.

KING

Do not entreat my grace no more, for he shall die the death.
Where is the execution-man him to bereave of breath?

Enter Execution.

EXECUTION

At hand, and if it like your grace, my duty to dispatch,
In hope that I, when deed is done, a good reward shall catch.

KING

Dispatch with sword this judge's life; extinguish fear and cares.
So done, draw thou his cursed skin straight over both his ears.
I will see the office done, and that before mine eyes.

EXECUTION

To do the thing my king commands I give the enterprise.

SISAMNES

Otian, my son, the king to death by law hath me condemned,
And you in room and office mine his grace's will hath placed;
Use justice, therefore, in this case, and yield unto no wrong,
Lest thou do purchase the like death ere ever it be long.

OTIAN

O father dear, these words to hear: that you must die by force,
Bedews my cheeks with stilled tears. The king hath no remorse.
The grievous griefs and strained sighs my heart doth break in twain,
And I deplore, most woeful child, that I should see you slain.
O false and fickle frowning dame, that turneth as the wind,

430 **miss** his crimes.
435 **At hand** (I'm) right here.
438 **draw** flay.
439 **the office** your task.
440 **I...enterprise** I devote myself.
446 **stilled** silent.
449 **false...dame** i.e. Fortune.

Is this the joy in father's age thou me assignest to find?
O doleful day, unhappy hour, that loving child should see;
His father dear before his face thus put to death should be!
Yet, father, give me blessing thine, and let me once embrace
Thy comely corpse in folded arms and kiss thy ancient face.

SISAMNES

O child, thou makes my eyes to run as rivers do, by stream.
My leave I take of thee, my son. Beware of this my beam.

KING

Dispatch even now, thou man of death; no longer seem to stay!

EXECUTION

Come, Master Sisamnes, come on your way.
My office I must pay; forgive therefore my deed.

SISAMNES

I do forgive it thee, my friend; dispatch therefore with speed.

Smite him in the neck with a sword to signify his death.

PRAXASPES

Behold, O king, how he doth bleed, being of life bereft.

KING

In this wise he shall not yet be left.
Pull his skin over his ears to make his death more vile.
A wretch he was, a cruel thief, my commons to beguile!

Flay him with a false skin.

OTIAN

What child is he of nature's mould could bide the same to see,
His father flayed in this wise? O, how it grieveth me!

KING

Otian, thou seest thy father dead, and thou art in his room;
If thou beest proud, as he hath been, even thereto shalt thou come.

OTIAN

O king, to me this is a glass; with grief in it I view
Example that unto your grace I do not prove untrue.

PRAXASPES

Otian, convey your father hence to tomb where he shall lie.

OTIAN

And if it please your lordship, it shall be done by and by.
Good execution-man, for need, help me with him away.

EXECUTIONER

I will fulfil, as you to me did say.

They take him away.

454 **comely** lovely/noble.
455 **by stream** in floods.
456 **beam** sin. (An allusion to Matthew 7:1–5, 'Judge not, that you may not be judged. For with what judgment you judge, you shall be judged: and with what measure you mete, it shall be measured to you again. And why seest thou the mote that is in thy brother's eye; and seest not the beam that is in thy own eye? ... Thou hypocrite, cast out first the beam in thy own eye, and then shalt thou see to cast out the mote out of thy brother's eye.')
459 **My ... pay** I must perform my role.
465 **of nature's mould** of natural creation.
469 **glass** mirror.
472 **by and by** at once.

KING
My lord, now that my Grace hath seen that finished is this deed,
To question mine give 'tentive care, and answer make with speed:
Have not I done a gracious deed, to redress my commons' woe?
PRAXASPES
Yea, truly, if it please your grace, you have indeed done so.
But now, O king, in friendly wise I counsel you in this,
Certain vices for to leave that in you placed is:
The vice of drunkenness, O king, which doth you sore infect,
With other great abuses which I wish you to detect.
KING
Peace, my lord! What needeth this? Of this I will not hear.
To palace now I will return, and thereto make good cheer.
God Bacchus he bestows his gifts, we have good store of wine,
And also that the ladies be both passing brave and fine.
But stay, I see a lord now come, and eke a valiant knight.
What news, my lord? To see you here my heart it doth delight.

Enter Lord and Knight to meet the King.

LORD
No news, O king; but of duty come to wait upon your grace.
KING
I thank you, my lord and loving knight. I pray you with me trace.
My lords and knight, I pray ye tell, I will not be offended,
Am I worthy of any crime once to be reprehended?
PRAXASPES
The Persians much do praise your grace, but one thing discommend,
In that to wine subject you be, wherein you do offend,
Sith that the might of wine's effect doth oft subdue your brain.
My counsel is, to please their hearts, from it you would refrain.
LORD
No, no, my lord, it is not so. For this of prince they tell,
For virtuous proof and princely facts Cyrus he doth excel.
By that his grace by conquest great the Egyptians did convince,
Of him report abroad doth pass to be a worthy prince.
KNIGHT
In person of Croesus I answer make: we may not his grace compare
In whole respect for to be like Cyrus, the king's father,
In so much your grace hath yet no child as Cyrus left behind,
Even you I mean, Cambises King, in whom I favour find.
KING
Croesus said well in saying so. But, Praxaspes, tell me why
That to my mouth in such a sort thou should avouch a lie,

476 **give 'tentive care** pay careful attention.
479 **wise** manner.
480 **Certain . . . is** to abandon certain vices that are natural to you.
485 **Bacchus** the god of wine.
486 **passing brave** surpassingly/superlatively elegant.
490 **with me trace** walk with me.
501 **Croesus** (595–547BC), king of Lydia, defeated and killed by Cyrus, Cambises' father.

Of drunkenness me thus to charge. But thou with speed shalt see
Whether that I a sober king or else a drunkard be.
I know thou hast a blissful babe, wherein thou dost delight;
Me to revenge of these thy words I will go wreak this spite:
When I the most have tasted wine, my bow it shall be bent,
At heart of him even then to shoot is now my whole intent.
And, if that I his heart can hit, the king no drunkard is;
If heart of his I do not kill, I yield to thee in this.
Therefore, Praxaspes, fetch to me thy youngest son with speed.
There is no way, I tell thee plain, but I will do this deed!

PRAXASPES

Redoubted prince, spare my sweet child; he is mine only joy!
I trust your grace to infant's heart no such thing will employ.
If that his mother hear of this, she is so nigh her flight,
In clay her corpse will soon be shrined to pass from world's delight.

KING

No more ado; go fetch me him. It shall be as I say.
And if that I do speak the word, how dare ye once say nay?

PRAXASPES

I will go fetch him to your grace; but so, I trust, it shall not be.

KING

For fear of my displeasure great, go fetch him unto me.
Is he gone? Now, by the gods, I will do assay.
My lord, therefore fill me some wine, I heartily you pray;
For I must drink to make my brain somewhat intoxicate.
When that the wine is in my head, O, trimly I can prate!

LORD

Here is the cup with filled wine, thereof to take repast.

KING

Give it me to drink it off, and see no wine be waste.

Drink.

Once again enlarge this cup, for I must taste it still. *Drink.*
By the gods, I think of pleasant wine I cannot take my fill!
Now drink is in, give me my bow and arrows from sir knight;
At heart of child I mean to shoot, hoping to cleave it right.

KNIGHT

Behold, O king, where he doth come, his infant young in hand.

PRAXASPES

O mighty king, your grace's behest with sorrow I have scanned,
And brought my child fro mother's knee before you to appear,
And she thereof no whit doth know that he in place is here.

KING

Set him up, my mark to be. I will shoot at his heart.

519 **so . . . flight** so close to death.
525 **assay** both 'put this to the test' and 'take a first drink'.
523 **trimly . . . prate** I can chatter finely.
531 **enlarge** refill.
532 **I cannot . . . fill** I cannot get enough.
536 **scanned** fulfilled.
539 **mark** target.

PRAXASPES
I beseech your grace not so to do! Set this pretence apart.
Farewell, my dear and loving babe! Come, kiss thy father dear.
A grievous sight to me it is to see thee slain even here.
Is this the game now from the king for giving counsel good,
Before my face with such despite to spill my son's heart-blood?
O heavy day to me this is, and mother in like case!

YOUNG CHILD
O father, father, wipe your face;
I see the tears run from your eye.
My mother is at home sewing of a band.
Alas, dear father, why do you cry?

KING
Before me as a mark now let him stand;
I will shoot at him my mind to fulfil.

YOUNG CHILD
Alas, alas, father, will you me kill?
Good Master king, do not shoot at me; my mother loves me best of all. *Shoot.*

KING
I have despatched him! Down he doth fall!
As right as a line his heart I have hit.
Nay, thou shalt see, Praxaspes, stranger news yet:
My knight, with speed his heart cut out and give it unto me.

KNIGHT
It shall be done, O mighty king, with all celerity.

LORD
My lord Praxaspes, this had not been but your tongue must be walking;
To the king of correction you must needs be talking!

PRAXASPES
No correction, my lord, but counsel for the best.

KNIGHT
Here is the heart, according to your grace's behest.

KING
Behold, Praxaspes, thy son's own heart! O, how well the same was hit.
After this wine to do this deed I thought it very fit.
Esteem thou maist right well thereby no drunkard is the king,
That in the midst of all his cups could do this valiant thing.
My lord and knight, on me attend; to palace we will go,
And leave him here to take his son when we are gone him fro.

ALL
With all our hearts we give consent to wait upon your grace. [*Exit.*]

PRAXASPES
A woeful man, O Lord, am I, to see him in this case!

540 **Set . . . apart.** Put aside this pretence.
545 **heavy** sorrowful.
545 **like case** the same situation.
549 **a band** a ribbon or tie for clothing.
559–560 **this . . . talking!** This would not have happened had it not been for your babbling tongue: you just couldn't stop yourself from chastising the king!

My days, I deem, desires their end; this deed will help me hence.
To have the blossoms of my field destroyed by violence!

Enter Mother.

MOTHER
Alas, alas! I do hear tell the king hath killed my son!
If it be so, woe worth the deed that ever it was done.
It is even so! My lord I see, how by him he doth weep.
What meant I, that from hands of him this child I did not keep?
Alas, husband and lord, what did you mean to fetch this child away?

PRAXASPES
O lady wife, I little thought for to have seen this day.

MOTHER
O blissful babe! O joy of womb! Heart's comfort and delight!
For counsel given unto the king is this thy just requite?
O heavy day and doleful time, these mourning tunes to make!
With blubbered eyes, into mine arms from earth I will thee take,
And wrap thee in mine apron white. But, oh my heavy heart;
The spiteful pangs that it sustains would make it in two to part,
The death of this my son to see! O heavy mother now,
That from thy sweet and sugared joy to sorrow so should'st bow.
What grief in womb did I retain before I did thee see;
Yet at the last, when smart was gone, what joy were't thou to me;
How tender was I of thy food, for to preserve thy state?
How stilled I thy tender heart at times early and late?
With velvet paps I gave thee suck with issue from my breast,
And danced thee upon my knee to bring thee unto rest.
Is this the joy of thee I reap? O king of tiger's brood!
O tiger's whelp, had'st thou the heart to see this child's heart-blood?
Nature enforceth me, alas, in this wise to deplore,
To wring my hands; O wellaway, that I should see this hour!
Thy mother yet will kiss thy lips, silk-soft and pleasant white,
With wringing hands lamenting for to see thee in this plight.
My lording dear, let us go home, our mourning to augment.

PRAXASPES
My lady dear, with heavy heart to it I do consent,
Between us both the child to bear unto our lordly place. *Exeunt.*

Enter Ambidexter.

AMBIDEXTER
Indeed, as ye say, I have been absent a long space.
But is not my cousin Cutpurse with you in the meantime?
To it, to it, cousin, and do your office fine!

571 **My days** My life.
574 **woe worth** curse.
580 **requite** reward.
589 **How...state?** How carefully did I serve you food to nourish you?
591 **paps** breasts.
595 **wise** manner.
596 **wellaway** alas.
601 **lordly place** noble palace.
602 **space** time.
604 **To it** Go on!
604 **do...fine** perform your task ably. (Ambidexter pretends to address a thief working his way through the audience.)

How like you Sisamnes for using of me?
He played with both hands, but he sped ill-favouredly!
The king himself was godly up-trained;
He professed virtue, but I think it was feigned.
He plays with both hands, good deeds and ill;
But it was no good deed Praxaspes' son for to kill.
As he for the good deed on the judge was commended,
For all his deeds else he is reprehended.
The most evil-disposed person that ever was,
All the state of his life he would not let pass:
Some good deeds he will do, though they be but few:
The like things this tyrant Cambises doth show:
No goodness from him to none is exhibited,
But still malediction abroad is distributed;
And yet ye shall see in the rest of his race
What infamy he will work against his own grace.
Whist, no more words! Here comes the king's brother.

Enter Lord Smirdis, with Attendance and Diligence.

SMIRDIS
The king's brother by birth am I, issued from Cyrus' loins;
A grief to me it is to hear of this the king's repines.
I like not well of those his deeds that he doth still frequent;
I wish to God that other ways his mind he could content.
Young I am, and next to him, no mo of us there be.
I would be glad a quiet realm in this his reign to see.

ATTENDANCE
My lord, your good and willing heart the gods will recompense,
In that your mind so pensive is, for those his great offence.
My lord, his grace shall have a time to pair and to amend.
Happy is he that can escape and not his race offend.

DILIGENCE
If that wicked vice he could refrain, from wasting wine forebear,
A moderate life he would frequent, amending this his square.

AMBIDEXTER
My lord, and if your honour it shall please,
I can inform you what is best for your ease:
Let him alone, of his deeds do not talk,
Then by his side ye may quietly walk;
After his death you shall be king.
Then may you reform each kind of thing.

606 **he sped ill-favouredly!** he had some bad luck!
613–615 **The most . . . do** i.e. even the worst of people cannot go through life without doing some good deeds.
617 **No . . . exhibited** He does no good deeds to anyone.
618 **malediction . . . distributed** evil (in word and deed) is spread widely around.
619 **race** journey/life.
621 **Whist!** Hush!
623 **repines** complaints/anxieties.
626 **mo** more (I am his only relative).
630 **pair** repair/put right.
632 **from . . . forbear** to resist destructive wine.
633 **A moderate . . . square** he would live a moderate life, restored to good order.

In the meantime live quietly, do not with him deal;
So shall it redound much to your weal.

SMIRDIS
Thou sayest true, my friend; that is the best.
I know not whether he love me or do me detest.

ATTENDANCE
Lean from his company all that you may.
I, faithful Attendance, will your honour obey;
If against your honour he take any ire,
His grace is as like to kindle his fire
To your honour's destruction as otherwise.

DILIGENCE
Therefore, my lord, take good advice,
And I, Diligence, your case will so tender,
That to his grace your honour shall be none offender.

SMIRDIS
I thank you both, entire friends; with my honour still remain.

AMBIDEXTER
Behold where the king doth come with his train!

Enter King and a Lord.

KING
O lording dear and brother mine, I joy your state to see,
Surmising much what is the cause you absent thus from me.

SMIRDIS
Pleaseth your grace, no absence I, but ready to fulfil
At all assays, my prince and king, in that your grace me will.
What I can do in true defence to you, my prince, aright,
In readiness I always am to offer forth my might.

KING
And I the like to you again do here avouch the same.

ALL
For this your good agreement here, now praised be God's name!

AMBIDEXTER
But hear ye, noble prince; hark in your ear,
It is best to do as I did declare.

KING
My lord and brother Smirdis, now this is my mind and will:
That you to court of mine return and there to tarry still
Till my return within short space your honour for to greet.

641 **weal** benefit/well-being.
644 **Lean ... may.** Stay out of his company as much as you can.
650 **I ... tender** I will speak for you (at court).
655 **Surmising much** Wondering greatly.
656–657 **no absence ... will** I am no absentee, but ready in all things, my prince ... to do whatever you want me to.
660 **And ... same.** And I swear the same to you in return.

SMIRDIS

At your behest so will I do, till time again we meet.
My leave I take from you, O king; even now I do depart.

Exeunt Smirdis, Attendance, and Diligence.

KING

Farewell, lord and brother mine; farewell with all my heart!
My lord, my brother Smirdis is of youth and manly might,
And in his sweet and pleasant face my heart doth take delight.

LORD

Yea, noble prince, if that your grace before his honour die,
He will succeed, a virtuous king, and rule with equity.

KING

As you have said, my lord, he is chief heir next my grace,
And, if I die tomorrow, next he shall succeed my place.

AMBIDEXTER

And if it please your grace, O king, I heard him say:
For your death unto the god[s] day and night he did pray;
He would live so virtuously and get him such a praise
That Fame by trump his due deserts in honour should upraise.
He said your grace deserved had the cursing of all men;
That ye should never after him get any praise again.

KING

Did he speak thus of my grace in such despiteful wise?
Or else dost thou presume to fill my princely ears with lies?

LORD

I cannot think it in my heart that he would report so.

KING

How sayest thou? Speak the truth: was it so or no?

AMBIDEXTER

I think so, if it please your grace, but I cannot tell.

KING

Thou playest with both hands now, I perceive well!
But, for to put all doubts aside, and to make him lose his hope,
He shall die by dint of sword or else by choking rope.
Shall he succeed when I am gone, to have more praise than I?
Were he father, as brother mine, I swear that he shall die!
To palace mine I will therefore, his death for to pursue. *Exit.*

AMBIDEXTER

Are ye gone? Straightway I will follow you.
How like ye now, my masters? Doth not this gear cotton!
The proverb old is verified: 'soon ripe and soon rotten'.
He will not be quiet till his brother be killed;
His delight is wholly to have his blood spilled.

689 **dint** stroke.

691 **Were . . . mine** Even if he were my father, rather than my brother.

694 **Doth . . . cotton!** Doesn't this business prosper!

Mary, sir, I told him a notable lie.
If it were to do again, I durst not do it, I!
Marry, when I had done, to it I durst not stand,
Thereby ye may perceive I use to play with each hand.
But, how now, cousin Cutpurse, with whom play you?
Take heed, for his hand is groping even now!
Cousin, take heed, if you do secretly grope;
If ye be taken, cousin, ye must look through a rope. *Exit.*

Enter Lord Smirdis, alone.

SMIRDIS
I am wand'ring alone, here and there to walk;
The court is so unquiet, in it I take no joy.
Solitary to myself now I may talk.
If I could rule, I wist what to say.

Enter Cruelty and Murder, with bloody hands.

CRUELTY
My co-equal partner Murder, come away;
From me long thou mayest not stay.

MURDER
Yes, from thee I may stay, but not thou from me;
Therefore I have a prerogative above thee.

CRUELTY
But in this case we must together abide.
Come, come, Lord Smirdis I have spied!
Lay hands on him with all festination,
That on him we may work our indignation.

SMIRDIS
How now, my friends? What have you to do with me?

MURDER
King Cambises hath sent us unto thee,
Commanding us straightly, without mercy or favour,
Upon thee to bestow our behaviour,
With cruelty to murder you, and make you away.

Strike him in diverse places.

SMIRDIS
Yet pardon me, I heartily you pray!
Consider, the king is a tyrant tyrannous,

699 **If...I!** (It was so audacious that) if I had to do it again, I wouldn't dare!
700 **I durst...stand** I didn't dare persist (i.e. he couldn't swear that the story was true when the king challenged him on it).
705 **look...rope** i.e. be hanged.
709 **I wist** I don't know.
713 **prerogative** power/advantage.
715 **festination** speed.
720 **straightly** immediately.

And all his doings be damnable and pernicious:
Favour me therefore; I did him never offend.

A little bladder of vinegar pricked.

CRUELTY
No favour at all. Your life is at an end!
Even now I strike, his body to wound.
Behold, now his blood springs out on the ground!

MURDER
Now he is dead, let us present him to the king.

CRUELTY
Lay to your hand, away him to bring. *Exeunt.*

Enter Ambidexter.

AMBIDEXTER
O the Passion of God, yonder is a heavy court!
Some weeps, some wails, and some make great sport.
Lord Smirdis by Cruelty and Murder is slain;
But, Jesus, for want of him how some do complain!
If I should have had a thousand pound I could not forbear weeping.
Now Jesus have his blessed soul in keeping.
Ah good Lord, to think on him, how it doth me grieve;
I cannot forbear weeping, ye may me believe. *Weep.*
O my heart, how my pulses do beat,
With sorrowful lamentations I am in such a heat!
Ah, my heart, how for him it doth sorrow!
Nay, I have done, in faith, now; and God give ye good morrow!
Ha, ha! Weep? Nay, laugh; with both hands to play!
The king through his cruelty hath made him away;
But hath not he wrought a most wicked deed,
Because king after him he should not proceed,
His own natural brother; and having no more,
To procure his death by violence sore?
In spite, because his brother should never be king,
His heart, being wicked, consented to this thing.
Now he hath no more brothers nor kindred alive;
If the king use this gear still, he cannot long thrive.

Enter Hob and Lob.

HOB
God's hat, neighbour, come away; it's time to market to go.

LOB
God's vast, neighbour, zay ye zo?

s.d. The stage direction neatly demonstrates how the bloodstain would be produced.
731 **Lay ... hand** Set your hands to work.
743 **God ... morrow!** Goodbye!
748 **no more** no other heir.
753 **use ... still** carries on like this.
754 **come away** hurry up!
755 **God's vast** God's fast. (Like the characters in *Gammer Gurton's Needle*, Hob and Lob speak with cod-rustic accents (nowadays often termed 'Mummerset') in which f's are sounded as v's and s's as z's.)

The clock hath stricken vive, ich think, by'r Laken!
Bum vay, vrom sleep cham not very well waken.
But, neighbour Hob, neighbour Hob, what have ye to zell?

HOB
Bum troth, neighbour Lob, to you Ich'll tell:
Chave two goslings and a chine of pork;
There is no vatter between this and York;
Chave a pot of strawberries, and a calf's head
A zennight zince tomorrow, it hath been dead.

LOB
Chave a score of eggs, and of butter a pound;
Yesterday a nest of goodly young rabbits I vound;
Chave vorty things mo, of more and of less;
My brain is not very good them to express.
But, God's hat, neighbour, wots't what?

HOB
No, not well, neighbour; wot's that?

LOB
Bum vay, neighbour, Master king is a zrewd lad;
Zo God help me, and holidam, I think the vool be mad!
Zome zay he deal cruelly, his brother he did kill,
And also a goodly young lad's heart-blood he did spill.

HOB
Vorbod of God, neighbour! Has he played zuch a voolish deed?

AMBIDEXTER
Goodman Hob and Goodman Lob, God be your speed!
As you two towards market do walk,
Of the king's cruelty I did hear you talk:
I ensure you he is a king most vile and pernicious,
His doings and life are odious and vicious.

LOB
It were a good deed zomebody would break his head.

HOB
Bum vay, neighbour Lob, I chould he were dead!

AMBIDEXTER
So would I, Lob and Hob, with all my heart.
(Now with both hands will you see me play my part?)
Ah, ye whoreson traitorly knaves,
Hob and Lob, out upon you, slaves!

756 **ich** rustic form of 'I'.
756 **by'r Laken!** by Our Lady (a mild oath).
757 **Bum vay** By my faith (another oath).
757 **cham** I am (a contraction of 'Ich am').
759 **Bum troth** By my troth ('on my honour')
760 **Chave** I have.
760 **a chine** a cheaper cut from the back of the pig.
763 **A zennight . . . tomorrow** a seven-night since tomorrow (a week ago tomorrow, i.e. six days ago).
764 **a score** twenty.
768 **wots't what?** do you know what?
770 **zrewd** shrewd (cursed/ill-tempered/contrary—like a shrew).
771 **holidam** Our Holy Mother.
774 **Vorbod** 'Forbad/forbidden by God', or possibly a contraction of the oath 'for the body of God'.

LOB

And thou call'st me knave, thou art another;
My name is Lob, and Hob my next neighbour.

AMBIDEXTER

Hob and Lob! Ah, ye country patches!
Ah, ye fool; ye have made wrong matches;
Ye have spoken treason against the king's grace.
For it I will accuse ye before his face;
Then for the same ye shall be martyred.
At the least ye shall be hanged, drawn, and quartered!

HOB

O gentleman, ye shall have two pear-pies and tell not of me!

LOB

By God, a vat goose chill give thee.
I think no hurt, by my vather's soul, I zwear!

HOB

Chave lived well all my lifetime, my neighbours among,
And now chould be loath to come to zuch wrong;
To be hanged and quartered; the grief would be great.

LOB

A foul evil on thee, Hob! Who bid thee on it treat?
Vor it was thou that first did him name.

HOB

Thou liest like a varlet and thou zaist the zame;
It was zuch a foolish Lob as thou!

LOB

Speak many words, and, by Cod's nails I vow,
Upon thy pate my staff I will lay!

AMBIDEXTER

By the Mass, I will cause them to make a fray.
Yea, Lob, thou sayest true: all came through him!

LOB

Bum vay, thou Hob, a little would make me thee trim!
Give thee a zwap on thy nose till thy heart ache!

HOB

If thou darest, do it; else, man, cry creek;
I trust, before thou hurt me,
With my staff chill make a Lob of thee!

Here let them fight with their staves, not come near another by three or four yards; the Vice set them on as hard as he can; one of their wives come out,

788 **patches** fools/clowns.
789 **ye . . . matches** you have picked the wrong opponent.
800 **Who . . . treat?** Who asked you to talk about it?
802 **Thou . . . zame** You lie like a servant/wretch if you say that.
805 **pate** head.
806 **fray** fight.
808 **a little . . . trim** say another word and I will beat you.
809 **zwap** blow.
810 **cry creek** say you give up (to cry 'creek' was to admit defeat in games).

and all to beat the Vice. He run away. Enter Marian May-be-Good, Hob's wife, running in with a broom, and part them.

MARIAN

O the body of me, husband Hob, what mean ye to fight?
For the Passion of God, no more blows smite.
Neighbours and friends so long, and now to fall out?
What, in your age to seem so stout?
If I had not parted ye, one had killed another.

LOB

I had not cared, I swear by God's Mother!

MARIAN

Shake hands again at the request of me;
As ye have been friends, so friends still be.

HOB

Bum troth, cham content and zaist word, neighbour Lob.

LOB

I am content; agreed, neighbour Hob!

Shake hands and laugh heartily one at another.

MARIAN

So, get you to market, no longer stay.
And with yonder knave let me make a fray.

HOB

Content, wife Marian; chill doo as thou dost say.
But buss me, ich pray thee, at going away!

Exeunt Hob, Lob.

MARIAN

Thou whoreson knave and prick-eared boy, why didst thou let them fight?
If one had killed another here, couldst thou their deaths requite?
It bears a sign by this thy deed a cowardly knave thou art,
Else wouldst thou draw that weapon thine, like a man, them to part.

AMBIDEXTER

What, Marian May-be-Good, are you come prattling?
Ye may hap get a box on the ear with you tattling!
If they had killed one another, I had not cared a pease.

Here let her swinge him in her broom; she gets him down, and he her down, thus one on the top of another make pastime.

MARIAN

Ah, villain, myself on thee I must ease!
Give me a box on the ear? That will I try.

816 **stout** courageous.
821 **cham . . . word** I'm content if you just say the word.
826 **buss** kiss.
828 **prick-eared** villainous (having had his ear cut as a result of being nailed to a pillory in punishment for a crime).
829 **requite** repay/reverse.
832 **tattling** the printed text has 'talking', but as Craik notes, the rhyme suggests 'tattling' was intended.
833 **a pease** a pea or pea-plant.
833.1 The stage direction offers the cue for comic sexual 'business' here.
834 **myself . . . ease** both the intended, 'I must take revenge', and the unintended 'take sexual pleasure'.

Who shall be master, thou shalt see by and by!

AMBIDEXTER

O, no more, no more, I beseech you heartily!
Even now I yield and give you the mastery.

Run his way out while she is down.

MARIAN

Ah, thou knave, dost thou throw me down and run thy way?
If he were here again, oh, how I would him pay!
I will after him and, if I can him meet,
With these my nails his face I will greet. [*Exit.*]

Enter Venus leading out her son, Cupid, blind: he must have a bow and two shafts, one headed with gold and th'other headed with lead.

VENUS

Come forth, my son; unto my words attentive ears resign;
What I pretend, see you frequent, to force this game of mine.
The king a kinswoman hath, adorned with beauty store;
And I wish that Diana's gifts they twain shall keep no more,
But use my silver sugared game their joys for to augment.
When I do speak, to wound his heart, Cupid my son, consent,
And shoot at him the shaft of love that bears the head of gold,
To wound his heart, in lovers' wise his grief for to unfold.
Though kin she be unto his grace, that nature me expel,
Against the course thereof he may in my game please me well.
Wherefore, my son, do not forget; forthwith pursue the deed!

CUPID

Mother, I mean for to obey as you have whole decreed;
But you must tell me, mother dear, when I shall arrow draw,
Else your request to be attained will not be worth a straw.
I am blind and cannot see, but still do shoot by guess;
The poets well, in places store, of my might do express.

VENUS

Cupid my son, when time shall serve that thou shalt do this deed,
Then warning I to thee will give; but see thou shoot with speed.

[Enter a] Lord, [a] Lady, [and a] Waiting-maid.

842.1 **shafts** arrows. (Cupid's arrows brought either happiness (the gold ones) or sorrow (lead) in love.)
843 **resign** turn.
844 **What . . . mine** Make sure that you do what I tell you, to further my plans.
845 **beauty store** abundant beauty.
846 **I wish . . . more** I wish that the two of them no longer be chaste.
847 **silver sugared game** the sweet, noble game (of sexual love).
850 **in lovers' . . . unfold** to make him speak of his desire as lovers' do.
851 **That . . . expel** And so nature abhors amorous love (between them).
856 **Else . . . straw** otherwise your request will be worthless.
858 **poets . . . express** poets speak in many places of my capacities (i.e. both his potency and his blindness).

LORD

Lady dear, to king akin, forthwith let us proceed
To trace abroad the beauty fields, as erst we had decreed;
The blowing buds whose savoury scents our sense will much delight,
The sweet smell of musk white rose to please the appetite,
The chirping birds whose pleasant tunes therein shall here record,
That our great joy we shall it find in field to walk abroad,
On lute and cittern there to play a heavenly harmony;
Our ear shall hear, heart to content, our sports to beaut[if]y.

LADY

Unto your words, most comely lord, myself submit do I;
To trace with you in field so green I mean not to deny.

Here trace up and down, playing.

MAID

And I, your waiting-maid, at hand with diligence will be,
For to fulfil with heart and hand when you shall command me.

Enter King, Lord, and Knight.

KING

Come on, my lord and knight; abroad our mirth let us employ.
Since he is dead, this heart of mine in corpse I feel it joy.
Should brother mine have reigned king when I had yielded breath?
A thousand brothers I rather had, to put them all to death!
But, O behold, where I do see a lord and lady fair;
For beauty she most worthy is to sit in prince's chair.

VENUS

Shoot forth, my son! Now is the time that thou must wound his heart.

CUPID

Content you, mother; I will do my part.

Shoots there; and go out Venus and Cupid.

KING

Of truth, my lord, in eye of mine all ladies she doth excel.
Can none report what dame she is, and to my grace it tell?

LORD

Redoubted prince, pleaseth your grace, to you she is akin,
Cousin-german, nigh of birth, by mother's side come in.

KNIGHT

And that her waiting-maiden is, attending her upon.
He is a lord of prince's court, and will be there anon.
They sport themselves in pleasant field, to former used use.

862 **To . . . decreed** To walk through the beautiful fields, as we agreed earlier that we would.
863 **blowing** blossoming.
867 **cittern** a guitar-like stringed instrument.
870.1 **trace** walk.
884 **Cousin-german** first cousin (the child of an uncle and aunt).
887 **to . . . use** as the custom is.

KING

My lord and knight, of truth I speak, my heart it cannot choose
But with my lady I must speak, and so express my mind.
My lord and ladies walking there, if you will favour find,
Present yourselves unto my grace, and by my side come stand.

FIRST LORD

We will fulfil, most mighty king, as your grace doth command.

KING

Lady dear, intelligence my grace hath got of late,
You issued out of mother's stock and kin unto my state.
According to rule of birth you are cousin-german mine;
Yet do I wish that further of this kindred I could find;
For Cupid he, that eyeless boy, my heart hath so enflamed,
With beauty you me to content the like cannot be named;
For, since I entered in this place and on you fixed mine eyes,
Most burning fits about my heart in ample wise did rise.
The heat of them such force doth yield, my corpse they scorch, alas,
And burns the same with wasting heat, as Titan doth the grass.
And sith this heat is kindled so, and fresh in heart of me,
There is no way but of the same the quencher you must be.
My meaning is that beauty yours my heart with love doth wound;
To give me love, mind to content; my heart hath you out found;
And you are she must be my wife, else shall I end my days.
Consent to this and be my queen, to wear the crown with praise.

LADY

If it please your grace, O mighty king, you shall not this request.
It is a thing that Nature's course doth utterly detest,
And high it would the god[s] displease, of all that is the worst.
To grant your grace to marry so, it is not I that durst.
Yet humble thanks I render now unto you, mighty king,
That you vouchsafe to great estate so gladly would me bring.
Were it not it were offence, I would it not deny,
But such great honour to achieve my heart I would apply.
Therefore, O king, with humble heart in this I pardon crave;
My answer is, in this request your mind ye may not have.

KING

May I not? Nay, then, I will; by all the gods I vow!
And I will marry thee as wife. This is mine answer now.
Who dare say nay what I pretend? Who dare the same withstand
Shall lose his head, and have report traitor through my land.
There is no nay. I will you have, and you my queen shall be!

893 **intelligence . . . late** I have recently learned that.

897–898 **Cupid . . . named** Cupid has so inflamed my heart with desire for your beauty that I cannot think of anything comparable.

902 **wasting** withering.

902 **Titan** the sun.

909 **not** not (make).

911 **high** greatly.

912 **it . . . durst** I would not dare to do that.

916 **But . . . apply** I would eagerly pursue that goal (if it wasn't such an offence).

921 **Who . . . pretend?** Who dares to refuse what I order?

922 **have . . . traitor** be declared a traitor.

LADY

Then, mighty king, I crave your grace to hear the words of me:
Your counsel take of lordings' wit, the laws aright peruse;
If I with safe may grant this deed, I will it not refuse.

KING

No, no! What I have said to you, I mean to have it so.
For counsel theirs, I mean not, I, in this respect to go;
But to my palace let us go the marriage to prepare;
For, to avoid my will in this, I can it not forbear.

LADY

O God, forgive me, if I do amiss;
The king by compulsion enforceth me this.

MAID

Unto the gods for your estate I will not cease to pray,
That you may be a happy queen, and see most joyful day.

KING

Come on, my lords; with gladsome hearts let us rejoice with glee;
Your music show to joy this deed at the request of me!

BOTH

For to obey your Grace's words our honours do agree. *Exeunt.*

Enter Ambidexter.

AMBIDEXTER

O the Passion of me! Marry, as ye say, yonder is a royal court!
There is triumphing and sport upon sport,
Such loyal lords, with such lordly exercise,
Frequenting such pastime as they can devise,
Running at tilt, jousting, with running at the ring,
Masking and mumming, with each kind of thing;
Such dancing, such singing, with musical harmony;
Believe me, I was loath to absent their company.
But will you believe? Jesu, what haste they made till they were married!
Not for a million of pounds one day longer they would have tarried!
O, there was a banquet, royal and super-excellent;
Thousands and thousands at that banquet was spent.
I muse of nothing but how they can be married so soon;
I care not if I be married before tomorrow at noon,
If marriage be a thing that so may be had.
How say you, maid; to marry me will ye be glad?
Out of doubt, I believe it is some excellent treasure;
Else to the same belongs abundant pleasure.

925 **Your...peruse** Seek the advice of your lords, and consult the laws correctly.
926 **with safe** with (legal) safety.
928 **For...go** I do not intend to ask their advice.
933 **estate** situation/well-being.
938 **Marry** Indeed.
939 **triumphing** ceremonial celebrations.
942 **Running...ring** chivalric sports.
943 **Masking and mumming** indoor pastimes involving disguises, dancing, and dicing.
948 **super-excellent** superlative/better than excellent.
953 **How...maid?** addressed to a member of the audience.
955 **Else...belongs** Or else marriage involves.

Yet with mine ears I have heard some say,
'That ever I was married, now cursed be the day!'
Those be they that with cursed wives be matched.
That husband for hawks' meat of them is up-snatched,
Head broke with a bed-staff, face all to-be-scratched,
'Knave!' 'Slave!' and 'Villain!' a coiled coat now and then
When the wife hath given it, she will say, 'Alas, good man!'
Such were better unmarried, my masters, I trow,
Than all their life after to be matched with a shrew.

Enter Preparation.

PREPARATION
With speed I am sent all things to prepare,
My message to do as the king did declare.
His grace doth mean a banquet to make,
Meaning in this place repast for to take.
Well, the cloth shall be laid, and all things in readiness,
To court to return when done is my business.

AMBIDEXTER
A proper man and also a fit
For the king's estate to prepare a banquet!

PREPARATION
What, Ambidexter? Thou art not unknown.
A mischief on all good faces, so that I curse not mine own!
Now, in the knave's name, shake hands with me,

AMBIDEXTER
Well said, goodman pouch-mouth; your reverence I see;
I will teach ye, if your manners no better be.
Ah, ye slave; the king doth me a gentleman allow;
Therefore I look that to me ye should bow.

Fight.

PREPARATION
Good Master Ambidexter, pardon my behaviour;
For this your deeds you are a knave, for your labour!

AMBIDEXTER
Why, ye stale counterly villain, nothing but 'knave'?

Fight.

PREPARATION
I am sorry your mastership offended I have;
Shake hands, that between us agreement may be.

958 **cursed** shrewish.
959 **That...up-snatched** such husbands are quickly gobbled up (by their wives) as hawks do their food.
960 **to-be-scratched** an emphatic form of 'scratched'.
961 **coiled** beaten.
974 **A mischief...faces** A curse on every handsome face (a jocular oath).
976 **goodman pouch-mouth** mister big-mouth.
978 **doth...allow** has created me a gentleman.
979 **look** expect.
982 **counterly** villainous (worthy of The Counter, a London prison).

I was over-shot with myself, I do see.
Let me have your help this furniture to provide.
The king from this place will not long abide.

Set the fruit on the board.

AMBIDEXTER
Content, it is the thing that I would wish.
I myself will go fetch one dish.

Let the Vice fetch a dish of nuts, and let them fall in the bringing of them in.

PREPARATION
Cleanly, Master Ambidexter; for fair on the ground they lie.

AMBIDEXTER
I will have them up again by and by.

PREPARATION
To see all in readiness I will put you in trust;
There is no nay, to the court needs I must.

Exit Preparation.

AMBIDEXTER
Have ye no doubt but all shall be well.
Marry, sir, as you say, this gear doth excel!
All thing is in a readiness, when they come hither,
The king's grace and the queen both together.
I beseech ye, my masters, tell me, is it not best
That I be so bold as to bid a guest?
He is as honest a man as ever spurred cow,
My cousin Cutpurse, I mean; I beseech ye, judge you.
Believe me, cousin, if to be the king's guest ye could be taken,
I trust that offer will never be forsaken.
But, cousin, because to that office ye are not like to come,
Frequent your exercises: a horn on your thumb,
A quick eye, a sharp knife, at hand a receiver.
But then take heed, cousin, ye be a cleanly conveyor.
Content yourself, cousin; for this banquet you are unfit,
When such as I at the same am unworthy to sit.

Enter [*King, Queen, and their train.*]

985 **I . . . myself** I went too far (in my behaviour).

986 **provide** prepare.

990 **Cleanly** (Do it) properly.

993 **There . . . must** There's no alternative, I have to go to the court.

995 **this . . . excel!** this business is going very well!

999 **bid a guest** invite someone in (Ambidexter considers inviting his (imaginary?) cousin Cutpurse to the banquet).

1003 **forsaken** ignored.

1004 **office** role (i.e. guest at the King's feast).

1005 **Frequent . . . thumb** Keep to your chosen profession (as thief): (keep your) horn-thimble (used with a pocket-knife to cut the strings on purses) on your thumb.

1006 **at . . . receiver** have your receiver (accomplice) nearby (to make off with the purse).

1007 **a cleanly conveyor** one who steals efficiently.

KING
My queen and lords, to take repast let us attempt the same.
Here is the place; delay no time, but to our purpose frame.

QUEEN
With willing hearts your whole behest we mind for to obey.

ALL
And we, the rest of prince's train, will do as you do say.

Sit at the banquet.

KING
Me think mine ears doth wish the sound of music's harmony;
Here, for to play before my grace, in place I would them spy.

Play at the banquet.

AMBIDEXTER
They be at hand, sir, with stick and fiddle;
They can play a new dance, called 'Hey-diddle-diddle'.

KING
My queen, perpend: what I pronounce, I will not violate;
But one thing which my heart makes glad I mind to explicate:
You know in court up-trained is a lion very young;
Of one litter two whelps beside, as yet not very strong.
I did request one whelp to see, and this young lion fight;
But lion did the whelp convince by strength of force and might.
His brother whelp, perceiving that the lion was too good,
And he by force was like to see the other whelp his blood,
With force to lion he did run, his brother for to help.
A wonder great it was to see that friendship in a whelp!
So then the whelps between them both the lion did convince;
Which thing to see before mine eyes did glad the heart of prince.

At this tale told, let the Queen weep.

QUEEN
These words to hear makes stilling tears issue from crystal eyes.

KING
What, dost thou mean, my spouse; to weep for loss of any price?

QUEEN
No, no, O king; but, as you see friendship in brother's whelp:
When one was like to have reprise, the other yielded help.
And was this favour showed in dogs to shame of royal king?
Alack, I wish these ears of mine had not once heard this thing.
Even so should you, O mighty king, to brother been a stay,
And not, without offence to you, in such wise him to slay.

1011 **to . . . frame** organize yourselves as I have directed.
1018 **perpend** reflect (on what I say).
1021 **whelps** dogs.
1023 **convince** defeat.
1025 **he** the lion.
1025 **by force . . . blood** shed the other whelp's blood.
1033 **to have reprise** to suffer damage/punishment.
1036 **should . . . stay** you should have been a support to your brother.

In all assays it was your part his cause to have defended,
And, whosoever had him misused, to have them reprehended.
But faithful love was more in dog than it was in your grace.

KING

O cursed caitiff, vicious and vile! I hate thee in this place!
This banquet it is [at] an end; take all these things away.
Before my face thou shalt repent the words that thou dost say.
O wretch most vile, didst thou the cause of brother mine so tender
The loss of him should grieve thy heart; he being none offender?
It did me good his death to have, so will it to have thine.
What friendship he had at my hands, the same even thou shalt find.
I give consent, and make avow, that thou shalt die the death.
By Cruel's sword and Murder fell, even thou shalt lose thy breath.
Ambidexter, see with speed to Cruelty ye go;
Cause him hither to approach, Murder with him also.

AMBIDEXTER

I am ready for to fulfil,
If that it be your grace's will.

KING

Then nought oblight my message given; absent thyself away.

AMBIDEXTER

Then in this place I will no longer stay.
If that I durst, I would mourn your case;
But, alas! I dare not, for fear of his grace.

Exit Ambidexter.

KING

Thou cursed jill, by all the gods I take an oath and swear,
That flesh of thine these hands of mine in pieces small could tear!
But thou shalt die by dint of sword: there is no friend ne fee
Shall find remorse at prince's hand to save the life of thee.

QUEEN

O mighty king and husband mine, vouchsafe to hear me speak,
And licence give to spouse of thine her patient mind to break.
For tender love unto your grace my words I did so frame;
For pure love doth heart of king me violate and blame.
And to your grace is this offence that I should purchase death?
Then cursed time that I was queen, to shorten this my breath!
Your grace doth know by marriage true I am your wife and spouse,
And one to save another's health at troth-plight made our vows;
Therefore, O king, let loving queen at thy hand find remorse,
Let pity be a mean to quench that cruel raging force,

1038 **assays** matters/quarrels.
1044 **didst . . . tender** did you care for my brother's cause so much?
1049 **Cruel's** Cruelty's.
1054 **nought oblight** do not forget.
1056 **your** (spoken to the Queen).
1058 **jill** wench.
1060 **friend ne fee** (plea from a) friend or bribe.
1066 **is . . . death?** is this offence so great that I should die for it?
1069 **one . . . troth-plight** we swore to care for each other's well-being at our betrothal.

And pardon, plight from prince's mouth, yield grace unto your queen,
That amity with faithful zeal may ever be us between.

KING

Ah, caitiff vile; to pity thee my heart it is not bent;
Ne yet to pardon your offence it is not mine intent.

FIRST LORD

Our mighty prince, with humble suit of your grace this I crave,
That this request it may take place, your favour for to have.
Let mercy yet abundantly the life of queen preserve,
Sith she in most obedient wise your grace's will doth serve.
As yet your grace but while with her hath had cohabitation,
And sure this is no desert why to yield her indignation.
Therefore, O king, her life prolong, to joy her days in bliss!

SECOND LORD

Your grace shall win immortal fame in granting unto this.
She is a queen whose goodly hue excels the royal rose,
For beauty bright Dame Nature she a large gift did dispose.
For comeliness who may compare? Of all she bears the bell.
This should give cause to move your grace to love her very well.
Her silver breast in those your arms to sing the songs of love,
Fine qualities most excellent to be in her you prove;
A precious pearl of price to prince, a jewel passing all!
Therefore, O king, to beg remorse on both my knees I fall;
To grant her grace to have her life, with heart I do desire.

KING

You villains twain; with raging force ye set my heart on fire!
If I consent that she shall die, how dare ye crave her life?
You two to ask this at my hand doth much enlarge my strife.
Were it not for shame, you two should die that for her life do sue.
But favour mine from you is gone, my lords, I tell you true.
I sent for Cruelty of late; if he would come away,
I would commit her to his hands, his cruel part to play.
Even now I see where he doth come; it doth my heart delight.

Enter Cruelty and Murder.

CRUELTY

Come, Murder, come, let us go forth with might;
Once again the king's commandment we must fulfil.

MURDER

I am contented to do it with a good will.

KING

Murder and Cruelty, for both of you I sent,
With all festination your offices to frequent.

1072 **plight** promised.
1074 **bent** inclined.
1080 **while** only for a short time.
1086 **she...bell** she wins the prize (i.e. is most beautiful of all).
1090 **of price** of supreme value.
1090 **passing** surpassing.
1095 **enlarge** increase.
1105 **With...frequent** To perform your roles with all speed.

Lay hold on the queen, take her to your power,
And make her away within this hour.
Spare for no fear; I do you full permit.
So I from this place do mean for to flit.

BOTH
With courageous hearts, O king, we will obey.

KING
Then come, my lords, let us depart away.

BOTH THE LORDS
With heavy hearts we will do all your grace doth say.

Exeunt King and Lords.

CRUELTY
Come, lady and queen; now art you in our handling;
In faith, with you we will use no dandling.

MURDER
With all expedition I, Murder, will take place;
Though thou be a queen, ye be under my grace.

QUEEN
With patience I will you both obey.

CRUELTY
No more words, but go with us away.

QUEEN
Yet, before I die, some psalm to God let me sing.

BOTH
We be content to permit you that thing.

QUEEN
Farwell, you ladies of the court, with all your masking hue,
I do forsake these broidered guards and all the fashions new,
The court and all the courtly train wherein I had delight.
I banished am from happy sport, and all by spiteful spite;
Yet with a joyful heart to God a psalm I mean to sing,
Forgiving all [men] and the king of each kind of thing.

Sing and exeunt.

Enter Ambidexter, weeping.

AMBIDEXTER
Ah, ah, ah, ah; I cannot choose but weep for the queen!
Nothing but mourning now at the court there is seen.
O, O, my heart, my heart! O, my bum will break!
Very grief so torments me that scarce I can speak.
Who could but weep for the loss of such a lady?

1109 **flit** depart.
1114 **dandling** soft treatment or pampering.
1121 **masking hue** either 'your disguising cosmetics' or 'the bright colours you wear for masques (courtly entertainments)'.
1122 **broidered guards** embroidered borders (of gowns).
1130 **Very** True.

That cannot I do, I swear by mine honesty;
But, Lord, so the ladies mourn, crying 'Alack!'
Nothing is worn now but only black.
I believe all [the] cloth in Watling Street to make gowns would not serve,
If I make a lie, the devil let ye starve!
All ladies mourn, both young and old,
There is not one that weareth a point's worth of gold.
There is a sort for fear for the king do pray
That would have him dead, by the Mass, I dare say.
What a king was he that hath used such tyranny!
He was akin to Bishop Bonner, I think verily,
For both their delights was to shed blood,
But never intended to do any good.
Cambises put a judge to death, that was a good deed,
But to kill the young child was worse; to proceed
To murder his brother, and then his own wife;
So help me God and holidam, it is pity of his life!
Hear ye, I will lay twenty thousand pound
That the king himself doth die by some wound;
He hath shed so much blood that his will be shed.
If it come to pass, in faith, then he is sped.

Enter the King, without a gown, a sword thrust up into his side, bleeding.

KING

Out, alas! What shall I do? My life is finished!
Wounded I am by sudden chance; my blood is minished.
Gog's heart, what means might I make my life to preserve?
Is there nought to be my help, nor is there nought to serve?
Out upon the court and lords that there remain;
To help my grief in this my case will none of them take pain?
Who but I, in such a wise, his death wound could have got?
As I on horseback up did leap, my sword from scabbard shot,
And ran me thus into the side, as you right well may see.
A marvel's chance unfortunate, that in this wise should be.
I feel myself a-dying now; of life bereft am I;
And Death hath caught me with his dart, for want of blood I spy.

1135 **Watling Street** the old Roman road from London (and ultimately St Albans) to Canterbury.
1138 **point's worth** the weight of a ribbon for tying up hose.
1139–1140 **There . . . dead** There are some people who pray for the king's health through fear, who would secretly prefer him dead.
1142 **Bishop Bonner** Edmund Bonner (*c.*1500–69), bishop of London during the reign of the Catholic Mary Tudor, was responsible for the trial and execution of Protestant martyrs in London. Following the accession of Elizabeth I, he was tried for refusing to take the oath of supremacy, and spent the rest of his life in prison.
1149 **lay** wager.
1152 **sped** justly rewarded/sent on his way.
1153 **Out** Curse it.
1154 **minished** diminished/lost.
1162 **marvel's** marvellous/extraordinary.

Thus, gasping, here on ground I lie. For nothing I do care.
A just reward for my misdeeds my death doth plain declare.

Here let him quake and stir.

AMBIDEXTER
How now, noble king? Pluck up your heart.
What, will you die, and from us depart?
Speak to me and ye be alive.
He cannot speak. But behold, how with Death he doth strive.
Alas, good king! Alas, he is gone.
The devil take me if for him I make any moan.
I did prognosticate of his end, by the Mass!
Like as I did say, so is it come to pass.
I will be gone; if I should be found here,
That I should kill him it would appear.
For fear with his death they do me charge,
Farewell, my masters, I will go take barge;
I mean to be packing; now is the tide.
Farewell, my masters, I will no longer abide!

Exit Ambidexter.

Enter three Lords.

FIRST LORD
Behold, my lord, it is even so as he to us did tell.
His grace is dead, upon the ground, by dint of sword most fell.
SECOND LORD
As he in saddle would have leapt, his sword from sheath did go,
Goring him up into the side; his life was ended so.
THIRD LORD
His blood so fast did issue out that nought could him prolong;
Yet, before he yielded up the ghost, his heart was very strong.
FIRST LORD
A just reward for his misdeeds the God above hath wrought,
For certainly the life he led was to be counted nought.
SECOND LORD
Yet a princely burial he shall have, according to his estate;
And more of him here at this time we have not to dilate.
THIRD LORD
My lords, let us take him up, and carry him away.
BOTH
Content we are with one accord to do as you do say.

Exeunt all.

1166.1 **quake and stir** spasm and tremble.
1169 **and** if.
1172 **moan** lamentation.
1173 **prognosticate of** prophesy.
1176 **That . . . him** That I killed.
1182 **fell** cruel.
1188 **counted nought** judged as worthless/evil.
1190 **dilate** speak/expound.

EPILOGUS

Right gentle audience, here have you perused
The tragical history of this wicked king:
According to our duty we have not refused,
But to our best intent expressed everything.
We trust none is offended for this our doing.
Our author craves likewise, if he have squared amiss,
By gentle admonition to know where the fault is.
His good will shall not be neglected to amend the same.
Praying all to bear therefore with this simple deed
Until the time serve a better he may frame;
Thus yielding you thanks, to end we decreed
That you so gently have suffered us to proceed,
In such patient wise as to hear and see;
We can but thank ye therefore, we can do no more, we.
As duty binds us, for our noble queen let us pray,
And for her honourable Council, the truth that they may use,
To practise justice, and defend her grace each day,
To maintain God's word they may not refuse,
To correct all those that would her grace and grace's laws abuse;
Beseeching God over us she may reign long,
To be guided by truth and defended from wrong.

Amen quod Thomas Preston.
Imprinted at London by John Allde.

6 **squared amiss** fashioned anything wrongly/misjudged.

8 **His . . . same.** He (the author) will happily strive to improve the play.

10 **Until . . . frame** Until time allows him to produce a better one.

22.1 **quod** says.

Damon and Pythias

(1564–1565)

RICHARD EDWARDS

(?1525–1566)

THE PLAYWRIGHT

Richard Edwards was born in about 1525 in Somerset. He entered Corpus Christi College, Oxford in 1539/40, graduating BA in 1544. In the following August he was elected a probationer fellow of the college, and held a full fellowship there from late 1544 to 1547–8. He had moved to Christ Church, Oxford by 1550, where he held a studentship and lectured in logic, before taking up a position at the royal court as a yeoman of the chamber and gentleman of the Chapel Royal by 1554. He was appointed Master of the Children of the Chapel in 1561, a post he held until his death on 31 October 1566.

Edwards is best known for two plays on the theme of male friendship. The first of these, *Damon and Pythias*, based on a Greek legend retold by Cicero, was performed both at court and at Lincoln's Inn, one of the London Inns of Court where lawyers were trained, over the Christmas season of 1564–5, and was acted, as the title page of the printed edition suggests, by the Chapel children. It was evidently popular, as it was revived after Edwards' death, for a performance at Merton College, Oxford in 1568, before being printed by Richard Johns in 1571. Edwards' second play, *Palamon and Arcite*, was a dramatized version of Chaucer's *Knight's Tale*, which would also form the basis of Shakespeare's *Two Noble Kinsmen* half a century later. Although no text survives, it was known to have been performed in two parts over successive evenings in Christ Church Hall when Elizabeth I visited Oxford in 1566. The Queen was evidently amused by the play, as she is recorded as having given Edwards 'great thanks' for the production and to have 'laughed full heartily' afterwards with the actors, who included the future archbishop of York, Toby Matthew (*ODNB*).

Edwards also wrote a number of poems, which were printed along with verses by other writers, some of which Edwards had set to music, in a collection entitled *The Paradise of Dainty Devices*, published in 1576.

THE PLAY

The play is set in the court of the classical tyrant Dionysius of Syracuse (Dionysius I (*c.*432–367BC), ruler of part of what is now Sicily), a ruler whose court frequently appeared in the literature of the period, as it brought together political absolutism, in the form of the despotic king, with a range of political and intellectual positions, represented by the philosophers Plato, Aristippus, and Dion, all of whom visited his court, or those of his son, Dionysius II, at one point or another during their reigns. The action concerns the enduring, self-sacrificing love of the two friends, Damon and Pythias, which is variously contrasted with the time-serving self-love of the sycophantic courtly parasite, Carisophus, the more measured, sophisticated self-interest exhibited by the philosopher Aristippus, the capricious whims of the tyrant Dionysius himself, and the pragmatism of the various servants (Stephano, Will, and Jack) and labourers (Snap the porter, Grim the collier, and Gronno the executioner) who make up the play's small cast. The story of the two friends willing to die for each other was a byword for amicability in the Renaissance, and was frequently cited in works seeking to laud the value of platonic male affection. Edwards might have found his inspiration to dramatize the tale in the account of the young men's story in Sir Thomas Elyot's popular educational handbook for princes and aristocrats, *The Book Named the Governor* (1531) (see Walker, *Writing under Tyranny*).

The play is a powerful endorsement of the classical ideal of male friendship as the highest form of human love. Given that it was performed by the Chapel children, it is likely that any potential for homoeroticism would have been implicit rather than explicit in its first performances. It also deploys a number of themes and tropes from classical comedy, including the sly parasite, and the witty servant or slave, who acts as a foil to the idealism or naivety of his employers, a role here performed not only by Damon and Pythias' servant, Stephano, but also by the court lackeys Will and Jack. Additional comic potential might have been gained if, as Ros King suggests, Edwards himself played Grim the Collier, the physically imposing representative of the non-courtly class, who is humiliatingly 'shaved' by Will and Jack.

As King has argued, it is likely that the play was performed at court before a series of 'houses': painted canvas representations of the city walls of Syracuse and Dionysus' palace, stretched over wooden frames, while the Muses may have been revealed singing on their rock by the lifting and lowering of a curtain.

I have used the 1571 edition, printed by Richard Johnes as the basis for the following text, also consulting Ros King's edition in *The Works of Richard Edwards*, listed under further reading.

FURTHER READING

Elliott, jr, John R., 'Richard Edwards', The *Oxford Dictionary of National Biography*, <http://www.oxforddnb.com/view/article/8552> (accessed 6 June 2013).

King, Ros, ed., *The Works of Richard Edwards* (Manchester: Manchester University Press, 2001).

Richards, Jennifer, 'Male Friendship and Counsel in Richard Edwards' *Damon and Pythias*', in Thomas Betteridge and Greg Walker, eds., *The Oxford Handbook of Tudor Drama* (Oxford: Oxford University Press, 2012), 293–308.

Walker, Greg, *Writing Under Tyranny: English Literature and the Henrician Reformation* (Oxford: Oxford University Press, 2005).

The excellent comedy of two the most faithfullest
Friends, Damon and Pythias.
Newly imprinted as the same was shown before
the Queen's Majesty by the children of Her Grace's
Chapel, except the Prologue which is somewhat altered
for the proper use of them that hereafter
shall have occasion to play it, either in
private or open audience. Made
by Master Edwards, then being
Master of the Children.
1571.

Imprinted at
London in Fleet Lane by Richard Johns,
and are to be sold at his shop, joining to the southwest
door of Paul's Church.

THE PROLOGUE

On every side whereas I glance my roving eye,
Silence in all ears bent I plainly do espy.
But if your eager looks do long such toys to see
As heretofore in comical wise were wont abroad to be,
Your lust is lost, and all the pleasures that you sought
Is frustrate quite of toying plays. A sudden change is wrought,
For lo, our author's muse, that masked in delight,
Hath forced his pen against his kind no more such sports to write.
Muse he that lust (right worshipful), for chance hath made this change,
For that to some he seemed too much in young desires to range;
In which, right glad to please, seeing that he did offend,
Of all he humbly pardon craves; his pen that shall amend.
And yet (worshipful audience) thus much I dare avouch,
In comedies, the greatest skill is this, rightly to touch

1 **whereas** where.
2 **bent** straining/inclined (eager for the play to start).
3–5 **if... lost** if you long to see such trivial entertainment as has previously been played publicly in comedies, your desire is thwarted.
6 **Is... plays** you'll be utterly denied, if it's trivial games you want.
7 **masked in delight** hid himself in pleasure.
8 **his kind** his (or his pen's) nature.
9 **Muse... worshipful** ponder this if you wish, sirs.
13 **avouch** swear.
14–15 **rightly... quick** accurately to describe satirically/expose with painful rigour.

All things to the quick; and eke to frame each person so
That by his common talk you may his nature rightly know.
A roister ought not preach (that were too strange to hear!),
But as from virtue he doth swerve, so ought his words appear.
The old man is sober, the young man rash, the lover triumphing in joys,
The matron grave, the harlot wild and full of wanton toys;
Which all in one course they no wise do agree,
So correspondent to their kind their speeches ought to be.
Which speeches well pronounced, with action lively framed,
If this offend the lookers on, let Horace then be blamed,
Which hath our author taught at school, from whom he doth not swerve
In all such kind of exercise decorum to observe.
Thus much for his defence he sayeth, as poets erst have done,
Which heretofore in comedies the self-same race did run.
But now for to be brief, the matter to express
Which here we shall present is this: *Damon and Pythias*;
A rare example of friendship true, it is no legend-lie,
But a thing once done indeed, as histories do descry,
Which done of yore in long time past, yet present shall be here,
Even as it were in doing now, so lively it shall appear.
Lo, here in Syracuse, th'ancient town which once the Romans won,
Here Dionysius' palace, within whose court this thing most strange was done.
Which matter, mixed with mirth and care, a just name to apply,
As seems most fit we have it termed 'a tragical comedy',
Wherein talking of courtly toys, we do protest this flat,
We talk of Dionysius' court, we mean no court but that:
And that we do so mean, who wisely calleth to mind
The time, the place, the authors, here most plainly shall it find.
Lo, this I speak for our defence, lest of others we should be shent.
But, worthy audience, we you pray, take things as they be meant;
Whose upright judgment we do crave, with heedful ear and eye,
To hear the cause and see th'effect of this new tragical comedy. *Exit.*

15 **eke to frame** also to describe/represent.
16 **common** familiar.
17 **a roister** a roisterer or pleasure-seeking rogue.
18 **as... appear** his speech should reflect the way(s) that he deviates from virtue.
20 **wanton toys** flirtatious tricks.
23 **lively framed** carefully crafted (to be true to life).
24 The Roman Quintus Horatius Flaccus (65–8BC), whose *Ars Poetica* (*The Art of Poetry*) argued that the words spoken ought to be fitting to the character speaking them (the principal of decorum).
27 **erst** hitherto.
28 **self-same... run** have followed the same path (in having to apologize for using fitting language for vicious characters).
31 **legend-lie** false fable.
32 **descry** reveal.
33 **of yore** of old.
34 **as... now** appearing as if it was happening now.
37 **Which... apply** Which story, mingling laughter and sorrow, to give it a fitting name.
38 This is perhaps, as King suggests, the first use of the term 'tragicomedy' in English drama.
39 **flat** plainly/at the outset.
43 **of** by.
43 **shent** blamed/punished. The prologue is denying that any satire of the contemporary English court is intended (and thereby, of course, subtly implying that it might be).

The Speakers' Names:

ARISTIPPUS, a pleasant gentleman.
CARISOPHUS, a parasite.
DAMON and PYTHIAS, two gentlemen of Greece.
STEPHANO, servant to Damon and Pythias.
WILL, Aristippus' lackey.
JACK, Carisophus' lackey.
SNAP, the porter.
DIONYSIUS, the King.
EUBULUS, the King's councillor.
GRONNO, the hangman.
GRIM, the collier (a provider of coal and charcoal for the court).
[THE MUSES.]

Here entereth Aristippus.

ARISTIPPUS
Too strange, perhaps, it seems to some,
That I, Aristippus, a courtier am become;
A philosopher of late, not of the meanest name,
But now to the courtly behaviour my life I frame.
Muse he that list, to you of good skill
I say that I am a philosopher still.
Lovers of wisdom is termed 'philosophie',
Then who is a philosopher so rightly as I?
For in loving of wisdom, proof doth this try,
That *frustra sapit, qui non sapit sibi.*
I am wise for myself; then tell me of troth,
Is not that great wisdom, as the world goeth?
Some philosophers in the street go ragged and torn
And feed on vile roots, whom boys laugh to scorn;
But I in fine silks haunt Dionysius' palace,
Wherein with dainty fare myself I do solace.
I can talk of philosophy as well as the best,
But the strait kind of life I leave to the rest.
And I profess now the courtly philosophy:
To crouch, to speak fair, myself I apply,
To feed the King's humour with pleasant devices,

Aristippus of Cyrene (*c*.435–*c*.356BC), was the founder of the Cyrenaic school of philosophy, which aimed at deriving pleasure from every possible situation, conforming circumstances to his own needs, and keeping an even temperament despite changes of fortune.

parasite one who lives off the hospitality and generosity of others.

lackey menial servant.

Snap actually seems to perform the role of a constable.

Eubulus means 'good counsellor'.

The nine goddesses who inspire the arts and sciences: Calliope for epic poetry, Clio for history, Euterpe for lyric poetry, Thalia for comedy and pastoral verse, Melpomene for tragedy, Terpsichore for dance, Erato for amorous verse, Polyhymnia for sacred verse, and Urania for astronomy.

3 **meanest name** lowest reputation.

4 **frame** adapt.

5 **Muse...list** Wonder at this if you wish.

7 ***philosophie*** in Greek, '*philo-sophi*' are literally 'wisdom-lovers'.

9 **proof...try** experience tests (and proves).

10 ***frustra...sibi*** he knows nothing who does not know himself.

11 **of troth** truly.

12 **as...goeth** as things stand in the world today.

14 **roots** vegetables. (Diogenes the Cynic famously lived on a mean diet of root vegetables.)

15 **whom** i.e. such men.

18 **strait** strict/poor.

20 **crouch** bow low.

20 **myself I apply** dedicate myself.

For which I am called *regius canis*.
But wot ye who named me first the king's dog?
It was the rogue Diogenes, that vile grunting hog!
Let him roll in his tub to win a vain praise,
In the court pleasantly I will spend all my days,
Wherein what to do I am not to learn;
What will serve mine own turn I can quickly discern.
All my time at school I have not spent vainly,
I can help one; is not that a good point of philosophy?

Here entereth Carisophus.

CARISOPHUS
I beshrew your fine ears! Since you came from school,
In the court you have made many a wise man a fool;
And though you paint out your feigned philosophy,
So God help me, it is but a plain kind of flattery,
Which you use so finely in so pleasant a sort,
That none but Aristippus now makes the king sport.
Ere you came hither, poor I was somebody;
The king delighted in me, now I am but a noddy.

ARISTIPPUS
In faith, Carisophus, you know yourself best;
But I will not call you noddy but only in jest.
And thus I assure you, though I came from school
To serve in this court, I came not yet to be the king's fool,
Or to fill his ears with servile scurrility:
That office is yours, you know it right perfectly.
Of parasites and sycophants you are a grave bencher;
The king feeds you often from his own trencher.
I envy not your state, nor yet your great favour,
Then grudge not at all if in my behaviour
I make the king merry with pleasant urbanity,
Whom I never abused to any man's injury.

CARISOPHUS
By Cock, sir, yet in the court you do best thrive,
For you get more in one day than I do in five.

ARISTIPPUS
Why man, in the court do you not see
Rewards given for virtue to every degree?
To reward the unworthy, that world is done:
The court is changed. A good thread hath been spun

22 ***regius canis*** the king's dog.
25 **tub** Diogenes lived in a barrel to demonstrate his rejection of worldly comforts and values.
27 **I...learn** I'm not slow in learning.
28 **What...turn** What will benefit me.
31 **beshrew** curse.
33 **paint out** describe flatteringly.
35 **sort** manner.
38 **noddy** fool.
45 **a grave bencher** a fine judge.
46 **trencher** plate.
51 **By Cock** a euphemism for 'by God'.
54 **every degree** all ranks of society.
56–58 **good...picked** Aristippus claims that previously all kinds of absurd nonsense ('dog's wool') was rewarded, not for its qualities, but just

Of dog's wool heretofore; and why? Because it was liked,
And not for that it was best trimmed and picked.
But now men's ears are finer, such gross toys are not set by,
Therefore to a trimmer kind of mirth myself I apply;
Wherein though I please, it cometh not of my desert,
But of the king's favour.

CARISOPHUS

It may so be; yet in your prosperity
Despise not an old courtier—Carisophus is he—
Which hath long time fed Dionysius' humour,
Diligently to please, still at hand; there was never rumour
Spread in this town of any small thing but I
Brought it to the king in post by and by.
Yet now I crave your friendship, which, if I may attain,
Most sure and unfeigned friendship I promise you again;
So we two linked in friendship, brother and brother,
Full well in the court may help one another.

ARISTIPPUS

By'r Lady, Carisophus, though you know not philosophy,
Yet surely you are a better courtier than I;
And yet I not so evil a courtier that will seem to despise
Such an old courtier as you, so expert and so wise.
But whereas you crave mine, and offer your friendship so willingly,
With heart I give you thanks for this your great courtesy,
Assuring of friendship both with tooth and nail,
Whiles life lasteth, never to fail.

CARISOPHUS

A thousand thanks I give you, O friend Aristippus.

ARISTIPPUS

O friend Carisophus!

CARISOPHUS

How joyful am I, sith I have to friend Aristippus now.

ARISTIPPUS

None so glad of Carisophus' friendship as I, I make God a vow;
I speak as I think, believe me.

CARISOPHUS

Sith we are now so friendly joined, it seemeth to me
That one of us help each other in every degree.
Prefer you my cause when you are in presence;
To further your matters to the king let me alone in your absence.

because Dionysius happened to like that sort of thing then.

60 **trimmer** smarter.

61 **it...desert** it's not for my own merits.

65 **humour** inclination/tastes.

66 **still** always.

68 **in post** swiftly, like a messenger.

70 **again** in return.

73 **By'r Lady** By Our Lady (i.e. the Virgin Mary).

75 **I...evil** I am not so poor.

79 **with tooth and nail** utterly.

83 **sith** since.

87 **in every degree** in all matters.

88 **Prefer...presence** Advance my fortunes when you are in the king's presence: perhaps literally in his presence chamber, where he hears petitions and greets guests.

ARISTIPPUS
Friend Carisophus, this shall be done as you would wish,
But I pray you tell me thus much by the way,
Whither now from this place will you take your journey?

CARISOPHUS
I will not dissemble, that were against friendship;
I go into the city some knaves to nip;
For talk with their goods to increase the king's treasure.
In such kind of service I set my chief pleasure.
Farewell, friend Aristippus, now for a time. *Exit.*

ARISTIPPUS
Adieu, friend Carisophus. In good faith now,
Of force I must laugh at this solemn vow.
Is Aristippus linked in friendship with Carisophus?
Quid cum tanto asino, talis philosophus?
They say, '*Morum similitudo consiliat amicitias*';
Then how can this friendship between us two come to pass?
We are as like in conditions as Jack Fletcher and his bolt;
I brought up in learning, but he is a very dolt
As touching good letters, but otherwise such a crafty knave,
If you seek a whole region, his like you cannot have:
A villain for his life, a varlet dyed in grain.
You lose money by him if you sell him for one knave, for he serves for twain:
A flattering parasite, a sycophant also,
A common accuser of men, to the good an open foe.
Of half a word he can make a legend of lies,
Which he will avouch with such tragical cries
As though all were true that comes out of his mouth.
Whereas indeed, to be hanged by and by,
He cannot tell one tale but twice he must lie.
He spareth no man's life to get the king's favour,
In which kind of service he hath got such a savour
That he will never leave. Methink, then, that I
Have done very wisely to join in friendship with him, lest perhaps I,
Coming in his way, might be nipped; for such knaves in presence
We see oft times put honest men to silence.
Yet I have played with his beard in knitting this knot,

93 **against** contrary too.

94–95 **I...treasure** He will rob some lowborn folk ('nip' some 'knaves') by falsely accusing them of crimes and then confiscating their property in the king's name (for a share of the spoils).

99 **force** necessity.

101 ***Quid...philosophus?*** What would a philosopher have to do with such an ass?

102 ***Morum...amicitias*** Friendship is built on similarity of nature.

104 **Jack...bolt** the arrow-maker and his arrow.

105–106 **a...letters** a complete idiot concerning good learning.

107 **seek** search through.

107 **like** equal.

108 **a...grain** a knave through and through.

109 **You...twain** You'd lose out if you sold him as a rogue, as he's knavish enough for two.

113 **avouch** swear are true.

118–119 **In...leave** He's developed such a taste for that kind of knavery that he'll never cease it.

123 **played...knot** lied to his face by swearing this friendship.

I promised friendship; but—you love few words—I spake it, but I meant it not.
Who marks this friendship between us two,
Shall judge of the worldly friendship without any more ado.
It may be a right pattern thereof, but true friendship indeed
Of nought but of virtue doth truly proceed.
But why do I now enter into philosophy,
Which do profess the fine kind of courtesy?
I will hence to the court with all haste I may;
I think the king be stirring, it is now bright day.
To wait at a pinch still in sight I mean,
For wot ye what? A new broom sweeps clean!
As to high honour I mind not to climb.
So I mean in the court to lose no time;
Wherein, happy man be his dole, I trust that I
Shall not speed worst, and that very quickly. *Exit.*

Here entereth Damon and Pythias, like mariners.

DAMON
O Neptune, immortal be thy praise,
For that so safe from Greece we have passed the seas
To this noble city, Syracuse, where we
The ancient reign of the Romans may see,
Whose force Greece also heretofore hath known,
Whose virtue the shrill trump of fame so far hath blown.

PYTHIAS
My Damon, of right high praise we ought to give
To Neptune and all the gods, that we safely did arrive.
The seas, I think, with contrary winds never raged so;
I am even yet so seasick that I faint as I go.
Therefore let us get some lodging quickly. But where is Stephano?

Here entereth Stephano.

STEPHANO
Not far hence. A pox take these mariner knaves.
Not one would help me to carry this stuff; such drunken slaves
I think be accursed of the gods' own mouths.

DAMON
Stephano, leave thy raging, and let us enter Syracusae,
We will provide lodging, and thou shalt be eased of thy burden by and by.

125 **marks** observes closely.
126 **Shall ... friendship** Shall see what merely worldly/expedient friendships are like.
127 **right pattern** true model.
133–134 **To ... broom** To wait around in the king's sight until something crops up that he needs help with, for, don't you know, a new broom ... (i.e. as the newest courtier, he will be thought to do the job best.)
137 **happy ... dole** every man (should be) happy with his fate/portion.
138 **speed** prosper.
143 Damon anachronistically talks of Syracuse's 'ancient' history here as a sixteenth-century visitor might, whereas the story supposedly takes place in the 'Greek' period, with the Roman conquest (of 212BC) yet to happen.
144 **trump** trumpet.
153 **Syracusae** use of the Latin form here allows the rhyme with 'by'.

STEPHANO

Good master, make haste, for I tell you plain,
This heavy burden puts poor Stephano to much pain.

PYTHIAS

Come on thy ways, thou shalt be eased, and that anon. *Exit (all).*

Here entereth Carisophus.

CARISOPHUS

It is a true saying that oft hath been spoken,
'The pitcher goeth so long to the water, that it cometh home broken'.
My own proof this hath taught me, for truly, sith I
In the city have used to walk very slyly,
And to creep into men's bosoms some talk for to snatch,
By which into one trip or other I might trimly them catch,
And so accuse them; now, not with one can I meet
That will join in talk with me. I am shunned like a devil in the street.
My credit is cracked where I am known; but I hear say
Certain strangers are arrived: they were a good prey
If happily I might meet with them. I fear not I
But in talk I should trip them, and that very finely.
Which thing, I assure you, I do for mine own gain,
Or else I would not plod thus up and down, I tell you plain.
Well, I will for a while to the court, to see
What Aristippus doth; I would be loath in favour he should overrun me;
He is a subtle child, he flattereth so finely, that I fear me
He will lick the fat from my lips, and so outwear me.
Therefore I will not be long absent, but at hand,
That all his fine drifts I may understand. *Exit.*

Here entereth Will and Jack.

WILL

I wonder what my master Aristippus means nowadays,
That he leaveth philosophy and seeks to please
King Dionysius with such merry toys.
In Dionysius' court now he only joys,
As trim a courtier as the best,
Ready to answer, quick in taunts, pleasant to jest;
A lusty companion to devise with fine dames,
Whose humour to feed his wily wit he frames.

JACK

By Cock, as you say, your master is a minion;
A foul coil he keeps in this court; Aristippus alone

162 **creep...bosoms** get close to/feign friendship with men.
163 **trimly** quickly/smartly.
166 **My...cracked** My reputation is ruined.
168 **I fear not** I don't doubt that.
173 **overrun** outdo.
174 **a subtle child** a cunning young man.
175 **He...lips** steal what is due to me, even down to the last speck of fat.
176 **at hand** close by.
186 **minion** favourite.
187 **a foul coil** a foul disturbance he creates.

Now rules the roost with his pleasant devices,
That, I fear he will put out of conceit my master Carisophus.

WILL

Fear not that, Jack, for, like brother and brother
They are knit in true friendship, the one with the other.
They are fellows, you know, and honest men both,
Therefore the one to hinder the other they will be loath.

JACK

Yea, but I have heard say there is falsehood in fellowship.
In the court sometimes one gives another finely the slip,
Which, when it is spied, it is laughed out with a scoff,
And with sporting and playing quickly shaken off.
In which kind of toying thy master hath such a grace,
That he will never blush, he hath a wooden face.
But, Will, my master hath bees in his head,
If he find me here prating, I am but dead.
He is still trotting in the city, there is somewhat in the wind;
His looks bewray his inward troubled mind.
Therefore I will be packing to the court by and by;
If he be once angry, Jack shall cry, 'woe the pie!'

WILL

By'r Lady, if I tarry long here, of the same sauce shall I taste.
For my master sent me on an errand, and bade me make haste;
Therefore we will depart together. *Exeunt.*

Here entereth Stephano.

STEPHANO

Oft-times I have heard, before I came hither,
That no man can serve two masters together;
A sentence so true as most men do take it,
At any time false that no man can make it.
And yet, by their leave that first have it spoken,
How that may prove false, even here I will open.
For I, Stephano, lo, so named by my father,
At this time serve two masters together,
And love them alike; the one and the other
I duly obey, I can do no other.
A bondman I am, so nature hath wrought me.

189 **he...conceit** he'll displace all thought of Carisophus (from Dionysius' head).

199 **hath...face** expressionless (when he wants to give nothing away).

200 **hath...head** is troubled/angry.

201 **prating** gossiping.

202 **somewhat** something.

203 **bewray** reveal.

205 **'woe the pie!'** King notes that 'lamb pie' was proverbial for a thrashing, so Jack is probably lamenting the thrashing he'd receive for dawdling.

206 **of...taste** I'll get the same treatment.

208.1 ***Exeunt*** Exit everyone.

210 **no...together** see Matthew 6:24 ('No man can serve two masters; for either he will hate the one and love the other, or he will sustain the one and despise the other. You cannot serve God and mammon [worldly wealth].')

213 **by their leave** with their permission.

214 **open** reveal/demonstrate.

219 **a bondman** a slave, 'bound' to a master for life, or until granted his freedom.

One Damon of Greece, a gentleman, bought me.
To him I stand bound, yet serve I another,
Whom Damon my master loves as his own brother;
A gentleman too, and Pythias he is named,
Fraught with virtue, whom vice never defamed.
These two, since at school they fell acquainted,
In mutual friendship at no time have fainted,
But loved so kindly and friendly each other,
As though they were brothers by father and mother.
Pythagoras' learning these two have embraced,
Which both are in virtue so narrowly laced,
That all their whole doings do fall to this issue:
To have no respect but only to virtue.
All one in effect, all one in their going,
All one in their study, all one in their doing;
These gentlemen both, being of one condition,
Both alike of my service have all the fruition.
Pythias is joyful if Damon be pleased;
If Pythias is served, then Damon is eased.
Serve one, serve both; so near, who would win them?
I think they have but one heart between them.
In travelling countries we three have contrived
Full many a year, and this day arrived
At Syracusae in Sicilia, that ancient town,
Where my masters are lodged, and I up and down
Go seeking to learn what news here are walking,
To hark of what things the people are talking.
I like not this soil, for as I go plodding,
I mark there two, there three, their heads always nodding
In close, secret wise still whispering together.
If I ask any question, no man doth answer,
But shaking their heads, they go their ways speaking.
I mark how with tears their wet eyes are leaking.
Some strangeness there is that breedeth this musing.
Well, I will to my masters, and tell of their using,
That they may learn, and walk wisely together.
I fear we shall curse the time we came hither. *Exit.*

Here entereth Aristippus and Will.

224 **Fraught** freighted/full of.
226 **fainted** failed.
229 **Pythagoras** the Greek philosopher, Pythagoras of Samos (*c*.570–*c*.495BC), who taught among other things that true friends are united as if they were one person.
230 **narrowly laced** tightly bound (together).
235 **condition** nature.
236 **have...fruition** enjoy the fruits.
238 **eased** comforted.
239 **win** divide.
245 **what...walking** what news is circulating.
249 **In...whispering** In private, secret fashion, always whispering.
253 **breedeth this musing** causes this anxious thought.
254 **using** behaviour.

ARISTIPPUS
Will, didst thou hear the ladies so talk of me?
What aileth them? From their nips shall I never be free?
WILL
Good faith, sir, all the ladies in the court do plainly report
That without mention of them you can make no sport;
They are your plain-song to sing descant upon.
If they were not, your mirth were gone.
Therefore, master, jest no more with women in any wise.
If you do, by Cock, you are like to know the price.
ARISTIPPUS
By'r Lady, Will, this is good counsel; plainly to jest
Of women, proof hath taught me it is not the best.
I will change my copy; howbeit I care not a quince,
I know the galled horse will soonest wince.
But learn thou secretly what privily they talk
Of me in the court; among them slyly walk,
And bring me true news thereof.
WILL
I will, sir; master, thereof have no doubt; for I,
Where they talk of you, will inform you perfectly.
ARISTIPPUS
Do so, my boy. If thou bring it finely to pass,
For thy good service thou shalt go in thine old coat at Christmas. *Exeunt.*

Enter Damon, Pythias, Stephano.

DAMON
Stephano, is all this true that thou hast told me?
STEPHANO
Sir, for lies hitherto ye never controlled me.
O that we had never set foot on this land
Where Dionysius reigns with so bloody a hand!
Every day he showeth some token of cruelty;
With blood he hath filled all the streets in the city.
I tremble to hear the people's murmuring,
I lament to see his most cruel dealing.
I think there is no such tyrant under the sun;
O, my dear masters, this morning what hath he done!
DAMON
What is that? Tell us quickly.
STEPHANO
As I this morning passed in the street,

259 **nips** barbed comments.
261 **They...upon** They are the bass-melody over which you devise your higher pitched variations (i.e. they are the subject of all your witty conversation).
264 **Cock** God (euphemism).
267 **I...copy** I'll change my tune.
267 **a quince** a bitter fruit (i.e. I care very little).
268 **the...wince** it's the horse you touch on a sore place ('gall') that will be quickest to kick out. (He claims that it's because his jibes have struck home that the ladies criticize him.)
275 **For...Christmas** This may be an aside. Aristippus seems to say Will's reward will be *not* to receive a new livery coat at Christmas, a standard gift for servants in Tudor times (i.e. he'll get no reward).
277 **controlled me** had to punish me.
280 **token** sign/evidence.
286 **passed** walked.

With a woeful man going to his death did I meet.
Many people followed, and I of one secretly
Asked the cause why he was condemned to die,
[He] whispered in mine ear, 'Nought hath he done but thus:
In his sleep he dreamed he had killed Dionysius;
Which dream told abroad, was brought to the king in post,
By whom, condemned for suspicion, his life he hath lost.'
Marcias was his name, as the people said.

PYTHIAS

My dear friend Damon, I blame not Stephano
For wishing we had not come hither, seeing it is so,
That for so small cause such cruel death doth ensue.

DAMON

My Pythias, where tyrants reign, such cases are not new,
Which fearing their own state for great cruelty,
To sit fast as they think, do execute speedily
All such as any light suspicion have tainted.

STEPHANO

With such quick carvers I list not be acquainted!

DAMON

So are they never in quiet, but in suspicion still.
When one is made away, they take occasion another to kill;
Ever in fear, having no trusty friend, void of all people's love,
And in their own conscience a continual hell they prove.

PYTHIAS

As things by their contraries are always best proved,
How happy then are merciful princes, of their people beloved.
Having sure friends everywhere, no fear doth touch them,
They may safely spend the day pleasantly, at night *secure dormiunt in utramque aurem.*
O my Damon, if choice were offered me, I would choose to be Pythias,
As I am, Damon's friend, rather than to be King Dionysius.

STEPHANO

And good cause why; for you are entirely beloved of one,
And as far as I hear, Dionysius is beloved of none.

DAMON

That state is most miserable; thrice happy are we
Whom true love hath joined in perfect amity;
Which amity first sprung (without vaunting be it spoken that is true)
Of likeness of manners, took root by company, and now is conserved by virtue.
Which virtue always through worldly things do not frame,
Yet doth she achieve to her followers immortal fame;
Whereof, if men were careful, for virtue's sake only
They would honour friendship, and not for commodity.

292 **told abroad** spoken about publicly.
292 **in post** swiftly.
294 This story is related in Plutarch's 'Life of Dion' (See King, p. 125).
299 **fast** securely (on their thrones).
300 **light** trivial.
301 **quick carvers** speedy butchers.
302 **never ... still** never at peace, but always suspicious.
305 **prove** create/experience.
309 ***secure ... aurem*** they sleep soundly, free of worries.
316 **vaunting** boasting.
318 **virtue ... frame** virtue doesn't prosper through worldly things (i.e. it doesn't bring wealth)

But such as for profit in friendship do link,
When storms come, they slide away sooner than a man will think.
My Pythias, the sum of my talk falls to this issue:
To prove no friendship is sure but that which is grounded on virtue.

PYTHIAS

My Damon, of this thing there needs no proof to me,
The gods forbid but that Pythias with Damon in all things should agree.
For why is it said, '*Amicus alter ipse*',
But that true friends should be two in body but one in mind,
As it were transformed into another, which, against kind
Though it seem, yet in good faith, when I am alone
I forget I am Pythias, methink I am Damon.

STEPHANO

That could I never do, to forget myself; full well I know,
Wheresoever I go, that I am pauper Stephano.
But I pray you, sir, for all your philosophy,
See that in this court you walk very wisely.
You are but newly come hither; being strangers, ye know,
Many eyes are bent on you, in the streets as ye go.
Many spies are abroad, you cannot be too circumspect.

DAMON

Stephano, because thou art careful of me, thy master, I do thee praise;
Yet think this for a surety: no state to displease
By talk or otherwise my friend and I intend. We will here
As men that come to see the soil and manners of all men of every degree.
Pythagoras said that this world was like a stage,
Whereon many play their parts: the lookers-on the sage
Philosophers are, saith he, whose part is to learn
The manners of all nations, and the good from the bad to discern.

STEPHANO

Good faith, sir, concerning the people, they are not gay,
And as far as I see, they be mummers, for nought they say
For the most part, whatsoever you ask them.
The soil is such, that to live here I cannot like.

DAMON

Thou speakest according to thy learning, but I say,
Omne solum forti patria: a wise man may live everywhere.
Therefore, my dear friend Pythias,
Let us view this town in every place,
And then consider the people's manners also.

PYTHIAS

As you will, my Damon; but how say you, Stephano,
Is it not best, ere we go further, to take some repast?

328 ***Amicus alter ipse*** a (true) friend is a second self.

330–331 **against ... seem** though it seems contrary to nature.

336 **walk very wisely** act cautiously.

340 **careful of** full of concern for.

343 **the soil** the nature of the country.

348 **not gay** not much to look at.

349 **mummers** actors in a dumbshow.

353 ***Omne ... patria*** literally 'every soil/land is home to the wise'.

STEPHANO

In faith, I like this question, sir; for all your haste,
To eat somewhat I pray you, think it no folly;
It is high dinner-time, I know by my belly.

DAMON

Then let us to our lodging depart. When dinner is done
We will view this city as we have begun. *Exeunt.*

Here entereth Carisophus.

CARISOPHUS

Once again in hope of good wind, I hoist up my sail;
I go into the city to find some prey for mine avail.
I hunger while I may see these strangers that lately
Arrived. I were safe if once I might meet them happily.
Let them bark that lust at this kind of gain,
He is a fool that for his profit will not take pain.
Though it be joined with other men's hurt, I care not at all.
For profit I will accuse any man, hap what shall.
But soft, sirs, I pray you hush, what are they that comes here?
By their apparel and countenance some strangers they appear.
I will shroud myself secretly, even here for a while,
To hear all their talk that I may them beguile.

Here entereth Damon and Stephano.

STEPHANO

A short horse soon curried; my belly waxeth thinner,
I am as hungry now as when I went to dinner.
Your philosophical diet is so fine and small
That you may eat your dinner and supper at once, and not surfeit at all.

DAMON

Stephano, much meat breeds heaviness; thin diet makes thee light.

STEPHANO

I may be lighter thereby, but I shall never run the faster.

DAMON

I have had sufficiently discourse of amity,
Which I had at dinner with Pythias; and his pleasant company
Hath fully satisfied me; it doth me good to feed mine eyes on him.

STEPHANO

Course or discourse, your course is very coarse; for all your talk
You had but one bare course, and that was pike, rise, and walk.
And surely, for all your talk of philosophy,
I never heard that a man with words could fill his belly.

365 **mine avail** my profit.
367 **I were safe** I'd have achieved my goal.
368 **Let . . . gain** Let those who want to criticize this kind of profiting do so.
372 **soft** quiet.
374 **shroud** conceal.
376 **A . . . curried** A small horse is soon groomed (proverbial).
376 **waxeth** grows.
380 **heaviness** dullness/sleep.
380 **light** bright/cheerful.
386 **pike . . . walk** pick at the dish, get up and leave (with a pun on 'pike' the fish).

'Feed your eyes', quoth you? The reason from my wisdom swerveth;
I stared on you both, and yet my belly starveth.

DAMON

Ah, Stephano, small diet maketh a fine memory.

STEPHANO

I care not for your crafty sophistry,
You two are fine, let me be fed like a gross knave still.
I pray you license me for a while to have my will,
At home to tarry while you take view of this city.
To find some odd victuals in a corner I am very witty.

DAMON

At your pleasure, sir; I will wait on myself this day.
Yet attend upon Pythias, which for a purpose tarrieth at home;
So doing, you wait upon me also.

STEPHANO

With wings on my feet I go.

[*Exit.*]

DAMON

Not in vain the poet saith, '*Naturam furca expelles, tamen usque recurret*',
For, train up a bondman never to so good a behaviour,
Yet in some point of servility he will savour;
As this Stephano, trusty to me his master, loving and kind,
Yet touching his belly a very bondman I him find.
He is to be borne withal, being so just and true;
I assure you, I would not change him for no new.
But methinks this is a pleasant city;
The seat is good, and yet not strong, and that is great pity.

CARISOPHUS

I am safe, he is mine own!

DAMON

The air subtle and fine, the people should be witty
That dwell under this climate in so pure a region;
A trimmer plat I have not seen in my peregrination.
Nothing misliketh me in this country,
But that I heard such muttering of cruelty.
Fame reporteth strange things of Dionysius,
But kings' matters, passing our reach, pertain not to us.

CARISOPHUS

'Dionysius', quoth you? Since the world began,
In Sicilia never reigned so cruel a man.

389 **The...swerveth** My mind rejects that argument.

396 **To...witty.** I'm eager to hunt out some (more) food.

400 **With...feet** like Mercury, the swift, winged-footed messenger of the gods.

401 ***Naturam...recurret*** You can dig out nature (lit. with a fork) but it comes straight back in.

403 **in...savour** he'll always show evidence (lit. taste) of his base origins/nature.

406 **He...withal** He must be tolerated.

409 **The ....strong** The lie of the land is sound, but not very secure militarily.

410 **He...own!** I've got him!

413 **A...peregrination** I've not seen a neater layout (literally, map of the town) in all my travelling.

417 **passing...us** being beyond our place in society, don't concern us.

A despiteful tyrant to all men; I marvel, I
That none makes him away, and that suddenly.

DAMON

My friend, the gods forbid so cruel a thing,
That any man should lift up his sword against the king;
Or seek other means by death him to prevent
Whom to rule on earth the mighty gods have sent.
But, my friend, leave off this talk of King Dionysius.

CARISOPHUS

Why, sir, he cannot hear us!

DAMON

What then? *An nescis longas regibus esse manus?*
It is no[t] safe talking of them that strikes afar off.
But, leaving kings' matters, I pray you show me this courtesy,
To describe in few words the state of this city.
A traveller I am, desirous to know
The state of each country wherever I go;
Not to the hurt of any state, but to get experience thereby.
It is not for nought that the poet doth cry,
'Die mihi musa, virum captcae post tempora Troiae
Multorum hominum mores qui vidit et urbes.'
In which verses, as some writers do scan,
The poet describeth a perfect wise man.
Even so, I, being a stranger, addicted to philosophy,
To see the state of countries myself I apply.

CARISOPHUS

Sir, I like this intent, but may I ask your name without scorn?

DAMON

My name is Damon, well known in my country, a gentleman born.

CARISOPHUS

You do wisely to search the state of each country
To bear intelligence thereof whither you lust. (He is a spy!)
Sir, I pray you, have patience a while, for I have to do hereby.
View this weak part of this city as you stand, and I very quickly
Will return to you again, and then will I show
The state of all this country, and of the court also. *Exit.*

DAMON

I thank you for your courtesy. This chanceth well, that I
Met with this gentleman so happily,

420–421 **I ... away** I'm astonished no one assassinates him.
424 **prevent** check/forestall.
428 ***An ... manus?*** Do you not know that kings have long hands?
429 **that ... off** who can strike from distance.
436–437 ***Die ... urbes*** 'Speak to me, Muse, about the man who, after the capture of Troy, saw the customs and towns of many men/peoples.' A version of the opening of Homer's *Odyssey*; 'the man' being Odysseus.
438 **scan** interpret.
440 **addicted** devoted.
442 **without scorn** seriously/without causing offence.
444 **search** investigate.
445 **bear ... lust** carry away news/information to wherever you like.
446 **have ... hereby** have something to do nearby.
451 **happily** fortunately.

Which, as it seemeth, misliketh something,
Else he would not talk so boldly of the king,
And that to a stranger. But lo, where he comes in haste!

Here entereth Carisophus and Snap.

CARISOPHUS
This is the fellow, Snap; snap him up; away with him!

SNAP
Good fellow, thou must go with me to the court.

DAMON
To the court, sir, and why?

CARISOPHUS
Well, we will dispute that before the king. Away with him quickly!

DAMON
Is this the courtesy you promised me, and that very lately?

CARISOPHUS
Away with him, I say.

DAMON
Use no violence; I will go with you quietly.

Exeunt omnes.
Here entereth Aristippus.

ARISTIPPUS
Ah, sirrah, by'r Lady, Aristippus likes Dionysius' court very well,
Which in passing joys and pleasures doth excel.
Where he hath *Dapsiles cenas, geniales lectos, et auro*
Fulgentem tyranni zonam.
I have plied the harvest, and struck when the iron was hot.
When I spied my time, I was not squeamish to crave, God wot,
But with some pleasant toy I crept into the king's bosom,
For which Dionysius gave me *Auri talentum magnum*;
A large reward for so simple services.
What, then? The king's praise standeth chiefly in bountifulness,
Which thing, though I told the king very pleasantly,
Yet can I prove it by good writers of great antiquity.
But that shall not need at this time, since that I have abundantly.
When I lack hereafter, I will use this point of philosophy.
But now, whereas I have felt the king's liberality;
As princely as it came, I will spend it as regally.
Money is current, men say, and 'current' comes of '*currendo*';
Then will I make money run, as his nature requireth, I trow.

460.1 ***Exeunt omnes.*** Exit everyone.
461 **sirrah** a variant of 'sir' used for servants and social inferiors.
462 **passing** surpassing/superior.
463–464 ***Dapsiles . . . zonam*** 'Delightful suppers, bridal beds, and bright gold kingly money-belts.' As King notes, the court thus offers food, sex, and money, everything a worldly epicure might want.
465 **plied . . . hot** i.e. seized the opportunities for profit while I could.
466 **I . . . crave** I didn't hesitate to beg for favours, God knows.
467 **with . . . bosom** (subtly) won the king's favour with some pleasing jest or gift.
468 ***Auri talentum magnum*** 'A great talent of gold'—a talent being a (substantial) measure of weight.
470 **The . . . bountifulness** A king's reputation rests mostly on his generosity ('magnificence', a kind of generosity of spirit and largesse was one of the kingly virtues celebrated by Aristotle in his *Ethics*).
477 **is current** moves about/circulates.
477 ***currendo*** running (Latin).
478 **I trow** I swear.

For what becomes a philosopher best
But to despise money above the rest;
And yet not so despise it, but to have in store
Enough to serve his own turn, and somewhat more?
With sundry sports and taunts yesternight I delighted the king,
That with his loud laughter the whole court did ring.
And I thought he laughed not merrier than I when I got this money.
But, mumbudget, for Carisophus I espy,
In haste to come hither. I must handle the knave finely.

Here entereth Carisophus.

O Carisophus, my dearest friend, my trusty companion,
What news with you? Where have you been so long?

CARISOPHUS
My best beloved friend Aristippus, I am come at last;
I have not spent all my time in waste.
I have got a prey, and that a good one, I trow.

ARISTIPPUS
What prey is that? Fain would I know.

CARISOPHUS
Such a crafty spy I have caught, I dare say,
As never was in Sicilia before this day;
Such a one as viewed every weak place in the city,
Surviewed the haven and each bulwark; in talk very witty,
And yet by some words himself he did bewray.

ARISTIPPUS
I think so in good faith, as you did handle him.

CARISOPHUS
I handled him clerkly, I joined in talk with him courteously;
But when we were entered I let him speak his will, and I
Sucked out thus much of his words, that I made him say plainly
He was come hither to know the state of the city;
And not only this, but that he would understand
The state of Dionysius' court and of the whole land.
Which words when I heard, I desired him to stay
Till I had done a little business of the way,
Promising him to return again quickly; and so did convey
Myself to the court for Snap the tipstaff, which came and upsnatched him,
Brought him to the court, and in the porter's lodge dispatched him.
After I ran to Dionysius, as fast as I could
And bewrayed this matter to him which I have you told.
Which thing when he heard, being very merry before,
He suddenly fell in a dump and, foaming like a boar,

482 **serve...turn** meet his needs.
486 **mumbudget** hush!
487 **finely** carefully/subtly.
s.d. The stage direction is printed two lines later in the 1571 text.
493 **Fain** eagerly.
497 **Surviewed** Surveyed.
498 **bewray** revealed/betrayed himself.
500 **clerkly** skilfully/like a scholar.
501 **when...entered** once we'd begun.
509 **tipstaff** an officer of the court.
514 **dump** depression.

At last he swore in great rage that he should die,
By the sword or the wheel, and that very shortly.
I am too shamefast, for my travail and toil
I crave nothing of Dionysius, but only his spoil.
Little hath he about him but a few moth-eaten crowns of gold,
Cha pouched them up already, they are sure in hold.
And now I go into the city, to say sooth,
To see what he hath at his lodging to make up my mouth.

ARISTIPPUS

My Carisophus, you have done good service; but what is the spy's name?

CARISOPHUS

He is called Damon, born in Greece, from whence lately he came.

ARISTIPPUS

By my troth, I will go see him, and speak with him too, if I may.

CARISOPHUS

Do so, I pray you; but yet by the way,
As occasion serveth, commend my service to the king.

ARISTIPPUS

Dictum sapienti sat est: friend Carisophus, shall I forget that thing?
No, I warrant you, though I say little to your face,
I will lay one month for you to Dionysius when I am in place.
If I speak one word for such a knave, hang me! *Exit.*

CARISOPHUS

Our fine philosopher, our trim learned elf,
Is gone to see as false a spy as himself.
Damon smatters as well as he of crafty philosophy,
And can turn cat in the pan very prettily;
But Carisophus hath given him such a mighty check,
As I think in the end will break his neck.
What care I for that? Why would he then pry
And learn the secret estate of our country and city?
He is but a stranger, by his fall let others be wise.
I care not who fall, so that I may rise.
As for fine Aristippus, I will keep in with him.
He is a shrewd fool to deal withal; he can swim.
And yet, by my troth, to speak my conscience plainly,

516 **the wheel** a device that breaks the bones.
517 **shamefast** modest.
518 **spoil** the property confiscated from Damon.
520 **Cha...hold** I've pocketed them already, they're safely stored. (Carisophus briefly falls into the colloquial form 'cha' for 'I have', used commonly by rustic characters, as in *Gammer Gurton's Needle*).
521 **to say sooth** to speak truly.
522 **make...mouth** fill my mouth (i.e. make good the shortfall between what he has already seized and what he'd like to have).
526–527 **but...serveth** as you do so, when the chance arises.
528 ***Dictum...est*** a word to the wise is enough.
530 **lay one month** King suggests this is a misprint for 'lay on [i.e. work hard] with my mouth for you'. Alternatively the intention might be, 'lay [on for] a whole month'.
531 **If...me!** an aside.
532 **learned elf** sly youngster.
534 **smatters** talks superficially.
535 **can...prettily** can flip things over/prove that black is white very elegantly.
536 **given...check** delivered him a blow.
543 **he can swim** he knows how to look after himself/prosper.

I will use his friendship to mine own commodity.
While Dionysius favoureth him, Aristippus shall be mine;
But if the king once frown on him, then good night Tomaline!
He shall be as strange as though I never saw him before.
But I tarry too long, I will prate no more.
Jack, come away!

JACK
At hand, sir.

CARISOPHUS
At Damon's lodging if that you see
Any stir to arise, be still at hand by me.
Rather than I will lose the spoil, I will blade it out. [*Exit.*]

Here entereth Pythias and Stephano.

PYTHIAS
What strange news are these? Ah, my Stephano,
Is my Damon in prison, as the voice doth go?

STEPHANO
It is true, O cruel hap; he is taken for a spy;
And, as they say, by Dionysius' own mouth condemned to die.

PYTHIAS
To die? Alas! For what cause?

STEPHANO
A sycophant falsely accused him; other cause there is none.
That, O Jupiter, of all wrongs the revenger,
Seest thou this unjustice, and wilt thou stay any longer
From heaven to send down thy hot consuming fire
To destroy the workers of wrong which provoke thy just ire?
Alas, master Pythias, what shall we do,
Being in a strange country, void of friends and acquaintance too?
Ah, poor Stephano, hast thou lived to see this day,
To see thy true master unjustly made away?

PYTHIAS
Stephano, seeing the matter is come to this extremity,
Let us make virtue our friend of mere necessity.
Run thou to the court and understand secretly
As much as thou canst of Damon's cause, and I
Will make some means to entreat Aristippus;
He can do much, as I hear, with King Dionysius.

STEPHANO
I am gone, sir. Ah, I would to God my travail and pain
Might restore my master to his liberty again! [*Exit.*]

PYTHIAS
Ah woeful Pythias! Sith now I am alone,
What way shall I first begin to make my moan?

545 **commodity** benefit.
547 **good night Tomaline** a slang term for 'It's all over'.
549 **prate** chatter.
551 **if...me** if you see any trouble brewing, stay always at my side.
552 **blade it lout** fight with a sword.
554 **as...go** as the rumour says.
555 **cruel hap** cruel chance/fortune.
560 **stay** wait.
566 **made away** murdered.
567 **extremity** extreme situation.
576 **make my moan** to complain.

What words shall I find apt for my complaint?
Damon, my friend, my joy, my life, is in peril. Of force I must now faint.
But, music, as in joyful times thy merry notes did borrow,
So now lend me thy yearnful tunes to utter my sorrow.

Here Pythias sings and the regals play.

Awake, ye woeful wights,
That long have wept in woe;
Resign to me your plaints and tears.
My hapless hap to show.
My woe no tongue can tell,
No pen can well descry;
O, what a death is this to hear,
Damon, my friend must die.

The loss of worldly wealth
Man's wisdom may restore,
And physic hath provided too
A salve for every sore;
But my true friend once lost,
No art can well supply;
Then what a death is this to hear,
Damon, my friend must die.

My mouth refuse the food,
That should my limbs sustain;
Let sorrow sink into my breast,
And ransack every vein;
You Furies all at once
On me your torments try;
Why should I live, since that I hear
Damon, my friend must die.

Gripe me, you greedy griefs
And present pangs of death;
You Sisters three, with cruel hands,
With speed come stop my breath;
Shrine me in clay alive,
Some good man stop mine eye;
Death, come now, seeing I hear,
Damon, my friend must die.

He speaketh this after the song:

578 **Of…faint.** Of necessity I must now despair.
580 **yearnful** sorrowful.
580.1 **regals** portable pipe organs.
581 **wights** folk.
583 **Resign** Give up
583 **plaints** lamentations.
584 **hapless hap** unlucky fortune.
586 **descry** declare.
591 **physic** medicine.
592 **salve…sore** ointment for every ailment.
594 **No…supply** No kind of skill can restore his loss.
601 **Furies** the Erinyes, classical female spirits of vengeance.
605 **Gripe** grip violently.
607 **Sisters three** the Fates, who control human destiny.
609 **Shrine…clay** bury me.

In vain I call for death, which heareth not my complaint.
But what wisdom is this, in such extremity to faint?
Multum juvat in re mala animus bonus.
I will to the court myself to make friends, and that presently.
I will never forsake my friend in time of misery—
But do I see Stephano amazed hither to run?

Here entereth Stephano.

[STEPHANO]
O Pythias, Pythias, we are all undone!
Mine own ears have sucked in mine own sorrow;
I heard Dionysius swear that Damon should die tomorrow.

PYTHIAS
How camest thou so near the presence of the king
That thou mightest hear Dionysius speak this thing?

STEPHANO
By friendship I got into the court, where in great audience
I heard Dionysius with his own mouth give this cruel sentence,
By these express words: that Damon the Greek, that crafty spy,
Without further judgment tomorrow should die.
Believe me, Pythias, with these ears I heard it myself.

PYTHIAS
Then how near is my death also! Ah, woe is me!
Ah my Damon, another myself, shall I forego thee?

STEPHANO
Sir, there is no time of lamenting now; it behoveth us
To make means to them which can do much with Dionysius,
That he be not made away ere his cause be fully heard. For we see
By evil report things be made to princes far worse than they be.
But lo, yonder cometh Aristippus, in great favour with King Dionysius,
Entreat him to speak a good word to the king for us,
And in the mean season I will to your lodging to see all things safe there. *Exit.*

PYTHIAS
To that I agree; but let us slip aside his talk to hear.

Here entereth Aristippus.

ARISTIPPUS
Here is a sudden change indeed, a strange metamorphosis,
This court is clean altered. Who would have thought this?
Dionysius, of late so pleasant and merry,
Is quite changed now into such melancholy
That nothing can please him. He walketh up and down,
Fretting and chafing; on every man he doth frown.

615 ***Multum . . . bonus.*** A good spirit is a great thing when things are bad.
624 **in great audience** among a great crowd.
630 **forego** lose.
633 **cause** case.
637 **mean season** meantime.
640 **clean** completely.

In so much that, when I in pleasant words began to play,
So sternly he frowned on me, and knit me up so short;
I perceive it is no safe playing with lions but when it please them;
If you claw where it itch not, you shall disease them,
And so perhaps get a clap. Mine own proof taught me this,
That it is very good to be merry and wise.
The only cause of this hurly-burly is Carisophus, that wicked man,
Which lately took Damon for a spy, a poor gentleman,
And hath incensed the king against him so despitefully
That Dionysius hath judged him tomorrow to die.
I have talked with Damon, whom though in words I found very witty,
Yet was he more curious than wise in viewing this city.
But truly, for aught I can learn, there is no cause why
So suddenly and cruelly he should be condemned to die.
Howsoever it be, this is the short and long,
I dare not gainsay the king, be it right or wrong.
I am sorry, and that is all I may or can do in this case;
Nought availeth persuasion where froward opinion taketh place.

PYTHIAS

Sir, if humble suits you would not despise,
Then bow on me your pitiful eyes.
My name is Pythias, in Greece well known,
A perfect friend to that woeful Damon,
Which now a poor captive in this court doth lie,
By the king's own mouth, as I hear, condemned to die;
For whom I crave your mastership's goodness,
To stand his friend in this his great distress.
Nought hath he done worthy of death; but very fondly,
Being a stranger, he viewed this city
For no evil practices but to feed his eyes.
But, seeing Dionysius is informed otherwise,
My suit is to you, when you see time and place,
To assuage the king's anger and to purchase his grace;
In which doing you shall not do good to one only,
But you shall further two, and that fully.

ARISTIPPUS

My friend, in this case I can do you no pleasure.

PYTHIAS

Sir, you serve in the court, as fame doth tell.

ARISTIPPUS

I am of the court indeed, but none of the council.

648 **claw** scratch.
648 **disease** upset/anger.
649 **clap** blow.
649 **proof** experience.
651 **hurly-burly** turmoil.
657 **aught** anything.
662 **where . . . place** where stubborn/peevish opinions hold sway.
663 **suits** petitions/requests.
664 **bow on** turn towards.
670 **stand** act as.
671 **fondly** foolishly.
673 **evil . . . to** malicious reason, except to.
676 **purchase his grace** win his good will.
678 **further two** benefit the two of us.
680 **as . . . tell** as is well known.
681 **none . . . council** not a formal member of the king's council—which offers him political advice.

PYTHIAS
As I hear, none is in greater favour with the king than you at this day.

ARISTIPPUS
The more in favour, the less I dare say.

PYTHIAS
It is a courtier's praise to help strangers in misery.

ARISTIPPUS
To help another and hurt myself, it is an evil point of courtesy!

PYTHIAS
You shall not hurt yourself to speak for the innocent.

ARISTIPPUS
He is not innocent whom the king judgeth nocent.

PYTHIAS
Why, sir, do you think this matter past all remedy?

ARISTIPPUS
So far past that Dionysius hath sworn Damon tomorrow shall die.

PYTHIAS
This word my trembling heart cutteth in two.
Ah, sir, in this woeful case what wist I best to do?

ARISTIPPUS
Best to content yourself when there is no remedy;
He is well relieved that foreknoweth his misery;
Yet, if any comfort be, it resteth in Eubulus,
The chiefest counsellor about King Dionysius,
Which pitieth Damon's case in this great extremity,
Persuading the king from all kind of cruelty.

PYTHIAS
The mighty gods preserve you for this word of comfort.
Taking my leave of your goodness, I will now resort
To Eubulus, that good counsellor. But hark, methink I hear a trumpet blow.

ARISTIPPUS
The king is at hand, stand close in the press. Beware; if he know
You are friend to Damon, he will take you for a spy also.
Farewell, I dare not be seen with you.

Here entereth King Dionysius, Eubulus
the Councillor, and Gronno the Hangman.

DIONYSIUS
Gronno, do my commandment, strike off Damon's irons by and by,
Then bring him forth; I myself will see him executed presently.

GRONNO
O mighty king, your commandment will I do speedily.

684 **It...praise** It would benefit a courtier's reputation.
685 **it...courtesy!** that's perverse diplomacy!
687 **nocent** guilty.
691 **what...do?** what should I do for the best?
693 **relieved** comforted.
695 **counsellor** advisor—as distinct from a formal councillor, although Eubulus seems to be both.
696 **Which pitieth** Who pities.
704 **irons** chains.

DIONYSIUS
Eubulus, thou hast talked in vain, for sure he shall die.
Shall I suffer my life to stand in peril of every spy?

EUBULUS
That he conspired against your person, his accuser cannot say;
He only viewed your city, and will you for that make him away?

DIONYSIUS
What he would have done, the guess is great; he minded me to hurt
That came so slyly to search out the secret estate of my court.
Shall I still lie in fear? No, no, I will cut off such imps betime,
Lest that to my farther danger too high they climb.

EUBULUS
Yet have the mighty gods immortal fame assigned
To all worldly princes which in mercy be inclined.

DIONYSIUS
Let Fame talk what she list, so I may live in safety.

EUBULUS
The only mean to that is to use mercy,

DIONYSIUS
A mild prince the people despiseth.

EUBULUS
A cruel king the people hateth.

DIONYSIUS
Let them hate me, so they fear me.

EUBULUS
That is not the way to live in safety.

DIONYSIUS
My sword and power shall purchase my quietness.

EUBULUS
That is sooner procured by mercy and gentleness.

DIONYSIUS
Dionysius ought to be feared.

EUBULUS
Better for him to be well beloved.

DIONYSIUS
Fortune maketh all things subject to my power.

EUBULUS
Believe her not, she is a light goddess; she can laugh and lour.

DIONYSIUS
A king's praise standeth in the revenging of his enemy.

EUBULUS
A greater praise to win him by clemency.

711 **What . . . great** What he would have done is a matter for great speculation.
713 **still** always.
713 **I . . . betime** I will cut back these young shoots early.
718 **mean to that** way to do that.
721 **so** so long as.
723 **purchase my quietness** buy me safety.
728 **light** fickle.
728 **lour** frown.

DIONYSIUS
To suffer the wicked [to] live, it is no mercy.
EUBULUS
To kill the innocent, it is great cruelty.
DIONYSIUS
Is Damon innocent, which so craftily undermined Carisophus
To understand what he could of King Dionysius?
Which surviewed the haven and each bulwark in the city
Where battery might be laid; what way best to approach? Shall I
Suffer such a one to live that worketh me such despite?
No, he shall die; then I am safe. A dead dog cannot bite.
EUBULUS
But yet, O mighty king, my duty bindeth me
To give such counsel as with your honour may best agree.
The strongest pillars of princely dignity,
I find this: justice with mercy and prudent liberality;
The one judgeth all things by upright equity,
The other rewardeth the worthy, flying each extremity.
As to spare those which offend maliciously,
It may be called no justice, but extreme injury;
So upon suspicion of each thing not well proved,
To put to death presently whom envious flattery accused,
It seemeth of tyranny; and upon what fickle ground all tyrants do stand
Athens and Lacedemon can teach you, if it be rightly scanned.
And not only these citizens, but who curiously seeks
The whole histories of all the world, not only of Romans and Greeks,
Shall well perceive of all tyrants the ruinous fall,
Their state uncertain: beloved of none but hated of all.
Of merciful princes to set out the passing felicity
I need not; enough of that even these days do testify.
They live devoid of fear, their sleeps are sound, they dread no enemy,
They are feared and loved, and why? They rule with justice and mercy,
Extending justice to such as wickedly from justice have swerved;
Mercy unto those who in opinion of simpleness have mercy deserved.
Of liberty nought I say, but only this thing:
Liberty upholdeth the state of a king,
Whose large bountifulness ought to fall to this issue:
To reward none but such as deserve it for virtue.
Which merciful justice if you would follow, and provident liberality,
Neither the caterpillars of all courts (*et fruges consumere nati*),

735 **haven** harbour.
736 **Where...laid** Defensive wall where artillery might be situated.
740 **To...agree** To advise you of the best way to maintain your honour.
742 **liberality** largesse.
744 **flying** avoiding.
749 **seemeth of** appears to be.
750 **Athens and Lacedemon** Athens, birthplace of civic democracy, and Sparta, reputedly among the best ordered of states.
750 **scanned** interpreted.
751 **who curiously seeks** whoever searches through.
755 **passing felicity** superior/perfect happiness.
759 **swerved** deviated.
762 **upholdeth** supports.
763 **fall...issue** lead to this end.
766 **caterpillars** parasites.
766 ***et fruges consumere nati*** born to consume all the fruits.

Parasites with wealth puffed up, should not look so high;
Nor yet for this simple fact poor Damon should die.

DIONYSIUS
With pain mine ears have heard this vain talk of mercy.
I tell thee, fear and terror defendeth kings only:
Till he be gone whom I suspect, how shall I live quietly,
Whose memory with chilling horror fills my breast day and night violently?
My dreadful dreams of him bereaves my rest; on bed I lie
Shaking and trembling, as one ready to yield his throat to Damon's sword.
This quaking dread nothing but Damon's blood can stay;
Better he die than I to be tormented with fear alway.
He shall die, though Eubulus consent not thereto:
It is lawful for kings as they list all things to do.

Here Gronno and Snap bring in Damon, and Pythias meeteth him by the way.

PYTHIAS
O my Damon!

DAMON
O my Pythias! Seeing death must part us, farewell forever.

PYTHIAS
O Damon, O my sweet friend!

SNAP
Away from the prisoner! What a press have we here!

GRONNO
As you commanded, O mighty king, we have brought Damon.

DIONYSIUS
Then go to; make ready, I will not stir out of this place
Till I see his head strucken off before my face.

GRONNO
It shall be done, sir. Because your eyes have made such ado
I will knock down this your lantern, and shut up your shop-window too.

DAMON
O mighty king, whereas no truth my innocent life can save,
But that so greedily you thirst my guiltless blood to have,
Albeit (even for thought) for ought against your person;
Yet now I plead not for life, ne will I crave your pardon,
But seeing in Greece my country, where well I am known,
I have worldly things fit for mine alliance when I am gone,
To dispose them, ere I die, if I might obtain leisure,
I would account it, O king, for a passing great pleasure,
Not to prolong my life thereby, for which I reckon not this,
But to set my things in a stay. And surely I will not miss,

772 **Whose memory** Whose (image in my) memory.
775 **stay** prevent.
778 **as . . . do** to do anything they like.
780.1 **press** crowd.
782 **go to** get on with it.
784 **made much ado** caused all this trouble (by spying).
785 **knock . . . too** knock off your head and so shut your eyes, proverbially 'the windows of the soul'.
788 **for** in.
788 **Albeit . . . person** Albeit I have done nothing against you, even in thought.
791 **fit . . . alliance** that ought to go to my friends and family.
794 Presumably a flick of his fingers or other gesture here accompanies 'this'.
795 **set . . . stay** put my affairs in order.
795 **miss** fail.

Upon the faith which all gentlemen ought to embrace,
To return again, at your time to appoint, to yield my body here in this place.
Grant me, O king, such time to despatch this injury,
And I will not fail when you appoint even here my life to pay.

DIONYSIUS
A pleasant request! As though I could trust him absent
Whom in no wise I cannot trust being present!
And yet, though I sware the contrary, do that I require:
Give me a pledge for thy return, and have thine own desire.
(He is as near now as he was before!)

DAMON
There is no surer nor greater pledge than the faith of a gentleman.

DIONYSIUS
It was wont to be, but otherwise now the world doth stand;
Therefore do as I say, else presently yield thy neck to the sword.
If I might with my honour, I would recall my word.

PYTHIAS
Stand to your word, O king, for kings ought nothing say
But that they would perform in perfect deeds alway.
A pledge you did require when Damon his suit did move,
For which with heart and stretched hands most humble thanks I give;
And that you may not say but Damon hath a friend
That loves him better than his own life, and will do to his end,
Take me, mighty king; my life I pawn for his.
Strike off my head if Damon hap at his day to miss.

DIONYSIUS
What art thou that chargest me with my word so boldly here?

PYTHIAS
I am Pythias, a Greek born, which hold Damon my friend full dear.

DIONYSIUS
Too dear perhaps to hazard thy life for him. What fondness moveth thee?

PYTHIAS
No fondness at all, but perfect amity.

DIONYSIUS
A mad kind of amity! Advise thyself well; if Damon fail at his day,
Which shall be justly appointed, wilt thou die for him, to me his life to pay?

PYTHIAS
Most willingly, O mighty king. If Damon fail, let Pythias die.

DIONYSIUS
Thou seemest to trust his words that pawnest thy life so frankly.

798 **despatch this injury** put right this injustice (of killing him while his affairs are not settled).
801 **wise** way.
802 **though** even if.
803 **pledge** someone who will act as guarantor.
804 **(He...before!)** i.e. he's not really any nearer what he wants (as no one will offer to pledge their life for his return).
805 **faith** honesty.
806 **It...stand** That used to be true, but the world is different now.
808 **If ...honour** If I could do so and not lose honour.
811 **his...move** make his request.
816 **hap...miss** happens to miss his appointment.
819 **What...thee?** What folly motivates you?
824 **pawnest** pledges.

PYTHIAS
What Damon saith, Pythias believeth assuredly.

DIONYSIUS
Take heed, for life worldly men break promise in many things.

PYTHIAS
Though worldly men do so, it never haps amongst friends.

DIONYSIUS
What callest thou friends? Are they not men; is not this true?

PYTHIAS
Men they be, but such men as love one another only for virtue.

DIONYSIUS
For what virtue dost thou love this spy, this Damon?

PYTHIAS
For that virtue which yet to you is unknown.

DIONYSIUS
Eubulus, what shall I do? I would despatch this Damon fain,
But this foolish fellow so chargeth me, that I may not call back my word again.

EUBULUS
The reverent majesty of a king stands chiefly in keeping his promise.
What you have said, this whole court beareth witness.
Save your honour, whatsoever you do.

DIONYSIUS
For saving mine honour, I must forbear my will? Go to!
Pythias, seeing thou tookest me at my word, take Damon to thee;
For two months he is thine. Unbind him, I set him free.
Which time once expired, if he appear not the next day by noon,
Without further delay thou shalt lose thy life, and that full soon.
Whether he die by the way, or lie sick in his bed,
If he return not then, thou shalt either hang or lose thy head.

PYTHIAS
For this, mighty king, I yield immortal thanks. O joyful day!

DIONYSIUS
Gronno, take him to thee; bind him, see him kept in safety;
If he escape, assure thyself for him thou shalt die.
Eubulus, let us depart to talk of this strange thing within.

EUBULUS
I follow. *Exit [following Dionysius].*

GRONNO
Damon, thou servest the gods well today; be thou of comfort.
As for you, sir, I think you will be hanged in sport.
You heard what the king said; I must keep you safely;
By Cock, so I will, you shall rather hang than I.
Come on your way.

PYTHIAS
My Damon, farewell; the gods have thee in keeping.

833 **chargeth** insistently requests.
837 **I . . . to!** must I go without what I want? That's ridiculous! (But he quickly changes his mind, perhaps after exchanging looks with Eubulus.)
842 **by the way** on the journey here.
847 **within** indoors.

DAMON
O my Pythias, my pledge, farewell; I part from thee weeping.
But joyful at my day appointed I will return again,
When I will deliver thee from all trouble and pain.
Stephano will I leave behind me to wait upon thee in prison alone,
And I, whom fortune hath reserved to this misery, will walk home.
Ah my Pythias, my pledge, my life, my friend, farewell.

PYTHIAS.
Farewell, my Damon.

DAMON
Loath am I to depart, sith sobs my trembling tongue doth stay.
O music, sound my doleful plaints when I am gone my way. [*Exit.*]

GRONNO
I am glad he is gone, I had almost wept too. Come, Pythias;
So God help me, I am sorry for thy foolish case;
Wilt thou venture thy life for a man so fondly?

PYTHIAS
It is no venture; my friend is just, for whom I desire to die.

GRONNO
Here is a madman, I tell thee! I have a wife, whom I love well,
And if ich would die for her, chould ich were in hell!
Wilt thou do more for a man than I would for a woman?

PYTHIAS
Yea, that I will.

GRONNO
Then come on your ways, you must to prison in haste;
I fear you will repent this folly at last.

PYTHIAS
That shalt thou never see. But O music, as my Damon requested thee,
Sound out thy doleful tunes in this time of calamity. *Exit.*

Here the regals play a mourning song, and Damon cometh in, in mariner's apparel, and Stephano with him.

DAMON
Weep no more Stephano, this is but destiny.
Had not this happed, yet I know I am born to die;
Where or in what place the gods know alone,
To whose judgment myself I commit. Therefore leave off thy moan,
And wait upon Pythias in prison till I return again,
In whom my joy, my care, and life doth only remain.

STEPHANO
O my dear master, let me go with you; for my poor company
Shall be some small comfort in this time of misery.

DAMON
O Stephano, hast thou been so long with me

859 **reserved to** appointed to/set aside for.
862 **stay** hold back.
866 **venture** risk.
869 **chould ich** I would (rather) I.

And yet dost not know the force of true amity?
I tell thee once again, my friend and I are but one:
Wait upon Pythias, and think thou art with Damon.
Whereof I may not now discourse, the time passeth away;
The sooner I am gone, the shorter shall be my journey.
Therefore farewell, Stephano, commend me to my friend Pythias,
Whom I trust to deliver in time out of this woeful case.

STEPHANO

Farewell my dear master, since your pleasure is so.
O cruel hap! O poor Stephano!
O cursed Carisophus, that first moved this tragedy!
But what a noise is this? Is all well within, trow ye?
I fear all be not well within. I will go see.
Come out, you weasel; are you seeking eggs in Damon's chest?
Come out, I say, wilt thou be packing? By Cock, you were best.

CARISOPHUS

How durst thou, villain, to lay hands on me?

STEPHANO

Out, sir knave, or I will send ye.
Art thou not content to accuse Damon wrongfully,
But wilt thou rob him also, and that openly?

CARISOPHUS

The king gave me the spoil; to take mine own wilt thou let me?

STEPHANO

Thine own, villain? Where is thine authority?

CARISOPHUS

I am authority of myself, dost thou not know?

STEPHANO

By'r Lady, that is somewhat; but have you no more to show?

CARISOPHUS

What if I have not?

STEPHANO

Then for an earnest penny take this blow!
I shall bum-baste you, you mocking knave; chill put 'pro' in my purse for this time.

CARISOPHUS

Jack, give me my sword and target.

JACK

I cannot come to you, master, this knave doth me let. Hold, master.

STEPHANO

Away, Jackanapes, else I will colpheg you by and by.

---

897 Weasels were known for sucking eggs in birds' nests, hence were proverbial for sneak thieves.
898 **wilt . . . best** will you come out? By God, you'd better!
899 **durst** dare.
903 **to . . . me?** will you prevent me collecting what is my own property?
907.1 **penny** a token of greater payment to follow.
908 **bum-baste** thrash your arse.
908 **chill . . . time** King suggests, 'I'll put an IOU in my wallet for now', 'pro' being Latin for 'instead of', i.e. Stephano threatens to postpone the greater beating for another time.
909 **target** small shield.
910 **me let** prevents me.
911 **Hold** Wait.
911 **Away . . . by.** Clear off, you tricky rogue (lit. monkey), I'll batter ('colpheg' is a corruption of 'colaphize') you later.

Ye slave, I will have my pennyworths of thee therefore, if I die. About, villain!

CARISOPHUS

O citizens, help to defend me!

STEPHANO

Nay, they will rather help to hang thee.

CARISOPHUS

Good fellow, let us reason of the matter quietly. Beat me no more!

STEPHANO

Of this condition I will stay, if thou swear, as thou art an honest man,
Thou wilt say nothing to the king of this when I am gone.

CARISOPHUS

I will say nothing. Here is my hand, as I am an honest man.

STEPHANO

Then say on thy mind. I have taken a wise oath on him, have I not, trow ye?
To trust such a false knave upon his honesty?
'As he is an honest man' (quoth you?) he may bewray all to the king.
And break his oath for this never a whit. But, my franion, I tell you this one thing:
If you disclose this, I will devise such a way
That whilst thou livest thou shalt remember this day.

CARISOPHUS

You need not devise for that, for this day is printed in my memory;
I warrant you I shall remember this beating till I die.
But seeing of courtesy you have granted that we should talk quietly,
Methinks in calling me knave you do me much injury.

STEPHANO

Why so, I pray thee, heartily?

CARISOPHUS

Because I am the king's man; keeps the king any knaves?

STEPHANO

He should not, but what he doth it is evident by thee.
And as far as I can learn or understand,
There is none better able to keep knaves in all the land.

CARISOPHUS

O sir, I am a courtier; when courtiers shall hear tell
How you have used me, they will not take it well.

STEPHANO

Nay, all right courtiers will ken me thank; and wot you why?
Because I handled a counterfeit courtier in his kind so finely.
What, sir? All are not courtiers that have a counterfeit show;
In a troop of honest men some knaves may stand, ye know,
Such as by stealth creep in under the colour of honesty,
Which sort, under that cloak, do all kinds of villainy.

912 **I will... villain!** I'll have my money's worth (of revenge) of you for this (theft), if it's the last thing I do. Turn round, you villain!
915 **reason of** discuss.
916 **Of** On.
916 **stay** stop.
922 **never a whit** not at all.
922 **franion** a lover or reckless rogue.
926 **warrant** promise.
935 **used** treated.
936 **will... thank** tell me of their gratitude.
937 **in... finely** so perfectly as his nature deserved.
940 **the colour of** the pretence of.

A right courtier is virtuous, gentle, and full of urbanity,
Hurting no man, good to all, devoid of villainy;
But such as thou art, fountains of scurrility and vain delights.
Though you hang by the courts, you are but flatt'ring parasites;
As well deserving the right name of courtesy
As the coward knight the true praise of chivalry.
I could say more, but I will not, for that I am your well-willer.
In faith, Carisophus, you are no courtier but a caterpillar,
A sycophant, a parasite, a flatterer, and a knave.
Whether I will or no, these names you must have.
How well you deserve this, by your deeds it is known,
For that so unjustly thou hast accused poor Damon,
Whose woeful case the gods help alone.

CARISOPHUS
Sir, are you his servant, that you pity his case so?

STEPHANO
No, bum troth, goodman Grumb, *his* name is Stephano;
I am called Onaphets, if needs you will know.
(The knave beginneth to sift me, but I turn my name in and out,
Cretiso cum Cretense, to make him a lout.)

CARISOPHUS
What mumble you with yourself, Master Onaphets?

STEPHANO
I am reckoning with myself how I may pay my debts.

CARISOPHUS
You have paid me more than you did owe me.

STEPHANO
Nay, upon a farther reckoning, I will pay you more, if I know
Either you talk of that is done, or by your sycophantical envy
You prick forth Dionysius the sooner that Damon may die.
I will so pay thee that thy bones shall rattle in thy skin.
Remember what I have said: Onaphets is my name. *Exit.*

CARISOPHUS
The sturdy knave is gone, the devil him take!
He hath made my head, shoulders, arms, sides, and all to ache.
Thou whoreson villain boy, why didst thou wait no better?
As he paid me, so will I not die thy debtor.

JACK
Master, why do you fight with me? I am not your match, you see;
You durst not fight with him that is gone, and will you wreak your anger on me?

945 **hang by** hang around.
948 **well-willer** well-wisher.
956 **bum...Grumb** by my faith, master groom (lackey) (colloquial).
957 **Onaphets** the false name is, of course, 'Stephano' backwards.
958 **beginneth to sift me** is beginning to discover who I really am.
959 ***Cretiso cum Cretense*** I play the Cretan with a Cretan (i.e. lie to a liar: Cretans were proverbial liars), to honour him.
965 **prick forth** encourage.
970 **wait** attend me.
971 **As...debtor.** In the same manner he paid me, I'll not owe you anything (i.e. he starts to beat Jack).

CARISOPHUS
Thou villain, by thee I have lost mine honour,
Beaten with a cudgel like a slave, a vagabond, or a lazy lubber,
And not given one blow again. Hast thou handled me well?

JACK
Master, I handled you not, but who did handle you very handsomely, you can tell.

CARISOPHUS
Handsomely, thou crack-rope?

JACK
Yea, sir, very handsomely, I hold you a groat;
He handled you so handsomely that he left not one mote in your coat.

CARISOPHUS
O, I had firked him trimly, thou villain, if thou hadst given me my sword.

JACK
It is better as it is, master, believe me at a word.
If he had seen your weapon, he would have been fiercer,
And so perhaps beat you worse, I speak it with my heart;
You were never at the dealing of fence-blows, but you had four away for your part.
It is but your luck, you are man good enough;
But the Welsh Onaphets was a vengeance knave, and rough.
Master, you were best go home and rest in your bed,
Methinks your cap waxeth too little for your head.

CARISOPHUS
What, doth my head swell?

JACK
Yea, as big as a cod's head, and bleeds too.

CARISOPHUS
I am ashamed to show my face with this hue.

JACK
No shame at all; men have been beaten far better than you.

CARISOPHUS
I must go to the chirurgeon's. What shall I say, when I am a-dressing?

JACK
You may say truly you met with a knave's blessing. *Exeunt.*

Here entereth Aristippus.

ARISTIPPUS
By mine own experience I prove true that many men tell:
To live in court not beloved, better be in hell!
What crying out, what cursing, is there within of Carisophus,
Because he accused Damon to King Dionysius.
Even now he came whining and crying into the court for the nonce,

975 **lubber** rogue.
976 **handled** treated.
978 **crack-rope** a villain who'll hang.
979 **I . . . groat** I bet you a groat (a coin worth four-pence).
979 **mote** speck of dust.
980 **I . . . trimly** I'd have thrashed him soundly.
984 **fence-blows** sword-strokes.
984 **you had . . . part** you took four blows to every one delivered.
986 Jack assumes that Stephano's strange false name must mean he is Welsh.
986 **vengeance** extremely violent.
988 **waxeth** grows.
991 **chirurgeon's** surgeon's.
991 **when . . . a-dressing?** while my wounds are being dressed?
993 **that** what.
997 **for the nonce** especially for that purpose.

Showing that one Onaphets had broke his knave's sconce.
Which strange name when they heard, every man laughed heartily,
And I by myself scanned his name secretly;
For well I knew it was some mad-headed child
That invented this name, that the log-headed knave might be beguiled.
In tossing it often with myself to and fro,
I found out that 'Onaphets' backward spelled Stephano.
I smiled in my sleeve, how to see by turning his name he dressed him,
And how for Damon his master's sake with a wooden cudgel he blessed him.
None pitied the knave, no man nor woman; but all laughed him to scorn.
To be thus hated of all, better unborn!
Far better Aristippus hath provided, I trow;
For in all the court I am beloved both of high and low.
I offend none, insomuch that women sing this to my great praise.
'*Omnis Aristippum decuit color, et locus et res*.'
But in all this jollity one thing 'mazeth me,
The strangest thing that ever was heard or known
Is now happened in this court by that Damon,
Whom Carisophus accused. Damon is now at liberty,
For whose return Pythias his friend lieth in prison, alas, in great jeopardy.
Tomorrow is the day, which day by noon if Damon return not, earnestly
The king hath sworn that Pythias should die;
Whereof Pythias hath intelligence very secretly,
Wishing that Damon may not return till he hath paid
His life for his friend. Hath it been heretofore ever said
That any man for his friend would die so willingly?
O noble friendship! O perfect amity!
Thy force is here seen, and that very perfectly.
The king himself museth hereat, yet he is far out of square
That he trusteth none to come near him; not his own daughters will he have
Unsearched to enter his chamber, which he hath made barbers his beard to shave,
Not with knife or razor, for all edge-tools he fears,
But with hot burning nutshells they singe off his hairs.
Was there ever man that lived in such misery?
Well, I will go in, with a heavy and pensive heart, too,
To think how Pythias, this poor gentleman, tomorrow shall die. *Exit.*

Here entereth Jack and Will.

JACK
Will, by mine honesty, I will mar your monkey's face if you so fondly prate.

998 **sconce** head.
1002 **log-headed** block-headed.
1003 **tossing it** turning it over in the mind.
1005 **in my sleeve** privately.
1005 **dressed** tricked.
1012 ***Omnis . . . res.*** Every colour, place and thing suited Aristippus. (A quotation from Horace. See King, p. 155).
1013 **'mazeth** amazes/puzzles.
1020 **intelligence** has heard word.
1026 **museth hereat** wonders at this.
1026 **far . . . square** unsettled.
1029 **edge-tools** tools with sharp edges (that might be used to assassinate him).
1034 **I . . . prate** I'll spoil your monkey face (with a slap) if you chatter so foolishly.

WILL
Jack, by my troth, seeing you are without the court gate,
If you play Jackanapes in mocking my master and despising my face,
Even here with a pantacle I will you disgrace;
And though you have a far better face than I,
Yet who is better man of us two these fists shall try,
Unless you leave your taunting.

JACK
Thou began'st first; didst thou now not say even now
That Carisophus my master was no man but a cow
In taking so many blows, and gave never a blow again?

WILL
I said so indeed; he is but a tame ruffian,
That can swear by his flask and touch-box and God's precious lady,
And yet will be beaten with a faggot-stick.
These barking whelps were never good biters,
Ne yet great crakers were ever great fighters.
But seeing you egg me so much, I will somewhat more recite:
I say Carisophus, thy master, is a flatt'ring parasite,
Gleaning away the sweet from the worthy in all the court.
What tragedy hath he moved of late? The devil take him, he doth much hurt.

JACK
I pray you, what is Aristippus, thy master? Is not he a parasite too,
That with scoffing and jesting in the court makes so much ado?

WILL
He is no parasite, but a pleasant gentleman, full of courtesy.
Thy master is a churlish lout, the heir of a dung-fork; as void of honesty
As thou art of honour.

JACK
Nay, if you will needs be prating of my master still,
In faith I must cool you, my friend dapper Will.
Take this at the beginning!

WILL
Praise well your winning,
My pantacle is as ready as yours.

JACK
By the mass, I will box you.

WILL
By Cock, I will fox you.

JACK
Will, was I with you?

WILL
Jack, did I fly?

1035 **without** outside.
1037 Will suggests that, since they are outside the court now, and so not subject to its discipline, he'll take off his shoe (his pantofle or overshoe) and beat him with it.
1040 **leave** stop.
1044 **touch-box** box for touch-powder for muskets.
1045 **faggot-stick** a small stick from a bundle used for lighting a fire.
1047 **crakers** boasters.
1048 **egg** encourage.
1051 **moved of late?** set in motion recently?
1059 **Praise... winning** wait until you've won before boasting.
1061.1 **was... you?** did you feel that?

JACK
Alas, pretty cockerel, you are too weak.

WILL
In faith, doting dottrel, you will cry 'creak'!

Here entereth Snap.

SNAP
Away you crack-ropes, are you fighting at the court gate?
And I take you here again, I will swinge you both; what! *Exit.*

JACK
I beshrew Snap the tipstaff, that great knave's heart that hither did come,
Had he not been, you had cried ere this, '*Victus, victa victum*'.
But seeing we have breathed ourselves, if ye list,
Let us agree like friends, and shake each other by the fist.

WILL
Content am I, for I am not malicious; but on this condition:
That you talk no more so broad of my master as here you have done.
But who have we here? 'Tis *Cobex epi* coming yonder.

JACK
Will, let us slip aside and view him well.

Here entereth Grim the Collier, whistling.

GRIM
What devil! Ich ween the porters are drunk, will they not dup the gate today?
Take in coals for the king's own mouth! Will nobody stir, I say?
Ich might have lain tway hours longer in my bed,
Cha tarried so long here that my teeth chatter in my head.

JACK
Will, after our falling out wilt thou laugh merrily?

WILL
Ay, marry, Jack, I pray thee heartily.

JACK
Then follow me, and hem in a word now and then.
What brawling knave is there at the court gate so early?

WILL
It is some brainsick villain, I durst lay a penny.

JACK
Was it you, sir, that cried so loud, I trow;

1063 **doting dottrel** silly fool (literally a plover, a bird so slow-witted as to be easily caught).
1063 To cry out 'crick' or 'creak' was to concede defeat.
1065 **And** If.
1065 **swinge** thrash.
1066 **beshrew** curse.
1067 ***Victus, victa victum*** variants of '(I'm) vanquished'.
1068 **breathed** got our breath back.
1069 **shake . . . fist** shake hands.
1071 **broad** rudely.
1072 ***Cobex epi*** King suggests a misprint for '*colax epi*': 'coals on top', i.e. a man carrying a sack of coal.
1074 **Ich ween** I think. Grim speaks in the same cod-rustic dialect as the characters in *Gammer Gurton's Needle*.
1074 **dup** do up (open).
1075 Grim misapplies the term used for food brought to court for the king's use, applying it to his coals; a slip that Jack will pick him up on.
1076 **tway** two.
1079 **marry** certainly.
1080 **hem** throw in (lit. cough in).
1082 **lay** bet.

And bid us take in coals for the king's mouth even now?

GRIM

'Twas I indeed.

JACK

Why, sir, how dare you speak such petty treason?
Doth the king eat coals at any season?

GRIM

Here is a gay world; boys now sets old men to school!
I said well enough. What, Jack-sauce, think'st cham a fool?
At bakehouse, buttery-hatch, kitchen, and cellar,
Do they not say 'for the king's mouth'?

WILL

What, then, goodman collier?

GRIM

What then? Seeing without coals they cannot finely dress the king's meat,
May I not say, 'take in coals for the king's mouth', though coals he do not eat?

JACK

James Christ, came ever from a collier an answer so trim?
You are learned, are you not, father Grim?

GRIM

Grim is my name indeed; cham not learned, and yet the king's collier.
This vorty winter cha been to the king a servitor.
Though I be not learned, yet cha mother-wit enough, whole and some.

WILL

So it seems, you have so much mother-wit, that you lack your father's wisdom.

GRIM

Mass, cham well beset; here's a trim cast of murleons.
What be you, my pretty cockerels, that ask me these questions?

JACK

Good faith, master Grim, if such merlins on your pouch may light,
They are so quick of wing that quickly they can carry it out of your sight;
And though we are cockerels now, we shall have spurs one day,
And shall be able perhaps to make you a capon.
But to tell you the truth, we are the porter's men, which early and late
Wait on such gentlemen as you, to open the court gate.

GRIM

Are ye servants then?

WILL

Yea, sir; are we not pretty men?

GRIM

'Pretty men', quoth you? Nay, you are strong men,
Else you could not bear these breeches.

1088 **Jack-sauce** cheeky fellow.
1089 **bakehouse** the larder door.
1091 **dress . . . meat** prepare the king's food.
1093 **trim** fine (ironic).
1096 **vorty** forty.
1097 **cha . . . some** I've enough natural wit, when all things are considered.
1099 **beset** set upon.
1099 **trim . . . murleons** a fine set of merlins (small hunting birds).
1101 **on . . . light** might land on your purse/wallet.
1103 **we . . . spurs** grow from young game-cocks to adult fighting-cocks, equipped with sharp spikes on their feet.
1104 **capon** a castrated cock.
1107.1 **pretty** proper/suitable but also 'small'.
1109.1 **great hose** large baggy trousers.

WILL

Are these such great hose?
In faith, goodman collier, you see with your nose!
By mine honesty, I have but one lining in one hose, but seven ells of rug.

GRIM

This is but a little, yet it makes thee seem a great bug.

JACK

How say you, goodman collier, can you find any fault here?

GRIM

Nay, you should find fault, marry, here's trim gear!
Alas, little knave, dost not sweat? Thou goest with great pain,
These are no hose, but water-bougets, I tell thee plain;
Good for none but such as have no buttocks.
Did you ever see two such little robin ruddocks
So laden with breeches? Chill say no more, lest I offend.
Who invented these monsters first, did it to a ghostly end,
To have a male ready to put in other folks' stuff.
We see this evident by daily proof.
One preached of late not far hence, in no pulpit but in a wain-cart,
That spake enough of this; but for my part
Chill say no more; your own necessity
In the end will force you to find some remedy.

JACK

Will, hold this railing knave with a talk when I am gone;
I will fetch him his filling ale for his good sermon. [*Exit.*]

WILL

Go thy way, father Grim, gaily well you do say.
It is but young men's folly that list to play
And mask awhile in the net of their own device.
When they come to your age, they will be wise.

GRIM

Bum troth, but few such roisters come to my years at this day;
They be cut off betimes ere they have gone half their journey.
I will not tell why; let them guess that can, I mean somewhat thereby.

Enter Jack with a pot of wine, and a cup to drink on.

[JACK]

Father Grim, because you are stirring so early,

1110 **you see...nose!** have a look with your nose—an insulting invitation to sniff his backside.
1111 **seven...rug** over eight metres of cloth: an absurd amount for even the most fashionable hose for so small a boy.
1112 **bug** hobgoblin.
1114 **trim gear** fine clothing (ironic).
1115 **Thou...pain** It must be an effort to walk (in such trousers).
1116 **water-bougets** great leather pouches slung over a horse or cow to carry water.
1118 **robin ruddocks** robin redbreasts—little birds.
1120 **to ghostly end** for a spiritual/holy purpose.
1121 **male...stuff** a bag or pocket to carry others goods.
1123 **in a wain-cart** on the back of a wagon, i.e. a travelling preacher or someone on their way to be hanged.
1127 **hold** delay.
1128 **his filling ale** perhaps: his fill of ale—enough to get him drunk.
1131 **mask...device** take part in a play of their own devising. (Will suggests Grim should not worry, as they are just messing about as young boys like to do.)
1133 **Bum troth** By my honour!
1134–1135 **They...thereby.** Perhaps an allusion to early death from sexually transmitted disease as King suggests.
1135.1 **on** from.

I have brought you a bowl of wine to make you merry.

GRIM

Wine? Marry, this is welcome to colliers! Chill swap't off by and by.
Chwas stirring so early that my very soul is dry.

JACK

This is stoutly done; will you have it warmed, father Grim?

GRIM

No, it is warm enough; it is very luscious and trim.
'Tis musselden, ich ween; of fellowship let me have another spurt,
Ich can drink as easily now as if I sat in my shirt.

JACK

By Cock, and you shall have it; but I will begin, and that anon,
Je bit a vous mon compagnon.

GRIM

Jai vous pledge, petit zawne!

JACK

Can you speak French? Here is a trim collier, by this day!

GRIM

What man? Ich learned this when Ich was a soldier;
When Ich was a lusty fellow, and could yerk a whip trimly,
Better than these boy-colliers, that come to the court daily,
When there were not so many captious fellows as now,
That would torrup men for every trifle, I wot not how;
As there was one Damon, not long since taken for a spy;
How justly I know not, but he was condemned to die.

WILL

This wine hath warmed him, this comes well to pass.
We shall know all now, for *in vino veritas.*
Father Grim, who accused this Damon to King Dionysius?

GRIM

A vengeance take him; 'twas a gentleman, one Master Crowsphus.

WILL

'Crowsphus'! You clip the king's language, you would have said 'Carisophus'.
But I perceive now either the wind is at the south
Or else your tongue cleaveth to the roof of your mouth.

GRIM

A murrain take thick wine, it so intoxicate my brain
That to be hanged by and by I cannot speak plain.

1138 **Chill ... by.** I'll quickly drink that off.

1140 **stoutly** bravely.

1142 **'Tis ... spurt** It's Muscatel, I think, for friendship's sake let me have another swig.

1145 ***Je ... compagnon.*** King suggests '*Je bois a vous ...*': 'I drink to you, my good fellow'.

1146 ***Jai ... zawne!*** 'I pledge you' (drink this to you) 'my little zany'. A zany is a clownish character in the *commedia dell'arte*: if this is the point of the reference, it is a very early reference to the *commedia* in England.

1149 **yerk** crack.

1151 **captious** quarrelsome.

1152 **torrup** perhaps Grim, getting steadily more drunk, slurs 'trip up' into a single word.

1155 **this ... pass** this is going well.

1156 ***in vino veritas*** in wine is truth.

1159 **clip** mar, like a coin clipper who trims the edges from a coin to melt down the shavings.

1162 **murrain** plague.

JACK

You speak knavishly plain, seeing my master you do mock.
In faith, ere you go, I will make you a lobcock.
Father Grim, what say they of this Damon abroad?

GRIM

All men are sorry for him, so help me God.
They say a false knave 'cused him to the king wrongfully,
And he is gone, and should be here tomorrow to die,
Or else his fellow which is in prison his room shall supply.
Chill not be his half for vorty shillings, I tell you plain,
I think Damon be too wise to return again.

WILL

Will no man speak for them in this woeful case?

GRIM

No, chill warrant you, one master Stippus is in place
Where he may do good, but he frames himself so,
Whatsoever Dionysius willeth, to that he will not say no.
'Tis a subtle vox, he will not tread on thorns for none;
A merry harecop 'tis, and a pleasant companion,
A right courtier, and can provide for one.

JACK

Will, how like you this gear? Your master Aristippus also
At this collier's hand hath had a blow!
But in faith, father Grim, cannot ye colliers
Provide for yourselves far better than courtiers?

GRIM

Yes, I trow; black colliers go in threadbare coats,
Yet so provide they that they have the fair white groats.
Ich may say in counsel, though all day I moil in dirt,
Chill not change lives with any in Dionysius' court;
For though their apparel be never so fine,
Yet sure their credit is far worse than mine.
And, by Cock, I may say, for all their high looks,
I know some sticks full deep in merchants' books;
And deeper will fall in, as fame me tells.
As long as instead of money they take up hawks' hoods and bells,
Whereby they fall into a swelling disease, which colliers do not know;
'T hath a mad name; it is called, ich ween, *centum pro cento*.
Some other in courts make others laugh merrily,
When they wail and lament their own estate secretly.

1165 **lobcock** a rustic idiot.
1168 **'cused** accused.
1170 **his room...supply** shall take his place.
1171 **Chill...half** I'd not be in his place (lit. act on his behalf).
1175 **he...so** makes sure he behaves in such a way.
1177 **'Tis...none** A wily fox, he'll not pain himself on anyone's behalf.
1178 **A merry...'tis** Here's a hare-brained fellow.
1179 **and...one** (but) he can look after himself.
1180 **gear** business.
1186 **in counsel** just between us.
1186 **moil** stain myself.
1191 **full...books** are deeply in debt to merchants.
1192 **as...tells** as rumour has it.
1193 **take...bells** i.e. spend all their borrowed money on hawking and other pleasures.
1195 ***centum pro cento*** 'cent for cent', i.e. 100 per cent interest.
1197 **estate** situation.

Friendship is dead in court, hypocrisy doth reign;
Who is in favour now, tomorrow is out again.
The state is so uncertain that I, by my will,
Will never be courtier, but a collier still.

WILL

It seemeth that colliers have a very trim life.

GRIM

Colliers get money still. Tell me of troth,
Is not that a trim life now as the world goeth?
All day though I toil with my main and might,
With money in my pouch I come home merry at night,
And sit down in my chair by my wife, fair Alison,
And turn a crab in the fire, as merry as Pope Joan.

JACK

That Pope was a merry fellow, of whom folk talk so much.

GRIM

Had to be merry withal, had gold enough in his hutch.

JACK

Can gold make men merry? They say, 'who can sing so merry a note,
As he that is not able to change a groat?'

GRIM

Who sings in that case, sings never in tune. I know for my part
That a heavy pouch with gold makes a light heart;
Of which I have provided for a dear year good store.
And these benters, I trow, shall anon get me more.

WILL

By serving the court with coals, you gained all this money?

GRIM

By the court only, I assure ye.

JACK

After what sort, I pray thee tell me?

GRIM

Nay, there bate me an ace (quod Bolton);
I can wear a horn and blow it not.

JACK

By'r Lady, the wiser man!

GRIM

Shall I tell you by what sleight I got all this money?
Then ich were a noddy indeed! No, no, I warrant ye;
Yet in few words I tell you this one thing,

1203 **get money still** always make money.

1205 **main** strength.

1208 **crab** crab apple.

1208 **Pope Joan** An apocryphal pope who was discovered to be a woman in disguise, subject of a well-known story in the Middle Ages.

1210 **hutch** chest. Grim seems not have realized Joan was a woman.

1211–1212 **'who . . . groat?'** i.e. who is as happy as someone with no money—and so no money worries?

1215 **provided . . . store** saved some money to provide for difficult times ahead.

1216 **benters** debentures: warrants for payment from the crown.

1219 **After what sort?** In what way?

1219.1 A probably apocryphal allusion to one John Bolton, a courtier to Henry VIII, who reputedly always asked the king to 'abate him' an ace—let him lose a low card first, to give him a better chance. Grim is saying he'll keep his advantage here by not revealing his methods.

1220 **I . . . not.** I can keep quiet when I want.

1222 **ich . . . noddy** I'd be a fool.

He is a very fool that cannot gain by the king.

WILL

Well said, father Grim; you are a wily collier and a brave,
I see now there is no knave like to the old knave.

GRIM

Such knaves have money when courtiers have none.
But tell me, is it true that abroad is blown?

JACK

What is that?

GRIM

Hath the king made those fair damsels his daughters
To become now fine and trim barbers?

JACK

Yea, truly, to his own person.

GRIM

Good fellows, believe me, as the case now stands,
I would give one sack of coals to be washed at their hands.
If Ich came so near them, for my wit chould not give three chips
If Ich could not steal one swap at their lips.

JACK

Will, this knave is drunk, let us dress him.
Let me rifle him so that he have not one penny to bless him,
And steal away his debentures too.

WILL

Content! Invent the way and I am ready.

JACK

Faith, and I will make him a noddy.
Father Grim, if you pray me well, I will wash you and shave you too,
Even after the same fashion as the king's daughters do.
In all points as they handle Dionysius, I will dress you trim and fine.

GRIM

Chould vain learn that. Come on then, chill give thee a whole pint of wine
At tavern for thy labour, when cha money for my benters here.

Here Will fetcheth a barber's basin, a pot with water, a razor and cloths and a pair of spectacles.

JACK

Come, mine own father Grim, sit down.

GRIM

Mass, to begin withal, here is a trim chair.

JACK

What, man? I will use you like a prince. Sir boy, fetch me my gear.

WILL

Here, sir.

1228 **that . . . blown?** what is being said everywhere?
1235 **swap** kiss.
1236 **dress him** clean him out (lit. prepare him like meat for the table).
1237 **rifle him** pick his purse.
1238.1 **Content!** I'm happy with that!
1243 **Chould vain** I'd be eager to.

JACK

Hold up, Father Grim.

GRIM

Me-seem my head doth swim!

JACK

My costly perfumes make that.—Away with this, sir boy; be quick,
Aloyse, aloyse!—How pretty it is; is not here a good face?
A fine owl's eyes, a mouth like an oven.
Father, you have good butter-teeth full seen.
You were weaned, else you would have been a great calf.
Ah, trim lips to sweep a manger! Here is a chin,
As soft as the hoof of an horse!

GRIM

Doth the king's daughters rub so hard?

JACK

Hold your head straight, man, else all will be marred.
By'r Lady, you are of good complexion:
A right Croydon sanguine. Beshrew me,
Hold up, father Grim. Will, can you bestir yet?

GRIM

Methinks after a marvellous fashion you do besmear me.

JACK

It is with *unguentum* of *Daucus-Maucus*, that is very costly;
I give not this washing-ball to everybody.
After you have been dressed so finely at my hand,
You may kiss any lady's lips within this land.
Ah, you are trimly washed! How say you, is not this trim water?

GRIM

It may be wholesome, but it is vengeance sour.

JACK

It scours the better. Sir boy, give me my razor.

WILL

Here at hand, sir.

GRIM

God's arms; 'tis a chopping knife, 'tis no razor!

JACK

It is a razor, and that a very good one;
It came lately from Palermo, it cost me twenty crowns alone.

1249 **Me-seem** It seems to me.
1251 **Aloyse** King suggests 'aloynez': 'carry it away' is intended. Jack slips Grim's purse to Will who is told to hurry it away and hide it.
1252 Owls are notoriously blind in daylight, despite having large eyes; ovens have proverbially wide mouths.
1253 **good...seen** good back-teeth (but also yellow), when looked at properly.
1254 **calf** a fool/young cow. Jack implies if Grim hadn't grown his back teeth he'd have been a great idiot.
1260 **A right...sanguine** a ruddy complexion from Croydon, a town south of the Thames.
1261 **Hold...Grim.** Curse me, hold your chin up.
1261 **can...yet?** Can you hurry up? (Jack is still trying to distract Grim's attention while they pick his purse).
1262 **after...me** you're lathering my face in a very odd way.
1263 ***unguentum* of *Daucus-Maucus*** ointment of carrot-marrot (a nonsensical 'lotion').
1264 **washing-ball** soap.
1267 **trim water** perhaps, as King suggests, they are washing his face in urine.
1268 **vengeance sour** smells absolutely horrible.
1270.1 **God's arms** a mild oath.
1272 **Palermo** a city in northern Sicily.
1272 **crowns** gold coins.

Your eyes dazzle after your washing, these spectacles put on.
Now view this razor, tell me, is it not a good one?

GRIM
They be gay barnacles, yet I see never the better.

JACK
Indeed they be a young sight, and that is the matter;
But I warrant you this razor is very easy.

GRIM
Go to, then; since you begun, do as please ye.

JACK
Hold up, father Grim.

GRIM
Oh, your razor doth hurt my lip!

JACK
No, it scrapeth off a pimple to ease you of the pip.
I have done now, how say you? Are you not well?

GRIM
Cham lighter than ich was, the truth to tell.

JACK
Will you sing after your shaving?

GRIM
Mass, content; but chill be polled first, ere I sing.

JACK
Nay, that shall not need; you are polled near enough for this time.

GRIM
Go to then lustily, I will sing in my man's voice.
Chave a troubling base buss.

JACK
You are like to bear the bob, for we will give it;
Set out your bussing base, and we will quiddle upon it.

Grim singeth bass.

Jack sings

To-nidden and to-nidden.

Will sings

To-nidden and toodle, toodle do-nidden,
Is not Grim the collier most finely shaven?

GRIM
Why, my fellows, think Ich am a cow, that you make such toying?

1275 **gay barnacles** nice shells/spectacles.
1276 **be . . . sight** perhaps 'suitable for younger eyes' (King).
1280 **the pip** a disease.
1284 **Mass . . . first** By the Mass, I'm happy with that, but I'll have my hair cut first.
1285 'Polling' and 'shaving' are also colloquial terms for robbery.
1287 **Chave . . . buss.** Literally Grim seems to say, 'I've a disturbing bass voice', but he may be confusing his musical parts and be trying to claim to be both a 'treble' (high) and a bass (low) singer.
1288 **bear . . . it** 'carry the chorus' (but also 'be fooled'), as we will lead you in.
1289 **quiddle** descant/elaborate playfully.
1290 **To-nidden** perhaps a nonsensical chorus, perhaps a variant of noddy, or niddy-noddy: a fool, or, as King suggests, a corruption of the Latin *tondeo*: 'I prune or shave'.
1293 **a cow** a dupe.

JACK
Nay, by'r Lady, you are no cow, by your singing;
Yet your wife told me you were an ox.

GRIM
Did she so? 'tis a pestens quean; she is full of such mocks.
But go to, let us sing out our song merrily.

The Song at the shaving of the Collier.

JACK
Such barbers God send you at all times of need.

WILL
That can dress you so finely, and make such quick speed.

JACK
Your face like an inkhorn now shineth so gay.

WILL
That I with your nostrils of force must needs play;
With to-nidden and to-nidden.

JACK
With to-nidden and toodle, toodle do-nidden,
Is not Grim the collier most finely shaven?

WILL
With shaving you shine like a pestle of pork.

JACK
Here is the trimmest hog's flesh from London to York.

WILL
It would be trim bacon to hang up awhile.

JACK
To play with this hoglin of course I must smile,
With to-nidden and to-nidden.

WILL
With to-nidden and toodle, etc.

GRIM
Your shaving doth please me, I am now your debtor.

WILL
Your wife now will buss you, because you are sweeter.

GRIM
Near would I be polled, as near as cham shaven.

WILL
Then out of your jerkin needs must you be shaken.
With to-nidden and to-nidden, etc.

GRIM
It is a trim thing to be washed in the court.

1295 **ox** castrated bull.

1296 **pestens quean** cursed (Grim means 'pestilent') whore.

1301 **of force** necessarily (to play with his nostrils might imply leading Grim by the nose, i.e. against his will).

1305 **pestle** haunch or ham.

1308 **hoglin** little pig.

1312 **buss** kiss.

1313 **Near... shaven.** I want to have my hair cut as short/closely as I've been shaven.

1314 **jerkin** short jacket.

WILL
Their hands are so fine that they never do hurt.

GRIM
Me-think Ich am lighter than ever Ich was.

WILL
Our shaving in the court hath brought this to pass.
With to-nidden and to-nidden.

JACK
With to-nidden and toodle, toodle do-nidden,
Is not Grim the collier most finely shaven? *Finis.*

GRIM
This is trimly done; now chill pitch my coals not far hence,
And then at the tavern shall bestow whole tway pence. [*Exit.*]

JACK
Farewell, cock. Before the collier again do us seek,
Let us into the court to part the spoil, share and share [a]like.

WILL
Away then. *Exit.*

Here entereth Grim.

GRIM
Out alas, where shall I make my moan?
My pouch, my benters and all is gone.
Where is that villain that did me shave?
H'ath robbed me, alas, of all that I have.

Here entereth Snap.

SNAP
Who crieth so at the court gate?

GRIM
I, the poor collier that was robbed of late.

SNAP
Who robbed thee?

GRIM
Two of the porter's men that did shave me.

SNAP
Why, the porter's men are no barbers.

GRIM
A vengeance take them, they are quick carvers.

SNAP
What stature were they of?

GRIM
As little dapper knaves, as they trimly could scoff.

1322.1 **Finis** The end.
1323 **pitch** throw/drop off.
1324 **bestow...pence** spend two pence (on drink).
1326 **part the spoil** divide the pickings.
1328 **Out** Woe is me!
1331 **H'ath** He has.
1337 **quick carvers** swift operators.

SNAP
They are lackeys, as near as I can guess them.

GRIM
Such lackeys make me lack; an halter beswing them!
Cham undone, they have my benters too.

SNAP
Dost thou know them if thou seest them?

GRIM
Yea, that I do.

SNAP
Then come with me; we will find them out, and that quickly.

GRIM
I follow, mast' tipstaff; they be in the court, it is likely.

SNAP
Then cry no more, come away. *Exeunt.*

Here entereth Carisophus and Aristippus.

CARISOPHUS
If ever you will show your friendship, now is the time,
Seeing the king is displeased with me, of my part without any crime.

ARISTIPPUS
It should appear it comes of some evil behaviour,
That you so suddenly are cast out of favour.

CARISOPHUS
Nothing have I done but this: in talk I over-thwarted Eubulus
When he lamented Pythias' case to King Dionysius,
Which tomorrow shall die but for that false knave Damon;
He hath left his friend in the briars, and now is gone.
We grew so hot in talk, that Eubulus protested plainly,
Which held his ears open to parasitical flattery.
And now in the king's ear like a bell he rings,
Crying that flatterers have been the destroyers of kings;
Which talk in Dionysius' heart hath made so deep impression,
That he trusteth me not as heretofore in no condition.
And some words brake from him, as though that he
Began to suspect my truth and honesty,
Which you of friendship I know will defend, howsoever the world goeth.
My friend, for my honesty will you not take an oath?

ARISTIPPUS
To swear for your honesty, I should lose mine own.

CARISOPHUS
Should you so, indeed? I would that were known.
Is your void friendship come thus to pass?

1341 **an halter** a noose.
1345 **mast'** master.
1351 **over-thwarted** crossed/quarrelled with.
1354 **left . . . briars** abandoned him in trouble.
1360 **in no condition** under any circumstances.
1364 **take an oath** i.e. swear to Dionysius that Carisophus is honest.
1367 **void** empty.

ARISTIPPUS
I follow the proverb: *Amicus usque ad arras.*
CARISOPHUS
Where can you say I ever lost mine honesty?
ARISTIPPUS
You never lost it, for you never had it, as far as I know.
CARISOPHUS
Say you so, friend Aristippus, whom I trust so well?
ARISTIPPUS
Because you trust me, to you the truth I tell.
CARISOPHUS
Will you not stretch one point to bring me in favour again?
ARISTIPPUS
I love no stretching; so I may breed mine own pain.
CARISOPHUS
A friend ought to shun no pain to stand his friend in stead.
ARISTIPPUS
Where true friendship is, it is so in very deed.
CARISOPHUS
Why, sir, hath not the chain of true friendship linked us two together?
ARISTIPPUS
The chiefest link lacked thereof, it must needs dissever.
CARISOPHUS
What link is that? Fain would I know.
ARISTIPPUS
Honesty.
CARISOPHUS
Doth honesty knit the perfect knot in true friendship?
ARISTIPPUS
Yea, truly, and that knot so knit will never slip.
CARISOPHUS
Belike, then, there is no friendship but between honest men?
ARISTIPPUS
Between the honest only; for, *Amicitia inter bonos*, sayeth a learned man.
CARISOPHUS
Yet evil men use friendship in things unhonest, where fancy doth serve.
ARISTIPPUS
That is no friendship but a lewd liking; it lasts but a while.
CARISOPHUS
What is the perfectest friendship among men that ever grew?
ARISTIPPUS
Where men love one another, not for profit, but for virtue.

1368 ***Amicus ... arras*** a friend (only) as far as the altar (i.e. until the soul is threatened).
1374 **breed . . . pain** bring about my own pain (Aristippus is perhaps thinking of being stretched on the rack).
1375 **stand . . . stead** support/speak up for.
1378 **The . . . dissever.** It couldn't avoid snapping, it lacked the most important/strongest link.
1384 ***Amicitia inter bonos*** Friendship among good men.
1386 **lewd liking** dishonest affection.

CARISOPHUS

Are such friends both alike in joy and also in smart?

ARISTIPPUS

They must needs, for in two bodies they have but one heart.

CARISOPHUS

Friend Aristippus, deceive me not with sophistry;
Is there no perfect friendship, but where is virtue and honesty?

ARISTIPPUS

What a devil then meant Carisophus,
To join in friendship with fine Aristippus,
In whom is as much virtue, truth, and honesty
As there are true feathers in the Three Cranes of the Vintry?
Yet these feathers have the shadow of lively feathers, the truth to scan,
But Carisophus hath not the shadow of an honest man.
To be plain, because I know thy villainy
In abusing Dionysius to many men's injury,
Under the cloak of friendship I played with his head,
And sought means how thou with thine own fancy might be led.
My friendship thou soughtest for thine own commodity,
As worldly men do, by profit measuring amity;
Which I perceiving, to the like myself I framed,
Wherein I know of the wise I shall not be blamed.
If you ask me, '*Quare*?'
I answer, '*Quia prudentis est multum disumulare*.'
To speak more plainer, as the proverb doth go,
In faith, Carisophus, *cum Cretense cretiso*.
Yet a perfect friend I show myself to thee in one thing:
I do not dissemble now I say I will not speak for thee to the king.
Therefore sink in thy sorrow, I do not deceive thee;
A false knave I found thee, a false knave I leave thee. *Exit.*

CARISOPHUS

He is gone. Is this friendship, to leave his friend in the plain field?
Well I see now, I myself have beguiled
In matching with that false fox in amity,
Which hath me used to his own commodity;
Which, seeing me in distress, unfeignedly goes his ways.
Lo, this is the perfect friendship among men nowadays,
Which kind of friendship toward him I used secretly,
And he with me the like hath requited me craftily.
It is the gods' judgment, I see it plainly,
For all the world may know, *incidi in foveam quam feci*.

1389 **smart** pain/suffering.
1395 **In whom** i.e. in Carisophus.
1396 **the Three Cranes** was a well-known inn on the banks of the Thames.
1397 **Yet... scan** at least the feathers on the inn-sign are an image of real ones, when truly considered.
1405 **to... framed** adapted myself to the same plan.
1406 **of the wise** by wise folk.
1407 ***Quare?*** Why?
1408 ***Quia... disumulare.*** Because it is wise greatly to dissimulate.
1410 ***cum Cretense cretiso*** I play the Cretan with Cretans, i.e. to liars I lie.
1415 **plain field** open battlefield.
1424 ***incidi... feci*** I fell into the hole I dug myself.

Well, I must content myself, none other help I know,
Until a merrier gale of wind may hap to blow. *Exit.*

Enter Eubulus.

EUBULUS

Who deals with kings in matters of great weight,
When froward will doth bear the chiefest sway,
Must yield of force. There need no subtle sleight,
No painted speech the matter to convey.
No prayer can move when kindled is the ire;
The more ye quench, the more increased the fire.
This thing I prove in Pythias' woeful case,
Whose heavy hap with tears I do lament.
The day is come when he, in Damon's place,
Must lose his life; the time is fully spent.
Nought can my words now with the king prevail,
Against the wind and striving stream I sail.
For die thou must, alas, thou silly Greek.
Ah, Pythias, now come is thy doleful hour;
A perfect friend, none such a world to seek.
Though bitter death shall give thee sauce full sour,
Yet for thy faith enrolled shall be thy name
Among the gods within the book of fame.
Who knoweth his case and will not melt in tears?
His guiltless blood shall trickle down anon.

Then the Muses sing.

Alas, what hap hast thou, poor Pythias, now to die?
Woe worth the man which for his death hath given us cause to cry.

EUBULUS

Methink I hear, with yellow, rented hairs,
The Muses frame their notes my state to moan;
Among which sort, as one that mourneth with heart,
In doleful times myself will bear a part.

MUSES

Woe worth the man which for his death . . . etc.

EUBULUS

With yellow, rented hairs, come on, you Muses nine;
Fill now my breast with heavy tunes, to me your plaint resign;
For Pythias I bewail, which presently must die,
Woe worth the man which for his death hath given us cause . . . etc.

MUSES

Woe worth the man which for his . . . etc.

1428–1429 **When . . . force** When peevish/perverse will dominates things, must of necessity give up.
1434 **heavy hap** sorry situation.
1438 **striving** strongly flowing.
1439 **silly** poor/innocent.
1441 **none . . . seek** one couldn't find your like anywhere in the world.
1448 **Woe worth** Woe betides.
1449 **rented** torn (though grief).

EUBULUS

Was ever such a man that would die for his friend?
I think even from the heavens above the gods did him down send
To show true friendship's power, which forced thee now to die.
Woe worth the man which for thy death . . . etc.

MUSES

Woe worth the man . . . etc.

EUBULUS

What tiger's whelp was he that Damon did accuse?
What faith hast thou which for thy friend thy death doth not refuse?
O heavy hap hadst thou to play this tragedy!
Woe worth the man which for thy death . . . etc.

MUSES

Woe worth the man . . . etc.

EUBULUS

Thou young and worthy Greek, that showeth such perfect love,
The gods receive thy simple ghost into the heavens above.
Thy death we shall lament with many a weeping eye.
Woe worth the man, which for his death . . . etc.

MUSES

Woe worth the man, which for thy death hath given us cause to cry.

FINIS.

EUBULUS

Eternal be your fame, ye Muses, for that in misery
Ye did vouchsafe to strain your notes to walk.
My heart is rent in two with this miserable case;
Yet am I charged by Dionysius' mouth to see this place
At all points ready for the execution of Pythias.
Need hath no law, will I or nil I, it must be done,
But lo, the bloody minister is even here at hand.
Gronno, I came hither now to understand
If all things are well appointed for the execution of Pythias.
The king himself will see it done here in this place.

GRONNO

Sir, all things are ready; here is the place, here is the hand, here is the sword;
Here lacketh none but Pythias, whose head at a word,
If he were present, I could finely strike off.
You may report that all things are ready.

EUBULUS

I go with an heavy heart to report it. Ah woeful Pythias,
Full near now is thy misery. [*Exit.*]

GRONNO

I marvel very much under what constellation

1466 **heavy hap** sad chance.
1475 **Ye . . . walk.** You exerted yourselves to sing.
1478 **At all points** In each particular circumstance.
1479 **will . . . I** whether I want it or not.

All hangmen are born, for they are hated of all, beloved of none;
Which hatred is showed by this point evidently:
The hangman always dwells in the vilest place of the city.
That such spite should be, I know no cause why,
Unless it be for their office's sake, which is cruel and bloody.
Yet some men must do it to execute laws.
Methink they hate me without any just cause.
But I must look to my toil; Pythias must lose his head at one blow,
Else the boys will stone me to death in the street as I go.
But hark, the prisoner cometh, and the king also;
I see there is no help, Pythias his life must forego.

Here entereth Dionysius and Eubulus.

[DIONYSIUS]
Bring forth Pythias, that pleasant companion,
Which took me at my word and became pledge for Damon.
It pricketh fast upon noon, I do him no injury
If now he lose his head, for so he requested me
If Damon return not, which now in Greece is full merry.
Therefore shall Pythias pay his death, and that by and by.
He thought belike, if Damon were out of the city,
I would not put him to death, for some foolish pity;
But seeing it was his request, I will not be mocked: he shall die.
Bring him forth. *Here entereth Snap.*

[SNAP]
Give place; let the prisoner come by! Give place.

DIONYSIUS
How say you, sir; where is Damon, your trusty friend?
You have played a wise part, I make God a vow!
You know what time a day it is; make you ready.

PYTHIAS
Most ready I am, mighty king, and most ready also
For my true friend Damon this life to forego,
Even at your pleasure.

DIONYSIUS
A true friend? A false traitor, that so breaketh his oath!
Thou shalt lose thy life, though thou be never so loath.

PYTHIAS
I am not loath to do whatsoever I said,
Nor at this present pinch of death am I dismayed.
The gods now I know have heard my fervent prayer,
That they have reserved me to this passing great honour,
To die for my friend, whose faith even now I do not mistrust.
My friend Damon is no false traitor, he is true and just.

1495 **for . . . sake** because of their job.
1498 **look . . . toil** concentrate on my task.
1504 **pricketh fast** hurries towards.
1507 **by and by** very soon.
1508 **belike** probably/perhaps.
1511 **Give place** Make way!

But sith he is no god but a man, he must do as he may,
The wind may be contrary, sickness may let him, or some misadventure by the way.
Which the eternal gods turn all to my glory,
That fame may resound how Pythias for Damon did die.
He breaketh no oath which doth as much as he can.
His mind is here, he hath some let, he is but a man.
That he might not return, of all the gods I did require,
Which now to my joy do grant my desire.
But why do I stay any longer, seeing that one man's death
May suffice, O king, to pacify thy wrath?
O thou minister of justice, do thine office by and by,
Let not thy hand tremble, for I tremble not to die.
Stephano, the right pattern of true fidelity,
Commend me to thy master, my sweet Damon, and of him crave liberty
When I am dead, in my name; for thy trusty services
Hath well deserved a gift far better than this.
O my Damon, farewell now forever, a true friend, to me most dear;
Whiles life doth last, my mouth shall still talk of thee,
And when I am dead, my simple ghost, true witness of amity,
Shall hover about the place where so ever thou be.

DIONYSIUS

Eubulus, this gear is strange; and yet because
Damon hath falsed his faith, Pythias shall have the law.
Gronno, despoil him, and eke dispatch him quickly.

GRONNO

It shall be done. Since you came into this place,
I might have strucken off seven heads in this space.
By'r Lady, here are good garments, these are mine, by the Rood!
It is an evil wind that bloweth no man good.
Now, Pythias, kneel down, ask me blessing like a pretty boy,
And with a trice thy head from thy shoulders I will convey.

Here entereth Damon, running, and stays the sword.

[DAMON]

Stay, stay, stay! For the king's advantage, stay!
O mighty king, mine appointed time is not yet fully past;
Within the compass of mine hour, lo, here I come at last.
A life I owe; a life I will you pay.
O my Pythias, my noble pledge, my constant friend;
Ah, woe is me, for Damon's sake how near were thou to thy end!
Give place to me, this room is mine, on this stage must I play.

1528 **let** delay/hinder.
1533 **I did require** I prayed.
1539 **right pattern** perfect example.
1547 **gear** matter.
1548 **falsed** betrayed.
1549 **despoil** strip.
1551 **space** time.
1552 **these are mine** by tradition the executioner claimed the victim's outer garments as his fee.
1552 **by the Rood!** by the Holy Cross!
1556 **Stay!** Stop!
1558 **compass** limits.
1562 **Give place** Give up your place.

Damon is the man, none ought but he to Dionysius his blood to pay.

GRONNO

Are you come, sir? You might have tarried, if you had been wise,
For your hasty coming you are like to know the price.

PYTHIAS

O thou cruel minister, why didst not thou thine office?
Did I not beg thee make haste in any wise?
Hast thou spared to kill me once, that I may die twice?
Not to die for my friend is present death to me; and alas,
Shall I see my sweet Damon slain before my face?
What double death is this? But, O mighty Dionysius,
Do true justice now; weigh this aright, thou noble Eubulus;
Let me have no wrong; as now stands the case,
Damon ought not to die, but Pythias.
By misadventure, not by his will, his hour is past; therefore I,
Because he came not at his just time, ought justly to die.
So was my promise; so was thy promise, O king,
All this court can bear witness of this thing.

DAMON

Not so, O mighty king; to justice it is contrary
That for another man's fault the innocent should die.
Nor yet is my time plainly expired, it is not fully noon
Of this my day appointed, by all the clocks in the town.

PYTHIAS

Believe no clock, the hour is past by the sun.

DAMON

Ah, my Pythias, shall we now break the bonds of amity?
Will you now overthwart me, which heretofore so well did agree?

PYTHIAS

My Damon, the gods forbid but we should agree;
Therefore agree to this: let me perform the promise made for thee.
Let me die for thee; do me not that injury
Both to break my promise and to suffer me to see thee die
Whom so dearly I love. This small request grant me,
I shall never ask thee more; my desire is but friendly.
Do me this honour, that fame may report triumphantly
That Pythias for his friend Damon was contented to die.

DAMON

That you were contented for me to die, fame cannot deny;
Yet fame shall never touch me with such a villainy
To report that Damon did suffer his friend Pythias for him guiltless to die.
Therefore content thyself, the gods requite thy constant faith,

1566 **didst . . . office?** complete your job.
1567 **in any wise** in all respects.
1569 **present** instant.
1572 **weigh this aright** judge this correctly.
1575 **misadventure** accident.
1585 **overthwart** contradict.
1597 **requite** reward.

None but Damon's blood can appease Dionysius' wrath.
And now, O mighty king, to you my talk I convey;
Because you gave me leave my worldly things to stay;
To requite that good turn, ere I die, for your behalf this I say:
Although your regal state Dame Fortune decketh so,
That like a king in worldly wealth abundantly ye flow,
Yet fickle is the ground whereon all tyrants tread,
A thousand sundry cares and fears do haunt their restless head.
No trusty band, no faithful friends do guard thy hateful state,
And why? Whom men obey for deadly fear, sure them they deadly hate.
That you may safely reign, by love get friends whose constant faith
Will never fail. This counsel gives poor Damon at his death.
Friends are the surest guard for kings, gold in time does wear away,
And other precious things do fade, friendship will never decay.
Have friends in store therefore, so shall you safely sleep;
Have friends at home, of foreign foes so need you take no keep.
Abandon flatt'ring tongues, whose clacks truth never tell;
Abase the ill, advance the good, in whom dame Virtue dwells;
Let them your playfellows be. But, O, you earthly kings,
Your sure defence and strongest guard stands chiefly in faithful friends.
Then get you friends by liberal deeds; and here I make an end.
Accept this counsel, mighty king, of Damon, Pythias' friend.
O my Pythias, now farewell forever; let me kiss thee ere I die.
My soul shall honour thee, thy constant faith above the heavens shall fly.
Come, Gronno, do thine office now; why is thy colour so dead?
My neck is so short that thou wilt never have honesty in striking off this head.

DIONYSIUS

Eubulus, my spirits are suddenly appalled, my limbs wax weak;
This strange friendship amazeth me so that I can scarce speak.

PYTHIAS

O mighty king, let some pity your noble heart move;
You require but one man's death, take Pythias, let Damon live.

EUBULUS

O unspeakable friendship!

DAMON

Not so, he hath not offended, there is no cause why
My constant friend, my Pythias, for Damon's sake should die.
Alas, he is but young, he may do good to many.
Thou coward minister, why dost thou not let me die?

GRONNO

My hand with sudden fear quivereth.

PYTHIAS

O noble king, show mercy upon Damon, let Pythias die!

1599 **my talk I convey** I direct my speech.
1602 **decketh** decorates/adorns.
1604 **fickle** unstable.
1608 **get** win.
1612 **in store** in abundance.
1613 **of...keep** then you won't need to worry about foreign enemies.
1614 **clacks** chattering.
1619 **of** from.
1622 **why...dead?** why is your face so grey/pale?
1624 **appalled** paralysed.
1624 **wax** grow.
1628 **unspeakable** unbelievable.

DIONYSIUS

Stay, Gronno, my flesh trembleth. Eubulus, what shall I do?
Were there ever such friends on earth as were these two?
What heart is so cruel that would divide them asunder?
O noble friendship, I must yield; at thy force I wonder.
My heart this rare friendship hath pierced to the root,
And quenched all my fury. This sight hath brought this about,
Which thy grave counsel, Eubulus, and learned persuasion could never do.
O noble gentlemen, the immortal gods above
Hath made you play this tragedy, I think, for my behove.
Before this day I never knew what perfect friendship meant.
My cruel mind to bloody deeds was full and wholly bent;
My fearful life I thought with terror to defend.
But now I see there is no guard [like] unto a faithful friend,
Which will not spare his life at time of present need.
O happy kings, [who] within your courts have two such friends indeed!
I honour friendship now, which that you may plainly see,
Damon, have thou thy life, from death I pardon thee;
For which good turn, I crave, this honour do me lend,
O friendly heart, let me link with you, to you make me the third friend.
My court is yours; dwell here with me, by my commission large
Myself, my realm, my wealth, my health, I commit to your charge.
Make me a third friend, more shall I joy in that thing,
Than to be called, as I am, Dionysius the mighty king.

DAMON

O mighty king, first for my life most humble thanks I give;
And next I praise the immortal gods that did your heart so move
That you would have respect to friendship's heavenly lore,
Foreseeing well he need not fear which hath true friends in store.
For my part, most noble king, as a third friend, welcome to our friendly society;
But you must forget you are a king, for friendship stands in true equality.

DIONYSIUS

Unequal though I be in great possessions,
Yet full equal shall you find me in my changed conditions.
Tyranny, flattery, oppression, lo, here I cast away;
Justice, truth, love, friendship shall be my joy.
True friendship will I honour unto my life's end;
My greatest glory shall be to be counted a perfect friend.

PYTHIAS

For this your deed, most noble king, the gods advance your name.
And since to friendship's lore you list your princely heart to frame,
With joyful heart, O king, most welcome now to me,
With you will I knit the perfect knot of amity,
Wherein I shall instruct you so, and Damon here your friend,

1637 **force** strength.
1642 **behove** benefit.
1644 **bent** inclined.
1651 **good turn** in return.
1653 **commission large** complete grant.
1654 **charge** control.

That you may know of amity the mighty force, and eke the joyful end;
And how that kings do stand upon a fickle ground,
Within whose realm at time of need no faithful friends are found.

DIONYSIUS
Your instruction will I follow; to you myself I do commit.
Eubulus, make haste to fet new apparel, fit for my new friends.

EUBULUS
I go with joyful heart. O happy day! *Exit.*

GRONNO
I am glad to hear this word. Though their lives they do not lese,
It is no reason the hangman should lose his fees;
These are mine, I am gone with a trice. *Exit.*

Here entereth Eubulus with new garments.

DIONYSIUS
Put on these garments now; go in with me, the jewels of my court.

DAMON AND PYTHIAS
We go with joyful hearts.

STEPHANO
O Damon, my dear master, in all this joy remember me.

DIONYSIUS
My friend Damon, he asketh reason.

DAMON
Stephano, for thy good service be thou free.

Exeunt Dion[ysius]

STEPHANO
Most happy, pleasant, joyful, and triumphant day!
Poor Stephano now shall live in continual joy;
Vive le roi, with Damon and Pythias, in perfect amity.
Vive tu, Stephano, in thy pleasant liberality;
Wherein I joy as much as he that hath a conquest won;
I am a free man, none so merry as I now under the sun.
Farewell my lords, now the gods grant you all the sum of perfect amity,
And me long to enjoy my long-desired liberty. *Exit.*

Here entereth Eubulus beating Carisophus.

[EUBULUS]
Away, villain! Away, you flatt'ring parasite!
Away, the plague of this court! Thy filed tongue that forged lies,
No more here shall do hurt. Away, false sycophant! Wilt thou not?

CARISOPHUS
I am gone, sir, seeing it is the king's pleasure.
Why whip ye me alone? A plague take Damon and Pythias, since they came hither

1678 **fet** fetch.
1680 **lese** lose.
1682 **These** Pythias' clothes.
1682 **with a trice** in an instant.
1685 **he asketh reason** his request is reasonable.
1688 ***Vive le roi*** Long live the king!
1689 ***Vive tu*** Long live you.
1695 **filed** smooth/flattering.

I am driven to seek relief abroad, alas, I know not whither.
Yet, Eubulus, though I be gone, hereafter time shall try;
There shall be found, even in this court, as great flatterers as I.
Well, for a while I will forgo the court, though to my great pain,
I doubt not but to spy a time when I may creep in again. *Exit.*

EUBULUS

The serpent that eats men alive, flattery, with all her brood,
Is whipped away in princes' courts, which yet did never good.
What force, what mighty power true friendship may possess,
To all the world Dionysius' court now plainly doth express;
Who, since to faithful friends he gave his willing ear,
Most safely sitteth on his seat, and sleeps devoid of fear.
Purged is the court of vice since friendship entered in,
Tyranny quails, he studieth now with love each heart to win;
Virtue is had in price and hath his just reward,
And painted speech, that gloseth for gain, from gifts is quite debarred.
One loveth another now for virtue, not for gain;
Where virtue doth not knit the knot, there friendship cannot reign;
Without the which no house, no land, nor kingdom can endure,
As necessary for man's life as water, air, and fire,
Which frameth the mind of man all honest things to do.
Unhonest things friendship ne craveth, nor yet consents thereto.
In wealth a double joy, in woe a present stay,
A sweet companion in each state true friendship is alway.
A sure defence for kings, a perfect trusty band,
A force to assail, a shield to defend the enemy's cruel hand;
A rare and yet the greatest gift that god can give to man;
So rare that scarce four couple of faithful friends have been since the world began.
A gift so strange and of such price, I wish all kings to have;
But chiefly yet, as duty bindeth, I humbly crave,
True friendship and true friends, full fraught with constant faith,
The giver of all friends, the Lord grant her, most noble Queen Elizabeth.

FINIS.

THE LAST SONG

The strongest guard that kings can have,
Are constant friends their state to save.
True friends are constant, both in word and deed,
True friends are present, and help at each need;
True friends talk truly, they glose for no gain,
When treasure consumeth, true friends will remain.

1700 **try** test.
1712 **had in price** truly valued.
1713 **gloseth** flatters.
1720 **present** constant.
1723 **defend** protect against.
1728 **full fraught** fully laden
1729 Elizabeth I.
1734 **glose . . . gain** do not flatter for any gain.
1735 **When treasure consumeth** When all wealth is spent.

True friends for their true prince refuseth not their death;
The Lord grant her such friends, most noble Queen Elizabeth.

Long may she govern in honour and wealth,
Void of all sickness, in most perfect health;
Which health to prolong, as true friends require,
God grant she may have her own heart's desire;
Which friends will defend with most steadfast faith;
The Lord grant her such friends, most noble Queen Elizabeth,

FINIS.

The Three Ladies of London

(1581–1584)

ROBERT WILSON

(1540s?–1600)

THE PLAYWRIGHT

Robert Wilson's date and place of birth and the nature of his education are not known. He was probably born in the 1540s, possibly in London. The first record of a place of residence dates from 1579, when he was living in the London parish of St Botolph's without Bishopsgate. By this time he was married, although his wife's name is unknown. They had two children who died in early infancy, and a third, a daughter, Sara, born in 1586, who survived.

The first record of Wilson's career identifies him, in 1572, as an actor in the Earl of Leicester's Men. He evidently stayed with the Earl's company through the 1570s and by 1581 was also writing plays for them. His acting skills, particularly his forte for improvisational comedy, gained him a national reputation to match that of the celebrated clown, Richard Tarlton, such that his name seems to have become a byword for witty improvisation. The scholar, Gabriel Harvey, writing to Edmund Spenser in 1579, described having to speak extemporarily in public as 'play[ing] Wilson's or Tarlton's part', and as late as 1598, Francis Meres was remarking in his *Palladis Tamia*, that 'our witty Wilson... for learning and extemporal wit in his faculty is without compare or compeer'. When, in 1583, a new company, the Queen's Men, was formed, drawing its actors from the best men in all the existing troupes, Wilson's was among the first names selected, along with that of Tarlton himself.

The first of Wilson's plays to survive is *The Three Ladies of London*, probably written in 1581 for Leicester's Men (with himself in the role of the clown, Simplicity), and printed three years later. He may have written an earlier work, *Short and Sweet*, around 1579, although it isn't clear whether a contemporary allusion to 'Wilson's short and sweet' refers to a play of that name or to Wilson's writing style more generally. He certainly wrote a sequel to *The Three Ladies*, *The Three Lords and Three Ladies of London*, in 1588, and *Three Ladies* itself was reprinted in a revised edition in 1592, revealing that the earlier play was evidently popular and (because a crucial reference to time is updated in the new text (see below)), probably still being performed at this time.

In January 1586 Wilson travelled to the Netherlands to deliver letters to his old patron, the Earl of Leicester, and was rewarded for performing while he was there, but there is no further record of his acting with the Queen's Men after this, implying, perhaps, that he turned his hand to writing full time from this point on. He is named on the title page as the author of *The Cobbler's Prophecy* (1594), and may also have written the subsequent *Pedlar's Prophecy* (1595), which appeared anonymously. Each of these plays is built around an eponymous witty clown figure, so it may be that Wilson retained an aspiration to act in them, even if he was no longer formally attached to a company. He may also have been the author of an anti-Catholic prose tract, *Martin Mar-Sixtus*, published in 1591, which lists its author only as 'R. W.' Thereafter his name appears more certainly in the diary of the theatrical impresario Philip Henslowe as a collaborator in the writing of eleven now lost plays during the spring and summer of 1598, and as one of the authors of *Sir John Oldcastle* in 1599. It is plausible that his role was to provide comic scenes in these plays, while other writers concentrated on more serious material. Wilson died in November 1600 and was buried in St Giles Cripplegate, in London.

THE PLAY

From a modern perspective, *The Three Ladies of London* might appear something of an anomaly. A curious hybrid of moral interlude and city comedy, it can seem strangely old fashioned in a decade that would see the arrival of *Tamburlaine* and *The Spanish Tragedy*. But it is probably a better index of what was popular, and indeed innovative in its own way, in the Tudor theatres of the 1580s than the avant-garde experiments that were just around the corner. It is not that Wilson was ignorant of the more fashionable classical genres that were finding favour with scholarly writers such as Jasper Heywood and John Lyly. He explicitly considers—and rejects—them in the Prologue in favour of more modest, popular fare. His play will not, he says, be a hellish, Senecan tragedy like *Thyestes* ('We search not Pluto's pensive pit, nor taste of Limbo lake . . . / We speak not of the powers divine, ne yet of furious sprites [*spirits*]'), nor will it be a martial history ('We do not show of warlike fight, as sword and shield to shake') or pastoral comedy ('We do not seek high hills to climb, nor talk of love's delights. / We do not here present to you the thresher with his flail'). What he offers instead is a moral play in the mode of mid-Tudor interludes such as Ulpian Fulwell's *Like Will to Like* (1568) or George Wappul's *The Tide Tarrieth for No Man* (1576). This highly flexible form of drama combined a conventional allegorical framework, with its rise and eventual fall of personified vices, with the capacity to address sharply contemporary social issues. Hence Wilson is able to tilt at topics such as urban poverty, unemployment, overcrowded housing, vicious slum landlords, and the politics of race and immigration in the course of a play that has seeming moral abstractions such as Love, Conscience, and Simplicity (foolish innocence) among its central characters.

At the heart of *The Three Ladies* is the controversial issue of usury, the form of moneylending at exorbitant rates of interest that was both the chief motor and a baleful consequence of the burgeoning capitalist economy of Tudor London. In the early 1580s, England's capital was a rapidly expanding centre of global trade and industrial production, attracting merchants and artisans from across the known world in search of work and profit, and needing to accommodate them in a limited and often decaying housing stock. The consequences were overcrowding, profiteering, exploitation, and not infrequent violence, as class preyed on class and individual upon individual in search of either bare survival or the sizeable profits to be made from renting out property or lending money to those who lacked it. The play's principal villain is thus money itself: Lady Lucre, whose corrupting influence lies behind all the other scams and crimes represented. All the vices and virtues seek her aid or patronage, and eventually fall under her spell. The merchant Mercadore smuggles goods and borrows money, never meaning to repay it, and, along with the lawyer, Creticus, commits adultery with Lucre (symbolizing her corrupt influence over trade and the legal system); Dissimulation, Simony, and Fraud all work in her service, the first cutting the throat of Hospitality on her orders, the last persuading honest craftsmen to produce shoddy goods to exalt his name. Thus the bonds of neighbourliness and the good reputation of the City are destroyed in the savage scramble for cash. Finally Conscience and Love are thrown out of their home and forced to take it back on a short-term lease for four times the previous rent, driving them to borrow at interest from Lucre to meet the payments. As a consequence, Love is tricked into marrying Dissimulation, a union which turns her literally into a two-faced monstrosity (the actor wears a vizard or mask bearing the second face on the back of his head), while Conscience is equally literally 'spotted' on her face (the staining or corruption of conscience personified) by ink from Lucre's 'box of abominations'. The latter's influence even spreads overseas, for a number of the scenes in which Mercadore borrows from the Jewish moneylender Gerontus are set in Turkey, although little effort is made to suggest a Turkish, or even foreign, ambiance.

The play thus allegorizes the very real crimes and misdemeanours of contemporary London, giving the moral lessons on offer a very concrete and tangible sense of societal collapse and moral and physical threat. As Lloyd Kermode eloquently summarizes, 'the interplay of geography and ethnicity, morality and practicality, gender and power, class and corruption in *Three Ladies* insists that we consider carefully Wilson's combination of telling us a moral tale and showing us an embattled community' (Kermode, pp. 36–37). The final scene, however, reverts to a more obviously abstract and allegorical mode. The punishments handed out by Judge Nemo owe more to the divine justice of Doomsday than any sentence available to a Tudor assize. Simplicity (probably played by Wilson himself) is whipped around the stage, as befits his status as a menial victim of others' schemes, but Lucre is despatched 'to the lowest hell, / Where the infernal sprites and damned ghosts do dwell' (17.60–61), Love is made perpetually subject to the biting worm of conscience ('Thou shalt be dying, yet never dead, but pining still [*forever*] in endless pain'), and even Conscience, who confessed her guilt, is sent to prison to await the judgement of a higher court. The allegorical nature of these punishments, coupled with the Judge's self-defeating name ('Nemo' is Latin for 'no one'), is perhaps the final indication of the seriousness with which Wilson treats the problems created by Lucre and Usury. Only in the next world can such abuses be punished and rectified, for no one in Tudor London is capable of the task.

The character of Gerontus, the Jewish moneylender, has attracted considerable interest. In what is at times a fiercely xenophobic play (witness the vicious caricature of Mercadore, with his comic 'Italian' accent) and a generally anti-Semitic age, the Turkish Jew is represented very sympathetically. He is honest in his dealings, cannot believe that anyone would be so duplicitous as to abandon their religion for money, and ultimately releases Mercadore from the repayment of his debt rather than forcing him to undergo what he assumes will be the trauma of conversion to Islam (although Mercadore, believing in nothing but self-interest, does not actually care either way). In his complexity Gerontus looks forward to other, better-known, Jewish figures in later Tudor plays, the villainous but engaging Barabas in Marlowe's *The Jew of Malta* (1589–90) and Shylock in Shakespeare's *The Merchant of Venice* (1596–98). (Like Marlowe's Malta, Wilson's Turkey is a land where 'Jews seek to excel in Christianity and Christians in Jewishness' (14.48); like Shylock, Gerontus lends money to a Christian, and for the same sum and term, 3,000 ducats for three months.) But Wilson's play looks back as well as forward; for the portrayal of Gerontus also echoes that of the Jew Jonathas in the Croxton *Play of the Sacrament*, suggesting that there was always a more sophisticated and nuanced tradition of representing Jews in English drama than the broadly anti-Semitic portraits of the mystery plays might imply.

There are no records of performances of *The Three Ladies* prior to the printing of the 1584 quarto, and no reference to the play in the Stationers' Register that would help to date its composition, but Simony's reference to taxes paid to the Pope in Rome, and specifically to the levy known as Peter's Pence (II. l. 266–9: 'it is but lately since the Pope received this fine, / Not much more than twenty-six years, it was in Queen Mary's time'), would seem to place it about twenty-six years after the revival of Peter's Pence in the winter of 1554 (i.e. in 1581). A reference to the play in Stephen Gosson's *Play's Confuted in Five Actions* (1582) would seem to confirm that date, as would the fact that, when *Three Ladies* was revised for reprinting in 1592, 'twenty-six years' was altered to 'thirty-three'. Usury was a hot topic in 1581, having been the subject of a royal proclamation of 19 May which confirmed, in response to 'doubts and questions raised abroad [i.e. publicly]' that the terms of the Act Against Usury of 1571 still stood, limiting the rate of interest which could be legally charged to 10%.

The play is written in a mixture of irregular couplets, the fourteen-syllable lines known as fourteeners, and the occasional passage of prose. Some of the stage directions suggest that the surviving editions were based on playhouse prompt copies. A direction in scene 17, for example, indicates that the actor playing Lucre needs to perform a quick change offstage in order to return again in the role of Love ('*Let Lucre make ready for Love quickly, and come with Diligence*' (following l. 62)), which only makes sense if the writer knew roughly how many actors he had at his disposal and what their doubling pattern would be (Kermode calculates that seven actors are the minimum number required, but three of them have to be adept at playing the demanding female roles of Lucre, Love, and Conscience). Similarly in scene 16 the opening direction indicates that it is better to have two Beadles available for the scene, but that it can be made to work with only one ('*Enter Serviceable Diligence, the Constable, and Simplicity, with an Officer* [*Beadle*] *to whip him, or two, if you can.*')

The 1584 quarto, which I have used as the base text for this edition, is not divided into acts or scenes, beyond an indication of a first and second act, corresponding to scenes one and two. I have followed Kermode's edition (see below) in dividing the action into scenes, ending each when the stage clears.

FURTHER READING

Bevington, David, *Tudor Drama and Politics* (Cambridge, MA: Harvard University Press, 1968).

Jowitt, Claire, 'Robert Wilson's *The Three Ladies of London* and its Theatrical and Cultural Contexts', in Thomas Betteridge and Greg Walker, eds., *The Oxford Handbook of Tudor Drama* (Oxford: Oxford University Press, 2012), 309–22.

Kathman, David, 'Wilson, Robert (*d.* 1600)', *Oxford Dictionary of National Biography* (Oxford: Oxford University Press, 2004); <http://www.oxforddnb.com/view/article/29682>, accessed 6 June 2013.

Kermode, Lloyd Edward, ed., *Three Renaissance Usury Plays* (Manchester: Manchester University Press, 2009).

Lunney, Ruth, *Marlowe and the Popular Tradition: Innovation in English Drama before 1595* Revels Plays Companions Library (Manchester: Manchester University Press, 2002).

McMillan, Scott and Sally-Beth MacLean, *The Queen's Men and Their Plays* (Cambridge: Cambridge University Press, 1998).

A right excellent and famous Comedy called
the Three Ladies of London.
Wherein is notably declared and set forth how by the means of Lucre,
Love and Conscience is so corrupted that the one is married to Dissimulation,
the other fraught with all abomination.

A Perfect Pattern for All Estates to look into, and a work right
worthy to be marked.
Written by R.W. as it hath been publicly played.

At London, Printed by Roger Warde,
dwelling near Holbourn Conduit,
at the sign of the Talbot. 1584.

[*Dramatis Personae:*

LADY LOVE
LADY CONCIENCE
LADY LUCRE
DISSIMULATION, FRAUD, SIMONY and USURY (servants to Lady Lucre)
COGGING (servant to Disimulation)
SIMPLICITY (a miller)
MERCADORE (an Italian merchant)
ARTIFEX, an artisan
CRETICUS (a lawyer)
SINCERITY
HOSPITALITY
SIR NICHOLAS NEMO
PETER PLEASEMAN (a parson)
GERONTUS (a Jewish usurer from Turkey)
TOM BEGGAR and WILY WILL (beggars)
A JUDGE OF TURKEY
SERVICEABLE DILIGENCE (a constable)
JUDGE NEMO,
COURT CLERK,
COURT CRIER,
One or more BEADLES (officers of the court).]

is are.
marked noted.
talbot a kind of large hound used for hunting.
Lucre money.
Simony the crime of buying and selling ecclesiastical offices (the name comes from Simon Magus, who tried to buy the power of healing from Christ's Apostles, see Acts 8:9–24).
Usury lending money at (usually outrageously high) interest.
Cogging trickery.
Simplicity meaning in this context something like 'foolish innocence'.
Mercadore properly 'Mercatore': merchant.
Creticus a variant of 'the Cretan', playing on the classical proverb that said all Cretans were liars.
Nicholas Nemo Nicholas 'Nobody'.

THE PROLOGUE

To sit on honour's seat, it is a lofty reach,
To seek for praise by making brags oft-times doth get a breach.
We list not ride the rolling racks that dims the crystal skies,
We mean to set no glimmering glance before your courteous eyes.
We search not Pluto's pensive pit, nor taste of Limbo lake,
We do not show of warlike fight, as sword and shield to shake.
We speak not of the powers divine, ne yet of furious sprites,
We do not seek high hills to climb, nor talk of love's delights.
We do not here present to you the thresher with his flail,
Ne do we here present to you the milkmaid with her pail.
We show not you of country toil, as hedger with his bill,
We do not bring the husbandman to lop and top with skill.
We play not here the gardener's part, to plant, to set, and sow,
You marvel, then, what stuff we have to furnish out our show.
Your patience yet we crave a while, till we have trimmed our stall,
Then young and old come and behold our wares, and buy them all.
Then, if our wares shall seem to you well-woven, good, and fine,
We hope we shall your custom have again another time.

FINIS.

The First Act. [Scene 1]

Enter Fame, sounding before Love and Conscience.

LOVE

Lady Conscience, what shall we say to our estates? To whom shall we complain?
Or how shall we abridge such fates as heapeth up our pain?
'Tis Lucre now that rules the rout, 'tis she is all in all;
'Tis she that holds her head so stout; in fine, 'tis she that works our fall.
O Conscience, I fear, I fear a day
That we by her and Usury shall quite be cast away.

CONSCIENCE

Indeed, I fear the worst, for every man doth sue,

1 **lofty reach** high aspiration.
2 **doth . . . breach** causes contention.
3 **list . . . racks** don't desire to ride the moving banks of clouds.
4 **glimmering glance** glittering ore.
5 **Pluto's pensive pit** Hades.
5 **Limbo lake** hint of the lakes of Limbo (the region of hell reserved for the souls of those virtuous folk born before the Christian era and the unbaptized).
7 **sprites** ghosts.
11 **hedger . . . bill** the maker of hedges with his curved blade.
12 **the husbandman . . . top** the farmer to prune and cut back.
15 **trimmed** prepared.
15.1 **Finis** The end.
s.d. Because the 1584 quarto only notes the start of the first two acts, I follow Kermode's practice, dividing the play into scenes.
sounding blowing a trumpet.
1 **what . . . estates?** what shall we do about the state we are in?
2 **abridge . . . pain?** stop the processes that increase our woes.
3 **rout** crowd.
3 **all in all** all powerful.
4 **in fine . . . fall** to sum things up, it is she who causes our ruin.

And comes from countries strange and far, of her to have a view.
Although they ought to seek true Love and Conscience clear;
But Love and Conscience few do like that lean on Lucre's chair.
Men ought be ruled by us, we ought in them bear sway,
So should each neighbour live by other in good estate alway.

LOVE

For Lucre men come from Italy, Barbary, Turkey,
From Jewry; nay, the pagan himself
Endangers his body to gape for her pelf.
They forsake mother, prince, country, religion, kith, and kin,
Nay, men care not what they forsake, so Lady Lucre they win;
That we poor ladies may sigh to see our states thus turned and tossed,
And worse and worse is like to be, where Lucre rules the roost.

CONSCIENCE

You say the truth, yet God, I trust, will not admit it so,
That Love and Conscience by Lucre's lust shall catch an overthrow.

FAME

Good ladies, rest content, and you, no doubt, shall see
Them plagued with painful punishment for such their cruelty.
And if true Love and Conscience live from Lucre's lust lascivious,
Then Fame a triple crown will give, which lasteth ay victorious.

CONSCIENCE

God grant that Conscience keep within the bounds of right,
And that vile Lucre do not haunt her heart with deadly spite.

LOVE

And grant, O God, that Love be found in city, town, and country,
Which causeth wealth and peace abound, and pleaseth God Almighty.

FAME

But, ladies, is't your pleasure to walk abroad a while,
And recreate yourselves with measure, your sorrows to beguile?

CONSCIENCE

Pass on, good Fame, your steps do frame, on you we will attend,
And pray to God that holds the rod, our states for to defend.

Exeunt.

The Second Act. [Scene 2.]

Enter Dissimulation, having on a farmer's long coat and a cap, and his poll and beard painted motley.

[11] **we ... sway** we ought to be the dominant influence over them.
[12] **always** always.
[13] **Barbary** North Africa.
[14] **Jewry** Judea/Palestine.
[15] **gape ... pelf** greedily seek her riches.
[16] **kith, and kin** friends and family.
[17] **so** so long as.
[19] **rules the roost** governs everything.
[20] **admit** permit.
[21] **catch an overflow** be overthrown/ruined.
[24] **live from** keep clear of.
[25] **ay** eternally.
[30] **abroad** outside.
[31] **with measure** moderately.
[32] **Pass ... attend** Lead the way ... and we will follow.
[33] **holds the rod** has the capacity to punish.
[33.1] **poll ... motley** head/scalp ... multi-coloured.

DISSIMULATION

Nay, no less than a farmer, a right honest man,
But my tongue cannot stay me to tell what I am:
Nay, who is it that knows me not by my parti-coloured head?
They may well think that see me, my honesty is fled.
Tush, a fig for honesty! Tut, let that go,
Sith men, women, and children my name and doings do know.
My name is Dissimulation, and no base mind I bear,
For my outward effects my inward zeal do declare,
For men do dissemble with their wives, and their wives with them again,
So that in the hearts of them I always remain.
The child dissembles with his father, the sister with her brother,
The maiden with her mistress, and the young man with his lover.
There is dissimulation between neighbour and neighbour, friend and friend, one with another,
Between the servant and his master, between brother and brother.
Then, why make you it strange that ever you knew me,
Seeing so how I range throughout every degree?
But I forget my business: I'll towards London as fast I can,
To get entertainment of one of the three ladies, like an honest man.

Enter Simplicity like a miller, all mealy, with a wand in his hand.

SIMPLICITY

They say there is preferment in London to have:
Mass, and there be, I'll be passing and brave.
Why, I'll be no more a miller, because the maidens call me Dusty-poll;
One thumps me on the neck, and another strikes me on the nol,
And you see I am a handsome fellow: mark the comporknance of my stature.
Faith, I'll go seek peradventures, and be a serving-creature.

DISSIMULATION

Whither away, good fellow? I pray thee, declare.

SIMPLICITY

Marry, I'll 'clare thee: to London; would thou didst go there.

DISSIMULATION

What if I did? Would it be better for thee?

SIMPLICITY

Aye, marry should it, for I love honest company.

DISSIMULATION

Agreed, there is a bargain; but what shall I call thee?

[4] **my... fled** I've lost my honesty/public reputation.
[5] **Tush... honesty!** Pah, honesty is worthless!
[6] **Sith** Since.
[8] **effects** appearance.
[15] **why... me** why pretend you don't know me.
[16] **every degree** every social class.
[18] **entertainment of** employment from.
[18.1] **all mealy** covered in meal/flour.
wand stick.
[19] **preferment** employment/patronage.
[20] **Mass... brave.** By the mass, if there is I'll become superlative and splendid.
[22] **nol** top of the head.
[23] **comporknance** a mistake for 'comportment'.
[24] **peradventures** possibilities.
[25] **Whither away?** Where are you going?
[26] **Marry... thee** Indeed ('marry'), I'll declare to you.
[28] **Aye... it** Yes... it should.
[29] **there... bargain** we have an agreement.

SIMPLICITY
'Cause thou art an honest man, I'll tell thee: my name is Simplicity.
DISSIMULATION
A name agreeing to thy nature... but stay, here comes more company.

Enter Fraud with a sword and buckler, like a ruffian.

FRAUD
'Huff' once aloft, and I may hit in the right vein,
Where I may beguile easily without any great pain,
I will flaunt it and brave it after the lusty swash:
I'll deceive thousands. What care I who lie in the lash?
DISSIMULATION
What, Fraud? Well met! Whither travellest thou this way?
FRAUD
To London, to get entertainment there, if I may,
Of the three ladies Lucre, Love, and Conscience.
I care not whom I serve, the devil, so I may get pence.
SIMPLICITY
O Fraud! I know thee for a deceitful knave,
And art thou gotten so *baniacion* and brave?
I knew thee when thou dwellest at a place called Gravesend,
And the guests knew thee too, because thou wast not their friend;
For when thou shouldst bring reckoning to the guests,
Thou would, but twice so much, and swear it cost thy dame no less.
So thou didst deceive them and thy dame too.
And because they spied thy knavery, away thou didst go.
Then thou didst go into Hertfordshire, to a place called Ware,
And because horses stood at hay for a penny a night there,
So that thou couldst get nothing that kind of way,
Thou didst grease the horses' teeth, that they should not eat hay:
Then thou wouldst tell the rider his horse no hay would eat.
Then the man would say, 'Give him some other kind of meat'.
'Sir, shall I give him oats, vetches, peas, barley, or bread?'

30 **'cause** because.
31 **stay** wait.
31.1 **buckler** small shield.
31.1 **ruffian** a discharged soldier/street-fighter.
32–35 **'Huff'... lash?** 'Huff'/'Huffa' was a traditional cry of the 'gallant' or swaggering swordsman. Fraud's scheme is to pretend to be a swordsman to win the confidence of his intended victims: 'All I need do is cry out "Huff" and, so long as I make it sound authentic, and do it where there's no risk of really getting hurt, I'll flaunt and swagger like a swashbuckler... What do I care who I leave in debt?'
36 **Well met!** Good to see you!
39 **so** so long as.
41 ***baniacion*** meaning unclear. The 1591 edition alters the word to the equally problematic 'boniacion'. Perhaps a nonce French variant of 'ban', to summon peremptorily, or 'bon', fine/elegant, is intended (Simplicity is seeking a suitable word for Fraud's haughty manner), or more parochially, a variant of 'bone-ache', acting as if you have a venereal disease.
42 **Gravesend** a town on the south bank of the Thames east of London, a popular stopping point for travellers.
44 **reckoning** the bill. (Simplicity remembers Fraud as a waiter in an inn run by a woman ('thy dame').)
45 **but... much** but asked for double the price.
47 **spied thy knavery** saw your tricks.
48 **Ware** another town well used by travellers, about a day's journey from London on the main north road.
49 **because... there** because horses could be fed on hay for only a penny a night (i.e. too cheaply to allow for profitable scams).
51 **should not** were unable to.
53 **meat** food.
54 **vetches** beans.
54 **peas... bread** all more expensive provender than hay.

But whate'er thou gavest him, thou stolest three quarters, when he was in bed.
And now thou art so proud with thy filching and cosening art.
But I think one day thou wilt not be proud of the rope and the cart.
Take a wise fellow's counsel, Fraud, leave thy cosening and filching.

FRAUD
Thou whoreson rascal swad, avaunt! I'll bang thee for thy brawling.
How darest thou defame a gentleman that hath so large a living?

SIMPLICITY
A goodly gentleman ostler! I think none of all you will believe him.

FRAUD
What a clench-poop drudge is this. I can forbear him no more.

Let Fraud make as though he would strike him, but let Dissimulation step between them.

DISSIMULATION
My good friend Fraud, refrain, and care not therefore.
'Tis Simplicity, that patch; he knoweth not good from bad,
And to stand in contention with him, I would think you were mad.
But tell me, Fraud, tell me, hast thou been an ostler in thy days?

FRAUD
Tut, I have proved an hundred such ways;
For when I could not thrive by all other trades,
I became a squire to wait upon jades.
But then was then, and now is now. But let that pass:
I am, as thou seest me; what care I the devil what I was?

DISSIMULATION
You say you go to London? In faith, have with you then.

SIMPLICITY
Nay, come and go with me, good, honest man.
For if thou go with him, he will teach thee all his knavery.
There is none will go with him that hath any honesty...
A bots on thy motley beard! I know thee; thou art Dissimulation!
And hast thou got an honest man's coat to 'semble this fashion?
I'll tell thee what, thou wilt even 'semble and cog with thine own father.
A couple of false knaves together, a thief and a broker.
Thou makes townsfolks believe thou art an honest man: in the country
Thou dost nothing but cog, lie, and foist with Hypocrisy.
You shall be hanged together, and go alone together for me,

56 **cosening** stealing/tricking.
57 **the rope...cart** the hangman's cart and noose.
59–60 **Thou...living?** Be off with you, you rustic oaf, you villainous son of a whore. I'll beat you for this abuse. How dare you insult a gentleman of such a good income?
61 **A...ostler!** A gentleman stable-boy!
62 **clench-poop drudge** chattering foolish slave.
63 **care not therefore** don't worry/take offence at this.
64 **patch** clown.
65 **in contention** arguing.
66 **hast...days?** were you once a stable-boy?
67 **proved** made a living.
69 **jades** old, worn-out horses.
70 **let that pass** forget about that.
71 **what devil** what the devil do I care.
72 **have with you** I'll come with you.
76 **A bots on** curse (lit. a parasitical disease of animals).
77 **got** stolen.
77 **'semble** dissemble.
78 **cog** trick (lit. to cheat when dicing).
79 **broker** pimp.
81 **foist** cheat.

For if I should go, the folks would say we were knaves all three.

Enter Simony and Usury, hand in hand.

SIMONY
Friend Usury, I think we are well near at our journey's end.
But knowest thou whom I have espied?

USURY
No.

SIMONY
Fraud, our great friend.

USURY
And I see another that is now come into my remembrance.

SIMONY
Who is that?

USURY
Marry, Master Davy Dissimulation, a good helper, and our old acquaintance.

SIMPLICITY
Now all the cards in the stock are dealt about,
The four knaves in a cluster comes ruffling out.

SIMONY
What, Fraud and Dissimulation, happily found out!
I marvel what piece of work you two go about.

FRAUD
Faith, sir, we met by chance, and towards London are bent.

USURY
And to London we hie, it is our chiefest intent,
To see if we can get entertainment of the ladies or no.

DISSIMULATION
And for the selfsame matter even thither we go.

SIMONY
Then we are luckily well-met; and, seeing we wish all for one thing,
I would we our wills and wishing might win.

SIMPLICITY
Yes, they will be sure to win the devil and all,
Or else they'll make a man to spew out his gall.
O that vile Usury, he lent my father a little money, and for breaking one day
He took the fee-simple of his house and mill quite away;
And yet he borrowed not half a quarter as much as it cost.
But I think if he had had but a shilling it had been lost.
So he killed my father with sorrow, and undoed me quite.
And you deal with him, sirs, you shall find him a knave full of spite.

88 **stock…about** pack are dealt out.
89 A knave is equivalent to the modern Jack in a pack of cards.
89 **comes ruffling** come swaggering.
92 **bent** heading.
93 **we hie** we are heading/hurrying.
97 **I would…win** I hope we get what we want and wish for.
99 **spew…gall** vomit up his stomach.
100–102 **and for…cost** and (just) because he missed his repayment date by a day, he took the legal ownership…completely away, even though the loan was less than an eighth the value (of the house and mill).
103 **if…shilling** even if he had only borrowed twelve pence.
104 **undoed me quite** ruined me completely.
105 **And** If.

And Simony, *I-per-se-I* Simony, too, he is a knave for the nonce:
He loves to have twenty livings at once;
And if he let an honest man, as I am, to have one,
He'll let it so dear that he shall be undone.
And he seeks to get parsons' livings into his hand,
And puts in some odd dunce that to his payment will stand:
So, if the parsonage be worth forty or fifty pound a year,
He will give one twenty nobles to mumble service once a month there.

SIMONY AND USURY BOTH
What rascal is he that speaketh by us such villainy?

DISSIMULATION
Sirs, he was at us erewhile too. It is no matter, it is a simple soul called Simplicity.

Enter Love and Conscience.

But here come two of the ladies; therefore make ready.

FRAUD
But which of us all shall first break the matter?

DISSIMULATION
Marry, let Simony do it, for he finely can flatter.

USURY
Nay, sirs, because none of us shall have pre-eminence above other,
We will sing in fellowship together, like brother and brother.

SIMONY
Of truth, agreed, my masters: let it be so.

SIMPLICITY
Nay, and they sing, I'll sing too.

THE SONG

[ALL THE MEN]
Good ladies, take pity and grant our desire.

CONSCIENCE'S REPLY
Speak boldly, and tell me what is't you require.

THEIR REPLY
Your service, good ladies, is what we do crave.

HER REPLY
We like not, nor list not, such servants to have.

THEIR REPLY
If you entertain us, we trusty will be;

106 **Simony...Simony** Simony, in himself/Simony is unique. From '*a per se a*', the letter 'a' on its own.
106 **for the nonce** fit for the purpose.
107 **livings** ecclesiastical positions/incomes.
109 **let...undone** rent it out so expensively that the renter will be ruined.
110–113 **he seeks...there** he buys up the right to appoint the vicar to as many churches as he can, then appoints an uneducated man who will do the job poorly (mumble his way through the service) for a pittance, so, if the living is worth £40/£50 annually, he will pay him only 20 nobles (a coin worth one third of a pound sterling) and keep the rest himself.
114 **by us** about us.
115 **erewhile** just now.
117 **break the matter** broach the subject.

But if you refrain us, then most unhappy.
We will come, we will run, we will bend at your beck,
We will ply, we will hie, for fear of your check.

HER REPLY

You do feign, you do flatter, you do lie, you do prate;
You will steal, you will rob, you will kill in your hate.
I deny you, I defy you, then cease of your talking,
I refrain you, I disdain you; therefore, get you walking.

CONSCIENCE

What, Fraud, Dissimulation, Usury, and Simony,
How dare you for shame presume so boldly
As once to show yourselves before Love and Conscience,
Not yielding your lewd lives first to repentance?
Think you not that God will plague you for your wicked practices,
If you intend not to amend your vile lives so amiss?
Think you not God knows your thoughts, words, and works,
And what secret mischiefs in the hearts of you lurks?
Then how dare you offend his heavenly majesty
With your dissembling deceit, your flattery, and your usury?

FRAUD

Tut, sirs, seeing Lady Conscience is so scrupulous,
Let us not speak to her, for I see it is frivolous.
But what say you, Lady Love; will you grant us favour?

LOVE

I'll no such servants, so ill of behaviour,
Servants more fitter for Lucre than Love,
And happy are they which refrain for to prove
Shameless, pitiless, graceless, and quite past honesty;
Then who of good conscience but will hate your company?

USURY

Here is scrupulous Conscience and nice Love indeed.
Tush! If they will not, others will; I know we shall speed.

SIMPLICITY

But, lady, I stand still behind, for I am none of their company.

CONSCIENCE

Why, what art thou? O, I know: thou art Simplicity.

SIMPLICITY

I'faith, I am Simplicity, and would fain serve ye.

CONSCIENCE

No, I may have no fools to dwell with me.

SIMPLICITY

Why then, Lady Love, will you have me then?

LOVE

Aye, Simplicity, thou shalt be my man.

128 **refrain** reject.
130 **check** criticism.
131 **prate** speak nonsense.
150 **refrain...prove** prevent themselves becoming.
154 **Tush!** Pah!
154 **speed** prosper.
155 **I...company** I am not one of their gang.
157 **would fain** would be pleased to.

SIMPLICITY
But shall I be your goodman

LOVE
Aye, my good man, indeed.

SIMPLICITY
Aye, but I would be your goodman, and swap up a wedding with good speed.

LOVE
No, Love may not marry in any case with Simplicity.
But if thou wilt serve me, I'll receive it willingly.
And if thou wilt not, what remedy?

SIMPLICITY
Yes, I will serve ye; but will ye go into dinner, for I am hungry?

LOVE
Come, Lady Conscience, pleaseth you to walk home from this company?

CONSCIENCE
With right good will, for their sights pleaseth not me.

Exeunt Lady Love and Conscience.

SIMPLICITY
Fraud is the clubbish knave, and Usury the hard-hearted knave,
And Simony the diamond-dainty knave,
And Dissimulation the spiteful knave of spade.
Come there any mo knaves? Come there any mo?
I see four knaves stand in a row.

Let Fraud run at him, and let Simplicity run in, and come out again straight.

FRAUD
Away, drudge! Be gone quickly.

SIMPLICITY
I wous, do thrust out my eyes with a lady.

Exit Simplicity.

USURY
Did you ever see gentlemen so rated at before?
But it skills not, I hope one day to turn them both out of door.

SIMONY
We were arrantly flouted, railed at, and scoffed in our kind.

161 **goodman** husband.
162 **swap up** arrange.
165 **what remedy?** what can we do?
169–171 Simplicity continues the playing cards simile, punning on each suit in turn: **clubbish**: rough and violent, **diamond-dainty**: perhaps meanly fastidious.
172 **mo** more.
Simplicity...straight Simplicity runs offstage and then runs back onstage immediately.
175 **I...lady.** Meaning uncertain. Kermode suggests **I wous** might be a version of the archaic, **iwis**: 'certainly'. The text may be corrupt, but the context implies that Simplicity, having been chased off by Fraud, is either being emphatic ('You bet I'll run away, poke out my eyes and call me a woman if I don't') or trying to be insulting ('I'll run, rather than have my eyes poked out by a woman like you').
176 **rated at** insulted.
177 **skills not** doesn't matter.
178 **arrantly...kind** grossly insulted...for our characters.

That same Conscience is a vile terror to man's mind.
Yet, faith, I care not, for I have borne many more than these
When I was conversant with the clergy beyond the seas.
And he that will live in this world must not care what such say,
For they are blossoms blown down, not to be found after May.

FRAUD

Faith, care that care will, for I care not a point.
I have shift it hitherto, and whilst I live I will jeopard a joint;
And at my death I will leave my inheritor behind
That shall be of the right stamp to follow my mind.
Therefore, let them prate till their hearts ache, and spit out their evil:
She cannot quail me, if she came in likeness of the great devil.

DISSIMULATION

Mass, Fraud, thou hast a doughty heart to make a hangman off,
For thou hast good skill to help men from the coff.
But we were arrantly flouted, yet I thought she had not known me;
But I perceive, though Dissimulation do disguise him, Conscience can see.
What though Conscience perceive it, all the world cannot beside,
Tush, there be a thousand places where we ourselves may provide.
But look, sirs, here cometh a lusty lady towards us in haste;
But speak to her, if you will, that we may be all placed.

Enter Lady Lucre.

USURY

I pray thee do, for thou art the likeliest to speed.

DISSIMULATION

Why then, I'll to it with a stomach in hope of good speed.
Fair lady, all the gods of good fellowship kiss ye (I would say 'bless ye'!)

LUCRE

Thou art very pleasant, and full of thy rope-ripe (I would say 'rhetoric'.)

DISSIMULATION

Lady, you took me at the worst: I beseech you therefore
To pardon my boldness, offending no more.

LUCRE

We do; the matter is not great. But what wouldest thou have?
How shall I call thee, and what is't thou dost crave?

[183] **blossoms blown down** short-lived phenomena, like blossom in May.

[184] **I ... point** I don't care a thing (a point is literally a lace used to tie hose up).

[185] **shift it** I've provided for myself ('shifted it') thus far in my life.

[185] **jeopard a joint** risk a limb (or two).

[187] **of ... mind** someone of the same mind who'll carry on my work.

[189] **quail ... if** frighten me, even if.

[190] **to make ... off** to see off the hangman.

[191] **coff** can mean bribe, and 'corf' a basket or cage, so the point may be either ironic: the only way Fraud could really see off the hangman is by bribing him, as he's skilled in that (i.e. he isn't really as doughty/brave as he claims), or, more supportively, that he has the skill to free all the hangman's prisoners from their cage.

[194] **What though** But what if.

[194] **all ... beside** no one else is able to.

[195] **may provide** can make a living.

[199] **to ... speed** set to it with relish, in hope of success.

[200] **I would say** I should have said (Dissimulation corrects his slip of the tongue.)

[201] Lucre responds with a double-entendre, **rope-ripe** meaning both bombastic in speech and ready for hanging.

[202] **you ... worst** you took advantage of me/ deliberately chose the worst of my meanings.

DISSIMULATION

I am called Dissimulation, and my earnest request
Is to crave entertainment for me and the rest,
Whose names are Fraud, Usury, and Simony,
Great carers for your health, wealth, and prosperity.

LUCRE

Fraud, Dissimulation, Usury, and Simony,
Now truly I thank you for proffering your service to me.
You are all heartily welcome, and I will appoint straightway,
Where each one in his office in great honour shall stay.
But, Usury, didst thou never know my grandmother, the old Lady Lucre of Venice?

USURY

Yes, madam, I was servant unto her, and lived there in bliss.

LUCRE

But why camest thou into England, seeing Venice is a city
Where Usury by Lucre may live in great glory?

USURY

I have often heard your good grandmother tell
That she had in England a daughter, which her far did excel;
And that England was such a place for Lucre to bide,
As was not in Europe and the whole world beside.
Then, lusting greatly to see you and the country, she being dead,
I made haste to come over to serve you in her stead.

LUCRE

Gramercy, Usury; and I doubt not but that you shall live here as pleasantly;
Aye, and pleasanter, too, if it may be. But, Simony, from whence came ye, tell me?

SIMONY

My birth, nursery, and bringing-up hitherto hath been in Rome, that ancient religious city.
On a time the monks and friars made a banquet, whereunto they invited me,
With certain other some English merchants, which belike were of their familiarity;
So, talking of many matters, amongst others one began to debate
Of the abundant substance still brought to that state.
Some said the increase of their substance and wealth
Came from other princes, and was brought thither by stealth.
But the friars and monks, with all the ancient company,
Said that it first came and is now upholden by me, Simony;
Which the English merchants gave ear to. Then they flattered a little too much,
As Englishmen can do for advantage, when increase it doth touch;
And being a-shipboard merry, and overcome with drink on a day,
The wind served, they hoist sail, and so brought me away;
And landing here, I heard in what great estimation you were,
Made bold to your honour to make my repair.

221 **in . . . beside** a better place than any other in Europe, or indeed the world.
224 **Gramercy** Many thanks (from the French, '*grand merci*').
227 **On a time** once.
228 **which . . . familiarity** who they probably knew.
230 **substance** wealth.
236 **when . . . touch** when it concerns profit.
238 **served** was blowing in the right direction.
239 **estimation** reputation.
240 **Made . . . repair** Was bold enough to come to you.

LUCRE
Well, Simony, I thank thee. But as for Fraud and Dissimulation,
I know their long continuance, and after what fashion.
Therefore, Dissimulation, you shall be my steward,
An office that every man's case by you must be preferred.
And you, Fraud, shall be my rent-gatherer, my letter of leases, and my purchaser of land,
So that many old bribes will come to thy hand.
And, Usury, because I know you be trusty, you shall be my secretary,
To deal amongst merchants, to bargain and exchange money.
And Simony, because you are a sly fellow, and have your tongue liberal,
I will place you over such matters as are ecclesiastical.
And though we appoint sundry offices, where now ye are in,
Yet jointly we mean to use you together oft-times in one thing.

ALL
Lady, we rest at your command in ought we can or may.

LUCRE
Then, Master Davy, to my palace haste thee away,
And will Crafty Conveyance, my butler, to make ready
The best fare in the house to welcome thee and thy company.
But stay, Dissimulation, I myself will go with thee.
Gentlemen, I'll go before; but pray, in any case,
So soon as ye please resort to my place.

Exeunt Dissimulation and Lucre.

SIMONY
I warrant you, lady, we will not long absent be.

USURY
Fellow Simony, this fell out pat, so well as heart could wish.
We are cunning anglers; we have caught the fattest fish.
I perceive it is true that her grandmother told,
Here is good to be done by use of silver and gold.
And sith I am so well settled in this country,
I will pinch all, rich and poor, that come to me.

SIMONY
And sirrah, when I was at Rome, and dwelt in the friary,
They would talk how England yearly sent over a great mass of money,
And that this little island was more worth to the Pope
Than three bigger realms which had a great deal more scope.

242 **I...fashion** I know their histories, and the manner of their lives.
244 **every...preferred** everyone who has a suit to me will have to come through you (giving ample opportunity for bribes).
249 **have...liberal** are a great gossip.
251–252 **though...thing** although you each have your separate jobs, I'll also use you together on many occasions.
254 **Master Davy** Dissimulation.
255 **will Crafty Conveyance** tell Sly-dealing.
257 **stay** wait.
261 **fell out pat** worked perfectly.
266 **pinch all** squeeze everyone.
267 **sirrah** a variant of 'sir', used usually with servants and inferiors.
270 **had...scope** were geographically larger.

For here were smoke-pence, Peter-pence, and Paul-pence to be paid,
Besides much other money that to the Pope's use was made.
Why, it is but lately since the Pope received this fine,
Not much more than twenty-six years, it was in Queen Mary's time.
But I think England had never known what this gear had meant,
If Friar Austin from the Pope had not hither been sent;
For the Pope, hearing it to be a little island, sent him with a great army over,
And winning the victory, he landed about Rye, Sandwich, or Dover.
Then he erected laws, having the people in subjection,
So for the most part, England hath paid tribute so long.
I, hearing of the great store and wealth in the country,
Could not choose but persuade myself the people loved Simony.

USURY

But stay your talk till some other time; we forget my lady.

SIMONY

Of troth you say true, for she bad us make haste;
But my talk, methought, savoured well, and had a good taste.

Exeunt ambo.

[Scene 3.]

Enter Mercadore, like an Italian Merchant.

MERCADORE

I judge in my mind-a dat me be not vary far
From da place where dwells my Lady Lucre.
But here come an shentlymane-a, so he do.

Enter Dissimulation.

Shentleman, I pray you heartily, let me speak you.
Pray you, do you not know a shentleman dat Master Davy do call?

DISSIMULATION

Yes, marry, do I. I am he, and what would you withal?

MERCADORE

Good-a my friend Master Davy, help me, pray you heartily,
For a some-a acquaintance-a with Madonna Lucre, your lady.

271 **smoke-pence...Paul-pence** colloquial terms for ecclesiastical taxes. Smoke-pence or smoke-money was a levy of one penny per person in a parish paid to the vicar; Peter's Pence another levy, gathered on 1 August each year (the feast day of St Peter ad Vincula) for the upkeep of the Papacy (the See of St Peter). Paul-pence may be Simony's invention to match Peter-pence, but Kermode suggests it is a pun on poll tax, another tax levied per 'poll' or head.

273 **fine** levy.

274 Henry VIII's government abolished all these taxes paid to Rome in the 1530s, but they were briefly restored in the reign of Mary I (1554–9), before Elizabeth I's administration ended them again.

275 **gear had meant** business involved.

276 **Friar Austin** St Augustine of Canterbury, who led the mission from Rome which converted England in 597AD.

278 **Rye, Sandwich, or Dover** ports in Kent.

280 **tribute** a tax paid to an overlord or conqueror.

291 **bad us** instructed us to.

280.1 ***Exeunt ambo.*** (They) leave together.

1 The quarto represents Mercadore's 'Italian' accent phonetically, hence many words end with an additional 'a'.

1 **vary** very.

3 **an shentlymane-a** a gentleman.

5 **dat ...call** i.e. who is called.

6 **what...withal?** what do you want?

8 **Madonna** Madam (Italian).

[DISSIMULATION]
Sir, upon condition I will, therefore I would you should know
That on me and my fellows you must largely bestow,
Whose names are Fraud, Usury, and Simony, men of great credit and calling,
And to get my lady's goodwill and theirs it is no small thing.
But tell me, can you be content to win Lucre by Dissimulation?

MERCADORE
Ah, good-a my friend, do axe-a me no shush a question,
For he dat will live in the world must be of the world sure;
And de world will love his own, so long as the world endure.

DISSIMULATION
I commend your wit, sir; but here comes my lady.

Enter Lucre.

MERCADORE
Come hither; here's two, tree crowns for de speak me.

DISSIMULATION
Well, sir, I thank you. I will go speak for you.

LUCRE
Master Davy Dissimulation, what new acquaintance have ye gotten there?

DISSIMULATION
Such a one, madam, that unto your state hath great care;
And surely in my mind the gentleman is worthy
To be well-thought on for his liberality, bounty, and great care to seek ye.

LUCRE
Gentleman, you are heartily welcome. How are you called, I pray you tell us?

MERCADORE
Madonna, me be a mershant, and be called Signor Mercadore.

LUCRE
But, I pray you, tell me what countryman?

MERCADORE
Me be, Madonna, an Italian.

LUCRE
Yet let me trouble ye; I beseech ye whence came ye?

MERCADORE
For *salva vostra buona grazia*, me come from Turkey.

LUCRE
Gramercy; but Signor Mercadore, dare you not to undertake
Secretly to convey good commodities out of this country for my sake?

MERCADORE
Madonna, me do for love of you tink no pain too mush,
And to do anyting for you me will not grush:
Me will-a forsake-a my fader, moder, king, country, and more dan dat;

10 **you . . . bestow** you must give (bribes) generously to.
14 **axe-a . . . shush** ask me no such (i.e. there's no need to ask me).
18 **tree . . . me** three crowns (gold coins) to speak for (recommend) me.
29 ***salva . . . grazia*** saving your good grace (Italian).
31 **Secretly . . . commodities** are you willing to smuggle goods.
32 **tink** think.
33 **grush** grudge.

Me will lie and forswear meself for a quarter so much as my hat.
What is dat for love of Lucre me dare or will not do?
Me care not for all the world, the great devil, nay, make my God angry for you.

LUCRE

You say well, Mercadore; yet Lucre by this is not thoroughly won.
But give ear, and I will show what by thee must be done.
Thou must carry over wheat, peas, barley, oats, and vetches, and all kind of grain,
Which is well sold beyond sea, and bring such merchants great gain.
Then thou must carry beside leather, tallow, beef, bacon, bell-metal, and everything,
And for these good commodities trifles into England thou must bring;
As bugles to make bables, coloured bones, glass beads to make bracelets withal,
For every day gentlewomen of England do ask for such trifles from stall to stall.
And you must bring more, as amber, jet, coral, crystal, and every such bauble
That is slight, pretty, and pleasant: they care not to have it profitable.
And if they demand wherefore your wares and merchandise agree,
You must say jet will take up a straw, amber will make one fat,
Coral will look pale when you be sick, and crystal staunch blood.
So with lying, flattering, and glosing you must utter your ware,
And you shall win me to your will, if you can deceitfully swear.

MERCADORE

Tink ye not dat me have carried over corn, leader, beef and bacon too, all tis while?
And brought heder many babbles dese countrymen to beguile?
Yes, shall me tell you, Madonna, I, me and my countrymans, have sent over
Bell-metal for make ordnance, yea, and ordnance itself beside,
Dat my country and oder countries be so well furnish as dis country, and has never been spied.

LUCRE

Now I perceive you love me, and if you continue in this still;
You shall not only be with me, but command me when and where you will.

MERCADORE

Lady, for to do all dis and more for you me be content;
But I tink some skall knave will put a bill in da Parliament
For dat such-a tings shall not be brought here.

38 **thoroughly won** completely persuaded.
40 **carry over** take overseas.
42 **leather ... everything** all of these commodities were subject to export tax, and so prone to smuggling. A similar list of goods appears in Nicholas Udall's *Respublica*, III, 6.
44 **bables** coloured beads to make toys and decorations for clothing.
46 **as** (things such) as.
47 **slight** small.
47 **they ... profitable** the women buy only worthless pretty stuff, they don't care about the inherent value of things.
48 **wherefore ... agree** what these things are good for.
49–50 **jet ... blood** when rubbed, jet will attract light objects such as straws: a trivial purpose. The others seem to play into popular superstitions: perhaps amber will aid one to become pregnant, coral will act as a warning of sickness, and crystal prevent blood-loss (Kermode notes that it was actually thought to prevent stomach problems).
51 **glosing** false interpretation.
51 **utter** sell.
53 **leader** leather.
53 **tis** this.
56 **make ordnance** for making cannons.
56–57 **beside ... spied** as well, so that mine and other countries are secretly as well supplied with cannon (as England). Probably intended as the most treacherous form of smuggling, endangering national security.
59 **command me** have me at your service.
61 **skall knave** scald/scurvy villain.

LUCRE

Tush, Mercadore, I warrant thee, thou needest not to fear.
What and one do? There is some other will flatter, and say
They do no hurt to the country, and with a sleight fetch that bill away.
And if they do not, so that by Act of Parliament it be passed,
I know you merchants have many a sleight and subtle cast,
So that you will by stealth bring over great store,
And say it was in the realm a long time before.
For being so many of these trifles here, as there are at this day,
You may increase them at pleasure, when you send over sea;
And do but give the searcher an odd bribe in his hand,
I warrant you, he will let you 'scape roundly with such things in and out the land.
But, Signor Mercadore, I pray you walk in with me,
And as I find you kind to me, so will I favour ye.

MERCADORE

Me tank you, my good lady. But, Master Dissimulation, here is for your fellows, Fraud, Usury, and Simony, and say me give it dem.

Exeunt Lucre and Mercadore.

DISSIMULATION

Aye, marry, sir, these bribes have (welcome) been.
Good faith, I perceive, Dissimulation, Fraud, Usury, and Simony shall live,
In spite of Love and Conscience, though their hearts it doth grieve.
Mass, masters, he that cannot lie, cog, dissemble, and flatter nowadays,
Is not worthy to live in the world, nor in the court to have praise.

Enter Artifex, an Artificer.

ARTIFEX

I beseech you, good Master Dissimulation, befriend a poor man
To serve Lady Lucre; and sure, sir, I'll consider it hereafter, if I can.

DISSIMULATION

What, consider me? Dost thou think that I am a bribe-taker?
Faith, it lies not in me to further thy matter.

ARTIFEX

Good Master Dissimulation, help me; I am almost quite undone.
But yet my living hitherto with Conscience I have won;
But my true working, my early rising, and my late going to bed
Is scant able to find myself, wife, and children dry bread.
For there be such a sort of strangers in this country
That work fine to please the eye, though it be deceitfully;
And that which is slight, and seems to the eye well,
Shall sooner than a piece of good work be proffered to sell.

63 **warrant** promise.
64 **What and one do?** What if someone does?
67 **sleight . . . cast** scheme and cunning ploy.
72 **searcher** customs officer.
73 **'scape roundly** get away completely.
78 Added from the 1592 quarto.
79 **live** prosper.
84 **consider it** remember it (and reward you).
86 **further thy matter** aid your suit.
91 **strangers** foreign (craftsmen).
92 **work . . . deceitfully** produce attractive-looking goods, which are actually no good.

And our Englishmen be grown so foolish and nice,
That they will not give a penny above the ordinary price.

DISSIMULATION
Faith, I cannot help thee; 'tis my fellow Fraud must pleasure thee.
Here comes my fellow Fraud, speak to him, and I'll do what I can.

Enter Fraud.

ARTIFEX
I beseech you be good unto me, right honest gentleman.

FRAUD
Why and whereto? What wouldest thou have me do?

ARTIFEX
That my poor estate you will so much prefer
As to get me to be a workman to Lady Lucre.
And, sir, I doubt not but to please you so well for your pain
That you shall think very well of me, if I in her service remain.

DISSIMULATION
Good fellow Fraud, do so much; for I see he is very willing to live,
And some piece of work to thee for thy pains he will give.

FRAUD
Well, upon that condition I will; but I care not so much for his gifts
As that he will by my name declare how he came by his great thrifts,
And that he will set out in every kind of thing
That Fraud is a good husband, and great profit doth bring.
Therefore the next piece of work that thou dost make,
Let me see how deceitful thou wilt do it for my sake.

ARTIFEX
Yes, I will, sir; of that be you sure:
I'll honour your name, while life doth endure.

DISSIMULATION
Fellow Fraud, here comes a citizen, as I deem.

FRAUD
Nay, rather a lawyer, or some pettifogger he doth seem.

Enter a Lawyer [*Creticus*].

LAWYER
Gentlemen, my earnest suit is to desire ye
That unto your lady's service you would help me,
For I am an attorney of the law, and pleader at the bar,
And have a great desire to plead for Lady Lucre.
I have been earnest, sir, as is needful in such a case,
For fear another come before me and obtain my place.
I have pleaded for Love and Conscience till I was weary;

95 **nice** silly.
103 **please** reward.
108 **he... thrifts** he tells everyone how it was Fraud that allowed him to save money.
110 **a good husband** a thrifty worker (i.e. Artifex must debase his trade by persuading others that it is sound economics to make shoddy goods).
115 **deem** judge.
116 **pettifogger** dodgy lawyer.
119 **pleader... bar** barrister/lawyer.

I had many clients, and many matters that made my purse light and my heart heavy.
Therefore let them plead for Conscience that list, for me,
I'll plead no more for such as brings nothing but beggary.

DISSIMULATION
Sir, upon this condition, that you will keep men in the law
Ten or twelve years for matters that are not worth a straw,
And that you will make an ill matter seem good and firmable indeed,
Faith, I am content for my part you shall speed.

FRAUD
Nay, fellow, thou knowest that Simony and Usury hath an ill-matter in law at this time;
Now, if thou canst handle the matter so subtle and fine
As to plead that ill-matter good and firmable at the bar,
Then thou shalt show thyself worthy to win Lady Lucre.
Therefore tell me if you can or will do it or no.
If you do it, be sure to get my lady's goodwill, ere you go.

DISSIMULATION
By my honesty, well-remembered, I had quite forgot;
'Tis about that a fortnight ago fell out, the matter I wot.

LAWYER
Tush, sir, I can make black white, and white black again.
Tut, he that will be a lawyer must have a thousand ways to feign;
And many times we lawyers do one befriend another,
And let good matters slip. Tut, we agree like brother and brother.
Why, sir, what shall let us to wrest and turn the law as we list,
Seeing we have them printed in the palms of our fist?
Therefore doubt you not, but make bold report
That I came and will plead their ill-cause in good kind of sort.

FRAUD
Of troth, how likest thou this fellow, Dissimulation?

DISSIMULATION
Marry, I like him well. He is a cunning clerk, and one of our profession.
But come, sir, go with us, and we will prefer you.

ARTIFEX
Good Master Fraud, remember me.

FRAUD
Leave thy prating; I will, I tell thee.

ARTIFEX
Good Master Dissimulation, think on me.

DISSIMULATION
Thou art too importunate and greedy.

FRAUD
Come after dinner, or some other time, when we are at leisure.

Dissim[*ulation*], *Fraud, and Lawyer exeunt.*

125 **that list** who want to.
127 **keep...law** tie up suitors in legal cases.
129 **firmable** able to be confirmed in law.
138 **'Tis...wot** It started about two weeks ago, I know the case.
142 **let...slip** let sound cases get lost.
143 **what...wrest** what shall prevent us from twisting.

ARTIFEX

Come after dinner, or some other time? I think so indeed,
For full little do they think of a poor man's need.
These fellows will do nothing for pity and love,
And thrice happy are they that hath no need them to prove.
God, he knows the world is grown to such a stay
That men must use Fraud and Dissimulation too, or beg by the way.
Therefore I'll do as the most doth; the fewest shall laugh me to scorn,
And be a fellow amongst good fellows to hold, by St Luke's horn! *Exit.*

[Scene 4]

Enter Simplicity and Sincerity.

SINCERITY

Good Cousin Simplicity, do somewhat for me.

SIMPLICITY

Yes, faith, Cousin Sincerity, I'll do anything for thee.
What wouldst for me to do for thee, canst tell that?
Mass, I cannot tell what shouldst do for me, except thou wouldst give
me a new hat.

SINCERITY

Alas! I am not able to give thee a new.

SIMPLICITY

Why, I marvel then how thou dost do:
Dost thou get thy living amongst beggars, from door to door?
Indeed, Cousin Sincerity, I had thought thou wast not so poor.

SINCERITY

Nay, Cousin Simplicity, I got my living hardly, but yet I hope just,
And with good conscience too, although I am restrained from my lust.
But this is it, Cousin Simplicity, I would request you to do for me,
Which is to get Lady Love and Lady Conscience's hand to a letter,
That by their means I may get some benefice, to make me live the better.

SIMPLICITY

Yes, I'll do so much for thee, cousin; but hast thou any here?

SINCERITY

Aye, behold, they are ready-drawn, if assigned they were.

Let Simplicity make as though he read it, and look quite over; meanwhile let Conscience enter.

158 **no...prove** no need to put them to the test.
159 **stay** state.
160 **the way** the roadside.
161–162 **Therefore...horn!** So I'll follow the majority, fewer will laugh at me that way, and I'll throw in my lot with the rogues, by St Luke's horn! (A mild oath, reflecting Luke 1:68–9: 'Blessed be the Lord God of Israel; because he hath visited and wrought the redemption of his people: and hath raised up an horn of salvation to us, in the house of David his servant'.)

3 **What...me** what do you want me.
9 **hardly** through hard labour.
9 **just** justly/honestly.
10 **am...lust** don't always get what I want.
12 **get...letter** to sign a letter for me.
13 **benefice** ecclesiastical post.
14 **any** any such letter(s).
15.1 **make...over** i.e. he pretends to read it, although he obviously cannot.

SIMPLICITY
Let me see, cousin, for I can read.
Mass, 'tis bravely done; didst thou it indeed?
Mistress Conscience, I have a matter to bequest you to.

CONSCIENCE
What is't? I doubt not but 'tis some wise thing, if it be for you.

SIMPLICITY
Marry, my cousin Sincerity wad besire to scribe these papers here,
That he may get some preferment, but I know not where.

CONSCIENCE
Be these your letters? What would you have me do, and how shall I call ye?

SINCERITY
Lady, my name is Sincerity.

CONSCIENCE
And from whence come ye?

SINCERITY
I came from Oxford, but in Cambridge I studied late;
Having nothing, thought good if I could to make better my state;
But if I had, instead of divinity, the law, astronomy, astrology,
Physiognomy, palmestry, arithmetic, logic, music, physic, or any such thing,
I had not doubted, then, but to have had some better living.
But divines that preach the word of God sincerely and truly
Are in these days little or nothing at all set by.
God grant the good preachers be not taken away for our unthankfulness!
There never was more preaching and less following, the people live so amiss.
But what is he that may not on the Sabbath-day attend to hear God's word,
But he will rather run to bowls, sit at the alehouse, than one hour afford,
Telling a tale of Robin Hood, sitting at cards, playing at kettles, or some other vain thing,
That I fear God's vengeance on our heads it will bring.
God grant amendment! But, Lady Conscience, I pray,
In my behalf unto Lucre do what ye may.

SIMPLICITY
Mass, my cousin can say his book well; I had not thought it.
He's worthy to have a benefice, and it will hit.

CONSCIENCE
God be blessed, Sincerity, for the good comfort I have of thee.
I would it lay in us to pleasure such, believe me.
We will do what we can; but *ultra posse non est esse*, you know:
It is Lucre that hath brought us poor souls so low.
For we have sold our house, we are brought so poor,
And fear by her shortly to be shut out of door.

17 **bravely** elegantly.
18 **bequest** mistake for 'request'.
20 **wad . . . scribe** mistake for 'would desire you to inscribe'.
24 **late** most recently.
27 **physic** medicine.
30 **set by** respected.
35 **kettles** skittles.
39 **can . . . well** learn his part/reveal his learning.
40 **and . . . hit** if he can get one.
42 **I would . . . such** I wish it was in our power to give people such as you what you want.
43 ***ultra . . . esse*** we cannot do more than we are able.

Yet to subscribe our name we will with all our heart.
Perchance for our sakes something she will impart.
Come hither, Simplicity; let me write on thy back.

SIMPLICITY
Here is the right picture of that fellow that sits in the corner.

Enter Hospitality, while she is writing.

HOSPITALITY
Lady, methinks you are busy.

CONSCIENCE
I have done, sir. I was setting my hand to a letter to Lucre for our friend Sincerity.
But I would Lady Love were here too.

HOSPITALITY
She is at home with me; but, if it please, so much in her behalf I will do.

CONSCIENCE
I pray you heartily, and it shall suffice the turn well enou'.
Good Simplicity, once more thy body do bow.

SIMPLICITY
I think I shall serve to be a washing-block for you.
I would do it for you, but I am afraid yonder boy will mock me.

HOSPITALITY
No; I warrant thee.

CONSCIENCE
Here, take thy letters, Sincerity; and I wish them prosperous to thee.

SINCERITY
I yield you most hearty thanks, my good lady.

HOSPITALITY
Lady Conscience, pleaseth it you to walk home to dinner with me?

CONSCIENCE
I give you thanks, my good friend Hospitality;
But I pray, sir, have you invited to dinner any stranger?

HOSPITALITY
No, sure; none but Lady Love, and three or four honest neighbours.

SIMPLICITY
Mass, my lady is gotten to dinner already.
I believe she rose at ten o'clock, she is so hungry.
What, and I should come to dinner, hast thou any good cheer.

HOSPITALITY
I have bread and beer, one joint of meat, and welcome, thy best fare.

SIMPLICITY
Why, art thou called Hospitality, and hast no better cheer than that?
I'll tell thee, if thou hast no more meat for so many, they'll ne'er be fat.

48 **impart** give you.
50 **that ... corner** perhaps a reference to a fool or dunce in the classroom, i.e. 'I must look an absolute fool bent double like this'. The potential for sexual comedy is also apparent when Hospitality enters and sees them.
53 **would** wish.
54 **if ... do** I'll sign on her behalf if you like.
55 **I pray ... enou'.** Please do, that will do well enough.
56 **bow** bend over.
57 **washing-block** the board against which clothes were beaten in washing.
68 **cheer** provision/feast.
69 **welcome ... fare** a good welcome is the best fare (proverbial).

What, if my cousin, nay, I myself alone, to dinner should come,
Where should my lady and the rest dine, for I could eat up every crumb?
Thou art an old miser; dost thou keep no better fare in thy house?
Hast no great bag-pudding, nor hog's-face that is called souse?

HOSPITALITY
My friend, hospitality doth not consist in great fare and banqueting,
But in doing good unto the poor and to yield them some refreshing;
Therefore, thou and Sincerity will come and take part,
Such as I have I'll give you with a free and willing heart.

Exeunt Hospitality and Conscience.

SIMPLICITY
He speaks well, cousin; let's go to dinner with him.
The old man shall not think but we will pleasure him.
Faith, he might have richer fellows than we to take his part,
But he shall never have better eating fellows, if he would swelt his heart.
Here be them that will eat with the proudest of them.
I am sure my mother said I could eat so much as five men.
Nay, I have a gift for eating, I tell ye,
For our maids would never believe I put all the meat in my belly.
But I have spied a knave, my Lady Lucre's cogging man.
Give me your letters, cousin; I'll prefer ye, if I can.

Enter Dissimulation.

SINCERITY
Dissimulation! Out upon him, he shall be no spokeman for me.

SIMPLICITY
Why then, you are a fool, Cousin Sincerity.
Give me 'em; I tell ye, I know he'll do it for me.

SINCERITY
Seeing thou wilt have it, here receive it; but yet it grieves my heart
That this dissembling wretch should speak on my part.

SIMPLICITY
Hear ye, sir, I would request [you] to 'liver this letter
To your good wholesome mistress, Lady Lucre.

DISSIMULATION
Where hadst thou it, tell me?

SIMPLICITY
Marry, of my Cousin Sincerity.

DISSIMULATION
Why, I have nothing to do in it; 'tis not to me thou shouldst come;
I have not to do with Sincerity's matters: 'tis my fellow Simony's room.

75 **Hast . . . souse?** Haven't you any haggis (entrails boiled in a bag made from a sheep's stomach) or hogshead, called souse when pickled.

78 **thou** (if) you.

83 **if . . . heart** no matter hard he tries (lit. 'even if he tries until his heart swoons/fails').

90 **spokeman** spokesman.

95 **'liver** deliver.

97 **Where . . . it?** Where did you get this?

98 **of** from.

100 **room** job.

SINCERITY

Thou art akin to the lawyer; thou wilt do nothing without a fee!
But thou, Fraud, Usury, nor yet Simony shall do nothing for me.
And thou wilt do it, do it; and thou wilt not, choose,
Both thee and their dealing I hate and refuse.

DISSIMULATION

Why, and I am not bound to thee so far as knave go,
And therefore, in despite of thee and thy cousin, there thy letters be.
What, thinkest thou by captious words to make me do it?
Let them deliver your letters that hath a stomach to it.

SIMPLICITY

Faith, cousin, he's such a testern and proud, 'sembling knave,
That he'll do nothing 'less some bribery he have.
There's a great many such promoting knaves, that gets their living
With nothing else but facing, lying, swearing, and flattering.
Why, he has a face like a black dog, and blusheth like the back-side of a chimney.
'Twas not for nothing thy godfathers a cogging name gave thee.

Enter Lady Lucre.

But here comes his mistress, Lady Lucre.
Now, cousin, I'll 'liver your letter.
Mistress, Lady Lucre, here's a letter for ye.

LUCRE

Hast thou a letter for me?

SIMPLICITY

Yes, by Saint Mary.
How say you, cousin? She reads your letter;
And you can flatter, perhaps you shall speed better.

SINCERITY

Thou speakest the truth, Simplicity; for flatterers nowadays
Live gentlemen-like, and with prating get praise.

LUCRE

Sir, I have read the tenor of your letter, wherein I find
That, at the request of Love and Conscience, I should show myself kind
In bestowing some spiritual living on ye: parsonage or benefice.
It seems it stands greatly in need, as appears by this.
And, trust me, I would do for you; but it lies not in me,
For I have referred all such matters to my servant Simony.
You must speak to him, and if you can get his goodwill,
Then be sure of mine, their minds to fulfil.

103 **And** If.
106 He puts them on the ground.
107 **captious** carping.
108 **that . . . it** who have the taste for it.
109 **testern . . . knave** Simplicity probably means 'a testy and dissembling knave', but misspeaks. A teston was an old debased coin.
110 **'less** unless.
112 **facing** audacity.
113 **has . . . chimney** i.e. is shameless, black dogs and chimneys are proverbially so black no one can see them blush.
127 **it . . . me** it's not in my power.
130 **their . . . fulfil** to satisfy their (Love and Conscience's) wishes.

SINCERITY

Lady, I shall never get his goodwill, because I want ability,
For he will do nothing except I bring money.
And if you grant it not, then 'tis past all doubt
I shall be never the better, but go quite without.

DISSIMULATION

Madam, I can tell you what you may give,
Not hurting yourself, whereby he may live,
And without my fellow Simony's consent,
If to follow my mind you are any whit bent.

LUCRE

Pray thee, what is it? Thou knowest while for their house I am in bargaining,
And it be never so little, I must seem to do something.

DISSIMULATION

Why, have you not the parsonage of St Nihil to bestow?
If you give him that, Simony shall never know.

LUCRE

Indeed, thou sayest true. Draw near, Sincerity.
Lo, for their sakes I will bestow frankly on thee;
I'll give thee the parsonage of Saint Nihil to pleasure them withal,
And such another to it, if thou watch till it fall.

SIMPLICITY

My lady axes you when you will take possession of your house, and lend the rest of the money.

LUCRE

What, are they so hasty? Belike they spent it merrily.

SIMPLICITY

Faith, no; for they would eat it, if they could get it, when they are a-hungry.

(*Speaking to Sincerity.*)

But you may be happy, for you have sped well today.
You may thank God and good company that you came this way.
The parsonage of St Michael's: by'r Lady, if you have nothing else,
You shall be sure of a living, beside a good ring of bells.
Cousin, I'll tell thee what thou shalt do; sell the bells, and make money.

SINCERITY

Thou mayest well be Simplicity, for thou showest thy folly.
I have a parsonage, but what? Of St Nihil; and 'Nihil' is nothing.
Then, where is the church, or any bells for to ring?
Thou understandest her not, she was set for to flout.

131 **want** lack.
132 **except** unless.
138 **any whit bent** in the least way inclined.
139 Lucre reveals that she is in negotiation to take Love and Conscience's house as collateral security on a loan of which they have received the first instalment. So she needs to appear generous to them.
140 **And...little** Even if it is minuscule.
141 **St Nihil** Saint Nothing.
144 **bestow frankly** give liberally.
146 **And...fall** And another one like it as well, if you wait until it falls vacant.
147 **axes** asks.
148 **Belike** Seemingly.
151 Simplicity has misheard 'Nihils' for 'Michaels'.
151 **by'r Lady** By Our Lady (the Virgin Mary), an oath.
152 **good...bells** a good peal of bells in the bell-tower.
157 **set...flout** intending to shame me.

I thought, coming in their names, I should go without.
'Tis easy to see that Lucre loves not Love and Conscience;
But God, I trust, will one day yield her just recompense.

SIMPLICITY
Cousin, you said that something to me you would give
When you had gotten preferment of Lucre to live;
And I trust you will remember your poor cousin Simplicity.
You know to Lady Conscience and ev'rybody I did speak for you.

SINCERITY
Good Simplicity, hold thy peace: my state is yet nought.
I will help thee, sure, if ever I get ought.
But here comes Sir Nicholas Nemo; to him I will go,
And see if for their sakes he will anything bestow.

Enter Sir Nicholas Nemo.

NEMO
You come from Love and Conscience, as seemeth me here,
My special good friends, whom I account of most dear,
And you are called Sincerity; your state shows the same.
You are welcome to me for their sakes, and for your own name.
And for their sakes you shall see what I will do for you
Without Dissimulation, Fraud, Usury, or Simony;
For they will do nothing without some kind of gain,
Such cankered corruption in their hearts doth remain.
But come in to dinner with me, and when you have dined,
You shall have...

Presently go out.

SINCERITY
'You shall have...'? But what, a living that is blown down with the wind?

SIMPLICITY
Now, cousin, dismember your friends, seeing two livings you have,
One that this man promised, and another that Lady Lucre gave.
Mass, you'll be a jolly man, and you had three or four more.
Let's beg apace, cousin, and we shall get great store.
Do thou get some more letters, and I'll get them scribed of Mistress Love and Conscience,
And we'll go beg livings together; we'll beg no small pence.
How sayest thou, Cousin Sincerity, wut do so mich?
If we can speak fair and 'semble, we shall be plaguey rich.

SINCERITY
Good Simplicity, content thee; I am never the better for this,

165 **my...nought** my situation/living is still nothing.

s.d. Kermode argues that Sir Nicholas is a different character to Judge Nemo who appears later, but the simpler option would seem to treat them as one. Nemo leaves without finishing his last sentence, but this might as well be the result of the lofty condescension of a judge talking to commoners as the mysterious fading away of an impoverished gentleman that Kermode suggests.

178.1 **Presently** Immediately.

179 **dismember** i.e. remember.

185 **wut...mich?** would you do so much/go that far?

186 **'semble** dissemble.

186 **plaguey** grossly (akin to 'stinking rich').

But must of force leave off, for I see how vain it is.
It boots not Sincerity to sue for relief:
So few regard [me,] that to me is a grief.
This was Nicholas Nemo, and 'No-Man' hath no place.
Then how can I speed well in this heavy case?
And no man bid me to dinner, when shall I dine?
Or how shall I find him? Where, when, and at what time?
Wherefore the relief I have had, and shall have, is small;
But to speak truth, the relief is nothing at all.
But come, Simplicity, let us go see what may be had.
Sincerity in these days was, sure, born to be sad.

SIMPLICITY
Come, let's go to dinner, cousin, for the gentleman, I think, hath almost dined,
But, and I do get victuals enough, I'll warrant you, I will not be behind.

SINCERITY
What, if thou canst not get it then, how wilt thou eat?

SIMPLICITY
Marry, on this fashion; with both hands at once; ye shall see, when I get meat.

SINCERITY
Why, his name was Nemo, and Nemo hath no being.

SIMPLICITY
I believe, cousin, you be not hungry that you stand prating.
Faith, I'll go do him a pleasure, because he hath need.
Why, and he will needs have meat eat, a' shall see how I'll feed.
I believe he will not bid me come again to him;
Mass, and he do, a' shall find a fellow that has his eating.

Exeunt ambo.

[Scene 5.]

Enter Usury and Conscience.

USURY
Lady Conscience, is there anybody within your house, can you tell?

CONSCIENCE
There is nobody at all, be ye sure; I know certainly well.

USURY
You know, when one comes to take possession of any piece of land,
There must not be one within, for against the order of law it doth stand.
Therefore I thought good to ask you, but I pray you think not amiss,

188 **of force** necessity.
189 **boots** benefits.
192 **heavy case** sad situation.
193 **And...bid** If no man invites.
202 **on this fashion** in this way.
204 **I...prating.** You cannot be hungry if you stand around chatting.
206 **and...feed** if he needs to have his food eaten, he'll see how I can eat.
208 **and he do...eating** if he ever invites me again he'll know he's met a man who knows how to eat.
3–4 **when...stand** the law says that one can only take possession of land that is unoccupied.

For both you and almost all others knows that an old custom it is.

CONSCIENCE

You say truth; take possession when you please; good leave I render ye.
Doubt you not; there is neither man, woman, nor child that will or shall hinder ye.

USURY

Why, then, I will be bold to enter. *Exit.*

CONSCIENCE

Who is more bold than Usury to venter?
He maketh the matter dangerous where is no need at all,
But he thinks it not perilous to seek every man's fall.
Both he and Lucre hath so pinched us we know not what to do.
Were it not for Hospitality, we knew not whither to go.
Great is the misery that we poor ladies abide,
And much more is the cruelty of Lucre and Usury beside,
O Conscience, thou art not accounted of; O Love, thou art little set by,
For almost everyone true love and pure conscience doth deny.
So hath Lucre crept into the bosom of man, woman, and child,
That every one doth practise his dear friend to beguile.
But God grant Hospitality be not by them over-pressed,
In whom all our stay and chiefest comfort doth rest.
But Usury hates Hospitality, and cannot him abide,
Because he for the poor and comfortless doth provide.
Here he comes that hath undone many an honest man,
And daily seeks to destroy, deface, and bring to ruin, if he can.
Now, sir, have you taken possession, as your dear lady willed you?

Enter Usury.

USURY

I have done it, and I think you have received your money.
But this to you: my lady willed me to bid you provide some other
house out of hand,
For she would not by her will have Love and Conscience to dwell in her land.
Therefore I would wish you to provide ye;
So ye should save charges, for a less house may serve ye.

CONSCIENCE

I pray you heartily, let us stay there, and we will be content
To give you ten pound a year, which is the old rent.

USURY

Ten pound a year? That were a stale jest,
If I should take the old rent to follow your request.
Nay, after forty pound a year you shall have it for a quarter,
And you may think, too, I greatly befriend ye in this matter.

10 **venter** offer for sale.
11 **dangerous** difficult.
16 **beside** as well.
17 **set by** valued.
21 **over-pressed** oppressed.
22 **stay** support.
29 **provide ... hand** quickly find somewhere else to live.
32 **less** smaller.
35 **stale jest** a poor, old joke.
37 **after ... quarter** I'll let you stay in the house for forty pounds a year, but only for three months.

But no longer than for a quarter to you I'll set it,
For perhaps my lady shall sell it, or else to some other will let it.

CONSCIENCE
Well, sith we are driven to this hard and bitter drift,
We accept it, and are contented to make bare and hard shift.

USURY
Then, get you gone, and see at a day your rent be ready.

CONSCIENCE
We must have patience perforce, seeing there is no remedy.

Exit Conscience.

USURY
What a fool was I! It repents me I have let it so reasonable;
I might so well have had after threescore as such a trifle;
For, seeing they were distressed, they would have given largely.
I was a right sot; but I'll be overseen no more, believe me.

Enter Mercadore.

MERCADORE
Ah, my good-a friend Master Usury! By my trot', you be very well met.
Me be much beholden unto you for your goodwill; me be in your debt.
But-a me take-a your part so much against a scald old churl, called Hospitality,
Did speak against you, and says you bring good honest men to beggary.

USURY
I thank [you], sir. Did he speak such evil of me as you now say?
I doubt not but to reward him for his treachery one day.

MERCADORE
But, I pray, tell-a me how fare-a my lady all dis while?

USURY
Marry, very [well], sir; and here she comes, if myself I do not beguile.

Enter Lucre.

LUCRE
What, Signor Mercadore; I have not seen you many a day.
I marvel what is the cause you kept so long away.

MERCADORE
Shall me say you, Madonna, dat me have had much business for you in hand,
For send away good commodities out of dis little country England.
Me have now sent over brass, copper, pewter, and many oder ting,
And for dat me shall ha for gentlewomans fine trifles, that great profit will bring.

LUCRE
I perceive you have been mindful of me, for which I thank ye.
But, Usury, tell me, how have you sped in that you went about?

41 **drift** course of action.
42 **to . . . shift** to make the best of the little that we have.
43 **at a day** within a day.
45 **so reasonable** at such a reasonable rent.
46 **threescore** sixty pounds (a year).
48 **sot** fool.
48 **overseen** lax.
49 **By my trot'** By my troth/my word!
56 **if . . . beguile** if I'm not mistaken.

USURY
Indifferently, lady, you need not to doubt.
I have taken possession, and because they were destitute,
I have let it for a quarter. My tale to conclude,
Marry, I have a little raised the rent, but it is but forty pound by the year.
But if it were to let now, I would let it more dear.

LUCRE
Indeed, 'tis but a trifle; it makes no matter:
I force not greatly, being but for a quarter.

MERCADORE
Madonna, me tell ye vat you shall do: let dem to stranger dat are content
To dwell in a little room, and to pay much rent,
For you know da Frenchmans and Flemings in dis country be many,
So dat they make shift to dwell ten houses in one very gladly;
And be content-a for pay fifty or threescore pound a year
For dat which da Englishmans say twenty mark is too dear.

LUCRE
Why, Signor Mercadore, think you not that I
Have infinite numbers in London that my want doth supply?
Beside in Bristow, Northampton, Norwich, Westchester, Canterbury,
Dover, Sandwich, Rye, Portsmouth, Plymouth, and many mo,
That great rents upon little room do bestow?
Yes, I warrant you; and truly I may thank the strangers for this,
That they have made houses so dear, whereby I live in bliss.
But, Signor Mercadore, dare you to travel undertake,
And go amongst the Moors, Turks, and pagans for my sake?

MERCADORE
Madonna, me dare go to de Turks, Moors, pagans, and more too:
What do me care and me go to da great devil for you?
Command-a me, madam, and you shall see plain,
Dat-a for your sake me refuse-a no pain.

LUCRE
Then, Signor Mercadore, I am forthwith to send ye
From hence to search for some new toys in Barbary and in Turkey;
Such trifles as you think will please wantons best,
For you know in this country 'tis their chiefest request.

MERCADORE
Indeed, de gentlewomans here buy so much vain toys
Dat me strangers laugh-a to tink wherein day have their joys.

71 **I . . . greatly** I don't greatly care.
72 **stranger** foreigners.
75 **So . . . gladly** So they will happily suffer living ten households/families to one house.
77 **mark** a mark was worth roughly two thirds of a pound sterling.
79 **that . . . supply** who pay me what I lack.
80 **Bristow** Bristol.
80 **Westchester** Chester.
82 **That . . . bestow?** Who pay high rents for tiny rooms. (Most of these towns were ports and industrial centres where large numbers of foreign workers might be found.)
85 **dare . . . undertake** do you dare to go on a journey.
88 **and me** if I.
91 **I am . . . ye** I will soon send you.
92 **toys** trifles.
93 **wantons** vain young women.
96 **to tink . . . joys** to think what they take pleasure in.

Fait', Madonna, me will search all da strange countries me can tell,
But me will have sush tings dat please dese gentlewomans vell.

LUCRE

Why, then, let us provide things ready to haste you away.

MERCADORE

A vostro commandamento, Madonna, me obey.

Exeunt.

[Scene 6]

Enter Simony and Peter Pleaseman, like a parson.

SIMONY

Now proceed with your tale, and I'll hear thee.

PETER

And so, sir, as I was about to tell you,
This same Presco and this same Cracko be both my parishioners now;
And, sir, they fell out marvellously together about you.
This same Cracko took your part, and said that the clergy
Was upholden by you, and maintained very worshipfully.
So, sir, Presco, he would not grant that in no case,
But said that you did corrupt the clergy, and dishonour that holy place.
Now, sir, I was weary to hear them at such great strife,
For I love to please men, so long as I have life.
Therefore I beseech your mastership to speak to Lady Lucre,
That I may be her chaplain, or else to serve her.

SIMONY

What is your name?

PETER

Sir Peter.

SIMONY

What more?

PETER

Forsooth, Pleaseman.

SIMONY

Then, your name is Sir Peter Pleaseman?

PETER

Aye, forsooth.

SIMONY

And please-woman too, now and then?

PETER

You know that *homo* is indifferent.

97 **Fait'** (In) faith.

100 ***A vostro commandamento*** At your service.

3 **Presco...Cracko** Kermode suggests these silly names might imply that Presco, who rejects Simony, is prescient, and Cracko, who embraces him, is 'crack-brained'.

14 Priests took the informal honorific title 'sir'

16 **Forsooth** Truly.

20 ***homo* is indifferent** in Latin the word *homo* (man) is ungendered. Sir Peter may be acknowledging the implied allegation of fornication ('well, I have to please everyone') or denying it ('like the word, I am indifferent to sex').

SIMONY
Now, surely, a good scholar in my judgment!
I pray, at what university were ye?

PETER
Of no university, truly. Marry, I have gone
To school in a college, where I have studied two or three places of divinity;
And all for Lady Lucre's sake, sir, you may steadfastly believe me.

SIMONY
Nay, I believe ye. But of what religion are you, can ye tell?

PETER
Marry, sir, of all religions, I know not myself very well.

SIMONY
You are a Protestant now, and I think to that you will grant?

PETER
Indeed, I have been a Catholic; marry, now for the most part, a Protestant.
But, and if my service may please her, hark in your ear, sir
I warrant you my religion shall not offend her.

SIMONY
You say well; but if I help you to such great preferment,
Would you be willing that for my pain
I shall have yearly half the gain?
For it is reason, you know, that if I help you to a living,
That you should unto me be somewhat beholding.

PETER
Aye, sir; and reason good. I'll be as your mastership please;
I care not what you do, so I may live at ease.

SIMONY
Then this man is answered. Sir Peter Pleaseman, come in with me,
And I'll prefer you straightway to my lady.

PETER
O sir, I thank ye. *Exeunt.*

[Scene 7]

Enter Simplicity, with a basket on his arm.

SIMPLICITY
You think I am going to market to buy roast meat, do ye not?
I thought so; but you are deceived, for I wot what I wot.
I am neither going to the butcher's to buy veal, mutton, or beef,
But I am going to a bloodsucker; and who is it? Faith, Usury, that thief.
Why, sirs, 'twas no marcle he undid my father, that was called Plain-Dealing,
When he has undone my lady, and Conscience too with his usuring.
I'll tell ye, sirs, trust him not, for he'll flatter *bonacion* and sore,

24 **places of divinity** clerical jobs.
28 **I...grant** I think you'll admit to that.
31 **my...her** i.e. I'll be whatever Lucre wants me to be.
2 **wot** know.
5 **marcle** miracle.
7 ***bonacion*** see note to Scene 2, line 41.
7 **sore** severely.

Till he has gotten the baker vantage; then he'll turn you out of door.

Enter Dissimulation.

DISSIMULATION
Simplicity, now of my honesty, very heartily well-met!

SIMPLICITY
What, Semblation, swear not; for thou swearest by that thou couldst not get.
Thou have honesty now? Thy honesty is quite gone.
Marry, thou hadst honesty at eleven of the clock, and [it] went from you at noon.
Why, how canst thou have honesty, when it dare not come nigh thee?
I warrant, Semblation, he that has less honesty than thou may defy thee.
Thou hast honesty, Sir Reverence? Come out, dog, where art thou;
Even as much honesty as had my mother's great hoggish sow!
No, faith, thou must put out my eye with honesty and thou hadst it here;
Hast not left it at the alehouse in gage for a pot of strong beer?

DISSIMULATION
Pray thee, leave prating, Simplicity, and tell me what thou hast there.

SIMPLICITY
Why, 'tis nothing for thee; thou dost not deal with such kind of ware.
Sirrah, there is no beceit in a bag-pudding, is there? Nor in a plain pudding [pie]?
But there is beceit, and knavery too, in thy fellow that is called Usury.
Sirrah, I'll tell thee... I wonnot tell thee... and yet I'll tell thee, now I 'member me, too.
Canst tell, or wouldst know whither with this parliament I go?
Faith, even to Suck-Swill, thy fellow Usury, I am sent,
With my Lady Love's gown, and Lady Conscience['s] too, for a quarter's rent.

DISSIMULATION
Alas! poor Lady Love, art thou driven so low?
Some little pittance on thee I'll bestow.
Hold, Simplicity, carry her three or four ducats from me,
And commend me to her even very heartily.

SIMPLICITY
Duck-eggs? Yes, I'll carry 'em, and 'twere as many as this would hold.

DISSIMULATION
Tush; thou knowest not what I mean. Take this, 'tis gold.

SIMPLICITY
Mass, 'tis gold indeed. Why wilt thou send away thy gold? Hast no more need?
I think thou art grown plaguey rich with thy dissembling trade.
But I'll carry my lady the gold, for this will make her well apaid.

DISSIMULATION
And, sirrah, carry Lady Love's gown back again; for my fellow Usury
Shall not have her gown. I am sure so much he will befriend me.

SIMPLICITY
But what shall Conscience's gown do? Shall I carry it back again too?

[8] **has...vantage** gets the advantage over you (as bakers proverbially always do, keeping a thirteenth loaf for themselves when they bake you twelve: hence, a 'baker's dozen').

[10] **Semblation** Dissimulation.

[21] **beceit** Simplicity's mistake for 'deceit' again.

[23] **wonnot** won't.

[24] **parliament** he means 'parament', a fine robe.

[29] **Hold** Wait.

[29] **ducats** gold coins.

DISSIMULATION
Nay, let Conscience's gown and skin to Usury go.
If nobody cared for Conscience more than I,
They would hang her up like bacon in a chimney to dry.

SIMPLICITY
Faith, I told thee thou caredst not for Conscience nor honesty.
I think, indeed, it will never be the death of thee.
But I'll go conspatch my arrant so soon as I can, I tell ye,
For now I ha' gold, I would fain have some good meat in my belly. *Exit.*

DISSIMULATION
Nay, I'll hie me after, that I may send back Lady Love's gown,
For I would not have Love bought quite out of town.
Marry, for Conscience; tut, I care not two straws;
Why I should take care for her, I know no kind of cause. *Exit.*

[Scene 8]

Enter Hospitality.

HOSPITALITY
O, what shall I say? Usury hath undone me, and now he hates me to the death,
And seeks by all means possible for to bereave me of breath.
I cannot rest in any place, but he hunts and follows me everywhere,
That I know no place to abide, I live so much in fear.
But, out, alas; here comes he that will shorten my days.

Enter Usury.

USURY
O, have I caught your old grey beard? You be the man whom the people so praise;
You are a frank gentleman, and full of liberality.
Why, who had all the praise in London or England, but Master Hospitality?
But I'll master you now, I'll hold you a groat.

HOSPITALITY
What, will you kill me?

USURY
No; I'll do nothing but cut thy throat.

HOSPITALITY
O help, help, help, for God's sake!

Enter Conscience, running apace.

CONSCIENCE
What lamentable cry was that I heard one make?

HOSPITALITY
O Lady Conscience, now or never help me!

39 **let...skin** and she herself (for all I care).
44 **conspatch my arrant** he means 'despatch (carry out) my errand'.
46 **hie** hurry.
5 **out** woe!
7 **frank** generous.
9 **hold** bet.

CONSCIENCE
Why, what wilt thou do with him, Usury?
USURY
What will I do with him? Marry, cut his throat, and then no more.
CONSCIENCE
O, dost thou not consider that thou shalt dearly answer
For Hospitality, that good member? Refrain it therefore.
USURY
Refrain me no refraining, nor answer me no answering;
The matter is answered well enough in this thing.
CONSCIENCE
For God's sake, spare him! For country's sake, spare him! For pity's sake, spare him!
For Love's sake, spare him! For Conscience's sake, forbear him!
USURY
Let country, pity, love, Conscience, and all go; in respect of myself
He shall die. Come, ye feeble wretch, I'll dress ye like an elf.
CONSCIENCE
But yet, Usury, consider the lamentable cry of the poor;
For lack of Hospitality fatherless children are turned out of door.
Consider again the complaint of the sick, blind, and lame,
That will cry unto the Lord for vengeance on thy head in his name.
Is the fear of God so far from thee that thou hast no feeling at all?
O, repent, Usury; leave Hospitality, and for mercy at the Lord's hand call.
USURY
Leave prating, Conscience, thou canst not mollify my heart.
He shall, in spite of thee and all other, feel his deadly smart.
Yet I'll not commit the murder openly,
But hale the villain into a corner, and so kill him secretly.
Come, ye miserable drudge, and receive thy death.
HOSPITALITY
Help, good lady, help! He will stop my breath.
CONSCIENCE
Alas! I would help thee, but I have not the power.
HOSPITALITY
Farewell, Lady Conscience; you shall have Hospitality in London nor
England no more.

Hale him in.

CONSCIENCE
O help! help, help, some good body!

Enter Dissimulation and Simplicity hastily.

16 **dearly answer** give a reckoning (either in heaven or in a court).
22 **in respect of myself** i.e. for my sake.
23 **I'll . . . elf** I'll treat you like a naughty little boy (i.e. beat him).
31 **his deadly smart** his death wound.
33 **hale** drag.

DISSIMULATION
Who is that calls for help so hastily?
CONSCIENCE
Out, alas! Thy fellow Usury hath killed Hospitality.
SIMPLICITY
Now, God's blessing on his heart. Why, 'twas time that he was dead;
He was an old churl, with never a good tooth in his head.
And he ne'er kept no good cheer that I could see;
For if one had not come at dinner-time, he should have gone away hungry.
I could never get my belly-full of meat;
He had nothing but beef, bread, and cheese for me to eat.
Now I would have had some pies, or bag-puddings with great lumps of fat;
But, I warrant ye, he did keep my mouth well enough from that.
Faith, and he be dead, he is dead; let him go to the devil, and he will;
Or if he will not go thither, let him even lie there still.
I'll ne'er make wamentation for an old churl,
For he has been a great while, and now 'tis time that he were out of the worl'.

Enter Lucre.

LUCRE
What, Conscience, thou look'st like a poor pigeon, pulled of late.
CONSCIENCE
What, Lucre, thou lookest like a whore, full of deadly hate.
LUCRE
Alas, Conscience, I am sorry for thee, but I cannot weep.
CONSCIENCE
Alas, Lucre, I am sorry for thee that thou canst no honesty keep.
But such as thou art, such are the attenders on thee,
As appears by thy servant Usury, that hath killed that good member Hospitality.
SIMPLICITY
Faith, Hospitality is killed, and hath made his will,
And hath given Dissimulation three trees upon an high hill.
LUCRE
Come hither, Dissimulation, and hie you hence, so fast as you may,
And help thy fellow Usury to convey himself out of the way.
Further, will the justices, if they chance to see him, not to know him,
Or, know him, not by any means to hinder him;
And they shall command thrice so much at my hand.
Go trudge, run; out, away! How, dost thou stand?
DISSIMULATION
Nay, good lady, send my fellow Simony;
For I have an earnest suit to ye.

51 **wamentation** lamentation, from the medieval word 'wayment'.
53 **pulled of late** who's just been plucked.
60 **hath...hill** has bequeathed to Dissimulation the gallows.
63 **Further...justices** And command the judges.
64 **know him** if they recognize him.
65 **And...hand** she gives him a bribe for the judges, promising triple that again if they do as she asks.
66 **Go trudge!** Off you go!
66 **How?** What?

LUCRE
Then, Simony, go, do what I have willed.

SIMONY
I run, Madam: your mind shall be fulfilled. *Exit.*

CONSCIENCE
Well, well, Lucre, *Audeo et taceo*: 'I see and say nothing';
But I fear the plague of God on thy head it will bring.

DISSIMULATION
Good lady, grant that Love be your waiting-maid.
For I think, being brought so low, she will be well apaid.

LUCRE
Speakest thou in good earnest, or dost thou but dissemble?
I know not how to have thee, thou art so variable.

DISSIMULATION
Lady, though my name be Dissimulation, yet I speak *bona fide* now.
If it please you my petitions to allow.

Enter Simony.

LUCRE
Stand by, I'll answer thee anon. What news, Simony,
Bringest thou of thy fellow Usury?

SIMONY
Marry, madam, good news; for Usury lies close,
Hid in a rich man's house, that will not let him loose,
Until they see the matter brought to a good end;
For Usury in this country hath many a good friend.
And late I saw Hospitality carried to burying.

LUCRE
I pray thee, tell me who were they that followed him?

SIMONY
There were many of the clergy, and many of the nobility,
And many right worshipful rich citizens,
Substantial, gracious, and very wealthy farmers.
But to see how the poor followed him, it was a wonder;
Never yet at any burial I have seen such a number.

LUCRE
But what say the people of the murder?

SIMONY
Many are sorry, and say 'tis great pity that he was slain.
But who be they? The poor beggarly people that so complain.
As for the other, they say 'twas a cruel, bloody fact,
But I perceive none will hinder the murderer for this cruel act.

LUCRE
'Tis well; I am glad of it. Now, Dissimulation, if you can get Love's good will,
I am contented with all my heart to grant there-until.

75 **have** take/respond to.
76 ***bona fide*** in good faith.
80 **close** concealed.
94 **fact** deed.
96 **there-until** to what you ask.

DISSIMULATION
I thank you, good lady, and I doubt not but she
With a little entreaty will thereto agree.

SIMPLICITY
Now I have it in my breeches, and very well can tell,
That I and my lady with Mistress Lucre shall dwell.
But if I be her serving-fellow, and dwell there,
I must learn to cog, lie, foist, and swear;
And surely I shall never learn. Marry, and 'twere to lie abed all day,
I know to that kind of living I should give a good 'ssay
Or if 'twere to eat one's meat, then I knew what I had to do.
How say ye, sirrah, can I not? I'll be judged by you.

LUCRE
Now to you, little mouse; did I not tell you before
That I should, ere 'twere long, turn you both out of door?
How say you, pretty soul, is't come to pass, yea or no?
I think I have pulled your peacock's plumes somewhat low.
And yet you be so stout as though you felt no grief.
But I know, ere it be long, you will come puling to me for relief.

CONSCIENCE
Well, Lucre, well; you know pride will have a fall.
What avantageth it thee to win the world, and lose thy soul withal?
Yet better it is to live with little, and keep a conscience clear,
Which is to God a sacrifice, and accounted of most dear.

LUCRE
Nay, Conscience, and you be bookish, I mean to leave ye;
And the cold ground to comfort your feet I bequeath ye.
Methink, you being so deeply learned may do well to keep a school.
Why, I have seen so cunning a clerk in time to prove a fool.

Exeunt Lucre and Simony.

SIMPLICITY
Sirrah, if thou shouldst marry my lady, thou wouldst keep her brave,
For I think now thou art a plaguey rich knave.

DISSIMULATION
Rich I am, but as for knave, keep to thyself.
Come, give me my lady's gown, thou ass-headed elf.

SIMPLICITY
Why, I'll go with thee, for I must dwell with my lady.

DISSIMULATION
Pack, hence, away! Jack Drum's entertainment: she will none of thee. *Exit.*

100 **I . . . breeches** I know it instinctively (equivalent of 'I feel it in my water').
103 **foist** cheat.
104 **and . . . day** if it were a matter of lying in bed all day.
105 **'ssay** assay (i.e. give a good trial to).
111 **pulled . . . low** i.e. killed your pride.
112 **stout** bold.
113 **puling** crying.
118 **and . . . bookish** if you're going to get scholarly.
120 **keep** open.
122 **keep her brave** support/maintain her splendidly.
124 **keep to thyself** apply that term to yourself.
127 **Pack** Move on.
127 **Jack Drum's entertainment** Jack or Tom Drum's entertainment was slang for being thrown out. There was a play of that name by John Marston, performed *c.*1600.
127 **she will none of thee** she doesn't want anything to do with you.

SIMPLICITY

This is as my cousin and I went to Master Nemo's house:
There was nobody to bid a dog drink, or to change a man a louse.
But Lady Conscience... Nay, whoo there; scratch that name away!
Can she be a lady that is turned out of all her beray?
Do not be called more lady and if you be wise,
For everybody will mock you, and say you be not worth two butterflies.

CONSCIENCE

What remedy, Simplicity? I cannot do withal.
But what shall we go do? Or whereto shall we fall?

SIMPLICITY

Why, to our victuals, I know nothing else we have to do;
And mark if I cannot eat twenty times as much as you.

CONSCIENCE

If I go lie in an inn, I shall be sore grieved to see
The deceit of the ostler, the polling of the tapster, as in most houses of lodging they be.
If in a brewer's house, at the over-plenty of water and the scarceness of malt I should grieve,
Whereby to enrich themselves all other with unsavoury thin drink they deceive;
If in a tanner's house, with his great deceit in tanning;
If in a weaver's house, with his great cosening in weaving.
If in a baker's house, with light bread and very evil working;
If in a chandler's, with deceitful weights, false measures, selling for a halfpenny that is scant worth a farthing;
And if in an alehouse, with the great resort of poor unthrifts, that with swearing at the cards consume their lives,
Having greater delight to spend a shilling that way than a groat at home to sustain their needy children and wives.
For which I judge it best for me to get some solitary place,
Where I may with patience this my heavy cross embrace,
And learn to seek broom, whereby to get my living,
Using that as a quiet mean to keep myself from begging.
Wherefore, Simplicity, if thou wilt do the like,
Settle thyself to it, and with true labour thy living do seek. *Exit Conscience.*

SIMPLICITY

No, faith, Mistress Conscience, I'll not; for, and I should sell broom,

128 **as** just like when.
129 **change...louse** pick a louse from your clothes.
130 **whoo...away!** woo, stop a moment, rub that name out.
131 **beray** he means 'array' (if she has lost all her clothes). To 'beray' is to befoul.
132 **Do...wise** If you are wise, no longer call yourself a lady.
134 **cannot do withal** cannot help matters.
135 **whereto...fall** what shall we turn our hands to (to earn a living).
136 **to our victuals** Simplicity puns that they should 'fall' to eating.
137 **mark** note.
139 **polling...tapster** the barman's robbery.
140 **at...grieve** I should lament the adulteration of the beer, through too much water and not enough malt.
142 **tanner's** leather-maker's.
143 **cosening** trickery.
144 **light** short-weight, through skimping on the ingredients.
145 **chandler's** grocer.
146 **a farthing** a coin worth a quarter of a penny.
147 **unthrifts** wasters.
151 **seek broom** gather the twigs from which brushes ('brooms') are made.

The maids would cosen me too competually with their old shoon.
And, too, I cannot work, and you would hang me out of the way;
For when I was a miller, Will did grind the meal while I did play.
Therefore I'll have as easy an occupation as I had when my father was alive.
Faith, I'll go even a-begging. Why, 'tis a good trade; a man shall be sure to thrive;
For I am sure my prayers will get bread and cheese, and my singing will get me drink.
Then shall not I do better than Mistress Conscience? Tell me as you think.
Therefore god Pan in the kitchen, and god Pot in the buttery,
Come and resist me, that I may sing with the more meliosity.
But, sirs, mark my cauled countenance when I begin.
But yonder is a fellow that gapes to bite me, or else to eat that which I sing.
Why, thou art a fool; canst thou not keep thy mouth strait together?
And when it comes, snap at it, as my father's dog would do at a liver.
But thou art so greedy,
That thou thinkest to eat it before it comes nigh thee.

Simplicity sings.

Simplicity sings it, and 'sperience doth prove,
No biding in London for Conscience and Love.
The country hath no peer,
Where Conscience comes not once a year;
And Love so welcome to every town,
As wind that blows the houses down.
Sing down a-down, down, down, down.
Simplicity sings it, and 'sperience doth prove,
No dwelling in London, no biding in London, for Conscience and Love.

SIMPLICITY
Now, sirrah, hast eaten up my song? And ye have, ye shall eat no more to-day,
For everybody may see your belly is grown bigger with eating up our play.
He has filled his belly, but I am never a whit the better,
Therefore I'll go seek some victuals; and 'member, for eating up my song you shall be my debtor. *Exit Simplicity.*

[Scene 9]

Enter Mercadore, the Merchant, and Gerontus, a Jew.

GERONTUS
But, Signor Mercadore, tell me, did ye serve me well or no,

156 **cosen...shoon** trick me all the time with their old shoes. 'Competually' is perhaps a compound of 'completely' and 'perpetually'. As Conscience's song in scene 10 reveals, broom-sellers often part-exchanged their wares for old shoes and other goods, so Simplicity fears he will always lose out in such deals.

157 **you...way** you would kill me to get rid of me.

163 **Pan** he mistakes the classical god Pan with the cooking implement of the same name, and assumes there must be a god called Pot to match.

163 **buttery** food-store.

164 **resist** i.e. assist.

164 **meliosity** mellifluousness.

165 **cauled** either his 'cabbage-like' or 'hooded' face.

166 **yonder...me** perhaps, as Kermode suggests, Simplicity addresses someone in their audience with their mouth hanging open.

167 **strait together** closed tightly.

171 **'sperience** experience.

172 **No biding** There's no living.

173 **hath no peer** is peerless (much better than anywhere else).

183 **'member** remember (this).

That, having gotten my money, would seem the country to forego?
You know I lent you two thousand ducats for three months' space,
And, ere the time came, you got another thousand by flattery and thy smooth face.
So, when the time came that I should have received my money,
You were not to be found, but was fled out of the country.
Surely, if we that be Jews should deal so one with another,
We should not be trusted again of our own brother;
But many of you Christians make no conscience to falsify your faith, and break your day.
I should have been paid at the month's end, and now it is two years you have been away.
Well, I am glad you be come again to Turkey; now I trust I shall receive the interest of you, so well as the principal.

MERCADORE

Ah, good-a Master Geronto, pray heartily, bear-a me a little while,
And me shall pay ye all, without any deceit or guile.
Me have much business for my pretty knacks to send to England.
Good sir, bear-a me for five days, me'll despatch your money out of hand.

GERONTUS

Signor Mercadore, I know no reason why, because you have dealt with me so ill.
Sure, you did it not for need, but of set purpose and will;
And, I tell ye, to bear with ye four or five days goes sore against my mind,
Lest you should steal away, and forget to leave my money behind.

MERCADORE

Pray heartily, do tink-a no such ting, my good friend-a me.
Be my trot' and fait', me pay you all, every penny.

GERONTUS

Well, I'll take your faith and troth once more, and trust to your honesty,
In hope that for my long tarrying you will deal well with me.
Tell me what ware you would buy for England, such necessaries as they lack?

MERCADORE

O no, lack some pretty fine toy, or some fantastic new knack;
For da gentlewomans in England buy much tings for fantasy.
You pleasure-a me, sir, vat me mean-a dear buy?

GERONTUS

I understand you, sir, but keep touch with me and I'll bring you to great store,
Such as I perceive you came to this country for;
As musk, amber, sweet powders, fine odours, pleasant perfumes, and many such toys,
Wherein I perceive consisteth that country gentlewomen's joys.
Besides, I have diamonds, rubies, emeralds, sapphires, smaradines, opals, onacles, jacinths, agates, turquoise, and almost of all kind of precious stones,
And many mo fit things to suck away money from such green-headed wantons.

2 **the . . . forego** leave the country (Gerontus accuses Mercadore of fleeing Turkey to avoid repaying a loan).
9 **break your day** default on repayment day.
11 **the principal** the sum loaned itself.
12 **pray . . . me** I beg you from my heart, bear with me.
14 **knacks** trifles.
15 **out of hand** immediately.
19 **steal** sneak.
24 **necessaries** essential goods.
27 **You . . . buy?** Will you help me to find what I want to buy?
28 **keep . . . store** just stay in touch with me (i.e. don't sneak away again) and I'll show you where there is an abundance of such things.
32 **smaradines** smaragdite (a green gem).
33 **onacles** onyx.
34 **fit** suitable.
34 **green-headed wantons** silly (greedy) girls.

MERCADORE
Faith-a, my good friend, me tank you most heartly alway.
Me shall-a content your debt within this two or tree day.
GERONTUS
Well, look you do keep your promise, and another time you shall command me.
Come, go we home, where our commodities you may at pleasure see. [*Exeunt.*]

[Scene 10]

Enter Conscience, with brooms at her back, singing as followeth:

New brooms, green brooms, will you buy any?
Come, maidens, come quickly, let me take a penny.

My brooms are not steeped,
But very well-bound:
My brooms be not crooked,
But smooth-cut and round.

I wish it should please you
To buy of my broom,
Then would it well ease me,
If market were done.

Have you any old boots,
Or any old shoon;
Pouch-rings or buskins
To cope for new broom?
If so you have, maidens,
I pray you bring hither,
That you and I friendly
May bargain together.

New brooms, green brooms, will you buy any?
Come, maidens, come quickly, let me take a penny.

Conscience speaketh

Thus am I driven to make a virtue of necessity;
And, seeing God almighty will have it so, I embrace it thankfully,
Desiring God to mollify and lessen Usury's hard heart,
That the poor people feel not the like penury and smart.
But Usury is made tolerable amongst Christians, as a necessary thing,
So that, going beyond the limits of our law, they extort, and many to misery bring.
But if we should follow God's law, we should not receive above that we lend,

37 **and...me** and you can use my services again later.
3 **steeped** soaked to make them seem suppler than they are.
10 **If...done** If we can agree a sale.
12 **shoon** shoes.
13 **pouch-rings** small rings for securing pouches.
13 **buskins** boots.
14 **cope** swap.
24 **the like** similar.
24 **smart** pain.
26 Usury was permitted under English law provided that the maximum interest charged was 10 per cent. Many usurers charged far higher rates, however.

For if we lend for reward, how can we say we are our neighbours' friend?
O, how blessed shall that man be that lends without abuse,
But thrice accursed shall he be that greatly covets use.
For he that covets over-much, insatiate is his mind,
So that to perjury and cruelty he wholly is inclined.
Wherewith they sore oppress the poor by divers sundry ways,
Which makes them cry unto the Lord to shorten cut-throats' days.
Paul calleth them thieves that doth not give the needy of their store,
And thrice accursed are they that take one penny from the poor.
But while I stand reasoning thus, I forget my market clean;
And sith God hath ordained this way, I am to use the mean.

Sing again.

Have ye any old shoes,
Or have ye any boots?
Have ye any buskins,
Or will ye buy any broom?

Who bargain or chop with Conscience?
What, will no customer come?

Enter Usury.

USURY
Who is it that cries brooms? What, Conscience, selling brooms about the street?

CONSCIENCE
What, Usury, it is great pity thou art unhanged yet.

USURY
Believe me, Conscience, it grieves me thou art brought so low.

CONSCIENCE
Believe me, Usury, it grieves me thou wast not hanged long ago;
For if thou hadst been hanged before thou slewest Hospitality,
Thou hadst not made me and thousands more to feel like poverty.

Enter Lucre.

LUCRE
Methought I heard one cry brooms along the door.

USURY
Aye, marry, madam; it was Conscience, who seems to be offended at me very sore.

LUCRE
Alas, Conscience, art thou become a poor broom-wife?

30 **use** usury/interest.
33 **sundry** many different.
35 **Paul** St Paul. Perhaps, as Kermode suggests, an interpretation of 2 Corinthians 9:9: 'As it is written: He hath dispersed abroad, he hath given to the poor: his justice remaineth for ever.' See also the Epistle of St James 2:6–9: 'But you have dishonoured the poor man... If then you fulfil the royal law, according to the scriptures, Thou shalt love thy neighbour as thyself; you do well. But if you have respect to persons, you commit sin, being reproved by the law as transgressors.'
37 **I forget...clean** I completely forget my trade.
38 **I...mean** I must follow this means of doing God's will.
43 **chop** will haggle or exchange.
50 **like** the same (degree of).
51 **along the door** from door to door.
53 **broom-wife** broom-seller.

CONSCIENCE
Alas, Lucre, wilt thou continue a harlot all days of thy life?
LUCRE
Alas, I think it is a grief to thee that thou art so poor.
CONSCIENCE
Alas, Lucre, I think it is no pain to thee that thou still playest the whore.
LUCRE
Well, well, Conscience, that sharp tongue of thine hath not been thy furtherance.
If thou hadst kept thy tongue, thou hadst kept thy friend, and not have had such hindrance.
But wottest thou who shall be married tomorrow? Love, with my Dissimulation;
For I think to bid the guests, they are by this time well-nigh gone;
And having occasion to buy brooms, I care not if I buy them all.
CONSCIENCE
Then, give me a shilling, and with a good will have them you shall.
LUCRE
Usury, carry in these brooms, and give them to the maid,
For I know of such store she will be well apaid. *Exit Usury with the brooms.*
Hold, Conscience, though thy brooms be not worth a quarter so much,
Yet to give thee a piece of gold I do it not grudge.
And if thou wouldst follow my mind, thou shouldst not live in such sort,
But pass thy days with pleasure, store of every kind of sport.
CONSCIENCE
I think you lead the world in a string, for everybody follows you.
And sith every one doth it, why may not I do it too?
For that I see your free heart and great liberality,
I marvel not that all people are so willing to follow ye.
LUCRE
Then, sweet soul, mark what I would have thee do for me.
That is, to deck up thy poor cottage handsomely;
And for that purpose I have five thousand crowns in store,
And when it is spent, thou shalt have twice as much more.
But only see thy rooms be neat when I shall thither resort
With familiar friends, to play and pass the time in sport.
For the deputy, constable, and spiteful neighbours do spy, pry, and eye about my house,
That I dare not be once merry within, but still mute like a mouse.

57 **hath...furtherance** has not helped you.
59 **wottest thou** do you know.
60 **I...gone** I intend to invite the guests to the feast, as the bride and groom are almost ready to leave for the service. (The quarto has 'gesse' here, but 'guests' seems to make more sense.)
61 **having...brooms** brooms might be needed to sweep the dining room in preparation for the feast, or as part of rituals of good luck such as 'jumping the broom'.
63 **such...apaid** she will be well served with such an abundance.
67 **in such sort** in this way.
68 **store...sport** abounding in all pleasures.
69 **in a string** by a leash.
71 **For...heart** Because I (now) see your generous heart.
77–78 **only...friends** just make sure that your rooms are clean when I want to visit with my close friends.
80 **still mute** always silent. (The implication is that Lucre wants to use Conscience's house for the immoral or criminal activities which the attentions of the constable and her neighbours make too dangerous in her own.)

CONSCIENCE
My good Lady Lucre, I will fulfil your mind in every kind of thing,
So that you shall be welcome at all hours, whomsoever you do bring.
And all the dogs in the town shall not bark at your doings, I trow;
For your full pretence and intent I do throughly know,
Even so well as if you had opened the very secrets of your heart,
For which I doubt not but to rest in your favour by my desert.
But here comes your man, Usury.

Enter Usury.

LUCRE
I'll send him home for the money.
Usury, step in, and bring me the box of all abomination that stands in the window.
It is little and round, painted with diverse colours, and is pretty to the show.

USURY
Madam, is there any superscription thereon?

LUCRE
Have I not told you the name? For shame, get you gone. [*Exit Usury.*]
Well, my wench, I doubt not but our pleasures shall excel,
Seeing thou hast got a corner fit, where few neighbours dwell,
And they be of the poorest sort, which fits our turn so right,
Because they dare not speak against our sports and sweet delight.
And if they should, alas, their words would nought at all be weighed,
And for to speak before my face they will be all afraid.

Enter Usury, with a painted box of ink in his hand.

USURY
Madam, I deem this same to be it, so far as I can guess.

LUCRE
Thou sayest the truth, 'tis it indeed; the outside shows no less.
But, Usury, I think Dissimulation hath not seen you since your coming home;
Therefore go see him, he will rejoice when to him you are shown.
It is a busy time with him, help to further him, if you can.

USURY
He may command me to attend at board to be his man. [*Exit Usury.*]

Here let Lucre open the box, and dip her finger in it, and spot Conscience's face, saying as followeth.

81 **fulfil ... thing** do whatever you want.
83 **trow** believe.
84 **throughly** thoroughly.
86 **desert** deserving.
90 **pretty ... show** pretty to look at.
91 **superscription** writing/label.
93 **our ... excel** we'll have a great time.
94–95 **thou ... right** you live in a very suitable nook, with few neighbours, and those all very poor, which is ideal for our purposes.
97 **their ... weighed** their complaints will not be listened to.
103 **help ... him** help him in what he is trying to do.
104 **attend ... man** wait at his table as his servant.
spot cover in ink spots.

LUCRE
Hold here, my sweet; and then over to see if any want.
The more I do behold this face, the more my mind doth vaunt.
This face is of favour, these cheeks are reddy and white;
These lips are cherry-red, and full of deep delight.
Quick-rolling eyes, her temples high, and forehead white as snow;
Her eyebrows seemly set in frame, with dimpled chin below.
O, how beauty hath adorned thee with every seemly hue,
In limbs, in looks, with all the rest proportion keeping due.
Sure, I have not seen a finer soul in every kind of part.
I cannot choose but kiss thee with my lips, that love thee with my heart.

CONSCIENCE
I have told the crowns, and here are just so many as you to me did say.

LUCRE
Then, when thou wilt thou may'st depart, and homewards take thy way.
And I pray thee, make haste in decking of thy room,
That I may find thy lodging fine when with my friend I come.

CONSCIENCE
I'll make speed, and where I have with brooms oft-times been roaming,
I mean henceforth not to be seen, but sit to watch your coming. *Exit Conscience.*

LUCRE
O, how joyful may I be that such success do find!
No marvel, for poverty and desire of Lucre do force them follow my mind.
Now may I rejoice in full contentation
That shall marry Love with Dissimulation.
And I have spotted Conscience with all abomination.
But I forget myself, for I must to the wedding,
Both vauntingly and flauntingly, although I had no bidding. *Exit Lucre.*

[Scene 11]

Enter Dissimulation and Cogging, his man, and Simony.

COGGING
Sir, although you be my master, I would not have you to upbraid my name,
But I would have you use the right skill and title of the same.
For my name is neither Scogging nor Scragging, but ancient Cogging.
Sir, my ancestors were five of the four worthies, and yourself are of my near kin.

105 **Hold . . . want** Hold your face that way . . . and now turn this way so I may see if I have missed anywhere.
106 **vaunt** exalt.
107 **favour** lovely.
109 **quick-rolling** vivacious, expressive.
110 **seemly . . . frame** perfectly positioned.
111 **seemly hue** fitting colour.
112 **proportion keeping due** keeping due proportion.
115 **told** counted.
117 **decking** preparing.
120 **watch** wait for.
122 **No marvel** It's no wonder.
123 **contentation** satisfaction.
127 **vauntingly . . . bidding** proudly and flamboyantly, although I am not invited.
3 **Scogging nor Scragging** 'scogging' may be an allusion to the fifteenth-century court fool, Scogin; a 'scragging' is a hanging or beating.
4 **worthies** there were actually Nine Worthies, who represented classical, biblical, and Christian heroes.

DISSIMULATION
Indeed thou say'st true, for Cogging is a kinsman to Dissimulation.
But, tell me, have you taken the names of the guests?

COGGING
Yea, sir.

DISSIMULATION
Let me hear after what fashion.

The names of the guests told by Cogging.

COGGING
There is, first and foremost, Master Forgery and Master Flattery, Master Perjury and Master Injury, Master Cruelty and Master Pickery, Master Bribery and Master Treachery, Master Wink-at-wrong and Master Headstrong, Mistress Privy-theft and Master Deep-deceit, Master Abomination and Mistress Fornication, his wife, Ferdinando False-weight and Frisset False-measure his wife.

DISSIMULATION
Stay; Fornication and Frisset False-measure?
They are often familiar with my Lady Lucre,
And one of them she accounts her friend.
Therefore they shall sit with the bride in the middest, and the men at each end.
Let me see; there are sixteen, even as many as well near is able
To dine in the summer-parlour at the playing-table;
Beside my fellow Fraud, and you, fellow Simony;
But I shall have a great miss of my fellow Usury.

SIMONY
Take no care for that; he came home yesterday even, no longer:
His pardon was quickly begged, and that by a courtier.
But, sirrah, since he came home, he had like to have slain Good Neighbourhood and Liberality,
Had not True Friendship stepped between them very suddenly.
But, sirrah, he hit True Friendship such a blow on the ear
That he keeps out of all men's sight, I think for shame or for fear.

DISSIMULATION
Now, of my troth, it is a pretty jest. Hath he made True Friendship hide his head?
Sure, if it be so, Good Neighbourhood and Liberality for fear are fled.

SIMONY
But, fellow Dissimulation, tell me what priest shall marry ye.

DISSIMULATION
Marry, that shall an old friend of mine, Master Doctor Hypocrisy.

SIMONY
Why, will you not have Sir Peter Pleaseman to supply that want?

6 **taken** listed.
8 **Pickery** pickpocketing/theft.
9 **Wink-at-wrong** turn a blind eye to crime.
12 **Stay** Wait.
15 **middest** the middle of the top table.
17 **playing-table** a summer parlour was an airy room used for entertaining in the summer months. The playing table may be that used for card games.
19 **I...miss** I shall miss greatly.
20 **even** evening.
22 **he...slain** he nearly killed.
26 **a pretty jest** a good trick.
30 **supply that want** fill that need/role.

DISSIMULATION

Indeed, Sir Peter is a good priest, but Doctor Hypocrisy is most ancient.
But, Cousin Cogging, I pray you go to invite the guests,
And tell them that they need not disturb their quietness.
Desire them to come at dinner-time and it shall suffice,
Because I know they will be loth so early to rise.
But at any hand, will Doctor Hypocrisy,
That he meet us at the church very early;
For I would not have all the world to wonder at our match.
It is an old proverb: ''tis good having a hatch before the door',
but I'll have a door before the hatch.

COGGING

Sir, I will about it as fast as I can hie.
I'll first to that scald bald-knave Doctor Hypocrisy. *Exit Cog*[*ging*].

SIMONY

But, fellow Dissimulation, how darest thou marry with Love, bearing no love at all?
For thou dost nothing but dissemble, then thy love must needs be small.
Thou canst not love but from the teeth forward.
Sure the wife that marries thee shall highly be preferred.

DISSIMULATION

Tush, tush, you are a merry man. I warrant you I know what I do,
And can yield a good reason for it, I may say unto you.
What, and if the world should change and run all on her side,
Then might I by her means still in good credit abide.
Thou knowest Love is ancient, and lives peaceably without any strife;
Then sure the people will think well of me because she is my wife.

SIMONY

Trust me, thou art as crafty to have an eye to the main-chance
As the tailor, that out of seven yards stole one and a half of durance.
He served at that time the devil in the likeness of Saint Katherine.
Such tailors will thrive, that out of a doublet and a pair of hose can steal their wife an
apron.
The doublet-sleeves three fingers were too short;
The Venetians came nothing near the knee.

DISSIMULATION

Then, for to make them long enough, I pray thee what did he?

SIMONY

Two pieces set an handful broad, to lengthen them withal;
Yet for all that below the knee by no means they could fall.

33 **they . . . quietness** they need not interrupt their slumbers.
36 **at . . . will** whatever you do, instruct.
38 **wonder . . . match** gawp at our wedding.
39 **hatch** a hatch was the lower half of a divided door. The implication seems to be that Dissimulation will be doubly safe. Rather than having an open half door, he'll keep his hatch behind a locked door.
44 **from . . . forward** i.e. in empty words with nothing behind them.
45 **preferred** favoured (ironic).
48 **What . . . side** What if everything went wrong for us?
52 **to . . . main-chance** to always keep the best option in view.
53 **durance** strong, 'enduring' cloth.
56 **three . . . short** were too short by the width of three fingers.
57 **Venetians** Venetian-style breeches.
59 **Two . . . broad** added two extra pieces of cloth a hands-width wide.

He, seeing that, desired the party to buy as much to make another pair;
The party did; yet, for all that, he stole a quarter there.

DISSIMULATION

Now, sure, I can him thank, he could his occupation!
My fellow Fraud would laugh to hear one dressed of such a fashion.
But, fellow Simony, I thank you heartily for comparing the tailor to me.
As who should say his knavery and my policy did not agree.

SIMONY

Not so, but I was the willinger to tell thee because I know it to be a true tale;
And to see how artificers do extol Fraud, by whom they bear their sale.
But come, let us walk, and talk no more of this.
Your policy was very good, and so, no doubt, was his.

Exeunt.

[Scene 12]

Enter Mercadore reading a letter to himself; and let Gerontus the Jew follow him, and speak as followeth.

GERONTUS

Signor Mercadore, why do you not pay me? Think you I will be mocked in this sort?
This is three times you have flouted me, it seems you make thereat a sport.
Truly, pay me my money, and that even now presently,
Or, by mighty Mahomet, I swear I will forthwith arrest ye.

MERCADORE

Ha, pray-a bare wit me tree or four days; me have much business in hand.
Me be troubled with letters, you see here, dat comes from England.

GERONTUS

Tush, this is not my matter; I have nothing therewith to do.
Pay me my money, or I'll make you, before to your lodging you go.
I have officers stand watching for you, so that you cannot pass by;
Therefore you were best to pay me, or else in prison you shall lie.

MERCADORE

Arrest me, dou scal knave? Marry, do, and if thou dare;
Me will not pay de one penny. Arrest me, do; me do not care.
Me will be a Turk; me came heder for dat cause;
Derefore me care not de so mush as two straws.

GERONTUS

This is but your words, because you would defeat me.
I cannot think you will forsake your faith so lightly.
But, seeing you drive me to doubt, I'll try your honesty;
Therefore be sure of this, I'll go about it presently. *Exit.*

61 **the party** the other party to the transaction: the buyer.
63 **he . . . occupation** he knew his job!
66 **policy** cunning.
1 **sort** manner.
3 **presently** immediately.
4 **Mahomet** the Prophet Muhammad: often represented as a Jewish idol in medieval and Tudor plays.
13 **Me will . . . cause** I will convert to Islam (and so avoid his debts); that's why I came here.
16 **lightly** easily.
17 **try** test.

MERCADORE
Marry, farewell and be hanged, s[h]itten, scald, drunken Jew.
I warrant ye, me shall be able very well to pay you.
My Lady Lucre have sent me here dis letter,
Praying me to cosen de Jew for love a' her.
Derefore me'll go to get-a some Turk apparel,
Dat me may cosen de Jew, and end dis quarrel. *Exit.*

[Scene 13]

Enter three beggars; that is to say, Tom Beggar, Wily Will, and Simplicity, singing.

THE SONG

To the wedding, to the wedding, to the wedding go we:
To the wedding a-begging, a-begging all three.

Tom Beggar shall brave it, and Wily Will too,
Simplicity shall knave it, wherever we go:
With lustly bravado, take care that care will,
To catch it and snatch it we have the brave skill.

Our fingers are lime-twigs, and barbers we be,
To catch sheets from hedges most pleasant to see;
Then to the alewife roundly we set them to sale,
And spend the money merrily upon her good ale.

To the wedding, to the wedding, to the wedding go we:
To the wedding a-begging, a-begging all three.

Finis.

TOM
Now truly, my masters, of all occupations under the sun, begging is the best;
For when a man is weary, then he may lay him down to rest.
Tell me, is it not a lord's life in summer to louse one under a hedge,
And then, leaving that game, may go clip and coll his Madge?
Or else may walk to take the wholesome air abroad for his delight,
When he may tumble on the grass, have sweet smells, and see many a pretty sight?
Why, an emperor for all his wealth can have but his pleasure,
And surely I would not lose my charter of liberty for all the king's treasure.

WILL
Shall I tell thee, Tom Beggar, by the faith of a gentleman, this ancient freedom
I would not forego,
If I might have whole mines of money at my will to bestow.

7 **lime-twigs** sticky (for stolen goods). Fowlers spread sticky lime over the branches of trees to trap birds.
7 **barbers** i.e. able to 'shave' and 'shear' (colloquial terms for 'rob').
8 **catch...hedges** washed bed-sheets were often hung out to dry over hedges, thus making them very vulnerable to theft.
15 **louse one** pick the lice from one's clothing.
16 **clip...Madge** embrace and kiss his woman.
20 **charter of liberty** this freedom.

Then, a man's mind should be troubled to keep that he had;
And you know it were not for me; it would make my valiant mind mad.
For now we neither pay Church-money, subsidies, fifteens, scot nor lot;
All the payings we pay is to pay the good ale-pot.

SIMPLICITY

But, fellow beggars, you cosen me, and take away all the best meat,
And leave me nothing but brown bread or fin of fish to eat.
When you be at the alehouse, you drink up the strong ale, and give me small beer;
You tell me 'tis better than the strong to make me sing clear.
Indeed, you know, with my singing I get twice so much as ye,
But, and you serve me so, you shall sing yourselves, and beg alone for me.

TOM

We stand prating here; come, let us go to the gate.
Mass, I am greatly afraid we are come somewhat too late.
Good gentle master porter, your reward do bestow
On a poor lame man, that hath but a pair of legs to go.

WILL

For the honour of God, good master porter, give somewhat to the blind,
That the way to the alehouse in his sleep cannot find.

TOM

For the good Lord's sake, take compassion on the poor.

Enter Fraud, with a basket of meat on his arm.

FRAUD

How now, sirs! You are vengeance hasty; can ye not tarry,
But stand bawling so at my lady's door?
Here, take it amongst you; yet 'twere a good alms-deed to give you nothing,
Because you were so hasty, and kept such a calling.

TOM

I beseech ye not so, sir, for we were very hungry;
That made us so earnest, but we are sorry we troubled ye.

SIMPLICITY

Look how greedy they be, like dogs that fall a snatching.
You shall see that I shall have the greatest alms, because I said nothing.
Fraud knows me, therefore he'll be my friend, I am sure of that.
They have nothing but lean beef; ye shall see, I shall have a piece that is fat.
Master Fraud, you have forgot me; pray ye, let me have my share.

FRAUD

Faith, all is gone; thou com'st too late. Thou seest to all is given there.
By the faith of a gentleman, I have it not; I would I were able to give thee more.

23 **to...had** to guard the wealth he possessed.

25 **Church-money...lot** taxes: the tithe was a levy of 10% annual income paid to the vicar, subsidies and fifteenths were taxes on wealth and property granted by parliament (the latter a levy of one fifteenth of the value of one's wealth), the scot and the lot were local taxes.

29 **small beer** weaker beer.

31 **get** earn.

32 **and...so** if you treat me like that.

36 **but...go** only one pair of legs to walk with.

37–38 **blind...find** a blind man who cannot find his way to the pub...while sleeping. These are not, of course, real disabilities worthy of alms.

40 **You...tarry** You're damned hasty; can't you wait?

43 **take...nothing** divide this among you, although it would be a good act of charity to give you nothing.

SIMPLICITY
O sir, I saw your arms hang out of a stable-door.
FRAUD
Indeed, my arms are at the painter's; belike, he hung them out to dry.
I pray thee, tell me what they were, if thou canst them descry.
SIMPLICITY
Marry, there was never a scutcheon, but there was two trees rampant,
And then over them lay a sour tree passant,
With a man like you in a green field pendant,
Having a hempen halter about his neck, with a knot under the left ear, because you are a younger brother.
Then, sir, there stands on each side, holding up the crease,
A worthy ostler's hand in a dish of grease.
Besides all this, on the helmet stands the hangman's hand,
Ready to turn the ladder, whereon your picture did stand.
Then under the helmet hung tables like chains, and for what they are I cannot devise,
Except it be to make you hang fast, that the crows might pick out your eyes.
FRAUD
What a swad is this? I had been better to have sent him to the back-door,
To have gotten some alms amongst the rest of the poor.
Thou prat'st thou canst not tell what, or else art not well in thy wit.
I am sure my arms are not blased so far abroad as yet.
SIMPLICITY
O yes, sir, your arms were known a great while ago,
For your elder brother Deceit did give those arms too.
Marry, the difference is all, which is the knot under the left ear.
The painter says, when he is hung, you may put out the knot without fear.
I am sure they were arms, for there was written in Roman letters round about the hempen collar:
'Given by the worthy valiant captain, Master Fraud, the ostler'.
Now, God be wi' ye, sir; I'll get me even close to the back-door.
Farewell, Tom Beggar and Wily Will; I'll beg with you no more. *Exit.*
TOM
O farewell, Simplicity, we are very loth to lose thy company.
FRAUD
Now he is gone, give ear to me. You seem to be sound men in every joint and limb,
And can ye live in this sort to go up and down the country a-begging?
O base minds! I trow I had rather hack it out by the highway-side,

54 **arms** coat of arms.
56 **descry** describe.
57 **scutcheon** shield.
57 **rampant** rearing up.
58 **a...passant** as if walking: the allusion is to the gallows tree.
59 **pendant** hanging.
60 **hempen halter** hemp noose.
60 **because...brother** The heir and his younger brothers quartered their arms differently.
62 **crease** crest.
64 **turn the ladder** push away the ladder.
65 **chains** chains of small weights.
66 **fast** still/securely.
67 **swad** country clown.
70 **blased...abroad** talked about so widely/inscribed so visibly.
74 **when...fear** When his elder brother is hanged, he can move the knot in his own shield to indicate he is now the oldest.
79 **loth** sorry.
80 **give ear** listen.
80 **sound** healthy/strong.
82 **hack...highway-side** make a living as a highwayman.

Than such misery and penury still to abide.
Sirs, if you will be ruled by me, and do what I shall say,
I'll bring ye where we shall have a notable fine prey.
It is so, sirs, that a merchant, one Mercadore, is coming from Turkey,
And it is my lady's pleasure that he robbed should be.
She hath sworn that we shall be all sharers alike,
And upon that willed me some such companions as you be to seek.

TOM
O worthy Captain Fraud, you have won my noble heart.
You shall see how manfully I can play my part.
And here's Wily Will, as good a fellow as your heart can wish,
To go a-fishing with a crank through a window, or to set lime-twigs to catch a pan, pot, or dish.

WILL
He says true; for I tell you, I am one that will not give back;
Not for a double shot out of a black Jack!
O sir, you bring us a-bed, when ye talk of this gear.
Come, shall we go, worthy Captain? I long till we be there.

FRAUD
Aye, let us about it, to provide our weapons ready,
And when the time serves, I myself will conduct ye.

TOM
O, valiantly spoken! Come, Wily Will, two pots of ale we'll bestow
On our captain courageously for a parting blow. *Exeunt.*

[Scene 14]

Enter the Judge of Turkey with Gerontus and Mercadore.

JUDGE
Sir Gerontus, because you are the plaintiff, you first your mind shall say.
Declare the cause you did arrest this merchant yesterday.

GERONTUS
Then, learned Judge, attend. This Mercadore, whom you see in place,
Did borrow two thousand ducats of me but for a five weeks' space.
Then, sir, before the day came, by his flattery he obtained one thousand more,
And promised me at two months' end I should receive my store.
But before the time expired, he was closely fled away,
So that I never heard of him at least this two years' day,
Till at the last I met with him, and my money did demand;
Who sware to me at five days' end he would pay me out of hand.

88 **be . . . alike** we'll get an equal share of his wealth.
89 **willed . . . seek** she told me to seek out some confederates like you.
93 **crank** hook.
95 **double . . . Jack** two swigs from a tar-covered beer-mug.
96 **you . . . a-bed** you bring us comfort.
101 **parting blow** farewell gift.
1 **the plaintiff** the complainant/prosecutor.
3 **attend** listen.
3 **in place** here.
6 **my store** the whole amount.
7 **closely** secretly.
8 **at . . . day** for at least two years.

The five days came, and three days more, then one day he requested.
I, perceiving that he flouted me, have got him thus arrested.
And now he comes in Turkish weeds to defeat me of my money,
But, I trow, he will not forsake his faith; I deem he hath more honesty.

JUDGE

Sir Gerontus, you know, if any man forsake his faith, king, country, and become a Mahomet,
All debts are paid. 'Tis the law of our realm, and you may not gainsay it.

GERONTUS

Most true, reverend Judge,
We may not; nor I will not against our laws grudge.

JUDGE

Signor Mercadore, is this true that Gerontus doth tell?

MERCADORE

My lord Judge, de matter and de circumstance be true, me know well;
But me will be a Turk, and for dat cause me came here.

JUDGE

Then, it is but folly to make many words. Signor Mercadore, draw near.
Lay your hand upon this book, and say after me.

MERCADORE

With a good will, my lord Judge; me be all ready.

GERONTUS

Not for any devotion, but for Lucre's sake of my money.

JUDGE

[*Mercadore repeating after him.*]

Say: 'I, Mercadore, do utterly renounce before all the world my duty to
my prince, my honour to my parents, and my good-will to my country.
Furthermore, I protest and swear to be true to this country during life,
and thereupon I forsake my Christian faith...'

GERONTUS

Stay there, most puissant judge. Signor Mercadore, consider what you do:
Pay me the principal; as for the interest, I forgive it you.
And yet the interest is allowed amongst you Christians, as well as in Turkey.
Therefore, respect your faith, and do not seek to deceive me.

MERCADORE

No point da interest, no point da principal.

GERONTUS

Then pay me the one half, if you will not pay me all.

MERCADORE

No point da half, no point denier. Me will be a Turk, I say.
Me be weary of my Christ's religion, and for dat me come away.

GERONTUS

Well, seeing it is so, I would be loth to hear the people say it was 'long of me

12 **flouted** mocked.
13 **weeds** clothes.
15 **Mahomet** Muslim.
16 **gainsay** deny.
22 **draw near** come here.
30 **puissant** powerful.
34 **No point** I care nothing for.
36 **denier** even the smallest copper coin.
38 **'long of me** my fault.

Thou forsakest thy faith. Wherefore I forgive thee frank and free;
Protesting before the judge and all the world never to demand penny nor halfpenny.

MERCADORE
O, Sir Gerontus, me take-a your proffer, and tank you most heartily.

JUDGE
But, Signor Mercadore, I trow ye will be a Turk for all this.

MERCADORE
Signor, no; not for all da good in da world me forsake-a my Christ.

JUDGE
Why, then, it is as Sir Gerontus said; you did more for the greediness of the money
Than for any zeal or goodwill you bear to Turkey.

MERCADORE
O sir, you make a great offence. You must not Judge-a my conscience.

JUDGE
One may judge and speak truth, as appears by this;
Jews seek to excel in Christianity, and Christians in Jewishness. *Exit.*

MERCADORE
Vell, vell; but me tank you, Sir Gerontus, with all my very heart.

GERONTUS
Much good may it do you, sir. I repent it not for my part.
But yet I would not have this bolden you to serve another so:
Seek to pay, and keep day with me, so a good name on you will go. *Exit.*

MERCADORE
You say vel, sir; it does me good dat me have cosened de Jew.
Faith, I would my Lady Lucre de whole matter now knew.
What is dat me will not do for her sweet sake?
But now me will provide my journey toward England to take.
Me be a Turk? No; it will make my Lady Lucre to smile,
When she knows how me did da scald Jew beguile. *Exit.*

[Scene 15]

Enter Lucre, and Love with a vizard, behind.

LUCRE
Mistress Love, I marvel not a little what coy conceit is crept into your head,
That you seem so sad and sorrowful, since the time you first did wed.
Tell me, sweet wench, what thou ailest, and if I can ease thy grief,
I will be prest to pleasure thee in yielding of relief.
Sure, thou makest me for to think something has chanced amiss.
I pray thee, tell me what thou ailest, and what the matter is.

LOVE
My grief, alas, I shame to show, because my bad intent
Hath brought on me a just reward, and eke a strange event.

39 **I...free** I absolve you of all debts, liberally and freely.
51 **bolden...so** encourage you to treat others like this.
56 **provide** prepare.
vizard, behind a mask on the back of her head, so she appears to have two faces.
1 **coy conceit** strange notion.
3 **what thou ailest** what ails you.
4 **prest** eager/ready.
7 **I...show** I am ashamed to reveal.
8 **eke** also.

Shall I be counted Love? Nay, rather lascivious Lust,
Because unto Dissimulation I did repose such trust.
But now I moan too late, and blush my hap to tell.
My head in monstrous sort, alas, doth more and more still swell.

LUCRE
Is your head then swollen, good Mistress Love? I pray you let me see.
Of troth it is, behold a face that seems to smile on me:
It is fair and well-favoured, with a countenance smooth and good;
Wonder is the worst, to see two faces in a hood.
Come, let's go, we'll find some sports to spurn away such toys.

LOVE
Were it not for Lucre, sure, Love had lost all her joys. *Exeunt.*

[Scene 16]

Enter Serviceable Diligence, the Constable, and Simplicity, with an Officer [Beadle] to whip him, or two, if you can.

SIMPLICITY
Why, but must I be whipped, Master Constable, indeed?
You may save your labour, for I have no need.

DILIGENCE
I must needs see thee punished; there is no remedy,
Except thou wilt confess, and tell me
Where thy fellows are become that did the robbery.

SIMPLICITY
Indeed, Master Constable, I do not know of their stealing,
For I did not see them since we went together a-begging.
Therefore pray ye, sir, be miserable to me, and let me go,
For I labour to get my living with begging, you know.

DILIGENCE
Thou wast seen in their company a little before the deed was done;
Therefore it is most likely thou knowest where they are become.

SIMPLICITY
Why, Master Constable, if a sheep go among wolves all day,
Shall the sheep be blamed if they steal anything away?

DILIGENCE
Aye, marry, shall he; for it is a great presumption
That, keeping them company, he is of like profession,
But despatch, sirs; strip him and whip him.
Stand not to reason the question.

SIMPLICITY
Indeed, 'twas Fraud, so it was, it was not I;

11 **my...tell** to reveal my destiny.
17 **some...toys** some entertainment to drive away such nonsense.
if you can if there are enough free actors.
5 **become** have gone.
7 **I...them** I have not seen them.
8 **miserable** he means 'commiserable': compassionate.
14 **Aye...he** Yes indeed, he shall.
15 **like** the same.
17 **Stand...question.** Don't stop to debate the point.

And here he comes himself. Ask him if I lie.

Enter Fraud.

DILIGENCE

What sayest thou, villain? I would advise thee hold thy tongue;
I know him to be a wealthy man and a burgess of the town.
Sir, and it please your mastership, here one slanders you with felony:
He saith you were the chief doer of a robbery.

FRAUD

What says the rascal? But you know
It standeth not with my credit to brawl;
But, good Master Constable, for his slanderous report
Pay him double, and in a greater matter command me you shall. *Exit.*

SIMPLICITY

Master Constable, must the countenance carry out the knave?
Why, then, if one will face folks out, some fine reparlment he must have.

[*Beadle put off his clothes.*]

BEADLE

Come, Sir Jack-sauce, make quick despatch at once;
You shall see how finely we will fetch the skin from your bones.

SIMPLICITY

Nay, but tell me whether you be right-handed or no?

BEADLE

What is that to thee? Why wouldst thou so fain know?

SIMPLICITY

Marry, if you should be both right-handed, the one would hinder the other;
Then it would not be done finely, according to order;
For if I be not whipped with credit, it is not worth a pin.
Therefore, I pray, Master Constable, let me be whipped upon my skin.

DILIGENCE

Whereon dost thou think they would whip thee, I pray thee declare,
That thou puttest us in mind, and takest such great care?

SIMPLICITY

I was afraid you would have worn out my clothes with whipping;
Then afterward I should go naked a-begging.

BEADLE

Have no doubt of that; we will favour thy clothes:
Thou shalt judge that thyself by feeling the blows.

Lead him once or twice about, whipping him, and so exit.

21 **burgess** magistrate or civic officer.

25 **It...brawl** It is not in keeping with my dignity to take part in disturbances.

27 **and...shall** and you can call on my services in more important matters later.

29 **Must...have** Does the face make the knave, then? (i.e. is the mere appearance of social standing and honesty enough these days?) Well then, if you want to defy folks to their faces, you just need some fine clothes (misspeaking 'reparlment' for 'apparelment').

29.1 **Beadle...clothes** the Beadle strips Simplicity.

30 **Come...once** Impudent rogue, let's get on with it.

33 **Why...know?** Why would you like to know that?

36 **with credit** decently.

39 **That...care** That you remind us and are so concerned about it.

42 **favour** take care with.

[Scene 17]

Enter Judge Nemo, the Clerk of the 'size, the Crier, and Serviceable Diligence: the Judge and Clerk being set, the Crier shall sound three times.

JUDGE
Serviceable Diligence, bring hither such prisoners as are in custody.

DILIGENCE
My diligence shall be applied very willingly. Pleaseth it you, there are but three prisoners, so far as I know,
Which are Lucre and Conscience, with a deformed creature much like Bifrons, the base daughter of Juno.

JUDGE
No? Where is that wretch Dissimulation?

DILIGENCE
He hath transformed himself after a strange fashion.

JUDGE
Fraud: where is he become?

DILIGENCE
He was seen in the streets, walking in a citizen's gown.

JUDGE
What is become of Usury?

DILIGENCE
He was seen at the Exchange very lately.

JUDGE
Tell me, when have you heard of Simony?

DILIGENCE
He was seen this day walking in Paul's, having conference and very great familiarity with some of the clergy.

JUDGE
Fetch Lucre and Conscience to the bar.

DILIGENCE
Behold, worthy judge, here ready they are.

Enter Lucre and Conscience.

JUDGE
Stand forth. Diligence, divide them asunder.

CLERK
Lucre, thou art indicted by the name of Lucre,
To have committed adultery with Mercadore the merchant and Creticus the lawyer.
Thou art also indicted for the robbery of Mercadore.
Lastly and chiefly, for the consenting to the murder of Hospitality.
What sayest thou, art thou guilty or not in these causes?

'size Court of Assize.
being set once they are in their seats.
sound cry out. Possibly 'hear ye, hear ye, hear ye' to announce the opening of the court.
3 **Bifrons** is literally 'two faces'. Diligence may have his mythology wrong regarding the 'low-born' daughter, though, as the two-faced God was Janus, who was associated with Juno as god of the changing year and thresholds.
9 **the Exchange** the money market.
11 **Paul's** St Paul's cathedral: a place for trade as well as religious services.
14 **Stand forth.** Step forward.

LUCRE

Not guilty. Where are mine accusers? They may shame to show their faces.
I warrant you, none comes, nor dare to discredit my name.
In despite of the teeth of them that dare, I speak in disdain.

JUDGE

Impudent; canst thou deny deeds so manifestly known?

LUCRE

In denial stands trial. I shame not; let them be shown.
It grinds my gall they should slander me on this sort.
They are some old, cankered, currish, corrupt carls, that gave me this report.
My soul craves revenge on such my secret foes,
And revengement I will have, if body and soul I lose.

JUDGE

Thy hateful heart declares thy wicked life.
In the abundance of thy abomination all evils are rife.
But what sayest thou, Conscience, to thy accusation,
That art accused to have been bawd unto Lucre, and spotted with all abomination?

CONSCIENCE

What should I say: nay? What would I say in this our naughty living?

LUCRE

Good Conscience, if thou love me, say nothing.

CLERK

Diligence, suffer her not to stand prating.

Let him put her aside.

JUDGE

What letter is that in thy bosom, Conscience?
Diligence, reach it hither.

Make as though he read it.

Conscience, speak on; let me hear what thou canst say,
For I know in singleness thou wilt a truth bewray.

CONSCIENCE

My good lord, I have no way to excuse myself.
She hath corrupted me by flattery and her accursed pelf.
What need further trial, sith I, Conscience, am a thousand witnesses?
I cannot choose but condemn us all in living amiss.
Such terror doth affright me, that living I wish to die:
I am afraid there is no spark left for me of God's mercy.

JUDGE

Conscience, where hadst thou this letter?

[22] **In...disdain.** I scorn those who do dare to their faces.
[25] **It...sort.** It irritates me that they can slander me in this way.
[26] **corrupt carls** diseased, doglike, corrupt churls/rogues.
[32] **bawd** pimp.
[36] **in...bosom** concealed in the front of your dress.
[37] **reach it hither** pass it here (to me).
[39] **in...bewray** when left to speak for yourself will reveal the truth.
[41] **pelf** money.
[43] **in living amiss** for sinful/criminal living.

CONSCIENCE
It was put into my bosom by Lucre,
Willing me to keep secret our lascivious living.
I cannot but condemn us all in this thing.

JUDGE
How now, malapert; stand you still in defence or no?
This letter declares thy guilty conscience. How sayest thou, is it not so?
Tell me, why standest thou in a maze? Speak quickly.
Hadst thou thy tongue so liberal, and now stand to study?

LUCRE
O Conscience, thou hast killed me. By thee I am overthrown.

JUDGE
It is happy that by Conscience thy abomination is known.
Wherefore I pronounce judgment against thee on this wise:
Thou shalt pass to the place of darkness, where thou shalt hear fearful cries;
Weeping, wailing, gnashing of teeth, and torment without end;
Burning in the lake of fire and brimstone, because thou canst not amend.
Wherefore, Diligence, convey her hence. Throw her down to the lowest hell,
Where the infernal sprites and damned ghosts do dwell;
And bring forth Love.

Exit Lucre and Diligence. Let Lucre make ready for Love quickly, and come with Diligence.

Declare the cause, Conscience, at large how thou comest so spotted,
Whereby many by thee hath been greatly infected;
For under the colour of Conscience thou deceived'st many,
Causing them to defile the temple of God, which is man's body.
A clean conscience is a sacrifice, God's own resting-place:
Why wast thou then corrupted so, and spotted on thy face?

CONSCIENCE
When Hospitality had his throat cut by Usury,
He oppressed me with cruelty and brought me to beggary,
Turning me out of house and home; and in the end
My gown, to pay my rent to him, I did send.
So, driven to that extremity, I have fallen to that you see;
Yet after judgment I hope of God's mercy.

JUDGE
O Conscience, shall cankered coin corrupt thy heart?
Or shall want in this world cause thee to feel everlasting smart?
O Conscience, what a small time thou hast on earth to live;
Why dost thou not, then, to God all honour give,
Considering the time is everlasting that thou shalt live in bliss,

48 **Willing me** who told me.
50 **malapert** presumptuous woman.
52 **in a maze** dumbfounded.
53 **Hadst... study?** Do you stand silent who was earlier speaking so freely?
56 **on this wise** in this manner.
62.1 **Let... quickly** Let the actor playing Lucre quickly change costume to play Love.
63 **at... spotted** in detail, how you became covered in spots.
74 **of** for.
76 **Or... smart?** Or shall worldly poverty prompt you to experience eternal pains?

If by thy life thou rise from death to judgment, mercy, and forgiveness?

Enter Love with Diligence.

Stand aside, Conscience. Bring Love to the bar.
What sayest thou to thy deformity; who was the cause?

LOVE

Lady Lucre.

JUDGE

Did Lucre choke thee so, that thou gavest thyself over unto Lust?
And did prodigal expenses cause thee in Dissimulation to trust?
Thou wast pure, Love, and art thou become a monster,
Bolstering thyself upon the lasciviousness of Lucre?
Love, answer for thyself; speak in thy defence.

LOVE

I cannot choose but yield, confounded by Conscience.

JUDGE

Then judgment I pronounce on thee. Because thou followed Lucre,
Whereby thou hast sold thy soul, to feel like torment with her,
Which torments comprehended are in the worm of Conscience,
Who, raging still, shall ne'er have end, a plague for thine offence.
Care shall be thy comfort, and sorrow thy life sustain,
Thou shalt be dying, yet never dead, but pining still in endless pain.
Diligence, convey her to Lucre: let that be her reward.
Because unto her cankered coin she gave her whole regard.
But, as for Conscience, carry her to prison,
There to remain until the day of the general session.
Thus we make an end,
Knowing that the best of us all may amend.
Which God grant to his goodwill and pleasure,
That we be not corrupted with the unsatiate desire of vanishing earthly treasure;
For covetousness is the cause of wresting man's conscience:
Therefore, restrain thy lust, and thou shalt shun the offence.

FINIS.

84 **choke** infect you with the deforming disease of choke or quinsy.

91 **to . . . her** you shall suffer the same torments as her.

92–93 **are . . . plague** are all contained within the worm of conscience, whose eternal attack will plague you.

94 **care** suffering.

96 **unto . . . regard** she thought of nothing but rotten money.

98 **general session** the meeting of the high court.

102 **unsatiate** insatiable.

Tamburlaine the Great

(1587?)

CHRISTOPHER MARLOWE

(1564–1593)

THE AUTHOR

Christopher Marlowe was arguably the best known, and certainly the most controversial playwright of the Tudor period. He was born in Canterbury in February 1564, the same year as Shakespeare's birth, and baptized on the 26th of that month, the second of nine children of a shoemaker, John Marlowe and his wife Katherine. He was educated at King's School in Canterbury, where he held a scholarship from Christmas 1578. In late 1580 he progressed to Corpus Christi College, Cambridge where he held a scholarship funded by Archbishop Matthew Parker, graduating BA in 1584 and MA in July 1587, before moving to London.

Marlowe's was no ordinary academic career, however, as the correspondence over the award of his MA reveals. The university authorities sought to withhold the degree, citing his irregular attendance over the previous years, and seemingly also in response to rumours that he had gone into exile in the French city of Reims, where English Catholics were educated for the priesthood. In response, the privy council wrote to the university to quash these rumours, declaring that 'in all his [Marlowe's] actions he had behaved himself orderly and discretely, whereby he had done her majesty good service, and deserved to be rewarded for his faithful dealing'. This (rare but not unprecedented) intervention on behalf of a young student has led to speculation that Marlowe's absences from Cambridge and his trips abroad were covert missions on behalf of the government, perhaps aimed at infiltrating the recusant community at Reims. The precise nature of Marlowe's 'good service' to his queen is impossible to discover, but it is clear that he was mixing in circles close to the government's spymaster, Sir Francis Walsingham, if not directly in his employ.

While still enrolled at Cambridge, Marlowe began his playwriting career. He almost certainly wrote *Dido, Queen of Carthage* (published in 1594) for performance at this time, and may have begun *Tamburlaine the Great* as well. The latter was probably first performed in London, by the Admiral's Men, in 1587, and, as he clearly intended, it announced Marlowe as a sensational new voice on the capital's stages. Its Prologue brashly announces the manifesto for a dramaturgical revolution, dismissing the work of his contemporaries as comic doggerel, the 'jigging veins of rhyming mother-wits,/And such conceits as clownage keeps in pay'. As McMillan and McLean suggest (*The Queen's Men and Their Plays*, pp. 121ff.), this seems to be an obvious swipe at the repertoire of the Queen's Men, the company that, since its formation in 1583, had dominated the London scene, and which specialized in plays in rhymed verse and copious comic business performed by the celebrated clowns Richard Tarlton, Robert Wilson, and their fellows. In place of this clown-driven theatre, the Prologue promises high seriousness, grandiloquence, and the theatre of power: 'We'll lead you to the stately tent of war,/Where you shall hear the Scythian Tamburlaine/Threatening the world with high astounding terms,/And scourging kingdoms with his conquering sword.'

These 'high astounding terms' were at the heart of Marlowe's writing. His use of unrhymed blank verse and a consciously resonant 'high' register, what Ben Jonson would later call 'Marlowe's mighty line' (and his critics would call mere bombast) brought a new kind of domineering rhetoric to the Elizabethan stage, calling for a new style of acting. In the celebrated Edward Alleyn, who would play all of Marlowe's heroes, the playwright found an actor capable of delivering that new style: magisterial, declamatory, and accompanied by a commanding, mobile presence, striding across the stage. Ben Jonson is again a useful guide to the effect of this style, writing in his *Discoveries* of Tamburlaine's 'scenical strutting and furious vociferation', while Joseph Hall would talk of his 'strutting steps'. The style would be parodied in the later 1590s as arcane and old-fashioned in the figure of 'ancient' (ensign) Pistol in Shakespeare's *Henry IV (part II)* and *Henry V*, but for a period it dominated the stage. Perfectly suited to represent Marlowe's audaciously ambitious, restless, unconventional heroes, each in his own way determined to defy conventional religion and morality and determine his own destiny, it would drive his further iconoclastic successes, *The Jew of Malta* (1592), *Edward II*, *The Massacre at Paris*, and, perhaps most obviously, *Dr Faustus* (all 1593?).

Marlowe was as contentious outside the theatre as he was in, falling foul of the authorities on more than one occasion before his violent and untimely death in 1593. He was arrested and briefly imprisoned in 1589 for his part in a brawl in which an innkeeper's son was killed, and arrested again in January 1592 for 'coining' (making counterfeit coins) while in the Netherlands. The latter crime may again have been part of shady business on behalf of the government, as no formal charges were brought against him in England. Most strikingly he was the subject of accusations of atheism, blasphemy, and homosexuality which again brought him to the attention of the privy council just before his death in 1593.

When on 5 May 1593 verses against foreign traders were pinned to the wall of the Dutch church in London, the government, fearing potential race riots, sought out their author. As the verses were signed 'Tamburlaine', attention turned not unnaturally to Marlowe and his associates. On 12 May the playwright Thomas Kyd was arrested, interrogated, and his rooms searched. Nothing was found to connect him to the verses, but the search did uncover a manuscript containing 'vile heretical conceits denying the deity of Jesus Christ our saviour'. Under interrogation Kyd claimed that this text was not his but Marlowe's, and must have been mistakenly 'shuffled' among his own papers when they shared a room two years earlier. The suggestion is not an unreasonable one, and the document itself was not as contentious as it first appeared. What no one involved seemed to realize was that it was not an original composition but notes copied from an orthodox printed book, John Proctour's *Fall of the Late Arian* (1549), which rehearsed atheist arguments in order to refute them. What makes it at least plausible that it was Marlowe's property rather than Kyd's was that, as Charles Nichol has shown, his headmaster at the King's School, John Gressop, owned a copy of the book. It would not have been out of character for the young Marlowe to have made notes of the most salacious and controversial views from a book that he had first seen while at school.

Events quickly outpaced the sober investigation of the facts, however. Perhaps under torture, Kyd began to recall a whole series of controversial views that Marlowe had allegedly expressed about religion and morality that diverted the attention of the authorities toward his former roommate, claims that he later repeated in two letters to his interrogators. 'It was his [Marlowe's] custom', Kyd claimed, 'to jest at the divine scriptures, jibe at prayers, and strive in argument to frustrate and confute what hath been spoke or writ by prophets and such holy men'. 'The first beginning of religion', he had allegedly declared, 'was only to keep men in awe'. A subsequent investigation, undertaken by one Richard Baines (hardly an impartial figure, as he had informed against Marlowe in the coining episode the previous year) uncovered further blasphemies: 'Moses was a juggler (conjuror)'; the Jews made the right choice in saving Barabbas; 'St John the

Evangelist was bedfellow to Christ and... used him as the sinners of Sodom'; 'all they that love not tobacco and boys are fools'. Marlowe was bound over to report to the privy council daily, but before the investigation could be completed, he was dead. On 30 May he was stabbed to death in a house in Deptford, east of London, by one Ingram Frizer, seemingly in an argument over the bill ('le reckoning'). The incident might appear a fitting end for a young man whose life had been spent courting controversy and argument. But the closer one looks, the less clear-cut the story seems to be. The 'tavern' in which the brawl occurred was actually no low dive but the home of a substantial property holder, one Eleanor Bull, and the encounter with Frizer was no chance argument but the end of a long day's eating and walking in the gardens with him and two other men, Nicholas Skeres and Robert Poley, each of whom had connections with petty crime, extortion, and Walsingham's spy network. Was Marlowe murdered on government orders as he was becoming too contentious to keep bailing out of trouble? Was he the victim of a sting or scam that went wrong? The evidence is insufficient to produce anything beyond a sense that there was more to these events than meets the eye, not least as Frizer himself was never fully punished. Perhaps this enigmatic, mysterious end, which has fascinated scholars and literary detectives ever since, was in its own way fitting for a playwright who thrived on challenging his audience's expectations and defying the commonplace.

THE PLAY

Tamburlaine is based on the life and career of the Mongol-Turkic military leader, Timur (1336–1405), who forged a powerful Muslim empire in what is now Iran, north-eastern Iraq, and large swathes of central Asia to the Ural mountains, slaughtering millions in the process. Timur's story was available to the playwright in a number of contemporary English sources, most obviously Thomas Fortescue's *The Forest or Collections of Histories* (1571) and George Whetstone's *The English Mirror* (1586). But Marlowe turns that bloody story into a spectacular account of the triumph of military *virtù* and the human will. Tamburlaine's rise from humble shepherd to king of Persia and overlord of the near and middle east is inexorable. Each of his enemies is easily crushed and humiliated, as much by his vaunting rhetoric of defiant power and self-praise as by his military skill. Indeed, as his battles are all conducted offstage, and little is said about his strategy or tactics, his triumphs can appear to be a direct result of the 'high astounding terms' of his speeches. This is not just the theatre of power, but theatre *as* power: dramatic performance as heroic action in the world.

The play's first audiences, familiar with the rise-and-fall pattern of moral drama, would probably have been waiting for the moment when Tamburlaine finally overreaches himself and falls, thereby exemplifying a moral or cultural lesson, and reaffirming the political status quo as the natural state of things. But that moment never comes. Tamburlaine defies dramatic precedent every bit as much as he defies the contemporary social structure by striving to conquer, and succeeding, over and over again, and remaining at the height of his powers at the end of the play. As Roma Gill observed (*Plays*, p. xiii), 'Tamburlaine is superhuman in his relentless ambition, and this sets him beyond considerations of ordinary morality. Marlowe asks not for a close, critical examination of character and motive, but only for amazement and wonder at his hero's exploits.' Thus, while the plight of his victims is clearly worthy of audience sympathy, the play contrives to focus attention not on them, but on the fixity of purpose in their conqueror. Even so gratuitous a case as the butchery of the Virgins of Damascus thus appears, in Marlowe's mischievously transgressive hands, an almost admirable instance of his hero's personal integrity. He had, after all, warned them: once the colour of his tents and banners had turned from red to black, there would be no mercy for anyone, however innocent.

Such a hero aspires to be superhuman, but risks becoming merely subhuman. And there is a hint of both in the key speech in Act II, in which Menaphon, half in admiration, half in terror, describes Tamburlaine as compounded of gems and celestial bodies, a killing machine on a cosmic scale set on a collision course with power ('twixt his manly pitch [shoulders]/A pearl more worth than all the world is placed,/Wherein by curious sovereignty of art/Are fixed his piercing instruments of sight,/Whose fiery circles bear encompassed/A heaven of heavenly bodies in their spheres,/That guides his steps and actions to the throne' (II.i.7–27)). The only moment when the hero seems to experience humanizing self-doubt comes in the lengthy speech in the final act (V.ii.72–128) in which he contemplates the beauty of Zenocrate, and wonders at his own love for her. But even this moment is quickly converted in Tamburlaine's conception into further evidence of his own superiority, as he concludes that such feelings simply mark out his own superiority, as 'That virtue solely is the sum of glory,/And fashions men with true nobility'.

While the play is rightly famed for its innovative rhetoric, it also employs a symbolism that links it to earlier forms of religious and secular drama. A number of its set pieces are highly spectacular and emblematic in their effects and import. The hero's transformation from shepherd to conqueror effected by a rapid change of costume from homespun smock to glittering armour; the entrance of the servants to Tamburlaine's victory banquet bearing crowns on dishes; the image of the Turkish emperor, Bajazeth, caged like a beast, and Tamburlaine's use of him as a footstool on which to step up to his own throne; the changing of the colours of his banners and tents from white to red to black: all of these are highly visual moments that deploy aesthetics as an adjunct to power in a way that both recalls the depiction of God in the mystery plays and the transformations of the protagonists of the moralities, but can seem very modern, indeed potentially fascistic to contemporary eyes.

The play seems to have been a major success on the stage. It was quickly followed by a sequel, *The Second Part of Tamburlaine the Great*, continuing the story of Timur's career and conquests up until his death. Critics have long wondered whether Marlowe always intended to write this continuation, and argue over whether the two plays constitute a single, unified work, but there seems no good reason to doubt the evidence of the prologue to the *Second Part*, which claims that it was the success of the first part that prompted the new work ('the general welcome's Tamburlaine received,/When he arrived last upon our stage/Hath made our poet pen his second part'). The evidence does not allow a clear picture of how many times it was played, but it appeared eight times in 1594–5 alone, and was played a further seven times in tandem with part two. In all there are records of twenty-two performances, and the extent to which the play was pastiched and parodied in later years suggest that there were many more. Both parts were printed together in the first published edition, that of 1590. For the text below I have used this 1590 edition of both parts of *Tamburlaine*, printed by Richard Jones (at the sign of the Rose and Crown, near Holborn Bridge), and have also consulted the modern editions by Gill and Dawson listed under further reading.

FURTHER READING

Dawson, Anthony, B., ed., *Tamburlaine Parts One and Two*, New Mermaids (London: A & C Black, 1997).

Dillon, Janette, '*Tamburlaine*' in Thomas Betteridge and Greg Walker, eds., *The Oxford Handbook of Tudor Drama* (Oxford: Oxford University Press, 2012), 584–98.

Gill, Roma, *The Plays of Christopher Marlowe* (Oxford: Oxford University Press, 1971).

Lunney, Ruth, *Marlowe and the Popular Tradition: Innovation in English Drama before 1595* (Manchester: Manchester University Press, 2002).

McMillan Scott and Sally-Beth MacLean, *The Queen's Men and Their Plays* (Cambridge: Cambridge University Press, 1998).

Nicholl, Charles, *The Reckoning: The Murder of Christopher Marlowe* (London: Jonathan Cape, 1992).

—— 'Marlowe, Christopher (*bap.* 1564, *d.* 1593)', *Oxford Dictionary of National Biography* (Oxford University Press, 2004); <http://www.oxforddnb.com/view/article/18079>, accessed 6 June 2013.

Shepherd, Simon, *Marlowe and the Politics of Elizabethan Theatre* (London: Palgrave Macmillan, 1986).

Vitkuss, Daniel, *Turning Turk: English Theatre and the Multicultural Mediterranean, 1570–1630* (New York and London: Palgrave Macmillan, 2003).

Whitfield White, Paul, *Marlowe, History and Sexuality: New Essays on Christopher Marlowe* (New York: AMS Press, 1998).

[The First Part of] Tamburlaine the Great
Who, from a Scythian shepherd, by his rare and wonderful conquests,
became a most puissant and mighty monarch,
and (for his tyranny and terror in war) was termed
The Scourge of God.
Divided into two Tragical Discourses, as they were sundry times showed
Upon stages in the City of London,
By the right honourable the Lord Admiral, his servants.

Now first and newly published.

London
Printed by Richard Jhones, at the sign
of the Rose and Crown near Holborne Bridge, 1590

To the Gentleman Readers and others that take pleasure in reading histories.

Gentlemen, and courteous readers whosoever: I have here published in print for your sakes, the two tragical discourses of the Scythian shepherd Tamburlaine, that became so great a conqueror and so mighty a monarch. My hope is that they will be now no less acceptable unto you to read after your serious affairs and studies than they have been (lately) delightful for many of you to see when the same were showed in London upon stages. I have (purposely) omitted and left out some fond and frivolous gestures, digressing and (in my poor opinion) far unmeet for the matter, which I thought might seem more tedious unto the wise than any way else to be regarded, though (haply) they have been of some vain-conceited fondlings greatly gaped at, what times they were showed upon the stage in their graced deformities: nevertheless, now to be mixtured in print with such matter of worth, it would prove a great disgrace to so honourable and stately a history. Great folly were it in me to commend unto your wisdoms either the eloquence of the author that writ them or the worthiness of the matter itself. I therefore leave unto your learned censures both the one and the other, and myself the poor printer of them unto your most courteous and favourable protection; which, if you vouchsafe to accept, you shall evermore bind me to employ what travail and service I can to the advancing and pleasuring of your excellent degree.

Yours, most humble at commandment,
R[ichard] J[ones], printer.

Scythian a kingdom in Central Asia. The historical Timur was born in the region of Samarkand in modern Uzbekistan.

The Lord Admiral's Men, a professional acting company sponsored by Charles Howard, 1st Earl of Nottingham, who played most frequently at the Rose Theatre in Southwark on the south bank of the Thames.

fond silly.
far unmeet very unsuitable.
haply perhaps.
fondlings vacuous fools.
censures judgements.
vouchsafe agree.

[*Dramatis personae:*

MYCETES, King of Persia.
COSROE, his brother.
MEANDER, THERIDAMAS, CENEUS, MENAPHON, and ORTYGIUS, Persian lords.
TAMBURLAINE, a Scythian shepherd.
TECHELLES AND USUMCASANE, his followers.
BAJAZETH, Emperor of the Turks.
KINGS of FEZ, MOROCCO and ARGIER, tributary kings to Bajazeth.
KING OF ARABIA (Alcidamus).
SOLDAN of Egypt.
GOVERNOR OF DAMASCUS,
AGYDAS, and MAGNETES, Median lords
CAPOLIN, an Egyptian.
PHILEMUS, a messenger.
A SPY.
ZENOCRATE, daughter to the Soldan of Egypt.
ANIPPE, her maid.
ZABINA, wife to Bajazeth,
EBEA, her maid.
VIRGINS of Damascus.
BASSOES, Lords, Citizens, Moors, Soldiers, and Attendants.]

THE PROLOGUE
From jigging veins of rhyming mother-wits,
And such conceits as clownage keeps in pay,
We'll lead you to the stately tent of war,
Where you shall hear the Scythian Tamburlaine
Threatening the world with high astounding terms,
And scourging kingdoms with his conquering sword.
View but his picture in this tragic glass,
And then applaud his fortunes as you please.

Actus I. Scaena i.

[*Enter*] *Mycetes, Cosroe, Meander, Theridamas, Ortygius, Ceneus, Menaphon, with others.*

MYCETES
Brother Cosroe, I find myself aggrieved;
Yet insufficient to express the same,
For it requires a great and thundering speech.
Good brother, tell the cause unto my lords;
I know you have a better wit than I.

COSROE
Unhappy Persia, that in former age
Hast been the seat of mighty conquerors,
That in their prowess and their policies
Have triumphed over Afric, and the bounds
Of Europe, where the sun dares scarce appear
For freezing meteors and congealed cold,
Now to be ruled and governed by a man
At whose birth-day Cynthia with Saturn joined,
And Jove, the Sun, and Mercury denied
To shed their influence in his fickle brain.
Now Turks and Tartars shake their swords at thee,
Meaning to mangle all thy provinces.

MYCETES
Brother, I see your meaning well enough,
And through your planets I perceive you think
I am not wise enough to be a king.
But I refer me to my noblemen,
That know my wit, and can be witnesses.
I might command you to be slain for this,
Meander, might I not?

MEANDER
Not for so small a fault, my sovereign lord.

Argier Algiers.
Soldan Sultan.
Bassoes Pashas.
1–2 **From . . . pay** From the sing-song verse of rhyming simpletons (i.e. those who have only the wit their mothers passed on to them) and the kinds of ideas that can only service slapstick comedy. (The claim is for the superiority of Marlowe's scholarly, unrhymed blank verse and solemn themes over popular contemporary verse-drama.)
7 **glass** mirror.
7.1 ***Actus . . . i.*** Act I. Scene i.
13 **Cynthia** the Moon. The suggestion is that fickleness (the Moon), mischance and stupidity (Saturn) presided over Mycetes' birth, while the more auspicious influences of the Jupiter, the Sun, and Mercury were denied him.

MYCETES
I mean it not, but yet I know I might.
Yet live, yea, live; Mycetes wills it so.
Meander, thou, my faithful counsellor,
Declare the cause of my conceived grief,
Which is, God knows, about that Tamburlaine,
That, like a fox in midst of harvest-time,
Doth prey upon my flocks of passengers;
And, as I hear, doth mean to pull my plumes.
Therefore 'tis good and meet for to be wise.

MEANDER
Oft have I heard your majesty complain
Of Tamburlaine, that sturdy Scythian thief,
That robs your merchants of Persepolis,
Trading by land unto the Western Isles,
And in your confines with his lawless train
Daily commits incivil outrages,
Hoping (misled by dreaming prophecies)
To reign in Asia, and with barbarous arms
To make himself the monarch of the East.
But, ere he march in Asia or display
His vagrant ensign in the Persian fields,
Your grace hath taken order by Theridamas,
Charged with a thousand horse, to apprehend
And bring him captive to your highness' throne.

MYCETES
Full true thou speak'st, and like thyself, my lord,
Whom I may term a Damon for thy love:
Therefore 'tis best, if so it like you all,
To send my thousand horse incontinent
To apprehend that paltry Scythian.
How like you this, my honourable lords?
Is it not a kingly resolution?

COSROE
It cannot choose, because it comes from you.

MYCETES
Then hear thy charge, valiant Theridamas,
The chiefest captain of Mycetes' host,
The hope of Persia, and the very legs
Whereon our state doth lean, as on a staff
That holds us up and foils our neighbour foes:
Thou shalt be leader of this thousand horse,
Whose foaming gall with rage and high disdain
Have sworn the death of wicked Tamburlaine.
Go frowning forth, but come thou smiling home,
As did Sir Paris with the Grecian dame.
Return with speed; time passeth swift away,
Our life is frail, and we may die today.

THERIDAMAS
Before the moon renew her borrowed light,
Doubt not, my lord and gracious sovereign,
But Tamburlaine and that Tartarian rout
Shall either perish by our warlike hands
Or plead for mercy at your highness' feet.

MYCETES
Go, stout Theridamas; thy words are swords,
And with thy looks thou conquerest all thy foes.
I long to see thee back return from thence,
That I may view these milk-white steeds of mine
All loaden with the heads of killed men,
And, from their knees even to their hoofs below,
Besmeared with blood that makes a dainty show.

THERIDAMAS
Then now, my lord, I humbly take my leave. *Exit.*

MYCETES
Theridamas, farewell ten thousand times.
Ah, Menaphon, why stay'st thou thus behind,
When other men press forward for renown?
Go Menaphon, go into Scythia,
And foot by foot follow Theridamas.

COSROE
Nay, pray you, let him stay, a greater [task]
Fits Menaphon than warring with a thief.
Create him pro-rex of all Africa,
That he may win the Babylonians' hearts,
Which will revolt from Persian government
Unless they have a wiser king than you.

32 **flocks of passengers** merchants travelling through my realms.
33 **doth . . . plumes** intends to pluck away my honours.
37 **Persepolis** the Persian capital.
38 **Western Isles** Britain and Ireland.
39 **in your confines** within your borders.
39 **train** retinue.
45 **vagrant ensign** wandering banner.
50 **Damon** for the story of the faithful friends Damon and Pythias, see Edwards's play of that name in this volume.
52 **incontinent** without delay.
56 **choose** be otherwise.
66 **Grecian dame** Helen of Troy (not, perhaps, an auspicious simile).
71 **Tartarian rout** Tartar/Scythian rabble.
74 **stout** brave/strong.
78 **loaden** laden.
80 **dainty** excellent.
89 **pro-rex** viceroy.

MYCETES
'Unless they have a wiser king than you'?
These are his words; Meander, set them down.

COSROE
And add this to them, that all Asia
Lament to see the folly of their king.

MYCETES
Well, here I swear by this my royal seat ...

COSROE
You may do well to kiss it then.

MYCETES
... Embossed with silk as best beseems my state,
To be revenged for these contemptuous words.
O, where is duty and allegiance now?
Fled to the Caspian or the Ocean main?
What, shall I call thee brother? No, a foe;
Monster of nature, shame unto thy stock,
That dar'st presume thy sovereign for to mock.
Meander, come; I am abused, Meander. *Exit*

Manent Cosroe and Menaphon.

MENAPHON
How now, my lord! What, mated and amazed
To hear the king thus threaten like himself?

COSROE
Ah, Menaphon, I pass not for his threats;
The plot is laid by Persian noblemen
And captains of the Median garrisons
To crown me emperor of Asia.
But this it is that doth excruciate
The very substance of my vexed soul,
To see our neighbours that were wont to quake
And tremble at the Persian monarch's name,
Now sit and laugh our regiment to scorn;
And that which might resolve me into tears,
Men from the farthest equinoctial line
Have swarmed in troops into the Eastern India,
Lading their ships with gold and precious stones,
And made their spoils from all our provinces.

MENAPHON
This should entreat your highness to rejoice,
Since Fortune gives you opportunity
To gain the title of a conqueror
By curing of this maimed empery.
Afric and Europe bordering on your land,
And continent to your dominions,
How easily may you with a mighty host,
Pass into Graecia, as did Cyrus once,
And cause them to withdraw their forces home,
Lest you subdue the pride of Christendom. *Sound.*

COSROE
But Menaphon, what means this trumpet's sound?

MENAPHON
Behold, my lord, Ortygius and the rest
Bringing the crown to make you emperor!

Enter Ortygius and C[eneus], bearing a crown, with other[s].

ORTYGIUS
Magnificent and mighty prince Cosroe,
We, in the name of other Persian states
And commons of this mighty monarchy,
Present thee with th'imperial diadem.

CENEUS
The warlike soldiers and the gentlemen,
That heretofore have filled Persepolis
With Afric captains taken in the field,
Whose ransom made them march in coats of gold,
With costly jewels hanging at their ears,
And shining stones upon their lofty crests,
Now living idle in the walled towns,
Wanting both pay and martial discipline,
Begin in troops to threaten civil war,

98 **You...then.** Punning on 'seat' as both 'throne' and 'arse' (presumably an aside).
106.1 ***Manent*** Remain (on stage).
107 **mated** stunned/defeated.
109 **pass** care.
111 **Median** Media in the north of the Persian territories.
113 **excruciate** torture.
117 **regiment** government/regime.
118 **resolve** dissolve.
119 **from...line** from the far equator.
126 **By...empery** By healing the wounded empire.
128 **continent** adjacent.
130 **Cyrus** Cyrus II, the founder of the Persian empire of the sixth century BC, who overran the Greek settlements of Asia Minor (Graecia).
132.1 **Sound** A trumpet blast.
137–138 **states...commons** noblemen and common people.
147 **Wanting** lacking.

And openly exclaim against their king.
Therefore, to stay all sudden mutinies,
We will invest your highness emperor;
Whereat the soldiers will conceive more joy
Than did the Macedonians at the spoil
Of great Darius and his wealthy host.

COSROE
Well, since I see the state of Persia droop
And languish in my brother's government,
I willingly receive th'imperial crown,
And vow to wear it for my country's good,
In spite of them shall malice my estate.

ORTYGIUS
And, in assurance of desired success,
We here do crown thee monarch of the East;
Emperor of Asia and Persia;
Great lord of Media and Armenia;
Duke of Africa and Albania,
Mesopotamia and of Parthia,
East India and the late-discovered isles;
Chief lord of all the wide vast Euxine Sea,
And of the ever-raging Caspian lake.

ALL
Long live Cosroe, mighty emperor!

COSROE
And Jove may never let me longer live
Than I may seek to gratify your love,
And cause the soldiers that thus honour me
To triumph over many provinces,
By whose desires of discipline in arms
I doubt not shortly but to reign sole king,
And with the army of Theridamas
(Whither we presently will fly, my lords,)
To rest secure against my brother's force.

ORTYGIUS
We knew, my lord, before we brought the crown,
Intending your investion so near
The residence of your despised brother,
The lords would not be too exasperate
To injure or suppress your worthy title;
Or, if they would, there are in readiness
Ten thousand horse to carry you from hence,
In spite of all suspected enemies.

COSROE
I know it well, my lord, and thank you all.

ORTYGIUS
Sound up the trumpets, then. God save the king!

Exeunt.

Actus I. Scaena ii.

[Enter] Tamburlaine leading Zenocrate, Techelles, Usumcasane, other Lords [Agydas, Magnetes], and Soldiers loaden with treasure.

TAMBURLAINE
Come lady, let not this appal your thoughts;
The jewels and the treasure we have ta'en
Shall be reserved, and you in better state
Than if you were arrived in Syria,
Even in the circle of your father's arms,
The mighty Soldan of Egyptia.

ZENOCRATE
Ah, shepherd, pity my distressed plight!
(If, as thou seemst, thou art so mean a man,)
And seek not to enrich thy followers
By lawless rapine from a silly maid,
Who, travelling with these Median lords
To Memphis, from my uncle's country of
Media,
Where, all my youth, I have been governed,
Have passed the army of the mighty Turk,
Bearing his privy-signet and his hand
To safe-conduct us thorough Africa.

MAGNETES
And, since we have arrived in Scythia,
Besides rich presents from the puissant Cham,
We have his highness' letters to command
Aid and assistance if we stand in need.

150 **stay** forestall.
153–154 **Than...host** When Alexander the Great of Macedon crushed Darius III of Persia at the battle of Issus (333BC).
159 **shall** who shall.
167 **Euxine Sea** Black Sea.
168 **Caspian lake** Caspian Sea.
170 **Jove** Jupiter.
180 **investion** investiture.
188.1 **Exeunt** All exit.

3 **reserved** preserved.
7 **mean** low-born.
9 **silly maid** innocent/simple virgin.
11 **Memphis** the ancient capital of Egypt, south of Cairo.
12 **governed** brought up (under her uncle's authority).
14 **Bearing...hand** carrying a letter of safe-conduct signed by the Turkish emperor's own hand and bearing his private seal (imprinted from his signet ring).
17 **the puissant Cham** the mighty khan (king of Tartary).

TAMBURLAINE
But now you see these letters and commands
Are countermanded by a greater man;
And through my provinces you must expect
Letters of conduct from my mightiness,
If you intend to keep your treasure safe.
But, since I love to live at liberty,
As easily may you get the Soldan's crown
As any prizes out of my precinct;
For they are friends that help to wean my state
Till men and kingdoms help to strengthen it,
And must maintain my life exempt from servitude.
But, tell me, madam, is your grace betrothed?
ZENOCRATE
I am, my lord, for so you do import.
TAMBURLAINE
I am a lord, for so my deeds shall prove;
And yet a shepherd by my parentage.
But, lady, this fair face and heavenly hue
Must grace his bed that conquers Asia,
And means to be a terror to the world,
Measuring the limits of his empery
By east and west, as Phoebus doth his course.
Lie here, ye weeds that I disdain to wear!
This complete armour and this curtle-axe
Are adjuncts more beseeming Tamburlaine.
And, madam, whatsoever you esteem
Of this success and loss unvalued,
Both may invest you empress of the East;
And these that seem but silly country swains
May have the leading of so great an host
As with their weight shall make the mountains quake,
Even as when windy exhalations,
Fighting for passage, tilt within the earth.
TECHELLES
As princely lions, when they rouse themselves,
Stretching their paws, and threatening herds of beasts,
So in his armour looketh Tamburlaine.
Methinks I see kings kneeling at his feet,
And he with frowning brows and fiery looks
Spurning their crowns from off their captive heads.
USUMCASANE
And making thee and me, Techelles, kings,
That even to death will follow Tamburlaine.
TAMBURLAINE
Nobly resolved, sweet friends and followers!
These lords, perhaps, do scorn our estimates,
And think we prattle with distempered spirits.
But, since they measure our deserts so mean,
That in conceit bear empires on our spears,
Affecting thoughts coequal with the clouds,
They shall be kept our forced followers
Till with their eyes they view us emperors.
ZENOCRATE
The gods, defenders of the innocent,
Will never prosper your intended drifts,
That thus oppress poor friendless passengers.
Therefore at least admit us liberty,
Even as thou hop'st to be eternized
By living Asia's mighty emperor.
AGYDAS
I hope our lady's treasure and our own
May serve for ransom to our liberties.
Return our mules and empty camels back,
That we may travel into Syria,
Where her betrothed lord, Alcidamus,
Expects the arrival of her highness' person.
MAGNETES
And wheresoever we repose ourselves,
We will report but well of Tamburlaine.

27 **precinct** territory.
28 **they...state** they (i.e. any prizes/booty he obtains) are the allies which (help me to) grow my authority.
32 **my...import** i.e. I call you 'my lord', as you seem to be one.
40 **ye weeds** you clothes (Tamburlaine here throws off his shepherd's clothes, either to don new armour brought by his men, or to reveal the armour he is already wearing).
41 **curtle-axe** cutlass.
42 **adjuncts more beseeming** accessories/equipment more fitting (for).
43–44 **whatsoever...loss unvalued** whatever you (currently) think of this outcome, and the loss of your priceless treasure.
46 **these...swains** these men, who seem but simple rustic shepherds.
49–50 **Even...earth** even as an earthquake shakes the mountains. (Earthquakes were thought to be caused by the movements of contrary winds warring or jousting ('tilting') underground.)
56 **Spurning** casting down.
60 **These...estimates** These (captured) lords perhaps scoff at our ambitions.
61 **distempered spirits** feverish minds.
62–64 **since...clouds** since they rate so poorly the merits of we, who plan to win empires on our spear-points, daring to aspire to the highest of thoughts.
68 **Will...drifts** Will never allow your plans to prosper.
71 **eternized** immortalized.

TAMBURLAINE
Disdains Zenocrate to live with me?
Or you, my lords, to be my followers?
Think you I weigh this treasure more than you?
Not all the gold in India's wealthy arms
Shall buy the meanest soldier in my train.
Zenocrate, lovelier than the love of Jove,
Brighter than is the silver Rhodope,
Fairer than whitest snow on Scythian hills,
Thy person is more worth to Tamburlaine
Than the possession of the Persian crown,
Which gracious stars have promised at my birth.
A hundred Tartars shall attend on thee,
Mounted on steeds swifter than Pegasus.
Thy garments shall be made of Median silk,
Enchased with precious jewels of mine own,
More rich and valurous than Zenocrate's.
With milk-white harts upon an ivory sled
Thou shalt be drawn amidst the frozen pools,
And scale the icy mountains' lofty tops,
Which with thy beauty will be soon resolved.
My martial prizes, with five hundred men,
Won on the fifty-headed Volga's waves,
Shall we all offer to Zenocrate,
And then myself to fair Zenocrate.

TECHELLES
What now; in love?

TAMBURLAINE
Techelles, women must be flattered;
But this is she with whom I am in love.

Enter a Soldier.

SOLDIER
News, news!

TAMBURLAINE.
How now, what's the matter?

SOLDIER
A thousand Persian horsemen are at hand,
Sent from the king to overcome us all.

TAMBURLAINE
How now, my lords of Egypt, and Zenocrate;
Now must your jewels be restored again,
And I, that triumphed so, be overcome?
How say you, lordings, is not this your hope?

AGYDAS
We hope yourself will willingly restore them.

TAMBURLAINE
Such hope, such fortune, have the thousand horse.
Soft ye, my lords and sweet Zenocrate,
You must be forced from me ere you go.
A thousand horsemen; we five hundred foot?
An odds too great for us to stand against.
But are they rich, and is their armour good?

SOLDIER
Their plumed helms are wrought with beaten gold,
Their swords enamelled, and about their necks
Hang massy chains of gold down to the waist;
In every part exceeding brave and rich.

TAMBURLAINE
Then shall we fight courageously with them,
Or look you I should play the orator?

TECHELLES
No; cowards and faint-hearted runaways
Look for orations when the foe is near;
Our swords shall play the orators for us.

USUMCASANE
Come, let us meet them at the mountain-top,
And with a sudden and an hot alarum
Drive all their horses headlong down the hill.

TECHELLES
Come, let us march.

TAMBURLAINE
Stay, Techelles; ask a parley first.

The Soldiers enter.

Open the mails, yet guard the treasure sure.
Lay out our golden wedges to the view,
That their reflections may amaze the Persians;
And look we friendly on them when they come.

87 **silver Rhodope** the Rhodope mountains in modern Bulgaria, famed for their silver mines.
93 **Pegasus** the legendary winged horse.
95 **Enchased** decorated.
96 **Valurous** valuable.
100 **resolved** dissolved/melted.
102 **fifty-headed Volga's waves** the fifty tributaries of the mighty river Volga.
112 **How now** What do you think?
118 **Soft ye** Be quiet.
125 **massy** heavy.
126 **brave** splendid.
128 **I ... orator** in this context, 'should I sue for peace?'
133 **hot alarum** urgent call to arms.
137 **mails** panniers/baggage.
138 **wedges** ingots.

But, if they offer word or violence,
We'll fight, five hundred men-at-arms to one,
Before we part with our possession.
And 'gainst the general we will lift our swords,
And either lanch his greedy thirsting throat,
Or take him prisoner, and his chain shall serve
For manacles till he be ransomed home.

TECHELLES
I hear them come. Shall we encounter them?

TAMBURLAINE
Keep all your standings, and not stir a foot:
Myself will bide the danger of the brunt.

Enter Theridamas, with others.

THERIDAMAS
Where is this Scythian Tamburlaine?

TAMBURLAINE
Whom seek'st thou, Persian? I am Tamburlaine.

THERIDAMAS
Tamburlaine!
A Scythian shepherd so embellished
With nature's pride and richest furniture!
His looks do menace heaven and dare the gods.
His fiery eyes are fixed upon the earth,
As if he now devised some stratagem,
Or meant to pierce Avernus' darksome vaults
To pull the triple-headed dog from hell.

TAMBURLAINE
Noble and mild this Persian seems to be,
If outward habit judge the inward man.

TECHELLES
His deep affections make him passionate.

TAMBURLAINE
With what a majesty he rears his looks!
In thee, thou valiant man of Persia,
I see the folly of thy emperor.
Art thou but captain of a thousand horse,
That by characters graven in thy brows,
And by thy martial face and stout aspect,
Deserv'st to have the leading of an host?
Forsake thy king, and do but join with me,
And we will triumph over all the world.
I hold the Fates bound fast in iron chains,
And with my hand turn Fortune's wheel about;
And sooner shall the sun fall from his sphere
Than Tamburlaine be slain or overcome.
Draw forth thy sword, thou mighty man-at-arms,
Intending but to raze my charmed skin,
And Jove himself will stretch his hand from heaven
To ward the blow and shield me safe from harm.
See, how he rains down heaps of gold in showers,
As if he meant to give my soldiers pay!
And, as a sure and grounded argument
That I shall be the monarch of the East,
He sends this Soldan's daughter, rich and brave,
To be my queen and portly emperess.
If thou wilt stay with me, renowned man,
And lead thy thousand horse with my conduct,
Besides thy share of this Egyptian prize,
Those thousand horse shall sweat with martial
spoil
Of conquered kingdoms and of cities sacked.
Both we will walk upon the lofty cliffs;
And Christian merchants, that with Russian stems
Plough up huge furrows in the Caspian Sea,
Shall vail to us as lords of all the lake.
Both we will reign as consuls of the earth,
And mighty kings shall be our senators.
Jove sometime masked in a shepherd's weed;
And, by those steps that he hath scaled the heavens,
May we become immortal like the gods.
Join with me now in this my mean estate,
(I call it mean, because, being yet obscure,
The nations far-removed admire me not,)

145 **lanch** lance/pierce.
150 **brunt** assault.
155 **furniture** equipment/armour.
159–160 **pierce...hell** violate the gates of hell and pull Cerberus from his den. (Avernus was the lake marking the entrance to Hades, Cerberus the triple-headed dog who guarded it.)
162 **If...man** If outward appearances reveal inner character.
169 **stout aspect** heroic appearance.
170 **an host** a (whole) army.
173–174 **the fates...about** the Fates, *Moirai* (Greek) or *Parcai* (Roman), were three goddesses who determined each person's destiny. Fortune was depicted as a blind goddess who randomly turned a wheel, thereby raising up and casting down those tied to it.
178 **raze** shave/graze.
180 **ward** fend off.
186 **portly** stately/dignified.
188 **with my conduct** under my direction.
193 **stems** vessels (lit. the bow and stern posts of ships).
195 **vail** lower their sails.
198 **sometime masked** sometimes disguised himself.
203 **nations far-removed** distant nations.

And when my name and honour shall be spread
As far as Boreas claps his brazen wings,
Or fair Boötes sends his cheerful light,
Then shalt thou be competitor with me,
And sit with Tamburlaine in all his majesty.

THERIDAMAS
Not Hermes, prolocutor to the gods,
Could use persuasions more pathetical.

TAMBURLAINE
Nor are Apollo's oracles more true
Than thou shalt find my vaunts substantial.

TECHELLES
We are his friends, and, if the Persian king
Should offer present dukedoms to our state,
We think it loss to make exchange for that
We are assured of by our friend's success.

USUMCASANE
And kingdoms at the least we all expect,
Besides the honour in assured conquests,
Where kings shall crouch unto our conquering swords,
And hosts of soldiers stand amazed at us,
When with their fearful tongues they shall confess:
These are the men that all the world admires.

THERIDAMAS
What strong enchantments tice my yielding soul;
Ah, these resolved, noble Scythians!
But shall I prove a traitor to my king?

TAMBURLAINE
No, but the trusty friend of Tamburlaine.

THERIDAMAS
Won with thy words, and conquered with thy looks,
I yield myself, my men, and horse to thee,
To be partaker of thy good or ill,
As long as life maintains Theridamas.

TAMBURLAINE
Theridamas, my friend, take here my hand,
Which is as much as if I swore by heaven,
And called the gods to witness of my vow.
Thus shall my heart be still combined with thine,
Until our bodies turn to elements,
And both our souls aspire celestial thrones.
Techelles and Casane, welcome him.

TECHELLES
Welcome, renowned Persian, to us all.

USUMCASANE
Long may Theridamas remain with us.

TAMBURLAINE
These are my friends, in whom I more rejoice
Than doth the king of Persia in his crown;
And, by the love of Pylades and Orestes,
Whose statues we adore in Scythia,
Thyself and them shall never part from me
Before I crown you kings in Asia.
Make much of them, gentle Theridamas,
And they will never leave thee till the death.

THERIDAMAS
Nor thee nor them, thrice-noble Tamburlaine,
Shall want my heart to be with gladness pierced,
To do you honour and security.

TAMBURLAINE
A thousand thanks, worthy Theridamas.
And now, fair madam, and my noble lords,
If you will willingly remain with me,
You shall have honours as your merits be;
Or else you shall be forced with slavery.

AGYDAS
We yield unto thee, happy Tamburlaine.

TAMBURLAINE
For you, then, madam, I am out of doubt.

205 **Boreas** the north wind.
206 **Boötes** a constellation in the northern sky whose largest star is Arcturus.
207 **competitor** partner.
209 **Hermes** god of eloquence, was the messenger and spokesman (prolocutor) of the gods.
210 **pathetical** moving/persuasive.
212 **vaunts** boasts/claims.
223 **tice** entice.
234 **still** forever.
242 **Pylades and Orestes** the friends who murder Orestes' mother Clytemnestra and her lover Aegisthus in Aeschylus' *Oresteia*.
246 **Make much of them** Treat them well.
248 **Nor** neither.
249–250 **Shall...honour** I shall gladly pierce my heart, if it should be necessary, to do you honour.
256 **happy** fortunate/blessed.

ZENOCRATE
I must be pleased perforce; wretched Zenocrate!

Exeunt.

Actus II. Scaena i.

[Enter] Cosroe, Menaphon, Ortygius, [and Ceneus], with other Soldiers.

COSROE
Thus far are we towards Theridamas,
And valiant Tamburlaine, the man of fame,
The man that in the forehead of his fortune
Bears figures of renown and miracle.
But tell me, that hast seen him, Menaphon,
What stature wields he, and what personage?

MENAPHON
Of stature tall, and straightly fashioned,
Like his desire, lift upwards and divine;
So large of limbs, his joints so strongly knit,
Such breadth of shoulders as might mainly bear
Old Atlas' burden; 'twixt his manly pitch,
A pearl more worth than all the world is placed,
Wherein by curious sovereignty of art
Are fixed his piercing instruments of sight,
Whose fiery circles bear encompassed
A heaven of heavenly bodies in their spheres,
That guides his steps and actions to the throne
Where honour sits invested royally;
Pale of complexion, wrought in him with passion,
Thirsting with sovereignty and love of arms;
His lofty brows in folds do figure death,
And in their smoothness, amity and life;
About them hangs a knot of amber hair,
Wrapped in curls, as fierce Achilles' was,
On which the breath of heaven delights to play,
Making it dance with wanton majesty.
His arms and fingers long and sinewy,
Betokening valour and excess of strength;
In every part proportioned like the man
Should make the world subdued to Tamburlaine.

COSROE
Well hast thou portrayed in thy terms of life
The face and personage of a wondrous man.
Nature doth strive with Fortune and his stars
To make him famous in accomplished worth,
And well his merits show him to be made
His fortune's master and the king of men,
That could persuade, at such a sudden pinch,
With reasons of his valour and his life,
A thousand sworn and overmatching foes.
Then, when our powers in points of swords are joined,
And closed in compass of the killing bullet,
Though strait the passage and the port be made
That leads to palace of my brother's life,
Proud is his fortune if we pierce it not.
And, when the princely Persian diadem
Shall overweigh his weary, witless head,
And fall like mellowed fruit, with shakes of death,
In fair Persia noble Tamburlaine
Shall be my regent, and remain as king.

ORTYGIUS
In happy hour we have set the crown
Upon your kingly head, that seeks our honour
In joining with the man ordained by heaven
To further every action to the best.

CENEUS
He that with shepherds and a little spoil
Durst, in disdain of wrong and tyranny,
Defend his freedom 'gainst a monarchy,
What will he do supported by a king,
Leading a troop of gentlemen and lords,
And stuffed with treasure for his highest thoughts!

COSROE
And such shall wait on worthy Tamburlaine.
Our army will be forty thousand strong,

258 **perforce** of necessity.
3 **in . . . fortune** an allusion to the notion that one's fate was written on one's forehead.
5 **that hast** you who have.
6 **What . . . personage?** How is he built, and what is he like?
8 **lift** lifted.
10 **mainly** strongly/entirely.
11 **Atlas' burden** the Titan, Atlas, carried the world on his shoulders ('pitch').
21 **His . . . folds** When he frowns.
26 **wanton** careless.
27 **sinewy** 1590 has 'snowy'. I follow Gill's suggested amendment.
28 **Betokening** Indicating.
31 **Well . . . life** lively description.
37 **at . . . pinch** in an emergency.
41 **closed . . . bullet** advanced within gunshot range of each other.
42–44 **Though . . . not.** Though the passage and gate that lead to my brother's heart (the 'palace' of his body) are narrow, he'll be a very lucky man if we do not manage to pierce it.

When Tamburlaine and brave Theridamas
Have met us by the river Araris;
And all conjoined to meet the witless king,
That now is marching near to Parthia,
And, with unwilling soldiers faintly armed,
To seek revenge on me and Tamburlaine;
To whom, sweet Menaphon, direct me straight.

MENAPHON
I will, my lord. *Exeunt.*

Actus II. Scaena ii.

[Enter] Mycetes, Meander, with other Lords and Soldiers.

MYCETES
Come, my Meander, let us to this gear.
I tell you true, my heart is swoll'n with wrath
On this same thievish villain Tamburlaine,
And of that false Cosroe, my traitorous brother.
Would it not grieve a king to be so abused,
And have a thousand horsemen ta'en away?
And, which is worse, to have his diadem
Sought for by such scald knaves as love him not?
I think it would. Well, then, by heavens I swear,
Aurora shall not peep out of her doors,
But I will have Cosroe by the head,
And kill proud Tamburlaine with point of sword.
Tell you the rest, Meander: I have said.

MEANDER
Then, having passed Armenian deserts now,
And pitched our tents under the Georgian hills,
Whose tops are covered with Tartarian thieves,
That lie in ambush, waiting for a prey,
What should we do but bid them battle straight,
And rid the world of those detested troops?
Lest, if we let them linger here awhile,
They gather strength by power of fresh supplies.
This country swarms with vile outrageous men
That live by rapine and by lawless spoil,
Fit soldiers for the wicked Tamburlaine;
And he that could with gifts and promises
Inveigle him that led a thousand horse,
And make him false his faith unto his king,
Will quickly win such as be like himself.
Therefore cheer up your minds, prepare to fight.
He that can take or slaughter Tamburlaine,
Shall rule the province of Albania;
Who brings that traitor's head, Theridamas,
Shall have a government in Media,
Beside the spoil of him and all his train.
But, if Cosroe (as our spials say,
And as we know) remains with Tamburlaine,
His highness' pleasure is that he should live,
And be reclaimed with princely lenity.

[Enter a Spy.]

SPY
An hundred horsemen of my company,
Scouting abroad upon these champion plains,
Have viewed the army of the Scythians,
Which make report it far exceeds the king's.

MEANDER
Suppose they be in number infinite,
Yet, being void of martial discipline,
All running headlong, greedy after spoils,
And more regarding gain than victory,
Like to the cruel brothers of the earth,
Sprung of the teeth of dragons venomous,
Their careless swords shall lance their fellows' throats,
And make us triumph in their overthrow.

MYCETES
Was there such brethren, sweet Meander, say,
That sprung of teeth of dragons venomous?

MEANDER
So poets say, my lord.

MYCETES
And 'tis a pretty toy to be a poet.

63 **Araris** Gill suggests the Araxes, that flows into the Caspian Sea.
65 **Parthia** a kingdom in what is now north-east Iran.
66 **faintly** poorly.
1 **let...gear** let's get on with this business.
8 **scald** scurvy/wretched.
10 **Aurora** goddess of dawn.
15 Armenia bordered on the Caspian from the west. Georgia was to the north of Armenia.
18 **straight** immediately.
23 **spoil** robbery.
31 **Albania** a region on the Caspian Sea according to the maps Marlowe was familiar with.
35 **spials** spies.
38 **lenity** leniency.
40 **plains** flat grasslands.
48 **Sprung...venomous** In Greek myth, the Phoenician hero Cadmus threw a dragon's teeth on the ground, from which sprang an army of warriors. He was able to distract them into slaughtering each other by tossing a gemstone into their midst.
54 **pretty toy** pleasing trifle.

Well, well, Meander, thou art deeply read;
And having thee, I have a jewel sure.
Go on, my lord, and give your charge, I say;
Thy wit will make us conquerors to-day.

MEANDER

Then, noble soldiers, to entrap these thieves
That live confounded in disordered troops,
If wealth or riches may prevail with them,
We have our camels laden all with gold,
Which you that be but common soldiers
Shall fling in every corner of the field;
And, while the base-born Tartars take it up,
You, fighting more for honour than for gold,
Shall massacre those greedy-minded slaves.
And when their scattered army is subdued,
And you march on their slaughtered carcasses,
Share equally the gold that bought their lives,
And live like gentlemen in Persia.
Strike up the drum, and march courageously,
Fortune herself doth sit upon our crests.

MYCETES

He tells you true, my masters, so he does.
Drums, why sound ye not when Meander speaks?

Exeunt.

Actus II. Scaena iii

[*Enter*] *Cosroe, Tamburlaine, Theridamas, Techelles, Usumcasane, Ortygius, with others.*

COSROE

Now, worthy Tamburlaine, have I reposed
In thy approved fortunes all my hope.
What think'st thou, man, shall come of our attempts?
For, even as from assured oracle,
I take thy doom for satisfaction.

TAMBURLAINE

And so mistake you not a whit, my lord;
For fates and oracles, heaven have sworn
To royalize the deeds of Tamburlaine,
And make them blessed that share in his attempts.
And doubt you not but, if you favour me,
And let my fortunes and my valour sway
To some direction in your martial deeds,
The world will strive with hosts of men-at-arms
To swarm unto the ensign I support.
The host of Xerxes, which by fame is said
To drink the mighty Parthian Araris,
Was but a handful to that we will have.
Our quivering lances, shaking in the air,
And bullets, like Jove's dreadful thunderbolts,
Enrolled in flames and fiery smouldering mists,
Shall threat the gods more than Cyclopian wars;
And with our sun-bright armour, as we march,
We'll chase the stars from heaven, and dim their eyes
That stand and muse at our admired arms.

THERIDAMAS

You see, my lord, what working words he hath;
But, when you see his actions top his speech,
Your speech will stay, or so extol his worth
As I shall be commended and excused
For turning my poor charge to his direction.
And these his two renowned friends, my lord,
Would make one thirst and strive to be retained
In such a great degree of amity.

TECHELLES

With duty [and] with amity we yield
Our utmost service to the fair Cosroe.

COSROE

Which I esteem as portion of my crown.
Usumcasane and Techelles both,
When she that rules in Rhamnus' golden gates,
And makes a passage for all prosperous arms,
Shall make me solely emperor of Asia,
Then shall your meeds and valours be advanced
To rooms of honour and nobility.

TAMBURLAINE

Then haste, Cosroe, to be king alone,
That I with these my friends and all my men
May triumph in our long-expected fate.
The king your brother is now hard at hand

2 **approved** tried and tested.
5 **I . . . satisfaction** I accept your judgements as certain truth.
8 **royalize** celebrate/literally make royal.
12 **to some direction** have some influence.
14 **the ensign I support** the banner I carry.
16 **To . . . Araris** the army of Xerxes I of Persia was said to have been be so large that it drank the river dry.
21 **Cyclopian** the Cyclopes were a race of one-eyed giants who forged the thunderbolts used by Jupiter in the gods' war against the Titans.
25 **working** persuasive.
27 **Your . . . stay** you'll be lost for words.
33 **[and]** 1590 has 'not'.
37 **Rhamnus** in Attica (Greece) was the site of a shrine to Nemesis, goddess of vengeance.
40 **meeds** merits.
41 **rooms** positions/roles.
45 **hard at hand** close by.

Meet with the fool, and rid your royal shoulders
Of such a burden as outweighs the sands
And all the craggy rocks of Caspia.

[*Enter a Messenger.*]

MESSENGER
My lord, we have discovered the enemy
Ready to charge you with a mighty army.

COSROE
Come, Tamburlaine; now whet thy winged sword,
And lift thy lofty arm into the clouds,
That it may reach the king of Persia's crown,
And set it safe on my victorious head.

TAMBURLAINE
See where it is, the keenest curtle-axe
That e'er made passage thorough Persian arms!
These are the wings shall make it fly as swift
As doth the lightning or the breath of heaven,
And kill as sure as it swiftly flies.

COSROE
Thy words assure me of kind success.
Go, valiant soldier, go before, and charge
The fainting army of that foolish king.

TAMBURLAINE
Usumcasane and Techelles, come,
We are enough to scare the enemy,
And more than needs to make an emperor.

[*Exeunt.*]

[Actus II. Scaena iv.]

[*Enter*] *To the Battle, and Mycetes comes out alone with his crown in his hand, offering to hide it.*

MYCETES
Accursed be he that first invented war!
They knew not, ah, they knew not (simple men),
How those were hit by pelting cannon-shot
Stand staggering like a quivering aspen-leaf
Fearing the force of Boreas' boisterous blasts.
In what a lamentable case were I,
If nature had not given me wisdom's lore.
For kings are clouts that every man shoots at,
Our crown the pin that thousands seek to cleave.
Therefore in policy I think it good
To hide it close; a goodly stratagem,
And far from any man that is a fool.
So shall not I be known; or if I be,
They cannot take away my crown from me.
Here will I hide it in this simple hole.

Enter Tamburlaine.

TAMBURLAINE
What, fearful coward, straggling from the camp,
When kings themselves are present in the field?

MYCETES
Thou liest.

TAMBURLAINE
Base villain, darest thou give me the lie?

MYCETES
Away; I am the king! Go, touch me not.
Thou break'st the law of arms unless thou kneel,
And cry me 'Mercy, noble king!'

TAMBURLAINE
Are you the witty king of Persia?

MYCETES
Aye, marry, am I. Have you any suit to me?

TAMBURLAINE
I would entreat you to speak but three wise words.

MYCETES
So I can, when I see my time.

TAMBURLAINE
Is this your crown?

MYCETES
Aye; didst thou ever see a fairer?

TAMBURLAINE
You will not sell it, will ye?

MYCETES
Such another word, and I will have thee executed.
Come, give it me.

TAMBURLAINE
No; I took it prisoner.

MYCETES
You lie; I gave it you.

60 **kind** natural (no more than he thinks he deserves).
s.d. **offering** trying.
3 **How those** Those who.
5 **Boreas'** the north wind's.
6 **case** situation.
8 **clouts** targets (in archery), cloths held to the target by a pin (see next line).
10–11 **in...close** I think it politically sensible to hide it very secretly.
19 **Base...lie?** Low-born wretch, do you dare to call me a liar?
24 **marry** indeed.

TAMBURLAINE
Then 'tis mine.
MYCETES
No; I mean I let you keep it.
TAMBURLAINE
Well, I mean you shall have it again.
Here, take it for a while; I lend it thee
Till I may see thee hemmed with armed men;
Then shalt thou see me pull it from thy head.
Thou art no match for mighty Tamburlaine. *[Exit.]*
MYCETES
O gods, is this Tamburlaine the thief?
I marvel much he stole it not away.

Sound trumpets to the battle; and he runs in.

[Actus II. Scaena v.]

[Enter] Cosroe, Tamburlaine, Theridamas, Menaphon, Meander, Ortygius, Techelles, Usumcasane, with others.

TAMBURLAINE
Hold thee, Cosroe; wear two imperial crowns;
Think thee invested now as royally,
Even by the mighty hand of Tamburlaine,
As if as many kings as could encompass thee
With greatest pomp had crowned thee emperor.
COSROE
So do I, thrice-renowned man-at-arms;
And none shall keep the crown but Tamburlaine.
Thee do I make my regent of Persia,
And general-lieutenant of my armies.
Meander, you, that were our brother's guide,
And chiefest counsellor in all his acts,
Since he is yielded to the stroke of war,
On your submission we with thanks excuse,
And give you equal place in our affairs.
MEANDER
Most happy emperor, in humblest terms
I vow my service to your majesty,
With utmost virtue of my faith and duty.
COSROE
Thanks, good Meander. Then Cosroe reign,
And govern Persia in her former pomp.
Now send embassage to thy neighbour kings,
And let them know the Persian king is changed,
From one that knew not what a king should do
To one that can command what 'longs thereto.
And now we will to fair Persepolis,
With twenty thousand expert soldiers.
The lords and captains of my brother's camp
With little slaughter take Meander's course,
And gladly yield them to my gracious rule.
Ortygius and Menaphon, my trusty friends,
Now will I gratify your former good,
And grace your calling with a greater sway.
ORTYGIUS
And as we ever aimed at your behoof,
And sought your state all honour it deserved,
So will we with our powers and our lives
Endeavour to preserve and prosper it.
COSROE
I will not thank thee, sweet Ortygius;
Better replies shall prove my purposes.
And now, Lord Tamburlaine, my brother's camp
I leave to thee and to Theridamas,
To follow me to fair Persepolis;
Then will we march to all those Indian mines
My witless brother to the Christians lost,
And ransom them with fame and usury.
And, till thou overtake me, Tamburlaine
(Staying to order all the scattered troops,)
Farewell, lord regent and his happy friends.
I long to sit upon my brother's throne.
MEANDER
Your majesty shall shortly have your wish,
And ride in triumph through Persepolis. *Exeunt.*

Manent Tamb[urlaine], Tech[elles], Ther[idamas], and Usum[casane].

TAMBURLAINE
'And ride in triumph through Persepolis!'
Is it not brave to be a king, Techelles?
Usumcasane and Theridamas,
Is it not passing brave to be a king,
And ride in triumph through Persepolis?

33 **keep it** look after it for a (short) time.
41.1 **in** offstage.
20 **embassage** ambassadors.
23 **'longs** belongs.
30–31 **will . . . sway** we will reward your earlier good service, and honour your position with greater authority.
32 **behoof** advantage/benefit.
43 **ransom . . . usury** win them back to our honour and profit.
51 **brave** wonderful.
53 **passing** exceedingly ('surpassing').

TECHELLES
O, my lord, it is sweet and full of pomp!
USUMCASANE
To be a king is half to be a god.
THERIDAMAS
A god is not so glorious as a king:
I think the pleasure they enjoy in heaven,
Cannot compare with kingly joys in earth;
To wear a crown enchased with pearl and gold,
Whose virtues carry with it life and death;
To ask and have, command and be obeyed;
When looks breed love, with looks to gain the prize,
Such power attractive shines in princes' eyes.
TAMBURLAINE
Why, say, Theridamas, wilt thou be a king?
THERIDAMAS
Nay, though I praise it, I can live without it.
TAMBURLAINE
What say my other friends; will you be kings?
TECHELLES
Aye, if I could, with all my heart, my lord.
TAMBURLAINE
Why, that's well said, Techelles; so would I;
And so would you, my masters, would you not?
USUMCASANE
What, then, my lord?
TAMBURLAINE
Why, then, 'Casane, shall we wish for aught
The world affords in greatest novelty,
And rest attemptless, faint, and destitute?
Methinks we should not. I am strongly moved,
That if I should desire the Persian crown,
I could attain it with a wondrous ease:
And would not all our soldiers soon consent,
If we should aim at such a dignity?
THERIDAMAS
I know they would with our persuasions.
TAMBURLAINE
Why, then, Theridamas, I'll first assay
To get the Persian kingdom to myself;
Then thou for Parthia; they for Scythia and Media;
And, if I prosper, all shall be as sure
As if the Turk, the Pope, Afric, and Greece,
Came creeping to us with their crowns a-piece.
TECHELLES
Then shall we send to this triumphing king,
And bid him battle for his novel crown?
USUMCASANE
Nay, quickly, then, before his room be hot.
TAMBURLAINE
'Twill prove a pretty jest, in faith, my friends.
THERIDAMAS
A jest to charge on twenty thousand men?
I judge the purchase more important far.
TAMBURLAINE
Judge by thyself, Theridamas, not me;
For presently Techelles here shall haste
To bid him battle ere he pass too far,
And lose more labour than the gain will quit.
Then shalt thou see this Scythian Tamburlaine
Make but a jest to win the Persian crown.
Techelles, take a thousand horse with thee,
And bid him turn him back to war with us,
That only made him king to make us sport.
We will not steal upon him cowardly,
But give him warning and more warriors.
Haste thee, Techelles; we will follow thee.
What saith Theridamas?
THERIDAMAS.
Go on, for me. *Exeunt.*

Actus II. Scaena vi.

[Enter] Cosroe, Meander, Ortygius, [and] Menaphon, with other Soldiers.

COSROE
What means this devilish shepherd to aspire
With such a giantly presumption,
To cast up hills against the face of heaven,
And dare the force of angry Jupiter?
But, as he thrust them underneath the hills,
And pressed out fire from their burning jaws,

60 **enchased** set.
61 **virtues** powers.
72–74 **shall . . . destitute** shall we wish for everything new and rich that the world has to offer, yet be content never to try for it, and remain weak and poor?
81 **assay** attempt.
86 **their . . . a-piece** each with their crowns.
89 **before . . . hot** before he warms to his position.
90 **pretty** pleasing.
92 **purchase** business.
94 **presently** immediately.
96 **And . . . quit** And the task requires more effort than it is worth.
101 **That . . . sport** we who made him king only as a joke.
102 **steal upon him** creep up on him.
3–6 **To . . . jaws** another reference to the Titans' war with the gods. The latter piled Mounts Pelion and Ossa together to try to reach Olympus, but Jupiter routed them and buried them beneath the volcano, Mt Etna in Sicily.

So will I send this monstrous slave to hell,
Where flames shall ever feed upon his soul.

MEANDER

Some powers divine, or else infernal, mixed
Their angry seeds at his conception;
For he was never sprung of human race,
Since with the spirit of his fearful pride
He dares so doubtlessly resolve of rule,
And by profession be ambitious.

ORTYGIUS

What god, or fiend, or spirit of the earth,
Or monster turned to a manly shape,
Or of what mould or mettle he be made,
What star or fate soever govern him,
Let us put on our meet encountering minds,
And, in detesting such a devilish thief,
In love of honour and defence of right,
Be armed against the hate of such a foe,
Whether from earth, or hell, or heaven he grow.

COSROE

Nobly resolved, my good Ortygius;
And, since we all have sucked one
wholesome air,
And with the same proportion of elements
Resolve, I hope we are resembled,
Vowing our loves to equal death and life.
Let's cheer our soldiers to encounter him,
That grievous image of ingratitude,
That fiery thirster after sovereignty,
And burn him in the fury of that flame
That none can quench but blood and empery.
Resolve, my lords and loving soldiers, now
To save your king and country from decay.
Then strike up, drum; and all the stars that make
The loathsome circle of my dated life,
Direct my weapon to his barbarous heart,
That thus opposeth him against the gods,
And scorns the powers that govern Persia!

[*Exeunt.*]

[Actus II. Scaena vii.]

Enter to the battle, and, after the battle, enter Cosroe wounded, Theridamas, Tamburlaine, Techelles, Usumcasane, with others.

COSROE

Barbarous and bloody Tamburlaine,
Thus to deprive me of my crown and life!
Treacherous and false Theridamas,
Even at the morning of my happy state,
Scarce being seated in my royal throne,
To work my downfall and untimely end!
An uncouth pain torments my grieved soul;
And death arrests the organ of my voice,
Who, entering at the breach thy sword
hath made,
Sacks every vein and artier of my heart.
Bloody and insatiate Tamburlaine!

TAMBURLAINE

The thirst of reign and sweetness of a crown,
That caused the eldest son of heavenly Ops
To thrust his doting father from his chair
And place himself in the empyreal heaven,
Moved me to manage arms against thy state.
What better precedent than mighty Jove?
Nature, that framed us of four elements
Warring within our breasts for regiment,
Doth teach us all to have aspiring minds.
Our souls, whose faculties can comprehend
The wondrous architecture of the world,
And measure every wandering planet's
course,
Still climbing after knowledge infinite,
And always moving as the restless spheres,
Wills us to wear ourselves, and never rest,
Until we reach the ripest fruit of all,
That perfect bliss and sole felicity,
The sweet fruition of an earthly crown.

THERIDAMAS

And that made me to join with Tamburlaine.

13–14 **He . . . ambitious.** He dares with such certainty to aim for dominion, and openly/by his very nature be ambitious.

19 **put . . . minds** ready our thoughts for battle.

25–27 **sucked . . . resembled** breathed the same . . . air, and will melt into the same elements (when we die), I believe we are no different.

37 **dated** predestined/limited.

7 **uncouth** strange/unknown.

9 **Who** i.e. Death.

10 **Sacks . . . artier** pillages every . . . artery.

13–14 **eldest . . . chair** Jupiter, whose mother was Ops, usurped his father, Saturn's Olympian throne.

15 The outermost sphere of the universe, known as the empyrean.

18 **framed . . . elements** made us from the four elements: water, air, earth, and fire.

For he is gross and like the massy earth
That moves not upwards, nor by princely deeds
Doth mean to soar above the highest sort.

TECHELLES
And that made us, the friends of Tamburlaine,
To lift our swords against the Persian king.

USUMCASANE
For as when Jove did thrust old Saturn down,
Neptune and Dis gained each of them a crown,
So do we hope to reign in Asia,
If Tamburlaine be placed in Persia.

COSROE
The strangest men that ever nature made!
I know not how to take their tyrannies.
My bloodless body waxeth chill and cold,
And with my blood my life slides through my
wound.
My soul begins to take her flight to hell,
And summons all my senses to depart.
The heat and moisture, which did feed each other,
For want of nourishment to feed them both,
Is dry and cold; and now doth ghastly Death
With greedy talents gripe my bleeding heart,
And like a Harpy tires on my life
Theridamas and Tamburlaine, I die:
And fearful vengeance light upon you both! [*Dies.*]

He [*Tamburlaine*] *takes the crown, and puts it on.*

TAMBURLAINE
Not all the curses which the Furies breathe
Shall make me leave so rich a prize as this.
Theridamas, Techelles, and the rest,
Who think you now is king of Persia?

ALL
Tamburlaine! Tamburlaine!

TAMBURLAINE
Though Mars himself, the angry god of arms,
And all the earthly potentates conspire
To dispossess me of this diadem,
Yet will I wear it in despite of them,
As great commander of this eastern world,
If you but say that Tamburlaine shall reign.

ALL
Long live Tamburlaine, and reign in Asia!

TAMBURLAINE
So; now it is more surer on my head
Than if the gods had held a parliament,
And all pronounced me king of Persia. [*Exeunt.*]

Finis Actus 2.

Actus III. Scaena i.

[*Enter*] *Bajazeth, the Kings of Fez, Morocco, and Argier, with others, in great pomp.*

BAJAZETH
Great kings of Barbary, and my portly bassoes,
We hear the Tartars and the eastern thieves,
Under the conduct of one Tamburlaine,
Presume a bickering with your emperor,
And think to rouse us from our dreadful siege
Of the famous Grecian Constantinople.
You know our army is invincible:
As many circumcised Turks we have,
And warlike bands of Christians renied,
As hath the ocean or the Terrene sea
Small drops of water when the moon begins
To join in one her semi-circled horns.
Yet would we not be braved with foreign power,
Nor raise our siege before the Grecians yield,
Or breathless lie before the city-walls.

KING OF FEZ
Renowned emperor and mighty general,
What if you sent the bassoes of your guard
To charge him to remain in Asia,
Or else to threaten death and deadly arms
As from the mouth of mighty Bajazeth?

31–32 **he . . . upwards** anyone who does not aspire to rise is gross, like the lumpen earth.
37 **Neptune and Dis** Jupiter's brothers Neptune and Dis (Pluto) became kings of the oceans and the underworld respectively when Jupiter seized the throne.
42 **waxeth** grows.
49 **talents gripe** talons grip.
50 **tires** preys (like a falcon). Harpies were mythical beasts with women's heads and the bodies of birds of prey, which inflicted punishment on those whom the gods wished to suffer.
52 **light** alight/fall.
67.1 ***Finis Actus 2*** End of Act Two.
1 **Barbary** the region on the north African coast.
1 **portly bassoes** stately pashas (a Turkish official of high rank).
3 **conduct** leadership.
9 **Christians renied** renegade Christians.
10 **Terrene** Mediterranean.
11–12 **when . . . horns** when the moon is full (and the tides are high).
13 **braved with** defied by.
18 **charge** command.

BAJAZETH

Hie thee, my basso, fast to Persia;
Tell him thy lord, the Turkish emperor,
Dread lord of Afric, Europe, and Asia,
Great king and conqueror of Graecia,
The ocean, Terrene, and the coal-black sea,
The high and highest monarch of the world,
Wills and commands (for say not I entreat)
Not once to set his foot in Africa,
Or spread his colours in Graecia,
Lest he incur the fury of my wrath.
Tell him I am content to take a truce,
Because I hear he bears a valiant mind;
But if, presuming on his silly power,
He be so mad to manage arms with me,
Then stay thou with him, say, I bid thee so.
And if, before the sun have measured heaven
With triple circuit, thou re-greet us not,
We mean to take his morning's next arise
For messenger he will not be reclaimed,
And mean to fetch thee in despite of him.

BASSO

Most great and puissant monarch of the earth,
Your basso will accomplish your behest,
And show your pleasure to the Persian,
As fits the legate of the stately Turk. *Exit Bass*[*o*].

KING OF ARGIER

They say he is the king of Persia;
But, if he dare attempt to stir your siege,
'Twere requisite he should be ten times more,
For all flesh quakes at your magnificence.

BAJAZETH

True, Argier; and tremble at my looks.

KING OF MOROCCO

The spring is hindered by your smothering host;
For neither rain can fall upon the earth,
Nor sun reflex his virtuous beams thereon,
The ground is mantled with such multitudes.

BAJAZETH

All this is true as holy Mahomet,
And all the trees are blasted with our breaths.

KING OF FEZ

What thinks your greatness best to be achieved
In pursuit of the city's overthrow?

BAJAZETH

I will the captive pioneers of Argier
Cut off the water that by leaden pipes
Runs to the city from the mountain Carnon.
Two thousand horse shall forage up and down,
That no relief or succour come by land;
And all the sea my galleys countermand.
Then shall our footmen lie within the trench,
And with their cannons, mouthed like
Orcus' gulf,
Batter the walls, and we will enter in;
And thus the Grecians shall be conquered. *Exeunt.*

Actus III. Scaena ii.

[*Enter*] *Agydas, Zenocrate, Anippe, with others.*

[AGYDAS]

Madam Zenocrate, may I presume
To know the cause of these unquiet fits
That work such trouble to your wonted rest?
'Tis more than pity such a heavenly face
Should by heart's sorrow wax so wan and pale,
When your offensive rape by Tamburlaine
(Which of your whole displeasures should
be most)
Hath seemed to be digested long ago.

ZENOCRATE

Although it be digested long ago,
As his exceeding favours have deserved,
And might content the queen of heaven as well
As it hath changed my first-conceived disdain;
Yet, since, a farther passion feeds my thoughts
With ceaseless and disconsolate conceits,
Which dye my looks so lifeless as they are,
And might, if my extremes had full events,
Make me the ghastly counterfeit of death.

21 **Hie** Hurry.
33 **silly** simple/weak.
38 **his** the sun's.
50 **The . . . host** an army so vast it smothers the earth and so prevents the arrival of spring.
52 **reflex** cast.
58 **will** order.
58 **captive pioneers** specialist troops, skilled in mining.
63 **countermand** command.
65 **Orcus' gulf** the gates of hell.
6 **rape** abduction.
8 **digested** recovered from.
11 **queen of heaven** Juno.
16 **if . . . events** if my extreme fears were realised.
17 **counterfeit** likeness.

AGYDAS
Eternal heaven sooner be dissolved,
And all that pierceth Phoebus' silver eye,
Before such hap fall to Zenocrate.

ZENOCRATE
Ah, life and soul, still hover in his breast,
And leave my body senseless as the earth,
Or else unite you to his life and soul,
That I may live and die with Tamburlaine!

Enter Tamburlaine [unnoticed], with Techelles and others.

AGYDAS
With Tamburlaine? Ah, fair Zenocrate,
Let not a man so vile and barbarous,
That holds you from your father in despite,
And keeps you from the honours of a queen,
Being supposed his worthless concubine,
Be honoured with your love but for necessity.
So now the mighty Soldan hears of you,
Your highness needs not doubt but in short time
He will with Tamburlaine's destruction,
Redeem you from this deadly servitude.

ZENOCRATE
Leave to wound me with these words,
And speak of Tamburlaine as he deserves.
The entertainment we have had of him
Is far from villainy or servitude,
And might in noble minds be counted princely.

AGYDAS
How can you fancy one that looks so fierce,
Only disposed to martial stratagems?
Who, when he shall embrace you in his arms,
Will tell how many thousand men he slew;
And, when you look for amorous discourse,
Will rattle forth his facts of war and blood,
Too harsh a subject for your dainty ears.

ZENOCRATE
As looks the sun through Nilus' flowing stream,
Or when the morning holds him in her arms,
So looks my lordly love, fair Tamburlaine;
His talk much sweeter than the Muses' song
They sung for honour 'gainst Pierides,
Or when Minerva did with Neptune strive;
And higher would I rear my estimate
Than Juno, sister to the highest god,
If I were matched with mighty Tamburlaine.

AGYDAS
Yet be not so inconstant in your love,
But let the young Arabian live in hope
After your rescue to enjoy his choice.
You see, though first the king of Persia,
Being a shepherd, seemed to love you much,
Now in his majesty he leaves those looks,
Those words of favour, and those comfortings,
And gives no more than common courtesies.

ZENOCRATE
Thence rise the tears that so distain my cheeks,
Fearing his love through my unworthiness.

Tamburlaine goes to her, and takes her away lovingly by the hand, looking wrathfully on Agydas, and says nothing.

AGYDAS
Betrayed by fortune and suspicious love,
Threatened with frowning wrath and jealousy,
Surprised with fear of hideous revenge,
I stand aghast; but most astonied
To see his choler shut in secret thoughts,
And wrapt in silence of his angry soul.
Upon his brows was portrayed ugly death,
And in his eyes the fury of his heart,
That shone as comets, menacing revenge,
And cast a pale complexion on his cheeks.
As when the seaman sees the Hyades

[19] **all . . . eye** all that meets the silver eye of the sun.
[35] **Leave to wound** Stop wounding me.
[37] **entertainment** hospitality/treatment.
[40] **fancy** love.
[45] **facts** feats.
[47] **Nilus** the river Nile.
[52] The nine daughters of King Pierus challenged the Muses in a song contest. When they lost, they were transformed into birds. Minerva/Athena and Neptune/Poseidon challenged each other over the right to be patron deity of the city of Athens.
[53] **rear my estimate** raise my reputation.
[57] **the young Arabian** the prince to whom Zenocrate is betrothed (see I.ii.32–3).
[65] **Fearing his love** Fearing I have lost his love.
[68] **surprised** ambushed/assaulted.
[69] **astonied** astonished/stunned.
[70] **choler** anger.
[74] **comets** were seen as forewarnings of disaster.
[76] **Hyades** a star cluster whose appearance was believed to presage rain.

Gather an army of Cimmerian clouds
(Auster and Aquilon with winged steeds,
All sweating, tilt about the watery heavens,
With shivering spears enforcing thunder-claps,
And from their shields strike flames of lightning,)
All fearful folds his sails, and sounds the main,
Lifting his prayers to the heavens for aid
Against the terror of the winds and waves:
So fares Agydas for the late-felt frowns,
That send a tempest to my daunted thoughts,
And make my soul divine her overthrow.

Enter Techelles with a naked dagger.

TECHELLES
See you, Agydas, how the king salutes you.
He bids you prophesy what it imports. *Exit.*

AGYDAS
I prophesied before, and now I prove
The killing frowns of jealousy and love.
He needed not with words confirm my fear,
For words are vain where working tools present
The naked action of my threatened end.
It says, Agydas, thou shalt surely die,
And of extremities elect the least;
More honour and less pain it may procure,
To die by this resolved hand of thine
Than stay the torments he and heaven have sworn.
Then haste, Agydas, and prevent the plagues
Which thy prolonged fates may draw on thee.
Go wander free from fear of tyrant's rage,
Removed from the torments and the hell
Wherewith he may excruciate thy soul;
And let Agydas by Agydas die,
And with this stab slumber eternally. [*Stabs himself.*]

[*Re-enter Techelles, with Usumcasane*]

TECHELLES
Usumcasane, see how right the man
Hath hit the meaning of my lord the king.

USUMCASANE
Faith, and Techelles, it was manly done;
And, since he was so wise and honourable,
Let us afford him now the bearing hence,
And crave his triple-worthy burial.

TECHELLES
Agreed, Casane; we will honour him.

[*Exeunt, bearing out the body.*]

Actus III. Scaena iii.

[Enter] Tamburlaine, Techelles, Usumcasane, Theridamas, Basso, Zenocrate, [Anippe], with others.

TAMBURLAINE
Basso, by this thy lord and master knows
I mean to meet him in Bithynia.
See, how he comes! Tush, Turks are full of brags,
And menace more than they can well perform.
He meet me in the field, and fetch thee hence?
Alas, poor Turk, his fortune is too weak
T'encounter with the strength of Tamburlaine.
View well my camp, and speak indifferently;
Do not my captains and my soldiers look
As if they meant to conquer Africa?

BASSO
Your men are valiant, but their number few,
And cannot terrify his mighty host.
My lord, the great commander of the world,
Besides fifteen contributory kings,
Hath now in arms ten thousand janissaries,
Mounted on lusty Mauritanian steeds,
Brought to the war by men of Tripoli;
Two hundred thousand footmen that have served
In two set battles fought in Graecia;
And for the expedition of this war,
If he think good, can from his garrisons
Withdraw as many more to follow him.

77 **Cimmerian** pitch black.
78 **Auster and Aquilon** the Roman south and north winds.
79 **tilt** joust.
82 **sounds the main** tests the depth of the sea.
87 **divine** foretell.
8 **hit** understood.
9 **Faith** a contraction of '(Yes,) in faith', a mild oath.
2 **Bithynia** a province on the Black Sea coast of what is now north-west Turkey.
3 **Tush** a dismissive, contemptuous expression.
14 **contributory** tributary/subordinate.
15 **janissaries** elite Turkish guardsmen (actually infantry rather than cavalry).
16 **Mauritania** a province in north-west Africa famed for its horses.
19 **set** full-scale/pitched.
20 **expedition** swift conclusion.

TECHELLES
The more he brings, the greater is the spoil.
For, when they perish by our warlike hands,
We mean to set our footmen on their steeds,
And rifle all those stately janissars.

TAMBURLAINE
But will those kings accompany your lord?

BASSO
Such as his highness please; but some must stay
To rule the provinces he late subdued.

TAMBURLAINE
[To the Lords]
Then fight courageously, their crowns are yours;
This hand shall set them on your conquering heads,
That made me emperor of Asia.

USUMCASANE
Let him bring millions infinite of men,
Unpeopling Western Africa and Greece,
Yet we assure us of the victory.

THERIDAMAS
Even he, that in a trice vanquished two kings
More mighty than the Turkish emperor,
Shall rouse him out of Europe, and pursue
His scattered army till they yield or die.

TAMBURLAINE
Well said, Theridamas; speak in that mood,
For 'will' and 'shall' best fitteth Tamburlaine,
Whose smiling stars give him assured hope
Of martial triumph ere he meet his foes.
I that am termed the scourge and wrath of God,
The only fear and terror of the world,
Will first subdue the Turk, and then enlarge
Those Christian captives which you keep as slaves,
Burdening their bodies with your heavy chains,
And feeding them with thin and slender fare;
That naked row about the Terrene sea,
And, when they chance to rest or breathe a space,
Are punished with bastones so grievously
That they lie panting on the galleys' side,
And strive for life at every stroke they give.
These are the cruel pirates of Argier,
That damned train, the scum of Africa,
Inhabited with straggling runagates,
That make quick havoc of the Christian blood.
But, as I live, that town shall curse the time
That Tamburlaine set foot in Africa.

Enter Bajazeth with his Bassoes and contributory Kings [of Fez, Morocco, and Argier, with Zabina and Ebea.]

BAJAZETH
Bassoes and janissaries of my guard,
Attend upon the person of your lord,
The greatest potentate of Africa.

TAMBURLAINE
Techelles and the rest, prepare your swords;
I mean t'encounter with that Bajazeth.

BAJAZETH
Kings of Fez, Morocco, and Argier,
He calls me Bajazeth, whom you call lord;
Note the presumption of this Scythian slave.
I tell thee, villain, those that lead my horse
Have to their names titles of dignity;
And dar'st thou bluntly call me 'Bajazeth'?

TAMBURLAINE
And know thou, Turk, that those which lead my horse
Shall lead thee captive thorough Africa;
And dar'st thou bluntly call me 'Tamburlaine'?

BAJAZETH
By Mahomet my kinsman's sepulchre,
And by the holy Alcoran, I swear
He shall be made a chaste and lustless eunuch,
And in my sarell tend my concubines.
And all his captains, that thus stoutly stand,
Shall draw the chariot of my emperess,
Whom I have brought to see their overthrow!

26 **rifle** pillage.
29 **late subdued** recently conquered.
36 **in a trice** an instant.
41 **fitteth** suit.
42 **smiling stars** favourable fortunes.
46 **enlarge** release.
52 **bastones** cudgels.
54 **every stroke** of the oars. The reference is to the Turkish practice of manning their galleys with captured Christian slaves.
56 **train** gang.
57 **runagates** runaways/renegades.
70 **t'encounter** battle.
80 **Mahomet** the prophet Muhammad.
81 **Alcoran** Koran.
83 **sarell** seraglio/harem.

TAMBURLAINE
By this my sword that conquered Persia,
Thy fall shall make me famous through the world!
I will not tell thee how I'll handle thee,
But every common soldier of my camp
Shall smile to see thy miserable state.

KING OF FEZ
What means the mighty Turkish emperor,
To talk with one so base as Tamburlaine?

KING OF MOROCCO
Ye Moors and valiant men of Barbary.
How can ye suffer these indignities?

KING OF ARGIER
Leave words, and let them feel your lances' points,
Which glided through the bowels of the Greeks.

BAJAZETH
Well said, my stout contributory kings!
Your threefold army and my hugey host
Shall swallow up these base-born Persians.

TECHELLES
Puissant, renowned, and mighty Tamburlaine,
Why stay we thus, prolonging of their lives?

THERIDAMAS
I long to see those crowns won by our swords,
That we may rule as kings of Africa.

USUMCASANE
What coward would not fight for such a prize?

TAMBURLAINE
Fight all courageously, and be you kings:
I speak it, and my words are oracles.

BAJAZETH
Zabina, mother of three braver boys
Than Hercules, that in his infancy
Did pash the jaws of serpents venomous;
Whose hands are made to gripe a warlike lance,
Their shoulders broad for complete armour fit,
Their limbs more large and of a bigger size
Than all the brats y-sprung from Typhon's loins;
Who, when they come unto their father's age,
Will batter turrets with their manly fists;
Sit here upon this royal chair of state,
And on thy head wear my imperial crown,
Until I bring this sturdy Tamburlaine
And all his captains bound in captive chains.

ZABINA
Such good success happen to Bajazeth!

TAMBURLAINE
Zenocrate, the loveliest maid alive,
Fairer than rocks of pearl and precious stone,
The only paragon of Tamburlaine;
Whose eyes are brighter than the lamps of heaven,
And speech more pleasant than sweet harmony;
That with thy looks canst clear the darkened sky,
And calm the rage of thundering Jupiter;
Sit down by her, adorned with my crown,
As if thou were't the empress of the world.
Stir not, Zenocrate, until thou see
Me march victoriously with all my men,
Triumphing over him and these his kings,
Which I will bring as vassals to thy feet.
Till then, take thou my crown, vaunt of my worth,
And manage words with her, as we will arms.

ZENOCRATE
And may my love, the king of Persia,
Return with victory and free from wound!

BAJAZETH
Now shalt thou feel the force of Turkish arms,
Which lately made all Europe quake for fear.
I have of Turks, Arabians, Moors, and Jews,
Enough to cover all Bithynia.
Let thousands die; their slaughtered carcasses
Shall serve for walls and bulwarks to the rest;
And as the heads of Hydra, so my power,
Subdued, shall stand as mighty as before.
If they should yield their necks unto the sword,
Thy soldiers' arms could not endure to strike
So many blows as I have heads for them.
Thou know'st not, foolish-hardy Tamburlaine,
What 'tis to meet me in the open field,
That leave no ground for thee to march upon.

99 **hugey** huge.
110 **pash** break.
109–110 **Hercules ... venomous** Hercules was said to have strangled two snakes when he was still in his cradle.
114 **Typhon** the hundred-dragon-headed giant, was the most fearsome creature in Greek mythology, dubbed 'the father of monsters'.
117 **chair of state** throne.
124 **paragon** equal.
135–136 **vaunt ... her** boast of my worthiness and combat verbally with her.
145 **Hydra** the serpent-headed hydra had the ability to grow a new head for each one that was chopped off.
150 **foolish-hardy** foolhardy.

TAMBURLAINE
Our conquering swords shall marshal us the way
We use to march upon the slaughtered foe,
Trampling their bowels with our horses' hoofs,
Brave horses bred on the white Tartarian hills.
My camp is like to Julius Caesar's host,
That never fought but had the victory.
Nor in Pharsalia was there such hot war
As these my followers willingly would have.
Legions of spirits, fleeting in the air,
Direct our bullets and our weapons' points,
And make your strokes to wound the senseless air;
And when she sees our bloody colours spread,
Then Victory begins to take her flight,
Resting herself upon my milk-white tent.
But come, my lords, to weapons let us fall;
The field is ours, the Turk, his wife, and all.

Exit, with his followers.

BAJAZETH
Come, kings and bassoes, let us glut our swords,
That thirst to drink the feeble Persians' blood.

Exit, with his followers.

ZABINA
Base concubine, must thou be placed by me
That am the empress of the mighty Turk?

ZENOCRATE
Disdainful Turkess, and unreverend boss,
Call'st thou me concubine, that am betrothed
Unto the great and mighty Tamburlaine?

ZABINA
To Tamburlaine, the great Tartarian thief!

ZENOCRATE
Thou wilt repent these lavish words of thine
When thy great basso-master and thyself
Must plead for mercy at his kingly feet,
And sue to me to be your advocate.

ZABINA
And sue to thee? I tell thee, shameless girl,
Thou shalt be laundress to my waiting-maid.
How lik'st thou her, Ebea; will she serve?

EBEA
Madam, she thinks perhaps she is too fine;
But I shall turn her into other weeds,
And make her dainty fingers fall to work.

ZENOCRATE
Hear'st thou, Anippe, how thy drudge doth talk?
And how my slave, her mistress, menaceth?
Both for their sauciness shall be employed
To dress the common soldiers' meat and drink;
For we will scorn they should come near ourselves.

ANIPPE
Yet sometimes let your highness send for them
To do the work my chambermaid disdains.

They sound the battle within, and stay.

ZENOCRATE
Ye gods and powers that govern Persia,
And made my lordly love her worthy king,
Now strengthen him against the Turkish Bajazeth,
And let his foes, like flocks of fearful roes
Pursued by hunters, fly his angry looks,
That I may see him issue conqueror!

ZABINA
Now, Mahomet, solicit God himself,
And make him rain down murdering shot from heaven,
To dash the Scythians' brains, and strike them dead,
That dare to manage arms with him
That offered jewels to thy sacred shrine
When first he warred against the Christians!

To the battle again.

ZENOCRATE
By this the Turks lie weltering in their blood,
And Tamburlaine is lord of Africa.

ZABINA
Thou art deceived. I heard the trumpets sound,

153 **marshal . . . way** clear the way for us (as a marshal would part the crowds in a hall).
159 **Pharsalia** the site of Julius Caesar's battle with Pompey the Great in 48BC.
163 **your . . . air** 1590 has 'our strokes' and 'senseless lure'.
164 **colours** banners.
173 **unreverend boss** rude fat woman.
185 **weeds** clothes.
188 **menaceth** threatens.
189 **sauciness** impudence.
190 **dress . . . meat** prepare their food.
193.1 **They . . . stay.** Trumpets (and shouting) sound offstage, then stop.
197 **roes** roe deer.
199 **issue** emerge (from the battle).
205.1 **To . . . again.** Further martial trumpets sound.
206 **weltering** wallowing.

As when my emperor overthrew the Greeks,
And led them captive into Africa.
Straight will I use thee as thy pride deserves;
Prepare thyself to live and die my slave.

ZENOCRATE
If Mahomet should come from heaven and swear
My royal lord is slain or conquered,
Yet should he not persuade me otherwise
But that he lives and will be conqueror.

Bajazeth flies, and he [Tamburlaine] pursues him. The battle short, and they enter. Bajazeth is overcome.

TAMBURLAINE
Now, king of bassoes, who is conqueror?

BAJAZETH
Thou, by the fortune of this damned foil.

TAMBURLAINE
Where are your stout contributory kings?

Enter Techelles, Theridamas, Usumcasane.

TECHELLES
We have their crowns; their bodies strew the field.

TAMBURLAINE
Each man a crown! Why, kingly fought, i'faith.
Deliver them into my treasury.

ZENOCRATE
Now let me offer to my gracious lord
His royal crown again so highly won.

TAMBURLAINE
Nay, take the Turkish crown from her, Zenocrate,
And crown me emperor of Africa.

ZABINA
No, Tamburlaine; though now thou gat the best,
Thou shalt not yet be lord of Africa.

THERIDAMAS
Give her the crown, Turkess, you were best.

He takes it from her, and gives it Zenocrate.

ZABINA
Injurious villains, thieves, runagates,
How dare you thus abuse my majesty?

THERIDAMAS
Here, madam, you are empress; she is none.

TAMBURLAINE
Not now, Theridamas; her time is past.
The pillars that have bolstered up those terms,
Are fall'n in clusters at my conquering feet.

ZABINA
Though he be prisoner, he may be ransomed.

TAMBURLAINE
Not all the world shall ransom Bajazeth.

BAJAZETH
Ah, fair Zabina, we have lost the field;
And never had the Turkish emperor
So great a foil by any foreign foe.
Now will the Christian miscreants be glad,
Ringing with joy their superstitious bells,
And making bonfires for my overthrow.
But, ere I die, those foul idolaters
Shall make me bonfires with their filthy bones;
For, though the glory of this day be lost,
Afric and Greece have garrisons enough
To make me sovereign of the earth again.

TAMBURLAINE
Those walled garrisons will I subdue,
And write myself great lord of Africa.
So from the East unto the furthest West
Shall Tamburlaine extend his puissant arm.
The galleys and those pilling brigandines,
That yearly sail to the Venetian gulf,
And hover in the Straits for Christians' wreck,
Shall lie at anchor in the Isle Asant,
Until the Persian fleet and men-of-war,
Sailing along the oriental sea,
Have fetched about the Indian continent,
Even from Persepolis to Mexico,
And thence unto the Straits of Gibraltar;
Where they shall meet and join their force in one,
Keeping in awe the Bay of Portingale,

211 **straight** very soon.
216.1 **Bajazeth . . . overcome.** Tamburlaine pursues Bajazeth across the stage, then trumpets briefly sound, before the two re-enter, and Tamburlaine captures him.
218 **foil** defeat.
229 **you were best** that would be the best thing for you to do.
234 **pillars . . . terms** carved statuary busts on columns ('pillars').
253 **pilling brigandines** pillaging pirate ships.
256 **Isle Asant** Zante, off the coast of mainland Greece.
263 **Portingale** Portugal.

And all the ocean by the British shore;
And by this means I'll win the world at last.

BAJAZETH
Yet set a ransom on me, Tamburlaine.

TAMBURLAINE
What, think'st thou Tamburlaine esteems thy gold?
I'll make the kings of India, ere I die,
Offer their mines to sue for peace to me,
And dig for treasure to appease my wrath.
Come, bind them both, and one lead in the Turk;
The Turkess let my love's maid lead away.

They bind them.

BAJAZETH
Ah, villains, dare you touch my sacred arms?
O Mahomet! O sleepy Mahomet!

ZABINA
O cursed Mahomet, that mak'st us thus
The slaves to Scythians, rude and barbarous!

TAMBURLAINE
Come, bring them in; and for this happy conquest
Triumph, and solemnize a martial feast. *Exeunt.*

Finis Actus Tertii.

Actus IV. Scaena i.

[Enter the] Soldan of Egypt with three or four Lords, Capolin, [and a Messenger].

SOLDAN
Awake, ye men of Memphis; hear the clang
Of Scythian trumpets; hear the basilisks,
That, roaring, shake Damascus' turrets down!
The rogue of Volga holds Zenocrate,
The Soldan's daughter, for his concubine,
And, with a troop of thieves and vagabonds,
Hath spread his colours to our high disgrace,
While you, faint-hearted, base Egyptians,
Lie slumbering on the flowery banks of Nile,
As crocodiles that unaffrighted rest
While thundering cannons rattle on their skins.

MESSENGER
Nay, mighty Soldan, did your greatness see
The frowning looks of fiery Tamburlaine,
That with his terror and imperious eyes
Commands the hearts of his associates,
It might amaze your royal majesty.

SOLDAN
Villain, I tell thee, were that Tamburlaine
As monsterous as Gorgon, prince of hell,
The Soldan would not start a foot from him.
But speak, what power hath he?

MESSENGER
Mighty lord,
Three hundred thousand men in armour clad,
Upon their prancing steeds, disdainfully
With wanton paces trampling on the ground;
Five hundred thousand footmen threatening shot,
Shaking their swords, their spears, and iron bills,
Environing their standard round, that stood
As bristle-pointed as a thorny wood;
Their warlike engines and munition
Exceed the forces of their martial men.

SOLDAN
Nay, could their numbers countervail the stars,
Or ever-drizzling drops of April showers,
Or withered leaves that autumn shaketh down,
Yet would the Soldan by his conquering power
So scatter and consume them in his rage,
That not a man should live to rue their fall.

CAPOLIN
So might your highness, had you time to sort
Your fighting men, and raise your royal host;
But Tamburlaine by expedition
Advantage takes of your unreadiness.

SOLDAN
Let him take all th'advantages he can.
Were all the world conspired to fight for him,
Nay, were he devil, as he is no man,
Yet in revenge of fair Zenocrate,
Whom he detaineth in despite of us,
This arm should send him down to Erebus,
To shroud his shame in darkness of the night.

278.1 *Finis Actus Tertii.* End of the Third Act.
2 **basilisks** great cannons.
12 **did...see** if you could see.
18 **Gorgon** the demon Demogorgon.
19 **start** move.
20 **power** troops.
25 **iron bills** billhooks/halberds.
26 **Environing** encircling.
28 **munition** siege weapons and supplies.
30 **countervail** equal in numbers.
33 **by expedition** swift action.
45 **Erebus** Hades.

MESSENGER
Pleaseth your mightiness to understand,
His resolution far exceedeth all.
The first day when he pitcheth down his tents,
White is their hue, and on his silver crest
A snowy feather spangled-white he bears,
To signify the mildness of his mind,
That, satiate with spoil, refuseth blood.
But, when Aurora mounts the second time,
As red as scarlet is his furniture;
Then must his kindled wrath be quenched with blood,
Not sparing any that can manage arms.
But, if these threats move not submission,
Black are his colours, black pavilion;
His spear, his shield, his horse, his armour, plumes,
And jetty feathers, menace death and hell;
Without respect of sex, degree, or age,
He razeth all his foes with fire and sword.

SOLDAN
Merciless villain, peasant, ignorant
Of lawful arms or martial discipline.
Pillage and murder are his usual trades:
The slave usurps the glorious name of war.
See, Capolin, the fair Arabian king,
That hath been disappointed by this slave
Of my fair daughter and his princely love,
May have fresh warning to go war with us,
And be revenged for her disparagement. [*Exeunt.*]

Actus IV. Scaena ii.

[Enter] Tamburlaine, Techelles, Theridamas, Usumcasane, Zenocrate, Anippe, two Moors drawing Bajazeth in his cage, and his wife [Zabina] following him.

TAMBURLAINE
Bring out my footstool.

They take him [*Bajazeth*] *out of the cage.*

BAJAZETH
Ye holy priests of heavenly Mahomet,
That, sacrificing, slice and cut your flesh,
Staining his altars with your purple blood,
Make heaven to frown, and every fixed star
To suck up poison from the moorish fens,
And pour it in this glorious tyrant's throat!

TAMBURLAINE
The chiefest god, first mover of that sphere
Enchased with thousands ever-shining lamps,
Will sooner burn the glorious frame of heaven
Than it should so conspire my overthrow.
But, villain, thou that wishest this to me,
Fall prostrate on the low disdainful earth,
And be the footstool of great Tamburlaine,
That I may rise into my royal throne.

BAJAZETH
First shalt thou rip my bowels with thy sword,
And sacrifice my heart to death and hell,
Before I yield to such a slavery.

TAMBURLAINE
Base villain, vassal, slave to Tamburlaine,
Unworthy to embrace or touch the ground
That bears the honour of my royal weight;
Stoop, villain, stoop! Stoop; for so he bids
That may command thee piecemeal to be torn,
Or scattered like the lofty cedar-trees
Struck with the voice of thundering Jupiter.

BAJAZETH
Then, as I look down to the damned fiends,
Fiends, look on me; and thou, dread god of hell,
With ebon sceptre strike this hateful earth,
And make it swallow both of us at once!

He [*Tamburlaine*] *gets up upon him to his chair.*

TAMBURLAINE
Now clear the triple region of the air,
And let the majesty of heaven behold
Their scourge and terror tread on emperors.
Smile, stars that reigned at my nativity,
And dim the brightness of your neighbour lamps;
Disdain to borrow light of Cynthia!
For I, the chiefest lamp of all the earth,
First rising in the east with mild aspect,
But fixed now in the meridian line,

53 **refuseth** will not shed.
54 **Aurora mounts** the dawn rises.
55 **is his furniture** are his trappings (banners and tents).
61 **jetty** jet black.
72 **disparagement** the insult done to her [Zenocrate].
9 **Enchased** Studded, as with gems.
23 **piecemeal...torn** to be torn into tiny pieces.
30 **triple...air** the atmosphere was thought to be divided into three zones depending on their distance from the earth.
35 **Cynthia** the moon (which was thought a source of light in this period).
38 **fixed...line** fixed forever at its zenith, on the north-south equivalent of the equator.

Will send up fire to your turning spheres,
And cause the sun to borrow light of you.
My sword struck fire from his coat of steel,
Even in Bithynia, when I took this Turk;
As when a fiery exhalation,
Wrapt in the bowels of a freezing cloud,
Fighting for passage, makes the welkin crack,
And casts a flash of lightning to the earth.
But, ere I march to wealthy Persia,
Or leave Damascus and th'Egyptian fields,
As was the fame of Clymene's brain-sick son
That almost brent the axle-tree of heaven,
So shall our swords, our lances, and our shot
Fill all the air with fiery meteors;
Then, when the sky shall wax as red as blood,
It shall be said I made it red myself,
To make me think of naught but blood and war.

ZABINA

Unworthy king, that by thy cruelty
Unlawfully usurp'st the Persian seat,
Dar'st thou, that never saw an emperor
Before thou met my husband in the field,
Being thy captive, thus abuse his state,
Keeping his kingly body in a cage,
That roofs of gold and sun-bright palaces
Should have prepared to entertain his grace?
And treading him beneath thy loathsome feet,
Whose feet the kings of Africa have kissed?

TECHELLES

You must devise some torment worse, my lord,
To make these captives rein their lavish tongues.

TAMBURLAINE

Zenocrate, look better to your slave.

ZENOCRATE

She is my handmaid's slave, and she shall look
That these abuses flow not from her tongue.
Chide her, Anippe.

ANIPPE

Let these be warnings for you, then, my slave,
How you abuse the person of the king;
Or else I swear to have you whipped stark nak'd.

BAJAZETH

Great Tamburlaine, great in my overthrow,
Ambitious pride shall make thee fall as low,
For treading on the back of Bajazeth,
That should be horsed on four mighty kings.

TAMBURLAINE

Thy names, and titles, and thy dignities
Are fled from Bajazeth and remain with me,
That will maintain it 'gainst a world of kings.
Put him in again.

BAJAZETH

Is this a place for mighty Bajazeth?
Confusion light on him that helps thee thus.

TAMBURLAINE

There, whiles he lives, shall Bajazeth be kept;
And where I go be thus in triumph drawn.
And thou, his wife, shalt feed him with the scraps
My servitors shall bring thee from my board;
For he that gives him other food than this
Shall sit by him, and starve to death himself:
This is my mind, and I will have it so.
Not all the kings and emperors of the earth,
If they would lay their crowns before my feet,
Shall ransom him, or take him from his cage.
The ages that shall talk of Tamburlaine,
Even from this day to Plato's wondrous year,
Shall talk how I have handled Bajazeth.
These Moors, that drew him from Bithynia
To fair Damascus, where we now remain,
Shall lead him with us wheresoe'er we go.
Techelles, and my loving followers,
Now may we see Damascus's lofty towers,
Like to the shadows of Pyramides
That with their beauties grace the Memphian fields.
The golden stature of their feathered bird,
That spreads her wings upon the city-walls,
Shall not defend it from our battering shot:
The townsmen mask in silk and cloth of gold,
And every house is as a treasury;

43 **exhalation** vapour.
45 **welkin** sky.
49–50 **Clymene's . . . heaven** Phaeton, the sun of Apollo and Clymene, stole his father's sun-chariot and, unable to control the fiery steeds, scorched ('brent') half the earth before he could be stopped.
51 **shot** muskets.
68 **look better to** control more closely.
74 **nak'd** naked (monosyllabic).
84 **light** fall.
88 **board** table.
96 **Plato's wondrous year** the year in the far future when, according to Plato's *Timaeus*, all the planets will return to their original locations in the heavens.
103 **Pyramides** pyramids (pronounced with four syllables)
105–106 **their . . . city-walls** the sacred Egyptian ibis.

The men, the treasure, and the town are ours.

THERIDAMAS

Your tents of white now pitched before the gates,
And gentle flags of amity displayed,
I doubt not but the governor will yield,
Offering Damascus to your majesty.

TAMBURLAINE

So shall he have his life, and all the rest.
But if he stay until the bloody flag
Be once advanced on my vermilion tent,
He dies, and those that kept us out so long;
And, when they see me march in black array,
With mournful streamers hanging down their
heads,
Were in that city all the world contained,
Not one should scape, but perish by our swords.

ZENOCRATE

Yet would you have some pity for my sake,
Because it is my country and my father's.

TAMBURLAINE

Not for the world, Zenocrate, if I have sworn.
Come, bring in the Turk. *Exeunt.*

Actus IV. Scaena iii.

[Enter] Soldan, [King of] Arabia, Capolin, with streaming colours, and Soldiers.

SOLDAN

Methinks we march as Meleager did,
Environed with brave Argolian knights,
To chase the savage Calydonian boar,
Or Cephalus, with lusty Theban youths,
Against the wolf that angry Themis sent
To waste and spoil the sweet Aonian fields.
A monster of five hundred thousand heads,
Compact of rapine, piracy, and spoil,
The scum of men, the hate and scourge of God,
Raves in Egyptia, and annoyeth us.
My lord, it is the bloody Tamburlaine,
A sturdy felon, and a base-bred thief,
By murder raised to the Persian crown,
That dares control us in our territories.
To tame the pride of this presumptuous beast,
Join your Arabians with the Soldan's power;
Let us unite our royal bands in one,
And hasten to remove Damascus' siege.
It is a blemish to the majesty
And high estate of mighty emperors,
That such a base usurping vagabond
Should brave a king, or wear a princely crown.

KING OF ARABIA

Renowned Soldan, have you lately heard
The overthrow of mighty Bajazeth
About the confines of Bithynia?
The slavery wherewith he persecutes
The noble Turk and his great emperess?

SOLDAN

I have, and sorrow for his bad success;
But, noble lord of great Arabia,
Be so persuaded that the Soldan is
No more dismayed with tidings of his fall,
Than in the haven when the pilot stands
And views a stranger's ship rent in the winds,
And shivered against a craggy rock.
Yet in compassion to his wretched state,
A sacred vow to heaven and him I make,
Confirming it with Ibis' holy name,
That Tamburlaine shall rue the day, the hour,
Wherein he wrought such ignominious wrong
Unto the hallowed person of a prince,
Or kept the fair Zenocrate so long,
As concubine, I fear, to feed his lust.

KING OF ARABIA

Let grief and fury hasten on revenge;
Let Tamburlaine for his offences feel
Such plagues as heaven and we can pour on him.
I long to break my spear upon his crest,
And prove the weight of his victorious arm;
For fame, I fear, hath been too prodigal
In sounding through the world his partial praise.

120 **streamers** banners.
164.1 **colours** banners.
1–3 **Meleager . . . boar** Meleager of Calydon (Greece) led a party of Greek (Argolian) heroes in the hunt for a monstrous boar sent by Artemis, as described in book ix of Homer's *Iliad*.
4–6 **Cephalus . . . fields** the story of the Theban (Aonian) hero Cephalus and his hunt for the beast (not necessarily a wolf) is described in book vii of Ovid's *Metamorphoses*. Themis is a prophetic figure of justice in Greek mythology.
8 **Compact of** constructed of.
22 **brave** defy.
25 **confines** borders.
28 **his bad success** Bajazeth's ill fortunes.
33–34 **in . . . rock** when the pilot (guide) stands in the harbour watching a foreign ship wrecked (i.e. it's not his problem).
47 **prove** test.
48–49 **fame . . . praise** fame has been too lavish in spreading overly favourable praise of him though the world.

SOLDAN
Capolin, hast thou surveyed our powers?

CAPOLIN
Great emperors of Egypt and Arabia,
The number of your hosts united is:
A hundred and fifty thousand horse,
Two hundred thousand foot, brave men-at-arms,
Courageous and full of hardiness,
As frolic as the hunters in the chase
Of savage beasts amid the desert woods.

KING OF ARABIA
My mind presageth fortunate success;
And, Tamburlaine, my spirit doth foresee
The utter ruin of thy men and thee.

SOLDAN
Then rear your standards; let your sounding drums
Direct our soldiers to Damascus' walls.
Now Tamburlaine, the mighty Soldan comes,
And leads with him the great Arabian king,
To dim thy baseness and obscurity,
Famous for nothing but for theft and spoil;
To raze and scatter thy inglorious crew
Of Scythians and slavish Persians. *Exeunt.*

Actus IV. Scaena iv.

A banquet, and to it cometh Tamburlaine all in scarlet, Theridamas, Techelles, Usumcasane, [and Zenocrate], the Turk [Bajazeth, drawn in his cage, Zabina], with others.

TAMBURLAINE
Now hang our bloody colours by Damascus,
Reflexing hues of blood upon their heads,
While they walk quivering on their city walls,
Half-dead for fear before they feel my wrath.
Then let us freely banquet, and carouse
Full bowls of wine unto the god of war,
That means to fill your helmets full of gold,
And make Damascus' spoils as rich to you
As was to Jason Colchis' golden fleece.
And now, Bajazeth, hast thou any stomach?

BAJAZETH
Aye, such a stomach, cruel Tamburlaine, as
I could willingly feed upon thy blood-raw heart.

TAMBURLAINE
Nay, thine own is easier to come by; pluck out that and 'twill serve thee and thy wife. Well, Zenocrate, Techelles, and the rest, fall to your victuals.

BAJAZETH
Fall to, and never may your meat digest!
Ye Furies, that can mask invisible,
Dive to the bottom of Avernus' pool,
And in your hands bring hellish poison up,
And squeeze it in the cup of Tamburlaine.
Or winged snakes of Lerna, cast your stings,
And leave your venoms in this tyrant's dish?

ZABINA
And may this banquet prove as ominous
As Progne's to th'adulterous Thracian king
That fed upon the substance of his child.

ZENOCRATE
My lord, how can you suffer these
Outrageous curses by these slaves of yours?

TAMBURLAINE
To let them see, divine Zenocrate,
I glory in the curses of my foes,
Having the power from the empyreal heaven
To turn them all upon their proper heads.

TECHELLES
I pray you give them leave, madam; this speech is a goodly refreshing for them.

THERIDAMAS
But, if his highness would let them be fed, it would do them more good.

56 **frolic** merry/festive.
57 **desert** wild/deserted.
58 **presageth fortunate success** predicts good fortune.
2 **Reflexing** Casting.
9 **Jason . . . fleece** the Greek hero Jason led the Argonauts to claim the golden fleece of Colchis (in modern Georgia). The story is related in the *Argonautica* of Apollonius of Rhodes.
15 **fall to your victuals** tuck into your food.
18 **Avernus' pool** the lake marking the entrance to Hades.
21 **winged . . . Lerna** the blood of the snake-headed Hydra of Lerna (south of Argos), the monster killed by Hercules as the second of his twelve labours, was highly poisonous.
24–25 **Progne . . . child.** The Thracian king Tereus raped and mutilated his wife Procne's sister Philomela. When Procne discovered the truth she killed their son, Itys, and served him to his unwitting father as a meal.
30 **empyreal** highest.
31 **proper** own.

TAMBURLAINE
Sirrah, why fall you not to? Are you so daintily brought up, you cannot eat your own flesh?
BAJAZETH
First, legions of devils shall tear thee in pieces.
USUMCASANE
Villain, knowest thou to whom thou speakest?
TAMBURLAINE
O, let him alone. Here, eat, sir; take it from my sword's point, or I'll thrust it to thy heart.

He takes it and stamps upon it.

THERIDAMAS
He stamps it under his feet, my lord.
TAMBURLAINE
Take it up, villain, and eat it; or I will make thee slice the brawns of thy arms into carbonadoes and eat them.
USUMCASANE
Nay, 'twere better he killed his wife, and then she shall be sure not to be starved, and he be provided for a month's victual beforehand.
TAMBURLAINE
Here is my dagger. Despatch her while she is fat; for if she live but a while longer she will fall into a consumption with fretting, and then she will not be worth the eating.
THERIDAMAS
Dost thou think that Mahomet will suffer this?
TECHELLES
'Tis like he will, when he cannot let it.
TAMBURLAINE
Go to; fall to your meat. What, not a bit? Belike he hath not been watered to-day; give him some drink.

They give him water to drink, and he flings it on the ground.

Fast, and welcome, sir, while hunger make you eat.
How now, Zenocrate; doth not the Turk and his wife make a goodly show at a banquet?
ZENOCRATE
Yes, my lord.
THERIDAMAS
Methinks 'tis a great deal better than a consort of music.
TAMBURLAINE
Yet music would do well to cheer up Zenocrate.
Pray thee, tell why art thou so sad? If thou wilt have a song, the Turk shall strain his voice; but why is it?
ZENOCRATE
My lord, to see my father's town besieged,
The country wasted where myself was born,
How can it but afflict my very soul?
If any love remain in you, my lord,
Or if my love unto your majesty
May merit favour at your highness' hands,
Then raise your siege from fair Damascus' walls,
And with my father take a friendly truce.
TAMBURLAINE
Zenocrate, were Egypt Jove's own land,
Yet would I with my sword make Jove to stoop.
I will confute those blind geographers
That make a triple region in the world,
Excluding regions which I mean to trace,
And with this pen reduce them to a map,
Calling the provinces, cities, and towns,
After my name and thine, Zenocrate.
Here at Damascus will I make the point,
That shall begin the perpendicular:
And wouldst thou have me buy thy father's love
With such a loss? Tell me, Zenocrate.
ZENOCRATE
Honour still wait on happy Tamburlaine;
Yet give me leave to plead for him, my lord.
TAMBURLAINE
Content thyself, his person shall be safe,

36 **Sirrah** a variant of 'sir' used to address servants and inferiors.
44 **brawns** muscles.
44 **carbonadoes** strips for frying/roasting.
51 **a consumption** wasting disease.
54 **let** prevent.
57 **Fast... eat.** You're welcome to fast, sir, until hunger makes you eat.
61 **consort of music** a troupe of musicians.
77 **make... world** a world divided into Europe, Asia, and Africa.
79 **this pen** i.e. his sword.
82–83 **Here... perpendicular** I will redraw the maps to place (my capital) Damascus at the centre.
87 **leave** permission.

And all the friends of fair Zenocrate,
If with their lives they will be pleased to yield,
Or may be forced to make me emperor;
For Egypt and Arabia must be mine.
Feed, you slave; thou mayst think thyself happy to be fed from my trencher.

BAJAZETH
My empty stomach, full of idle heat,
Draws bloody humours from my feeble parts,
Preserving life by hastening cruel death.
My veins are pale; my sinews hard and dry;
My joints benumbed; unless I eat, I die.

ZABINA
Eat, Bajazeth; let us live in spite of them, looking some happy power will pity and enlarge us.

TAMBURLAINE
Here, Turk; wilt thou have a clean trencher?

BAJAZETH
Aye, tyrant, and more meat.

TAMBURLAINE
Soft, sir, you must be dieted; too much eating will make you surfeit.

THERIDAMAS
So it would, my lord, 'specially having so small a walk and so little exercise.

Enter a second course, of crowns.

TAMBURLAINE
Theridamas, Techelles, and Casane, here are the cates you desire to finger, are they not?

THERIDAMAS
Aye, my lord: but none save kings must feed with these.

TECHELLES
'Tis enough for us to see them, and for Tamburlaine only to enjoy them.

TAMBURLAINE
Well, here is now to the Soldan of Egypt, the King of Arabia, and the Governor of Damascus.
Now, take these three crowns, and pledge me, my contributory kings. I crown you here:
Theridamas, king of Argier; Techelles, king of Fez; and Usumcasane, king of Morocco.
How say you to this, Turk? These are not your contributory kings.

BAJAZETH
Nor shall they long be thine, I warrant them.

TAMBURLAINE
Kings of Argier, Morocco, and of Fez,
You that have marched with happy Tamburlaine
As far as from the frozen place of heaven
Unto the wat'ry morning's ruddy bower,
And thence by land unto the torrid zone,
Deserve these titles I endow you with
By valour and by magnanimity.
Your births shall be no blemish to your fame,
For virtue is the fount whence Honour springs,
And they are worthy she investeth kings.

THERIDAMAS
And, since your highness hath so well vouchsafed,
If we deserve them not with higher meeds
Than erst our states and actions have retained,
Take them away again, and make us slaves.

TAMBURLAINE
Well said, Theridamas. When holy Fates
Shall stablish me in strong Egyptia,
We mean to travel to th'antarctic pole,
Conquering the people underneath our feet,
And be renowned as never emperors were.
Zenocrate, I will not crown thee yet,
Until with greater honours I be graced. [*Exeunt.*]

Finis Actus quarti.

Actus V. Scaena i.

[*Enter*] *the Governor of Damascus, with three or four Citizens, and four Virgins with branches of laurel in their hands.*

GOVERNOR
Still doth this man, or rather god of war,
Batter our walls and beat our turrets down;
And to resist with longer stubbornness,

94 **trencher** platter.
95–97 **My . . . death.** The heart draws to itself the humours it needs from the rest of the body, thus killing it from the extremities inwards.
100 **looking** hoping that.
101 **enlarge** free.
104 **Soft** Hush.
109 **cates** delicacies.
122 **I warrant them** i.e. I guarantee it.
133 **vouchsafed** granted.
134–135 **with . . . retained** with even greater deeds than we have hitherto performed.

Or hope of rescue from the Soldan's power,
Were but to bring our wilful overthrow,
And make us desperate of our threatened lives.
We see his tents have now been altered
With terrors to the last and cruel'st hue.
His coal-black colours, everywhere advanced,
Threaten our city with a general spoil;
And, if we should with common rites of arms
Offer our safeties to his clemency,
I fear the custom proper to his sword,
Which he observes as parcel of his fame,
Intending so to terrify the world,
By any innovation or remorse
Will never be dispensed with till our deaths.
Therefore, for these our harmless virgins' sakes,
Whose honours and whose lives rely on him,
Let us have hope that their unspotted prayers,
Their blubbered cheeks, and hearty humble moans,
Will melt his fury into some remorse,
And use us like a loving conqueror.

FIRST VIRGIN

If humble suits or imprecations
(Uttered with tears of wretchedness and blood
Shed from the heads and hearts of all our sex,
Some made your wives, and some your children,)
Might have entreated your obdurate breasts
To entertain some care of our securities
Whiles only danger beat upon our walls,
These more than dangerous warrants of our death
Had never been erected as they be,
Nor you depend on such weak helps as we.

GOVERNOR

Well, lovely virgins, think our country's care,
Our love of honour, loath to be enthralled
To foreign powers and rough imperious yokes,
Would not with too much cowardice or fear,
Before all hope of rescue were denied,
Submit yourselves and us to servitude.
Therefore, in that your safeties and our own,
Your honours, liberties, and lives were weighed
In equal care and balance with our own,
Endure as we the malice of our stars,
The wrath of Tamburlaine and power of wars;
Or be the means the overweighing heavens
Have kept to qualify these hot extremes,
And bring us pardon in your cheerful looks.

SECOND VIRGIN

Then here, before the majesty of heaven
And holy patrons of Egyptia,
With knees and hearts submissive we entreat
Grace to our words and pity to our looks,
That this device may prove propitious,
And through the eyes and ears of Tamburlaine
Convey events of mercy to his heart.
Grant that these signs of victory we yield
May bind the temples of his conquering head,
To hide the folded furrows of his brows,
And shadow his displeased countenance
With happy looks of ruth and lenity.
Leave us, my lord, and loving countrymen:
What simple virgins may persuade, we will.

GOVERNOR

Farewell, sweet virgins, on whose safe return
Depends our city, liberty, and lives.

Exeunt [*all except the Virgins.*]

Actus V. Scaena ii.

[*Enter*] *Tamburlaine, Techelles, Theridamas, Usumcasane, with others; Tamburlaine all in black and very melancholy.*

TAMBURLAINE

What, are the turtles frayed out of their nests?
Alas, poor fools, must you be first shall feel
The sworn destruction of Damascus?
They knew my custom; could they not as well
Have sent ye out when first my milk-white flags,
Through which sweet Mercy threw her gentle beams,
Reflexed them on their disdainful eyes,
As now, when fury and incensed hate
Flings slaughtering terror from my coal-black tents,
And tells for truth submission comes too late?

FIRST VIRGIN

Most happy king and emperor of the earth,
Image of honour and nobility,

10 **general spoil** complete destruction.
14 **parcel** a central part.
20 **unspotted** pure.
21 **blubbered** tear-stained
21 **hearty** heart-felt.
24 **imprecations** prayers.
45 **overweighing** governing/judging.
59 **lenity** mercy.
1 **turtles frayed** turtle doves frightened.
11 **happy** fortunate.

For whom the powers divine have made the world,
And on whose throne the holy Graces sit;
In whose sweet person is comprised the sum
Of Nature's skill and heavenly majesty;
Pity our plights; O, pity poor Damascus!
Pity old age, within whose silver hairs
Honour and reverence evermore have reigned;
Pity the marriage-bed, where many a lord,
In prime and glory of his loving joy,
Embraceth now with tears of ruth and blood
The jealous body of his fearful wife,
Whose cheeks and hearts, so punished with conceit,
To think thy puissant never-stayed arm
Will part their bodies, and prevent their souls
From heavens of comfort yet their age might bear,
Now wax all pale and withered to the death,
As well for grief our ruthless governor
Hath thus refused the mercy of thy hand,
(Whose sceptre angels kiss and Furies dread,)
As for their liberties, their loves, or lives!
O, then, for these, and such as we ourselves,
For us, for infants, and for all our bloods,
That never nourished thought against thy rule,
Pity, O, pity, sacred emperor,
The prostrate service of this wretched town;
And take in sign thereof this gilded wreath,
Whereto each man of rule hath given his hand,
And wished, as worthy subjects, happy means
To be investors of thy royal brows
Even with the true Egyptian diadem!

TAMBURLAINE
Virgins, in vain you labour to prevent
That which mine honour swears shall be performed.
Behold my sword; what see you at the point?

FIRST VIRGIN
Nothing but fear and fatal steel, my lord.

TAMBURLAINE
Your fearful minds are thick and misty, then,
For there sits Death; there sits imperious Death,
Keeping his circuit by the slicing edge.
But I am pleased you shall not see him there;
He now is seated on my horsemen's spears,
And on their points his fleshless body feeds.
Techelles, straight go charge a few of them
To charge these dames, and show my servant Death,
Sitting in scarlet on their armed spears.

OMNES
O, pity us!

TAMBURLAINE
Away with them, I say, and show them Death!

They take them away.

I will not spare these proud Egyptians,
Nor change my martial observations
For all the wealth of Gihon's golden waves,
Or for the love of Venus, would she leave
The angry god of arms and lie with me.
They have refused the offer of their lives,
And know my customs are as peremptory
As wrathful planets, death, or destiny.

Enter Techelles.

What, have your horsemen shown the virgins Death?

TECHELLES
They have, my lord, and on Damascus' walls
Have hoisted up their slaughtered carcasses.

TAMBURLAINE
A sight as baneful to their souls, I think,
As are Thessalian drugs or mithridate:
But go, my lords, put the rest to the sword.

Exeunt [*all except Tamburlaine.*]

Ah, fair Zenocrate; divine Zenocrate,
'Fair' is too foul an epithet for thee,
That in thy passion for thy country's love,
And fear to see thy kingly father's harm,
With hair dishevelled wipe'st thy watery cheeks;
And, like to Flora in her morning's pride,

14 **Graces** the three daughters of Jupiter, goddesses of charm, beauty, and creativity.
23 **jealous** anxious.
24 **punished with conceit** tormented with the thought.
26–27 **prevent...bear** forestall many happy years they might otherwise expect to live.
40 **happy means** fortunate opportunity.
47 **thick and misty** dull and confused.
49 **Keeping his circuit** Maintaining his jurisdiction (like a travelling 'circuit judge').
53 **charge** command (with later pun on cavalry charge).
54 **show** reveal.
55.1 **OMNES** All (the Virgins).
60 **Gihon** a river in Eden.
62 **god of arms** Mars, god of war.
69 **baneful** deadly.
70 **Thessalian...mithridate** Thessaly is on the eastern seaboard of Greece. Mithridate, named after its supposed inventor, King Mithridates VI of Pontus, was usually famed as an antidote to poison.
77 **Flora** goddess of Spring and flowers.

Shaking her silver tresses in the air,
Rain'st on the earth resolved pearl in showers,
And sprinklest sapphires on thy shining face,
Where Beauty, mother to the Muses, sits,
And comments volumes with her ivory pen,
Taking instructions from thy flowing eyes;
Eyes, when that Ebena steps to heaven,
In silence of thy solemn evening's walk,
Making the mantle of the richest night,
The moon, the planets, and the meteors, light;
There angels in their crystal armours fight
A doubtful battle with my tempted thoughts
For Egypt's freedom and the Soldan's life,
His life that so consumes Zenocrate;
Whose sorrows lay more siege unto my soul
Than all my army to Damascus' walls;
And neither Persia's sovereign nor the Turk
Troubled my senses with conceit of foil
So much by much as doth Zenocrate.
What is beauty, saith my sufferings, then?
If all the pens that ever poets held
Had fed the feeling of their masters' thoughts,
And every sweetness that inspired their hearts,
Their minds, and muses on admired themes;
If all the heavenly quintessence they still
From their immortal flowers of poesy,
Wherein, as in a mirror, we perceive
The highest reaches of a human wit;
If these had made one poem's period,
And all combined in beauty's worthiness,
Yet should there hover in their restless heads
One thought, one grace, one wonder, at the least,
Which into words no virtue can digest.
But how unseemly is it for my sex,
My discipline of arms and chivalry,
My nature, and the terror of my name,
To harbour thoughts effeminate and faint!
Save only that in beauty's just applause,
With whose instinct the soul of man is touched;
And every warrior that is rapt with love
Of fame, of valour, and of victory,
Must needs have beauty beat on his conceits:
I thus conceiving, and subduing both,
That which hath stopped the tempest of
the gods,
Even from the fiery-spangled veil of heaven,
To feel the lovely warmth of shepherds' flames,
And march in cottages of strewed reeds,
Shall give the world to note, for all my birth,
That virtue solely is the sum of glory,
And fashions men with true nobility...
Who's within there?

Enter two or three [servants].

Hath Bajazeth been fed to-day?

ATTENDANTS
Aye, my lord.

TAMBURLAINE
Bring him forth; and let us know if the town be
ransacked. *[Exeunt servants.]*

Enter Techelles, Theridamas, Usumcasane, and others.

TECHELLES
The town is ours, my lord, and fresh supply
Of conquest and of spoil is offered us.

TAMBURLAINE
That's well, Techelles. What's the news?

TECHELLES
The Soldan and the Arabian king together
March on us with such eager violence,
As if there were no way but one with us.

TAMBURLAINE
No more there is not, I warrant thee, Techelles.

They bring in the Turk [Bajazeth in his cage, and Zabina.]

79 **resolved** dissolved pearls (i.e. dew/tears).
84 **Ebena** Ebon/black: perhaps a personification of night.
95 **conceit of foil** the thought of defeat.
101 **muses** meditations.
102 **quintessence they still** the essence they distil.
106 **made...period** been combined in one single poem.
119 **beat...conceits** besiege his thoughts.
106–127 **If...nobility** The general sense of this rambling passage is clear (no one can fully define love; and love is an unfitting subject for a warrior like Tamburlaine anyway, yet every great soul admires beauty, and every warrior is obsessed by the love of honour and victory; yet he, Tamburlaine, has managed to master both loves, even that love that has stopped the storming gods in their tracks, who, for love, have descended into humble shepherd's disguise, etc. so Tamburlaine, whose birth was so low, shows the world that inner strength (the Italian concept of manly *virtù*) is the true mark of greatness). The syntax is, however, strained and hard to pin down in places, suggestive of the state of Tamburlaine's troubled mind. (Gill and others plausibly suggest replacing the awkward phrase, 'stopped the tempest of the gods' with 'stooped the topmost (or 'chiefest') of the gods'.)
138 **As...us** As if there was only one way to deal with us.

THERIDAMAS
We know the victory is ours, my lord;
But let us save the reverend Soldan's life
For fair Zenocrate that so laments his state.

TAMBURLAINE
That will we chiefly see unto, Theridamas,
For sweet Zenocrate, whose worthiness
Deserves a conquest over every heart.
And now, my footstool, if I lose the field,
You hope of liberty and restitution?
Here let him stay, my masters, from the tents,
Till we have made us ready for the field.
Pray for us, Bajazeth; we are going.

Exeunt [*all except Bajazeth and Zabina.*]

BAJAZETH
Go, never to return with victory!
Millions of men encompass thee about,
And gore thy body with as many wounds!
Sharp forked arrows light upon thy horse!
Furies from the black Cocytus' lake,
Break up the earth, and with their fire-brands
Enforce thee run upon the baneful pikes!
Volleys of shot pierce through thy charmed skin,
And every bullet dipped in poisoned drugs!
Or roaring cannons sever all thy joints,
Making thee mount as high as eagles soar!

ZABINA
Let all the swords and lances in the field
Stick in his breast as in their proper rooms!
At every pore let blood come dropping forth,
That lingering pains may massacre his heart,
And madness send his damned soul to hell!

BAJAZETH
Ah, fair Zabina, we may curse his power,
The heavens may frown, the earth for anger quake;
But such a star hath influence in his sword
As rules the skies and countermands the gods
More than Cimmerian Styx or Destiny.
And then shall we in this detested guise,
With shame, with hunger, and with horror stay,
Griping our bowels with retorqued thoughts,
And have no hope to end our ecstasies.

ZABINA
Then is there left no Mahomet, no God,
No fiend, no fortune, nor no hope of end
To our infamous, monstrous slaveries.
Gape earth, and let the fiends infernal view
A hell as hopeless and as full of fear
As are the blasted banks of Erebus,
Where shaking ghosts with ever-howling groans
Hover about the ugly ferryman,
To get a passage to Elysium.
Why should we live? O, wretches, beggars, slaves!
Why live we, Bajazeth, and build up nests
So high within the region of the air,
By living long in this oppression,
That all the world will see and laugh to scorn
The former triumphs of our mightiness
In this obscure infernal servitude?

BAJAZETH
O life, more loathsome to my vexed thoughts
Than noisome parbreak of the Stygian snakes,
Which fills the nooks of hell with standing air,
Infecting all the ghosts with cureless griefs!
O dreary engines of my loathed sight,
That see my crown, my honour, and my name
Thrust under yoke and thraldom of a thief,
Why feed ye still on day's accursed beams,
And sink not quite into my tortured soul?
You see my wife, my queen, and emperess,
Brought up and propped by the hand of Fame,
Queen of fifteen contributory queens,
Now thrown to rooms of black abjection,
Smeared with blots of basest drudgery,
And villainess to shame, disdain, and misery.
Accursed Bajazeth, whose words of ruth,
That would with pity cheer Zabina's heart,

155 **Cocytus** Coctys, the river of wailing, is a principal river of Hades.
157 **Enforce thee run** Drive you to run against.
163 **as … rooms** as their natural homes.
171 **Cimmerian Styx** the black river Styx in Hades, by which the gods swore their oaths.
174 **retorqued thoughts** thoughts which forever turn back on themselves.
175 **ecstasies** frantic fears and rages.
181 **banks of Erebus** the outer zone of Hades, where souls wait for Charon to ferry them across the Acheron (or in some accounts the Styx) to Hades itself and Elysium.
193 **parbreak** vomit.
193 **of the Stygian** of the Styx/hellish.
194 **standing** stagnant.
196 **dreary … sight** i.e. his eyes.
201 **emperess** pronounced with three syllables.
206 **villainess** female slave.

And make our souls resolve in ceaseless tears,
Sharp hunger bites upon and gripes the root
From whence the issues of my thoughts
do break!
O poor Zabina; O my queen, my queen!
Fetch me some water for my burning breast,
To cool and comfort me with longer date,
That, in the shortened sequel of my life,
I may pour forth my soul into thine arms
With words of love, whose moaning intercourse
Hath hitherto been stayed with wrath and hate
Of our expressless banned inflictions.

ZABINA

Sweet Bajazeth, I will prolong thy life
As long as any blood or spark of breath
Can quench or cool the torments of my grief.

She goes out.

BAJAZETH

Now, Bajazeth, abridge thy baneful days,
And beat the brains out of thy conquered head,
Since other means are all forbidden me,
That may be ministers of my decay.
O highest lamp of ever-living Jove,
Accursed day, infected with my griefs,
Hide now thy stained face in endless night,
And shut the windows of the lightsome heavens!
Let ugly Darkness with her rusty coach,
Engirt with tempests, wrapped in pitchy clouds,
Smother the earth with never-fading mists,
And let her horses from their nostrils breathe
Rebellious winds and dreadful thunder-claps,
That in this terror Tamburlaine may live,
And my pined soul, resolved in liquid air,
May still excruciate his tormented thoughts!
Then let the stony dart of senseless cold
Pierce through the centre of my withered heart,
And make a passage for my loathed life!

He brains himself against the cage.
Enter Zabina.

ZABINA

What do mine eyes behold; my husband dead?
His skull all riven in twain, his brains dashed out,
The brains of Bajazeth, my lord and sovereign!
O Bajazeth, my husband and my lord!
O Bajazeth! O Turk! O emperor!
Give him his liquor? Not I. Bring milk and fire, and
my blood I bring him again. Tear me in pieces,
give me the sword with a ball of wild-fire upon it.
Down with him; down with him! Go to my child;
away, away, away! Ah, save that infant, save him,
save him! I, even I, speak to her. The sun was down:
streamers white, red, black, here, here, here! Fling
the meat in his face. Tamburlaine, Tamburlaine!
Let the soldiers be buried. Hell, death, Tamburlaine,
hell! Make ready my coach, my chair, my jewels;
I come, I come, I come!

She runs against the cage, and brains herself.
[Enter] Zenocrate with Anippe.

ZENOCRATE

Wretched Zenocrate, that live'st to see
Damascus' walls dyed with Egyptians' blood,
Thy father's subjects and thy countrymen;
The streets strewed with dissevered joints of men,
And wounded bodies gasping yet for life.
But most accursed, to see the sun-bright troop
Of heavenly virgins and unspotted maids
(Whose looks might make the angry god of arms
To break his sword and mildly treat of love)
On horsemen's lances to be hoisted up,
And guiltlessly endure a cruel death;
For every fell and stout Tartarian steed,
That stamped on others with their thundering
hoofs,
When all their riders charged their quivering
spears,
Began to check the ground and rein themselves,
Gazing upon the beauty of their looks.
Ah, Tamburlaine, were't thou the cause of this,

214 **longer date** longer life.
219 **expressless banned inflictions** unspeakable, cursed sufferings.
223 **abridge** cut short.
232 **pitchy** tar black.
237 **pined** tortured.
237 **resolved** dissolve.
238 **excruciate** torture.
269 **fell** fierce.
271 **charged** set (ready to charge).
272 **check... themselves** paw the ground and hold back.

That term'st Zenocrate thy dearest love?
Whose lives were dearer to Zenocrate
Than her own life, or aught save thine own love.
But see, another bloody spectacle!
Ah, wretched eyes, the enemies of my heart,
How are ye glutted with these grievous objects,
And tell my soul more tales of bleeding ruth.
See, see, Anippe, if they breathe or no.

ANIPPE
No breath, nor sense, nor motion, in them both.
Ah, madam, this their slavery hath enforced,
And ruthless cruelty of Tamburlaine!

ZENOCRATE
Earth, cast up fountains from thy entrails,
And wet thy cheeks for their untimely deaths;
Shake with their weight in sign of fear and grief!
Blush, heaven, that gave them honour at
their birth,
And let them die a death so barbarous!
Those that are proud of fickle empery
And place their chiefest good in earthly pomp,
Behold the Turk and his great emperess!
Ah, Tamburlaine my love, sweet Tamburlaine,
That fight'st for sceptres and for slippery crowns,
Behold the Turk and his great emperess!
Thou that in conduct of thy happy stars,
Sleep'st every night with conquest on thy brows,
And yet wouldst shun the wavering turns of war,
In fear and feeling of the like distress,
Behold the Turk and his great emperess!
Ah mighty Jove and holy Mahomet,
Pardon my love! O, pardon his contempt
Of earthly fortune and respect of pity;
And let not conquest, ruthlessly pursued,
Be equally against his life incensed
In this great Turk and hapless emperess!
And pardon me that was not moved with ruth
To see them live so long in misery.
Ah, what may chance to thee, Zenocrate?

ANIPPE
Madam, content yourself, and be resolved,
Your love hath Fortune so at his command,
That she shall stay, and turn her wheel no more,
As long as life maintains his mighty arm
That fights for honour to adorn your head.,

Enter a Messenger [*Philemus*].

ZENOCRATE
What other heavy news now brings Philemus?

PHILEMUS
Madam, your father, and the Arabian king,
The first affecter of your excellence,
Come now, as Turnus 'gainst Aeneas did,
Armed with lance into the Egyptian fields,
Ready for battle 'gainst my lord the king.

ZENOCRATE
Now shame and duty, love and fear presents
A thousand sorrows to my martyred soul.
Whom should I wish the fatal victory,
When my poor pleasures are divided thus,
And racked by duty from my cursed heart?
My father and my first-betrothed love
Must fight against my life and present love;
Wherein the change I use condemns my faith,
And makes my deeds infamous through the world.
But as the gods, to end the Trojans' toil,
Prevented Turnus of Lavinia,
And fatally enriched Aeneas' love,
So, for a final issue to my griefs,
To pacify my country and my love,
Must Tamburlaine by their resistless powers,
With virtue of a gentle victory,
Conclude a league of honour to my hope.
Then, as the powers divine have pre-ordained,
With happy safety of my father's life,
Send like defence of fair Arabia.

They sound to the battle; and Tamburlaine enjoys the victory: after Arabia enters wounded.

281 **bleeding ruth** pitiful suffering.
297 **in conduct** under the guidance.
303–304 **his contempt... pity** his contempt... for any concern for pity.
313 **stay** stop still.
316 **heavy** sad.
318 **affecter** lover.
319 **as... did** In books ix–xii of Virgil's *Aeneid*, Turnus was the first suitor of Lavinia, daughter to the Italian king Latinus. When Aeneas landed in Italy and claimed Lavinia for himself, Turnus marched against him, but was defeated.
329 **the change... faith** my defection destroys my reputation for constancy.
332 **Prevented... Lavinia** Took Lavinia from Turnus.
333 **enriched** enriched (through the death of Turnus).
338 **league of honour** honourable (peace) treaty.

KING OF ARABIA

What cursed power guides the murdering hands
Of this infamous tyrant's soldiers,
That no escape may save their enemies,
Nor fortune keep themselves from victory?
Lie down Arabia, wounded to the death,
And let Zenocrate's fair eyes behold
That, as for her thou bear'st these wretched arms,
Even so for her thou diest in these arms,
Leaving thy blood for witness of thy love.

ZENOCRATE

Too dear a witness for such love, my lord!
Behold Zenocrate, the cursed object,
Whose fortunes never mastered her griefs;
Behold her, wounded in conceit for thee,
As much as thy fair body is for me.

KING OF ARABIA

Then shall I die with full contented heart,
Having beheld divine Zenocrate,
Whose sight with joy would take away my life
As now it bringeth sweetness to my wound,
If I had not been wounded as I am.
Ah, that the deadly pangs I suffer now
Would lend an hour's licence to my tongue,
To make discourse of some sweet accidents
Have chanced thy merits in this worthless bondage,
And that I might be privy to the state
Of thy deserved contentment and thy love.
But, making now a virtue of thy sight,
To drive all sorrow from my fainting soul,
Since death denies me further cause of joy,
Deprived of care, my heart with comfort dies,
Since thy desired hand shall close mine eyes. [*He dies.*]

Enter Tamburlaine, leading the Soldan; Techelles, Theridamas, Usumcasane, with others.

TAMBURLAINE

Come, happy father of Zenocrate,
A title higher than thy Soldan's name.
Though my right hand have thus enthralled thee,
Thy princely daughter here shall set thee free;
She that hath calmed the fury of my sword,
Which had ere this been bathed in streams of blood
As vast and deep as Euphrates or Nile.

ZENOCRATE

O sight thrice-welcome to my joyful soul,
To see the king, my father, issue safe
From dangerous battle of my conquering love.

SOLDAN

Well met, my only dear Zenocrate,
Though with the loss of Egypt and my crown.

TAMBURLAINE

'Twas I, my lord, that gat the victory;
And therefore grieve not at your overthrow,
Since I shall render all into your hands,
And add more strength to your dominions
Than ever yet confirmed th'Egyptian crown.
The god of war resigns his room to me,
Meaning to make me general of the world.
Jove, viewing me in arms, looks pale and wan,
Fearing my power should pull him from his throne.
Where'er I come the Fatal Sisters sweat,
And grisly Death, by running to and fro
To do their ceaseless homage to my sword.
And here in Afric, where it seldom rains,
Since I arrived with my triumphant host,
Have swelling clouds, drawn from wide-gaping wounds,
Been oft resolved in bloody purple showers,
A meteor that might terrify the earth,
And make it quake at every drop it drinks.
Millions of souls sit on the banks of Styx,
Waiting the back-return of Charon's boat;
Hell and Elysium swarm with ghosts of men
That I have sent from sundry foughten fields
To spread my fame through hell and up to heaven.
And see, my lord, a sight of strange import,
Emperors and kings lie breathless at my feet;
The Turk and his great empress, as it seems,
Left to themselves while we were at the fight,
Have desperately despatched their slavish lives;
With them Arabia, too, hath left his life:
All sights of power to grace my victory.

362–366 **Would . . . love** If only I had an hour's respite to talk with you about what has happened to you (literally, to your merits) during your imprisonment, so I might know you are as comfortable as you deserve to be, and understand where your love is directed.
381 **of** against.
388 **confirmed** supported.
393 **Fatal Sisters** the Fates.
398–399 **Have . . . showers** clouds have sucked up the blood of the fallen, and delivered it again as bloody rain.
402–403 **sit . . . boat** wait to be ferried across the river Styx into Hades.
405 **foughten fields** fields of battle.

And such are objects fit for Tamburlaine,
Wherein, as in a mirror, may be seen
His honour, that consists in shedding blood
When men presume to manage arms with him.

SOLDAN
Mighty hath God and Mahomet made thy hand,
Renowned Tamburlaine, to whom all kings
Of force must yield their crowns and emperies.
And I am pleased with this my overthrow,
If, as beseems a person of thy state,
Thou hast with honour used Zenocrate.

TAMBURLAINE
Her state and person want no pomp, you see;
And for all blot of foul inchastity,
I record heaven, her heavenly self is clear.
Then let me find no further time to grace
Her princely temples with the Persian crown;
But here these kings that on my fortunes wait,
And have been crowned for proved worthiness
Even by this hand that shall establish them,
Shall now, adjoining all their hands with mine,
Invest her here the Queen of Persia.
What saith the noble Soldan, and Zenocrate?

SOLDAN
I yield with thanks and protestations
Of endless honour to thee for her love.

TAMBURLAINE
Then doubt I not but fair Zenocrate
Will soon consent to satisfy us both.

ZENOCRATE
Else should I much forget myself, my lord.

THERIDAMAS
Then let us set the crown upon her head,
That long hath lingered for so high a seat.

TECHELLES
My hand is ready to perform the deed;
For now her marriage-time shall work us rest.

USUMCASANE
And here's the crown, my lord; help set it on.

TAMBURLAINE
Then sit thou down, divine Zenocrate;
And here we crown thee Queen of Persia,
And all the kingdoms and dominions
That late the power of Tamburlaine subdued.
As Juno, when the giants were suppressed,
That darted mountains at her brother Jove,
So looks my love, shadowing in her brows
Triumphs and trophies for my victories;
Or as Latona's daughter, bent to arms,
Adding more courage to my conquering
mind.
To gratify thee, sweet Zenocrate,
Egyptians, Moors, and men of Asia,
From Barbary unto the Western India,
Shall pay a yearly tribute to thy sire;
And from the bounds of Afric to the banks
Of Ganges shall his mighty arm extend.
And now, my lords and loving followers,
That purchased kingdoms by your martial
deeds,
Cast off your armour, put on scarlet robes,
Mount up your royal places of estate,
Environed with troops of noblemen,
And there make laws to rule your provinces:
Hang up your weapons on Alcides' post;
For Tamburlaine takes truce with all the world.
Thy first-betrothed love, Arabia,
Shall we with honour, as beseems, entomb
With this great Turk and his fair emperess.
Then, after all these solemn exequies,
We will our celebrated rites of marriage
solemnize.

[*Exeunt.*]

Finis Actus Quinti.

424 **want** lack.
426 **I record heaven** I call heaven as witness.
443 **work** bring.
450 See note to II.vi.6.
453 **Latona's ... arms** Diana, in hunter's garb.
464 **places of estate** thrones of state.
465 **Environed** Surrounded.
467 **Alcides' post** the doorpost of the temple of Hercules.
472 **exequies** funeral ceremonies.

Endymion

(1588)

JOHN LYLY
(1554–1606)

THE AUTHOR

John Lyly was born in Kent, the eldest of eight children of the notary public Peter Lyly and his wife Jane Burgh of Burgh Hall, North Yorkshire. His grandfather was the humanist schoolmaster and grammarian William Lily (*c.*1468–1522), the first high master of St Paul's School and author of the bestselling grammar textbook of the early sixteenth century. Lyly may well have studied at the King's School, Canterbury before taking a BA (1573) and MA (1575) at Magdalen College, Oxford. He then moved to London where he wrote his celebrated prose work, *Euphues, the Anatomy of Wit* (printed in 1578), the tale of a stylish, witty Italian scholar who makes his way in the world through his brilliance. *Euphues* quickly established Lyly as the most fashionable author of his generation. A sequel, *Euphues and His England* (1580) followed, in which the hero visits England, and offers extended praise of Elizabeth I.

Lyly joined the household of Edward de Vere, 17th Earl of Oxford at this time, and also began writing plays for companies of child actors patronized by Oxford which performed at court and in private theatres such as Blackfriars and the playhouse used by the choirboys of St Paul's Cathedral. These plays, beginning with *Campaspe* and *Sappho and Phao*, all retell moralized versions of classical tales in the heavily rhetorical, ornate style that Lyly developed in *Euphues* and which, as a result, became known as 'euphuism'. The late 1580s and early 1590s were years of extraordinary success for Lyly, in which he wrote a number of other plays performed at court, including *Midas* (performed in 1589), *Love's Metamorphoses* (not printed until 1601) and *Endymion* itself, which was first performed at court in 1588, but not printed until 1591. By the late 1590s, however, the fashion for euphuism had waned, and the style was the butt of considerable mockery by the new generation of playwrights, including Shakespeare, who parodied Lyly's carefully balanced, repetitive style in a number of plays, including *The First Part of King Henry IV*, where Falstaff declaims in euphuistic style, that 'I do not speak to thee in drink, but in tears; not in pleasure, but in passion; not in words only, but in woes also' (Act II, Scene V, ll. 418–20). For all his mockery, however, Shakespeare was evidently influenced by Lyly's work, especially in early plays such as *Love's Labour's Lost*, with its schoolroom jokes and parodies, and *A Midsummer Night's Dream*, which shares something of *Endymion*'s languorous mood of love-longing and delight in courtly and pastoral settings. By the 1630s the hostility to Lyly's style had disappeared, and Edward Blount was able to publish a collection of his plays, *Six Court Comedies* (1632), which celebrated the playwright as 'witty, comical, facetiously-quick and unparalleled'.

Lily's own fortunes were on the decline by the later 1590s, in part prompted by an unwise foray into political satire with the pamphlet *Pap with an Hatchet* (*c.*1589), written in defence of the ecclesiastical establishment in the fierce dispute known as the Martin Marprelate Controversy.

What finished his dramatic career, however, was the end of the children's theatre companies in 1590. He died in London in November 1606, leaving a wife and at least three children.

THE PLAY

The story of *Endymion*, such as it is, retells a variant of the mythical tale, extant in various classical sources (including Ovid and Lucian), of the shepherd with whom the moon goddess (variously Cynthia, Diana, or Selene) falls in love, and whom she causes to fall into an eternal sleep, so that only she can visit him and enjoy his love. In this version, however, it is Endymion who loves Cynthia from afar rather than vice versa. As Elizabeth I was sometimes figured in poetry and art as Cynthia or Diana, this version flatters the virtue and constancy of the Virgin Queen without implying any improper desires on her part. The association also allows Lyly to work a dextrous and playful double allusion, simultaneously hinting through the subtitle, 'The Man in the Moon', that his story is just a trivial fable ('a tale of the man in the moon' was a popular term for a tall story or fantasy), yet simultaneously hinting that, in dealing with Cynthia and her courtiers, it alluded to contemporary events and the Queen herself.

Like all of Lyly's plays, *Endymion* is a drama of ideas and aesthetics rather than action. Written in the highly rhetorical euphuistical style, the play parallels and balances ideas, characters, and images on the stage, just as, on a linguistic level it balances words and tropes. *Endymion* is a play about love, in that it explores the themes of platonic and physical love, desire and friendship, comparing and contrasting the unrequited love of Endymion for Cynthia, the devoted friendship of Eumenides for Endymion, and the variously unrequited or misdirected passions of Tellus (for Endymion), Eumenides (for Semele), Corsites (for Tellus), and the comic suit of the foolish braggart Sir Thopas (ostensibly for Dipsas, but he is primarily in love with himself). Each of the characters represents a particular attitude or quality, sometimes on a mythical, universal scale, as their names imply. Thus Eumenides (whose name is taken from the Greek *eumenes*) is a figure of 'goodwill', while Geron (Greek for 'aged') is a wise old man. Similarly, Cynthia is both a virtuous goddess, a queen, and the moon itself, as her command of the elements and her association with celestial forces reveals, while Tellus (named after an earth goddess) represents a less virtuous, more passionate woman, but also, at times, the earth itself, its fecundity and inconstancy, contrasted to the calmer, chaste powers of the moon.

Whether the play is a specific allegorical or symbolic treatment of political events or allegiances, or simply a general romance with overtones flattering to the Queen, remains an open question. A number of critics have argued that its central figure is a coded reference to courtiers who were excluded from Elizabeth's favour and were seeking to regain it. Thus R. Warwick Bond suggests that Endymion represents Robert Dudley, 1st Earl of Leicester, while David Bevington suggests he is Lyly's patron, the Earl of Oxford. Similarly the case has been advanced that Tellus is an unflattering figure of Mary Queen of Scots (see Bevington, p. 29). But none of these suggestions has won widespread support. More obviously the play reveals its origins as a children's play in its schoolroom in-jokes about grammar, its evident delight in witty answers, and frequent citation of maxims and phrases from the classical texts with which schoolboys would have been familiar from their lessons.

The play requires a number of elaborate stage props, and may have used 'houses' of painted cloth or canvas for its initial performances at court and St Paul's. The fountain guarded by Geron, and into which Eumenides looks to see the oracular message concerning Endymion's curse, would need to be represented onstage, as would the grassy 'lunary' bank on which the hero falls asleep. The latter would, presumably need to be concealed at some point, unless the prone

Endymion is to be visible throughout the play. Most of the actors would have been children, although, given the jokes about his height, Sir Thopas (like Grim the Collier in *Cambises*) might have been intended for an adult actor, perhaps even Lyly himself.

The play was first printed in 1591 by I. Charlewood for the Widow Broom. I have used this edition as the base text for what follows, also consulting the modern editions listed under further reading.

FURTHER READING

Bond, R. Warwick, ed., *The Complete Works of John Lyly*, 3 vols. (Oxford: Clarendon Press, 1902).

Hunter, George K. *John Lyly: The Humanist as Courtier* (London: Routledge and Kegan Paul, 1962).

—— 'Lyly, John (1554–1606)', *Oxford Dictionary of National Biography* (Oxford: Oxford University Press, 2004) <http://www.oxforddnb.com/view/article/1725>, accessed 6 June 2013.

Kesson, Andy, *John Lyly and Early Modern Authorship* (Manchester: Manchester University Press, 2013).

Lyly, John, *Endymion*, ed. David Bevington (Manchester: Manchester University Press, 1996).

Pincombe, Michael, *John Lyly* (Manchester: Manchester University Press, 1996).

Thomas, Susan D., '*Endymion* and its Sources', *Comparative Drama* xxx (1978): 35–52.

Scragg, Leah, 'John Lyly, *Endymion*' in Thomas Betteridge and Greg Walker, eds., *The Oxford Handbook to Tudor Drama* (Oxford: Oxford University Press, 2012), 323–37.

Walker, Greg, 'Courtship and Counsel: John Lyly's *Campaspe*' in M. Hattaway, ed., *The Blackwell Companion to English Renaissance Literature and Culture*, 2nd edn. (Oxford: Blackwell, 2010), 320–28.

Endymion: The Man in the Moon

Played before the Queen's Majesty
at Greenwich on Candlemas day at night,
by the Children of Paul's

At London
Printed by I. Charlewood,
For the Widow Broome.
1591

THE PRINTER TO THE READER

Since the plays in Paul's were dissolved, there are certain Comedies come to my hands by chance, which were presented before Her Majesty at several times by the children of Paul's. This is the first, and if in any place it shall displease, I will take more pains to perfect the next. I refer it to thy indifferent judgement to peruse, whom I would willingly please. And, if this may pass with thy good liking, I will then go forward to publish the rest. In the mean time, let this have thy good word for my better encouragement. Farewell.

The Prologue

Most high and happy Princess, we must tell you a tale of the Man in the Moon, which, if it seem ridiculous for the method, or superfluous for the matter, or for the means incredible, for three faults we can make but one excuse: it is a tale of the Man in the Moon.

It was forbidden in old time to dispute of Chimera, because it was a fiction. We hope in our times none will apply pastimes, because they are fancies; for there liveth none under the sun that know what to make of the Man in the Moon. We present neither comedy, nor tragedy, nor story, nor anything, but that whosoever heareth may say this: Why, here is a tale of the Man in the Moon.

Candlemas the Feast of the Purification of the Virgin Mary, 2 February. Bevington suggests that the year in question was probably 1588, the only year that a payment was made for a performance by the boys of St Paul's at Greenwich between 1580 and 1591.

Paul's The children's companies, including that of St Paul's Cathedral choir, were prohibited from playing in the private theatres at St Paul's and Blackfriars in 1590, in part because their repertoire was thought to be dangerously satirical; at which point they may have sold their scripts to the printer. Broome registered Lyly's *Endymion*, *Gallathea*, and *Midas* in 1591. Her husband, William Broome, had printed editions of Lyly's *Campaspe* and *Sappho and Phao* prior to his death earlier in the same year.

indifferent impartial.

Princess Queen Elizabeth.

tale . . . Moon colloquially, an unbelievable story or fable.

Chimera a mythical beast with the heads of a lion, dragon and goat.

apply pastimes try to interpret seriously or politically ('apply') what is just an entertainment ('pastimes').

fancies (merely) products of the imagination.

[*Dramatis Personae*:

ENDYMION, in love with Cynthia
EUMENIDES, friend of Endymion; in love with Semele
CORSITES, a lord; in love with Tellus
ZONTES and PENELION, other lords
GERON, a wise old man, estranged husband of Dipsas
PYTHAGORAS, the Greek philosopher
GYPTES, an Egyptian soothsayer
SIR TOPHAS, a braggart
SAMIAS, page to Endymion
DARES, page to Eumenides
EPITON, Page to Sir Tophas
MASTER CONSTABLE
TWO WATCHMEN
CYNTHIA, the Queen
TELLUS, in love with Endymion
FLOSCULA, friend of Tellus and Endymion
SEMELE, a lady, loved by Eumenides
SCINTILLA and FAVILLA, waiting-maids; friends of Samias and Dares
DIPSAS, a witch
BAGOA, servant of Dipsas
FAIRIES
THREE LADIES and an OLD MAN in the Dumb-show.]

Actus Primus, Scaena prima.
(Endymion, Eumenides.)

ENDYMION
I find, Eumenides, in all things both variety to content and satiety to glut, saving only in my affections, which are so stayed, and withal so stately, that I can neither satisfy my heart with love, nor mine eyes with wonder. My thoughts, Eumenides, are stitched to the stars, which being as high as I can see, thou mayest imagine how much higher they are than I can reach.

EUMENIDES
If you be enamoured of anything above the moon, your thoughts are ridiculous, for that things immortal are not subject to affections; if allured or enchanted with these transitory things under the moon, you show yourself senseless, to attribute such lofty titles to such love-trifles.

Eumenides from the Greek *eumenes*, 'well-wishing': Eumenides is a type of the good friend.
Geron the name means 'old man' in Greek.
Gyptes from the slang for of 'Egyptian' or 'Gypsy'.
Sir Tophas a variant of the classical *miles gloriosus* or bragging, cowardly knight. His name is probably taken from Chaucer's tale of *Sir Thopas* in *The Canterbury Tales*.
Epiton a follower, echoing the Greek *epitemnein*, 'cut short'. The contrast in size between the tiny Epiton and the larger, perhaps adult, Sir Thopas is part of the joke. Shakespeare reprises the relationship in that of 'the fantastical shepherd', Don Armado and his page Moth ('mote') in *Love's Labour's Lost*.
Cynthia another name for Diana, goddess of the moon.
Tellus named after the earth deity of the same name, here representing worldly values.
Floscula from the Latin *flosculus*, 'little flower'.
Semele named after the daughter of Cadmus in Greek mythology, who was consumed as a result of overzealous desire for her lover Jupiter.
Scintilla and Favilla from the Latin for 'spark' and 'hot embers' respectively.
Dipsas her name is probably taken from the old bawd in Ovid's *Amores*.
Bagoa probably a female variant of Bagoas, the name of a guardian in the *Amores*.
Actus . . . prima. Act One, Scene One.
s.d. The play follows Continental, neoclassical practice in listing at the outset the names of the characters appearing in the scene, regardless of when they actually enter the action.
2 **stayed** fixed.
4 **stitched to the stars** i.e. set upon an unobtainable goal.
6 **above the moon** in Renaissance cosmology things beyond the sphere of the moon were celestial and unchanging, those lower than the moon ('sublunary') mutable, transitory, and mortal.
7 **for that** because.

ENDYMION
My love is placed neither under the moon nor above.

EUMENIDES
I hope you be not sotted upon the man in the moon.

ENDYMION
No; but settled either to die or possess the moon herself.

EUMENIDES
Is Endymion mad, or do I mistake? Do you love the moon, Endymion?

ENDYMION
Eumenides, the moon.

EUMENIDES
There was never any so peevish to imagine the moon either capable of affection or shape of a mistress; for as impossible it is to make love fit to her humour, which no man knoweth, as a coat to her form, which continueth not in one bigness whilst she is measuring. Cease off, Endymion, to feed so much upon fancies. That melancholy blood must be purged which draweth you to a dotage no less miserable than monstrous.

ENDYMION
My thoughts have no veins, and yet unless they be let blood, I shall perish.

EUMENIDES
But they have vanities, which being reformed, you may be restored.

ENDYMION
O, fair Cynthia, why do others term thee inconstant whom I have ever found unmovable? Injurious time, corrupt manners, unkind men, who, finding a constancy not to be matched in my sweet mistress, have christened her with the name of wavering, waxing, and waning! Is she inconstant that keepeth a settled course, which since her first creation altereth not one minute in her moving? There is nothing thought more admirable or commendable in the sea than the ebbing and flowing; and shall the moon, from whom the sea taketh this virtue, be accounted fickle for increasing and decreasing? Flowers in their buds are nothing worth till they be blown, nor blossoms accounted till they be ripe fruit; and shall we then say they be changeable for that they grow from seeds to leaves, from leaves to buds, from buds to their perfection? Then, why be not twigs that become trees, children that become men, and mornings that grow to evenings, termed wavering, for that they continue not at one stay? Aye, but Cynthia, being in her fullness, decayeth, as not delighting in her greatest beauty, or withering when she should be most honoured. When malice cannot object anything, folly will, making that a vice which is the greatest virtue. What thing (my mistress excepted), being in the pride of her beauty and latter

11 **sotted upon** besotted with.
15 **peevish** perverse.
16–17 **fit . . . humour** suit her disposition.
17–18 **coat . . . measuring** Eumenides imagines the moon as a customer being measured for a new coat, who, owing to her continual waxing and waning, never keeps the same shape or size.
19 **melancholy blood** medically, blood over-burdened with black bile, believed to cause melancholy. Letting or purging blood was believed to restore the body to a healthy equilibrium.
20 **dotage** foolish obsession.
22 **vanities** vain thoughts.
26 **waxing and waning** growing and declining.
31 **nothing . . . blown** thought worthless until they blossom.
35 **at one stay** in one position or condition.
36–37 **Cynthia . . . beauty** Cynthia (the moon), as soon as she is at her full, begins to diminish, as if she did not delight in her most beautiful state.
38–39 **What thing** What thing (is there . . . that).

minute of her age, that waxeth young again? Tell me, Eumenides, what is he that, having a mistress of ripe years and infinite virtues, great honours and unspeakable beauty, but would wish that she might grow tender again, getting youth by years, and never-decaying beauty by time; whose fair face neither the summer's blaze can scorch, nor winter's blast chap, nor the numbering of years breed altering of colours? Such is my sweet Cynthia, whom time cannot touch because she is divine, nor will offend because she is delicate.

O Cynthia, if thou shouldst always continue at thy fullness, both gods and men would conspire to ravish thee. But thou, to abate the pride of our affections, dost detract from thy perfections, thinking it sufficient if once in a month we enjoy a glimpse of thy majesty; and then, to increase our griefs, thou dost decrease thy gleams, coming out of thy royal robes, wherewith thou dazzlest our eyes, down into thy swathe clouts, beguiling our eyes; and then...

EUMENIDES

Stay there, Endymion; thou that committest idolatry wilt straight blaspheme if thou be suffered. Sleep would do thee more good than speech; the moon heareth thee not, or if she do, regardeth thee not.

ENDYMION

Vain Eumenides, whose thoughts never grow higher than the crown of thy head, Why troublest thou me, having neither head to conceive the cause of my love, [n]or heart to receive the impressions? Follow thou thine own fortunes, which creep on the earth, and suffer me too to fly to mine, whose fall, though it be desperate, yet shall it come by daring. Farewell. [*Exit.*]

EUMENIDES

Without doubt Endymion is bewitched, otherwise in a man of such rare virtues there could not harbour a mind of such extreme madness. I will follow him, lest in this fancy of the moon he deprive himself of the sight of the sun. *Exit.*

Actus Primus, Scaena secunda
(Tellus, Floscula.)

TELLUS

Treacherous and most perjured Endymion, is Cynthia the sweetness of thy life and the bitterness of my death? What revenge may be devised so full of shame as my thoughts are replenished with malice? Tell me, Floscula, if falseness in love can possibly be punished with extremity of hate. As long as sword, fire, or poison may be hired, no traitor to my love shall live unrevenged. Were thy oaths without number, thy kisses without measure, thy sighs without end, forged to deceive a poor credulous virgin, whose simplicity had been worth thy favour and better fortune? If the gods sit unequal beholders of injuries, or laughers at lovers' deceits, then let mischief be as well forgiven in women as perjury winked at in men.

42–43 **getting... years** getting younger again with each passing year.
52 **swathe clouts** swaddling clothes.
53 **Stay** Stop.
53–54 **if... suffered** if I allow you to.
5 **thy oaths** aimed at Endymion.

FLOSCULA

Madam, if you would compare the state of Cynthia with your own, and the height of Endymion his thoughts with the meanness of your fortune, you would rather yield than contend, being between you and her no comparison; and rather wonder than rage at the greatness of his mind, being affected with a thing more than mortal.

TELLUS

No comparison, Floscula? And why so? Is not my beauty divine, whose body is decked with fair flowers, and veins are vines, yielding sweet liquor to the dullest spirits; whose ears are corn, to bring strength, and whose hairs are grass, to bring abundance? Doth not frankincense and myrrh breathe out of my nostrils, and all the sacrifice of the gods breed in my bowels? Infinite are my creatures, without which neither thou, nor Endymion, nor any could love or live.

FLOSCULA

But know you not, fair lady, that Cynthia governeth all things? Your grapes would be but dry husks, your corn but chaff, and all your virtues vain, were it not Cynthia that preserveth the one in the bud and nourisheth the other in the blade, and by her influence both comforteth all things, and by her authority commandeth all creatures. Suffer, then, Endymion to follow his affections, though to obtain her be impossible, and let him flatter himself in his own imaginations, because they are immortal.

TELLUS

Loath I am, Endymion, thou shouldst die, because I love thee well; and that thou shouldst live, it grieveth me, because thou lovest Cynthia too well. In these extremities, what shall I do? Floscula, no more words; I am resolved. He shall neither live nor die.

FLOSCULA

A strange practice, if it be possible.

TELLUS

Yes, I will entangle him in such a sweet net that he shall neither find the means to come out, nor desire it. All allurements of pleasure will I cast before his eyes, insomuch that he shall slake that love which he now voweth to Cynthia, and burn in mine, of which he seemeth careless. In this languishing between my amorous devices and his own loose desires, there shall such dissolute thoughts take root in his head, and over his heart grow so thick a skin, that neither hope of preferment, nor fear of punishment, nor counsel of the wisest, nor company of the worthiest, shall alter his humour, nor make him once to think of his honour.

FLOSCULA

A revenge incredible, and if it may be, unnatural.

TELLUS

He shall know the malice of a woman to have neither mean nor end; and of a woman deluded in love to have neither rule nor reason. I can do it; I must, I will! All his virtues will I shadow with vices; his person (ah, sweet person!)

12 **meanness** lowliness.
14 **affected** in love with.
33 **practice** plot/plan.
36 **slake** satiate/quench.
37 **careless** indifferent.
44 **mean** moderation.
46 **person** body.

shall he deck with such rich robes as he shall forget it is his own person; his sharp wit (ah, wit too sharp that hath cut off all my joys!) shall he use in flattering of my face and devising sonnets in my favour. The prime of his youth and pride of his time shall be spent in melancholy passions, careless behaviour, untamed thoughts and unbridled affections.

FLOSCULA

When this is done, what then? Shall it continue till his death, or shall he dote forever in this delight?

TELLUS

Ah, Floscula, thou rendest my heart in sunder in putting me in remembrance of the end.

FLOSCULA

Why, if this be not the end, all the rest is to no end.

TELLUS

Yet suffer me to imitate Juno, who would turn Jupiter's lovers to beasts on the earth, though she knew afterwards they should be stars in heaven.

FLOSCULA

Affection that is bred by enchantment is like a flower that is wrought in silk, in colour and form most like, but nothing at all in substance or savour.

TELLUS

It shall suffice me if the world talk that I am favoured of Endymion.

FLOSCULA

Well, use your own will, but you shall find that love gotten with witchcraft is as unpleasant as fish taken with medicines unwholesome.

TELLUS

Floscula, they that be so poor that they have neither net nor hook will rather poison dough than pine with hunger; and she that is so oppressed with love that she is neither able with beauty nor wit to obtain her friend, will rather use unlawful means than try intolerable pains. I will do it. *Exit.*

FLOSCULA

Then about it. Poor Endymion, what traps are laid for thee because thou honourest one that all the world wondereth at. And what plots are cast to make thee unfortunate that studiest of all men to be the faithfulest. *Exit.*

Actus Primus, Scaena Tertia
(Dares, Samias, Sir Tophas, Epiton)

DARES

Now our masters are in love up to the ears, what have we to do but to be in knavery up to the crowns?

54 **in sunder** asunder/in two.
57 **Juno** wife of Jupiter, who transformed a number of her husband's lovers into lowly beasts or plants, only for other gods to rescue and stellify them in due course.
60 **savour** scent.
61 **talk** talks (i.e. if it is only believed that Endymion loves her).
63 **taken . . . unwholesome** caught with poison.
65 **poison dough** i.e. catch fish with poisoned lumps of dough (because they cannot afford a line and hook).
67 **try** experience.
68 **about it** get on with it.
2 **the crowns** the top of the head.

SAMIAS

Oh, that we had Sir Tophas, that brave squire, in the midst of our mirth, and *ecce autem*, will you see the devil? *Enter Sir Tophas.*

TOPHAS

Epi!

EPITON

Here, sir.

TOPHAS

I brook not this idle humour of love; it tickleth not my liver, from whence the love-mongers in former ages seemed to infer it should proceed.

EPITON

Love, sir, may lie in your lungs, and I think it doth, and that is the cause you blow and are so pursy.

TOPHAS

Tush, boy, I think it but some device of the poet to get money.

EPITON

A poet; what's that?

TOPHAS

Dost thou not know what a poet is?

EPITON

No.

TOPHAS

Why, fool, a poet is as much as one should say . . . a poet. But soft, yonder be two wrens; shall I shoot at them?

EPITON

They are two lads.

TOPHAS

Larks or wrens, I will kill them.

EPITON

Larks? Are you blind? They are two little boys.

TOPHAS

Birds or boys, they are both but a pittance for my breakfast; therefore have at them, for their brains must as it were embroider my bolts.

SAMIAS

Stay your courage, valiant knight, for your wisdom is so weary that it stayeth itself.

DARES

Why, Sir Tophas, have you forgotten your old friends?

TOPHAS

Friends? *Nego argumentum.*

SAMIAS

And why not friends?

4 ***ecce autem*** but behold!
7 **brook not** have no patience for.
7 The liver was thought to be the seat of the passions.
10 **pursy** short of breath.
15 **soft** hush.
16 **wrens** tiny birds (i.e. Samias and Dares).
21 **embroider my bolts** decorate my bird-bolts (blunted arrows used to hunt small birds).
25 ***Nego argumentum.*** I deny your argument! (A schoolroom debating term.)

TOPHAS

Because *amicitia* (as in old annals we find) is *inter pares*. Now, my pretty companions, you shall see how unequal you be to me; but I will not cut you quite off, you shall be my half-friends for reaching to my middle; so far as from the ground to the waist I will be your friend.

DARES

Learnedly. But what shall become of the rest of your body, from the waist to the crown?

TOPHAS

My children, *quod supra vos nihil ad vos*; you must think the rest immortal, because you cannot reach it.

EPITON

Nay, I tell ye, my master is more than a man.

DARES

And thou less than a mouse.

TOPHAS

But what be you two?

SAMIAS

I am Samias, page to Endymion.

DARES

And I Dares, page to Eumenides.

TOPHAS

Of what occupation are your masters?

DARES

Occupation, you clown! Why, they are honourable and warriors.

TOPHAS

Then are they my prentices.

DARES

Thine? And why so?

TOPHAS

I was the first that ever devised war, and therefore by Mars himself had given me for my arms a whole armoury; and thus I go, as you see, clothed with artillery. It is not silks, milksops, nor tissues, nor the fine wool of Seres, but iron, steel, swords, flame, shot, terror, clamour, blood, and ruin that rock asleep my thoughts, which never had any other cradle but cruelty. Let me see, do you not bleed?

DARES

Why so?

TOPHAS

Commonly my words wound.

27 ***amicitia...pares*** friendship, as old chronicles show us, is between equals.

28 **unequal** Tophas interprets the maxim literally, as a question of equal height.

33 ***quod...vos*** that which is above you is nothing to you (proverbial).

41 **Occupation...warriors.** As aristocratic warriors they have no need of the sort of menial trade which 'occupation' can imply.

42 **prentices** apprentices.

44 **Mars** the god of War.

46 **clothed with artillery** covered with weapons.

46 **milksops** (you) feeble youths.

46 **tissues** fine cloth, interweaved with gold or silver thread.

46 **Seres** the Seres were an eastern people cited in Virgil's *Georgics* for their fine silken wool.

SAMIAS

What then do your blows?

TOPHAS

Not only wound, but also confound.

SAMIAS

How darest thou come so near thy master, Epi? Sir Tophas, spare us.

TOPHAS

You shall live; you, Samias, because you are little; you, Dares, because you are no bigger; and both of you, because you are but two; for commonly I kill by the dozen, and have for every particular adversary a peculiar weapon.

SAMIAS

May we know the use, for our better skill in war?

TOPHAS

You shall. Here is a bird-bolt for the ugly beast, the blackbird.

DARES

A cruel sight.

TOPHAS

Here is the musket for the untamed or, as the vulgar sort term it, the 'wild' mallard.

SAMIAS

O desperate attempt!

EPITON

Nay, my master will match them.

DARES

Aye, if he catch them.

TOPHAS

Here is a spear and shield, and both necessary, the one to conquer, the other to subdue or overcome the terrible trout, which, although he be under the water, yet tying a string to the top of my spear and an engine of iron to the end of my line, I overthrow him, and then herein I put him.

SAMIAS

O wonderful war! (Dares, didst thou ever hear such a dolt?)

DARES

All the better; we shall have good sport hereafter, if we can get leisure.

SAMIAS

Leisure? I will rather lose my master's service than his company. Look how he struts. But what is this? Call you it your sword?

TOPHAS

No, it is my scimitar; which I, by construction, often studying to be compendious, call my smiter.

DARES

What, are you also learned, sir?

53 **confound** destroy.
63 **desperate attempt** warlike enterprise.
68 **engine of iron** iron device (i.e. a fishhook). The **spear and shield** are a fishing rod and basket.
74 **scimitar** a curved oriental blade.
74–75 **which . . . smiter** which I define, seeking to be succinct, as my 'smiter' (which is both a more succinct word and also indicates its function).

TOPHAS

Learned? I am all Mars and *Ars*.

SAMIAS

Nay, you are all mass and ass.

TOPHAS

Mock you me? You shall both suffer, yet with such weapons as you shall make choice of the weapon wherewith you shall perish. Am I all a mass or lump; is there no proportion in me? Am I all ass; is there no wit in me? Epi, prepare them to the slaughter.

SAMIAS

I pray, sir, hear us speak! We call you mass, which your learning doth well understand is 'all man', for *mas, maris* is a man. Then '*as*' (as you know) is a weight, and we for your virtues account you a weight.

TOPHAS

The Latin hath saved your lives, the which a world of silver could not have ransomed. I understand you, and pardon you.

DARES

Well, Sir Tophas, we bid you farewell, and at our next meeting we will be ready to do you service.

TOPHAS

Samias, I thank you; Dares, I thank you; but especially I thank you both.

SAMIAS

Wisely. Come, next time we'll have some pretty gentlewomen with us to walk, for without doubt with them he will be very dainty.

DARES

Come, let us see what our masters do; it is high time. *Exeunt.*

TOPHAS

Now will I march into the field, where, if I cannot encounter with my foul enemies, I will withdraw myself to the river, and there fortify for fish, for there resteth no minute free from fight. *Exit.*

Actus Primus, Scaena Quarta
(Tellus, Floscula, Dipsas.)

TELLUS

Behold, Floscula, we have met with the woman by chance that we sought for by travel. I will break my mind to her without ceremony or circumstance, lest we lose that time in advice that should be spent in execution.

FLOSCULA

Use your discretion. I will in this case neither give counsel nor consent, for there cannot be a thing more monstrous than to force affection by sorcery, neither do I imagine anything more impossible.

77 **all . . . *Ars*** a master of both war and the arts.
84 **maris** Latin for male, hence 'masculine'.
84 ***'as'*** a Roman coin, initially weighing twelve ounces.
85 **weight** perhaps, as Bevington suggests, playing on the Middle English 'wight', a manly warrior.
93 **it . . . time** it's about time we were with them.
95 **fortify** prepare/strengthen myself.
1–2 **woman . . . travel** both, 'this is the very woman we were travelling to see' and 'the woman we were labouring ('travailing') to find'.
2 **break my mind** reveal my thoughts.
3 **advice** discussion.

TELLUS

Tush, Floscula, in obtaining of love what impossibilities will I not try? And for the winning of Endymion what impieties will I not practise? Dipsas, whom as many honour for age as wonder at for cunning, listen in few words to my tale, and answer in one word to the purpose, for that neither my burning desire can afford long speech, nor the short time I have to stay many delays. Is it possible by herbs, stones, spells, incantation, enchantment, exorcisms, fire, metals, planets, or any practise, to plant affection where it is not, and to supplant it where it is?

DIPSAS

Fair lady, you may imagine that these hoary hairs are not void of experience, nor the great name that goeth of my cunning to be without cause. I can darken the sun by my skill and remove the moon out of her course; I can restore youth to the aged and make hills without bottoms; there is nothing that I cannot do but that only which you would have me do: and therein I differ from the gods, that I am not able to rule hearts; for, were it in my power to place affection by appointment, I would make such evil appetites, such inordinate lusts, such cursed desires, as all the world should be filled both with superstitious heats and extreme love.

TELLUS

Unhappy Tellus, whose desires are so desperate that they are neither to be conceived of any creature nor to be cured by any art!

DIPSAS

This I can: breed slackness in love, though never root it out. What is he whom you love, and what she that he honoureth?

TELLUS

Endymion, sweet Endymion, is he that hath my heart; and Cynthia, too, too fair Cynthia, the miracle of nature, of time, of fortune, is the lady that he delights in, and dotes on every day, and dies for ten thousand times a day.

DIPSAS

Would you have his love either by absence or sickness aslaked? Would you that Cynthia should mistrust him, or be jealous of him without colour?

TELLUS

It is the only thing I crave, that, seeing my love to Endymion, unspotted, cannot be accepted, his truth to Cynthia (though it be unspeakable) may be suspected.

DIPSAS

I will undertake it, and overtake him, that all his love shall be doubted of, and therefore become desperate. But this will wear out with time, that treadeth all things down but truth.

9 **cunning** learning/wisdom.
10 **for that** because.
13 **planets** the use of astrology.
15 **hoary** white.
16 **the great...cunning** the great reputation that I have for my skills.
16–17 **I...course** These were feats claimed by Medea in Ovid's *Metamorphosis*, and would later be claimed by Prospero in Shakespeare's *The Tempest*.
19 **that** (only in) that.
26 **breed slackness** create a diminution.
32 **without colour** without reason (lit. without any deception on his part).
33–34 **seeing...accepted** given that my pure love for him cannot be reciprocated.
34–35 **though...suspected** though it is indescribably deep, may be doubted.
36 **overtake** overpower.

Sol addresses to Cynthia; exclamations, questions (confessional)

TELLUS

Let us go.

DIPSAS

I follow. *Exeunt.*

Actus Secundus, Scaena Prima
(Endymion, Tellus)

ENDYMION

O fair Cynthia! O unfortunate Endymion! Why was not thy birth as high as thy thoughts, or her beauty less than heavenly? Or why are not thine honours as rare as her beauty, or thy fortunes as great as thy deserts? Sweet Cynthia, how wouldst thou be pleased; how possessed? Will labours, patient of all extremities, obtain thy love? There is no mountain so steep that I will not climb, no monster so cruel that I will not tame, no action so desperate that I will not attempt. Desirest thou the passions of love, the sad and melancholy moods of perplexed minds, the not-to-be-expressed torments of racked thoughts? Behold my sad tears, my deep sighs, my hollow eyes, my broken sleeps, my heavy countenance. Wouldst thou have me vowed only to thy beauty and consume every minute of time in thy service? Remember my solitary life almost these seven years. Whom have I entertained but mine own thoughts and thy virtues? What company have I used but contemplation? Whom have I wondered at but thee? Nay, whom have I not contemned for thee? Have I not crept to those on whom I might have trodden, only because thou didst shine upon them? Have not injuries been sweet to me, if thou vouchsafedst I should bear them? Have I not spent my golden years in hopes, waxing old with wishing, yet wishing nothing but thy love? With Tellus, fair Tellus, have I dissembled, using her but as a cloak for mine affections, that others, seeing my mangled and disordered mind, might think it were for one that loveth me, not for Cynthia, whose perfection alloweth no companion nor comparison.

In the midst of these distempered thoughts of mine, thou art not only jealous of my truth, but careless, suspicious, and secure; which strange humour maketh my mind as desperate as thy conceits are doubtful. I am none of those wolves that bark most when thou shinest brightest, but that fish (thy fish, Cynthia, in the flood Araris) which at thy waxing is as white as the driven snow, and at thy waning as black as deepest darkness. I am that Endymion, sweet Cynthia, that have carried my thoughts in equal balance with my actions, being always as free from imagining ill as enterprising; that Endymion whose eyes never esteemed anything fair but thy face, whose tongue termed nothing rare but thy virtues, and whose heart imagined nothing miraculous but thy government; yea, that Endymion who, divorcing himself from the

8 **racked** tortured.

14 **contemned** despised.

14 **crept to** fawned upon.

16 **vouchsafedst** declared.

19 **cloak** cover/deception. Endymion admits, rather damningly, that he has deceived Tellus into thinking he loved her, only to disguise the true object of his passion.

22 **distempered** troubled.

23 **secure** complacent/indifferent.

24 **thy...doubtful** your intentions are unreadable.

25 **that fish** in *Euphues* Lyly describes a fish, the scolopidus, that lives in the river Araris (perhaps the Arar or Saône in France) and changes colour as the moon waxes and wanes.

amiableness of all ladies, the bravery of all courts, the company of all men, hath chosen in a solitary cell to live, only by feeding on thy favour, accounting in the world, but thyself, nothing excellent, nothing immortal. Thus mayest thou see every vein, sinew, muscle, and artery of my love, in which there is no flattery nor deceit, error nor art. But soft, here cometh Tellus. I must turn my other face to her, like Janus, lest she be as suspicious as Juno.

Enter Tellus [Floscula and Dipsas].

TELLUS

Yonder I espy Endymion. I will seem to suspect nothing, but soothe him, that, seeing I cannot obtain the depth of his love, I may learn the height of his dissembling. Floscula and Dipsas, withdraw yourselves out of our sight, yet be within the hearing of our saluting. How now, Endymion, always solitary? No company but your own thoughts; no friend but melancholy fancies?

ENDYMION

You know, fair Tellus, that the sweet remembrance of your love is the only companion of my life, and thy presence, my paradise, so that I am not alone when nobody is with me, and in heaven itself when thou art with me.

TELLUS

Then you love me, Endymion?

ENDYMION

Or else I live not, Tellus.

TELLUS

Is it not possible for you, Endymion, to dissemble?

ENDYMION

Not, Tellus, unless I could make me a woman.

TELLUS

Why, is dissembling joined to their sex inseparable, as heat to fire, heaviness to earth, moisture to water, thinness to air?

ENDYMION

No, but found in their sex as common as spots upon doves, moles upon faces, caterpillars upon sweet apples, cobwebs upon fair windows.

TELLUS

Do they all dissemble?

ENDYMION

All but one.

TELLUS

Who is that?

ENDYMION

I dare not tell; for if I should say you, then would you imagine my flattery to be extreme; if another, then would you think my love to be but indifferent.

TELLUS

You will be sure I shall take no vantage of your words. But in sooth, Endymion, without more ceremonies, is it not Cynthia?

32 **government** conduct/demeanour.
38 **Janus** the two-faced god of gateways and doors.
50 **make me** turn myself into.
61 **ceremonies** prevarication/games.

ENDYMION

You know, Tellus, that of the gods we are forbidden to dispute, because their deities come not within the compass of our reasons; and of Cynthia we are allowed not to talk but to wonder, because her virtues are not within the reach of our capacities.

TELLUS

Why, she is but a woman.

ENDYMION

No more was Venus.

TELLUS

She is but a virgin.

ENDYMION

No more was Vesta.

TELLUS

She shall have an end.

ENDYMION

So shall the world.

TELLUS

Is not her beauty subject to time?

ENDYMION

No more than time is to standing still.

TELLUS

Wilt thou make her immortal?

ENDYMION

No, but incomparable.

TELLUS

Take heed, Endymion, lest like the wrestler in Olympia, that striving to lift an impossible weight, catched an incurable strain, thou, by fixing thy thoughts above thy reach, fall into a disease without all recure. But I see thou art now in love with Cynthia.

ENDYMION

No, Tellus, thou knowest that the stately cedar, whose top reacheth unto the clouds, never boweth his head to the shrubs that grow in the valley; nor ivy, that climbeth up by the elm, can ever get hold of the beams of the sun. Cynthia I honour in all humility, whom none ought or dare adventure to love, whose affections are immortal, and virtues infinite. Suffer me, therefore, to gaze on the moon, at whom, were it not for thyself, I would die with wondering.

Exeunt.

Actus Secundus, Scaena Secunda.
(Dares, Samias, Scintilla, Favilla)

DARES

Come, Samias, didst thou ever hear such a sighing, the one for Cynthia, the other for Semele, and both for moonshine in the water?

63 **of... reasons** we are forbidden to talk about the gods, as their divine natures are beyond our understanding.

69 **Vesta** Roman goddess of hearth and home, whose temple was tended by the Vestal virgins.

78 **recure** recovery/cure.

2 **moonshine... water** i.e. something unobtainable.

SAMIAS

Let them sigh, and let us sing. How say you, gentlewomen, are not our masters too far in love?

SCINTILLA

Their tongues, happily, are dipped to the root in amorous words and sweet discourses, but I think their hearts are scarce tipped on the side with constant desires.

DARES

How say you, Favilla, is not love a lurcher, that taketh men's stomachs away that they cannot eat, their spleen that they cannot laugh, their hearts that they cannot fight, their eyes that they cannot sleep, and leaveth nothing but livers to make nothing but lovers?

FAVILLA

Away, peevish boy; a rod were better under thy girdle than love in thy mouth. It will be a forward cock that croweth in the shell.

DARES

Alas, good old gentlewoman, how it becometh you to be grave!

SCINTILLA

Favilla, though she be but a spark, yet is she fire.

FAVILLA

And you, Scintilla, be not much more than a spark, though you would be esteemed a flame.

SAMIAS

It were good sport to see the fight between two sparks.

DARES

Let them to it, and we will warm us by their words.

SCINTILLA

You are not angry, Favilla?

FAVILLA

That is, Scintilla, as you list to take it.

SAMIAS

That, that!

SCINTILLA

This it is to be matched with girls, who coming but yesterday from making of babies, would before tomorrow be accounted matrons.

FAVILLA

I cry your matronship mercy. Because your pantables be higher with cork, therefore your feet must needs be higher in the insteps; you will be mine elder because you stand upon a stool and I on the floor.

SAMIAS

Good, good!

5 **happily** perhaps.

6 **scarce . . . side** not even lightly touched.

8 **lurcher** someone who deprives another of food by eating it all first.

12–13 **Away . . . shell.** Get away with you, perverse boy, you're better suited to a thrashing on the arse than to be talking about love. It's a precocious cockerel that crows while still in the egg.

21 **as . . . it** however you choose to interpret it.

22 **That, that!** Go on, go on!

24 **babies** dolls.

24 **accounted matrons** considered mature women.

25 **pantable** pantofles, shoes with high cork soles and heels.

DARES
Let them alone, and see with what countenance they will become friends.

SCINTILLA
Nay, you think to be the wiser, because you mean to have the last word.

SAMIAS
Step between them lest they scratch. In faith, gentlewomen, seeing we came out to be merry, let not your jarring mar our jests; be friends. How say you?

SCINTILLA
I am not angry, but it spited me to see how short she was.

FAVILLA
I meant nothing till she would needs cross me.

DARES
Then, so let it rest.

SCINTILLA
I am agreed.

FAVILLA
And I. Yet I never took anything so unkindly in my life.

SCINTILLA
'Tis I have the cause, that never offered the occasion.

DARES
Excellent, and right like a woman.

SAMIAS
A strange sight, to see water come out of fire.

DARES
It is their property to carry in their eyes fire and water, tears and torches, and in their mouths honey and gall.

SCINTILLA
You will be a good one if you live, but what is yonder formal fellow?

Enter Sir Tophas [and Epiton].

DARES
Sir Tophas, Sir Tophas, of whom we told you. If you be good wenches, make as though you love him, and wonder at him.

FAVILLA
We will do our parts.

DARES
But first let us stand aside, and let him use his garb, for all consisteth in his gracing.

TOPHAS
Epi!

EPITON
At hand, sir.

TOPHAS
How likest thou this martial life, where nothing but blood besprinkleth our bosoms? Let me see, be our enemies fat?

32 **jarring** wrangling.
34 **till . . me** until she had to go and pick a fight with me.
38 **'Tis . . . occasion.** I'm the injured party here, who never gave cause for offence.
40 **water . . . fire** i.e. tears created from anger.
47–48 **let . . . gracing** let him show us his manners, for (the joke) will rest on his attempts to be stylish.

EPITON

Passing fat: and I would not change this life to be a lord; and yourself passeth all comparison, for other captains kill and beat, and there is nothing you kill but you also eat.

TOPHAS

I will draw out their guts out of their bellies, and tear the flesh with my teeth, so mortal is my hate, and so eager my unstaunched stomach.

EPITON

My master thinks himself the valiantest man in the world if he kill a wren; so warlike a thing he accounteth to take away life, though it be from a lark.

TOPHAS

Epi, I find my thoughts to swell and my spirit to take wings, insomuch that I cannot continue within the compass of so slender combats.

SCINTILLA

Why, is he not mad?

SAMIAS

No, but a little vainglorious.

TOPHAS

Epi.

EPITON

Sir.

TOPHAS

I will encounter that black and cruel enemy that beareth rough and untewed locks upon his body, whose sire throweth down the strongest walls, whose legs are as many as both ours, on whose head are placed most horrible horns by nature as a defence from all harms.

EPITON

What mean you, master, to be so desperate?

TOPHAS

Honour inciteth me, and very hunger compelleth me.

EPITON

What is that monster?

TOPHAS

The monster *ovis*. I have said; let thy wits work.

EPITON

I cannot imagine it. Yet let me see, a black enemy with rough locks. It may be a sheep, and *ovis* is a sheep. His sire so strong? A ram is a sheep's sire, that being also an engine of war. Horns he hath, and four legs; so hath a sheep. Without doubt this monster is a black sheep. Is it not a sheep that you mean?

TOPHAS

Thou hast hit it: that monster will I kill and sup with.

SAMIAS

Come let us take him off. Sir Tophas, all hail.

53 **passeth** surpass.
60–61 **I . . . combats** I am no longer satisfied with such meagre battles.
67 **untewed locks** uncombed hair.
73 ***ovis*** sheep (Latin).
78 **sup with** eat.
79 **take him off** distract him.

TOPHAS

Welcome, children; I seldom cast mine eyes so low as to the crowns of your heads, and therefore pardon me that I spake not all this while.

DARES

No harm done. Here be fair ladies come to wonder at your person, your valour, your wit, the report whereof hath made them careless of their own honours, to glut their eyes and hearts upon yours.

TOPHAS

Report cannot but injure me, for that not knowing fully what I am, I fear she hath been a niggard in her praises.

SCINTILLA

No, gentle knight, report hath been prodigal, for she hath left you no equal, nor herself credit, so much hath she told, yet no more than we now see.

DARES

A good wench.

FAVILLA

If there remain as much pity toward women as there is in you courage against your enemies, then shall we be happy, who, hearing of your person, came to see it, and seeing it, are now in love with it.

TOPHAS

Love me, ladies? I easily believe it, but my tough heart receiveth no impression with sweet words. Mars may pierce it, Venus shall not paint on it.

FAVILLA

A cruel saying.

SAMIAS

There's a girl!

DARES

Will you cast these ladies away, and all for a little love? Do but speak kindly.

TOPHAS

There cometh no soft syllable within my lips; custom hath made my words bloody and my heart barbarous: that pelting word love, how waterish in my mouth; it carrieth no sound. Hate, horror, death, are speeches that nourish my spirits. I like honey, but I care not for the bees; I delight in music, but I love not to play on the bagpipes; I can vouchsafe to hear the voice of women, but to touch their bodies I disdain it as a thing childish and fit for such men as can digest nothing but milk.

SCINTILLA

A hard heart! Shall we die for your love and find no remedy?

TOPHAS

I have already taken a surfeit.

EPITON

Good master, pity them.

85 **Report...me** Rumour can only underestimate my prowess.
86 **niggard** miser.
99 **pelting** paltry.
99 **waterish** thin/unsatisfying (it is)
100 **it...sound** it does not resonate.
106 **I...surfeit.** I've already had too much (talk of love).

Sort of self-address, self-questioning soc

TOPHAS

Pity them, Epi? No, I do not think that this breast shall be pestered with such a foolish passion. What is that the gentlewoman carrieth in a chain?

EPITON

Why, it is a squirrel.

TOPHAS

A squirrel? O gods, what things are made for money!

DARES

Is not this gentleman over-wise?

FAVILLA

I could stay all day with him, if I feared not to be shent.

SCINTILLA

Is it not possible to meet again?

DARES

Yes, at any time.

FAVILLA

Then let us hasten home.

SCINTILLA

Sir Tophas, the god of war deal better with you than you do with the god of love.

FAVILLA

Our love we may dissemble, digest we cannot; but I doubt not but time will hamper you and help us.

TOPHAS

I defy time, who hath no interest in my heart. Come, Epi, let me to the battle with that hideous beast. Love is pap, and hath no relish in my taste because it is not terrible.

DARES

Indeed a black sheep is a perilous beast, but let us in till another time.

FAVILLA

I shall long for that time.

Exeunt.

Actus Secundus, Scaena Tertia
(Endymion, Dipsas, Bagoa)

ENDYMION

No rest, Endymion? Still uncertain how to settle thy steps by day or thy thoughts by night? Thy truth is measured by thy fortune, and thou art judged unfaithful because thou art unhappy. I will see if I can beguile myself with sleep, and if no slumber will take hold in my eyes, yet will I embrace the golden thoughts in my head, and wish to melt by musing; that as ebony, which no fire can scorch, is yet consumed with sweet savours, so my heart, which cannot be bent by the hardness of fortune, may be bruised by amorous desires. On

111 **what . . . money!** what will they think of next!
113 **shent** punished (by his master).
119 **digest we cannot** we cannot stomach it.
122 **pap** the mushy food given to babies.
5–6 **ebony . . . savours** ebony was reputed to be very hard to burn, but when it did it smouldered with a pleasant scent.

yonder bank never grew anything but lunary, and hereafter I will never have any bed but that bank. O Endymion, Tellus was fair. But what availeth beauty without wisdom? Nay, Endymion, she was wise. But what availeth wisdom without honour? She was honourable, Endymion; belie her not. Aye, but how obscure is honour without fortune. Was she not fortunate whom so many followed? Yes, yes, but base is fortune without majesty. Thy majesty, Cynthia, all the world knoweth and wondereth at, but not one in the world that can imitate it or comprehend it. No more, Endymion: sleep or die. Nay, die, for to sleep it is impossible; and yet, I know not how it cometh to pass, I feel such a heaviness both in mine eyes and heart that I am suddenly benumbed, yea, in every joint. It may be weariness, for when did I rest? It may be deep melancholy, for when did I not sigh? Cynthia! Aye, so I say, Cynthia! *He falls asleep.*

DIPSAS

Little dost thou know, Endymion, when thou shalt wake, for hadst thou placed thy heart as low in love as thy head lieth now in sleep, thou mightest have commanded Tellus, whom now, instead of a mistress, thou shalt find a tomb. These eyes must I seal up by art, not nature, which are to be opened neither by art nor nature. Thou that liest down with golden locks shalt not wake until they be turned to silver hairs; and that chin on which scarcely appeareth soft down shall be filled with bristles as hard as broom. Thou shalt sleep out thy youth and flowering time, and become dry hay before thou knowest thyself green grass; and ready by age to step into the grave when thou wakest, that wast youthful in the court when thou laidest thee down to sleep. The malice of Tellus hath brought this to pass, which if she could not have entreated of me by fair means, she would have commanded by menacing, for from her gather we all our simples to maintain our sorceries.

Fan with this hemlock over his face, and sing the enchantment for sleep, whilst I go in and finish those ceremonies that are required in our art. Take heed ye touch not his face, for the fan is so seasoned that whoso it toucheth with a leaf shall presently die, and over whom the wind of it breatheth, he shall sleep forever. *Exit.*

BAGOA

Let me alone; I will be careful. What hap hadst thou, Endymion, to come under the hands of Dipsas? O fair Endymion, how it grieveth me that that fair face must be turned to a withered skin and taste the pains of death before it feel the reward of love. I fear Tellus will repent that which the heavens themselves seemed to rue. But I hear Dipsas coming; I dare not repine, lest she make me pine, and rock me into such a deep sleep that I shall not awake to my marriage. *Enter Dipsas.*

DIPSAS

How now, have you finished?

BAGOA

Yea.

8 **lunary** the herb moonwart.
11 **belie her** misrepresent her.
23 **art** magical skill.
31–32 **for . . . simples** from Tellus (the earth) we gather all the herbs for our potions.
35 **seasoned** treated with poison.
38 **hap** fortune.
43 **pine** suffer.

DIPSAS

Well then, let us in; and see that you do not so much as whisper that I did this, for if you do, I will turn thy hairs to adders and all thy teeth in thy head to tongues. Come away, come away. *Exeunt.*

[*A Dumb-Show*]

[*Music sounds. Three ladies enter: one with a knife and a looking-glass, who, by the procurement of one of the other two, offers to stab Endymion as he sleeps; but the third wrings her hands, lamenteth, offering still to prevent it, but dares not. At last, the first lady looking in the glass, casts down the knife.* (*Exeunt.*)

Enters an ancient man with books with three leaves; offers the same twice. Endymion refuseth. He re[n]deth two, and offers the third, where he stands awhile; and then Endymion offers to take it. (*Exit.*)]

Actus Tertius, Scaena Prima
(Cynthia, Three Lords [Panelion, Corsites, and Zontes], Tellus, [Eumenides], [Semele])

CYNTHIA

Is the report true, that Endymion is stricken into such a dead sleep that nothing can either wake him or move him?

EUMENIDES

Too true, madam, and as much to be pitied as wondered at.

TELLUS

As good sleep and do no harm as wake and do no good.

CYNTHIA

What maketh you, Tellus, to be so short? The time was Endymion only was.

EUMENIDES

It is an old saying, madam, that a waking dog doth afar off bark at a sleeping lion.

SEMELE

It were good, Eumenides, that you took a nap with your friend, for your speech beginneth to be heavy.

EUMENIDES

Contrary to your nature, Semele, which hath been always accounted light.

CYNTHIA

What, have we here before my face these unseemly and malapert overthwarts! I will tame your tongues and your thoughts, and make your speeches answerable to your duties, and your conceits fit for my dignity, else will I banish you both my person and the world.

EUMENIDES

Pardon I humbly ask; but such is my unspotted faith to Endymion that

The dumbshow, which appears only in the version of the play in Blount's *Six Court Comedies* (1632), offers a visualization of the dream that Endymion will later describe.

rendeth tears.

5 **short** curt.

5–6 **The . . . was.** It used to be that Endymion was all you thought about.

11 **light** both 'trivial' and 'wanton'.

12–13 **malapert overthwarts** impertinent squabbles.

whatsoever seemeth a needle to prick his finger is a dagger to wound my heart.

CYNTHIA

If you be so dear to him, how happeneth it you neither go to see him, nor search for remedy for him?

EUMENIDES

I have seen him to my grief, and sought recure with despair, for that I cannot imagine who should restore him that is the wonder to all men. Your highness, on whose hands the compass of the earth is at command, though not in possession, may show yourself both worthy your sex, your nature, and your favour, if you redeem that honourable Endymion, whose ripe years foretell rare virtues, and whose unmellowed conceits promise ripe counsel.

CYNTHIA

I have had trial of Endymion, and conceive greater assurance of his age than I could hope of his youth.

TELLUS

But timely, madam, crooks that tree that will be a cammock, and young it pricks that will be a thorn; and therefore he that began without care to settle his life, it is a sign without amendment he will end it.

CYNTHIA

Presumptuous girl, I will make thy tongue an example of unrecoverable displeasure. Corsites, carry her to the castle in the desert, there to remain and weave.

CORSITES

Shall she work stories or poetries?

CYNTHIA

It skilleth not which. Go to, in both; for she shall find examples infinite in either what punishment long tongues have. Eumenides, if either the soothsayers in Egypt, or the enchanters in Thessaly, or the philosophers in Greece, or all the sages of the world can find remedy, I will procure it; therefore, dispatch with all speed. You, Eumenides, into Thessaly; you, Zontes, into Greece (because you are acquainted in Athens); you, Panelion, to Egypt; saying that Cynthia sendeth, and if you will, commandeth.

EUMENIDES

On bowed knee I give thanks, and with wings on my legs, I fly for remedy.

ZONTES

We are ready at your highness' command, and hope to return to your full content.

CYNTHIA

It shall never be said that Cynthia, whose mercy and goodness filleth the heavens with joys and the world with marvels, will suffer either Endymion or any to perish, if he may be protected.

EUMENIDES

Your majesty's words have been always deeds, and your deeds virtues. *Exeunt.*

24–25 **whose ripe...counsel** whose youth promises rare virtue and youthful ideas promise wisdom when he is older.
28 **cammock** a crooked tree.
34 **Shall...poetries?** Shall she embroider images of true events or fantasies?
35 **It skilleth not** It does not matter.
35 **Go to, in both!** Curse it, she shall do both!
36 **long tongues** those who don't know when to keep silent.
37 **Thessaly** a Greek state renowned for its sorcerers.
48 **Your...deeds** You have always kept your promises,

Actus Tertius, Scaena Secunda
(Corsites, Tellus)

CORSITES

Here is the castle, fair Tellus, in which you must weave, till either time end your days or Cynthia her displeasure. I am sorry so fair a face should be subject to so hard a fortune, and that the flower of beauty, which is honoured in courts, should here wither in prison.

TELLUS

Corsites, Cynthia may restrain the liberty of my body, of my thoughts she cannot. And therefore do I esteem myself most free, though I am in greatest bondage.

CORSITES

Can you then feed on fancy, and subdue the malice of envy by the sweetness of imagination?

TELLUS

Corsites, there is no sweeter music to the miserable than despair; and therefore the more bitterness I feel, the more sweetness I find. For so vain were liberty, and so unwelcome the following of higher fortune, that I choose rather to pine in this castle than to be a prince in any other court.

CORSITES

A humour contrary to your years and nothing agreeable to your sex: the one commonly allured with delights, the other always with sovereignty.

TELLUS

I marvel, Corsites, that you, being a captain, who should sound nothing but terror and suck nothing but blood, can find in your heart to talk such smooth words, for that it agreeth not with your calling to use words so soft as that of love.

CORSITES

Lady, it were unfit of wars to discourse with women, into whose minds nothing can sink but smoothness. Besides, you must not think that soldiers be so rough-hewn, or of such knotty mettle, that beauty cannot allure, and you, being beyond perfection, enchant.

TELLUS

Good Corsites, talk not of love, but let me to my labour. The little beauty I have shall be bestowed on my loom, which I now mean to make my lover.

CORSITES

Let us in, and what favour Corsites can show, Tellus shall command.

TELLUS

The only favour I desire is now and then to walk. *Exeunt.*

Actus Tertius, Scaena Tertia
(Sir Tophas and Epi[ton].)

TOPHAS

Epi!

EPITON

Here, sir.

16 **sound** talk of.

22 **knotty mettle** rough disposition.

TOPHAS

Unrig me. Hey ho!

EPITON

What's that?

TOPHAS

An interjection, whereof some are of mourning: as 'Eho! Vah!'

EPITON

I understand you not.

TOPHAS

Thou seest me?

EPITON

Aye.

TOPHAS

Thou hearest me?

EPITON

Aye.

TOPHAS

Thou feelest me?

EPITON

Aye.

TOPHAS

And not understandest me?

EPITON

No.

TOPHAS

Then am I but three-quarters of a noun substantive. But alas, Epi, to tell thee the truth, I am a noun adjective.

EPITON

Why?

TOPHAS

Because I cannot stand without another.

EPITON

Who is that?

TOPHAS

Dipsas.

EPITON

Are you in love?

TOPHAS

No, but love hath, as it were, milked my thoughts and drained from my heart the very substance of my accustomed courage; it worketh in my head like new wine, so as I must hoop my sconce with iron, lest my head break, and so I

3 **Unrig** Disarm/undress.

5 **interjection** in Renaissance rhetoric, a sudden expression prompted by a surge of passion in the speaker.

5 **'Eho! Vah!** *Eheu* ('alas!'), Ah!

15–16 **Then . . . adjective.** A schoolroom joke, see William Lilly's *Grammar*: 'a Noun Substantive is that which standeth by himself, and requireth not another word to be joined with him, to declare his signification.' 'A Noun Adjective is that which cannot stand by himself, in reason or signification, but requireth to be joined with another word.'

24 **sconce** head.

bewray my brains. But I pray thee first discover me in all parts, that I may be like a lover, and then will I sigh and die. Take my gun and give me a gown: *Cedant arma toga.*

EPITON

Here.

TOPHAS

Take my sword and shield and give me beard-brush and scissors. *Bella gerant alii tu Pari semper ama.*

EPITON

Will you be trimmed, sir?

TOPHAS

Not yet; for I feel a contention within me whether I shall frame the bodkin beard or the bush. But take my pike and give me pen, *dicere quae puduit, scribere iusiit amor.*

EPITON

I will furnish you, sir.

TOPHAS

Now, for my bow and bolts, give me ink and paper, for my smiter, a pen-knife; for *scalpellum, calami, atramentum, charta, libelli, sint semper studiis arma parata meis.*

EPITON

Sir, will you give over wars and play with that bauble called love?

TOPHAS

Give over wars? No, Epi, *militat omnis amans, et habet sua castra Cupido.*

EPITON

Love hath made you very eloquent, but your face is nothing fair.

TOPHAS

Non formosus erat, sed erat facundus Ulysses?

EPITON

Nay, I must seek a new master if you can speak nothing but verses.

TOPHAS

Quicquid conabar dicere versus erat! Epi, I feel all Ovid *De arte amandi* lie as heavy at my heart as a load of logs. Oh, what a fine thin hair hath Dipsas! What a pretty low forehead. What a tall and stately nose! What little hollow eyes! What great and goodly lips! How harmless she is, being toothless; her fingers fat and short, adorned with long nails like a bittern! In how sweet

25 **bewray** reveal/spill.

25 **discover . . . parts** disarm me completely.

27 ***Cedant arma toga.*** Let armour give way to the toga (see Cicero, *De Officiis*, I, 22, 77).

29–30 ***Bella . . . ama.*** Let others fight, you, Paris, should always love. An allusion to Ovid's *Heroides*, xiii.

32–33 **the bodkin . . bush** either a pointed beard or a wide one.

33–34 ***dicere . . . amor*** love urges one to write what one cannot speak of (Ovid, *Heroides*, iv, 10).

37–38 ***scalpellum . . . meis*** may pen-knife, quills, ink, paper and booklets be always apt weapons for my scholarly engagements. (A phrase adapted from the advice to schoolboys in Lilly and Colet's *A Short Introduction of Grammar* (1577).)

39 **bauble** trifle.

40 ***militat . . . Cupido.*** Every lover goes to battle, and Cupid has his own fortress (Ovid, *Amores*, i, 9).

42 ***Non . . . Ulysses?*** Ulysses was not fair, but he was eloquent (Ovid, *Ars Amatoria*, II, 123).

44 ***Quicquid . . . erat!*** Whatever I tried to say emerged as verse! (Ovid, *Tristia*, iv, 10). Sir Philip Sidney quotes the line in *The Apology for Poetry.*

44 ***De arte amandi*** the *Ars Amatoria* ('Concerning the Art of Love').

45–52 **Oh . . . jealous!** Sir Tophas' comic praise for traits generally seen as unattractive in women is echoed in Shakespeare's anti-Petrarchan sonnet 130, 'My mistress' eyes are nothing like the sun'.

48 **bittern** a wading bird.

a proportion her cheeks hang down to her breasts like dugs, and her paps to her waist like bags! What a low stature she is; and yet what a great foot she carrieth! How thrifty must she be in whom there is no waist! How virtuous is she like to be, over whom no man can be jealous!

EPITON

Stay, master, you forget yourself.

TOPHAS

O Epi, even as a dish melteth by the fire, so doth my wit increase by love.

EPITON

Pithily, and to the purpose! But what, begin you to nod?

TOPHAS

Good Epi, let me take a nap; for as some man may better steal a horse than another look over the hedge, so divers shall be sleepy when they would fainest take rest. *He sleeps.*

EPITON

Who ever saw such a woodcock! Love Dipsas? Without doubt all the world will now account him valiant, that ventureth on her whom none durst undertake. But here cometh two wags. *Enter Dares and Samias.*

SAMIAS

Thy master hath slept his share.

DARES

I think he doth it because he would not pay me my board-wages.

SAMIAS

It is a thing most strange: and I think mine will never return, so that we must both seek new masters, for we shall never live by our manners.

EPITON

If you want masters, join with me and serve Sir Tophas, who must needs keep more men, because he is toward marriage.

SAMIAS

What, Epi, where's thy master?

EPITON

Yonder, sleeping in love.

DARES

Is it possible?

EPITON

He hath taken his thoughts a hole lower, and saith, seeing it is the fashion of the world, he will vail bonnet to beauty.

SAMIAS

How is he attired?

49 **dugs** breasts.
50–51 **what...carrieth** what large feet she has.
51 **How...waist!** Punning on 'waste'.
54 **dish** a dish of food. Perhaps Tophas is thinking specifically of a dish of butter, but, as Epi's ironic comment suggests, the analogy seems bizarre.
55 **nod** fall asleep.
56–58 **for...rest** another absurd analogy: just as some will steal a horse while others dare only look at it, many will just feel sleepy when they should take a nap.
59 **woodcock** idiot (slang).
60–61 **that...undertake** who attempts to woo she who no one else would dare to.
61 **two wags** mischievous or witty fellows.
63 **board-wages** subsistence allowance.
67 **toward** planning on.
71 **taken...lower** lowered his aim (from war to love).
72 **vail bonnet** doff his cap.

EPITON
Lovely.

DARES
Whom loveth this amorous knight?

EPITON
Dipsas.

SAMIAS
That ugly creature? Why, she is a fool, a scold, fat, without fashion, and quite without favour.

EPITON
Tush, you be simple; my master hath a good marriage.

DARES
Good? As how?

EPITON
Why, in marrying Dipsas he shall have every day twelve dishes of meat to his dinner, though there be none but Dipsas with him: four of flesh, four of fish, four of fruit.

SAMIAS
As how, Epi?

EPITON
For flesh these: woodcock, goose, bittern, and rail.

DARES
Indeed, he shall not miss, if Dipsas be there.

EPITON
For fish these: crab, carp, lump, and pouting.

SAMIAS
Excellent, for of my word she is both crabbish, lumpish, and carping.

EPITON
For fruit these: fritters, medlars, artichokes, and lady-longings. Thus you see he shall fare like a king, though he be but a beggar.

DARES
Well, Epi, dine thou with him, for I had rather fast than see her face. But see, thy master is asleep; let us have a song to wake this amorous knight.

EPITON
Agreed.

SAMIAS
Content.

77 **a scold** a nagging shrew.
78 **quite without favour** wholly unattractive.
79 **simple** foolish/dim.
81 **to** at/for.
85 **woodcock...rail** a series of puns, implying: idiot, ninny, ugliness (see the earlier comment on the bittern's huge feet), and argument ('railing': the rail is a small wading bird).
86 **miss** lack (those things).
87 **crab...pouting** bad temper, nagging, lumpenness, and sulkiness (punning on the lump (*Cyclopterus lumpus*) and the pout or pouting (a variety of the genus *Trisopterus*), respectively.
89 **fritters** battered fruit (but also wastes of time), **medlars** an apple-like fruit (from the tree *Mespilus germanica*) but also, by implication, a wife who meddles in his life, **artichoke** an ugly woman (slang: 'artichoke'), and **lady-longings**, the apple known as 'lady's longing', suggesting a longing on his part for other ladies.

[THE FIRST SONG.

EPITON
Here snores Tophas,
That amorous ass,
Who loves Dipsas,
With face so sweet
Nose and chin meet.

ALL THREE
At sight of her each Fury skips
And flings into her lap their whips.

DARES
Holla, holla in his ear.

SAMIAS
The witch, sure, thrust her fingers there.

EPITON
Cramp him, or wring the fool by the nose.

DARES
Or clap some burning flax to his toes.

SAMIAS
What music's best to wake him?

EPITON
Bow-wow, let bandogs shake him!

DARES
Let adders hiss in's ear.

SAMIAS
Else earwigs wriggle there.

EPITON
No, let him batten; when his tongue
Once goes, a cat is not worse strung.

ALL THREE
But if he ope nor mouth nor eyes,
He may in time sleep himself wise.]

TOPHAS
Sleep is a binding of the senses, love a loosing.

EPITON
Let us hear him awhile.

TOPHAS
There appeared in my sleep a goodly owl, who, sitting upon my shoulder, cried 'Twit, twit'; and before mine eyes presented herself the express image of

93.1 The lyrics of the song appear only in Blount's *Six Court Comedies*.

100 **each Fury skips** each of the three Furies or Erinyes (Tisiphone, Megæra, Alecto), the classical spirits of revenge and torment, flees.

104 **Cramp** Pinch.

107 **bandogs** chained guard dogs.

108 **in's** in his.

109 **Else...there.** Or else put earwigs to wriggle in his ears.

110 **batten** grow fat (i.e. stay lying where he is).

110–111 **when...strung** if we wake him and he starts to sing or complain (as lovers do) he'll sound as bad as a caterwauling tomcat.

112 **ope nor** open neither.

114 **love a loosing** which frees (the mind to dream of) love.

Dipsas. I marvelled what the owl said, till at the last I perceived: 'T'wit, t'wit': 'To it, to it!' only by contraction admonished by this vision to make account of my sweet Venus.

SAMIAS

Sir Tophas, you have overslept yourself.

TOPHAS

No, youth, I have but slept over my love.

DARES

Love? Why, it is impossible that into so noble and unconquered a courage love should creep, having first a head as hard to pierce as steel, then to pass to a heart armed with shirt of mail!

EPITON

Aye, but my master, yawning one day in the sun, love crept into his mouth before he could close it, and there kept such a tumbling in his body that he was glad to untruss the points of his heart and entertain Love as a stranger.

TOPHAS

If there remain any pity in you, plead for me to Dipsas.

DARES

Plead? Nay, we will press her to it. Let us go with him to Dipsas, and there shall we have good sport. But, Sir Tophas, when shall we go? For I find my tongue voluble and my heart venturous, and all myself like myself.

SAMIAS

Come, Dares, let us not lose him until we find our masters, for as long as he liveth, we shall lack neither mirth nor meat.

EPITON

We will traverse. Will you go, sir?

TOPHAS

Aye, *pra sequar*. *Exeunt.*

Actus Tertius, Scaena Quarta
(Eumenides, Geron.)

EUMENIDES

Father, your sad music being tuned on the same key that my hard fortune is, hath so melted my mind that I wish to hang at your mouth's end t[i]ll my life end.

GERON

These tunes, gentleman, have I been accustomed with these fifty winters, having no other house to shroud myself but the broad heavens; and so familiar with me hath use made misery that I esteem sorrow my chiefest solace; and welcomest is that guest to me that can rehearse the saddest tale or the bloodiest tragedy.

118–120 **I perceived . . . Venus** I perceived that 'T'wit', by contraction meant 'to it' (get on with it!), and was urging me to address my beloved Venus (i.e. Dipsas, implausibly figured as the goddess of love).

125 **mail** chainmail.

128 **untruss the points** untie the draw-strings.

128 **entertain** play host to.

135 **traverse** journey.

136 **Aye, *pra sequar*.** Go ahead, I'll follow.

1 **Father** reverent sir (here a respectful title rather than the more brusque 'old man' that it can also denote).

2–3 **hang . . . end** listen to your words.

5–6 **and so . . . solace** and I have become so accustomed to misery that I now think of sorrow as my greatest comfort.

EUMENIDES
A strange humour. Might I inquire the cause?

GERON
You must pardon me if I deny to tell it, for knowing that the revealing of griefs is, as it were, a renewing of sorrow, I have vowed therefore to conceal them, that I might not only feel the depth of everlasting discontentment, but despair of remedy. But whence are you? What fortune hath thrust you to this distress?

EUMENIDES
I am going to Thessaly, to seek remedy for Endymion, my dearest friend, who hath been cast into a dead sleep almost these twenty years, waxing old and ready for the grave, being almost but newly come forth of the cradle.

GERON
You need not for recure travel far, for whoso can clearly see the bottom of this fountain shall have remedy for anything.

EUMENIDES
That, methinketh, is unpossible. Why, what virtue can there be in water?

GERON
Yes, whosoever can shed the tears of a faithful lover shall obtain anything he would. Read these words engraven about the brim,

EUMENIDES
Have you known this by experience, or is it placed here of purpose to delude men?

GERON
I only would have experience of it, and then should there be an end of my misery; and then would I tell the strangest discourse that ever yet was heard.

EUMENIDES
Ah, Eumenides!

GERON
What lack you, gentleman? Are you not well?

EUMENIDES
Yes, father, but a qualm that often cometh over my heart doth now take hold of me. But did never any lovers come hither?

GERON
Lusters, but not lovers; for often have I seen them weep, but never could I hear they saw the bottom.

EUMENIDES
Came there women also?

GERON
Some.

EUMENIDES
What did they see?

GERON
They all wept, that the fountain overflowed with tears, but so thick became the

12 **whence are you?** where are you going?
16 **recure** remedy.
18 **virtue** special power.
20 **would** desires.
23 **I...it** All I desire is to have experience of it.
27 **qualm** sickness.
29 **Lusters...lovers** Only those who lust, never true lovers.

water with their tears that I could scarce discern the brim, much less behold the bottom.

EUMENIDES

Be faithful lovers so scant?

GERON

It seemeth so, for yet heard I never of any.

EUMENIDES

Ah, Eumenides, how art thou perplexed! Call to mind the beauty of thy sweet mistress and the depth of thy never-dying affections. How oft hast thou honoured her, not only without spot, but suspicion of falsehood. And how hardly hath she rewarded thee without cause or colour of despite. How secret hast thou been these seven years, that hast not, nor once darest not, to name her for discontenting her. How faithful, that hath offered to die for her, to please her. Unhappy Eumenides!

GERON

Why, gentleman, did you once love?

EUMENIDES

Once? Aye, father, and ever shall.

GERON

Was she unkind, and you faithful?

EUMENIDES

She of all women the most froward, and I of all creatures the most fond.

GERON

You doted then, not loved, for affection is grounded on virtue, and virtue is never peevish; or on beauty, and beauty loveth to be praised.

EUMENIDES

Aye, but if all virtuous ladies should yield to all that be loving, or all amiable gentlewomen entertain all that be amorous, their virtues would be accounted vices, and beauties deformities; for that love can be but between two, and that not proceeding of him that is most faithful, but most fortunate.

GERON

I would you were so faithful that your tears might make you fortunate.

EUMENIDES

Yea, father, if that my tears clear not this fountain, then may you swear it is but a mere mockery.

GERON

So saith every one yet that wept.

EUMENIDES

Ah, I faint! I die! Ah, sweet Semele, let me alone, and dissolve, by weeping, into water.

GERON

This affection seemeth strange. If he see nothing, without doubt this

41 **not... suspicion** without even any suspicion.
44 **for discontenting her** for fear of angering her.
49 **froward** stubborn/perverse.
49 **fond** foolish/doting.
52 **all... loving** everyone who loves them (or says that they do)
55 **that... fortunate** true love can only exist between two lovers, and the man is (often) not the most faithful, but simply the luckiest.
60 **dissolve** let me dissolve.
62–63 **this dissembling passeth** he is an excellent ('surpassing') dissembler.

dissembling passeth, for nothing shall draw me from the belief.

EUMENIDES

Father, I plainly see the bottom, and there in white marble engraven these words: 'Ask one for all, and but one thing at all'.

GERON

O fortunate Eumenides (for so have I heard thee call thyself), let me see. I cannot discern any such thing! I think thou dreamest.

EUMENIDES

Ah, father, thou art not a faithful lover and therefore canst not behold it.

GERON

Then ask, that I may be satisfied by the event, and thyself blessed.

EUMENIDES

Ask? So I will. And what shall I do but ask, and whom should I ask but Semele, the possessing of whose person is a pleasure that cannot come within the compass of comparison; whose golden locks seem most curious when they seem most careless, whose sweet looks seem most alluring when they are most chaste, and whose words the more virtuous they are, the more amorous they be accounted? I pray thee, Fortune, when I shall first meet with fair Semele, dash my delight with some light disgrace, lest, embracing sweetness beyond measure, I take a surfeit without recure. Let her practise her accustomed coyness that I may diet myself upon my desires; otherwise the fullness of my joys will diminish the sweetness, and I shall perish by them before I possess them, Why do I trifle the time in words? The least minute being spent in the getting of Semele is more worth than the whole world; therefore let me ask... What now, Eumenides? Whither art thou drawn? Hast thou forgotten both friendship and duty, care of Endymion, and the commandment of Cynthia? Shall he die in a leaden sleep because thou sleepest in a golden dream? Aye, let him sleep ever, so I slumber but one minute with Semele. Love knoweth neither friendship nor kindred.

Shall I not hazard the loss of a friend for the obtaining of her for whom I would often lose myself? Fond Eumenides, shall the enticing beauty of a most disdainful lady be of more force than the rare fidelity of a tried friend? The love of men to women is a thing common and of course; the friendship of man to man infinite and immortal. Tush! Semele doth possess my love. Aye, but Endymion hath deserved it. I will help Endymion. I found Endymion unspotted in his truth. Aye, but I shall find Semele constant in her love. I will have Semele. What shall I do? Father, thy grey hairs are ambassadors of experience. Which shall I ask?

GERON

Eumenides, release Endymion; for all things, friendship excepted, are subject to Fortune. Love is but an eye-worm, which only tickleth the head with hopes

69 **Then...event** That your wish, if it is granted, will prove to me that you have seen the writing.

72 **most curious** intricately arranged.

75–77 **dash...recure** restrict my delight with some small impediment, in case, by experiencing the full delight of her person, I glut myself beyond remedy (with pleasure). (Eumenides imagines himself as the victim in a version of the mythological Semele's experience when she experienced the full glory of her lover Jupiter's divine majesty and was destroyed.)

80 **trifle** waste.

87 **hazard** gamble.

90 **common** mundane.

97 **eye-worm** an infection or malady of the eyes.

and wishes; friendship the image of eternity, in which there is nothing movable, nothing mischievous. As much difference as there is between beauty and virtue, bodies and shadows, colours and life, so great odds is there between love and friendship.

Love is a chameleon, which draweth nothing into the mouth but air, and nourisheth nothing in the body but lungs. Believe me, Eumenides, desire dies in the same moment that beauty sickens, and beauty fadeth in the same instant that it flourisheth. When adversities flow, then love ebbs; but friendship standeth stiffly in storms. Time draweth wrinkles in a fair face, but addeth fresh colours to a fast friend, which neither heat, nor cold, nor misery, nor place, nor destiny can alter or diminish. O friendship, of all things the most rare, and therefore most rare because most excellent, whose comforts in misery [are] always sweet, and whose counsels in prosperity are ever fortunate! Vain love, that only coming near to friendship in name, would seem to be the same or better in nature!

EUMENIDES

Father, I allow your reasons, and will therefore conquer mine own. Virtue shall subdue affections, wisdom lust, friendship beauty. Mistresses are in every place, and as common as hares in Athos, bees in Hybla, fowls in the air; but friends to be found are like the phoenix in Arabia, but one; or the *philadelphi* in Arays, never above two. I will have Endymion. Sacred fountain, in whose bowels are hidden divine secrets, I have increased your waters with the tears of unspotted thoughts, and therefore let me receive the reward you promise. Endymion, the truest friend to me, and faithfullest lover to Cynthia, is in such a dead sleep that nothing can wake or move him.

GERON

Dost thou see anything?

EUMENIDES

I see in the same pillar these words: 'When she, whose figure of all is the perfectest, and never to be measured; always one, yet never the same; still inconstant, yet never wavering, shall come and kiss Endymion in his sleep, he shall then rise, else never.' This is strange.

GERON

What see you else?

EUMENIDES

There cometh over mine eyes either a dark mist, or upon the fountain a deep thickness, for I can perceive nothing. But how am I deluded, or what difficult, nay, impossible, thing is this?

100 **colours and life** deceptive appearances and reality itself.

100 **odds** difference.

102 Chameleons were thought to live on air alone, nourishing themselves through breathing.

106 **stiffly** resolutely.

115 **hares ... Hybla** Mount Athos in northern Greece was noted for its hares and Hybla in Sicily for its fine honey, in Ovid's *Ars Amatoria*, II. 517.

116–117 **phoenix ... two** The legendary phoenix was a unique bird whose death prompted its reincarnation from its own ashes. Who or what the *Philadelphi* ('brotherly lovers') were, or where Arays is (probably not Arras in modern Belgium) is less clear. Bevington suggests they may be Lyly's invention.

126 **else never** otherwise he will never do so.

129 **thickness** fog.

GERON

Methinketh it easy.

EUMENIDES

Good father, and how?

GERON

Is not a circle of all figures the perfectest?

EUMENIDES

Yes.

GERON

And is not Cynthia of all circles the most absolute?

EUMENIDES

Yes.

GERON

Is it not impossible to measure her, who still worketh by her influence, never standing at one stay?

EUMENIDES

Yes.

GERON

Is she not always Cynthia, yet seldom in the same bigness; always wavering in her waxing or waning, that our bodies might the better be governed, our seasons the dailyer give their increase; yet never to be removed from her course, as long as the heavens continue theirs?

EUMENIDES

Yes.

GERON

Then who can it be but Cynthia, whose virtues, being all divine, must needs bring things to pass that be miraculous? Go, humble thyself to Cynthia; tell her the success, of which myself shall be a witness. And this assure thyself, that she that sent to find means for his safety will now work her cunning.

EUMENIDES

How fortunate am I, if Cynthia be she that may do it!

GERON

How fond art thou, if thou do not believe it.

EUMENIDES

I will hasten thither, that I may entreat on my knees for succour, and embrace in mine arms my friend.

GERON

I will go with thee, for unto Cynthia must I discover all my sorrows, who also must work in me a contentment.

EUMENIDES

May I now know the cause?

GERON

That shall be as we walk, and I doubt not but the strangeness of my tale will take away the tediousness of our journey.

137–138 **her . . . stay?** She who eternally governs earthly things by her astrological influence, never remaining in one place/form.

141–142 **seasons . . . increase** each season deliver its produce day by day.

153 **discover** reveal.

Tellus: speculative sol + self-address

EUMENIDES

Let us go.

GERON

I follow. *Exeunt.*

Actus Quartus, Scaena Prima
(Tellus, Corsites.)

TELLUS

I marvel Corsites giveth me so much liberty, all the world knowing his charge to be so high and his nature to be most strange, who hath so ill-treated ladies of great honour that he hath not suffered them to look out of windows, much less to walk abroad. It may be he is in love with me, for (Endymion, hard-hearted Endymion, excepted) what is he that is not enamoured of my beauty? But what respectest thou the love of all the world? Endymion hates thee. Alas, poor Endymion, my malice hath exceeded my love, and thy faith to Cynthia quenched my affections. Quenched, Tellus? Nay, kindled them afresh, insomuch that I find scorching flames for dead embers, and cruel encounters of war in my thoughts instead of sweet parleys. Ah, that I might once again see Endymion! Accursed girl, what hope hast thou to see Endymion, on whose head already are grown grey hairs, and whose life must yield to nature, before Cynthia end her displeasure. Wicked Dipsas, and most devilish Tellus, the one for cunning too exquisite, the other for hate too intolerable. Thou wast commanded to weave the stories and poetries wherein were showed both examples and punishments of tattling tongues, and thou hast only embroidered the sweet face of Endymion, devices of love, melancholy imaginations, and what-not out of thy work, that thou shouldst study to pick out of thy mind. But here cometh Corsites. I must seem yielding and stout, full of mildness, yet tempered with a majesty; for if I be too flexible, I shall give him more hope than I mean; if too froward, enjoy less liberty than I would. Love him I cannot, and therefore will practise that which is most contrary to our sex: to dissemble.

Enter Corsites.

CORSITES

Fair Tellus, I perceive you rise with the lark, and to yourself sing with the nightingale.

TELLUS

My lord, I have no playfellow but fancy. Being barred of all company, I must question with myself, and make my thoughts my friends.

CORSITES

I would you would account my thoughts also your friends, for they be such as are only busied in wondering at your beauty and wisdom; and some such as have esteemed your fortune too hard; and divers of that kind that offer to set you free, if you will set them free.

1–2 **his charge . . . high** either 'his responsibility so great', or 'his prisoner so important'.
2 **strange** reserved/formal.
4 **abroad** outside.
6 **what respectest thou** Tellus addresses herself here.
10 **parleys** talks.
18 **what-not** who knows what else.
23–24 Larks awoke very early, nightingales sang late at night.
28–29 **and some . . . hard** and some of my thoughts think your fate is too harsh.

TELLUS

There are no colours so contrary as white and black, nor elements so disagreeing as fire and water, nor anything so opposite as men's thoughts and their words.

CORSITES

He that gave Cassandra the gift of prophesying, with the curse that, spake she never so true, she should never be believed, hath I think poisoned the fortune of men, that uttering the extremities of their inward passions are always suspected of outward perjuries.

TELLUS

Well, Corsites, I will flatter myself and believe you. What would you do to enjoy my love?

CORSITES

Set all the ladies of the castle free, and make you the pleasure of my life. More I cannot do, less I will not.

TELLUS

These be great words, and fit your calling; for captains must promise things impossible. But will you do one thing for all?

CORSITES

Anything, sweet Tellus, that am ready for all.

TELLUS

You know that on the lunary bank sleepeth Endymion?

CORSITES

I know it.

TELLUS

If you will remove him from that place by force, and convey him into some obscure cave by policy, I give you here the faith of an unspotted virgin that you only shall possess me as a lover, and, in spite of malice, have me for a wife.

CORSITES

Remove him, Tellus? Yes, Tellus, he shall be removed, and that so soon as thou shalt as much commend my diligence as my force. I go.

TELLUS

Stay, will yourself attempt it?

CORSITES

Aye, Tellus, as I would have none partaker of my sweet love, so shall none be partners of my labours. But I pray thee go at your best leisure, for Cynthia beginneth to rise, and if she discover our love, we both perish, for nothing pleaseth her but the fairness of virginity. All things must be not only without lust but without suspicion of lightness.

TELLUS

I will depart, and go you to Endymion.

CORSITES

I fly, Tellus, being of all men the most fortunate. *Exit.*

34 **He** Apollo gave Cassandra the gift of being able to see the future as an inducement to be his lover, but, when she refused, added the curse that whenever she prophesied, she would not be believed.

41 **calling** vocation (as a soldier).

48 **policy** strategy/cunning.

57 **lightness** wantonness.

TELLUS

Simple Corsites, I have set thee about a task, being but a man, the gods themselves cannot perform, for little dost thou know how heavy his head lies, how hard his fortune. But such shifts must women have to deceive men, and under colour of things easy, entreat that which is impossible. Otherwise we should be cumbered with importunities, oaths, sighs, letters, and all implements of love, which to one resolved to the contrary are most loathsome. I will in, and laugh with the other ladies at Corsites' sweating. *Exit.*

Actus Quartus, Scaena Secunda
(Samias, Dares, and Epiton.)

SAMIAS

Will thy master never awake?

DARES

No, I think he sleeps for a wager. But how shall we spend the time? Sir Tophas is so far in love that he pineth in his bed and cometh not abroad.

SAMIAS

But here cometh Epi in a pelting chafe.

EPITON

A pox of all false proverbs, and were a proverb a page, I would have him by the ears!

SAMIAS

Why art thou angry?

EPITON

Why? You know it is said, 'The tide tarrieth no man'.

SAMIAS

True.

EPITON

A monstrous lie; for I was tied two hours, and tarried for one to unloose me.

DARES

Alas, poor Epi!

EPITON

Poor? No, no, you base-conceited slaves, I am a most complete gentleman, although I be in disgrace with Sir Tophas.

DARES

Art thou out with him?

EPITON

Aye, because I cannot get him a lodging with Endymion. He would fain take a nap for forty or fifty years.

DARES

A short sleep, considering our long life.

62 **shifts** expedients/tricks.
64 **cumbered** burdened.
66 **will in** go inside.
4 **pelting chafe** irritable temper.
8 **tarrieth no man** waits for no one.
12 **Poor?** Epi (deliberately?) mistakes Samias' sympathy for a social slur: that he is poor, and so no gentleman.
12 **base-conceited** low-minded.
14 **out** at odds.

SAMIAS
Is he still in love?

EPITON
In love? Why he doth nothing but make sonnets.

SAMIAS
Canst thou remember any one of his poems?

EPITON
Aye, this is one:
'The beggar, Love, that knows not where to lodge,
At last within my heart, when I slept,
He crept,
I waked, and so my fancies began to fodge.'

SAMIAS
That's a very long verse.

EPITON
Why, the other was short: the first is called from the thumb to the little finger, the second from the little finger to the elbow, and some he made to reach to the crown of his head, and down again to the sole of his foot. It is set to the tune of 'The Black Saunce'; *ratio est*, because Dipsas is a black saint.

DARES
Very wisely. But pray thee, Epi, how art thou complete; and being from thy master, what occupation wilt thou take?

EPITON
Know, my hearts, I am an absolute *microcosmus*, a petty world of myself: my library is my head, for I have no other books but my brains; my wardrobe on my back, for I have no more apparel than is on my body; my armoury at my fingers' end, for I use no other artillery than my nails; my treasure in my purse. *Sic omnia mea mecum porto.*

DARES
Good.

EPITON
Know, sirs, my palace is paved with grass, and tiled with stars, for *celo tegitur qui non habet urnam*: he that hath no house must lie in the yard.

SAMIAS
A brave resolution. But how wilt thou spend thy time?

EPITON
Not in any melancholy sort; for mine exercise I will walk horses.

DARES
Too bad.

EPITON
Why, is it not said: 'It is good walking when one hath his horse in his hand'?

25 **fodge** either to move (i.e. become more active) or to accord with each other.

27 **Why...finger** Epi describes the literal length of each poem, as if it were written on a scroll.

30 **'The Black Saunce'** 'The Black Sanctus', a parodic hymn.

30 ***ratio est*** the reason is.

31 **how...complete** in what way are you 'a *complete* gentleman' (as he claimed to be)?

36–37 ***Sic...porto.*** So I carry with me all that I possess (the snail's motto).

39–40 ***celo...urnam*** the heavens cover he who is without a burial urn (Lucan, *Pharsalia*, vii, 819).

44 **Why...hand?** The proverb intends rather that it is good to walk if you also have a horse to ride upon (i.e. if you have better options available). Epi takes it literally to mean it is good to hold onto a horse as you walk.

SAMIAS
Worse and worse! But how wilt thou live?

EPITON
By angling. O, 'tis a stately occupation to stand four hours in a cold morning, and to have his nose bitten with frost before his bait be mumbled with a fish.

DARES
A rare attempt! But wilt thou never travel?

EPITON
Yes, in a western barge, when with a good wind and lusty pugs, one may go ten miles in two days.

SAMIAS
Thou art excellent at thy choice. But what pastime wilt thou use? None?

EPITON
Yes, the quickest of all.

SAMIAS
What, dice?

EPITON
No, when I am in haste, one-and-twenty games at chess, to pass a few minutes.

DARES
A life for a little lord, and full of quickness.

EPITON
Tush, let me alone. But I must needs see if I can find where Endymion lieth, and then go to a certain fountain hard by, where they say faithful lovers shall have all things they will ask. If I can find out any of these, *ego et magister meus erimus in tuto*, I and my master shall be friends. He is resolved to weep some three or four pail-fulls to avoid the rheum of love that wambleth in his stomach.

Enter the Watch [*Master Constable* and Two *Watchmen*].

SAMIAS
Shall we never see thy master, Dares?

DARES
Yes; let us go now, for tomorrow Cynthia will be there.

EPITON
I will go with you; but how shall we see for the Watch?

SAMIAS
Tush, let me alone. I'll begin to them. Masters, God speed you!

FIRST WATCH
Sir boy, we are all sped already.

47 **mumbled with** nibbled by.

48 **A rare attempt!** An excellent answer! (Dares continues to mock Epi's bizarre claims.)

49 **western barge** a barge headed westward on the Thames was notoriously slow, as it was headed against the stream.

49 **lusty pugs** hearty sailors.

58–59 ***ego . . . tuto*** I and my master will be safely harboured.

60 **the rheum . . . wambleth** the fluid of love that rumbles.

64 **how . . . Watch?** How shall we be able to see it, for the watchmen are there to prevent us?

65 **God speed you!** God give you prosperity/health! (A conventional polite greeting.)

66 **sped** exhausted/ruined.

EPITON
So methinks, for they smell all of drink, like a beggar's beard.

DARES
But I pray, sirs, may we see Endymion?

SECOND WATCH
No, we are commanded in Cynthia's name that no man shall see him.

SAMIAS
No man? Why, we are but boys.

FIRST WATCH
Mass, neighbours, he says true, for if I swear I will never drink my liquor by the quart, and yet call for two pints, I think with a safe conscience I may carouse both.

DARES
Pithily, and to the purpose.

SECOND WATCH
Tush, tush, neighbours, take me with you.

SAMIAS
This will grow hot!

DARES
Let them alone.

SECOND WATCH
If I say to my wife, 'Wife, I will have no raisins in my pudding', she puts in currants. Small raisins are raisins, and boys are men: even as my wife should have put no raisins in my pudding, so shall there no boys see Endymion.

DARES
Learnedly.

EPITON
Let Master Constable speak; I think he is the wisest among you.

MASTER CONSTABLE
You know, neighbours, 'tis an old said saw, 'Children and fools speak true.'

ALL
True.

MASTER CONSTABLE
Well, there you see the men be the fools, because it is provided from the children.

DARES
Good.

MASTER CONSTABLE
Then, say I, neighbours, that children must not see Endymion, because children and fools speak true.

EPITON
O wicked application!

71 **Mass** By the Mass! (An old Catholic oath.)
70–73 **we . . . both** the analogy is not without a kind of shrewd sense. Samias has, by redefining himself as a boy, tried to evade the bar on men having access to Endymion. Similarly, the Watchmen might, while promising never to drink a quart of ale (a two-pint measure), drink the same amount in two separate pints with impunity.
75 **take . . . you** explain this to me.
76 **This . . . hot!** This'll end in a fight!
77 **Let them alone.** Let them get on with it.
79 **currants** small raisins.
83 **an . . . saw** an old and common proverb.
85 **provided from** proved by.
90 **application** conclusion (application of logic).

SAMIAS
Scurvily brought about!

FIRST WATCH
Nay, he says true, and therefore, till Cynthia have been here, he shall not be uncovered. Therefore, away!

DARES
A Watch, quoth you? A man may watch seven years for a wise word, and yet go without it. Their wits are all as rusty as their bills. But come on, Master Constable, shall we have a song before we go?

MASTER CONSTABLE
With all my heart.

[THE SECOND SONG.

THE TWO WATCHMEN
Stand! Who goes there?
We charge you appear
'Fore our constable here,
In the name of the Man in the Moon.
To us billmen relate
Why you stagger so late,
And how you come drunk so soon.

PAGES
What are ye, scabs?

WATCH
The Watch: this the Constable.

PAGES
A patch!

CONSTABLE
Knock 'em down unless they all stand.
If any run away,
'Tis the old watchman's play,
To reach him a bill of his hand.

PAGES
O gentlemen, hold,
Your gowns freeze with cold,
And your rotten teeth dance in your head;

EPITON
Wine, nothing shall cost ye;

SAMIAS
Nor huge fires to roast ye;

91 **Scurvily brought about!** Wretchedly argued!
95 **bills** bill-hooks/halberds, a standard weapon of watchmen.
97.1 Taken from Blount's *Six Court Comedies*.
105 **scabs** rogues.
107 **patch** fool.
110–111 **'Tis . . . hand.** It's the old watchman's trick to give him a whack with his billhook.
112 **hold** stop.
115–116 **Wine . . . roast ye** i.e. let us buy you a drink, and find you a roaring fire to sit beside.

DARES

Then soberly let us be led.

CONSTABLE

Come, my brown bills, we'll roar,
Bounce loud at tavern door,

OMNES

And i' the morning steal all to bed.

Exeunt.]

Actus Quartus, Scaena tertia
(Corsites solus)

CORSITES

I am come in sight of the lunary bank. Without doubt Tellus doteth upon me, and cunningly, that I might not perceive her love, she hath set me to a task that is done before it is begun. Endymion, you must change your pillow, and if you be not weary of sleep, I will carry you where at ease you shall sleep your fill. It were good that without more ceremonies I took him, lest, being espied, I be entrapped, and so incur the displeasure of Cynthia, who commonly setteth watch that Endymion have no wrong. *He lifts.*

What now, is your mastership so heavy? Or are you nailed to the ground? Not stir one whit? Then use all thy force, though he feel it and wake.

What, stone-still? Turned, I think, to earth with lying so long on the earth. Didst not thou, Corsites, before Cynthia, pull up a tree that forty years was fastened with roots and wreathed in knots to the ground? Didst not thou, with main force, pull open the iron gates which no ram or engine could move? Have my weak thoughts made brawn-fallen my strong arms, or is it the nature of love, or the quintessence of the mind, to breed numbness or litherness, or I know not what languishing in my joints and sinews, being but the base strings of my body? Or doth the remembrance of Tellus so refine my spirits into a matter so subtle and divine that the other fleshy parts cannot work whilst they muse? Rest thyself, rest thyself; nay, ren[d] thyself in pieces, Corsites, and strive, in spite of love, fortune, and nature, to lift up this dulled body, heavier than dead and more senseless than death. *Enter Fairies.*

But what are these so fair fiends that cause my hairs to stand upright and spirits to fall down? Hags? Out alas, nymphs, I crave pardon. Ay me, but what do I hear?

The Fairies dance, and with a song pinch him, and he falleth asleep.
They kiss Endymion and depart.

118 **my brown bills** my bill-men.
119 **roar, bounce** shout (and) knock.
119.1 ***Omnes*** everyone.
120 **steal all** everyone creep.
solus alone.
1 **doteth upon me** adores me.
9 **one whit** even a little.
12 **main force** great strength.
13 **ram or engine** battering-ram or siege engine.
14 **brawn-fallen** unmanned/reduced in strength.
15 **litherness** lassitude.
16 **base strings** lowest organs.
23 **Out alas!** Woe is me!

[THE THIRD SONG, BY FAERIES

Pinch him, pinch him, black and blue.
Saucy mortals must not view
What the Queen of Stars is doing,
Nor pry into our fairy wooing.

FIRST FAIRY

Pinch him blue.

SECOND FAIRY

And pinch him black.

THIRD FAIRY

Let him not lack
Sharp nails to pinch him blue and red,
Till sleep has rocked his addle head.

FOURTH FAIRY

For the trespass he hath done,
Spots o'er all his flesh shall run.
Kiss Endymion, kiss his eyes,
Then to our midnight hey-de-guise.]

[Actus Quartus, Scaena Quinta]
(Cynthia, Floscula, Semele, Panelion, Zontes, Pythagoras, Gyptes, Corsites.)

CYNTHIA

You see, Pythagoras, what ridiculous opinions you hold, and I doubt not but you are now of another mind.

PYTHAGORAS

Madam, I plainly perceive that the perfection of your brightness hath pierced through the thickness that covered my mind; insomuch that I am no less glad to be reformed than ashamed to remember my grossness.

GYPTES

They are thrice fortunate that live in your palace, where truth is not in colours but life, virtues not in imagination but execution.

CYNTHIA

I have always studied to have rather living virtues than painted gods, the body of truth than the tomb. But let us walk to Endymion; it may be it lieth in your arts to deliver him. As for Eumenides, I fear he is dead.

PYTHAGORAS

I have alleged all the natural reasons I can for such a long sleep.

GYPTES

I can do nothing till I see him.

CYNTHIA

Come, Floscula, I am sure you are glad that you shall behold Endymion.

FLOSCULA

I were blessed if I might have him recovered.

24.1 From Blount's *Six Court Comedies*.
27 **Queen of Stars** Cynthia.
33 **addle** addled/befuddled.
35 **Spots ... run** they cover him in spots.
37 **hey-de-guise** a country dance,
11 **alleged** described to you.

CYNTHIA
Are you in love with his person?

FLOSCULA
No, but with his virtue.

CYNTHIA
What say you, Semele?

SEMELE
Madam, I dare say nothing, for fear I offend.

CYNTHIA
Belike you cannot speak except you be spiteful. But as good be silent as saucy. Panelion, what punishment were fit for Semele, in whose speech and thoughts is only contempt and sourness?

PANELION
I love not, madam, to give any judgement. Yet, sith your highness commandeth, I think to commit her tongue close prisoner to her mouth.

CYNTHIA
Agreed. Semele, if thou speak this twelve-month, thou shalt forfeit thy tongue. Behold Endymion. Alas, poor gentleman, hast thou spent thy youth in sleep, that once vowed all to my service? Hollow eyes, grey hairs, wrinkled cheeks, and decayed limbs. Is it destiny or deceit that hath brought this to pass? If the first, who could prevent thy wretched stars? If the latter, I would I might know thy cruel enemy. I favoured thee, Endymion, for thy honour, thy virtues, thy affections; but, to bring thy thoughts within the compass of thy fortunes, I have seemed strange, that I might have thee stayed, and now are thy days ended before my favour begin. But whom have we here? Is it not Corsites?

ZONTES
It is, but more like a leopard than a man.

CYNTHIA
Awake him. How now, Corsites, what make you here? How came you deformed? Look on thy hands, and then thou seest the picture of thy face.

CORSITES
Miserable wretch, and accursed. How am I deluded? Madam, I ask pardon for my offence, and you see my fortune deserveth pity.

CYNTHIA
Speak on, thy offence cannot deserve greater punishment; but see thou rehearse the truth, else shalt thou not find me as thou wishest me.

CORSITES
Madam, as it is no offence to be in love, being a man mortal, so I hope can it be no shame to tell with whom, my lady being heavenly. Your majesty committed to my charge fair Tellus, whose beauty in the same moment took my heart captive that I undertook to carry her body prisoner. Since that time have I found such combats in my thoughts between love and duty, reverence and affection, that I could neither endure the conflict, nor hope for the conquest.

22 **sith** since.
28 **stars** fate.
30 **to bring... fortunes** to help you to fashion your hopes in accordance with your position (i.e. to forestall his hopes of her loving him).
31 **stayed** stopped you/held you back.
33 **like... man** i.e. spotted.
34 **what... here?** what are you doing?
38 **greater punishment** i.e. than it already has.
39 **rehearse** speak.

CYNTHIA

In love? A thing far unfitting the name of a captain, and (as I thought) the tough and unsmoothed nature of Corsites. But forth.

CORSITES

Feeling this continual war, I thought rather by parley to yield than by certain danger to perish. I unfolded to Tellus the depth of my affections, and framed my tongue to utter a sweet tale of love, that was wont to sound nothing but threats of war. She, too fair to be true and too false for one so fair, after a nice denial, practised a notable deceit, commanding me to remove Endymion from this cabin, and carry him to some dark cave; which I, seeking to accomplish, found impossible, and so by fairies or fiends have been thus handled.

CYNTHIA

How say you, my lords, is not Tellus always practising of some deceits. In sooth, Corsites, thy face is now too foul for a lover, and thine heart too fond for a soldier. You may see when warriors become wantons how their manners alter with their faces. Is it not a shame, Corsites, that, having lived so long in Mars' camp, thou shouldst now be rocked in Venus' cradle? Dost thou wear Cupid's quiver at thy girdle and make lances of looks? Well, Corsites, rouse thyself and be as thou hast been; and let Tellus, who is made all of love, melt herself in her own looseness.

CORSITES

Madam, I doubt not but to recover my former state, for Tellus' beauty never wrought such love in my mind as now her deceit hath despite; and yet to be revenged of a woman were a thing than love itself more womanish.

GYPTES

These spots, gentleman, are to be worn out, if you rub them over with this lunary, so that in the place where you received this maim you shall find a medicine.

CORSITES

I thank you for that. The gods bless me from love and these pretty ladies that haunt this green.

FLOSCULA

Corsites, I would Tellus saw your amiable face.

ZONTES

How spitefully Semele laugheth, that dare not speak.

CYNTHIA

Could you not stir Endymion with that doubled strength of yours?

CORSITES

Not so much as his finger, with all my force.

CYNTHIA

Pythagoras and Gyptes, what think you of Endymion? What reason is to be given, what remedy?

PYTHAGORAS

Madam, it is impossible to yield reason for things that happen not in compass

47 **forth** carry on.
50 **wont to** used to.
51 **nice** cunning.
64 **hath despite** has created hate.
65 **of** upon.
65 **than . . . womanish** more womanish than love itself.
77 **in compass** within the realm.

of nature. It is most certain that some strange enchantment hath bound all his senses.

CYNTHIA
What say you, Gyptes?

GYPTES
With Pythagoras, that it is enchantment, and that so strange that no art can undo it, for that heaviness argueth a malice unremovable in the enchantress, and that no power can end it, till she die that did it, or the heavens show some means more miraculous.

FLOSCULA
O Endymion, could spite itself devise a mischief so monstrous as to make thee dead with life, and living, being altogether dead? Where others number their years, their hours, their minutes, and step to age by stairs, thou only hast thy years and times in a cluster, being old before thou rememberest thou wast young.

CYNTHIA
No more, Floscula; pity doth him no good. I would anything else might; and I vow by the unspotted honour of a lady he should not miss it. But is this all, Gyptes, that is to be done?

GYPTES
All as yet. It may be that either the enchantress shall die or else be discovered. If either happen, I will then practise the utmost of my art. In the mean season, about this grove would I have a watch, and the first living thing that toucheth Endymion to be taken.

CYNTHIA
Corsites, what say you, will you undertake this?

CORSITES
Good madam, pardon me. I was overtaken too late. I should rather break into the midst of a main battle than again fall into the hands of those fair babies.

CYNTHIA
Well, I will provide others. Pythagoras and Gyptes, you shall yet remain in my court, till I hear what may be done in this matter.

PYTHAGORAS
We attend.

CYNTHIA
Let us go in. *Exeunt.*

Actus Quintus, Scaena Primus
(Samias, Dares.)

SAMIAS
Eumenides hath told such strange tales as I may well wonder at them, but never believe them.

82 **unremovable... enchantress** not even removable by the enchantress who cast the spell.
87 **stairs** gradual steps.
88 **in a cluster** all at once.
91 **he... it** he would not lack it.
94 **main season** meantime.
96 **taken** arrested.
98 **overtaken too late** overcome too recently (by the faeries).
99 **main** full-scale.

DARES

The other old man, what a sad speech used he, that caused us almost all to weep. Cynthia is so desirous to know the experiment of her own virtue, and so willing to ease Endymion's hard fortune, that she no sooner heard the discourse but she made herself in a readiness to try the event.

SAMIAS

We will also see the event. But whist, here cometh Cynthia with all her train. Let us sneak in amongst them.

Enter Cynthia, Floscula, Semele, Panelion, etc.
[*Eumenides, Zontes, Pyhtagoras, Gyptes*].

CYNTHIA

Eumenides, it cannot sink into my head that I should be signified by that sacred fountain, for many things are there in the world to which those words may be applied.

EUMENIDES

Good madam, vouchsafe but to try; else shall I think myself most unhappy that I asked not my sweet mistress.

CYNTHIA

Will you not yet tell me her name?

EUMENIDES

Pardon me, good madam, for if Endymion awake he shall, myself have sworn never to reveal it.

CYNTHIA

Well, let us to Endymion. I will not be so stately, good Endymion, not to stoop to do thee good, and if thy liberty consist in a kiss from me, thou shalt have it. And, although my mouth hath been heretofore as untouched as my thoughts, yet now to recover thy life, though to restore thy youth it be impossible, I will do that to Endymion which yet never mortal man could boast of heretofore, nor shall ever hope for hereafter. *She kisseth him.*

EUMENIDES

Madam, he beginneth to stir.

CYNTHIA

Soft, Eumenides; stand still.

EUMENIDES

Ah, I see his eyes almost open.

CYNTHIA

I command thee once again, stir not; I will stand behind him.

PANELION

What do I see? Endymion almost awake?

3 **old man** Geron.
4 **to know . . . virtue** test out her own powers (by trying Geron's idea that a kiss from her will cure Endymion).
6 **try the event** put the matter to trial.
7 **whist** hush.
8 **train** entourage.
9–10 **that . . . fountain** that the inscription on the fountain refers to me.
12 **vouchsafe but** agree only.
13 **my sweet mistress** (for) my mistress' love (rather than Endymion's recovery).
17 **stately** formal.
24 **Soft** Quiet.

EUMENIDES

Endymion, Endymion, art thou deaf or dumb, or hath this long sleep taken away thy memory? Ah, my sweet Endymion, seest thou not Eumenides, thy faithful friend, thy faithful Eumenides, who for thy safety hath been careless of his own content? Speak, Endymion. Endymion! Endymion!

ENDYMION

Endymion? I call to mind such a name.

EUMENIDES

Hast thou forgotten thyself, Endymion? Then do I not marvel thou rememberest not thy friend. I tell thee thou art Endymion and I Eumenides. Behold also Cynthia, by whose favour thou art awaked, and by whose virtue thou shalt continue thy natural course.

CYNTHIA

Endymion, speak. Sweet Endymion, knowest thou not Cynthia?

ENDYMION

O heavens, whom do I behold? Fair Cynthia, divine Cynthia?

CYNTHIA

I am Cynthia, and thou Endymion.

ENDYMION

'Endymion'? What do I hear? What, a grey beard, hollow eyes, withered body, decayed limbs, and all in one night?

EUMENIDES

One night? Thou hast here slept forty years, by what enchantress as yet it is not known, and behold, the twig to which thou laidest thy head is now become a tree. Callest thou not Eumenides to remembrance?

ENDYMION

Thy name I do remember by the sound, but thy favour I do not yet call to mind; only divine Cynthia, to whom time, fortune, destiny, and death are subject, I see and remember, and in all humility I regard and reverence.

CYNTHIA

You have good cause to remember Eumenides, who hath for thy safety forsaken his own solace.

ENDYMION

Am I that Endymion who was wont in court to lead my life, and in jousts, tourneys, and arms to exercise my youth? Am I that Endymion?

EUMENIDES

Thou art that Endymion, and I Eumenides. Wilt thou not yet call me to remembrance?

ENDYMION

Ah, sweet Eumenides, I now perceive thou art he, and that myself have the name of Endymion. But that this should be my body I doubt, for how could my curled locks be turned to grey hairs and my strong body to a dying weakness, having waxed old, and not knowing it.

CYNTHIA

Well, Endymion, arise. Awhile sit down, for that thy limbs are stiff and not able

31 **content** happiness.
32 **call to mind** remember.
36 **natural course** life.
43 **(the twig) to which** against.
45 **favour** face.

to stay thee, and tell what hast thou seen in thy sleep all this while, what dreams, visions, thoughts, and fortunes; for it is impossible but in so long time thou shouldst see things strange.

ENDYMION

Fair Cynthia, I will rehearse what I have seen, humbly desiring that when I exceed in length, you give me warning, that I may end. For to utter all I have to speak would be troublesome, although haply the strangeness may somewhat abate the tediousness.

CYNTHIA

Well, Endymion, begin.

ENDYMION

Methought I saw a lady passing fair, but very mischievous, who in the one hand carried a knife, with which she offered to cut my throat, and in the other a looking-glass, wherein, seeing how ill anger became ladies, she refrained from intended violence. She was accompanied with other damsels, one of which, with a stern countenance, and as it were with a settled malice engraven in her eyes, provoked her to execute mischief. Another, with visage sad, and constant only in sorrow, with her arms crossed, and watery eyes, seemed to lament my fortune, but durst not offer to prevent the force. I started in my sleep, feeling my very veins to swell and my sinews to stretch with fear, and such a cold sweat bedewed all my body that death itself could not be so terrible as the vision.

CYNTHIA

A strange sight. Gyptes, at our better leisure, shall expound it.

ENDYMION

After long debating with herself, mercy overcame anger, and there appeared in her heavenly face such a divine majesty, mingled with a sweet mildness, that I was ravished with the sight above measure, and wished that I might have enjoyed the sight without end. And so she departed with the other ladies, of which the one retained still an unmovable cruelty, the other a constant pity.

CYNTHIA

Poor Endymion, how wast thou affrighted. What else?

ENDYMION

After her, immediately appeared an aged man, with a beard as white as snow, carrying in his hand a book with three leaves, and speaking, as I remember, these words: 'Endymion, receive this book with three leaves, in which are contained counsels, policies, and pictures'. And with that he offered me the book, which I rejected; wherewith, moved with a disdainful pity, he rent the first leaf in a thousand shivers. The second time he offered it, which I refused also; at which, bending his brows, and pitching his eyes fast to the ground, as though they were fixed to the earth, and not again to be removed, then suddenly casting them up to the heavens, he tore in a rage the second leaf, and offered the book only with one leaf. I know not whether fear to offend or desire to know some strange thing moved me, I took the book, and so the old man vanished.

59 **stay** support.
63 **exceed in length** go on too long.
64 **haply** perhaps.
67 **passing fair** exceedingly beautiful.
72 **visage** face.
73 **with . . . crossed** a traditionally melancholic stance.
77 **at our . . . it** shall interpret it when we have more time.
85 **leaves** pages.
89 **shivers** fragments.
90 **pitching . . . ground** turning his eyes firmly toward the ground.

CYNTHIA

What didst thou imagine was in the last leaf?

ENDYMION

There, aye portrayed to life, with a cold quaking in every joint, I beheld many wolves barking at thee, Cynthia, who having ground their teeth to bite, did with striving bleed themselves to death. There might I see Ingratitude with an hundred eyes gazing for benefits, and with a thousand teeth gnawing on the bowels wherein she was bred. Treachery stood all clothed in white, with a smiling countenance, but both her hands bathed in blood. Envy, with a pale and meagre face (whose body was so lean that one might tell all her bones, and whose garment was so tattered that it was easy to number every thread) stood shooting at stars, whose darts fell down again on her own face. There might I behold drones or beetles, I know not how to term them, creeping under the wings of a princely eagle, who, being carried into her nest, sought there to suck that vein that would have killed the eagle. I mused that things so base should attempt a fact so barbarous, or durst imagine a thing so bloody, and many other things, madam, the repetition whereof may at your better leisure seem more pleasing. For bees surfeit sometimes with honey, and the gods are glutted with harmony, and your highness may be dulled with delight.

CYNTHIA

I am content to be dieted; therefore, let us in. Eumenides, see that Endymion be well tended, lest either eating immoderately or sleeping again too long, he fall into a deadly surfeit or into his former sleep. See this also be proclaimed: that whosoever will discover this practice shall have of Cynthia infinite thanks and no small rewards. *Exit.*

FLOSCULA

Ah, Endymion, none so joyful as Floscula of thy restoring.

EUMENIDES

Yes, Floscula, let Eumenides be somewhat gladder, and do not that wrong to the settled friendship of a man as to compare it with the light affection of a woman. Ah, my dear friend Endymion, suffer me to die with gazing at thee.

ENDYMION

Eumenides, thy friendship is immortal and not to be conceived; and thy good will, Floscula, better than I have deserved. But let us all wait on Cynthia. I marvel Semele speaketh not a word.

EUMENIDES

Because if she do, she loseth her tongue.

ENDYMION

But how prospereth your love?

EUMENIDES

I never yet spake word since your sleep.

102 **tell** count (with the fingers).
108 **fact** feat/act.
113 **tended** looked after.
114 **deadly surfeit** fatal illness brought on by overeating.
115 **discover this practice** reveal the truth about this matter.
119 **settled** fixed/constant.
121 **not...conceived** is beyond human understanding.

ENDYMION

I doubt not but your affection is old and your appetite cold.

EUMENIDES

No, Endymion, thine hath made it stronger, and now are my sparks grown to flames and my fancies almost to frenzies. But let us follow, and within we will debate all this matter at large. *Exeunt.*

Actus Quintus, Scaena Secunda
(Sir Tophas, Epiton)

TOPHAS

Epi, love hath jostled my liberty from the wall, and taken the upper hand of my reason.

EPITON

Let me then trip up the heels of your affection and thrust your good will into the gutter.

TOPHAS

No, Epi, Love is a lord of misrule and keepeth Christmas in my corpse.

EPITON

No doubt there is good cheer: what dishes of delight doth his lordship feast you with withal?

TOPHAS

First, with a great platter of plum porridge of pleasure, wherein is stewed the mutton of mistrust.

EPITON

Excellent love-lap.

TOPHAS

Then cometh a pie of patience, a hen of honey, a goose of gall, a capon of care, and many other viands, some sweet and some sour, which proveth love to be, as was said of it in old years, *dulce venenum.*

EPITON

A brave banquet.

TOPHAS

But, Epi, I pray thee feel on my chin; something pricketh me. What dost thou feel or see?

EPITON

There are three or four little hairs.

TOPHAS

I pray thee call it my beard. How shall I be troubled when this young spring shall grow to a great wood?

130 **at large** freely.

1 **jostled ... wall** pushed it from prime position (to 'take the wall' as one passed on the street was to claim superior status, making the other stand closer to the cart-way, where one could be splashed with mud or worse).

5 **keepeth Christmas** holds a long (twelve-day) party, characterized by misrule.

8–9 **stewed ... mutton** 'mutton' being a slang term for an older prostitute, and 'stew' being a brothel, there are clear sexual overtones to Tophas' mistrust.

10 **love-lap** love-food.

12 **viands** foods.

13 ***dulce venenum*** sweet venom.

14 **brave** splendid.

18 **young spring** thicket of young saplings.

EPITON

Oh, sir, your chin is but a quiller yet. You will be most majestical when it is full-fledged. But I marvel that you love Dipsas, that old crone.

TOPHAS

Agnosco veteris vestigia flamme. I love the smoke of an old fire.

EPITON

Why, she is so cold that no fire can thaw her thoughts.

TOPHAS

It is an old goose, Epi, that will eat no oats. Old kine will kick, old rats gnaw cheese, and old sacks will have much patching. I prefer an old cony before a rabbit-sucker, and an ancient hen before a young chicken-peeper.

EPITON

Argumentum ab antiquitate; my master loveth antique work.

TOPHAS

Give me a pippin that is withered like an old wife.

EPITON

Good, sir.

TOPHAS

Then, *a contrario sequitur argumentum*, give me a wife that looks like an old pippin.

EPITON

Nothing hath made my master a fool but flat scholarship.

TOPHAS

Knowest thou not that old wine is best?

EPITON

Yes.

TOPHAS

And thou knowest that like will to like?

EPITON

Aye.

TOPHAS

And thou knowest that Venus loved the best wine?

EPITON

So.

TOPHAS

Then I conclude that Venus was an old woman in an old cup of wine, for *est Venus in vinis, ignis in igne fuit*.

EPITON

O lepidum caput! O madcap master! You were worthy to win Dipsas, were

20 **a quiller** a chick/unfledged bird.
22 ***Agnosco...famme.*** I know the remnants of an old fire (Virgil, *The Aeneid*, IV, 23).
24 **kine** cattle.
25 **cony** rabbit.
26 **rabbit-sucker** suckling/baby rabbit.
26 **chicken-peeper** chick.
27 ***Argumentum ab antiquitate*** an argument from classical sources.
27 **antique work** both 'the classics' and an old woman.
28 **pippin** apple.
30 ***a...argumentum*** the truth follows from the opposite.
32 **flat** plain/clear.
35 **like...like** similar things attract each other.
39–40 ***est...fuit*** Venus in wine is fire in fire (Ovid, *Ars Amatoria*, i, 244).
41 ***O lepidum caput!*** Oh fine head!
41–42 **were...again** if she were twice her age.

she as old again, for in your love you have worn the nap of your wit quite off and made it threadbare. But soft, who comes here?

TOPHAS

My solicitors.

SAMIAS

All hail, Sir Tophas; how feel you yourself?

TOPHAS

Stately in every joint, which the common people term stiffness. Doth Dipsas stoop? Will she yield? Will she bend?

DARES

Oh, sir, as much as you would wish, for her chin almost toucheth her knees.

EPITON

Master, she is bent, I warrant you.

TOPHAS

What conditions doth she ask?

SAMIAS

She hath vowed she will never love any that hath not a tooth in his head less than she.

TOPHAS

How many hath she?

DARES

One.

EPITON

That goeth hard, master, for then you must have none.

TOPHAS

A small request, and agreeable to the gravity of her years. What should a wise man do with his mouth full of bones like a charnel-house? The turtle true hath ne'er a tooth.

SAMIAS

Thy master is in a notable vein, that will lose his teeth to be like a turtle.

EPITON

Let him lose his tongue too, I care not.

DARES

Nay, you must also have no nails, for she long since hath cast hers.

TOPHAS

That I yield too. What a quiet life shall Dipsas and I lead when we can neither bite nor scratch. You may see, youths, how age provides for peace.

SAMIAS

How shall we do to make him leave his love, for we never spake to her?

DARES

Let me alone. She is a notable witch, and hath turned her maid Bagoa to an aspen tree for bewraying her secrets.

44 **my solicitors** i.e. those he has asked to 'solicit' his case for him with Dipsas.
47 **stoop** bend to my request (but also literally stoop with age).
55 **That goeth hard** That's bad news.
57 **charnel-house** mausoleum.
57 **The turtle true** The faithful turtle-dove (symbol of love).
61 **cast** shed them (like an animal).
65 **Let me alone.** Leave it to me.
66 **bewraying** revealing.

TOPHAS

I honour her for her cunning. For now when I am weary of walking on two legs, what a pleasure may she do me to turn me to some goodly ass, and help me to four.

DARES

Nay, then I must tell you the truth. Her husband, Geron, is come home, who this fifty years hath had her to wife.

TOPHAS

What do I hear? Hath she an husband? Go to the sexton and tell him desire is dead, and will him to dig his grave. O heavens, an husband! What death is agreeable to my fortune?

SAMIAS

Be not desperate, and we will help you to find a young lady.

TOPHAS

I love no grissels; they are so brittle they will crack like glass, or so dainty that if they be touched they are straight of the fashion of wax. *Animus maioribus instat*? I desire old matrons. What a sight would it be to embrace one whose hair were as orient as the pearl, whose teeth shall be so pure a watchet that they shall stain the truest turquoise; whose nose shall throw more beams from it than the fiery carbuncle, whose eyes shall be environed about with redness exceeding the deepest coral, and whose lips might compare with silver for the paleness. Such a one if you can help me to, will by piecemeal curtail my affections towards Dipsas, and walk my swelling thoughts till they be cold.

EPITON

Wisely provided. How say you, my friends, will you angle for my master's cause?

SAMIAS

Most willingly.

DARES

If we speed him not shortly, I will burn my cap. We will serve him of the spades, and dig an old wife out of the grave that shall be answerable to his gravity.

TOPHAS

Youths, adieu; he that bringeth me first news shall possess mine inheritance. [*Exit.*]

DARES

What, is thy master landed?

EPITON

Know you not that my master is *liber tenens*?

72 **sexton** the official in charge of burials and the graveyard.

73–74 **is agreeable** could be appropriate to/commensurate with.

76 **grissels** Griseldas/young women (the well-known story of 'Patient Griselda', the subject of Chaucer's *Clerk's Tale*, portrayed the heroine as the notionally perfect, virtuous young woman).

77–78 ***Animus maioribus instat?*** My soul seeks greater subjects? (Ovid, *Ars Amatoria*, ii, 535)

79 **orient** shining/white.

79 **watchet** pale blue.

83 **by piecemeal** bit by bit.

84 **walk** exercise/train.

85 **angle** plan a remedy.

88 **speed him** provide for him/help him to prosper.

88 **of the** with.

89 **answerable to** fitting for.

92 **is...landed?** does he own lands?

93 ***liber tenens*** a landowner with a life-long freehold.

SAMIAS
What's that?

EPITON
A freeholder. But I will after him.

SAMIAS
And we to hear what news of Endymion for the conclusion. [*Exeunt.*]

Actus Quintus, Scaena tertia
(Panelion, Zontes.)

PANELION
Who would have thought that Tellus, being so fair by nature, so honourable by birth, so wise by education, would have entered into a mischief to the gods so odious, to men so detestable, and to her friend so malicious.

ZONTES
If Bagoa had not bewrayed it, how then should it have come to light? But we see that gold and fair words are of force to corrupt the strongest men, and therefore able to work silly women like wax.

PANELION
I marvel what Cynthia will determine in this cause.

ZONTES
I fear as in all causes: hear of it in justice, and then judge of it in mercy. For how can it be that she that is unwilling to punish her deadliest foes with disgrace, will revenge injuries of her train with death.

PANELION
That old witch, Dipsas, in a rage, having understood her practice to be discovered, turned poor Bagoa to an aspen tree. But let us make haste and bring Tellus before Cynthia, for she was coming out after us.

ZONTES
Let us go. *Exeunt.*

[Actus Quintus, Scaena quarta]
(Cynthia, Semele, Floscula, Dipsas, Endymion, Eumenides
[Geron, Pythagoras, Gyptes, and Sir Tophas.])

CYNTHIA
Dipsas, thy years are not so many as thy vices, yet more in number than commonly nature doth afford or justice should permit. Hast thou almost these fifty years practised that detested wickedness of witchcraft? Wast thou, so simple as for to know the nature of simples, of all creatures to be most sinful? Thou hast threatened to turn my course awry and alter by thy damnable art the government that I now possess by the eternal gods. But know thou, Dipsas, and let all the enchanters know, that Cynthia, being placed for light on earth, is also protected by the powers of heaven. Breathe out thou mayest words, gather thou mayest herbs, find out thou mayest stones agreeable to thine art, yet of no

[5] **of force** strong enough.
[6] **work silly women** shape innocent//foolish women.
[7] **marvel** wonder.
[3–4] **Wast . . . simples** (Who was) so foolish as to seek to understand the nature of potions.
[9] **mayest . . art** minerals and gems useful in potion-making.
[9–10] **no . . . appal** unable to dismay.

force to appal my heart, in which courage is so rooted and constant persuasion of the mercy of the gods so grounded, that all thy witchcraft I esteem as weak as the world doth thy case wretched.

This noble gentleman, Geron, once thy husband, but now thy mortal hate, didst thou procure to live in a desert, almost desperate. Endymion, the flower of my court and the hope of succeeding time, hast thou bewitched by art, before thou wouldst suffer him to flourish by nature.

DIPSAS

Madam, things past may be repented, not recalled. There is nothing so wicked that I have not done, nor anything so wished for as death. Yet among all the things that I committed, there is nothing so much tormenteth my rented and ransacked thoughts as that in the prime of my husband's youth I divorced him by my devilish art; for which, if to die might be amends, I would not live till tomorrow. If to live and still be more miserable would better content him, I would wish of all creatures to be oldest and ugliest.

GERON

Dipsas, thou hast made this difference between me and Endymion, that being both young, thou hast caused me to wake in melancholy, losing the joys of my youth, and him to sleep, not remembering youth.

CYNTHIA

Stay, here cometh Tellus; we shall now know all.

Enter Corsites, Tellus, Panelion, etc. [*Zontes*].

CORSITES

I would to Cynthia thou couldst make as good an excuse in truth as to me thou hast done by wit.

TELLUS

Truth shall be mine answer, and therefore I will not study for an excuse.

CYNTHIA

Is it possible, Tellus, that so few years should harbour so many mischiefs? Thy swelling pride have I borne, because it is a thing that beauty maketh blameless, which, the more it exceedeth fairness in measure, the more it stretcheth itself in disdain. Thy devices against Corsites I smile at, for that wits, the sharper they are, the shrewder they are. But this unacquainted and most unnatural practice with a vile enchantress against so noble a gentleman as Endymion I abhor as a thing most malicious, and will revenge as a deed most monstrous.

And as for you, Dipsas, I will send you into the desert amongst wild beasts, and try whether you can cast lions, tigers, boars, and bears into as dead a sleep as you did Endymion, or turn them to trees, as you have done Bagoa. But tell me,

13–14 **didst...desert** you plotted to force him to live in a wilderness (the area around the magical fountain, a wild, uninhabited place).

19 **rented** tattered.

32 **borne** tolerated.

33 **maketh blameless** excuses.

33–34 **the more...disdain** the more than normally beautiful one is, the more proud and disdainful one is likely to become.

34 **devices** plots/tricks.

35 **for that** because.

35 **unacquainted** so far un-encountered (i.e. worse than anything I've ever known).

40 **try** test.

Tellus, what was the cause of this cruel part, far unfitting thy sex, in which nothing should be but simpleness; and much disagreeing from thy face, in which nothing seemed to be but softness?

TELLUS

Divine Cynthia, by whom I receive my life and am content to end it, I can neither excuse my fault without lying, nor confess it without shame. Yet, were it possible that in so heavenly thoughts as yours there could fall such earthly motions as mine, I would then hope, if not to be pardoned without extreme punishment, yet to be heard without great marvel.

CYNTHIA

Say on, Tellus; I cannot imagine anything that can colour such a cruelty.

TELLUS

Endymion, that Endymion, in the prime of his youth, so ravished my heart with love, that to obtain my desires I could not find means, nor to recite them reason. What was she that favoured not Endymion, being young, wise, honourable, and virtuous? Besides, what metal was she made of (be she mortal) that is not affected with the spice, nay infected with the poison, of that not-to-be-expressed yet always-to-be-felt love which breaketh the brains and never bruiseth the brow, consumeth the heart and never toucheth the skin, and maketh a deep scar to be seen before any wound at all be felt. My heart, too tender to withstand such a divine fury, yielded to love. Madam, I, not without blushing, confess, yielded to love.

CYNTHIA

A strange effect of love, to work such an extreme hate. How say you, Endymion? All this was for love?

ENDYMION

I say, madam, then the gods send me a woman's hate.

CYNTHIA

That were as bad, for then by contrary you should never sleep. But on, Tellus; let us hear the end.

TELLUS

Feeling a continual burning in all my bowels and a bursting almost in every vein, I could not smother the inward fire, but it must needs be perceived by the outward smoke; and by the flying abroad of divers sparks, divers judged of my scalding flames.

Endymion, as full of art as wit, marking mine eyes (in which he might see almost his own), my sighs (by which he might ever hear his name sounded), aimed at my heart (in which he was assured his person was imprinted), and by questions wrung out that which was ready to burst out. When he saw the depth of my affections, he swore that mine in respect of his were as fumes to Etna,

42 **this . . . sex** this cruel deed, completely unnatural to womankind.

47–48 **there . . . mine** there might be such human/worldly emotions as I have.

50 **colour** excuse/present favourably.

53 **What was she** Who was it that did not? (i.e. everyone did).

57–58 **maketh . . . felt** there may be a printing error here, as the sense of the preceding argument would suggest that the wound should be felt before the scar is seen.

66 **bowels** stomach.

70–71 **marking . . . own)** observing my eyes (in which he could see his own image imprinted).

74 **he swore . . . Etna** he promised that my love for him was like a small fire compared to the volcano of Mount Etna of his love for me.

valleys to Alps, ants to eagles, and nothing could be compared to my beauty but his love and eternity. Thus drawing a smooth shoe upon a crooked foot, he made me believe that (which all of our sex willingly acknowledge) I was beautiful, and to wonder (which indeed is a thing miraculous) that any of his sex should be faithful.

CYNTHIA
Endymion, how will you clear yourself?

ENDYMION
Madam, by mine own accuser.

CYNTHIA
Well, Tellus, proceed; but briefly, lest taking delight in uttering thy love, thou offend us with the length of it.

TELLUS
I will, madam, quickly make an end of my love and my tale. Finding continual increase of my tormenting thoughts, and that the enjoying of my love made deeper wounds than the entering into it, I could find no means to ease my grief but to follow Endymion, and continually to have him in the object of mine eyes who had me slave and subject to his love. But in the moment that I feared his falsehood and fried myself most in mine affections, I found (ah, grief, even then I lost myself!) I found him in most melancholy and desperate terms cursing his stars, his state, the earth, the heavens, the world, and all for the love of...

CYNTHIA
Of whom? Tellus, speak boldly.

TELLUS
Madam, I dare not utter for fear to offend.

CYNTHIA
Speak, I say. Who dare take offence, if thou be commanded by Cynthia?

TELLUS
For the love of Cynthia.

CYNTHIA
For my love, Tellus? That were strange. Endymion, is it true?

ENDYMION
In all things, madam, Tellus doth not speak false.

CYNTHIA
What will this breed to in the end? Well, Endymion, we shall hear all.

TELLUS
I, seeing my hopes turned to mishaps, and a settled dissembling towards me, and an immovable desire to Cynthia, forgetting both myself and my sex, fell into this unnatural hate. For, knowing your virtues, Cynthia, to be immortal, I could not have an imagination to withdraw him; and finding mine own affections unquenchable, I could not carry the mind that any else should possess what I had pursued. For, though in majesty, beauty, virtue, and dignity I always humbled and yielded myself to Cynthia, yet in affections I esteemed

76 **drawing . . . foot** i.e. making something ugly or twisted seem fair.

89 **fried . . . affections** consumed myself in the flames of my own desire.

98 **What . . . end?** Whatever will this lead to?

101–102 **I could . . . him** I could not imagine ever getting him to withdraw his love from you.

103 **I could . . . mind** I could not bear the thought.

myself equal with the goddesses, and all other creatures, according to their states, with myself. For stars to their bigness have their lights, and the sun hath no more, and little pitchers, when they can hold no more, are as full as great vessels that run over. Thus, madam, in all truth, have I uttered the unhappiness of my love and the cause of my hate, yielding wholly to that divine judgment which never erred for want of wisdom, or envied for too much partiality.

CYNTHIA

How say you, my lords, to this matter? But what say you, Endymion, hath Tellus told truth?

ENDYMION

Madam, in all things, but in that she said I loved her and swore to honour her.

CYNTHIA

Was there such a time whenas for my love thou didst vow thyself to death, and in respect of it loathed thy life? Speak, Endymion; I will not revenge it with hate.

ENDYMION

The time was, Madam, and is, and ever shall be, that I honoured your highness above all the world; but to stretch it so far as to call it love I never durst. There hath none pleased mine eye but Cynthia, none delighted mine ears but Cynthia, none possessed my heart but Cynthia. I have forsaken all other fortunes to follow Cynthia, and here I stand ready to die, if it please Cynthia. Such a difference hath the gods set between our states that all must be duty, loyalty, and reverence; nothing (without it vouchsafe your highness) be termed love. My unspotted thoughts, my languishing body, my discontented life, let them obtain by princely favour that which to challenge they must not presume, only wishing of impossibilities; with imagination of which I will spend my spirits; and to myself, that no creature may hear, softly call it love. And if any urge to utter what I whisper, then will I name it honour. From this sweet contemplation if I be not driven, I shall live of all men the most content, taking more pleasure in mine aged thoughts than ever I did in my youthful actions.

CYNTHIA

Endymion, this honourable respect of thine shall be christened 'love' in thee, and my reward for it, favour. Persevere, Endymion, in loving me, and I account more strength in a true heart than in a walled city. I have laboured to win all, and study to keep such as have won; but those that neither my favour can move to continue constant, nor my offered benefits get to be faithful, the gods shall either reduce to truth, or revenge their treacheries with justice. Endymion, continue as thou hast begun, and thou shalt find that Cynthia shineth not on thee in vain.

108–109 **are . . . over** i.e. to be filled with desire is the same experience, regardless of how great one is.

116 **whenas** when.

127 **challenge** demand/ask for directly.

127–128 **only . . . spirits** I could only wish for what I knew to be impossible; and I will spend my thoughts so wishing.

130 **any . . . utter** ask me to say out loud.

134 **favour** will be my favour. (Cynthia, rather like Elizabeth I herself when she dealt with her male suitors, coyly fails to define exactly what this favour will involve, committing herself only to goodwill and patronage, but employing an eroticized language that might be read as hinting at more.)

135–136 **I . . . won** I have laboured to win the hearts of all my subjects, and strive to retain the love of all those I have won over.

138 **reduce to truth** make loyal by force.

ENDYMION
Your Highness hath blessed me, and your words have again restored my youth. Methinks I feel my joints strong, and these mouldy hairs to moult, and all by your virtue, Cynthia, into whose hands the balance that weigheth time and fortune are committed.

CYNTHIA
What, young again? Then it is pity to punish Tellus.

TELLUS
Ah, Endymion, now I know thee and ask pardon of thee. Suffer me still to wish thee well.

ENDYMION
Tellus, Cynthia must command what she will.

FLOSCULA
Endymion, I rejoice to see thee in thy former estate.

ENDYMION
Good Floscula, to thee also am I in my former affections.

EUMENIDES
Endymion, the comfort of my life, how am I ravished with a joy matchless, saving only the enjoying of my mistress.

CYNTHIA
Endymion, you must now tell who Eumenides shrineth for his saint.

ENDYMION
Semele, madam.

CYNTHIA
Semele? Eumenides, is it Semele, the very wasp of all women, whose tongue stingeth as much as an adder's tooth?

EUMENIDES
It is Semele, Cynthia, the possessing of whose love must only prolong my life.

CYNTHIA
Nay, sith Endymion is restored, we will have all parties pleased. Semele, are you content after so long trial of his faith, such rare secrecy, such unspotted love, to take Eumenides? Why speak you not? Not a word?

ENDYMION
Silence, madam, consents; that is most true.

CYNTHIA
It is true, Endymion. Eumenides, take Semele. Take her, I say.

EUMENIDES
Humble thanks, madam; now only do I begin to live.

SEMELE
A hard choice, madam, either to be married if I say nothing, or to lose my tongue if I speak a word. Yet do I rather choose to have my tongue cut out than my heart distempered: I will not have him.

CYNTHIA
Speaks the parrot? She shall nod hereafter with signs! Cut off her tongue, nay

142 **mouldy** ancient.
143 **virtue** 'power' as well as 'goodness'.
153 **shrineth...saint** i.e. who it is that he loves.
157 **only** alone can.
161 **Silence, madam, consents** it was a principle of law that silence in response to a suggestion could be interpreted to imply consent.
167 **She...signs!** She'll only be able to nod and gesture in future!

her head, that having a servant of honourable birth, honest manners and true love, will not be persuaded.

SEMELE

He is no faithful lover, madam, for then would he have asked his mistress.

GERON

Had he not been faithful, he had never seen into the fountain, and so lost his friend and mistress.

EUMENIDES

Thine own thoughts, sweet Semele, witness against thy words, for what hast thou found in my life but love? And as yet what have I found in my love but bitterness? Madam, pardon Semele, and let my tongue ransom hers.

CYNTHIA

Thy tongue, Eumenides? What, shouldst thou live wanting a tongue to blaze the beauty of Semele? Well, Semele, I will not command love, for it cannot be enforced. Let me entreat it.

SEMELE

I am content your highness shall command, for now only do I think Eumenides faithful, that is willing to lose his tongue for my sake; yet loath, because it should do me better service. Madam, I accept of Eumenides.

CYNTHIA

I thank you, Semele.

EUMENIDES

Ah, happy Eumenides, that hast a friend so faithful and a mistress so fair. With what sudden mischief will the gods daunt this excess of joy? Sweet Semele, I live or die as thou wilt.

CYNTHIA

What shall become of Tellus? Tellus, you know Endymion is vowed to a service from which death cannot remove him. Corsites casteth still a lovely look towards you. How say you, will you have your Corsites, and so receive pardon for all that is past?

TELLUS

Madam, most willingly.

CYNTHIA

But I cannot tell whether Corsites be agreed.

CORSITES

Aye, madam, more happy to enjoy Tellus than the monarchy of the world.

EUMENIDES

Why, she caused you to be pinched with fairies.

CORSITES

Aye, but her fairness hath pinched my heart more deeply.

CYNTHIA

Well, enjoy thy love. But what have you wrought in the castle, Tellus?

TELLUS

Only the picture of Endymion.

180 **sake . . . loath** I am loathed he should lose his tongue, as he should use it to serve me better (by praising her beauty, but also with possible bawdy implications).

183–184 **Ah . . . joy?** Fearing that he is now too happy, Eumenides fears the gods will punish him to bring him back to humility.

CYNTHIA

Then so much of Endymion as his picture cometh to, possess and play withal.

CORSITES

Ah, my sweet Tellus, my love shall be as thy beauty is: matchless.

CYNTHIA

Now it resteth, Dipsas, that if thou wilt forswear that vile art of enchanting, Geron hath promised again to receive thee; otherwise, if thou be wedded to that wickedness, I must and will see it punished to the uttermost.

DIPSAS

Madam, I renounce both substance and shadow of that most horrible and hateful trade, vowing to the gods continual penance, and to your highness obedience.

CYNTHIA

How say you, Geron; will you admit her to your wife?

GERON

Aye, with more joy than I did the first day, for nothing could happen to make me happy but only her forsaking that lewd and detestable course. Dipsas, I embrace thee.

DIPSAS

And I thee, Geron, to whom I will hereafter recite the cause of these my first follies.

CYNTHIA

Well, Endymion, nothing resteth now but that we depart. Thou hast my favour, Tellus her friend, Eumenides in paradise with his Semele, Geron content with Dipsas.

SIR TOPHAS

Nay, soft; I cannot handsomely go to bed without Bagoa.

CYNTHIA

Well, Sir Tophas, it may be there are more virtues in me than myself knoweth of, for Endymion I awaked, and at my words he waxed young. I will try whether I can turn this tree again to thy true love.

TOPHAS

Turn her to a true love or false, so she be a wench I care not.

CYNTHIA

Bagoa, Cynthia putteth an end to thy hard fortunes, for, being turned to a tree for revealing a truth, I will recover thee again, if in my power be the effect of truth.

TOPHAS

Bagoa, a bots upon thee!

CYNTHIA

Come, my lords, let us in. You, Gyptes and Pythagoras, if you cannot content yourselves in our court to fall from vain follies of philosophers to such virtues as are here practised, you shall be entertained according to your deserts, for Cynthia is no stepmother to strangers.

197 **cometh to** amounts to (i.e. you can contemplate only his image).

206 **course** path/life.

213 **I . . . Bagoa** presumably as she is now the only available single woman, albeit she is in the form of a tree.

221 **a bots . . . thee!** curse you! (A bots is an infection of horses.)

PYTHAGORAS
I had rather in Cynthia's court spend ten years than in Greece one hour.

GYPTES
And I choose rather to live by the sight of Cynthia than by the possessing of all Egypt.

CYNTHIA
Then follow.

EUMENIDES
We all attend.

Exeunt.

FINIS

The Epilogue

A man walking abroad, the Wind and Sun strove for sovereignty, the one with his blast, the other with his beams. The Wind blew hard; the man wrapped his garment about him harder. It blustered more strongly; he then girt it fast to him. 'I cannot prevail', said the Wind. The Sun, casting her crystal beams, began to warm the man; he unloosed his gown. Yet it shined brighter; he then put it off. 'I yield', said the Wind, 'for if thou continue shining, he will also put off his coat'.

Dread Sovereign, the malicious that seek to overthrow us with threats do but stiffen our thoughts and make them sturdier in storms. But if your highness vouchsafe with your favourable beams to glance upon us, we shall not only stoop, but with all humility lay both our hands and hearts at your majesty 's feet.

The short allegorical tale suggests, as what follows clarifies, that threats are much less effective than rewards in winning love and loyalty.

stoop bow.

The Spanish Tragedy

(*c.*1587–1592?)

THOMAS KYD

(1558–1594)

THE AUTHOR

Thomas Kyd was born in early November 1558, the son of the prominent London scrivener (copier of texts) Francis Kyd and his wife Anna. He studied at Merchant Taylors' School in London from 1565, under the headmastership of the well-known educationalist, Richard Mulcaster. There he would have performed in plays as part of his studies; and the boys also acted for paying audiences, making at least one appearance before Elizabeth I. Despite this early brush with drama, Kyd may have initially followed his father's profession (critics note admiringly his very neat writing hand). At some point after 1583, however, he joined the Queen's Men, the newly formed acting company made up of the best actors of the day, as a playwright. From a letter, we know that at some point around 1587 he also entered the service (in what capacity is unclear) of an unknown 'lord', perhaps Henry Herbert, second earl of Pembroke, to whose wife, Mary, countess of Pembroke, he dedicated his translation of Robert Garnier's *Cornelia* in 1594. He also produced a prose work, a translation from Tasso, which he named *The Householder's Philosophy*, in 1588, but of the large number of plays (including perhaps the earliest, ur-version of *Hamlet*) that he must have produced for the Queen's Men, and perhaps for other companies, no others are known to have survived.

The most sensational evidence of Kyd's life concerns the period, around 1591, when he shared rooms with his fellow playwright Christopher Marlowe (see the head-note to *Tamburlaine*, above). On 11 May 1593 the privy council, concerned to track down the author of a controversial tract or 'libel' against foreigners resident in London, instigated a search of Kyd's lodgings. There they found no evidence of the racist material, but did unearth a short text containing 'vile heretical conceits denying the divinity of Jesus Christ'. Kyd denied that this text was his, suggesting, perhaps under torture, that it must have belonged to Marlowe, and had somehow got mixed up with his papers when they shared a room ('shuffled with some of mine (unknown to me) by some occasion of writing in one chamber two years since'). Marlowe was subsequently arrested, but released without charge on 20 May. Ten days later he was dead, having been stabbed in the infamous brawl in a Deptford tavern. Kyd was also subsequently released, but seems never to have fully recovered from his experiences under interrogation. He died only a year later, and was buried on 15 August 1594.

THE PLAY

The dating of *The Spanish Tragedy* is uncertain. It was entered in the Stationers' Register on 6 October 1592, but this shows only that someone in possession of a text, in this case the printer Abel Jeffes, wanted to secure the legal right to print it. The play was probably written and first performed some years earlier, perhaps as early as 1582 on some estimates. Most critics, however, place it either around 1587 (on the grounds that it would surely have mentioned the defeat of the Spanish Armada, had it been written after 1588) or close to the time of its first recorded performance in early 1592, when Edward Allde printed the play for Edward White. Whenever it was created, however, it was a huge success, enjoying twenty performances in its first season at the Rose on Bankside, and further London revivals, and probably touring extensively in following years. It ran in all through eleven printed editions between 1592 and 1633, with performances recorded as far away as Frankfurt in Germany, where it was played by a touring English company in 1601. It was still being performed, with various 'additions' to update the text, some (probably now lost) written by Ben Jonson, well into the seventeenth century. That it was being quoted, pastiched, and parodied in other works (not least *Hamlet*, that shares Kyd's use of the ghost calling for vengeance, the Machiavellian villain, a witty, unhinged revenger, and a play-within-a-play) for even longer is telling evidence of its place in popular cultural memory.

Strangely, all of the early editions of the play were printed anonymously. It is only thanks to a reference in *The Apology for Actors* (1612), by Thomas Heywood (who, as a member of the Queen's Men in the 1590s might well have acted in the play) to 'Master Kyd in his Spanish Tragedy' that the play can be securely attributed to Kyd at all. While the reason for its initial anonymity is uncertain, however, the reasons for its popularity are clear. It brought the dynastic revenge plot, infernal imagery, and bloody denouement of the newly popular Senecan drama into the present day of Elizabethan politics, and then increased their sensationalism (see Heywood's *Thyestes*, above, for a good example of original Senecan drama in Elizabethan translation). As Philip Edwards noted, Kyd provides not one revenge plot, but four. The dead Andrea returns from Hades with the spirit of Revenge, hoping to bring retribution upon Balthazar, who killed him on the battlefield. His lover, the Spanish princess Bel-Imperia, resists a forced dynastic marriage to the same Balthazar, and seeks vengeance on him in Andrea's name by allying with Horatio, the son of the Spanish knight-marshal, Hieronimo. Balthazar and Bel-Imperia's brother, Lorenzo, in turn murder Horatio when they realise that Bel-Imperia has transferred her affections to him; and finally, Hieronimo, once he is assured of their identity (he is, after all, the chief legal officer of Spain, and must act with due regard for justice), pursues the murderers of his son in a bloody plot which wipes out virtually the entire Spanish and Portuguese successions.

The background to these machinations and carnage is a diplomatic situation not unlike that of Europe in the 1580s, when Kyd was probably writing the play. A new world order had been created in 1581 by the Spanish conquest of Portugal. By the terms of an imperious papal edict of 1493, Spain and Portugal had been allowed to divide overlordship of the globe between them, so this victory gave the Spanish king practical control of both the empires of the New World. Kyd's play explores this terrifying prospect in a drama that both flirts with the spectre of a Spanish-Portuguese superpower (it begins with the defeat of a Portuguese rebellion and the plotting of a dynastic marriage between Balthazar and Bel-Imperia that will make their union permanent), and suggests its fragility (it is the devious internecine plots of the Iberian princes that brings about their own destruction). But he also imbues his drama with a Senecan sense of a pre-ordained, supernaturally driven destiny pushing events to their bloody conclusion. Having Andrea's ghost and the personification of Revenge seated onstage throughout the action, coming forward to speak as a Chorus at the end of each act, keeps at the forefront of the audience's mind a sense that the working out of the plot is inevitable once the gods of the underworld have intervened, and that what Francis Bacon called the 'wild justice' of vengeance will eventually work itself out.

There are a number of problematic elements to the play text as we now have it. Two relate to the play's sensational, and very sanguine, denouement. The first concerns the language(s) in which the 'play-within-a-play' was performed. As Hieronimo describes it to the would-be actors, each player will speak their lines in a different language (IV.i. 168–9), one speaking Latin, another Greek, a third Italian, and the fourth French. Yet the printed text as we have it gives all of these speeches in English, providing an explanatory note that reads, 'Gentlemen, this play of Hieronimo in sundry languages was thought good to be set down in English more largely, for the easier understanding to every public reader'. Are we to assume that the original performances made good Hieronomo's plan, thereby rendering the scene near-incomprehensible for most of the audience? Or was the talk of 'unknown languages' merely a conceit, similar to that governing the play as a whole, in which everyone must be assumed to be speaking Spanish or Portuguese, while they actually speak in English? Critics have been divided on the subject. In the absence of a text with speeches in 'sundry languages', we can only work with the 'translated' text in this edition.

A more puzzling problem arises from Hieronimo's behaviour after the enactment of his revenge. Having revealed the body of Horatio hanging behind a curtain, he gives a lengthy account of who murdered whom and why, and invites the king and the newly bereaved father, the Viceroy, to experience the kinds of horror and grief which were inflicted upon him. Once he has finished, however, the king and Viceroy turn upon him and, seemingly redundantly, demand that he tells them his motives for committing such atrocities. He in turn announces that he will never do so, biting off his own tongue and killing the Duke and himself with a pen-knife to make good the claim. How can we reconcile the seeming inconsistency here? It is, perhaps, psychologically plausible that the witnesses to his lengthy, emotive speech are just too horrified to comprehend the details of what he has told them, and so need to hear it all again before they can 'process' it satisfactorily, and that an exasperated Hieronimo refuses to give them that satisfaction. But most critics have assumed that there is a problem with the text at this point, and that the play as we have it contains 'fossils' of two alternative versions: one in which Hieronimo gives a full confession of his crimes, and another, shorter version in which he does not, taking his motives with him to the grave. If this is so, one can only speculate over which was the earlier version, and why it was judged necessary to change it.

Another problem is created by the existence of the 'additions' to the play mentioned above. Contained in editions printed after 1602, these are of mixed quality, prompting most critics to conclude that they are not the 'additions' and 'new additions' which Philip Henslowe, the owner of the Rose, commissioned from Ben Jonson in September 1601 and June 1602 respectively. Two of them, a lengthy speech for Hieronimo in 'distracted' mode, and the well-known 'Painter' scene, are more substantial and have more literary and dramatic merit than the rest, and I have printed them in the edition that follows. What is clear, however, is that they repeat or closely echo material already in the 1592 text, and so were probably intended to replace existing scenes rather than simply to slot into the play as it already existed. Rather than try to second guess which material was to be cut, I have given both the additions and the adjacent scenes in their entirety below, allowing readers both to see what the play looked like in its earlier form, and to speculate on how it may have been adapted to incorporate the additions.

This edition is based on the earliest surviving Tudor text, that printed by Edward Allde for Edward White in London in 1592. I have added scene divisions for ease of reference, as the original text was divided solely into four acts. Why it did not follow convention and have five acts is unclear. Critics have argued that the overlong third act should actually be divided in two; but, as there is no compelling case for where to divide that act, and no surviving chorus that might mark the division, I have followed the 1592 text in having just four acts. In addition to using the 1592 text, I have also benefited from consulting the modern editions listed under further reading.

FURTHER READING

Erne, Lukas, *Beyond the Spanish Tragedy: A Study of the Works of Thomas Kyd* (Manchester: Manchester University Press, 2001).

Freeman, A., *Thomas Kyd: Facts and Problems* (Oxford: Clarendon Press, 1967).

Kyd, Thomas, *The Spanish Tragedy*, Revels edn., ed. Philip Edwards (London: Methuen, 1969).

—— *The Spanish Tragedy*, New Mermaid edn., 3rd edn., ed. J. R. Mulryne, with introduction and notes by Andrew Gurr (London: Methuen, 2009).

McMillan, Scott and Sally-Beth MacLean, *The Queen's Men and Their Plays* (Cambridge: Cambridge University Press, 1998).

Hillman, Richard, 'The Spanish Tragedy' in Thomas Betteridge and Greg Walker, eds., *The Oxford Handbook of Tudor Drama* (Oxford: Oxford University Press, 2012), 566–83.

Mulryne, J. R., 'Kyd, Thomas (*bap.* 1558, *d.* 1594)', *Oxford Dictionary of National Biography* (Oxford University Press, 2004) <http://www.oxforddnb.com/view/article/15816>, accessed 6 June 2013.

The Spanish Tragedy,
Containing the lamentable end of Don Horatio and Bel-Imperia, with the pitiful death of Old Hieronimo.

Newly corrected and amended of such gross faults as passed in the first impression

At London
Printed by Edward Allde for Edward White.

[*Dramatis Personae:*

GHOST of Andrea
REVENGE
KING OF SPAIN
CYPRIAN, Duke of Castile, brother to the king
LORENZO, Cyprian's son
BEL-IMPERIA, Cyprian's daughter
SPANISH GENERAL
VICEROY OF PORTUGAL
PEDRO, the viceroy's brother
BALTHAZAR, the viceroy's son
ALEXANDRO and VILLUPPO, lords of Portugal
PORTUGUESE AMBASSADOR
HIERONIMO, knight-marshal of Spain
ISABELLA, Hieronimo's wife
HORATIO, their son
PEDRINGANO, servant of Bel-Imperia
SERBERINE, servant of Balthazar
CHRISTOPHEL, servant to Lorenzo
PAGE/BOY, servant to Lorenzo
3 WATCHMEN
MESSENGER
DEPUTY
HANGMAN
MAID to Isabella
SERVANT
OLD MAN [SENEX/BAZULTO].
2 PORTUGUESE
3 CITIZENS
Soldiers, Halberdiers, Attendants, etc.
And, in 'The Painter scene', added in the 1602 edition:
JAQUES and PEDRO, servants to Hieronimo
THE PAINTER [BAZARDO].]

Actus Primus.
[Act I, Scene i.]

Enter the Ghost of Andrea, and with him Revenge.

GHOST
When this eternal substance of my soul
Did live imprisoned in my wanton flesh,
Each in their function serving other's need,
I was a courtier in the Spanish court.
My name was Don Andrea, my descent,
Though not ignoble, yet inferior far
To gracious fortunes of my tender youth,
For there, in prime and pride of all my years,
By duteous service and deserving love,
In secret I possessed a worthy dame,
Which hight sweet Bel-Imperia by name.
But in the harvest of my summer joys
Death's winter nipped the blossoms of my bliss,
Forcing divorce betwixt my love and me.
For in the late conflict with Portingale
My valour drew me into danger's mouth,
Till life to death made passage through my wounds.
When I was slain, my soul descended straight

Actus Primus Act 1.
10 **possessed** 'possession' here implies that their relationship was consummated sexually.
11 **Which hight** Who was called.
15 **late** recent.
15 **Portingale** Portugal.

To pass the flowing stream of Acheron;
But churlish Charon, only boatman there,
Said that, my rites of burial not performed,
I might not sit amongst his passengers.
Ere Sol had slept three nights in Thetis' lap
And slaked his smoking chariot in her flood,
By Don Horatio, our knight-marshal's son,
My funerals and obsequies were done.
Then was the ferryman of hell content
To pass me over to the slimy strond
That leads to fell Avernus' ugly waves.
There, pleasing Cerberus with honeyed speech,
I passed the perils of the foremost porch.
Not far from hence, amidst ten thousand souls,
Sat Minos, Aeacus, and Rhadamanth;
To whom no sooner 'gan I make approach,
To crave a passport for my wand'ring ghost,
But Minos in graven leaves of lottery
Drew forth the manner of my life and death.
'This knight', quoth he, 'both lived and died in love;
And for his love tried fortune of the wars;
And by war's fortune lost both love and life.'
'Why then,' said Aeacus, 'convey him hence
To walk with lovers in our field of love,
And spend the course of everlasting time
Under green myrtle-trees and cypress shades.'
'No, no,' said Rhadamanth, 'it were not well
With loving souls to place a martialist.
He died in war, and must to martial fields,
Where wounded Hector lives in lasting pain,
And Achilles' Myrmidons do scour the plain.'
Then Minos, mildest censor of the three,
Made this device to end the difference:
'Send him', quoth he, 'to our infernal king,
To doom him as best seems his majesty.'
To this effect my passport straight was drawn.
In keeping on my way to Pluto's court,
Through dreadful shades of ever-glooming night,
I saw more sights than thousand tongues can tell,
Or pens can write or mortal hearts can think.
Three ways there were: that on the right hand side
Was ready way unto the foresaid fields
Where lovers live and bloody martialists,
But either sort contained within his bounds;
The left hand path, declining fearfully,
Was ready downfall to the deepest hell,
Where bloody Furies shake their whips of steel,
And poor Ixion turns an endless wheel,
Where usurers are choked with melting gold,
And wantons are embraced with ugly snakes,
And murderers groan with never-killing wounds,
And perjured wights scalded in boiling lead,
And all foul sins with torments overwhelmed.
Twixt these two ways I trod the middle path,
Which brought me to the fair Elysian green,
In midst whereof there stands a stately tower,
The walls of brass, the gates of adamant.
Here finding Pluto with his Proserpine,
I showed my passport, humbled on my knee.
Whereat fair Proserpine began to smile,
And begged that only she might give me doom.
Pluto was pleased, and sealed it with a kiss.

19 **Acheron** the largest of the five rivers of the classical underworld, which the spirits of the dead must cross, rowed by the ferryman Charon, to enter Hades. This account of the underworld is based upon that in the sixth book of Virgil's *Aeneid*.

23 **Ere . . . lap** Sol is the sun, and Thetis a sea-nymph, so 'before three nights had passed'.

25 **knight-marshal** In England, the knight marshal was responsible for keeping justice within the 'verge' or environs of the royal court.

28 **strond** strand/shore.

29–30 **Avernus** was the lake that marked the gateway to the underworld, **Cerberus** the three-headed dog who was its guardian.

33 **Minos, Aeacus, Rhadamanth** the three judges of the underworld, who allot each soul his or her fate.

34 **'gan I** began I [to].

36–37 **Minos . . . death.** Minos is imagined drawing a sheet of paper narrating Andrea's story from an urn, as in a lottery.

46 **martialist** soldier.

48–49 **Hector . . . Myrmidons** Hector and Achilles were protagonists of Homer's *Iliad*. The Myrmidons were seasoned warriors loyal to Achilles.

51 **device** stratagem/suggestion.

52 **infernal king** Pluto, king of the underworld.

53 **doom** judge.

54 **straight was drawn** immediately drawn up.

59 **Three ways** paths (Kyd adds a third to Virgil's two).

60 **ready** a short/convenient.

63 **declining** descending.

65–66 **Furies . . . wheel** The Furies or Erinyes were winged female spirits of vengeance. Ixion was a mythical king who was bound to a fiery wheel in Hades for offending Zeus.

68 **wantons** sexual sinners.

70 **perjured wights** liars.

72 **Twixt** Between.

73 **fair Elysian green** the happy fields, abode of the heroic dead.

76 **Proserpine** Pluto's queen.

Forthwith, Revenge, she rounded thee in th'ear,
And bade thee lead me though the gates of horn,
Where dreams have passage in the silent night.
No sooner had she spoke, but we were here,
I wot not how, in twinkling of an eye.

REVENGE
Then know, Andrea, that thou arrived
Where thou shalt see the author of thy death,
Don Balthazar, the prince of Portingale,
Deprived of life by Bel-Imperia.
Here sit we down to see the mystery,
And serve for Chorus in this tragedy.

[Act I. Scene ii.]

Enter Spanish King, General, Castile, Hieronimo.

KING
Now say, Lord General: how fares our camp?

GENERAL
All well, my sovereign liege, except some few
That are deceased by fortune of the war.

KING
But what portends thy cheerful countenance,
And posting to our presence thus in hast?
Speak, man, hath fortune given us victory?

GENERAL
Victory, my liege, and that with little loss.

KING
Our Portingales will pay us tribute then?

GENERAL
Tribute, and wonted homage therewithal.

KING
Then blessed be heaven, and guider of the heavens,
From whose fair influence such justice flows!

CASTILE
O multum dilecte Deo, tibi militat aether,
Et conjuratae curvato poplit[e] gentes
Succumbunt: recti soror est victoria juris!

KING
Thanks to my loving brother of Castile.
But General, unfold in brief discourse
Your form of battle and your war's success,
That adding all the pleasure of thy news
Unto the height of former happiness,
With deeper wage and gentle dignity
We may reward thy blissful chivalry.

GENERAL
Where Spain and Portingale do jointly knit
Their frontiers, leaning on each other's bound,
There met our armies in their proud array:
Both furnished well, both full of hope and fear,
Both menacing alike with daring shows,
Both vaunting sundry colours of device,
Both cheerly sounding trumpets, drums and fifes,
Both raising dreadful clamours to the sky,
That valleys, hills, and rivers made rebound
And heaven itself was frighted with the sound.
Our battles both were pitched in squadron form,
Each corner strongly fenced with wings of shot;
But ere we joined and came to push of pike,
I brought a squadron of our readiest shot
From out our rearward to begin the fight:
They brought another wing to encounter us.
Meanwhile our ordinance played on either side,
And captains strove to have their valours tried.
Don Pedro, their chief horsemen's colonel,
Did with his cornet bravely make attempt
To break the order of our battle ranks:
But Don Rogero, worthy man of war,
Marched forth against him with our musketeers,
And stopped the malice of his fell approach.
While they maintain hot skirmish to and fro,
Both battles join and fall to handy blows,
Their violent shot resembling th'ocean's rage,

81 **rounded** whispered.
85 **wot** know.
1 **camp** army.
5 **posting** riding post (i.e. swiftly).
9 **Tribute...therewithal** i.e. the General's victory has prompted the Portuguese to submit once more to Spanish authority, pledging their loyalty (homage) as well as financial payments (tribute).
12–14 ***O multum...juris!*** 'O greatly beloved of God, for you the heavens make war / and the conspirators fall / on bended knee: victory is the sister of justice': an adaptation of Claudian's *On the Third Consulship of the Emperor Honorius*, 96–98.
20 **deeper wage** greater reward.
23 **bound** boundaries.
25 **furnished well** well equipped and supplied.
27 **vaunting...device** proudly bearing many colourful heraldic banners.
32–33 **Our...shot** each army formed up with its armoured infantry in squares in the centre and musketeers on the flanks.
34 **ere...pike** before the two blocks of pikemen came into hand-to-hand combat.
38 **our...side** the opposing artillery exchanged fire.
41 **cornet** a squadron of cavalry.
45 **fell** fierce.
47 **handy** hand-to-hand.

When, roaring loud, and with a swelling tide,
It beats upon the rampiers of huge rocks,
And gapes to swallow neighbour-bounding lands.
Now, while Bellona rageth here and there,
Thick storms of bullets ran like winter's hail,
And shivered lances dark the troubled air.
Pede pes et cuspide cuspis,
Arma sonant armis, vir petiturque viro.
On every side drop captains to the ground,
And soldiers, some ill-maimed, some slain outright:
Here falls a body sundered from his head,
There legs and arms lie bleeding on the grass,
Mingled with weapons and unbowelled steeds,
That scattering over-spread the purple plain.
In all this turmoil, three long hours and more,
The victory to neither part inclined,
Till Don Andrea, with his brave lanciers,
In their main battle made so great a breach
That, half dismayed, the multitude retired.
But Balthazar, the Portingales' young prince,
Brought rescue and encouraged them to stay.
Here-hence the fight was eagerly renewed,
And in that conflict was Andrea slain,
Brave man-at-arms, but weak to Balthazar.
Yet, while the prince, insulting over him,
Breathed out proud vaunts, sounding to our reproach,
Friendship and hardy valour joined in one
Pricked forth Horatio, our knight-marshal's son,
To challenge forth that prince in single fight.
Not long between these twain the fight endured,
But straight the prince was beaten from his horse
And forced to yield him prisoner to his foe.
When he was taken, all the rest fled,
And our carbines pursued them to death,
Till, Phoebus waning to the western deep,
Our trumpeters were charged to sound retreat.

KING
Thanks, good Lord General, for these good news.
And for some argument of more to come,
Take this and wear it for thy sovereign's sake.

Give him his chain.

But tell me now; hast thou confirmed a peace?

GENERAL
No peace, my liege, but peace conditional,
That, if with homage tribute be well paid,
The fury of your forces will be staid.
And to this peace their viceroy hath subscribed,

Give the King a paper.

And made a solemn vow that during life
His tribute shall be truly paid to Spain.

KING
These words, these deeds become thy person well.
But now, knight-marshal, frolic with thy king,
For 'tis thy son that wins this battle's prize.

HIERONIMO
Long may he live to serve my sovereign liege,
And soon decay unless he serve my liege!

A tucket afar off.

KING
Nor thou nor he shall die without reward.
What means this warning of this trumpet's sound?

GENERAL
This tells me that your grace's men of war,
Such as war's fortune hath reserved from death,
Come marching on towards your royal seat
To show themselves before your majesty,
For so gave I in charge at my depart.
Whereby by demonstration shall appear
That all (except three hundred or few more)
Are safe returned and by their foes enriched.

The army enters, Balthazar between Lorenzo and Horatio, captive.

50 **rampiers** ramparts.
52 **Bellona** Roman goddess of war.
54 **shivered** splintered.
55–56 ***Peded . . . viro.*** 'Foot against foot, and lance against lance, / Arms crash on arms and man is assailed by man.'
58 **ill-maimed** sorely wounded.
61 **inbowelled steeds** disembowelled horses.
65 **lanciers** lancers.
70 **Here-hence** from this point onward.
76 **Pricked forth** spurred on.
82 **carbines** musketeers.
83 **Phoebus . . . deep** the sun, declining into the western ocean (1592 has 'waving' for 'waning').
84 **charged** commanded.
86 **argument** token.
96 **frolic** be cheerful.
99.1 **tucket** trumpet blast.
100 **Nor** Neither.
106 **gave . . . depart** instructed them when I left them.

KING
A gladsome sight! I long to see them here.

They enter and pass by.

Was that the warlike prince of Portingale,
That by our nephew was in triumph led?

GENERAL
It was, my liege, the prince of Portingale.

KING
But what was he that on the other side
Held him by th'arm as partner of the prize?

HIERONIMO
That was my son, my gracious sovereign;
Of whom though from his tender infancy
My loving thoughts did never hope but well,
He never pleased his father's eyes till now,
Nor filled my heart with over-cloying joys.

KING
Go, let them march once more about these walls,
That, staying them, we may confer and talk
With our brave prisoner and his double guard.
Hieronimo, it greatly pleaseth us
That in our victory thou have a share
By virtue of thy worthy son's exploit.

Enter [army] again.

Bring hither the young prince of Portingale.
The rest march on, but, ere they be dismissed,
We will bestow on every soldier
Two ducats, and on every leader ten,
That they may know our largess welcomes them.

Exeunt all but Balthazar, Lorenzo, and Horatio.

Welcome, Don Balthazar, welcome nephew,
And thou, Horatio, thou art welcome too.
Young prince, although thy father's hard misdeeds
In keeping back the tribute that he owes
Deserve but evil measure at our hands,
Yet shalt thou know that Spain is honourable.

BALTHAZAR
The trespass that my father made in peace
Is now controlled by fortune of the wars:
And cards once dealt, it boots not ask why so.
His men are slain, a weakening to his realm,
His colours seized, a blot unto his name,
His son distressed, a corsive to his heart:
These punishments may clear his late offence.

KING
Aye, Balthazar, if he observe this truce,
Our peace will grow the stronger for these
wars.
Meanwhile, live thou, though not in liberty,
Yet free from bearing any servile yoke;
For in our hearing thy deserts were great.
And in our sight thyself art gracious.

BALTHAZAR
And I shall study to deserve this grace.

KING
But tell me, for their holding makes me doubt:
To which of these twain art thou prisoner?

LORENZO
To me, my liege.

HORATIO
To me, my sovereign.

LORENZO
This hand first took his courser by the reins.

HORATIO
But first my lance did put him from his horse.

LORENZO
I seized the weapon and enjoyed it first.

HORATIO
But first I forced him lay his weapons down.

KING
Let go his arm, upon my privilege!

Let him go.

Say, worthy prince, to whether didst thou
yield?

BALTHAZAR
To him in courtesy; to this perforce;
He spake me fair, this other gave me strokes;
He promised life, this other threatened death;
He won my love, this other conquered me;
And, truth to say, I yield myself to both.

120 **over-cloying** excessive.
130 **ducats** gold coins.
136 **evil measure** harsh punishment.
139 **controlled** disciplined.
140 **it boots not** it is pointless (to).
142 **colours** banners.
143 **corsive** corrosive/poison.
155 **courser** warhorse.
159 **privilege** authority.
160 **whether** which of them.

HIERONIMO
But that I know your grace is just and wise,
And might seem partial in this difference,
Enforced by nature and by law of arms,
My tongue should plead for young Horatio's right.
He hunted well that was a lion's death,
Not he that in a garment wore his skin;
So hares may pull dead lions by the beard.

KING
Content thee, marshal; thou shalt have no wrong,
And for thy sake thy son shall want no right.
Will both abide the censure of my doom?

LORENZO
I crave no better than your grace awards.

HORATIO
Nor I, although I sit beside my right.

KING
Then by judgment thus your strife shall end:
You both deserve and both shall have reward.
Nephew, thou tookst his weapons and his horse,
His weapons and his horse are thy reward.
Horatio, thou didst force him first to yield,
His ransom therefore is thy valour's fee:
Appoint the sum as you shall both agree.
But nephew, thou shalt have the prince in guard,
For thine estate best fitteth such a guest;
Horatio's house were small for all his train.
Yet, in regard thy substance passeth his,
And that just guerdon may befall desert,
To him we yield the armour of the prince.
How likes Don Balthazar of this device?

BALTHAZAR
Right well, my liege, if this proviso were:
That Don Horatio bear us company,
Whom I admire and love for chivalry.

KING
Horatio, leave him not that loves thee so.
Now let us hence, to see our soldiers paid,
And feast our prisoner as our friendly guest. *Exeunt.*

[Act I. Scene iii.]

Enter Viceroy, Alexandro, Villuppo.

VICEROY
Is our ambassador dispatched for Spain?

ALEXANDRO
Two days, my liege, are passed since his depart.

VICEROY
And tribute payment gone along with him?

ALEXANDRO
Aye, my good lord.

VICEROY
Then rest we here awhile in our unrest;
And feed our sorrows with inward sighs,
For deepest cares break never into tears.
But wherefore sit I in a regal throne?

Falls to the ground.

This better fits a wretch's endless moan.
Yet this is higher than my fortunes reach,
And therefore better than my state deserves.
Aye, aye, this earth, image of melancholy,
Seeks him whom fates adjudge to misery!
Here let me lie. Now am I at the lowest.
Qui iacet in terra non habet unde cadat.
In me con[s]umpsit vires fortuna nocendo,
Nil superest ut iam possit obesse magis.
Yes, Fortune may bereave me of my crown:
Here, take it now; let Fortune do her worst,
She shall now rob me of this sable weed.
O, no, she envies none but pleasant things.
Such is the folly of despiteful chance.
Fortune is blind and sees not my deserts,
So is she deaf and hears not my laments:
And, could she hear, yet is she wilful mad,
And therefore will not pity my distress.
Suppose that she could pity me, what then?
What help can be expected at her hands
Whose foot is standing on a rolling stone,

167 **might** I might.
172 **So . . . beard** proverbial.
174 **want** lack.
175 **censure . . . doom** verdict of my judgement.
177 **I . . . right** I think I have right on my side.
187 **train** attendants.
188–189 **in regard . . . desert** because your wealth is greater than his, and as fair reward should go where it is deserved.
15–17 ***Qui . . . magis.*** 'Whoever lies on the earth can fall no further./Fortune has no more power to hurt me. / Nothing more can injure me.' The first line echoes the medieval French theologian Alanus de Insulis' *liber parabolarum*, cap. 2, l.19, the second Seneca's *Agamemnon*, l. 698. Kyd may have devised the third himself.
20 **sable weed** black (mourning) clothing.
29 **Whose . . . stone** Fortune was conventionally depicted standing on a rolling stone to symbolize her inconstancy.

And mind more mutable then fickle winds?
Why wail I, then, where's hope of no redress?
O yes, complaining makes my grief seem less.
My late ambition hath distained my faith,
My breach of faith occasioned bloody wars;
Those bloody wars have spent my treasury,
And with my treasury my people's blood,
And with the blood my joy and best beloved,
My best beloved, my sweet and only son.
O, wherefore went I not to war myself?
The cause was mine; I might have died for both.
My years were mellow, but his young and green;
My death were natural, but his was forced.

ALEXANDRO
No doubt, my liege, but still the prince survives.

VICEROY
Survives? Aye, where?

ALEXANDRO
In Spain, a prisoner by mischance of war.

VICEROY
Then they have slain him for his father's fault.

ALEXANDRO
That were a breach to common law of arms.

VICEROY
They reck no laws that meditate revenge.

ALEXANDRO
His ransom's worth will stay from foul revenge.

VICEROY
No; if he lived, the news would soon be here.

VILLUPPO
My sovereign, pardon the author of ill news,
And I'll bewray the fortune of thy son.

VICEROY
Speak on, I'll guerdon thee, whate'er it be.
Mine ear is ready to receive ill news,
My heart grown hard gainst mischief's battery:
Stand up, I say, and tell thy tale at large.

VILLUPPO
Then hear that truth which these mine eyes have seen:
When both the armies were in battle joined.
Don Balthazar amidst the thickest troops,
To win renown, did wondrous feats of arms.
Amongst the rest I saw him hand-to-hand
In single fight with their lord general.
Till Alexandro, that here counterfeits
Under the colour of a duteous friend,
Discharged his pistol at the prince's back,
As though he would have slain their general:
But therewithal Don Balthazar fell down,
And when he fell, then we began to fly;
But, had he lived, the day had sure been ours.

ALEXANDRO
O wicked forgery; O traiterous miscreant!

VICEROY
Hold thou thy peace! But now, Villuppo, say:
Where then became the carcass of my son?

VILLUPPO
I saw them drag it to the Spanish tents.

VICEROY
Aye, aye, my nightly dreams have told me this.
Thou false, unkind, unthankful, traitorous beast,
Wherein had Balthazar offended thee,
That thou should betray him to our foes?
Was't Spanish gold that bleared so thine eyes
That thou couldst see no part of our deserts?
Perchance, because thou art Terceira's lord,
Thou hadst some hope to wear this diadem,
If first my son and then myself were slain?
But thy ambitious thought shall break thy neck.
Aye, this was it that made thee spill his blood,

Take the crown and put it on again.

But I'll now wear it till thy blood be spilt.

ALEXANDRO
Vouchsafe, dread sovereign, to hear me speak.

VICEROY
Away with him, his sight is second hell;
Keep him till we determine his death.
If Balthazar be dead, he shall not live.
Villuppo, follow us for thy reward.

Exit Viceroy.

33 **distained** stained/sullied.
48 **They... revenge.** The vengeful respect no laws.
49 **His... revenge.** The value of his ransom will deter them from killing him.
52 **bewray** reveal.
53 **guerdon** reward.
64 **colour** feigned image.
70 **forgery** deception.
70 **miscreant** villain.
80 **Terceira's lord** Lord of Terceira in the Azores, which still resisted Spanish rule in 1582. The Viceroy imagines that Alexandro plots to throw off Spanish rule and win the Portuguese throne for himself.

VILLUPPO

Thus have I with an envious forged tale
Deceived the king, betrayed mine enemy,
And hope for guerdon of my villainy. *Exit.*

[Act I. Scene iv.]

Enter Horatio and Bel-Imperia.

BEL-IMPERIA

Signior Horatio, this is the place and hour
Wherein I must entreat thee to relate
The circumstance of Don Andrea's death,
Who, living, was my garland's sweetest flower,
And in his death hath buried my delights.

HORATIO

For love of him and service to yourself,
I'll not refuse this heavy, doleful charge;
Yet tears and sighs, I fear, will hinder me.
When both our armies were enjoined in fight,
Your worthy chevalier amidst the thick'st,
For glorious cause still aiming at the fairest,
Was at the last by young Don Balthazar
Encountered hand-to-hand. Their fight was long,
Their hearts were great, their clamours menacing,
Their strength alike, their strokes both dangerous.
But wrathful Nemesis, that wicked power,
Envying at Andrea's praise and worth,
Cut short his life to end his praise and worth.
She, she herself, disguised in armour's mask,
As Pallas was before proud Pergamus,
Brought in a fresh supply of halberdiers,
Which paunched his horse and dinged him to the
 ground.
Then young Don Balthazar, with ruthless rage,
Taking advantage of his foe's distress,
Did finish what his halberdiers begun,
And left not till Andrea's life was done.
Then, though too late, incensed with just remorse,
I with my band set forth against the prince,
And brought him prisoner from his halberdiers.

BEL-IMPERIA

Would thou hadst slain him that so slew my love!
But then was Don Andrea's carcass lost?

HORATIO

No, that was it for which I chiefly strove,
Nor stepped I back till I recovered him.
I took him up, and wound him in mine arms,
And, welding him unto my private tent,
There laid him down and dewed him with my tears,
And sighed and sorrowed as became a friend.
But neither friendly sorrow, sighs, nor tears
Could win pale Death from his usurped right.
Yet this I did, and less I could not do:
I saw him honoured with due funeral.
This scarf I plucked from off his lifeless arm,
And wear it in remembrance of my friend.

BEL-IMPERIA

I know the scarf; would he had kept it still,
For, had he lived, he would have kept it still,
And worn it for his Bel-Imperia's sake:
For 'twas my favour at his last depart.
But now wear thou it both for him and me,
For after him thou hast deserved it best.
But, for thy kindness in his life and death,
Be sure, while Bel-Imperia's life endures,
She will be Don Horatio's thankful friend.

HORATIO

And, madam, Don Horatio will not slack
Humbly to serve fair Bel-Imperia.
But now, if your good liking stand thereto,
I'll crave your pardon to go seek the prince,
For so the duke your father gave me charge. *Exit.*

BEL-IMPERIA

Aye, go, Horatio, leave me here alone,
For solitude best fits my cheerless mood.
Yet what avails to wail Andrea's death,
From whence Horatio proves my second love?
Had he not loved Andrea as he did,
He could not sit in Bel-Imperia's thoughts.
But how can love find harbour in my breast,
Till I revenge the death of my beloved?
Yes, second love shall further my revenge.
I'll love Horatio, my Andrea's friend,
The more to spite the prince that wrought his end.
And where Don Balthazar, that slew my love,
Himself now pleads for favour at my hands,

16 **Nemesis** Greek goddess of retribution.

20 **As... Pergamus** In Homer's *Iliad*, Pallas Athene dons Zeus's armour to intervene in the siege of Troy (of which Pergamus was the citadel) several times (see, for example, books V and VIII).

22 **paunched** disembowelled.

22 **dinged** struck.

35 **welding** carrying.

He shall, in rigour of my just disdain,
Reap long repentance for his murderous deed,
For what wast else but murderous cowardice,
So many to oppress one valiant knight,
Without respect of honour in the fight?
And here he comes that murdered my delight.

Enter Lorenzo and Balthazar.

LORENZO
Sister, what means this melancholy walk?

BEL-IMPERIA
That for a while I wish no company.

LORENZO
But here the prince is come to visit you.

BEL-IMPERIA
That argues that he lives in liberty.

BALTHAZAR
No madam, but in pleasing servitude.

BEL-IMPERIA
Your prison then belike is your conceit.

BALTHAZAR
Aye, by conceit my freedom is enthralled.

BEL-IMPERIA
Then with conceit enlarge yourself again.

BALTHAZAR
What if conceit have laid my heart to gage?

BEL-IMPERIA
Pay that you borrowed and recover it.

BALTHAZAR
I die if it return from whence it lies.

BEL-IMPERIA
A heartless man, and live? A miracle!

BALTHAZAR
Aye, lady, love can work such miracles.

LORENZO
Tush, tush, my lord; let go these ambages,
And in plain terms acquaint her with your love.

BEL-IMPERIA
What boots complaint, when there's no remedy?

BALTHAZAR
Yes, to your gracious self must I complain,
In whose fair answer lies my remedy,
On whose perfection all my thoughts
attend,
On whose aspect mine eyes find beauty's bower,
In whose translucent breast my heart is lodged.

BEL-IMPERIA
Alas, my lord; there but words of course,
And but devise to drive me from this place.

She, going in, lets fall her glove, which Horatio, coming out, takes up.

HORATIO
Madam, your glove.

BEL-IMPERIA
Thanks, good Horatio; take it for thy pains. [*Exit.*]

BALTHAZAR
Signior Horatio stooped in happy time!

HORATIO
I reaped more grace than I deserved or hoped.

LORENZO
My lord, be not dismayed for what is past;
You know that women oft are humorous:
These clouds will overblow with little wind.
Let me alone, I'll scatter them myself.
Meanwhile let us devise to spend the time
In some delightful sports and revelling.

HORATIO
The king, my lords, is coming hither straight,
To feast the Portingale ambassador;
Things were in readiness before I came.

BALTHAZAR
Then here it fits us to attend the king,
To welcome hither our ambassador,
And learn my father and my country's health.

Enter the banquet, trumpets, the King, and Ambassador.

KING
See lord Ambassador, how Spain entreats
Their prisoner Balthazar, thy viceroy's son:
We pleasure more in kindness than in wars.

AMBASSADOR
Sad is our king, and Portingale laments,
Supposing that Don Balthazar is slain.

82 **belike...conceit** perhaps only imaginary.
84 **enlarge** free.
85 **to gage** in pledge/pawn.
90 **ambages** circumlocutions.
92 **What boots complaint** What good is complaining.
98 **words of course** clichés.
105 **humorous** emotionally unstable.
116 **entreats** treats.

BALTHAZAR *[Aside]*
So am I, slain by beauty's tyranny!
You see, my lord, how Balthazar is slain:
I frolic with the Duke of Castile's son,
Wrapped every hour in pleasures of the court,
And graced with favours of his majesty.

KING
Put off your greetings till our feast be done;
Now come and sit with us, and taste our cheer.

Sit to the banquet.

Sit down, young prince, you are our second guest;
Brother sit down, and nephew, take your place.
Signior Horatio, wait thou upon our cup,
For well thou hast deserved to be honoured.
Now, lordings, fall too: Spain is Portugal,
And Portugal is Spain, we both are friends;
Tribute is paid, and we enjoy our right.
But where is old Hieronimo, our marshal?
He promised us, in honour of our guest,
To grace our banquet with some pompous jest.

Enter Hieronimo with a drum, three knights, each with scutcheon; then he fetches three kings; they [the knights] take their crowns and them captive.

Hieronimo, this masque contents mine eye,
Although I sound well not the mystery.

HIERONIMO
The first armed knight that hung his scutcheon up

He takes the scutcheon and gives it to the King.

Was English Robert, Earl of Gloucester,
Who, when King Stephen bore sway in Albion,
Arrived with five and twenty thousand men
In Portingale, and, by success of war,
Enforced the king, then but a Saracen,
To bear the yoke of the English monarchy.

KING
My lord of Portingale, by this you see
That which may comfort both your king and you,
And make your late discomfort seem the less.
But say, Hieronimo, what was the next?

HIERONIMO
The second knight that hung his scutcheon up

He doth as he did before.

Was Edmund, Earl of Kent in Albion.
When English Richard wore the diadem,
He came likewise and razed Lisbon walls,
And took the king of Portingale in fight,
For which, and other such service done,
He after was created Duke of York.

KING
This is another special argument
That Portingale may deign to bear our yoke,
When it by little England hath been yoked.
But now, Hieronimo, what were the last?

HIERONIMO
The third and last, not least in our account,

Doing as before.

Was, as the rest, a valiant Englishman,
Brave John of Gaunt, the Duke of Lancaster,
As by his scutcheon plainly may appear:
He with a puissant army came to Spain
And took our King of Castile prisoner.

AMBASSADOR
This is an argument for our viceroy,
That Spain may not insult for her success,
Since English warriors likewise conquered Spain,
And made them bow their knees to Albion.

KING
Hieronimo, I drink to thee for this device,
Which hath pleased both the ambassador and me:
Pledge me, Hieronimo, if thou love the king.

Takes the cup of Horatio.

My lord, I fear we sit but over-long,

127 **taste our cheer** sample our hospitality.
132 **fall too** eat.
137 **pompous jest** spectacular entertainment.
137.1 **scutcheon** heraldic shield.
139 **I . . . mystery** I can't quite see its meaning.
140–146 **The first . . . monarchy.** It is not clear from where Kyd got this, unhistorical, story about the conquest of Lisbon (1147).
157 Edwards notes that Edmund Langley actually fought on the Portuguese side in the campaign of 1381–2.
167 John of Gaunt, Chaucer's patron, claimed the throne of Castile on the strength of his marriage to the Infanta Constance in 1371. With the support of Portugal he campaigned unsuccessfully in Spain in 1386 and 1387 but never achieved the kind of victory imagined here.
169 **insult for** boast of.
174 **Pledge me** Share a toast with me.

Unless our dainties were more delicate,
But welcome are to you the best we have.
Now let us in, that you may be dispatched;
I think our council is already set. *Exeunt omnes.*

[Act I. Scene v.]

ANDREA
Come we for this from depth of underground,
To see him feast that gave me my death's wound?
These pleasant sights are sorrow to my soul:
Nothing but league and love, and banqueting!

REVENGE
Be still, Andrea; ere we go from hence
I'll turn their friendship into fell despite,
Their love to mortal hate, their day to night,
Their hope into despair, their peace in war,
Their joys to pain, their bliss to misery.

Actus Secundus.
[Act II. Scene i.]

Enter Lorenzo and Balthazar.

LORENZO
My lord, though Bel-Imperia seem thus coy,
Let reason hold you in your wonted joy:
'In time the savage bull sustains the yoke,
In time all haggard hawks will stoop to lure,
In time small wedges cleave the hardest oak,
In time the flint is pierced with softest shower.'
And she in time will fall from her disdain,
And rue the sufferance of your friendly pain.

BALTHAZAR
'No, she is wilder, and more hard withal
Than beast or bird, or tree, or stony wall.'
But wherefore blot I Bel-Imperia's name?
It is my fault, not she, that merits blame.
My feature is not to content her sight;
My words are rude and work her no delight;
The lines I send her are but harsh and ill,
Such as do drop from Pan and Marsyas' quill;
My presents are not of sufficient cost;
And, being worthless, all my labour's lost.
Yet might she love me for my valiancy;
Aye, but that's slandered by captivity.
Yet might she love me to content her sire;
Aye, but her reason masters her desire.
Yet might she love me as her brother's friend;
Aye, but her hopes aim at some other end.
Yet might she love me to uprear her state;
Aye, but perhaps she hopes some nobler mate.
Yet might she love me as her beauty's thrall;
Aye, but I fear she cannot love at all.

LORENZO
My lord, for my sake leave these ecstasies,
And doubt not but we'll find some remedy.
Some cause there is that lets you not be loved:
First that must needs be known, and then removed.
What if my sister love some other knight?

BALTHAZAR
My summer's day will turn to winter's night.

LORENZO
I have already found a stratagem
To sound the bottom of this doubtful theme.
My lord, for once you shall be ruled by me;
Hinder me not whate're you hear or see.
By force or fair means will I cast about
To find the truth of all this question out.
Ho, Pedringano!

PEDRINGANO
Signior.

LORENZO
Vien qui presto! *Enter Pedringano.*

PEDRINGANO
Hath your lordship any service to command me?

179.1 **Exeunt omnes.** Exit everyone.
4 **league and love** alliance and friendship.
6 **fell despite** fierce malice.
1 **coy** reluctant.
2 **wonted** usual.
4 **In ... lure** All untrained hawks will learn to fly to the bait. (These lines borrow directly from sonnet 47 of Thomas Watson's *Hecatompathia* or *Passionate Century of Love* (1582).)
8 **rue the sufferance** pity the suffering.
10 Balthazar quotes Watson's sonnet 48 back at Lorenzo.
13 **feature** appearance.
14 **rude ... her** unsophisticated and cause her.
16 **Pan and Marsyas** These two gods foolishly challenged Apollo to a flute-playing contest, and lost.
19 **valiancy** bravery.
25 **uprear her state** improve her social position.
26 **hopes** hopes for.
27 **her beauty's thrall** slave to her beauty. 1592 has 'beauteous', but Jonson's *Poetaster* quotes the line as here.
36 **sound ... theme** discover the whole truth of this unclear matter.
41.1 ***Vien qui presto!*** Come here quickly (Italian).

LORENZO
Aye, Pedringano, service of import.
And, not to spend the time in trifling words,
Thus stands the case: it is not long, thou knowst,
Since I did shield thee from my father's wrath,
For thy conveyance in Andrea's love,
For which thou were't adjudged to punishment.
I stood betwixt thee and thy punishment,
And, since, thou knowest how I have favoured thee.
Now to these favours will I add reward,
Not with fair words, but store of golden coin,
And lands and living joined with dignities,
If thou but satisfy my just demand.
Tell truth and have me for thy lasting friend.

PEDRINGANO
Whate're it be your lordship shall demand,
My bounden duty bids me tell the truth,
If case it lie in me to tell the truth.

LORENZO
Then, Pedringano, this is my demand:
Whom loves my sister Bel-Imperia?
For she reposeth all her trust in thee.
Speak, man, and gain both friendship and reward.
I mean, whom loves she in Andrea's place?

PEDRINGANO
Alas, my lord, since Don Andrea's death
I have no credit with her as before,
And therefore know not if she love or no.

LORENZO
Nay, if thou dally, then I am thy foe,
And fear shall force what friendship cannot win.
Thy death shall bury what thy life conceals,
Thou diest for more esteeming her than me.

PEDRINGANO
Oh stay, my lord!

LORENZO
Yet speak the truth and I will guerdon thee,
And shield thee from whatever can ensue,
And will conceal whatever proceeds from thee.
But if thou dally once again, thou diest!

PEDRINGANO
If madam Bel-Imperia be in love...

LORENZO
What, villain, 'if's and 'and's?

PEDRINGANO
Oh stay, my lord, she loves Horatio!

Balthazar starts back.

LORENZO
What, Don Horatio, our knight-marshal's son?

PEDRINGANO
Even him, my lord.

LORENZO
Now say but how knowest thou he is her love,
And thou shalt find me kind and liberal.
Stand up, I say, and fearless tell the truth.

PEDRINGANO
She sent him letters which myself perused,
Full-fraught with lines and arguments of love,
Preferring him before Prince Balthazar.

LORENZO
Swear on this cross that what thou sayest is true,
And that thou wilt conceal what thou hast told.

PEDRINGANO
I swear to both, by Him that made us all.

LORENZO
In hope thine oath is true, here's thy reward.
But if I prove thee perjured and unjust,
This very sword whereon thou tookst thine oath
Shall be the worker of thy tragedy.

PEDRINGANO
What I have said is true, and shall for me
Be still concealed from Bel-Imperia.
Besides, your honour's liberality
Deserves my duteous service even till death.

LORENZO
Let this be all that thou shall do for me:
Be watchful when and where these lovers meet,
And give me notice in some secret sort.

PEDRINGANO
I will, my lord.

LORENZO
Then thou shalt find that I am liberal.
Thou knowest that I can more advance thy state

[47] **For thy conveyance** acting as (secret) broker/go-between.
[58] **If...me** If I am able.
[71] **stay** stop.
[72] **guerdon** reward.
[85] **full-fraught** heavily laden.
[87] **this cross** the hilt of his sword.
[100] **sort** manner.
[102] **liberal** generous.

Than she; be therefore wise and fail me not.
Go and attend her as thy custom is,
Lest absence make her think thou dost amiss.

Exit Pedringano.

Why, so, *tam armis quam ingenio*:
Where words prevail not, violence prevails.
But gold doth more than either of them both.
How likes Prince Balthazar this stratagem?

BALTHAZAR

Both well and ill. It makes me glad and sad:
Glad, that I know the hinderer of my love,
Sad, that I fear she hates me whom I love.
Glad, that I know on whom to be revenged;
Sad, that she'll fly me if I take revenge.
Yet must I take revenge or die myself;
For love resisted grows impatient.
I think Horatio be my destined plague:
First, in his hand he brandished a sword,
And with that sword he fiercely waged war,
And in that war he gave me dangerous wounds,
And by those wounds he forced me to yield,
And by my yielding I became his slave.
Now in his mouth he carries pleasing words,
Which pleasing words do harbour sweet conceits,
Which sweet conceits are limed with sly deceits,
Which sly deceits smooth Bel-Imperia's ears,
And through her ears dive down into her heart,
And in her heart set him, where I should stand.
Thus hath he ta'en my body by force,
And now by sleight would captivate my soul.
But in his fall I'll tempt the destinies,
And either lose my life or win my love.

LORENZO

Let's go, my lord; our staying stays revenge.
Do but follow me and gain your love:
Her favour must be won by his remove. *Exeunt.*

[Act II. Scene ii.]

Enter Horatio and Bel-Imperia.

HORATIO

Now, madam, since by favour of your love
Our hidden smoke is turned to open flame,
And that with looks and words we feed our thought
(Two chief contents where more cannot be had)
Thus in the midst of love's fair blandishments
Why show you sign of inward languishments?

Pedringano showeth all to the Prince and Lorenzo, placing them in secret.

BEL-IMPERIA

My heart, sweet friend, is like a ship at sea:
She wisheth port, where, riding all at ease,
She may repair what stormy times have worn,
And, leaning on the shore, may sing with joy
That pleasure follows pain, and bliss annoy.
Possession of thy love is th'only port
Wherein my heart, with fears and hopes long tossed,
Each hour doth wish and long to make resort,
There to repair the joys that it hath lost,
And, sitting safe, to sing in Cupid's choir
That sweetest bliss is crown of love's desire.

BALTHAZAR (ABOVE)

O sleep mine eyes, see not my love profaned.
Be deaf, my ears, hear not my discontent.
Die, heart, another joys what thou deservest!

LORENZO

Watch still mine eyes, to see this love disjoined,
Hear still mine ears, to hear them both lament,
Live, heart, to joy at fond Horatio's fall!

BEL-IMPERIA

Why stands Horatio speechless all this while?

HORATIO

The less I speak, the more I meditate.

BEL-IMPERIA

But whereon dost thou chiefly meditate?

HORATIO

On dangers past, and pleasures to ensue.

BALTHAZAR

On pleasures past, and dangers to ensue.

BEL-IMPERIA

What dangers and what pleasures dost thou mean?

HORATIO

Dangers of war and pleasures of our love.

LORENZO

Dangers of death, but pleasures none at all!

107 ***tam . . . ingenio*** as much [is won] by brains as by strength.
126 **limed** set with traps.
127 **smooth** flatter.

11 **and bliss annoy** and bliss follows irritation/hurt.
20 **joys** enjoys.
23 **fond** foolish.

BEL-IMPERIA
Let dangers go, thy war shall be with me,
But such a warring as breaks no bond of peace.
Speak thou fair words, I'll cross them with fair words,
Send thou sweet looks, I'll meet them with sweet looks,
Write loving lines, I'll answer loving lines,
Give me a kiss, I'll countercheck thy kiss:
Be this our warring peace, or peaceful war.

HORATIO
But gracious madam, then appoint the field
Where trial of this war shall first be made.

BALTHAZAR
Ambitious villain, how his boldness grows!

BEL-IMPERIA
Then be thy father's pleasant bower in the field,
Where first we vowed a mutual amity.
The court were dangerous, that place is safe.
Our hour shall be when Vesper 'gins to rise,
That summons home distressful travellers.
There none shall hear us but the harmless birds:
Happily the gentle nightingale
Shall carol us asleep ere we be ware,
And, singing with the prickle at her breast,
Tell our delight and mirthful dalliance.
Till then, each hour will seem a year and more.

HORATIO
But honey-sweet and honourable love,
Return we now into your father's sight:
Dangerous suspicion waits on our delight.

LORENZO
Aye, danger mixed with jealous despite
Shall send thy soul into eternal night! *Exeunt.*

[Act II. Scene iii.]

Enter the King of Spain, Portingale, Ambassador, Don Cyprian, etc.

KING
Brother of Castile, to the prince's love
What says your daughter Bel-Imperia?

DON CYPRIAN
Although she coy it, as becomes her kind,
And yet dissemble[s] that she loves the prince,
I doubt not, I, but she will stoop in time.
And, were she froward, which she will not be,
Yet herein shall she follow my advice,
Which is to love him or forgo my love.

KING
Then, lord Ambassador of Portingale,
Advise thy king to make this marriage up,
For strengthening of our late-confirmed league;
I know no better means to make us friends.
Her dowry shall be large and liberal;
Besides that she is daughter and half-heir
Unto our brother here, Don Cyprian,
And shall enjoy the moiety of his land,
I'll grace her marriage with an uncle's gift,
And this is it: in case the match go forward,
The tribute which you pay shall be released,
And, if by Balthazar she have a son,
He shall enjoy the kingdom after us.

AMBASSADOR
I'll make the motion to my sovereign liege,
And work it if my counsel may prevail.

KING
Do so, my lord, and, if he give consent,
I hope his presence here will honour us
In celebration of the nuptial day:
And let himself determine of the time.

AMBASSADOR
Wilt please your grace command me aught beside?

KING
Commend me to the king, and so farewell!
But where's Prince Balthazar, to take his leave?

AMBASSADOR
That is performed already, my good lord.

KING
Amongst the rest of what you have in charge,
The prince's ransom must not be forgot:
That's none of mine, but his that took him prisoner,
And well his forwardness deserves reward:
It was Horatio, our knight-marshal's son.

AMBASSADOR
Between us there's a price already pitched,
And shall be sent with all convenient speed.

45 **Vesper 'gins** Venus, the evening star, begins.
48 **Happily** Perhaps.
49 **ere...ware** before we (even) notice.
50 Nightingales were believed to press against thorns to increase the sorrow of their song.
3 **coy...kind** behaves reservedly, as is fitting for women.
6 **froward** stubborn.
16 **moiety** half.
28 **aught beside** anything else.
35 **forwardness** courage/initiative.
37 **pitched** agreed.

KING
Then once again farewell, my lord.

AMBASSADOR
Farewell, my lord of Castile, and the rest.

Exit.

KING
Now brother, you must make some little pains
To win fair Bel-Imperia from her will.
Young virgins must be ruled by their friends.
The prince is amiable, and loves her well;
If she neglect him and forgo his love,
She both will wrong her own estate and ours.
Therefore, whiles I do entertain the prince
With greatest pleasure that our court affords,
Endeavor you to win your daughter's thought.
If she give back, all this will come to naught.

Exeunt.

[Act II. Scene iv.]

Enter Horatio, Bel-Imperia, and Pedringano.

HORATIO
Now that the night begins with sable wings
To over-cloud the brightness of the sun,
And that in darkness pleasures may be done,
Come Bel-Imperia, let us to the bower,
And there in safety pass a pleasant hour.

BEL-IMPERIA
I follow thee, my love, and will not back,
Although my fainting heart controls my soul.

HORATIO
Why, make you doubt of Pedringano's faith?

BEL-IMPERIA
No, he is as trusty as my second self.
Go, Pedringano, watch without the gate,
And let us know if any make approach.

PEDRINGANO [*Aside*]
Instead of watching, I'll deserve more gold
By fetching Don Lorenzo to this match.

Exit Pedringano.

HORATIO
What means my love?

BEL-IMPERIA
I know not what myself,
And yet my heart foretells me some mischance.

HORATIO
Sweet, say not so, fair Fortune is our friend,
And heavens have shut up day to pleasure us.
The stars, thou seest, hold back their twinkling shine,
And Luna hides herself to pleasure us.

BEL-IMPERIA
Thou hast prevailed. I'll conquer my misdoubt,
And in thy love and counsel drown my fear.
I fear no more; love now is all my thoughts.
Why sit we not; for pleasure asketh ease?

HORATIO
The more thou sitst within these leafy bowers,
The more will Flora deck it with her flowers.

BEL-IMPERIA
Aye; but if Flora spy Horatio here,
Her jealous eye will think I sit too near.

HORATIO
Hark, madam, how the birds record by night,
For joy that Bel-Imperia sits in sight.

BEL-IMPERIA
No, Cupid counterfeits the nightingale,
To frame sweet music to Horatio's tale.

HORATIO
If Cupid sing, then Venus is not far:
Aye, thou art Venus, or some fairer star.

BEL-IMPERIA
If I be Venus, thou must needs be Mars;
And where Mars reigneth, there must needs
be wars.

HORATIO
Then thus begin our wars: put forth thy hand,
That it may combat with my ruder hand.

BEL-IMPERIA
Set forth thy foot to try the push of mine.

HORATIO
But first my looks shall combat against thee.

BEL-IMPERIA
Then ward thyself! I dart this kiss at thee.

50 **give back** turns her back on us/refuses to cooperate.
51 **sable** black.
10 **without** outside.
19 **Luna** the moon.
25 **Flora** Roman goddess of flowers and spring.
28 **record** sing.
38 **try** test.
40 **ward** guard.

HORATIO
Thus I retort the dart thou threw'st at me.

BEL-IMPERIA
Nay then, to gain the glory of the field,
My twining arms shall yoke and make thee yield.

HORATIO
Nay then, my arms are large and strong withal:
Thus elms by vines are compassed till they fall.

BEL-IMPERIA
O, let me go, for in my troubled eyes
Now mayest thou read that life in passion dies.

HORATIO
O, stay a while, and I will die with thee;
So shalt thou yield, and yet have conquered me.

BEL-IMPERIA
Who's there? Pedringano? We are betrayed!

Enter Lorenzo, Balthazar, Cerberin, Pedringano disguised.

LORENZO
My lord, away with her; take her aside.
O sir, forbear, your valour is already tried.
Quickly dispatch, my masters.

They hang him in the arbour.

HORATIO
What, will you murder me?

LORENZO
Aye, thus! And thus! These are the fruits of love.

They stab him.

BEL-IMPERIA
O, save his life and let me die for him!
O, save him brother; save him Balthazar!
I loved Horatio, but he loved not me.

BALTHAZAR
But Balthazar loves Bel-Imperia.

LORENZO
Although his life were still ambitious proud,
Yet is he at the highest now he is dead.

BEL-IMPERIA
Murder! Murder! Help, Hieronimo, help!

LORENZO
Come, stop her mouth! Away with her! *Exeunt.*

[Act II. Scene v.]

Enter Hieronimo in his shirt, etc.

HIERONIMO
What outcries pluck me from my naked bed,
And chill my throbbing heart with trembling fear,
Which never danger yet could daunt before?
Who calls Hieronimo? Speak, here I am.
I did not slumber; therefore t'was no dream.
No, no, it was some woman cried for help.
And here within this garden did she cry,
And in this garden must I rescue her.
But stay, what murderous spectacle is this?
A man hanged up, and all the murderers gone.
And in the bower, to lay the guilt on me!
This place was made for pleasure not for death.

He cuts him down.

Those garments that he wears I oft have seen.
Alas, it is Horatio, my sweet son!
O no, but he that whilom was my son.
O was it thou that call'dst me from my bed?
O speak, if any spark of life remain:
I am thy father. Who hath slain my son?
What savage monster, not of human kind,
Hath here been glutted with thy harmless blood,
And left thy bloody corpse dishonoured here,
For me, amidst these dark and dreadful shades,
To drown thee with an ocean of my tears?
O heavens, why made you night to cover sin?
By day this deed of darkness had not been.
O earth, why didst thou not in time devour
The vile profaner of this sacred bower?
O poor Horatio, what hadst thou misdone
To lese thy life ere life was new begun?
O wicked butcher, whatsoe'er thou wert,
How could thou strangle virtue and desert?

[41] **retort** return.
[45] **compassed** encircled.
[48] **I will die** with sexual implications, 'die' being slang for reaching orgasm.

[64] **naked bed** the bed slept in at night, rather than the daybed.
[9] **stay** wait.
[15] **whilom** once.
[29] **lese** lose.

Ay me, most wretched, that have lost my joy
In losing my Horatio, my sweet boy!

Enter Isabella.

ISABELLA
My husband's absence makes my heart to throb.
Hieronimo!

HIERONIMO
Here, Isabella. Help me to lament,
For sighs are stopped, and all my tears are spent.

ISABELLA
What world of grief ...? My son Horatio!
O where's the author of this endless woe?

HIERONIMO
To know the author were some ease of grief,
For in revenge my heart would find relief.

ISABELLA
Then is he gone? And is my son gone too?
O, gush out, tears, fountains and floods of tears!
Blow, sighs, and raise an everlasting storm;
For outrage fits our cursed wretchedness.

HIERONIMO
Sweet lovely rose, ill plucked before thy time,
Fair, worthy son, not conquered, but betrayed!
I'll kiss thee now, for words with tears are stayed.

ISABELLA
And I'll close up the glasses of his sight,
For once these eyes were only my delight.

HIERONIMO
Seest thou this handkercher besmeared with blood?
It shall not from me till I take revenge.
Seest thou those wounds that yet are bleeding fresh?
I'll not entomb them till I have revenged.
Then will I joy amidst my discontent,
Till then my sorrow never shall be spent.

ISABELLA
The heavens are just, murder cannot be hid;
Time is the author of both truth and right,
And time will bring this treachery to light.

HIERONIMO
Meanwhile, good Isabella, cease thy plaints,
Or, at the least, dissemble them awhile;
So shall we sooner find the practice out,
And learn by whom all this was brought about.
Come, Isabel, now let us take him up.

They take him up.

And bear him in from out this cursed place.
I'll say his dirge, singing fits not this case.
O aliquis mihi quas pulchrum ver educat herbas

Hieronimo sets his breast unto his sword.

Misceat, et nostro detur medicina dolori;
Aut, si qui faciunt [*animis*] *oblivia, succos*
Praebeat; ipse metam magnum quaecunque per
orbem
Gramina Sol pulchras [*effert in luminis oras*].
Ipse bibam quicquid meditatur saga veneni,
Quicquid et herbarum vi caeca nenia nectit:
Omnia perpetiar, lethum quoque, dum
semel omnis
Noster in extincto moriatur pectore sensus.
Ergo tua perpetuus sepelivit lumina somnus?
E,oriar tecum, sic, sic juvat ire sub umbras.
At tamen absistam properato cedere letho,
Ne mortem vindicta tuam tum nulla sequatur.

Here he throws it from him and bears the body away.

[Act II. Scene vi.]

ANDREA
Brought'st thou me hither to increase my pain?
I looked that Balthazar should have been slain;
But tis my friend Horatio that is slain,
And they abuse fair Bel-Imperia,
On whom I doted more than all the world,
Because she loved me more than all the world.

40 **were** would be.
45 **fits** is fitting for.
51 **handkercher** handkerchief.
60 **plaints** complaints.
67–79 ***O...sequatur.*** 'Let someone gather for me the herbs that the beautiful spring raises, and bring a medicine for our sorrow, or let him offer juices, if any bring forgetfulness to the brain. I shall gather the plants the sun draws into the world of light across the world. I shall drink whatever potion the cunning woman concocts, and whatever herbs the spell weaves with its secret power. I shall try all things, even death, until all feeling dies in my dead heart. Shall I never again see your eyes, O life of mine, and has eternal sleep sealed up your life light? I shall die with you. Thus, thus would it delight me to pass to the shadows below. But I shall resist surrender to an early death, in case no revenge should follow from your death.' Kyd offers a florid pastiche of a funeral hymn in the style of Ovid, Virgil, and Lucretius.
2 **looked** expected.

REVENGE
Thou talk'st of harvest when the corn is green;
The end is crown of every work well done;
The sickle comes not till the corn be ripe.
Be still, and ere I lead thee from this place,
I'll show thee Balthazar in heavy case.

Actus Tertius.

[Act III. Scene i.]

Enter Viceroy of Portingale, Nobles, Alexandro, Villuppo.

VICEROY
Infortunate condition of kings,
Seated amidst so many helpless doubts!
First, we are placed upon extremest height,
And oft supplanted with exceeding heat,
But ever subject to the wheel of chance;
And at our highest never joy we so
As we both doubt and dread our overthrow.
So striveth not the waves with sundry winds
As fortune toileth in the affairs of kings,
That would be feared, yet fear to be beloved,
Sith fear and love to kings is flattery.
For instance, lordings, look upon your king,
By hate deprived of his dearest son,
The only hope of our successive line.

FIRST NOBLE
I had not thought that Alexandro's heart
Had been envenomed with such extreme hate;
But now I see that words have several works,
And there's no credit in the countenance.

VILLUPPO
No, for, my lord, had you beheld the train
That feigned love had coloured in his looks
When he in camp consorted Balthazar,
Far more inconstant had you thought the sun,
That hourly coasts the centre of the earth,
Than Alexandro's purpose to the prince.

VICEROY
No more, Villuppo; thou hast said enough,
And with thy words thou sayest our wounded
thoughts.
Nor shall I longer dally with the world,
Procrastinating Alexandro's death.
Go, some of you, and fetch the traitor forth,
That as he is condemned he may die.

Enter Alexandro, with a Nobleman and Halberdiers.

SECOND NOBLE
In such extremes will nought but patience serve.

ALEXANDRO
But in extremes what patience shall I use?
Nor discontents it me to leave the world,
With whom there nothing can prevail but wrong.

SECOND NOBLE
Yet hope the best.

ALEXANDRO
'Tis Heaven my hope:
As for the earth, it is too much infect
To yield me hope of any of her mould.

VICEROY
Why linger ye? Bring forth that daring fiend,
And let him die for his accursed deed.

ALEXANDRO
Not that I fear the extremity of death,
For nobles cannot stoop to servile fear,
Do I, O king, thus discontented live;
But this, O this, torments my labouring soul,
That thus I die suspected of a sin
Whereof, as heavens have known my secret
thoughts,
So am I free from this suggestion.

VICEROY
No more, I say; to the tortures! When?
Bind him, and burn his body in those flames,

They bind him to the stake.

That shall prefigure those unquenched fires
Of Phlegethon prepared for his soul.

ALEXANDRO
My guiltless death will be avenged on thee.

[11] **heavy case** a desperate situation.
[2] **helpless doubts** fears for which there is no remedy.
[4] **heat** passion/anger.
[11] **Sith** Since.
[17–18] **words . . . countenance** words need not be related to deeds, and the face is no true guide to the mind.
[19] **train** deception.
[21] **consorted** kept the company of.
[37] **any . . . mould** any mortal creation.
[46] **suggestion** accusation.
[47] **When?** Hurry!
[50] **Phlegethon** a river of fire in Hades.

On thee, Villuppo, that hath maliced thus,
Or for thy meed hast falsely me accused.

VILLUPPO
Nay Alexandro, if thou menace me,
I'll lend a hand to send thee to the lake
Where those thy words shall perish with thy works,
Injurious traitor, monstrous homicide!

Enter Ambassador.

AMBASSADOR
Stay, hold a while,
And here, with pardon of his majesty,
Lay hands upon Villuppo!

VICEROY
Ambassador,
What news hath urged this sudden entrance?

AMBASSADOR
Know, sovereign lord, that Balthazar doth live.

VICEROY
What say'st thou? Liveth Balthazar, our son?

AMBASSADOR
Your highness's son, Lord Balthazar, doth live,
And, well entreated in the court of Spain,
Humbly commends him to your majesty.
These eyes beheld; and these my followers,
With these, the letters of the king's commend,

Gives him letters.

Are happy witnesses of his highness' health.

The King looks on the letters, and proceeds.

VICEROY [*reading*].
'Thy son doth live, your tribute is received,
Thy peace is made, and we are satisfied.
The rest resolve upon as things proposed
For both our honours and thy benefit.'

AMBASSADOR
These are his highness's further articles.

He gives him more letters.

VICEROY
Accursed wretch, to intimate these ills
Against the life and reputation
Of noble Alexandro! Come, my lord, unbind him.
Let him unbind thee that is bound to death,
To make a quital for thy discontent.

They unbind him.

ALEXANDRO
Dread lord, in kindness you could do no less,
Upon report of such a damned fact.
But thus we see our innocence hath saved
The hopeless life which thou, Villuppo, sought
By thy suggestions to have massacred.

VICEROY
Say, false Villuppo, wherefore didst thou thus
Falsely betray Lord Alexandro's life?
Him, whom thou knowest that no unkindness else
But even the slaughter of our dearest son,
Could once have moved us to have misconceived?

ALEXANDRO
Say, treacherous Villuppo, tell the king,
Or wherein hath Alexandro used thee ill?

VILLUPPO
Rent with remembrance of so foul a deed,
My guilty soul submits me to thy doom.
For, not for Alexandro's injuries,
But for reward and hope to be preferred,
Thus have I shamelessly hazarded his life.

VICEROY
Which, villain, shall be ransomed with thy death,
And not so mean a torment as we here
Devised for him who thou said'st slew our son,
But with the bitterest torments and extremes
That may be yet invented for thine end.

Alexandro seems to entreat.

Entreat me not! Go, take the traitor hence!

Exit Villuppo [*under guard.*]

And, Alexandro, let us honour thee
With public notice of thy loyalty.
To end those things articulated here
By our great lord, the mighty King of Spain,
We with our council will deliberate.
Come, Alexandro, keep us company. *Exeunt.*

53 **meed** reward.
55 **the lake** the lake at the entrance to Hades.
61 **urged** prompted.
79 **quital** payment in compensation.
98 **mean** moderate/mild.

[Act III. Scene ii.]

Enter Hieronimo.

HIERONIMO
O eyes, no eyes but fountains fraught with tears!
O life, no life but lively form of death;
O world, no world but mass of public wrongs,
Confused and filled with murder and misdeeds!
O sacred heavens, if this unhallowed deed;
If this inhuman and barbarous attempt;
If this incomparable murder thus
Of mine, but now no more my son,
Shall pass unrevealed, and unrevenged pass,
How should we term your dealings to be just,
If you unjustly deal with those that in your justice trust?
The night, sad secretary to my moans,
With direful visions wake my vexed soul,
And with the wounds of my distressful son
Solicit me for notice of his death.
The ugly fiends do sally forth of hell,
And frame my steps to unfrequented paths,
And fear my heart with fierce inflamed thoughts.
The cloudy day my discontents records,
Early begins to register my dreams
And drive me forth to seek the murtherer.
Eyes, life, world, heavens, hell, night, and day,
See, search, show, send, some man, some mean, that may…

A letter falleth.

What's here? A letter? Tush, it is not so!
A letter written to Hieronimo.

[Reads]

'For want of ink receive this bloody writ.
Me hath my hapless brother hid from thee:
Revenge thyself on Balthazar and him,
For these were they that murdered thy son.
Hieronimo, revenge Horatio's death,
And better fare than Bel-Imperia doth.'
What means this unexpected miracle?
My son slain by Lorenzo and the prince?
What cause had they Horatio to malign?
Or what might move thee, Bel-Imperia,
To accuse thy brother, had he been the mean?
Hieronimo, beware; thou art betrayed,
And to entrap thy life this train is laid.
Advise thee therefore, be not credulous:
This is devised to endanger thee,
That thou, by this, Lorenzo shouldst accuse,
And he, for thy dishonour done, should draw
Thy life in question, and thy name in hate.
Dear was the life of my beloved son,
And of his death behoves me to be avenged:
Then hazard not thine own, Hieronimo,
But live t'effect thy resolution.
I therefore will by circumstances try
What I can gather to confirm this writ,
And, harken near the Duke of Castile's house,
Close if I can with Bel-Imperia,
To listen more, but nothing to bewray.

Enter Pedringano.

Now, Pedringano!

PEDRINGANO
Now, Hieronimo!

HIERONIMO
Where's thy lady?

PEDRINGANO
I know not; here's my lord.

Enter Lorenzo.

LORENZO
How now, who's this? Hieronimo?

HIERONIMO
My lord.

PEDRINGANO
He asketh me for my lady Bel-Imperia.

LORENZO
What to do, Hieronimo? The duke my father hath,

[12] **sad…moans** the confidential servant who hears my moans.
[16] **sally forth** issue out of.
[17] **frame** direct.
[18] **fear** frighten/terrify.
[21] **murtherer** variant of 'murderer'.
[26] **bloody writ** a letter written in blood. A marginal note in the 1592 edition reads, 'red ink', suggesting the actor would allow the audience to see the ominous text.
[34] **malign** hate.
[38] **train** trap.
[39] **Advise…credulous** Act with care, don't believe this too readily.
[48–49] **try…gather** will seek out circumstantial evidence.
[51] **Close** Get close and talk to.
[52] **bewray** reveal.
[53] **Now** 'How now' ('how are you?')

Upon some disgrace a while removed her hence,
But if it be ought I may inform her of,
Tell me, Hieronimo, and I'll let her know it.

HIERONIMO
Nay, nay, my lord, I thank you, it shall not need.
I had a suit unto her, but too late,
And her disgrace makes me unfortunate.

LORENZO
Why so, Hieronimo? Use me.

HIERONIMO
O no, my lord, I dare not, it must not be,
I humbly thank your lordship.

LORENZO
Why then, farewell!

HIERONIMO
My grief no heart, my thoughts no tongue can tell.

Exit.

LORENZO
Come hither, Pedringano, seest thou this?

PEDRINGANO
My lord, I see it, and suspect it too.

LORENZO
This is that damned villain Serberine,
That hath, I fear, revealed Horatio's death.

PEDRINGANO
My lord, he could not, 'twas so lately done,
And since, he hath not left my company.

LORENZO
Admit he have not; his condition's such
As fear or flattering words may make him false.
I know his humour, and therewith repent
That e'er I used him in this enterprise.
But, Pedringano, to prevent the worst,
And 'cause I know thee secret as my soul,
Here, for thy further satisfaction, take thou this.

Gives him more gold.

And harken to me. Thus it is devised:
This night thou must, and prithee so resolve,
Meet Serberine at St. Luigi's Park,
Thou knowest 'tis here hard by behind the house;
There take thy stand, and see thou strike him sure,
For die he must, if we do mean to live.

PEDRINGANO
But how shall Serberine be there, my lord?

LORENZO
Let me alone, I'll send him to meet
The prince and me where thou must do this deed.

PEDRINGANO
It shall be done, my lord, it shall be done;
And I'll go arm myself to meet him there.

LORENZO
When things shall alter, as I hope they will,
Then shalt thou mount for this: thou knowest my mind.

Exit Pedringano.

Che le, Ieron! *Enter Page.*

PAGE
My lord?

LORENZO
Go, sirrah, to Serberine,
And bid him forthwith meet the prince and me
At St Luigi's Park, behind the house,
This evening, boy.

PAGE
I go, my lord.

LORENZO
But, sirrah, let the hour be eight o'clock.
Bid him not fail.

PAGE
I fly, my lord. *Exit.*

LORENZO
Now to confirm the complot thou hast cast
Of all these practices, I'll spread the watch,
Upon precise commandment from the king
Strongly to guard the place where Pedringano
This night shall murder hapless Serberine.
Thus must we work that will avoid distrust,
Thus must we practice to prevent mishap.

74–75 **his...false** his nature is such that... will get him to betray us.
76 **humour** character.
84 **here hard by** right next to here.
93 **shalt thou mount** I'll raise your fortunes.
93.1 ***Che le, Ieron!*** an odd phrase, possibly '*che la*' ('Who's there?' (Italian)) and 'Ieron' (perhaps the page's name).
94 **sirrah** a variant of 'sir', used to address servants and inferiors.
100 **complot** plan.
101 **spread the watch** position the night watch.
105 **we** those of us who (Lorenzo represents himself as an experienced Machiavellian schemer).

And thus one ill another must expulse.
This sly enquiry of Hieronimo
For Bel-Imperia breeds suspicion;
And thus suspicion bodes a further ill.
As for myself, I know my secret fault,
And so do they, but I have dealt for them.
They that for coin their souls endangered,
To save my life, for coin shall venture theirs.
And better 'tis that base companions die
Than by their life to hazard our good haps.
Nor shall they live, for me to fear their faith;
I'll trust myself, myself shall be my friend;
For die they shall: slaves are ordained to
no other end.

Exit.

[Act III. Scene iii.]

Enter Pedringano with a pistol.

PEDRINGANO
Now, Pedringano, bid thy pistol hold;
And hold on, Fortune, once more favour me.
Give but success to mine attempting spirit,
And let me shift for taking of mine aim.
Here is the gold, this is the gold proposed.
It is no dream that I adventure for,
But Pedringano is possessed thereof.
And he that would not strain his conscience
For him that thus his liberal purse hath stretched,
Unworthy such a favour may he fail,
And, wishing, want, when such as I prevail.
As for the fear of apprehension,
I know, if need should be, my noble lord
Will stand between me and ensuing harms.
Besides, this place is free from all suspect.
Here therefore will I stay and take my stand.

Enter the Watch.

FIRST WATCHMAN
I wonder much to what intent it is
That we are thus expressly charged to watch.

SECOND WATCHMAN
This by commandment in the king's own name.

THIRD WATCHMAN
But we were never wont to watch and ward
So near the duke his brother's house before.

SECOND WATCHMAN
Content yourself, stand close, there's
somewhat in't.

Enter Serberine.

SERBERINE
Here, Serberine, attend and stay thy pace;
For here did Don Lorenzo's page appoint
That thou by his command shouldst meet
with him.
How fit a place, if one were so disposed,
Methinks this corner is to close with one.

PEDRINGANO
Here comes the bird that I must seize upon;
Now, Pedringano, or never play the man!

SERBERINE
I wonder that his lordship stays so long,
Or wherefore should he send for me so late.

PEDRINGANO
For this, Serberine; and thou shalt ha't!

Shoots the dag.

So, there he lies; my promise is performed.

[Step forward] the Watch.

FIRST WATCHMAN
Hark, gentlemen, this is a pistol shot!

SECOND WATCHMAN
And here's one slain; stay the murderer!

PEDRINGANO
Now, by the sorrows of the souls in hell,

He strives with the Watch.

Who first lay hands on me, I'll be his priest!

112 **they** i.e. Serberine and Pedringano.
116 **to . . . haps** to put our well-being at risk.
4 **And . . . aim.** And leave the aiming to me.
9–11 **For . . . prevail.** Let he who won't act immorally for fear of being caught regret missing out on the rewards won by those who will.
15 **suspect** suspicion.
18 **thus . . . watch** specifically ordered to patrol here.
20 **ward** guard.
27 **close with one** ambush someone.
30 **stays** delays.
32 **ha't** have it.
32.1 **dag** a large pistol.
36 **stay** arrest.
37 **I'll . . . priest** i.e. I'll send him to heaven/hell.

THIRD WATCHMAN
Sirrah, confess, and therein play the priest.
Why hast thou thus unkindly killed the man?
PEDRINGANO
Why, because he walked abroad so late.
THIRD WATCHMAN
Come sir, you had been better kept your bed
Than have committed this misdeed so late.
SECOND WATCHMAN
Come, to the marshal's with the murderer!
FIRST WATCHMAN
On to Hieronimo's! Help me here
To bring the murdered body with us too.
PEDRINGANO
Hieronimo? Carry me before whom you will;
Whate'er he be, I'll answer him and you.
And do your worst, for I defy you all! *Exeunt.*

[Act III. Scene iv.]

Enter Lorenzo and Balthazar.

BALTHAZAR
How now, my lord, what makes you rise so soon?
LORENZO
Fear of preventing our mishaps too late.
BALTHAZAR
What mischief is it that we not mistrust?
LORENZO
Our greatest ills we least mistrust, my lord,
And unexpected harms do hurt us most.
BALTHAZAR
Why, tell me, Don Lorenzo, tell me, man,
If ought concerns our honour and your own.
LORENZO
Nor you nor me, my lord, but both in one;
But I suspect, and the presumption's great,
That by those base confederates in our fault
Touching the death of Don Horatio,
We are all betrayed to old Hieronimo.
BALTHAZAR
Betrayed, Lorenzo? Tush, it cannot be.
LORENZO
A guilty conscience urged with the thought
Of former evils, easily cannot err:
I am persuaded, and dissuade me not,
That all's revealed to Hieronimo.
And therefore know that I have cast it thus...

[Enter Page.]

But here's the page. How now? What news with thee?
PAGE
My lord, Serberine is slain.
BALTHAZAR
Who? Serberine, my man?
PAGE
Your Highness's man, my lord.
LORENZO
Speak, page; who murdered him?
PAGE
He that is apprehended for the fact.
LORENZO
Who?
PAGE
Pedringano.
BALTHAZAR
Is Serberine slain, that loved his lord so well?
Injurious villain, murderer of his friend!
LORENZO
Hath Pedringano murdered Serberine?
My lord, let me entreat you to take the pains
To exasperate and hasten his revenge
With your complaints unto my lord the king.
This their dissention breeds a greater doubt.
BALTHAZAR
Assure thee, Don Lorenzo, he shall die,
Or else his highness hardly shall deny.
Meanwhile, I'll haste the marshal sessions,
For die he shall for this damned deed.

Exit Balthazar.

LORENZO
Why, so, this fits our former policy;
And thus experience bids the wise to deal.

[38] Punning on another priestly function, to take confession
[39] **unkindly** unnaturally.
[40] **abroad** outdoors.
[3] **mistrust** suspect.
[10] **those...fault** those low-life accomplices in our crime.
[18] **cast it** planned things.
[30] **exasperate** intensify.
[34] **hardly shall deny** will be very harsh in denying the request.
[35] **marshal sessions** the meeting of the marshal's court.
[37] **fits...policy** suits the plan already laid.

I lay the plot, he prosecutes the point;
I set the trap, he breaks the worthless twigs,
And sees not that wherewith the bird was limed.
Thus hopeful men, that mean to hold their own,
Must look like fowlers to their dearest friends.
He runs to kill whom I have hope to catch,
And no man knows it was my reaching fetch.
'Tis hard to trust unto a multitude,
Or anyone, in mine opinion,
When men themselves their secrets will reveal.

Enter a Messenger with a letter.

LORENZO
Boy.

PAGE
My lord?

LORENZO
What's he?

MESSENGER
I have a letter to your lordship.

LORENZO
From whence?

MESSENGER
From Pedringano that's imprisoned.

LORENZO
So he is in prison then?

MESSENGER
Aye, my good lord.

LORENZO
What would he with us? He writes us here
To stand good lord and help him in distress.
Tell him I have his letters, know his mind;
And what we may, let him assure him of.
Fellow, be gone; my boy shall follow thee.

Exit Messenger.

This works like wax! Yet once more try thy wits.
Boy, go convey this purse to Pedringano,
Thou knowest the prison, closely give it him,
And be advised that none hear thereabout.
Bid him be merry still, but secret;
And, though the marshal sessions be today,
Bid him not doubt of his delivery.
Tell him his pardon is already signed,
And thereon bid him boldly be resolved,
For, were he ready to be turned off,
As 'tis my will the uttermost be tried,
Thou with his pardon shalt attend him still.
Show him this box, tell him his pardon's in't;
But open't not, and if thou lovest thy life,
But let him wisely keep his hopes unknown.
He shall not want while Don Lorenzo lives.
Away!

PAGE
I go, my lord, I run!

LORENZO
But, sirrah, see that this be cleanly done.

Exit Page.

Now stands our fortune on a tickle point,
And now or never ends Lorenzo's doubts.
One only thing is unaffected yet,
And that's to see the executioner.
But to what end? I list not trust the air
With utterance of our pretence therein,
For fear the privy whisp'ring of the wind
Convey our words amongst unfriendly ears,
That lie too open to advantages.
Et quel che voglio io, nessun lo sa,
Intendo io: quel che mi bastera. *Exit.*

[Act III. Scene v.]

Enter Boy with the box.

BOY
My master hath forbidden me to look in this box, and, by my troth, 'tis likely, if he had not warned

[41] **sees . . . limed** i.e. he does not see that I have planned all this.
[45] **reaching fetch** far-sighted scheme.
[56] **stand good lord** act as his patron.
[59] **works like wax** i.e. it moulds itself easily in the hands.
[61] **closely** secretly.
[65] **not . . . delivery** don't doubt he'll be released.
[68] **turned off** hanged.
[69] **'tis . . . tried** i.e. I wish him to seem content to be hanged (expecting to be rescued) until the very last minute (when it will be too late to confess the truth).
[76] **cleanly done** perfectly performed.
[77] **tickle** finely balanced/precarious.
[81] **list not** do not wish to.
[86–87] ***Et . . . bastera.*** 'And what I want, no one knows: I alone know, and that's enough for me' (Italian).

me, I should not have had so much idle time; for we men's-kind in our minority are like women in their uncertainty; that they are most forbidden, they will soonest attempt. So I now. By my bare honesty, here's nothing but the bare empty box! Were it not sin against secrecy, I would say it were a piece of gentleman-like knavery. I must go to Pedringano and tell him his pardon is in this box? Nay, I would have sworn it, had I not seen the contrary. I cannot choose but smile to think how the villain will flout the gallows, scorn the audience, and descant on the hangman, and all presuming of his pardon from hence. Will't not be an odd jest, for me to stand and grace every jest he makes, pointing my finger at this box, as who should say: 'Mock on, here's thy warrant!' Is't not a scurvy jest that a man should jest himself to death? Alas, poor Pedringano! I am in a sort sorry for thee, but, if I should be hanged with thee, I could not weep. *Exit.*

[Act III. Scene vi.]

Enter Hieronimo and the Deputy.

HIERONIMO
Thus must we toil in other men's extremes,
That know not how to remedy our own:
And do them justice, when unjustly we,
For all our wrongs, can compass no redress.
But shall I never live to see the day
That I may come by justice to the heavens,
To know the cause that may my cares allay?
This toils my body, this consumeth age,
That only I to all men just must be,
And neither gods nor men be just to me!

DEPUTY
Worthy Hieronimo, your office asks
A care to punish such as do transgress.

HIERONIMO
So is't my duty to regard his death
Who, when he lived, deserved my dearest blood.
But come; for that we came for, let's begin;
For here lies that which bids me to be gone.

Enter Officers, Boy, and Pedringano with a letter in his hand, bound.

DEPUTY
Bring forth the prisoner, for the court is set.

PEDRINGANO
Gramercy boy, but it was time to come,
For I had written to my lord anew
A nearer matter that concerneth him,
For fear his lordship had forgotten me.
But, sith he hath remembered me so well,
Come, come, come on; when shall we to this gear?

HIERONIMO
Stand forth, thou monster, murderer of men,
And here, for satisfaction of the world,
Confess thy folly and repent thy fault,
For there's thy place of execution.

PEDRINGANO
This is short work! Well, to your marshalship
First I confess, nor fear I death therefore,
I am the man, 'twas I slew Serberine.
But, sir, then you think this shall be the place
Where we shall satisfy you for this gear?

DEPUTY
Aye, Pedringano.

PEDRINGANO
No, I think not so.

HIERONIMO
Peace, impudent; for thou shalt find it so!
For blood with blood shall, while I sit as judge,
Be satisfied, and the law discharged.
And, though myself cannot receive the like,
Yet will I see that others have their right.

4–5 **men's-kind... uncertainty** men in their infancy are like women, who are inconsistent.
14 **descant on** abuse (i.e. improvise rudely on whatever he says).
19 **a scurvy jest** a poor/knavish joke.
21 **in a sort** sort of (but not really).
3–4 **when... redress** when we, for all the wrongs done to us, can devise no resolution of them.
7 **my cares allay** salve my sorrows.
11 **your office asks** your role demands.
13 **regard** care for.
16 **here** perhaps he touches his heart at this point.
18 **Gramercy** 'Thanks': contraction of '*grand merci*'.
20 **A nearer matter** On a more intimate matter.
23 **to this gear** get on with this business.
37 **the like** the same (i.e. justice).

Despatch, the fault approved and confessed,
And by our law he is condemned to die.

HANGMAN
Come on, sir, are you ready?

PEDRINGANO
To do what, my fine officious knave?

HANGMAN
To go to this gear.

PEDRINGANO
O, sir, you are too forward; thou wouldst fain furnish me with a halter, to disfurnish me of my habit. So should I go out of this gear, my raiment, into that gear, the rope. But, hangman, now I spy your knavery, I'll not change without boot; that's flat!

HANGMAN
Come, sir.

PEDRINGANO
So then, I must up?

HANGMAN
No remedy.

PEDRINGANO
Yes, but there shall be for my coming down.

HANGMAN
Indeed here's a remedy for that.

PEDRINGANO
How? Be turned off?

HANGMAN
Aye, truly. Come, are you ready? I pray you, sir, despatch; the day goes away.

PEDRINGANO
What, do you hang by the hour? If you do, I may chance to break your old custom.

HANGMAN
Faith, you have no reason, for I am like to break your young neck.

PEDRINGANO
Dost thou mock me, hangman? Pray God I be not preserved to break your knave's pate for this!

HANGMAN
Alas, sir, you are a foot too low to reach it, and I hope you will never grow so high while I am in office.

PEDRINGANO
Sirrah, dost see yonder boy with the box in his hand?

HANGMAN
What, he that points to it with his finger?

PEDRINGANO
Aye, that companion.

HANGMAN
I know him not; but what of him?

PEDRINGANO
Dost thou think to live till his old doublet will make thee a new truss?

HANGMAN
Aye, and many a fair year after, to truss up many an honester man than either thou or he.

PEDRINGANO
What hath he in his box, as thou think'st?

HANGMAN
Faith, I cannot tell, nor I care not greatly. Methinks you should rather harken to your soul's health.

PEDRINGANO
Why, sirrah hangman, I take it that that is good for the body is likewise good for the soul; and it may be in that box is balm for both.

HANGMAN
Well, thou art even the merriest piece of man's flesh that e'er groaned at my office-door.

PEDRINGANO
Is your roguery become an 'office', with a knave's name?

HANGMAN
Aye, and that shall all they witness that see you seal it with a thief's name.

PEDRINGANO
I prithee, request this good company to pray for me.

39 **Despatch** Get on with it.
43 **this gear** i.e. the scaffold.
44 **forward** eager.
44–45 **thou . . . habit** you would give me the noose in order to take from me my clothing (the hangman traditionally claimed the outer garments ('raiment') of the prisoner as his fee).
48 **without . . . flat!** without reward (punning perhaps on taking off his boots); that's certain!
49.2 **No remedy.** There's no alternative.
52 **turned off** hanged (pushed from his foothold).
60 **pate** skull.
68 **companion** fellow.
71 **truss** set of breeches.

HANGMAN
Aye, marry, sir, this is a good motion. My masters, you see here's a good fellow.

PEDRINGANO
Nay, nay, now I remember me, let them alone till some other time; for now I have no great need.

HIERONIMO
I have not seen a wretch so impudent!
O monstrous times, where murders are so light,
And where the soul that should be shrined in heaven
Solely delights in interdicted things,
Still wand'ring in the thorny passages
That intercepts itself of happiness!
Murder? O bloody monster! God forbid
A fault so foul should scape unpunished.
Despatch and see this execution done;
This makes me to remember thee, my son.

Exit Hieronimo.

PEDRINGANO
Nay soft, no haste!

DEPUTY
Why, wherefore stay you? Have you hope of life?

PEDRINGANO
Why, aye.

HANGMAN
As how?

PEDRINGANO
Why, rascal, by my pardon from the king.

HANGMAN
Stand you on that? Then you shall off with this.

He turns him off.

DEPUTY
So, executioner, convey him hence;
But let his body be unburied.
Let not the earth be choked or infect
With that which heaven condemns and men neglect.

Exeunt.

[Act III. Scene vii.]

Enter Hieronimo.

HIERONIMO
Where shall I run to breathe abroad my woes,
My woes whose weight hath wearied the earth?
Or mine exclaims that have surcharged the air
With ceaseless plaints for my deceased son?
The blust'ring winds, conspiring with my words,
At my lament have moved the leafless trees,
Disrobed the meadows of their flowered green,
Made mountains marsh with spring-tides of my tears,
And broken through the brazen gates of hell.
Yet still tormented is my tortured soul
With broken sighs and restless passions,
That, winged, mount, and hovering in the air,
Beat at the windows of the brightest heavens,
Soliciting for justice and revenge.
But they are placed in those empyrial heights,
Where, countermured with walls of diamond,
I find the place impregnable, and they
Resist my woes and give my words no way.

Enter Hangman with a letter.

HANGMAN
O lord, sir; God bless you, sir. The man, sir, Petergade, sir: he that was so full of merry conceits...

HIERONIMO
Well, what of him?

HANGMAN
O lord sir; he went the wrong way; the fellow had a fair commission to the contrary. Sir, here is his passport, I pray you, sir; we have done him wrong.

HIERONIMO
I warrant thee; give it me.

HANGMAN
You will stand between the gallows and me?

92 **let...time** tell them to wait until another time.
95 **light** flippant.
95-99 **the soul...happiness** i.e. the soul cannot find peace through confession and contrition, but still dwells on the crimes that keep it from heaven.
104 **soft** be quiet.
105 **wherefore you stay?** what are you waiting for?

1 **breathe abroad** speak publicly about.
3 **surcharged** overburdened.
15 **empyrial** heavenly.
16 **countermured** double-walled.
20 **Petergade** mispronunciation of 'Pedringano'.
28 **You...me?** You'll protect me from punishment (if it turns out we have hanged an innocent man)?

HIERONIMO
Aye, aye.

HANGMAN
I thank your lord worship.

Exit Hangman.

HIERONIMO
And yet, though somewhat nearer me concerns
I will, to ease the grief that I sustain,
Take truce with sorrow while I read on this. [*Reads*]
'My lord, I write, as mine extremes require,
That you would labour my delivery:
If you neglect, my life is desperate,
And in my death I shall reveal the truth.
You know, my lord, I slew him for your sake,
And was confederate with the prince and you;
Won by rewards and hopeful promises,
I holp to murder Don Horatio too.'
Holp he to murder mine Horatio?
And actors in th'accursed tragedy
Wast thou, Lorenzo, Balthazar, and thou,
Of whom my son, my son deserved so well?
What have I heard? What have mine eyes beheld?
O sacred heavens, may it come to pass
That such a monstrous and detested deed,
So closely smothered, and so long concealed,
Shall thus by this be venged or revealed?
Now see I, what I durst not then suspect,
That Bel-Imperia's letter was not feigned,
Nor feigned she, though falsely they have wronged
Both her, myself, Horatio, and themselves.
Now may I make compare twixt hers and this
Of every accident. I ne'er could find
Till now, and now I feelingly perceive,
They did what heaven unpunished should not leave.
O false Lorenzo, are these thy flattering looks?
Is this honour that thou didst my son?
And, Balthazar, bane to thy soul and me!
Was this the ransom he reserved for thee?
Woe to the cause of these constrained wars,
Woe to thy baseness and captivity,
Woe to thy birth, thy body and thy soul,
Thy cursed father, and thy conquered self!
And banned with bitter execrations be
The day and place where he did pity thee!
But wherefore waste I mine unfruitful words,
When naught but blood will satisfy my woes?
I will go plain me to my lord the king,
And cry aloud for justice through the court,
Wearing the flints with these my withered feet,
And either purchase justice by entreats
Or tire them all with my revenging threats. *Exit.*

[Act III. Scene viii.]

Enter Isabella and her Maid.

ISABELLA
So that you say this herb will purge the eyes,
And this the head?
Ah, but none of them will purge the heart.
No, there's no medicine left for my disease,
Nor any physic to recure the dead.

She runs lunatic.

Horatio! O, where's Horatio?

MAID
Good madam, affright not thus yourself
With outrage for your son Horatio;
He sleeps in quiet in the Elysian fields.

ISABELLA
Why did I not give you gowns and goodly things,
Bought you a whistle and a whipstalk too,
To be revenged on their villainies?

MAID
Madam, these humours do torment my soul.

ISABELLA
My soul? Poor soul, thou talks of things
Thou knowest not what. My soul hath silver wings,
That mount me up unto the highest heavens.
To heaven? Aye, there sits up Horatio,
Backed with a troop of fiery cherubins,
Dancing about his newly healed wounds,

27 **though...concerns** although something closer (to my heart) preoccupies my thoughts.
40 **holp** helped.
48 **smothered** hidden.
55 **accident** detail.
66 **banned** cursed.
70 **plain** complain.
73 **purchase...entreats** win justice through my entreaties.
5 **recure** cure/recover.
9 **Elysian fields** that part of Hades reserved for the virtuous.
11 **whipstalk** a whip for spinning a top. Isabella is speaking to Horatio as if he were a child.

Singing sweet hymns and chanting heavenly notes:
Rare harmony to greet his innocence,
That died, aye, died, a mirror in our days.
But say, where shall I find the men, the murderers,
That slew Horatio? Whither shall I run
To find them out that murdered my son?

Exeunt.

[Act III. Scene ix.]

Bel-Imperia at a window.

BEL-IMPERIA
What means this outrage that is offered me?
Why am I thus sequestered from the court?
No notice? Shall I not know the cause
Of these my secret and suspicious ills?
Accursed brother, unkind murderer,
Why bends thou thus thy mind to martyr me?
Hieronimo, why writ I of their wrongs,
Or why art thou so slack in thy revenge?
Andrea, O Andrea, that thou sawest
Me for thy friend Horatio handled thus,
And him for me thus causeless murdered.
Well, force perforce, I must constrain myself
To patience, and apply me to the time,
Till heaven, as I have hoped, shall set me free.

Enter Christophel.

CHRISTOPHEL
Come, Madam Bel-Imperia, this must not be.

Exeunt.

[Act III. Scene x.]

Enter Lorenzo, Balthazar and the Page.

LORENZO
Boy, talk no further; thus far things go well.
Thou art assured that thou sawest him dead?
PAGE
Or else, my lord, I live not.
LORENZO
That's enough.
As for his resolution at his end,
Leave that to him with whom he sojourns now.
Here, take my ring and give it Christophel,
And bid him let my sister be enlarged,
And bring her hither straight.

Exit Page.

This that I did was for a policy,
To smooth and keep the murder secret,
Which as a nine days wonder being o'er-blown,
My gentle sister will I now enlarge.
BALTHAZAR
And time, Lorenzo; for my lord the duke,
You heard, enquired for her yesternight.
LORENZO
Why, and, my lord, I hope you have heard me say
Sufficient reason why she kept away.
But that's all one. My lord, you love her?
BALTHAZAR
Aye.
LORENZO
Then in your love beware; deal cunningly;
Salve all suspicions; only soothe me up,
And, if she hap to stand on terms with us,
As for her sweetheart, and concealment so,
Jest with her gently; under feigned jest
Are things concealed that else would breed unrest.
But here she comes.

Enter Bel-Imperia.

LORENZO
Now, sister.
BEL-IMPERIA
Sister? No.
Thou art no brother, but an enemy,
Else wouldst thou not have used thy sister so:
First, to affright me with thy weapons drawn,
And with extremes abuse my company;
And then to hurry me like whirlwind's rage
Amidst a crew of thy confederates,
And clap me up where none might come at me,
Nor I at any, to reveal my wrongs.

21 **greet** weep for/honour.
22 **a mirror** an example (of perfection).
12 **force perforce** of necessity.
7 **enlarged** released.
11 **a nine ... o'er-blown** a temporary scandal now forgotten.
19–22 **Salve ... gently** calm her suspicions, just support whatever I say. And if she happens to challenge us over her lover's death, or her own imprisonment, make a gentle joke of it.
31 **clap ... me** lock me away where no one could come to me.

What madding fury did possess thy wits?
Or wherein is't that I offended thee?

LORENZO
Advise you better, Bel-Imperia;
For I have done you no disparagement,
Unless, by more discretion than deserved,
I sought to save your honour and mine own.

BEL-IMPERIA
Mine honour? Why, Lorenzo, wherein is't
That I neglect my reputation so
As you, or any, need to rescue it?

LORENZO
His highness and my father were resolved
To come confer with old Hieronimo
Concerning certain matters of estate
That by the viceroy was determined.

BEL-IMPERIA
And wherein was mine honour touched in that?

BALTHAZAR
Have patience, Bel-Imperia; hear the rest.

LORENZO
Me next in sight as messenger they sent
To give him notice that they were so nigh.
Now, when I came, consorted with the prince,
And unexpected in an arbour there
Found Bel-Imperia with Horatio.

BEL-IMPERIA
How then?

LORENZO
Why, then, remembering that old disgrace
Which you for Don Andrea had endured,
And now were likely longer to sustain
By being found so meanly accompanied,
Thought rather, for I knew no readier mean,
To thrust Horatio forth my father's way.

BALTHAZAR
And carry you obscurely somewhere else,
Lest that his highness should have found you there.

BEL-IMPERIA
Even so, my lord? And you are witness
That this is true which he entreateth of?
You, gentle brother, forged this for my sake?
And you, my lord, were made his instrument?
A work of worth, worthy the noting too!
But what's the cause that you concealed me since?

LORENZO
Your melancholy, sister, since the news
Of your first favourite Don Andrea's death,
My father's old wrath hath exasperate.

BALTHAZAR
And better was't for you, being in disgrace,
To absent yourself and give his fury place.

BEL-IMPERIA
But why had I no notice of his ire?

LORENZO
That were to add more fuel to your fire,
Who burnt like Etna for Andrea's loss.

BEL-IMPERIA
Hath not my father then enquired for me?

LORENZO
Sister, he hath; and this excused I thee.

He whispereth in her ear.

But, Bel-Imperia, see the gentle prince;
Look on thy love, behold young Balthazar,
Whose passions by the presence are increased,
And in whose melancholy thou may'st see
Thy hate, his love; thy flight, his following thee.

BEL-IMPERIA
Brother, you are become an orator,
I know not, I, by what experience,
Too politic for me, past all compare,
Since I last saw you. But content yourself,
The prince is meditating higher things.

BALTHAZAR
'Tis of thy beauty, then, that conquers kings,
Of those thy tresses, Ariadne's twines,
Wherewith my liberty thou hast surprised,
Of that thine ivory front, my sorrow's map,
Wherein I see no haven to rest my hope.

BEL-IMPERIA
To love and fear, and both at once, my lord,
In my conceit, are things of more import
Than women's wit are to be busied with.

35 **Advise you better** Think more clearly.
57 **meanly accompanied** in the company of a social inferior (the same 'offence' she had committed with Andrea).
58 **readier mean** easier way.
70 **My ... exasperate** has just increased my father's anger with you.
72 **give ... place** leave him alone with his anger.
75 **Etna** the Sicilian volcano.
89 **Ariadne's twines** the threads used by Ariadne to guide Theseus through the maze of the Minotaur, for which she was turned by Athene into a spider.
90 **surprised** ambushed.

BALTHAZAR
'Tis that I love thee.

BEL-IMPERIA
Whom?

BALTHAZAR
Bel-Imperia.

BEL-IMPERIA
But that I fear?

BALTHAZAR
Whom?

BEL-IMPERIA
Bel-Imperia.

LORENZO
Fear yourself?

BEL-IMPERIA
Aye, brother.

LORENZO
How?

BEL-IMPERIA
As those
That what they love are loath and fear to lose.

BALTHAZAR
Then, fair, let Balthazar your keeper be.

BEL-IMPERIA
No, Balthazar doth fear as well as we;
Et tremulo metui pavidum junxere timorem,
Et vanum stolidae proditionis opus. *Exit.*

LORENZO
Nay, and you argue things so cunningly,
We'll go continue this discourse at court.

BALTHAZAR
Led by the loadstar of heavenly looks,
Wends poor oppressed Balthazar,
As o'er the mountains walks the wanderer,
Incertain to effect his pilgrimage.

Exeunt.

[Act III. Scene xi.]

Enter two Portingales, and Hieronimo meets them.

FIRST PORTINGAL
By your leave, sir.

[*Additional lines from the 1602 edition.*

HIERONIMO
'Tis neither as you think, nor as you think,
Nor as you think, you're wide all:
These slippers are not mine, they were my son
Horatio's.
My son? And what's a son? A thing begot
Within a pair of minutes, thereabout;
A lump bred up in darkness, and doth serve
To balance those light creatures we call women,
And at nine months end creeps forth to light.
What is there yet in a son
To make a father dote, rave, or run mad?
Being born, it pouts, cries, and breeds teeth.
What is there yet in a son? He must be fed,
Be taught to go and speak. Aye, or yet,
Why might not a man love a calf as well,
Or melt in passion over a frisking kid
As for a son? Methinks a young bacon
Or a fine smooth little horse-colt
Should move a man as much as doth a son;
For one of these in very little time
Will grow to some good use, whereas a son,
The more he grows in stature and in years,
The more unsquared, unlevelled he appears,
Reckons his parents among the rank of fools,
Strikes cares upon their heads with his mad riots,
Makes them look old before they meet with age.
This is a son!
And what a loss were this, considered truly.
O, but my Horatio
Grew out of reach of those insatiate humours.
He loved his loving parents,
He was my comfort, and his mother's joy
The very arm that did hold up our house;
Our hopes were stored up in him.
None but a damned murderer could hate him.

102–103 ***Et...opus.*** 'They bound trembling fear to timorous dread, a foolish piece of stupid treason.'
104 **and** if.
109 **Incertain to effect** Uncertain how to perform.
1 **By...sir.** Excuse me, sir.
3 **wide all** all wide of the mark/wrong.
6 **thereabout** roughly speaking.
14 **go** walk.
16 **frisking kid** young goat.
17 **bacon** pig.
23 **unsquared, unlevelled** rough and irregular.

He had not seen the back of nineteen year,
When his strong arm unhorsed the proud prince
Balthazar;
And his great mind, too full of honour
Took him unto mercy,
That valiant but ignoble Portingale.
Well, heaven is heaven still.
And there's Nemesis, and Furies,
And things called whips,
And they sometimes do meet with murderers.
They do not always 'scape, that's some comfort.
Aye, aye, aye; and then time steals on,
And steals and steals, till violence leaps forth
Like thunder wrapped in a ball of fire,
And so doth bring confusion to them all.]
Good leave have you; nay, I pray you go,
For I'll leave you, if you can leave me so.

SECOND PORTINGALE
Pray you, which is the next way to my lord the Duke's?

HIERONIMO
The next way from me.

FIRST PORTINGALE
To the house, we mean.

HIERONIMO
O hard by; 'tis yon house that you see.

SECOND PORTINGALE
You could not tell us if his son were there?

HIERONIMO
Who, my lord Lorenzo?

FIRST PORTINGALE
Aye, sir.

He goeth in at one door and comes out at another.

HIERONIMO
O, forbear,
For other talk for us far fitter were.
But, if you be importunate to know
The way to him and where to find him out,
Then list to me, and I'll resolve your doubt.
There is a path upon your left hand side
That leadeth from a guilty conscience
Unto a forest of distrust and fear,
A darksome place and dangerous to pass,
There shall you meet with melancholy thoughts
Whose baleful humours if you but uphold,
It will conduct you to despair and death;
Whose rocky cliffs when you have once beheld,
Within a hugey dale of lasting night,
That, kindled with worlds of iniquities,
Doth cast up filthy and detested fumes;
Not far from thence where murderers have built
A habitation for their cursed souls,
There, in a brazen caldron fixed by Jove
In his fell wrath upon a sulpher flame,
Yourselves shall find Lorenzo bathing him
In boiling lead and blood of innocents.

FIRST PORTINGALE
Ha, ha, ha!

HIERONIMO
Ha, ha, ha!
Why, ha, ha, ha! Farewell, good ha, ha, ha! *Exit.*

SECOND PORTINGAL
Doubtless this man is passing lunatic,
Or imperfection of his age doth make him dote.
Come, let's away to seek my lord the Duke. [*Exeunt.*]

[Act III. Scene xii.]

Enter Hieronimo with a poniard in one hand and a rope in the other.

HIERONIMO
Now, sir, perhaps I come to see the king,
The king sees me, and fain would hear my suit:
Why, is this not a strange and seld-seen thing
That standers by with toys should strike me mute?
Go to, I see their shifts, and say no more.
Hieronimo, 'tis time for thee to trudge.
Down by the dale that flows with purple gore
Standeth a fiery tower; there sits a judge
Upon a seat of steel and molten brass,
And twixt his teeth he holds a fire-brand,
That leads unto the lake where he doth stand.
Away, Hieronimo, to him be gone:
He'll do thee justice for Horatio's death.

68 **uphold** sustain.
71 **hugey dale** huge valley.
85.1 **poniard** knife.
3 **seld-seen** seldom-seen.
4 **toys** trifles.
5 **shifts** schemes.
6 **trudge** leave/get going.

Turn down this path, thou shalt be with him straight;
Or this, and then thou needst not take thy
breath.
This way, or that way? Soft and fair, not so.
For, if I hang or kill myself, let's know
Who will revenge Horatio's murther then.
No, no; fie, no! Pardon me, I'll none of that.

He flings away the dagger and halter.

This way I'll take; and this way comes the king,

He takes them up again.

And here I'll have a fling at him, that's flat!
And, Balthazar, I'll be with thee to bring;
And thee, Lorenzo. Here's the king, nay, stay,
And here, aye here, there goes the hare away!

Enter King, Ambassador, Castile, and Lorenzo.

KING
Now show, Ambassador, what our viceroy saith:
Hath he received the articles we sent?

HIERONIMO
Justice! O, justice to Hieronimo!

LORENZO
Back! Seest thou not the king is busy?

HIERONIMO
Oh, is he so?

KING
Who is he that interrupts our business?

HIERONIMO
Not I.

[*Aside*]

Hieronimo, beware; go by, go by!

AMBASSADOR
Renowned king, he hath received and read
Thy kingly proffers and thy promised league,
And, as a man extremely overjoyed
To hear his son so princely entertained,
Whose death he had so solemnly bewailed,
This, for thy further satisfaction
And kingly love, he kindly lets thee know:
First, for the marriage of his princely son
With Bel-Imperia, thy beloved niece,
The news are more delightful to his soul
Than myrrh or incense to the offended heavens.
In person, therefore, will he come himself
To see the marriage rites solemnized,
And in the presence of the court of Spain
To knit a sure inextricable band
Of kingly love and everlasting league
Betwixt the crowns of Spain and Portingale,
There will he give his crown to Balthazar,
And make a queen of Bel-Imperia.

KING
Brother, how like you this our viceroy's love?

CASTILE
No doubt, my lord, it is an argument
Of honourable care to keep his friend,
And wondrous zeal to Balthazar, his son.
Nor am I least indebted to his grace,
That bends his liking to my daughter thus.

AMBASSADOR
Now last, dread lord, here hath his highness sent,
Although he send not that his son return,
His ransom due to Don Horatio.

HIERONIMO
Horatio? Who calls Horatio?

KING
And well remembered, thank his majesty.
Here, see it given to Horatio.

HIERONIMO
Justice! O justice! Justice, gentle king!

KING
Who is that? Hieronimo?

HIERONIMO
Justice! O justice! O my son, my son;
My son, whom naught can ransom or redeem!

LORENZO
Hieronimo, you are not well advised.

HIERONIMO
Away, Lorenzo; hinder me no more,
For thou hast made me bankrupt of my bliss.
Give me my son! You shall not ransom him.
Away! I'll rip the bowels of the earth,

He diggeth with his dagger.

And ferry over th'Elysian plains
And bring my son to show his deadly wounds.

[15] Hieronimo contemplates the knife and rope, rival means to take his own life and speed his passage to the king of the underworld.

[24] **there . . . away** there goes my quarry.
[31] **go by!** step aside/watch out!
[52] **argument** evidence of.

Stand from about me! I'll make a pickaxe of my
 poniard,
And here surrender up my marshalship;
For I'll go marshal up the fiends in hell,
To be avenged on you all for this.

KING
What means this outrage?
Will none of you restrain his fury?

HIERONIMO
Nay, soft and fair; you shall not need to strive;
Needs must he go that the devils drive. *Exit.*

KING
What accident hath happed Hieronimo?
I have not seen him to demean him so.

LORENZO
My gracious lord, he is with extreme pride
Conceived of young Horatio, his son,
And covetous of having himself
The ransom of the young prince, Balthazar,
Distract, and in a manner lunatic.

KING
Believe me, nephew, we are sorry for't;
This is the love that fathers bear their sons.
But, gentle brother, go give to him this gold,
The prince's ransom; let him have his due;
For what he hath, Horatio shall not want.
Happily Hieronimo hath need thereof.

LORENZO
But if he be thus helplessly distract,
'Tis requisite his office be resigned
And given to one of more discretion.

KING
We shall increase his melancholy so.
'Tis best that we see further in it first;
Till when, ourself will exempt the place.
And, brother, now bring in the ambassador,
That he may be a witness of the match
'Twixt Balthazar and Bel-Imperia,
And that we may prefix a certain time
Wherein the marriage shall be solemnized,
That we may have thy lord the viceroy here.

AMBASSADOR
Therein your Highness highly shall content
His majesty, that longs to hear from hence.

KING
On then, and hear you, lord Ambassador. *Exeunt.*

[*'The Painter Scene,' from the Additions of 1602*]
Enter Jaques and Pedro.

JAQUES
I wonder Pedro, why our master thus
At midnight sends us with our torches' light,
When man and bird and beast are all at rest,
Save those that watch for rape and bloody murder?

PEDRO
O Jaques, know thou that our master's mind
Is much distraught since his Horatio died,
And, now his aged years should sleep in rest,
His heart in quiet, like a desperate man,
Grows lunatic and childish for his son.
Sometimes, as he doth at his table sit,
He speaks as if Horatio stood by him,
Then, starting in a rage, falls on the earth,
Cries out, 'Horatio; Where is my Horatio?'
So that with extreme grief and cutting sorrow,
There is not left in him one inch of man.
See where he comes. *Enter Hieronimo.*

HIERONIMO
I pry through every crevice of each wall,
Look on each tree, and search through every brake,
Beat at the bushes, stamp our grandam earth,
Dive in the water, and stare up to heaven,
Yet cannot I behold my son Horatio.
How now? Who's there? Sprites? Sprites?

PEDRO
We are your servants that attend you, sir.

HIERONIMO
What make you with your torches in the dark?

PEDRO
You bid us light them, and attend you here.

HIERONIMO
No, no, you are deceived: not I, you are deceived.

88 **Distract** distracted/mentally unbalanced.
94 **Happily** perhaps.
98 **We...so.** Doing that would only increase his derangement.
100 **ourself...place** perhaps, 'we will temporarily exempt the office from the normal practice of replacing unfit holders'.
s.d. This scene in part echoes III.xiii that follows, with the role of Bazulto, the old man seeking justice for a murdered son, replaced by Bazardo the painter. It is unlikely that both scenes would have been played in the same performance, but both are given here as each has its own dramatic and artistic merits.
18 **brake** thicket.
19 **grandam** grandmother.
22 **Sprites?** Spirits/ghosts.
24 **What make you?** What are you doing?

Was I so mad to bid you light your torches now?
Light me your torches at the mid of noon,
Whenas the sun-god rides in all his glory:
Light me your torches then.

PEDRO
Then we burn daylight.

HIERONIMO
Let it be burnt; night is a murderous slut
That would not have her treasons to be seen,
And yonder pale-faced Hecate there, the moon,
Doth give consent to that is done in darkness,
And all those stars that gaze upon her face
Are aglets on her sleeve, pins on her train:
And those that should be powerful and divine,
Do sleep in darkness when they most should shine.

PEDRO
Provoke them not, fair sir, with tempting words.
The heavens are gracious, and your miseries
And sorrow makes you speak you know not what.

HIERONIMO
Villain, thou liest, and thou doest naught
But tell me I am mad. Thou liest, I am not mad.
I know thee to be Pedro, and he Jaques.
I'll prove it to thee, and were I mad, how could I?
Where was she that same night when my Horatio
Was murdered? She should have shone, search thou
the book.
Had the moon shone, in my boy's face there was a
kind of grace,
That I know, nay, I do know, had the murderer
seen him,
His weapon would have fall'n and cut the earth,
Had he been framed of naught but blood and death.
Alack, when mischief doth it knows not what,
What shall we say to mischief?

Enter Isabella.

ISABELLA
Dear Hieronimo, come in a-doors;
O seek not means so to increase thy sorrow.

HIERONIMO
Indeed, Isabella, we do nothing here,
I do not cry, ask Pedro and ask Jaques,
Not I indeed, we are very merry, very merry.

ISABELLA
How, be merry here? Be merry here?
Is not this the place, and this the very tree,
Where my Horatio died, where he was murdered?

HIERONIMO
Was ... do not say what; let her weep it out.
This was the tree, I set it of a kernel,
And when our hot Spain could not let it grow,
But that the infant and the human sap
Began to wither, duly twice a morning
Would I be sprinkling it with fountain water.
At last it grew and grew, and bore and bore,
Till at the length it grew a gallows, and did bear
our son.
It bore thy fruit and mine: O wicked, wicked plant.

One knocks within at the door.

See who knock[s] there.

PEDRO
It is a painter, sir.

HIERONIMO
Bid him come in, and paint some comfort.
For surely there's none lives but painted comfort.
Let him come in. One knows not what may
chance ...
God's will that I should set this tree? But even so
Masters ungrateful servants rear from naught,
And then they hate them that did bring them up.

Enter the Painter.

PAINTER
God bless you, sir.

HIERONIMO
Wherefore? Why, thou scornful villain,
How, where, or by what means should
I be blessed?

ISABELLA
What wouldst thou have, good fellow?

PAINTER
Justice, madam.

[29] **Whenas** When.
[31] **burn daylight** i.e. waste our time in something pointless.
[34] **Hecate** goddess of the moon and witchcraft.
[37] **aglets** broaches/ornaments.
[46] **I'll prove it** i.e. what he was saying about the moon and stars conniving in Horatio's murder.
[47] **she** the moon.
[48] **the book** the almanac charting the phases of the moon.
[52] **Had ... but** Even if he had been made up of nothing but.
[64] **set ... kernel** planted it as a nut.

HIERONIMO

O ambitious beggar, wouldst thou have that
That lives not in the world?
Why all the undelved mines cannot buy
An ounce of justice, 'tis a jewel so inestimable:
I tell thee, God hath engrossed all justice in his hands,
And there is none, but what comes from him.

PAINTER

O then I see that God must right me for my murdered son.

HIERONIMO

How, was thy son murdered?

PAINTER

Aye, sir, no man did hold a son so dear.

HIERONIMO

What, not as thine? That's a lie
As massy as the earth! I had a son,
Whose least unvalued hair did weigh
A thousand of thy sons, and he was murdered.

PAINTER

Alas, sir, I had no more but he.

HIERONIMO

Nor I, nor I, but this same one of mine
Was worth a legion, but all is one.
Pedro, Jaques, go in a-doors; Isabella go,
And this good fellow here and I
Will range this hideous orchard up and down,
Like to two lions reaved of their young.
Go in a-doors, I say.

Exeunt [Isabella. Pedro, Jacques]
The Painter and he sit down.

Come, let's talk wisely now. Was thy son murdered?

PAINTER

Aye, sir.

HIERONIMO

So was mine. How dost take it? Art thou not sometimes mad? Is there no tricks that comes before thine eyes?

PAINTER

O Lord, yes sir.

HIERONIMO

Art a painter? Canst paint me a tear, or a wound, a groan, or a sigh?
Canst paint me such a tree as this?

PAINTER

Sir, I am sure you have heard of my painting, my name's Bazardo.

HIERONIMO

Bazardo! Afore God, an excellent fellow! Look you sir, do you see: I'd have you paint me in my gallery, in your oil colours matted, and draw me five years younger than I am: do you see, sir, let five years go, let them go like the marshal of Spain, my wife Isabella standing by me, with a speaking look to my son Horatio, which should intend to this or some such like purpose: 'God bless thee, my sweet son', and my hand leaning upon his head, thus sir. Do you see? May it be done?

PAINTER

Very well, sir.

HIERONIMO

Nay, I pray mark me, sir. Then sir, would I have you paint me this tree, this very tree. Canst paint a doleful cry?

PAINTER

Seemingly, sir.

HIERONIMO

Nay, it should cry: but all is one. Well sir, paint me a youth, run through and through with villains' swords, hanging upon this tree. Canst thou draw a murderer?

PAINTER

I'll warrant you, sir: I have the pattern of the most notorious villains that ever lived in all Spain.

HIERONIMO

O let them be worse, worse: stretch thine art, and let their beards be of Judas his own colour, and let their eye-brows jutty over: in any case observe that. Then sir, after some violent noise, bring me

86 **all... mines** all the unexploited mines in the world.
94 **massy** massive/heavy.
99 **all is one** it doesn't matter.
102 **range** prowl.
103 **reaved** robbed.
111 **Canst** Can you.
118 **matted** dulled, like matt paint.
128 **mark** pay attention to.
131 **Seemingly** So that it seems real.
139 **colour** Judas was painted in Medieval and Renaissance art with red hair and beard.
140 **jutty over** overhang.

forth in my shirt, and my gown under mine arm, with my torch in my hand, and my sword reared up thus, and with these words: 'What noise is this? Who calls Hieronimo?' May it be done?

PAINTER

Yea, sir.

HIERONIMO

Well sir, then bring me forth, bring me through alley and alley, still with a distracted countenance going along, and let my hair heave up my night-cap. Let the clouds scowl, make the moon dark, the stars extinct, the winds blowing, the bells tolling, the owl shrieking, the toads croaking, the minutes jarring, and the clock striking twelve. And then at last, sir, starting, behold a man hanging, and tottering and tottering, as you know the wind will weave a man, and I with a trice to cut him down. And, looking upon him by the advantage of my torch, find it to be my son Horatio. There you may show a passion; there you may show a passion! Draw me like old Priam of Troy, crying, 'The house is a-fire, the house is a-fire', as the torch over my head. Make me curse, make me rave, make me cry, make me mad, make me well again, make me curse hell, invocate heaven, and in the end, leave me in a trance, and so forth.

PAINTER

And is this the end?

HIERONIMO

O no, there is no end: the end is death and madness. As I am never better than when I am mad: then methinks I am a brave fellow, then I do wonders: but reason abuseth me, and there's the torment, there's the hell. At the last, sir, bring me to one of the murderers, were he as strong as Hector, thus would I tear and drag him up and down.

He beats the Painter in, then comes out again with a book in his hand.

End of inserted scene.]

[Act III. Scene xiii.]

Enter Hieronimo with a book in his hand.

HIERONIMO

Vindicta mihi.
Aye, heaven will be revenged of every ill,
Nor will they suffer murder unrepaid.
Then stay, Hieronimo, attend their will,
For mortal men may not appoint their time.
'*Per scelus semper tutum est sceleribus iter.*'
Strike, and strike home, where wrong is offered thee,
For evils unto ills conductors be,
And death's the worst of resolution.
For he that thinks with patience to contend
To quiet life, his life shall easily end.
'*Fata si miseros juvant, habes selutem;*
Fata si vitam negant, habes sepulchrum.'
'If destiny thy miseries do ease,
Then hast thou health, and happy shalt thou be;
If destiny deny thee life, Hieronimo,
Yet shalt thou be assured of a tomb;'
If neither, yet let this thy comfort be:
Heaven covereth him that hath no burial.
And, to conclude, I will revenge his death!
But how? Not as the vulgar wits of men,
With open, but inevitable ills;
As by a secret, yet a certain mean,
Which under kindship will be cloaked best.
Wise men will take their opportunity,
Closely and safely fitting things to time;
But in extremes advantage hath no time;

155–156 **weave a man** swing a body.
156 **with a trice** in an instant.
160 **Draw...Troy** Paint me in the mode of Priam, King of Troy, bewailing the destruction of his city.
172 **were...Hector** even if he is as strong as the Trojan hero, Hector.
s.d. 174 **He...in** i.e. pursues him offstage, beating him.
1 ***Vindicta mihi.*** 'Vengeance is mine.' Hieronimo recalls Romans 12:19 ('Revenge is mine, I will repay, saith the Lord').
6 ***Per...iter.*** 'The safe way for crime is through (more) crime.' Hieronimo is reading an edition of Seneca. This is a quotation from his *Agamemnon*, l. 155.
7–9 **Strike...resolution.** The criminals will only go from one crime to another, so strike against them, the worst that can happen is death (and that will happen either way).
12–13 ***Fata...sepulchrum.*** From Seneca's *Troades*, 511–12. Hieronimo translates these lines in what follows.
24 **kindship** (the appearance of) friendship.
27 **in...time** in desperate situations there is no time to pick the best opportunity.

And therefore all times fit not for revenge.
Thus, therefore, will I rest me in unrest,
Dissembling quiet in unquietness,
Not seeming that I know their villainies,
That my simplicity may make them think
That ignorantly I will let all slip:
For ignorance, I wot, and well they know,
Remedium malorum iners est.
Nor ought avails it me to menace them,
Who, as a wintry storm upon a plain,
Will bear me down with their nobility.
No, no, Hieronimo, thou must enjoin
Thine eyes to observation, and thy tongue
To milder speeches than thy spirit affords,
Thy heart to patience, and thy hands to rest,
Thy cap to courtesy, and thy knee to bow,
Till to revenge thou know when, where and how.
How now? What noise, what coil is that you keep?

A noise within. Enter a Servant.

SERVANT
Here are a sort of poor petitioners
That are importunate, and it shall please you, sir,
That you should plead their cases to the king.

HIERONIMO
That I should plead their several actions?
Why, let them enter, and let me see them.

Enter three Citizens and an Old Man [*Bazulto*].

FIRST CITIZEN
So I tell you this, for learning and for law
There is not any advocate in Spain
That can prevail or will take half the pain
That he will, in pursuit of equity.

HIERONIMO
Come near, you men that thus importune me.
[*Aside*]
Now must I bear a face of gravity,
For thus I used, before my marshalship,
To plead the causes as corregidor.
Come on, sirs, what's the matter?

FIRST CITIZEN
Sir, an action.

HIERONIMO
Of battery?

FIRST CITIZEN
Mine of debt.

HIERONIMO
Give place.

SECOND CITIZEN
No, sir, mine is an action of the case.

THIRD CITIZEN
Mine an *ejectionae firmae* by a lease.

HIERONIMO
Content you sirs, are you determined
That I should plead your several actions?

FIRST CITIZEN
Aye, sir; and here's my declaration.

SECOND CITIZEN
And here is my bond.

THIRD CITIZEN
And here is my lease.

They give him papers.

HIERONIMO
But wherefore stands you, silly man, so mute,
With mournful eyes and hands to heaven upreared?
Come hither, father; let me know thy cause.

SENEX [*Bazulto*]
O worthy sir, my cause but slightly known
May move the hearts of warlike Myrmidons,
And melt the Corsic rocks with ruthful tears!

HIERONIMO
Say, father; tell me, what's thy suit?

BAZULTO
No, sir, could my woes
Give way unto my most distressful words,
Then should I not in paper, as you see,
With ink bewray what blood began in me.

34 **wot** know.
35 ***Remedium... est*** '(Ignorance) is a poor remedy for evil.' Seneca, *Oedipus*, 515.
36 **Nor... me** nor does it help me at all.
45 **What... keep?** What commotion are you making?
46 **sort** group.
49 **several actions** various lawsuits.
58 **corregidor** a Spanish magistrate, here used more generally to mean a lawyer.
60.1 **Give place.** Step aside.
61 **action... case** a special kind of writ allowing access to the court.
62 ***ejectionae*... lease** a writ to eject a tenant before his or her lease expires.
69.1 **Senex** Old man.
70 **but slightly known** even if it were known only in part.
71 **Myrmidons** the fierce followers of Achilles.
72 **Corsic rocks** rugged rocks of Corsica.

HIERONIMO
What's here? 'The humble supplication
Of Don Bazulto for his murdered son.'

BAZULTO
Aye, sir.

HIERONIMO
No, sir, it was my murdered son,
O, my son, my son, O, my son Horatio!
But mine or thine, Bazulto, be content.
Here, take my handkercher and wipe thine eyes,
Whiles wretched I in thy mishaps may see
The lively portrait of my dying self.

He draweth out a bloody napkin.

O, no, not this. Horatio, this was thine!
And when I dyed it in thy dearest blood,
This was a token 'twixt thy soul and me
That of thy death revenged I should be.
But here, take this, and this—what, my purse?
Aye, this, and that, and all of them are thine;
For all as one are our extremities.

FIRST CITIZEN
O, see the kindness of Hieronimo!

SECOND CITIZEN
This gentleness shows him a gentleman.

HIERONIMO
See, see, O, see thy shame, Hieronimo,
See here a loving father to his son.
Behold the sorrows and the sad laments
That he delivereth for his son's decease.
If love's effects so strives in lesser things,
If love enforce such moods in meaner wits,
If love express such power in poor estates,
Hieronimo, as when a raging sea,
Tossed with the wind and tide, o'erturneth then
The upper-billows, course of waves to keep,
Whilest lesser waters labour in the deep,
Then shamest thou not, Hieronimo, to neglect
The sweet revenge of thy Horatio?
Though on this earth justice will not be found,
I'll down to hell and in this passion
Knock at the dismal gates of Pluto's court,
Getting by force, as once Alcides did,
A troop of Furies and tormenting hags
To torture Don Lorenzo and the rest.
Yet, lest the triple-headed porter should
Deny my passage to the slimy strond,
The Thracian poet thou shalt counterfeit.
Come on, old father, be my Orpheus;
And, if thou canst no notes upon the harp,
Then sound the burden of thy sore heart's grief
Till we do gain that Proserpine may grant:
Revenge on them that murdered my son.
Then will I rent and tear them thus and thus,
Shivering their limbs in pieces with my teeth!

Tear the papers.

FIRST CITIZEN
Oh, sir, my declaration!

Exit Hieronimo and they after.

SECOND CITIZEN
Save my bond! *Enter Hieronimo.*

FIRST CITIZEN
Save my bond!

THIRD CITIZEN
Alas my lease, it cost me ten pound,
And you, my lord, have torn the same!

HIERONIMO
That cannot be, I gave it never a wound;
Show me one drop of blood fall from the same.
How is it possible I should slay it then?
Tush, no. Run after, catch me if you can!

Exeunt all but the Old Man [*Bazulto*].
Bazulto remains till Hieronimo enters again, who, staring him the face, speaks:

And art thou come, Horatio, from the depth,
To ask for justice in this upper earth?
To tell thy father thou art unrevenged?
To wring more tears from Isabella's eyes,
Whose lights are dimmed with overlong laments?

89 **'twixt** between.
95 **shows him** reveals him to be.
105–106 **upper-billows . . . deep** the surface currents ('upper-billows') are disrupted by the storm while lesser, deeper ones are able to continue their work below. Perhaps the point is that Hieronimo feels he has been sidetracked by his duties from his true purpose of revenge.
112 **Alcides** Hercules, the last of whose labours was to descend into Hades and bring out Cerberus, its three-headed canine guardian (the 'triple-headed porter').
117 **The Thracian poet** Orpheus, who descended into Hades to rescue his wife, Eurydice from Proserpine, queen of Hades.
119 **canst** know.

Go back, my son, complain to Aeacus;
For here's no justice. Gentle boy, be gone,
For justice is exiled from the earth.
Hieronimo will bear thee company.
Thy mother cries on righteous Rhadamanth
For just revenge against the murderers.

DON BAZULTO
Alas, my lord, whence springs this troubled speech?

HIERONIMO
But let me look on my Horatio.
Sweet boy, how art thou changed in death's black shade!
Had Proserpine no pity on thy youth,
But suffered thy fair crimson coloured spring
With withered winter to be blasted thus?
Horatio, thou are older than thy father:
Ah, ruthless father, that favour thus transforms.

DON BAZULTO
Ah, my good lord, I am not your young son.

HIERONIMO
What, not my son? Thou then a Fury art,
Sent from the empty kingdom of black night
To summon me to make appearance
Before grim Minos and just Rhadamanth,
To plague Hieronimo that is remiss
And seeks not vengeance for Horatio's death.

DON BAZULTO
I am a grieved man, and not a ghost,
That came for justice for my murdered son.

HIERONIMO
Aye, now I know thee, now thou namest thy son.
Thou art the lively image of my grief:
Within thy face my sorrows I may see.
Thy eyes are gummed with tears, thy cheeks are wan,
Thy forehead troubled, and thy mutt'ring lips
Murmur sad words abruptly broken off
By force of windy sighs thy spirit breathes;
And all this sorrow riseth for thy son.
And self-same sorrow feel I for my son.
Come in, old man; thou shalt to Isabel.
Lean on my arm; I thee, thou me shalt stay,
And thou, and I, and she will sing a song,
Three parts in one, but all of discords framed...
Talk not of chords! But let us now be gone,
For with a cord Horatio was slain.

Exeunt.

[Act III. Scene xiv.]

Enter King of Spain, the Duke, Viceroy, and Lorenzo, Balthazar, Don Pedro, and Bel-Imperia.

KING
Go, brother, it is the Duke of Castile's cause,
Salute the viceroy in our name.

CASTILE
I go.

VICEROY
Go forth, Don Pedro, for thy nephew's sake,
And greet the Duke of Castile.

DON PEDRO
It shall be so.

KING
And now to meet these Portuguese;
For, as we now are, so sometimes were these,
Kings and commanders of the western Indies.
Welcome, brave viceroy, to the court of Spain,
And welcome all his honourable train.
'Tis not unknown to us for why you come,
Or have so kingly crossed the seas:
Suffiseth it, in this we note the troth
And more than common love you lend to us.
So is it that mine honourable niece,
For it beseems us now that it be known,
Already is betrothed to Balthazar;
And, by appointment and our condescent,
Tomorrow are they to be married.
To this intent we entertain thyself,
Thy followers, their pleasure, and our peace.
Speak, men of Portingale, shall it be so?
If aye, say so; if not, say flatly no.

VICEROY
Renowned king, I come not, as thou thinkst,
With doubtful followers, unresolved men,
But such as have upon thine articles

138 **Aeacus** with Rhadamanth (l. 142) and Minos (l.156), one of the three judges of the underworld. See I.i, this play.
164 **wan** pale.
171 **thou...stay** you shall hold me up.
173 **of discords framed** made up of disharmonies.

11 **crossed the seas** Although Portugal and Spain share a land border, it may be that Kyd thought, from his experience of early-modern roads, that a sea voyage would be quicker.
17 **condescent** agreement.
22 **flatly** clearly/quickly.

Confirmed thy motion and contented me.
Know, sovereign, I come to solemnize
The marriage of thy beloved niece,
Fair Bel-Imperia, with my Balthazar—
With thee, my son, whom sith I live to see,
Here, take my crown, I give it to her and thee,
And let me live a solitary life,
In ceaseless prayers,
To think how strangely heaven hath thee preserved.

KING
See, brother, see, how nature strives in him!
Come, worthy viceroy, and accompany
Thy friend, with thine extremities.
A place more private fits this princely mood.

VICEROY
Or here or where your highness thinks it good.

Exeunt all but Castile and Lorenzo.

CASTILE
Nay, stay, Lorenzo; let me talk with you.
Seest thou this entertainment of these kings?

LORENZO
I do, my lord, and joy to see the same.

CASTILE
And knowest thou why this meeting is?

LORENZO
For her, my lord, whom Balthazar doth love,
And to confirm their promised marriage.

CASTILE
She is thy sister.

LORENZO
Who? Bel-Imperia?
Aye, my gracious lord, and this is the day
That I have longed so happily to see.

CASTILE
Thou wouldst be loath that any fault of thine
Should intercept her in her happiness?

LORENZO
Heavens will not let Lorenzo err so much.

CASTILE
Why then, Lorenzo, listen to my words:
It is suspected, and reported too,
That thou, Lorenzo, wrongst Hieronimo,
And in his suits toward his majesty
Still keepst him back and seeks to cross his suit.

LORENZO
That I, my lord?

CASTILE
I tell thee, son, myself have heard it said,
When to my sorrow I have been ashamed
To answer for thee, though thou art my son.
Lorenzo, knowest thou not the common love
And kindness that Hieronimo hath won
By his deserts within the court of Spain?
Or seest thou not the king my brother's care
In his behalf, and to procure his health?
Lorenzo, shouldst thou thwart his passions,
And he exclaim against thee to the king,
What honour were't in this assembly,
Or what a scandal were't among the kings
To hear Hieronimo exclaim on thee?
Tell me, and look thou tell me truly too,
Whence grows the ground of this report in court?

LORENZO
My lord, it lies not in Lorenzo's power
To stop the vulgar liberal of their tongues:
A small advantage makes a water-breach;
And no man lives that long contenteth all.

CASTILE
Myself have seen thee busy to keep back
Him and his supplications from the king.

LORENZO
Yourself, my lord, hath seen his passions,
That ill beseemed the presence of a king;
And, for I pitied him in his distress,
I held him thence with kind and courteous words,
As free from malice to Hieronimo
As to my soul, my lord.

CASTILE
Hieronimo, my son, mistakes thee then?

LORENZO
My gracious father, believe me, so he doth.
But what's a silly man, distract in mind,
To think upon the murder of his son?
Alas, how easy is it for him to err.
But, for his satisfaction and the world's,
'Twere good, my lord, that Hieronimo and I
Were reconciled, if he misconster me.

39 **Or** Either.
72 **Whence . . . report** What is the basis of this rumour.
73–75 **it . . . water-breach** I can't stop the proliferation of common gossip. Even the smallest hole will let in a flood (i.e. even a small fault can prompt extravagant gossip).
80 **ill beseemed** were ill-suited for.
92 **misconster** misconstrue/misinterpret.

CASTILE
Lorenzo, thou hast said, it shall be so.
Go, one of you, and call Hieronimo.

Enter Balthazar and Bel-Imperia.

BALTHAZAR
Come, Bel-Imperia, Balthazar's content,
My sorrow's ease and sovereign of my bliss,
Sith heaven hath ordained thee to be mine,
Disperse those clouds and melancholy looks,
And clear them up with those thy sun-bright eyes,
Wherein my hope and heaven's fair beauty lies!
BEL-IMPERIA
My looks, my lord, are fitting for my love,
Which, new begun, can show no brighter yet.
BALTHAZAR
New kindled flames should burn as morning sun.
BEL-IMPERIA
But not too fast, lest heat and all be done.
I see my lord my father.
BALTHAZAR
Truce, my love;
I will go salute him.
CASTILE
Welcome, Balthazar,
Welcome, brave prince, the pledge of Castile's peace,
And welcome Bel-Imperia. How now, girl,
Why com'st thou sadly to salute us thus?
Content thyself, for I am satisfied.
It is not now as when Andrea lived;
We have forgotten and forgiven that,
And thou art graced with a happier love.
But, Balthazar, here comes Hieronimo;
I'll have a word with him.

Enter Hieronimo and a Servant.

HIERONIMO
And where's the duke?
SERVANT
Yonder.
HIERONIMO
Even so.
What new device have they devised, trow? [*Aside*]
Pocas palabras! Mild as the lamb,
Is't I will be revenged? No, I am not the man.
CASTILE
Welcome, Hieronimo.
LORENZO
Welcome, Hieronimo.
BALTHAZAR
Welcome, Hieronimo.
HIERONIMO
My lords, I thank you for Horatio.
CASTILE
Hieronimo, the reason that I sent
To speak with you is this…
HIERONIMO
What, so short?
Then I'll be gone; I thank you for't.
CASTILE
Nay, stay, Hieronimo; go call him, son.
LORENZO
Hieronimo, my father craves a word with you.
HIERONIMO
With me, sir? Why, my lord, I thought you had done.
LORENZO
[*Aside*]
No; would he had!
CASTILE
Hieronimo, I hear
You find yourself aggrieved at my son,
Because you have not access unto the king,
And say 'tis he that intercepts your suits.
HIERONIMO
Why, is not this a miserable thing, my lord?
CASTILE
Hieronimo, I hope you have no cause,
And would be loath that one of your deserts,
Should once have reason to suspect my son,
Considering how I think of you myself.
HIERONIMO
Your son Lorenzo? Whom, my noble lord?
The hope of Spain? Mine honorable friend?
Grant me the combat of them, if they dare!

Draws out his sword.

I'll meet them face-to-face to tell me so.

117 **trow** truly.
118 ***Pocas palabras!*** Few words! (Hieronimo is getting into part).
136 **one of your deserts** someone of your deserving.

These be the scandalous reports of such
As loves not me, and hate my lord too much.
Should I suspect Lorenzo would prevent
Or cross my suit, that loved my son so well?
My lord, I am ashamed it should be said.

LORENZO
Hieronimo, I never gave you cause.

HIERONIMO
My good lord, I know you did not.

CASTILE
There then pause,
And, for the satisfaction of the world,
Hieronimo, frequent my homely house,
The Duke of Castile, Cyprian's ancient seat;
And when thou wilt, use me, my son, and it.
But here, before Prince Balthazar and me,
Embrace each other, and be perfect friends.

HIERONIMO
Aye, marry, my lord, and shall!
'Friends', quoth he? See, I'll be friends with you all!
Especially with you, my lovely lord;
For divers causes it is fit for us
That we be friends. The world is suspicious,
And men may think what we imagine not.

BALTHAZAR
Why this is freely done, Hieronimo.

LORENZO
And I hope old grudges are forgot.

HIERONIMO
What else? It were a shame it should not be so.

CASTILE
Come on, Hieronimo, at my request;
Let us entreat your company today. *Exeunt.*

HIERONIMO
Your lordship's to command.
Pha! Keep your way.
Chi mi fa più carezze che non suole,
Traditio mi ha, o tradir mi vuole.

Exit.

[Act III. Scene xv.]

Enter Ghost and Revenge.

GHOST
Awake Erichtho! Cerberus, awake!
Solicit Pluto, gentle Proserpine.
To combat, Acheron and Erebus in hell!
For ne'er by Styx and Phlegeton there came,
Nor ferried Charon to the fiery lakes,
Such fearful sights as poor Andrea sees?
Revenge awake!

REVENGE
Awake? For-why?

GHOST
Awake, Revenge, for thou art ill-advised
To sleep away what thou art warned to watch!

REVENGE
Content thyself, and do not trouble me.

GHOST
Awake, Revenge, if love, as love hath had,
Have yet the power of prevalence in hell!
Hieronimo with Lorenzo is joined in league,
And intercepts our passage to revenge.
Awake, Revenge, or we are woe-begone!

REVENGE
Thus worldings ground what they have dreamed upon.
Content thyself, Andrea; though I sleep,
Yet is my mood soliciting their souls.
Sufficeth thee that poor Hieronimo
Cannot forget his son Horatio.
Nor dies Revenge, although he sleep awhile;
For in unquiet, quietness is feigned,
And slumb'ring is a common worldly wile.
Behold, Andrea, for an instance how
Revenge hath slept; and then imagine thou
What 'tis to be subject to destiny.

Enter a Dumbshow.

156 **Aye, marry** Yes indeed.
162 **freely** generously.
178–179 ***Chi . . . vuole.*** He who gives me unexpected caresses will betray me, or wants to. (Italian).
1 **Erichtho** a Thessalian sorceress, said by Ovid to be a Fury.
3 **Acheron and Erebus** The river and darkness of Hades are seemingly evoked. The 1592 text has the seemingly nonsensical 'Achinon and Ericus'.
4 **Styx and Phlegeton** other rivers of Hades.
16 **Thus . . . upon.** Thus mortals base their beliefs on what they have merely dreamed.

GHOST
Awake, Revenge! Reveal this mystery.

REVENGE
The two first, the nuptial torches bore,
As brightly burning as the midday's sun;
But after them doth Hymen hie as fast,
Clothed in sable, and saffron robe,
And blows them out and quencheth them with blood,
As discontent that things continue so.

GHOST
Sufficeth me; thy meanings understood,
And thanks to thee and those infernal powers
That will not tolerate a lover's woe.
Rest thee; for I will sit to see the rest.

REVENGE
Then argue not; for thou hast thy request. *Exeunt.*

Actus Quartus
[Act IV. Scene i.]

Enter Bel-Imperia and Hieronimo.

BEL-IMPERIA
Is this the love thou bear'st Horatio?
Is this the kindness that thou counterfeits?
Are these the fruits of thine incessant tears?
Hieronimo, are these thy passions,
Thy protestations and thy deep laments,
That thou were't wont to weary men withal?
O unkind father! O deceitful world!
With what excuses canst thou show thyself,
With what dishonour, and the hate of men,
Thus to neglect the loss and life of him
Whom both my letters and thine own belief
Assures thee to be causeless slaughtered?
Hieronimo, for shame! Hieronimo,
Be not a history to after times
Of such ingratitude unto thy son.
Unhappy mothers of such children then,
But monstrous fathers, to forget so soon
The death of those whom they with care and cost
Have tendered so, thus careless should be lost.
Myself, a stranger in respect to thee,
So loved his life as still I wish their deaths.
Nor shall his death be unrevenged by me.
Although I bear it out for fashion's sake;
For here I swear in sight of heaven and earth,
Shouldst thou neglect the love thou shoudst retain,
And give over and devise no more,
Myself should send their hateful souls to hell
That wrought his downfall with extremest death!

HIERONIMO
But may it be that Bel-Imperia
Vows such revenge as she hath deigned to say?
Why then, I see that heaven applies our drift,
And all the saints do sit soliciting
For vengeance on those cursed murtherers.
Madam, 'tis true, and now I find it so.
I found a letter, written in your name,
And in that letter how Horatio died.
Pardon, O pardon, Bel-Imperia,
My fear and care in not believing it!
Nor think I thoughtless think upon a mean
To let his death be unrevenged at full.
And here I vow, so you but give consent
And will conceal my resolution,
I will ere long determine of their deaths
That causeless thus have murdered my son.

BEL-IMPERIA
Hieronimo, I will consent, conceal,
And ought that may effect for thine avail,
Join with thee to revenge Horatio's death.

HIERONIMO
On then, and whatsoever I devise,
Let me entreat you grace my practice,
For-why the plot's already in mine head.
Here they are!

Enter Balthazar and Lorenzo.

BALTHAZAR
How now, Hieronimo?
What, courting Bel-Imperia?

HIERONIMO
Aye, my lord,

30 **Hymen** the god of marriage, **hie** hurry.
33 **discontent** unhappy/unwilling.
14 **history ...times** an example to the future.
19 **tendered** looked after so tenderly.
31 **applies our drift** agrees with our intentions.
39–40 **Nor ... full.** And don't think that I am not thinking about revenge.
41 **so** if.
49 **grace my practice** take part in my scheme.
50 **For-why** Because.

Such courting as, I promise you,
She hath my heart, but you, my lord, have hers.

LORENZO
But now, Hieronimo, or never,
We are to entreat your help.

HIERONIMO
My help?
Why, my good lords, assure yourselves of me;
For you have given me cause,
Aye, by my faith, have you.

BALTHAZAR
It pleased you,
At the entertainment of the ambassador
To grace the king so much as with a show.
Now, were your study so well furnished
As, for the passing of the first night's sport,
To entertain my father with the like,
Or any such-like pleasing motion,
Assure yourself it would content them well.

HIERONIMO
Is this all?

BALTHAZAR
Aye, this is all.

HIERONIMO
While then I'll fit you; say no more.
When I was young I gave my mind
And plied myself to fruitless poetry,
Which, though it profit the professor nought,
Yet is it passing pleasing to the world.

LORENZO
And how for that?

HIERONIMO
Marry, my good lord, thus.
And yet, methinks you are too quick with us,
When in Toledo there I studied,
It was my chance to write a tragedy,
See here, my lords.

He shows them a book.

Which, long forgot, I found this other day.
Now, would your lordships favour me so much
As but to grace me with your acting it,
I mean each one of you to play a part.
Assure you it will prove most passing strange
And wondrous plausible to that assembly.

BALTHAZAR
What, would you have us play a tragedy?

HIERONIMO
Why, Nero thought it no disparagement,
And kings and emperors have ta'en delight
To make experience of their wit in plays.

LORENZO
Nay, be not angry, good Hieronimo,
The prince but asked a question.

BALTHAZAR
In faith, Hieronimo, and you be in earnest,
I'll make one.

LORENZO
And I another.

HIERONIMO
Now, my good lord, could you entreat
Your sister, Bel-Imperia, to make one;
For what's a play without a woman in it?

BEL-IMPERIA
Little entreaty shall serve me, Hieronimo,
For I must needs be employed in your play.

HIERONIMO
Why, this is well! I tell you, lordings,
It was determined to have been acted,
By gentlemen and scholars too,
Such as could tell what to speak.

BALTHAZAR
And now
It shall be played by princes and courtiers,
Such as can tell how to speak,
If, as it is our country manner,
You will but let us know the argument.

HIERONIMO
That shall I roundly. The chronicles of Spain
Record this written of a knight of Rhodes:

62 **were . . . furnished** if you have books in your study (that provide the matter for another show).
68 **I'll fit you** I'll give you what you want (with the hidden sense of, 'I'll pay you fittingly (for what you have done)').
71 **though . . . nought** while it doesn't profit the practitioner.
72 **passing** very.
74 **you . . . us** you already see where this is leading (with the additional sense, 'you are too quick/alive for my taste'). In his excitement, Hieronimo is larding his speeches with innuendos.
83 **plausible** agreeable/worthy of applause.
85 **Nero . . . disparagement** The tyrannical Roman emperor Nero didn't think it beneath his dignity to act in plays (a rather ominous precedent).
90–91 **and . . . one** if you're serious, I'll take a part.
104 **the argument** the plot of the play.
105 **roundly** immediately.

He was betrothed, and wedded at the length,
To one Perseda, an Italian dame,
Whose beauty ravished all that her beheld,
Especially the soul of Soliman,
Who at the marriage was the chiefest guest.
By sundry means sought Soliman to win
Perseda's love, and could not gain the same.
Then gan he break his passions to a friend,
One of his bashaws whom he held full dear.
Her had this bashaw long solicited,
And saw she was not otherwise to be won
But by her husband's death, this knight of Rhodes,
Whom presently by treachery he slew.
She, stirred with an exceeding hate therefore,
As cause of this, slew Soliman,
And, to escape the bashaw's tyranny,
Did stab herself. And this the tragedy.

LORENZO
O, excellent!

BEL-IMPERIA
But say, Hieronimo,
What then became of him that was the bashaw?

HIERONIMO
Marry thus: moved with remorse of his misdeeds,
Ran to a mountain top and hung himself.

BALTHAZAR
But which of us is to perform that part?

HIERONIMO
O, that will I, my lords, make no doubt of it.
I'll play the murderer, I warrant you;
For I already have conceited that.

BALTHAZAR
And what shall I?

HIERONIMO
Great Soliman, the Turkish emperor.

LORENZO
And I?

HIERONIMO
Erastus, the knight of Rhodes.

BEL-IMPERIA
And I?

HIERONIMO
Perseda, chaste and resolute.
And here, my lords, are several abstracts drawn,
For each of you to note your several parts,
And act it, as occasion's offered you.
You must provide a Turkish cap,
A black moustache and a falchion.

Gives paper to Balthazar.

You with a cross, like a knight of Rhodes.

Gives another to Lorenzo.

And, madam, you must attire yourself

He giveth Bel-Imperia another.

Like Phoebe, Flora, or the huntress,
Which to your discretion shall seem best.
And as for me, my lords, I'll look to one,
And with the ransom that the viceroy sent
So furnish and perform this tragedy
As all the world shall say Hieronimo
Was liberal in gracing of it so.

BALTHAZAR
Hieronimo, me thinks a comedy were better.

HIERONIMO
A comedy? Fie! Comedies are fit for common wits;
But to present a kingly troupe withal,
Give me a stately-written tragedy,
Tragedia cothurnata, fitting kings,
Containing matter, and not common things.
My lords, all this must be performed,
As fitting, for the first night's revelling.
The Italian tragedians were so sharp
Of wit that in one hour's meditation
They would perform anything in action.

LORENZO
And well it may, for I have seen the like
In Paris, 'mongst the French tragedians.

111 The plot of this play strongly resembles that of *Soliman and Perseda*, printed in London in 1592, the same year as *The Spanish Tragedy*. Critics have wondered whether that might also have been written by Kyd.

115 **bashaws** a corruption of 'pasha', a Turkish title of nobility.

131 **conceited** planned for.

141 **falchion** scimitar.

144 **Phoebe... huntress** Phoebe, Flora, or Diana (the huntress), the goddesses of the moon, flowers, and the moon and hunting.

150 **liberal** lavish.

155 ***Tragedia cothurnata*** Buskinned tragedy: the most serious of tragic forms.

156 **matter** serious material.

HIERONIMO
In Paris? Mass, and well remembered!
There's one thing more that rests for us to do.

BALTHAZAR
What's that, Hieronimo? Forget not anything.

HIERONIMO
Each one of us must act his part
In unknown languages,
That it may breed the more variety:
As you, my lord, in Latin, I in Greek,
You in Italian, and, for-because I know
That Bel-Imperia hath practised the French,
In courtly French shall all her phrases be.

BEL-IMPERIA
You mean to try my cunning then, Hieronimo.

BALTHAZAR
But this will be a mere confusion,
And hardly shall we all be understood.

HEIRONIMO
It must be so, for the conclusion
Shall prove the invention and all was good;
And I myself in an oration,
That I will have there behind a curtain,
And with a strange and wondrous show besides,
Assure yourself, shall make the matter known.
And all shall be concluded in one scene,
For there's no pleasure ta'en in tediousness.

BALTHAZAR [*To Lorenzo.*]
How like you this?

LORENZO
Why thus, my lord, we must resolve
To soothe his humours up.

BALTHAZAR
On then, Hieronimo; farewell till soon!

HIERONIMO
You'll ply this gear?

LORENZO
I warrant you.

Exeunt all but Hieronimo.

HIERONIMO
Why, so; now shall I see the fall of Babylon
Wrought by the heavens in this confusion.
And, if the world like not this tragedy,
Hard is the hap of old Hieronimo. *Exit.*

[Act IV. Scene ii.]

Enter Isabella with a weapon.

ISABELLA
Tell me no more! O monstrous homicides!
Since neither piety nor pity moves
The king to justice or compassion,
I will revenge myself upon this place
Where thus they murdered my beloved son.

She cuts down the arbour.

Down with these branches and these loathsome boughs
On this unfortunate and fatal pine.
Down with them, Isabella, rent them up,
And burn the roots from whence the rest is sprung.
I will leave not a root, a stalk, a tree,
A bough, a branch, a blossom, nor a leaf,
No, not a herb within this garden plot,
Accursed complot of my misery.
Fruitless forever may this garden be,
Barren the earth, and blissless whosoever
Imagines not to keep it unmanured.
An eastern wind comixed with noisome airs
Shall blast the plants and young saplings,
The earth with serpents shall be pestered,
And passengers, for fear to be infect,
Shall stand aloof, and, looking at it, tell,
'There murdered died the son of Isabel.'
Aye, here he died, and here I him embrace;
See where his ghost solicits with his wounds
Revenge on her that should revenge his death.
Hieronimo, make haste to see thy son,
For sorrow and despair hath cited me

164 **Mass** By the mass! (An oath.)
165 **rests** remains.
174 **try my cunning** test my skill.
189 **You'll . . . gear?** You'll take part in this business?
190 **Babylon** the Tower of Babel, brought down when God confused the languages of all those building it. ('Babel' and 'Babylon' were often used interchangeably in early-modern discourse.)
193 **Hard . . . hap** Ill is the fortune.
8 **rent** tear.
13 **complot** both 'location' and 'accomplice'.
17 **noisome** noxious.
20 **passengers** those passing by.

To hear Horatio plead with Rhadamanth.
Make haste, Hieronimo, to hold excused
Thy negligence in pursuit of their deaths
Whose hateful wrath bereaved him of his breath.
Ah nay, thou dost delay their deaths,
Forgive the murderers of thy noble son;
And none but I bestir me, to no end!
And, as I curse this tree from further fruit,
So shall my womb be cursed for his sake;
And with this weapon will I wound this breast,
That hapless breast that gave Horatio suck!

She stabs herself.

[Act IV. Scene iii.]

Enter Hieronimo; he knocks up the curtain. Enter the Duke of Castile.

CASTILE
How now, Hieronimo; where's your fellows,
That you take all this pain?

HIERONIMO
O sir, it is for the author's credit
To look that all things may go well.
But, good my lord, let me entreat your grace
To give the king the copy of the play:
This is the argument of what we show.

CASTILE
I will, Hieronimo.

HIERONIMO
One more thing, my good lord.

CASTILE
What's that?

HIERONIMO
Let me entreat your grace
That, when the train are passed into the gallery,
You would vouchsafe to throw me down the key.

CASTILE
I will, Hieronimo. *Exit Castile.*

HIERONIMO
What, are you ready, Balthazar?
Bring a chair and a cushion for the king.

Enter Balthazar with a chair.

Well done, Balthazar; hang up the title:
'Our scene is Rhodes'. What, is your beard on?

BALTHAZAR
Half on, the other is in my hand.

HIERONIMO
Despatch, for shame; are you so long?

Exit Balthazar.

Bethink thyself, Hieronimo,
Recall thy wits, recompt thy former wrongs
Thou hast received by murder of thy son,
And lastly, not least, how Isabel,
Once his mother and thy dearest wife,
All woe-begone for him, hath slain herself.
Behoves thee then, Hieronimo, to be revenged.
The plot is laid of dire revenge:
On then, Hieronimo; pursue revenge,
For nothing wants but acting of revenge!

Exit Hieronimo.

[Act IV. Scene iv.]

Enter Spanish King, Viceroy, the Duke of Castile, and their train.

KING
Now, viceroy, shall we see the tragedy
Of Soliman, the Turkish emperor,
Performed of pleasure by your son the prince,
My nephew, Don Lorenzo, and my niece.

VICEROY
Who, Bel-Imperia?

KING
Aye, and Hieronimo our marshal,
At whose request they deign to do't themselves.
These be our pastimes in the court of Spain.
Here, brother, you shall be the book-keeper:
This is the argument of that they show.

He giveth him a book.

knocks...curtain nails up the curtain (concealing Horatio's hanging body).
[7] **argument** plot.
[11] **train** king's party.
[16] **the title** a board informing the audience where the scene is set.
[19] **Despatch** Hurry up!
[20] **Bethink thyself** Think carefully.
[21] **recompt** recount/remember.
[29] **wants** is lacking.

(Gentlemen, this play of Hieronimo in sundry languages was thought good to be set down in English more largely, for the easier understanding to every public reader.)

Enter Balthazar, Bel-Imperia, and Hieronimo.

BALTHAZAR [*as Soliman*]
'Bashaw, that Rhodes is ours yield heavens the honour
And holy Mahomet, our sacred prophet.
And be thou graced with every excellence
That Soliman can give or thou desire!
But thy desert in conquering Rhodes is less
Than in reserving this fair Christian nymph,
Perseda, blissful lamp of excellence,
Whose eyes compel, like powerful adamant,
The warlike heart of Soliman to wait.'

KING
See, viceroy, that is Balthazar, your son,
That represents the Emperor Soliman.
How well he acts his amorous passion.

VICEROY
Aye, Bel-Imperia hath taught him that.

CASTILE
That's because his mind runs all on Bel-Imperia.

HIERONIMO [*as the Bashaw*]
'Whatever joy earth yields betide your Majesty.'

BALTHAZAR
'Earth yields no joy without Perseda's love.'

HIERONIMO
'Let then Perseda on your Grace attend.'

BALTHAZAR
'She shall not wait on me, but I on her!
Drawn by the influence of her lights, I yield.
But let my friend, the Rhodian knight, come forth:
Erasto, dearer than my life to me,
That he may see Perseda, my beloved.'

Enter Erasto [*Lorenzo*].

KING
Here comes Lorenzo: look upon the plot
And tell me, brother, what part plays he?

BEL-IMPERIA
'Ah, my Erasto, welcome to Perseda.'

LORENZO
'Thrice happy is Erasto that thou livest.
Rhodes' loss is nothing to Erasto's joy;
Sith his Perseda lives, his life survives.'

BALTHAZAR
'Ah, Bashaw, here is love between Erasto
And fair Perseda, sovereign of my soul.'

HIERONIMO
'Remove Erasto, mighty Soliman,
And then Perseda will be quickly won.'

BALTHAZAR
'Erasto is my friend; and, while he lives,
Perseda never will remove her love.'

HIERONIMO
'Let not Erasto live to grieve great Soliman.'

BALTHAZAR
'Dear is Erasto in our princely eye.'

HIERONIMO
'But, if he be your rival, let him die!'

BALTHAZAR
'Why, let him die; so love commandeth me.
Yet grieve I that Erasto should so die.'

HIERONIMO
'Erasto, Soliman saluteth thee,
And lets thee wit by me his highness's will,
Which is, thou shouldst be thus employed.

Stab him.

BEL-IMPERIA
'Ay, me, Erasto! See, Soliman, Erasto's slain!'

BALTHAZAR
'Yet liveth Soliman to comfort thee.
Fair queen of beauty, let not favour die,
But with a gracious eye behold his grief,
That with Perseda's beauty is increased,
If by Perseda grief be not released.'

BEL-IMPERIA
'Tyrant, desist soliciting vain suits,
Relentless are mine ears to thy laments,
As thy butcher is pitiless and base,
Which seized on my Erasto, harmless knight.
Yet by thy power thou thinkest to command,
And to thy power Perseda doth obey;
But, were she able, thus she would revenge

46 **adamant** the magnetic stone used in compasses.

79 **wit** know.

Thy treacheries on thee, ignoble prince.'

Stab him.

'And on herself she would be thus revenged.'

Stab herself.

KING
Well said, old marshal! This was bravely done!

HIERONIMO
But Bel-Imperia plays Perseda well.

VICEROY
Were this in earnest, Bel-Imperia,
You would be better to my son than so.

KING
But now what follows for Hieronimo?

HIERONIMO
Marry, this follows for Hieronimo:
Here break we off our sundry languages,
And thus conclude I in our vulgar tongue:
Haply you think, but bootless are your thoughts,
That this is fabulously counterfeit,
And that we do as all tragedians do,
To die today, for fashioning our scene,
The death of Ajax, or some Roman peer,
And, in a minute, starting up again,
Revive to please tomorrow's audience.
No, princes; know, I am Hieronimo,
The hopeless father of a hapless son,
Whose tongue is tuned to tell his latest tale,
Not to excuse gross errors in the play.
I see your looks urge instance of these words:
Behold the reason urging me to this:

Shows his dead son.

See here my show; look on this spectacle.
Here lay my hope, and here my hope hath end;
Here lay my heart, and here my heart was slain;
Here lay my treasure, here my treasure lost;
Here lay my bliss, and here my bliss bereft.
But hope, heart, treasure, joy, and bliss,
All fled, failed, died, yea, all decayed with this.
From forth these wounds came breath that gave me life;
They murdered me that made these fatal marks.
The cause was love, whence grew this mortal hate:
The hate, Lorenzo and young Balthazar;
The love, my son to Bel-Imperia.
But night, the coverer of accursed crimes,
With pitchy silence hushed these traitors' harms,
And lent them leave, for they had sorted leisure,
To take advantage in my garden plot
Upon my son, my dear Horatio.
There merciless they butchered up my boy,
In black, dark night, to pale, dim, cruel death.
He shrieks, I heard, and yet methinks I hear,
His dismal outcry echo in the air.
With soonest speed I hasted to the noise,
Where, hanging on a tree, I found my son
Through-girt with wounds and slaughtered, as you see.
And grieved I, think you, at this spectacle?
Speak, Portuguese, whose loss resembles mine:
If thou canst weep upon thy Balthazar,
'Tis like I wailed for my Horatio.
And you, my lord, whose reconciled son
Marched in a net and thought himself unseen,
And rated me for a brain-sick lunacy,
With 'God amend that mad Hieronimo.'
How can you brook our play's catastrophe?
And here behold this bloody handkercher,
Which at Horatio's death I weeping dipped
Within the river of his bleeding wounds.
It as propitious, see, I have reserved,
And never hath it left my bloody heart,
Soliciting remembrance of my vow
With these, O these accursed murderers!
Which now performed, my heart is satisfied.
And to this end the Bashaw I became,
That might revenge me on Lorenzo's life,
Who therefore was appointed to the part,
And was to represent the knight of Rhodes,
That I might kill him more conveniently.
So, viceroy, was this Balthazar, thy son,

101 **bravely** impressively.
108 **vulgar** native.
110 **fabulously** fictively (as in a fable).
113 **Ajax** the Trojan hero.
118 **latest** final.
135 **pitchy** pitch-black.
136 **sorted leisure** arranged the opportunity (to do the deed).
145 **Through-girt** Stabbed through/impaled.
151 **Marched . . . net** Worked deceptively/in camouflage.
152 **rated** berated/mocked.
154 **catastrophe** dramatic climax.
158 **It . . . reserved** I have kept it as a talisman (of his sacrifice).

That Soliman which Bel-Imperia
In person of Perseda murdered,
Solely appointed to that tragic part
That she might slay him that offended her.
Poor Bel-Imperia missed her part in this;
For, though the story saith she should have died,
Yet I of kindness and care for her,
Did otherwise determine of her end.
But love of him whom they did hate too much
Did urge her resolution to be such.
And princes, now behold Hieronimo,
Author and actor in this tragedy,
Bearing his latest fortune in his fist;
And will as resolute conclude his part
As any of the actors gone before.
And, gentles, thus I end my play.
Urge no more words, I have no more to say.

He runs to hang himself.

KING
O harken, viceroy; hold Hieronimo!
Brother, my nephew and thy son are slain!

VICEROY
We are betrayed? My Balthazar is slain!
Break ope the doors; run, save Hieronimo!
Hieronimo, do but inform the king of these events;
Upon mine honour, thou shalt have no harm.

HIERONIMO
Viceroy, I will not trust thee with my life,
Which I this day have offered to my son:
Accursed wretch, why stayest thou him that was resolved to die?

KING
Speak, traitor; damned, bloody murderer, speak!
For, now I have thee, I will make thee speak:
Why hast thou done this undeserving deed?

VICEROY
Why hast thou murdered my Balthazar?

CASTILE
Why hast thou butchered both my children thus?

HIERONIMO
O good words! As dear to me was Horatio
As yours, or yours, my lord, to you.
My guiltless son was by Lorenzo slain;
And by Lorenzo and that Balthazar
Am I at last revenged thoroughly,
Upon whose souls may heavens be yet avenged
With far greater far than these afflictions!

CASTILE
But who were thy confederates in this?

VICEROY
That was thy daughter Bel-Imperia;
For by her hand my Balthazar was slain,
I saw her stab him.

KING
Why speakest thou not?

HIERONIMO
What lesser liberty can kings afford
Than harmless silence? That afford it me.
Sufficeth I may not, nor I will not tell thee.

KING
Fetch forth the tortures.
Traitor as thou art, I'll make thee tell!

HIERONIMO
Indeed?
Thou maist torment me as his wretched son
Hath done in murd'ring my Horatio,
But never shalt thou force me to reveal
The thing which I have vowed inviolate.
And therefore, in despite of all thy threats,
Pleased with their deaths, and eased with their revenge,
First take my tongue, and afterwards my heart!

He bites out his tongue.

KING
O monstrous resolution of a wretch!
See, viceroy, he hath bitten forth his tongue
Rather than reveal what we required.

CASTILE
Yet can he write.

KING
And if in this he satisfy us not,
We will devise the extremest kind of death
That ever was invented for a wretch.

Then he [*Hieronimo*] *makes signs for a knife to mend his pen.*

219–220 **But . . . inviolate** Given that Hieronimo has already confessed fully, it is hard to imagine what more he is keeping secret.

CASTILE

O, he would have a knife to mend his pen.

VICEROY

Here, and advise thee that thou write the truth,
Look to my brother; save Hieronimo!

He, with a knife, stabs the Duke and himself.

KING

What age hath ever heard such monstrous deeds?
My brother and the whole succeeding hope
That Spain expected after my decease!
Go bear his body hence, that we may mourn
The loss of our beloved brother's death,
That he may be entombed, whate'er befall.
I am the next, the nearest, last of all.

VICEROY

And thou, Don Pedro, do the like for us:
Take up our hapless son, untimely slain;
Set me up with him, and he with woeful me,
Upon the main-mast of a ship unmanned,
And let the wind and tide haul me along
To Scylla's barking and untamed gulf,
Or to the loathsome pool of Acheron,
To weep my want for my sweet Balthazar.
Spain hath no refuge for a Portingale.

The trumpets sound a dead march, the King of Spain, mourning after his brother's body, and the King of Portingale, bearing the body of his son.

[Act IV. Scene v.]

Enter Ghost and Revenge.

GHOST

Aye, now my hopes have end in their effects,
When blood and sorrow finish my desires:
Horatio murdered in his father's bower,
Vile Serberine by Pedringano slain,
False Pedringano hanged by quaint device,
Fair Isabella by herself misdone,
Prince Balthazar by Bel-Imperia stabbed,
The Duke of Castile and his wicked son
Both done to death by old Hieronimo,
My Bel-Imperia fallen as Dido fell,
And good Hieronimo slain by himself.
Aye, these were spectacles to please my soul.
Now will I beg at lovely Proserpine
That, by the virtue of her princely doom,
I may consort my friends in pleasing sort,
And on my foes work just and sharp revenge.
I'll lead my friend Horatio through those fields
Where never-dying wars are still inured;
I'll lead fair Isabella to that train
Where pity weeps but never feeleth pain;
I'll lead my Bel-Imperia to those joys
That vestal virgins and fair queens possess.
I'll lead Hieronimo where Orpheus plays,
Adding sweet pleasure to eternal days.
But say, Revenge, for thou must help or none,
Against the rest how shall my hate be shown?

REVENGE

This hand shall hale them down to deepest hell,
Where none but Furies, bugs and tortures dwell.

GHOST

Then, sweet Revenge, do this at my request:
Let me judge and doom them to unrest;
Let loose poor Tityus from the vultures' gripe,
And let Don Cyprian supply his room;
Place Don Lorenzo on Ixion's wheel,
And let the lover's endless pains surcease,
Juno forget old wrath and grant him ease;

234 **whole succeeding hope** the entire succession.

245 **Scylla's . . . gulf.** The great rock between Sicily and Italy, next to the whirlpool Charybdis.

1 **have . . . effects** have ended in their desired outcomes.

5 **quaint device** cunning stratagem.

10 **Dido** Queen of Carthage, killed herself after losing the love of Aeneas.

13 **at** of.

14 **doom** judgement.

15 **consort . . . sort** gather with my friends in pleasant ways.

18 **inured** conducted, i.e. in the Elysian fields.

19 **train** condition of life.

25 **or none** or no one can.

28 **bugs** bugbears/monsters.

31 **gripe** talons.

32–44 Andrea imagines his enemies enduring the fates allotted to classical victims of divine wrath. Cyprian will take the place ('supply the room') of Tityus, the giant, who, for trying to rape Zeus' lover Leto, was tied to a rock in Hades where two vultures perpetually pecked out his liver, which miraculously replaced itself overnight. Lorenzo will replace Ixion, bound by Zeus to a flaming wheel for flirting with his queen, Hera. The Chimera was a mythical beast combining a lion, serpent, and goat. Sisyphus was condemned eternally to push a great stone uphill, only to see it roll back to the bottom again.

34 **surcease** be relieved.

Hang Balthazar about Chimera's neck,
And let him there bewail his bloody love,
Repining at our joys that are above.
Let Serberine go roll the fatal stone,
And take from Sysiphus his endless moan;
False Pedringano, for his treachery,
Let him be dragged through boiling Acheron,
And there live, dying still in endless flames,
Blaspheming gods and all their holy names.

REVENGE

Then haste we down to meet thy friends and foes;
To place thy friends in ease, the rest in woes.
For here though death hath end their misery,
I'll there begin their endless tragedy. *Exeunt.*

FINIS.

43 **dying still** dying forever.

Titus Andronicus

(1594?)

WILLIAM SHAKESPEARE

(1564–1616)

THE AUTHOR: SHAKESPEARE'S TUDOR YEARS

The life of William Shakespeare is probably too well known—and too much debated—to require extensive rehearsal here. As the best-known dramatist of his, or any other, age, his face and reputation are known across the world. His origins, if not exactly humble, were at least relatively modest. He was the third child born to John Shakespeare, a glove-maker, moneylender, and town official, and his wife Mary (née Arden) of Stratford-upon-Avon, Warwickshire. Christened in Holy Trinity church, Stratford, on 26 April, tradition, and a degree of romantic patriotism, place his birthday on 23 April, the feast of England's patron saint, St George. Having almost certainly studied at the local grammar school, the King's New School, he would have encountered a wide range of classical literature, including the drama of Plautus and Terence, in the classroom, as well as more contemporary plays in performance, for Stratford was a regular stopping point on the tour itineraries of a number of the professional acting companies, including the celebrated Queen's Men, from the 1580s onwards.

Shakespeare's early years are not well documented, leading to a good deal of speculation about how and where he made his living after leaving school. In 1582 he was certainly in Stratford, for on 27 November, while still a minor in the eyes of the law, he was granted a licence to marry Anne Hathaway, who was already pregnant with their first child, Susanna. Twins, a boy named Hamnet and a girl named Judith, followed in February 1585. The years from 1585 to 1592 are particularly poorly documented. Shakespeare may have stayed in Stratford and followed his father's trade, or, as a rival tradition suggests, spent time as 'a schoolmaster in the country'. When he next appears in the records, though, it is in London, and in the very different world of the professional theatre. He had also evidently been there for some time, as he was sufficiently well known to be the target of the satirist Robert Greene, who sneered, in his *Groatsworth of Wit* (1592) at an actor who had dared to try his hand at playwriting, and evidently made a success of it: 'an upstart crow, beautified with our feathers...as well able to bombast [stuff] out a blank verse as the best of you...in his own conceit the only shake-scene in a country'. Another publication of the same year, Thomas Nashe's *Pierce Penniless*, indicates the sort of plays that Shakespeare had a hand in, commenting with some exaggeration on the 'tens of thousands' of spectators who now shed tears at the fate of 'brave Talbot (the terror of the French)' in the theatres. The reference is to the first part of the *Henry VI* tetralogy, on which Nashe himself may well have collaborated.

By 1592, then, Shakespeare had not only begun a career as a professional actor (perhaps with Lord Strange's Men, or perhaps the Queen's Men), but had also successfully moved into writing as well, a career path that marked him out as very different to both scholar-playwrights such as Lyly and Marlowe, and others, such as Greene and Kyd, who made their living from writing alone. This was not unprecedented, as the comedian Robert Wilson had also doubled the careers of actor and playwright (see the head-note to *The Three Ladies of London*, above). But what aroused the ire of a writer like Greene was probably that, unlike Wilson, Shakespeare did not confine his ambitions to broadly popular moral plays such as *The Three Ladies*, but experimented also with the more scholarly and prestigious genres of classical comedy and tragedy as well. By 1592 he had probably written the early comedies, *Two Gentlemen of Verona* and *The Taming of the Shrew*, and perhaps also drafted his first tragedy, *Titus Andronicus*, at which point an outbreak of the plague closed the theatres until 1594. Rather than seeking another way to make acting pay for the duration of the closure, however, Shakespeare again defied convention and chose to focus on his writing, switching to narrative poetry with two long, classically inflected works, *Venus and Adonis* and *The Rape of Lucrece* (printed in 1593 and 1594 respectively), which he dedicated to a young man who would become his patron, and perhaps also his friend and lover, Henry Wriothesley, the third Earl of Southampton. Had Robert Greene not died in 1592, he would no doubt have been galled to discover that the upstart crow's foray into narrative verse was also a critical and commercial success.

The adaptability and ambition, the work ethic and commercial shrewdness evident in these early years were to be the hallmark of Shakespeare's professional career. In 1594, as soon as the playhouses reopened, he returned to playwriting, producing in a prolific couple of years, *Richard III*, *A Comedy of Errors*, *Love's Labour's Lost* (and probably *Love's Labour's Won*, ironically now lost), *Richard II*, *Romeo and Juliet*, and *A Midsummer Night's Dream*, and also sealing the relationship with the Lord Chamberlain's Men that would be maintained until his death. As not only the principal playwright but also (with the clown Will Kemp, the principal actor Richard Burbage, and others) a sharer (stakeholder) in the company, he would write on average two plays per year for their exclusive use thereafter, and have a share in their often substantial profits, investing much of the latter in property in his old home town, Stratford.

By the end of the Tudor century, Shakespeare had written many of the plays that are central to his canon: *The Merchant of Venice*, *Much Ado About Nothing*, the two parts of *Henry IV*, *Henry V*, and *The Merry Wives of Windsor* (all probably written between 1596 and 1598), then (between 1598 and 1600) *Julius Caesar*, *As You Like It*, *Twelfth Night*, and *Hamlet*, the play that pointed towards the next phase of his career, which would produce his major tragedies. By 1600 the Lord Chamberlain's Men had built and moved into their new home in the Globe Theatre, and Shakespeare himself was, while not yet the celebrated national figure that he would become, a major writer with a growing reputation. A number of his earlier plays had been printed in more or less authorized quarto editions with his name on the title pages, and other writers were regularly referring to him and his work in their own texts. If not quite at the pinnacle of his career (that would follow in the reign of James VI and I, when the Lord Chamberlain's Men would become the King's Men, and Shakespeare would write plays such as *King Lear*, *Macbeth*, *Antony and Cleopatra*, *The Winter's Tale*, and *The Tempest* for both the court and popular audiences, and for the new, indoor theatre that his company would invest in at Blackfriars), the Shakespeare of 1603 was already a writer with a body of work behind him that eclipsed that of earlier playwrights, and whose willingness to experiment with genres rivalled that of even Marlowe and the rising star, Ben Jonson. He would continue to write, both alone and in collaboration with other writers such as Middleton and Webster, until close to his death on 23 April 1616, dividing his time between his substantial properties in Stratford and a variety of more modest lodgings in London and its suburbs. He was buried in Holy Trinity church, Stratford, where a memorial can still be seen bearing his recognizable effigy. A more significant memorial appeared in 1623 in the form of a collected edition of his plays, the so-called First Folio (*Mr William Shakespeare's Comedies, Histories, and Tragedies*) which would establish both his canon and his global reputation.

THE PLAY

Titus Andronicus is a rare excursion for Shakespeare into the Senecan tragedy of blood and revenge. Representing an imaginary episode in the late history of the Roman Empire, it reveals the young playwright at his most visceral and flamboyant, pressing hard on the borders of absurdity and artificiality in pursuit of spectacular, grotesque effects. Indeed, the play displays a very evident desire not only to match, but to outdo the 'Senecan' atrocities and excesses staged by his contemporary tragedians. Where Kyd had his hero, Hieronimo, bite out his own tongue in *The Spanish Tragedy*, and Thomas Preston had the unjust judge Sisamnes flayed alive onstage in *Cambises* (see the versions of these plays elsewhere in this anthology), Shakespeare (and perhaps a collaborator, for a fellow playwright, George Peele, may have drafted the first act) goes several steps further in having a rape victim, virtuous Lavinia, the hero's daughter, appear onstage with her hands cut off and her tongue cut out, and her father, Titus, submit to having his own hand severed, before forcing a mother to eat the heads of her murdered sons baked in a pie. *Titus* is thus not for the squeamish.

It is also not a play for the purist, or for anyone dedicated to the idea of Shakespeare as a naturalistic playwright. Hence it has had a rather ambivalent relationship with the modern stage, being rarely performed until the latter half of the twentieth century, when audiences (and directors) had perforce become more familiar with the human capacity for atrocity and notions of the banality of evil. The playwright would, of course, experiment with atrocious acts in later, better-known, plays; most obviously with the blinding of Gloucester in *King Lear*, which similarly mixes extreme horror with macabre, black humour ('out vile jelly!' declares Cornwall, as he plucks out an eye; 'Go thrust him out at gates, and let him smell/His way to Dover' quips the Tamora-like Regan in response to the blinded man's pleas (*Lear*, III.vii.81 and 91–2)). But in *Lear* the horror is exacerbated by the otherwise naturalistic portrayal of Gloucester as a complex, flawed, but ultimately sympathetic character, such that we experience his suffering on a personal level, as well as recoiling from the macabre spectacle of the deed. We never get that close to the characters in *Titus*. So, while there is a great deal of suffering evident in this play, and a great deal of lamentation from those whom it touches, we tend to observe it rather than share it. Critics have tended to see this as a serious flaw in the play; evidence of a writer not yet fully in command of his medium. But it might perhaps be better thought of as a response to the very particular demands of this kind of pseudo-Senecan tragedy.

The first note of a performance of *Titus* comes in the diary of the theatrical impresario, Philip Henslowe, who records that the Earl of Sussex's Men played 'Titus and Ondronicus', probably at the Rose theatre on Bankside, on 23 and 28 January and 6 February 1594. Further performances are mentioned in June of the same year, this time by 'My Lord Admiral's Men and My Lord Chamberlain's Men' in the playhouse at Newington Butts, south of London. A further performance occurred on 1 January 1596 in Burley-on-the-Hill, the Rutland seat of Sir John Harrington of Exton, the cousin of the Elizabethan satirist and translator of the same name, probably again by the Chamberlain's Men ('*les commediens de Londres*'), after which point the records of pre-restoration performances end. The continued popularity of the play, even into the Jacobean period, is suggested, however, both by the printing of quarto editions in 1594, 1600, and 1611, and by Ben Jonson's rather caustic comment in the introduction to his *Bartholomew Fair* (1614) that some misguided playgoers still swore that 'Jeronimo' (Kyd's *Spanish Tragedy*) and 'Andronicus' are the best plays, and have been these thirty years.

Henslowe adds the annotation 'ne' next to the reference to 'Titus' in 1594, which normally indicates a new or substantially revised play, but scholars have been reluctant to date the play this late, preferring to think of it as one of Shakespeare's earliest works, possibly even predating his move to London (Hughes, p. 6), which he may have revised for those performances at the Rose and Newington Butts. Some support for this view might be found on the title page of the first printed text, the quarto published by John Danter in 1594. There the play is referred to as having been 'played by the Right Honourable the Earl of Derby, Earl of Pembroke, and Earl of Sussex, their servants'. If this is accurate, then one might assume performances at least as early as the period from 1592 to late 1593, when the Lord Admiral's Men were in their heyday.

Titus begins *in medias res*, with a dramatic confrontation between the rival claimants for the imperial throne, Saturninus and Basianus and their followers, who spill out from the doors at either side of the rear of the stage, and it continues with a scene in which the protagonist stubbornly insists on the right to slaughter the eldest son of Tamora, queen of the defeated Goths, thereby setting in motion the sequence of reprisals that drives the narrative. This is not imperial Rome at the height of its powers, but a city on the point of collapse, divided and threatened by barbaric forces without and corruption within. The play goes on to chart the destruction of the noble house of Andronicus, bulwark of Roman military might, at the hands of its barbaric enemies, the newly defeated Goths, the Andronici's revenge, and the fall of the treacherous Emperor Saturninus, before another Goth army, led by Lucius Andronicus restores a degree of order to proceedings. The events depicted are fictional, and may be derived, although probably not directly, from either a prose narrative, *A Noble Roman History of Titus Andronicus*, or from a ballad on the same theme, although, as with many works published in this period, it is not clear which came first. So whether the play borrowed from the prose work or the ballad, or vice versa, is unclear.

More certain are the play's less direct inspirations. In Seneca's *Thyestes* (see the English version by Jasper Heywood, this volume) Shakespeare would have found the story of a father whose two sons were murdered and served to him in a feast as part of a grotesque revenge plot. An even closer analogue of unwitting cannibalism occurs in the classical myth of King Tereus of Thrace, Queen Procne, and her sister Philomela, which the playwright would have encountered in Book vi of Ovid's *Metamorphoses* (a source on which Shakespeare would draw throughout his career). This narrative underpins the events of *Titus* both implicitly and explicitly, as various characters draw attention to the similarity of Lavinia's suffering to the fate of Philomela, who, having been raped by Tereus, has her tongue cut out to prevent her revealing his crime. She ingeniously depicts the deed in a tapestry, however, which she laboriously sews for her sister, prompting Procne to murder her son, Itys, and serve his flesh to his father at a feast. Finally, there are more indirect echoes of a number of contemporary Elizabethan revenge plays, most obviously Kyd's *Spanish Tragedy* (first published in 1592, see the head-note to the play, above), with its narrative of an upright judge driven to madness and ingenious bloody revenge by the murder of his son and the corruption of those in authority.

Some critics have seen the play's mixture of scholarly classical allusion and seemingly populist grotesquery as jarring (Hughes, p. 35), but what it probably suggests is that Elizabethan audiences understood and enjoyed the brutality of aspects of their classical inheritance every bit as much as its more civilized dimensions. The classical stories of Philomel and Procne, Thyestes and Prometheus, the centaurs' feast (see V.ii.203) and the violent deeds of the Titans, Giants, and Furies reverberate through not only this play but many another Elizabethan Senecan drama, providing writers with a vocabulary of horror that was as scholarly as it was visceral.

What has prompted critics to see this as very early Shakespeare is its seeming lack of those qualities they most admire in the mature Shakespeare: the prosodic and narrative control, the depth of characterization, and the seemingly effortless portrayal of the complexities of what it is to be human, to name only the most obvious. Other creative writers have shared this dismissive view of the play. The Restoration playwright Edward Ravenscroft described it as 'rather a heap of rubbish than a structure' (albeit in the preface to his own 'improved' version), while T. S. Eliot called it 'one of the stupidest and most uninspired plays ever written' ('Seneca in Elizabethan Translation', in *Selected Essays*, p. 23, Hughes, p. 34), citing the apparent irrelevance and wantonness of the violence as evidence. And undeniably *Titus* is a very ragged, and a very savagely inhumane play, not only in the extent of the atrocities which the characters inflict upon each other, but in the ways that the play presents them. The forty-five line speech (II.iv.11–57) in which Marcus descants upon the appearance of his niece Lavinia, '*her hands cut off and her tongue cut out, and ravished*' (as the stage direction describes her), defies all emotional plausibility in pursuit of its rhetorical effects. Rather than rush to her aid, Marcus (who is supposed to be one of the virtuous characters) observes her injuries with minute attention to detail, describing them with a delicate lyrical eloquence that is wholly inappropriate to the circumstances ('Ah, now thou turn'st away thy face for shame,/And notwithstanding all this loss of blood,/As from a conduit with three issuing spouts, / Yet do thy cheeks look red as Titan's face,/Blushing to be encountered with a cloud' (II.iv.28–32)), speaking about compassion rather than showing it (Hughes, p. 34; Betteridge, pp. 656–7). If taken naturalistically, the encounter would be obscene. But the aim is clearly not to offer a naturalistic representation of the human response to grotesque suffering, rather it is to seek a poetic register sufficiently lofty in tone and broad in scope to match that suffering. In this sense the passage perhaps resembles aspects of both Lyly and Marlowe's work more closely than it does the later Shakespeare's.

Other scenes can seem simply awkward on the page. That in which Titus, having been delivered both his own severed hand and the heads of his two dead sons by the villainous Aaron, carries the latter offstage in his remaining hand, while instructing the handless Lavinia to pick up the bag containing his hand in her teeth, risks appearing merely laughable if approached with a naturalistic eye. Likewise, the disguised Tamora's failed attempt to persuade Titus that she is the spirit of Revenge come from Hades can appear both motiveless and potentially silly. We want our stage villains to be more cunning and manipulating that the heroes, not less, and Tamora here seems to be a poor prefiguration of later villainesses such as Goneril and Regan and Lady Macbeth. Although in Aaron the Moor the play does have a more plausible version of the stage Machiavel, a descendant of Marlowe's Barabas (the eponymous Jew of Malta) and a prefiguration of Richard III, Iago, and Edmund (Hughes, p. 32), it can nonetheless appear a flawed experiment in tragedy, a little less than the sum of its parts. Thus A. W. Schlegel described it as a work which 'by an accumulation of cruelties and enormities, degenerated into the horrible and yet leaves no deep impression behind' (Schlegel, p. 442; Hughes, p. 36).

But there are more ways to approach tragedy than one. And, for all its lyricism and extended conceits, *Titus* is a play which asks to be witnessed as spectacle rather than appreciated as poetry or dissected for insights into character or motivation. It is thus no surprise that the most successful modern adaptations, such as Peter Brook's Stratford-upon-Avon production of 1955, or Julie Taymor's film, *Titus* (1999), adopted a symbolic vocabulary to match the artificiality of the verse, using red ribbons or twigs to symbolize Lavinia's bloody stumps, rather than seeking to titillate viewers with ever more shocking examples of ultra-realism.

A sense of how Titus may have looked on the Elizabethan stage is provided by an ink drawing of what appears to be the opening scene (its caption reads, 'Enter Tamora, pleading for her sons going to execution'), probably created by Henry Peacham, the future author of *The Art of Drawing* (1606) and *The Complete Gentleman* (1622), in 1594 or 1595, at which point he would have been around eighteen years old. There are problems with the image and its accompanying text. It appears to conflate more than one scene from the play as we have it, has two sons rather than one kneeling in supplication, and so may be a sketch for an imagined production rather than an accurate reproduction of a specific performance. But its combination of arresting gestures, classical and Tudor costumes (Titus wears a toga and laurel wreath, while the soldiers behind him sport Elizabethan armour and trail pikes, and Tamora seems to be wearing a sumptuous Renaissance gown), and the vivid blackness of Aaron's skin, all suggest the visual appeal and impact of the play onstage.

In this edition I have used the 1594 quarto as the base text, with additional material taken from the First Folio of 1623, and have referred to the modern editions listed below. For clarity, I have placed the added folio material within round brackets and any editorial additions within square ones. Given that the folio prints a substantial amount of new material, this has involved a number of subjective choices about what to add and when to leave the quarto text alone. In most cases I have followed the quarto, only adding from the folio when it seemed to clarify an otherwise uncertain meaning or bring something additional to the play. Where the folio simply offers an alternative, I have tended to follow the quarto, placing the folio material in a note. Hence in the final scene, where the folio adds new lines to speeches by the Boy (young Lucius) and Lucius, I have followed the quarto, rejecting in particular the four final lines added in the folio. There is a particular poignancy, I think, for a play so obsessed with animalistic cruelty and slaughter to end on a note of savage retribution rather than reconciliation: 'But throw her forth to beasts and birds to prey... And being dead, let birds on her take pity' (V.iii.197–8).

FURTHER READING

Aebischer, Pascale, *Shakespeare's Violated Bodies: Stage and Screen Performance* (Cambridge: Cambridge University Press, 2009).

Bate, Jonathan, *Shakespeare and Ovid* (Oxford: Clarendon Paperbacks, 1994).

Betteridge, Thomas, 'The Most Lamentable Roman Tragedy of Titus Andronicus: Shakespeare and Tudor Theatre' in Thomas Betteridge and Greg Walker, eds., *The Oxford Handbook of Tudor Drama* (Oxford: Oxford University Press, 2012), 653–68.

Dessen, Alan, *Shakespeare in Performance: Titus Andronicus* (Manchester: Manchester University Press, 1992).

Eliot, T. S., *Selected Essays, 1917–1932* (London: Faber & Faber, 1932).

Holland, Peter, 'Shakespeare, William (1564–1616)', *Oxford Dictionary of National Biography* (Oxford: Oxford University Press, 2004); <http://www.oxforddnb.com/view/article/25200>, accessed 6 June 2013.

Hughes, Alan, ed., *Titus Andronicus*, New Cambridge Shakespeare, updated edn. (Cambridge: Cambridge University Press, 2006).

Metz, G. Harold, *Shakespeare's Earliest Tragedy: Studies in Titus Andronicus* (Madison, NJ: Fairleigh Dickinson University Press, 1997).

Schlegel, A. W., *A Course of Lectures on Dramatic Art and Literature*, repr. edn., trans. John Black (New York: AMS, 1946).

Waith, Eugene M., ed., *Titus Andronicus*, Oxford World's Classics (Oxford: Oxford University Press, 1994).

Wilson, John Dover, ed., *Titus Andronicus*, New Cambridge Shakespeare (Cambridge: Cambridge University Press, 1968).

The most Lamentable Roman Tragedy of Titus Andronicus: As it was Played by the Right Honourable the Earl of Derby, Earl of Pembroke, and Earl of Sussex their Servants

London
Printed by John Danter,
and are to be sold by Edward White and Thomas Millington
At the little north door of Paul's
At the sign of the Gun
1594

[Dramatis Personae:

SATURNINUS, The Deceased Emperor's Eldest Son,
BASSIANUS, his brother,
TITUS ANDRONICUS, a victorious general,
MARCUS, Titus' brother, a tribune of the people,
LAVINIA, Titus' daughter,
LUCIUS, QUINTUS, MARTIUS, and MUTIUS, Titus' sons,
BOY [YOUNG LUCIUS], Lucius' son,
PUBLIUS, son of Marcus,
(SEPRONIUS), CAIUS, and VALENTINE, kinsmen of Titus,
AEMILIUS, a noble,
A CAPTAIN,
TAMORA, Queen of the Goths, later empress of Rome,
ALARBUS, Demetrius, and Chiron, her sons,
AARON, a Moor, Tamora's lover,
A MESSENGER,
A NURSE,
A CLOWN,
Senators, Tribunes, Lords, Soldiers, Attendants, and Soldiers.]

(Actus Primus. Scena Prima.)

Enter the Tribunes and Senators aloft. And then enter Saturninus and his followers at one door, and Bassianus and his followers (at the other), with drums and trumpets.

SATURNINUS
Noble Patricians, patrons of my right,
Defend the justice of my cause with arms,
And countrymen, my loving followers,
Plead my successive title with your swords.
I am his first-born son that was the last
That wore the imperial diadem of Rome,
Then let my father's honours live in me,
Nor wrong mine age with this indignity.

BASSIANUS
Romans, friends, followers, favourers of my right,
If ever Bassianus, Caesar's son,

Paul's St Pauls' Cathedral.
The Goths were a Germanic nation, one of the barbarian peoples involved in the fall of Rome.
Moor North African.
Actus . . . Prima. Act One, Scene One.
with drums and trumpets The folio has 'with drum and colours ("banners")'.

1 **Patricians** aristocrats.
4 **my successive title** right (to the imperial throne) by succession.
8 **wrong . . . indignity** don't insult my seniority (over my younger brother, Bassanius, by allowing his supporters to block my access to the Capitol).

Were gracious in the eyes of royal Rome,
Keep then this passage to the Capitol,
And suffer not dishonour to approach
The imperial seat, to virtue consecrate,
To justice, continence and nobility;
But let desert in pure election shine,
And Romans fight for freedom in your choice.

(Enter) Marcus Andronicus (aloft) with the crown.

[MARCUS]
Princes, that strive by factions and by friends,
Ambitiously for rule and empery,
Know that the people of Rome, for whom we stand
A special party, have by common voice,
In election for the Roman empery,
Chosen Andronicus, surnamèd Pius
For many good and great deserts to Rome.
A nobler man, a braver warrior
Lives not this day within the city walls.
He by the senate is accited home
From weary wars against the barbarous Goths,
That with his sons, a terror to our foes,
Hath yoked a nation strong, trained up in arms.
Ten years are spent since first he undertook
This cause of Rome, and chastised with arms
Our enemies' pride. Five times he hath returned
Bleeding to Rome, bearing his valiant sons
In coffins from the field; and at this day,
To the monument of the Andronici
Done sacrifice of expiation,
And slain the noblest prisoner of the Goths.
And now at last, laden with honour's spoils,
Returns the good Andronicus to Rome:
Renownèd Titus, flourishing in arms.
Let us entreat, by honour of his name,
Whom worthily you would have now succeed,
And in the Capitol and senate's right,
Whom you pretend to honour and adore,
That you withdraw you, and abate your strength;
Dismiss your followers, and, as suitors should,
Plead your deserts in peace and humbleness.

SATURNINUS
How fair the tribune speaks to calm my thoughts.

BASSIANUS
Marcus Andronicus, so I do affy
In thy uprightness and integrity,
And so I love and honour thee and thine,
Thy noble brother Titus and his sons,
And her to whom my thoughts are humbled all,
Gracious Lavinia, Rome's rich ornament,
That I will here dismiss my loving friends,
And to my fortunes and the people's favour
Commit my cause in balance to be weighed.

Exit Soldiers.

SATURNINUS
Friends that have been thus forward in my right,
I thank you all, and here dismiss you all,
And to the love and favour of my country
Commit myself, my person, and the cause.
Rome be as just and gracious unto me
As I am confident and kind to thee.
Open the gates, and let me in.

BASSIANUS
Tribunes, and me, a poor competitor.

They go up into the Senate house. Enter a Captain.

CAPTAIN
Romans, make way, the good Andronicus,
Patron of virtue, Rome's best champion,
Successful in the battles that he fights,

12 **Keep** guard.
12 **Capitol** the temple of Jupiter Capitolinus, thought in this period to be the seat of the Roman Senate.
14 **to virtue consecrate** (which is) dedicated to virtue.
15 **continence** self-discipline.
16 **let... shine** let a free vote reveal the most deserving candidate.
19 **empery** imperial authority.
21 **a special party** as a special representative (as a Tribune).
23 **Pius** Patriotic (a secular version of 'pious').
27 **accited** (re)called.
30 **yoked** enslaved.
31 **spent** used up.
35–38 **And at... Goths** most editors omit these lines, which are in the quarto but not the folio, as they seem to describe the sacrifice of Alarbus as already having taken place. Perhaps Shakespeare marked the lines for cutting but the printer failed to notice.
36 **Andronici** plural of 'Andronicus'.
42–43 **by... succeed** in respect for the candidate you wish to succeed (and who I'm sure you will want to be elected honourably).
45 **Whom you pretend** Which you claim.
46 **you withdraw... strength** withdraw yourselves from public gaze, stand down your soldiers.
50 **affy** have faith in.
59 **forward... right** outspoken/active in supporting my (rightful) claim.
64 **confident** trusting.
66 **competitor** co-petitioner/rival.

With honour and with fortune is returned
From where he circumscribed with his sword,
And brought to yoke the enemies of Rome.

Sound drums and trumpets. (A)nd then enter two of Titus' sons, (after them) two men bearing a coffin covered with black, then two other sons. (After them) Titus Andronicus, and then Tamora, the Queen of Goths and her two sons, Chiron and Demetrius, with Aaron the Moor, and others, as many as can be. (They) set down the coffin, and Titus speaks.

TITUS
Hail Rome, victorious in thy mourning weeds,
Lo, as the bark that hath discharged her freight,
Returns with precious lading to the bay
From whence at first she weighed her anchorage,
Cometh Andronicus, bound with laurel boughs,
To re-salute his country with his tears,
Tears of true joy for his return to Rome.
Thou great defender of this Capitol,
Stand gracious to the rites that we intend.
Romans, of five and twenty valiant sons,
Half of the number that King Priam had,
Behold the poor remains, alive and dead.
These that survive, let Rome reward with love;
These that I bring unto their latest home,
With burial amongst their ancestors.
Here Goths have given me leave to sheathe
my sword,
Titus, unkind and careless of thine own,
Why suffer'st thou thy sons unburied yet,
To hover on the dreadful shore of Styx?
Make way to lay them by their brethren.

They open the tomb.

There greet in silence, as the dead are wont,
And sleep in peace, slain in your country's wars.
O sacred receptacle of my joys,
Sweet cell of virtue and nobility,
How many sons of mine hast thou in store,
That thou wilt never render to me more.

LUCIUS
Give us the proudest prisoner of the Goths,
That we may hew his limbs, and on a pile
Ad manes fratrum, sacrifice his flesh
Before this earthy prison of their bones,
That so the shadows be not unappeased,
Nor we disturbed with prodigies on earth.

TITUS
I give him you, the noblest that survives,
The eldest son of this distressèd queen.

TAMORA
Stay, Roman brethren; gracious conqueror,
Victorious Titus, rue the tears I shed,
A mother's tears in passion for her son;
And if thy sons were ever dear to thee,
O, think my son to be as dear to me.
Sufficeth not that we are brought to Rome
To beautify thy triumphs and return
Captive to thee, and to thy Roman yoke;
But must my sons be slaughtered in the streets,
For valiant doings in their country's cause?
O, if to fight for king and commonweal
Were piety in thine, it is in these.
Andronicus, stain not thy tomb with
blood.
Wilt thou draw near the nature of the gods?
Draw near them then in being merciful;
Sweet mercy is nobility's true badge.
Thrice noble Titus, spare my first-born son.

TITUS
Patient yourself madam, and pardon me,
These are their brethren, whom you
Goths beheld

71 **circumscribed** cut back to their proper limits.
73 **weeds** garments.
74 **as...freight** like the trading ship which has unloaded its cargo.
76 **weighed her anchorage** lifted her anchors (i.e. from where she originally departed).
77 **laurel boughs** the laurel wreaths worn by victorious commanders.
80 **Thou...Capitol** Jupiter, who in his aspect as Jupiter Capitolinus, was protector of the Capitol.
82–83 **five...had** According to Homer, Priam, King of Troy, had fifty sons.
89 **unkind...own** unnatural and uncaring for your kin.
91 **Styx** the river which formed the barrier between the world of the living and Hades.
101 ***Ad manes fratrum*** To our brothers' ghosts.
103 **shadows** shades/ghosts.
104 **prodigies** omens/unnatural events.
107 **Stay** Wait.
113 **beautify thy triumphs** adorn your triumphal procession.
117 **commonweal** both the commonwealth and the common good.
124 **Patient yourself** be patient.

Alive and dead, and for their brethren slain,
Religiously they ask a sacrifice.
To this your son is marked, and die he must,
T'appease their groaning shadows that are gone.

LUCIUS

Away with him, and make a fire straight,
And with our swords upon a pile of wood
Let's hew his limbs till they be clean consumed.

Exit Titus' sons with Alarbus.

TAMORA

O cruel, irreligious piety!

CHIRON

Was ever Scythia half so barbarous.

DEMETRIUS

Oppose not Scythia to ambitious Rome.
Alarbus goes to rest; and we survive
To tremble under Titus' threatening look.
Then, madam, stand resolved, but hope withal,
The selfsame gods that armed the Queen of Troy,
With opportunity of sharp revenge
Upon the Thracian tyrant in his tent,
May favour Tamora the Queen of Goths
(When Goths were Goths, and Tamora was queen)
To quit the bloody wrongs upon her foes.

Enter the sons of Andronicus again.

LUCIUS

See, lord and father, how we have performed
Our Roman rites: Alarbus' limbs are lopped,
And entrails feed the sacrificing fire,
Whose smoke like incense doth perfume the sky.
Remaineth nought but to inter our brethren,
And with loud 'larums welcome them to Rome.

TITUS

Let it be so; and let Andronicus
Make this his latest farewell to their souls.

Sound trumpets, and lay the coffin in the tomb.

In peace and honour rest you here my sons,
Rome's readiest champions, repose you here in rest,
Secure from worldly chances and mishaps.
Here lurks no treason, here no envy swells,
Here grow no damned grudges, here are no storms,
No noise, but silence and eternal sleep.
In peace and honour rest you here, my sons.

Enter Lavinia.

LAVINIA

In peace and honour live lord Titus long,
My noble lord and father, live in fame.
Lo, at this tomb my tributary tears,
I render for my brethren's obsequies,
And at thy feet I kneel, with tears of joy
Shed on the earth, for thy return to Rome.
O, bless me here with thy victorious hand,
Whose fortunes Rome's best citizens applaud.

TITUS

Kind Rome, that hast thus lovingly reserved
The cordial of mine age to glad my heart,
Lavinia live, outlive thy father's days,
And fame's eternal date for virtue's praise.

MARCUS ANDRONICUS

Long live lord Titus, my beloved brother,
Gracious triumpher in the eyes of Rome.

TITUS

Thanks gentle tribune, noble brother Marcus.

MARCUS ANDRONICUS

And welcome, nephews, from successful wars;
You that survive, and you that sleep in fame.
Fair lords, your fortunes are alike in all,
That in your country's service drew your swords,
But safer triumph is this funeral pomp,
That hath aspired to Solon's happiness,
And triumphs over chance in honour's bed.

128 **To . . . marked** Your son is selected for this role.
130 **straight** immediately.
134 **Scythia** an ancient kingdom to the north of the Black Sea, notorious for its cruelty.
135 **Oppose** Compare.
139–141 **Queen . . . tent** Hecuba, Priam's queen, blinded the Thracian king Polymnestor when he killed her last surviving son, Polydoros (see book xiii of Ovid's *Metamorphoses*).
144 **quit** avenge/repay.
149 **Remaineth nought** Nothing remains to be done.
150 **'larums** fanfares.
162 **tributary tears** tears of tribute.
163 **obsequies** funeral rites.
169 **cordial** comfort.
170–171 **outlive . . . praise** outlive even the eternal life that fame grants to the celebration of virtue.
177 **alike in all** all alike.
180 **Solon's happiness** the Athenian statesman famously said that no man is happy until he is dead (and thus safe from misfortune).
181 **And . . . bed** And so can sleep forever with honour, safe from chance.

Titus Andronicus, the people of Rome,
Whose friend in justice thou hast ever been,
Send thee by me, their tribune and their trust,
This palliament of white and spotless hue,
And name thee in election for the empire,
With these our late-deceased emperor's sons.
Be *candidatus* then, and put it on,
And help to set a head on headless Rome.

TITUS
A better head her glorious body fits
Than his that shakes for age and feebleness.
What, should I don this robe and trouble you?
Be chosen with proclamations to-day,
Tomorrow yield up rule, resign my life,
And set abroad new business for you all?
Rome, I have been thy soldier forty years,
And led my country's strength successfully,
And buried one and twenty valiant sons,
Knighted in field, slain manfully in arms,
In right and service of their noble country.
Give me a staff of honour for mine age,
But not a sceptre to control the world,
Upright he held it, lords, that held it last.

MARCUS ANDRONICUS
Titus, thou shalt obtain and ask the empery.

SATURNINUS
Proud and ambitious tribune, canst thou tell.

TITUS
Patience, prince Saturninus.

SATURNINUS
Romans, do me right.
Patricians, draw your swords and sheathe them not
Till Saturninus be Rome's emperor.
Andronicus, would thou were't shipped to hell,
Rather than rob me of the people's hearts.

LUCIUS
Proud Saturnine, interrupter of the good
That noble-minded Titus means to thee.

TITUS
Content thee, prince, I will restore to thee
The people's hearts, and wean them from themselves.

BASSIANUS
Andronicus, I do not flatter thee,
But honour thee, and will do till I die.
My faction if thou strengthen with thy friends,
I will most thankful be; and thanks to men
Of noble minds is honourable meed.

TITUS
People of Rome, and people's tribunes here,
I ask your voices and your suffrages:
Will you bestow them friendly on Andronicus.

TRIBUNES
To gratify the good Andronicus,
And gratulate his safe return to Rome,
The people will accept whom he admits.

TITUS
Tribunes I thank you, and this suit I make,
That you create your emperor's eldest son,
Lord Saturnine, whose virtues will, I hope,
Reflect on Rome as Titan's rays on earth,
And ripen justice in this commonweal.
Then, if you will elect by my advice,
Crown him and say, 'long live our emperor'.

MARCUS ANDRONICUS
With voices and applause of every sort,
Patricians and plebeians, we create
Lord Saturninus Rome's great emperor,
And say 'long live our Emperor Saturnine'.

SATURNINUS
Titus Andronicus, for thy favours done
To us in our election this day
I give thee thanks in part of thy deserts,
And will with deeds requite thy gentleness.
And for an onset, Titus, to advance
Thy name and honourable family,
Lavinia will I make my empress,
Rome's royal mistress, mistress of my heart,
And in the sacred Pantheon her espouse.
Tell me Andronicus, doth this motion please thee?

185 **palliament** robe.
188 ***candidatus*** a candidate: literally 'one clothed in white'.
194–195 **resign ... all** create new work for you by dying (and prompting a fresh election).
199 **Knighted in field** in medieval chivalry a commander could knight heroic soldiers on the battlefield.
204 **thou ... empery** if you only ask for it, it is yours.
205 **canst thou tell** do you know that? (A contemptuous retort.)
212 **means** intends to do you.
217 **My ... friends** If you and your allies join my supporters.
219 **meed** reward.
221 **voices** votes.
224 **gratulate** celebrate.
225 **admits** chooses.
229 **Titan's** the sun's.
233 **of every sort** from every social class.
234 **plebeians** common people.
239 **thanks ... of** in (only) partial reward for.
240 **requite they gentleness** reward your nobility.
241 **onset** beginning/first act.
245 **in ... espouse** marry her in the temple of all the gods.

TITUS

It doth, my worthy lord, and in this match
I hold me highly honoured of your grace.
And here in sight of Rome to Saturnine,
King and commander of our commonweal,
The wide world's emperor, do I consecrate
My sword, my chariot, and my prisoners:
Presents well worthy Rome's imperial lord.
Receive them, then, the tribute that I owe,
Mine honour's ensigns humbled at thy feet.

SATURNINUS

Thanks, noble Titus, father of my life,
How proud I am of thee and of thy gifts
Rome shall record, and when I do forget
The least of these unspeakable deserts,
Romans, forget your fealty to me.

TITUS

Now, madam, are you prisoner to an emperor.
To him that, for your honour and your state,
Will use you nobly, and your followers.

SATURNINUS

A goodly lady, trust me, of the hue
That I would choose were I to choose anew.
Clear up, fair queen, that cloudy countenance,
Though chance of war hath wrought this change of cheer,
Thou comest not to be made a scorn in Rome.
Princely shall be thy usage every way,
Rest on my word, and let not discontent
Daunt all your hopes. Madam, he comforts you
Can make you greater than the queen of Goths.
Lavinia you are not displeased with this?

LAVINIA

Not I, my lord, sith true nobility
Warrants these words in princely courtesy.

SATURNINUS

Thanks, sweet Lavinia. Romans let us go.
Ransomless here we set our prisoners free,
Proclaim our honours, lords, with trumpet and drum.

BASSIANUS

Lord Titus, by your leave, this maid is mine.

TITUS

How sir? Are you in earnest, then, my lord?

BASSIANUS

Aye, noble Titus, and resolved withal
To do myself this reason and this right.

MARCUS ANDRONICUS

Suum cuique is our Roman justice;
This prince in justice seizeth but his own.

LUCIUS

And that he will, and shall, if Lucius live.

TITUS

Traitors avaunt! Where is the emperor's guard?
Treason my lord, Lavinia is surprised.

SATURNINUS

Surprised, by whom?

BASSIANUS

By him that justly may
Bear his betrothed from all the world away.

MUTIUS

Brothers, help to convey her hence away,
And with my sword I'll keep this door safe.

TITUS

Follow my lord, and I'll soon bring her back.

MUTIUS

My lord, you pass not here.

TITUS

What, villain boy,
Barr'st me my way in Rome?

MUTIUS

Help, Lucius, help!

(He [Titus] kills him.)

LUCIUS

My lord you are unjust, and more than so:
In wrongful quarrel you have slain your son.

TITUS

Nor thou, nor he, are any sons of mine;

255 **Mine honour's ensign** The symbols of my honour.
259 **unspeakable** beyond description.
261 He turns to address Tamora here.
264 **hue** colour/complexion.
267 **Though... cheer** Though the misfortunes of war have prompted this change of expression/mood.
270 **Rest... word** Trust my promise.
271 **he** he who.
274 **sith** since.
279 **maid** virgin (Lavinia).
283 ***Suum cuique*** To each his own.
286 **avaunt** be gone!
287 **surprised** ambushed/kidnapped. (Bassanius tries to carry her away.)
297 **Nor** Neither.

My sons would never so dishonour me.
Traitor, restore Lavinia to the emperor.

LUCIUS

Dead if you will, but not to be his wife;
That is another's lawful promised love.

Enter aloft the Emperor [Saturninus] with Tamora and her two sons and Aaron the Moor.

SATURNINUS

No, Titus, no, the emperor needs her not;
Nor her, nor thee, nor any of thy stock.
I'll trust by leisure him that mocks me once;
Thee never, nor thy traitorous haughty sons,
Confederates all thus to dishonour me.
Was there none else in Rome to make a stale
But Saturnine? Full well, Andronicus,
Agree these deeds with that proud brag of thine,
That said'st I begged the empire at thy hands.

TITUS

O monstrous, what reproachful words are these?

SATURNINUS

But go thy ways, go give that changing piece
To him that flourished for her with his sword.
A valiant son-in-law thou shalt enjoy,
One fit to bandy with thy lawless sons,
To ruffle in the commonwealth of Rome.

TITUS

These words are razors to my wounded heart.

SATURNINUS

And therefore, lovely Tamora, queen of Goths,
That like the stately Phoebe 'mongst her nymphs
Dost over-shine the gallant'st dames of Rome,
If thou be pleased with this my sudden choice,
Behold, I choose thee, Tamora, for my bride,
And will create thee empress of Rome.
Speak, Queen of Goths, dost thou applaud my choice?
And here I swear by all the Roman gods,
Sith priest and holy water are so near,
And tapers burn so bright, and everything
In readiness for Hymenaeus stand,
I will not re-salute the streets of Rome,
Or climb my palace, till from forth this place
I lead espoused my bride along with me.

TAMORA

And here in sight of heaven to Rome I swear,
If Saturnine advance the queen of Goths,
She will a handmaid be to his desires,
A loving nurse, a mother to his youth.

SATURNINUS

Ascend fair queen, Pantheon. Lords accompany
Your noble emperor and his lovely bride,
Sent by the heavens for Prince Saturnine,
Whose wisdom hath her fortune conquered:
There shall we consummate our spousal rites.

Exeunt omnes.

TITUS

I am not bid to wait upon this bride.
Titus, when wert thou wont to walk alone,
Dishonoured thus and challenged of wrongs.

Enter Marcus and Titus' sons.

MARCUS ANDRONICUS

O Titus see, O see what thou hast done:
In a bad quarrel slain a virtuous son.

TITUS

No, foolish tribune, no; no son of mine,
Nor thou, nor these, confederates in the deed,
That hath dishonoured all our family,
Unworthy brother, and unworthy sons.

LUCIUS

But let us give him burial as becomes,
Give Mutius burial with our brethren.

TITUS

Traitors away, he rests not in this tomb.
This monument five hundred years hath stood,
Which I have sumptuously re-edified:
Here none but soldiers and Rome's servitors

299 **restore** return.
304 **I'll . . . leisure** I'll take my time before I trust (again).
307 **stale** figure of mockery.
312 **changing piece** 'piece of small change'/'fickle slut'.
313 **flourished . . . sword** brandished (his sword).
315 **bandy** brawl.
316 **ruffle** swagger.
319 **Phoebe** goddess of the moon (an aspect of Diana).
327 **tapers** candles.
327–328 **everything . . . stand** everything is prepared for Hymen (god of marriage).
336 **Ascend . . . Pantheon.** Climb the steps of the Pantheon, the temple dedicated to all the gods.
340.1 ***Exeunt omnes.*** Exit everyone (except Titus).
341 **bid** invited.
343 **challenged** accused.
350 **as becomes** as befits him.

Repose in fame; none basely slain in brawls.
Bury him where you can, he comes not here.

MARCUS ANDRONICUS
My lord, this is impiety in you.
My nephew Mutius' deeds do plead for him,
He must be buried with his brethren.

TITUS' TWO SONS SPEAK
And shall, or him we will accompany.

TITUS
'And shall'? What villain was it that spake that word?

TITUS' SON [MARTIUS] SPEAKS
He that would vouch it in any place but here.

TITUS
What, would you bury him in my despite?

MARCUS ANDRONICUS
No, noble Titus, but entreat of thee
To pardon Mutius and to bury him.

TITUS
Marcus, even thou hast struck upon my crest,
And with these boys mine honour thou hast wounded.
My foes I do repute you every one,
So trouble me no more, but get you gone.

THIRD SON [LUCIUS]
He is not with himself, let us withdraw.

SECOND SON [MARTIUS]
Not I, till Mutius' bones be buried.

The brother and the sons kneel.

MARCUS ANDRONICUS
Brother, for in that name doth nature plead.

SECOND SON
Father, and in that name doth nature speak.

TITUS
Speak thou no more, if all the rest will speed.

MARCUS ANDRONICUS
Renowned Titus, more than half my soul.

LUCIUS
Dear father, soul and substance of us all.

MARCUS ANDRONICUS
Suffer thy brother Marcus to inter
His noble nephew here in virtue's nest,
That died in honour and Lavinia's cause.
Thou art a Roman, be not barbarous.
The Greeks upon advice did bury Ajax
That slew himself; and wise Laertes' son
Did graciously plead for his funerals.
Let not young Mutius, then, that was thy jcy,
Be barred his entrance here.

TITUS
Rise, Marcus, rise.
The dismall'st day is this that e'er I saw,
To be dishonoured by my sons in Rome.
Well, bury him, and bury me the next.

They put him in the tomb.

LUCIUS
There lie thy bones, sweet Mutius, with thy friends,
Till we with trophies do adorn thy tomb.
No man shed tears for noble Mutius,
He lives in fame that died in virtue's cause.

Exit all but Marcus and Titus.

MARCUS ANDRONICUS
My lord, to step out of these dreary dumps,
How comes it that the subtle queen of Goths,
Is of a sudden thus advanced in Rome.

TITUS
I know not Marcus, but I know it is
(Whether by device or no, the heavens can tell).
Is she not then beholding to the man
That brought her for this high good turn so far?

Enter the Emperor [Saturninus], Tamora and her two sons, with the Moor at one door. Enter at the other door Bassianus and Lavinia, with others.

SATURNINUS
So, Bassianus, you have played your prize.
God give you joy sir, of your gallant bride.

BASSIANUS
And you of yours, my lord, I say no more,
Nor wish no less; and so I take my leave.

356 **basely** ignobly.
363 **vouch** defend it.
375 **if...speed** if the rest of you want to live.
383–384 **wise...funerals** After careful consideration the Greeks gave Ajax a noble burial, although he committed suicide, having lost his mind. Odysseus (son of Laertes) argued for an honourable funeral.
391 **trophies** memorials.
394 **to step...dumps** to move on from these melancholy matters.
398 **by device** as part of some plan.
399 **beholding** indebted.
401 **played your prize** won your contest.

SATURNINUS
Traitor, if Rome have law, or we have power,
Thou and thy faction shall repent this rape.
BASSIANUS
Rape call you it, my lord, to seize my own,
My truth-betrothed love, and now my wife?
But let the laws of Rome determine all,
Meanwhile I am possessed of that is mine.
SATURNINUS
'Tis good, sir, you are very short with us.
But, if we live, we'll be as sharp with you.
BASSIANUS
My lord, what I have done as best I may,
Answer I must, and shall do with my life,
Only thus much I give your grace to know,
By all the duties that I owe to Rome,
This noble gentleman, lord Titus here,
Is in opinion and in honour wronged,
That in the rescue of Lavinia
With his own hand did slay his youngest son,
In zeal to you and highly moved to wrath,
To be controlled in that he frankly gave.
Receive him, then, to favour, Saturnine,
That hath expressed himself in all his deeds,
A father and a friend to thee and Rome.
TITUS
Prince Bassianus leave to plead my deeds,
'Tis thou, and those, that have dishonoured me.
Rome and the righteous heavens be my judge
How I have loved and honoured Saturnine.
TAMORA
My worthy lord, if ever Tamora
Were gracious in those princely eyes of thine,
Then hear me speak indifferently for all,
And at my suit pardon what is past.
SATURNINUS
What, madam, be dishonoured openly,
And basely put it up without revenge?
TAMORA
Not so, my lord, the gods of Rome forefend
I should be author to dishonour you.
But on mine honour dare I undertake
For good lord Titus' innocence in all,
Whose fury not dissembled speaks his griefs.
Then at my suit look graciously on him,
Lose not so noble a friend on vain suppose,
Nor with sour looks afflict his gentle heart.
My lord, be ruled by me, be won at last,

[*Aside*]

Dissemble all your griefs and discontents;
You are but newly planted in your throne,
Lest then the people, and patricians too,
Upon a just survey take Titus' part,
And so supplant you for ingratitude,
Which Rome reputes to be a heinous sin.
Yield at entreats, and then let me alone,
I'll find a day to massacre them all,
And raze their faction and their family,
The cruel father, and his traitorous sons,
To whom I sued for my dear son's life,
And make them know what 'tis to let a queen
Kneel in the streets and beg for grace in vain.

Come, come, sweet emperor, come,
Andronicus:
Take up this good old man, and cheer the heart,
That dies in tempest of thy angry frown.
SATURNINUS
Rise, Titus, rise, my empress hath prevailed.
TITUS
I thank your majesty, and her, my lord.
These words, these looks, infuse new life in me.
TAMORA
Titus, I am incorporate in Rome,
A Roman now adopted happily,
And must advise the emperor for his good,
This day all quarrels die, Andronicus.
And let it be mine honour, good my lord,
That I have reconciled your friends and you.

[410] **that** that which.
[411] **short** curt.
[418] **opinion** reputation
[422] **controlled** restrained.
[422] **frankly** freely.
[426] **leave . . . deeds** stop speaking up for my merits.
[427] **those** Marcus and his sons.
[435] **put it up** end the matter (literally sheath it, like a sword).
[436–437] **the gods . . . you** the gods forbid I should be the instigator of any dishonour to you.
[438] **undertake** stand guarantor.
[440] **Whose . . . griefs** His clearly genuine fury reveals his grief.
[442] **vain suppose** idle supposition.
[445] **won** persuaded.
[451] **at entreats** to entreaties.
[451] **let me alone** leave things to me.
[464] **incorporate in Rome** now part of Rome.

For you, Prince Bassianus I have passed
My word and promise to the emperor
That you will be more mild and tractable.
And fear not lords, and you Lavinia,
By my advice, all humbled on your knees,
You shall ask pardon of his majesty.

LUCIUS
We do, and vow to heaven and to his highness,
That what we did was mildly as we might,
Tendering our sister's honour and our own.

MARCUS ANDRONICUS
That on mine honour here I do protest.

SATURNINUS
Away and talk not; trouble us no more.

TAMORA
Nay, nay, sweet emperor, we must all be friends.
The tribune and his nephews kneel for grace,
I will not be denied, sweetheart look back.

SATURNINUS
Marcus, for thy sake, and thy brother's here,
And at my lovely Tamora's entreats,
I do remit these young men's heinous faults.
Stand up. Lavinia, though you left me like a churl,
I found a friend, and sure as death I swore
I would not part a bachelor from the priest.
Come, if the emperor's court can feast two brides,
You are my guest, Lavinia, and your friends.
This day shall be a love-day, Tamora.

TITUS
To-morrow, and it please your majesty
To hunt the panther and the hart with me,
With horn and hound we'll give your grace *bonjour*.

SATURNINUS
Be it so Titus, and gramercy too.

(Exeunt.)

(Actus Secunda. [Scena Prima.])

Flourish. Enter Aaron alone.

AARON
Now climbeth Tamora Olympus' top,
Safe out of fortune's shot, and sits aloft,
Secure of thunder's crack or lightning flash,
Advanced above pale envy's threatening reach.
As when the golden sun salutes the morn
And having gilt the ocean with his beams,
Gallops the zodiac in his glistering coach,
And overlooks the highest-peering hills:
So Tamora.
Upon her wit doth earthly honour wait,
And virtue stoops and trembles at her frown.
Then Aaron, arm thy heart, and fit thy thoughts
To mount aloft with thy imperial mistress,
And mount her pitch, whom thou in triumph long
Hast prisoner held, fettered in amorous chains,
And faster bound to Aaron's charming eyes
Than is Prometheus tied to Caucasus.
Away with slavish weeds and servile thoughts,
I will be bright and shine in pearl and gold,
To wait upon this new-made empress.
'To wait', said I? To wanton with this queen,
This goddess, this Semiramis, this nymph,
This siren that will charm Rome's Saturnine,
And see his shipwreck and his commonweal's.
Hello, what storm is this?

Enter Demetrius and Chiron braving.

477–478 **did...own** done as mildly as we could, given that our sister's honour and our own were threatened.
487 **left...churl** left me standing jilted, like a peasant.
492 **love-day** a day when disputes were formally settled.
493 **and** if.
495 **give...*bonjour*** salute you in the morning with 'good day'.
496 **gramercy** thanks ('*grand merci*'). Saturninus picks up on Titus' use of French.
s.d. Quarto has the scene continue by having Aaron remain onstage ('*Sound trumpets, manet* [i.e. remain] *Moor*').
Flourish The trumpets sound.
1 **climbeth...top** Tamora has ascended the peak of Mount Olympus, home of the gods.
7 **Gallops the zodiac** Gallops across the heavens.
14 **mount her pitch** meet her at the peak of her ascent (a term from falconry).
17 **Prometheus...Caucasus** Prometheus was chained by Jupiter to a rock in the Caucasus, where an eagle unceasingly pecked out his liver, in punishment for stealing fire from the gods to give to humankind.
22 **Semiramis** a legendarily beautiful, and lustful, Assyrian queen.
23 **siren** the Sirens were supernatural women who lured sailors to their deaths by the beauty of their song.
25.1 **braving** scuffling.

DEMETRIUS
Chiron, thy years want wit, thy wit wants edge
And manners, to intrude where I am graced,
And may, for aught thou know'st, affected be.

CHIRON
Demetrius, thou dost over-ween in all,
And so in this, to bear me down with braves,
'Tis not the difference of a year or two
Makes me less gracious, or thee more fortunate.
I am as able and as fit as thou
To serve and to deserve my mistress's grace,
And that my sword upon thee shall approve,
And plead my passions for Lavinia's love.

MOOR (AARON)
Clubs, clubs! These lovers will not keep the peace.

DEMETRIUS
Why, boy, although our mother, unadvised,
Gave you a dancing-rapier by your side,
Are you so desperate grown to threat your friends.
Go to; have your lath glued within your sheath,
Till you know better how to handle it.

CHIRON
Meanwhile, sir, with the little skill I have,
Full well shalt thou perceive how much I dare.

DEMETRIUS
Aye, boy, grow ye so brave?

They draw.

(AARON)
Why, how now lords?
So near the emperor's palace dare you draw,
And maintain such a quarrel openly?
Full well I wot the ground of all this grudge.
I would not for a million of gold
The cause were known to them it most concerns,
Nor would your noble mother for much more
Be so dishonoured in the court of Rome.
For shame, put up.

DEMETRIUS
Not I till I have sheathed
My rapier in his bosom, and withal
Thrust those reproachful speeches down his throat
That he hath breathed in my dishonour here.

CHIRON
For that I am prepared and full resolved,
Foul-spoken coward, that thunder'st with thy tongue,
And with thy weapon nothing dare'st perform.

(AARON)
Away, I say.
Now, by the gods that warlike Goths adore,
This petty brabble will undo us all.
Why, lords, and think you not how dangerous
It is to jet upon a prince's right?
What, is Lavinia then become so loose,
Or Bassianus so degenerate,
That for her love such quarrels may be broached
Without controlment, justice, or revenge?
Young lords beware, and should the empress know
This discord's ground, the music would not please.

CHIRON
I care not, I, knew she and all the world;
I love Lavinia more than all the world.

DEMETRIUS
Youngling, learn thou to make some meaner choice;
Lavinia is thine elder brother's hope.

(AARON)
Why, are ye mad, or know ye not, in Rome,
How furious and impatient they be,
And cannot brook competitors in love?
I tell you lords, you do but plot your deaths
By this device.

CHIRON
Aaron, a thousand deaths would I propose,
To achieve her whom I love.

AARON
To achieve her how?

DEMETRIUS
Why makest thou it so strange?

26 **want** lack.
28 **affected be** be loved.
29 **over-ween in all** presume too much in all things.
30 **braves** boastful threats.
35 **approve** prove.
37 **Clubs, clubs!** A fight, a fight! (The call to arms of London apprentices.)
39 **dancing rapier** an ornamental sword used by dancers.
41 **Go to** Come off it!
41 **lath** a wooden play-sword.
48 **wot the ground** know the basis.
53 **put up** put away your swords.
54 **withal** also.
62 **brabble** squabble.
64 **jet . . . right** boast about a prince's property.
69–70 **should . . . please** if Tamora knew what you were arguing about, her response ('song') wouldn't please you.
71 **knew she** if she knew.
73 **Youngling** Boy.
73 **meaner** humbler.
81 **Why . . . strange?** Why do you pretend not to understand me?

She is a woman, therefore may be wooed;
She is a woman, therefore may be won;
She is Lavinia, therefore must be loved.
What, man? More water glideth by the mill
Than wots the miller of, and easy it is
Of a cut loaf to steal a shive, we know.
Though Bassianus be the emperor's brother.
Better than he have worn Vulcan's badge.

(AARON)
Aye, and as good as Saturninus may.

DEMETRIUS
Then why should he despair that knows to
court it
With words, fair looks, and liberality.
What, hast not thou full often struck a doe,
And borne her cleanly by the keeper's nose?

(AARON)
Why then, it seems some certain snatch or so
Would serve your turns.

CHIRON
Aye, so the turn were served.

DEMETRIUS
Aaron, thou hast hit it.

(AARON)
Would you had hit it too,
Then should not we be tired with this ado.
Why, hark ye, hark ye: and are you such fools
To square for this? Would it offend you, then,
That both should speed?

CHIRON
Faith, not me.

DEMETRIUS
Nor me, so I were one.

AARON
For shame, be friends, and join for that you jar,
'Tis policy and stratagem must do
That you affect, and so must you resolve
That what you cannot as you would achieve,
You must perforce accomplish as you may.
Take this of me, Lucrece was not more chaste
Than this Lavinia, Bassianus' love.
A speedier course than lingering languishment
Must we pursue, and I have found the path,
My lords, a solemn hunting is in hand,
There will the lovely Roman ladies troop.
The forest walks are wide and spacious,
And many unfrequented plots there are,
Fitted by kind for rape and villainy.
Single you thither then this dainty doe,
And strike her home by force, if not by words:
This way, or not at all, stand you in hope.
Come, come, our empress, with her sacred wit
To villainy and vengeance consecrate,
Will we acquaint with all that we intend,
And she shall file our engines with advice
That will not suffer you to square yourselves,
But to your wishes' height advance you both.
The emperor's court is like the house of fame,
The palace full of tongues, of eyes, and ears.
The woods are ruthless, dreadful, deaf, and dull;
There speak and strike, brave boys, and take your turns;
There serve your lusts, shadowed from
heaven's eye,
And revel in Lavinia's treasury.

CHIRON
Thy counsel, lad, smells of no cowardice.

86 **Than . . . of** Than the miller knows about.
87 **shive** slice.
89 **Vulcan's badge** the emblem of the cuckold. Vulcan's wife, Venus, had an affair with Mars (although, unfortunately for the analogy, she was caught out).
91 **court it** play the courtier/suitor.
93 **struck** killed.
94 **borne . . . by** carried her neatly past.
95–96 **it . . . turns** it seems a quickly grabbed share (of her)—punning on 'a swift copulation'—would be good enough for you.
96.1 **so . . . served** if the sexual act was served up.
97 **thou . . . it** you've got it right.
97.1 **Would . . . too** If only you'd achieved what you want (with bawdy anatomical overtones to 'hit' and 'it').
98 **ado** fuss.
100 **square** fight ('square up' to each other).
101 **That . . . speed** If both of you could prosper.
102.1 **so . . . one** as long as I am one of those (who prospers).
103 **join . . . jar** ally together to get what you are arguing over.
104–105 **must . . . affect** must achieve what you desire.
106–107 **That what . . . may** That which you cannot achieve in the way you want, you need to achieve how you can.
108 **Take . . . me** Believe me in this.
108 **Lucrece** the Roman woman raped by King Tarquin, whose story is retold in Shakespeare's narrative poem, *The Rape of Lucrece*, first published, like *Titus Andronicus*, in 1594.
112 **is in hand** being planned.
115 **unfrequented plots** deserted areas.
116 **fitted by kind** naturally suitable.
117 **Single you thither** Drive her alone (a hunting term).
121 **consecrate** dedicated.
123–125 **file . . . both** refine our plans that will prevent you arguing among yourselves, but satisfy your ambitions in full.
126 **house of fame** an allusion to Chaucer's narrative poem, *The House of Fame*, in which the palaces of Fame and Rumour are depicted with news and gossip pouring in and out at the whims of their owners.
128 **dull** silent.

DEMETRIUS
Sit fasaut nefas, till I find the stream
To cool this heat, a charm to calm these fits,
Per Styga, per manes vehor.

Exeunt.

[Act II. Scene ii.]

Enter Titus Andronicus, and his three sons, making a noise with hounds and horns, (and Marcus).

TITUS
The hunt is up, the moon is bright and grey,
The fields are fragrant, and the woods are green.
Uncouple here, and let us make a bay,
And wake the emperor and his lovely bride,
And rouse the prince, and ring a hunter's peal,
That all the court may echo with the noise.
Sons, let it be your charge, as it is ours,
To attend the emperor's person carefully.
I have been troubled in my sleep this night,
But dawning day new comfort hath inspired.

Here a cry of hounds, and wind horns in a peal: then enter Saturninus, Tamora, Bassianus, Lavinia, Chiron, Demetrius, and their attendants.

TITUS
Many good morrows to your majesty,
Madam, to you as many, and as good,
I promised your grace a hunter's peal.

SATURNINUS
And you have rung it lustily my lords,
Somewhat too early for new-married ladies.

BASSIANUS
Lavinia, how say you?

LAVINIA
I say no,
I have been broad awake two hours and more.

SATURNINUS
Come on, then, horse and chariots let us have,
And to our sport. Madam, now shall you see
Our Roman hunting.

MARCUS ANDRONICUS
I have dogs, my lord,
Will rouse the proudest panther in the chase,
And climb the highest promontory top.

TITUS ANDRONICUS
And I have horse will follow where the game
Makes way, and run like swallows o'er the plain.

DEMETRIUS
Chiron, we hunt not we with horse nor hound,
But hope to pluck a dainty doe to ground.

Exeunt.

[Act II. Scene iii.]

Enter Aaron alone.

(AARON)
He that had wit would think that I had none,
To bury so much gold under a tree,
And never after to inherit it.
Let him that thinks of me so abjectly
Know that this gold must coin a stratagem,
Which, cunningly effected, will beget
A very excellent piece of villainy.
And so repose, sweet gold, for their unrest
That have their alms out of the empress' chest.

Enter Tamora alone to the Moor.

TAMORA
My lovely Aaron, wherefore look'st thou sad,
When everything doth make a gleeful boast?
The birds chant melody on every bush,
The snakes lie rolled in the cheerful sun,
The green leaves quiver with the cooling wind
And make a chequered shadow on the ground.
Under their sweet shade, Aaron, let us sit
And, whilst the babbling echo mocks the hounds,
Replying shrilly to the well-tuned horns,
As if a double hunt were heard at once,
Let us sit down and mark their yellowing noise.
And after conflict such as was supposed
The wandering prince and Dido once enjoyed,

133 ***Sit fasaut nefas*** Whether it is right or wrong.
135 ***Per... vehor*** I am carried through Stygian realms among the ghosts.
3 **uncouple** release (the hounds).
3 **a bay** a great cry of hounds.
7 **charge** responsibility.
wind blow.
17 **broad** wide.
23–24 **where... way** wherever the prey runs.
6 **Which... beget** Which, if I can execute it skilfully, will bring about.
8 **repose** lie there.
20 **mark... noise** listen to their yelping.
22 In book iv of Virgil's *Aeneid*, Aeneas (the wandering prince) and Dido, while hunting, take shelter from a storm in a cave, and consummate their love.

When with a happy storm they were surprised
And curtained with a counsel-keeping cave,
We may, each wreathed in the other's arms,
Our pastimes done, possess a golden slumber,
Whiles hounds and horns, and sweet melodious birds,
Be unto us as is a nurse's song
Of lullaby, to bring her babe asleep.

(AARON)
Madam, though Venus govern your desires,
Saturn is dominator over mine.
What signifies my deadly-standing eye,
My silence, and my cloudy melancholy,
My fleece of woolly hair that now uncurls,
Even as an adder when she doth unroll
To do some fatal execution?
No madam, these are no venereal signs,
Vengeance is in my heart, death in my hand,
Blood and revenge are hammering in my head.
Hark, Tamora, the empress of my soul,
Which never hopes more heaven than rests in thee,
This is the day of doom for Bassianus,
His Philomel must lose her tongue to-day,
Thy sons make pillage of her chastity,
And wash their hands in Bassianus' blood.
See'st thou this letter? Take it up, I pray thee,
And give the king this fatal plotted scroll.
Now question me no more, we are espied.
Here comes a parcel of our hopeful booty,
Which dreads not yet their lives' destruction.

Enter Bassianus and Lavinia.

TAMORA
Ah, my sweet Moor, sweeter to me than life.

(AARON)
No more, great empress, Bassianus comes.
Be cross with him, and I'll go fetch thy sons
To back thy quarrels, whatsoe'er they be.

BASSIANUS
Who have we here? Rome's royal empress,
Unfurnished of her well-beseeming troop?
Or is it Diane, habited like her,
Who hath abandoned her holy groves
To see the general hunting in this forest?

TAMORA
Saucy controller of our private steps,
Had I the power that some say Diane had,
Thy temples should be planted presently
With horns, as was Actaeon's, and the hounds
Should drive upon thy new-transformed limbs,
Unmannerly intruder as thou art.

LAVINIA
Under your patience, gentle empress,
'Tis thought you have a goodly gift in horning,
And to be doubted that your Moor and you
Are singled forth to try experiments.
Jove shield your husband from his hounds to-day,
'Tis pity they should take him for a stag.

BASSIANUS
Believe me, queen, your swarthy Cimmerian,
Doth make your honour of his body's hue,
Spotted, detested, and abominable.
Why are you sequestered from all your train,
Dismounted from your snow-white goodly steed,
And wandered hither to an obscure plot,
Accompanied but with a barbarous Moor,
If foul desire had not conducted you?

LAVINIA
And being intercepted in your sport,
Great reason that my noble lord be rated
For sauciness. I pray you, let us hence,
And let her joy her raven-coloured love;

24 **counsel-keeping** secret.
31 **Venus** the goddess of love and **Saturn** god of misfortune and melancholy respectively.
37 **venereal signs** signs of lust/desire.
43 For the story of Philomel, see head-note, and book vii of Ovid's *Metamorphoses* for the full story.
49 **parcel** portion.
54 **back thy quarrels** support you in your argument.
56 **Unfurnished . . . troop** Unaccompanied by her appropriate followers.
57 **habited** clothed.
60 **Saucy controller** Insolent critic.
64 When the huntsman, Actaeon, unwittingly saw the goddess Diana bathing, she punished his transgression by transforming him into a stag, and his own hounds tore him to pieces.
66 **Under your patience** With your permission.
67 **gift in horning** a talent for bestowing horns/cuckolding.
68 **to be doubted** it is suspected.
69 **Are . . . experiments** Have sneaked away together to test it out.
71 **'Tis pity** It would be a pity if.
72–73 **your . . . hue** your dark-skinned black barbarian turns your reputation the same colour as his skin.
74 **Spotted** Stained.
75 **sequestered . . . train** hidden away from your retinue.
80 **intercepted** interrupted.
81–82 **Great . . . sauciness** That's why you criticize my husband for insolence.
82 **let us hence** let's go.
83 **joy** please/enjoy.

This valley fits the purpose passing well.

BASSIANUS

The king my brother shall have note of this.

LAVINIA

Aye, for these slips have made him noted long;
Good king to be so mightily abused!

(TAMORA)

Why, I have patience to endure all this.

Enter Chiron and Demetrius.

DEMETRIUS

How now, dear sovereign, and our gracious mother;
Why doth your highness look so pale and wan?

(TAMORA)

Have I not reason, think you, to look pale,
These two have 'ticed me hither to this place,
A barren, detested vale you see it is;
The trees, though summer, yet forlorn and lean,
O'ercome with moss and baleful mistletoe.
Here never shines the sun, here nothing breeds,
Unless the nightly owl or fatal raven;
And when they showed me this abhorred pit,
They told me here at dead time of the night,
A thousand fiends, a thousand hissing snakes,
Ten thousand swelling toads, as many urchins,
Would make such fearful and confused cries
As any mortal body hearing it
Should straight fall mad, or else die suddenly.
No sooner had they told this hellish tale,
But straight they told me they would bind me here,
Unto the body of a dismal yew,
And leave me to this miserable death.
And then they called me foul adulteress,
Lascivious Goth, and all the bitterest terms
That ever ear did hear to such effect.
And, had you not by wondrous fortune come,
This vengeance on me had they executed.
Revenge it, as you love your mother's life,
Or be ye not henceforth called my children.

DEMETRIUS

This is a witness that I am thy son.

[*They*] *stab him.*

CHIRON

And this for me struck home, to show my strength.

LAVINIA

Aye, come Semiramis, nay, barbarous Tamora,
For no name fits thy nature but thy own.

TAMORA

Give me the poniard, you shall know, my boys,
Your mother's hand shall right your mother's wrong.

DEMETRIUS

Stay madam, here is more belongs to her.
First thrash the corn, then after burn the straw.
This minion stood upon her chastity,
Upon her nuptial vow, her loyalty,
And with that painted hope braves your mightiness.
And shall she carry this unto her grave?

CHIRON

And if she do, I would I were an eunuch.
Drag hence her husband to some secret hole,
And make his dead trunk pillow to our lust.

TAMORA

But when ye have the honey ye desire,
Let not this wasp outlive us both to sting.

CHIRON

I warrant you madam, we will make that sure.
Come mistress, now perforce we will enjoy
That nice-preserved honesty of yours.

LAVINIA

O Tamora, thou bear'st a woman's face…

TAMORA

I will not hear her speak, away with her.

LAVINIA

Sweet lords, entreat her hear me but a word.

DEMETRIUS

Listen, fair madam, let it be your glory
To see her tears, but be your heart to them
As unrelenting flint to drops of rain.

LAVINIA

When did the tiger's young ones teach the dam?
O, do not learn her wrath, she taught it thee.

84 **passing** exceedingly.

86 **have…long** have made him notorious for a long time. Quarto has 'Queen' for this and the next speech heading for Tamora.

92 **'ticed** enticed.

97 **fatal** ill-omened.

101 **urchins** hedgehogs.

107 **dismal yew** yew trees were often planted in graveyards, hence their 'dismal' reputation.

120 **poniard** dagger.

122 **Stay** Hold back (from killing Lavinia).

122 **belongs to her** to be done to her.

124 **minion stood upon** strumpet made a fuss about.

126 **braves** defies.

135 **nice-preserved honesty** fastidiously preserved virginity.

142 **dam** mother.

143 **learn** teach.

The milk thou suck'st from her did turn to marble,
Even at thy teat thou hadst thy tyranny.
Yet every mother breeds not sons alike,
Do thou entreat her show a woman's pity?

CHIRON
What, wouldst thou have me prove myself a bastard?

LAVINIA
'Tis true, the raven doth not hatch a lark,
Yet have I heard, O, could I find it now,
The lion, moved with pity, did endure
To have his princely paws pared all away.
Some say that ravens foster forlorn children
The whilst their own birds famish in their nests.
O, be to me, though thy hard heart say no,
Nothing so kind but something pitiful.

TAMORA
I know not what it means, away with her.

LAVINIA
O let me teach thee for my father's sake,
That gave thee life when well he might have slain thee;
Be not obdurate, open thy deaf ears.

TAMORA
Hadst thou in person ne'er offended me,
Even for his sake am I pitiless.
Remember boys, I poured forth tears in vain
To save your brother from the sacrifice,
But fierce Andronicus would not relent;
Therefore away with her, and use her as you will,
The worse to her, the better loved of me.

LAVINIA
O Tamora, be called a gentle queen,
And with thine own hands kill me in this place,
For 'tis not life that I have begged so long;
Poor I was slain when Bassianus died.

TAMORA
What begg'st thou then, fond woman? Let me go.

LAVINIA
'Tis present death I beg, and one thing more
That womanhood denies my tongue to tell.
O, keep me from their worse than killing lust,
And tumble me into some loathsome pit
Where never man's eye may behold my body.
Do this and be a charitable murderer.

TAMORA
So should I rob my sweet sons of their fee.
No, let them satisfy their lust on thee.

DEMETRIUS
Away, for thou hast stayed us here too long.

LAVINIA
No grace, no womanhood? Ah, beastly creature,
The blot and enemy to our general name.
Confusion fall...

CHIRON
Nay then, I'll stop your mouth. Bring thou her husband;
This is the hole where Aaron bid us hide him.

TAMORA
Farewell, my sons, see that you make her sure,
Ne'er let my heart know merry cheer indeed
Till all the Andronici be made away.
Now will I hence to seek my lovely Moor,
And let my spleenful sons this trull deflower.

Enter Aaron with two of Titus' sons [Quintus and Martius].

(AARON)
Come on, my lords, the better foot before,
Straight will I bring you to the loathsome pit
Where I espied the panther fast asleep.

QUINTUS
My sight is very dull, whate'er it bodes.

MARTIUS
And mine, I promise you, were't not for shame
Well could I leave our sport to sleep awhile.

QUINTUS
What, art thou fall'n? What subtle hole is this,
Whose mouth is covered with rude-growing briers,
Upon whose leaves are drops of new-shed blood
As fresh as morning dew distilled on flowers?
A very fatal place it seems to me.

145 **hadst** gained.
152 **paws pared** claws trimmed (the story is from Aesop's *Fables*).
153 **foster forlorn children** rear foundlings.
156 **Nothing...pitiful** Not that kind, but at least a little pitying.
172 **fond** foolish.
173 **present** immediate.
183 **our general name** our collective reputation as women.
184 **Conclusion fall** Let chaos reign.
187 **make her sure** make her safe/be sure to kill her.
191 **spleenful** lustful.
191 **trull** slut.
192 **the...before** put your best foot forward.

Speak, brother, hast thou hurt thee with the fall?

MARTIUS

O brother, with the dismall'st object hurt
That ever eye with sight made heart lament.

AARON

Now will I fetch the king to find them here,
That he thereby may give a likely guess
How these were they that made away his brother.

Exit.

MARTIUS

Why dost not comfort me, and help me out
From this unhallowed and blood-stained hole.

QUINTUS

I am surprised with an uncouth fear,
A chilling sweat o'er-runs my trembling joints;
My heart suspects more than mine eye can see.

MARTIUS

To prove thou hast a true-divining heart,
Aaron and thou look down into this den
And see a fearful sight of blood and death.

QUINTUS

Aaron is gone, and my compassionate heart
Will not permit mine eyes once to behold
The thing whereat it trembles by surmise.
O, tell me who it is, for ne'er till now
Was I a child to fear I know not what.

MARTIUS

Lord Bassianus lies bereaved in blood,
All on a heap like to a slaughtered lamb,
In this detested dark, blood-drinking pit.

QUINTUS

If it be dark, how dost thou know 'tis he.

MARTIUS

Upon his bloody finger he doth wear
A precious ring that lightens all the hole;
Which, like a taper in some monument,
Doth shine upon the dead man's earthy cheeks,
And shows the ragged entrails of the pit.
So pale did shine the moon on Pyramus
When he by night lay bathed in maiden blood.
O brother, help me with thy fainting hand,
If fear hath made thee faint as me it hath,
Out of this fell devouring receptacle,
As hateful as Cocytus' misty mouth.

QUINTUS

Reach me thy hand, that I may help thee out,
Or, wanting strength to do thee so much good,
I may be plucked into the swallowing womb
Of this deep pit, poor Bassianus' grave.
I have no strength to pluck thee to the brink.

MARTIUS

Nor I no strength to climb without thy help.

QUINTUS

Thy hand once more, I will not loose again
Till thou art here aloft or I below.
Thou canst not come to me; I come to thee!

Enter the Emperor [*Saturninus*] *and Aaron, the Moor.*

SATURNINUS

Along with me; I'll see what hole is here,
And what he is that now is leaped into it.
Say, who art thou that lately didst descend
Into this gaping hollow of the earth.

MARTIUS

The unhappy son of old Andronicus,
Brought hither in a most unlucky hour,
To find thy brother Bassianus dead.

SATURNINUS

My brother dead? I know thou dost but jest,
He and his lady both are at the lodge
Upon the north side of this pleasant chase;
'Tis not an hour since I left him there.

MARTIUS

We know not where you left him all alive,
But, out alas, here have we found him dead.

Enter Tamora, [*Titus*] *Andronicus, and Lucius.*

204 **with . . . hurt** with the most dismal vision of misery.
209 **dost not** do you not.
211 **surprised . . . fear** overcome by an uncanny fear.
214 **thou . . . heart** i.e. that your fears are truly prophetic.
219 **whereat . . . surmise** it trembles even in imagining it.
223 **on** in.
229 **earthy** grey/earth coloured.
231 For the story of Pyramus, who was slain by a lion on his way to meet his lover, Thisbe, see book iv of Ovid's *Metamorphoses*, and the parodic interlude performed by the rude mechanicals in Shakespeare's own *A Midsummer Night's Dream*.
236 **Cocytus' misty mouth** the smoky mouth of the Cocytus, one of the rivers of Hades.
243 **loose** let go.
246 **Along with me** Follow me.
255 **chase** hunting park.
258 **out** woe.

TAMORA
Where is my lord the king?

SATURNINUS
Here Tamora, though grieved with killing grief.

TAMORA
Where is thy brother Bassianus?

SATURNINUS
Now to the bottom dost thou search my wound.
Poor Bassianus here lies murdered.

TAMORA
Then all too late I bring this fatal writ.
The complot of this timeless tragedy,
And wonder greatly that man's face can fold
In pleasing smiles such murderous tyranny.

She giveth Saturninus a letter.
Saturninus reads the letter.

'And if we miss to meet him handsomely,
Sweet huntsman (Bassianus 'tis we mean),
Do thou so much as dig the grave for him;
Thou know'st our meaning. Look for thy reward
Among the nettles at the elder tree
Which overshades the mouth of that same pit
Where we decreed to bury Bassianus.
Do this, and purchase us thy lasting friends.'

KING [SATURNINUS]
O, Tamora was ever heard the like?
This is the pit, and this the elder-tree.
Look, sirs, if you can find the huntsman out
That should have murdered Bassianus here.

AARON
My gracious lord here is the bag of gold.

KING
Two of thy whelps, fell curs of bloody kind,
Have here bereft my brother of his life.
Sirs, drag them from the pit unto the prison,
There let them bide until we have devised
Some never-heard-of torturing pain for them.

TAMORA
What are they in this pit? O wondrous thing!
How easily murder is discovered.

TITUS
High emperor, upon my feeble knee
I beg this boon with tears not lightly shed,
That this fell fault of my accursed sons—
Accursed, if the fault be proved in them...

KING
If it be proved? You see it is apparent.
Who found this letter, Tamora; was it you?

TAMORA
Andronicus himself did take it up.

TITUS
I did, my lord, yet let me be their bail,
For by my father's reverend tomb I vow,
They shall be ready at your highness's will
To answer their suspicion with their lives.

KING
Thou shalt not bail them; see thou follow me.
Some bring the murdered body, some the murderers.
Let them not speak a word; the guilt is plain,
For, by my soul, were there worse end than death
That end upon them should be executed.

TAMORA
Andronicus, I will entreat the king.
Fear not thy sons, they shall do well enough.

TITUS
Come, Lucius, come; stay not to talk with them.

(*Exeunt.*)

[Act II. Scene iv.]

Enter the Empress's sons with Lavinia, her hands cut off, and her tongue cut out, and ravished.

DEMETRIUS
So now go tell, and if thy tongue can speak,
Who 'twas that cut thy tongue and ravished thee.

CHIRON
Write down thy mind, bewray thy meaning so,
And if thy stumps will let thee play the scribe.

DEMETRIUS
See how with signs and tokens she can scrowl.

262 **search** probe.
264 **writ** text.
265 **complot** plot.
266 **fold** hide.
268 **miss** fail.
268 **handsomely** conveniently.
275 **purchase us** win us as.
289 **boon** favour.
290 **fell fault** evil crime.
298 **their suspicion** the suspicions against them.
3 **bewray** reveal.
5 **scrowl** write.

CHIRON
Go home, call for sweet water, wash thy hands.
DEMETRIUS
She hath no tongue to call, nor hands to wash,
And so let's leave her to her silent walks.
CHIRON
And 'twere my case, I should go hang myself.
DEMETRIUS
If thou hadst hands to help thee knit the cord.

Exeunt [*Chiron and Demetrius*].
(*Wind horns.*) *Enter Marcus from hunting.*

MARCUS
Who is this, my niece that flies away so fast?
Cousin, a word; where is your husband?
If I do dream, would all my wealth would wake me.
If I do wake, some planet strike me down,
That I may slumber in eternal sleep.
Speak, gentle niece, what stern, ungentle hands
Have lopped and hewed and made thy body bare
Of her two branches, those sweet ornaments
Whose circling shadows kings have sought to sleep in,
And might not gain so great a happiness
As half thy love. Why dost not speak to me?
Alas, a crimson river of warm blood,
Like to a bubbling fountain stirred with wind,
Doth rise and fall between thy rosèd lips,
Coming and going with thy honey breath.
But sure some Tereus hath deflowered thee,
And, lest thou shouldst detect him, cut thy tongue.
Ah, now thou turn'st away thy face for shame,
And notwithstanding all this loss of blood,
As from a conduit with three issuing spouts,
Yet do thy cheeks look red as Titan's face,
Blushing to be encountered with a cloud.
Shall I speak for thee? Shall I say 'tis so?
O that I knew thy heart, and knew the beast,
That I might rail at him to ease my mind!
Sorrow concealed, like an oven stopped,
Doth burn the heart to cinders where it is.
Fair Philomela, why she but lost her tongue,
And in a tedious sampler sewed her mind.
But, lovely niece, that mean is cut from thee;
A craftier Tereus, cousin, hast thou met,
And he hath cut those pretty fingers off
That could have better sewed than Philomel.
O had the monster seen those lily hands,
Tremble like aspen-leaves upon a lute,
And make the silken strings delight to kiss them,
He would not then have touched them for his life.
Or had he heard the heavenly harmony
Which that sweet tongue hath made,
He would have dropped his knife and fell asleep,
As Cerberus at the Thracian poet's feet.
Come let us go, and make thy father blind,
For such a sight will blind a father's eye.
One hour's storm will drown the fragrant meads,
What will whole months of tears thy father's eyes?
Do not draw back, for we will mourn with thee,
O could our mourning ease thy misery.

Exeunt.

Actus Tertius. [Scena Prima.]

Enter the Judges and Senators and Tribunes with Titus' two sons, bound, passing on the stage to the place of execution, and Titus going before, pleading.

TITUS
Hear me, grave fathers, noble tribunes, stay.
For pity of mine age, whose youth was spent
In dangerous wars, whilst you securely slept,
For all my blood in Rome's great quarrel shed,
For all the frosty nights that I have watched,
And for these bitter tears which now you see
Filling the aged wrinkles in my cheeks,
Be pitiful to my condemned sons,
Whose souls are not corrupted as 'tis thought.
For two and twenty sons I never wept,

[9] **And…case** If I were in that situation.
[10] **knit** tie.
[13] **would all…me** I'd give everything I own to wake up.
[26] **sure** without doubt.
[26] See note to II.iii.43 and head-note.
[27] **detect him** reveal his crime.
[36] **like…stopped** like a sealed clay oven
[39] **tedious sampler** long-laboured embroidery.
[40] **that…thee** that method (of revealing the truth) is deprived you (literally cut off).
[51] **As…feet** As the triple-headed dog Cerberus did when Orpheus charmed him with his lyre.
[4] **quarrel** wars.
[5] **watched** stood watch/guarded the frontiers.

Because they died in honour's lofty bed;

[Titus] Andronicus lieth down, and the Judges pass by him.

For these, tribunes, in the dust I write
My heart's deep languor and my soul's sad tears.
Let my tears stanch the earth's dry appetite,
My sons' sweet blood will make it shame;
and blush.
O earth, I will befriend thee more with rain
That shall distil from these two ancient ruins
Than youthful April shall with all his showers.
In summer's drought I'll drop upon thee still,
In winter with warm tears I'll melt the snow
And keep eternal spring-time on thy face,
So thou refuse to drink my dear sons' blood.

Enter Lucius with his weapon drawn.

O reverend tribunes, O gentle, aged men,
Unbind my sons, reverse the doom of death,
And let me say (that never wept before)
My tears are now prevailing orators.

LUCIUS
O noble father, you lament in vain,
The tribunes hear you not, no man is by,
And you recount your sorrows to a stone.

TITUS
Ah Lucius, for thy brothers let me plead;
Grave tribunes, once more I entreat of you.

LUCIUS
My gracious lord, no tribune hears you speak.

TITUS
Why 'tis no matter, man, if they did hear
They would not mark me, (O), if they did mark
They would not pity me, yet plead I must,
And bootless unto them.
Therefore I tell my sorrows to the stones,
Who, though they cannot answer my distress,
Yet in some sort they are better than the tribunes,
For that they will not intercept my tale.
When I do weep, they humbly at my feet
Receive my tears, and seem to weep with me,
And, were they but attired in grave weeds,
Rome could afford no tribune like to these.
A stone is soft as wax, tribunes more hard than
stones;
A stone is silent and offendeth not,
And tribunes with their tongues doom men to
death.
But wherefore stand'st thou with thy weapon
drawn?

LUCIUS
To rescue my two brothers from their death,
For which attempt the judges have pronounced
My everlasting doom of banishment.

TITUS
O happy man, they have befriended thee!
Why, foolish Lucius, dost thou not perceive
That Rome is but a wilderness of tigers?
Tigers must prey, and Rome affords no prey
But me and mine; how happy art thou then
From these devourers to be banished.
But who comes with our brother Marcus here?

Enter Marcus and Lavinia.

MARCUS
Titus, prepare thy aged eyes to weep,
Or if not so, thy noble heart to break.
I bring consuming sorrow to thine age.

TITUS
Will it consume me? Let me see it then.

MARCUS
This was thy daughter.

TITUS
Why, Marcus, so she is.

LUCIUS
Ay me! This object kills me.

14 **stanch** quench.
15 **shame** be ashamed.
17 **two ancient ruins** his eyes.
22 **So thou** If only you will.
24 **doom** judgement.
25 **that** he who.
26 **prevailing orators** persuasive speakers.
28 **by** near (they have all left).
34 **mark** pay attention to.
36 **bootless** fruitlessly.
39 **sort** ways.
40 **intercept** interrupt.
43 **grave weeds** sombre clothes.
44 **afford** provide.
48 **wherefore** why?
64 **object** sight.

TITUS
Faint-hearted boy, arise and look upon her.
Speak, Lavinia, what accursed hand
Hath made thee handless in thy father's sight?
What fool hath added water to the sea,
Or brought a faggot to bright-burning Troy?
My grief was at the height before thou camest,
And now like Nilus it disdaineth bounds.
Give me a sword, I'll chop off my hands too,
For they have fought for Rome, and all in vain;
And they have nursed this woe in feeding life.
In bootless prayer have they been held up,
And they have served me to effectless use.
Now all the service I require of them
Is that the one will help to cut the other.
'Tis well, Lavinia, that thou hast no hands,
For hands to do Rome service is but vain.

LUCIUS
Speak, gentle sister, who hath martyred thee?

MARCUS
O that delightful engine of her thoughts,
That blabbed them with such pleasing eloquence,
Is torn from forth that pretty hollow cage,
Where like a sweet melodious bird it sung
Sweet varied notes, enchanting every ear.

LUCIUS
O say thou for her, who hath done this deed?

MARCUS
O thus I found her, straying in the park,
Seeking to hide herself, as doth the deer
That hath received some unrecuring wound.

TITUS
It was my deer; and he that wounded her
Hath hurt me more than had he killed me dead.
For now I stand as one upon a rock,
Environed with a wilderness of sea,
Who marks the waxing tide grow wave by wave,
Expecting ever when some envious surge
Will in his brinish bowels swallow him.
This way to death my wretched sons are gone;
Here stands my other son, a banished man,
And here my brother weeping at my woes.
But that which gives my soul the greatest spurn
Is dear Lavinia, dearer than my soul.
Had I but seen thy picture in this plight
It would have madded me; what shall I do
Now I behold thy lively body so?
Thou hast no hands to wipe away thy tears,
Nor tongue to tell me who hath martyred thee.
Thy husband he is dead, and for his death
Thy brothers are condemned, and dead by this.
Look, Marcus, ah, son Lucius, look on her!
When I did name her brothers, then fresh tears
Stood on her cheeks, as doth the honey-dew
Upon a gathered lily almost withered.

MARCUS
Perchance she weeps because they killed her husband;
Perchance because she knows them innocent.

TITUS
If they did kill thy husband, then be joyful,
Because the law hath ta'en revenge on them.
No, no, they would not do so foul a deed;
Witness the sorrow that their sister makes.
Gentle Lavinia, let me kiss thy lips,
Or make some sign how I may do thee ease.
Shall thy good uncle, and thy brother Lucius,
And thou, and I, sit round about some fountain,
Looking all downwards to behold our cheeks,
How they are stained like meadows yet not dry,
With miry slime left on them by a flood?
And in the fountain shall we gaze so long
Till the fresh taste be taken from that clearness
And made a brine-pit with our bitter tears?
Or shall we cut away our hands like thine?
Or shall we bite our tongues and in dumb shows
Pass the remainder of our hateful days?
What shall we do? Let us that have our tongues

69 **faggot** bundle of firewood (i.e. who has added a superfluous sorrow to someone already consumed with sorrows).
71 **like . . . bounds** like the river Nile it scorns its banks (the annual flooding of the Nile valley was proverbial).
76 **effectless** fruitless.
82 **engine . . . thoughts** her tongue, the device (engine) that served her thoughts (by expressing them).
90 **unrecuring** incurable.
95 **Who . . . grow** Who watches the swelling tide rise.
96 **envious surge** cruel wave.
97 **brinish bowels** salty innards.
101 **spurn** kick.
109 **dead by this** already dead by now.
114 **Perchance** Perhaps.
121 **do thee ease** comfort you.
128 **clearness** fresh water.
131 **dumb shows** mimes.

Plot some device of further misery,
To make us wondered at in time to come.

LUCIUS
Sweet father, cease your tears, for at your grief
See how my wretched sister sobs and weeps.

MARCUS
Patience, dear niece; good Titus, dry thine eyes.

TITUS
Ah Marcus, Marcus, brother well I wot
Thy napkin cannot drink a tear of mine,
For thou, poor man, hast drowned it with thine own.

LUCIUS
Ah, my Lavinia, I will wipe thy cheeks.

TITUS
Mark, Marcus, mark; I understand her signs;
Had she a tongue to speak, now would she say
That to her brother which I said to thee.
His napkin, with his true tears all be-wet,
Can do no service on her sorrowful cheeks.
O what a sympathy of woe is this,
As far from help as Limbo is from bliss.

Enter Aaron the Moor, alone.

(AARON)
Titus Andronicus, my lord the emperor
Sends thee this word, that if thou love thy sons,
Let Marcus, Lucius, or thyself, old Titus,
Or any one of you, chop off your hand
And send it to the king. He for the same
Will send thee hither both thy sons alive,
And that shall be the ransom for their fault.

TITUS
O gracious emperor, O gentle Aaron,
Did ever raven sing so like a lark,
That gives sweet tidings of the sun's up-rise?
With all my heart I'll send the emperor my hand.
Good Aaron wilt thou help to chop it off?

LUCIUS
Stay father, for that noble hand of thine,
That hath thrown down so many enemies,
Shall not be sent. My hand will serve the turn;
My youth can better spare my blood than you,
And therefore mine shall save my brothers' lives.

MARCUS
Which of your hands hath not defended Rome,
And reared aloft the bloody battle-axe,
Writing destruction on the enemy's castle?
O, none of both but are of high desert.
My hand hath been but idle, let it serve
To ransom my two nephews from their death,
Then have I kept it to a worthy end.

(AARON)
Nay, come, agree whose hand shall go along,
For fear they die before their pardon come.

MARCUS
My hand shall go.

LUCIUS
By heaven, it shall not go.

TITUS
Sirs, strive no more, such withered herbs as these
Are meet for plucking up, and therefore mine.

LUCIUS
Sweet father, if I shall be thought thy son,
Let me redeem my brothers both from death.

MARCUS
And for our father's sake, and mother's care,
Now let me show a brother's love to thee.

TITUS
Agree between you, I will spare my hand.

LUCIUS
Then I'll go fetch an axe.

MARCUS
But I will use the axe. *Exeunt.*

TITUS
Come hither, Aaron, I'll deceive them both.
Lend me thy hand, and I will give thee mine.

(AARON)
If that be called deceit, I will be honest,
And never whilst I live deceive men so.
But I'll deceive you in another sort,
And that you'll say ere half an hour pass.

He cuts off Titus' hand.
Enter Lucius and Marcus again.

139 **wot** know.
143 **Mark** Observe.
147 **Can...service** Is of no help.
148 **a sympathy...woe** a sharing of identical woes.
149 **As...bliss** As far as is Limbo, the antechamber of Hell where the souls of the un-baptized await their fate, from heaven.
156 **ransom...fault** expiation of their crimes.
164 **serve the turn** do the job.
170 **none...desert** neither of you lacks great honour.
178 **meet** ripe/most appropriate.
189 **sort** way.

TITUS
Now stay your strife, what shall be is dispatched.
Good Aaron, give his majesty my hand,
Tell him it was a hand that warded him
From thousand dangers; bid him bury it.
More hath it merited; that let it have.
As for my sons, say I account of them
As jewels purchased at an easy price,
And yet dear too, because I bought mine own.

AARON
I go, Andronicus, and for thy hand
Look by and by to have thy sons with thee.
Their heads I mean. O how this villainy
Doth fat me with the very thoughts of it.
Let fools do good, and fair men call for grace;
Aaron will have his soul black, like his face. *Exit*

TITUS
O, here I lift this one hand up to heaven,
And bow this feeble ruin to the earth.
If any power pities wretched tears,
To that I call. What, wouldst thou kneel with me?
Do then, dear heart, for heaven shall hear our
prayers,
Or with our sighs we'll breath the welkin dim
And stain the sun with fog, as sometime clouds
When they do hug him in their melting bosoms.

MARCUS
O brother, speak with possibility,
And do not break into these deep extremes.

TITUS
Is not my sorrow deep, having no bottom?
Then be my passions bottomless with them.

MARCUS
But yet let reason govern thy lament.

TITUS
If there were reason for these miseries,
Then into limits could I bind my woes.
When heaven doth weep, doth not the
earth o'erflow?
If the winds rage, doth not the sea wax mad,
Threatening the welkin with his big-swoll'n face?
And wilt thou have a reason for this coil?
I am the sea. Hark how her sighs do flow;
She is the weeping welkin, I the earth;
Then must my sea be movèd with her sighs,
Then must my earth with her continual tears
Become a deluge, overflowed and drowned,
For why my bowels cannot hide her woes,
But like a drunkard must I vomit them.
Then give me leave, for losers will have leave,
To ease their stomachs with their bitter tongues.

Enter a messenger with two heads and a hand.

MESSENGER
Worthy Andronicus, ill art thou repaid
For that good hand thou sent'st the emperor.
Here are the heads of thy two noble sons,
And here's thy hand in scorn to thee sent back.
Thy griefs, their sports; thy resolution mocked,
That woe is me to think upon thy woes,
More than remembrance of my father's death.

(*Exit*.)

MARCUS
Now let hot Etna cool in Sicily,
And be my heart an ever-burning hell.
These miseries are more than may be borne.
To weep with them that weep doth ease some deal,
But sorrow flouted at is double death.

LUCIUS
Ah, that this sight should make so deep
a wound,
And yet detested life not shrink thereat.
That ever death should let life bear his name,

195 **that...have** at least let it have that (burial).
197 **easy** cheap.
201 **Their...mean** spoken as an aside.
202 **fat** satisfy delightfully.
208 **thou** Lavinia.
210 **with...dim** cloud the sky with our sighs.
211 **as sometime clouds** as clouds sometimes do.
213–214 **speak...extremes** talk about real things, don't indulge these wild thoughts.
221 **wax mad** grow wild.
223 **coil** chaos.
229 **For why** because.
233 **ill** evilly.
237–238 **Thy griefs...woes** they jest at your grief and mock your resolve; so much so that I am overcome with sorrow to think of your miseries.
240 **Etna** the Sicilian volcano.
243 **some deal** a little.
244 **flouted at** jeered at.
246 **And...thereat** i.e. it is surprising that it has not killed him.
247–248 **That...breathe** i.e. this living death cannot bear the name of life.

Where life hath no more interest but to breathe.

MARCUS
Alas, poor heart, that kiss is comfortless
As frozen water to a starvèd snake.

TITUS
When will this fearful slumber have an end?

MARCUS
Now farewell, flattery, die Andronicus;
Thou dost not slumber, see thy two sons' heads,
Thy warlike hand, thy mangled daughter here;
Thy other banished son, with this dear sight
Struck pale and bloodless, and thy brother, I,
Even like a stony image, cold and numb.
Ah, now no more will I control thy griefs,
Rent off thy silver hair, thy other hand
Gnawing with thy teeth, and be this dismal sight
The closing up of our most wretched eyes.
Now is a time to storm; why art thou still?

TITUS
Ha, ha, ha!

MARCUS
Why dost thou laugh? It fits not with this hour.

TITUS
Why, I have not another tear to shed.
Besides, this sorrow is an enemy,
And would usurp upon my watery eyes
And make them blind with tributary tears.
Then which way shall I find Revenge's cave?
For these two heads do seem to speak to me
And threat me, I shall never come to bliss
Till all these mischiefs be returned again
Even in their throats that have committed them.
Come, let me see what task I have to do;
You heavy people circle me about
That I may turn me to each one of you,
And swear unto my soul to right your wrongs.
The vow is made. Come, brother, take a head,
And in this hand the other I will bear;
Lavinia thou shalt be employed in these arms;
Bear thou my hand, sweet wench, between thy teeth.
As for thee, boy, go, get thee from my sight;
Thou art an exile, and thou must not stay.
Hie to the Goths and raise an army there,
And if you love me as I think you do,
Let's kiss and part, for we have much to do.

Exeunt. (Manet Lucius).

LUCIUS
Farewell, Andronicus, my noble father,
The wofullest man that ever lived in Rome.
Farewell, proud Rome, till Lucius come again;
He loves his pledges dearer than his life.
Farewell, Lavinia, my noble sister;
O, would thou wert as thou tofore hast been!
But now nor Lucius nor Lavinia lives
But in oblivion and hateful griefs.
If Lucius live, he will requite your wrongs,
And make proud Saturnine and his empress
Beg at the gates like Tarquin and his queen.
Now will I to the Goths and raise a power,
To be revenged on Rome and Saturnine.

Exit.

[ActIII. Scene ii.]

A banquet. Enter [Titus]Andronicus, Marcus, Lavinia and the Boy [Young Lucius].

TITUS
So, so, now sit, and look you eat no more
Than will preserve just so much strength in us
As will revenge these bitter woes of ours.
Marcus, unknit that sorrow-wreathen knot:
Thy niece and I, poor creatures, want our hands,
And cannot passionate our tenfold grief

249 **kiss** Lavinia kisses him here.
250 **starvèd** dying of thirst.
251 **slumber** sleep/nightmare.
255 **dear** dreadful.
259–260 **Rent...teeth** Tear out your silver hair while gnawing your remaining hand with your teeth.
268 **tributary tears** tears of tribute to sorrow.
275 **heavy** sorrowful.
280 **thou...arms** you shall have a role in this war.
284 **Hie** Hurry.
286.1 **Manet** Remain.
292 **tofore** previously.
293 **nor** neither.
295 **requite** repay.
297 **Tarquin** the king who raped Lucrece was expelled from Rome (to 'beg at the gates', i.e. outside the walls).
298 **a power** an army.
s.d. This scene is found only in the Folio.
4 **unknit...knot** unfold your folded arms (a sign of melancholy).
5 **want** lack.
6 **passionate** demonstrate passionately.

With folded arms. This poor right hand of mine
Is left to tyrannize upon my breast;
Who, when my heart, all mad with misery,
Beats in this hollow prison of my flesh,
Then thus I thump it down.
Thou map of woe, that thus dost talk in signs,
When thy poor heart beats with outrageous beating,
Thou canst not strike it thus to make it still.
Wound it with sighing, girl, kill it with groans;
Or get some little knife between thy teeth,
And just against thy heart make thou a hole
That all the tears that thy poor eyes let fall
May run into that sink, and soaking in,
Drown the lamenting fool in sea-salt tears.

MARCUS
Fie, brother, fie! Teach her not thus to lay
Such violent hands upon her tender life.

TITUS
How now; has sorrow made thee dote already?
Why, Marcus, no man should be mad but I.
What violent hands can she lay on her life?
Ah, wherefore dost thou urge the name of hands,
To bid Aeneas tell the tale twice o'er
How Troy was burnt and he made miserable?
O, handle not the theme, to talk of hands,
Lest we remember still that we have none.
Fie, fie, how franticly I square my talk,
As if we should forget we had no hands
If Marcus did not name the word of hands!
Come, let's fall to; and, gentle girl, eat this.
Here is no drink! Hark, Marcus, what she says:
I can interpret all her martyred signs.
She says she drinks no other drink but tears,
Brewed with her sorrow, meshed upon her cheeks.
Speechless complainer, I will learn thy thought;
In thy dumb action will I be as perfect
As begging hermits in their holy prayers.
Thou shalt not sigh, nor hold thy stumps to heaven,
Nor wink, nor nod, nor kneel, nor make a sign,
But I of these will wrest an alphabet
And by still practice learn to know thy
meaning.

BOY [YOUNG LUCIUS]
Good grandsire, leave these bitter deep laments;
Make my aunt merry with some pleasing tale.

MARCUS
Alas, the tender boy, in passion moved,
Doth weep to see his grandsire's heaviness.

TITUS
Peace, tender sapling; thou art made of tears,
And tears will quickly melt thy life away.

Marcus strikes the dish with a knife.

What dost thou strike at, Marcus, with thy knife?

MARCUS
At that that I have killed, my lord: a fly.

TITUS
Out on thee, murderer! Thou kill'st my heart.
Mine eyes are cloyed with view of tyranny;
A deed of death done on the innocent
Becomes not Titus' brother. Get thee gone,
I see thou art not for my company.

MARCUS
Alas, my lord, I have but killed a fly.

TITUS
But how if that fly had a father and mother?
How would he hang his slender gilded wings,
And buzz lamenting doings in the air!
Poor harmless fly,
That with his pretty buzzing melody
Came here to make us merry, and thou hast
killed him.

17 **just against** right next to.
20 **the lamenting fool** i.e. her heart.
21 **Fie** Tut.
23 **dote** act foolishly.
26–28 **urge . . . miserable** make her tell her dreadful story again (to explain why she has no hands), like Dido who asked Aeneas to retell the whole story of the destruction of Troy to her in book ii of Virgil's *Aeneid*.
29 **handle . . . theme** don't discuss that.
31 **square** frame/shape.
34 **fall to** tuck in.
36 **martyred signs** mutilated gestures.
38 **Brewed . . . cheeks** a metaphor from ale-making: brewing and mashing are parts of the fermentation process.
40–41 **In . . . prayers** I will learn to read your speechless signs as well as a hermit learns his prayers.
43 **wink** close your eyes.
44–45 **I . . . practice** I'll derive an alphabet from your gestures by continual practice.
54 **Out on thee** Curse you.
55 **Mine . . . tyranny** I have seen enough acts of tyranny.
57 **Becomes not** Is not appropriate for.
60 **how** what.

MARCUS
Pardon me, sir, it was a black, ill-favoured fly,
Like to the empress's Moor; therefore I killed him.

TITUS
O, O, O!
Then pardon me for reprehending thee,
For thou hast done a charitable deed.
Give me thy knife, I will insult on him,
Flattering myself as if it were the Moor
Come hither purposely to poison me.
There's for thyself, and that's for Tamora.
Ah, sirrah!
Yet I think we are not brought so low
But that between us we can kill a fly
That comes in likeness of a coal-black Moor.

MARCUS
Alas, poor man, grief has so wrought on him
He takes false shadows for true substances.

TITUS
Come, take away. Lavinia, go with me;
I'll to thy closet, and go read with thee
Sad stories chancèd in the times of old.
Come, boy, and go with me, thy sight is young,
And thou shalt read when mine begin to dazzle.

(*Exeunt.*)

Actus Quartus. [Scena Prima.]

Enter young Lucius, and Lavinia running after him, and the Boy flies from her with his books under his arm. [Then]enter Titus and Marcus.

(BOY) [YOUNG LUCIUS]
Help, grandsire, help! My aunt Lavinia
Follows me everywhere, I know not why.
Good uncle Marcus, see how swift she comes.
Alas, sweet aunt, I know not what you mean.

MARCUS
Stand by me, Lucius; do not fear thine aunt.

TITUS
She loves thee, boy, too well to do thee harm.

BOY
Aye, when my father was in Rome she did.

MARCUS
What means my niece Lavinia by these signs?

TITUS
Fear her not, Lucius; somewhat doth she mean.
See, Lucius, see how much she makes of thee;
Some-whither would she have thee go with her.
Ah, boy, Cornelia never with more care
Read to her sons than she hath read to thee
Sweet poetry and Tully's *Orator*.

MARCUS
Canst thou not guess wherefore she plies
thee thus?

BOY
My lord, I know not, I, nor can I guess,
Unless some fit or frenzy do possess her;
For I have heard my grandsire say full oft
Extremity of griefs would make men mad.
And I have read that Hecuba of Troy
Ran mad through sorrow; that made me to fear,
Although, my lord, I know my noble aunt
Loves me as dear as e'er my mother did,
And would not but in fury fright my youth,
Which made me down to throw my books, and fly,
Causeless, perhaps. But pardon me, sweet aunt,
And, madam, if my uncle Marcus go,
I will most willingly attend your ladyship.

MARCUS
Lucius, I will.

TITUS
How now, Lavinia? Marcus, what means this?
Some book there is that she desires to see.
Which is it, girl, of these? Open them, boy.
But thou art deeper read and better skilled;
Come and take choice of all my library,
And so beguile thy sorrow, till the heavens
Reveal the damned contriver of this deed.

66 **ill-favoured** ugly.
75 **sirrah** slave (more generally a term used of servants and inferiors).
81 **take away** i.e. the food.
82 **thy closet** private inner chamber.
83 **chancèd** that happened.
85 **mine...dazzle** my eyes begin to blur.
Boy quarto has '*puer*', Latin for 'boy'.
9–10 **somewhat...thee** she wants something...see how much attention she pays you.
12 **Cornela** the mother and educator of the Gracchi, boys who grew up to be famous Roman tribunes.
14 ***Orator*** Cicero's *On the Ideal Orator*, used as a standard rhetorical textbook in the Renaissance.
15 **wherefore** why.
18 **full oft** many times.
20 **Hecuba of Troy** Queen Hecuba went mad after blinding King Polymnestor (see note to I.i.141).
26 **Causeless** Unnecessarily.
27 **go** will come too.

Why lifts she up her arms in sequence thus?

MARCUS

I think she means that there was more than one
Confederate in the fact; aye, more there was;
Or else to heaven she heaves them for revenge.

TITUS

Lucius, what book is that she tosseth so?

BOY

Grandsire, 'tis Ovid's *Metamorphoses.*
My mother gave it me.

MARCUS

For love of her that's gone,
Perhaps she culled it from among the rest.

TITUS

Soft, so busily she turns the leaves.

[*Help her.*]

What would she find? Lavinia, shall I read?
This is the tragic tale of Philomel,
And treats of Tereus' treason and his rape;
And rape, I fear, was root of thine annoy.

MARCUS

See, brother, see; note how she quotes the leaves.

TITUS

Lavinia, were't thou thus surprised, sweet girl,
Ravished and wronged, as Philomela was,
Forced in the ruthless, vast, and gloomy woods?
See, see! Aye, such a place there is, where we did
hunt,
(O, had we never, never hunted there!)
Patterned by that the poet here describes,
By nature made for murders and for rapes.

MARCUS

O, why should nature build so foul a den
Unless the gods delight in tragedies?

TITUS

Give signs, sweet girl, for here are none
but friends,
What Roman lord it was durst do the deed.
Or slunk not Saturnine, as Tarquin erst,
That left the camp to sin in Lucrece's bed?

MARCUS

Sit down, sweet niece; brother, sit down by me.
Apollo, Pallas, Jove, or Mercury
Inspire me, that I may this treason find.
My lord, look here; look here, Lavinia:

He writes his name with his staff, and guides it with feet and mouth.

This sandy plot is plain; guide, if thou canst,
This after me. I have writ my name
Without the help of any hand at all.
Cursed be that heart that forced us to this shift!
Write thou, good niece, and here display at last
What God will have discovered for revenge.
Heaven guide thy pen to print thy sorrows plain,
That we may know the traitors and the truth.

She takes the staff in her mouth, and guides it with her stumps, and writes.

TITUS

O, do ye read, my lord, what she hath writ?
'*Stuprum*. Chiron. Demetrius.'

MARCUS

What, what? The lustful sons of Tamora
Performers of this heinous, bloody deed?

TITUS

Magni Dominator poli,
Tam lentus audis sclera, tam lentus vides?

MARCUS

O, calm thee, gentle lord; although I know
There is enough written upon this earth
To stir a mutiny in the mildest thoughts,
And arm the minds of infants to exclaims.
My lord, kneel down with me; Lavinia, kneel;
And kneel, sweet boy, the Roman Hector's hope;

37 **in sequence** first one then the other.
39 **Confederate . . . fact** Conspirator in the rape.
43–44 **For . . . rest.** Perhaps she has chosen it for love of her?
45 **Soft** Hush.
s.d. Both the 1594 quarto and the folio print this as part of Marcus' speech, but as previous editors suggest it looks more like a stage direction that Marcus should try to help Lavinia to read the book.
49 **annoy** injury.
50 **quotes** reads over.
56 **Patterned . . . describes** One just like the place the poet describes here.
62–63 **Or . . . camp** Or was it not Saturnine who, like Tarquin before him, sneaked from his army's camp.
65 **Apollo . . . Mercury** the gods of prophecy, wisdom, and justice, and the messenger of the gods respectively.
68 **plain** flat.
71 **that forced . . . shift** who brought us to this expedient.
78 ***Stuprum*** Rape (Latin).
81–82 ***Magni . . . vides?*** Ruler of great heaven, are you so slow to hear these crimes, and to see them? An adaptation of lines from Seneca's *Phaedra*.
86 **arm . . . exclaims** stir even babes in arms to cry out.
88 **the Roman . . . hope** the heir of Titus, the Roman equivalent of Hector of Troy.

And swear with me, as with the woeful fere
And father of that chaste dishonoured dame,
Lord Junius Brutus sware for Lucrece's rape,
That we will prosecute by good advice
Mortal revenge upon these traitorous Goths,
And see their blood, or die with this reproach.

TITUS
'Tis sure enough, and you knew how.
But if you hunt these bear-whelps, then beware:
The dam will wake, and if she wind you once;
She's with the lion deeply still in league,
And lulls him whilst she playeth on her back.
And when he sleeps will she do what she list.
You are a young huntsman, Marcus; let alone;
And come, I will go get a leaf of brass
And with a gad of steel will write these words,
And lay it by. The angry northern wind
Will blow these sands, like Sibyl's leaves, abroad,
And where's your lesson, then? Boy, what say you?

BOY
I say, my lord, that if I were a man,
Their mother's bed-chamber should not be safe
For these base bondmen to the yoke of Rome.

MARCUS
Aye, that's my boy! Thy father hath full oft
For his ungrateful country done the like.

BOY
And, uncle, so will I, and if I live.

TITUS
Come, go with me into mine armoury.
Lucius, I'll fit thee; and withal my boy
Shalt carry from me to the empress' sons
Presents that I intend to send them both.
Come, come, thou'lt do thy message, wilt thou not?

BOY
Aye, with my dagger in their bosoms, grandsire.

TITUS
No, boy, not so; I'll teach thee another course.
Lavinia, come. Marcus, look to my house,
Lucius and I'll go brave it at the court.
Aye, marry, will we, sir; and we'll be waited on.

Exeunt [Titus, Lavinia, and Young Lucius].

MARCUS
O heavens, can you hear a good man groan
And not relent, or not compassion him?
Marcus, attend him in his ecstasy,
That hath more scars of sorrow in his heart
Than foemen's marks upon his battered shield;
But yet so just that he will not revenge.
Revenge, the heavens, for old Andronicus!

Exit.

[Act IV. Scene ii.]

Enter Aaron, Chiron, and Demetrius at one door; and at the other door, Young Lucius and another with a bundle of weapons, and verses writ upon them.

CHIRON
Demetrius, here's the son of Lucius;
He hath some message to deliver us.

AARON
Aye, some mad message from his mad grandfather.

BOY
My lords, with all the humbleness I may
I greet your honours from Andronicus;
And pray the Roman gods confound you both!

DEMETRIUS
Gramercy, lovely Lucius; what's the news?

BOY [*Aside*]
That you are both deciphered, that's the news,
For villains marked with rape. May it please you,
My grandsire, well advised, hath sent by me
The goodliest weapons of his armoury

[89] **fere** husband.
[91] **Junius Brutus** having heard Lucrece's account of her rape, swore vengeance and drove Tarquin from Rome, thus helping to establish the Roman Republic.
[95] **and** if.
[96] **bear-whelps** cubs.
[97] **if...once** if she once sniffs your scent.
[98] **the lion** Saturninus, the imperial lion.
[100] **she...list** she does as she pleases.
[101] **let alone** leave it.
[103] **gad** pointed spike.
[105] **Sybil's leaves** the prophetic Sibyl would at times inscribe her prophecies on leaves, allowing them to blow away.
[109] **base bondmen** low-born slaves.
[114] **I'll...boy** I'll equip you, and you and my boy shall.
[120] **look to** guard.
[121] **brave it** display ourselves.
[122] **Aye, marry** Yes indeed.
[124] **compassion** feel compassion for.
[125] **ecstasy** madness.
[128] **yet so** yet is so.
[7] **Gramercy** Many thanks.
[8] **deciphered** revealed.

To gratify your honourable youth,
The hope of Rome; for so he bade me say;
And so I do, and with his gifts present
Your lordships, that, whenever you have need
You may be armèd and appointed well:
And so I leave you both—
like bloody villains. [*aside*]

Exit [*Young Lucius and servant.*]

DEMETRIUS
What's here? A scroll; and written round about.
Let's see;
'*Integer vitae, scelerisque purus,*
Non eget Mauri iaculis, nec arcu.'

CHIRON
O, 'tis a verse in Horace; I know it well:
I read it in the grammar long ago.

AARON
Aye, just; a verse in Horace; right, you have it.
Now, what a thing it is to be an ass!
Here's no sound jest; the old man hath found their guilt
And sends them weapons wrapped about with lines
That wound, beyond their feeling, to the quick.
But were our witty empress well afoot
She would applaud Andronicus' conceit.
But let her rest in her unrest awhile.
And now, young lords, was't not a happy star
Led us to Rome, strangers and more than so,
Captives, to be advanced to this height?
It did me good before the palace gate
To brave the tribune in his brother's hearing.

DEMETRIUS
But me more good to see so great a lord
Basely insinuate and send us gifts.

AARON
Had he not reason, Lord Demetrius?
Did you not use his daughter very friendly?

DEMETRIUS
I would we had a thousand Roman dames
At such a bay, by turn to serve our lust.

CHIRON
A charitable wish and full of love!

AARON
Here lacks but your mother for to say amen.

CHIRON
And that would she for twenty thousand more.

DEMETRIUS
Come, let us go and pray to all the gods
For our beloved mother in her pains.

AARON
Pray to the devils; the gods have given us over.

Trumpets sound.

DEMETRIUS
Why do the emperor's trumpets flourish thus?

CHIRON
Belike for joy the emperor hath a son.

DEMETRIUS
Soft, who comes here?

Enter a Nurse, with a blackamoor child.

NURSE
(Good) morrow, lords.
O, tell me, did you see Aaron the Moor?

AARON
Well, more or less, or ne'er a whit at all,
Here Aaron is; and what with Aaron now?

NURSE
O gentle Aaron, we are all undone!
Now help, or woe betide thee evermore!

AARON
Why, what a caterwauling dost thou keep!
What dost thou wrap and fumble in thine arms?

NURSE
O, that which I would hide from heaven's eye,
Our empress's shame, and stately Rome's disgrace!
She is delivered, lords; she is delivered.

AARON
To whom?

20–21 **'*Integer... arcu.*'** 'The man of honest life and free of crime needs not the javelins or bow of the Moor.'
23 The line is quoted in the Latin *Grammar* of William Lily, commonly used in English schools.
24 **just** that's right (ironic).
28 **That... quick** That wound them to the core, although they feel nothing.
29 **well afoot** on her feet (she is in labour in bed).
30 **conceit** clever ploy.
31 **unrest** travails.
32 **happy** fortunate.
36 **brave** defy.
38 **Basely insinuate** Humbly ingratiate himself.
42 **At... bay** At our mercy (like cornered deer).
50 **Belike** Probably.
51 **Soft** Quiet.
51.1 **a blackamoor child** a black baby.
53 **ne'er a whit** not a bit.
54 **what with** what do you want with.
55 **undone** ruined.
61 **she is delivered** she has given birth.

NURSE
I mean, she is brought a-bed.

AARON
Well, God give her good rest! What hath he sent her?

NURSE
A devil.

AARON
Why, then she is the devil's dam; a joyful issue!

NURSE
A joyless, dismal, black, and sorrowful issue.
Here is the babe, as loathsome as a toad
Amongst the fair-faced breeders of our clime.
The empress sends it thee, thy stamp, thy seal,
And bids thee christen it with thy dagger's point.

AARON
Zounds, ye whore, is black so base a hue?
Sweet blowse, you are a beauteous blossom, sure.

DEMETRIUS
Villain, what hast thou done?

AARON
That which thou canst not undo.

CHIRON
Thou hast undone our mother.

AARON
Villain, I have done thy mother.

DEMETRIUS
And therein, hellish dog, thou hast undone.
Woe to her chance, and damned her loathed choice;
Accursed the offspring of so foul a fiend!

CHIRON
It shall not live.

AARON
It shall not die.

NURSE
Aaron, it must; the mother wills it so.

AARON
What? Must it, nurse? Then let no man but I
Do execution on my flesh and blood.

DEMETRIUS
I'll broach the tadpole on my rapier's point.
Nurse, give it me; my sword shall soon dispatch it.

AARON
Sooner this sword shall plough thy bowels up.
Stay, murderous villains; will you kill your brother?
Now, by the burning tapers of the sky,
That shone so brightly when this boy was got,
He dies upon my scimitar's sharp point
That touches this, my first-born son and heir.
I tell you, younglings, not Enceladus,
With all his threatening band of Typhon's brood,
Nor great Alcides, nor the god of war,
Shall seize this prey out of his father's hands.
What, what, ye sanguine, shallow-hearted boys;
Ye white-limed walls; ye alehouse painted signs!
Coal-black is better than another hue,
In that it scorns to bear another hue;
For all the water in the ocean
Can never turn the swan's black legs to white,
Although she lave them hourly in the flood.
Tell the empress from me, I am of age
To keep mine own, excuse it how she can.

DEMETRIUS
Wilt thou betray thy noble mistress thus?

AARON
My mistress is my mistress; this myself,
The vigour and the picture of my youth.
This before all the world do I prefer;
This, maugre all the world, will I keep safe,
Or some of you shall smoke for it in Rome.

DEMETRIUS
By this our mother is forever shamed.

CHIRON
Rome will despise her for this foul escape.

65 **issue** result.
66 **issue** birth/child.
68 **Amongst . . . clime** Among the fair-skinned children of this climate.
69 **thy stamp, thy seal** it's your mark, your signature.
71 **Zounds** contraction of 'God's wounds', an oath.
72 **blowse** fat, red-faced woman.
76 **done** had sex with (slang).
78 **Woe . . . chance** Curse her luck.
85 **broach** impale.
90 **got** conceived.
93–94 **Enceladus . . . Typhon** two giants who warred on the Olympian gods.
95 **Alcides** Hercules.
95 **god of war** Mars.
97 **sanguine** red-faced.
98 **white-limed . . . signs** whitewashed walls (echoing Christ's condemnation of hypocrites as 'whited sepulchres') and mere images of men.
99–100 **Coal-black . . . hue** Black paint cannot be changed to another colour (whereas adding black to any other turns that paint black).
103 **lave . . . flood** wash them every hour in the river.
108 **vigour** i.e. the life, or, more plausibly, a variant of 'figure': the very image.
110 **maugre** despite.
111 **smoke** burn.
113 **escape** escapade.

NURSE
The emperor in his rage will doom her death.
CHIRON
I blush to think upon this ignomy.
AARON
Why, there's the privilege your beauty bears;
Fie, treacherous hue that will betray with blushing
The close enacts and counsels of the heart!
Here's a young lad framed of another leer;
Look, how the black slave smiles upon the father,
As who should say, 'Old lad, I am thine own.'
He is your brother, lords, sensibly fed
Of that self-blood that first gave life to you,
And from that womb where you imprisoned were
He is enfranchised and come to light.
Nay, he is your brother by the surer side,
Although my seal be stamped in his face.
NURSE
Aaron, what shall I say unto the empress?
DEMETRIUS
Advise thee, Aaron, what is to be done,
And we will all subscribe to thy advice.
Save thou the child, so we may all be safe.
AARON
Then sit we down, and let us all consult.
My son and I will have the wind of you.
Keep there: now talk at pleasure of your safety.
DEMETRIUS
How many women saw this child of his?
AARON
Why, so, brave lords, when we join in league
I am a lamb, but if you brave the Moor,
The chafed boar, the mountain lioness,
The ocean swells not so as Aaron storms.
But say again; how many saw the child?
NURSE
Cornelia the midwife and myself,
And no one else but the delivered empress.
AARON
The empress, the midwife, and yourself?
Two may keep counsel when the third's away.
Go to the empress, tell her this I said.

He kills her.

'Squeak squeak!' So cries a pig preparèd
to the spit.
DEMETRIUS
What mean'st thou, Aaron? Wherefore didst thou
this?
AARON
O Lord, sir, 'tis a deed of policy.
Shall she live to betray this guilt of ours,
A long-tongued babbling gossip? No, lords, no.
And now be it known to you my full intent.
Not far, one Muliteus lives, my countryman;
His wife but yester-night was brought to bed;
His child is like to her, fair as you are.
Go pack with him, and give the mother gold,
And tell them both the circumstance of all,
And how by this their child shall be advanced,
And be receivèd for the emperor's heir,
And substituted in the place of mine
To calm this tempest whirling in the court,
And let the emperor dandle him for his own.
Hark ye, lords; ye see I have given her physic,
And you must needs bestow her funeral;
The fields are near, and you are gallant grooms.
This done, see that you take no longer days,
But send the midwife presently to me.
The midwife and the nurse well made away,
Then let the ladies tattle what they please.
CHIRON
Aaron, I see thou wilt not trust the air
With secrets.

115 **ignomy** ignominy.
116 **there's...bears** that's the benefit of your 'beautiful' (white) skin (you can blush).
118 **close enacts** secret resolutions.
119 **framed...leer** made up of another complexion.
122–123 **sensibly...self-blood** demonstrably nourished by that same blood.
125 **enfranchised** released.
126 **by...side** on the more certain (maternal) side.
129 **Advise thee** Consider/think.
130 **subscribe** agree.
131 **so** so long as.
133 **will...you** will stay downwind (as in hunting): i.e. we'll sit where we can see what you are doing.
138 **chafed** enraged.
144 **Two...away** proverbial.
146 **'Squeak squeak!'** he mocks her death-cries.
148 **deed of policy** shrewd calculation.
150 **long-tongued** loose-tongued.
153 **to bed** into labour.
155 **pack** conspire.
161 **dandle** bounce him on his knee.
162 **physic** medicine.
163 **bestow** provide.
164 **gallant grooms** strong lads.
166 **presently** immediately.
167 **made away** disposed of.
168 **tattle** gossip.

DEMETRIUS
For this care of Tamora,
Herself and hers are highly bound to thee.

Exeunt [Demetrius and Chiron, with the Nurse's body].

AARON
Now to the Goths, as swift as swallow flies;
There to dispose this treasure in mine arms,
And secretly to greet the empress's friends.
Come on, you thick-lipped slave, I'll bear you hence;
For it is you that puts us to our shifts.
I'll make you feed on berries and on roots,
And feed on curds and whey, and suck the goat,
And cabin in a cave, and bring you up
To be a warrior, and command a camp.

Exit.

[Act IV. Scene iii.]

Enter Titus, old Marcus, young Lucius, and other gentlemen [Publius, Sempronius, Caius] with bows, and Titus bears the arrows with letters at the ends of them.

TITUS
Come, Marcus, come; kinsmen, this is the way.
Sir boy, now let me see your archery;
Look ye draw home enough, and 'tis there straight.
Terras Astraea reliquit:
Be you remembered, Marcus, she's gone, she's fled.
Sirs, take you to your tools. You, cousins, shall
Go sound the ocean, and cast your nets;
Happily you may catch her in the sea;
Yet there's as little justice as at land.
No; Publius and Sempronius, you must do it;
'Tis you must dig with mattock and with spade,
And pierce the inmost centre of the earth.
Then, when you come to Pluto's region,
I pray you, deliver him this petition;
Tell him it is for justice and for aid
And that it comes from old Andronicus,
Shaken with sorrows in ungrateful Rome.
Ah, Rome! Well, well; I made thee miserable
What time I threw the people's suffrages
On him that thus doth tyrannize o'er me.
Go, get you gone; and pray be careful all,
And leave you not a man-of-war unsearched.
This wicked emperor may have shipped her hence;
And, kinsmen, then we may go pipe for justice.

MARCUS
O Publius, is not this a heavy case,
To see thy noble uncle thus distract?

PUBLIUS
Therefore, my lords, it highly us concerns
By day and night to attend him carefully,
And feed his humour kindly as we may,
Till time beget some careful remedy.

MARCUS
Kinsmen, his sorrows are past remedy.
Join with the Goths, and with revengeful war
Take wreak on Rome for this ingratitude,
And vengeance on the traitor Saturnine.

TITUS
Publius, how now? How now, my masters?
What, have you met with her?

PUBLIUS
No, my good lord, but Pluto sends you word
If you will have Revenge from hell, you shall.
Marry, for Justice, she is so employed,
He thinks, with Jove in heaven, or somewhere else,
So that perforce you must needs stay a time.

176 **puts...shifts** tests our mettle.
179 **cabin** live roughly.
180 **a camp** an army.
3 **Look...straight** Be sure to draw back the bow back far enough and it'll be sure to get there.
4 ***Terras Astraea reliquit*** 'Astraea [the daughter of Jupiter and goddess of Justice] has departed the earth' (from book i of Ovid's *Metamorphoses*). The departure of Astraea marked the end of the Golden Age and the beginning of the Age of Iron.
7 **sound** test the depth of/search.
8 **happily** maybe.
11 **mattock** pick-axe.
13 **Pluto's region** Hades.
19–20 **What...me** When I gave the people's vote to him who now makes me suffer (i.e. Saturninus).
22 **man-of-war** warship.
24 **pipe** whistle (fruitlessly).
25 **heavy case** sad situation.
26 **distract** distracted/mad.
29 **feed his humour** humour his moods.
30 **beget** brings forth.
31 **past remedy** beyond cure. A line beginning 'But' may have been lost after this one.
33 **wreak** revenge.
38 **Revenge** the personification of Revenge (who appears as a character in Kyd's *The Spanish Tragedy*).
39 **for** as for.
41 **stay a time** wait a while for her.

TITUS
He doth me wrong to feed me with delays.
I'll dive into the burning lake below,
And pull her out of Acheron by the heels.
Marcus, we are but shrubs, no cedars we,
No big-boned men, framed of the Cyclops' size,
But metal, Marcus, steel to the very back,
Yet wrung with wrongs more than our backs can bear.
And, sith there's no justice in earth nor hell,
We will solicit heaven and move the gods
To send down Justice for to wreak our wrongs.
Come, to this gear. You are a good archer, Marcus.

He gives them the arrows.

'*Ad Jovem*,' that's for you; here, '*Ad Apollinem*';
'*Ad Martem*', that's for myself.
Here, boy, 'To Pallas': here, 'To Mercury':
'To Saturn'. Caius, not to Saturnine;
You were as good to shoot against the wind.
To it, boy. Marcus, loose when I bid.
Of my word, I have written to effect
There's not a god left unsolicited.

MARCUS
Kinsmen, shoot all your shafts into the court:
We will afflict the emperor in his pride.

TITUS
Now, masters, draw. O, well said, Lucius!
Good boy; in Virgo's lap; give it Pallas.

MARCUS
My lord, I aim a mile beyond the moon;
Your letter is with Jupiter by this.

TITUS
Ha, ha! Publius, Publius, what hast thou done?
See, see, thou hast shot off one of Taurus' horns.

MARCUS
This was the sport, my lord: when Publius shot,
The Bull, being galled, gave Aries such a knock
That down fell both the Ram's horns in the court;
And who should find them but the empress's villain?
She laughed, and told the Moor he should not choose
But give them to his master for a present.

TITUS
Why, there it goes: God give his lordship joy!

Enter the Clown, with a basket, and two pigeons in it.

News, news from heaven! Marcus, the post is come.
Sirrah, what tidings? Have you any letters?
Shall I have justice? What says Jupiter?

CLOWN
O, the gibbet-maker? He says that he hath taken them down again, for the man must not be hanged till the next week.

TITUS
But what says Jupiter, I ask thee?

CLOWN
Alas, sir, I know not Jupiter; I never drank with him in all my life.

TITUS
Why, villain, art not thou the carrier?

CLOWN
Aye, of my pigeons, sir, nothing else.

TITUS
Why, didst thou not come from heaven?

CLOWN
From heaven? Alas, sir, I never came there; God forbid I should be so bold to press to heaven in my young days. Why, I am going with my pigeons to the tribunal plebs, to take up a matter of brawl betwixt my uncle and one of the emperial's men.

44 **Acheron** a river of Hades. Phlegethon was the burning *river* of Hades, which Titus may have in mind here.
46 **Cyclops** one-eyed giants.
47 **steel . . . back** we're made of steel, through and through.
52 **Come . . . gear.** Let's get on with this business.
54 The arrows are marked in Latin: 'To Jupiter', 'To Apollo', and 'To Mars'.
57 **You . . . good** That would be as much use.
58 **loose** shoot.
59 **to effect** to good effect.
63 **well said** well shot.
64 **Virgo's lap** the constellation Virgo, here an aspect of Astraea.
64 **Pallas** Athena, goddess of wisdom.
66 **by this** by now.
68 **Taurus** the constellation/zodiac sign of Taurus, the bull.
70 **galled** stung.
70 **Aries** the constellation/sign of the ram.
72 **villain** servant (i.e. having the horns, Aaron could thus cuckold his master, Saturninus).
79 **gibbet-maker** he mishears 'Jupiter' as 'Gibbeter'.
85 **carrier** messenger/postman.
91 **tribunal plebs** mistake for '*Tribunus plebis*': tribune of the people.
91–92 **to . . . betwixt** to pursue a case of affray between.
92 **emperial's** i.e. emperor's.

MARCUS
Why, sir, that is as fit as can be to serve for your oration; and let him deliver the pigeons to the emperor from you.

TITUS
Tell me, can you deliver an oration to the emperor with a grace?

CLOWN
Nay, truly, sir, I could never say grace in all my life.

TITUS
Sirrah, come hither, make no more ado,
But give your pigeons to the emperor.
By me thou shalt have justice at his hands.
Hold, hold; meanwhile here's money for
thy charges.
Give me pen and ink. Sirrah, can you with a grace deliver a supplication?

CLOWN
Aye, sir.

TITUS
Then here is a supplication for you. And when you come to him, at the first approach you must kneel, then kiss his foot, then deliver up your pigeons, and then look for your reward. I'll be at hand, sir; see you do it bravely.

CLOWN
I warrant you, sir, let me alone.

TITUS
Sirrah, hast thou a knife? Come, let me see it.
Here, Marcus, fold it in the oration;
For thou hast made it like an humble suppliant.
And when thou hast given it the emperor,
Knock at my door, and tell me what he says.

CLOWN
God be with you, sir; I will.

Exit.

TITUS
Come, Marcus, let us go. Publius, follow me.

Exeunt.

[Act IV. Scene iv.]

Enter Emperor and Empress [Saturninus and Tamora], and her two sons. The Emperor brings the arrows in his hand that Titus shot at him.

SATURNINUS
Why, lords, what wrongs are these! Was ever seen
An emperor in Rome thus overborne,
Troubled, confronted thus; and for the extent
Of egall justice, used in such contempt?
My lords, you know, [as know] the mightful gods,
However these disturbers of our peace
Buzz in the people's ears, there nought hath passed
But even with law against the wilful sons
Of old Andronicus. And what and if
His sorrows have so overwhelmed his wits?
Shall we be thus afflicted in his wreaks,
His fits, his frenzy, and his bitterness?
And now he writes to heaven for his redress.
See, here's to Jove, and this to Mercury;
This to Apollo; this to the god of war;
Sweet scrolls to fly about the streets of Rome!
What's this but libelling against the senate,
And blazoning our injustice everywhere?
A goodly humour, is it not, my lords?
As who would say, in Rome no justice were.
But if I live, his feignèd ecstasies
Shall be no shelter to these outrages,
But he and his shall know that justice lives
In Saturninus' health, whom, if he sleep,
He'll so awake as he in fury shall
Cut off the proud'st conspirator that lives.

TAMORA
My gracious lord, my lovely Saturnine,
Lord of my life, commander of my thoughts,
Calm thee, and bear the faults of Titus' age,
The effects of sorrow for his valiant sons
Whose loss hath pierced him deep and scarred his
heart;
And rather comfort his distressèd plight
Than prosecute the meanest or the best

[94] **oration** petition.
[97] **with a grace** elegantly.
[99] **ado** fuss.
[102] **Hold** Wait.
[111] **let me alone** leave it to me.
[2] **overborne** oppressed.
[3–4] **for...justice** for administering impartial justice.
[7] **Buzz** Whisper/spread rumours.
[7–8] **nought...law** nothing has been done that was not in keeping with the law.
[18] **blazoning** publicly denouncing.
[24] **if he sleep** if he (Saturninus himself) seems to be dormant/placid now.
[33] **the meanest...best** any of the Andronici, high or low.

For these contempts.

(Aside)

Why, thus it shall become
High-witted Tamora to glose with all:
But, Titus, I have touched thee to the quick;
Thy life-blood out, if Aaron now be wise,
Then is all safe, the anchor's in the port.

Enter Clown.

How now, good fellow, wouldst thou
speak with us?

CLOWN
Yea, forsooth, and your mistress-ship be emperial.

TAMORA
Empress I am, but yonder sits the emperor.

CLOWN
'Tis he. God and Saint Stephen give you good den.
I have brought you a letter and a couple of pigeons here.

He [Saturninus] reads the letter.

SATURNINUS
Go, take him away, and hang him presently.

CLOWN
How much money must I have?

TAMORA
Come, sirrah, you must be hanged.

CLOWN
Hanged! by'r lady, then I have brought up a neck to a fair end.

Exit [under guard].

SATURNINUS
Despiteful and intolerable wrongs!
Shall I endure this monstrous villainy?
I know from whence this same device proceeds.
May this be borne, as if his traitorous sons,
That died by law for murder of our brother,
Have by my means been butchered wrongfully?
Go, drag the villain hither by the hair;
Nor age nor honour shall shape privilege.
For this proud mock I'll be thy slaughterman,
Sly frantic wretch, that holp'st to make me great
In hope thyself should govern Rome and me.

Enter Nu(n)tius, Aemilius.

What news with thee, Aemilius?

AEMILIUS
Arm, my lords! Rome never had more cause.
The Goths have gathered head, and with a power
Of high-resolved men, bent to the spoil,
They hither march amain under conduct
Of Lucius, son to old Andronicus;
Who threats, in course of this revenge, to do
As much as ever Coriolanus did.

SATURNINUS
Is warlike Lucius general of the Goths?
These tidings nip me, and I hang the head
As flowers with frost or grass beat down with
storms.
Aye, now begin our sorrows to approach.
'Tis he the common people love so much;
Myself hath often overheard them say,
When I have walked like a private man,
That Lucius' banishment was wrongfully,
And they have wished that Lucius were their
emperor.

TAMORA
Why should you fear? Is not your city strong?

SATURNINUS
Aye, but the citizens favour Lucius,
And will revolt from me to succour him.

TAMORA
King, be thy thoughts imperious like thy name.
Is the sun dimmed that gnats do fly in it?
The eagle suffers little birds to sing
And is not careful what they mean thereby,
Knowing that with the shadow of his wings

36 **High-witted . . . glose** shrewd Tamora to deceive everyone.
38 **Thy life-blood out** Once your blood is spilled.
41 **and** if.
43 **good den** good evening.
48 **by'r lady** by Our Lady.
57 **shape privilege** prompt special treatment.
59 **holp'st** helped.
Nu(n)tius '(as) messenger'
63–66 **The Goths . . . Lucius** The Goths have gathered their strength, and with an army of determined men, focused upon pillage, they are marching here swiftly under the command of Lucius.
68 **Coriolanus** Caius Marcius, given the honorific name, 'Coriolanus', was exiled from Rome but returned at the head of an army of their enemies, the Volscians. Shakespeare would write his version of the story in *c.*1607.
70 **nip** injure, as a flower is damaged by frost.
71 **As** Like.
76 **wrongfully** unjust.
84 **is not careful** does not care.

He can at pleasure stint their melody.
Even so mayst thou the giddy men of Rome.
Then cheer thy spirit, for know thou, emperor,
I will enchant the old Andronicus
With words more sweet and yet more dangerous
Than baits to fish, or honey-stalks to sheep,
When as the one is wounded with the bait,
The other rotted with delicious feed.

SATURNINUS
But he will not entreat his son for us.

TAMORA
If Tamora entreat him, then he will;
For I can smooth and fill his aged ear
With golden promises that, were his heart
Almost impregnable, his old ears deaf,
Yet should both ear and heart obey my tongue.
Go thou before to be our ambassador,
Say that the emperor requests a parley
Of warlike Lucius, and appoint the meeting
Even at his father's house, the old Andronicus.

SATURNINUS
Aemilius, do this message honourably,
And if he stand on hostage for his safety,
Bid him demand what pledge will please him best.

AEMILIUS
Your bidding shall I do effectually. *Exit.*

TAMORA
Now will I to that old Andronicus,
And temper him with all the art I have
To pluck proud Lucius from the warlike Goths.
And now, sweet emperor, be blithe again
And bury all thy fear in my devices.

SATURNINUS
Then go successantly, and plead to him. *Exeunt.*

Actus Quintus [Scena Prima].

Enter Lucius with an army of Goths, with drums and soldiers.

LUCIUS
Approvèd warriors, and my faithful friends,
I have received letters from great Rome
Which signifies what hate they bear their emperor
And how desirous of our sight they are.
Therefore, great lords, be as your titles witness,
Imperious and impatient of your wrongs,
And wherein Rome hath done you any scath,
Let him make treble satisfaction.

FIRST GOTH
Brave slip, sprung from the great Andronicus,
Whose name was once our terror, now our comfort,
Whose high exploits and honourable deeds
Ingrateful Rome requites with foul contempt,
Be bold in us; we'll follow where thou lead'st,
Like stinging bees in hottest summer's day
Led by their master to the flowered fields,
And be avenged on cursèd Tamora.
And as he saith, so say we all with him.

LUCIUS
I humbly thank him, and I thank you all.
But who comes here, led by a lusty Goth?

Enter a Goth, leading of Aaron with his child in his arms.

[SECOND] GOTH
Renownèd Lucius, from our troops I strayed
To gaze upon a ruinous monastery,
And, as I earnestly did fix mine eye
Upon the wasted building, suddenly
I heard a child cry underneath a wall.
I made unto the noise, when soon I heard
The crying babe controlled with this discourse:
'Peace, tawny slave, half me and half thy dam,
Did not thy hue bewray whose brat thou art.
Had nature lent thee but thy mother's look,
Villain, thou mightst have been an emperor;
But where the bull and cow are both milk-white,
They never do beget a coal-black calf.
Peace, villain, peace!' (Even thus he rates the babe)
'For I must bear thee to a trusty Goth
Who, when he knows thou art the empress's babe,

86 **at pleasure ... melody** end their song whenever he likes.
87 **giddy** silly.
91 **honey-stalks** red clover, poisonous to sheep if eaten in large quantities.
102 **Of** With.
105 **if ... hostage** if he insists upon a hostage.
107 **effectually** diligently.
109 **temper** work on.
113 **successantly** perhaps a variant of 'successfully'.
1 **Approved** Tried and tested.
7 **scath** injury.
9 **slip** scion.
13 **Be bold** Have confidence.
27 **tawny** dusky.
28 **bewray** reveal.
33 **rates** berates.

Will hold thee dearly for thy mother's sake.'
With this, my weapon drawn, I rushed upon him,
Surprised him suddenly, and brought him hither
To use as you think needful of the man.

LUCIUS
O worthy Goth, this is the incarnate devil
That robbed Andronicus of his good hand,
This is the pearl that pleased your empress' eye;
And here's the base fruit of his burning lust.
Say, wall-eyed slave, whither wouldst thou convey
This growing image of thy fiend-like face?
Why dost not speak? What, deaf? Not a word?
A halter, soldiers; hang him on this tree.
And by his side his fruit of bastardy.

AARON
Touch not the boy; he is of royal blood.

LUCIUS
Too like the sire for ever being good.
First hang the child, that he may see it sprawl;
A sight to vex the father's soul withal.

AARON
Get me a ladder. Lucius, save the child,
And bear it from me to the empress.
If thou do this, I'll show thee wondrous things,
That highly may advantage thee to hear.
If thou wilt not, befall what may befall,
I'll speak no more but 'Vengeance rot you all!'

LUCIUS
Say on, and if it please me which thou speak'st
Thy child shall live, and I will see it nourished.

AARON
'And if it please thee'? Why, assure thee, Lucius,
'Twill vex thy soul to hear what I shall speak;
For I must talk of murders, rapes, and massacres,
Acts of black night, abominable deeds,
Complots of mischief, treason, villainies
Ruthful to hear, yet piteously performed.
And this shall all be buried by my death
Unless thou swear to me my child shall live.

LUCIUS
Tell on thy mind; I say thy child shall live.

AARON
Swear that he shall, and then I will begin.

LUCIUS
Who should I swear by? Thou believest no god.
That granted, how canst thou believe an oath?

AARON
What if I do not? As, indeed, I do not;
Yet, for I know thou art religious
And hast a thing within thee called conscience,
With twenty popish tricks and ceremonies
Which I have seen thee careful to observe,
Therefore I urge thy oath, for that I know
An idiot holds his bauble for a god
And keeps the oath which by that god he swears,
To that I'll urge him; therefore thou shalt vow
By that same god, what god soe'er it be,
That thou adorest and hast in reverence,
To save my boy, to nourish and bring him up;
Or else I will discover nought to thee.

LUCIUS
Even by my god I swear to thee I will.

AARON
First know thou, I begot him on the empress.

LUCIUS
O most insatiate and luxurious woman!

AARON
Tut, Lucius, this was but a deed of charity
To that which thou shalt hear of me anon.
'Twas her two sons that murdered Bassianus;
They cut thy sister's tongue and ravished her,
And cut her hands and trimmed her as thou saw'st.

LUCIUS
O detestable villain; call'st thou that trimming?

AARON
Why, she was washed and cut and trimmed, and 'twas
Trim sport for them that had the doing of it.

[39] **needful ... man** the man deserves.
[44] **wall-eyed** having bulging eyes with lots of the white showing.
[51] **sprawl** in its death-throes.
[53] Most modern editions give this line to Lucius, but both the 1594 quarto and the folio give it to Aaron. If it is his line, the meaning may be, 'bring a ladder and I'll climb it myself and be hanged, and tell you my secrets too, if only you will let the baby go', which would fit with Lucius' response at ll. 59–60.
[66] **Ruthful .. performed** Lamentable to hear about, yet performed in ways still more worthy of pity.
[74] **for** as.
[76] **popish** Catholic (and so superstitious in Protestant eyes).
[79] **bauble** a fool's stick.
[85] **discover nought** reveal nothing.
[88] **luxurious** lustful.
[90] **To** Compared to.
[93] **trimmed her** cut her up, as a butcher does a carcass.
[96] **Trim sport** Good fun.

LUCIUS
O barbarous, beastly villains, like thyself!

AARON
Indeed, I was their tutor to instruct them.
That codding spirit had they from their mother,
As sure a card as ever won the set;
That bloody mind, I think, they learned of me,
As true a dog as ever fought at head.
Well, let my deeds be witness of my worth.
I trained thy brethren to that guileful hole
Where the dead corpse of Bassianus lay.
I wrote the letter that thy father found,
And hid the gold within the letter mentioned,
Confederate with the queen and her two sons.
And what not done that thou hast cause to rue
Wherein I had no stroke of mischief in it?
I played the cheater for thy father's hand,
And when I had it, drew myself apart
And almost broke my heart with extreme laughter.
I pried me through the crevice of a wall
When, for his hand, he had his two sons' heads,
Beheld his tears, and laughed so heartily
That both mine eyes were rainy like to his.
And when I told the empress of this sport,
She swooned almost at my pleasing tale,
And for my tidings gave me twenty kisses.

[FIRST] GOTH
What, canst thou say all this, and never blush?

AARON
Aye, like a black dog, as the saying is.

LUCIUS
Art thou not sorry for these heinous deeds?

AARON
Aye, that I had not done a thousand more.
Even now I curse the day. And yet, I think,
Few come within the compass of my curse,
Wherein I did not some notorious ill,
As kill a man, or else devise his death,
Ravish a maid, or plot the way to do it,
Accuse some innocent and forswear myself,
Set deadly enmity between two friends,
Make poor men's cattle break their necks,
Set fire on barns and hay-stacks in the night,
And bid the owners quench them with their tears.
Oft have I digged up dead men from their graves
And set them upright at their dear friends' doors,
Even when their sorrows almost were forgot;
And on their skins, as on the bark of trees,
Have with my knife carved in Roman letters,
'Let not your sorrow die, though I am dead.'
Tut, I have done a thousand dreadful things
As willingly as one would kill a fly,
And nothing grieves me heartily indeed
But that I cannot do ten thousand more.

LUCIUS
Bring down the devil; for he must not die
So sweet a death as hanging presently.

AARON
If there be devils, would I were a devil,
To live and burn in everlasting fire,
So I might have your company in hell,
But to torment you with my bitter tongue!

LUCIUS
Sirs, stop his mouth, and let him speak no more.

Enter Aemilius [*preceded by the Third Goth*].

[THIRD] GOTH
My lord, there is a messenger from Rome
Desires to be admitted to your presence.

LUCIUS
Let him come near.
Welcome, Aemilius what's the news from
Rome?

AEMILIUS
Lord Lucius, and you princes of the Goths,
The Roman emperor greets you all by me;
And, for he understands you are in arms,
He craves a parley at your father's house,
Willing you to demand your hostages,
And they shall be immediately delivered.

[FIRST] GOTH
What says our general?

LUCIUS
Aemilius, let the emperor give his pledges

99 **codding** mocking.
100 **set** game. i.e. she is the best card in the pack in that vein.
102 **at head** near the bull's head in a bull-baiting, where the fiercest dogs were placed.
104 **trained** lured.
109–110 **what . . . it** i.e. there's nothing that causes you sorrow that I did not have some mischievous part in.
111 **cheater** trickster.
114 **pried me** peeped.
122 **like . . . dog** black dogs are not seen to blush.
126–127 **Few . . . ill** There are few who I curse that I do not inflict some terrible cruelty upon.

Unto my father and my uncle Marcus,
And we will come. March away.

Flourish. Exeunt.

[Act V. Scene ii.]

Enter Tamora and her two sons, disguised.

TAMORA
Thus, in this strange and sad habiliment,
I will encounter with Andronicus
And say I am Revenge, sent from below
To join with him and right his heinous wrongs.
Knock at his study, where they say he keeps
To ruminate strange plots of dire revenge;
Tell him Revenge is come to join with him,
And work confusion on his enemies.

They knock, and Titus opens his study door.

TITUS
Who doth molest my contemplation?
Is it your trick to make me ope the door
That so my sad decrees may fly away,
And all my study be to no effect?
You are deceived, for what I mean to do
See here in bloody lines I have set down;
And what is written shall be executed.

TAMORA
Titus, I am come to talk with thee.

TITUS
No, not a word; how can I grace my talk,
Wanting a hand to give that accord?
Thou hast the odds of me; therefore no more.

TAMORA
If thou didst know me, thou wouldst talk with me.

TITUS
I am not mad; I know thee well enough.
Witness this wretched stump, witness these crimson lines,
Witness these trenches made by grief and care,
Witness the tiring day and heavy night,
Witness all sorrow, that I know thee well
For our proud empress, mighty Tamora.
Is not thy coming for my other hand?

TAMORA
Know thou, sad man, I am not Tamora;
She is thy enemy, and I thy friend.
I am Revenge, sent from the infernal kingdom
To ease the gnawing vulture of thy mind
By working wreakful vengeance on thy foes.
Come down, and welcome me to this world's light;
Confer with me of murder and of death.
There's not a hollow cave or lurking-place,
No vast obscurity or misty vale,
Where bloody murder or detested rape
Can couch for fear, but I will find them out;
And in their ears tell them my dreadful name,
Revenge, which makes the foul offender quake.

TITUS
Art thou Revenge, and art thou sent to me
To be a torment to mine enemies?

TAMORA
I am; therefore come down, and welcome me.

TITUS
Do me some service ere I come to thee.
Lo, by thy side where Rape and Murder stands;
Now give me some surance that thou art Revenge,
Stab them, or tear them on thy chariot-wheels;
And then I'll come and be thy wagoner,
And whirl along with thee about the globes.
Provide thee two proper palfreys, black as jet,
To hale thy vengeful wagon swift away,
And find out murderers in their guilty caves.
And when thy car is loaden with their heads
I will dismount, and by the wagon-wheel

1 **sad habiliment** sombre costume.
5 **keeps** stays secluded.
8 **work confusion on** bring ruin to.
11 **sad decrees** serious proclamations.
14 **bloody lines** lines written in (his own) blood.
17–18 **how . . . accord?** How can I accompany my talk with the appropriate gestures (an important element in rhetoric) that must accompany them, lacking a hand?
19 **Thou . . . me** You have the advantage over me (having two hands yourself).
23 **trenches** lines and wrinkles in his skin.
23 **care** worry.
31 **gnawing vulture** like that eternally gnawing Prometheus' liver (see note to II.i.17).
33 Titus's study is presumably located on the balcony over the rear of the playhouse stage.
36 **obscurity** dark place.
38 **couch** hide.
46 **surance** assurance.
48 **wagoner** charioteer.
49 **the globes** the spheres of heaven.
50 **proper palfreys** suitable horses.
51 **hale** haul.
53 **car** chariot.

Trot, like a servile footman, all day long,
Even from [Hyperion]'s rising in the east
Until his very downfall in the sea.
And day by day I'll do this heavy task,
So thou destroy Rapine and Murder there.

TAMORA
These are my ministers, and come with me.

TITUS
Are these thy ministers? What are they called?

TAMORA
Rapine and Murder; therefore called so,
'Cause they take vengeance of such kind of men.

TITUS
Good lord, how like the empress' sons they are,
And you the empress! But we worldly men
Have miserable, mad, mistaking eyes.
O sweet Revenge, now do I come to thee;
And, if one arm's embracement will content thee,
I will embrace thee in it by and by.

TAMORA
This closing with him fits his lunacy.
Whate'er I forge to feed his brain-sick fits,
Do you uphold and maintain in your speeches,
For now he firmly takes me for Revenge,
And, being credulous in this mad thought,
I'll make him send for Lucius his son,
And whilst I at a banquet hold him sure,
I'll find some cunning practice out of hand
To scatter and disperse the giddy Goths,
Or at the least make them his enemies.
See, here he comes, and I must ply my theme.

TITUS
Long have I been forlorn, and all for thee.
Welcome, dread Fury, to my woeful house.
Rapine and Murder, you are welcome too.
How like the empress and her sons you are!
Well are you fitted, had you but a Moor.
Could not all hell afford you such a devil?
For well I wot the empress never wags
But in her company there is a Moor;
And, would you represent our queen aright,
It were convenient you had such a devil.
But welcome as you are. What shall we do?

TAMORA
What wouldst thou have us do, Andronicus?

DEMETRIUS
Show me a murderer, I'll deal with him.

CHIRON
Show me a villain that hath done a rape,
And I am sent to be revenged on him.

TAMORA
Show me a thousand that have done thee wrong,
And I will be revenged on them all.

TITUS
Look round about the wicked streets of Rome;
And when thou find'st a man that's like thyself,
Good Murder, stab him; he's a murderer.
Go thou with him; and when it is thy hap
To find another that is like to thee,
Good Rapine, stab him; he's a ravisher.
Go thou with them, and in the emperor's court
There is a queen, attended by a Moor;
Well mayst thou know her by thy own proportion,
For up and down she doth resemble thee.
I pray thee, do on them some violent death;
They have been violent to me and mine.

TAMORA
Well hast thou lessoned us; this shall we do.
But would it please thee, good Andronicus,
To send for Lucius, thy thrice-valiant son,
Who leads towards Rome a band of warlike Goths,
And bid him come and banquet at thy house?
When he is here, even at thy solemn feast,
I will bring in the empress and her sons,
The emperor himself and all thy foes,
And at thy mercy shalt they stoop and kneel,

56 **[Hyperion]'s** a Titan associated with the sun, here intended as the sun itself. The 1594 quarto and the folio both have the apparently meaningless 'Epeon' here.
59 **So** So long as.
60 **ministers** agents.
63 **'Cause** Because.
65 **worldly** mortal.
69 **by and by** soon. (He leaves the balcony at this point to re-enter at stage level for his next speech.)
70 **closing** agreeing.
71 **forge** think up.
72 **uphold and maintain** support and agree with.
76 **hold him sure** keep him where I can see him.
77 **I'll...hand** I'll improvise some subtle scheme
80 **ply my theme** go to work on my scheme.
82 **Fury** the Furies or Erinyes were the Greek spirits of vengeance.
87 **wags** moves.
89 **would you represent** if you want to impersonate.
103 **ravisher** rapist.
106 **proportion** shape.
110 **lessoned** taught.

And on them shalt thou ease thy angry heart.
What says Andronicus to this device?

Enter Marcus.

TITUS
Marcus, my brother, 'tis sad Titus calls.
Go, gentle Marcus, to thy nephew Lucius;
Thou shalt inquire him out among the Goths.
Bid him repair to me, and bring with him
Some of the chiefest princes of the Goths.
Bid him encamp his soldiers where they are.
Tell him the emperor and the empress too
Feast at my house, and he shall feast with them.
This do thou for my love, and so let him,
As he regards his aged father's life.

MARCUS
This will I do, and soon return again.

TAMORA
Now will I hence about thy business,
And take my ministers along with me.

TITUS
Nay, nay, let Rape and Murder stay with me;
Or else I'll call my brother back again,
And cleave to no revenge but Lucius.

TAMORA
What say you, boys? Will you bide with him,
Whiles I go tell my lord the emperor
How I have governed our determined jest?
Yield to his humour, smooth and speak him fair,
And tarry with him till I turn again.

TITUS
I know them all, though they suppose me mad,
And will o'er-reach them in their own devices.
A pair of cursed hell-hounds and their dam!

DEMETRIUS
Madam, depart at pleasure; leave us here.

TAMORA
Farewell, Andronicus: Revenge now goes
To lay a complot to betray thy foes. [*Exit.*]

TITUS
I know thou dost; and, sweet Revenge, farewell.

CHIRON
Tell us, old man, how shall we be employed?

TITUS
Tut, I have work enough for you to do.
Publius, come hither, Caius, and Valentine!

[*Enter Publius, Caius, and Valentine.*]

PUBLIUS
What is your will?

TITUS
Know you these two?

PUBLIUS
The empress' sons, I take them, Chiron and Demetrius.

TITUS
Fie, Publius, fie, thou art too much deceived;
The one is Murder, Rape is the other's name;
And therefore bind them, gentle Publius.
Caius and Valentine, lay hands on them.
Oft have you heard me wish for such an hour,
And now I find it; therefore bind them sure,
And stop their mouths, if they begin to cry. *Exit.*

CHIRON
Villains, forbear; we are the empress's sons.

PUBLIUS
And therefore do we what we are commanded.
Stop close their mouths, let them not speak a word.
Is he sure bound? Look that you bind them fast.

Enter Titus Andronicus with a knife, and Lavinia with a basin.

TITUS
Come, come, Lavinia; look, thy foes are bound.
Sirs, stop their mouths, let them not speak to me;
But let them hear what fearful words I utter.
O villains, Chiron and Demetrius,
Here stands the spring whom you have stained with mud,
This goodly summer with your winter mixed.
You killed her husband, and for that vile fault
Two of her brothers were condemned to death,
My hand cut off and made a merry jest;
Both her sweet hands, her tongue, and that more dear

124 **repair** come.
129 **so let him** let him do so too.
132 **hence** leave here.
136 **cleave . . . Lucius** trust no channel of vengeance but him.
139 **our determined gest** the trick we planned? (Said aside to her sons.)
141 **turn again** return.
143 **o'er-reach** outdo.
154 **I take them** I take them to be.
160 **sure** securely.
164 **Stop close** Seal tightly.
165 **fast** tightly.
170 **spring** stream/fountain.

Than hands or tongue, her spotless chastity,
Inhuman traitors, you constrained and forced.
What would you say, if I should let you speak?
Villains, for shame you could not beg for grace.
Hark, wretches, how I mean to martyr you:
This one hand yet is left to cut your throats,
Whilst that Lavinia 'tween her stumps doth hold
The basin that receives your guilty blood.
You know your mother means to feast with me,
And calls herself Revenge, and thinks me mad.
Hark, villains, I will grind your bones to dust,
And with your blood and it I'll make a paste,
And of the paste a coffin I will rear
And make two pasties of your shameful heads,
And bid that strumpet, your unhallowed dam,
Like to the earth, swallow her own increase.
This is the feast that I have bid her to,
And this the banquet she shall surfeit on;
For worse than Philomel you used my daughter,
And worse than Procne I will be revenged.
And now prepare your throats. Lavinia, come,
Receive the blood; and when that they are dead
Let me go grind their bones to powder small
And with this hateful liquor temper it;
And in that paste let their vile heads be baked.
Come, come, be every one officious
To make this banquet which I wish may prove
More stern and bloody than the Centaurs' feast.

He cuts their throats.

So now bring them in, for I'll play the cook,
And see them ready 'gainst their mother comes.

Exeunt.

[Act V. Scene iii.]

Enter Lucius, Marcus, and the Goths [with Aaron guarded].

LUCIUS
Uncle Marcus, since it is my father's mind
That I repair to Rome, I am content.

[FIRST] GOTH
And ours with thine, befall what fortune will.

LUCIUS
Good uncle, take you in this barbarous Moor,
This ravenous tiger, this accursed devil;
Let him receive no susten'nce; fetter him
Till he be brought unto the empress' face
For testimony of her foul proceedings.
And see the ambush of our friends be strong;
I fear the emperor means no good to us.

AARON
Some devil whisper curses in mine ear,
And prompt me that my tongue may utter forth
The venomous malice of my swelling heart!

LUCIUS
Away, inhuman dog; unhallowed slave!
Sirs, help our uncle to convey him in.

[Exeunt Goths, with Aaron.] Sound trumpets. Enter Emperor and Empress with Tribunes and others.

The trumpets show the emperor is at hand.

SATURNINUS
What, hath the firmament more suns than one?

LUCIUS
What boots it thee to call thyself a sun?

MARCUS
Rome's emperor, and nephew, break the parley;
These quarrels must be quietly debated.
The feast is ready which the careful Titus
Hath ordained to an honourable end,
For peace, for love, for league, and good to Rome.
Please you, therefore, draw nigh, and take your places.

SATURNINUS
Marcus, we will.

(Hautboys.) Trumpets sounding. Enter Titus like a cook, placing the dishes, and Lavinia with a veil over her face. [Enter also young Lucius, and others.]

[177] **constrained** took violently.
[188] **a coffin . . . rear** I will make a pie-crust.
[189] **pasties** pies.
[191] **increase** offspring. The earth both generates life and absorbs it again on its death.
[192] **bid** invited.
[195] See note to II.iii.43 and head-note.
[201] **officious** busy.
[203] **Centaurs' feast** the wedding feast of King Pirithous of Lapith and his bride Hippodamia ended in slaughter when the Centaurs, enraged by wine, tried to rape the bride and other guests.
[205] **'gainst** in preparation for when.
[3] **befall . . . will** whatever results.
[18] **What . . . thee** What does it benefit you.
[19] **break** commence.
[23] **league** alliance.
Hautboys Oboes.

TITUS
Welcome, my gracious lord; welcome, dread queen;
Welcome, ye warlike Goths; welcome, Lucius;
And welcome all. Although the cheer be poor,
'Twill fill your stomachs; please you eat of it.

SATURNINUS
Why art thou thus attired, Andronicus?

TITUS
Because I would be sure to have all well
To entertain your highness and your empress.

TAMORA
We are beholding to you, good Andronicus.

TITUS
And if your highness knew my heart, you were.
My lord the emperor, resolve me this:
Was it well done of rash Virginius
To slay his daughter with his own right hand,
Because she was enforced, stained, and deflowered?

SATURNINUS
It was, Andronicus.

TITUS
Your reason, mighty lord?

SATURNINUS
Because the girl should not survive her shame,
And by her presence still renew his sorrows.

TITUS
A reason mighty, strong, and effectual;
A pattern, precedent, and lively warrant
For me, most wretched, to perform the like.
Die, die, Lavinia, and thy shame with thee;
And, with thy shame, thy father's sorrow die!

He kills her.

SATURNINUS
What hast thou done, unnatural and unkind?

TITUS
Killed her, for whom my tears have made me blind.
I am as woeful as Virginius was,
And have a thousand times more cause than he
To do this outrage; and it now is done.

SATURNINUS
What, was she ravished? Tell who did the deed.

TITUS
Will't please you eat? Will't please your highness feed?

TAMORA
Why hast thou slain thine only daughter thus?

TITUS
Not I, 'twas Chiron and Demetrius;
They ravished her, and cut away her tongue;
And they, 'twas they, that did her all this wrong.

SATURNINUS
Go fetch them hither to us presently.

TITUS
Why, there they are both, baked in that pie,
Whereof their mother daintily hath fed,
Eating the flesh that she herself hath bred.
'Tis true, 'tis true; witness my knife's sharp point.

He stabs the Empress.

SATURNINUS
Die, frantic wretch, for this accursèd deed!

[*Stabs Titus.*]

LUCIUS
Can the son's eye behold his father bleed?
There's meed for meed, death for a deadly deed!

[*Stabs Saturninus.*]

MARCUS
You sad-faced men, people and sons of Rome,
By uproar severed, like a flight of fowl
Scattered by winds and high tempestuous gusts,
O, let me teach you how to knit again
This scattered corn into one mutual sheaf,
These broken limbs again into one body.

ROMAN LORD
Let Rome herself be bane unto herself,
And she whom mighty kingdoms curtsey to,
Like a forlorn and desperate castaway
Do shameful execution on herself.
But if my frosty signs and chaps of age,

28 **cheer** food.
35 **resolve me thus** settle this question for me.
38 The Roman patrician Virginius killed his own daughter after she was raped by the judge Appius. The story is found in numerous sources, including Chaucer's *Physician's Tale*.
42 **effectual** persuasive.
43 **pattern** model.
43 **lively** living.
44 **like** same.
64 **meed** reward.
69 **mutual** unified.
s.d. The 1594 quarto gives this speech to an unnamed lord, the folio to 'Goth'. Modern editors have tended to give it to Aemelius, or to change 'Let' to 'Lest' and let Marcus' speech run on, which makes more sense intellectually, but the evidence of both quarto and folio would suggest that this was originally conceived as a separate speech.
71 **bane unto herself** her own nemesis.
75 **chaps** (sunken) cheeks.

Grave witnesses of true experience,
Cannot induce you to attend my words,
Speak, Rome's dear friend, as erst our ancestor,
When with his solemn tongue he did discourse
To love-sick Dido's sad attending ear
The story of that baleful burning night
When subtle Greeks surprised King Priam's Troy.
Tell us what Sinon hath bewitched our ears,
Or who hath brought the fatal engine in
That gives our Troy, our Rome, the civil wound.
My heart is not compact of flint nor steel,
Nor can I utter all our bitter grief,
But floods of tears will drown my oratory
And break my utterance, even in the time
When it should move you to attend me most,
Lending your kind commiseration.
Here's Rome's young captain, let him tell the tale;
Your hearts will throb and weep to hear him speak.

LUCIUS

Then, noble auditory, be it known to you
That cursed Chiron and Demetrius
Were they that murdered our emperor's brother;
And they it were that ravished our sister.
For their fell faults our brothers were beheaded;
Our father's tears despised, and basely cozened
Of that true hand that fought Rome's quarrel out,
And sent her enemies unto the grave.
Lastly, myself unkindly banished,
The gates shut on me, and turned weeping out
To beg relief among Rome's enemies,
Who drowned their enmity in my true tears
And oped their arms to embrace me as a friend.
I am the turned-forth, be it known to you,
That have preserved her welfare in my blood,
And from her bosom took the enemy's point,
Sheathing the steel in my adventurous body.
Alas, you know I am no vaunter, I;
My scars can witness, dumb although they are,
That my report is just and full of truth.
But, soft, methinks I do digress too much,
Citing my worthless praise. O, pardon me,
For when no friends are by, men praise themselves.

MARCUS

Now is my turn to speak. Behold this child;
Of this was Tamora delivered,
The issue of an irreligious Moor,
Chief architect and plotter of these woes.
The villain is alive in Titus' house,
And, as he is, to witness this is true.
Now judge what course had Titus to revenge
These wrongs, unspeakable, past patience,
Or more than any living man could bear.
Now you have heard the truth, what say you,
Romans?
Have we done aught amiss, show us wherein,
And from the place where you behold us pleading,
The poor remainder of Andronici
Will, hand in hand, all headlong hurl ourselves,
And on the ragged stones beat forth our souls,
And make a mutual closure of our house.
Speak, Romans, speak; and if you say we shall,
Lo, hand in hand, Lucius and I will fall.

AEMILIUS

Come, come, thou reverend man of Rome,
And bring our emperor gently in thy hand,
Lucius, our emperor; for well I know
The common voice do cry it shall be so.

MARCUS

Lucius, all hail, Rome's royal emperor!
Go, go into old Titus' sorrowful house
And hither hale that misbelieving Moor,
To be adjudged some direful slaughtering death
As punishment for his most wicked life.
Lucius, all hail, Rome's gracious governor!

78 **Rome's dear friend** Lucius.
78 **erst** once.
82 Another reference to the moment in Virgil's *Aeneid* when Dido makes Aeneas, the legendary founder of Rome ('our ancestor'), retell the story of the fall of Troy (see III.ii.27–8).
83 **what Sinon** what modern version of Sinon, the deceitful Greek who persuaded the Trojans to bring the horse into the city.
84 **fatal engine** murderous device (the equivalent of the Trojan horse).
86 **compact of** made up of.
89 **break** interrupt.
89 **in the time** at that moment.
94 **auditory** listeners.
98 **fell faults** cruel crimes.
100 **Of** Cheated out of.
100 **out** from start to finish.
102 **unkindly** unnaturally/unjustly.
104 **relief** for alms.
107 **the turned-forth** the exile.
111 **vaunter** boaster.
116 **by** nearby.
123 **what course** what other route.
127 **Have...amiss** If we have done anything wrong.
131 **beat...souls** i.e. end our lives.
132 **make...house** bring a universal end to our dynasty.
133 **shall** should.
141 **hale** drag.
141 **misbelieving** false-believing (i.e. not Christian).

LUCIUS
Thanks, gentle Romans. May I govern so,
To heal Rome's harms and wipe away her woe.
But, gentle people, give me aim awhile,
For nature puts me to a heavy task.
Stand all aloof; but, uncle, draw you near
To shed obsequious tears upon this trunk.
O take this warm kiss on thy pale cold lips,
These sorrowful drops upon thy blood-slain face,
The last true duties of thy noble son!

MARCUS
Tear for tear, and loving kiss for kiss,
Thy brother Marcus tenders on thy lips.
O were the sum of these that I should pay
Countless and infinite, yet would I pay them.

LUCIUS
Come hither, boy, come, come, and learn of us
To melt in showers. Thy grandsire loved thee well;
Many a time he danced thee on his knee,
Sung thee asleep, his loving breast thy pillow.
Many a story hath he told to thee,
And bid thee bear his pretty tales in mind,
And talk of them when he was dead and gone.

MARCUS
How many thousand times hath these poor lips,
When they were living, warmed themselves on thine.
O now, sweet boy, give them their latest kiss;
Bid him farewell; commit him to the grave;
Do them that kindness and take leave of them.

(BOY) [YOUNG LUCIUS]
O grandsire, grandsire, even with all my heart.
Would I were dead, so you did live again!
O Lord, I cannot speak to him for weeping;
My tears will choke me if I ope my mouth.

[*Re-enter Attendants with Aaron.*]

ROMAN
You sad Andronici, have done with woes.
Give sentence on this execrable wretch
That hath been breeder of these dire events.

LUCIUS
Set him breast-deep in earth and famish him;
There let him stand, and rave, and cry for food.
If anyone relieves or pities him,
For the offence he dies. This is our doom.
Some stay to see him fastened in the earth.

AARON
Ah, why should wrath be mute and fury dumb?
I am no baby, I, that with base prayers
I should repent the evils I have done.
Ten thousand worse than ever yet I did
Would I perform, if I might have my will.
If one good deed in all my life I did,
I do repent it from my very soul.

LUCIUS
Some loving friends convey the emperor hence,
And give him burial in his father's grave.
My father and Lavinia shall forthwith
Be closed in our household's monument.
As for that heinous tiger, Tamora,
No funeral rite, nor man in mourning weed,
No mournful bell shall ring her burial;
But throw her forth to beasts and birds to prey.
Her life was beastly and devoid of pity,
And being dead, let birds on her take pity.

Exeunt.

Finis the Tragedy of Titus Andronicus.

145 **so** i.e. graciously.
147 **give ... awhile** guide me (as in archery, where one near to the target indicates where each shot strikes).
148 **puts me to** gives me.
149 **Stand all aloof** Everyone stand back.
150 **obsequious** funereal.
150 **trunk** corpse.
152 **blood-slain** 'dead and bloody'? Seemingly Shakespeare's own coinage.
156 **were** even if.
159 **To melt in showers** i.e. to weep copiously.
164 The folio has 'Meet and agreeing with thine infancy; / In that respect, then, like a loving child, / Shed yet some small drops from thy tender spring, / Because kind nature doth require it so: / Friends should associate friends in grief and woe: / Bid him farewell; commit him to the grave; / Do him that kindness, and take leave of him' in place of the last two lines.
167 **latest** final.
169 **them** Titus's lips.
177 **famish** starve.
180 **doom** judgement.
192 **closed ... monument** sealed in the family mausoleum.
196 **prey** prey upon.
198 The folio adds the following final lines: 'See justice done on Aaron, that damned Moor, / By whom our heavy haps had their beginning: / Then, afterwards, to order well the state, / That like events may ne'er it ruinate.'
Finis Here ends.

The Comedy of Errors

(1589–1594?)

WILLIAM SHAKESPEARE

(1564–1616)

THE AUTHOR

For Shakespeare's life and Tudor career, see the head-note to *Titus Andronicus*, earlier in this volume.

THE PLAY

Errors is generally assumed to be one of Shakespeare's earliest plays (as well as his shortest), one of a group that includes the comedies, *The Taming of the Shrew*, *Two Gentlemen of Verona*, and *Love's Labour's Lost*, along with the tragedy *Titus Andronicus* and the *Henry VI* plays. But quite how early it was is a matter of debate. For some editors its slapstick comedy and heavy reliance on classical models have suggested the work of an inexperienced playwright yet to discover his own voice, while for others the complexity of plotting and deft weaving of the play's various generic elements have implied the work of a more confident, mature writer. The only secure date is provided by its first recorded performance, on 28 December 1594 (see below). But there is also what looks like a reference to the French Wars of Religion in Dromio of Syracuse's punning comment on the kitchen-maid 'Nell', whose forehead, he says, is, like France, 'armed and reverted, making war against her hair [with a pun on 'heir']' (III.ii.116–7). The allusion would seem to be to the war between the Protestant Henry of Navarre, whom Henry III had named as his heir, and the French Catholic forces who wished to prevent his succession, which broke out formally in 1589 and effectively ended when Henry converted to Catholicism and took the throne as Henry IV in July 1593. For the reference to work, the play would have to have been written while the French civil conflict was still current news. Thus, because the theatres were closed by an outbreak of plague between July 1592 and Autumn 1593, editors have tended to place the play either in the period 1589–mid-1592, making it possibly Shakespeare's earliest comedy, or between late 1593 and December 1594, putting it more squarely in the author's early maturity, alongside works such as *A Midsummer Night's Dream* and *Romeo and Juliet*.

Whenever it was written, the play enjoyed its only recorded Tudor performance on the night of 28 December 1594, Holy Innocents Day, in the great hall of Gray's Inn, one of the London Inns of Court where lawyers were trained.[1] We know about this occasion, not because the performance was a great success, but because the evening seems to have been shambolic. Shakespeare's company,

[1] The only other known performance was at the court of James VI and I, again on Holy Innocents Day, in 1604. The lack of any record of playhouse performances, coupled with the play's brevity, might suggest that it was especially written for the Gray's Inn performance, or for a production at court (where the Lord Chamberlain's Men performed unnamed 'comedies or interludes' on 26 and 27 December that same year), and was never intended for the public stage.

the recently formed Lord Chamberlain's Men, were booked to play at the end of a long night of dramatic entertainments, as part of the Inn's Christmas revels. But things did not go quite to plan. The evening was supposed to start with a performance on a specially built stage in the hall, in which the gentlemen of the Inn seem to have been the main actors. But 'the great presence of lords, ladies, and worshipful personages' far exceeded the available seats, and was 'so exceeding great that there was no convenient room for those that were actors'. As a result, 'there arose such a disordered tumult and crowd upon the stage that there was no opportunity to effect that which was intended'. Once the 'ambassador' from another Inn, the Inner Temple, and his entourage had left,

> The throngs and tumult did somewhat cease, although so much of them continued as was able to disorder and confound any good inventions whatsoever. In regard whereof, as also for that [i.e. *because*] the sports intended were especially for the gracing of the Templarians, it was thought good not to offer anything of account, saving dancing and revelling with gentlewomen; and after such sports, a *Comedy of Errors* (like to Plautus his *Menaechmus*) was played by the Players. So that night was begun, and continued to the end, in nothing but confusion and errors; whereupon it was ever afterwards called 'The Night of Errors'.[2]

This account, written much later, but surely based on contemporary testimony, is a sobering reminder of the ambivalent status of the professional stage at this time. Far from being the centrepiece of the evening's entertainment, the visit of the Lord Chamberlain's Men (later described by the same writer, probably not wholly ironically, as 'a company of base and common fellows') was booked as a comic after-show treat to entertain the gathering, once those events which were thought to be significant ('of account') were completed. It was only the failure of the main performance, and the neat coincidence of the play's theme with the shambolic nature of the evening, that thrust the players into the spotlight in this narrative.

As the description noticed, Shakespeare borrowed much of the plot of *Errors* from the work of the Roman playwright Plautus (Titus Maccius Plautus (*c.*254–184 BC)), whose comedies, filled with witty slaves, lustful, greedy masters, and violent comic incident, he would have been familiar with from his schooldays. From Plautus' farcical comedy, the *Menaechmi* ('the men named Menaechmus') Shakespeare took the story of a man (here renamed Antipholus) arriving unheralded and unknowingly in the home town of his lost twin (in Plautus it is Epidamnum rather than Ephesus), and of the various incidents of mistaken identity that this creates. Sensing the potential to increase the confusion, and the consequent 'errors', however, he adds a second set of twins to the plot, giving each man an identical slave named Dromio, and so increasing exponentially both the implausibility and the complexity of the plot. To this narrative he also added the set-piece scene of the husband locked out of his own home while his wife entertains an interloper, mistakenly thinking it is him, which is taken from another of Plautus' plays, the *Amphitryon*, where Jupiter takes on the appearance of the eponymous husband in order to have sex with his wife, while Mercury, disguised as the slave Sosia, keeps the real slave and husband locked outside. Finally, Shakespeare gives the frantic comic narrative a frame story, in the tale of Egeon, the old father searching for his lost sons, who has fallen foul of the law condemning anyone from Syracuse found within Ephesian territory, and so spends the whole play under sentence of death, until he is finally released and reunited in the final act, not only with his sons, but with the wife he thought was drowned over thirty years earlier. This latter plot, which adds to the play a more sombre, emotionally rich texture, is drawn from the very different genre of romance, with its capacity to encompass sadness, redemption, and wonder in the face of the inexplicable. Specifically, he borrowed the idea of a husband and wife separated in a shipwreck, from which the wife, thought drowned, is washed ashore in Ephesus, where she joins a religious sisterhood, only to be later

[2] This account is taken from the *Gesta Grayorum* (1688), a history of entertainments at Gray's Inn.

reunited with her wandering husband when he visits the city, from the classical romance *Apollonius of Tyre*, which he would have known from the version in John Gower's *Confessio Amantis* (1380), to which he would return towards the end of his career for the plot of *Pericles*.

Far from being a simple comedy, then, *Errors* is a generically rich and relatively complex play, in which motifs drawn from romance (miraculous coincidences, wrecks at sea, the division and reunion of families, the questing hero) are deftly mingled with those of the much more cynical form of late Tudor city comedy (the shrewish wife, the cheating husband, complex commercial dealings, debts incurred and defaulted upon, 'credit' won and lost, commodities (a ring, a gold chain) exchanged and seemingly stolen), and knock-about farce (see Whitworth, pp. 48–9). What also distinguishes it from pure farce is the emotional depth which Shakespeare hints at in his characters. Egeon, Adriana, Luciana, and the two sets of twins, are all at times genuinely and eloquently moved by the situations in which they find themselves. Issues that might have been handled more perfunctorily, as simply background to the plot—Egeon's plight or Antipholus of Syracuse's search for his lost relatives—are in this play the cues for moments of serious introspection and self-doubt. Thus Antipholus of Syracuse is already disturbed and conflicted by the loss of his family, and seemingly on the verge of disorientation, before the events of the plot spin him into complete confusion: 'He that commends me to mine own content, / Commends me to the thing I cannot get. / I to the world am like a drop of water, / That in the ocean seeks another drop, / Who, falling there to find his fellow forth, / (Unseen, inquisitive) confounds himself. / So I, to find a mother and a brother, / In quest of them (unhappy) lose myself.' (I.ii.33–40).

Interestingly, the earliest surviving text of the play (that printed in the First Folio of 1623), which may have been based upon Shakespeare's own manuscript copy or 'foul papers', refers to the twins in a number of speech headings, not by their city of origin, but as Antipholus *sereptus*' (perhaps from the Latin, *surripere*: to snatch or abduct) and Antipholus '*Erotes*' and '*Erratis*' (which editors have read as variants of the Latin *errare*: to wander). This suggests that the playwright thought of the drama as driven, like many a knightly romance, by a quest, in which one child is 'snatched away' by fate or chance, and the other spends his life 'wandering' in search of him. This seems confirmed by the balance of the play. For, where Plautus reads his way into the plot through the experience of the local twin, Manaechmus the citizen and householder, beset by a parasitical neighbour and married to a wife he does not love, who suddenly becomes alienated from his own world when his relatives and friends start to accuse him of doing and saying things of which he has no memory, Shakespeare, in the spirit of the quest romance, cues his audience to experience events through the eyes of the questing twin, Antipholus of Syracuse. The latter is a knight errant manqué, a man already displaced and disoriented, seeking a fixed point on which to anchor himself, for whom things become only more overtly deranged when he finds himself in a strange city where everyone already seems to know him. What for Plautus was a play that explored the frightening experience of the civic and domestic dispossession of a substantial citizen, for Shakespeare was a drama of perplexing search and foreign adventure for an innocent abroad. Hence perhaps, as Whitworth notes (p. 56), where Plautus gives the balance of his speeches to the citizen twin, in Shakespeare's play it is the introspective traveller who is given all six soliloquies, while his brother, the man of action, quick to anger and quick to blame others for the inexplicable events around him, has none.

Shakespeare also subtly but significantly altered the tone and focus of his Plautine model in other ways. He reduced the role of the Courtesan, and the significance (and overt sexuality) of her relationship with the local twin, placing greater emphasis instead on the latter's wife Adriana, giving her a confidante, Luciana, with whom she can discuss her feelings, and developing her from a stereotypical jealous, shrewish spouse of classical comedy into a more complex, sympathetic figure who clearly loves her erring husband, despite his insensitivity and infidelities. The shifting of the location of the action from the relatively obscure (to Elizabethan audiences at least) city of Epidamnum (Durazzo/Durrës in modern Albania) to Ephesus (a port on the

Mediterranean coast of Asia Minor—modern Turkey), the location of the reunion of husband and wife in *Apollonius of Tyre*, also has its consequences. The latter was well known to Christian audiences as the city visited by St Paul in Acts 18 and 19, where the citizens were said to 'follow...curious arts' (Acts 19:19) and, according to the Geneva Bible, to practise exorcism and 'conjuring'. This probably explains Antipholus of Syracuse's sense that the city is 'full of cozenage [*deception*] / [such] as nimble jugglers [*conjurors*] that deceive the eye, / Dark-working sorcerers that change the mind, / Soul-killing witches that deform the body' (I.ii.97–100). And, as a number of editors note, Adriana and Luciana seem to know well Paul's letter to the Ephesians, with its stern injunctions regarding the duties of husbands and wives ('So also ought men to love their wives as their own bodies. He that loveth his wife, loveth himself. For no man ever hated his own flesh; but nourisheth and cherisheth it' (Ephesians 5:28–9)) and to have taken it to heart. For their discussion of the local Antipholus' treatment of his wife, and Adriana's rebukes to him, seem to echo its tone and language in a number of places (see, for example, II.ii.110–14). Shakespeare's Ephesus, then, like his play as a whole, is a place both richly exotic and strangely familiar, both dangerous and homely, in which implausible events come to seem commonplace, and commonplace things: family ties, personal identity, marriage vows, and civic and personal standing and obligations, are subjected to extraordinary stress.

In the absence of any earlier printed versions, I have used the 1623 first folio text as my base text, also consulting the modern editions by Foakes, Dorsch, and Whitworth listed under further reading. In a number of places (indicated in the notes) I have returned to the original folio reading rather than accepting modern editorial changes where the folio seems to make plausible sense. As the folio text is divided only into acts, I have added scene divisions in accordance with longstanding editorial practice.

FURTHER READING

Cartwright, Kent, 'Language, Magic, the Dromios, and *The Comedy of Errors*', *Shakespeare Quarterly* 60 (2009), 47–72.

Dorsch, T. S., ed., *The Comedy of Errors*, The New Cambridge Shakespeare (Cambridge: Cambridge University Press, 1988).

van Elk, Martine, 'Urban Misidentification in *The Comedy of Errors* and the Cony-Catching Pamphlets', *Studies in English Literature* 43 (2003), 323–46.

—— '"This sympathized one day's error": Genre, Representation and Subjectivity in *The Comedy of Errors*', *Shakespeare Quarterly* 60 (2009), 47–72.

Findlay, Alison, 'Ceremony and Selfhood in *The Comedy of Errors*' (c.1592) in Thomas Betteridge and Greg Walker, eds., *The Oxford Handbook of Tudor Drama* (Oxford: Oxford University Press, 2012), 338–54.

Foakes, R. A., ed., *The Comedy of Errors*, The Arden Shakespeare (London: Methuen 1968).

Kern Paster, Gail, *The Idea of the City in the Age of Shakespeare* (Athens, GA: University of Georgia Press, 1985).

Kinney, Arthur F., 'Shakespeare's *The Comedy of Errors* and the Nature of Kinds', *Studies in Philology* 85 (1988), 29–52.

Riehle, Wolfgang, *Shakespeare, Plautus and the Humanist Tradition* (Cambridge: Cambridge University Press, 1990).

Whitworth, Charles, ed., *The Comedy of Errors*, Oxford World's Classics (Oxford: Oxford University Press, 2002).

The Comedy of Errors

[Dramatis Personae:

SOLINUS, Duke of Ephesus,
EGEON, a merchant of Syracuse, father of the Antipholus twins,
ANTIPHOLUS, of Ephesus,
ANTIPHOLUS, of Syracuse,
DROMIO, of Ephesus, servant to Antipholus of Ephesus,
DROMIO, of Syracuse, twin brother of Dromio of Ephesus, servant to Antipholus of Syracuse,
ADRIANA, wife of Antipholus of Ephesus,
LUCIANA, sister to Adriana,
LUCE, maid to Adriana,
ANGELO, a goldsmith,
BALTHASAR, a merchant,
A COURTESAN,
DOCTOR PINCH, a schoolmaster and exorcist,
FIRST MERCHANT,
SECOND MERCHANT,
EMILIA, Abbess of Ephesus,
JAILOR, Officers, Headsman, and other attendants.]

Actus Primu. Scena Prima.

Enter the Duke of Ephesus [Solinus] with the merchant of Syracuse [Egeon], Jailor and Attendants

MERCHANT [EGEON]
Proceed Solinus, to procure my fall,
And by the doom of death end woes and all.

DUKE
Merchant of Syracuse, plead no more.
I am not partial to infringe our laws;
The enmity and discord which of late
Sprung from the rancorous outrage of your duke,
To merchants, our well-dealing countrymen,
Who wanting guilders to redeem their lives,
Have sealed his rigorous statutes with their bloods,
Excludes all pity from our threat'ning looks.
For since the mortal and intestine jars
'Twixt thy seditious countrymen and us,
It hath in solemn synods been decreed,
Both by the Syracusians and ourselves,
T'admit no traffic to our adverse towns:
Nay, more, if any born at Ephesus
Be seen at any Syracusian marts and fairs:
Again, if any Syracusian born
Come to the bay of Ephesus, he dies:
His goods confiscate to the duke's dispose,
Unless a thousand marks be levied
To quit the penalty, and to ransom him.
Thy substance, valued at the highest rate,
Cannot amount unto a hundred marks,
Therefore by law thou art condemned to die.

MERCHANT
Yet this my comfort: when your words are done,
My woes end likewise with the evening sun.

DUKE
Well, Syracusian, say in brief the cause

Syracuse a seaport in Sicily.
Luce seeemingly the same character as the kitchen maid whom Dromio of Syracuse refers to as 'Nell' at III.ii.104.
Courtesan Prostitute.
Actus... Prima Act One, Scene One.
1 **fall** downfall.
2 **doom** judgement.
4 **partial** inclined.
6 **rancorous outrage** malicious violence.
7 **well-dealing** honest/fair-trading.
8 **wanting guilders** lacking coins.
9 **sealed... bloods** confirmed his fierce laws with their deaths.
11 **intestine jars** internal conflicts.
12 **seditious** treacherous/turbulent.
13 **synods** councils.
15 **T'admit... towns** To allow no trade between our warring cities.
17 **marts** markets.
20 **to... dispose** for the Duke to dispose of.
21–22 **levied... penalty** paid to cancel the sentence.
23 **substance** wealth.

Why thou departedst from thy native home?
And for what cause thou cam'st to Ephesus?

MERCHANT

A heavier task could not have been imposed,
Than I to speak my griefs unspeakable:
Yet that the world may witness, that my end
Was wrought by nature, not by vile offence,
I'll utter what my sorrows give me leave.
In Syracusa was I born, and wed
Unto a woman, happy but for me;
And by me, had not our hap been bad:
With her I lived in joy, our wealth increased
By prosperous voyages I often made
To Epidamnium; till my factor's death,
And he great store of goods at random leaving,
Drew me from kind embracements of my spouse;
From whom my absence was not six months old,
Before herself (almost at fainting under
The pleasing punishment that women bear)
Had made provision for her following me,
And soon, and safe, arrived where I was.
There had she not been long but she became
A joyful mother of two goodly sons.
And, which was strange, the one so like the other
As could not be distinguished but by names.
That very hour, and in the self-same inn,
A poor mean woman was delivered
Of such a burden, male twins both alike.
Those, for their parents were exceeding poor,
I bought, and brought up to attend my sons.
My wife, not meanly proud of two such boys,
Made daily motions for our home return.
Unwilling I agreed. Alas, too soon we
came aboard!
A league from Epidamnum had we sailed
Before the always wind-obeying deep
Gave any tragic instance of our harm.
But longer did we not retain much hope;
For what obscured light the heavens did grant
Did but convey unto our fearful minds
A doubtful warrant of immediate death;
Which though myself would gladly have embraced,
Yet the incessant weepings of my wife,
Weeping before for what she saw must come,
And piteous plainings of the pretty babes
That mourned for fashion, ignorant what to fear,
Forced me to seek delays for them and me,
And this it was (for other means was none)
The sailors sought for safety by our boat,
And left the ship, then sinking-ripe, to us.
My wife, more careful for the latter-born,
Had fastened him unto a small spare mast,
Such as seafaring men provide for storms;
To him one of the other twins was bound,
Whilst I had been like heedful of the other.
The children thus disposed, my wife and I,
Fixing our eyes on whom our care was fixed,
Fastened ourselves at either end the mast,
And floating straight, obedient to the stream,
Was carried towards Corinth, as we thought.
At length the sun gazing upon the earth,
Dispersed those vapours that offended us,
And by the benefit of his wished light
The seas waxed calm, and we discovered
Two ships from far making amain to us.
Of Corinth that, of Epidaurus this;
But ere they came, O let me say no more,
Gather the sequel by that went before.

31 **heavier** harder/sadder.
34 **offence** crime.
38 **hap** luck.
41 **Epidamnium** Epidamnus, a port on the Adriatic coast of Albania.
41 **factor** commercial agent.
42 **at random** spread around (different ports).
43 **kind embracements** natural loving embraces.
46 **pleasing...bear** pregnancy.
49 **but** before.
54 **mean** low-class.
55 **such a** a similar.
57 **attend** serve.
58 **meanly** slightly.
59 **motions** requests.
61 **a league** just over three miles.
62 **deep** sea.
63 **instance** indication.
67 **doubtful warrant** dreadful forewarning.
71 **plainings** complaints.
72 **for fashion** in imitation.
74 **And...none** And this is how it happened, for there was no alternative.
75 **boat** lifeboat.
76 **sinking ripe** on the point of sinking.
77 **latter-born** (slightly) younger son.
81 **heedful of** careful about.
85 **stream** current.
88 **vapours** storm clouds.
90 **waxed** grew.
91 **amain** full speed.
93 **ere** before.
94 **Gather...before** Understand what was to happen by what happened before.

DUKE
Nay, forward old man, do not break off so,
For we may pity, though not pardon thee.

MERCHANT
O had the gods done so, I had not now
Worthily termed them merciless to us.
For, ere the ships could meet by twice five leagues,
We were encountered by a mighty rock,
Which being violently borne upon,
Our helpful ship was splitted in the midst;
So that in this unjust divorce of us,
Fortune had left to both of us alike,
What to delight in, what to sorrow for.
Her part, poor soul, seeming as burdened,
With lesser weight, but not with lesser woe,
Was carried with more speed before the wind,
And in our sight they three were taken up
By fishermen of Corinth, as we thought.
At length another ship had seized on us,
And knowing whom it was their hap to save,
Gave healthful welcome to their shipwrecked guests,
And would have reft the fishers of their prey,
Had not their bark been very slow of sail;
And therefore homeward did they bend
their course.
Thus have you heard me severed from my bliss,
That by misfortunes was my life prolonged,
To tell sad stories of my own mishaps.

DUKE
And for the sake of them thou sorrowest for,
Do me the favour to dilate at full,
What hath befallen of them and thee till now.

MERCHANT
My youngest boy, and yet my eldest care,
At eighteen years became inquisitive
After his brother; and importuned me
That his attendant (so his case was like,
Reft of his brother, but retained his name)
Might bear him company in the quest of him,
Whom, whilst I laboured of a love to see,
I hazarded the loss of whom I loved.
Five summers have I spent in furthest Greece,
Roaming clean through the bounds of Asia,
And coasting homeward, came to Ephesus,
Hopeless to find, yet loath to leave unsought
Or that or any place that harbours men.
But here must end the story of my life,
And happy were I in my timely death,
Could all my travels warrant me they live.

DUKE
Hapless Egeon, whom the fates have marked
To bear th'extremity of dire mishap!
Now trust me, were it not against our laws,
Against my crown, my oath, my dignity
(Which princes would, they may not disannul),
My soul would sue as advocate for thee.
But, though thou art adjudged to the death,
And passed sentence may not be recalled
But to our honour's great disparagement:
Yet I will favour thee in what I can.
Therefore, merchant, I'll limit thee this day
To seek thy life by beneficial help.
Try all the friends thou hast in Ephesus,
Beg thou, or borrow, to make up the sum,

95 **forward** carry on.
98 **termed** called.
99 **ere…leagues** while the ships were still over thirty miles apart (an unlikely distance).
101 **Which…upon** We being violently dashed against it.
102 **splitted…midst** our mast was severed in the middle.
103–105 **So…for.** Thus separated, we each had an equal share in joy (one son and one servant child safe with us) and in misery (another son and servant lost).
112 **And…save** Once they knew who they had the good fortune to have rescued.
114 **reft** robbed.
115 **bark** ship.
116 **bend their course** make their way.
121 **dilate at full** tell the full story.
126–127 His servant was in a similar situation, wondering about his lost brother and eager to search for him. 'But retained his name' seems to summarize the situation, explained more carefully in Plautus, that the father had changed the names of his son and servant to those of their lost brothers in their memory. Hence the confusion when they arrive in Ephesus.
129–130 **whilst…loved** while I was eager to see (the lost child), I was mindful of the risk of losing the one I had.
132 **clean** completely.
133 **coasting homeward** returning homeward along the coast.
134–135 **loath…men** I was loathe to leave (Ephesus) unsearched, or anywhere else where people live.
139 **Hapless** Unfortunate.
143 **Which…disannul** That which princes command, they cannot later ignore.
147 **But…disparagement** Except with great loss of honour/authority to me.
149 **I'll…day** I'll grant you until the end of today.

And live: if no, then thou art doomed to die.
Jailor, take him to thy custody.

JAILOR
I will, my lord.

MERCHANT
Hopeless and helpless doth Egeon wend,
But to procrastinate his lifeless end. *Exeunt*

[Act I. Scene ii.]

Enter Antipholus [of Syracuse], a [First] Merchant and Dromio [of Syracuse].

FIRST MERCHANT
Therefore give out you are of Epidamnum,
Lest that your goods too soon be confiscate.
This very day a Syracusian merchant
Is apprehended for arrival here,
And not being able to buy out his life,
According to the statute of the town,
Dies ere the weary sun set in the west.
There is your money that I had to keep.

ANTIPHOLUS OF SYRACUSE
Go bear it to the Centaur, where we host,
And stay there Dromio, till I come to thee.
Within this hour it will be dinner-time;
Till that I'll view the manners of the town,
Peruse the traders, gaze upon the buildings,
And then return and sleep within mine inn,
For with long travel I am stiff and weary.
Get thee away.

DROMIO OF SYRACUSE
Many a man would take you at your word,
And go indeed, having so good a mean.

Exit Dromio

ANTIPHOLUS OF SYRACUSE
A trusty villain, sir, that very oft,
When I am dull with care and melancholy,
Lightens my humour with his merry jests.
What, will you walk with me about the town,
And then go to my inn and dine with me?

FIRST MERCHANT
I am invited sir to certain merchants,
Of whom I hope to make much benefit.
I crave your pardon; soon at five o'clock,
Please you, I'll meet with you upon the mart,
And afterward consort you till bedtime.
My present business calls me from you now.

ANTIPHOLUS OF SYRACUSE
Farewell till then. I will go lose myself,
And wander up and down to view the city.

FIRST MERCHANT
Sir I commend you to your own content. *Ex[it.]*

ANTIPHOLUS OF SYRACUSE
He that commends me to mine own content,
Commends me to the thing I cannot get.
I to the world am like a drop of water,
That in the ocean seeks another drop,
Who, falling there to find his fellow forth,
(Unseen, inquisitive) confounds himself.
So I, to find a mother and a brother,
In quest of them (unhappy) lose myself.

Enter Dromio of Ephesus.

Here comes the almanac of my true date:
What now? How chance thou art returned so soon?

DROMIO OF EPHESUS
Returned so soon, rather approached too late!
The capon burns, the pig falls from the spit;
The clock hath strucken twelve upon the bell:
My mistress made it one upon my cheek.

156–157 **wend ... end** make his way, only to postpone his death. ***Exeunt.*** Exit all.
The folio gives '*Enter Antipholus Erotes*', which modern editors suggest is a corruption of Antipholus '*errans*' or '*erratus*': 'the wanderer' (see head-note).
1 **give out** tell people.
2 **Lest that** In case.
8 **that ... keep** that I was looking after for you.
9 **the Centaur** an inn.
9 **host** are lodging.
12 **manners** nature.
18 **so ... mean** so much money (a means to run off and never return).
19 **villain** servant.
25 **benefit** profit.
27 **mart** market square.
28 **consort you** keep you company.
32 **I ... content** I'll leave you to your own contentment.
38 **confounds** dissolves/loses.
40 **In ... (unhappy)** in (unsuccessful) search for them.
41 **almanac ... date** the book from which I can calculate my own age (Dromio shares a birthday with Antipholus). More generally: here's the fellow who reminds me who I am.
44 **capon** chicken.
46 **made it one** struck me once (with a pun on the clock striking twelve).

She is so hot because the meat is cold;
The meat is cold because you come not home;
You come not home because you have no stomach;
You have no stomach, having broke your fast:
But we that know what 'tis to fast and pray,
Are penitent for your default today.

ANTIPHOLUS OF SYRACUSE
Stop in your wind, sir, tell me this I pray,
Where have you left the money that I gave you?

DROMIO OF EPHESUS
O, sixpence, that I had a Wednesday last
To pay the saddler for my mistress's crupper?
The saddler had it sir, I kept it not.

ANTIPHOLUS OF SYRACUSE
I am not in a sportive humour now:
Tell me, and dally not, where is the money?
We being strangers here, how dare'st thou trust
So great a charge from thine own custody.

DROMIO OF EPHESUS
I pray you, jest sir as you sit at dinner.
I from my mistress come to you in post;
If I return I shall be post indeed.
For she will score your fault upon my pate
Methinks your maw, like mine, should be your clock,
And strike you home without a messenger.

ANTIPHOLUS OF SYRACUSE
Come Dromio, come, these jests are out of season;
Reserve them till a merrier hour than this.
Where is the gold I gave in charge to thee?

DROMIO OF EPHESUS
To me sir? Why, you gave no gold to me.

ANTIPHOLUS OF SYRACUSE
Come on, sir knave, have done your foolishness,
And tell me how thou hast disposed thy charge.

DROMIO OF EPHESUS
My charge was but to fetch you from the mart
Home to your house, the Phoenix sir, to dinner.
My mistress and her sister stays for you.

ANTIPHOLUS OF SYRACUSE
Now, as I am a Christian, answer me:
In what safe place you have bestowed my money?
Or I shall break that merry sconce of yours
That stands on tricks, when I am undisposed;
Where is the thousand marks thou hadst of me?

DROMIO OF EPHESUS
I have some marks of yours upon my pate,
Some of my mistress's marks upon my shoulders,
But not a thousand marks between you both.
If I should pay your worship those again,
Perchance you will not bear them patiently.

ANTIPHOLUS OF SYRACUSE
Thy mistress's marks? What mistress, slave, hast thou?

DROMIO OF EPHESUS
Your worship's wife, my mistress at the Phoenix.
She that doth fast till you come home to dinner,
And prays that you will hie you home to dinner.

ANTIPHOLUS OF SYRACUSE
What, wilt thou flout me thus unto my face,
Being forbid? There take you that, sir knave.

[Beats him.]

DROMIO OF EPHESUS
What mean you, sir? For God's sake, hold your hands!
Nay, and you will not sir, I'll take my heels.

Exit Dromio of Ephesus.

ANTIPHOLUS OF SYRACUSE
Upon my life, by some device or other,
The villain is o'er-raught of all my money.

49 **stomach** appetite.
50 **having... fast** having already breakfasted. (Dromio assumes that his master has spent the morning, and perhaps all night, with the Courtesan).
52 **Are... default** we do the penance (by having to fast) for your absence.
53 **Stop... wind** Hold your breath/shut up!
56 **crupper** leather saddle-strap.
58 **sportive humour** playful mood.
60–61 **how... custody** How dare you not keep hold of so large a sum of money yourself.
63 **in post** post-haste/at top speed.
64–65 **be... pate** like a tavern-post, I'll have the bill chalked up ('scored') on my head ('pate').
66 **your... clock** your stomach should tell you when it is mealtime.
68 **out of season** badly timed.
72 **have done** cease.
73 **charge** task.
76 **stays** wait.
79 **sconce** head.
80 **That... undisposed** That persists with joking when I am not in the mood.
90 **hie** hurry.
94 **and** if.
94 **take my heels** run away.
95 **device** trick.
96 **is o'er-raught** has robbed me (lit. has reached over and grabbed).

They say this town is full of cozenage:
As nimble jugglers that deceive the eye,
Dark-working sorcerers that change the mind,
Soul-killing witches that deform the body,
Disguised cheaters, prating mountebanks;
And many such-like liberties of sin.
If it prove so, I will be gone the sooner.
I'll to the Centaur to go seek this slave.
I greatly fear my money is not safe.

Exit

Actus Secundus. [Scene i.]

Enter Adriana, wife to Antipholus [of Syracuse], with Luciana, her sister.

ADRIANA
Neither my husband nor the slave returned,
That in such haste I sent to seek his master?
Sure, Luciana, it is two o'clock.

LUCIANA
Perhaps some merchant hath invited him,
And from the mart he's somewhere gone to dinner.
Good sister, let us dine and never fret;
A man is master of his liberty;
Time is their master, and, when they see time,
They'll go or come; if so, be patient, sister.

ADRIANA
Why should their liberty than ours be more?

LUCIANA
Because their business still lies out o'door.

ADRIANA
Look, when I serve him so, he takes it [ill].

LUCIANA
Oh, know he is the bridle of your will.

ADRIANA
There's none but asses will be bridled so.

LUCIANA
Why, headstrong liberty is lashed with woe.
There's nothing situate under heaven's eye
But hath his bound, in earth, in sea, in sky.
The beasts, the fishes, and the winged fowls
Are their males' subjects, and at their controls.
Men, more divine, the masters of all these,
Lords of the wide world and wild watery seas,
Indued with intellectual sense and souls,
Of more pre-eminence than fish and fowls,
Are masters to their females, and their lords,
Then let your will attend on their accords.

ADRIANA
This servitude makes you to keep unwed.

LUCIANA
Not this, but troubles of the marriage-bed.

ADRIANA
But were you wedded, you would bear some sway.

LUCIANA
Ere I learn love, I'll practise to obey.

ADRIANA
How if your husband start some otherwhere?

LUCIANA
Till he come home again, I would forbear.

ADRIANA
Patience unmoved! No marvel though she pause,
They can be meek that have no other cause.
A wretched soul, bruised with adversity,
We bid be quiet when we hear it cry.
But were we burdened with like weight of pain,
As much or more would we ourselves complain.
So thou, that hast no unkind mate to grieve thee,

97 **cozenage** deception.
98 **jugglers** magicians.
101 **prating mountebanks** chattering charlatans.
102 **liberties of sin** sinful offences. Modern editors often change 'liberties' to 'libertines', but this does not seem necessary.
The folio has '*Wife to Antipholus Seruptus*', i.e. '*surreptus*', 'snatched/abducted'.
3 **Sure** See.
6 **fret** worry.
8 **when . . . time** whenever they want.
11 **still . . . o'door** always takes them out of the house.
12 **when . . . [ill]** when I do the same to him, he takes it badly. The folio has 'thus' for 'ill', but the rhyme suggests the latter.
13 **the bridle . . . will** the one who disciplines your will.
16 **situate** located.
17 **But . . . bound** That doesn't have limits.
20 **more divine** closer to God.
22 **Indued** Endowed.
22–23 **Indued . . . fowls** see Genesis 1:26: 'And he said: Let us make man to our image and likeness: and let him have dominion over the fishes of the sea, and the fowls of the air, and the beasts, and the whole earth, and every creeping creature that moveth upon the earth.'
25 **attend . . . accords** wait for their consent. See Ephesians 5:23: 'Because the husband is the head of the wife, as Christ is the head of the church.'
28 **bear some sway** have some authority.
30 **start some otherwhere** turns elsewhere (i.e. has an affair).
31 **forbear** tolerate it.
32 **No . . . pause** No wonder she hesitates (to marry).
33 **cause** choice.
36 **like weight** a similar degree.

With urging helpless patience wouldst relieve me;
But if thou live to see like right bereft,
This fool-begged patience in thee will be left.

LUCIANA
Well, I will marry one day, but to try.
Here comes your man; now is your husband nigh.

Enter Dromio of Ephesus.

ADRIANA
Say, is your tardy master now at hand?

DROMIO OF EPHESUS
Nay, he's at two hands with me, and that my two ears can witness.

ADRIANA
Say, didst thou speak with him? Know'st thou his mind?

DROMIO OF EPHESUS
Aye, aye, he told his mind upon mine ear.
Beshrew his hand, I scarce could understand it.

LUCIANA
Spake he so doubtfully, thou couldst not feel his meaning?

DROMIO OF EPHESUS
Nay, he struck so plainly I could too well feel his blows; and withal so doubtfully that I could scarce understand them.

ADRIANA
But say, I prithee, is he coming home?
It seems he hath great care to please his wife!

DROMIO OF EPHESUS
Why mistress, sure my master is horn-mad.

ADRIANA
Horn-mad, thou villain?

DROMIO OF EPHESUS
I mean not cuckold-mad,
But sure, he is stark mad.
When I desired him to come home to dinner,
He asked me for a thousand marks in gold.
''Tis dinner-time', quoth I; 'My gold', quoth he.
'Your meat doth burn', quoth I; 'My gold', quoth he.
'Will you come?' quoth I; 'My gold', quoth he.
'Where is the thousand marks I gave thee villain?'
'The pig', quoth I, 'is burned'; 'My gold', quoth he.
'My mistress, sir', quoth I. 'Hang up thy mistress!
I know not thy mistress, out on thy mistress!'

LUCIANA
Quoth who?

DROMIO OF EPHESUS
Quoth my master. 'I know', quoth he, 'no house, no wife, no mistress!' So that my errand, due unto my tongue, I thank him, I bare home upon my shoulders: for in conclusion, he did beat me there.

ADRIANA
Go back again, thou slave, and fetch him home.

DROMIO OF EPHESUS
Go back again and be new beaten home?
For God's sake send some other messenger.

ADRIANA
Back slave, or I will break thy pate across.

DROMIO OF EPHESUS
And he will bless that cross with other beating:
Between you I shall have a holy head.

ADRIANA
Hence, prating peasant, fetch thy master home.

DROMIO OF EPHESUS
Am I so round with you, as you with me,
That like a football you do spurn me thus?
You spurn me hence, and he will spurn me hither,
If I last in this service, you must case me in leather.

Exit

40–41 **if...left** if you experienced a similar unjust betrayal, you'd (soon) stop this foolish begging me to have patience.
42 **but to try** just to test that out.
44 **is...hand?** is your late/slow master now here?
45–46 **he's...witness** i.e. his ears have been beaten with Antipholus' two hands.
47 **mind** intentions.
49 **Beshrew** Curse.
50–51 **so...meaning** so ambiguously you could not sense/understand his intentions.
53 **withal so doubtfully** at the same time so awfully.
55 **I prithee** I pray you.
57 **horn-mad** enraged like a bull or goat, ready to charge (but with the additional meaning of 'mad like a cuckold', to which Adriana takes exception).
59 **cuckold-mad** enraged like a cuckold (husband of an adulterous wife).
63 **quoth** said.
68 **Hang...mistress!** Forget your mistress! (lit. 'your mistress be hanged!').
69 **out on** enough about.
81 **holy** both 'much blessed' and 'beaten full of holes'.
82 **Hence, prating** Get out, chattering.
83 **round** rude (with a pun on 'spherical').
84 **spurn** knock me away.
86 **you...leather** i.e. like a football.

LUCIANA
Fie how impatience loureth in your face:
ADRIANA
His company must do his minions grace,
Whilst I at home starve for a merry look?
Hath homely age th'alluring beauty took
From my poor cheek? Then he hath wasted it.
Are my discourses dull? Barren my wit?
If voluble and sharp discourse be marred,
Unkindness blunts it more than marble hard.
Do their gay vestments his affections bait?
That's not my fault, he's master of my state.
What ruins are in me that can be found
By him not ruined? Then is he the ground
Of my defeatures. My decayed fair,
A sunny look of his, would soon repair.
But (too unruly deer,) he breaks the pale,
And feeds from home; poor I am but
his stale.
LUCIANA
Self-harming jealousy, fie, beat it hence!
ADRIANA
Unfeeling fools can with such wrongs dispense.
I know his eye doth homage other-where,
Or else what lets it but he would be here?
Sister, you know he promised me a chain,
Would that alone a love he would detain,
So he would keep fair quarter with his bed.
I see the jewel best enamellèd
Will lose his beauty; yet the gold bides still
That others touch; and often touching will
Wear gold, and no man hath a name
B[ut] falsehood and corruption doth it shame.
Since that my beauty cannot please his eye,
I'll weep (what's left) away, and weeping die.
LUCIANA
How many fond fools serve mad jealousy? *Exeunt*

[Act II. Scene ii.]

Enter Antipholus [of Syracuse].

ANTIPHOLUS OF SYRACUSE
The gold I gave to Dromio is laid up
Safe at the Centaur, and the heedful slave
Is wandered forth, in care to seek me out,
By computation and mine host's report.
I could not speak with Dromio since at first
I sent him from the mart. See, here he comes.

Enter Dromio Syracusia [of Syracuse].

How now, sir, is your merry humour altered?
As you love strokes, so jest with me again:
You know no Centaur? You received no gold?
Your mistress sent to have me home to dinner?
My house was at the Phoenix? Wast thou mad,
That thus so madly thou didst answer me?
DROMIO OF SYRACUSE
What answer sir? When spake I such a word?
ANTIPHOLUS OF SYRACUSE
Even now, even here, not half an hour since.
DROMIO OF SYRACUSE
I did not see you since you sent me hence
Home to the Centaur with the gold you gave me.
ANTIPHOLUS OF SYRACUSE
Villain, thou didst deny the gold's receipt,
And told'st me of a mistress, and a dinner.

87 **loureth** frowns.
88 **do...grace** please/honour his harlots.
91 **discourses** conversations.
93–94 **If...hard.** If my fluency and witty conversation are ruined, it's his unkindness that has blunted them, worse than hard marble would.
95 **Do...bait?** Do his mistresses' fine clothes provoke his desires?
96 **he's...state** i.e. he determines what I wear.
98–99 **he...defeatures** he is the cause of my disfigurement.
99–100 **My...repair.** A sunny look from him would soon restore my faded beauty.
101–102 **But...stale.** Like an unruly deer he jumps the fence of his enclosure and takes his pleasures elsewhere. I'm just his stooge/a laughing stock (for him and his lovers).
103 **beat it hence!** drive it away!
104 **can...dispense** can endure such wrongs.
105 **his...other-where** he looks with desire elsewhere.
106 **lets** prevents.
108–109 **Would...bed** That would be enough to keep my love, if he would play fair in his bed.
110–114 This is a difficult passage, and possibly corrupt. As it stands, even with the emendation of 'by' to 'but' Adriana seems to change her mind at least once. The argument seems to run: 'even the most costly jewellery loses its lustre [perhaps thinking of the Courtesan], but true gold [herself?] endures however many people touch it. And [yet?] even gold wears away with frequent handling; and no man's reputation can survive when lying and corruption dishonour it.'
114 **B[ut]** folio has 'By'.
117 **fond** mad.
The folio has '*Enter Antipholus Erotas*' (see head-note).
2 **heedful** attentive.
4 **By...report** At least this is what I guess from the circumstances and from what the inn-keeper tells me.
8 **As...again** If you love being beaten, jest with me again.

For which I hope thou felt'st I was displeased.

DROMIO OF SYRACUSE
I am glad to see you in this merry vein,
What means this jest? I pray you master tell me?

ANTIPHOLUS OF SYRACUSE
Yea, dost thou jeer and flout me in the teeth?
Think'st thou I jest? Hold, take thou that, and that.

Beats Dro[mio].

DROMIO OF SYRACUSE
Hold sir, for God's sake! Now your jest is earnest,
Upon what bargain do you give it me?

ANTIPHOLUS OF SYRACUSE
Because that I familiarly sometimes
Do use you for my fool, and chat with you,
Your sauciness will jest upon my love,
And make a common of my serious hours.
When the sun shines, let foolish gnats make sport,
But creep in crannies, when he hides his beams;
If you will jest with me, know my aspect,
And fashion your demeanour to my looks,
Or I will beat this method in your sconce.

DROMIO OF SYRACUSE
'Sconce' call you it? So you would leave battering, I had rather have it a head, and you use these blows long, I must get a sconce for my head, and ensconce it too, or else I shall seek my wit in my shoulders. But I pray sir, why am I beaten?

ANTIPHOLUS OF SYRACUSE
Dost thou not know?

DROMIO OF SYRACUSE
Nothing sir, but that I am beaten.

ANTIPHOLUS OF SYRACUSE
Shall I tell you why?

DROMIO OF SYRACUSE
Aye sir, and wherefore; for they say, 'every why hath a wherefore'.

ANTIPHOLUS OF SYRACUSE
Why, first for flouting me, and then, wherefore, for urging it the second time to me.

DROMIO OF SYRACUSE
Was there ever any man thus beaten out of season,
When in the why and the wherefore is neither rhyme nor reason?
Well sir, I thank you.

ANTIPHOLUS OF SYRACUSE
Thank me sir, for what?

DROMIO OF SYRACUSE
Marry sir, for this something that you gave me for nothing.

ANTIPHOLUS OF SYRACUSE
I'll make you amends next, to give you nothing for something. But say, sir, is it dinner-time?

DROMIO OF SYRACUSE
No, sir, I think the meat wants that I have.

ANTIPHOLUS OF SYRACUSE
In good time sir, what's that?

DROMIO OF SYRACUSE
Basting.

ANTIPHOLUS OF SYRACUSE
Well sir, then 'twill be dry.

DROMIO OF SYRACUSE
If it be sir, I pray you eat none of it.

ANTIPHOLUS OF SYRACUSE
Your reason?

DROMIO OF SYRACUSE
Lest it make you choleric, and purchase me another dry basting.

22 **jeer...teeth** mock and defy me to my face.
25 **Upon what bargain** For what reason.
26-27 **Because...fool** Because I sometimes jest with you.
28 **sauciness** insolence.
29 **make...hours** treat my serious moments as if I was available for anyone to jest with.
30-33 **When...looks** i.e. gnats know that when the sun shines they can fly about, but when it is hidden they have to find cracks to hide in. (Similarly,) if you want to joke with me, learn to judge my moods, and suit your behaviour to them.
34 **sconce** head.
35 **So** If.
36 **and** if.
37 **sconce** Dromio puns on sconce as both 'head' and 'fortification'
43-44 **'every...wherefore'** a proverbial phrase.
47 **out of season** when he shouldn't be.
51 **Marry** Indeed.
55 **the meat...have** the meat is lacking something that I have (had).
57 **Basting** punning on 'beating' and the process of moistening meat with its own juices during cooking.
61 **choleric** angry. An angry disposition was thought to be the result of too much 'choler' (hot and dry humour) in one's system.

ANTIPHOLUS OF SYRACUSE
Well sir, learn to jest in good time, there's a time for all things.

DROMIO OF SYRACUSE
I durst have denied that, before you were so choleric.

ANTIPHOLUS OF SYRACUSE
By what rule sir?

DROMIO OF SYRACUSE
Marry sir, by a rule as plain as the plain bald pate of Father Time himself.

ANTIPHOLUS OF SYRACUSE
Let's hear it.

DROMIO OF SYRACUSE
There's no time for a man to recover his hair that grows bald by nature.

ANTIPHOLUS OF SYRACUSE
May he not do it by fine and recovery?

DROMIO OF SYRACUSE
Yes, to pay a fine for a periwig, and recover the lost hair of another man.

ANTIPHOLUS OF SYRACUSE
Why is Time such a niggard of hair, being (as it is) so plentiful an excrement?

DROMIO OF SYRACUSE
Because it is a blessing that he bestows on beasts, and what he hath scanted them in hair he hath given them in wit.

ANTIPHOLUS OF SYRACUSE
Why, but there's many a man hath more hair
than wit.

DROMIO OF SYRACUSE
Not a man of those but he hath the wit to lose his hair.

ANTIPHOLUS OF SYRACUSE
Why, thou didst conclude hairy men plain dealers
without wit.

DROMIO OF SYRACUSE
The plainer dealer, the sooner lost; yet he loseth it in a kind of jollity.

ANTIPHOLUS OF SYRACUSE
For what reason?

DROMIO OF SYRACUSE
For two; and sound ones too.

ANTIPHOLUS OF SYRACUSE
Nay not sound I pray you.

DROMIO OF SYRACUSE
Sure ones then.

ANTIPHOLUS OF SYRACUSE
Nay, not sure in a thing falsing.

DROMIO OF SYRACUSE
Certain ones then.

ANTIPHOLUS OF SYRACUSE
Name them.

DROMIO OF SYRACUSE
The one, to save the money that he spends in tiring: the other, that at dinner they should not drop in his porridge.

ANTIPHOLUS OF SYRACUSE
You would all this time have proved, there is no time for all things.

DROMIO OF SYRACUSE
Marry and did sir: namely, no time to recover hair lost by Nature.

ANTIPHOLUS OF SYRACUSE
But your reason was not substantial, why there is no time to recover.

DROMIO OF SYRACUSE
Thus I mend it: Time himself is bald, and therefore to the world's end, will have bald followers.

ANTIPHOLUS OF SYRACUSE
I knew 'twould be a bald conclusion. But soft, who wafts us yonder?

Enter Adriana and Luciana.

72 **by...recovery** a legal means of passing on property to an heir when the law would not normally allow it.
74 Wigs were made from human hair. There may be a pun on 'heir' too, given the allusion to fine and recovery.
75 **niggard** miser.
76 **excrement** outgrowth.
78 **scanted** short-changed.
81 As editors note, there may be an allusion to venereal disease here, one of the consequences of which was losing one's hair.
82 **plain...wit** honest men without sophistication.
86 Where Dromio uses 'sound' to mean good reasons, Antipholus puns on 'sound' as 'healthy/whole', which the man with venereal disease will not be.
88 **in...falsing** in an unreliable thing.
92 **tiring** preparing his hair. (The folio has 'trying'.)
102 **bald** poor/simple.
102–103 **But...yonder?** Hush, who's that over there beckoning us?

ADRIANA

Aye, aye, Antipholus, look strange and frown,
Some other mistress hath thy sweet aspects.
I am not Adriana, nor thy wife.
The time was once when thou, unurged,
wouldst vow
That never words were music to thine ear,
That never object pleasing in thine eye,
That never touch well welcome to thy hand;
That never meat sweet-savoured in thy taste,
Unless I spake, or looked, or touched, or carved to
thee.
How comes it now, my husband, O how
comes it,
That thou art thus estranged from thyself?
'Thyself' I call it, being strange to me;
That, undividable incorporate
Am better than thy dear self's better part.
Ah, do not tear away thyself from me,
For know, my love, as easy mayest thou fall
A drop of water in the breaking gulf,
And take unmingled that same drop again
Without addition or diminishing,
As take from me thyself and not me too.
How dearly would it touch me to the quick,
Should'st thou but hear I were licentious?
And that this body, consecrate to thee,
By ruffian lust should be contaminate?
Wouldst thou not spit at me and spurn at me,
And hurl the name of husband in my face,
And tear the stained skin off my harlot-brow,
And from my false hand cut the wedding-ring,
And break it with a deep-divorcing vow?
I know thou canst, and therefore see thou do it.
I am possessed with an adulterate blot,
My blood is mingled with the crime of lust.
For if we two be one, and thou play false,
I do digest the poison of thy flesh,
Being strumpeted by thy contagion.
Keep then fair league and truce with thy true bed,
I live unstained, thou un-dishonoured.

ANTIPHOLUS OF SYRACUSE

Plead you to me, fair dame? I know you not.
In Ephesus I am but two hours old,
As strange unto your town as to your talk;
Who, every word by all my wit being scanned,
Want wit in all one word to understand.

LUCIANA

Fie brother, how the world is changed with you.
When were you wont to use my sister thus?
She sent for you by Dromio home to dinner.

ANTIPHOLUS OF SYRACUSE

By Dromio?

DROMIO OF SYRACUSE

By me?

ADRIANA

By thee, and this thou didst return from him:
That he did buffet thee, and in his blows,
Denied my house for his, me for his wife.

ANTIPHOLUS OF SYRACUSE

Did you converse sir with this gentlewoman?
What is the course and drift of your compact?

DROMIO OF SYRACUSE

I sir? I never saw her till this time.

ANTIPHOLUS OF SYRACUSE

Villain thou liest, for even her very words,
Didst thou deliver to me on the mart.

DROMIO OF SYRACUSE

I never spake with her in all my life.

ANTIPHOLUS OF SYRACUSE

How can she thus then call us by our names,
Unless it be by inspiration?

ADRIANA

How ill agrees it with your gravity
To counterfeit thus grossly with your slave,
Abetting him to thwart me in my mood.
Be it my wrong you are from me exempt,
But wrong not that wrong with a more contempt.

105 **hath ...aspects** gets your sweeter looks.
107 **unurged** without being asked.
116–117 **That...part.** I, who, an indivisible part of you, am more than your best part.
120 **breaking gulf** turbulent (divided) ocean.
124 **touch...quick** wound me in the innermost, most sensitive part.
125 **licentious** unfaithful sexually.
136–138 **if...contagion** as we are one flesh, I 'catch' your whoredom by association.
139 **fair league** an honest alliance.
142–145 **In...understand.** I have only been in this city two hours and am as unfamiliar with it as with what you are saying, and, having listened carefully to every word you have said, lack the wit to understand a single one.
155 **What...compact?** What is the nature and extent of your conspiracy with her?
161 **inspiration** divine guidance.
162 **How...gravity** How unfitting it is to your status.
165–166 **Be...contempt.** I accept I may be to blame for your estrangement from me, but don't worsen things with a greater insult.

Come I will fasten on this sleeve of thine;
Thou art an elm, my husband, I a vine,
Whose weakness married to thy stronger state,
Makes me with thy strength to communicate.
If aught possess thee from me, it is dross,
Usurping ivy, brier, or idle moss;
Who all for want of pruning, with intrusion
Infect thy sap, and live on thy confusion.

ANTIPHOLUS OF SYRACUSE
To me she speaks, she moves me for her theme.
What, was I married to her in my dream?
Or sleep I now, and think I hear all this?
What error drives our eyes and ears amiss?
Until I know this sure uncertainty,
I'll entertain the offered fallacy.

LUCIANA
Dromio, go bid the servants spread for dinner.

DROMIO OF SYRACUSE
O for my beads, I cross me for a sinner.
This is the fairy land, O spite of spites,
We talk with goblins, owls, and sprites;
If we obey them not, this will ensue:
They'll suck our breath, or pinch us black and blue

LUCIANA
Why prat'st thou to thyself and answer'st not?
Dromio, thou Dromio, thou snail, thou slug, thou sot!

DROMIO OF SYRACUSE
I am transformed master, am I not?

ANTIPHOLUS OF SYRACUSE
I think thou art, in mind, and so am I.

DROMIO OF SYRACUSE
Nay master, both in mind and in my shape.

ANTIPHOLUS OF SYRACUSE
Thou hast thine own form.

DROMIO OF SYRACUSE
No, I am an ape.

LUCIANA
If thou art changed to aught, 'tis to an ass.

DROMIO OF SYRACUSE
'Tis true she rides me, and I long for grass.
'Tis so, I am an ass, else it could never be
But I should know her as well as she knows me.

ADRIANA
Come, come, no longer will I be a fool,
To put the finger in the eye and weep;
Whilst man and master laugh my woes to scorn.
Come sir, to dinner. Dromio, keep the gate.
Husband I'll dine above with you today,
And shrive you of a thousand idle pranks.
Sirrah, if any ask you for your master,
Say he dines forth, and let no creature enter.
Come sister. Dromio, play the porter well.

ANTIPHOLUS OF SYRACUSE
Am I in earth, in heaven, or in hell?
Sleeping or waking, mad or well-advised?
Known unto these, and to myself disguised?
I'll say as they say, and persever so;
And in this mist at all adventures go.

DROMIO OF SYRACUSE
Master, shall I be porter at the gate?

ADRIANA
Aye, and let none enter, lest I break your pate.

LUCIANA
Come, come, Antipholus, we dine too late.

Exeunt.

Actus Tercius. Scena Prima.

Enter Antipholus of Ephesus, his man Dromio, Angelo the Goldsmith and Balthazar the Merchant.

ANTIPHOLUS OF EPHESUS
Good Signor Angelo, you must excuse us all,
My wife is shrewish when I keep not hours.
Say that I lingered with you at your shop
To see the making of her carcanet,

170 **Makes...communicate** Lets me share your strength.
171–174 **If...confusion.** If anything takes possession of you away from me... it, for lack of pruning, breaks into you, infects you, and feeds on your destruction.
175 **she moves...theme** I am the subject of her argument.
180 **I'll...fallacy** I'll go along with this mad suggestion.
182 **beads...me** prayer beads, I make the sign of the cross.
184 **sprites** spirits/ghosts.
188 **sot** idiot.
192 **form** shape.
194 **I...grass** I long for my freedom (to be put out to grass).
198 **To...weep** To cry over something silly, like a child who has poked him- or herself in the eye.
200 **keep the gate** guard the door.
201 **above** upstairs (perhaps indicating that the next scene was played with the dining party 'above' on a balcony and Antipholus and Dromio of Ephesus on the stage floor).
202 **shrive** hear your confession and give penance.
203 **Sirrah** a variant of 'sir' used to servants and inferiors.
204 **he dines forth** he's dining out.
209–210 **I'll...go.** I'll go along with this ('persevere'), whatever happens next in this confusion.
2 **shrewish...hours** bad-tempered when I am late.
4 **carcanet** a necklace, often set with jewels (the 'chain' mentioned later).

And that tomorrow you will bring it home.
But here's a villain that would face me down
He met me on the mart, and that I beat him,
And charged him with a thousand marks in gold,
And that I did deny my wife and house.
Thou drunkard, thou, what didst thou mean by this?

DROMIO OF EPHESUS
Say what you will sir, but I know what I know.
That you beat me at the mart, I have your hand to show.
If the skin were parchment, and the blows you gave were ink,
Your own handwriting would tell you what I think.

ANTIPHOLUS OF EPHESUS
I think thou art an ass.

DROMIO OF EPHESUS
Marry, so it doth appear
By the wrongs I suffer, and the blows I bear.
I should kick, being kicked, and, being at that pass,
You would keep from my heels, and beware of an ass.

ANTIPHOLUS OF EPHESUS
You're sad, Signor Balthazar. Pray God our cheer
May answer my good will, and your good welcome here.

BALTHAZAR
I hold your dainties cheap sir, and your welcome dear.

ANTIPHOLUS OF EPHESUS
O Signor Balthazar, either at flesh or fish,
A table full of welcome makes scarce one dainty dish.

BALTHAZAR
Good meat, sir, is, common; that every churl affords.

ANTIPHOLUS OF EPHESUS
And welcome more common, for that's nothing but words.

BALTHAZAR
Small cheer and great welcome makes a merry feast.

ANTIPHOLUS OF EPHESUS
Aye, to a niggardly host, and more sparing guest.
But though my cates be mean, take them in good part,
Better cheer may you have, but not with better heart.
But soft, my door is locked. Go bid them let us in.

DROMIO OF EPHESUS
Maud, Bridget, Marian, Cicely, Gillian, Ginn!

DROMIO OF SYRACUSE
Mome, malt-horse, capon, coxcomb, idiot, patch!
Either get thee from the door; or sit down at the hatch.
Dost thou conjure for wenches, that thou call'st for such store
When one is one too many. Go, get thee from the door.

DROMIO OF EPHESUS
What patch is made our porter? My master stays in the street.

DROMIO OF SYRACUSE
Let him walk from whence he came, lest he catch cold on's feet.

ANTIPHOLUS OF EPHESUS
Who talks within there? Ho, open the door!

DROMIO OF SYRACUSE
Right sir, I'll tell you when, and you tell me wherefore.

ANTIPHOLUS OF EPHESUS
Wherefore? For my dinner. I have not dined today.

DROMIO OF SYRACUSE
Nor today here you must not, come again when you may.

ANTIPHOLUS OF EPHESUS
What art thou that keep'st me out from the house I owe?

DROMIO OF SYRACUSE
The porter for this time, sir, and my name is Dromio.

6 **face me down** insist to my face (despite my denial).
12 **I...show** the mark of your hand on my head as evidence.
17 **being...pass** being in that awkward situation.
18 **You...from** You should avoid.
19 **sad** serious/sombre.
19–20 **our...will** our hospitality will match my goodwill towards you.
21 **I...dear.** I value your welcome much higher than your food.
23 **A table...dish** i.e. you'll not get much nourishment out of welcome alone.
24 **that...affords** any fool can provide food.
26 **Small cheer** Few provisions.
26 **Small...feast** proverbial.
28 **cates be mean** provisions are modest.
29 **Better...have** you might find better food elsewhere.
30 **But soft** Be quiet a moment/What's this?
32 **Mome...patch!** Idiot, (brewer's) workhorse, eunuch, fool...clown! (As once Dromio is inside and the other out, they do not see each other.)
33 **sit...hatch** sit by the hatch through which alms are distributed to the poor (to see if any scraps are sent out).
34 **such store** so many (of them).
36 **What...porter?** What fool is acting as our porter?
37 **cold on's feet** a cold in his feet.
39 **and...wherefore** if you tell me why I should.
42 **owe** own.

DROMIO OF EPHESUS
O villain! Thou hast stolen both mine office and my name.
The one ne'er got me credit, the other mickle blame.
If thou hadst been Dromio today in my place,
Thou wouldst have changed thy face for a name, or thy name for an ass.

Enter Luce.

LUCE
What a coil is there, Dromio? Who are those at the gate?
DROMIO OF EPHESUS
Let my master in, Luce.
LUCE Faith no, he comes too late,
And so tell your master.
DROMIO OF EPHESUS O Lord, I must laugh,
Have at you with a proverb: Shall I set in my staff?
LUCE
Have at you with another, that's 'When? Can you tell?'
DROMIO OF SYRACUSE
If thy name be called Luce, Luce thou hast answered him well.
ANTIPHOLUS OF EPHESUS
Do you hear, you minion, you'll let us in, I hope?
LUCE
I thought to have asked you.
DROMIO OF SYRACUSE
And you said no.
DROMIO OF EPHESUS
So come help . . . Well struck, there was blow for blow.
ANTIPHOLUS OF EPHESUS
Thou baggage, let me in!
LUCE Can you tell for whose sake?
DROMIO OF EPHESUS
Master, knock the door hard.
LUCE Let him knock till it ache.
ANTIPHOLUS OF EPHESUS
You'll cry for this, minion, if I beat the door down.
LUCE
What needs all that, and a pair of stocks in the town?

Enter Adriana.

ADRIANA
Who is that at the door that keeps all this noise?
DROMIO OF SYRACUSE
By my troth, your town is troubled with unruly boys.
ANTIPHOLUS OF EPHESUS
Are you there, wife? You might have come before.
ADRIANA
Your wife, sir knave? Go, get you from the door.
DROMIO OF EPHESUS
If you went in pain, master, this 'knave' would go sore.
ANGELO
Here is neither cheer sir, nor welcome; we would fain have either.
BALTHAZAR
In debating which was best, we shall part with neither.
DROMIO OF EPHESUS
They stand at the door, master; bid them welcome hither.
ANTIPHOLUS OF EPHESUS
There is something in the wind that we cannot get in.
DROMIO OF EPHESUS
You would say so, master, if your garments were thin.
Your cake here is warm within: you stand here in the cold.
It would make a man mad as a buck to be so bought and sold.

44 **mine office** my job.
45 **mickle** (too) much.
46–47 **If . . . ass.** You wouldn't have wanted to have my name earlier today (when he was getting beaten).
48 **What . . . there** What is the commotion there?
51 **Shall . . . staff?** Shall I break open the door with my staff? (Proverbially, to set in one's staff was to make oneself at home).
52 **'When . . . tell?'** (defiantly) 'When will you do that? Do tell us'.
54 **I hope** I trust. There may be a line missing following this, which would make more sense of Luce's reply.
60 **What . . . town?** I won't need (to do) that, since there are stocks in the town (for imprisoning the likes of you in).
62 **boys** rascals.
65 **If . . . sore.** another difficult line. Perhaps 'If you retreat hurt now, master, her calling you 'knave' will be another humiliation'.
66 **we . . . either** we'd happily have either one.
67 **part** depart.
69 **something . . . wind** something strange going on.
72 **so . . . sold** treated so badly.

ANTIPHOLUS OF EPHESUS
Go fetch me something, I'll break ope the gate.
DROMIO OF SYRACUSE
Break any breaking here, and I'll break your knave's pate.
DROMIO OF EPHESUS
A man may break a word with you sir, and words are but wind;
Aye, and break it in your face, so he break it not behind.
DROMIO OF SYRACUSE
It seems thou want'st breaking; out upon thee, hind!
DROMIO OF EPHESUS
Here's too much: 'Out upon thee'! I pray thee let me in.
DROMIO OF SYRACUSE
Aye, when fowls have no feathers and fish have no fin.
ANTIPHOLUS OF EPHESUS
Well, I'll break in: go borrow me a crow.
DROMIO OF EPHESUS
A crow without feather, master, mean you so?
For a fish without a fin, there's a fowl without a feather.
If a crow help us in, sirrah, we'll pluck a crow together.
ANTIPHOLUS OF EPHESUS
Go get thee gone, fetch me an iron crow.
BALTHAZAR
Have patience sir, O let it not be so,
Herein you war against your reputation,
And draw within the compass of suspect
Th'unviolated honour of your wife.
Once this: your long experience of your wisdom,
Her sober virtue, years, and modesty,
Plead on her part some cause to you unknown.
And doubt not sir, but she will well excuse
Why at this time the doors are made against you.
Be ruled by me, depart in patience,
And let us to the Tiger all to dinner,
And about evening come yourself alone,
To know the reason of this strange restraint.
If by strong hand you offer to break in
Now, in the stirring passage of the day,
A vulgar comment will be made of it;
And that supposèd by the common rout
Against your yet ungallèd estimation,
That may with foul intrusion enter in,
And dwell upon your grave when you are dead.
For slander lives upon succession;
Forever housed where it gets possession.
ANTIPHOLUS OF EPHESUS
You have prevailed, I will depart in quiet,
And in despite of mirth mean to be merry.
I know a wench of excellent discourse,
Pretty and witty: wild, and yet, too, gentle.
There will we dine. This woman that I mean,
My wife (but, I protest without desert)
Hath oftentimes upbraided me withal.
To her will we to dinner. Get you home
And fetch the chain, by this I know 'tis made.
Bring it, I pray you, to the Porpentine,
For there's the house. That chain will I bestow
(Be it for nothing but to spite my wife)
Upon mine hostess there. Good sir, make haste:
Since mine own doors refuse to entertain me,
I'll knock elsewhere, to see if they'll disdain me.
ANGELO
I'll meet you at that place some hour hence.
ANTIPHOLUS OF EPHESUS
Do so. This jest shall cost me some expense. *Exeunt.*

[Act III. Scene ii.]

Enter Luciana with Antipholus of Syracuse.

[73] **ope** open.
[75] **break a word** have a conversation.
[76] **so...behind** i.e. so long as he doesn't break wind ('fart') in your face.
[77] **thou...hind!** you need disciplining ('breaking in', like a young horse); be off with you, churl!
[80] **a crow** a crowbar.
[83] **pluck a crow** carry on an argument (proverbial).
[87] **draw...suspect** draw into suspicion.
[93] **made** shut.
[95] **Tiger** an inn.
[99] **stirring passage** busy part.
[100] **A vulgar...it** common people will gossip.
[101–102] **And...estimation** Whatever the common mob suspects against your so far unsullied reputation.
[105] **lives upon succession** lives on down the generations.
[113] **Hath...withal** Has often accused me (unjustly) of having an affair with.
[115] **by this** by this time.
[118] **but** if only.
The folio mistakenly has 'Juliana' here.

LUCIANA

And may it be that you have quite forgot
A husband's office? Shall, Antipholus
Even in the spring of love, thy love-springs rot?
Shall love, in building, grow so ruinate?
If you did wed my sister for her wealth,
Then for her wealth's sake use her with more kindness.
Or, if you like elsewhere, do it by stealth,
Muffle your false love with some show of blindness;
Let not my sister read it in your eye.
Be not thy tongue thy own shame's orator.
Look sweet, be fair, become disloyalty;
Apparel vice like virtue's harbinger.
Bear a fair presence, though your heart be tainted;
Teach sin the carriage of a holy saint.
Be secret-false: what need she be acquainted?
What simple thief brags of his own attain[t]?
'Tis double wrong to truant with your bed
And let her read it in thy looks at board.
Shame hath a bastard fame, well managed;
Ill deeds are doubled with an evil word.
Alas, poor women, make us but believe
(Being compact of credit) that you love us,
Though others have the arm, show us the sleeve.
We in your motion turn, and you may move us.
Then, gentle brother, get you in again;
Comfort my sister, cheer her, call her wife;
'Tis holy sport to be a little vain
When the sweet breath of flattery conquers strife.

ANTIPHOLUS OF SYRACUSE

Sweet mistress; what your name is else I know not,
Nor by what wonder you do hit of mine.
Less in your knowledge and your grace you show not
Than our earth's wonder, more than earth divine.
Teach me, dear creature, how to think and speak;
Lay open to my earthy-gross conceit,
Smothered in errors, feeble, shallow, weak,
The folded meaning of your words' deceit.
Against my soul's pure truth, why labour you
To make it wander in an unknown field?
Are you a god? Would you create me new?
Transform me then, and to your power I'll yield.
But if that I am I, then well I know,
Your weeping sister is no wife of mine,
Nor to her bed no homage do I owe.
Far more, far more to you do I decline.
O train me not, sweet mermaid, with thy note
To drown me in thy sister['s] flood of tears.
Sing, siren, for thyself, and I will dote.
Spread o'er the silver waves thy golden hairs,
And as a bed I'll take them, and there lie;
And in that glorious supposition think
He gains by death that hath such means to die.
Let love, being light, be drowned if she sink.

LUCIANA

What, are you mad, that you do reason so?

ANTIPHOLUS OF SYRACUSE

Not mad, but mated; how, I do not know.

LUCIANA

It is a fault that springeth from your eye.

ANTIPHOLUS OF SYRACUSE

For gazing on your beams, fair sun, being by.

LUCIANA

Gaze where you should, and that will clear your sight.

ANTIPHOLUS OF SYRACUSE

As good to wink, sweet love, as look on night.

LUCIANA

Why call you me love? Call my sister so.

[2] **office** role/responsibilities.
[3] **love-springs** tender shoots of love.
[4] **in building** while it is still developing.
[8] **Muffle** Blindfold.
[10] **Be...orator.** Don't let your own tongue proclaim your shame.
[11] **Look...disloyalty** Be treacherous elegantly.
[12] **Apparel...harbinger** Dress vice like virtue's herald.
[14] **carriage** demeanour.
[15] **what...acquainted?** why does she need to know?
[16] **attain[t]** shame.
[18] **board** mealtimes.
[19] **Shame...managed** Shameful deeds, if you handle them well, can have a kind of illegitimate honour.
[22] **Being...credit** As we are made up of trust/credulousness.
[24] **motion** orbit.
[30] **hit of mine** guess my name.
[34] **earthy-gross conceit** dull human understanding.
[36] **folded** hidden.
[44] **decline** incline.
[45] **train** snare.
[45] **note** song. Mermaids lured sailors to their deaths through their enticing song.
[54] **mated** confounded (check-mated, as in chess).
[57] **Gaze...should** i.e. look to your wife.
[58] **wink** close your eyes altogether.

ANTIPHOLUS OF SYRACUSE
Thy sister's sister.
LUCIANA That's my sister.
ANTIPHOLUS OF SYRACUSE No:
It is thyself, mine own self's better part.
Mine eye's clear eye, my dear heart's dearer heart,
My food, my fortune, and my sweet hope's aim;
My sole earth's heaven, and my heaven's claim.
LUCIANA
All this my sister is, or else should be.
ANTIPHOLUS OF SYRACUSE
Call thyself sister, sweet, for I am thee.
Thee will I love, and with thee lead my life;
Thou hast no husband yet, nor I no wife.
Give me thy hand.
LUCIANA
O soft sir, hold you still.
I'll fetch my sister, to get her good will.

Exit.

Enter Dromio of Syracuse.

ANTIPHOLUS OF SYRACUSE
Why, how now Dromio, where run'st thou so fast.
DROMIO OF SYRACUSE
Do you know me sir? Am I Dromio?
Am I your man? Am I myself?
ANTIPHOLUS OF SYRACUSE
Thou art Dromio, thou art my man, thou art thyself.
DROMIO OF SYRACUSE
I am an ass, I am a woman's man, and
besides myself.
ANTIPHOLUS OF SYRACUSE
What woman's man? And how besides thyself?
DROMIO OF SYRACUSE
Marry sir, besides myself, I am due to a woman: one that claims me, one that haunts me, one that will have me.
ANTIPHOLUS OF SYRACUSE
What claim lays she to thee?
DROMIO OF SYRACUSE
Marry sir, such claim as you would lay to your horse, and she would have me as a beast; not that I being a beast, she would have me, but that she being a very beastly creature, lays claim to me.
ANTIPHOLUS OF SYRACUSE
What is she?
DROMIO OF SYRACUSE
A very reverent body; aye, such a one as a man may not speak of, without he say sir-reverence. I have but lean luck in the match, and yet is she a wondrous fat marriage.
ANTIPHOLUS OF SYRACUSE
How dost thou mean, 'a fat marriage'?
DROMIO OF SYRACUSE
Marry sir, she's the kitchen wench, and all grease, and I know not what use to put her to, but to make a lamp of her, and run from her by her own light. I warrant, her rags and the tallow in them will burn a Poland winter. If she lives till doomsday, she'll burn a week longer than the whole world.
ANTIPHOLUS OF SYRACUSE
What complexion is she of?
DROMIO OF SYRACUSE
Swart like my shoe, but her face nothing half like so clean kept, for why she sweats. A man may go over-shoes in the grime of it.
ANTIPHOLUS OF SYRACUSE
That's a fault that water will mend.
DROMIO OF SYRACUSE
No sir, 'tis in grain, Noah's flood could not do it.
ANTIPHOLUS OF SYRACUSE
What's her name?
DROMIO OF SYRACUSE
Nell, sir. But her name and three quarters, that's

75 **besides myself** deranged.
77 **due** promised.
86 **reverent body** holy person.
87 **sir-reverence** contraction of 'saving your reverence': an apology for something offensive to follow.
88 **lean** poor.
95 **a Poland winter** a long winter, as in Poland.
98 **Swart** Black.
98–100 **nothing . . . it.** Not kept half so clean, because she sweats. A man can walk over the depth of his shoes in her sweat.
102 **in grain** ingrained/permanent.
104 The character described would seem to be the 'Luce' of III.i. Either Dromio is making up this name for the sake of the joke on 'ell' to follow, or Shakespeare changed her name and did not go back to correct himself.

an ell and three quarters, will not measure her from hip to hip.

ANTIPHOLUS OF SYRACUSE
Then she bears some breadth?

DROMIO OF SYRACUSE
No longer from head to foot than from hip to hip. She is spherical like a globe; I could find out countries in her.

ANTIPHOLUS OF SYRACUSE
In what part of her body stands Ireland?

DROMIO OF SYRACUSE
Marry sir, in her buttocks, I found it out by the bogs.

ANTIPHOLUS OF SYRACUSE
Where Scotland?

DROMIO OF SYRACUSE
I found it by the barrenness, hard in the palm of the hand.

ANTIPHOLUS OF SYRACUSE
Where France?

DROMIO OF SYRACUSE
In her forehead, armed and reverted, making war against her hair.

ANTIPHOLUS OF SYRACUSE
Where England?

DROMIO OF SYRACUSE
I looked for the chalky cliffs, but I could find no whiteness in them. But I guess it stood in her chin, by the salt rheum that ran between France and it.

ANTIPHOLUS OF SYRACUSE
Where Spain?

DROMIO OF SYRACUSE
Faith I saw it not, but I felt it hot in her breath.

ANTIPHOLUS OF SYRACUSE
Where America, the Indies?

DROMIO OF SYRACUSE
Oh sir, upon her nose, all o'er embellished with rubies, carbuncles, sapphires; declining their rich aspect to the hot breath of Spain, who sent whole armadoes of caracks to be ballast at her nose.

ANTIPHOLUS OF SYRACUSE
Where stood Belgia, the Netherlands?

DROMIO OF SYRACUSE
Oh sir, I did not look so low. To conclude, this drudge or diviner, laid claim to me, called me Dromio, swore I was assured to her, told me what privy marks I had about me, as the mark of my shoulder, the mole in my neck, the great wart on my left arm, that I, amazed, ran from her as a witch. And I think if my breast had not been made of faith, and my heart of steel, She had transformed me to a curtal dog, and made me turn i' the wheel.

ANTIPHOLUS OF SYRACUSE
Go hie thee presently, post to the road,
And if the wind blow any way from shore,
I will not harbour in this town to-night.
If any bark put forth, come to the mart,
Where I will walk till thou return to me.
If everyone knows us, and we know none,
'Tis time I think to trudge, pack and be gone.

DROMIO OF SYRACUSE
As from a bear a man would run for life,
So fly I from her that would be my wife. *Exit*

ANTIPHOLUS OF SYRACUSE
There's none but witches do inhabit here,
And therefore 'tis high time that I were hence.
She that doth call me husband, even my soul

105 **an . . . quarters** an ell is a measurement of 45 inches, so an ell and three quarters is approximately six and a half feet/two metres.

116–117 **reverted . . . hair** turned in on itself. See the head-note for the potential significance of the reference to France warring against its own hair/heir for the dating of *Errors*.

120 A white complexion was considered beautiful, so this woman is distinctly not 'chalky'.

121 **salt rheum** snot.

125–126 **upon . . . sapphires** i.e. her nose was covered with spots and scabs, like gemstones brought back from the Indies.

126–127 **rich aspect** hooked shape.

127–128 **whole . . . nose** whole fleets of galleons to be filled with freight at her nostrils.

129 **Belgia, the Netherlands** the Low Countries.

131 **drudge or diviner** scullion or witch (one who uses divination).

132 **assured** promised.

136–137 **if . . . steel** i.e. if I had not been a good Christian (alluding to Ephesians 6:13–14: '[T]ake unto you the armour of God . . . in the evil day, and to stand in all things perfect . . . having your loins girt about with truth, and having on the breastplate of justice').

137–138 **transformed . . . wheel** turned me into a dock-tailed dog and made me turn the spit-wheel. (Dogs were sometimes used to rotate spits in kitchens.)

139 **Go . . . road** Immediately, hurry to the harbour.

142 **If . . . forth** If any vessel is leaving (port).

145 **trudge** get moving.

Doth for a wife abhor. But her fair sister,
Possessed with such a gentle sovereign grace,
Of such enchanting presence and discourse,
Hath almost made me traitor to myself.
But, lest myself be guilty to self-wrong,
I'll stop mine ears against the mermaid's song.

Enter Angelo with the chain.

ANGELO
Master Antipholus.

ANTIPHOLUS OF SYRACUSE
Aye, that's my name.

ANGELO
I know it well sir. Lo, here is the chain.
I thought to have ta'en you at the Porpentine,
The chain unfinished made me stay thus long.

ANTIPHOLUS OF SYRACUSE
What is your will that I shall do with this?

ANGELO
What please yourself sir. I have made it for you.

ANTIPHOLUS OF SYRACUSE
Made it for me, sir? I bespoke it not.

ANGELO
Not once, nor twice, but twenty times you have.
Go home with it, and please your wife withal;
And soon at supper-time I'll visit you,
And then receive my money for the chain.

ANTIPHOLUS OF SYRACUSE
I pray you, sir, receive the money now,
For fear you ne'er see chain nor money more.

ANGELO
You are a merry man sir, fare you well. *Exit*

ANTIPHOLUS OF SYRACUSE
What I should think of this, I cannot tell.
But this I think, there's no man is so vain,
That would refuse so fair an offered chain.
I see a man here needs not live by shifts,
When in the streets he meets such golden gifts.
I'll to the mart, and there for Dromio stay;
If any ship put out, then straight away. *Exit*

Actus Quartus. Scena Prima.

Enter a [Second] Merchant, Goldsmith [Angelo], and an Officer.

SECOND MERCHANT
You know since Pentecost the sum is due,
And since I have not much importuned you;
Nor now I had not, but that I am bound
To Persia, and want guilders for my voyage.
Therefore make present satisfaction,
Or I'll attach you by this officer.

ANGELO
Even just the sum that I do owe to you,
Is growing to me by Antipholus,
And in the instant that I met with you,
He had of me a chain. At five o'clock
I shall receive the money for the same.
Pleaseth you walk with me down to his house,
I will discharge my bond, and thank you too.

Enter Antipholus of Ephesus and Dromio [of Ephesus] from the Courtesan's.

OFFICER
That labour may you save; see where he comes.

ANTIPHOLUS OF EPHESUS
While I go to the goldsmith's house, go thou
And buy a rope's end, that will I bestow
Among my wife and her confederates,
For locking me out of my doors by day.
But soft, I see the goldsmith. Get thee gone;
Buy thou a rope and bring it home to me.

DROMIO OF EPHESUS
I buy a thousand pound a year, I buy a rope. *Exit.*

159 **ta'en** overtaken/met.
159 **Porpentine** Porcupine (another inn).
163 **bespoke** commissioned.
169 **more** again.
174 **needs . . . shifts** doesn't need to struggle to make a living.
1 **Pentecost** Whitsun, seven weeks after Easter.
4 **bound to Persia** leaving for Persia.
5 **make present satisfaction** pay me the sum owed.
6 **attach** arrest.
8 **growing** owed/coming.
17 **bestow among** i.e. use to beat.
21 Editors have struggled with this line, suggesting the joke is that a rope will 'repay' all those who have kept Antipholus from his home, as Dromio later quips. Hence it is worth a lot of money. More plausibly the joke refers to the thousand 'pounds' or blows Dromio receives each year from his master, hence the cruel irony of sending him to buy a rope's end. Editors have rejected this reading on the grounds that 'pound' was not used in this sense in this period: but a number of medieval instances, and Shakespeare's own usage in *Troilus and Cressida* (1609?), would seem to overcome that objection ('He would pun/pound thee into shivers with his fist, as a sailor breaks a biscuit' II.i.39). See *OED*, s.v. 'pound'.

ANTIPHOLUS OF EPHESUS
A man is well holp up that trusts to you.
I promised your presence, and the chain,
But neither chain nor goldsmith came to me.
Belike you thought our love would last too long
If it were chained together, and therefore came not.

ANGELO
Saving your merry humour, here's the note
How much your chain weighs to the utmost carat,
The fineness of the gold, and chargeful fashion,
Which doth amount to three odd ducats more
Than I stand debted to this gentleman.
I pray you see him presently discharged,
For he is bound to sea, and stays but for it.

ANTIPHOLUS OF EPHESUS
I am not furnished with the present money.
Besides I have some business in the town.
Good signor, take the stranger to my house,
And with you take the chain, and bid my wife
Disburse the sum on the receipt thereof.
Perchance I will be there as soon as you.

ANGELO
Then you will bring the chain to her yourself.

ANTIPHOLUS OF EPHESUS
No, bear it with you, lest I come not time enough.

ANGELO
Well, sir, I will. Have you the chain about you?

ANTIPHOLUS OF EPHESUS
And if I have not sir, I hope you have.
Or else you may return without your money.

ANGELO
Nay come, I pray you sir, give me the chain.
Both wind and tide stays for this gentleman,
And I, to blame, have held him here too long.

ANTIPHOLUS OF EPHESUS
Good lord, you use this dalliance to excuse
Your breach of promise to the Porpentine.
I should have chid you for not bringing it,
But like a shrew you first begin to brawl.

SECOND MERCHANT
The hour steals on, I pray you, sir, dispatch.

ANGELO
You hear how he importunes me. The chain!

ANTIPHOLUS OF EPHESUS
Why give it to my wife, and fetch your money.

ANGELO
Come, come, you know I gave it you even now.
Either send the chain, or send me by some token.

ANTIPHOLUS OF EPHESUS
Fie, now you run this humour out of breath,
Come, where's the chain, I pray you let me see it.

SECOND MERCHANT
My business cannot brook this dalliance,
Good sir ,say whe'er you'll answer me or no:
If not, I'll leave him to the officer.

ANTIPHOLUS OF EPHESUS
I answer you? What should I answer you?

ANGELO
The money that you owe me for the chain.

ANTIPHOLUS OF EPHESUS
I owe you none till I receive the chain.

ANGELO
You know I gave it you half an hour since.

ANTIPHOLUS OF EPHESUS
You gave me none; you wrong me much to say so.

ANGELO
You wrong me more sir in denying it.
Consider how it stands upon my credit.

SECOND MERCHANT
Well officer, arrest him at my suit.

OFFICER
I do, and charge you in the duke's name to
obey me.

ANGELO
This touches me in reputation.
Either consent to pay this sum for me,
Or I attach you by this officer.

ANTIPHOLUS OF EPHESUS
Consent to pay thee that I never had?
Arrest me, foolish fellow, if thou darest.

ANGELO
Here is thy fee; arrest him, officer.

22 **holp up** helped out (ironic).
25 **Belike** Perhaps.
28 **utmost** last.
29 **chargeful fashion** chargeable workmanship.
34 **I... money.** I don't have the money at the moment.
41 **time enough** in the required time.
49 **Your... Porpentine** Your failure to meet me at the Porpentine, as we had arranged.
51 **shrew** scolding/argumentative woman.
52 **The... dispatch.** Time is flying, please get on with it, sir.
57 **you... breath** you're taking this joke too far.
59 **cannot... dalliance** cannot abide this delay.
60 **whe'er** whether.

I would not spare my brother in this case,
If he should scorn me so apparently.

OFFICER
I do arrest you sir, you hear the suit.

ANTIPHOLUS OF EPHESUS
I do obey thee, till I give thee bail.
But sirrah, you shall buy this sport as dear
As all the metal in your shop will answer.

ANGELO
Sir, sir, I will have law in Ephesus,
To your notorious shame; I doubt it not.

Enter Dromio of Syracuse, from the bay.

DROMIO OF SYRACUSE
Master, there is a bark of Epidamnum,
That stays but till her owner comes aboard,
And then sir she bears away. Our fraughtage sir,
I have conveyed aboard, and I have bought
The oil, the balsamum, and aqua-vitae.
The ship is in her trim, the merry wind
Blows fair from land. They stay for nought at all,
But for their owner, master, and yourself.

ANTIPHOLUS OF EPHESUS
How now, a madman? Why, thou peevish sheep,
What ship of Epidamnum stays for me?

DROMIO OF SYRACUSE
A ship you sent me to, to hire waftage.

ANTIPHOLUS OF EPHESUS
Thou drunken slave, I sent thee for a rope,
And told thee to what purpose and what end.

DROMIO OF SYRACUSE
You sent me for a rope's end as soon!
You sent me to the bay sir, for a bark.

ANTIPHOLUS OF EPHESUS
I will debate this matter at more leisure,
And teach your ears to list me with more heed.
To Adriana villain; hie thee straight.
Give her this key, and tell her in the desk
That's covered o'er with Turkish tapestry
There is a purse of ducats, let her send it.
Tell her I am arrested in the street,
And that shall bail me. Hie thee slave, be gone.
On officer, to prison, till it come.

Exeunt [all but Dromio].

DROMIO OF SYRACUSE
To Adriana? That is where we dined,
Where Dowsabel did claim me for her husband.
She is too big, I hope, for me to compass,
Thither I must, although against my will;
For servants must their masters' minds fulfil. *Exit*

[Act IV. Scene ii.]

Enter Adriana and Luciana.

ADRIANA
Ah, Luciana, did he tempt thee so?
Might'st thou perceive austerely in his eye,
That he did plead in earnest, yea or no?
Looked he or red or pale, or sad or merrily?
What observation made'st thou in this case,
Of his heart's meteors tilting in his face?

LUCIANA
First he denied you had in him no right.

ADRIANA
He meant he did me none; the more my spite!

LUCIANA
Then swore he that he was a stranger here.

ADRIANA
And true he swore, though yet forsworn he were.

LUCIANA
Then pleaded I for you.

ADRIANA
And what said he?

87 **fraughtage** baggage.
89 **balsamum, and aqua-vitae** balsam/balm and distilled alcohol (medicines for the voyage?)
90 **in her trim** with sails ready to be set.
95 **hire waftage** buy passage.
98 **a rope's...soon** a beating, more likely.
102 **hie thee straight** hurry straight there.
110 **Dowsabel** the pretty young girl/strumpet (ironic) from the French '*douce et belle*'.
111 **I hope...compass** I think, for me to embrace/think about.
113 **their...fulfil** obey their masters' wishes.
2 **austerely** strictly (i.e. being serious about this).
4 **or** either.
5–6 **What...face?** What could you tell about the passionate movements of his heart (literally, the jousting comets of his heart) from his facial expressions?
7 **he ...right** he denied you had any rightful claim to him.
8 **He...spite!** He meant he did me no right, to my greater vexation!
10 **true he swore** i.e. we never see him in his own house.

LUCIANA
That love I begged for you, he begged of me.
ADRIANA
With what persuasion did he tempt thy love?
LUCIANA
With words that in an honest suit might move.
First he did praise my beauty, then my speech.
ADRIANA
Didst speak him fair?
LUCIANA
Have patience I beseech.
ADRIANA
I cannot, nor I will not, hold me still.
My tongue, though not my heart, shall have his will.
He is deformèd, crooked, old and sere,
Ill-faced, worse bodied, shapeless everywhere;
Vicious, ungentle, foolish, blunt, unkind,
Stigmatical in making, worse in mind.
LUCIANA
Who would be jealous, then, of such a one?
No evil lost is wailed when it is gone.
ADRIANA
Ah, but I think him better than I say,
And yet would herein others' eyes were worse.
Far from her nest the lapwing cries away;
My heart prays for him, though my tongue do curse.

Enter Dromio of Syracuse.

DROMIO OF SYRACUSE
Here: go... the desk... the purse... Sweet, now make haste!
LUCIANA
How hast thou lost thy breath?
DROMIO OF SYRACUSE
By running fast.
ADRIANA
Where is thy master, Dromio? Is he well?
DROMIO OF SYRACUSE
No, he's in Tartar limbo, worse than hell.
A devil in an everlasting garment hath him,
One whose hard heart is buttoned up with steel;
A fiend, a fury, pitiless and rough;
A wolf, nay worse, a fellow all in buff,
A back friend, a shoulder-clapper, one that countermands
The passages of alleys, creeks and narrow lands;
A hound that runs counter, and yet draws dry-foot well;
One that before the judgement carries poor souls to hell.
ADRIANA
Why man, what is the matter?
DROMIO OF SYRACUSE
I do not know the matter, he is 'rested on the case.
ADRIANA
What, is he arrested? Tell me at whose suit.
DROMIO OF SYRACUSE
I know not at whose suit he is arrested, well;
But he's in a suit of buff which 'rested him, that can I tell.
Will you send him, mistress, redemption: the money in his desk?
ADRIANA
Go fetch it, sister. This I wonder at, *Exit Luciana*
That he, unknown to me, should be in debt.
Tell me, was he arrested on a band?

14 **With... move.** That might, if his suit was honest, be persuasive.
16 **Didst... fair?** Did you speak kindly/affectionately to him?
19 **sere** shrivelled up.
21 **ungentle** ignoble.
21 **unkind** unnatural.
22 **Stigmatical in making** Deformed in his shape.
24 **No... gone.** We never cry for something horrible when we have lost it.
26 **would... worse** i.e. I wish others couldn't see his faults so clearly.
27 **Far... away** Like the lapwing (who runs from her nest to lead predators away from her eggs) her words are decoys to her true feelings.
29 Dromio seems to be checking through his instructions in his head to be sure he has them correct ('sweet') while he runs to the house.
32 **Tartar limbo** the prison ('limbo') of Tartarus (the classical hell).
33 **everlasting garment** a garment of the durable material (sometimes leather, sometimes a woollen substitute) called 'durance' from which uniforms were made.
36 **buff** a coarse, hard-wearing leather uniform.
37–39 **A back... well** All variations on an arresting officer: one who, while claiming to be a friend, is a foe behind your back (with a pun on someone who 'claps' you on the shoulder, as the officer has done to Antipholus); one who ambushes folk trying to escape down narrow lanes, allies, and passages; a hunting dog who runs around ('counter' to the direction of the chase) to get in front of the quarry; and yet can track it by the scent left by its feet well too.
41–42 **what... case** Adriana asks what is going on; Dromio quibbles that he does not know the precise nature of the charge (the 'matter' of the case), but knows Antipholus was arrested on an ad hoc warrant (''rested on the case') rather than under a specified law.
45 **he's... tell** I know the one who arrested him wore a suit of buff.
49 **on a band** for breaking a bond.

DROMIO OF SYRACUSE
Not on a band, but on a stronger thing:
A chain, a chain... Do you not hear it ring?

ADRIANA
What, the chain?

DROMIO OF SYRACUSE
No, no, the bell. 'Tis time that I were gone.
It was two ere I left him, and now the clock strikes one.

ADRIANA
The hours come back? That did I never hear.

DROMIO OF SYRACUSE
Oh yes, if any hour meet a sergeant, a turns back for very fear.

ADRIANA
As if time were in debt! How fondly dost thou reason.

DROMIO OF SYRACUSE
Time is a very bankrupt, and owes more than he's worth to season.
Nay, he's a thief too, have you not heard men say
That time comes stealing on by night and day?
If a be in debt and theft, and a sergeant in the way,
Hath he not reason to turn back an hour in a day?

Enter Luciana.

ADRIANA
Go Dromio, there's the money, bear it straight,
And bring thy master home immediately.
Come sister, I am pressed down with conceit:
Conceit, my comfort and my injury. *Ex*[*eunt.*]

[Act IV. Scene iii.]

Enter Antipholus of Syracuse.

ANTIPHOLUS OF SYRACUSE
There's not a man I meet but doth salute me
As if I were their well-acquainted friend,
And every one doth call me by my name.
Some tender money to me, some invite me;
Some other give me thanks for kindnesses;
Some offer me commodities to buy.
Even now a tailor called me in his shop
And showed me silks that he had bought for me,
And therewithal took measure of my body.
Sure these are but imaginary wiles,
And Lapland sorcerers inhabit here.

Enter Dromio of Syracuse.

DROMIO OF SYRACUSE
Master, here's the gold you sent me for. What, have you got the picture of old Adam new-apparelled?

ANTIPHOLUS OF SYRACUSE
What gold is this? What Adam dost thou mean?

DROMIO OF SYRACUSE
Not that Adam that kept the Paradise, but that Adam that keeps the prison; he that goes in the calf's skin, that was killed for the Prodigal; he that came behind you sir, like an evil angel, and bid you forsake your liberty.

ANTIPHOLUS OF SYRACUSE
I understand thee not.

DROMIO OF SYRACUSE
No? Why, 'tis a plain case: he that went like a bass viol in a case of leather; the man, sir, that when gentlemen are tired gives them a sob, and 'rests them; he, sir, that takes pity on decayed men and

56 **sergeant** arresting officer.
56 **a** he.
57 **fondly** foolishly.
58 **more... season** uncertain: perhaps 'more than he's worth at any given time' or 'more than it would be worth to make him acceptable' (to 'season' him, as with salt and pepper).
60 **stealing** punning on 'thieving' and 'creeping'.
65 **pressed... conceit** oppressed with thoughts (both fears and hopes).
1 **salute** greet.
4 **tender** offer.
5 **invite me** i.e. to their homes.
10 **imaginary wiles** tricks of the imagination.
11 **Lapland sorcerers** Lapland was famed for witchcraft and wizardry.
12–13 **What... new-apparelled?** Another difficult line. The sense is, 'what have you done with the officer whom I saw arresting you just now?' The reference is to the fallen Adam, clothed in skins for his expulsion from Eden. Perhaps the connection is that the officer suggests to Dromio the likeness of 'the offending Adam' in his buff coat, and he wonders how Antipholus has achieved the god-like feat of both clothing him and expelling him so quickly.
16–17 **he... Prodigal** Another riff on the officer's buff leather coat. 'He who walks around in the skin of the calf slaughtered for the Prodigal son. (See Luke 15: 23–4: 'And bring hither the fatted calf, and kill it, and let us eat and make merry: because this my son... was lost, and is found'.)
21 **bass viol** a large stringed instrument.
23 Punning on 'sob': a break given to rest tired horses, and 'arrest'. Dromio is clearly enjoying this game of coining euphemistic descriptions of the officer.
23 **decayed** bankrupt.

gives them suits of durance; he that sets up his rest
to do more exploits with his mace than a morris-pike.

ANTIPHOLUS OF SYRACUSE

What? Thou mean'st an officer?

DROMIO OF SYRACUSE

Aye sir, the sergeant of the band; he that brings any
man to answer it that breaks his band. One that
thinks a man always going to bed, and saith,
God give you good rest.

ANTIPHOLUS OF SYRACUSE

Well, sir, there rest in your foolery.
Is there any ship puts forth tonight? May we be gone?

DROMIO OF SYRACUSE

Why, sir, I brought you word an hour since that the
bark *Expedition* put forth to night, and then, were you
hindered by the sergeant, to tarry for the hoy *Delay*.
Here are the angels that you sent for to deliver you.

ANTIPHOLUS OF SYRACUSE

The fellow is distract, and so am I,
And here we wander in illusions.
Some blessed power deliver us from hence.

Enter a Courtesan.

COURTESAN

Well met, well met, Master Antipholus.
I see sir, you have found the goldsmith now.
Is that the chain you promised me today?

ANTIPHOLUS OF SYRACUSE

Satan avoid; I charge thee, tempt me not.

DROMIO OF SYRACUSE

Master, is this Mistress Satan?

ANTIPHOLUS OF SYRACUSE

It is the devil.

DROMIO OF SYRACUSE

Nay, she is worse, she is the devil's dam. And
here she comes in the habit of a light wench, and
thereof comes that the wenches say, 'God damn me'.
That's as much to say, 'God make me a light wench'.
It is written, they appear to men like angels of light;
light is an effect of fire, and fire will burn; ergo,
light wenches will burn. Come not near her.

COURTESAN

Your man and you are marvellous merry sir.
Will you go with me, we'll mend our dinner here?

DROMIO OF SYRACUSE

Master, if you do, expect spoon-meat, or bespeak
a long spoon.

ANTIPHOLUS OF SYRACUSE

Why Dromio?

DROMIO OF SYRACUSE

Marry he must have a long spoon that must eat with
the devil.

ANTIPHOLUS OF SYRACUSE

Avoid then, fiend, what tell'st thou me of supping?
Thou art, (as you are all) a sorceress.
I conjure thee to leave me and be gone.

COURTESAN

Give me the ring of mine you had at dinner,
Or for my diamond the chain you promised,
And I'll be gone sir, and not trouble you.

DROMIO OF SYRACUSE

Some devils ask but the parings of one's nail,
a rush, a hair, a drop of blood, a pin, a nut, a
cherry-stone, but she, more covetous, would have

[24] **suits of durance** hard-wearing prison clothes/lawsuits involving lengthy sentences (requiring 'endurance').
[24–25] **he … morris-pike** he who stakes everything he has (with another pun on 'rest'/'arrest') on performing more with his staff of office ('mace') than a soldier does with his 'Moorish' pike.
[28] **sergeant … band** punning on a sergeant as the leader of a troop ('band') of soldiers and the man who arrests people for defaulting on 'bonds'.
[29–30] **One … rest.** He who says 'I wish you a good rest (arrest)' as if he thought everyone was going to bed.
[34] **put forth** leaves harbour.
[35] **hoy** (good) ship.
[36] **angels** gold coins.
[37] **distract** distracted/mad.
[43] **avoid** be gone. (Christ's words to Satan in Matthew 4:1, according to the Geneva Bible.)
[46] **dam** mother.
[47–48] **habit … say** clothes/appearance of a wanton girl/strumpet, and that's why such girls say.
[50] **It … light** see 2 Corinthians 11:14, 'for Satan himself transformeth himself into an angel of light'.
[51] **ergo** therefore.
[52] **burn** was a slang term for passing on venereal diseases. Dromio's mock syllogism 'proves' that prostitutes will give a man syphilis.
[54] **we'll … dinner** complete the dinner we started earlier.
[55] **expect … bespeak** expect soft food edible with a spoon, or call for.
[57] **he … devil** proverbial (i.e. if you dine with the devil, be very careful).
[58] **what … supping?** why do you talk to me of dining?
[64–66] **parings … cherry-stone** things that might be used in spells or potions.

a chain. Master be wise, and if you give it her,
the devil will shake her chain, and fright us with it.

COURTESAN
I pray you, sir, my ring, or else the chain.
I hope you do not mean to cheat me so?

ANTIPHOLUS OF SYRACUSE
Avaunt thou witch! Come Dromio, let us go.

DROMIO OF SYRACUSE
'Fly pride', says the peacock; Mistress that you know.

[*Exeunt.*]

COURTESAN
Now, out of doubt Antipholus is mad,
Else would he never so demean himself.
A ring he hath of mine worth forty ducats,
And for the same he promised me a chain;
Both one and other he denies me now.
The reason that I gather he is mad
(Besides this present instance of his rage)
Is a mad tale he told today at dinner,
Of his own doors being shut against his entrance.
Belike his wife, acquainted with his fits,
On purpose shut the doors against his way.
My way is now to hie home to his house,
And tell his wife that, being lunatic,
He rushed into my house and took perforce
My ring away. This course I fittest choose,
For forty ducats is too much to lose. [*Exit.*]

[Act IV. Scene iv.]

Enter Antipholus of Ephesus with a Jailor [Officer].

ANTIPHOLUS OF EPHESUS
Fear me not, man, I will not break away.
I'll give thee, ere I leave thee, so much money
To warrant thee as I am 'rested for.
My wife is in a wayward mood today,
And will not lightly trust the messenger,
That I should be attached in Ephesus;
I tell you, 'twill sound harshly in her ears.

Enter Dromio of Ephesus with a rope's-end.

Here comes my man, I think he brings the money.
How now sir? Have you that I sent you for?

DROMIO OF EPHESUS
Here's that I warrant you will pay them all.

ANTIPHOLUS OF EPHESUS
But where's the money?

DROMIO OF EPHESUS
Why sir, I gave the money for the rope.

ANTIPHOLUS OF EPHESUS
Five hundred ducats, villain, for a rope?

DROMIO OF EPHESUS
I'll serve you, sir, five hundred at the rate.

ANTIPHOLUS OF EPHESUS
To what end did I bid thee hie thee home?

DROMIO OF EPHESUS
To a rope's-end sir, and to that end am I returned.

ANTIPHOLUS OF EPHESUS
And to that end sir, I will welcome you.

[*Threatens to beat him.*]

OFFICER
Good sir, be patient.

DROMIO OF EPHESUS
Nay 'tis for me to be patient, I am in adversity.

OFFICER
Good now, hold thy tongue.

DROMIO OF EPHESUS
Nay, rather persuade him to hold his hands.

ANTIPHOLUS OF EPHESUS
Thou whoreson, senseless villain!

DROMIO OF EPHESUS
I would I were senseless, sir, that I might not feel your blows.

ANTIPHOLUS OF EPHESUS
Thou art sensible in nothing but blows, and so is an ass.

DROMIO OF EPHESUS
I am an ass indeed, you may prove it by my
long ears. I have served him from the hour
of my nativity to this instant, and have nothing
at his hands for my service but blows. When

[72] **Fly...peacock** Peacocks were proverbially proud. Dromio suggests that a prostitute complaining about being cheated is as hypocritical as a peacock warning against pride.
[73] **out of doubt** certainly.
[74] **so demean himself** behave like this.
[86] **perforce** by force.
[87] **This...choose** This I choose as the best course of action.
[5–7] **will...ears** she will not readily believe Dromio's story that I have been arrested in my home town. It will sound odd to her.

[10] **pay them all** repay them all (with a beating).
[14] **I'll...rate.** I'll sell you five hundred ropes' ends if you will pay that much for one.
[15] **To what end** For what purpose.
[23] **would** wish.
[24] **Thou...blows** You understand/respond to nothing but blows.
[26] **long ears** possibly punning on 'long years' of service.

I am cold, he heats me with beating; when I am warm, he cools me with beating; I am waked with it when I sleep; raised with it when I sit; driven out of doors with it when I go from home; welcomed home with it when I return; nay I bear it on my shoulders, as a beggar wont her brat; and I think when he hath lamed me, I shall beg with it from door to door.

Enter Adriana, Luciana, Courtesan, and a schoolmaster called Pinch.

ANTIPHOLUS OF EPHESUS
Come, go along, my wife is coming yonder.

DROMIO OF EPHESUS
Mistress *respice finem*: respect your end;
Or, rather, t[o] prophecy like the parrot, 'Beware the rope's end'.

ANTIPHOLUS OF EPHESUS
Wilt thou still talk? *Beats Dro[mio].*

COURTESAN
How say you now? Is not your husband mad?

ADRIANA
His incivility confirms no less.
Good Doctor Pinch, you are a conjurer,
Establish him in his true sense again,
And I will please you what you will demand.

LUCIANA
Alas, how fiery and how sharp he looks.

COURTESAN
Mark how he trembles in his ecstasy.

PINCH
Give me your hand, and let me feel your pulse.

ANTIPHOLUS OF EPHESUS
There is my hand, and let it feel your ear.

PINCH
I charge thee, Satan, housed within this man
To yield possession to my holy prayers,
And to thy state of darkness hie thee straight;
I conjure thee by all the saints in heaven.

ANTIPHOLUS OF EPHESUS
Peace, doting wizard, peace! I am not mad.

ADRIANA
Oh that thou were't not, poor distressed soul.

ANTIPHOLUS OF EPHESUS
You minion you, are these your customers?
Did this companion with the saffron face
Revel and feast it at my house today,
Whilst upon me the guilty doors were shut,
And I denied to enter in my house?

ADRIANA
O husband, God doth know you dined at home,
Where would you had remained until this time,
Free from these slanders and this open shame.

ANTIPHOLUS OF EPHESUS
Dined at home? Thou villain, what sayest thou?

DROMIO OF EPHESUS
Sir, sooth to say, you did not dine at home.

ANTIPHOLUS OF EPHESUS
Were not my doors locked up, and I shut out?

DROMIO OF EPHESUS
Perdie, your doors were locked, and you shut out.

ANTIPHOLUS OF EPHESUS
And did not she herself revile me there?

DROMIO OF EPHESUS
Sans fable, she herself reviled you there.

ANTIPHOLUS OF EPHESUS
Did not her kitchen-maid rail, taunt, and scorn me?

DROMIO OF EPHESUS
Certes she did; the kitchen vestal scorned you.

Antipholus of Ephesus

And did not I in rage depart from thence?

DROMIO OF EPHESUS
In verity you did; my bones bear witness,
That since have felt the vigour of his rage.

ADRIANA
Is't good to soothe him in these contraries?

[31] **it** beating.
[34] **wont** does.
[38] ***respice finem*** lit. 'think on your end' a *memento mori*.
[39] **t[o]** the folio has 'the'.
[44] **a conjurer** an exorcist. As a schoolmaster, Pinch might be thought learned enough to use the Latin prayers and spells to expel evil spirits.
[46] **please you** reward you with.
[48] **Mark** Note.
[55] **Peace, doting wizard** Silence, foolish wizard.
[57] **minion** whore.
[58] **saffron** yellow/sallow.
[63] **would** if only.
[68] **Perdie** By God (*par Dieu*)/truly.
[70] ***Sans* fable** Without telling stories (i.e. truly).
[72] **Certes** Certainly.
[72] **vestal** virgin/servant (ironic).
[76] **soothe...contraries** appease him in his delusions.

PINCH
It is no shame, the fellow finds his vein,
And yielding to him, humours well his frenzy.
ANTIPHOLUS OF EPHESUS
Thou hast suborned the goldsmith to arrest me.
ADRIANA
Alas, I sent you money to redeem you
By Dromio here, who came in haste for it.
DROMIO OF EPHESUS
Money by me? Heart and goodwill you might,
But surely, master, not a rag of money.
ANTIPHOLUS OF EPHESUS
Went'st not thou to her for a purse of ducats?
ADRIANA
He came to me and I delivered it.
LUCIANA
And I am witness with her that she did.
DROMIO OF EPHESUS
God and the rope-maker bear me witness,
That I was sent for nothing but a rope.
PINCH
Mistress, both man and master is possessed,
I know it by their pale and deadly looks.
They must be bound and laid in some dark room.
ANTIPHOLUS OF EPHESUS
Say, wherefore didst thou lock me forth today,
And why dost thou deny the bag of gold?
ADRIANA
I did not, gentle husband, lock thee forth.
DROMIO OF EPHESUS
And, gentle master, I received no gold.
But I confess, sir, that we were locked out.
ADRIANA
Dissembling villain, thou speak'st false in both.
ANTIPHOLUS OF EPHESUS
Dissembling harlot, thou art false in all,
And art confederate with a damned pack
To make a loathsome, abject scorn of me.
But with these nails I'll pluck out these false eyes,
That would behold in me this shameful sport.

Enter three or four, and offer to bind him: He strives.

ADRIANA
O bind him, bind him, let him not come near me.
PINCH
More company, the fiend is strong within him.
LUCIANA
Ay me, poor man, how pale and wan he looks.
ANTIPHOLUS OF EPHESUS
What, will you murder me, thou gaoler thou?
I am thy prisoner, wilt thou suffer them
To make a rescue?
OFFICER
Masters, let him go;
He is my prisoner, and you shall not have him.
PINCH
Go, bind this man, for he is frantic too.
ADRIANA
What wilt thou do, thou peevish officer?
Hast thou delight to see a wretched man
Do outrage and displeasure to himself?
OFFICER
He is my prisoner, if I let him go,
The debt he owes will be required of me.
ADRIANA
I will discharge thee ere I go from thee.
Bear me forthwith unto his creditor,
And, knowing how the debt grows, I will pay it.
Good master doctor, see him safe conveyed
Home to my house; O most unhappy day.
ANTIPHOLUS OF EPHESUS
O most unhappy strumpet!
DROMIO OF EPHESUS
Master, I am here entered in bond for you.
ANTIPHOLUS OF EPHESUS
Out on thee villain, wherefore dost thou mad me?
DROMIO OF EPHESUS
Will you be bound for nothing? Be mad, good master,
cry the devil.

77 **finds his vein** understands his train of thought.
82–83 **Heart . . . money.** You might have heart and goodwill from me, but I've not got even a bit of money.
88 **is** are.
98 **art confederate** (you) are conspiring.
101.1 **offer** attempt.
101.1 **strives** fights (with them).
103 **More company** Fetch more men.
111 **peevish** stubborn/spiteful.
118 **knowing . . . grows** once I know how the debt was created (and how much it amounts to).
122 **entered in bond** tied up (punning on 'guarantee a bond').
123 **wherefore . . . me?** why must you enrage me so?
125 **cry the devil** call upon the devil (to free us).

LUCIANA
God help poor souls, how idly do they talk.
ADRIANA
Go, bear him hence; sister, go you with me.
Say now, whose suit is he arrested at?

Exeunt. Manent Officer, Adriana, Luciana, and Courtesan.

OFFICER
One Angelo a goldsmith; do you know him?
ADRIANA
I know the man. What is the sum he owes?
OFFICER
Two hundred ducats.
ADRIANA
Say, how grows it due?
OFFICER
Due for a chain your husband had of him.
ADRIANA
He did bespeak a chain for me, but had it not.
COURTESAN
Whenas your husband, all in rage, today
Came to my house, and took away my ring,
(The ring I saw upon his finger now),
Straight after did I meet him with a chain.
ADRIANA
It may be so, but I did never see it.
Come, jailor, bring me where the goldsmith is,
I long to know the truth hereof at large.

Enter Antipholus of Syracuse, with his rapier drawn, and Dromio of Syracuse.

LUCIANA
God for thy mercy, they are loose again.
ADRIANA
And come with naked swords!
Let's call more help to have them bound again.

Run all out.

OFFICER
Away, they'll kill us!

Exeunt omnes, as fast as may be, frighted.

ANTIPHOLUS OF SYRACUSE
I see these witches are afraid of swords.
DROMIO OF SYRACUSE
She that would be your wife now ran from you.
ANTIPHOLUS OF SYRACUSE
Come to the Centaur, fetch our stuff from thence.
I long that we were safe and sound aboard.
DROMIO OF SYRACUSE
Faith, stay here this night, they will surely do us no harm. You saw they speak us fair, give us gold, me thinks they are such a gentle nation that, but for the mountain of mad flesh that claims marriage of me, I could find in my heart to stay here still, and turn witch.
ANTIPHOLUS OF SYRACUSE
I will not stay tonight for all the town;
Therefore away, to get our stuff aboard. *Exeunt.*

Actus Quintus. Scena Prima.

Enter the [Second] Merchant and the goldsmith [Angelo].

ANGELO
I am sorry, sir, that I have hindered you,
But I protest he had the chain of me,
Though most dishonestly he doth deny it.
SECOND MERCHANT
How is the man esteemed here in the city?
ANGELO
Of very reverend reputation, sir,
Of credit infinite, highly beloved.
Second to none that lives here in the city,
His word might bear my wealth at any time.
SECOND MERCHANT
Speak softly, yonder as I think, he walks.

Enter Antipholus and Dromio of Syracuse again.

ANGELO
'Tis so: and that self chain about his neck
Which he forswore (most monstrously) to have.

127 **bear him hence** carry him away.
128.1 *Manent* (the following should) remain.
133 **bespeak** commission.
134 **Whenas** when.
140 **at large** in full.
142 **naked** unsheathed.
144.1 *Exeunt*... **frighted.** Exit everyone, as quickly as they can, terrified.
154 **turn** become a.
4 **How... esteemed** What is his reputation/credit.
8 **His... wealth** He could borrow as much as I am worth on the strength of his word alone.
10 **self** same.

Good sir, draw near to me, I'll speak to him.
Signor Antipholus, I wonder much
That you would put me to this shame and trouble,
And not without some scandal to yourself,
With circumstance and oaths, so to deny
This chain, which now you wear so openly.
Beside the charge, the shame, imprisonment,
You have done wrong to this my honest friend,
Who but for staying on our controversy,
Had hoisted sail, and put to sea today.
This chain you had of me; can you deny it?

ANTIPHOLUS OF SYRACUSE
I think I had, I never did deny it.

SECOND MERCHANT
Yes, that you did sir, and forswore it too.

ANTIPHOLUS OF SYRACUSE
Who heard me to deny it or forswear it?

SECOND MERCHANT
These ears of mine, thou know'st did hear thee.
Fie on thee wretch, 'tis pity that thou liv'st
To walk where any honest man resort.

ANTIPHOLUS OF SYRACUSE
Thou art a villain to impeach me thus.
I'll prove mine honour, and mine honesty
Against thee presently, if thou darest stand.

SECOND MERCHANT
I dare, and do defy thee for a villain.

They draw. Enter Adrian, Luciana, the Courtesan, and others.

ADRIANA
Hold, hurt him not for God's sake, he is mad.
Some get within him, take his sword away.
Bind Dromio too, and bear them to my house.

DROMIO OF SYRACUSE
Run master, run, for God's sake take a house,
This is some priory. In, or we are spoiled.

Exeunt [Antipholus and Dromio of Syracuse] to the priory. Enter Lady Abbess [Emilia].

EMILIA
Be quiet people, wherefore throng you hither?

ADRIANA
To fetch my poor distracted husband hence.
Let us come in, that we may bind him fast,
And bear him home for his recovery.

ANGELO
I knew he was not in his perfect wits.

SECOND MERCHANT
I am sorry now that I did draw on him.

EMILIA
How long hath this possession held the man?

ADRIANA
This week he hath been heavy, sour, sad,
And much different from the man he was.
But till this afternoon his passion
Ne'er brake into extremity of rage.

EMILIA
Hath he not lost much wealth by wreck of sea,
Buried some dear friend? Hath not else his eye
Strayed his affection in unlawful love,
A sin prevailing much in youthful men,
Who give their eyes the liberty of gazing.
Which of these sorrows is he subject to?

ADRIANA
To none of these, except it be the last,
Namely, some love that drew him oft from home.

EMILIA
You should for that have reprehended him.

ADRIANA
Why so I did.

EMILIA
Aye, but not rough enough.

ADRIANA
As roughly as my modesty would let me.

EMILIA
Haply in private.

ADRIANA
And in assemblies too.

EMILIA
Aye, but not enough.

16 **circumstance** excuse(s).
20 **but...controversy** if he hadn't had to delay owing to our argument.
31 **presently...stand** immediately, if you dare defend yourself (in a duel).
34 **within him** in close to him (inside his guard).
36 **take a house** take shelter in some house.
37 **In...spoiled.** Get inside, or we're done for.
45 **sad** sombre/grave.
49 **by wreck of sea** by the wreck of one of his ships at sea.
50 **Hath...eye** Or has his eye not.
60 **Haply in private** Probably only in private.

ADRIANA
It was the copy of our conference.
In bed he slept not for my urging it,
At board he fed not for my urging it.
Alone it was the subject of my theme.
In company I often glanced it;
Still did I tell him it was vile and bad.

EMILIA
And thereof came it that the man was mad!
The venom clamours of a jealous woman
Poisons more deadly than a mad dog's tooth.
It seems his sleeps were hindered by thy railing,
And therefore comes it that his head is light.
Thou say'st his meat was sauced with thy upbraidings,
Unquiet meals make ill digestions.
Thereof the raging fire of fever bred,
And what's a fever but a fit of madness?
Thou say'st his sports were hindered by thy brawls.
Sweet recreation barred, what doth ensue
But moody and dull melancholy,
Kinsman to grim and comfortless despair;
And at her heels a huge infectious troop
Of pale distemperatures and foes to life?
In food, in sport, and life-preserving rest
To be disturbed, would mad or man or beast.
The consequence is, then, thy jealous fits
Have scared thy husband from the use of wits.

LUCIANA
She never reprehended him but mildly,
When he demeaned himself rough, rude, and wildly.
Why bear you these rebukes, and answer not?

ADRIANA
She did betray me to my own reproof,
Good people enter and lay hold on him.

EMILIA
No, not a creature enters in my house.

ADRIANA
Then let your servants bring my husband forth.

EMILIA
Neither; he took this place for sanctuary,
And it shall privilege him from your hands,
Till I have brought him to his wits again,
Or lose my labour in assaying it.

ADRIANA
I will attend my husband, be his nurse,
Diet his sickness, for it is my office,
And will have no attorney but myself.
And therefore, let me have him home with me.

EMILIA
Be patient, for I will not let him stir
Till I have used the approved means I have,
With wholesome syrups, drugs, and holy prayers,
To make of him a formal man again.
It is a branch and parcel of mine oath,
A charitable duty of my order.
Therefore depart, and leave him here with me.

ADRIANA
I will not hence, and leave my husband here.
And ill it doth beseem your holiness
To separate the husband and the wife.

EMILIA
Be quiet and depart; thou shalt not have him.

LUCIANA
Complain unto the duke of this indignity.

ADRIANA
Come, go, I will fall prostrate at his feet,
And never rise until my tears and prayers
Have won his grace to come in person hither,
And take perforce my husband from the abbess.

SECOND MERCHANT
By this I think, the dial points at five:
Anon, I'm sure the duke himself in person
Comes this way to the melancholy vale;
The place of death and sorry execution,
Behind the ditches of the abbey here.

62 **It . . . conference.** It was the subject of all our talk.
65 **Alone . . . theme.** It was all I talked about.
66 **glanced** hinted at.
67 **Still** Perpetually.
69 **venom clamours** poisonous cries.
73 **upbraidings** rebukes.
74 **Unquiet . . . digestions** Disturbed meals make for poor digestion.
77 **brawls** arguments.
82 **distemperatures** illnesses.
84 **would mad . . . beast** enrage either man or beast.
90 **She . . . reproof** She led me to criticize myself.
95 The right of sanctuary gave legal refuge to anyone who sought it.
97 **assaying it** attempting it.
100 **no attorney** no one to do it on my behalf.
104 **syrups** medicines.
105 **formal** proper.
106 **branch and parcel** an important part.
107 **order** sisterhood.
110 **ill . . . holiness** it is unbefitting your holy office.
118 **the dial . . . five** the clock shows five o'clock.
120 **vale** valley.
121 **sorry** sad.

ANGELO
Upon what cause?

SECOND MERCHANT
To see a reverend Syracusian merchant,
Who put unluckily into this bay
Against the laws and statutes of this town,
Beheaded publicly for his offence.

ANGELO
See where they come. We will behold his death.

LUCIANA
Kneel to the duke before he pass the abbey.

Enter the Duke of Ephesus and the merchant of Syracuse [Egeon], bare head[ed], with the Headsman and other officers.

DUKE
Yet once again proclaim it publicly:
If any friend will pay the sum for him,
He shall not die, so much we tender him.

ADRIANA
Justice, most sacred duke, against the abbess!

DUKE
She is a virtuous and a reverend lady,
It cannot be that she hath done thee wrong.

ADRIANA
May it please your grace, Antipholus, my husband,
Whom I made lord of me and all I had,
(At your important letters), this ill day
A most outrageous fit of madness took him,
That desp'rately he hurried through the street,
With him his bondman, all as mad as he,
Doing displeasure to the citizens,
By rushing in their houses, bearing thence
Rings, jewels, anything his rage did like.
Once did I get him bound, and sent him home,
Whil'st to take order for the wrongs I went
That here and there his fury had committed,
Anon, I wot not by what strong escape,
He broke from those that had the guard of him,
And with his mad attendant and himself,
Each one with ireful passion, with drawn swords
Met us again, and madly bent on us,
Chased us away till, raising of more aid,
We came again to bind them. Then they fled
Into this abbey, whither we pursued them;
And here the abbess shuts the gates on us,
And will not suffer us to fetch him out,
Nor send him forth that we may bear him hence.
Therefore, most gracious duke, with thy command
Let him be brought forth, and borne hence for help.

DUKE
Long since thy husband served me in my wars,
And I to thee engaged a prince's word,
When thou did'st make him master of thy bed,
To do him all the grace and good I could.
Go, some of you, knock at the abbey gate,
And bid the Lady Abbess come to me:
I will determine this before I stir.

Enter a Messenger.

MESSENGER
O mistress, mistress, shift and save yourself,
My master and his man are both broke loose,
Beaten the maids a-row, and bound the doctor,
Whose beard they have singed off with brands of fire,
And ever as it blazed, they threw on him
Great pails of puddled mire to quench the hair.
My master preaches patience to him, and the while
His man with scissors nicks him like a fool.
And sure (unless you send some present help)
Between them they will kill the conjurer.

ADRIANA
Peace fool, thy master and his man are here,
And that is false thou dost report to us.

MESSENGER
Mistress, upon my life, I tell you true,
I have not breathed almost since I did see it.
He cries for you, and vows if he can take you,
To scorch your face, and to disfigure you.

Cry within.

129.1 **Headsman** Executioner.
132 **tender him** will do for him.
137–138 **Whom ... letters** Whom I married at your importunate urging (by letter).
141 **bondman** slave.
146–147 **Whil'st ... committed** While I went around trying to discover (and put right) the inconveniences he had caused here and there.
148 **I ... escape** I know not by what violent/extraordinary means of escape.
152 **bent on us** charging towards us.
153 **raising ... aid** having gathered more helpers.
161 **Long since** Many years ago.
167 **determine ... stir** settle this matter before I leave here.
170 **a-row** one after the other.
173 **puddled mire** dirty water.
175 **nicks ... fool** madly snips his hair.

Hark, hark, I hear him mistress. Fly, be gone!

DUKE

Come, stand by me, fear nothing. Guard with halberds!

ADRIANA

Ay me, it is my husband. Witness you
That he is borne about invisible,
Even now we housed him in the abbey here,
And now he's there, past thought of human reason.

Enter Antipholus of Ephesus and Dromio of Ephesus.

ANTIPHOLUS OF EPHESUS

Justice, most gracious duke, O grant me justice,
Even for the service that long since I did thee,
When I bestrid thee in the wars, and took
Deep scars to save thy life; even for the blood
That then I lost for thee, now grant me justice.

MERCHANT OF SYRACUSE [EGEON]

Unless the fear of death doth make me dote,
I see my son Antipholus, and Dromio.

ANTIPHOLUS OF EPHESUS

Justice (sweet prince) against that woman there.
She whom thou gav'st to me to be my wife;
That hath abusèd and dishonoured me,
Even in the strength and height of injury.
Beyond imagination is the wrong
That she this day hath shameless thrown on me.

DUKE

Discover how, and thou shalt find me just.

ANTIPHOLUS OF EPHESUS

This day, great duke, she shut the doors upon me,
While she with harlots feasted in my house.

DUKE

A grievous fault. Say woman, didst thou so?

ADRIANA

No, my good lord. Myself, he, and my sister,
Today did dine together; so, befall my soul
As this is false he burdens me withal.

LUCIANA

Ne'er may I look on day, nor sleep on night,
But she tells to your highness simple truth.

ANGELO

O perjured woman! They are both forsworn.
In this the madman justly chargeth them.

ANTIPHOLUS OF EPHESUS

My liege, I am advised what I say,
Neither disturbed with the effect of wine,
Nor heady-rash provoked with raging ire,
Albeit my wrongs might make one wiser mad.
This woman locked me out this day from dinner;
That goldsmith there, were he not packed with her,
Could witness it, for he was with me then,
Who parted with me to go fetch a chain,
Promising to bring it to the Porpentine,
Where Balthazar and I did dine together.
Our dinner done, and he not coming thither,
I went to seek him. In the street I met him,
And in his company that gentleman.
There did this perjured goldsmith swear me down
That I this day of him received the chain,
Which, God he knows, I saw not. For the which,
He did arrest me with an officer.
I did obey, and sent my peasant home
For certain ducats. He with none returned.
Then fairly I bespoke the officer
To go in person with me to my house.
By th'way we met my wife, her sister, and a rabble more
Of vile confederates. Along with them
They brought one Pinch, a hungry lean-faced villain;
A mere anatomy, a mountebank,
A threadbare juggler, and a fortune-teller,
A needy, hollow-eyed, sharp-looking wretch;
A living dead man. This pernicious slave,
Forsooth, took on him as a conjurer:
And, gazing in mine eyes, feeling my pulse,
And with no-face (as 'twere) outfacing me,

185 **Guard with halberds!** Protect us with your poleaxes!
189 **past . . . reason** it's impossible to know how.
192 **bestrid thee** stood over your fallen body.
203 **Discover how** Tell me how.
208–209 **so . . . withal** I pledge my soul that what he accuses me of is false.
214 **I am . . . say** I speak with due care and seriousness.
216 **heady-rash provoked** provoked to passionate rashness.
219 **packed** conspiring.
227 **swear me down** swore to my face.
231 **peasant** servant (Dromio).
233 **fairly I bespoke** asked the officer politely.
238 **A mere . . . mountebank** A human skeleton, a con-man.
242 **took . . . conjurer** began to act as a conjuror.
244 **with . . . me** defied (out-faced) me with his (scrawny) non-face.

Cries out I was possessed. Then all together
They fell upon me, bound me, bore me thence,
And in a dark and dankish vault at home
There left me and my man, both bound together,
Till, gnawing with my teeth my bonds asunder,
I gained my freedom; and immediately
Ran hither to your grace; whom I beseech
To give me ample satisfaction
For these deep shames, and great indignities.

ANGELO
My lord, in truth, thus far I witness with him:
That he dined not at home, but was locked out.

DUKE
But had he such a chain of thee, or no?

ANGELO
He had, my lord; and when he ran in here,
These people saw the chain about his neck.

MERCHANT
Besides, I will be sworn these ears of mine
Heard you confess you had the chain of him,
After you first forswore it on the mart,
And thereupon I drew my sword on you.
And then you fled into this abbey here,
From whence I think you are come by miracle.

ANTIPHOLUS OF EPHESUS
I never came within these abbey walls,
Nor ever didst thou draw thy sword on me.
I never saw the chain, so help me heaven.
And this is false you burden me withal.

DUKE
Why, what an intricate impeach is this?
I think you all have drunk of Circe's cup.
If here you housed him, here he would have been.
If he were mad, he would not plead so coldly.
You say he dined at home, the goldsmith here
Denies that, saying... Sirrah, what say you?

DROMIO OF EPHESUS
Sir, he dined with her there, at the Porpentine.

COURTESAN
He did, and from my finger snatched that ring.

ANTIPHOLUS OF EPHESUS
'Tis true, my liege, this ring I had of her.

DUKE
Saw'st thou him enter at the abbey here?

COURTESAN
As sure, my liege, as I do see your grace.

DUKE
Why, this is strange. Go call the abbess hither.
I think you are all mated, or stark mad.

Exit one to the Abbess.

EGEON
Most mighty duke, vouchsafe me speak a word.
Haply I see a friend will save my life,
And pay the sum that may deliver me.

DUKE
Speak freely Syracusian, what thou wilt.

EGEON
Is not your name, sir, called Antipholus?
And is not that your bondman Dromio?

DROMIO OF EPHESUS
Within this hour I was his bondman sir,
But he, I thank him, gnawed in two my cords,
Now am I Dromio, and his man unbound.

EGEON
I am sure you both of you remember me.

DROMIO OF EPHESUS
Ourselves we do remember sir, by you.
For lately we were bound as you are now.
You are not Pinch's patient, are you, sir?

EGEON
Why look you strange on me? You know
me well.

ANTIPHOLUS OF EPHESUS
I never saw you in my life till now.

EGEON
O, grief hath changed me since you saw me last,
And careful hours with time's deformed hand
Have written strange defeatures in my face:
But tell me yet, dost thou not know my voice?

252 **satisfaction** redress.
261 **forswore** denied.
269 **what... impeach** what contradictory testimony.
270 **of Circe's cup** the potion of the witch Circe, who transformed Odysseus's crew into swine (see book x of Homer's *Odyssey*).
272 **coldly** calmly.
275 **her there** the Courtesan.
281 **all mated** terminally confused.
one someone.
292 **Ourselves... you.** You remind us of ourselves (as you are bound, as we were).
295 **strange** strangely/unrecognizing.
298 **careful hours** hours filled with care/worry.
299 **defeatures** disfigurements.

ANTIPHOLUS OF EPHESUS
Neither.

EGEON
Dromio, nor thou?

DROMIO OF EPHESUS
No trust me sir, nor I.

EGEON
I am sure thou dost?

DROMIO OF EPHESUS
Aye, sir, but I am sure I do not, and whatsoever a man denies, you are now bound to believe him.

EGEON
Not know my voice! O time's extremity,
Hast thou so cracked and splitted my poor tongue
In seven short years that here my only son
Knows not my feeble key of untuned cares?
Though now this grainèd face of mine be hid
In sap-consuming winter's drizzled snow,
And all the conduits of my blood froze up,
Yet hath my night of life some memory,
My wasting lamps some fading glimmer left,
My dull deaf ears a little use to hear.
All these old witnesses, I cannot err,
Tell me thou art my son, Antipholus.

ANTIPHOLUS OF EPHESUS
I never saw my father in my life.

EGEON
But seven years since, in Syracusa, boy,
Thou know'st we parted, but perhaps, my son,
Thou sham'st to acknowledge me in misery.

ANTIPHOLUS OF EPHESUS
The duke, and all that know me in the city,
Can witness with me that it is not so.
I ne'er saw Syracusa in my life.

DUKE
I tell thee, Syracusian, twenty years
Have I been patron to Antipholus,
During which time he ne'er saw Syracusa.
I see thy age and dangers make thee dote.

Enter the Abbess [Emilia] with Antipholus and Dromio of Syracuse.

EMILIA
Most mighty duke, behold a man much wronged.

All gather to see them.

ADRIANA
I see two husbands, or mine eyes deceive me.

DUKE
One of these men is *genius* to the other.
And so of these, which is the natural man,
And which the spirit? Who deciphers them?

DROMIO OF SYRACUSE
I, sir, am Dromio; command him away.

DROMIO OF EPHESUS
I, sir, am Dromio; pray let me stay.

ANTIPHOLUS OF SYRACUSE
Egeon art thou not, Or else his ghost?

DROMIO OF SYRACUSE
O, my old master, who hath bound him here?

EMILIA
Whoever bound him, I will loose his bonds,
And gain a husband by his liberty.
Speak, old Egeon, if thou be'st the man
That had'st a wife once, called Emilia,
That bore thee at a burden two fair sons?
O, if thou be'st the same Egeon, speak,
And speak unto the same Emilia.

DUKE
Why, here begins his morning story right.
These two Antipholuses, these two so like,
And these two Dromios, one in semblance,
Besides her urging of her wreck at sea,
These are the parents to these children,
Which accidently are met together.

EGEON
If I dream not, thou art Emilia.
If thou art she, tell me where is that son
That floated with thee on the fatal raft?

EMILIA
By men of Epidamnum, he and I
And the twin Dromio, all were taken up;
But by and by, rude fishermen of Corinth

301 **Neither** Not that either.
306 **bound** another pun on 'obliged/tied up'.
310 **my...cares** my feeble voice, made discordant by worries.
311 **grainèd** wrinkled/lined.
312 **sap-consuming...snow** i.e. a white beard.
313 **all...up** all my veins dried up/shrunken.
314 **hath...memory** I retain some memory at the end of my life.
322 **in misery** in my misery.
332 ***genius*** identical companion spirit or familiar.
334 **Who deciphers them?** Who can tell them apart?
343 **at a burden** in one labour.
346 **here...right** this confirms the start of the story he told me this morning.
348 **one in semblance** identical in appearance.

By force took Dromio and my son from them,
And me they left with those of Epidamnum.
What then became of them I cannot tell,
I to this fortune that you see me in.

DUKE
Antipholus, thou cam'st from Corinth first.

ANTIPHOLUS OF SYRACUSE
No, sir, not I; I came from Syracuse.

DUKE
Stay, stand apart, I know not which is which.

ANTIPHOLUS OF EPHESUS
I came from Corinth, my most gracious lord,

DROMIO OF EPHESUS
And I with him.

ANTIPHOLUS OF EPHESUS
Brought to this town by that most famous warrior,
Duke Menaphon, your most renownèd uncle.

ADRIANA
Which of you two did dine with me today?

ANTIPHOLUS OF SYRACUSE
I, gentle mistress.

ADRIANA
And are not you my husband?

ANTIPHOLUS OF EPHESUS
No, I say nay to that.

ANTIPHOLUS OF SYRACUSE
And so do I; yet did she call me so.
And this fair gentlewoman, her sister here,
Did call me brother. What I told you then,
I hope I shall have leisure to make good,
If this be not a dream I see and hear.

ANGELO
That is the chain, sir, which you had of me.

ANTIPHOLUS OF SYRACUSE
I think it be, sir, I deny it not.

ANTIPHOLUS OF EPHESUS
And you, sir, for this chain arrested me.

ANGELO
I think I did, sir, I deny it not.

ADRIANA
I sent you money, sir, to be your bail
By Dromio; but I think he brought it not.

DROMIO OF EPHESUS
No, none by me.

ANTIPHOLUS OF SYRACUSE
This purse of ducats I received from you,
And Dromio, my man, did bring them me.
I see we still did meet each other's man,
And I was ta'en for him, and he for me,
And thereupon these errors are arose.

ANTIPHOLUS OF EPHESUS
These ducats pawn I for my father here.

DUKE
It shall not need, thy father hath his life.

COURTESAN
Sir, I must have that diamond from you.

ANTIPHOLUS OF EPHESUS
There, take it, and much thanks for my good cheer.

EMILIA
Renownèd duke, vouchsafe to take the pains
To go with us into the abbey here,
And hear at large discoursèd all our fortunes.
And all that are assembled in this place,
That by this sympathizèd one day's error
Have suffered wrong, go, keep us company,
And we shall make full satisfaction.
Thirty-three years have I but gone in travail
Of you, my sons, and till this present hour
My heavy burden ne'er deliverèd.
The duke, my husband and my children both,
And you, the calendars of their nativity,
Go to a gossips' feast and go with me,
After so long grief, such festivity!

DUKE
With all my heart, I'll gossip at this feast.

Exeunt omnes. Manet the two Dromios and the two brothers [Antipholus].

DROMIO OF SYRACUSE
Master, shall I fetch your stuff from shipboard?

ANTIPHOLUS OF EPHESUS
Dromio, what stuff of mine hast thou embarked?

DROMIO OF SYRACUSE
Your goods that lay at host, sir, in the Centaur.

390 **These...here.** I offer these ducats in ransom for my father.
392 **diamond** i.e. the ring.
398 **sympathizèd...error** shared day of error.
401–402 **Thirty-three...you** I have been in labour with you these thirty-three years.
405 **calendars...nativity** those who record their date of birth (as they share it).
406 **gossips' feast** a banquet for godparents (god-sib(ling)s) to celebrate a baptism.
410 **embarked** loaded aboard.

ANTIPHOLUS OF SYRACUSE
He speaks to me; I am your master, Dromio.
Come, go with us; we'll look to that anon.
Embrace thy brother there, rejoice with him.

Exeunt [Antipholus of Syracuse and Antipholus of Ephesus].

DROMIO OF SYRACUSE
There is a fat friend at your master's house,
That kitchened me for you today at dinner.
She now shall be my sister, not my wife.

DROMIO OF EPHESUS
Methinks you are my glass, and not my brother.
I see by you I am a sweet-faced youth.
Will you walk in, to see their gossiping?

DROMIO OF SYRACUSE
Not I, sir, you are my elder.

DROMIO OF EPHESUS
That's a question, how shall we try it?

DROMIO OF SYRACUSE
We'll draw cuts for the senior, till then, lead thou first.

DROMIO OF EPHESUS
Nay then, thus:
We came into the world like brother and brother,
And now let's go hand in hand, not one before another. *Exeunt.*

FINIS.

413 **anon** soon/later.
416 **kitchened me** trapped me in the kitchen.
418 **glass** mirror (image).
422 **try** test/settle.
423 **cuts** lots.

BIBLIOGRAPHY

Beadle, Richard and Alan J. Fletcher, eds., *The Cambridge Companion to Medieval English Theatre*, 2nd edn. (Cambridge: Cambridge University Press, 2007).

Beckwith, Sarah, *Signifying God: Social Relation and Symbolic Act in the York Corpus Christi Play* (Chicago: University of Chicago Press, 2001).

Betteridge, Thomas and Greg Walker, eds., *The Oxford Handbook of Tudor Drama* (Oxford: Oxford University Press, 2012).

Burns, Edward, *Character: Acting and Being on the Pre-Modern Stage* (London: Macmillan, 1989).

Cartelli, Thomas, *Marlowe, Shakespeare and the Economy of Theatrical Experience* (Philadelphia: University of Pennsylvania Press, 1991).

Cartwright, Kent, *Theatre and Humanism: English Drama in the Sixteenth Century* (Cambridge: Cambridge University Press, 1999).

Cox, John D. and David Scott Kastan, eds., *A New History of Early English Drama* (New York: Columbia University Press, 1997).

Dawson, Anthony B. and Paul Yachnin, *The Culture of Playgoing in the English Renaissance* (Cambridge: Cambridge University Press, 2001).

Dessen, Alan C., *Elizabethan Drama and the Viewer's Eye* (Chapel Hill: University of North Carolina Press, 1977).

—— *Shakespeare and the Late Moral Plays* (Lincoln: University of Nebraska Press, 1986).

Dillon, Janette, *The Cambridge Introduction to Early English Theatre* (Cambridge: Cambridge University Press, 2006).

—— *The Language of Space in Court Performance, 1400–1625* (Cambridge: Cambridge University Press, 2010).

Greenblatt, Stephen, *Shakespearean Negotiations: The Circulation of Social Energy in Renaissance England* (Oxford: Clarendon Press, 1988).

Happè, Peter and Wim Hüsken, eds., *Interludes and Early Modern Society* (Amsterdam: Rodopi, 2007).

Hattaway, Michael, ed., *The Blackwell Companion to English Renaissance Literature and Culture*, 2nd edn. (Oxford: Blackwell, 2010).

Hill-Vásquez, Heather, *Sacred Plays: The Politics of Response in the Middle English Religious Drama* (Washington DC: Catholic University of America Press, 2007).

Holland, Peter and Stephen Orgel, eds., *From Script to Stage in Early Modern England* (Basingstoke: Palgrave Macmillan, 2004).

Hutson, Lorna, *The Invention of Suspicion: Law and Mimesis in Shakespeare and Renaissance Drama* (Oxford: Oxford University Press, 2007).

Jones, Robert C., *Engagement with Knavery: Point of View in Richard III, The Jew of Malta, Volpone and The Revenger's Tragedy* (Durham, NC: Duke University Press, 1986).

Kendall, Ritchie D., *The Drama of Dissent: The Radical Poetics of Nonconformity, 1380–1590* (Chapel Hill: University of North Carolina Press, 1986).

Lunney, Ruth, *Marlowe and the Popular Tradition: Innovation in the English Drama before 1595* (Manchester: Manchester University Press, 2002).

McMillin, Scott and Sally-Beth McLean, *The Queen's Men and their Plays* (Cambridge: Cambridge University Press, 1998).

McMullan, Gordon and David Matthews, eds., *Reading the Medieval in Early Modern England* (Cambridge: Cambridge University Press, 2007).
Milling, Jane, 'The Development of a Professional Theatre, 1540–1660', in Jane Milling and Peter Thomson, eds. *The Cambridge History of British Theatre, I: Origins to 1660* (Cambridge: Cambridge University Press, 2004), 139–77.
Norland, Howard B., *Drama in Early Tudor Britain, 1485–1558* (Lincoln: University of Nebraska Press, 1995).
O'Connell, Michael, *The Idolatrous Eye: Iconoclasm and Theatre in Early-Modern England* (Oxford: Oxford University Press, 2000).
Orgel, Stephen, *The Illusion of Power: Political Theatre in the English Renaissance* (Berkeley: University of California Press, 1975).
Shepherd, Simon, *Theatre, Body, Pleasure* (London: Routledge, 2006).
States, Bert O., *Great Reckonings in Little Rooms: On the Phenomenology of the Theater* (Berkeley: University of California Press, 1985).
—— *The Pleasure of the Play* (Ithaca, NY: Cornell University Press, 1994).
Streitberger, W., *Court Revels, 1485–1559* (Toronto: University of Toronto Press, 1994).
Twycross, Meg, ed., *Festive Drama* (Woodbridge: D.S. Brewer, 1996).
Walker, Greg, *The Politics of Performance in Early Renaissance Drama* (Cambridge: Cambridge University Press, 1998).
—— *Medieval Drama: An Anthology* (Oxford: Blackwell, 2000).
—— 'The Renaissance in Britain' in Patrick Collinson, ed., *The Short Oxford History of the British Isles: The Sixteenth Century* (Oxford: Oxford University Press, 2002), 145–87.
—— *Reading Literature Historically: Drama and Poetry from Chaucer to the Reformation* (Edinburgh: Edinburgh University Press, 2013).